The Handbook of Computers and Computing

The Handbook of Computers and Computing

Edited by

Arthur H. Seidman
Pratt Institute

Ivan Flores
Baruch College
City University of New York

VNR VAN NOSTRAND REINHOLD COMPANY

Manufactured in the United States of America

Published by Van Nostrand Reinhold Company Inc.
135 West 50th Street
New York, New York 10020

Van Nostrand Reinhold Company Limited
Molly Millars Lane
Wokingham, Berkshire RG11 2PY, England

Van Nostrand Reinhold
480 Latrobe Street
Melbourne, Victoria 3000, Australia

Macmillan of Canada
Division of Gage Publishing Limited
164 Commander Boulevard
Agincourt, Ontario MIS 3C7, Canada

15 14 13 12 11 10 9 8 7 6 5 4 3 2 1

Library of Congress Cataloging in Publication Data
Main entry under title:

The Handbook of computers and computing.

   Includes index.
1. Electronic   digital   computers—Handbooks,   manuals,
etc. 2. Programming (Electronic computers)—Handbooks,
manuals, etc. 3. Programming languages (Electronic computers)—Handbooks, manuals, etc. I. Seidman, Arthur H.
II. Flores, Ivan.
QA76.5.H3544   1984   001.64   83-16942
ISBN 0-442-23121-0

Contributors

Peter Abel / British Columbia Institute of Technology

Paul W. Abrahams / Consultant

Salvatore d'Ambra / American International Group

Ashok K. Agrawala / University of Maryland

Edward L. Averill / Honeywell Aerospace Defense Group

David R. Baldauf / IBM Corporation

Boris Beizer / Data Systems Analysts, Inc.

Walter S. Brainerd / UNICOMP, University of New Mexico

A. Paul Brokaw / Analog Devices, Inc.

Bill Burton / Teratek Company

John M. Cameron / Data General Corporation

Roy L. Chafin / Human Factors Specialist

Ned Chapin / InfoSci Inc.

Wayne Clary / Data Systems Associates

Ivan Flores / Baruch College, City University of New York

Howard Frank / Contel Information Services, Inc.

Paul Gubitosa / National Council on Compensation Insurance

V. C. Hamacher / University of Toronto

George Hannauer / Electronic Associates, Inc.

J. K. Hassan / IBM Corporation

William J. Harrison / Fireman's Fund Insurance Companies

Dennis James Heiman / IDR Inc.

Avrum E. Ikzkowitz / Data General Corporation

William Jennings / Synesort, Inc.

Ben Klein / City University of New York

Lloyd Kusak / Hewlett-Packard

Morris E. Levine / College of Staten Island, City University of New York

Harold Lorin / IBM Corporation

James B. Maginnis / Drexel University

Kurt Maly / University of Minnesota

Michael Montalbano / IBM Corporation

D. S. Owings / Pratt Institute

Gordon C. Padwick / Teradyne Inc.

Seymour V. Pollack / Washington University, St. Louis

Ronald D. Potter / Robot Systems, Inc.

Harry H. Poole / Poole Associates

Guy Rabbat / IBM Corporation

Julian Reitman / United Technologies

Charles L. Saxe / Tektronix Inc.

Arthur H. Seidman / Pratt Institute

Donald R. Shaw / Business Counselors, Inc.

Rita C. Summers / IBM Los Angeles Scientific Center

Christopher Terry / Microsystems

D. G. Vranesic / University of Toronto

Myles Walsh / CBS, Inc.

Steven W. Weingart / Language Processors Inc.

Martin Weinless / Baruch College, City University of New York

Thomas J. Wheeler / U.S. Army Communications Electronics Command

Nam S. Woo / University of Maryland

Mary N. Youssef / IBM Corporation

S. G. Zaky / University of Toronto

Vladimir Zwass / Fairleigh Dickinson University

Preface

This is an era of tremendous growth centered on the computer revolution. Four decades ago only a handful of people were working with computers. Today the work of a half-million people is directly associated with them. There is hardly a person whose life is not touched by computers.

A field in which fast growth is the byword leads to many specialties; each specialty develops its own subspecialty. The individual computer scientist finds little difficulty in concentrating attention on a smaller and smaller aspect of a chosen area. But, as one's view becomes circumscribed, the ability to understand and interact with the other computer scientists diminishes and one loses track of the field in general.

The Handbook of Computers and Computing describes the fast changes in particular areas of computer science. Each chapter provides a thorough introduction to one topic. The book is an overview of progress in computer science. It will help the reader to catch up with developments he or she may not have had the time to keep in touch with.

AUDIENCE

This volume is addressed to a number of major groups of users, among which are the following:

Electrical Engineers

Engineering design has changed considerably in the past decades. No longer does the engineer see the complete project as well as its details. Activity is compartmentalized into one or two of a number of areas. Interest may range from the bottom of the scale—looking into the physics and chemistry of the materials from which components are fabricated—through circuitry at any level of integration, to the far end of the spectrum—large systems of multiple computers. Or one may be concerned with the design of devices. The *Handbook* describes advances in all of these areas. Further, it relates hardware design to how computers are being used.

Bringing the computer's power to bear on the design procedure can indeed be fruitful. The design and layout of printed circuit boards, for instance, involve so many points, wires and constraints that they are now impossible to accomplish manually with any degree of optimality; hence circuit board layout has become almost completely automated.

Hardware System Designers

The sheer number and type of hardware subsystems has proliferated. In putting together a system, whether it be a robot or television game, it is important for the system designer to understand what subsystems are available. How do these subsystems interface? What are the choices for the languages which activate the system? What are the alternatives in cost, durability and flexibility for a particular subsystem choice?

Programmers

The programmer learns programming craft imbedded in a particular language. When asked to use another language because of the limitations of a project design, a programmer must quickly acquire the rudiments of that new language. Most programming texts assume a naive programmer and develop the language entirely from scratch. The chapters in this volume discuss each language from a professional point of view. Anyone familiar with computers can quickly acquire the flavor of the language, referring to the reference manual for a particular machine to get the details of its dialect.

The programmer must also consider the system to

which the program relates. For instance, the proper choice of a data structure for an application may expedite program construction considerably. Not all languages provide a complete range of data structures, so it is important to distinguish those which do. This volume brings the programmer up to date on the kinds of software systems with which various programs might interface.

System Applications Specialists

The people who analyze the needs of particular applications can choose from a growing set of tested tools. Procedures which formerly were derived intuitively now have the authority of formal proof. For example, there was a time the application designer was concerned with how records in a file get sorted. Today a sort is performed almost automatically. Still, the sort user must interface files and the application program with the sort, call it and present the results. As more computing power and utility packages become available, the system implementer can bring them to bear to solve an application as an integrated whole rather than in separate parts.

Professional System-Users

More computer systems are directly available to technical and nontechnical professional users. The knowledge needed for nontechnical users, such as airline reservations clerks, is trivial; they need know only which buttons to press to get information into and out of the system. The professional who spends many working hours interacting with a computer system uses it as a multifunctional tool and should understand each available function.

The technical writer is, or should be, using a word processing system. To gain full advantage of the word processor, to save time and make text preparation more exciting, a technical writer should understand all the features available.

Designers, business analysts, economists and many other professionals use computer systems; the more they know about them, the easier it is to get full measure from them. Grasp of system operation together with an appreciation for a programming language can double productivity. The operating system switches from one application system to another. Understanding the operating system—the services it provides, how to invoke them, what makes modules and files compatible and what utilities are available—opens up considerable untapped resources for combining modules to complete complicated tasks.

Installation Managers

The installation is a service organization. The services it provides should be easily available and cost-effective for all users. The installation manager seeks ways to satisfy users and employees and to make sure that the computer is operating at full tilt as much of the time as possible. The integrity and security of programs and data kept in the installation is vital. Managing the installation, keeping users and operators happy, is itself a tall order; the manager's need to keep up with the state of the art as well adds a further complication which this *Handbook* may alleviate.

Consultants

The consultant sells *knowledge* to clients and puts it to work in their behalf. Often a project straddles several areas; the consultant may be less informed about one or two of these areas. This volume is a source for further information and pointers to research outside of his or her own speciality.

Students

The student with an undergraduate background in computer science may not be content with the two extremes of textbooks. The introductory text starts the beginner learning a particular topic; the advanced text conveys a small portion of information of specialized importance in great detail. The chapters in this book start at a moderate level of background and describe the state of the art from there.

Inventors

The inventor puts together technology in a new and novel way. More and more inventions use computer technology to their benefit. The courts have recognized that software may often be copyrighted and occasionally be patented. The *Handbook* provides a single source for advances in technology in computer science and points to sources for further research. In this way, the inventor can tell if a combination of technology is unique or has already seen the light of day.

ORGANIZATION

The *Handbook* is organized into six subject areas: components, devices, hardware systems, languages, software systems, and procedures.

I. Components

Two decades have passed since discrete components were used in computers. Still miniaturization has not reached its ultimate. Each year we pack more and more circuits into less and less area. The first five chapters discuss the extent of this miniaturization process and the changes made in circuitry and their interconnection.

Chapter 1 looks at **logic circuits** which make up the computer. Chapter 2 shows how circuits are combined to form **logic families** which perform particular functions. There are a considerable number of such families; this chapter conveys the major differences among them. **Memory** is at the heart of the computer. Chapter 3 is devoted to the operation of various types of memories and to advances in their design. Chapter 4 examines the alternatives for the design of the **microprocessor,** the other important element in the computer system. How much or how little of the microprocessor may be put on a single chip? With what other chips does the microprocessor mate on the microprocessor PC board and how? Chapter 5, on **very large scale integration,** explores the limits to which miniaturization is being carried and expectations for reliability and cost.

II. Devices

Part II is devoted to equipment which stores data and converts them into a form palatable to humans or vice versa. The important aspects of some devices are reviewed and referenced in Chapter 6 on **peripheral devices.**

As more computers are incorporated into larger pieces of equipment, the ability for the computer to control mechanical, hydraulic and electrical devices becomes important. The topic of Chapter 7 is **analog to digital** and **digital to analog conversion.** Conversion devices make it possible to incorporate digital microcomputers into automobiles, air conditioners and security systems, contributing to the universality of computers.

The **terminal** is of prime importance to the user to talk with the computer and enter data, the topic of Chapter 8. When the display is deficient, it impedes the work of the operator, the most costly component in the human/computer symbiosis. What design factors are of importance and what improvements are in the offing?

Terminals are sometimes more conveniently located at a distance from the computer which services them. Often the distance is greater than a pair of twisted wires effectively spans. The answer is **modems** and **multiplexers** described in Chapter 9.

We depend for the bulk of our communication with other humans on vocalization and **voice comprehension.** This talent is only beginning to emerge for the computer. Chapter 10 examines this area.

III. Hardware Systems

Part III deals with aggregations of components. Often ignored as such is the desktop calculator, or even the hand-held type, made of almost the same components as the microcomputer and the minicomputer. Miniaturization has made it difficult to determine when a calculator becomes a micro and when a micro becomes a mini, as shown in Chapter 11 on **desktop computors.**

Although the differences between computers are much smaller than might be expected, it's important to understand what they are and what they mean to the designer and user. Chapter 12 discusses **computer organization.** Since the architecture relies heavily on the instruction set, command sequencing and addressing modes, these topics are given thorough attention here. The functional systems which comprise the computer—the central processor control, I/O, arithmetic and main memory—are considered. Interfacing and timing are not neglected.

Microprogramming makes it possible for a single machine to look like different computers and different architectures. Chapter 13 is devoted to the principles of microprogramming.

While the main thrust in the technology has been the development and profusion of digital computers, there are still tasks better done in analog form. Chapter 14 examines the operation of **analog** and **hybrid computers** and their interfacing to digital computers.

Computers are such complex devices that it is difficult to understand how they can be fabricated and tested exhaustively and yet be sold at such reasonable cost. The answer is **automatic test equipment** (ATE), discussed in detail in Chapter 15. At the heart of modern ATE is a computer. It applies voltages to all the connections and checks all the components and subsystems individually in such a short time that the whole process is economically feasible. Each chip, module and printed circuit board is tested in a similar fashion as assembly progresses. By thus testing larger and larger subassemblies exhaustively, we keep the number of tests of complete assemblies to a minimum. ATE is hence an application of computers to make possible better and less costly computers.

Another combination of devices and software modules is the **small business computer system.** It supercedes manual processing of accounting data, providing profitibility and frequently additional planning tools as an un-expected bonus. But choosing and putting together a suit-able system is fraught with the danger of misdesign and even failure. Chapter 16 addresses these problems.

Perhaps the greatest future growth will come as robots are perfected. Here a combination of mechanical and electrical systems produces a "creature" capable of movement and perception. These systems are tied to-gether with a conceptual system, the computer. Expen-sive though they are, robots can replace people in situa-tions which are

- Dangerous;
- Boring;
- Beyond human strength;
- Too complicated for one person;
- Requiring of inordinate dexterity.

Robotics is discussed in Chapter 17.

IV. Languages

This Part is rather large. But consider that all the pro-gramming which makes the computer a usable device is performed in some language. A huge amount of infor-mation created by a large number of people has been in-corporated into these programs. It is important to under-stand what alternatives are available to the practicing programmer.

Chapter 18 introduces **programming languages** and describes their similarities and differences. It looks at their many features to explain the proliferation of lan-guages. One chapter follows for each important program-ming language. Though not meant to take the place of a textbook, each chapter describes the features which make the covered language important.

All languages have pros and cons and there is often lee-way to choose one over another. There is hardly a lan-guage which does not have a **dialect**—a variation of the language which works on only one computer or group of computers. A language with few dialects is sometimes most suitable. Then it is truly transportable and can be used on a variety of computers. Each language has rea-sons for its popularity and success.

A chapter is devoted to each language as follows: Chapter 19—**FORTRAN**; Chapter 20—**COBOL**; Chap-ter 21—**PL/I**; Chapter 22—**APL**; Chapter 23—**BASIC**; Chapter 24—**PASCAL**; Chapter 25—**RPG**; Chapter 26—**ADA**; Chapter 27—**Assembly Language**; Chapter 28—**Job Control Language.**

JCL (Chapter 28) controls the flow of jobs in the large computer system. For the programmer who works with a large installation, it is a handicap not to be familiar with this language.

Part IV concludes with Chapter 29, on **compilers**—translators which create machine code. A compiler's ef-ficiency and construction are of importance in making a final choice for a programming language.

V. Software Systems

Assuming that we have a general purpose digital com-puter on hand, it can become a highly specialized, rapid and accurate tool to help us with our laborious clerical, scientific and accounting tasks. It is the program and the software which make this change possible.

No programming language runs the computer directly. At the very nub of everything is the **operating system,** discussed in Chapter 30. Nothing is quite so important in maintaining the efficiency and effectiveness of an appli-cation program, except when the program resides in a dedicated hardware system.

Chapter 31 examines **data structure** as seen by the pro-gram. There are many data structure alternatives and reasons for adopting one or another. The amount of in-formation in a large corporation is mind boggling. These needs are embraced by **data base technology,** which con-trols and keeps secure this storehouse of information as discussed in Chapter 32.

Bringing the application program from idea to fruition is an immensely important task. For this reason, the next three chapters are devoted to this topic. Chapter 33, on **software engineering,** describes the theoretical tech-niques developed in the last few years for making project creation and management more tractable. Chapter 34, **systems synthesis,** shows how factors such as program-mer personality, project leader philosophy and manage-ment policy affect the job. Chapter 35, **structured meth-odology,** describes how these tools are applied to a practical, real life project.

Time and distance are two problems that go into sys-tem makeup. Chapter 36 is dedicated to **on-line systems** that share the computer's time among different program-mers and operators and enable the programmer and com-puter to find a solution within a specified interval of time.

The other factor, distance, is so important that it gets two chapters. Chapter 37 examines the simplest part of the requirement, transporting information from a remote terminal or computer to another computer over dis-tance—**telecommunications.** How do systems talk to each other and recognize their "fellows"? The formalities required before programs in different computers can talk are called *protocols* and are explained here. What additional software (and hardware) is needed? How do we avoid conflict with working programs yet service incoming messages without losing data?

Once we have the ability to hook computers together, advantages can be gained by grouping computers which might need to talk to each other. We now have **teleprocessing networks** which are steadily gaining in importance; these are discussed in Chapter 38.

The next four chapters are aimed at particular types of programs. These may be furnished as separate modules—as stand-alone programs—or they may be designed to interface with other modules in comprehensive applications. There is hardly a system that does not require ordering or **sorting,** hence a full discussion is forthcoming in Chapter 39. **Word processing,** the topic of Chapter 40, is gaining momentum and soon it will be difficult to write without recourse to a word processor. But structuring information and words sometimes is not nearly as effective as presenting a picture. **Graphics,** a growing field with built-in problems, is discussed in Chapter 41.

Chapter 42 is about **CICS,** the Customer Information Control System, an IBM product. CICS is a programming system which supports clerical work terminals. All kinds of applications require daily entry of vast amounts of information. A CICS entry system provides menus and prompts to initially untrained operators, who can immediately do needed work because all alternatives have been foreseen by the programmers. CICS facilitates

- Creating display screens;
- Distinguishing between titles and entry fields;
- Validating data;
- Communicating with a host program;
- Regulating incoming telecommunication lines;
- Coordinating many terminals;
- Writing data to the proper program;
- And lots more.

Part V closes with Chapter 43, on **simulation.** Few people realize its importance for representing real world systems and events and then using the computer implemented model to predict the effect of changes on the system. Only the slightest intimation of the importance of this tool is seen by how many managers use VisiCalc, a financial "spreadsheet" which shows what happens as the values of variables change in the prediction formula.

Digital computer simulation provides the ultimate tool in prediction as described in this chapter.

VI. Procedures

The catchall phrase "procedures" truly describes how we go about doing things. Part VI starts with Chapter 44, on **numerical methods**— techniques to convert a scientific problem from a series of formulas to a set of procedures.

This activity precedes programming. During or after programming, **documentation** is a necessity as described in Chapter 45.

A consideration which should be observed from hardware system assemblage onwards through all program and system design work is a regard for the human user. Human engineering or **ergonomics,** suiting the system to the user, is discussed in Chapter 46.

Chapter 47, on **security,** describes how we make the installation safe. The company invests many millions in its computers, auxiliary equipment, a place to house it, air conditioning, the records, tape and disks which store its precious information, the programs it develops and the people who run the installation. How do we protect this investment?

Chapter 48, on **algorithms,** discusses the makeup of programming procedures in terms which are easily converted to a complex language. Perhaps it would go better with the chapters on programming languages, but this chapter does describe programming *procedures.*

Once a firm has installed equipment of considerable size and is running a large number of production jobs, an important question is how well the overall system is functioning. Tuning and balancing the system to extract the very last "bang per buck" is a highly specialized art. Under the heading of **software performance** are many tools, both hardware and software, to help monitor a running system and to predict actions to optimize it—the topic of Chapter 49.

Everything is wrapped up in Chapter 50, on **installation management.** The manager of the computer installation decides many user questions, creates installation policy, recommends equipment, sets up procedures and hires staff.

The Handbook of Computers and Computing has grown out of an emerging need. We hope that it satisfies this need, at least in part. New chapters will be added with each revision to reflect the changing state of affairs in a society which now includes the computer as an indispensable helpmate.

ACKNOWLEDGMENTS

The authors wish to express their gratitude to all those who have helped so unselfishly in this project. We can never repay Mrs. Lee Seidman for her support during our greatest trial. The people at Van Nostrand Reinhold gave unflinchingly: Larry Hager encouraged us unendingly; Walter Brownfield put up with bickering over details; and the production staff coordinated the complicated logistics of composition and proofing. Arlene Abend came through again with the gorgeous jacket. We thank you all.

Arthur H. Seidman
Ivan Flores

Contents

The Handbook of Computers and Computing

I
Components

1
Logic Circuits

Morris E. Levine

The College of Staten Island
The City University of New York

1.1 INTRODUCTION

Although digital systems, such as the computer, can become very complex, fundamentally they are based upon some quite simple building blocks that are repeated many times within a system. In this chapter we shall develop the basic building blocks employed in digital systems.

The digital system is a binary system: it has two, and only two, states. The two states may be a transistor in saturation or in cutoff, a lamp on or off, a magnet with north or south magnetic polarity, the presence or absence of a hole in a punched card or tape, or a switch in either one of two positions. Arithmetic employing digital techniques is based upon the binary, or base 2, numerical system. Digital functions and operations are based upon an algebra of logic developed by the mathematician George Boole approximately 100 years ago.

1.2 NUMBER SYSTEMS AND BINARY ARITHMETIC

Number Systems

Binary arithmetic (base 2) employs the same principles as decimal arithmetic. It has two values, 0 and 1. As in decimal arithmetic, additional levels of numbers are based upon the position concept. Derivatives of binary arithmetic are **octal** (base 8) which has eight values (0 to 7) and **hexadecimal** (base 16) which has sixteen values

(0 to 9 followed by A, B, C, D, E, and F). Table 1.1 shows the equivalencies between binary, octal, hexadecimal and decimal.

Table 1.1. Decimal, Binary, Octal, and Hexadecimal Numbers

Decimal	Binary	Octal	Hexadecimal
0	0	0	0
1	01	1	1
2	10	2	2
3	11	3	3
4	100	4	4
5	101	5	5
6	110	6	6
7	111	7	7
8	1000	10	8
9	1001	11	9
10	1010	12	A
11	1011	13	B
12	1100	14	C
13	1101	15	D
14	1110	16	E
15	1111	17	F
16	10000	20	10
17	10001	21	11
18	10010	22	12
etc.			

EXAMPLE 1.1. Express the number 10110.011_2 in powers of 2. 10

SOLUTION:

$$10110.011_2 = 1 \times 2^4 + 0 \times 2^3 + 1 \times 2^2 + 1 \times 2^1$$
$$+ 0 \times 2^0 + 0 \times 2^{-1} + 1 \times 2^{-2} + 1 \times 2^{-3}$$

binary point   binary point

$$= 16 + 0 + 4 + 2 + 0 + 0 + 0.25 + 0.125$$
$$= 22.375_{10}$$

This also illustrates the method of conversion to base 10, or decimal.

To convert from decimal to binary, the number is split at its decimal point. Successive division by 2 with tabulation of the remainder is applied to the integer part. Multiplication by 2 of the fractional part, with tabulation of the integer parts, yields the **binary fraction**.

EXAMPLE 1.2. Convert 22.375_{10} to its binary equivalent.

SOLUTION:

```
2 |22
2 |11 + 0
2 | 5 + 1
2 | 2 + 1
2 | 1 + 0
    0 + 1   = 10110 reading up
```

$$0.375 \times 2 = 0.750 = 0.750 + 0$$
$$0.750 \times 2 = 1.50 = 0.50 + 1$$
$$0.50 \times 2 = 1.00 = 0.00 + 1 \quad = .011 \text{ reading down}$$

$$22.375_{10} = 10110.011_2$$

Fractional decimals sometimes lead to repeating binaries.

EXAMPLE 1.3. $0.3_{10} = ?_2$.

SOLUTION:

$$0.3 \times 2 = 0.6 = 0.6 + 0$$
$$0.6 \times 2 = 1.2 = 0.2 + 1$$
$$0.2 \times 2 = 0.4 = 0.4 + 0$$
$$0.4 \times 2 = 0.8 = 0.8 + 0$$
$$0.8 \times 2 = 1.6 = 0.6 + 1$$
$$0.6 \times 2 = 1.2 = 0.2 + 1 \quad = 0.010011 \ldots _2 \text{ reading down}$$

Table 1.2. Binary Addition Tables

For 2 Bits		For 3 Bits	
Sum	Carry	Sum	Carry
$0 + 0 = 0$	0	$0 + 0 + 0 = 0$	0
$0 + 1 = 1$	0	$0 + 0 + 1 = 1$	0
$1 + 0 = 1$	0	$0 + 1 + 0 = 1$	0
$1 + 1 = 0$	1	$0 + 1 + 1 = 0$	1
		$1 + 0 + 0 = 1$	0
		$1 + 0 + 1 = 0$	1
		$1 + 1 + 0 = 0$	1
		$1 + 1 + 1 = 1$	1

Addition.

The **addition tables** used are shown in Table 1.2.

EXAMPLE 1.4. Perform the following problem in addition:

$$101101$$
$$+ 110110$$

SOLUTION:

$$101101 = 45_{10}$$
$$110110 = 54_{10}$$
$$1100011 = 99_{10}$$

Subtraction

Several techniques are used: direct subtraction using the subtraction table; 1s (ones) complement; 2s (twos) complement. **Subtraction tables** used in direct subtraction are shown in Table 1.3.

Direct subtraction.

EXAMPLE 1.5. Perform the following problem in subtraction:

$$10110$$
$$-01101$$

SOLUTION:

$$10110 \quad\quad 22_{10}$$
$$-01101 \quad\quad -13_{10}$$
$$01001 \quad\quad 9_{10}$$

Table 1.3. Binary Subtraction Tables

For 2 Bits	Difference	Borrow	For 3 Bits	Difference	Borrow
$0 - 0 =$	0	0	$0 - 0 - 0 =$	0	0
$0 - 1 =$	1	1	$0 - 0 - 1 =$	1	1
$1 - 0 =$	1	0	$0 - 1 - 0 =$	1	1
$1 - 1 =$	0	0	$0 - 1 - 1 =$	0	1
			$1 - 0 - 0 =$	1	0
			$1 - 0 - 1 =$	0	0
			$1 - 1 - 0 =$	0	0
			$1 - 1 - 1 =$	1	1

1s Complement subtraction. To perform this subtraction, the **1s complement** of a binary number must be obtained. This is done by subtracting it from a number containing all ones. In practice, this is accomplished by replacing 1s with 0s and 0s with 1s; for example:

$$\text{binary number} \qquad 01101$$

$$\text{ones complement} \qquad 10010$$

To subtract, add the 1s complement of the subtrahend to the minuend. If the difference is a positive number, an overflow 1 will appear. This is now added to the sum (end around carry) to give the resultant difference. When the difference is negative, a 0 results in the overflow column. The result of the addition is the difference, but in 1s complement form and negative.

EXAMPLE 1.6. Perform the following subtractions using ones complement subtraction:

(a) $10110 - 01101$ (b) $01101 - 10110$

SOLUTION:

(a) $10110 - 01101$

The 1s complement of 01101 is 10010.

```
              10110         22₁₀
             +10010        -13₁₀
      end   1  01000
      around ──→  +1
      carry       1001      + 9₁₀
```

(b) $01101 - 10110$

The 1s complement of 10110 is 01001.

```
              01101         13₁₀
             +01001        -22₁₀
            0  01110
 negative            Take complement.
 number     10001      = -9₁₀
```

2s Complement subtraction. The **2s complement** is one more than the 1s complement. Subtraction is performed as in 1s complement subtraction. With an overflow 1, the result is complete and no end around carry is required. With a negative result (overflow = 0), the final result is negative in 2s complement form.

EXAMPLE 1.7. Perform the following subtractions with 2s complement subtraction:

(a) $10110 - 01101$ (b) $01101 - 10110$

SOLUTION:

The 2s complement of $01101 = 10010 + 1 = 10011$.

```
              10110         22₁₀
             +10011         13₁₀
            1  01001       + 9₁₀
```

(b) $01101 - 10110$

The 2s complement of $10110 = 01001 + 1 = 01010$.

```
              01101          13
             +01010         -22
            0  10111  =     - 9 in 2s complement form
```

The 2s complement of $10111 = 01000 + 1 = 01001$.

Signed Arithmetic

In signed arithmetic the level of the most significant bit indicates the sign. A "0" indicates a positive and a "1" indicates a negative number.

0110 1110	positive number
1001 0110	negative number

Negative numbers are in 2s complement form.

EXAMPLE 1.8. Perform the following additions with signed numbers: (a) 0000 1011 + 0001 0111; (b) 1111 0100 + 1100 1010; (c) 0100 0001 + 0100 0001.

SOLUTION:

$$\begin{array}{llr}
\text{(a)} & 0000\ 1011 & +11 \\
& +0001\ 0111 & +23 \\
\hline
& 0010\ 0010 & +34 \\
\end{array}$$

$$\begin{array}{llr}
\text{(b)} & 1111\ 0100 & -12 \\
& 1100\ 1010 & -54 \\
\hline
\text{ignore 1} & 1011\ 1110 & -66 \\
\end{array}$$

If we try to add two numbers that are too large, there is a change in sign in the most significant bit of the sum.

$$\begin{array}{llr}
\text{(c) } 0100\ 0001 & +65 \\
0100\ 0001 & +65 \\
\hline
1000\ 0010 & -126 \text{ (incorrect)} \\
\\
1001\ 0101 & -107 \\
1001\ 0101 & -107 \\
\hline
1\ 0010\ 1010 & +\ 26 \text{ (incorrect)} \\
\end{array}$$

Computers using 2s complement addition are programmed to recognize this and correct the result.

Multiplication and Division

These follow the same rules and techniques used in decimal arithmetic. The **multiplication table** is found in Table 1.4.

Table 1.4.
Multiplication Table

$0 \times 0 = 0$
$0 \times 1 = 0$
$1 \times 0 = 0$
$1 \times 1 = 1$

EXAMPLE 1.9. Perform the following problems in multiplication and division:

(a) 1101 × 101   (b) 100 0011 ÷ 101

SOLUTION:

$$\begin{array}{lr}
\text{(a)} \quad 1101 & (13 \times 5)_{10} \\
\underline{\quad\ 101} & \\
1101 & \\
0000 & \\
\underline{1101} & \\
1000001 & = (65)_{10} \\
\end{array}$$

(b) 1000011 ÷ 101 $(61 \div 5)_{10}$

$$\begin{array}{r}
1100 \\
101\overline{)1000011} \\
\underline{101} \\
110 \\
\underline{101} \\
111 \\
\underline{101} \\
10 \\
\end{array}$$

→ 1101

$67_{10} \div 5_{10} = 13_{10} \ R\ 2_{10}$

$$\frac{1000011}{101} = 1100 + R10$$

The Octal Number System

The octal number system (Table 1.1) is a derivative of the binary number system and uses the digits 0 to 7. Its use results in economy of written storage space and error reduction. Conversion from binary to octal is readily achieved by separating the binary number into groups of 3 bits from the binary point in both directions, and replacing them with their octal equivalent. (Note: each binary grouping must have 3 bits. When needed, additional 0s can be added to complete a group of 3.)

EXAMPLE 1.10. Convert to octal: 11011101.1110011.

SOLUTION:

$$\begin{array}{ccccccc}
011 & 011 & 101. & 111 & 001 & 100 \\
3 & 3 & 5\ . & 7 & 1 & 4 \\
\end{array}$$

(Note the bits added at both ends to complete the groups of three.)

Conversion from octal to decimal follows the same methods used in binary to decimal conversion.

EXAMPLE 1.11. Convert the following octal number to decimal: 347.31_8.

SOLUTION:

$$347.31_8 = 3 \times 8^2 + 4 \times 8^1 + 7 \times 8^0$$

octal point   octal point

$$+ 3 \times 8^{-1} + 1 \times 8^{-2} = 231.3906_{10}.$$

The Hexadecimal Number System

This uses 16 digits: 0 to 9 and A, B, C, D, E, F (Table 1.1). Its equivalent in binary is binary groups of four and is even more economical than octal. A group of 4 bits is called a **nibble** and a group of 8 bits a **byte.** The equivalent is shown in Example 1.12 (Note that each binary grouping must have four bits. Leading or following zeros must be added to complete the groups.)

EXAMPLE 1.12. Convert to hexadecimal the following binary number: 10011011011000011111. Convert also to decimal.

SOLUTION:

0010   0110 1101 1000. 0111 1100

2   6   D   8 .   7   C

(Note bits added at both ends to complete groups of 4.)

$$26D8.7C_{16} = 2 \times 16^3 + 6 \times 16^2 + 13 \times 16^1 + 8$$
$$\times 16^0 + 7 \times 16^{-1} + 12 \times 16^{-2} = 9944.0468_{10}$$

1.3 BASIC LOGIC CIRCUITS AND TRUTH TABLES

Logic gates are combinations of diodes, transistors and resistors which operate in one of two logic states to generate the two **logic levels, 1** and **0,** used in digital systems. Most logic circuits operate with the output transistor either in saturation or in cutoff, called **saturated logic.**

The AND Gate

The **AND gate** is a coincidence gate. Its output is a 1 when all its inputs are at 1. Because it uses the symbology of Boolean algebra, the AND gate's operation gives the

Table 1.5. 3 Input AND Gate

A	B	C	D
0	0	0	0
0	0	1	0
0	1	0	0
0	1	1	0
1	0	0	0
1	0	1	0
1	1	0	0
1	1	1	1

appearance of algebraic multiplication. For a 3 input AND gate with inputs A, B and C, and output D, we can write:

$$A \times B \times C = D \qquad (1.1a)$$
$$\text{or } A \cdot B \cdot C = D \qquad (1.1b)$$
$$\text{or } ABC = D \qquad (1.1c)$$

Output D will be a 1 when A, B and C are *all* equal to 1. Figure 1.1 gives the logic symbol for a 3 input AND gate.

The operation of gates is frequently shown by means of **truth tables** which give the gate output for all possible combinations of the inputs. Table 1.5 gives the truth table for the 3 input AND gate of Figure 1.1.

The OR Gate

The **OR gate** generates an output of 1 when *any one* of its inputs is a 1. In terms of Boolean algebra, this gate's operation looks like arithmetic addition, but it differs from arithmetic because the gate can only have an output of 1. For a three input OR gate, with inputs A, B and C, we can write:

$$A + B + C = D \qquad (1.2)$$

Output D will be a 1 when A, B or C or **any** combination of A, B or C are at 1. Figure 1.2 gives the logic symbol

Figure 1.1. Logic symbol for a 3 input AND gate.

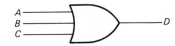

Figure 1.2. Logic symbol for a 3 input OR gate.

Table 1.6.
3 Input OR Gate

A	B	C	D
0	0	0	0
0	0	1	1
0	1	0	1
0	1	1	1
1	0	0	1
1	0	1	1
1	1	0	1
1	1	1	1

Figure 1.4. Inverter logic symbol.

Table 1.7.
Inverter
Truth Table

A	$\overline{A}$
0	1
1	0

for a 3 input OR gate. The truth table for a 3 input OR gate is given in Table 1.6.

The Buffer

The **buffer,** whose logic symbol, the triangle, shown in Figure 1.3, is a circuit which serves either as an isolator or as a power booster. There is no change in logic level when a signal is transmitted through a buffer.

The Inverter or Complementer

The **inverter** gives an output **opposite** to that of the input. Its output is shown by a bar above the input to indicate inversion. Its logic symbol is the triangle followed by or led by a bubble, as shown in Figure 1.4, and its truth table is given in Table 1.7.

NAND and NOR Gates

The **NAND,** an AND followed by an inverter, and the **NOR,** an OR followed by an inverter, have much greater universality than the AND or OR gates. The logic symbols for the NAND and NOR gates are given in Figures 1.5a and b; they are the symbols of Figures 1.1 and 1.2 followed by bubbles. These gates' truth tables are provided in Table 1.8.

Figure 1.3. Buffer logic symbol.

Negative Logic

In specifying logic levels it is common practice to specify logic 1 as more positive than logic 0. There are cases, however, in which a designer specifies logic 0 as more positive than logic 1. For example, in a TTL 2 input AND gate it is common practice to specify logic 1 as the more positive voltage ($\approx$5 volts) and logic 0 as the more negative ($\approx$0 volts) voltage. The truth tables corresponding to $AB = C$ are given in Table 1.9.

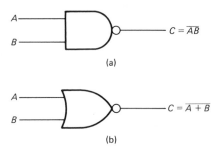

Figure 1.5. Logic symbols for (a) NAND and (b) NOR gates.

Table 1.8. NAND and NOR Gate Truth Tables

2 Input NAND			2 Input NOR		
A	B	$C = \overline{AB}$	A	B	$C = \overline{A + B}$
0	0	1	0	0	1
0	1	1	0	1	0
1	0	1	1	0	0
1	1	0	1	1	0

Table 1.9. Positive Logic for a 2 Input AND Gate

Logic Levels			Voltage Levels		
A	*B*	*C = AB*	*A*	*B*	*C*
0	0	0	0 V	0 V	0 V
0	1	0	0 V	+5 V	0 V
1	0	0	+5 V	0 V	0 V
1	1	1	+5 V	+5 V	+5 V

**Table 1.10.
2 Input OR
Negative Logic**

A	*B*	*C*
1	1	1
1	0	1
0	1	1
0	0	0

If in the same system we define 0 V as logic "1" and +5 V as logic "0," the logic levels portion of Table 1.9 converts to Table 1.10 and we define the system as a "negative logic" system.

Reading Table 1.10 upwards, we see that the 2 input AND converts to a 2 input OR gate. Following the same procedure we can draw the following conclusions for identical circuits:

Positive logic	Negative logic
AND	OR
OR	AND
NAND	NOR
NOR	NAND

Complex Logic Circuits

Figure 1.6 is a diagram of a **complex logic circuit.** The operation of such a circuit is more easily understood when at each point the logic equations are expressed in terms of the input variables.

1.4 BOOLEAN ALGEBRA AND MINIMIZATION

It can readily be shown that the expression for *F* in Figure 1.6 is not in its simplest, or minimized, form. The techniques available for minimization are:

1. Boolean formulas.
2. Karnaugh mapping.
3. Computer minimization (Quine-McClusky).

Boolean Formulas for the Simplification of Logic Diagrams

Logic circuits can be simplified by the use of formulas such as those which follow in this section. The technique is summarized in the following systematic procedure:

1. If there are parentheses in the equations, expand using conventional algebraic methods and priorities. Treat variables and inverted variables as separate terms.
2. Look for simplification using the Boolean formulas

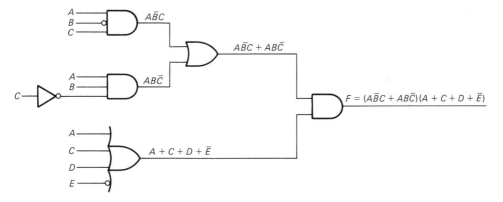

Figure 1.6. Example of a logic circuit.

(Eq. 1.3) which follow. Note that exponents do not exist (Eq. 1.3.4a) and levels greater than 1 do not exist (Eq. 1.3.1c).

3. Look for common terms and factor as in conventional algebra. Treat variables and inverted variables as separate terms.
4. Note that 1 + anything = 1 (Eq. 1.3.5c) and 0 × anything = 0 (Eq. 1.3.4d).
5. Apply DeMorgan's law (Eq. 1.3.7) wherever possible.
6. Repeat, beginning at step 1.

BOOLEAN FORMULAS

$$
\left.
\begin{array}{l}
0 + 0 = 0 \\
0 + 1 = 1 \\
1 + 1 = 1
\end{array}
\right\} \text{ OR}
$$

(1.3.1a)
(1.3.1b)
(1.3.1c)

$$
\left.
\begin{array}{l}
0 \cdot 0 = 0 \\
0 \cdot 1 = 0 \\
1 \cdot 1 = 1
\end{array}
\right\} \text{ AND}
$$

(1.3.2a)
(1.3.2b)
(1.3.2c)

$$
\left.
\begin{array}{l}
\overline{0} = 1 \\
\overline{1} = 0 \\
\overline{0} = 0 \\
\overline{1} = 1
\end{array}
\right\} \begin{array}{l}\text{Inversion or}\\ \text{Complement}\end{array}
$$

(1.3.3a)
(1.3.3b)
(1.3.3c)
(1.3.3d)

$$
\left.
\begin{array}{l}
A \cdot A = A \\
A \cdot \overline{A} = 0 \\
A \cdot 1 = A \\
A \cdot 0 = 0
\end{array}
\right\} \text{ AND}
$$

(1.3.4a)
(1.3.4b)
(1.3.4c)
(1.3.4d)

$$
\left.
\begin{array}{l}
A + A = A \\
A + \overline{A} = 1 \\
A + 1 = 1 \\
A + 0 = A
\end{array}
\right\} \text{ OR}
$$

(1.3.5a)
(1.3.5b)
(1.3.5c)
(1.3.5d)

$$\overline{\overline{A}} = A \qquad (1.3.6)$$

$$
\left.
\begin{array}{l}
A + B = \overline{\overline{A}\,\overline{B}} \\
\\
A \cdot B = \overline{\overline{A} + \overline{B}}
\end{array}
\right\} \text{ DeMorgan's law}^{*}
$$

(1.3.7a)

(1.3.7b)

$$A + AB = A \qquad (1.3.8)$$

$$A + \overline{A}B = A + B \qquad (1.3.9)$$

$$ABC = AB(C) = A(BC) \qquad (1.3.10)$$

$$AB = BA \qquad (1.3.11)$$

$$A + B = B + A \qquad (1.3.12)$$

*Note that whereas in Eq. 1.3.6 the two overbars above the A effectively cancel each other, in Eq. 1.3.7 they do not. To cancel, they must be of the same width.

$$A(B + C) = AB + AC \qquad (1.3.13)$$

$$(A + BC) = (A + B)(A + C) \qquad (1.3.14)$$

$$A\overline{B} + \overline{A}B = \overline{\overline{A}\,\overline{B} + AB} \qquad (1.3.15)$$

$$
\begin{aligned}
(A + B + C) &= A + (B + C) \\
&= (A + B) + C = (A + C) + B
\end{aligned} \qquad (1.3.16)
$$

$$AB + \overline{AB}C = AB + C \qquad (1.3.17)$$

$$AB + \overline{AB} = 1 \qquad (1.3.18)$$

$$(A + B)(A + \overline{B}) = A \qquad (1.3.19)$$

$$AB + A\overline{B}C = AB + AC \qquad (1.3.20)$$

$$(A + B)(A + \overline{B} + C) = (A + B)(A + C) \qquad (1.3.21)$$

$$\overline{A}\,\overline{B} + \overline{A}B + A\overline{B} = \overline{A} + \overline{B} \qquad (1.3.22)$$

DeMorgan's Law

DeMorgan's law, Eqs. 1.3.7, yields very useful formulas. They make possible solutions of logic equations with AND/NAND logic when the circuit calls for OR/NOR functions and vice versa. It makes possible solutions of circuits with only one form of logic when the circuit or system configuration calls for both forms.

These equations are in general form and extend to multilevel expressions. They can be applied to the complete equation or to any part of it. The fundamental rules are:

1. Replace AND with OR (or OR with AND).
2. Complement variables.
3. Complement total result.

EXAMPLE 1.13. Using DeMorgan's law, express the following combined equation only in OR/NOR logic:

$$F = A\overline{B}C + BC(A + \overline{D}) + (D + E)(A + \overline{B}).$$

SOLUTION:

Apply DeMorgan's law to only the AND part of the expression:

$$F = \overline{(\overline{A} + \overline{\overline{B}} + C)} + \overline{(\overline{B} + \overline{C})} + \overline{(\overline{A} + D)}$$

Reduces to B

$$+ \overline{(D + E)} + \overline{(\overline{A} + \overline{\overline{B}})}$$

Minimization of Complex Circuit by Boolean Formulas

EXAMPLE 1.14. Minimize the circuit of Figure 1.6.

SOLUTION:

$$(A\bar{B}C + AB\bar{C})(A + C + D + \bar{E}) = F$$

Multiplying out

$$F = AA\bar{B}C + AAB\bar{C} + A\bar{B}CC + AB\bar{C}C$$
$$+ \ A\bar{B}CD + AB\bar{C}D + A\bar{B}C\bar{E} + AB\bar{C}\,\bar{E}$$
$$= A\bar{B}C + AB\bar{C} + A\bar{B}C + 0 + A\bar{B}CD$$
$$+ \ AB\bar{C}D + A\bar{B}C\bar{E} + AB\bar{C}\,\bar{E}$$

by Eqs. 1.3.4a and 1.3.4b.

$$F = A\bar{B}C + AB\bar{C} + A\bar{B}CD + AB\bar{C}D$$
$$+ \ A\bar{B}C\bar{E} + AB\bar{C}\,\bar{E}$$

by Eqs. 1.3.5a. This equation applies to both simple and complex expressions.

$$F = A\bar{B}C(1 + D + \bar{E}) + AB\bar{C}(1 + D + \bar{E})$$

by factoring.

$$F = A\bar{B}C + AB\bar{C}$$

by Eq. 1.3.5d. This equation applies to both simple and complex expressions.

1.5 MINIMIZATION USING MAPPING TECHNIQUES: THE KARNAUGH MAP

The **Karnaugh map** is a simple and effective method of minimizing Boolean equations, particularly if the number of variables is four or less. The Boolean equation for the logic circuit must be expressed in the form of a sum of product terms and 1s put in the corresponding appropriate boxes.

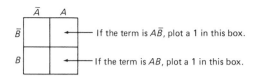

Figure 1.7. A two variable Karnaugh map.

Two Variable Map

The inputs are A, B, and their complements (Figure 1.7). Ones in adjacent boxes yield a reduction of one variable.

EXAMPLE 1.15. Minimize the circuit of Figure 1.8 using the Karnaugh map.

SOLUTION:

From the logic diagram (Figure 1.8) we can write

$$A\bar{B} + AB = A(B + \bar{B}) = A(1) = A$$

by Eqs. 1.3.5b and 1.3.4c.

From the Karnaugh map we see adjacent vertical 1s. Adjacent 1s (either vertical or horizontal) in a two variable map lead to minimization by the elimination of one variable, in this case B.

EXAMPLE 1.16. Minimize $A\bar{B} + \bar{A}B$

SOLUTION:

The function cannot be simplified by the reduction of a variable because the 1s are not "adjacent" vertically or horizontally (Figure 1.9a). However, the complement of the expression can be obtained by inserting 0s in the missing boxes and then treating them as though they were a given function, but then complementing the final result as shown in Figure 1.9b. That this is correct can be seen from the truth table of Figure 1.9c, in which the functions agree for all possible combinations of the input variables.

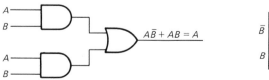
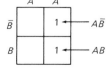

Figure 1.8. Logic circuit and Karnaugh map for $A\bar{B} + AB$.

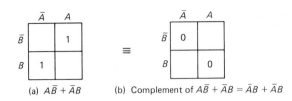

(a) $A\overline{B} + \overline{A}B$

(b) Complement of $A\overline{B} + \overline{A}B = \overline{A}B + \overline{A}B$

A	B	$\overline{A}$	$\overline{B}$	$A\overline{B}$	$\overline{A}B$	$A\overline{B} + \overline{A}B$	AB	$\overline{A}\overline{B}$	$AB + \overline{A}\overline{B}$	$\overline{A}\overline{B} + \overline{A}B$
0	0	1	1	0	0	0	0	1	1	0
0	1	1	0	0	1	1	0	0	0	1
1	0	0	1	0	0	1	0	0	0	1
1	1	0	0	1	0	0	1	0	1	0

(c) Truth table: $A\overline{B} + \overline{A}B = \overline{A}\overline{B} + AB$

Figure 1.9. Karnaugh maps for $A\overline{B} + \overline{A} B$ and truth tables.

Three Variable Map

The inputs are A, B C and their complements. The map plots as shown in Figure 1.10. Ones in two adjacent boxes yield a reduction of one variable, and four 1s in adjacent boxes (horizontally or in the form of a square) result in the reduction of two variables. The columns $\overline{A}\,\overline{B}$ and $A\overline{B}$ are adjacent. A 1 in a box may be used more than once.

Examples of reduction from the map are

$$\overline{A}B\overline{C} + \overline{A}BC = \overline{A}B \tag{1.4a}$$

$$\overline{A}B\overline{C} + AB\overline{C} = B\overline{C} \tag{1.4b}$$

$$\overline{A}B\overline{C} + \overline{A}BC + A\overline{C} + A\overline{B}\overline{C} = \overline{C} \tag{1.4c}$$

$$\overline{A}B\overline{C} + \overline{A}BC + AB\overline{C} + ABC = B \tag{1.4d}$$

$$A\overline{B}\overline{C} + A\overline{B}C + \overline{A}B\overline{C} + \overline{A}BC = \overline{B} \tag{1.4e}$$

$$AB\overline{C} + ABC + \overline{A}BC = AB + BC \tag{1.4f}$$

$$\overline{A}B\overline{C} + \overline{A}BC + AB\overline{C} + A\overline{B}C$$
$$= \overline{A}\overline{B}C + \overline{A}B\overline{C} + ABC + A\overline{B}\overline{C} \tag{1.4g}$$

Four Variable Map

The four variable map, with inputs A, B, C, D and their complement plots as shown in Figure 1.11. In the four variable map, two adjacent boxes result in a reduction of one variable. Four adjacent boxes, vertical, horizontal or in the form of a square yields a reduction in two variables. Eight adjacencies, horizontal or vertical, reduces the variables by three. Rows $\overline{C}D$ and $C\overline{D}$ are adjacent as are columns $\overline{A}\overline{B}$ and $A\,\overline{B}$. Any box may be used more than once.

Examples of reductions with the four variable map are

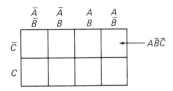

Figure 1.10. A three variable Karnaugh map.

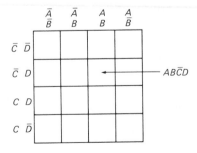

Figure 1.11. A four variable Karnaugh map.

Table 1.11.
Half Adder Truth Table

A	+	B	→	S	C
0		0		0	0
0		1		1	0
1		0		1	0
1		1		0	1

Table 1.12.
Full Adder Truth Table

A	+	B	+	C_i	→	S	C_o
0		0		0		0	0
0		0		1		1	0
0		1		0		1	0
0		1		1		0	1
1		0		0		1	0
1		0		1		0	1
1		1		0		0	1
1		1		1		1	1

$$\overline{AB}\overline{CD} + AB\overline{CD} = B\overline{CD} \tag{1.5a}$$

$$\overline{AB}\overline{CD} + \overline{AB}C\overline{D} = \overline{AB}\,\overline{C} \tag{1.5b}$$

$$\overline{AB}C + \overline{AB}\overline{CD} + \overline{AB}C\overline{D} = \overline{AB} \tag{1.5c}$$

$$\overline{A}B + AB = B \tag{1.5d}$$

$$A + C = \overline{AC} \tag{1.5e}$$

More than Four Variables

With more than four variables, mapping minimization is possible but becomes increasingly difficult because it requires multiple maps. Computer solutions are possible with the Quine-McClusky method.

2.6 ARITHMETIC CIRCUITS

Half Adder (HA)

A **half adder** adds the least significant bits in addition. The truth table for the addition of two inputs, A and B, is given as Table 1.11 in which $A + B = S$ (sum) and C (carry).
The logic equations are

$$S = \overline{A}B + A\overline{B} = A \oplus B \tag{1.6a}$$

$$C = AB \tag{1.6b}$$

Sum S also can be expressed as

$$S = \overline{AB} + AB = A \oplus B \tag{1.6c}$$

Figure 1.12. Logic symbol for an exclusive-OR gate.

The expression for S has important other applications, such as in the half subtractor, error checking, comparison, and in parity generation and checking. It is called the **exclusive OR.** The logic symbol for the exclusive-OR gate is given in Figure 1.12.

Full Adder (FA)

The **full adder** is needed for any bit other than the least significant bit. It adds A, B, and C_i, the carry from the preceding column to give an output S (sum) and C_o (carry out to the next colunn). The truth table for the full adder is given in Table 1.12.

The logic equation for the full adder, obtained from Table 1.12, are:

$$S = \overline{A}\,\overline{B}C_i + \overline{A}B\overline{C}_i + A\overline{B}\,\overline{C}_i + ABC_i \tag{1.7a}$$

$$C_o = \overline{A}BC_i + A\overline{B}C_i + AB\overline{C}_i + ABC_i \tag{1.7b}$$

Sum S cannot be simplified, but can be expressed in complementary form:

$$S = \overline{AB}\,\overline{C}_i + \overline{A}BC_i + AB\overline{C}_i + A\overline{B}C_i \tag{1.7c}$$

Carry C_o can be minimized to:

$$C_o = AB + AC_i + BC_i \tag{1.7d}$$

Equations 1.7 are in combination OR/NOR and AND/NAND form. Application of DeMorgan's theorem permits modification so that only one form of logic need be used and simplifies implementation with integrated circuits.

Table 1.13.
Half Subtractor Truth Table

X	−	Y	→	D	B
0		0		0	0
0		1		1	1
1		0		1	0
1		1		0	0

Half Subtractor (HS)

A **half subtractor** is the logic solution to the problem of subtracting one input from a second input. This occurs as the least significant bit in subtraction. The truth table is given in Table 1.13 for inputs $X - Y = D$ (difference) and B (borrow). The logic equations are:

$$D = X \oplus Y \tag{1.8a}$$

$$B = \overline{X}Y \tag{1.8b}$$

Full Subtractor (FS)

The **full subtractor** is used for subtraction of any bit, other than the least significant bit. It solves the problem of $X - Y - B_i$ (where B_i is a borrow-in from preceding column) to give an output D (difference) and B_o (borrow out to the next column). The truth table for the full subtractor is given in Table 1.14. The logic equations for the full subtractor, from Table 1.14, are:

Table 1.14.
Full Subtractor Truth Table

X	−	Y	−	B_i	→	D	B_o
0		0		0		0	0
0		0		1		1	1
0		1		0		1	1
0		1		1		0	1
1		0		0		1	0
1		0		1		0	0
1		1		0		0	0
1		1		1		1	1

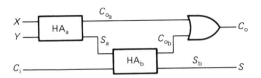

Figure 1.13. Full adder implemented with half adders.

$$D = \overline{X}\,\overline{Y}B_i + \overline{X}Y\overline{B}_i + X\overline{Y}\,\overline{B}_i + XYB_i \tag{1.9a}$$

$$B_o = \overline{X}\,\overline{Y}B_i + \overline{X}Y\overline{B}_i + \overline{X}YB_i + XYB_i \tag{1.9b}$$

The solution for D is the same as for the sum S in the full adder and can also be expressed in identical complementary form:

$$D = \overline{X}\,\overline{Y}\,\overline{B}_i + \overline{X}YB_i + XY\overline{B}_i + X\overline{Y}B_i \tag{1.9c}$$

$$\text{and } B_o = \overline{X}B_i + \overline{X}Y + YB_i \tag{1.9d}$$

Full Adder with Half Adders

The full adder can be implemented with a logic configuration using two half adders and an OR gate (Figure 1.13).

Full Adder: Serial

To make a multibit adder adding two multibit numbers X and Y, the circuit of Figure 1.14 is frequently used. It operates on the principle used in hand addition: adding one pair of bits at a time. It is economical, requiring only one full adder, but it is slow. Inputs X and Y are serial representations of the numbers, with the bits introduced serially (least significant bit first).

Full Adder: Parallel

This multibit adder is shown in Figure 1.15. It is expensive and needs one full adder (FA) for each bit; however,

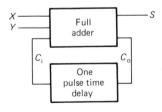

Figure 1.14. Serial full adder.

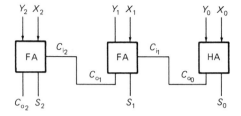

Figure 1.15. Parallel full adder.

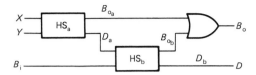

Figure 1.16. Full subtractor implemented with half subtractors.

it is extremely fast. There is still some delay in carry propagation, which may be corrected by a carry look-ahead circuit.

Full Subtractor with Half Subtractors

This can be implemented with two half subtractors and an OR (Figure 1.16).

1.7 THE FLIPFLOP (FF)

The **flipflop** (FF), or **bistable multivibrator** (MV), is a digital building block with two stable states, 1 and 0. It forms the basis for memory, counters, frequency dividers, and shift registers. The flipflops most commonly found in digital work are circuit configurations which require essentially equal amounts of energy to convert from one state to the other. There are regenerative devices, such as the silicon controlled rectifier (SCR) and two-transistor regenerative pairs, which require considerably different amounts of energy to transfer between the stable states. Their usage in common digital applications, however, is quite rare.

The Basic NAND/NOR Cross-Coupled FF

The basic FF configuration consists of two cross-coupled gates (NAND or NOR), as shown in Figures 1.17a and b. Figures 1.17c and d give the logic symbols and Figures 1.17e and f provide the truth tables. For the NAND FF to activate input S or R (force either to change states), one or the other input must be driven to logic 0. This condition is shown by the small circles at inputs S and R (Figure 1.17c). The output responds nearly immediately (there is a small delay owing to gate propagation time) to the forcing level. In the stable state, S and R must be at logic 1; the timing diagram of Figure 1.17g shows this. While it is electrically possible to make Q and $\overline{Q}$ both go

to logic 1 simultaneously by making S and R go to 0 together, this is an undesired condition, to be avoided by the system designer. For the NOR bistable, the forcing conditions are for S and R to go to logic 1 with S and R = 0 for stable conditions.

It is normal practice to consider $Q = 1$, $\overline{Q} = 0$ the set condition, and $Q = 0$ and $\overline{Q} = 1$ the reset condition. In Figures 1.17a and b, the forcing levels can be inverted if desired by inserting inverters at the input terminals. The term **latch** is also used for the flipflop.

The Clocked, or Gated, FF

These FFs are used for controlling the time for the transfer of data into temporary storage or memory. Data is transferred from S-R to Q-$\overline{Q}$ only when the clock enables the gates and FF. Figure 1.18 shows the characteristics of these FFs.

D (Data or Delay) Latch

This is shown in Figure 1.19. An inverter between S and R eliminates the not-allowed (NA) condition of the previous FFs. Output Q follows D (data) and the data appears at the output delayed after the clock pulse. This FF requires only single rail (single input) data. The previous FFs required double rail (double input) data.

The Master-Slave (M-S) FF

This is composed of two clocked FFs with an inverted clock to the **slave,** as shown in Figure 1.20 (NAND FFs). When the clock goes to logic 1, the **master** is enabled and data is transferred to $Q_M - \overline{Q}_M$, but not through the slave because the slave is disabled. When the clock returns to logic zero, data is transferred to Q_S-$\overline{Q}_S$. Delayed by one clock pulse, the data gets to the output at the trailing edge of the clock pulse as the clock goes to logic 0. This event is shown by the circle at the clock pulse input of the logic symbol (Figure 1.20b).

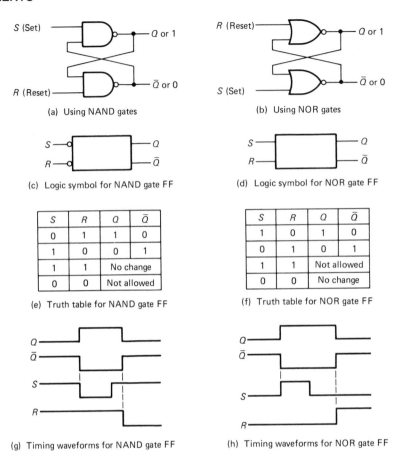

Figure 1.17. Basic cross-coupled flipflops.

T or Toggle FF

As shown in Figure 1.21, the **toggle FF** may be obtained from the M-S FF by cross-connecting S to $\overline{Q}$ and R to Q. This FF toggles (changes state) at the trailing edge of each clock pulse and the clock frequency is divided by 2.

The J-K FF

The **J-K FF** (NAND FFs) (Figure 1.22) is a master-slave FF that has multiple input R and S gates and combines the properties of the T and R-S master-slave FFs.

The Universal FF

The universal FF exists in many different forms. As Figure 1.23 shows, it consists of a J-K FF and has direct PR (preset) and CLR (clear) inputs. The PR and CLR inputs

supersede all other inputs and function as soon as they are activated. Outputs Q and $\overline{Q}$ follow PR and CLR (subject to transistor propagation delay). To activate the PR and CLR inputs, they must be forced to logic 0.

1.8 SEQUENTIAL COUNTERS AND CIRCUITS

The Binary Ripple Counter

The **binary ripple counter** is obtained by cascading a series of T flipflops. Figure 1.24a is the diagram of a three stage binary counter. Also given, in Figure 1.24b, are the waveforms at each of the outputs. The final row gives the count state expressed as a binary number in the form $Q_C Q_B Q_A$. The count progresses, or ripples, down the counter with each stage providing its own propagation delay.

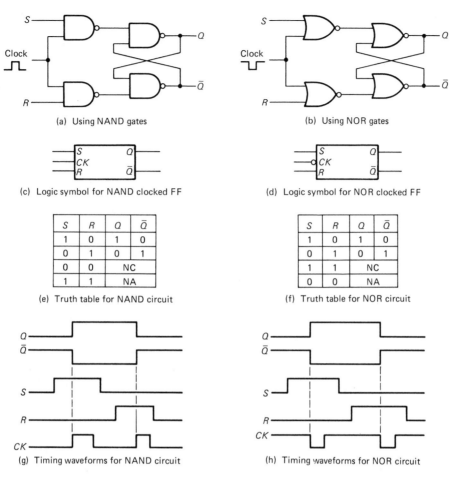

(a) Using NAND gates

(b) Using NOR gates

(c) Logic symbol for NAND clocked FF

(d) Logic symbol for NOR clocked FF

S	R	Q	$\bar{Q}$
1	0	1	0
0	1	0	1
0	0	NC	
1	1	NA	

(e) Truth table for NAND circuit

S	R	Q	$\bar{Q}$
1	0	1	0
0	1	0	1
1	1	NC	
0	0	NA	

(f) Truth table for NOR circuit

(g) Timing waveforms for NAND circuit

(h) Timing waveforms for NOR circuit

Figure 1.18. Clocked flipflop.

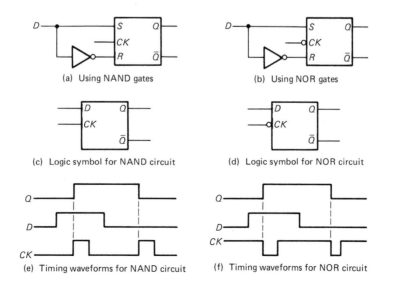

(a) Using NAND gates

(b) Using NOR gates

(c) Logic symbol for NAND circuit

(d) Logic symbol for NOR circuit

(e) Timing waveforms for NAND circuit

(f) Timing waveforms for NOR circuit

Figure 1.19. Clocked flipflop.

17

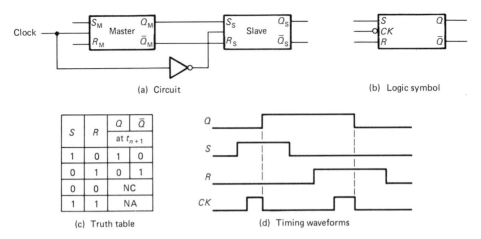

(a) Circuit

(b) Logic symbol

S	R	Q	Q̄
		at t_{n+1}	
1	0	1	0
0	1	0	1
0	0	NC	
1	1	NA	

(c) Truth table

(d) Timing waveforms

Figure 1.20. Master-slave flipflop.

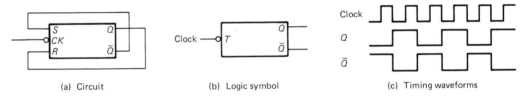

(a) Circuit

(b) Logic symbol

(c) Timing waveforms

Figure 1.21. Toggle (T) flipflop.

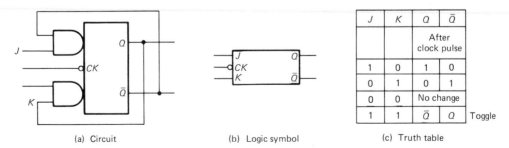

(a) Circuit

(b) Logic symbol

J	K	Q	Q̄
		After clock pulse	
1	0	1	0
0	1	0	1
0	0	No change	
1	1	Q̄	Q	Toggle

(c) Truth table

Figure 1.22. A J-K flipflop.

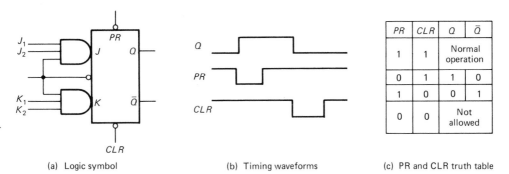

PR	CLR	Q	$\bar{Q}$
1	1	Normal operation	
0	1	1	0
1	0	0	1
0	0	Not allowed	

(a) Logic symbol   (b) Timing waveforms   (c) PR and CLR truth table

Figure 1.23. The universal flipflop.

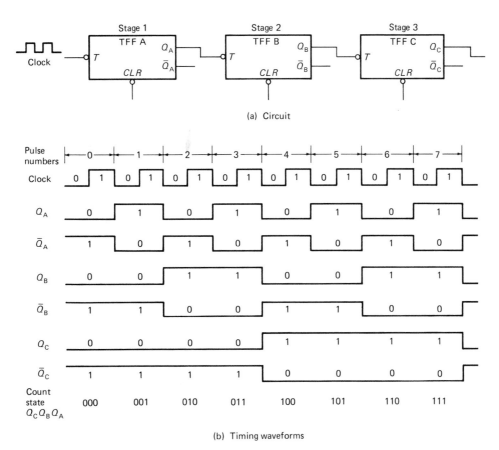

(a) Circuit

(b) Timing waveforms

Figure 1.24. The binary ripple counter. (From Morris E. Levine, *Digital Theory and Practice Using Integrated Circuits,* © 1978, p. 167. Reprinted by permission of Prentice-Hall, Inc.)

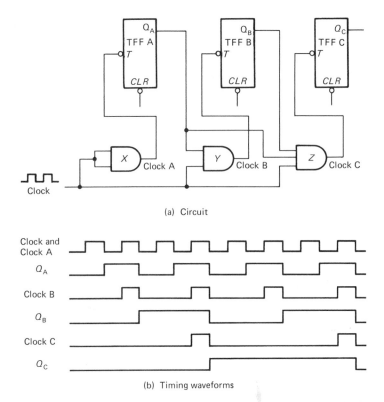

(a) Circuit

(b) Timing waveforms

Figure 1.25. The binary synchronous counter. (From Morris E. Levine, *Digital Theory and Practice Using Integrated Circuits,* © 1978, p. 172. Reprinted by permission of Prentice-Hall, Inc.)

The Binary Synchronous Counter

In the binary ripple counter the progressive delay in data propagation down the counter, because of the transistor switching time, leads to undesired glitches (noise) and decoding failures when coincidences between the stage counts are required. To overcome these undesirable effects, the **binary synchronous counter** (Figure 1.25) is used. It acts to gate the clock into each of the stages at the same time so that the stages change state simultaneously.

Properties of Binary Counters

For *n* stages:

1. The Q levels count up in binary from $0000 \ldots 0_n$ to $1111 \ldots 1_n$ (0 to $2^n - 1$).
2. The $\overline{Q}$ levels count down from $1111 \ldots 1_n$ to $0000 \ldots 0_n$ in binary.

3. The period, p, at the k'th stage $= 2^k \times p_{clock}$.
4. The frequency, f, at the k'th stage $= f \div 2^k$.
5. There are 2^n count states.

EXAMPLE 1.17. A 7 stage binary counter has a clock frequency of 1.28 MHz. What is its output frequency and its maximum count?

SOLUTION:

$$2^7 = 128$$

$$f_{out} = f_{clock} \div 128 = 1.28 \times 10^6 \div 128 = 10,000 \text{ Hz}$$

$$\text{Maximum count} = 111\ 1111_2 = 127_{10}$$

MOD-N Counter

When it is desired to obtain frequency division by other than a binary value, or to count in a sequence other than direct binary, sequential counters are built using *R-S* or

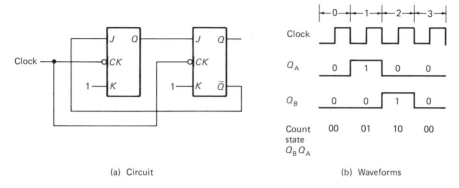

(a) Circuit   (b) Waveforms

Figure 1.26. A MOD-3 counter.

J-K clocked FFs. Their next state is controlled by R-S or J-K inputs whose levels are determined by the current state.

Figure 1.26 illustrates a MOD-3 ($N = 3$) counter. In MOD-N terminology, symbol N means that there are N count states and that the output frequency equals the input frequency divided by N. Because the count capability of an n stage binary counter is $2^n - 1$, a MOD-N counter requires n stages.

$$2^n > N > 2^{n-1} \qquad (1.10)$$

To build an MOD-N counter, it is necessary that count states be omitted. The counter can be realized by any combination or sequence of count states as determined by Eq. 1.10 and $2^n - N$. In general, the designer designs for component economy. In the MOD-3 counter of Figure 1.26, there are three count states and $f_B = f_{clock} \div 3$. One count state, 11, which occurs in the second stage, is omitted in this design. It is possible that during startup, or the generation of noise, the counter may get into such an undesired state. With a correct design the counter will recover into the correct sequence within a few counts. If it does not recover, steps must be taken in the design to ensure that the counter cannot ever get into an unrecoverable, unwanted, sequence.

MOD-N Counter: MOD-10.

As presented in Figure 1.27, the MOD-10 (decade) counter counts up in the normal binary sequence from 0 to 9 (0000 to 1001) and repeats; it is therefore called an **NBCD** or, more commonly, a **BCD counter.** (NBCD = natural binary coded decimal; BCD = binary coded decimal.) The term BCD is not truly correct; there are many other ways of building MOD 10 counters which have binary coded decimal sequences as well. The MOD-10 counter is also called an

8421 counter because it can be shown that if D = 8, C = 4, B = 2, and A = 1, the sum of the count states weighted in this manner yields correct decimal values. Numerous other weighted decimal counters have been developed, but the counter of Figure 1.27 has become quite popular as the IC type 54/7490 counter. There are six unwanted states: 1010 to 1111. As is seen from the count sequence diagram (Figure 1.27c), should they occur, the counter self-recovers within one or two counts.

1.9 SHIFT REGISTERS AND SHIFT COUNTERS

A **shift register** is a sequential series of FFs whose state, after the application of a shift pulse, is controlled by, and has the same level, as do adjacent FFs. The shift register has many applications:

1. Shifting data one position right or left.
2. Data transmission:
   a. Conversion of parallel data to serial data.
   b. Conversion of serial data to parallel data.
   c. Change serial data rate (buffering).
   d. Temporary data storage.
3. Controlled delay of data.
4. Circulating shift register for data refresh.
5. Pulse counter.
6. Element of stack or push-pull memory.

Static Shift Register with R-S, J-K, or D FFs

This is a common configuration that has all the properties just listed. It is composed of successive R-S, J-K, or D clocked FFs as shown in Figure 1.28. In this shift register:

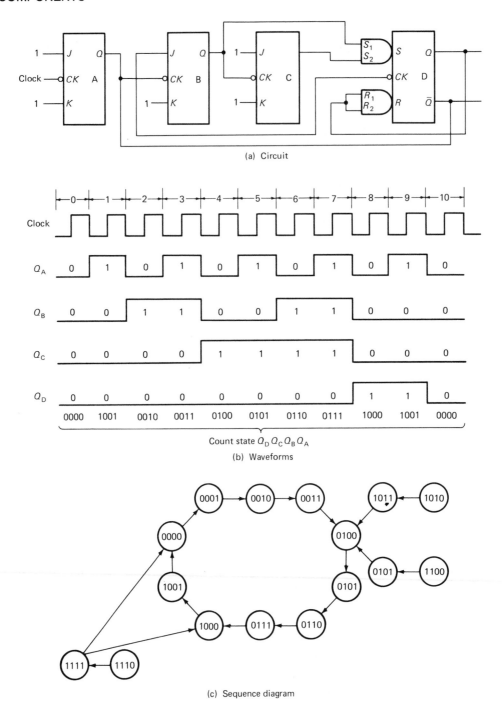

(a) Circuit

(b) Waveforms

(c) Sequence diagram

Figure 1.27. A MOD-10 (decimal) counter. (From Morris E. Levine, *Digital Theory and Practice Using Integrated Circuits*, © 1978, pp. 184, 186. Reprinted by permission of Prentice-Hall, Inc.)

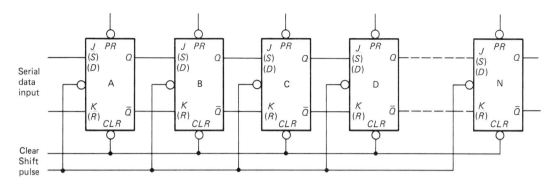

Figure 1.28. A static shift register employing *R-S*, *J–K*, or *D* flipflops.

1. Serial data can be inputted at J_A-K_A.
2. Serial data can be outputted at Q_N-$\overline{Q}_N$.
3. Parallel data can be inputted at the *PR* inputs.
4. Parallel data can be outputted at the *Q* outputs.
5. Buffering can be obtained by inputting the register serially at J_A-K_A at one clock rate and outputting it serially at Q_N-$\overline{Q}_N$ at a different clock rate.
6. Data can be stored temporarily in the register in either serial or parallel form or any combination of both.
7. Data is delayed from input to output by *N* times the clock period.
8. By connecting the output Q_N-$\overline{Q}_N$ to the input J_A-K_A, a circulating shift register is realized. It can be used both to store data and to circulate it to the output at periodic intervals for refresh applications and data storage.
9. With only one stage of the circulating shift register at a logic level different from all other stages, the shift register can be used as a self-decoding pulse (clock) counter.
10. If the outputs are cross-connected to the input (Q_N to K_A, $\overline{Q}_N$ to J_A), the shift register becomes the twisted-ring, or Johnson, counter which divides the clock frequency by 2*N*.

Two Phase PMOS Dynamic Shift Register

Figure 1.29 shows a **two phase dynamic shift register** element made with **PMOS technology.** MOS technology

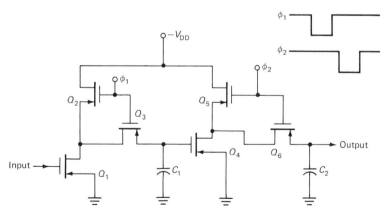

Figure 1.29. Two phase dynamic MOS shift register. (From Morris E. Levine, *Digital Theory and Practice Using Integrated Circuits,* © 1978, p. 211. Reprinted by permission of Prentice-Hall, Inc.)

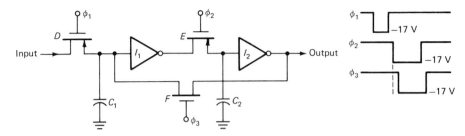

Figure 1.30. A MOS static shift register. (From Morris E. Levine, *Digital Theory and Practice Using Integrated Circuits*, © 1978, p., 212. Reprinted by permission of Prentice-Hall, Inc.)

lends itself to fabrication with small silicon units and large scale repetitive elements. In this shift register, capacitors C_1 and C_2 are **parasitic capacitors** associated with Q_3 and Q_6. Transistors Q_1-Q_2 form an inverter. When ϕ_1 goes negative, Q_2 and Q_3 are enabled and C_1 is charged to the invert of the input. A short time later, the inverter Q_4-Q_5 and Q_6 are enabled by ϕ_2, charging C_2 to the input level. Because of internal leakages, the charges on C_1 and C_2 slowly diminish. Hence the data must be periodically refreshed. Such shift registers operate at frequencies between 10 KHz and 5 MHz.

MOS Static Shift Register

Figure 1.30 shows an **MOS static shift register.** At high frequencies the two phases, ϕ_1 and ϕ_2, make it operate like the dynamic shift register of Figure 1.29. This phase ϕ_3 is generated on-chip and transistor F is enabled, completing a path to make a cross-coupled bistable similar to Figure 1.17, the basic bistable. Shift registers of this type lend themselves to economy of chip area, repetitiveness, and require very low power to operate.

Compatability of *n*-Channel and *p*-Channel MOS

When MOS shift registers were first developed, *p*-channel technology was available and *n*-channel technology was not. The shift registers of Figures 1.27 and 1.28 are not compatible with the IC logic families in common use, such as TTL and CMOS. This can be overcome with a shift in the voltage levels at which the registers operate (between +5 and −12 volts instead of between 0 and −17 volts) or by means of level converters. More recently, NMOS, which is compatible with the common IC

logic families, has been developed and NMOS shift registers (and memories) have become available.

1.10 PULSE GENERATORS: THE SCHMITT TRIGGER

Self-Repetitive Pulse Generators

Pulse generators for digital systems most frequently are of the astable multivibrator form. They generate waveforms that shift repetitively between logic 1 and logic 0. Basically they consist of two inverters self-driven alternately between cutoff and saturation without the need for external triggering, except possibly for synchronization. Several forms are illustrated in Figure 1.31.

In Figure 1-31a, the two transistor free-running multivibrator is shown. The period is given by:

$$T \approx 0.7(R_{B_1}C_1 + R_{B_2}C_2) \text{ s} \qquad (1.11)$$

In the symmetrical multivibrator $R_{B_1} = R_{B_2} = R_B$ and $C_1 = C_2 = C$. Then,

$$T \approx 1.4(RC) \text{ s} \qquad (1.12)$$

EXAMPLE 1.18. Determine the period and frequency of a free-running multivibrator in which $R_{B_1} = 10 \text{ k}\Omega$, $R_{B_2} = 20 \text{ k}\Omega$, $C_1 = 0.1 \text{ }\mu\text{F}$, and $C_2 = 0.2 \text{ }\mu\text{F}$.

SOLUTION:

$$T \approx 0.7(10,000 \times 0.1 \times 10^{-6}$$
$$+ 20,000 \times 0.2 \times 10^{-6}) \text{ s}$$
$$\approx 3.5 \times 10^{-3} \text{ s} = 3.5 \text{ ms}$$
$$f \approx 1/T = 280 \text{ Hz}$$

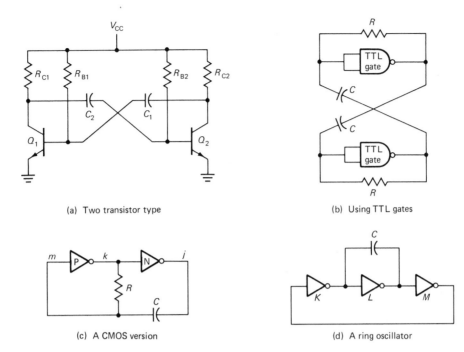

(a) Two transistor type

(b) Using TTL gates

(c) A CMOS version

(d) A ring oscillator

Figure 1.31. Astable (free running) generators. (From Morris E. Levine, *Digital Theory and Practice Using Integrated Circuits,* © 1978, pp. 220, 227. Reprinted by permission of Prentice-Hall, Inc.

EXAMPLE 1.19. Repeat Ex. 1.18 but for the symmetrical multivibrator in which $R = 10$ kΩ and $C = 0.2$ μ F.

SOLUTION:

$$T \approx 1.4(10{,}000 \times 0.2 \times 10^{-6})$$

$$\approx 2.8 \times 10^{-3} \text{ s}$$

$$f \approx 1/T = 350 \text{ Hz}$$

Figure 1.31b shows a free-running TTL gate (such as the 7400) used in an astable multivibrator. Resistors R are voltage feedback biasing resistors which put the gates into the active region. The gates are cross-coupled through capacitor C to form an ac regenerative pair.

Figure 1.31c shows an astable multivibrator which functions well with CMOS logic. The circuit acts to charge and discharge C, switching as the threshold voltage (approximately one-half the supply voltage) is crossed. In this circuit,

$$T \approx 1.4(RC) \text{ s} \qquad (1.13)$$

Figure 1.31d is a circuit consisting of three inverters and is called the **ring oscillator.** The frequency is determined by the switching time of the inverters and the time needed to charge and discharge capacitor C.

The oscillators shown in Figure 1.31 do not have particularly good frequency stability with respect to variations in the power supply voltage and in temperature. For greater stability, quartz crystal stabilized oscillators are used.

The Monostable

The **monostable** is a circuit configuration which generates a single pulse of predetermined time upon application of a triggering pulse. Whereas the bistable fundamentally consists of two inverter gates cross-dc-coupled, and the astable two gates ac coupled, the monostable has one connection dc coupled and the other ac coupled.

Integrated circuits have been developed to generate these single pulses. They are available in two basic types:

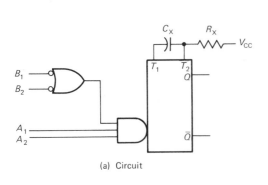

(a) Circuit

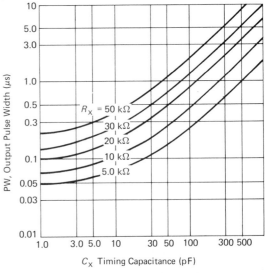

C_X Timing Capacitance (pF)

(b) Output pulse vs. timing capacitor

Figure 1.32. A retrigerable IC monostable MV, type 8601/9601. (From Morris E. Levine, *Digital Theory and Practice Using Integrated Circuits,* © 1978, pp. 234, 235. Reprinted by permission of Prentice-Hall, Inc.)

1. Nonretriggerable (54/74121).
2. Retriggerable (9601/8601).

In the nonretriggerable type, pulse triggering occurs at a set input voltage level and is not related to the rise time of the input pulse. Once fired, the outputs are independent of input changes. The time of the pulse is determined by the external R and C components. In the retriggerable type, the pulse width is also determined by external R and C, but it can be retriggered by a new input pulse. Figure 1.32a is the logic diagram of the retriggerable IC type 9601/8601. Figure 1.32b gives the time of the output pulse for small values of C_X. For large values of C_X, the time is given by Eq. 1.14. For $C_X > 1000$ pF,

$$T = 0.32\, R_X C_X \left(1 + \frac{0.7}{R_X}\right) \text{ ns} \qquad (1.14)$$

where $R_X = $ kΩ and $C_X = $ pF

The 555 Timer

The **555 timer** is an integrated circuit that can be used as an astable or as a monostable multivibrator. It has many applications in digital systems and has attained great popularity. It has excellent frequency stability with respect to power supply variation. The circuit acts to charge and discharge an external capacitor between ground, $\frac{1}{3}V_{CC}$ and $\frac{2}{3}V_{CC}$ (where V_{CC} is the supply voltage), depending upon the application, with time determined by external resistors. It has good output driving capability and can sink up to 200 mA; its diagram is shown in Figure 1.33a.

1. Monostable operation, Figure 1.33b. Capacitor C charges through timing resistor R_A up to $\frac{2}{3}V_{CC}$, and then is discharged. The monostable time is given by

$$T = 1.1(RC) \text{ s} \qquad (1.15)$$

where R is in ohms and C is in farads.

2. Astable operation, Figure 1.33c. The capacitor charges through R_A and R_B to $\frac{2}{3}V_{CC}$ and then is dis-

Figure 1.33. The 555 timer. (From Morris E. Levine, *Digital Theory and Practice Using Integrated Circuits,* © 1978, p. 237. Reprinted by permission of Prentice-Hall, Inc.)

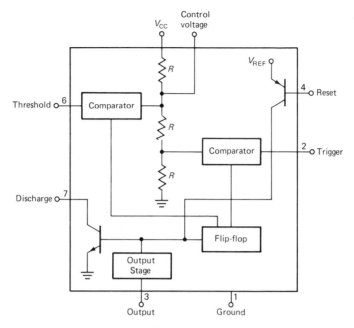

Control
voltage

V_{CC}

V_{REF}

4 Reset

Threshold 6

Comparator

R

R

R

Comparator

2 Trigger

Discharge 7

Flip-flop

Output
Stage

3
Output

1
Ground

(a) Internal circuit

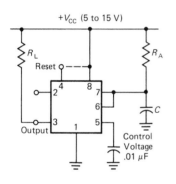

$+V_{CC}$ (5 to 15 V)

R_L

Reset

2

3
Output

4   8
         7
         6
1   5

R_A

C

Control
Voltage
.01 µF

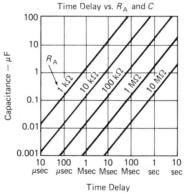

Time Delay vs. R_A and C

Capacitance — µF

R_A

1 kΩ
10 kΩ
100 kΩ
1 MΩ
10 MΩ

Time Delay

(b) Monostable operation

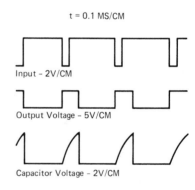

t = 0.1 MS/CM

Input – 2V/CM

Output Voltage – 5V/CM

Capacitor Voltage – 2V/CM

R_A = 9.1 kΩ, C = .01 µF, R_L = 1 kΩ

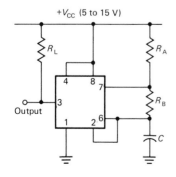

$+V_{CC}$ (5 to 15 V)

R_L

4   8
         7

3
Output

1   2   6

R_A

R_B

C

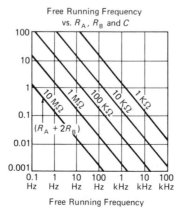

Free Running Frequency
vs. R_A, R_B and C

10 MΩ
1 MΩ
100 KΩ
10 KΩ
1 KΩ

$(R_A + 2R_B)$

Free Running Frequency

(c) Astable operation

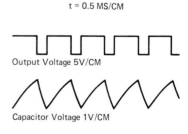

t = 0.5 MS/CM

Output Voltage 5V/CM

Capacitor Voltage 1V/CM

R_A = 4 kΩ, R_B = 3 kΩ, R_L = 1 kΩ

Figure 1.34. A 2 input NAND gate with Schmitt trigger.

charged to $\frac{1}{3}V_{CC}$ through R_B. The frequency, f, is given by

$$f = \frac{1}{T} = \frac{1.44}{(R_A + 2R_B)C} \text{ Hz} \qquad (1.15a)$$

and the duty cycle, D, by

$$D = \frac{\text{Time low}}{\text{Total time}} = \frac{R_B}{R_A + 2R_B} \qquad (1.16b)$$

The Schmitt Trigger

The **Schmitt trigger** is a regenerative circuit which triggers at a set input voltage level to provide a rapid change in output level, independent of the rise time of the input voltage. It is used to convert a slowly rising input voltage to a rapidly changing output voltage for system voltage conditioning standardization. The regenerative design makes the Schmitt trigger switch rapidly on both polarities of signals, upgoing and downgoing. Almost always there is a difference in level between upgoing and downgoing, giving a **hysteresis** property to the circuit, providing noise immunity and rejection. This is indicated by a hysteresis loop within a gate designed for Schmitt trigger functioning, as shown in Figure 1.34.

1.11 BINARY CODES

To interface between the everyday world and the world of the binary system, many sets of binary codes have been developed. Some of these are considered below.

NBCD, BCD, 8421

BCD (or NBCD or 8421) is a 4-bit code for representing the decimal numbers 0 to 9. It counts in the natural binary sequence from 0 to 9 (0000 to 1001). Decimal numbers when expressed in BCD have each digit expressed in its BCD equivalent. This makes it much easier to decode when compared with direct binary representation.

EXAMPLE 1.20. Express 943.27 in BCD code.

SOLUTION:

$$\underbrace{9}_{1001} \ \underbrace{4}_{0100} \ \underbrace{3}_{0011} \ . \ \underbrace{2}_{0010} \ \underbrace{7}_{0111}$$

While direct binary arithmetic is not possible in BCD, errors can be easily detected and corrections made.

Excess-3

Excess-3 is a 4 bit code for expressing the decimal numbers 0 to 9 in which the code values are 3 more than the BCD code of the previous section. The code for excess-3 is given in Table 1.15. No number in excess-3 has all 0s, which provides for error checking. The nines complements in decimal are ones complement in excess-3. This code is used in nines complement subtraction.

Ring Counter Code

Ring counter code is a 10 bit code in which only one bit differs from all the others. It is given in Table 1.16.

Parity Code

Parity code is an error checking code in which all numbers are transmitted with an even number of 1s (even parity) or an odd number of 1s (odd parity), as determined by the system design. In these codes, the character determines the code itself but an additional bit, the parity bit, is added (either a 1 or a 0) to convert the total coded character into one with the desired parity. An error in a single bit of a character during data transmission is detectable with a parity checker. Parity generators or checkers are shown in Figure 1.35.

Table 1.15. Excess-3 Code

Decimal	0	1	2	3	4	5	6	7	8	9
Excess-3	0011	0100	0101	0110	0111	1000	1001	1010	1011	1100

Table 1.16. The Ring Counter Code

Decimal	Ring Counter Code	Decimal	Ring Counter Code
0	10000 00000	5	00000 10000
1	01000 00000	6	00000 01000
2	00100 00000	7	00000 00100
3	00010 00000	8	00000 00010
4	00001 00000	9	00000 00001

The Gray Code

The **Gray code** is used on shift encoders, or positioners, to determine the angular location with a minimum of error.[*] This code changes at only one bit position in changing from one value to the next value. Multibit Gray shaft encoders (up to 15 bits) are used. Because $2^{14} = 4096$, it is possible to determine the angular position of a shaft within with an error no greater than $\pm 0.1°$.

$$\frac{360°}{4096} \approx 0.1°$$

The Gray code is provided in Table 1.17.

EXAMPLE 1.21. Convert 1001_2 to its Gray code equivalent.

[*]A card encoded with the Gray code is mounted on the shaft and its coded position is determined optically.

SOLUTION:

$$\text{Binary} \begin{array}{ccccc} \rightarrow(0) & 1 & 0 & 0 & 1 \\ \oplus & \oplus & \oplus & \oplus & \end{array}$$
$$\text{extra } 0$$
$$\quad 1 \quad 1 \quad 0 \quad 1 = 1101_{\text{Gray}}$$

Alphanumeric Codes

1. ASCII: *A*merican *S*tandard *C*ode for *I*nformation *E*xchange. A 7 bit code that can code 2^7 or 128 characters.
2. EBCDIC: *E*xtended *B*inary *C*ode for *D*ecimal *I*nter-change. An 8 bit code that can code 2^8 or 256 characters.

1.12 DECODING AND ENCODING

Decoding

To recover information sent in binary coded form, it is necessary to decode it. This is essentially an AND function with the binary coded data providing the inputs to the AND gate. A coded 1 is a direct input to the AND and a coded 0 is an inverted input to the AND gate.

For example, suppose we have a three stage binary counter, with stages A, B and C, and it is desired to decode (have a separate and unique pulse) at each of the count states or count intervals. The circuit diagram of the counter is given in Figure 1.36a. The decoding and gates are provided in Figure 1.36b and the waveforms and decoding in Figure 1.36c.

In MOD-N counters, where unused states exist, it is

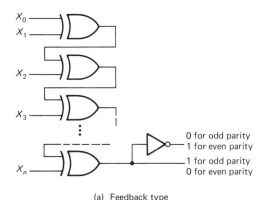

(a) Feedback type

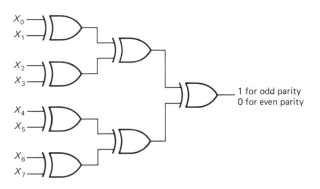

(b) Tree type

Figure 1.35. Examples of parity generators/checkers.

Table 1.17. 4 Bit Gray Code

Decimal	Gray	Decimal	Gray	Decimal	Gray	Decimal	Gray
0	0000	4	0110	8	1100	12	1010
1	0001	5	0111	9	1101	13	1011
2	0011	6	0101	10	1111	14	1001
3	0010	7	0100	11	1110	15	1000

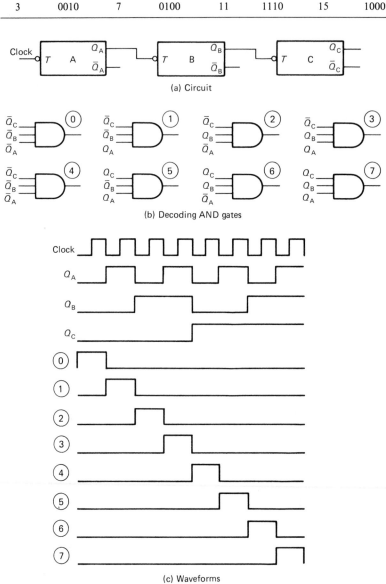

Figure 1.36. Decoding a 3 stage binary counter. (From Morris E. Levine, *Digital Theory and Practice Using Integrated Circuits,* © 1978, p. 267. Reprinted by permission of Prentice-Hall, Inc.)

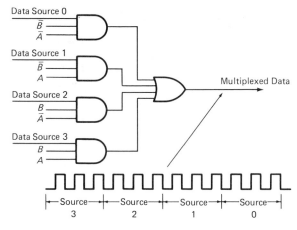

Figure 1.37. A 4 line multiplexer. (From Morris E. Levine, *Digital Theory and Practice Using Integrated Circuits,* © 1978, p. 267. Reprinted by permisson of Prentice-Hall, Inc.)

possible to make use of this information as a "don't care" condition and assigning it a 1 or 0 and then using this level to minimize the decoding. The Karnaugh map helps greatly with 4 bit codes. When this technique is used, fewer than four input gates are required to decode many of the counts of a BCD counter (Fig. 1.26) despite the four FFs. The five stage twisted-ring counter can be decoded with ten 2-input AND gates, one for each of its wanted count states, despite having five stages and at first appearance requiring ten 2-input AND gates.

Encoding

This is the opposite of decoding and is required in code forming or code conversion. This is fundamentally an OR operation, as illustrated in Ex. 1.22.

EXAMPLE 1.22. X is an arbitrary 2 bit code. Convert it to Y, an arbitrary 3 bit code.

X	Y	
	AB	CDE
1	11	100
2	01	001
3	00	011
4	10	111

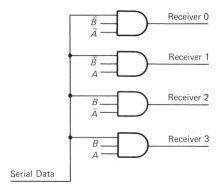

Figure 1.38. A demultiplexer. (From Morris E. Levine, *Digital Theory and Practice Using Integrated Circuits,* © 1978, p. 267. Reprinted by permission of Prentice-Hall, Inc.)

SOLUTION:

$$C = 1 + 4 = AB + A\overline{B} = A$$
$$D = 3 + 4 = \overline{A}\,\overline{B} + A\overline{B} = \overline{B}$$
$$E = 2 + 3 + 4 = \overline{A}B + \overline{A}\,\overline{B} + A\overline{B} = \overline{A} + \overline{B}$$

1.13 MULTIPLEXING AND DEMULTIPLEXING

Multiplexing

When one desires to time-share more than one data-stream on a single transmission line, the process is called **multiplexing.** In accomplishing this, separate time slots are separated by decoding and the decoded time slots are used to gate in the data sources successively. This process is shown in Figure 1.37 for a four message system.

Demultiplexing

Demultiplexing is the reverse of multiplexing in that the messages are separated and sent to their appropriate destinations. This process is shown in Figure 1.38.

REFERENCES

Bartee, T. D., *Digital Computer Fundamentals,* 4th Ed. New York: McGraw-Hill Book Co., 1977.

Flores, I., *Computer Logic.* Englewood Cliffs, NJ: Prentice-Hall, 1960.

Greenfield, J. D., *Practical Digital Design Using ICs.* New York: John Wiley and Sons, 1977.

IEEE Standard Graphic Symbols for Logic Diagrams. (Two-state devices) IEEE State 91-1973; (ANSI Y 32.14-1973) Aug. 1973.

Kaufman, M., and A. H. Seidman, *Handbook of Electronics Calculations for Engineers and Technicians.* New York: McGraw-Hill Book Co., 1979. Chapter 13.

Kline, R. M., *Digital Computer Design.* Englewood Cliffs, NJ: Prentice-Hall, 1977.

Levine, M. E., *Digital Theory and Practice Using Integrated Circuits.* Englewood Cliffs, NJ: Prentice-Hall, 1978.

Marcus, M. P., *Switching Circuits for Engineers.* Englewood Cliffs, NJ: Prentice-Hall, 1975.

Nagle, H. T., B. D. Carroll, and J. D. Irwin, *An Introduction to Computer Logic.* Englewood Cliffs, NJ: Prentice-Hall, 1975.

Peatman, J. B., *The Design of Digital Systems,* New York: McGraw-Hill Book Co., 1972.

2
IC Logic Families

Morris E. Levine

The College of Staten Island
The City University of New York

Arthur H. Seidman

Pratt Institute

2.1 INTRODUCTION

Chapter 1 discusses many different logic functions. When digital electronics was in its infancy, these logic functions were implemented with discrete components: resistors, capacitors, vacuum tubes and transistors. The concept of integrating components into a single unit always existed, but was not practically feasible until the silicon planar transistor was invented. Only then did it become possible to manufacture many transistors and resistors simultaneously in a common substrate of silicon and to interconnect them. At first, these circuits were simple and resembled the circuits which had been successfully used with discrete devices. With improvements in metallurgy and manufacturing techniques, new, improved, and more complex circuits were developed with continuously improved performance.

2.2 CHOICE OF A LOGIC FAMILY

To solve the problems in the use and application of **integrated circuits (ICs)**, different families of logic circuits have been developed. These include **transistor transistor logic (TTL, T²L)**, **complementary MOSFET logic (CMOS)**, **emitter coupled logic (ECL)**, and **integrated injection logic (IIL, I²L)**. In the design of circuits and systems employing integrated circuits, the following factors have to be considered in the selection of a logic family:

1. Availability of logic functions in the family.
2. Complex functions available.
3. Power supply voltage and stability.
4. Single or multiple power supplies.
5. Power dissipation.
6. Propagation delay.
7. Logic swing.
8. Noise immunity.
9. Noise generation.
10. Interfacing with other families.
11. Cost.
12. Temperature range.
13. Wired-collector logic capability.
14. Fan-in.
15. Fan-out.
16. Cross-coupling.
17. Output source and sink current capability.
18. Speed-power product.

2.3 DEFINITIONS

Some definitions of important terms used in characterizing IC logic families are provided in this section.

Saturated and Nonsaturated Operation

In logic families employing **bipolar junction transistors (BJTs)**, such as transistor transistor logic, transistors may operate with both the collector-base and base-emitter junctions forward biased when conducting current (ON). This is illustrated in Figure 2.1a for an *npn* transistor. The collector-base junction is forward biased because the *n* collector region is negative with respect to the *p* base region. Similarly, the base-emitter junction is forward biased since the *p* base is positive with respect to the *n* emitter. A transistor in this condition is said to be operated as a **saturated switch.**

Because the collector-base and base-emitter junctions are forward biased, charge (electrons for an *npn* transistor) is emitted from both the emitter *and* collector into the base region when the transistor is ON (conducting current). When the transistor is turned off, the charge stored in the base must be removed. This takes a finite time, called *storage time*. As a result, a decrease in the rate (operating speed) of switching the transistor on and off exists.

Operating as a **nonsaturated switch,** the collector-base junction is reverse biased and the base-emitter junction is forward biased when the transistor is conducting current (Figure 2.1b). This results in a faster operating speed than possible with a saturated switch.

Propagation Delay

When an input signal is applied to a gate, the output signal is delayed in time. This behavior stems primarily from the inherent delays in the transistor (e.g., storage time) and from the distributed circuit and load capacitance.

As an example, a typical response, v_{out}, of an inverter to an input pulse, v_{in}, with finite rise and fall times is illustrated in Figure 2.2. The output pulse is delayed with

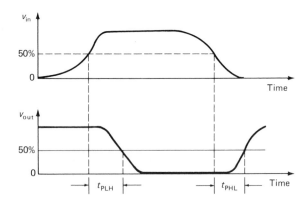

Figure 2.2. Defining propagation delay, t_{PD}.

respect to the input pulse. Specifying the delay times with respect to the 50% points of the leading and trailing edges of the input and output waveforms, t_{PHL} is the time delay for a high at the input to a low at the output of the transistor. Similarly, t_{PLH} is the time delay from a low at the input to a high at the output. The propagation delay, t_{PD}, is defined as the average of t_{PHL} and t_{PLH}:

$$t_{PD} = (t_{PHL} + t_{PLH})/2 \qquad (2.1)$$

Power-Delay Product

The power-delay product (also called the *speed-power product*) is a figure of merit that may be used in comparing different logic families. The power-delay product is equal to the product of the propagation delay, t_{PD}, and the power dissipated (usually under static conditions) in the gate, P_D:

$$\text{power-delay product} = t_{PD}P_D \text{ joules} \qquad (2.2)$$

Generally, a gate with a low value of propagation delay has a high value of power dissipation, and vice versa.

Fan-In

The fan-in of a gate is the number of inputs that may be applied to the gate. For example, the NAND gate in Figure 2.3a has a fan-in of 4. The fan-in is limited by input capacitance and the leakage current of the input transistors.

Fan-Out

The fan-out of a gate is the maximum number of similar gates that a gate can drive. For example, Figure 2.3b

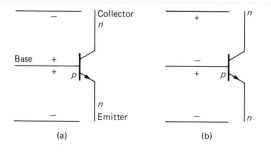

Figure 2.1. Transistor biasing for (a) saturated and (b) nonsaturated operation.

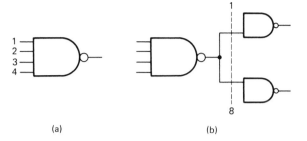

Figure 2.3. An example of a NAND gate having a (a) fan-in of 4 and (b) fan-out of 8.

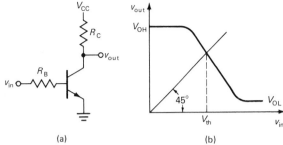

Figure 2.4. Determining noise immunity of an inverter. (a) Circuit. (b) Transfer characteristic.

shows a gate having a fan-out of 8. Fan-out is limited by the maximum current the driving transistor can handle and by load capacitance.

If current flows in the driving transistor during fan out, the driving transistor acts as a **current sink.** If no current flows in the driving transistor, it acts like a **current source.**

Noise Immunity

Logic gates and systems can be disturbed by unwanted signals or noise. These signals appear as a result of electromagnetic or electrostatic coupling to the interconnecting paths within the system. They also appear as a result of power supply variations or as a result of large currents that cause excessive voltage drops in the system interconnections. In the case of gates, this "noise" voltage can cause a momentary undesired logic level. The effect on flipflops is that an undesired state can be developed. For counters, undesired count states can exist. In the case of shift registers and memories, incorrect data can be stored.

The ability of a logic gate or family to reject noise is expressed as **noise immunity,** or **noise margin,** in volts. In the simplest case, its magnitude is determined by the difference between the input voltage level, V_{th} (threshold voltage), at which the gate output transfers between its high output level, V_{OH}, and low output level, V_{OL}.

Figure 2.4 shows a simple transistor inverter and its *transfer characteristic,* which is a plot of the output voltage, v_{out}, as a function of input voltage, v_{in}. The **threshold voltage,** V_{th} is defined as the voltage at which $v_{in} = v_{out}$. It is obtained by drawing a 45 degree line from the origin. The intersection of this line with the transfer curve, in the rapidly changing transition section of the curve, is V_{th}.

If the inverter of Figure 2.4a drives a second inverter, the ability of the coupled inverters to reject noise depends upon the difference in the voltage level of the first inverter

and the threshold voltage:

$$\text{High level noise immunity} = V_{OH} - V_{th} \quad (2.3)$$

$$\text{Low level noise immunity} = V_{th} - V_{OL} \quad (2.4)$$

In the more general cases concerning guaranteed worst-case noise margins for a logic family, one has to consider the following factors in the inverter circuit (similar considerations apply to other circuits in the various IC logic families):

1. That not all transistors have the same base-emitter turn-on voltage, and this voltage is a function of temperature.
2. Tolerance of base resistor, R_B.
3. That high output level V_{OH} can vary as the output sources additional inverters. Voltage V_{OH} under these conditions also is a function of the tolerance of the collector resistor, R_C.
4. That the low output level V_{OL}, which is the voltage representing a logic 0, is dependent upon the sink current the transistor may have to carry.

Noise margins are determined from the band diagram of Figure 2.5, the following definitions apply:

$V_{OH(min)} = $ minimum output voltage

    the gate accepts as a logic 1   (2.5)

$V_{IH(min)} = $ minimum input voltage

    the gate accepts as a logic 1   (2.6)

$V_{OL(max)} = $ maximum output voltage

    the gate accepts as a logic 0   (2.7)

$V_{IL(max)} = $ maximum input voltage

    the gate accepts as a logic 0   (2.8)

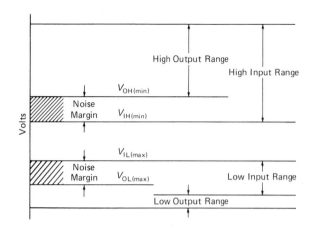

Figure 2.5. Band diagram for determining noise margin.

From Figure 2.5, we can write

High level noise margin $= V_{OH(min)} - V_{TH(min)}$ (2.9)

Low level noise margin $= V_{IL(max)} - V_{OL(max)}$ (2.10)

Wired Collector Logic

The connection shown in Figure 2.6, in which the outputs of two gates are wired together, is used quite frequently in logic systems. It provides a free extra level of logic, which is useful for multiplexing and memory expansion.

When the output of either inverter I or inverter II in Figure 2.6 is driven into saturation, the resultant low determines the level at point C, which also goes low. We can write a truth table in terms of D, E, and C and between A, B, and C, as indicated in Table 2.1. From the truth table, the following logic equations may be written:

$$C = \overline{C + E} \text{ (Nor function)} \quad (2.7)$$

$$C = AB \text{ (AND function)} \quad (2.8)$$

Table 2.1. Wired Collector Logic

D	E	A	B	C
0	0	1	1	1
0	1	1	0	0
1	0	0	1	0
1	1	0	0	0

From these equations, the connection in Figure 2.6 is known by various names such as wired-NOR, implied-AND, and dot-AND. To show that wired-collector logic is being used, the dashed-line logic symbol is superimposed at the junction point, as shown in Figure 2.7a and b.

Figure 2.7 assumes that the output impedance of the logic gate is high and that the connection between the two gates can be made safely. For some logic families with low output impedances (TTL totem-pole output and CMOS), this is not possible. In such a case, two techniques are available to permit wired-collector logic.

1. Gates are available with open, or bare, collectors. To obtain wired-collector logic, the collectors are tied together and a common load resistor is connected to the supply voltage.
2. Tri-state logic gates are available. These gates have three states: the standard 0 and 1 and a third state which disengages the gate from the system.

Tri-State Logic

In tri-state logic, the third state is an open circuit. A tri-state (or 3 state) device allows the connection of the outputs of devices in parallel without affecting circuit oper-

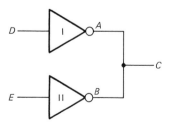

Figure 2.6. Wired collector logic.

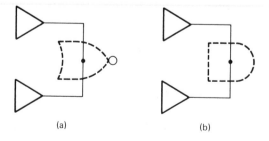

(a)   (b)

Figure 2.7. Wired collector logic symbols. (a) Wired-NOR. (b) Implied-AND.

ation. An example of a tri-state inverter and its truth table is provided in Figure 2.8. When the enable signal corresponds to logic 0, the circuit operates as a normal inverter: if v_{in} is a logic 0, v_{out} is a logic 1, and vice versa. If, however, the circuit is enabled (enable = 1), the output is an open circuit regardless of the states of the input signal.

2.4 TRANSISTOR TRANSISTOR LOGIC

Of the major families of logic in use, perhaps transistor transistor logic (TTL, T^2L) is the most widely used. The reasons for this popularity include the following:

1. Some hundreds of chips are available that provide such logic functions as NAND, NOT, counters and shift registers.
2. The cost of chips is relatively low.
3. There are many manufacturers making TTL chips.
4. With the various available versions of TTL, switching speeds from 20 MHz to 125 MHz are available.

There are two major series of TTL chips: the 5400 and 7400 series. The 5400 series is designed for military applications in which the operating temperature ranges from $-55°C$ to $+125°C$. In commercial applications, the 7400 series is used; its operating range is from $0°C$ to $+70°C$. Some typical logic functions are summarized in Table 2.2.

The majority of TTL chips are available in a 14 and 16 pin dual-in-line package (DIP). A few chips, such as a 1 of 16 data selector (54/74150), are available in a 24 pin package. An example of a 14 pin package and its pin outs for the 54/7400 quad 2 input NAND gate is illustrated in Figure 2.9.

Standard TTL

The schematic of a standard TTL 2 input NAND gate and its truth table are illustrated in Figure 2.10. Satu-

Table 2.2. Typical TTL Logic Functions

Logic Function	Part Number
Quad 2 input NAND gate	54/7400
Quad 2 input NOR gate	54/7402
Hex inverter	54/7404
Quad 2 input AND gate	54/7408
8 input NAND gate	54/7430
BCD to 7 segment decoder-driver	54/7447
Dual JK flipflop	54/7476
4 bit full adder	54/7483
Decade counter	54/7490
5 bit shift register	54/7496

rated logic is used and the power supply is fixed at $+5$ V. Input transistor Q_1 is a multiemitter transistor where each emitter and the base acts like a diode.

If input A and/or B is at a logic zero (maximum value of voltage corresponding to a logic 0 in TTL is 0.8 V), the base of Q_1 is at a maximum of 0.7 V (base-emitter voltage) plus 0.8 V (maximum value for a logic 0), or 1.5 V. To turn on Q_3, 2.1 V is required (0.7 V for the base-collector junction of Q_1, and 0.7 V each for the base-emitter junctions of Q_2 and Q_3). Transistor Q_3 is therefore OFF and Q_4 is ON; this corresponds to a logic 1 at the output.

When inputs A *and* B are both at a logic 1 (minimum value for a logic 1 in TTL is 2.4 V), the base emitter junctions of Q_1 are reverse biased. The base voltage of Q_1 now rises to 2.1 V, a sufficient voltage to turn Q_3 ON, which corresponds to a logic 0. Thus, the circuit functions as a NAND gate.

The output stage in Figure 2.10 is called a *totem pole amplifier*. During the transition from a logic 1 to a logic 0, or vice versa, a high current flows in Q_3, Q_4, and diode D. (The purpose of the diode is to limit this transition

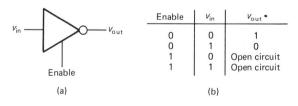

Enable	v_{in}	v_{out}
0	0	1
0	1	0
1	0	Open circuit
1	1	Open circuit

(a)　　　　　　　　(b)

Figure 2.8. Example of tri-state inverter. (a) Logic symbol. (b) Truth table.

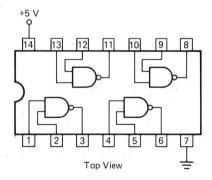

Top View

Figure 2.9. Pin connections for a 54/7400 quad 2 input NAND gate in a dual-in-line package (DIP).

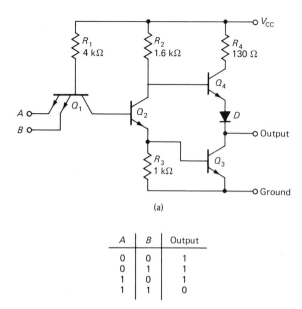

(a)

A	B	Output
0	0	1
0	1	1
1	0	1
1	1	0

(b)

Figure 2.10. Standard TTL 2 input NAND gate. (a) Circuit. (b) Truth table.

current.) Owing to the high transition current, often called a *current spike,* it is necessary to connect a bypass capacitor from the +5 V terminal to ground to minimize line noise. Generally, a small disc capacitor with short leads in the range of from 0.01 to 0.1 μF is used for this purpose.

Wire dotting with a totem pole output is not permitted. Instead, an open-collector version of the gate is used, as illustrated in Figure 2.11. A pullup resistor, typically 2.2

kΩ, is connected between the open collector and the +5 V supply terminal.

To minimize noise, unused inputs of a gate should be "pulled up" by connecting them to the +5 V supply in series with a 1 KΩ resistor. Texas Instruments, a major manufacturer of such devices, recommends that no more than 25 unused inputs be connected to the same resistor.

High Speed TTL (HTTL)

If the resistance values in standard TTL (Figure 2.10) are reduced, high speed TTL (HTTL) is realized. The effect of reducing the resistance values in the circuit is to decrease the time needed to charge and discharge stray and load capacitances. The circuit logic is saturating and the low value resistances result in an increase in the power dissipation per gate.

An example of a HTTL 3 input NAND gate is given in Figure 2.12. In addition to the reduced resistance values, each input is connected to clamping diodes. This is necessary to reduce transmission line effects which can be a problem when the input signal has fast rise and fall times. The output stage uses a Darlington pair, comprised of transistors Q_3 and Q_4. This circuit improves gate speed and provides a low output impedance. HTTL chips are available with a full complement of gates and are pin compatible with standard TTL.

Schottky TTL (STTL)

Standard and high speed TTL circuits operate as saturated switches. In Schottky TTL, the transistors are prevented from saturating and the storage time is thereby

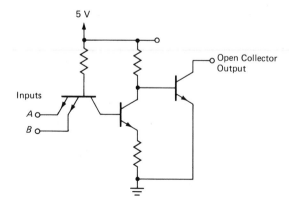

Figure 2.11. Simplified schematic of an open-collector 2 input NAND gate.

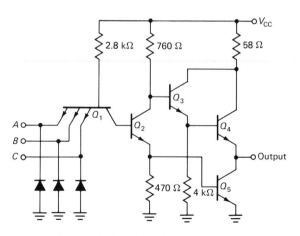

Figure 2.12. A HTTL 3 input NAND gate.

eliminated. To realize nonsaturation operation, the base-collector junction of transistors is clamped by a Schottky diode.

A **Schottky diode** is a diode having a metal semiconductor junction. It is a fast operating device and has a forward voltage drop of approximately 0.4 V. (For a *p-n* junction, such as a diode or a base-emitter junction of a transistor, the forward voltage drop is 0.7 V.) A Schottky diode connected across the collector and base of an *npn* transistor is illustrated in Figure 2.13a. This combination is easily fabricated in IC technology and the resultant device is called a *Schottky transistor* (Figure 2.13b). Saturation is avoided because some of the base current is shunted by the diode which conducts and clamps the collector-base junction by approximately 0.4 V. This voltage is too low for the collector to emit electrons into the base.

A Schottky 2 input NAND gate is shown in Figure 2.14. It is similar to HTTL but with all transistors replaced by Schottky transistors, except transistor Q_4. Because Q_4 never is allowed to saturate, there is no need to use a clamping diode. The input clamping diodes also have been replaced with Schottky diodes.

Low Power Schottky TTL (LSTTL)

Low power Schottky TTL (Figure 2.15) is similar to Schottky TTL except for the high value resistances used to reduce gate dissipation by a factor close to 10 over STTL. The propagation delay is only twice that of STTL. A comparison of the various families of TTL, including Fairchild's FAST transistor transistor logic, is provided in Table 2.3. The performance of advanced families of TTL are given in Table 2.4. The majority of advanced TTL is available in a full complement of logic functions.

Schmitt Trigger

There are occasions when an input signal to a gate is noisy. Owing to this noise, there is ambiguity when a gate

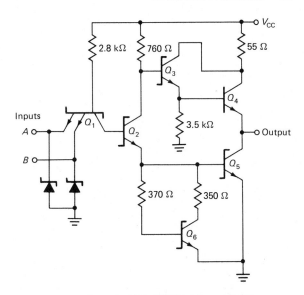

Figure 2.14. Schottky TTL (STTL) 2 input NAND gate.

switches on or off. This is illustrated in Figure 2.16a, where a noisy input pulse is impressed to 1 input of a 2 input NAND gate; the second input is maintained at a logic 1. The output, which switches on and off with the noise, is shown in Figure 2.16b.

A Schmitt trigger gate eliminates ambiguity in operation. The Schmitt trigger will not turn on until a specified positive threshold voltage, $V(+)$ is reached. Similarly, it will not turn off until the input voltage drops to a lower

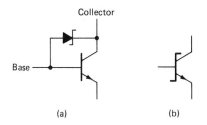

Figure 2.13. Nonsaturation operation. (a) Clamping collector-base junction with a Schottky diode. (b) Electrical symbol for a Schottky transistor.

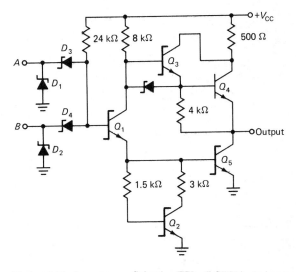

Figure 2.15. Low power Schottky TTL (LSTTL) 2 input NAND gate.

Table 2.3. TTL Family Comparisons

Logic Family Gates	Propagation Delay (ns)	Power Dissipation (mW)	Low Level Noise Margins (mV)	High Level Noise Margins (mV)
TTL 54/74 Standard series	t_{pLH}[b] 22 t_{pHL}[c] 15	110	400	400
HHTL, 54/74H	t_{pLH} 10 t_{pHL} 10	200	400	400
STTL, 54/74S	t_{pLH} 4.5 t_{pHL} 5.0	180	300	500
LSTTL, 54/74LS	t_{pLH} 10 t_{pHL} 10	22	300	500
FTTL,[a] 54/74F	t_{pLH} 4.0 t_{pHL} 3.5	51	300	500

[a]FTTL—Fairchild FAST TTL family.
[b]t_{pLH}—Propagation delay from low to high output transition.
[c]t_{pHL}—Propagation delay from high to low output transition.

Table 2.4. Advanced TTL Family Comparisons

Manufacturer	Family	Typical Power Per Gate (mW)	Typical Propagation Delay Per Gate (ns) 15 pF Load	50 pF Load	Typical Maximun Toggle Frequency (MHz)	Part Types To Be Built Initially	Initial Price Premium	Features
Fairchild Camera and Instrument Corp.	FAST	4	2	3	130	50 most popular standard-Schottky parts: 11 small-scale, the rest medium and large scale integrated	20% above Schottky	Isoplanar 11 process, Current-mirrored outputs for higher drive capability, Schottky-clamped inputs, Short circuit protection, Three-gain-stage gate designs
National Semiconductor Corp.	LS[2]	2	5–6	7–8	32	All low power Schottky	20% above low power Schottky	Higher noise immunity (800 mV)
Raytheon Co.	Advanced Schottky (54/74 AS)	20	1.5	2.2	200	Gates, flipflops, and MSI or standard Schottky	25% to 30% above Schottky	Higher output drive capability
Texas Instruments Inc.	Advanced Schottky (54/74 AS)	22	1.5	2.8	200	No exact duplication of standard Schottky—20 to 22 new arithmetic functions	15% to 30% above Schottky	Output current sink boosted to 40 mA in many parts, New 300-mil, 24 pin DIP, Ion implant, no diffusion, Low temperature coefficient
	Advanced low power Schottky (54/74 ALS)	1	4	6	50	25 popular SSI and MSI low power Schottky parts	15% to 30% above low power Schottky	Plug compatible with LS, new 300 mil, 24 pin DIP, all ion implant

Source: *Electronics.*

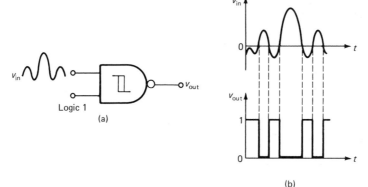

(b)

Figure 2.16. Effect of noise. (a) Noisy signal applied to a NAND gate. (b) Input and output waveforms.

threshold voltage, $V(-)$. The difference between $V(+)$ and $V(-)$ is called the *hysteresis voltage*. If a Schmitt trigger NAND gate (denoted by hysteresis symbol in Figure 2.17a) is used (dual 4 input, 54/7413), then there is no ambiguity in the output voltage as illustrated in Figure 2.17b. Also available are the Schmitt quad 2 input NAND gate (54/74132) and the hex Schmitt inverter (54/7414).

2.5 CMOS LOGIC

CMOS (Complementary Metal Oxide Semiconductor) logic, although not as fast as some of the other logic families, has several attractive features. These include

1. Operation over a wide voltage range, typically from +3 to +15 V.

2. Large fan-out capability.
3. Exhibits a noise margin which is approximately equal to one-half the supply voltage.
4. Does not create current spikes.
5. Dissipates nearly zero power under quiescent (unchanging signals) condition.
6. Low in cost.
7. Available in hundreds of logic function. (Some of these functions are summarized in Table 2.5.)

CMOS chips are available in 14, 16, and 24 pin dual-in-line packages, as they are for TTL.

Basic Structure

The basis for CMOS logic is the **enhancement mode metal oxide semiconductor field effect transistor (MOS-**

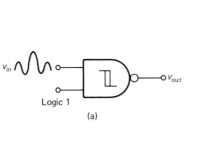

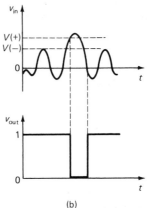

(a)

(b)

Figure 2.17. A Schmitt trigger NAND gate. (a) Circuit. (b) Input and output waveforms.

Table 2.5. Typical CMOS Logic Functions

Logic Function	Part Number
Quad 2 input NOR gate	4001
Quad 2 input NAND gate	4011
Dual 4 stage shift register	4015
14 stage ripple counter	4020
8 stage shift register	4021
Triple 3 input NAND gate	4023
Dual JK flipflop	4027
BCD to decimal converter	4028
Triple serial adder	4032

FET). A cross-sectional view and electrical symbol for an n-channel enhancement mode MOSFET are given in Figure 2.18. Referring to Figure 2.18a, two n regions are diffused into a p-type silicon substrate. The letter p indicates holes (positive charges) and the letter n indicates electrons (negative charges). Slightly overlapping the n regions is a thin layer of silicon dioxide (SiO_2), which acts as an insulator, or dielectric. On top of the SiO_2 layer a conductor, such as aluminum, is deposited. Leads connected to the n regions are called the source (S) and drain (D); a lead connected to the conductor is called the gate (G). Generally, the substrate is connected to the source.

In operation, the drain terminal is held positive with respect to the source terminal. If the gate is returned to the source, no current flows between the drain and source terminals. To allow current to flow, the gate is made positive with respect to the source. Because the gate-SiO_2-p region below the SiO_2 layer acts as a capacitor, electrons are induced (a channel of electrons is formed) in the region between the drain and source (Figure 2.18c). If the gate voltage is equal to, or greater than, the threshold voltage (a few volts), current flows.

The cross-sectional view and electrical symbol for a p-channel enhancement mode MOSFET are shown in Fig-

ure 2.19. For this device, the substrate is n-type and the diffused regions are p-type. In operation, the drain is held negative with respect to the source. For current to flow, the gate is made negative with respect to the source, and a channel of positive charges (holes) is induced between the source and drain (Figure 2.19c). If the gate is returned to the source, no drain current flows.

In the CMOS (complementary MOSFET) structure, the n- and p-channel enhancement MOSFETs are constructed in the same silicon chip, as illustrated in Figure 2.20. This structure is the basis for the INVERTER, and NOR and NAND gates. Owing to the high input resistance of a CMOS gate, static charge picked up by the gate, which acts as one plate of a capacitor, can build up. Eventually, the gate will be permanently damaged. To prevent this from happening, CMOS gate inputs are protected with diodes.

Inverter

The schematic of a CMOS inverter, truth table, and transfer characteristics are shown in Figure 2.21. When $v_{in} = 0$ V, corresponding to a logic 0, the p-channel MOSFET is ON (the gate-source voltage $= -V_{DD}$ volts) and the n-channel device is OFF; therefore, the output $= V_{DD}$ volts, which corresponds to a logic 1. When the input is V_{DD} volts, the p-channel gate-source voltage is equal to zero and is therefore OFF and the n-channel device is ON. Hence, $v_{out} = 0$ V (logic zero).

If the two MOSFETs were ideal, when one transistor is ON and the other is OFF, the current in the transistors would be zero, resulting in zero dissipation. Actually, a minute leakage current flows in the transistors.

When a signal is supplied to an inverter or gate, the power dissipation increases with frequency. This stems from the fact that across any gate, there is some capacitance, C. Capacitance C arises from stray and input ca-

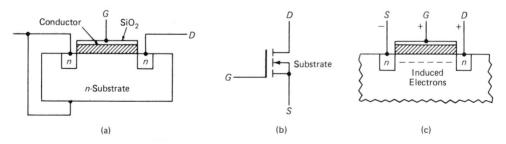

Figure 2.18. An n-channel enhancement mode MOSFET. (a) Cross-sectional view. (b) Electrical symbol. (c) Induced electrons.

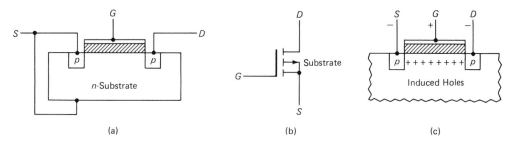

Figure 2.19. A p-channel enhancement mode MOSFET. (a) Cross-sectional view. (b) Electrical symbol. (c) Induced holes.

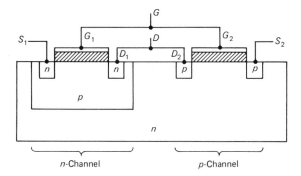

Figure 2.20. Cross-sectional view of the CMOS structure.

pacitances of other CMOS gates. The power dissipation, P_D is:

$$P_D = CV_{DD}^2 f \tag{2.9}$$

where V_{DD} is the drain supply voltage and f is the frequency of operation.

The transfer curve (a plot of output versus input voltage) indicates that the inverter changes state when $v_{in} = V_{DD}/2$ volts (Figure 2.21c). This is strictly true only if the p- and n-channel devices are perfectly matched. Whether the devices are perfectly matched or not, the noise margin of CMOS logic is superior to other logic families.

NOR Gate

The circuit of a 2 input CMOS NOR gate and its truth table are provided in Figure 2.22. Two n-channel MOS-FETs are in parallel and two p-channel MOSFETs are in series. If input A and/or B is at a logic 1, the n-channel devices are ON and the p-channel devices are OFF; the output, therefore, is at a logic 0. When A and B are both at a logic 0, the n-channel devices are OFF and the p-channel devices are ON; the output, therefore, is a logic 1.

The fan-in, for example, may be expanded to 3 by adding an n-channel device in parallel with Q_1 and Q_2 and a

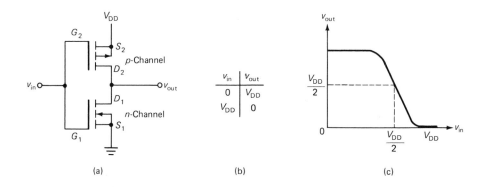

Figure 2.21. A CMOS inverter. (a) Circuit. (b) Truth table. (c) Transfer characteristics.

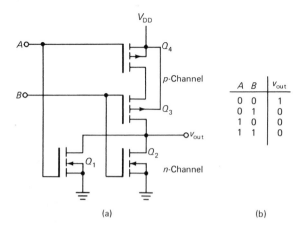

A	B	V_{out}
0	0	1
0	1	0
1	0	0
1	1	0

(a)   (b)

Figure 2.22. A 2 input CMOS NOR gate. (a) Circuit. (b) Truth table.

p-channel device in series with Q_3 and Q_4. The gates of the additional devices are connected to form a third input terminal, C.

NAND Gate

A 2 input NAND gate and its truth table are provided in Figure 2.23. In this circuit, the n-channel devices are in series and the p-channel devices are in parallel. If A and/or B is at a logic 0, the n-channel MOSFETs are OFF and the p-channel MOSFETs are ON; the output, therefore, is at a logic 1. If both A and B are at a logic 1, the

n-channel devices are ON and the p-channel devices are OFF; this yields a logic 0 at the output. Similar to the NOR gate, the fan-in may be expanded by adding n-channel MOSFETs in series and p-channel MOSFETs in parallel.

Transmission Gate

Unique to CMOS logic, the transmission gate of Figure 2.24 acts as a bilateral switch. When C is at a logic 1, the input is connected to the output; if C is at a logic 0, the input and output are disconnected. The transmission gate may be used for digital and analog signals.

Types of CMOS Logic

Three different types of CMOS logic are available. These are the A series, the B series, and the SOS (silicon on sapphire) devices. The A series is the common type of CMOS logic. It is inexpensive and has the greatest number of logic chips available. An improvement over the A series is the B (buffered) series. Pairs of inverters are added internally to all outputs. One significant advantage of the B over the A series is its improved signal response.

In SOS technology, the circuits are built on a sapphire substrate. This reduces distributed capacitance and results in an improvement in switching speed. SOS, however, is costlier than the A or B series of devices.

2.6 EMITTER COUPLED LOGIC

Emitter coupled logic (ECL) is a nonsaturating logic family capable of ultra high speed operation. Devices with propagation delays less than a nanosecond are avail-

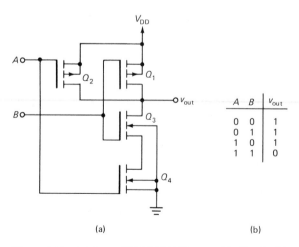

A	B	V_{out}
0	0	1
0	1	1
1	0	1
1	1	0

(a)   (b)

Figure 2.23. A 2 input CMOS NAND gate. (a) Circuit. (b) Truth table.

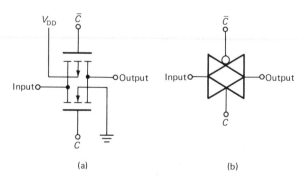

(a)   (b)

Figure 2.24. Basic CMOS transmission gate. (a) Circuit. (b) Logic symbol.

able. At these speeds, transmission line techniques have to be employed. Grounding and lead dress become especially important. For these reasons, ECL should not be used unless high speed switching requirements dictate its use or hardness to radiation is required. Table 2.6 lists the characteristics of 0.75, 1, and 2 ns delay circuits.

Important features of ECL include

1. Nonsaturating logic.
2. Highest operating speed of any IC logic family.
3. NOR and OR outputs for basic gate.
4. Possibility of developing gate arrays.
5. Availability of implied-OR function.
6. Nonpresence of current switching spikes.
7. Relatively high power dissipation with respect to other families of logic.
8. Possible high fan-out.

ECL OR/NOR Gate

A basic 3 input ECL OR/NOR gate and its logic symbol are provided in Figure 2.25. The negative voltage,

$-V_R$, at the base of Q_4 is generally derived from a temperature compensated voltage reference source. Emitter followers Q_5 and Q_6 provide the necessary dc level shifting for a logic 1 level of -0.75 V and a logic 0 level of -1.55 V. The power supply used for the circuit is -5.2 V.

Assume that inputs A, B, and C are at a logic 0 (-1.55 V). Transistors Q_1, Q_2, and Q_3 are nonconducting. Current I, which is constant, therefore flows in Q_4. The drop across R_{OR} minus the base-emitter voltage of Q_5 yields an OR output of -1.55 V, corresponding to a logic 0. Because no current flows in R_{NOR}, the voltage across the NOR output corresponds to the base-emitter voltage of Q_6, or approximately -0.75 V, which is a logic 1.

If A, B, or/and C are at a logic 1, current flows in R_{NOR} and Q_4 is nonconducting. The OR output is now equal to -0.75 V (logic 1) and the NOR output equals -1.55 V (logic 0). The truth table for the circuit is provided in Table 2.7.

Because of the high input resistance of a transistor in an ECL gate and the low output resistance of the emitter followers, the dc fan-in and fan-out can be high. The fan-

Table 2.6. ECL Characteristics

Features (Typical)	Gate Delay (ns)		
	0.75	1	2
Bias regulator parameters			
voltage compensation	(100K, 11C)[a]		(F95K)[a]
temperature compensation	(100K)[a]		(F95K)[a]
tracking, power supply and/or temperature	temp. only(11C)[a]	(MECLIII)[a]	(F10K, MECL10K)[a]
Built-in output load resistors	no	no	no
Built-in input pulldown resistors	yes	yes	yes
Input loading current	350 μA	350 μA	240 μA
Output current	>20 mA	>20 mA	>20 mA
Transmission line application	yes	yes	yes
Dc loading, fan out	>50	>50	>75
Input capacitance	2.0 pF	3.3 pF	2.9 pF
Output impedance	7 Ω	5 Ω	7 Ω
Gate edge speed (t_T, t_f)	0.7 ns	1 ns	3.5 ns
Flipflop toggle speed	1 GHz	500 MHz	125 MHz
Gate power dissipation	40 mW	60 mW	25 mW
Power speed product	30 pJ	60 pJ	50 pJ
Package availability			
flat package	yes	no	yes
dual-in-line	yes	yes	yes

[a]Motorola Inc. is the prime source for MECL, 10K, and MECL III. Fairchild is the prime source for F10K, F95K, F100K, and F11C.

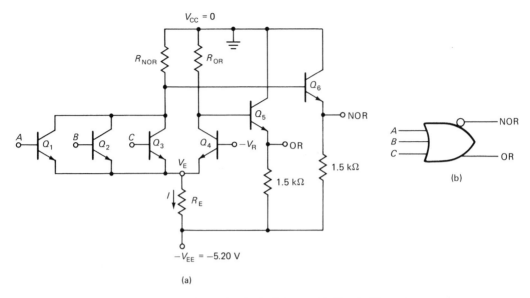

Figure 2.25. A basic 3 input ECL OR/NOR gate. (a) Circuit. (b) Logic symbol.

in and fan-out, however, is limited at high switching speeds owing to the input and output capacitances of the transistors.

Gate Arrays

In a gate array, an example of **large scale integration (LSI),** hundreds to thousands of gate functions are available in a single chip. An example is Motorola's Macrocell

Table 2.7. Truth Table for 3 Input ECL OR/NOR Gate

A	B	C	OR	NOR
0	0	0	0	1
0	0	1	1	0
0	1	0	1	0
0	1	1	1	0
1	0	0	1	0
1	0	1	1	0
1	1	0	1	0
1	1	1	1	0

gate array in which three basic cell types are available to the user. These include 48 major, 32 interface, and 26 output cells (Table 2.8). Each cell is customized by the user and the interconnection of cells is made possible by horizontal and metal interconnect channels.

An example of a Macrocell array mounted in a 68-lead chip carrier is given in Figure 2.26. "M" indicates a major, "I" an interface, and "O" an output cell.

2.7 INTEGRATED INJECTION LOGIC

Integrated injection logic (IIL, I^2L) is a saturating bipolar logic which is not available as a family of chips per se, such as TTL, but is employed in LSI circuits. Its features include

1. Lowest power delay product of any major logic family.
2. High packing density.
3. Low voltage and power operation.
4. Limited fan out.
5. Low current gain.

A subjective comparison of IIL and other logic families is provided in Table 2.9 and a comparison of speed and power dissipation is given in Figure 2.27.

Table 2.8. Basic Macrocell Array Features

106 total cells—48 major, 32 interface, and 26 output cells.
Up to 1,192 equivalent gates if full adders and latches are used in all the cells.
Up to 904 equivalent gates if flip flops and latches are used in all the cells.
Die size—221 $\times$ 249 mils.
Power dissipation—4 W typical.
4.4 mW per equivalent gate (for 904 gates and 4 W).
Interface cell delay—0.9 ns typ (1.3 ns max).
Major cell delay—0.9 to 1.3 ns typ (1.3 to 1.8 ns max).
Output cell delay—1.5 ns typ (2.2 ns max).
Any output cell (up to a total of 8) can drive a 25 Ω load.
All output cells can drive 50 Ω loads.
Edge speed—1.5 ns typ 20 to 80% (1 ns min).
85 Macros in cell library—54 macros for major cells, 14 macros for interface cells, 17 macros for output
  cells.
Ambient temperature range with heat sink and 1000 lfpm air flow = 0 to 70°C.
Θ_{JA} = 15°C/W with heat sink and 1000 lfpm air flow.
Absolute maximum function temperature, T_J = 165°C.
Voltage compensated, V_{EE} = −5.2 V ±10%.
MECL 10K compatible.

Basic Operation

The basic IIL circuit is illustrated in Figure 2.28a. Transistor Q_1, connected in the common base configuration, limits a constant current (constant current source). Its collector is connected to the base of Q_2, which has multiple collectors (two are shown in Figure 2.28a). Instead of Q_1 being drawn, the current source symbol is used, as indicated in Figure 2.28b.

Assume that v_{in} is at 0.1 V, which represents a logic 0. Because at a base voltage of 0.1 V, Q_2 cannot conduct (it requires 0.7 V), current I flows into the device (which is in a logic 0 state) connected to the input. If a logic 1 (0.7 V) is connected to the input, transistor Q_2 conducts and the voltage at C_1 and C_2 with respect to ground is approximately 0.1 V (logic 0). The basic circuit of Figure 2.28, therefore, operates as an inverter.

IIL Gates

An example of a 2 input NAND gate is shown in Figure 2.29. The base of Q_2 provides a wired AND function, that is $B = XY$. Because Q_2 is an inverter, at either collector, one obtains the NAND function, $\overline{XY}$. If both AND and NAND functions are required, an inverter connected to one of the collectors provides the AND function.

A NOR gate may be realized by paralleling two in-

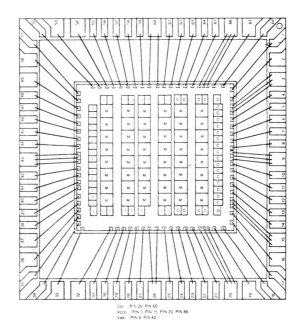

Vcc   PIN 26 PIN 60
Vcco   PIN 3 PIN 15 PIN 20 PIN 66
Vee   PIN 9 PIN 43

Figure 2.26. A Macrocell array mounted in a 68-lead chip carrier.

verters, as illustrated in Figure 2.30. Both the OR and NOR functions can be achieved by connecting an inverter to one set of the collectors. In addition to these

Table 2.9. Subjective Comparison of Major Logic Families

	S/C TTL	ECL	FL	NMOS	CMOS	CMOS/ SOS
Cell density	0	−	+ +	+ +	0	+
Switching speed	+	+ +	0	0	−	+ +
Static power dissipation	−	− −	+	−	+ +	+ +
Dynamic power dissipation	+	+	+ +	+	0	+
Speed power product	0	0	+ +	+	0	+ +
Output drive capability	+	+	0	0	−	− −
Noise immunity	+	0	− −	0	+ +	+ +
Temperature range	+	+	+	−	0	−
Neutron damage	0	+ +	−	+	+	+ +
Long term ionization damage	+	+ +	+	− −	−	− −
Transient logic upset level	0	0	+	0	+	+ +

+ + Superior, + Good, 0 Average, − Below average, − − Weak.
Source: IEE Transactions on Nuclear Science, vol. NS-24, Dec. 1977.

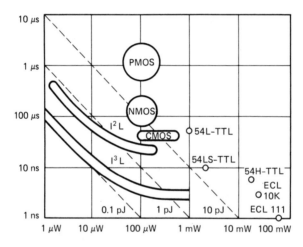

Figure 2.27. Comparison of speed and power capabilities of various logic families. I^3L is an advanced form of I^2L. (Courtesy Fairchild Camera and Instrument Corp.)

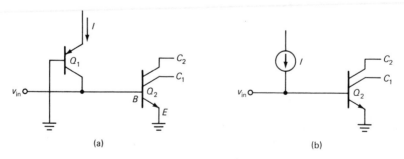

Figure 2.28. Basic IIL circuit. (a) Schematic. (b) Transistor Q_1 replaced by a current source symbol.

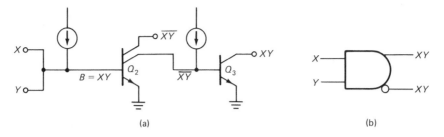

(a)   (b)

Figure 2.29. A 2 input IIL NAND/AND gate. (a) Circuit. (b) Logic symbol.

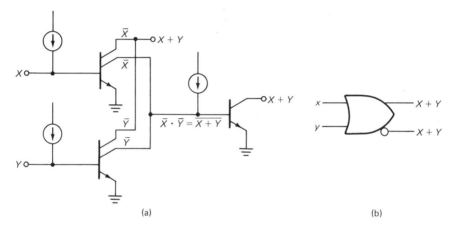

(a)   (b)

Figure 2.30. A 2 input IIL NOR/OR gate. (a) Circuit. (b) Logic symbol.

basic gates, other functions that may be realized using IIL include the exclusive-OR, AND-OR-INVERT (AOI), and flipflops.

REFERENCES

Comer, D. J., *Electronic Design with Integrated Circuits.* Reading, MA: Addison-Wesley, 1981.

Deene, B., K. Muchow, and A. Zeppa, *Introduction to Digital Techniques.* New York: John Wiley & Sons, 1979.

Garrett, L. S., "Integrated-Circuit Digital Logic Families," *IEEE Spectrum,* Oct., Nov., Dec. 1970.

Greenfield, J., *Practical Digital Design Using IC's,* 2nd Ed. New York: John Wiley & Sons, 1983.

Kaufman, M., and A. H. Seidman, *Handbook for Electronics Engineering Technicians.* New York: McGraw-Hill Book Co., 1976.

Kaufman, M., and A. H. Seidman, *Handbook of Electronics Calculations.* New York: McGraw-Hill Book Co., 1979.

Lancaster, D., *CMOS Cookbook.* Indianapolis: Howard W. Sams, 1977.

Lancaster, D., *TTL Cookbook.* Indianapolis: Howard W. Sams, 1974.

Levine, M. E., *Digital Theory and Practice Using Integrated Circuits.* Englewood Cliffs, NJ: Prentice-Hall, 1978.

Millman, J., *Microelectronics.* New York: McGraw-Hill Book Co., 1979.

Sedra, A. S., and K. C. Smith, *Microelectronic Circuits.* New York: Holt, Rinehart and Winston, 1982.

Seidman, A. H., *Integrated Circuits Applications Handbook.* New York: John Wiley & Sons, 1983.

3
Computer Memories

James Dennis Heiman

IDR Inc.

3.1 INTRODUCTION

The computer would indeed be a very limited tool if it were not for the computer's memory. A computer without memory is like a car without wheels. The **CPU,** or **central processing unit,** has great potential; but this potential cannot be realized without memory for storage of programs, data, calculations or intermediate results. For this reason, every computer usually has some form of memory attached to the system.

Memory is used in all types of computer systems including mainframes, minicomputers, microprocessors, single chip microcomputers and pocket calculators. The amount of memory varies according to the application, ranging from a single word to more than a million words. There is also a wide variety of memory types being used.

The need for the many memory types currently being used can be explained by engineering tradeoffs related to cost, speed, size and power. These tradeoffs are based upon the particular computer system under consideration. It would be undesirable to use a bulky memory design in a large computer mainframe because overall system size and power requirements would be affected. It is unnecessary to use high speed memory in a pocket calculator design, where speed is usually not important but price is very important. In other applications, low power memory is essential for battery operated toys, games or computer systems.

Owing to the great variety of memory types available, we have divided the available memory parts into two general categories: **read/write** and **read-only** memory. Al-

ready memories exist that overlap this simple classification system. Within the read/write memory group, for example, we have the subgroups of semiconductor and core memory. Two types of semiconductor read/write memory are currently being used: **static RAM** and **dynamic RAM.** Read-only memory can be subdivided into user programmable devices such as **PROM, EEPROM,** or factory programmed parts called **ROM.** This classification system is illustrated in Figure 3.1.

3.2 Definitions

There are a number of terms used in the following sections that will be explained at this point:

- **Memory** generally refers to actual computer hardware where data, programs or calculations are stored.
- **Memory address** is a particular location out of a larger memory array. Usually one memory address contains one word of data.
- A **bit** is one binary digit whose value is either true or false (one or zero). A **word** is one data packet of information for the computer; it is usually composed of many bits. Computers exist that use 1 bit words, 4 bit words, 8 bit words, 16 bit words and 32 bit words. Handling computer data in 8 bit words has been so common that the 8 bit word has its own name, the **byte.** Half of a byte is called a **nibble** (4 bits).
- Because *memory size* is an important aspect of system performance, it is useful to have a convenient way to

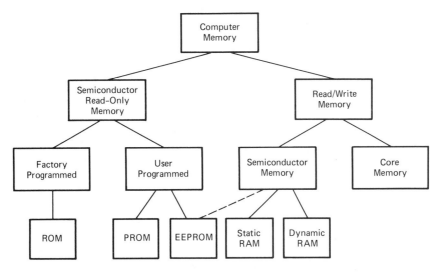

Figure 3.1. Memory classification scheme.

describe the size of a memory. At the individual part level, a device may be described as containing 65,536 bits or, alternately, it may be called an "8K by 8" memory. Most memory system sizes are described as a certain number of words. It is assumed that the word size is geared to the particular computer that is used with the memory. System sizes are given in *K increments,* or roughly 1,000 word blocks. (The exact size of a 1K block is 1,024 words, which is 2^{10}.) In small systems, memory sizes of 2K, 8K, 16K and 64K are common. Larger systems may use 100K and larger memories. Bulk storage systems of 1 **megabit,** or one million bits, are not unusual.

- *Speed* is another important parameter of memory systems. **Access time** is a measure of the time required to read or write the data contained at a particular address in the memory. This time can range from a few **nanoseconds (ns)** to **microseconds (μs),** and bulk systems can require **milliseconds (ms)** for one access. (A nanosecond is one billionth of a second; a microsecond is one millionth of a second; and a millisecond is one thousandth of a second.)
- A **bus** structure is typically used to connect the memory system to the computer. A bus is a collection of individual lines that are grouped together by function. The bus usually runs throughout the entire system. Sometimes a bus path is two way, as during read/write functions; another type of bus may be one way. An **address bus** is typically a one way bus while the **data bus** is two way. The address bus lines form the number of the particular

memory address of interest, while the data bus might contain the data word found at that address.

- *Power consumption* is an indication of the amount of waste heat generated in the memory system. Semiconductor memories typically require 5 volt direct current (dc) power to operate. A very small percentage of this energy is used to generate the output signals of the memory. The rest of the power is consumed by the memory device and is dissipated as heat.
- The *temperature range* of operation defines the safe operating region for a particular memory part. The range specified is the ambient air temperature around the device while it is in operation. Typical commercial-grade memories are geared to a range of 0°C to 70°C while military-grade units usually are rated -55°C to 125°C. Such ranges are specified so that safe operating temperatures within the devices can be maintained.
- **Packaging** generally refers to the method used to encapsulate the semiconductor die within a case that is easily used in a system, usually on a printed circuit (PC) board. Various techniques are currently in use. The *dual in line package,* or DIP, is the most popular, involving a case of plastic or ceramic. *Flat packages* have been used in a number of military products where compactness is important. Currently, *leadless carriers* are also being made by a number of manufacturers.
- **Pinouts** refers to the signal assignments of each pin or lead, of a memory device. The actual memory part might be a square die that is smaller than $\frac{3}{10}$ inch on each side. This die could be attached to a 16 pin DIP

integrated circuit (IC). Each pin has a separate function and name.

- *Reliability* and *quality control* refer to testing, measurements and calculations performed by a manufacturer to ensure that the customer receives parts that will operate correctly and reliably. Reliability calculations by the end customer give an indication of the *failure rate* of a device, or of the entire system. Typically, this reliability indication is given as the "mean time between failures," or the **MTBF** in hours. MTBF is influenced by the operating environment, for example, temperature; by the complexity of the device; and by the number of pin connections inside the device.

3.3 READ/WRITE MEMORY

The work horse of a typical general purpose computer is the read/write memory. This is true whether the computer is a mainframe, minicomputer, or a microprocessor. Any general purpose computer requires memory space to hold programs, store calculated results, and save processed information. Since results must somehow get "out" and new information or new programs must get "in," it is not unusual to find some sort of **input/output (I/O)** device attached to the computer. Because I/O devices are slow compared to the computer's speed, read/write memories are also used as buffers so that the computer's full speed capabilities can be optimized. Special-purpose processors may have some of these characteristics as well.

Of the various types of read/write memories available, the two most popular are **semiconductor RAM** and **magnetic core.** These two types account for the overwhelming majority of all computer memories in use today. Various other memory technologies are being used as read/write memories, but many of these have limited application or are still in development. Magnetic bubble memories, optical memories, delay line memories, and nonvolatile semiconductor memories are examples of read/write memories that fall into this second grouping. Because of the explosive nature of the computer memory market, it is impossible to predict what will happen to the individual market shares of each type of memory. Some may become more important as prices drop, as has happened with semiconductor RAM; others may fade or find favor in certain applications. (Three leading manufacturers, Rockwell International, Texas Instruments, and National Semiconductor stopped manufacturing bubble memories in 1981.)

3.4 SEMICONDUCTOR RAM

Semiconductor RAM refers to semiconductor integrated circuit memories that can be used in a write mode as well as in a read mode. The acronym RAM is a misnomer that has persisted, but it is understood to mean read/write devices. "RAM" stands for *random access memory,* which means that random addresses can be presented to the memory; therefore, data can be written and read in any desired order. This contrasts with a *serial access device,* such as a delay line or shift register memory, which operates in sequential order. The term RAM is not used for *read-only memories* (ROM), although a ROM can also be random access. Current popular usage limits the term RAM to semiconductor read/write memories.

Semiconductor RAM has commanded an increasingly larger share of the total memory market, in terms of both percentage of bits installed and percentage of sales. An ideal memory is random access, fast, low cost and nonvolatile, and consumes minimal power. Semiconductor memories have been shown to be extremely cost-effective as compared with magnetic core memories in most, if not all, of these areas.

Various small semiconductor RAM devices have been available with access times well under 100 ns and larger devices are fast approaching the 100 ns range. Costs are dropping rapidly as integrated circuit design techniques yield larger memories in smaller and smaller chip areas. Usually cost calculations are given as "cost per bit" so that easy comparisons can be made. For instance, 64K dynamic RAM memories are approaching 10 millicents (10 thousandths of a penny) per bit. Power dissipation or consumption is currently below 10 microwatts (μW) per bit for some semiconductor RAM types, and 1 μW/bit devices are already being proposed. Uninterruptable power supplies and battery backup systems have endowed even semiconductor RAM memory applications with cost-effectiveness when a nonvolatile system is required.

As already noted, there are two main types of semiconductor RAM memories: static and dynamic. These devices have fundamental differences in the way data is stored within an individual bit cell.

Static RAM

Static RAM memories are semiconductor integrated circuits that behave like a collection of logic flipflops (Chapter 1).

Each memory cell can latch, or store, data in a stable state. This state can be held indefinitely as long as proper power supply levels are maintained. Data can be read at any time.

Currently available static RAMs are composed of thousands of individual data cells. These cells are organized in various memory configurations. Popular memory structures are 1K by 4, 1K by 8, and 2K by 8. These numbers refer to the number of words and the size of each word in bits, respectively.

Static RAM cell design is worth examining in order to understand the difference between this and dynamic RAM. The structure of a typical MOS static RAM cell is pictured in Figure 3.2. (Compare this design with the flipflop composed of bipolar transistors and resistors shown in Figure 3.3.) The upper two FET transistors in the MOS static cell perform the same bias function as the two resistors (R_1) in the flipflop. The two cross-coupled transistors in the lower part of the circuits perform the latching function. Input data forces one transistor to be saturated, or fully turned on, while the other transistor is cut off, or turned off. This static state will not change unless the input data changes.

Examining this cell arrangement points out some of the drawbacks of the static operation of the cell. Size is a concern because the cell is composed of many individual components. These components' size becomes critical when an IC design involves 16,000 cells on one chip. Practical memory densities depend on cell size, wafer yields, and demand. Future increases in static RAM density are closely tied to design innovations that yield smaller memory cells.

Another drawback of the static RAM memory is that power must be consumed in order to maintain the latched state. Every cell is using some power because of the biased transistors in the cell circuit. This is true even when the cell is not being accessed.

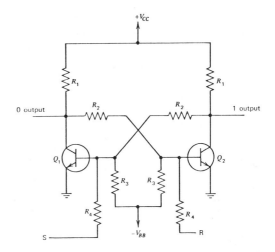

Figure 3.3. Typical flipflop employing bipolar junction transistors (BJTs).

One obvious advantage of the static RAM design is the simplicity of using these parts in a system. Pin connections of a typical RAM are shown in Figure 3.4. The 2114 is a 1K by 4 static RAM that has been very popular. Many 2114 parts can be grouped together with simple support logic to form larger memory systems.

A block diagram of the 2114 is shown in Figure 3.5. This part has ten address lines that are used to address 1,024 words. Because the computer is based on the binary number system, the ten address lines form 2^{10}, or 1,024, possible conditions. Each addressed word is 4 bits wide. Thus there is a total of 4,096 cells in the 2114 RAM. The address lines are only used to select one set of four data cells.

Data is stored in, or read from, the memory cells via the four I/O lines. In order to provide stable signals

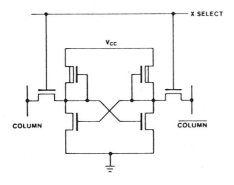

Figure 3.2. A basic static RAM storage Cell.

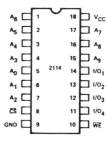

Figure 3.4. Typical pin connections for a static RAM. (Courtesy Synertek, Inc.)

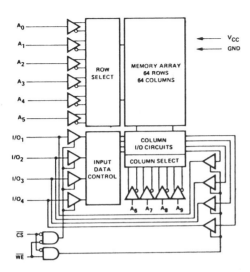

Figure 3.5. Block diagram of a static RAM. (Courtesy Synertek, Inc.)

within the memory cell array, the four I/O lines are buffered, as shown on the block diagram. The address lines are usually tied to the computer or memory system address bus, while the I/O data lines are tied to the data bus.

The remaining pin connections shown on the block diagram are used for control and power. The **chip select line** ($\overline{CS}$) is an input used to enable a particular part, or group of parts, out of a larger memory array. For example, a 16K by 8 memory can be formed from thirty-two 2114 static RAM parts. Only two parts are selected during any single read or write sequence.

The *write enable* input line $\overline{WE}$ is used to determine whether a "write" or "read" operation is taking place. The write enable signal is generated from the computer system. When chip select is active, a write pulse on the write enable line is used to store data within the memory cell array. The data buffers are switched to input mode during a write sequence. During a read sequence, write enable is inactive and the data buffers are switched to output mode. The internal cell data is outputted to the computer data bus during a read operation.

The V_{CC} and "ground" lines are used to supply power to the memory IC. Power consumption varies slightly with the mode of operation of the static RAM. The 2114 static RAM uses 5 V dc power and typical power consumption is 500 mW.

Dynamic RAM

Dynamic RAM memories are semiconductor integrated circuits that operate like a bank of capacitors. Each cell either holds a charge or it is empty, determining the "zero" and "one" states. The dynamic nature of these parts requires that each memory cell must be recharged or "refreshed" before the charge dissipates.

Dynamic RAM is far more popular than static RAM for large mainframe computer applications. The reasons for this popularity can be traced to fundamental design differences between the static RAM cell and the dynamic RAM cell. The net result of these differences is that dynamic RAM yields a cheaper memory system cost.

The dynamic RAM cell is less complex than a static cell because it does not use a latch to store data. A parasitic capacitor is formed in the integrated circuit and this becomes the storage element, as pictured in Figure 3.6. The single transistor switch is used to isolate or select one particular cell from the entire memory array. Because the basic dynamic cell design is simple and contains few elements, it is possible to achieve much higher densities than with static cell designs.

A typical memory system may be formed from many 16K word dynamic RAM parts. These parts are usually structured as "16K by 1," or 16,384 words of only one bit. Larger memory words are made by ganging as many chips as required. This allows greater flexibility for system designers to organize memory systems with a small or wide data bus (i.e., 16K by 8, or 16K by 16, or 16K by 32). Circuit boards that are extremely cost-effective for large mainframes are easily created with densely packed dynamic RAM parts.

Power dissipation is another function in which dynamic RAM has an advantage over static RAM. Because the dynamic RAM cell does not use a latched design to hold data as do static RAM parts, the power consumed by each cell is negligible when it is not being accessed. Most power is consumed during a read or a write operation; a small amount of power is used during the refresh cycle.

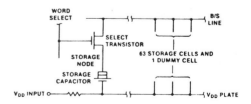

Figure 3.6. A basic dynamic RAM storage cell.

Because most computer memories access only one location at a time, peak power is consumed by only a small segment of the total memory system.

Indeed, the average power dissipation of the total memory system is very low when using dynamic RAM. This lower power dissipation affects two computer system design areas. First, power consumed by computer memories is dissipated as heat. Reliable operation of the computer system depends upon cool operation, so such heat must be purged by ventilation, fans, or air conditioning. Low power dissipation leads to smaller cooling requirements or more compact systems. Second, power supply volume also is a function of the power requirements of the computer system. Smaller power supplies can be used if the system requirements are lowered because of reduced memory power needs.

One disadvantage of using dynamic RAM is the need to refresh the entire memory array in a certain period (usually two milliseconds, or two thousandths of a second). There are a number of techniques for implementing the refresh mode with external logic within the memory system. Refresh is achieved by cycling the lower half of the address bus so that every cell receives a charge pulse. This small amount of extra hardware is cost-effective because the single refresh address generator is shared by the entire memory array. Recent versions of "64K by 1" dynamic RAM have been manufactured with built-in refresh hardware (i.e., pin 1 refresh); prices, however, are slightly higher than for standard parts. Mainframe computer memory systems will probably continue to use external refresh hardware because of the lower net system cost.

Two examples of modern dynamic RAM memory parts are Motorola's MCM6664 and MCM6665 integrated circuits, both 64K memories. The MCM6664 part contains built-in refresh circuitry which is driven by a simple external clock, while the MCM6665 part must be refreshed by external logic. A pin-assignment diagram for these pin parts is shown in Figure 3.7.

These dynamic RAM parts contain 65,536 one bit words and require a sixteen bit address word (i.e., $2^{16} = 65,536$). The address word is formed by a multiplex technique, whereas two 8 bit words are input in two steps from the eight address lines labelled A0 through A7. This 8 bit word must be formed by external logic that interfaces the computer memory bus to the memory system.

The D and Q lines are the data input and output lines. Depending upon the system design, these lines may be tied together or separated. Many applications call for a

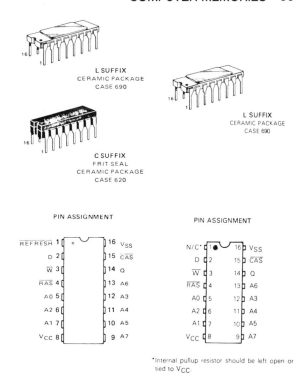

Figure 3.7. The MC6664/6665 64K dynamic RAM pin connections. Left: MC6664; right: 6665. (Courtesy Motorola, Inc.)

bidirectional data bus and the D and Q are tied together. Certain pipeline memory techniques may dictate that the D and Q lines be separated for faster system throughput. In larger memory systems, the address bus is shared by all the dynamic RAM parts in the memory array. The data bus is separated into individual data bits where each bit is associated with one RAM.

The $\overline{RAS}$ and $\overline{CAS}$ lines are used for timing and control purposes. A low level on the $\overline{W}$ line is used to signify that a write operation is being performed. The V_{CC} pin is used for 5 V power input, while V_{SS} is held at ground.

Pin 1 is used for refresh on the MCM6664, while the MCM6665 does not use pin 1 for refresh. The pin 1 refresh technique uses an internal 8 bit counter to generate the required 128 refresh addresses. Use of this pin requires a low-state clock pulse on the refresh line while the $\overline{RAS}$ signal is sent to a high state. The refresh clock increments the refresh address with each clock pulse. This is a fairly straightforward technique and is inexpensive to implement with external logic. The main disadvantage of this part is the additional internal refresh logic. This slight increase in complexity means that the pin 1 refresh part is higher in cost.

The alternate refresh technique is available on both the MCM6664 and the MCM6665 dynamic RAM parts. This technique uses the $\overline{RAS}$ and $\overline{CAS}$ lines to control the refresh mode. the $\overline{RAS}$ line is sent low, while the $\overline{CAS}$ line is sent high and the refresh address is presented from external logic to the dynamic RAM memory array. All 128 refresh addresses must be presented within two milliseconds, as is the case for the self-refresh mode.

System cost analysis can determine which dynamic RAM part is more cost-effective for a particular application. The tradeoff basically revolves around the higher part price for the pin 1 refresh parts and the simple external refresh hardware versus the cheaper price of the external refresh parts and the complex external refresh hardware. For large computer memory systems, the lower cost parts tend to be more attractive.

3.5 CORE MEMORY

Magnetic core memory was the most popular read/write memory used in computers before semiconductor memories became cost-effective. Core memory usage is still predominant in certain areas, such as military computers and aerospace applications. Old mainframe computers retired by computer center upgrades have found their way to emerging Third World countries, so that core replacement markets are still strong in these areas. In general, core memory has been displaced by semiconductor memory except in applications where the memory must be nonvolatile.

The basic principle of the magnetic core memory is fairly simple. A single round magnetic core is pictured in Figure 3.8. The magnetic core is shaped like a doughnut and is made from ferromagnetic material. One characteristic of this material is that it can "store flux" in a manner that is similar to the way a magnet "stores flux"

and has a north and south pole. Referring to the core pictured, current flowing through the wire can go in either direction. This current flow causes flux to be set up in either a clockwise or counterclockwise direction around the wire at the center of the core. If we let the current flow direction represent a "zero" or a "one" for current flow "in" or "out," we have a method of storing a 0 or 1 in the flux state, illustrated in Figure 3.9. This is similar to a "write" function.

Now that we have a method of storing information, we need a method of reading the "stored flux" value. The principle of current flow setting up flux direction in a magnetic core has a reverse principle, that a change in flux in a magnetic field can induce current flow in a wire. If we try to change the flux state of a core, we can find out what the original state was. In order to do a "read" operation, we can do a dummy "write" operation and sense the original flux state. We would have to follow this step with another write operation to restore the core to the original state. This is known as **destructive readout** and **restore** respectively.

Actual core memory systems use these principles of op-

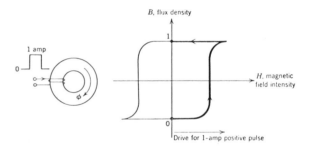

Positive drive (from 0 to 1).

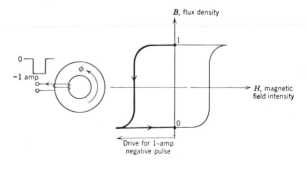

Negative drive (from 1 to 0).

Figure 3.9. Magnetic core flux storage.

Figure 3.8. A ferrite core memory element.

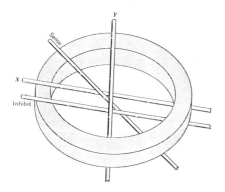

Figure 3.10. Magnetic core system employing 4 wires.

current needed for storing a "one" so no change occurs. Because the selected core always "sees" the full required current (i.e. one-half from X and one-half from Y), a 1 would always be stored, but this is not desired. An inhibit line is added to cancel one-half of the selection current when it is desired to store a 0.

The operation sequence requires that a "dummy read" operation be performed to set the core to the zero state. A write operation can then be performed with the help of this inhibit line so that either a 1 or a 0 can be stored. A read operation is performed by doing a "dummy write" to 0 while monitoring the sense line. After the write operation is performed, a restore operation rewrites the data back to the core array.

Practical core memory design is concerned with the particulars of choosing the optimum current value for each select line and problems of noise and crosstalk. Manufacturing considerations also determine the number of wires used in a core memory array and the technique of arranging these wires. A 3D core memory plane is pictured in Figure 3.11. Note that only 18 wires are needed to control the 64 cores—8 X-lines, 8 Y-lines, 1 sense line, and 1 inhibit line. Each bit in the memory word is formed by stacking planes of cores with one plane for each bit. A 16K by 8 core memory can be formed by 128 X-lines, 128 Y-lines, 8 sense lines, and 8 inhibit lines for a total of 272 lines. This could be formed from eight 16K core planes stacked into one package.

eration, but the complex organization of practical memory systems requires slightly enhanced selection techniques. Practical core memory systems contain many thousands of core elements. It is impractical to wire each individual core with a separate group of wires. Typically, a four wire scheme is used as pictured in Figure 3.10.

Although there are different ways to organize core memory systems, we will only examine the 3D method in detail. The four wire core technique uses X-Y coincident selection to select one core out of a larger array. Using a square matrix technique, one Y-line and one X-line are each activated with one-half the required current to store a "one" flux state. Unselected cores only see one-half the

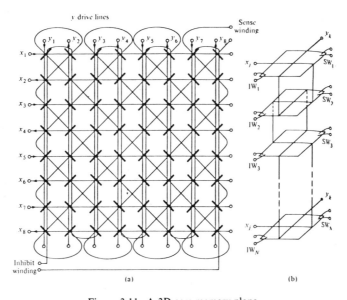

Figure 3.11. A 3D core memory plane.

Core memory systems have a wide range of access times. High speed core systems may run as fast as 500 ns per cycle, while typical minicomputer general purpose core systems may run at one μs (1000 ns) cycle times. Actual access times may run up to twice as fast, with some products available that operate at 250 ns.

It is interesting to contrast the difference between semiconductor and core memories when examining cycle times and access time. Many semiconductor RAMs can be accessed sequentially at a fast rate such that the memory access time and the fastest possible cycle time are equal. A magnetic core system will always have a longer cycle time than access time because of the need to perform dummy read and restore operations with every write or read operation. Magnetic core system speeds depend upon the basic core element flux time characteristics. Core switching speed is dependent upon the ferrite core material. Core technology has matured to the point where further speed enhancements are not being pushed by high demand.

Semiconductor technology has been enhanced by size reductions and photographic innovations. The semiconductor market has been demanding larger and faster parts almost as soon as new parts are introduced. The semiconductor RAM market has shown no signs of slowing down whereas core demands peaked a number of years ago.

In general, core memory systems tend to be more expensive than semiconductor systems of the equivalent size. Because of the large switching currents involved, core memories usually use more power than semiconductor RAM parts. Semiconductor parts are fabricated on a die that is a fraction of a square inch; by this standard 250 mils (0.25 inch) by 250 mils is considered a large part. Core memory arrays are formed from individual cores and wires which tend to be bulky and larger than semiconductor parts.

3.6 READ-ONLY MEMORY

Semiconductor read-only memory, or **ROM,** is used in computer memories where the memory data must remain fixed. ROMs are used for various memory applications such as fixed program storage, look-up tables, and code conversions. A ROM does not usually change after being placed in a circuit and it does not use a write pulse or data input buffers. Because of the simplicity of the ROM structure, very dense cell arrays can be formed on a chip. These dense parts are very cost effective over alternate techniques of read-only storage.

ROM applications abound in every class size of computer. Mainframe computer and minicomputers use ROMs for **bootstrap** loader programs which serve to bring up the computer from a "cold start." Many microprocessors in home computers execute a ROM based version of a BASIC intepreter in order to run BASIC programs. Special purpose processors may have their whole executable program stored in ROM while using a small RAM for a read/write scratchpad.

Certain licensed programs are easier to control if they are circulated in ROM versions instead of magnetic tape, disk, or paper tape. This technique is widely used in programmable TV game cartridges. Some military computer applications use ROM look-up tables for radar signature analysis or frequency selection for radio tuning. Texas Instrument's "Speak and Spell" uses plug-in ROM packs to generate a library of spoken words. There are many advantages to using ROMs for these tasks.

There are primarily three types of read-only memory. **ROM** refers to parts that are "masked" or coded by the manufacturer. A PROM is a semiconductor part that is obtained from the manufacturer in an unprogrammed state and the user programs or "burns" the desired code into the part. A PROM is programmed outside of the circuit where it is to be used and many commercial available machines, called prom programmers or prom burners, are used to program the various families of PROMs that are available. A relatively new part called an **electrically erasable PROM, or EEPROM,** is also being used for ROM applications. The EEPROM can be altered while being used in a logic board by using special power circuits and write pulse generators. The EEPROM can work like a read/write semiconductor memory while retaining the nonvolatile nature of ROMs and PROMs.

ROM

A ROM is a factory programmed semiconductor read-only memory that is formed from a cell array masked to a particular 0/1 arrangement. The "mask" is artwork that reflects the code pattern submitted by the buyer. This mask artwork is used in one of the IC manufacturing steps to form transistor connections that become the internal data bits of the ROM.

One example of a large MOS ROM is the Signetics 2664. The 2664 is a 65,536 bit static ROM that is organized as 8K words of 8 bits. The block diagram and pin configuration of the 2664 appear in Figure 3.12. This part is a 24 pin IC that uses 5 V power.

There are basically five sections in the 2664. The heart

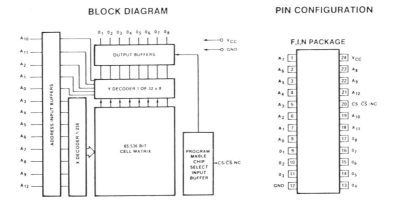

Figure 3.12. Block diagram and pin connection for a 64K ROM. (Courtesy Signetics, Inc.)

of the chip is the 65,536 bit memory array. This array is masked with a ROM data pattern. The desired word in the array is selected by the X and Y decoders. The 13 address lines are the inputs to these two decoders. As the address is decoded, the output word is presented to the output buffers.

The chip select line is used to enable or disable the tri-state mode of the output buffers. This tri-state feature is useful in forming a memory data bus when multiple memory parts are used. The eight output lines come from the output buffers.

Because the ROM is programmed by a factory manufacturing step, there is no need to have additional circuitry in the chip that is only used for programming. ROM parts are cheaper than field-programmable parts, but there may be a tooling charge for generating the ROM mask.

PROM

Because factory masked ROMs are usually cost-effective only for large quantity orders, alternatives to the ROM have been developed. A PROM, or programmable ROM, can be field-programmed by the user. Various manufacturers offer PROM programming machines that can be used to burn, or program, the desired code into the PROM and they can also be used to verify the PROM contents.

A PROM is cost-effective for development work, prototype units, pilot production runs, and small volume manufacturing. The PROM integrated circuit has a higher unit cost that an equivalent ROM, but the PROM has no tooling charges associated with it. A PROM does

require the investment in a PROM programmer (or one can be leased, rented or borrowed) and there is some time and labor associated with the programming step.

PROMs are so popular that they are available in a variety of logic families. There are two types of PROMs being used—erasable and nonerasable. One type of nonerasable PROM uses fusible links that are blown open and once blown cannot be changed. The erasable PROMs, such as MOS ultraviolet (UV) erasable, or UV EPROMs, trap charge in cells to represent the data. This charge can be released by exposing the IC die to UV light. The PROM, or EPROM, is erased by a few minutes exposure to the light, and can be reprogrammed after erasure.

The 2716 is a MOS UV EPROM that is organized as 2,048 words of 8 bits (2K × 8). It is electrically programmed but is erased with ultraviolet light. It is packaged in a 24 pin IC as shown in Figure 3.13. This part is usually programmed out of the circuit with a PROM programmer. It can be erased by shining UV light through the transparent lid for less than 30 minutes.

EEPROM

A number of manufacturers have announced a new type of PROM that is electrically erasable. This EEPROM can be programmed or erased while it is still in the circuit and used like a nonvolatile read/write memory. There are some timing constraints that cause the part to need more time for erasure or programming than is needed to read data from the part.

The Intel 2816 is an example of an EEPROM. It is a 24 pin IC that is organized as 2K × 8 in a manner that

The HN462716 is a 2048 word by 8 bit erasable and electrically programmable ROMs. This device is packaged in a 24-pin, dual-in-line package with transparent lid. The transparent lid allows the user to expose the chip to ultraviolet light to erase the bit pattern, whereby a new pattern can then be written into the device.

- Single Power Supply .... +5V ±5%;
- Simple Programming ....Program Voltage: +25V DC
  Programs with One 50ms Pulse
- Static .... No Clocks Required
- Inputs and Outputs TTL Compatible During Both Read and Program Modes
- Fully Decoded-on Chip Address Decode
- Access Time .... 450ns Max.
- Low Power Dissipation ......555mW Max. Active Power
  213mW Max. Standby Power
- Three State Output .... OR- Tie Capability
- Interchangeable with Intel 2716

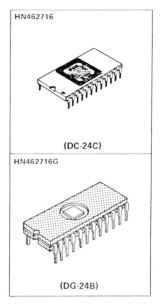

HN462716

(DC-24C)

HN462716G

(DG-24B)

■ BLOCK DIAGRAM

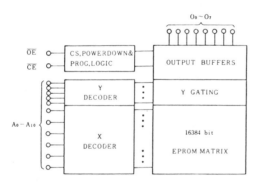

■ PIN ARRANGEMENT

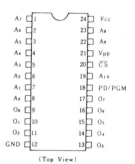

(Top View)

Figure 3.13. An example of a 2K × 8 UV PROM. (Courtesy Hitachi)

is similar to the 2716 part. This part can be read like a ROM and bulk-erased like a UV EPROM. In addition, the 2816 also has a word or byte erase mode.

With EEPROMs, programs can be modified in the field without unsoldering and removing parts from circuit boards. It is still not clear where the EEPROM will find the most popularity.

REFERENCES

Memory Manuals

Advanced Micro Devices
Dynamic Memory Support Handbook (AM2960 Series).
Sunnyvale, CA, 1981.

Fairchild Camera and Instrument Corporation,
Bipolar Memory Data Book.
Mountain View, CA, 1979.

Harris Corporation,
Bipolar and CMOS Memory Data Book.
Melbourne, FL, 1978.

Hitachi America Limited,
IC Memories.
San Jose, CA, 1980.

Hearst Business Communications, Inc.,
UTP Division,
IC Master.
Garden City, NY, 1982 (published annually).

Intel Corporation,
Memory Design Handbook.
Santa Clara, CA, 1980.

Mostek Corporation,
Memory Data Book and Designers' Guide.
Carrollton, TX, 1980.

Motorola Technical Information Center (Motorola Inc.),
Motorola Memory Data Manual.
Austin, TX, 1980.

National Semiconductor Corporation,
Memory Applications Handbook.
Santa Clara, CA, 1979.

Signetics Corporation,
Signetics Bipolar and MOS Memory Data Manual.
Sunnyvale, CA, 1979.

Synertek Inc.,
MOS Data Catalog.
Santa Clara, CA, 1979.

Texas Instruments Inc.
Semiconductor Group,
The MOS Memory Data Book.
Dallas, TX, 1980.

Recommended Periodicals

Computer Design, Computer Design Publishing Company,
Littleton, MA. Published monthly.

Digital Design, Morgan-Grampian Publishing Company,
Boston, MA. Published monthly.

EDN, Cahners Publishing Company,
Boston, MA. Published biweekly.

Electronic Design, Hayden Publishing Company,
Rochelle Park, NJ. Published biweekly.

Electronic Engineering Times, CMP Publications,
Manhasset, NY. Published biweekly.

IEEE Computer, IEEE Computer Society,
Los Alamitos, CA. Published monthly.

IEEE Micro, IEEE Computer Society,
Los Alamitos, CA. Published quarterly.

IEEE Spectrum, IEEE
New York, NY. Published monthly.

Mini-Micro Systems, Cahners Publishing Companu,
Boston, MA. Published monthly.

4
Microprocessors

Charles L. Saxe

Tektronix Inc.

4.1 INTRODUCTION

This chapter is designed to provide an introduction to microprocessors for the reader who has some basic knowledge of Boolean algebra and digital logic (see Chapter 1). For a real world reference and to ensure availability of more detailed information, a well known and established microprocessor has been chosen as a basis for description. This processor, the Motorola M6800 is currently produced by several semiconductor manufacturers. The 6800 is one processor among a half dozen or more devices of similar capabilities and price. It was selected because of its well designed and easy-to-understand architecture and great wealth of supporting documentation. Throughout the chapter, important features of other processors will be described and compared with those of the 6800.

It is difficult to provide a universal definition of **microprocessor** because the term has been used to describe a wide range of devices that vary greatly in capabilities. Generally speaking, however, it refers to a significant amount of digital computer hardware integrated into a monolithic large scale integrated (LSI) circuit. As is the case with any digital computer, the most fundamental use of a microprocessor is to perform a series of manipulations specified by a programmer on some data stored in a memory. These data manipulations can consist of almost any function imaginable, with the data itself originating in any device connected to the microprocessor. This data manipulation capability forms the basis of the microprocessor's ability to perform a wide range of functions, from business oriented data processing to the control of complex machinery. In these applications, the microprocessor replaces larger and much more expensive computer systems or complex hardwired control logic. In addition, the microprocessor has created new markets for its use by virtue of its small size and low power requirements. Such applications include video games and handheld calculators.

4.2 ORGANIZATION

A simplified block diagram of the 6800 is provided in Figure 4.1. This diagram is not intended to show the actual physical layout of components in the 6800, but is meant to illustrate data flow within the architecture. The 6800 falls into the architectural class of computers called **von Neumann machines.** The distinguishing feature of this type of machine is its ability to store programs and data in the same memory. Currently, the vast majority of computers, both large and small, are of the von Neumann type. This characteristic, which facilitates very efficient use of memory, will be more easily understood as the reader progresses into the chapter.

Processor operation can be broken down into various processes:

- **Instruction fetch,** during which an instruction is taken from memory and placed in the **instruction register (IR).** This instruction specifies precisely which data manipulation functions are to be performed during the next phase of operation, called **execution.** The instruction also contains information concerning the location of the data that is to be manipulated during execution.

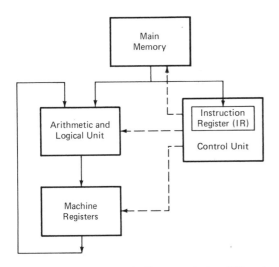

Figure 4.1. Simplified block diagram of the 6800 microprocessor.

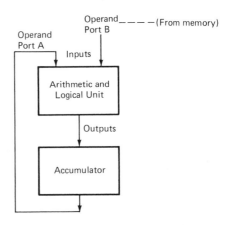

Figure 4.2. Accumulator based architecture.

- **Decoding** the foregoing information and controlling the hardware resources available in the microprocessor to perform the required data manipulation, both functions being performed by the **control unit.** After the instruction has been decoded, the **data words** to be used (also called **operands**) are fetched, and the manipulation performed. The result is then stored as directed by the original instruction.

Accumulator Based Architecture

The 6800 follows a tradition leading back to the earliest minicomputer in its approach to addressing operands (data). What is being referred to here is often called an **accumulator based architecture.** In such an architecture, one operand for an instruction is always received from, or headed to, the **accumulator** (ACCUM). An example of this type of configuration is shown in Figure 4.2. The top block in the figure represents the **arithmetic and logical unit (ALU),** which is that portion of a microprocessor that performs the actual arithmetic and logic operations. The ALU has two input ports (A and B) and one output port on which the result of such operations as $A + B$ and $A - B$ appear. Attached to the ALU output is an **accumulator register** whose output is returned to input port A of the ALU.

This configuration has some very positive features, the most significant of which is efficient use of memory. This desired end is realized because instructions which utilize two operands need only specify one memory address, since the accumulator always holds the second. Another positive feature is an increase in speed over instructions that would specify two memory addresses because memory references consume a considerable amount of instruction execution time. A third feature is the ease with which programs can be written for such an architecture.

For example, consider the program in Example 4.1, which finds the sum of four values in memory locations W, X, Y and Z, and stores the result in memory location R.

EXAMPLE 4.1

Operation Code	Operand	Comment
LDAA	W	Load ACCUM with value in W.
ADDA	X	Add to ACCUM value in X.
ADDA	Y	Add to ACCUM value in Y.
ADDA	Z	Add to ACCUM value in Z.
STAA	R	Store to location R value in ACCUM.

The LDAA W instruction causes the contents of memory location W to be placed in the accumulator. (LDAA, ADDA, and so on, are examples of **mnemonics.**) ADDA X causes the contents of location X to be added to the value in the accumulator with the result remaining there. The next two ADDAs cause Y and Z to be added to give the sum of W + X + Y + Z that resides in the accumulator. The STAA R instruction then causes this sum to be stored in memory location R. It should be noted that the LDAA W causes no change to the value stored in W. Likewise with the ADDA X, and so on. The only memory location whose value has changed is R. The accumulator of course is changed often, but it is not used for permanent storage. Rather, it is merely a scratchpad for holding intermediate results.

The Digital Equipment Corporation PDP-8 is an example of a minicomputer containing a single accumulator. The 6800 in fact has a number of the architectural characteristics of the PDP-8, but in many cases has enhanced these features to improve machine efficiency, or ease of programming. One such improvement is the inclusion of two accumulators in the 6800 as opposed to the PDP-8's one. It is worth noting here that several large microprocessor manufacturers are beginning to produce an even more powerful class of microprocessors. Such machines will have not 2 accumulators, but an array of about 16 (often called a **register stack**) and will provide the programmer with a much more extensive set of instructions. As they appear, these machines will be competitive in processing power with the large minicomputers and should be widely available at low cost in the very near future.

The two accumulators in the 6800 are called accumulator A (ACCUM A) and accumulator B (ACCUM B). As just stated, most instructions use the value in one of these accumulators as one operand. The other operand (if required) is specified in one of six ways (by the programmer) as allowed by the six addressing modes of the machine.

Instruction Sequencing

As previously mentioned, programs consist of groups of *instructions* which perform a variety of data manipulations. An important secondary operation that must be performed by the computer is keeping track of which instruction is being executed at any given time and determining the location of the next instruction when the present one is completed. This task is simplified through the use of a register called the **program counter (PC).** The PC is initialized before execution of a given program to contain the memory address of the first instruction in the program. Thereafter, the PC is updated automatically following each instruction's execution to point to the next.

The update operation is accomplished in one of two ways. If the instruction currently being executed is a data manipulation (e.g., ADD, SUBTRACT), the next instruction to be executed will immediately follow the current one in memory. The length of the current instruction is therefore added to the program counter to form the address of the next instruction. The second case is one in which the current instruction is a **branch.** Branches are used by the programmer to cause the computer to select, as its next instruction, one not necessarily following the present one. Indeed, a branch can cause an instruction stored anywhere in memory to be fetched next.

There are basically two types of branches: conditional and unconditional. **Conditional branches** are used to change the flow of instructions based on the result of a data manipulation. The conditional branch format is as follows:

OPCODE   ADDRESS

The Operation Code (OPCODE) specifies the type of instruction (in this case, the type of branch), and the ADDRESS defines the location of the next instruction should the required branch condition be met. If this condition is not met, the instruction immediately following the branch is executed next.

The second type of branch, the **unconditional branch,** has the same format as the conditional branch. These branches (also called **jump** instructions) do not require that a condition be met, but unconditionally redirect instruction fetch to a new area of memory.

The program and associated flow chart (Figure 4.3) of Example 4.2 are designed to demonstrate the functions of conditional branches and iterative loops. (Note that each of the six instructions in the example is given a number from 1 to 6. This numbering is used here and throughout the chapter only to identify the instructions in the text and has nothing to do with the actual machine representation of the program.)

EXAMPLE 4.2

Instruction Number	OPCODE	Operand*	Comment
1.	LDAB	#0	Load ACCUM B with 0.
2.	LDAA	#−5	Load ACCUM A with −5.
3. LOOP	ADDB	X	Add value in X to ACCUM B.
4.	ADDA	#1	Add 1 to ACCUM A.
5.	BNE	LOOP	Branch to LOOP if ACCUM A ≠ 0.
6.		Rest of program	

*The pound sign (#) indicates immediate addressing and is explained in Section 4.3.

The purpose of the program is to multiply the value in memory location X by 5, leaving the result in ACCUM B. This is accomplished by adding the value in X to ACCUM B five times. ACCUM A is used as what is

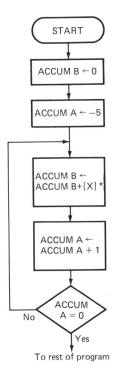

*[X] : Brackets mean "contents of" memory location X.

Figure 4.3. Flow chart for a conditional branch.

often called a **loop** or **iteration** counter. That is, a group of instructions will be executed more than once and a software counter keeps track of the number of repetitions.

Instructions 1 and 2 initialize accumulator B and A with 0 and −5 respectively. The 0 is put into ACCUM B in order to have a clear scratchpad in which to perform multiplication. The −5 in ACCUM A is used as the initial iteration count which will be incremented by 1 each time an add of memory location X is performed. When ACCUM A becomes 0, the loop will have been executed five times and the program will terminate.

Instruction 3 is the first one within the loop. This ADDB instruction adds the value in memory location X to ACCUM B, after which instruction 4 increments the iteration counter (ACCUM A) by 1. In instruction 5, the OPCODE "BNE" means "branch if not equal (to zero)." In other words, if the last instruction, 4, resulted in a value not equal to zero, a jump to LOOP is performed.

When ACCUM A finally becomes zero, the BNE results in a no-branch to instruction 6 for a termination of the algorithm.

4.3 ADDRESSING MODES

The 6800 permits several modes of addressing, but like many microprocessors in its class, it is somewhat more limited in this area than many programmers would like. Several useful modes such as autoincrement, indirect, and use of a base register displacement are not included in the 6800 but are in its successor, the 68000. The following are definitions of those modes included in the 6800 as well as several others commonly found in microprocessors:

Immediate Addressing

Format:

OPCODE
7   0

OPERAND
7   0

The first byte (8 bits) of an "immediate" instruction is the OPCODE. As stated previously, OPCODE specifies the type of operation to be performed. The second byte is one of the operands. The other operand, if one is required, is located in one of the accumulators.

EXAMPLE 4.3

	OPCODE	OPERAND
In English:	ANDA (Immediate)	14_{10}
In binary:	1000 0100	0000 1110
	7 0	7 0
In hexadecimal:		$(84\ OE)_{16}$

This instruction ANDs accumulator A with the value 14_{10} and puts the result into ACCUM A. The "in binary" representation is the actual string of ones and zeros that would be stored in memory to represent this instruction. Instructions and data are often shown on paper in hexadecimal (see Chapter 1) because it is more compact and easier to read.

The binary representation shows that the OPCODE is 1000 0100. This bit string not only specifies the type of operation (AND), but also includes information as to which accumulator (A) and addressing mode (Immediate) is to be used:

Extended Addressing

Format:

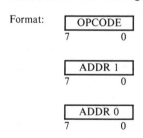

The OPCODE is followed by two bytes that are interpreted as a 16 bit address pointing to one of 65,536 locations in memory. The 8 bits contained in this location will either become an operand or the destination. The following three examples illustrate this addressing mode:

EXAMPLE 4.4

In English:	ADDA (Extended)	1024_{10}

In binary:	1001 1011	0000 0100 0000 0000

In HEX:	9B	0400

This instruction adds the contents of memory location 1024_{10} to ACCUM A leaving the result in this accumulator. The contents of the memory location are left unchanged.

EXAMPLE 4.5

In English:	STAA (Extended)	1025_{10}

In binary:	1011 0111	000 0100 0000 0001

In HEX:	B7	0401

This instruction stores the contents of ACCUM A in location 1025_{10}. The accumulator is left unchanged.

EXAMPLE 4.6

In English:	ROR (Extended)	1026_{10}

In binary:	0111 0110	0000 0100 0000 0010

In HEX:	76	0402

The **ROR** mnemonic means **rotate right.** Its function is to perform a 1 bit right shift of the data in the addressed location. In this case, the addressed memory location is 1026_{10}. The result of the shift remains in the addressed memory location.

Direct Addressing

Format:

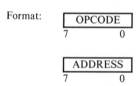

Direct addressing is essentially the same as extended. The only difference is that the most significant 8 bits of the 16 bit operand address are assumed to be zeros. The addressing range is therefore location 0 to 225_{10}, or 256 bytes instead of the full 64K, where K = 1024. If an operand is located within the first 256 bytes of memory, a direct address is preferable to an extended one because direct instructions consume less memory (2 bytes rather than 3), and execute more quickly.

Indexed Addressing

This mode of addressing is often used to sequence through an array of data. A dedicated 16 bit register called the **index register** is used as a pointer to any location in memory. The instruction format, which looks exactly like a direct instruction, has as its second byte an 8 bit offset. Instead of being interpreted as an operand address, this offset is first added to the contents of a 16 bit index register (with the offset right justified). This yields a 16 bit address that is used to address the desired operand.

Suppose a 100_{10} byte array of data begins at location 100_{10} and goes to location 199_{10}. To access the array one byte at a time, the sum of the offset and index register is set to 100. This can be accomplished by clearing the index register to zero and using an indexed instruction of the form

$$\text{OPCODE (Indexed)} \qquad (100)_{10}$$

This instruction can access all elements in order by simply incrementing the index register between accesses. The increment function is easily performed by a dedicated 1 byte instruction called **INX** (**increment index register**).

Implied Addressing

Implied instructions in the 6800 are only 1 byte long. The format is

These instructions indicate a machine register as the operand. For example, the **CLRA (clear ACCUM A)** instruction sets all 8 bits of the accumulator A to zero.

Relative Addressing

Relative instructions have the same format as the indexed type:

The 8 bit offset in this case is added to the contents of the program counter and the sum is interpreted as a 16 bit address. Many computers allow relative addressing for all types of instructions, but the 6800 permits this mode of addressing on branching only.

An advantage of a relative branch over one in the extended mode is its smaller size (2 bytes as compared to 3 for extended). The seemingly major limitation of only being able to jump to one of 256 locations around the current program locations is not really a major one because most jumps in a program are short in distance and within reach of relative branches. For cases in which a longer jump is required, an unconditional extended or indexed mode Jump instruction is available.

Indirect Addressing (Not Available in the 6800)

Indirect instructions normally have an operand address as part of the instruction, as in 6800 extended mode. But instead of interpreting this address as a memory pointer to the operand desired, it is treated as the pointer to the *address* of the operand.

This type of addressing is particularly useful in addressing arrayed data, much like indexed addressing. Because the actual address pointing to an array can be stored separately from the program in memory, a large number of array pointers can be used. This addressing mode is currently available in few microprocessors. One machine that does have it is the 6100, produced by Intersil and Harris.

Register-Indirect Addressing

This method of addressing (not available in the 6800) is sometimes available in machines having a register stack (see Section 4.5). The format might be

where the REG field points to one of 16 registers. The value in the indicated register is used as the desired operand's memory address. This provides the programmer up to 16 array pointers—not as flexible as indirect, but certainly better than no indirect addressing at all.

Autoincrement

Autoincrement (also not available in the 6800) is not an addressing mode in itself, but a function tied closely to memory addressing. It is found in some larger machines, as well as the 6100 microprocessor, and functions in the 6100 as follows. Each time a memory location from 010_8 to 017_8 is used as an address, it is incremented by one. This allows indexing through an array without a special instruction for incrementing an index register or array pointer. This results in fast running array oriented programs. **Autodecrement,** the complement to autoincrement, is also found in the 6100.

4.4 INTRODUCTION TO ASSEMBLY LANGUAGE

As we have seen, the computer control unit executes only one representation of an instruction—1s and 0s. Programs written in this fashion are extremely hard for a human to read or produce; therefore, many substitute computer programming languages have been developed. The lowest "level" (or closest to machine) language available to most computers is **assembly language.** When one writes a program in assembly code, English-like statements, instead of binary code, are used. A special program called an **assembler** (provided with the machine) is designed to take the assembly statements and convert them to machine code. Some assemblers are able to run on the subject machine and others are written to run on various other computers. In the latter case, the assembler is called a **cross-assembler.**

Assembly language is unique among programming languages in its one to one correspondence between the machine code statements produced by the assembler, and the original assembly statements.[*] In general, each line of assembly code assembles into one machine statement. The most significant functions performed by the assembler are to allow programmers to use English words in place of binary numbers and to allow the substitution of English-like mnemonics for binary OPCODEs. Because of the one to one relationship, assembly language permits all the programming flexibilities of machine code while eliminating the drudgery of communicating with ones and zeros.

There are three basic types of assembly statements:

1. Normal instructions.
2. Data statements.
3. Pseudoinstructions.

Normal instructions are machine language instructions in an English format. As mentioned above, they translate into only one machine instruction. The assembly format for such an instruction is as follows:

LABEL   MNEMONIC   OPERAND

The **label** is an alphanumeric character string that is used to "name" the instruction for future reference. It is assigned the value of the memory address in which the subject instruction is to reside. A label can therefore be used as the operand (branch address) of a branch instruction to cause a branch to the instruction "named" by the label.

The **mnemonic** is an alphanumeric character string that is used to replace the 8 bit OPCODE. The *operand* is the subject of the mnemonic and can either be a numeric value or a character string called a **symbol.** Numeric values can be expressed in binary, decimal, or octal with the following notations:

Numeric Value	Base
DIGITS	Decimal (base 10)
$ DIGITS	Hexidecimal (base 16)

[*]See Chapter 27 for a more detailed treatment of assembly language.

Numeric Value	Base
@ DIGITS	Octal (base 8)
% DIGITS	Binary (base 2)

For example, to express the binary value 1010_2 as an operand, one uses %1010. For a hexadecimal $9AF_{16}$, $9AF is the operand. Digits with no preceding character are assumed to be decimal. Symbols are character strings which are assigned a numeric value elsewhere in the program. In assembly language, a symbol can be used to replace any numeric value including operands and addresses. Symbols are assigned values using a **data statement.**

When a data statement is processed by the assembler, no instruction is produced. Instead, one or more bytes of memory are reserved, a constant value may be placed in those locations, and a name (label) may be given to the first location. For example, the 6800 assembler statement **RMB (reserve memory byte)** can be used as follows:

DATA1   RMB   3

This RMB instructs the assembler to reserve 3 bytes beginning with the first location following the previous instruction, naming the first location DATA1. No particular data is placed in these locations. If the programmer desires initialization of a memory location with a constant value, **FCB (form constant byte)** may be used, as illustrated below:

SIX   FCB   6

The next available location is assigned the name SIX by the assembler and will contain the binary value 00000110. Most assemblers include data statements of this type, in addition to others. Careful reading of the appropriate programming manual is necessary to fully appreciate their usage.

The final type of assembly statement mentioned is the **pseudoinstruction.** These are used to give instructions to the assembler itself. They produce no machine instructions or data output. Examples are ORG and END, which simply tell the assembler where to start the program in memory and when the last statement has been processed. Their use is illustrated:

ORG $100
Instruction #1
.
.
Instruction #n
END

This ORG statement causes instruction #1 to be placed starting in location 100_{16}. When the END statement is reached, the assembly procedure stops.

The assembler also permits convenient use of the various addressing modes. The 6800 assembler accepts these single characters in place of the mode names.

Addressing Mode	Address Mode Character
IMMEDIATE	#
INDEXED	X
RELATIVE	*
EXTENDED	None required
DIRECT	None required

The following example illustrates the use of the # sign as an indication of immediate addressing:

LDAA   # $FF

This instruction causes accumulator A to be loaded with the immediate operand $FF. If no address mode character is used, the extended or direct mode is assumed by the assembler. Direct is chosen where the address falls in the range of 0 to 255_{10} (8 bits). In cases where more than 8 bits are required, the extended mode is used.

The program of Figure 4.4 and program listing of Figures 4.5 and 4.6 illustrate a complete assembly language program along with the machine code generated by the assembler.

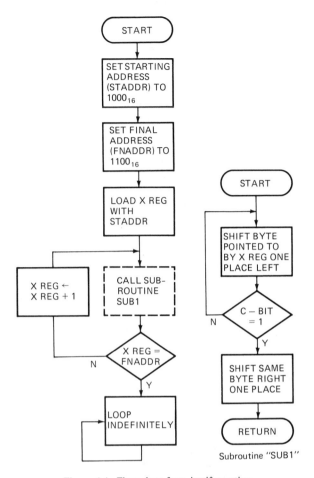

Figure 4.4. Flow chart for a justify routine.

4.5 INSTRUCTION SET

The number of instructions included in an instruction set can vary widely from processor to processor. The 6800 includes 72 whereas the bipolar 8X300 has only 8. The 8X300, however, is nearly ten times faster than the 6800 and is capable of executing programs of the same complexity with an increased programming effort. As is the case with hardware logic, only a small set of functions are necessary to perform any logical or arithmetic operation. But, as any logic designer knows well, it is far more convenient to have in one's arsenal some predefined combinations of functions that are tailored to common applications. In a general sense, microprocessor instructions can be divided into the following five categories:

- Logical.
- Arithmetic.
- Sequence control.
- Special control.
- Input/output (I/O).

Machine Status Bits

Almost all microprocessors have instructions representing each of the five classes. The first two classes, logical and arithmetic, are used to perform data manipulation operations. The data result produced by these instructions is left in either a machine register or a memory location. Another effect of executing a data manipulation instruc-

```
 1.* MAIN PROGRAM TO LEFT JUSTIFY TABLE FROM 1000 to 1100

 2.  STADDR    EQU     $1000     EQUATE STARTING ADDRESS WITH HEX 1000

 3.  FNADDR    EQU     $1100     EQUATE FINAL ADDRESS WITH HEX 1100

 4.            LDX     #STADDR   LOAD INDEX REG WITH 1000

 5.  MAIN      JSR     SUB1

 6.            CPX     #FNADDR   COMPARE INDEX REG WITH 1100

 7.            BEQ     DONE      IF X REG CONTAINS 1100 JUMP TO DONE

 8.            INX               INCREMENT X REG

 9.            BRA     MAIN      JUMP TO MAIN

10.  DONE      BRA     DONE      LOOP HERE INDEFINITELY


11.* SUBROUTINE TO LEFT JUSTIFY BYTE AT MEMORY LOCATION POINTED

12.* TO BY INDEX REGISTER

13.  SUB1      ASL     $00,X     SHIFT BYTE IN TABLE LEFT ONCE

14.            BCS     FIX       BRANCH IF "1" SHIFTED INTO CARRY-BIT

15.            BRA     SUB1      BRANCH BACK FOR MORE SHIFTS

16.  FIX       ROR     $00,X     CORRECT FOR EXTRA SHIFT

17.            RTS               RETURN
```

Figure 4.5. Justify routine program listing.

tion is the modification of one or more machine status bits. The 6800 includes five such bits, called **flags:**

- Zero (Z).
- Carry (C).
- Negative (N).
- Overflow (V).
- Half carry (H).

Not all instructions modify all of the above status bits. Instead, each instruction modifies only selected status bits

Assembly Statements			Hex Address	Machine Code
STADDR	EQU	$1000		
FNADDR	EQU	$1100		
	LDX	$STADDR	0000	CE 0000
MAIN	JSR	SUB1	0003	BD 0010
	CPX	$FNADDR	0006	8C 1100
	BEQ	DONE	0009	27 03
	INX		000B	08
	BRA	MAIN	000C	20 F5
DONE	BRA	DONE	000E	20 FE
SUB1	ASL	$00,X	0010	68 00
	BCS	FIX	0012	25 02
	BRA	SUB1	0014	20 FA
FIX	ROR	$00,X	0016	66 00
	RTS		0018	39

Figure 4.6. Justify routine machine code.

as shown in Tables 4.1, 2, 3, and 4. These bits are generally interpreted as follows:

Z-bit: If an ALU operation produces a result of zero, the Z bit is set to 1. If the operation produces a non-zero result, the Z-bit is cleared.

C-bit: The **carry bit** is interpreted in two ways. As the name indicates, the carry bit is set during arithmetic operations if the most significant bit of the adder (located within the ALU) produces a carryout. The C-bit is also modified during Shift or Rotate (Circular Shift) instructions. In this case, the bit shifted out of the end position is transferred to the carry bit. (This process is described later in this section.)

N-bit: If the result of an instruction is negative (2s complement negative implies that the most significant bit equals 1), then the N-bit is set to 1; otherwise, it is cleared.

V-bit: The **overflow bit** is set to 1 if the result of an arithmetic operation results in a 2s complement overflow.

H-bit: The H-bit is modified only by ADD instructions and represents the value of the carryout of the fourth bit (from the right) of the adder.

It should be noted that a status bit, once modified by an instruction execution, will remain at the same value until another instruction execution causes it to change.

The **machine status bits** are included in the architecture for two reasons:

1. They are used as branch conditions. The 6800 permits conditional branching based only on status bit values, singly or in logical combinations.
2. They are used as participants in data manipulation operations. The carry bit dominates in this usage because it acts as a connecting link between multiple step operations such as multiple length addition, subtraction and circular shifts.

Logical Instructions

Some of the logic instructions included in the 6800 are

(*Continues on p. 72*)

Table 4.1. Accumulator and Memory Instructions

OPERATIONS	MNEMONIC	IMMED OP	~	=	DIRECT OP	~	=	INDEX OP	~	=	EXTND OP	~	=	IMPLIED OP	~	=	BOOLEAN/ARITHMETIC OPERATION (All register labels refer to contents)	H	I	N	Z	V	C
Add	ADDA	8B	2	2	9B	3	2	AB	5	2	BB	4	3				A + M → A	↕	●	↕	↕	↕	↕
	ADDB	CB	2	2	DB	3	2	EB	5	2	FB	4	3				B + M → B	↕	●	↕	↕	↕	↕
Add Acmltrs	ABA													1B	2	1	A + B → A	↕	●	↕	↕	↕	↕
Add with Carry	ADCA	89	2	2	99	3	2	A9	5	2	B9	4	3				A + M + C → A	↕	●	↕	↕	↕	↕
	ADCB	C9	2	2	D9	3	2	E9	5	2	F9	4	3				B + M + C → B	↕	●	↕	↕	↕	↕
And	ANDA	84	2	2	94	3	2	A4	5	2	B4	4	3				A · M → A	●	●	↕	↕	R	●
	ANDB	C4	2	2	D4	3	2	E4	5	2	F4	4	3				B · M → B	●	●	↕	↕	R	●
Bit Test	BITA	85	2	2	95	3	2	A5	5	2	B5	4	3				A · M	●	●	↕	↕	R	●
	BITB	C5	2	2	D5	3	2	E5	5	2	F5	4	3				B · M	●	●	↕	↕	R	●
Clear	CLR							6F	7	2	7F	6	3				00 → M	●	●	R	S	R	R
	CLRA													4F	2	1	00 → A	●	●	R	S	R	R
	CLRB													5F	2	1	00 → B	●	●	R	S	R	R
Compare	CMPA	81	2	2	91	3	2	A1	5	2	B1	4	3				A − M	●	●	↕	↕	↕	↕
	CMPB	C1	2	2	D1	3	2	E1	5	2	F1	4	3				B − M	●	●	↕	↕	↕	↕
Compare Acmltrs	CBA													11	2	1	A − B	●	●	↕	↕	↕	↕
Complement, 1's	COM							63	7	2	73	6	3				$\overline{M}$ → M	●	●	↕	↕	R	S
	COMA													43	2	1	$\overline{A}$ → A	●	●	↕	↕	R	S
	COMB													53	2	1	$\overline{B}$ → B	●	●	↕	↕	R	S
Complement, 2's	NEG							60	7	2	70	6	3				00 − M → M	●	●	↕	↕	①	②
(Negate)	NEGA													40	2	1	00 − A → A	●	●	↕	↕	①	②
	NEGB													50	2	1	00 − B → B	●	●	↕	↕	①	②
Decimal Adjust, A	DAA													19	2	1	Converts Binary Add. of BCD Characters into BCD Format	●	●	↕	↕	↕	③
Decrement	DEC							6A	7	2	7A	6	3				M − 1 → M	●	●	↕	↕	④	●
	DECA													4A	2	1	A − 1 → A	●	●	↕	↕	④	●
	DECB													5A	2	1	B − 1 → B	●	●	↕	↕	④	●
Exclusive OR	EORA	88	2	2	98	3	2	A8	5	2	B8	4	3				A ⊕ M → A	●	●	↕	↕	R	●
	EORB	C8	2	2	D8	3	2	E8	5	2	F8	4	3				B ⊕ M → B	●	●	↕	↕	R	●
Increment	INC							6C	7	2	7C	6	3				M + 1 → M	●	●	↕	↕	⑤	●
	INCA													4C	2	1	A + 1 → A	●	●	↕	↕	⑤	●
	INCB													5C	2	1	B + 1 → B	●	●	↕	↕	⑤	●
Load Acmltr	LDAA	86	2	2	96	3	2	A6	5	2	B6	4	3				M → A	●	●	↕	↕	R	●
	LDAB	C6	2	2	D6	3	2	E6	5	2	F6	4	3				M → B	●	●	↕	↕	R	●
Or, Inclusive	ORAA	8A	2	2	9A	3	2	AA	5	2	BA	4	3				A + M → A	●	●	↕	↕	R	●
	ORAB	CA	2	2	DA	3	2	EA	5	2	FA	4	3				B + M → B	●	●	↕	↕	R	●
Push Data	PSHA													36	4	1	A → M_{SP}, SP − 1 → SP	●	●	●	●	●	●
	PSHB													37	4	1	B → M_{SP}, SP − 1 → SP	●	●	●	●	●	●
Pull Data	PULA													32	4	1	SP + 1 → SP, M_{SP} → A	●	●	●	●	●	●
	PULB													33	4	1	SP + 1 → SP, M_{SP} → B	●	●	●	●	●	●
Rotate Left	ROL							69	7	2	79	6	3				M	●	●	↕	↕	⑥	↕
	ROLA													49	2	1	A	●	●	↕	↕	⑥	↕
	ROLB													59	2	1	B	●	●	↕	↕	⑥	↕
Rotate Right	ROR							66	7	2	76	6	3				M	●	●	↕	↕	⑥	↕
	RORA													46	2	1	A	●	●	↕	↕	⑥	↕
	RORB													56	2	1	B	●	●	↕	↕	⑥	↕
Shift Left, Arithmetic	ASL							68	7	2	78	6	3				M	●	●	↕	↕	⑥	↕
	ASLA													48	2	1	A	●	●	↕	↕	⑥	↕
	ASLB													58	2	1	B	●	●	↕	↕	⑥	↕
Shift Right, Arithmetic	ASR							67	7	2	77	6	3				M	●	●	↕	↕	⑥	↕
	ASRA													47	2	1	A	●	●	↕	↕	⑥	↕
	ASRB													57	2	1	B	●	●	↕	↕	⑥	↕
Shift Right, Logic	LSR							64	7	2	74	6	3				M	●	●	R	↕	⑥	↕
	LSRA													44	2	1	A	●	●	R	↕	⑥	↕
	LSRB													54	2	1	B	●	●	R	↕	⑥	↕
Store Acmltr.	STAA				97	4	2	A7	6	2	B7	5	3				A → M	●	●	↕	↕	R	●
	STAB				D7	4	2	E7	6	2	F7	5	3				B → M	●	●	↕	↕	R	●
Subtract	SUBA	80	2	2	90	3	2	A0	5	2	B0	4	3				A − M → A	●	●	↕	↕	↕	↕
	SUBB	C0	2	2	D0	3	2	E0	5	2	F0	4	3				B − M → B	●	●	↕	↕	↕	↕
Subtract Acmltrs.	SBA													10	2	1	A − B → A	●	●	↕	↕	↕	↕
Subtr. with Carry	SBCA	82	2	2	92	3	2	A2	5	2	B2	4	3				A − M − C → A	●	●	↕	↕	↕	↕
	SBCB	C2	2	2	D2	3	2	E2	5	2	F2	4	3				B − M − C → B	●	●	↕	↕	↕	↕
Transfer Acmltrs	TAB													16	2	1	A → B	●	●	↕	↕	R	●
	TBA													17	2	1	B → A	●	●	↕	↕	R	●
Test, Zero or Minus	TST							6D	7	2	7D	6	3				M − 00	●	●	↕	↕	R	R
	TSTA													4D	2	1	A − 00	●	●	↕	↕	R	R
	TSTB													5D	2	1	B − 00	●	●	↕	↕	R	R

	H	I	N	Z	V	C

LEGEND:

OP	Operation Code (Hexadecimal);	+	Boolean Inclusive OR;
~	Number of MPU Cycles;	⊙	Boolean Exclusive OR;
=	Number of Program Bytes;	$\overline{M}$	Complement of M;
+	Arithmetic Plus;	→	Transfer Into;
−	Arithmetic Minus;	0	Bit = Zero;
·	Boolean AND;	00	Byte = Zero;
M_{SP}	Contents of memory location pointed to be Stack Pointer;		

Note − Accumulator addressing mode instructions are included in the column for IMPLIED addressing

CONDITION CODE SYMBOLS:

H	Half-carry from bit 3;
I	Interrupt mask
N	Negative (sign bit)
Z	Zero (byte)
V	Overflow, 2's complement
C	Carry from bit 7
R	Reset Always
S	Set Always
↕	Test and set if true, cleared otherwise
●	Not Affected

Table 4.2. Index Register and Stack Manipulation Instructions

POINTER OPERATIONS	MNEMONIC	IMMED			DIRECT			INDEX			EXTND			IMPLIED			BOOLEAN/ARITHMETIC OPERATION	H	I	N	Z	V	C
		OP	~	#	OP	~	#	OP	~	#	OP	~	#	OP	~	#		5	4	3	2	1	0
Compare Index Reg	CPX	8C	3	3	9C	4	2	AC	6	2	BC	5	3				$X_H - M, X_L - (M+1)$	•	•	⑦	‡	⑦	•
Decrement Index Reg	DEX													09	4	1	$X - 1 \rightarrow X$	•	•	•	‡	•	•
Decrement Stack Pntr	DES													34	4	1	$SP - 1 \rightarrow SP$	•	•	•	•	•	•
Increment Index Reg	INX													08	4	1	$X + 1 \rightarrow X$	•	•	•	‡	•	•
Increment Stack Pntr	INS													31	4	1	$SP + 1 \rightarrow SP$	•	•	•	•	•	•
Load Index Reg	LDX	CE	3	3	DE	4	2	EE	6	2	FE	5	3				$M \rightarrow X_H, (M + 1) \rightarrow X_L$	•	•	⑨	‡	R	•
Load Stack Pntr	LDS	8E	3	3	9E	4	2	AE	6	2	BE	5	3				$M \rightarrow SP_H, (M + 1) \rightarrow SP_L$	•	•	⑨	‡	R	•
Store Index Reg	STX				0F	5	2	EF	7	2	FF	6	3				$X_H \rightarrow M, X_L \rightarrow (M + 1)$	•	•	⑨	‡	R	•
Store Stack Pntr	STS				9F	5	2	AF	7	2	BF	6	3				$SP_H \rightarrow M, SP_L \rightarrow (M + 1)$	•	•	⑨	‡	R	•
Indx Reg → Stack Pntr	TXS													35	4	1	$X - 1 \rightarrow SP$	•	•	•	•	•	•
Stack Pntr → Indx Reg	TSX													30	4	1	$SP + 1 \rightarrow X$	•	•	•	•	•	•

(Courtesy Motorola, Inc.)

Table 4.3. Jump and Branch Instructions

OPERATIONS	MNEMONIC	RELATIVE			INDEX			EXTND			IMPLIED			BRANCH TEST	H	I	N	Z	V	C
		OP	~	#	OP	~	#	OP	~	#	OP	~	#		5	4	3	2	1	0
Branch Always	BRA	20	4	2										None	•	•	•	•	•	•
Branch If Carry Clear	BCC	24	4	2										$C = 0$	•	•	•	•	•	•
Branch If Carry Set	BCS	25	4	2										$C = 1$	•	•	•	•	•	•
Branch If = Zero	BEQ	27	4	2										$Z = 1$	•	•	•	•	•	•
Branch If ≥ Zero	BGE	2C	4	2										$N \oplus V = 0$	•	•	•	•	•	•
Branch If > Zero	BGT	2E	4	2										$Z + (N \oplus V) = 0$	•	•	•	•	•	•
Branch If Higher	BHI	22	4	2										$C + Z = 0$	•	•	•	•	•	•
Branch If ≤ Zero	BLE	2F	4	2										$Z + (N \oplus V) = 1$	•	•	•	•	•	•
Branch If Lower Or Same	BLS	23	4	2										$C + Z = 1$	•	•	•	•	•	•
Branch If < Zero	BLT	2D	4	2										$N \oplus V = 1$	•	•	•	•	•	•
Branch If Minus	BMI	2B	4	2										$N = 1$	•	•	•	•	•	•
Branch If Not Equal Zero	BNE	26	4	2										$Z = 0$	•	•	•	•	•	•
Branch If Overflow Clear	BVC	28	4	2										$V = 0$	•	•	•	•	•	•
Branch If Overflow Set	BVS	29	4	2										$V = 1$	•	•	•	•	•	•
Branch If Plus	BPL	2A	4	2										$N = 0$	•	•	•	•	•	•
Branch To Subroutine	BSR	8D	8	2											•	•	•	•	•	•
Jump	JMP				6E	4	2	7E	3	3				See Special Operations	•	•	•	•	•	•
Jump To Subroutine	JSR				AD	8	2	BD	9	3				See Special Operations	•	•	•	•	•	•
No Operation	NOP										02	2	1	Advances Prog. Cntr. Only	•	•	•	•	•	•
Return From Interrupt	RTI										3B	10	1		⑩					
Return From Subroutine	RTS										39	5	1	See Special Operations	•	•	•	•	•	•
Software Interrupt	SWI										3F	12	1	See Special Operations	•	•	•	•	•	•
Wait for Interrupt	WAI										3E	9	1		•	⑪	•	•	•	•

(Table courtesy Motorola, Inc.)

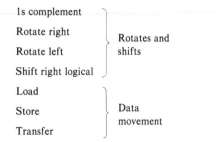

- 1s complement ⎫
- Rotate right ⎬ Rotates and shifts
- Rotate left ⎪
- Shift right logical ⎭
- Load ⎫
- Store ⎬ Data movement
- Transfer ⎭

The Boolean functions perform their respective operations bit by bit on the operand(s). Consider the case in which ACCUM A holds the value 01100110_2 and the following AND immediate ANDA instruction is executed:

$$\text{ANDA} \ \# \ \$55$$

The AND of the following two numbers is taken and the result is placed in ACCUM A:

01010101	Immediate operand
01100110	Initial value of ACCUM A
01000100	Final value of ACCUM A

The two OR instructions (inclusive, exclusive) function in an analogous manner, whereas the clear instruction uti-

Table 4.4. Condition Code Register Manipulation Instructions

| OPERATIONS | MNEMONIC | IMPLIED | | | BOOLEAN OPERATION | COND. CODE REG. | | | | | |
		OP	~	#		5 H	4 I	3 N	2 Z	1 V	0 C
Clear Carry	CLC	0C	2	1	0 → C	●	●	●	●	●	R
Clear Interrupt Mask	CLI	0E	2	1	0 → I	●	R	●	●	●	●
Clear Overflow	CLV	0A	2	1	0 → V	●	●	●	●	R	●
Set Carry	SEC	0D	2	1	1 → C	●	●	●	●	●	S
Set Interrupt Mask	SEI	0F	2	1	1 → I	●	S	●	●	●	●
Set Overflow	SEV	0B	2	1	1 → V	●	●	●	●	S	●
Acmltr A → CCR	TAP	06	2	1	A → CCR			⑫			
CCR → Acmltr A	TPA	07	2	1	CCR → A	●	●	●	●	●	●

CONDITION CODE REGISTER NOTES:

(Bit set if test is true and cleared otherwise)

1	(Bit V)	Test: Result = 10000000?
2	(Bit C)	Test: Result = 00000000?
3	(Bit C)	Test: Decimal value of most significant BCD Character greater than nine? (Not cleared if previously set.)
4	(Bit V)	Test: Operand = 10000000 prior to execution?
5	(Bit V)	Test: Operand = 01111111 prior to execution?
6	(Bit V)	Test: Set equal to result of N⊕C after shift has occurred.
7	(Bit N)	Test: Sign bit of most significant (MS) byte = 1?
8	(Bit V)	Test: 2's complement overflow from subtraction of MS bytes?
9	(Bit N)	Test: Result less than zero? (Bit 15 = 1)
10	(All)	Load Condition Code Register from Stack. (See Special Operations)
11	(Bit I)	Set when interrupt occurs. If previously set, a Non-Maskable Interrupt is required to exit the wait state.
12	(All)	Set according to the contents of Accumulator A.

(Courtesy Motorola, Inc.)

lizes only one operand by clearing its value to 0, be it in an accumulator or memory.

The second subdivision of logic instructions is "rotates and shifts." These instructions utilize only one operand by shifting the bits one position to the right or left. A **rotate** differs from a **shift** in the way the end bit position is handled. First, consider the **shift right logical (LSR)** instruction. The operand (ACCUM or a memory location) is concatenated with the carry bit as shown below:

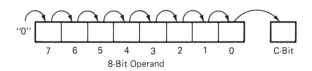

8-Bit Operand

The value in each bit position is shifted one place to the right. As is the case with any logic instruction, the shift-in bit position is set to 0. Notice that the least significant bit is shifted out into the carry bit. This preserves the value of this bit, permitting both testing of its value (branch-on carry), or multiple length shifting.

In contrast to logical shift right, the rotate right

(ROR) instruction operates as shown below:

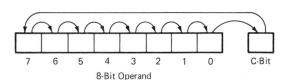

8-Bit Operand

Here the carry bit is shifted into bit 7 of the 8 bit operand. Because the 9 bit word rotates in a circular fashion around the 9 bit register, a Rotate operation is often called a **circular shift**. Repeating the circular shift nine times results in no change to the original 8 bit operand. Rotate left operates in the same fashion, except that the direction of shift is to the left.

The last subdivision of logical instructions is the **data movement** type. This subgroup includes these instructions:

- Load,
- Store,
- Transfer.

The **load** instruction brings an operand from memory and places it in an accumulator. In microprocessors with a register stack, this definition is extended to imply a memory to register transfer of the operand. The **store** instruction operates in reverse, and transfers an operand from an accumulator to memory. The **transfer** instruction simply transfers the value of one accumulator to another.

Arithmetic Instructions

Some arithmetic instructions included in the 6800 are

Add	Shift left arithmetic
Add with carry	Shift right arithmetic
2s complement	Subtract
Increment	Subtract with carry (borrow)
Decrement	

These arithmetic instructions provide not only the capability to perform addition and subtraction, but these same operations in multiple precision, as well as multiples and divides, are available. **Multiple precision** is a technique for increasing the accuracy of an operand by using more than one byte for its representation.

A single byte operand (8 bits) can take on only 1 of 256 values whereas a two byte operand (16 bits) can have 1 of 65,536 values. Single precision add and subtract operations are performed directly on 2s complement operands using the add and subtract instructions. Multiple precision adds and subtracts are performed by using the same instructions along with the add with carry and subtract with carry instructions. For example, consider the following double precision addition:

EXAMPLE 4.7

As the diagram illustrates, the least significant half of the two operands are added (using the ADD instruction). The carry produced by the add is placed automatically in the C-bit. The most significant halves of the two operands, as well as the C-bit, are then added together (using

the add with carry instruction) to produce the most significant half of the result. Again, the carryout is placed in the C-bit. This technique can be extended to as many bytes of precision as required. Multilength subtraction is performed in the same manner using the subtract and subtract with carry instructions.

The arithmetic shift instructions are useful in programming more complex mathematical operations, such as multiply and divide. These two functions are not available in the 6800 as instructions, but can be performed utilizing short routines. Hardware multiplication is, however, available in a few machines. Next generation 16 bit microprocessors will include much more along these lines, including possibly floating point instructions.

The **arithmetic shift right** (ASR) instruction operates in a manner that is often called "shift right with sign fill." Unlike the logical shift right (LSR), which fills the vacated most significant bit with a zero, the arithmetic shift retains the sign bit but otherwise shifts in the same manner. The following example illustrates ASR instruction operand before and after execution:

EXAMPLE 4.8

	OPERAND (2s Complement)	Decimal Value
Before shift	1101 1100	-36
After shift	1110 1110	-18

The reader may have noticed that the operand of value -36_{10} when shifted right produced a result of -18_{10}, a division by two. This is a general property of the arithmetic shifts and forms the fundamental basis for multiply, divide, and floating point operations. **Arithmetic left shift** (ASL) functions in a similar manner, but in reverse.

Sequence Control Instructions

The sequence control instructions are designed to permit the branching functions described in Section 4.2 (Instruction Sequencing) as well as "subroutining". **Subroutining**

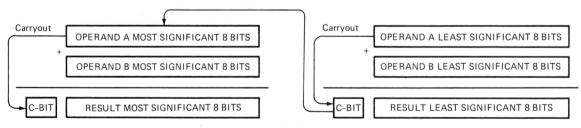

Diagram for Example 4.7.

is a technique of using subprograms to make more efficient use of memory space and allow programming to be done in a structured manner. The following is a partial list of sequence control instructions included in the 6800:

Instruction	Mnemonic	Type
Jump	JMP	Unconditional branches
Branch always	BRA	
Branch if carry set	BCS	
Branch if carry clear	BCC	Conditional branches
Branch if = 0	BEQ	
Branch if ≥ 0	BGE	
Jump to subroutine	JSR	
Branch to subroutine	BSR	Subroutine linkage
Return from subroutine	RTS	

Unconditional Branches

These instructions cause instruction fetch to be directed to a new area of memory unconditionally. The jump (JMP) operates in the indexed or extended mode, and therefore has the following format:

OPCODE
7   0

ADDR 1
7   0

ADDR 0
7   0

For the extended mode, the OPCODE is followed by two bytes (16 bits) of address which point to one memory location in the 65K address space. The instruction executed after the JMP will be the one starting at this memory location.

The **branch always (BRA)** instruction operates in only the relative mode and is therefore formatted as follows:

OPCODE
7   0

OFFSET
7   0

The 8 bit 2s complement offset is added to the program counter. This produces a branch to a location within 1 of 256 locations around the current location. Note that a 2s

complement offset can have values from 10000000_2 to 01111111_2, or in decimal, -128 to $+127$.

Conditional Branches

A **conditional branch** is an instruction that either results in a branch to a new location or not, based on the result of a test specified by the OPCODE. In the 6800, all branch tests are combinations of the machine status bits. An example of a 6800 conditional branch is the **branch if carry set (BCS)**, formatted as follows:

OPCODE
7   0

OFFSET
7   0

If the carry bit is set, the 8 bit OFFSET is added to the PC. If it is not set, the instruction following the BCS is executed. "Branch if carry clear" operates in a similar manner, except that the branch only takes place if the carry bit is 0.

Some conditional branches rely on more than one status bit. An example is "branch if greater than or equal" (BGE). It can be easily verified that an ALU result greater than or equal to zero will leave the N and V status bits having values that satisfy the relationship:

$$N \vee V = 0$$

The BGE therefore tests for this relation. If it holds true, the branch is taken. The other conditional branches test different conditions, and therefore check different status bit relationships.

Subroutine Linkage

A subroutine is a subprogram defined by the programmer to perform a function that is repeated. An example of subroutine usage is an arithmetic operation, like multiply. Here, there is no multiply instruction which means that the programmer must write a multiply subprogram. To execute this multiply like an instruction, a way of branching to the multiply routine each time it is to be performed and returning to the next instruction after the multiply is finished must be devised. This capability is provided on most computers in the form of subroutine linkage instructions.

Fundamental to the use of subroutines is the concept of a **last-in, first-out (LIFO)** stack. A LIFO stack is an array of data in which the last data entered is the first data that can be retrieved. LIFO stacks can be implemented in two ways: hardware and software. In the hardware stack, all data entered or retrieved must pass through the top location (ϕ in the diagram shown below).

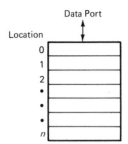

The first word entered goes into Location ϕ. When the second word is entered, the data in ϕ is "pushed" down into location 1 before the new data goes into ϕ. When a third word is entered, the first two words are pushed down, and so on. Retrieval of data occurs in exactly the opposite order. Each time a word is read off the top of the stack, all data words in the stack are "popped" up one location (i.e., 2 to 1, 3 to 2, 4 to 3, etc.). Note that all the stack user need do is indicate "push" or "pop" to the stack to transfer data in or out of location ϕ. All other locations are transferred automatically by stack hardware.

The software stack performs the same function as a hardware stack, but instead of operating out of dedicated stack hardware, it is able to operate out of the processor's memory. The 6800 (as well as many other microprocessors), uses a software stack for several functions, including subroutine linkage. The key to the 6800 software stack operation is a 16 bit pointer register called the **stack pointer** (**SP**). The SP points to the location of the stack's top. Instead of moving the data up or down in the stack, the data is left in place and the stacktop is moved by changing the value in the SP. The following rules apply in reading from or writing to the stack:

1. When a word is to be added to the stack, the data is first written to the location pointed to by the SP, after which the SP is decremented by 1.
2. When a word is to be read off the stack, the SP is first incremented by 1, after which the data is read off the stack.

Consider the following example where the SP points to location 8 in memory and the data "19" is added to the stack:

EXAMPLE 4.9

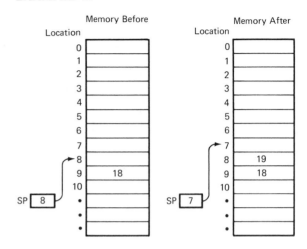

Note that the stacktop moves from location 8 to 7. If another write operation places the value 26 on the top of the stack, the SP and memory would appear as follows:

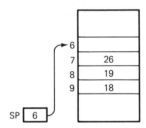

Again the SP is decremented. Read operations first move the stacktop down by one and then extract the data from the location pointed to by the SP. For example, a single read would now derive the value 26 and leave the following configuration of SP and memory:

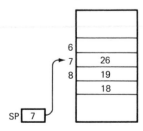

The 26 still resides in Memory Location 7 but does not belong to the stack, which now starts at 8.

In returning to the subject of subroutine operation in the 6800, it will now be shown how a software LIFO stack is utilized. There are two instructions that allow branching to subroutines, one of which is **jump to subroutine (JSR)**. This instruction operates in the extended or indexed modes and therefore has the format shown below.

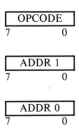

Consistent with these modes, a 16 bit effective address is computed. This address is interpreted as the starting location of the subroutine being called. Before the effective address is placed in the PC, the current value of the PC plus 3 (length in bytes of JMS instruction) is placed on the LIFO stacktop. The stacktop now contains the address of the instruction which follows the JMS. This can later be used to return to the main program when the subroutine is completed.

The other subroutine call instruction, **branch to subroutine (BSR),** operates in the program relative mode only. The BSR OPCODE is therefore followed by a one byte offset which is added to the current value of the PC to calculate the 16 bit starting address of the subroutine. Because the BSR instruction is 2 bytes long, the current PC plus 2 is placed on the stacktop, after which the 16 bit effective address is transferred to the PC. The next instruction executed will therefore be the first instruction of the subroutine.

Once a subroutine is completed, the return address on the stacktop must be transferred to the PC to effect a branch back to the main "calling" program. This is accomplished with the **return from subroutine (RTS)** instruction. Because no effective address need be computed for **RTS,** the instruction length is only 1 byte, the OPCODE.

The example program shown in Figure 4.5 illustrates the use of JMS and RTS. This program, when executed, will cause **leftmost zero suppression** on all data bytes in locations 1000_{16} to 1100_{16}. This type of function is commonly used in the programming of floating point arithmetic operations in returning all results to scientific notation. Leftmost zero suppression produces the following kind of result:

Before	After
0110 1111	1101 1110
0011 1101	1111 0100
0010 1000	1010 0000
etc.	

As can be seen, each byte is shifted left until all leading 0s are eliminated.

Flowcharts for the justify routine are shown in Figure 4.4. The left flowchart, the **calling** routine, illustrates the table indexing functions that are required in accessing each element of the array that is to be left justified. The right flowchart illustrates the justification procedure itself. Initially, the calling routine places in the index (X) register the address of the first table location, 1000_{16}. The subroutine, SUB1, is then called to left justify the memory location pointed to by the X register. This is accomplished by repeatedly shifting the data in this memory location arithmetically left until the carry becomes set.

Once this occurs, the algorithm has performed one too many left shifts and then performs one rotate right (ROR) to correct the overshifting. Following this correction, a return from subroutine is executed, returning control to the calling routine. After receiving control, the calling routine first checks the value of the X register to see if it contains the address of the last table location to be justified (1100_{16}). If it does, the calling program halts. If not, the value in the X-register is increased by one and the subroutine is called again. This procedure is repeated until all table values have been left justified.

The 6800 assembly language program listing shown in Figure 4.5 implements the above algorithm. As was the case in previous examples, the numbers to the left of each assembly statement are only for the purposes of describing the program in the text. Assembly statement 1 is a comment card. The * in the leftmost column tells the assembler not to assemble this statement. Data statements 2 and 3 equate the symbols STADDR and FNADDR with the table starting and finishing addresses 1000_{16} and 1100_{16} respectively. This produces no machine code, but simply permits the programmer to use the character strings STADDR and FNADDR instead of the numbers 1000 and 1100 in writing the rest of the program.

For example, the next instruction, LDX # STADDR, which is used to initialize the X-register with the table starting address (1000_{16}) is exactly the same as LDX # $1000 because STADDR has been equated with $1,000. Statement 5 causes a transfer of control to subroutine SUB1, which performs the left justify on the location pointed to by the X register. Following return from subroutine, the X register is compared to the final table address (FNADDR) with an **immediate compare index register** (**CPX**) instruction. During this instruction, the CPX two byte immediate operand is subtracted from the value contained in the X-register. Based on this subtraction, the Z-, N-, and V-bits are set. Note however, that the X register contents are left unchanged, because the purpose of CPX is only to compare the two values and set the status bits, not to modify any memory or register contents.

If the two values compared above are equal, the Z-bit is set to 1 and the BEQ of statement 7 causes a jump to DONE (statement 10). This instruction, DONE BRA DONE, is a branch to itself and will loop at this location indefinitely. If the two values compared are unequal, the X register is incremented by 1 (statement 8) and a branch to MAIN (statement 5) is performed, causing another table entry to be left justified.

Special Control

All computers have some (or many) internal state flip-flops that are affected by instruction execution. On the 6800, the C-,N-,V-,H-, and Z-status bits are good examples. Most microprocessors have special instructions permitting manipulation of these states under direct program control. The 6800 provides the following special control instructions:

Instruction	Mnemonic
Clear carry	CLC
Clear interrupt mask	CLI
Clear overflow	CLV
Set carry	SEC
Set interrupt mask	SEI
Set overflow	SEV
Accum A→CCR	TAP
CCR→Accum A	TPA

The **clear carry** (**CLC**) and **clear overflow** (**CLV**) clear the C-bit and V-bit, respectively, when executed. These instructions, like the remaining six above, do not require any effective address and are therefore 1 byte in length. **Set carry** (**SEC**) and **set overflow** (**SEV**) both set their respective status bits. Another bit controlled by an instruction above, but not mentioned previously, is the **interrupt mask** bit, which will be described in detail in Section 4.6 under Interrupt Structures. At this point, suffice it to say that the interrupt mask bit is set and cleared by SEI and CLI instructions respectively. On the 6800, all status bits are grouped into a single byte register to allow program

control of all status bits simultaneously. The status byte has the following format:

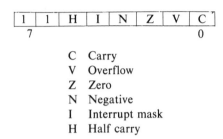

1	1	H	I	N	Z	V	C

7   0

C Carry
V Overflow
Z Zero
N Negative
I Interrupt mask
H Half carry

Because there are only 6 status bits, the most significant 2 bits of the status byte are 1s. Two instructions are available on the 6800 that permit transfer of the ACCUM A contents to the status byte, and vice versa. The first is ACCUM A→CCR. This transfers the contents of the Accumulator A to the status byte (also called **condition code register**). The CCR→ACCUM A instruction works in reverse by taking the status byte contents and transferring them to the accumulator.

Input Output (I/O) Instructions

In order to be useful, a microprocessor must have the ability both to send data to and receive data from external devices. Two basic elements are required to perform these operations. First, an interface must exist through which this data can flow and, second, the microprocessor must include instructions which enable the programmer to direct the data transfers. Interfacing will be discussed in Section 4.6 as it applies to memories, and I/O instructions will be described next.

Some microprocessors include instructions often described as "dedicated I/O instructions." By "dedicated" it is meant that they are used exclusively for input and output. As an example of this, consider the Intel 8085 Output (OUT) instruction with the following format:

OPCODE

7   0

PORT

7   0

The 8 bit OPCODE is followed by an 8 bit PORT address that can be valued from 0 to 255. Execution of the OUT instruction causes the contents of the 8085 accumulator to be transferred across the I/O interface along with the

8 bit PORT address. It is possible to have many devices connected to this interface, but only the one that recognizes the PORT address as its "device address" will accept the transmitted data. The 8085 also provides an **input (IN)** instruction with the same format. It works in a similar fashion but is used to transfer data from an I/O device to the accumulator.

Some microprocessors include no dedicated I/O instructions. These machines are able to conduct I/O operations with a technique called **memory mapped I/O.** In this case, an I/O device appears as a memory address so that all instructions that read from, or write to, memory can act as I/O instructions. This technique has some distinct advantages, the main one being the great amount of versatility it allows.

Suppose, for example, a 6800 programmer wants to add to ACCUM A an 8 bit value that can be retrieved from a device located at memory location $8FC8_{16}$. The single instruction

ADDA $8FC8

will cause the desired action, making it unneccessary to both input the data word and then add it to the accumulator.

The main disadvantage of memory mapped I/O is that the memory addresses dedicated to I/O addressing are no longer available for memory space. This is often of little concern, however, because most microprocessors have 65K and larger address spaces.

4.6 HARDWARE CONFIGURATIONS

Microprocessors are often used with two types of memory: **read-only memory (ROM)** and **read-write random access memory (RAM)** (see Chapter 3 for a further discussion). ROM, as its name suggests, can be read by the microprocessor, but not written into. ROM is often used to hold control programs on a permanent basis for such devices as disk drives and microwave ovens. ROMs are available in two basic formats: mask programmable and user programmable (PROM).

Mask programmable ROMs are programmed before manufacture by customization of a single IC mask layer. It is therefore necessary for the buyer to specify the program when ordering the devices. Normally, a significant startup fee is charged for this mask design, but the quantity price of this type ROM is low.

User programmable ROM is available in several versions including fusible-link and erasable (**EPROM**). Fusible-link PROM consists of memory elements containing fine wires that can be blown open (fused) by passing a large current through them. Each memory bit is programmed to a 0 or 1 by fusing or not fusing the associated link. This procedure can be performed automatically by a machine called a **ROM programmer.**

Erasable PROM consists of an array of MOS transistors with floating gates. A charge can be placed on these gates that will remain there for as long as ten years or more. The advantage of this type of memory is that they can be erased in one of several ways, depending on the type device being used. EPROMs are rather expensive, but are useful in prototyping ROM based systems.

Currently, almost all available ROMs are "random access" devices. Random access implies that all locations are directly addressable and an equal amount of time is required to access all. Most RAMs are also random access devices. A RAM is usually "volatile," which means that data stored in them will remain only as long as power is applied. RAMs are available in two basic versions: **static** and **dynamic.** Static RAMs are arrays of cross-coupled flipflops which by nature retain their state as long as power is applied. Dynamic RAMs are arrays of capacitors buffered by MOS transistors. These devices depend on the capacitors to hold charge which has a tendency to leak off in about 5 milliseconds. Special control circuitry (on-or-off chip) is used to "refresh" the data before it leaks off and is lost. Dynamic RAMS are therefore more complex to use in a system, but they have the advantage of being more dense (more bits per chip).

Integrated memory devices (ROMs and RAMs) are available from most microprocessor manufacturers in forms that are compatable with the input/output structure of the various microprocessors themselves. This compatibility is better understood by first considering the I/O structure of two machines: the 6800 and the 8085.

Input/Output (I/O) Structures

6800 I/O structure. In all, the 6800 has 40 pins (Figure 4.7). Of these, the following are related directly to the interfacing of memory.

D0–D7 Eight data lines used to send and receive 8 bit data words.

R/W: Read/write line when high indicates that the processor is doing a memory read and when low, a write.

VMA: Valid memory address indictes that a memory operation is occurring when it is high.

```
 1 ⊏ VSS    O Reset ⊐ 40
 2 ⊏ Halt        TSC ⊐ 39
 3 ⊏ φ1        N.C. ⊐ 38
 4 ⊏ IRQ         φ2 ⊐ 37
 5 ⊏ VMA        DBE ⊐ 36
 6 ⊏ NMI       N.C. ⊐ 35
 7 ⊏ BA        R/W ⊐ 34
 8 ⊏ Vcc         D0 ⊐ 33
 9 ⊏ A0          D1 ⊐ 32
10 ⊏ A1          D2 ⊐ 31
11 ⊏ A2          D3 ⊐ 30
12 ⊏ A3          D4 ⊐ 29
13 ⊏ A4          D5 ⊐ 28
14 ⊏ A5          D6 ⊐ 27
15 ⊏ A6          D7 ⊐ 26
16 ⊏ A7         A15 ⊐ 25
17 ⊏ A8         A14 ⊐ 24
18 ⊏ A9         A13 ⊐ 23
19 ⊏ A10        A12 ⊐ 22
20 ⊏ A11        VSS ⊐ 21
```

Figure 4.7. Pin assignments for the 6800. (Courtesy of Motorola, Inc.)

$\phi1, \phi2$: Two clock signals supplied to the microprocessor by the system; $\phi1$ is the inverse of $\phi2$.

The eight data lines (D0–D7) are referred to as a bidirectional data bus. It is called "bidirectional" because data is transferred both to and from the microprocessor on this bus. To accomplish this, the 6800 is capable of switching its bus drivers to a high impedance state so that memories and other devices can send data to the microprocessor.

Figure 4.8a shows the timing of a 6800 write operation. The R/W line goes to 0 to indicate a write operation and the VMA goes to 1 to indicate that a memory location is being accessed. At the same time, 16 bits of address go out over the address bus A0–A15. Later into the cycle, after some time is allowed for the memory or I/O device to recognize its address, the data goes out on the data bus. Note that the falling edge of $\phi2$ occurs during the data out period so that it can be used by the receiving device to clock this data.

Figure 4.8b shows the timing diagram for a read operation. This time R/W goes to 1, VMA is again 1, and the address of the location being read appears on the address bus. At the end of the cycle, the 6800 assumes that the memory or I/O device places its data on the bus so that it can be clocked in by the trailing edge of $\phi2$.

8085 I/O structure.

Like the 6800, the 8085 has 40 I/O pins, 16 of which are used as an address bus. Unlike the 6800, there is no separate 8 bit data bus; instead, the 8 least significant address lines are used for three types

of transfer: data in, data out, and address out. A block diagram of the 8085 is provided in Figure 4.9.

The following I/O lines are involved in I/O and memory transfers:

A8–A15:   Eight most significant address lines.
AD0–AD7:   Eight multiplexed lines used to transfer data in and out, in addition to address out.
ALE: Address-latch-enable pulses high while address is applied to AD0–AD7.
$\overline{RD}$:   Read pulses low during microprocessor read operations.
$\overline{WR}$:   Write pulses low during microprocessor write operations.
Status lines: Several status lines including IO/$\overline{M}$, S0, S1 assist in interfacing. These lines indicate the microprocessor's state and the type of transfer taking place.

The important thing to recognize from the above interface definitions is that the three-way address/data in/data out multiplexing technique has important implications in interfacing to memories or I/O devices. First, consider the timing requirements for a typical memory device as shown in Figure 4.10. Here it can be seen that the address must be applied to a memory during the entire cycle and cannot be removed until the data "ripples" (no clock is required) out of the memory. Because this is almost always the case, it implies that the 8085 I/O structure dictates the need for an external 8 bit address latch, while the 6800 does not.

To understand how an address latch is used, consider a typical 8085 memory read operation (Figure 4.11). First, the most significant byte of address appears on A8–A15, and the least significant byte of address appears on AD0–AD7. Address-latch-enable (ALE) is pulsed high to clock the least significant byte of address into an external address register. The full 16 bits of address are now stable (half out of the address register and half from A8–A15) and will remain so throughout the read cycle. The address lines AD0–AD7 are now free to accept data out of the memory when it becomes available.

One can now ask why one microprocessor would multiplex data and address lines when another would keep them separate. The answer, of course, is that multiplexing lines saves pins and allows a manufacturer to add features that could not otherwise be provided. This can be seen in the 8085 with its inclusion of extra I/O functions such as two serial communications lines and a greater number of interrupt lines than are found on the 6800.

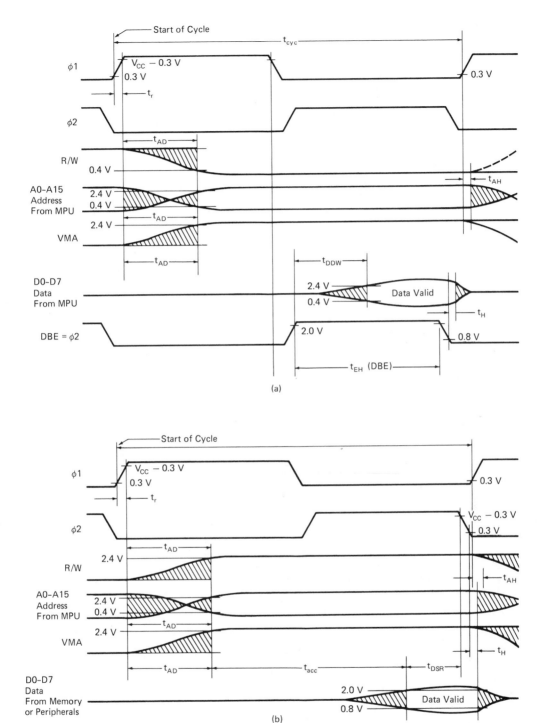

Figure 4.8. Timing diagrams for the 6800. (a) Write operation. (b) Read operation. (Courtesy of Motorola, Inc.)

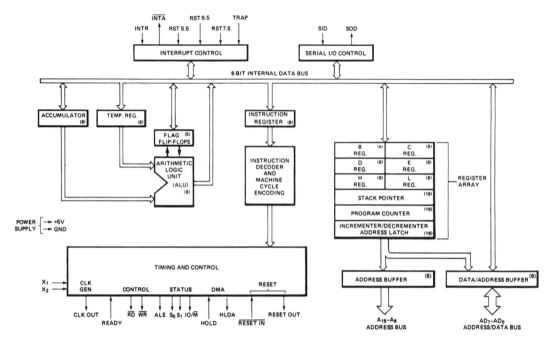

Figure 4.9. Block diagram of the 8085 microprocessor. (Courtesy of Intel, Inc.)

Interrupt Structures

The previous two sections have described how data can be transferred into or out of a microprocessor. These data transfers are only part of the device interfacing problem, however. In addition to devising a way to transfer data, the microprocessor system designer often needs to synchronize the timing of the transfers to the requirements of the I/O device. If, for example, a device only sends

data at specific time intervals (e.g., 30 times per second), the microprocessor must be able to do data transfer-in operations at the specific time that the data is available. One way to accomplish this is to have the processor continually test the I/O device to see if it is ready to send data. The processor can do this by reading a status line from the device (mapped to a memory location). When the status line indicates that device data is available, the microprocessor can perform the read operation.

This type of interface timing works well and has been

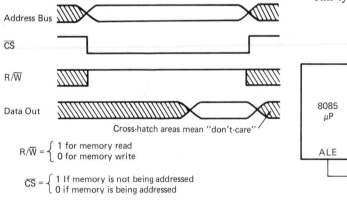

Figure 4.10. 8085 memory timing for a read operation.

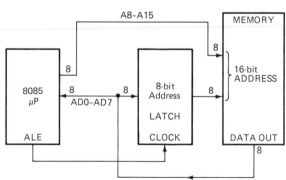

Figure 4.11. 8085 I/O structure with external address latches.

implemented many times, but has one distinct disadvantage. During the time the microprocessor is "polling" the status line, it is not available to perform other, and perhaps more useful functions. There is much to be gained in eliminating the need for polling because it often requires more time than the actual data transfers.

One way to eliminate polling is to use the interrupt structure available on most microprocessors. An **interrupt,** as its name implies, causes the processor to interrupt the program currently being executed and temporarily to execute another program called an **interrupt routine.** In the case above in which an I/O device sends data 30 times per second, the device would raise the microprocessor's interrupt input each time it has data available. This would cause an interrupt routine that has been designed to read data from the device to be executed. Following the data-read, the processor would be available to perform other functions until more device data is available.

Interrupts function in much the same way as subroutines with regard to their use of a stack to link into and out of subprograms. On most microprocessors, including the 6800, the same stack is used for both. When an interrupt is received by the 6800 on its interrupt-request ($\overline{\text{IRQ}}$) line, the contents of the program counter and other machine registers are written onto the top of the software stack. A 16 bit interrupt address is then taken from two dedicated memory locations, FFFC and FFFD$_{16}$, and loaded into the program counter. The next instruction executed after an interrupt is received is therefore the first instruction of the interrupt routine.

The interrupt routine is, of course, just a subprogram designed to perform whatever functions the system designer desires in order to service the interrupt. After interrupt servicing is completed, a return to the main program is affected by execution of a return-from-interrupt (RTI) instruction, which restores the program counter and other machine registers to the values on the stacktop.

One additional function is performed during the execution of interrupts. Because it would often be undesirable to have more interrupts during the processing of an interrupt, an interrupt mask bit located in the status byte (see Section 4.5) is automatically disabled soon after an $\overline{\text{IRQ}}$ is received. This prevents additional interrupts on the $\overline{\text{IRQ}}$ line from being recognized by the processor. As soon as the return from interrupt is executed, the interrupt mask bit is restored to its value preceding the interrupt. It should be mentioned again that the mask bit can be modified under program countrol by the CLI and SEI instructions.

In general, microprocessors have varying degrees of interrupt capability. One very powerful structure is called the **multilevel interrupt.** Such a structure permits many simultaneous interrupts to occur on a group of interrupt lines. Each interrupt line is assigned a priority by the microprocessor, causing multiple interrupts to be processed one at a time in order of priority. Multilevel interrupt structures can be achieved on many current generation microprocessors with the help of some external hardware. Next-generation machines are expected to provide more of this capability internally.

Direct Memory Access (DMA)

Occasions arise when it would be desirable to interface a microprocessor to a device that sends data at rates too fast for the processor to receive and store in memory. To accomplish such transfers, another interfacing technique has been developed. This method, **direct memory access (DMA),** permits an I/O device to send data directly to memory without going through the processor, thereby permitting data transfers to occur at the full speed of memory. How this is accomplished depends heavily on the microprocessor in question. Generally, the I/O device raises a DMA-request input to the microprocessor, which in turn brings all its address and data bus drivers to a high impedance state following completion of the current instruction. The I/O device then has sole access to memory for an amount of time depending on the type of microprocessor.

DMA certainly requires a substantial amount of logic external to the processor to determine which areas in memory are to be written into, and how much data is to be transferred. This hardware can be located in either the I/O device or in the processor itself. Microprocessor manufacturers have helped to make such hardware cost-effective by making available DMA controller LSI chips that are compatible with many processors. These devices can generally be hooked onto the I/O bus of a microprocessor and will handle numerous common DMA applications.

4.7 SELECTION CRITERIA FOR MICROPROCESSOR APPLICATIONS

A fundamental question that must be answered when beginning the design of a microprocessor-based system: "What, if any, microprocessor should be used?" There are scores of different microprocessors available, many of which are similar in capabilities (Table 4.5). Likewise,

Table 4.5. Microprocessor Comparison—Selected 8 and 16 Bit Machines

	6800	6809	8085	Z80	1802	Z8000	8086	68000
External data bus size (bits)	8	8	8	8	8	16	16	16
Internal data size (bits)	8	8	8	8	8	16	16	32
Maximum[1] operand size (bits)	8	16	16	16	8	32	16	32
Multi-operand instruction	no	no	no	block moves/ search	no	string manipulation	string manipulation	multi register moves
Address space (expansion)	65K	65K	65K	65K	65K	8(64)M	1M	16M
Package size (pins)	40	40	40	40	40	40	40	64
Number[2] clocks needed	2	1	1	1	1	1	1	1
Power supply voltages (V)	+5	+5	+5	+5	+5	+5	+5	+5

[1]The 8 bit microprocessors listed here offer very limited 16 bit instructions.
[2]Versions of some of these microprocessors have internal clock options.

there are many aspects of these microprocessors which need to be compared in order to make the best selection. Some of the more important aspects to consider are the following:

• Throughput.
• Available support hardware.
• Available support software.
• Power consumption.
• Second sourcing.
• Reliability.
• Cost.

The first step in doing a comparative analysis is to be sure the problem is well defined. The results of such an analysis can be no better than the original problem definition. Included in this definition should be a detailed specification for the algorithm to be performed by the processor, and also a definition of the hardware interfacing requirements. These inclusions will play a large part in specifying the amount of "throughput" required to adequately perform the application. **Throughput,** which refers to the amount of processing that can be done per unit time, is a function of the processor's instruction set, word length and clock rate. Unfortunately, there is no simple way to quantify throughput. What is normally done to compare two or more machines is to write a special program that resembles in some important ways the algorithm to be executed in the application. This program, often called a "benchmark," is then implemented in the instruction sets of the machines to be compared. Execution speed can then be calculated because instruction speeds are always specified. This technique is usually used when the microprocessor is expected to be operating near its full capacity.

Often times, however, the processor is only utilized to a fraction of its capacity. If this fraction is small, it is likely that either a less powerful microprocessor or perhaps hardwired logic should be considered for the task. For this reason, it is important that these studies are performed early in the design cycle. Another important consideration that may help eliminate some microprocessors from consideration is power consumption. If, for example, the application requires very low power consumption, a CMOS technology microprocessor might be the only type that fulfills this requirement.

The criteria for selection discussed thus far consider whether or not a microprocessor can perform the required task. Other considerations relate more to the ability of the hardware and software systems designers to build the product efficiently. Such useful items as high level software support and compatible peripheral components can greatly reduce the labor involved in designing a microprocessor based system. Software support can vary all the way from a simple cross-assembler and program debugging routine to high level languages such as FORTRAN, COBOL or PASCAL. Software support is very important because it has a large effect on the amount of time required to program the application.

Hardware support also varies widely among microprocessors. Because many different kinds of peripheral components are available, it is most important to examine the interface requirements to determine whether some of these components can be used. A good example is an interface to a video display (including common TV). Designed from discrete ICs, this interface can require dozens of components. But with microprocessor peripheral components, this interface can be reduced to just a few LSI ICs and some passive components. The same holds true for DMA controllers, serial interface controllers (e.g., TTY interfaces), in addition to other kinds of interfaces. The cost-effectiveness of these components is generally high if the functions they perform match the system specifications.

Other factors that will help specify the best machine are the availability of multiple sourcing for microprocessor components, reliability specifications, and cost. If, for example, the final product needs to meet high reliability standards like MIL-SPEC-883B, and meet second sourcing requirements as well, the number of available microprocessors will be greatly reduced. Finally, of course, for a product to be practical, all its components, including the microprocessor, must fall within some cost boundaries.

4.8 FUTURE TRENDS

There is a definite and fast moving trend toward putting more and more processing power on a single processor chip. Word widths are presently 16 bits on the newest machines and 32 bits is becoming available. In addition, other kinds of hardware are being added to microprocessor chips to minimize the number of external components needed. Included in these additions are RAM, ROM, analog to digital converters (A/D) and digital to analog converters (D/A). At present, there is no end in sight to these improvements, making increasingly more sophisticated products possible at lower cost. We can predict with high confidence that this advancement in technology will impact greatly on the entire field of electronics, and most other areas of technology as well.

REFERENCES

Hilburn, J. L., and Julich, P. M., *Microcomputers/Microprocessors*. Englewood Cliffs, NJ: Prentice-Hall, 1976.

Korn, G. A., *Minicomputers for Engineers and Scientists*. New York: McGraw-Hill Book Co., 1973.

Kraft, G. D., and W. N. Toy, *Mini/Microcomputer Hardware Design*. Englewood Cliffs, NJ: Prentice-Hall, 1979.

Krutz, R. L., *Microprocessors and Logic Design*. New York: John Wiley & Sons, 1980.

Lenk, J. D., *Handbook of Microprocessors, Microcomputers, and Minicomputers*. Englewood Cliffs, NJ: Prentice-Hall, 1979.

Levanthal, L. A., *Introduction to Microprocessors: Software, Hardware, Programming*. Englewood Cliffs, NJ: Prentice-Hall, 1978.

Sippl, C. J., *Microcomputer Handbook*. New York: Petrocelli/Charter, 1977.

Soucek, B., *Microprocessors and Microcomputers*. New York: John Wiley & Sons, 1976.

5
VLSI Concepts

J. K. Hassan
Guy Rabbat
IBM Corporation

5.1 INTRODUCTION

This chapter discusses the hardware and software concepts of **very large scale integration (VLSI).** The chapter is concerned with the effect of VLSI on computer architecture, chip design in VLSI, VLSI technologies, design automation, and software engineering in VLSI.

5.2 COMPUTER ARCHITECTURE

An **embedded computer system** may be defined as a computer system which controls a very large hardware complex. Any real-time control system fits into this category. The difficulties in the design of large scale embedded computer systems fall into two areas:

1. The requirement of real time control, criticality, high performance, and fault tolerance, which stress the available technology to its limits.
2. Sophisticated, complicated computer architectures, such as pipelining, interleaved memory, and parallel processing, which have to satisfy the imposed requirements, and usually lead to very expensive designs.

Further difficulties in developing large scale embedded computer systems arise from the largeness of the systems. The activities of the systems are so varied and complex that they are beyond the grasp of a single individual. Because each subsystem requires special design experience, it is usually developed and maintained by experts who

have little knowledge of the other subsystems. Consequently, some final decisions on primitives (essential system characteristics) are made for one subsystem without a consideration of the overall system requirement.

Another important problem to be faced in the development of large-scale computer systems is ever changing system environments. When a system's application or the technology changes, the system has to be modified to adapt to the changes. However, systems are usually designed without provision for future evolution. Therefore, when the system evolves, changes are incorporated in an ad hoc manner. As a result, the integrity of the system is undermined. In large scale critical real time systems, another difficulty imposed on the development process is the real-time constraint and the criticality of the system.

Despite the foregoing problems, difficulties in the design of large scale embedded computer systems have been alleviated by the rapid advances in two areas.

The emergence of VLSI technology has promised the availability of a million switching elements on a single silicon chip by the year 1985. For example, powerful distributed systems can be formed by interconnecting a large number of inexpensive VLSI single chip computers. The available parallelism in these systems can provide fast response time for real time control.

Moreover, through the exploitation of the inherent redundancy in these systems, fault tolerance can be achieved by the technique of graceful degradation. By the implementation of algorithms in special purpose VLSI chips, fast execution time of the corresponding functions can be provided. Further, the large number of switching elements in a VLSI chip allows the incorporation of more intelligence into different functional units, such as memory and I/O modules. These intelligent functional units can perform a large amount of local processing and, hence, can remove bottlenecks in the system. For these reasons, VLSI technology can resolve many difficulties in designing large-scale embedded computer systems.

5.3 VLSI TECHNOLOGY AND COMPUTER ARCHITECTURE—TRENDS

Basically, there are two different architectural directions for VLSI based computers to proceed. The first one is to put more and more functions on a chip, as well as to make the chip run faster and faster. By integrating the CPU, memory, and input/output circuitry of an older design that previously required several chips onto a single chip, one obtains a single chip computer architecture. Because the development of single-chip stand alone computers is plagued by the need for compatibility with prior designs, architectural progress in this direction is relatively slow.

The other architectural direction takes a fresh look at new technology and many recently emerged computer applications. It exploits to the advantage of VLSI technology the fact that a complex CPU, or even a full single-chip microcomputer, costs only a few dollars. It therefore becomes economical to design a system using a multiplicity of microcomputers that provides more processing power than would be possible, or practical, using a single CPU with traditional architecture. Essentially, this direction considers the interconnection of VLSI chips, which can be either general-purpose single chip computers or special purpose VLSI chips, to form highly concurrent computer systems. This direction implies the exploration of many new architectural concepts and algorithm designs, and the opening of many new computer applications.

One serious drawback of VLSI technology is the limited number of pins on the chip. While VLSI chips provide an exponentially growing number of gates, the number of pins remains almost constant. Experimental data shows that if the number of circuits on a chip is proportional to the volume of a sphere, then the number of pins that is required to serve these circuits is proportional to the surface of the sphere. As a result, communication becomes a very difficult design problem in the interconnection of VLSI chips. Owing to the insufficient communication power and the high design cost of VLSI chips, the

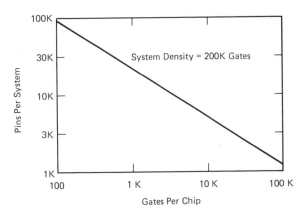

Figure 5.1. Pins per chip decrease as the number of gates per chip increases.

development of computer systems employing VLSI technology thus implies many architectural concepts that depart sharply from past and present practices.

5.4 SINGLE CHIP COMPUTERS

For conventional computer systems, in which the processor and memory are implemented in separate IC chips, communication between processor and memory remains a major and difficult design problem when high bandwidth is required. The difficulties stem from different loading capacities which result in the delay power product of a connection within a single IC chip being much smaller than the delay power products of the connectors for separate chips. At present, the difference ratio is more than two orders of magnitude and will become larger as proper scaling of MOS circuitry leads to faster and smaller circuits that operate at lower power levels.

Microprocessors

The role of bit slice microprocessors in providing a multicomputer system with dynamic reconfiguration capabilities should be examined. These capabilities allow reconfiguration, under software control, of the system hardware into a variable number of processors of different characteristics (such as word size and instruction set). Such capabilities have many potential uses in multiprogramming, parallel processing, and fault tolerant systems. Reconfiguration capability introduces a number of issues concerning processor function modularization which do not arise in fixed architecture.

Large computers generally have computing power in excess of what a single user can efficiently utilize. Thus some means of shared usage is customary, a multiprocessing system usually being employed. Allowing computing resources to be shared among the programs of many users increases the global efficiency of usage, that is, computing resources are not idle as often as they would be with a single user.

Because such a shared computer must meet the needs of many users, it generally follows that the computing environment that it supports must be general purpose. However, this computing environment, optimized over many widely differing requirements, may not be very efficient for any particular one. The overhead implied by the inefficiency of a general purpose computer for any particular task and the overhead required to support a multiprogramming system can become a substantial portion of the total cost of computation.

Smaller computers may be used in ways which eliminate some of this overhead. For fixed computing requirements, the computing resources provided can be chosen to satisfy the user's needs at optimal cost. With only a single user, the software overhead can also be kept low. In fact, with fixed computing requirements, single user utilization of a small computer can be very efficient.

However, most computer users do not have fixed needs. Even a commercial installation, running only production jobs, will still run jobs with a wide range of computational requirements. Even a single task may involve different amounts of its computer's processing capability at various stages in execution.

The problem of providing an efficient solution to a variety of computing needs has been recognized before, and a number of attempts at solving it have been made. The general direction of these solutions has been to provide a pool of computing power, from which a user draws only an amount necessary to meet his or her own computing requirements.

Until recently, computing technology did not permit other solutions to the problem. The fixed architectures of most computers do not permit effective combination of one computer with another. Yet the problem remains: the need to provide an extended range of computing power to solve a variety of problems efficiently.

5.5 HARDWARE ALGORITHMS

The advent of VLSI technology has stimulated renewed interest in a fundamental issue in the context of LSI: what to put into a chip? Because they have a regular geometry based on the repetition of simple cells, memory devices are natural candidates for VLSI implementation. But there is always some communication and system overhead for utilizing a pure memory device in the total system architecture. An improvement in this situation is possible if both memory and logic can be combined to build a special purpose processor to take over some of the specialized functions of the CPU, reduce system bottlenecks, and simplify the overall communication and control structure. The basic problem seems to be the identification of tasks that can be built into special purpose VLSI chips.

Nonnumeric processing is one area which could benefit tremendously from VLSI. Nonnumeric processing includes those specialized operations that are not very well suited for a classical ALU. Some examples are string processing, sorting, merging, text and word processing, data base search and updates, and graph processing. The software algorithms currently used on conventional system are not sufficient to meet expected performance criteria in most applications involving large volumes of data. There is a need to develop special purpose hardware algorithms for these applications.

In developing specialized hardware for VLSI implementation, one has to remember the technological constraints. The idea is to use an algorithmic approach suitable for VLSI that reduces communication, rather than computation, and that approach is based on the replication of a basic function in space or time. Replication *in space* leads to cellular structure of simple cells, whereas replication *in time* leads to parallelism, or pipelining, on several data streams. The need to reduce communication overhead leads to a regular geometry for cell organization.

5.6 CIRCUIT TECHNOLOGY

Factors such as speed, power, cost reliability, custom design versus off the shelf, and degree of risk must all be considered during the decision making process which selects a specific integrated circuit (IC) technology. The feature which is called "chip architecture" must also be considered, because of its effect in areas such as system performance, design flexibility, and engineering changes. Chip architecture consists of IC design and layout plus application features such as mask, or fused link, programmable logic functions.

VLSI appears to be controversial and complex in its definition, but Price of Amdahl defines it as follows: greater than 1K per chip; or greater than 10K bits of

Table 5.1. Chronology of Chip Architecture

Very High			Random Gate Logic	Gate Array Bit Slice
High Speed		Random Gate Logic	ROM Bit Slice	Micro-processor PLA
Medium Speed	Random Gate Logic	Gate Array ROM	Micro-processor	

1960   1965   1970   1975   1980

|←—— SSI ——→|←— MSI —→|←———— LSI ————→|

Table 5.3. Chip Density Definitions

	Logic	Memory
SSI	< 10 Gates	< 100 Bits
MSI	10–100 Gates	100–1000 Bits
LSI	> 100 Gates	> 1000 Bits

duction of the microprocessor, which ushered in the era of low cost computing. The full capability of LSI could now be realized by means of software programmable functions. Medium speed applications were served by single chip MOS processors and high speed applications by bipolar bit-slice processor building blocks.

For very high speed applications, the gate array was revived. A pioneer in this approach was Amdahl Corporation, who used subnanosecond 100 gate array chips in the CPU of the 470 V-Series computer systems. In the latter part of the 1970s, programmable logic arrays (PLAs) were introduced and used in a variety of applications. PLA and ROM performance ranged from me-

static RAM; or greater than 50K bits of dynamic RAM; or less than 24 micrometer minimum feature size. (See Tables 5.1-3 and Figures 5.1, 2.)

For logic chips, the performance figure of merit is the signal propagation delay through a gate from input to output. This range is from greater than 10 ns for medium speed to less than 1 ns for very high speed gates. For memory chips, the performance figure of merit is the read access time (the delay from a valid address at the input to valid data at the output). The range is from greater than 100 ns for medium speed to less than 10 ns for very high speed memory.

In the early 1970s, circuit innovations made possible the realization of large (1K bits and up) high speed bipolar ROMs, which were rapidly put to use in diverse applications including code conversion, table lookup, arithmetic logic and control logic (the last especially in central processors where ROMs were required to match logic speeds in the processor). This period also saw the intro-

Table 5.2. Chip Performance Architectures

	Logic	Memory
Medium Speed	> 10 ns	> 100 ns
High Speed	1–10 ns	10–100 ns
Very High Speed	< 1 ns	< 10 ns

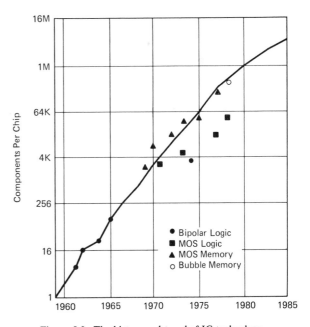

Figure 5.2. The history and trend of IC technology.

dium to high speed, but for very high speed LSI, usage was and is limited largely to gate arrays. Recent users of very high speed gate arrays have included Control Data Corporation, 168 gates per chip; Hitachi Ltd, 550 gates per chip; IBM, 5,000 gates per chip; and Cray Research Inc., who, bucking the trend to LSI, designed a 16 gate MSI array to satisfy their system requirements.

High reliability is brought about primarily by the reduction of interconnections between chips. Placing more gates, and hence more interconnections, on the chip results in an inherently more reliable system owing to the longer mean time to failure of on-chip interconnections. Additionally, mean time to repair can be minimized by use of LSI. The fewer the number of chips in the system, the easier and faster it is to isolate a failing component and replace it.

High speed is likewise realized by the ability to put more interconnections on the chip. The capacitance of on-chip interconnections is significantly lower than that of off-chip interconnections. For a given switching current, therefore, on-chip interconnections can be switched between signal levels more rapidly than can off-chip interconnections.

Small size and low parts count are further benefits of using LSI. Together, they help reduce the total number and length of interconnections between chips, with concomitant improvements in realiability and speed. Low cost is perhaps the most notable benefit of LSI. However, in large computers, the cost of LSI (not including main memory) is a small fraction of total system cost. It is therefore of less importance than the previously described benefits.

5.7 BIPOLAR MASTERSLICE

The demand for new data processing systems which have higher performance, smaller system size, lower cost, and higher reliability continues to increase. High speed LSIs are indispensable to meet these requirements. However, they bring many problems to the fore as their integration level is increased.

First, existing high speed circuits, such as emitter coupled logic (ECL), can meet performance objectives, but they dissipate a lot of power. When many ECL circuits are integrated in a chip, increased power dissipation necessitates the use of a special, expensive cooling system. Therefore, high speed circuits with low power dissipation are desirable for LSIs. But they, in turn, demand advanced bipolar processes to realize low power dissipation and high performance.

Second, as the circuits in a chip are increased by advanced LSI technology, standard LSI products cannot satisfy the system designer's requirements in regard to their performance and functionality. Therefore, high speed system oriented LSIs are the solution to the requirement for high performance systems. These LSIs, however, require a large quantity of different kinds of parts, and a high development budget. Moreover, the development for these LSIs eventually occupies a large part of the system development time. Therefore, it is desirable to develop system oriented LSIs with short turnaround time and a low development cost.

One approach involves **bipolar gate arrays,** or **masterslices.** A gate array chip contains an array of identical and unconnected gates, or logic sites, in which there are identical arrangements of transistors, diodes, and resistors for forming logic functions. There are also a number of input/output gates or sites for chip to chip interconnection. Custom logic functions are realized by the interconnection pattern (meta level masks) used on the array chip. Only custom interconnection patterning (gate or site wiring) is required to complete the chip.

The purpose of array chips is to provide many custom codes (designs) with the shortest possible design time, lowest design cost, and high confidence in a correct design outcome. Because only the selection of gates or sites and their routing (interconnection) in accord with a desired logic function are required to customize an array, the amount of design required per chip code is significantly reduced. Further, because the generic array chips are essentially predesigned, prefabricated, and stocked ready for metal patterning (interconnection), the number of chip fabrication steps required to complete the custom chip is reduced. Since the amount of both design and fabrication is reduced with array chips, the time, cost and risk in custom design are correspondingly reduced.

Array chips are used mostly because of their short design time, low design cost, and low schedule risk. However, existing gate arrays and masterslices have disadvantages in low transistor utilization and high power dissipation. To overcome these disadvantages, new masterslice LSIs have been developed featuring a low energy logic, fabrication by the polysilicon self-aligned process, transistor array masterslice, computer aided design, and applicability to large computers. In these LSIs, transistor utilization and power dissipation are improved by the low energy logic through a series gate structure, collector dotting, and emitting dotting.

Improved performance for data processing systems depends mainly on advances in circuit delay time and chip integration level. Figure 5.3 shows the relation between circuit delay time and chip integration level corresponding to energy level per gate. The energy levels shown in the figure are achieved when maximum power dissipation in a chip is limited to 1 watt. For example, a small computer with 10,000 gates can be integrated in a chip only when gates with 10 ns delay can be realized with 0.1 milliwatts operational power (i.e., 1 pJ). Allowable power dissipation per chip cannot be increased much more because of cooling system limitations. Therefore, low energy circuits are required to realize very large scale integration.

5.8 GATE ARRAYS AND CAD

To cope with VLSI on chips, effective design strategies and **computer aids for design** (**CAD**) are emerging. Array

chips, design strategies, and CAD all contribute to reducing the time, cost, and risk in VLSI chip design.

Design Time, Effort and Confidence with Arrays

Early in 1978, the turnaround time with a 200 gate array was 14 weeks. Design and silicon processing times were about one-half that for comparable nonarray bipolar chips. Within one year, the design people had drastically reduced their design time for arrays so that the complete logic-to-models cycle was reduced to 11 weeks. Today, designers are using arrays with 1,000 or more gates while the interval from logic to models or production remains 11 weeks.

The three major activities in going from logic description to array chip models or production are design, pro-

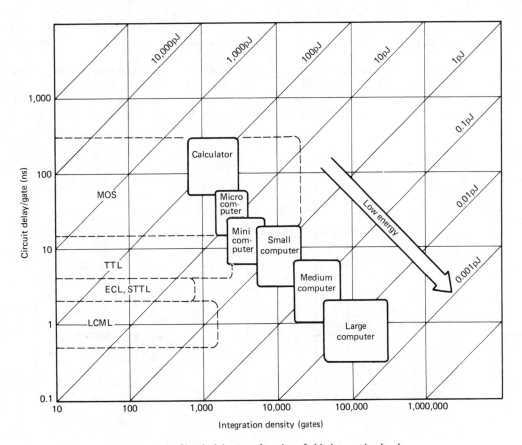

Figure 5.3. Circuit delay as a function of chip integration level.

cessing (masks and chip metallization), and packaging and testing. With the array chips, models and production are synonomous. The same masks, stocked wafers, process line, packages, and test programs are used for both models and for production. Clearly, large investments in special dedicated facilities for masking and processing arrays could again cut the logic-to-models time in half.

To sum up, the design cycle results with array chips are:

1. Confidence of 90 percent in a correct outcome (logic to models) within 11 weeks.
2. The per code design effort or cost is one designer-month.
3. The design cycle time and cost are practically independent of array size.

These are the results using general VLSI design strategies and a comprehensive set of CAD tools that are easily adapted to array, polycell, and other styles of chip design.

5.9 PLA AND MACRO DESIGN

The ability of the semiconductor industry to produce chips with higher and higher circuit densities has created a challenge for the product designer: to utilize this capacity and still develop chips rapidly at reasonable cost.

A multifaceted approach to VLSI design is offered by **programmable logic array (PLA)** structures, or macros (Figure 5.4). This approach consists of a hardware/software modeling technique, use of laser personalizable PLAs for rapid modeling of PLA macros, and a method for repairing design errors (which may hide other errors) on the actual VLSI wafers with a laser tool. A two pass VLSI design is, therefore, highly probable to minimize the number of errors.

Achieving a cost effective VLSI chip design with a two year design cycle requires that chip function be maximized while the time and number of iterations through the design cycle are minimized. However, as the degree of integration increases to thousands or tens of thousands of circuits per chip, it becomes more difficult to ensure that the desired function is correct, and that the final chip performs that function after the first, or even succeeding, design passes. This is especially true when the design is optimized for circuit density and performance, for example, changing the mask layout of a circuit so that it fits within a geometrical bound and still retains its electrical characteristics. This type of design is known as "custom design."

Among the custom chips now available are the Motorola 68000 and the Zilog Z8000 microprocessors. Today's microprocessors have from 25,000 to 70,000 transistors, the latter certainly representing more than 10,000

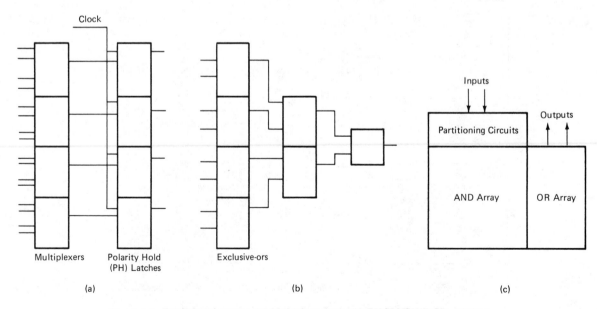

Figure 5.4. Examples of macros. (a) Multiple register. (b) EXCLUSIVE-OR. (c) PLA.

circuits. The question arises as to whether the VLSI design capability of the semiconductor industry can keep pace with its ability to fabricate an ever increasing number of logic gates on a chip. According to estimates, today's design cost for a VLSI chip is approximately $100 per gate. As our capability to put more gates on a chip increases, we must improve our design abilities; otherwise the growth of VLSI and the semiconductor industry itself will be seriously limited.

For the foregoing reasons, and the need to achieve densities higher than those obtainable from a masterslice design, a technique based on the PLA, and known as **macro design,** is utilized. This technique is one part of a multifaceted approach to achieving successful VLSI designs, and it is one of obviously many approaches that can be pursued. VLSI design is a rapidly evolving body of knowledge and the above approaches are still in an evolutionary stage.

Macro design is based on the observation that circuits with a high degree of logic connectivity will fit closely together when physically implemented. These aggregations of circuits are called **macros.** Examples of macros are a multiplexer-register, an EXCLUSIVE-OR tree, and most important—the PLA (Figure 5.4). In PLA design, multiple logic functions are implemented in array form, analogous to the personalization of words in a read only memory. PLA macros consist of three sections (Figure 5.4c):

1. *Partitioning circuits*—in their simplest form providing the true and complement functions for each input, i.e., A, $\overline{A}$, and are known as 1 bit decoders.

2. *AND array*—rows of AND circuits whose inputs can be selectively connected (personalized) to any combination of outputs from the partitioning circuits.

3. *OR array*—columns of OR circuits whose inputs are selectively connected to any combination of outputs from the AND array.

Any function in product term canonical form, e.g., $f\hat{1} = AB + CD + AE = \ldots$, is suitable for implementation "as is" in a PLA. Each product term becomes a row within an AND array, and personalizing the OR array determines which product terms make up the function. A "match" or selection of a product term occurs when the logical state of the PLA's inputs correspond to the connection of that product term's crosspoints (Figure 5.5). In FET technologies, AND and OR arrays are implemented with NOR circuits. Because PLA logic is always in canonical product term form, minimization techniques similar to the Quine-McCluskey method can be applied with computer programs.

Generally, logic design may be defined as the transformation of a specification into logic primitives (AND, OR, INVERT, and so on), and storage elements (LATCHES, MEMORY). The objective is to obtain an accurate transformation using a minimum number of elements. This logic description is either recorded on handdrawn diagrams and then entered into a computer data base, or entered directly into the data base graphically.

The regular structure of the PLA macro makes a tabular format convenient for specifying and recording the logic function. The format used is a matrix in which the columns are the AND array input and the OR array out-

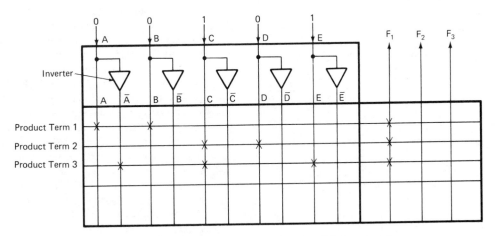

Figure 5.5. Example of a product term (number 3) being selected.

put lines of the macro, and the rows are the product terms. The logic functions of the PLA macro are defined by the following symbols:

1. In the AND array:

   I—match on a logical 1.
   0—match on a logical 0.

   .—match on either a logical 1 or 0 (don't care state).

2. In the OR array:

   I—set output to logical 1 if any input product term is selected, or to logical 0 if no input product terms are selected.
   .—ignore this product term.

The AND array symbols are for input partitioning circuits which are 1 bit (or 1 input) decoders. Additional symbols specify partitioning circuits which are 2 to 4 bit (or 2 input) decoders, but they will not be defined here. An example of PLA logic documented in this notation is shown in Figure 5.6.

The matrix is numbered from left to right, and from top to bottom, as indicated on the top and left sides of the figure. Consider the third row. Product term 3 will be selected when column 5 is a logic 0 and column 6 is a logic 1. In this event, output columns 13, 15, and 16 will each represent logic 1 conditions.

The PLA macro logic specification describes the logic functions within the macro itself. However, the interconnections of the PLAs to the other macros on the chip, and the circuit connections within the other macros, must also be specified to describe fully the logical function of the chip. This global representation of the chip uses the IBM standardized logic specification language to form a data base for documentation, simulation, test pattern generation, and checking.

5.10 SUPERCONDUCTING TECHNOLOGY

The significance of VLSI has been emphasized throughout this chapter. High logic power $\approx$ 10K circuits per chip, and high memory capacity $\approx$ 1 Mbits per chip, are among its promises. If these chips are packaged densely, then it is reasonable to expect, in principle at least, that faster general purpose computers will be manufactured. The performance of such computers is measured in **millions of instructions per second (MIPS)**. For instance, IBM's newest computer, the 3081, is rated at approximately 10 MIPS, which represents an improvement over its predecessor, the 3033, by nearly a factor of 2. These systems are based on LSI technologies.

In the VLSI era, the following questions can be posed while speculating on the future of computers: (1) Can a factor of 10 or more improvement in performance be achieved? (2) What VLSI technology is likely to realize that goal? (3) Are there readily identifiable obstacles which significantly hinder that goal? While it is easy to ask these and perhaps other questions, no one possesses a crystal ball for predicting the future and providing complete answers. Computers are complex systems which are built by large groups of people trained in diverse disciplines such as physics, engineering, and computer science.

General Requirements and Limitations

To improve the performance of logic devices we have three choices. The first is to reduce the size of the silicon transistors. This has been pursued vigorously, leading to present VLSI technologies. For instance, recently, a MOSFET with channel length of 0.3 micrometer and intrinsic switching speed of approximately 30 picoseconds has been reported. The second choice is to make transistors from other semiconducting materials which have higher mobilities. This is manifested in the rapidly growing GaAs transistor effort, which has demonstrated a switching speed of 17 ps, and further improvements are anticipated by a combination of smaller structures and lower operating temperatures. The third choice is to invent new transistors using novel operating principles. A recipe for inventing new types of transistors is available and industry forecasts indicate, for example, that quasi-

```
                AND-array        OR-array
                 inputs          outputs
              ┌─────────┐      ┌──────┐
                    111          11111    Column
              123456789012       34567  } numbers
              ────────────       ─────    1- 17
           ┌  1  ...I........     IIIII
           │  2  ....I.......     II.I.
           │  3  ....0I......     I.II.
           │  4  ......I.....     I..I.
  Product  │  5  ....000I....     .III.
  terms    ┤  6  .....00.I...     .I.I.
  1-11     │  7  ....0.0.0I..     ..II.
           │  8  ..........I.     ...I.
           │  9  ..0.........     IIIII
           │  10 .0.........0     IIIII
           └  11 I...........     ...I.
```

Figure 5.6. Example of a PLA representation.

particles and pairs may be the ingredients in superconducting transistors which will serve as minority and majority carriers in bipolar transistors. Another possibility, which has been demonstrated separately, is the QUITRON, which is a transistor-like superconducting switch based on heavy injection of quasiparticles to break pairs and the subsequent suppression to 0 of the superconducting gap.

The success of these new devices and those not yet invented will hinge on whether or not they fulfill specific requirements discussed below. The limits of digital information processing depend on chip power dissipation, heat removal from packages, the role interconnections play in VLSI, and the physical limitations of the devices themselves as they are scaled down in size. With the likelihood that semiconducting transistors are being pushed to their limits, inventing new devices may no longer be a choice but a necessity; this may be the only avenue left which will lead to the realization of an ultrahigh performance machine.

In the era during which VLSI tools exist, we may find ourselves compelled to depart from the traditional mode, that of building systems from existing devices, and instead adopt a new mode, that of specifying the system characteristics first, and then invent device and package technologies which meet those specifications.

The following is an attempt to apply this new mode to the design of a hypothetical general purpose computer capable of 500 MIPS. This is an example used to unravel the limitations and constraints that must be accommodated by the device and package technologies we will have to invent for this system. This exercise leads to the conclusion that superconducting devices will inevitably play a significant role in future systems owing to their intrinsically low power dissipation. Although performance enhancement by means of optimized architecture is not precluded, we assume for our example that the architecture of the IBM 3081 still prevails.

Given the objective of a 500 MIPS mainframe, the CPU would require a cycle time $\tau_{cpu} \approx 660$ ps, assuming 3 cycles are needed to execute an instruction. The designer requires approximately 300K logic circuits, each having an average delay $\tau_1 \approx 0.1\tau_{cpu} \approx 66$ ps, and a cache capacity of 64KB at a cycle time $\tau_c \approx \tau_{cpu}$ and an access time $\tau_{ca} \approx \frac{1}{3}\tau_{cpu} \approx 220$ ps. Also needed is a main memory capacity of 250 to 500 MB at a cycle time $\tau_M \approx 6.6$ ns.

Assuming that the cache path delay is the bottleneck of the system, and if 50 percent of this delay, 330 ps, is due to the propagation of the address and data signals at approximately 100 ps/cm, we require a three dimensional package of about 1 cm^3 to contain the cache memory chips, logic chips, and their interconnections. Because it is necessary to dissipate power in order to carry out the logic operations, an inevitable temperature rise, ΔT, in this package results. This rise has to be maintained at a tolerable level; otherwise, the system will either operate erratically or cease to operate altogether.

Clearly, devices dissipating more than 1 mW (readily available fast transistors) lead to a total power dissipation on the order of 1000 W within our 1 cm^3 package—a challenge to heat removal specialists. Cooling of actual VLSI chips by forced convection using liquids at optimum flow rates is limited to tens of watts per cm^2. Assuming that $\frac{2}{3}\tau_M \approx 4.4$ ns is the propagation delay within the main memory package, and $\frac{1}{3}\tau_M \approx 2.2$ ns is the main memory chip access time, the package would have a volume approximately $(12 \text{ cm})^3$. Realizing this package with existing devices at a 1 Mbit/chip density would result in the dissipation of hundreds of kilowatts in such a small volume. Supplying this amount of regulated power, its cost per year, and its removal from the package pose other challenges.

The circuit delay is given by

$$\tau_1 = \tau_d + \tau_{load} \qquad (5.1)$$

where τ_d is the intrinsic switching delay of the device; τ_{load} is the delay which results when driving a useful load, and depends on the fan out number and the wire length needed. This load could be resistive, when matched transmission lines are used; capacitive, as in the case of transistor circuits; or inductive as in the case of Josephson memory circuits. In most cases, τ_{load} dominates. It is therefore clear from the above analysis that in order to realize our objective (500 MIPS), the device we need to invent must possess the following physical properties: (1) ultrafast switching speed, i.e., ≈ 20 ps; (2) extremely low power dissipation on the order of a few μW; and (3) ultrahigh density.

Engineering Requirements

While the above physical requirements are necessary, they are not sufficient. There are other engineering requirements which must be fulfilled in order to manufacture the memory and logic chips at a reasonable cost (yield), and ensure error-free operation as well. The devices, logic circuits, and memory cells are not identical.

Their parameters vary to a degree or so as a result of imperfect line width control at the mask level, imprecise alignment between the various levels, nonreproducible exposure and development of the resists, variations in the doping, material imperfections, variations in critical film thicknesses, bias variations, intrinsic noise, fluctuations in the environment, and so on.

The VLSI chip design represents the combined effort of various people who deal with devices, circuits, process development, and characterization, and materials. All have the common goal of achieving high chip yield,

$$Y_c = (Y_{cir})(Y_{proc}) \qquad (5.2)$$

The device and circuit properties determine Y_{cir}, whereas the process related defects, shorts, opens, and so on determine Y_{proc}. The designers start with distributions of all these parameters and carry out statistical circuit analysis until they arrive at an optimum chip design. This process often involves many iterations, compromises, and trade-offs between performance and chip yield. Sometimes certain approaches are abandoned when insurmountable problems and inadequacies are discovered.

Certain device and circuit properties are known to give better yields than others. The properties which play significant roles are the following: devices with three terminals; high gain, inversion; nonlatching; good isolation between the input and output stages; high nonlinearity; high discrimination between the levels representing binary 1 and 0; high noise immunity; and the ability to standardize the levels. Figure 5.7 illustrates graphically a few such desirable properties. The dashed region represents all possible variations in the device.

In Figure 5.7a, the 1 state I_1 remains stable as long as the input is at the 0 level, I_0. In the illustrated case, level I_0 can vary significantly between 0 and a threshold value, I_{tr}, without affecting the stable state I_1, indicating good noise immunity and good tolerance to parameter variations. As the input exceeds the threshold, the device abruptly switches to the other stable state, I_0. From this illustration, it is clear that such a nonlinear element possesses these desirable qualities: absence of hysteresis; ability to standardize levels; high discrimination ratio, $I_1/I_0 \gg 1$ and $I_{tr}/I_0 \gg 1$. Nonhysteretic devices operate in the nonlatching mode, which has many advantages, for example, the ability to invert. Esaki diodes and Josephson junctions belong to the class of hysteretic devices which operate in the latching mode.

Noninverting devices have the input-output characteristic shown in Figure 5.7b, i.e., the output is in the 0 state as long as the input is also in the 0 state, and the output

switches to the 1 state when an input larger than the threshold is applied. Devices capable of inversion have a fundamental advantage crucial to circuit design: they can be used to construct multi-input NOR circuits from which all logic and memory operations can be implemented.

For example, if the inputs A, B and C are applied to a NOR circuit, the result is the output

$$\overline{A + B + C} \qquad (5.3)$$

which upon inverting yields $A + B + C$, the OR function. To obtain the AND function, $\overline{A}$, $\overline{B}$, and $\overline{C}$ are applied to the NOR circuit, yielding ABC. In the latter case De Morgan's theorem is applied, i.e.,

$$\overline{\overline{A} + \overline{B} + \overline{C}} = \overline{ABC} \qquad (5.4)$$

On the other hand, the noninverting circuit allows construction of multiinput OR function, and with some restrictions, the AND function. It is, however, unable to implement the necessary invert function.

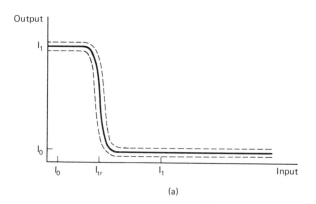

(a)

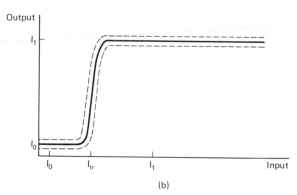

(b)

Figure 5.7. Input/output characteristics of nonlinear devices. (a) Inverting. (b) Noninverting.

Transistors have many of the desirable properties represented by Figure 5.7a whereas Esaki diodes do not. Because they lack those transistor-like properties that engineers require, Esaki diodes have not qualified as computer elements, even though they can be made faster and denser, and dissipate lower power than transistors.

5.11 THE PROSPECTS FOR FUTURE SEMICONDUCTOR TRANSISTORS

The performance of transistor circuits is measured by their power dissipation $p_1 = IV$, their average delay $\tau_1 = (C_d + C_L)V/2I$, and switching energy $E_1 = p_1\tau_1 = \frac{1}{2}(C_d + C_L)V$, where C_d and C_L are respectively the device and load capacitances, V is the voltage swing, and I is the device current. Miniaturization leads to improved device performance, mainly as a result of reducing the capacitance since the voltage is constrained as to be nearly constant by the nonlinearity and noise immunity requirements. The reduction in device area and the increase in the number of circuits lead to an increase in current density, power density, and total chip power.

The possible enhancement in device and circuit performance is realizable by pushing transistor technologies to their limits at the expense of power dissipation, increased device and wiring resistance, electromigration, hot electron and breakdown phenomena, punchthrough, large fluctuation in impurity concentration, and yield. By means of submicrometer lithographic techniques, transistors with impressive speeds have been reported. For instance, silicon MOSFET with a channel length of 0.3 μm has an intrinsic switching speed of 30 ps with a power dissipation of 1.3 mW. GaAs MESFET with a channel length of 0.6 μm has a switching speed of 30 ps, dissipating 1.9 mW at room temperature, and a speed of 17 ps when cooled to 77° K. While these fast transistors will undoubtedly be found in numerous applications, their high power dissipation may not satisfy one of the major physical requirements, i.e., low power dissipation, for our hypothetical ultrahigh performance computer.

5.12 MOS TECHNOLOGY

In MOS technology, methodology is proposed for designing VLSI devices and processes for high density, high performance circuits. The procedure involves scaling down the devices' lateral and vertical dimensions and supply voltage while increasing the substrate doping, all by the same scaling factor S. Scaled devices take higher currents, with lower capacitance, and a power delay product that is reduced by the factor S^3. In practice, however, voltage supplies are not scaled down for various reasons, such as a need for TTL compatibility and to preserve operating margins. The power delay product could only be reduced by a factor in the range S to S^2.

Nonscalability of voltages combined with shrinking of devices' lateral dimensions result in a number of high field effects on device characteristics. Some of these effects are related to physical properties, such as carrier velocity saturation. Others can be reduced by proper process techniques, such as threshold voltage geometry dependence. Shrinking the vertical dimensions enhances the role of parasitic resistance and capacitance in affecting device currents. It also makes the thickness of the inversion channel an important parameter for thin gate oxide devices.

For scaled devices, a number of factors have a major role in defining terminal behavior. Among these are:

1. Velocity saturation of mobile channel charge.
2. Source and drain ohmic and contact resistances.
3. Screening of finite inversion channel thickness.
4. Hot electron and high voltage limitations.

What makes these effects significant is that they are mostly dependent on material physical properties, and as such, innovations in processing techniques will not have major impact on them. Another effect, also important for small devices, is the dependence of threshold voltage on geometry.

5.13 GALLIUM ARSENIDE TECHNOLOGY

During the past few years, there has been growing interest in the use of gallium arsenide in high speed digital integrated circuits. This attention is due to the intrinsic advantages arising from high electron mobility in this material, combined with the availability of a semiinsulating substrate. Very high switching speeds, approaching those of Josephson junction devices, have been demonstrated for GaAs logic employing short channel (0.6 μm) Schottky gate metal semiconductor FETs (MESFETs). Propagation delays as low as 17.5 ps at 77° K or $\tau_D = 30$ ps at room temperature have been reported. Maximum clock frequencies of 5.5 GHz have also been observed on binary frequency dividers. However, high level integration has yet to be achieved with most of these approaches.

While future system applications of gigabit digital circuits will likely be possible at all levels of integration, an ever expanding range of applications is now being achieved as complexity increases through the LSI range and into the VLSI range. This will allow such systems as signal processors, microwave frequency synthesizers, and high speed analog to digital converters to be built on a single chip in more efficient architectures than are currently achievable. In addition, it is desirable in high-speed integrated circuits to build at the highest possible level of integration. Off-chip interfacing through packages and transmission lines introduces propagation delay, and is costly in power dissipation. Therefore, a competitive, practical and versatile GaAs IC design should provide compatibility with LSI/VLSI density and power requirements, while maintaining propagation delays at least below 200 ps per gate.

Issues common to all LSI/VLSI circuits technologies are low power, high density, and extremely high process and functional yields. The depletion mode GaAs MESFET technology has long been used for the fabrication of microwave transistors. When GaAs was first considered for IC implementation, it was expected that depletion mode (normally on) MESFET technologies would be incompatible with LSI requirements, because of high power dissipation and gate areas. However, low pinchoff voltage ($\sim$1V) depletion mode MESFETs can overcome these limitations if sufficient pinchoff voltage uniformity can be realized.

A reproducible ion implantation technology in GaAs has recently been developed. This technology provides MESFETs with the uniformity in pinchoff voltage required for LSI circuits. Localized ion implantation also permits the use of planar instead of mesa fabrication methods. Because of these technological advances, low pinchoff voltage depletion mode MESFET logic has been able to achieve low power dissipation and high circuit density with little sacrifice in speed, thereby overcoming many of the former objections to the feasibility of GaAs LSI circuits.

The cutoff frequency, f_r, of a FET, $g_m(2\pi C_{gs})$, is dependent on the transconductance, g_m, which is proportional to either the electron mobility, μ_e, or the saturated drift velocity, V_s. The gate source capacitance, C_{gs}, is approximately equal for Si and GaAs MESFETs. Theoretical predictions of the performance margin to be expected over silicon FETs (MESFET or NMOS) depend critically on which model is believed to apply correctly to a very large scale integrated circuit.

The mobility model predicts about six times higher g_m for GaAs than silicon for equivalent device geometries, while the velocity saturation model implies only a factor of 1.5 to 2 difference in g_m at high electric fields. The mobility model certainly applies to very low pinchoff (threshold) voltage devices ($V_p < 0.5$ V) while the velocity saturation model is applicable to high pinchoff voltage (> 2 V) devices such as discrete microwave MESFETs operating as Class A amplifiers for gate lengths of the order of 1 μm.

The switching FET used for low power GaAs logic has a pinchoff (threshold) voltage of $\sim$1 V, intermediate between the values that ensure pure mobility and pure saturation regions. Because the device switches between "on" and "off" states, it operates in a mobility controlled region for a fraction of a cycle, and in saturation for another fraction. Velocity overshoot of electrons accelerated in the high mobility conduction band central valley before they transfer to the lower mobility satellite valleys tends to increase switching speeds. The effect of this is more appreciable for short gate ($\sim$0.5 μm) devices.

In view of the complexity of the models, it becomes attractive to compare GaAs and Si FET devices in a practical manner. Figure 5.8 shows experimental curves of saturated drain current versus gate voltage at fixed drain voltage for GaAs MESFETs of 0.5 and 1.0 μm gate lengths, for 1.0 μm Si MESFETs, and for n-channel MOSFETs (NMOS) of 0.7 and 1.3 μm channel lengths. All the curves are nearly parabolic at the origin and tend to become linear only at high gate voltage, owing to current saturation. However, logic devices for VLSI circuits are, or will be, required to operate at moderate voltage swings (> 1 V) between "off" and "on" states, where the curves are nearly parabolic.

In Figure 5.8, both the GaAs and Si devices exhibit approximate square low drain current vs. gate voltage characteristics, $I_{ds} = K(V_{gs} - V_p)^2$. The values of K, however, are different as would be predicted from a comparison of transconductance. Drain currents also differ by about a factor of six because of the higher GaAs mobility. Silicon NMOS devices outperform Si MESFETs because the gate oxide can be made quite thin (200 to 300Å), much thinner than the MESFET gate depletion region. Therefore, the capacitive coupling of the gate is larger for the MOSFET than it is for the MESFET. However, the K factor for the 0.7 μm NMOS device is still nearly 2 times smaller than the K factor for the 1.0 μm GaAs MESFET, and over 3 times smaller than K for the 0.5 μm GaAs MESFET.

The $\sim$3 times higher transconductance of GaAs FETs as compared to Si devices can be exploited to obtain higher speed, lower power dissipation, or a combination

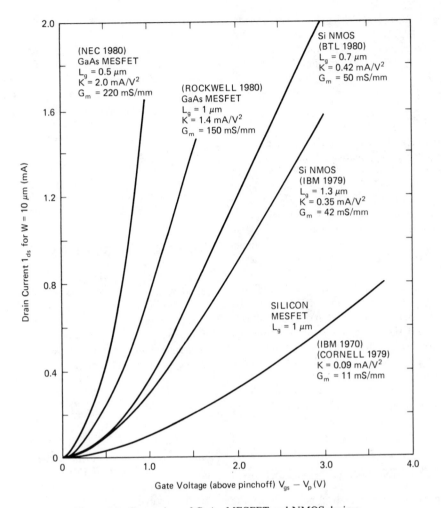

Figure 5.8. Comparison of GaAs, MESFET and NMOS devices.

of both. For higher speed, one would retain "large" voltage swings and use the higher transconductance to attain high slew rates. For low power dissipation, one would reduce the magnitude of the voltage swings and keep the currents unchanged.

In general, both options are impractical because very high currents may exceed the permitted power dissipation, and too low a voltage swing may not allow for sufficient noise margins. Therefore, the advantages arising from high device transconductance are exploited for a combination of higher speed and lower power dissipation. The balance between the two is determined, to a great

extent, by the choice of logic family, with adjustments from device design. The first GaAs ICs were made with **buffered FET logic (BFL)**, which achieved high speed ($\sim$ 34 ps/gate) with a moderately high power dissipation ($\sim$ 40 mW/gate). On the contrary, **direct coupled logic (DCL)** using enhancement mode FETs is capable of very low power dissipation, but it suffers from difficulties in obtaining high yield because of the very low noise margins (the voltage swings are constrained to be < 5.0 V).

Schottky diode FET logic (SDFL) offers a good compromise. Speeds are still high ($\sim$ 60 ps/gate) but the power dissipation is very moderate (< 1 mW/gate) and, therefore, acceptable for LSI/VLSI. The voltage swings of $\sim$ 1 V used in SDFL are quite compatible with current GaAs technology capabilities. The most complex IC made with GaAs, a 1,008 gate multiplier, has been fabricated using SDFL.

5.14 CAD SYSTEMS

As integrated circuit complexities increase, many existing computer aided design methods must be replaced with an integrated system to support VLSI circuit and system design. Hierarchical **computer aided design (CAD)** systems are very important. The system supports both functional and physical design from initial specification and system synthesis to simulation, mask layout, verification and documentation, and evolutionary changes as new technologies are developed and design strategies defined.

Computer aided design refers to a collection of software tools integrated into a system to provide the integrated circuit designer with step by step assistance during each phase of the design. Although many decisions are made by the software people during the design process, important hardware decisions are the designer's responsibility. The computer aids, or tools, simply provide the designer with a rapid and orderly method for consolidating and evaluating design ideas and relieve the designer of numerous routine and mechanistic steps.

5.15 SURVEY OF AUTOMATED INTERCONNECTION TECHNIQUES

A **signal net** consists of a set of fixed points where the signal will pass. A chip contains a set of such signal nets. The interconnection problem consists of finding paths in the chip so that (1) each net is made electrically common, and (2) all nets are electrically isolated from each other. There are several important parameters and constraints associated with the physical and geometric aspects of these interconnections, some of which will now be informally defined.

A **layer** is a fabrication plane of a chip used for interconnections. In some technologies, interconnections are restricted to a single "metal" layer, while in others two or more layers are used. For single layer technologies, it is sometimes possible for one wire to cross another by going under it employing some other medium, such as polysilicon, or by way of diffusion. For multilayer car-

riers, connections between layers are made by a **via** (plated through hole), or contact.

The main reason the interconnection problem is difficult to solve is constricted space. Each layer of a carrier has a fixed wire capacity. Once a certain percentage of this capacity is taken, it becomes extremely difficult to synthesize a path between two arbitrary points.

The interconnection problem can be divided into four subproblems: wire segment generation, ordering, layering, and routing. In this chapter, our primary concern will be with routing, namely finding a path for interconnecting two points—a point to a wire, or a wire to a wire. Prior to discussing the routing problem, we will first review briefly the other three subproblems.

Wire Segment Generation

Most routing algorithms deal with the problem of connecting two entities, such as two points, or a point and a wire. Hence, given an n point net, the net is usually first divided into $(n - 1)$ wire segments, each of which connects two points. This can be done in several ways. The first is to chain the n points, i.e., to find a permutation p of the signal points 1, 2, . . . , n so that

$$\sum_{i=1}^{n-1} d_{p(i),p(i+1)}$$

is minimum, where $p(i)$ is the ith point in the permutation and $d_{p(i),p(i+1)}$ is the distance between point $p(i)$ and $p(i+1)$. Unfortunately, this problem is equivalent to the traveling salesperson problem and results in a nondeterministic polynomial (NP).

The second most common means for wire segment generation is constructing a minimal spanning tree. The third technique, which is also NP complete, is to form a Steiner tree. These three concepts are illustrated in Figure 5.9. Note that wire segments are used only to define pairs of points to be connected. The actual path taken is usually not the one defined by the wire segment. In fact, the pair of points may end up being connected indirectly, e.g., both being connected to a common via.

Wire segment generation is also useful in predicting wire demand or density prior to routing. For example, consider the routing grid and two points A and B to be connected, as shown in Figure 5.10. Here we can assign at most one wire to each grid segment. Two minimum length rectilinear paths are shown by the heavy lines. In

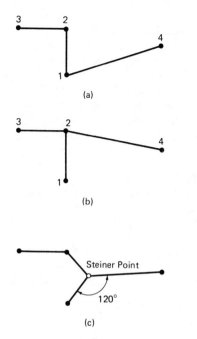

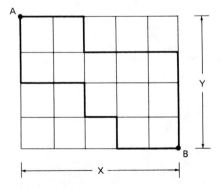

Figure 5.9. Wire segment generation. (a) Minimum chain connection. (b) Minimum spanning tree. (c) Steiner tree.

general, for X columns and Y rows, there are $\left(\dfrac{X+Y}{X}\right)$ minimal length paths between A and B. From this result, one can easily compute the probability that a given grid segment will be used in a minimal length path, assuming each path is equally likely. Given all the wire segments, one can now determine a density map indicating the rel-

ative a priori demand on each grid segment of a carrier available for routing. Such a map can be used to determine the routing of points A and B.

Ordering

Wires are usually routed sequentially; hence, wire segments must be put into some order prior to routing. There are two common types of ordering schemes: **static** and **dynamic.** A *static* ordering scheme determines an a priori sequence in which to process the wire segments. Ordering appears to be much more important for single layer routing than for multilayer routing. Though no clearcut "best" ordering procedure has yet been found, a good "rule of thumb" is to order wire segments in increasing order of $v = \Delta x + \alpha \Delta y$, where Δx (Δy) is the length of the x (y) projection of the wire segment, and α is a "skew" parameter and is dependent on the carrier geometry. This criterion encourages that shorter connections be considered first, and that horizontal and vertical lines precede lines of the same length which are not horizontal or vertical.

In *dynamic ordering,* selecting the next wire segment to be routed is based upon the results of routing the previous wire segments. For example, consider a partially routed net and in the net a point p, which is not yet connected to another point and which is the closest to some point q (pad or via) in the partially connected net. Points p and q define the next wire segment to be processed. It is generally believed that dynamic ordering produces better results than static ordering, but requires considerably more computation time.

Layering

Layering deals with the assignment of wire segments to layers. Layering is not required for single layer carriers. For two layer carriers, preferred direction layers are usually desirable, i.e., only horizontal wires are routed on one layer and vertical wires on the other. Horizontal and vertical segments can be interconnected by means of a via. Hence, a wire segment for a net is automatically "layered" when routed. When the two layers do not have the same electrical properties, after routing wire segments can be reassigned to the preferred layer as long as no shorts occur.

Multilayer carriers, which are coming into production, can be processed either as a series of single layer carriers, or as pairs of preferred layer carriers. The major problem

Figure 5.10. Two minimal length paths between A and B.

with preferred layer routing is the need for vias, though this means of routing appears to produce higher interconnection densities than those achieved by using two non-preferred layers.

Routing

Routing is concerned with finding paths between points in a signal net. Routing algorithms fall into four categories: maze, line, channel, and graph. Maze and line routers only are considered.

Maze routers.   One model of the routing environment is shown in Figure 5.11a. Here, a grid system where at most one signal wire can be placed in each cell is shown. The grid is scaled so that the center to center distances for the wires meet the constraints imposed by the technology's ground rules. In Figure 5.11b, the cells which

contain wires are indicated by cross-hatching. These cells are referred to as blockages.

Assume it is desired to find a path from A to B. This problem corresponds to that of finding a path through a maze. The most used procedure for solving this problem is the **Lee algorithm.** This algorithm finds a minimal cost path in a maze between two points, if such a path exists. Cost can be quite general, and can depend on such factors as length, density, and turns. The algorithm consists of a labeling process, in which a cell is assigned a label $i + 1$ if it is unlabeled, not blocked, and is adjacent to a cell labeled i. Starting with cell A containing the label 0, the labels shown in Figure 5.11b are obtained. This process terminates when cell B is labeled. To find a path, one need only retrace back from B to A, going from a cell having a label $i + 1$ to one having a label i.

The Lee algorithm is an extremely effective tool and is universally used. In order to reduce storage demand, it has been shown that instead of the labeling sequence 1,

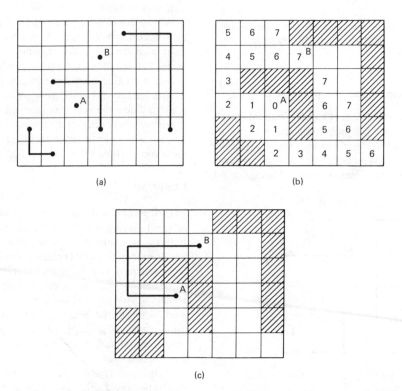

Figure 5.11. Maze routing. (a) Original layout on a grid. (b) Lee algorithm computed. (c) Path A-B.

2, 3, 4, 5, . . . , one can use the sequence 1, 1, 2, 2, 1, 1, 2, 2, ... Hence, only a few bits per cell are necessary, the number of bits being independent of the size of the grid system.

Several techniques exist for attempting to speed up the Lee algorithm. One is to put a constraining window around points A and B, and not allow the labels to extend past this window. This can reduce computation by about 50 percent. Finally, one can modify this technique by expanding in the direction of rows and columns, rather than radially outward in the shape of a diamond as occurs for the procedure described when no blockages exist.

Two main drawbacks with the Lee algorithm are its relatively large demands for computer storage and computation time. To alleviate these problems, researchers have looked for other techniques for routing. However, in order to reduce computation time, researchers have considered embedding the Lee algorithm into hardware, such as a VLSI chip.

Line routers are path construction algorithms which do not employ a grid system. Paths consist of an alternating sequence of horizontal and vertical line segments on a single layer. Each segment is represented by a 3 tuple, e.g., a horizontal wire segment represented by (x_1, y_1, x_2) where (x_1, y_1) is the coordinate of the leftmost point on the wire and x_2 is the x coordinate of the rightmost point. Horizontal wire segments are normally stored in a well structured manner, for example, sorted according to their y coordinate value, and then by their x_1 value. Vertical line segments would be similarly stored. In addition, a fast procedure exists for checking as to whether two line segments intersect. Paths are found by constructing a sequence of connected line segments starting from the two points A and B to be interconnected. When one segment of one of the sequences intersects a segment in the other sequence, a path is created.

5.16 DATA BASE CONSIDERATIONS

The evolution of silicon technology over the past decade has been so rapid that the development of computer aids has not maintained pace with it. Existing design methods cannot cope with presently feasible scales of integration. Many CAD tools are outdated and some projects for developing new ones have become obsolete even before completion. Layout in particular seems destined to be a bottleneck in the design cycle. The Intel 8086 microprocessor, for example, required 13 man-years merely for

layout design, yet it cannot be regarded as an isolated problem.

Anyone in VLSI design must agree that conceptual integrity is the most important consideration in system design. From the first conception to the last test, designers must be sensitive to the effects a decision has on all future design tasks. During the design process, the design itself is to be stored as data on computers. Thus the integrity of a design is, in fact, the integrity of its data base. Decisions regarding data base design should precede overall program design as well as the individual design states contained within the covering program. Questions like: "What data is needed, when is it needed, by which program?" should be answered. The answers will lead to a tentative data base configuration.

Design automation data can be divided into two types: design and library. This division is not based on a difference in logical or physical representation, but on how the data is utilized. **Library data** is utilized in a "read-only mode" by the program subsystems. The data is not changed during a design process. It is accessed by pointer references, and program subsystems may copy pertinent parts of the library.

Library data can also be divided into two types: data stored in the master library, and data stored in the user library. The master library is built, maintained, and updated by a group of authorized people and protected against alterations by users. Many designs may reference data of this type. It typically represents standard components, complete with their simulation models and mask geometry. The user library contains data entered by the user and specific to his or her own design, for example, a layout structure defined by the user.

Design data is the set of data that describes the actual state of the design. This set can also be divided into two classes: (1) design data available to all program subsystems and (2) design data exclusively pertaining to a particular program subsystem. The two classes are called *common design data* and *private design data* respectively. Circuit topology data is a typical example of common design data. It defines how modules—generic name for components and subsystems—are interconnected. These data are reflected in a structure known as the *potential graph*.

5.17 CELL DESIGN

The main steps in developing an integrated circuit are functional design, physical design, and generation of test and fabrication data. *Functional design* starts with a specification of the intended behavior of the circuit and results in a schematic. *Design verification* (simulation on various levels such as register transfer, gate, circuit) makes sure that the designated network exhibits the intended behavior. The next step—*physical design*—deals with the physical implementation of the circuitry on the wafer.

For each component, the device geometry has to be found and then the components placed and interconnected using as little silicon area as possible. Placement and routing are closely coupled problems; placement has a heavy impact on the possibilities for routing, and the space used for wire determines the final positions of the components. This interdependence of placement and routing renders the layout problem difficult not only for the human designer, but also for computer programs. Physical design has to be verified for adherence to design rules and to make sure that the circuit implemented is consistent with the functional specification. In a final step, the data collected during the functional and physical design stages are used to generate control information for mask making or for direct exposure of the wafer to electron beams for testing.

The layout design problem is as follows. Given a two layer wiring board in general, components or circuit modules are mounted on the first side of the board, each with connector pins; then connections through holes (vias) tie into wiring patterns on the opposite side of the board. Each set of pins to be electrically connected in common, called a *signal net* or a *power line*, can be connected by wiring patterns in each layer by way of vias. The layout problem is to decide on the position of each component and find the routing of each signal net and power line that will satisfy a given specification. The ultimate layer design goal is to provide an automatic design system that achieves complete net connectivity while meeting all physical and electrical constraints.

5.18 DESIGN VERIFICATION AND TESTING

The scale and performance of logic systems, especially in the computer field, have been improved by advancing VLSI design and fabrication technologies. CAD tools have made possible not only the development of VLSI circuits in a short turnaround time, but also the execution of rigid timing designs of the circuits for higher performance. Verifying each design step for logic systems has become an important technology in the overall VLSI design process. Hardware and software simulations are particularly effective in verifying a designed system:

1. They enable us easily to determine whether the intended functions to the VLSI circuit will be attained by the present design or not.
2. They make it possible to simulate the timing of the circuit exactly by taking the active device parameters and loading conditions into account. Micromodeling and microsimulation work effectively here.
3. They enable us to evaluate the electrical characteristics as subject to the fluctuations of fabrication parameters and operational conditions.

REFERENCES

Colclaser, R. A., *Microelectronics: Processing and Device Design*. New York: John Wiley & Sons, 1980.

Einspruch, N. G., ed., *VLSI Electronics: Microstructure Science*. New York: Academic Press, 1982.

McGreivy, D. G., and K. A. Pickar, *VLSI Technologies—Through the 80s and Beyond*. Silver Spring, MD: IEEE Computer Society Press, 1982. Mead, C., and L. Conway, *Introduction to VLSI Systems*. Reading, MA: Addison-Wesley, 1980.

Rabbat, G., ed., *Hardware and Software Concepts in VLSI*. New York: Van Nostrand Reinhold, 1983.

Rice, R., *VLSI Support Technologies (Computer-Aided Design, Testing, and Packaging)*. Silver Spring, MD: IEEE Computer Society Press, 1982.

Rice, R., *VLSI—The Coming Revolution in Applications and Design*. Silver Spring, MD: IEEE Computer Society Press, 1980.

II
DEVICES

6
Peripheral Devices

Lloyd Kusak

Hewlett-Packard

6.1 INTRODUCTION

If we look into a typical modern computer system installation, the majority of the space is occupied by equipment
other than the computer itself. The other equipment, or
peripheral devices, is used to augment the performance
of the computer by permitting data to be transmitted to
it rapidly or by providing it with a large capacity for storage that is readily and quickly accessible. Peripheral devices naturally seem to fall into two categories: those
which assist in the process of transmitting data to and
from the computer (input/output devices) and those
whose principal function is to store large quantities of
data (mass storage devices).

In the category of I/O (input/output) devices, we have
those which are closely related to manual functions.
These include on-line typewriters, cathode ray tube displays, card reading and punching equipment, and various
forms of optical record and magnetic ink reading equipment. Equipment that more automatically transmits data
to the computer system includes various types of teleprocessing devices which connect computers to the telephone
system, and analog and digital I/O methods which monitor and control production processes. Mass storage devices almost always use a magnetic iron oxide recording
medium as a much lower cost means of permanently storing very large amounts of data which can be made conveniently accessible to the computer.

The basic architecture for connecting peripheral devices to a computer is shown in Figure 6.1. A computer
is provided with a number of I/O channels for connecting
a device control unit, or controller. With most systems,

several controllers may be attached to a single I/O channel and each controller has the capacity of controlling a
single type of device, i.e., magnetic tape, card readers, or
line printers. Typically, the controller operates eight peripherals on that channel. Less frequently, one sees controllers capable of controlling as few as four devices and
as many as thirty-two.

It is important to match the capability of a peripheral
device to the capability of its channel. All the I/O channels on some computers have an equal capacity for high
transfer rate, direct memory access (DMA), and interrupts. With other computer systems, DMA capacity, for
example, is available only on certain selected channels.
With such a computer system, high speed devices such as
disks, drums and tape drives, for example, must be connected to the high speed channels. Slower devices, such
as typewriters, card readers and cathode ray tube (CRT)
displays may be connected to lower speed channels. The
lower speed channels generally operate on an interrupt
basis. That is to say, anytime some information is ready,
such as a character, a byte or a word, the main computer
processor interrupts its program and goes to a program
to collect the data item being presented on the channel
that interrupted it.

When several devices on the same channel can cause
an interrupt (or a request for service from the computer),
some means must be provided to identify the interrupting
device. Two methods are provided for this function. With
one method, the computer interrogates each device until
it finds the one requiring service. In the other method, a
hardware register on the I/O channel is provided to contain an identifying bit for each device. When the device

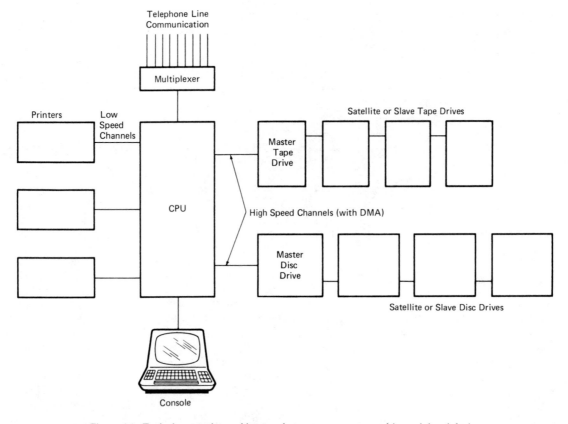

Figure 6.1. Typical connecting architecture between a computer and its peripheral devices.

interrupts, an appropriate bit is set and the computer is able to identify the interrupting device immediately. When the computer responds, the bit is cleared (set to 0) and the device can again interrupt.

An added attribute of such a system is that the computer programmer may choose to ignore such interrupts in the program by using a register that contains an **interrupt mask.** The mask contains a bit for each position that corresponds to a device, in just the same fashion as the interrupt register. However, interrupts are recognized only for devices for which a bit has been set in the mask register. Therefore, if the programmer wishes to ignore other interrupts, he or she sets a zero value for all the other bit positions.

Higher speed devices (which use transfer rates at over 10,000 bytes per second) require the use of DMA or buffered I/O. DMA permits (as its name implies) direct access to memory without requiring interrupts or service

from the CPU to accept each byte and store it in memory. It is as though there is a small central processing unit (CPU) on that I/O channel which performs this function. The main CPU is required to initiate this function, but once DMA has started, the CPU can go about its other programs. In fact, several DMA transfers can take place simultaneously, thus enhancing substantially the performance of the computing system.

DMA rates are related to the cycle time of the main processor. Typically, a one microsecond (1 μs) cycle time machine can transfer at a rate of a million (10^6) bytes per second, a 500 nanosecond machine would go at 2 million bytes per second, etc. From the point of view of the peripheral device, DMA provides a capability for the CPU to transfer data at speeds that can match the peripheral device.

A third form of interface, used with typewriters and CRTs, is the **multiplexer.** The multiplexer appears to the computer as a single device, rather than a controller with several slave devices. In terms of explaining its operation simply, the multiplexer acts to accept individual characters from each of several CRTs and passes the resultant string of characters in a buffer to the main CPU. While the main CPU builds a character stream for each device in memory, the multiplexer assembles the next character for each device in its own buffer, checking each for validity. At the next character time interval, the whole buffer is again transferred to main memory.

Because each class of device has its unique set of characteristics, a capability exists within the CPU and its I/O channels to accommodate those characteristics. Usually, high speed devices are connected to high speed channels and low speed devices to low speed channels. Although with many systems it is possible to connect a device as slow as a typewriter to a DMA channel, this would be considered a poor use of the DMA function.

6.2 MASS STORAGE DEVICES

The term **mass storage devices** is used for equipment that provides lower cost storage in contrast with the read-write storage which is normally the memory of the computer. Storage media of this type almost always use magnetic oxide technology—disks, drums, magnetic tape drives, floppy disks and cartridge tape drives. In all cases, a uniform layer of magnetic iron oxide is placed over a substrate which may be a disk platter, a strip of mylar plastic, or a circular sheet of mylar plastic as in a floppy disc.

Typically, the read/write mechanism to store information on this media is generated by ordering the magnetic flux in a predetermined manner to indicate the presence or absence of binary information. In all cases, this type of storage does not require any power to maintain the information; consequently, a reel of tape or a disk cartridge may be removed from the tape or disk drive and stored on a shelf for a substantial length of time without loss or alteration of data. By contrast, active memories within a computer will lose their contents if power to the computer is turned off. Active memories are said to be **volatile** (see Chap. 3.)

6.3 MAGNETIC TAPE DRIVES

The principal advantage of magnetic tape is its large storage capacity at relatively low cost and the good storage characteristics of the medium on which the data are recorded. The principal disadvantage of magnetic tape is that data can be accessed only on a serial basis and that this access is slower than that to disks or computer memory. A major feature of standard magnetic tape is that the leading manufacturer, IBM, has established a standard recording format which is accepted by all members of the data processing community.

Standard reels of magnetic tape contain up to 2,400 feet of tape that is ½ inch wide. Tape is also available in 1,200, 600, 400, and 200 foot lengths for convenience of use. At a density of 800 BPI (bits per inch), a 2,400 foot reel of tape could theoretically hold 23 million characters. The medium is reusable and can be erased and remagnetized as many as 10,000 times. Data stored on the tape will remain indefinitely unless exposed to excessive heat or fluctuating magnetic fields, which can erase the data.

The recording material is a combination of a magnetic iron oxide substance and a binder about ½ mil in thickness. It is put on a plastic mylar tape which is about 1 mil ($\frac{1}{1000}$ inch) in thickness. Each manufacturer attempts to achieve the most desirable combination of *high permeability* (ease of recording), *high retentivity* (retention of recorded data) and *high coercivity* (resistance to stray fields). Usually there are tradeoffs among these characteristics, influenced by both the oxide layer and the binding agent.

After the tape is manufactured, it is tested for a number of characteristics. Normally, the manufacturer certifies it for zero permanent errors at a given density if it meets that specification. This means that data has been successfully recorded and recaptured throughout the length of the tape without the discovery of any permanent errors. If the tape fails the test at the highest density, an attempt will be made to certify it at some lower density. If it fails to pass the latter test, the tape is rejected as unsuitable for recording digital data.

The better magnetic tapes have a layer of *conductive* material on the back of the tape. This coating reduces the buildup of static charges when the tape is being used in a very dry environment. The most common problem with tapes is that the magnetic oxide material becomes relocated from one area of the tape to another. This can cause microscopic bumps which alter signal strength significantly as the tape passes under the read head. Other problem sources are contamination by dirt and loss of dimensional stability because of humidity and high temperature. Often the electronics of the tape drive are less susceptible to malfunction owing to a wide variation of temperature and humidity, than is the tape itself.

Recording Mechanism

The recording technique for magnetic tape is similar in principle to that for other forms of magnetic storage, i.e., disks or drums. The **write head** is a form of electromagnet wherein a current is manipulated to generate a series of magnetized spots on the tape which correspond to the presence or absence of data.

In the **read** process, as the tape passes the read/write head, the changing flux on the tape induces a voltage in the coil winding. The voltage so induced is amplified and converted back into its original digital form.

A recording head functions as a small transformer with one winding. As shown in Figure 6.2, it is constructed of two pieces which are wound separately and bonded together with some gap material in between. When a current flows through the C-shaped portion of the recording head, a magnetic flux is generated and flows preferably through the tape to the pole piece of the read/write head, instead of flowing through the gap material. Most versions of tape drives record nine tracks in parallel so that a read/write head consists of nine individual recording stations. Eight of the nine tracks record 8 bits, or 1 byte, of information in parallel, and the remaining track is used to record parity bits.

Recording densities use the terminology of bits per inch along the longitudinal track. In reality, this means that the actual density is that number of bytes, or frames, per inch (BPI). Earlier versions of tape drives recorded in densities of 556 BPI and 200 BPI. In some older computer installations, such drives are still in use. Other densities are 1600 and 6250 BPI; at present, the most commonly used densities are 800 and 1600 BPI.

Recording Formats

A number of techniques is used for generating the bit patterns to be stored on the tape. The most common of these are **NRZI (nonreturn zero inversion)** and **PE (phase encoding)**. NRZI is used on tape recording at densities at 800 BPI or less; PE is used for recording on 1600 BPI drives. The two individual techniques are illustrated by the wave pattern shown in Figure 6.3.

In the NRZI format, a flux change takes place only when 1 bit is recorded. This has the advantage in that if a flux change is missed, the succeeding bits are still recognized correctly because a change in flux always represents a bit. In the PE format, a 0 bit is recognized by a flux change in one direction while a 1 bit is recognized by a flux change in the opposite direction. This means that within the distance in which a bit is to be recorded, a flux transition must take place at the beginning so that a flux change in the proper direction will take place within that bit cell. This requires twice as many transitions for an equivalent amount of data as are involved in NRZI format. The PE recording format, however, has the advantage in that errors in the preceding bit patterns are not propagated into succeeding data.

Phase encoding also provides a self-clocking capability in that distinct pulses must be generated for each bit cell position. Consequently, if there is a change in the longitudinal dimension of the tape, the self-clocking feature of the PE recording format automatically compensates for it.

Data is recorded on tape as a series of records separated by **inter-record gaps (IRG)**, as indicated in Figure 6.4. A physical **record** consists of one or more bytes

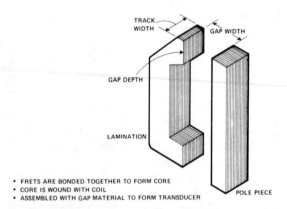

• FRETS ARE BONDED TOGETHER TO FORM CORE
• CORE IS WOUND WITH COIL
• ASSEMBLED WITH GAP MATERIAL TO FORM TRANSDUCER

Figure 6.2. A tape recording head is basically a small transformer with a single winding.

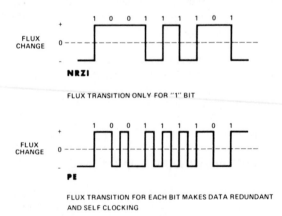

Figure 6.3. Recording formats for the NRZI and PE modes.

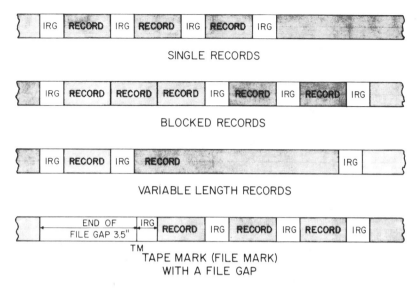

Figure 6.4. Data is stored on tape in individual physical records separated by an interrecord gap (IRG).

stored in series. It is theoretically possible to load one reel of tape with one continuous record of information. However, the computer addresses information on the tape by physical record number; and, for this reason, the record length must be kept to a reasonable size. The IRG is usually a ½ to ¾ inch length of blank space on the tape with the purpose of providing a tape length sufficient to permit the tape transport mechanism to come to a halt from its full speed operation, and to start up again from its halted position and return to full speed. In other words, the tape transport must be able to decelerate from full speed to a halt and reverse the process all within the length of the IRG.

A record can be conceived as an 80-column card image containing 80 characters of information. Records can range in size from a single character up to as many characters as can be configured by the specific computer. A recording format holding only 80 characters is somewhat wasteful in that in this case $\frac{1}{10}$ inch contains meaningful data for every ¾ inch of blank space (800 BPI density). Consequently, logical records may be blocked together to form one physical record on the tape. The **blocking factor** indicates the number of logical records stored within one physical record. A file's end is marked by an end of file mark.

There is a tape marker a few feet inward from each end usually a silver strip about ¾ × ⅛ inch in dimension.

It is sensed by the tape drive as being the physical limitation for writing on the tape. The few feet at each end which are not used for recording are allowed so that the tape can be wound on the reel.

In addition to a parity check for each byte of recorded data in a nine-track tape, two other check characters are provided, called a **longitudinal redundancy check character (LRCC)** and **cyclic redundancy check character (CRCC)**. Seven track tape drive formats use only the LRCC. Each record is followed by the CRCC (for nine-track tapes) and an LRCC. During a nine track write operation, the CRCC is developed in the CRC register in the tape drive controller. It is written on the tape 4 byte spaces after the end of the record. The value of the CRCC is calculated on the basis of a polynomial such that the probability of the CRCC missing an error is very low.

The LRC character is an odd or even parity count of all the bits in each track of that record. In a nine track format (Figure 6.5), the count of the bits in the preceding CRCC is included in the LRCC computation. The LRCC is written 4 byte spaces after the CRCC or 4 byte spaces after the last data item in the record for seven track formats. In nine track formats, the parity bit generates an odd count. In seven track drives, the parity count is odd if binary data are written, but even if BCD data are recorded.

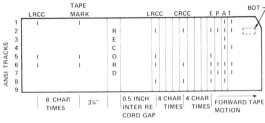

- ONE BYTE PER CHARACTER ON TAPE
- ALL NINE-TRACK OPERATIONS USE ODD VERTICAL (LATERAL) PARITY
- TRACK WIDTH .043 INCH
- SPACING .055 INCH CENTER TO CENTER

Figure 6.5. A nine track 800 cpi NRZI format.

Transport Mechanism

Two transport mechanisms are in common use at the present time. The lower speed mechanism uses a tension arm concept for controlling the movement of the tape between the reel and the read/write head. The purpose of the tension arm is to allow the feeding of short tape increments to the read/write portion without requiring that the complete reel be started and stopped for each minor motion at the read/write station. This frees the mechanism from the requirement of many quick movements of the reel whose inertia would be too great to permit the quickness of response required for any reasonable tape reading speed. Electronic circuitry within the tape drive senses the need for more tape and initiates motion of the reel as necessary.

At the read/write station, the movement of the tape is controlled by one or more capstans and pinch rollers. The capstans are low in inertia so that they may be quickly brought up to the design speed of the tape drive. In Figure 6.6, both single and dual capstans are shown.

With the single capstan, direction of motion is provided by the bidirectional movement of the capstan and the fact that the tape is mounted, with slight tension, around 180° of its circumference. Because this mechanism has fewer moving parts and requires no pinch roller adjustment, it is appearing more frequently in the newer tape drives.

The dual capstan mechanism depends on pinch rollers to provide a sufficient grip on the tape to move it back and forth across the read/write station. Each capstan permits motion in one direction only. Obviously only one pinch roller at a time can grip the tape for motion control. When the pinch roller is not active, it releases its pressure

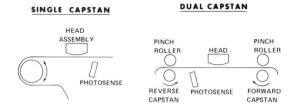

Figure 6.6. Single and dual capstan control of speed.

on the tape, permitting the tape to slip past the roller's location.

Figure 6.7 shows a typical tape recording head and guide assembly. Ideally, spring-loaded ceramic washers are provided at the tape guide stations because of their resistance to wear from many passes of the tape medium. The tape will more easily scratch and score a metal surface; such a surface is more prone to snag a tape and cause a break. The normal course of the tape is to pass over a tape cleaner, an erase head, a write head, and finally a read head.

This is a typical configuration and there may be many variations among manufacturers. However, the sequence of functions is usually consistent among them. It is important to provide a cleaning function before the tape reaches the read/write station; an erase function assures a clear tape before new data are recorded. The read function, if it follows the write function, can be used to verify what has been written on the tape.

Because the inertia of the entire reel of tape is too great to be accelerated quickly for each read or write function,

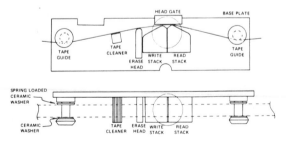

- SINGLE MOUNTING PLATE ASSURES PROPER ALIGNMENT
- GUIDE – HEAD SPACING IS STANDARD IBM
- CERAMIC WASHERS REDUCE WEAR
- SPRING LOADED WASHER PUSHES TAPE TO REFERENCE EDGE
- ERASE HEAD ASSURES BLANK TAPE
- TAPE CLEANER NEAR HEAD
- HEAD GATE REDUCES CROSSTALK

Figure 6.7. A typical tape head.

slack is maintained between the tape reel and the read/ write station. The capstans at the read/write station then need only to pull on the slack tape as it is needed. Two types of mechanisms are used to take up the slack, or feed it, as required. One mechanism uses tension arms; the other uses vacuum columns (Figure 6.8).

The tension arm design depends on the capability of the system to sense the need for more tape and release it by moving the tension arm to reduce the tape tension. As the slack is used up, the tape reel will unreel at one time several inches of tape, which will immediately be taken up into the tension arm mechanism. The opposite action takes place where the tape is being fed from the read/ write station; i.e., the tension arm system takes up the slack, and as the capacity to hold the slack reaches its limit, the tape is passed onto the tape reel. Tape drives using this design operate at speeds up to 50 inches per second. At densities of 1600 BPI, they can pass data at 80 kilobytes per second.

The other very common design for taking up tape slack in tape transport mechanisms makes use of vacuum columns (Figure 6.8). The tape slack droops inside the chamber between predetermined upper and lower limits. Small inlets are provided near the lower and upper ends of each chamber to permit an airstream to blow across to sense the position of the lower loop of the tape within the

chamber. This information is transmitted to the circuitry of the tape drive and will automatically feed more tape into the chamber when the loop reaches its upper point. The action ceases as soon as the loop reaches its lower-most point. Tape drives using this mechanism operate at speeds up to 200 inches per second and, at densities of 1600 BPI, and can transmit information at a rate of 320 kilobytes per second.

6.4 DISK STORAGE SYSTEMS

Disk systems physically resemble record players in their design as well as in the general principle of their opera-tion. Information is stored on the surface of the disk and accessed by a sensing device at the end of a moving arm which has access to any desired part of the information on the platter. The information stored on the record player disk is contained in tracks which are of a spiral nature; the record player needle actually touches the sur-face of the record to receive its information.

The information on the disk in a computer system has its information stored on concentric tracks. The read/ write mechanism on conventional information disks does not touch the surface but "flies" just a few microinches above it. The recording medium, rather than being phys-ical grooves in the surface, is a layer of magnetic iron oxide which contains spots magnetized in a manner rec-ognizable as data by the reading mechanism. Also, unlike the disks in a record player, the disks for a computing system are always enclosed in some protective device. They may appear as a single disk, or as a permanent as-sembly of as many as 10 disks.

Information is recorded on disks in typically as many as 800 concentric tracks on each surface. The informa-tion is allocated by **sector,** which is the smallest address-able portion on the disk. A typical sector contains 256 bytes. Reading and writing of information on the disk take place a sector at a time. Therefore, if some infor-mation in the middle of the sector is to be updated, the entire sector of information must be read into the com-puter, the appropriate information updated, then the en-tire sector rewritten onto the disk. The bit density along the track can be as high as 6,500 bits per inch. Therefore, storage capacities of 12,000 to 20,000 bytes per track are common. Rotation speeds of commercial disks vary, but a very common rate is 3600 rpm. Therefore, the transfer rate of information from the disk to the computer can be 12,000 bytes in a $\frac{1}{60}$ second, or roughly 720,000 bytes per second. Because there is some variation in track density

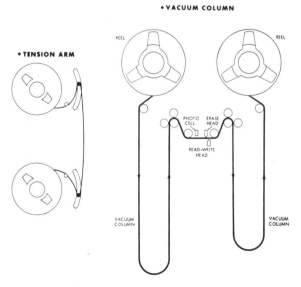

Figure 6.8. Tension arm and vacuum column methods for con-trolling motion of tape past the read/write station.

and rpm rates among manufacturers, some commercial models will transfer data at over a million bytes per second.

The read/write mechanism is composed of a small electromagnet whose flux is controlled electronically so that lines of magnetism are generated on the storage media to correspond to the presence or absence of a bit. In one recording format, the presence of a bit is indicated by the lines of flux running in one direction and its absence is indicated by the lines of flux running in an opposite direction (Figure 6.9). Bits are stored in serial fashion along the track until an end of sector is indicated.

With many disk systems, the end of sector location is indicated by slots on the outer portion of the disk; these slots are sensed by the circuitry of the disk drive. With other disk systems, an entire surface is devoted to format the disk, which indicates magnetically to the disk drive where each sector and each track are located. The recording head flies as close as possible to the surface of the disk without actually touching it. The distance between the surface of the disk and the read/write head can be as close as 20 microinches, much less than the thickness of a human hair. To obtain a proper perspective, we can compare the size of the read/write head to Boeing 747 jet aircraft: it would be like attempting to fly the aircraft an inch above the surface of the ground. Therefore it is extremely important to keep dust particles out of the space which contains the disk cartridge and the reading and writing mechanism. The dust particles represent large ob-

jects which might scratch the disk surface if the head hits one of them. (Figure 6.10).

Because the density of information on the disk increases inversely to the distance of the read/write head above the disk, there is a very strong incentive to develop mechanisms that will fly as close to the surface of the disk as possible. Most read/write heads are of the flying head variety, and they are so-named because they rely on the pressure from a boundary layer of air rotating with the disk to maintain the proper height of the read/write head from the disk surface. A very light spring within the head mechanism provides some downward pressure on the head. The opposite, balancing pressure from the boundary layer steadies the head so that it flies at the correct height when the disk surface is in rotation.

Drives appear in two varieties: moving head and fixed head. Indeed, there are some disk drives that may have two or four moving heads to service two or four tracks of information simultaneously. With the moving head disk, the read/write head must be positioned over the appropriate track before the information can be transferred between the disk drive and the computer. In addition, if a particular sector is required, the disk must rotate until the correct sector is beneath the read/write head. Because of these two actions, there is a seek-time and a rotational delay time during which nothing happens. As soon as the beginning of the addressed sector is sensed, the transfer of information begins.

The seek-time and rotational delay problem is some-

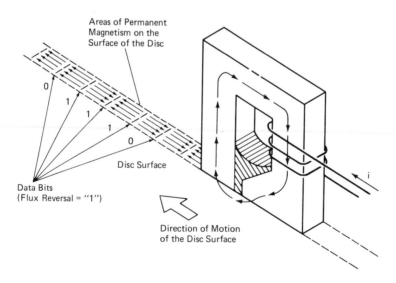

Figure 6.9. Schematic of a read/write mechanism for a disk system.

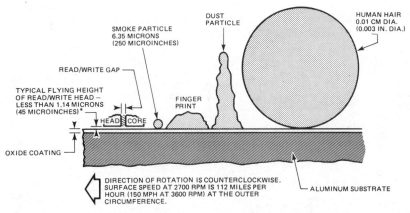

Figure 6.10. Head/media critical elements.

times reduced by multiplatter disks, fixed head disks, or with drums. With multiplatter disks, a single read/write mechanism, which has a comb-like structure, addresses the same track on all of the platters simultaneously (Figure 6.11). In a 10 platter drive, for example, there are 20 tracks of information available for the same track position. Consequently, less track switching is required because the volume of information is much larger.

With fixed head disks and drums, the latter of which also have read/write heads over each track, a read/write mechanism is provided so that no arm movement is necessary to move in one direction to another. All the tracks are available, and the only delay before a specific sector of information is transferred will be a rotational delay. Typical seek-time delays range from 10 to 50 milliseconds; with a 3600 rpm system, the average rotational delay is 8⅓ milliseconds. Consequently, elimination of seek-times will very substantially enhance the performance of a disk system. However, the costs of such systems are substantially greater than the moving head variety for the amount of information stored, and they are not nearly as common.

The normal construction of a disk drive system is such that all the recording mechanisms are included within the drive. The cartridge or multiplatter unit is usually encased within a plastic housing. In the case of a single platter cartridge, the housing is usually permanently mounted around the disk, but a capability is provided to pry open a slot for an opening through which the read/write heads can access the rotating surface. With the multiple cartridge, a cover is provided which locks over the entire unit (Figure 6.12). When the unit is mounted onto the drive, a twist lock releases the cover which is subsequently removed. The cover of the drive is then closed to create a relatively dust free environment within which the recording media and read/write heads operate.

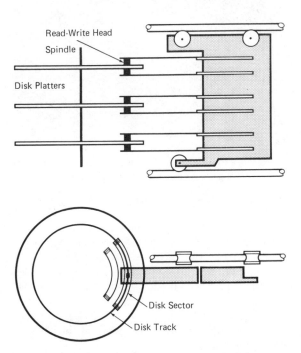

Figure 6.11(a). Accessing data in a multiplatter disk system: schematic representation.

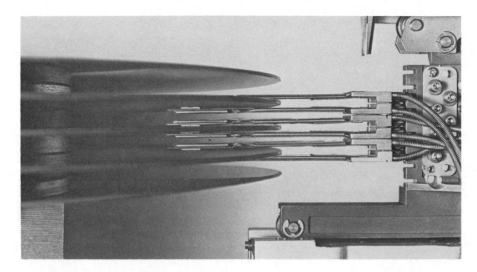

Figure 6.11(b). Read/write heads are shown in place accessing information on six disk surfaces.

Figure 6.12. Multiplatter disk cartridge containing ten platters with data storage on 20 surfaces. (Courtesy IBM Corporation)

It is obviously important to provide filters on the disk mechanism that will maintain as dust free an environment as possible within the disk enclosure. For this purpose, some disk systems use two sets of filters, one to filter out normal sized dust particles and the second to filter out the smallest particles possible (Figure 6.13). In addition, positive air pressure is maintained inside the enclosure to inhibit the entrance of any dust particles through any possible unsealed opening.

A recent development in disk technology is inclusion of read/write heads with the disk cartridge. These car-

tridges are obviously more expensive to manufacture; however, the completely enclosed system provides a minimum of opportunity for any impurity or dust particle from entering into the enclosure containing the read/write mechanism. The read/write heads with such a system may be even closer to the read-write surface than in the systems just discussed; this permits recording at very high densities. A single platter disk of this type can store over 100 million bytes of information.

Disk technology continues to be limited by the density with which data can be recorded along a track (currently

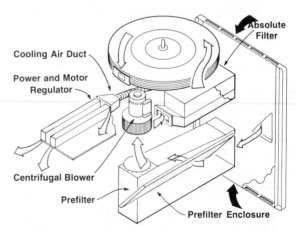

Figure 6.13. Outline of air flow used for cooling a disk enclosure.

about 11,000 BPI) and the track density (about 800 tracks per inch). The present mode of recording stores exactly the same amount of information along the innermost track as it does on the outermost track. The amount of information per track, therefore, is limited by the innermost track capacity. Because of the demands of the data processing community for ever larger-capacity disks, there is considerable activity to increase recording densities. Several manufacturers believe that capacities can be increased by as much as a factor of 10 within the next five to ten years. In the meantime, solid state memories are becoming less expensive each year. However, the dominance of the disk drive as a storage medium seems assured for the forseeable future.

6.5 DRUMS

The recording technology for drums is exactly the same as for disk drives. Information is stored on a series of tracks on the surface of the drum. Read/write heads are provided over each track and, because the entire system is permanently enclosed, recording densities are possible which are greater than those of moving head disk drives. Drums typically rotate at 3600 rpm; but because they are usually smaller in diameter, the transfer rate of information is somewhat lower than that of the more modern disks. As with disks, information on drums is addressed on a sector basis. Sector size is usually predetermined by the hardware manufacturer and ranges from 128 bytes to 512 bytes.

The big advantage of the drum is that it is a head per track device. Hence no seek time is required, only latency. This substantially reduces the average access time. Drums have another advantage, which is that they can be almost completely sealed from the outside atmosphere so that they are much less subject to a hostile environment. Some manufacturers, in order to ensure the cleanliness of the atmosphere around the read/write disk mechanism, include a bottle of compressed air which bleeds slowly into the chamber to maintain a positive pressure within it. This assures a very clean atmosphere almost continuously.

Because drums can be built with greater ruggedness and the chambers within which the recording mechanism is located can be well insulated from the outside atmosphere, they are more usable in difficult environmental conditions than are disks. Consequently, many process control systems, where the equipment is required to function in a factory environment, will be found with drums rather than with disks. The drum also has fewer mechan-

ical moving parts than the disk so that its life expectancy is normally greater than that of a disk. Furthermore, a cylinder onto which the recording medium is deposited can be machined almost perfectly cylindrical and smooth. It is mechanically much more difficult to manufacture a very flat surface which is required for a disk, another factor that makes life expectancies of drums exceed those of disks.

The main disadvantage of a drum system as compared with disks is that an equivalent amount of information is substantially more costly to store on drums. Therefore, with most commercial systems, where the equipment is in an office-like environment, disks rather than drums tend to be used.

6.6 FLEXIBLE DISKS

The **flexible disk, diskette,** or **floppy disk** is a small version of the standard cartridge disk. The recording medium is a layer of magnetic iron oxide deposited on a circular sheet of mylar plastic which resembles a 45 rpm record. Two sizes of these recording media are commonly in use: one is just under 8 inches in diameter, and the other is 5¼ inches in diameter. In both cases, the unit is enclosed in a plastic envelope, and the entire unit is mounted onto the drive. Rotating speeds are much less than those of conventional disks, typically 360 rpm. The read/write heads that are recording or reading information actually ride in contact with the surface of the disk much as they do in a tape drive mechanism or a voice tape recorder. Storage capacities of floppy disks range from 77,000 bytes of information for a 5¼ inch disk up to 1.2 million bytes of information for an 8 inch disk.

The newer floppy disk drives lift the recording mechanism above the surface when there is no reading or writing action. This reduces the wear which would otherwise shorten the useful life of the media and the recording head. Current floppy drives use track densities of up to 96 TPI (tracks per inch). A 48 TPI 64 track configuration using a bit density of 6,250 per inch, with an innermost track diameter of 5 inches, could store about 800,000 bytes per surface. Allowing for gaps between sectors, the actual amount is somewhat less.

6.7 OTHER MASS STORAGE DEVICES

Although disk and tape drives are the most commonly used large storage devices, two other classes of devices also are available. The more common one is the tape cartridge or tape cassette, which has a storage capacity of up to 250,000 bytes. The less common one is called simply a **mass storage system** (CDC [Control Data Corporation] nomenclature) or a **mass storage facility** (IBM nomenclature). The mass storage systems have data storage capacities for many billions of bytes.

In the mass storage systems, data is stored on a strip of tape about 3 inches wide and up to 770 inches long. The tape is wound inside a module about 3½ inches long and about 1¾ inches in diameter. The cartridges are stored in a honeycomb-like shelf structure. Under computer program control, an access arm retrieves the desired cartridge from its storage slot, moves it to its appropriate read station, unwinds the tape, and proceeds to read it. The time to perform this function is in the range of 2 to 5 seconds. The system is therefore suitable only with a faster access system (i.e., disk drive) where large volumes can be transferred for later access to individual records. The mass storage units with their billions of byte capacities provide a capability for storing vast quantities of data on an on-line basis. Even though access is slower than to a disk mass storage, it provides the capacity of very many tape drives without the need for mounting individual reels to reach a given file.

In the CDC configuration, units are offered with a capacity of 2052 cartridges, each of which can store 8 million bytes of data. The recording density within the cartridge is 6,250 BPI, and at a tape movement rate of 129 ips, a transfer rate of 806,000 bytes per second is achieved.

The IBM system is offered in conjunction with a large disk system, such as the Model 3330. Data are stored on the tape cell system as an image of a file on the disk pack, and two tape cells contain the capacity of a Model 3336 disk cartridge (100 million bytes). Mass storage systems are available in modules of 706 up to 4,720 tape cells.

The tape cartridge, or cassette, is commonly used with CRT terminals, and with many desktop computers. The several types in use include the cassette that is found in the portable voice tape recorder and a cartridge specifically designed for use with computer-oriented equipment.

The cartridge appears in a standard sized and a miniature version. The design of the cartridge is such that only a very small part of tape is exposed to minimize exposure to dust and other detrimental environmental effects. In its standard size, the tape cartridge is enclosed in a case approximately 6 inches by 4 inches. It contains about 300 feet of ¼ inch wide tape and a capacity of slightly over 200,000 bytes. A typical data transfer rate is 2,850 characters per second for a read operation and

950 char./sec. for writing. During a write operation, most cartridge tape systems automatically backspace a record and read back the just-written data for check purposes. Hence the write operation is much slower.

In its miniature version, the cartridge measures about 3 × 2½ inches. The tape is 140 feet long and ¼ inch in width. Typical tape transfer rates are 2750 bytes per second. Tape capacities range from 90,000 up to over 250,000 bytes. Data are stored sequentially on two tracks.

Magnetic tape technology is being actively developed to improve the capacity of cartridge systems because of their convenience and portability. Developmental versions of cartridge drives exist which record data on 16 tracks at 10,000 BPI and contain up to 600 feet in a standard size cartridge. With this format, capacities of several million bytes are possible in a conveniently portable unit.

6.8 PRINTING DEVICES

The major product of the work of a computing system is presented in the form of hard-copy printed results. Although there are efforts being made to reduce the so-called paper glut by use of direct inquiry devices, the printed page is still the most common medium for presenting results. Some type of printer is virtually a standard part of every computer system.

Printers tend to fall into two classes: the low speed keyboard oriented devices and the much higher speed printing-only devices. With lower cost computing systems, the keyboard oriented system acts as a console to the computer system, in addition to serving as the standard printer. In very large data processing systems, a computer may be equipped with several devices of each type. The entire system may be orchestrated by the computer's operating system to select each device as it is available for listing results.

Keyboard Devices

Most keyboard oriented devices are derived from the standard typewriter. One of the very common devices in this category is the teletypewriter. It was originally designed to communicate with the telephone-teletype network so that a manufacturer who chose to use this device as the console for a computer system did not have to redesign the interface at the printing station. The interface for the device is an industry standard (RS-232), which is also available with most computers. One of the more common teletypewriters (ASR-33), which operates at 10 characters per second (cps), has a carriage width of 72 characters. A significant attribute of the device is that it can come equipped with a side-mounted paper tape reader and punch. This results in a low cost system with printing as well as paper tape handling capabilities.

Later versions of the teletypewriter operate at higher speeds (typically 30 cps) and use a wider carriage (up to 120 characters). Larger configurations of data terminal stations have appeared with a CRT display, a thermal printer, and an interface to a modem which links it to the telephone network. This same station can be linked directly to a computer system via the standard RS-232 interface.

Several manufacturers, in addition to the Teletype Corporation, have entered the field to produce keyboard oriented terminals. IBM offers the Model 1052 printer-keyboard which is very similar in physical appearance to a typewriter. It operates at 15.5 characters per second, allows a carriage width of 125 characters with character spacing at 10 characters per inch and line spacing at 6 per inch. Another version, the Model 3210, uses a modified Selectric typewriter. The format and printing speed of the latter machine are identical to that of the 1052, i.e., 15.5 cps, 125 character carriage, 10 characters per inch, and 6 lines per inch. A faster console oriented device is available in the form of the Model 3215 printer-keyboard. This device prints at a rate of 85 characters per second. It permits 126 characters per line, has a character spacing of 10 to the inch and a line spacing of 6 per inch. It also comes equipped with a cover over the printing mechanism for modest sound suppression.

Most of the independent suppliers of keyboard-printer devices offer them with an RS-232 interface so that they are readily connectable to any computer or time sharing facility which is equipped with it. Devices that print at up to 120 characters per second use some form of engraved character mechanism from which the character is formed. This may be designed, as in a typewriter, as a character connected to each arm that is activated by a keystroke. In the IBM Selectric typewriter, a print ball mechanism is used. With other printers, a plastic print wheel is used. When printing speeds of greater than 120 characters per second are offered, the printing mechanism forms the character from a **dot matrix** stylus. The character field may be formed from a matrix ranging from 7 × 9 dots up to 9 × 15. The matrix printer has the capability of printing characters of varying sizes,

weights, and styles and even of printing line drawings when printing control is provided for individual dots in the matrix.

Line Printers

Line printers, incorporating a much more rugged design, are used for even larger volumes of paper output. The most common features of these machines are printing speeds ranging between 500 and 2000 lines per minute and a 132 column line print width. A print density of 10 characters per inch and a choice of 6 or 8 lines per inch appear to be a de facto industry standard.

Additional standard features of conventional line printers are control functions to move to a new page (top of form), new half page location, automatically skip a line, and to suppress line skips to allow overprinting. When a number of lines is to be skipped, or if a new page is to be moved up, the higher speed printers utilize a dual speed feature that permits movement at rates up to 75 inches per second to the new print position. Most of the larger printers also are equipped with a soundproofing cover that may be power operated.

Line printers also offer several choices of character sets. Between 48 and 52 characters are provided as a standard. This may include all the capital letters, numbers, and some commonly used characters such as a period and comma. Because the characters are mounted in several sets on the printing mechanism (drum, ribbon, etc.), where there is a smaller number of characters, they can be repeated more frequently. Consequently, the printer can operate at greater speeds. Printers appear with as few as 13 characters in a character set (IBM 1443 Model NI) up to a 96 character set. The larger character set includes both upper and lower case characters, numerics, as well as a variety of special characters.

Printing Mechanisms

The most common mechanical construction in line printers is the **train mechanism** illustrated in Figure 6.14. Print characters are contained in a chain (or train) which is moved continuously at a rapid rate by two geared pulleys. Circuitry within the printer senses when the correct character appears at the desired print position on the page. At that point, a hammer strikes the page. This action presses the paper against a ribbon and against the character located at that position. The result leaves an

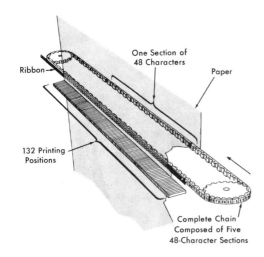

Figure 6.14. A print train mechanism for conventional line printers. (Courtesy IBM Corporation)

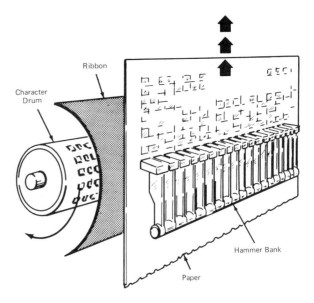

Figure 6.15. Drum printer mechanism. (Courtesy Creative Strategies, Inc.)

impression of that character. As the chain continues to move transversely across the page, additional characters are printed as they reach the position required by the commands of the computer. When the requirements of the printed line are fulfilled, the printer carriage control moves the page to the next line position.

The principle of the drum printer, illustrated in Figure 6.15, is very similar to that of the train printer. All the characters in the specified character set are engraved along the circumference of the drum, and if 132 print positions are available, this is repeated for each column. With very high speed printers, or if an abbreviated character set is used, the set may be repeated more than once for each column print position. With this construction, the drum need only make ½ or ⅓ of a complete revolution in order to print the entire line.

Both the train and drum printer construction can be utilized to produce printing speeds of over 1,000 lines per minute. The main point of contention between the two methods of construction lies in the output characteristics of the printed line when they are out of adjustment. A poorly adjusted drum printer generates a wavy line; a poorly adjusted train printer results in uneven character spacing. The former is generally the more noticeable, and consequently more objectionable. However, the drum printer has the advantage of simpler construction and generally easier maintenance.

Another method of printer operation uses a modification of the train printing principle. As shown in Figure 6.16, a steel band containing the printer character is

moved transversely across a printer line by a pair of pulleys, in exactly the same way as is done with the train printer. However, there is a smaller number of hammers available for striking the page to generate the printed line. The set of hammers that is available is mounted on a carriage and it moves across the line position to print

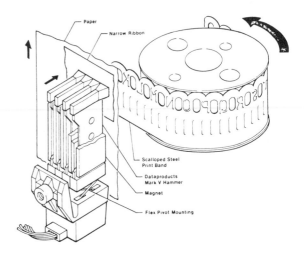

Figure 6.16. Band printing mechanism. (Courtesy Data Products Corporation)

the desired character whenever it appears at the desired position as a result of the band motion.

Attributes of this construction are its lower cost (compared to a train printer) and lower printing speed. However, because of variable timing combinations of hammer and printer band movements, it is possible to vary the character spacing. An example of such a printer is the Control Data Model 9380 series, which prints at 10 or 15 characters per inch.

Still another modification of the impact printing function utilizes a **daisy wheel** mechanism, illustrated in Figure 6.17. All of the characters available for printing are embossed on paddle-shaped plates mounted in slots within a print wheel. A modification of this construction takes the form of a single plastic (or metal) print wheel with the characters engraved near the outer edge. The entire mechanism moves from one print position to the next across the print line. At each position, the print wheel rotates until the selected character is in the print position. At that time, a hammer strikes to generate the character on the paper.

The term *serial printer* is used for devices of this type because they generate only one character at a time, serially, across the print line. Printers using this principle operate at speeds ranging from 15 to 60 cps. The print quality, however, is very good. An advantage is that the print wheel can be readily replaced whenever any wear appears.

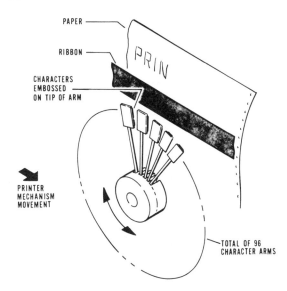

Figure 6.17. Daisy wheel print mechanism. (Courtesy Data Products Corporation)

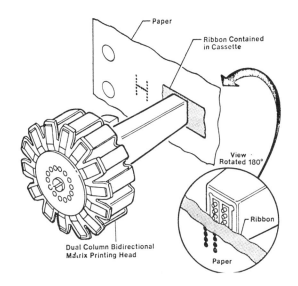

Figure 6.18. Dot matrix printing mechanism. (Courtesy Data Products Corporation)

A very common mechanism (introduced earlier in this Section) now being used in lower cost serial printers is the dot matrix, shown in Figure 6.18. These printers operate in the neighborhood of 200 characters per second. As we have seen, the character is formed out of a dot matrix which ranges from a 7×9 up to a 9×15 format of individual pins that strike the paper. The print head moves across the page and logic within the printer causes the appropriate pins to strike to form the character. Although the printed characters are of good quality, the individual dots are obviously discernible, and to some users, not as elegant as characters formed from a print drum or print wheel.

The dot matrix printer can also be used to generate graphical output. Printers of this type contain additional logic to address individual pin positions of the dot matrix. Computer systems with a capability for graphics generation contain programming logic to translate plotter-style commands to logic functions to output individual print pin positions for plotting graphs. Resolution, of course, is limited to that available on the printer, and with a character format using a 9 position width, a line of print would contain 9×132 or 1,188 plotting points.

Several versions of nonmechanical printers are available and are generally used in special purpose systems. The principle of the **thermal printer** is illustrated in Figure 6.19. The concept is very similar to that of a dot matrix printing system. The printing head moves across a

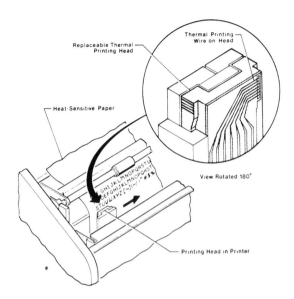

Figure 6.19. A thermal printer system. (Courtesy Data Products Corporation)

print line and characters are generated thermally from a column of dot positions in the print head. Such printers can also be used for graphics generation with computers possessing that capability. Printers of this type are very quiet in their operation and they can be built at somewhat lower cost as compared to a mechanical printer. They do require a heat sensitive paper, and only one copy at a time can be generated. Moreover, the printed characters on thermal paper fade noticeably in a period of a few months, so that this paper is not suitable for permanent storage. The main advantage of thermal printers is their relatively low cost and portability due to their light weight.

Several manufacturers have developed printers using an **ink jet** printing technique. A fairly complex plumbing system is needed to circulate and pressurize the ink that is ejected on the page to generate a character. The ink is aimed at the desired position on the paper by a printing "gun" operating like an electron gun in a cathode ray tube. Excess ink is collected in a gutter below the printer position and recirculated for reuse. Printers of this type have some attributes of both the dot matrix and thermal printers. They can readily generate characters of varying sizes, change the slope of the printed character, and alter its height-to-width ratio as well. Ink jet printers are also very quiet; their noise output is similar to a continuous series of brush strokes. As with thermal printers, only one copy at a time can be produced. However, ink jet print is

as permanent as copy from an impact line printer, thus suitable for long term storage.

The highest speed line printer currently offered is a **laser electrophotographic** device. Printers using this principle can operate at rates around 10,000 lines per minute. The printer utilizes a laser light beam which sweeps across a photoconductor drum to generate characters requested by the computer (Figure 6.20). The beam is turned on and off to generate a stream of dots which build the characters on the printed line in successive sweeps. In one commercial version, seven lines at a time sweep across the page to generate characters. Another version uses a system that sweeps a single line at a time, but at a much faster rate. The images on the drum are transferred to the printer paper and treated (fused) to generate a permanent copy.

Printers of the laser type contain computer-type memories which may store as many as 50 to 60 pages of information for transfer onto paper. These printers generate good quality copy, which is also permanent. Like other nonmechanical printers, only one copy at a time can be produced, but the very high speed of these devices readily overcomes that disadvantage.

6.9 CARD EQUIPMENT

Much of the data that is entered into the computer is transmitted by means of the punched card. Indeed, the idea of the punched card predates the computer. The punched card was invented by Dr. Herman Hollerith in

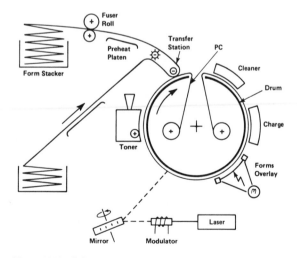

Figure 6.20. Schematic of steps used in the printing process of an IBM Model 3800 printing system. (Courtesy IBM Corporation)

the late 1800s to help tabulate the U.S. census. As the 1880 census was being tabulated, it became apparent that, because of the expanding population, the 1890 census would not be completed before it became time to collect data for the next census. The Bureau of the Census held a contest to find a more rapid way to tabulate the data and this resulted in the invention of the punched card.

Although there have been alternate designs, the dimensions and information layout of the standard 80 column card have changed very little over a long time. The standard card is shown in Figure 6.21. It is 7⅞ inches long and 3¼ inches wide. There are versions that appear in lengths up to 11 inches. Data on the standard card are stored in as many as 80 columns and 12 rows, and are represented by small rectangular holes (Figure 6.22). One convention labels the row numbers by assigning 12 to the top row, 11 to the next row and the numeric values for the other rows.

Numeric information requires a punch only in the row representing that number; a negative value is indicated by placing a punch in the row 12 in addition to a punch for the number in its representative row. Alphabetic information, as well as special characters, is represented by two or three punches in the appropriate row for that column. For example, a comma is indicated by a punch in rows 0, 3 and 8; a $ sign is represented by punches in rows 11, 3 and 8.

Binary data also can be stored on the 80 column card, provided special card punching equipment is available.

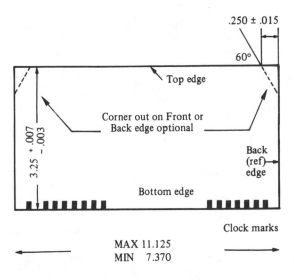

For punch card applications length of form must be 7.375 ± 0.005 inches.

Figure 6.21. Standard card dimensions and clock marks on the bottom edge (9 edge) for optical readers.

The format that is used can vary depending on the word size of the computer. For example, 3 columns containing 12 positions each can represent a 36 bit word. Because most computers now use a format that uses a multiple or simple fraction of a 32 bit word, 32 positions, of the avail-

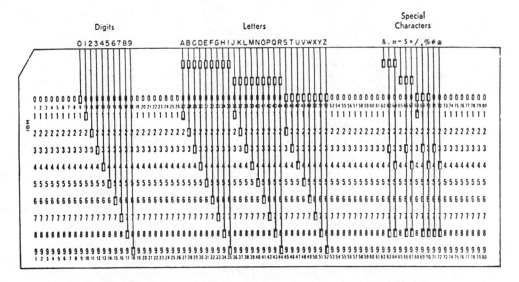

Figure 6.22. Arrangement of information on an 80-column card. (Courtesy IBM Corporation)

able 36, may be used for the data word or instruction; the other four may be used as check bits. In addition, a number of columns on the card may be used for starting address for the data on the card, the number of words, and a check sum of all the data on the card. As a specific example, the IBM Model 1130 computer can read and punch cards in column binary format. The 1130 is a 16 bit machine, so that an instruction word occupies 1⅛ columns on the card.

The same 80 column card format is used in a version that can be employed by an optical card reader. Clock marks are placed at the lower edge of the card to indicate to the reader the position at which data is to be read. The optical reader senses the change in light reflecting at the point where a punch or a pencil mark is made. Some card readers do not require the clock marks at the bottom of the card and, instead, rely on the distance from the leading edge of the card to indicate the column number.

Because the presence of a punch, or a pencil mark, is sensed in the same manner, optical readers can read cards that have intermixed punches and marks. This is a useful attribute in that prepunched cards can be used in many applications, such as job ticket accounting, inventories by department, where the common information is prepunched and the specific information is added by hand.

A version of the small punched card (Figure 6.23) is used with business computers in medium to small applications. The card measures 3¼ × 2⅝ inches and stores 96 characters of information. The card utilizes small round holes, rather than the rectangular holes of the 80 column card. Space is available in three rows at the top of the card to allow for a printout of the data stored on the card. The data are stored, as punched holes, in three rows of 32 columns each. Only six rows are used to represent a character or a number in a BCD format; multiple punches are used to add up to a numeric value: i.e., the 1, 2 and 4 row will be punched to indicate a value of 7. This is a saving of space over the format used in the 80 column card which uses a decimal format for numeric data.

There are many designs used for the mechanics of card punching and reading equipment. Attention is focussed intently on handling the cards in a gentle manner. If the edge of the card becomes slightly damaged, it can cause a severe jam in the reading mechanism, which in turn can interrupt the processing of a very powerful piece of computing equipment.

The early card readers, most present medium to low speed readers, and most punches rely on the cards being stacked face down in a hopper, or stacker, as shown in Figure 6.24. A metal plate, equal in thickness to the card, moves behind the card stack and pushes the cards one at a time towards the read or the punch station. As the card passes the read station, in the case of a mechanical reader, holes are sensed by brushes to determine the presence or absence of punches. With high speed readers (over 1,000 cards per minute), this sensing is done opti-

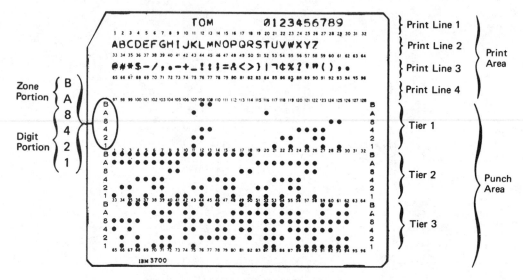

Figure 6.23. Data arrangement on an IBM 96 column card.

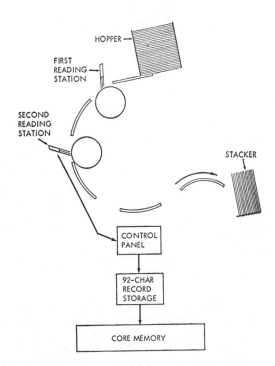

HOPPER

FIRST
READING
STATION

SECOND
READING
STATION

STACKER

CONTROL
PANEL

92-CHAR
RECORD
STORAGE

CORE MEMORY

Figure 6.24. Schematic of card read mechanism. (Courtesy IBM Corporation)

cally, i.e., by the detection of light transmitted through the punched hole. The optical mark readers, however, detect the punched hole, or pencil mark, by a change in light reflectivity. As shown in Figure 6.24, it is common to read the same position of the card at two reading stations to ensure its validity. If there is a difference in the data presented between stations, the card in question may be routed to a different stacker.

Higher speed card readers allow for loading 2,000 or more cards in a horizontal feed fashion. The cards, loaded as a block, move toward the read station face-forward, standing on the lower, or 9 inch edge. A light pressure maintained by a spring mechanism presses the card stack against the reader. Within a ½ inch of the card select mechanism, a flow of air is introduced to separate the cards before they are picked for reading.

It is a very common practice among many card punchers to design a read station inside a punch unit to verify the correctness of the data punched in the cards. As with the card read function, an alternate hopper or stacker is provided for mispunched cards.

Card punch and card reading equipment is available in a large variety of capacities and combinations. Stand-

alone card readers are available to read cards at rates in excess of 1,000 cards per minute. Because of the greater mechanical complexity of a card punch function, card punch units have reached a limit of about 500 cards per minute. There is, of course, less incentive to build high speed punches because there are other, higher speed, lower cost, storage media available in the form of magnetic tapes and disks.

In addition to the "conventional" individual card readers and punches, various combinations of both card readers and punches are available. As an example, the IBM model 2501-B2 is a combination unit, capable of reading cards at 1,000 per minute and punching them at 300 per minute. Another combination unit, the IBM Model 2596, is used with smaller computer systems. This unit reads and punches 96 column cards, prints the data contents of each card on the card, and allows for selective stacking an output from both the read and punch units.

Special purpose card readers also exist for limited card input applications. Optical readers generally operate at lower speeds and are designed for reading only a few hundred cards per day. Other card readers are designed for reading only one card at a time. These are suitable for applications in which a card is used with a unit of production. Each time the product is tested, the card may be placed in the reader for automatic identification; the test results can then be automatically collected and stored with high assurance of reliability.

6.10 PAPER TAPE EQUIPMENT

Paper tape readers and punches are found most frequently with small computer systems which rely on this type of equipment in place of card readers or punches, in installations where it is necessary to process paper tapes generated by teletypewriters, and in machine tool applications. Paper tape appears in widths ranging from $\frac{11}{16}$ inch to 1 inch. The recording medium is usually a medium weight paper, but for applications whose permanence is necessary, the paper can be fortified with a rubber-like compound. Instead of paper, mylar plastic also may be used. In some instances, the plastic also may be coated with a thin layer of aluminum.

The $\frac{11}{16}$ inch tape uses a 5 level code (also called **Baudot code,** after its developer). Because 5 levels are not sufficient to represent all the letters and numbers, two special characters are used to designate the patterns that follow: one, to represent numbers plus some special characters, and the other to represent letters. The 5 level code is being supplanted by the ASCII code, both in the telegraphic industry, and, particularly, in the computer industry. A paper width of ⅞ inch is used for 6 and 7 level codes; a full inch width is necessary for 8 level code. With the 8 level code, parity checking can be included within each character.

Paper tape readers range in speed from 10 characters per second, as with the side mounted reader on the Teletype Corporation's ASR-33, to over 1,000 characters per second with stand-alone readers. The slower speed readers (100 characters per second or less) rely on mechanical "fingers" to detect the presence of holes in the tape. The higher speed readers sense the holes optically by using photoelectric cells to detect the transmission of light. The mechanical method of reading tends to be more reliable in that it does not rely on the optical density of the paper. In machine tool applications, in particular, oil may make the paper translucent, or foreign material may clog the holes in the paper, either with the result of erroneous readings. Obviously the mechanical reader is less prone to these problems.

Because of their greater complexity, punches operate at much lower speeds. At the low end in terms of speed is the sidemounted punch on the ASR-33. Stand-alone punches operate in the range of 100 to 150 characters per second. Both readers and punches have a variety of ways of handling the paper tape medium. Paper may be fed from a reel, or in the case of fan-fold paper, it is taken up from a holder. A takeup reel is also occasionally used. Other optional features include a capability to handle tapes of more than one width, as well as a capability to backspace and overpunch a character already punched incorrectly. Although originally designed for ASCII or Baudot code, under program control any bit pattern can be generated by a punch. This includes binary information which can be used to store compiled programs to be read into the computer when needed.

6.11 CHARACTER RECOGNITION INPUT UNITS

Because a great deal of data is printed for uses other than input to computer systems, it is appropriate that character readers exist for high speed data input. Two systems that fulfill this function are **magnetic character readers** and various forms of **document readers.** Magnetic character readers are used extensively in the banking industry in that a vast number of checks and deposit slips are magnetically encoded. Document readers possess a variety of characteristics: some versions exist to read only paper strips of 3 to 3½ inches wide from cash registers; others can read a standard printed page.

Magnetic Character Readers

A standard font for magnetic characters has been established by the American Bankers Association. This font, E13B, reads characters formed in a 10 × 7 matrix, as shown in Figure 6.25. Only 14 characters are established in the standard. The unusual patterns of the characters had been selected so that if the document is out of line, it is possible to reconstitute the character from the segments that are read. In Figure 6.25, an example is shown in which the upper and lower portions of a character are reconstituted.

Typical magnetically coded documents range in size from 2.5 to 4.25 inches wide and 5.75 to 8.875 inches long. Documents can be processed at rates up to 2,400 per minute. The documents can be separated into separate stackers on the basis of a given symbol, or they may even be sorted by account number. With many readers, docu-

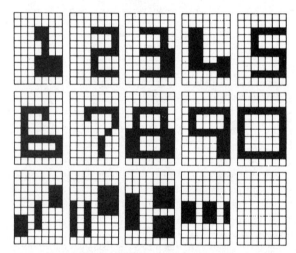

Each magnetic character passing the read head in the reader is sensed and examined. The reader looks for key recognition shapes and characteristics. If the character is slightly out of position as it passes under the read head, the signals sent to the matrix form what is called a folded character. The reader automatically unfolds the pattern by shifting it vertically to check for recognition.

Folded Character
Pattern in Matrix

Character Pattern
Shifted in Matrix

Figure 6.25. Matrix patterns of E13B characters used by magnetic ink character readers. (Courtesy IBM Corporation)

ments of varying dimensions and thicknesses can be intermixed.

Added attributes of some of the larger document readers include a capability to print an 8 digit number and/or a full endorsement on the back of each check. In addition, a microfilming feature may be provided to record images of selected documents. A typical film cassette contains 2,000 feet of 16 millimeter film and can store up to 380,000 typical check images.

Optical Character Readers

A number of character fonts has been designed for convenient and unambiguous input by various document readers. These fonts are quite similar to fonts normally used so that they are quite easily recognized by the human reader. For machine reading purposes, the characters have been slightly modified to make them more distinct from each other.

As with magnetic ink readers, the optical character is formed in a matrix of bit patterns within which the character itself is situated. Logic within the document reader recognizes the character and transmits it either to the computer, if it is connected directly, or to an attached tape drive, which may be read by the computer at a later time. When a character is not recognized, it may be rescanned a number of times in an attempt at recognition.

If this fails, the character may be transmitted to the operator's console, together with adjacent character, so that a correction can be typed in. With some readers, it is also possible to make corrections on an offline basis after the entire document has been scanned.

As indicated in Figure 6.26, a number of character fonts is in use among several manufacturers of optical mark readers. Included among them is a standardized handprinted character set. The handprinted characters must adhere to a reasonably strict geometric pattern to avoid ambiguity, and they must be drawn with a reasonably soft pencil to be clearly readable. Various fonts have been developed for different segments of industry; for example, the Selfchek 73 font is used with credit plate imprinters. Others are used on standard line printers equipped with a special print train.

The term "turnaround document reader" applies to devices that will read printed copy generated by still other devices. This implies that the printed page could be used as a form of off-line data storage; that is, its data could be re-entered into a computer system.

Document readers are often designed for special purposes, such as reading cash register tapes, credit card imprints, on up to full sized line printer pages. Reading speeds vary widely and are usually a function of page size and number of characters per page. For example, the IBM Model 3881 can read up to 100 3 × 3-inch docu-

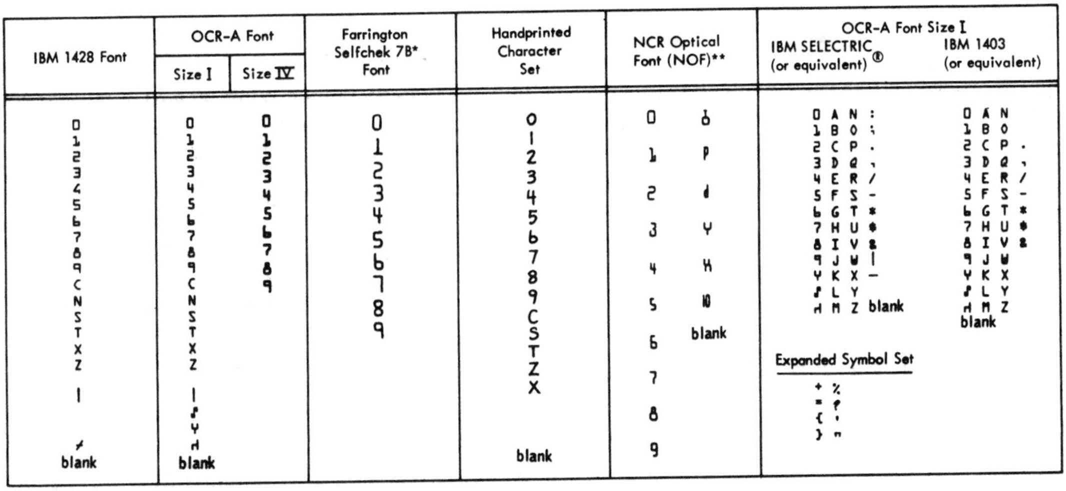

IBM 1428 Font	OCR-A Font		Farrington Selfchek 7B* Font	Handprinted Character Set	NCR Optical Font (NOF)**		OCR-A Font Size I	
	Size I	Size IV					IBM SELECTRIC (or equivalent)®	IBM 1403 (or equivalent)
0 1 2 3 4 5 6 7 8 9 C N S T X Z I blank	0 1 2 3 4 5 6 7 8 9 C N S T X Z blank	0 1 2 3 4 5 6 7 8 9	0 1 2 3 4 5 6 7 8 9	0 1 2 3 4 5 6 7 8 9 C S T Z X blank	0 1 2 3 4 5 6 7 8 9	(symbols) blank	0 A N : 1 B O ; 2 C P . 3 D Q , 4 E R / 5 F S - 6 G T * 7 H U 8 I V 9 J W K X L Y M Z blank Expanded Symbol Set	0 A N 1 B O 2 C P . 3 D Q , 4 E R / 5 F S - 6 G T * 7 H U 8 I V 9 J W K X L Y M Z blank

*Farrington Selfchek 7B shown by permission of Farrington Manufacturing Co.
**NCR Optical Font shown by permission of National Cash Register Co.

Note: Characters and symbols are shown reduced in size.

Figure 6.26. Fonts, letters and symbols used by manufacturers of document readers. (Courtesy IBM Corporation)

ments per minute but only 66 8½ × 11-inch documents per minute. Many document readers can number serially pages that have been read, as well as keep a count of them.

6.12 DISPLAY DEVICES

Display devices, or more specifically, cathode ray tubes (CRTs), are undergoing a very substantial evolution at the present time. The first CRTs were principally a replacement for the typewriter commonly used in a computer console or time share terminal. Display devices possess a very wide range of display capacities and an even wider range of "intelligent" capabilities.

CRTs can be obtained with a very minimum of capabilities beyond communicating with a computer and displaying the information being transmitted to or from the computer. The term "dumb terminal" or "glass typewriter" has frequently been used for such a device. The most commonly available CRTs have a display capacity of 24 lines of 80 characters each. The units contain a memory for storing the characters of information that are displayed on the screen. If the memory is limited to the number that can be displayed on the screen, then, as new lines of information are entered at the bottom, all other lines on the screen will move up and the topmost lines lost. When memory exceeds the screen size, the displayed information can be scrolled past the screen and recovered when the scrolling direction is reversed.

Visual display systems are typically attached to individual I/O channels of a computer or multiplexer. Where a number of displays is used, a display system may be organized with a controller which in turn communicates with several CRTs. In this way, a single computer channel can accommodate several CRTs. Most CRT displays provide 24 lines of 80 characters each; some provide an additional status line.

Display areas can vary from as little as 9 × 5 inches up to about 10 × 10 inches. Keyboards attached to the display stations also show some variation. They may be obtained with a numeric keypad only, typewriter alphanumeric keyboard only, or both the numeric and typewriter keypad. Very frequently, the keyboard is attached to the CRT by a 3 to 4 foot cable so that display and keyboard may be more conveniently arranged for use by console operators.

In addition to possessing additional memory, the "smart" terminals also may come equipped with tape cartridges for data storage, attached hard copy printers, and an ability to transmit data in line or block mode. Ter-

minals equipped with tape cartridges may store over 100,000 bytes of data per cartridge. Terminals can be used for data entry on an off-line mode. The data can then be transmitted from the cartridge to the computer at a much greater rate than would be possible by direct operator entry.

CRTs with attached hard copy printers permit a selective printout of the data transmitted to the CRT. Typically, the attached printer is a device that can act as a stand-alone hard copy terminal. Recently, CRTs have appeared with built-in thermal printers that share electronics components with the CRT. The combined system can be manufactured less expensively than a separate CRT and hard-copy printer.

Almost all CRT devices operate with a bit-serial interface which can be used for communication between devices several hundred feet apart, as well as with the telephone system. Transmission rates range from 10 cps up to 960 cps. The lower capability terminals transmit in a character by character mode; the more sophisticated terminals can transmit a line at a time, or an entire screen at a time (page or block mode).

Graphics Terminals

Display devices featuring a graphics capability represent a major increase in sophistication over the usual CRT terminal devices. These terminals frequently possess an alphanumeric display capability as well. This dual capability is achieved through separate memories for the display of graphical and normal alphanumeric information. Graphics and alphanumerics are almost always used interactively by engineers, designers, and businesspersons in such applications as automobile styling and in displaying sales and production information.

The screen in a graphics display terminal is divided into a matrix of dots, each of which is individually addressable. Screens vary in size from 3 × 4 inches to 13½ × 18 inches (23 inches diagonal). Dot matrix sizes range from as low as 300 × 200 up to 4096 × 4096. The latter size implies an ability to address more than 16 million points. The screen may be of the permanent phosphor type, which does not require continuous refreshing, or the nonpermanent type, which requires both an internal memory and a repetitive refresh cycle that functions between 40 and 50 times per second to avoid flicker.

Light pens also are used with the larger CRTs for special functions. These functions depend on the pen being pointed to a spot on the screen; under program control, special functions such as expanding a drawing, entering a standard module, or deleting a portion of the drawing may be performed. Location of the light pen is actually determined through the screen: a light dot moves very rapidly across the screen, a line at a time, until the light pen detects it. The light dot moves too rapidly to be detected by the human eye; consequently, the impression of a "light pen" is created. A common type of light pen uses fiber optics to transmit light from the screen to the logic in the graphics display unit.

Two modes to generate drawings are implemented internally by the logic of the display units. In one mode, drawings are generated as a set of vectors which can be drawn very rapidly (as much as 8,000 inches per second for the Tektronix 4016). Straight lines can, of course, be drawn very rapidly. Circles and curved lines must be drawn as a succession of short segments, which can be short enough to give the unaided eye the impression of a perfectly smooth curve. Where the display is of the refresh type, the image on the screen is stored in read/write memory, individual dots are set or cleared using a graphics writing software system. FORTRAN-like statements are used to indicate points to be plotted or skipped; these points may be located by previous statements which perform functions such as generating circles or bar charts.

REFERENCES

Bylander, E. G., *Electronic Displays.* New York: McGraw-Hill Book Co., 1979.

Dutta-Mazumder, D., *Digital Computers' Memory Technology.* New York: John Wiley & Sons, 1980.

Eadie, D., *A User's Guide to Computer Peripherals.* Englewood Cliffs, NJ: Prentice-Hall, 1982.

Flores, I., *Peripheral Devices.* Englewood Cliffs, NJ: Prentice-Hall, 1973.

Hanson, P. L., *Operating Data Entry Systems.* Englewood Cliffs, NJ: Prentice-Hall, 1977.

Hohenstein, C. L., *Computer Peripherals for Minicomputers, Microprocessors, and Personal Computers.* New York: McGraw-Hill Book Co., 1980.

Kane, G., *The CRT Controller Handbook.* Berkeley CA: Osborne/McGraw-Hill, 1980.

National Business Forms Association, *Minicomputer Printer Handbook,* 3rd edition. Alexandria, VA, 1980.

Osborne, A., *I/O Processor Handbook.* Berkeley, CA: Osborne/McGraw-Hill, 1980.

Sherr, S., *Video and Digital Electronic Displays.* New York: John Wiley & Sons, 1982.

Wilkinson, B., *Computer Peripherals.* New York: Crane, Russak, 1981.

7
A/D and D/A Conversion

A. Paul Brokaw

Analog Devices Inc.

7.1 INTRODUCTION

The large computing installations processing numerical input data and producing prodigious numerical outputs represent only a fraction of the computing power in use. Great numbers of digital processors and computers are employed in real time applications where at least some of the desired input and output signals are not in numerical or discrete form. These signals must be transformed from their continuous variable form to discrete digital form for computer processing, and from digital computer outputs to quasi-continuous output levels.

Addressing the first problem, that of quantizing continuous signals, examine Figure 7.1. This figure illustrates graphically the **analog to digital,** or **A/D,** function. The analog input signal range is shown along the horizontal axis and the corresponding digital outputs are shown along the vertical axis. To simply illustrate the principle involved, the figure assumes a 3 bit converter. That is, the analog input range is divided into eight intervals and analog signals falling into these intervals are mapped into corresponding digital output codes. The 0 code (000) is generally associated with 0 input signal and some or all of the first interval of the analog input range. Generally, the converter is made so that it changes output codes in the middle of each input interval, as in Figure 7.1. As a result, the code for 1 (001) spans the edge of the first interval, the 2 code (010) spans the edge of the second interval, and so forth.

Because 3 bits can represent at most eight input levels, and one of these codes represents zero, the eighth interval or full scale value of the analog input is not represented by a code. The code for 7 (111) spans the upper edge of the seventh interval but does not represent the full scale input value because of the half interval "offset" to *span* zero.

Many A/D converters are made to convert analog signals into digital words of 8 or more bits to give a resolution of one part in 256 or more. Nevertheless, the all 1s code will span an interval which ends one-half interval below the full-scale value. The width of an interval of analog input signal corresponds to a change in output code of one **least significant bit** (**LSB**). For this reason, the width of the analog input signal intervals is generally referred to as an **LSB weight,** or just as an **LSB.**

Analog signals, usually in the form of a voltage, can be applied to an A/D converter and the resulting digital outputs can be used as inputs to a digital controller or computer. The input signal is measured against a full scale input range, or reference. The digital output of the converter is essentially dimensionless and must be related to the analog input signal by a knowledge of the full scale reference of the converter.

7.2 PARALLEL A/D CONVERSION

A conceptually simple method of implementing the A/D function is shown in Figure 7.2. A reference voltage, E_{REF}, equal to the desired full scale voltage, is applied to a resistor voltage divider network. The values of the resistors are chosen to produce at the nodes of the network the voltages which correspond to the code transitions in Figure 7.1.

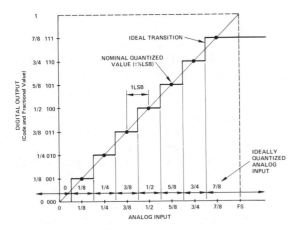

Figure 7.1. Conversion relationship for an ideal A/D converter. (Courtesy Analog Devices Inc.)

The applied input voltage, V_{in}, is compared to the voltages at these nodes by a collection of analog comparators. Each comparator has a digital output, which is 1 or 0, depending on the polarity of the voltage applied differentially to its input. The digital output of the comparator changes between 1 and 0 as the input signal passes through 0. The converter's analog input signal is compared to the transition voltages by a comparator connected to each. The output of each comparator connected to a voltage that is less than the input signal will switch, while the outputs of those connected to a higher voltage

will not switch. The resulting pattern of 1s and 0s at the eight comparator outputs is condensed to a one-of-eight 3 bit code by the logic, which provides the actual converter output.

Because this converter tests the input against each of the possible transition points simultaneously, it is known as a **parallel converter.** Since the output appears almost immediately in response to application of, or change in, the input signal, these converters are also called **flash converters.**

If the output of a flash converter is taken in standard binary code, a problem may arise as the input signal changes rapidly. For example, the code transition from 011 → 100 at half scale may proceed by way of a momentary intermediate value, such as 111. That is, the transition may be 011 → 111 → 100. Although the false intermediate value is only transitory, it may occur while data is being read from the converter by the system using the data.

This will result in a large error, nearly equal to half scale. Such problems may be circumvented by use of a **Gray code** (see Chapter 1), as shown in Figure 7.2.

The Gray code is arranged so that, in a counting sequence, adjacent codes differ at one, and only one, of their bit positions. As a result, there are no intermediate codes between adjacent values in a counting sequence. Therefore, slight variations in timing when transferring A/D output data will result in no more than one LSB weight difference in the transferred data and no spurious outputs will be generated. The flash converter of Figure 7.2 is arranged to produce a Gray code output.

An alternative to the use of Gray code is to provide the comparators with a latching signal to freeze their outputs and transfer the result to the n bit binary conversion logic. This logic output can also be latched so that a normal binary coded output can be synchronized with data collection to avoid spurious codes.

A more serious complication of parallel conversion methods arises when greater resolution is required. Parallel converters associate an analog comparator and some additional logic circuitry with each of the possible output codes to be produced, except zero. For a 3 bit code, seven comparators are required. For a 4 bit converter, 15 comparators are needed and, in general, for an n bit converter $2^n - 1$ comparators are required. Unlike digital systems, which grow in complexity in proportion to the number of bits, or at worst to n^2, flash converters grow as 2^n, doubling in size with each additional bit of resolution.

Flash converters are available up to the 8 bit level. Their cost, high power dissipation, and other practical dif-

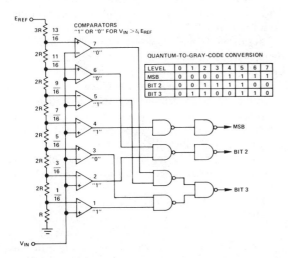

Figure 7.2. A parallel 3 bit A/D converter with Gray code output. (Courtesy Analog Devices Inc.)

ficulties limit their use to applications in which very fast response is mandatory. Typical applications are video conversions, such as radar signals, and transient recording. These applications generally employ high speed buffers and **direct memory access (DMA)** techniques to make data available for computation.

7.3 INTEGRATING CONVERTERS

An alternative to parallel conversion is the **integrating converter.** Integrating converters contrast with flash converters in that they are inexpensive, relatively simple to apply, and are available in high (14 or even 16 bit) resolution, but they are extremely slow. The most popular type of integrating converter is the **dual slope** A/D, an example of which is illustrated by Figure 7.3.

This circuit measures the input voltage, V_{in}, applied to a buffer amplifier at the left by means of an integrator implemented by the center amplifier. The integrator output is zeroed by the switch across capacitance C. Then, the buffered input signal is applied to the integrator input resistor and the shorting switch is opened. The voltage at the output of the integrating amplifier rises in proportion to the time integral of the buffer output signal. The control logic interrupts the integration after an interval fixed by counting a predetermined number of clock cycles. At this point the integrator output voltage is proportional to the average buffer output voltage.

The control logic next causes the integrator to be reconnected to the reference voltage input, which provides the full scale value for the converter. The converter is configured so that the polarity of the reference voltage is opposite to that of the buffered input signal. Consequently, the integral of the reference is of opposite polarity and the integrator output begins to return toward 0. The control logic restarts the clock from 0, or some preset value, and counts clock pulses until the comparator detects that the output of the integrator has returned to 0. At this moment, the time integral of the reference voltage is equal to the integral of the input voltage and the count is held and transferred to the output buffer.

To understand how this count is made to represent the value of the input voltage, compare the equations in the figure with this description of the operation. The input signal integration will last for a fixed time with the buffer output voltage as the independent variable. The reference voltage integration proceeds with a fixed voltage for a variable length of time (related, of course, to the starting value). Because the control logic uses the comparator to determine when the integrals are equal, the variable time will be proportional to the average value of the buffer output voltage.

The elegance of this scheme becomes more apparent when one observes that the exact time constant of the integrator, and even the linearity of the integrator, are almost irrelevant as long as it repeatedly retraces its "integration path." Moreover, the clock frequency needs only to be approximately controlled as long as it remains unchanged during a measurement. To a remarkable degree of accuracy, the ratio of the counts during the first and second integration is the same as the ratio of the reference voltage to the voltage out of the buffer amplifier. Notice that this output is actually composed of a mixture of the input voltage and the reference. The addition of a component of reference voltage to the input signal offsets the input signal range by one-half full scale for the values shown in Figure 7.3.

This allows the dual slope integrator, which is basically a unipolar measurement scheme (requiring the reference and the measured voltage to have opposite sign), to accommodate bipolar input signals. When the total count controlling the fixed interval integration in relation to the reference voltage is properly chosen, the scale of the count used for the output can be made to match convenient units. And with the choice of a starting value for the output count different from zero, the result can be offset to accommodate the input voltage offset and bipolar range.

The great advantage of integrating converters over parallel converters is their simplicity. The converter analog circuit of Figure 7.3 is essentially the same whatever the resolution of the converter. The complexity of the digital circuitry is roughly related to n, the number of bits, and grows in proportion to n. Although the highest reso-

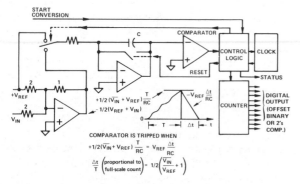

Figure 7.3. Dual ramp A/D converter for bipolar input. (Courtesy Analog Devices Inc.)

lution integrating converters require certain refinements, the appeal of integrating schemes is the relative simplicity of realizing high resolution.

In order to obtain high accuracy, as distinct from resolution, the precision required of the circuitry doubles with each additional bit of resolution. This inescapable requirement is one of the fundamental distinctions between digital and analog circuitry. Accuracy, in terms of bits in a digital system, can be increased almost without limit by the aggregation of circuitry which is basically no different in kind or quality from less accurate circuits. Increasing the accuracy of an analog system, however, requires not only more but "better" analog components. Each added bit of accuracy raises by a factor of 2 the performance required of some, if not all, of the analog portions of the system.

The penalty paid for the use of integrating converters in high resolution applications is their inherent speed limitation. Imagine, for instance, that a 12 bit converter is required. The variable time integration period must have an available range of 2^{12} or 4,096 counts in order to accommodate the desired resolution. Strictly speaking, the fixed interval of integration need not equal this value, but it must be in the same range. Assume then that the two integrations must have an available time span given by about 8,000 counts. Bandwidth requirements of the integrator and comparator will, in a typical case, limit the clock to 0.5 megahertz or less. The implication of these two factors is that a measurement cycle may last as long as 16 milliseconds. Higher resolution converters may take even longer, because not only will the number of counts increase but the clock frequency may have to be reduced to obtain the improved accuracy.

Integrating converters are used in applications having a desired low signal bandwidth, such as digital panel meters. Because the input signal is integrated during the fixed measurement interval, high frequency components of input signal are "filtered" and certain types of noise are removed from the signal. Measurements can be commenced in synchronism with interfering signals, most notably 60 Hz power line interference, to further reduce the sensitivity to unwanted frequency components of the input signal.

Note that integrating converters measure during a finite interval which has a well defined start. Integrating converters can be made so that they automatically measure periodically under internal control. In computer controlled applications, however, the measurement is usually started by an external signal applied to a start conversion control line. This signal is readily provided to the converter from a digital output derived from a decoded address line, and selected to correspond to the converter, combined (ANDed) with the system WRITE signal. A dummy WRITE to the selected address initiates a conversion.

The actual time required for a conversion may easily vary over a two-to-one range, depending upon the analog signal input level. An **end of conversion (EOC)** signal is usually provided by the converter to indicate that a conversion has been completed, as indicated by the integrator output reaching zero, and that the new digital output data is ready. The EOC may be used as a system interrupt or assigned an address and simply read as a digital input to the computer to test for completion of a conversion.

7.4 SUCCESSIVE APPROXIMATION CONVERSION

The integrating and flash converters represent extremes in terms of the tradeoff between speed, complexity, and resolution. An alternative which moderates between these schemes is the **successive approximation (SA) converter.** The SA converter is one of a class of converters which employs a digital to analog converter (DAC), a comparator, and some control logic to operate the DAC. Various codes are applied to the digital input of the DAC and the resulting sequence of analog output signals is compared with the analog signal which is to be measured. The analog output of the DAC which most nearly matches the analog input signal is identified and the digital code which produced it is output as the result of the A/D conversion.

A member of this class which is conceptually a little simpler than the SA A/D is the **tracking converter** of Figure 7.4. In this converter, a comparator examines an analog input signal and the output of a digital to analog converter. If the input is larger than the DAC output, the control logic causes the counter to increase the magnitude of the "number" applied to the DAC, and thereby increase the analog signal out of the DAC. When the DAC's output signal exceeds the analog input, the counter is reversed and the DAC output is reduced. As a result, the counter will "dither" around a value which causes the DAC output to approximate the input. A slightly more sophisticated comparator arrangement can be used to stabilize the counter at the "closest" value and change count only as the input changes.

The tracking A/D is useful for continuous monitoring of slowly changing signals. If the signal changes rapidly,

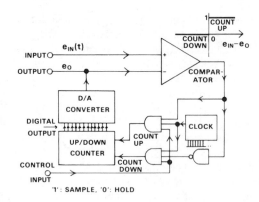

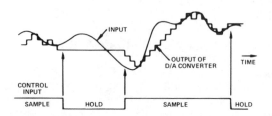

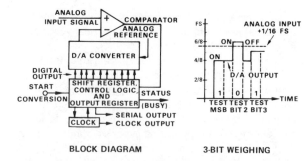

Figure 7.5. Successive approximation ADC. (Courtesy Analog Devices Inc.)

weight which is initially unknown will be found to be between 45 and 46 units, so the scale will not tip. The effect of this test is to divide the full scale range in two and to determine that the unknown falls in the upper half of it. By leaving the half scale reference weight in the pan, the problem is changed to one of determining the residue by which the unknown exceeds half scale.

Next, the residue is tested to determine whether it is in the lower or upper half of the top half of the full scale range. In other words, the quarter scale weight determines which of the top two quarters of full scale contains the unknown. In this case, the unknown is less than 48 units so the balance tips and the unknown is determined to be between ½ and ¾ of full scale. The quarter scale weight is removed, and the problem is now reduced to searching the third quarter for the unknown value. The unknown is again tested to see if it is in the upper or lower

Figure 7.4. Tracking sample hold ADC. (Courtesy Analog Devices Inc.)

however, this converter begins to behave very much like an integrating converter. That is, the output of the DAC will ramp from the "old" signal value to some "new" value at a rate limited by the settling time of the DAC and/or the clock frequency. For multiplexed or rapidly changing data, the tracking A/D is relatively slow.

A similar circuit, however, can be used to perform A/D conversions at a relatively high rate of speed. The similarity of Figure 7.5 to the tracking converter should be apparent. In Figure 7.5, however, the up/down counter and control logic is replaced by a successive approximation register. This logic uses a successive approximation algorithm (sometimes known as a *binary search*) to cause the output of the DAC to converge on the value of the analog input.

The strategy for a successive approximation measurement is illustrated in Figure 7.6. Imagine that it is desired to measure an unknown weight by means of a balance scale and a collection of reference weights. The magnitudes of the reference weights form a binary sequence and their sum total, plus an additional LSB, represents the full scale value or range of the possible measurement. The unknown is first compared to the largest weight (32 units) which equals half of full scale. In this case, the

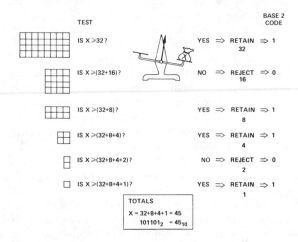

Figure 7.6. Strategy for a successive approximation measurement. (Courtesy Analog Devices Inc.)

half of the quarter with the ⅛ scale reference weight. After this test, the unknown will have been determined to fall between ⅝ and 6/8 of full scale. Again, the test weight does not cause the balance to tip and it remains in the pan.

As the weighings continue, the remaining uncertainty about the unknown is halved with each test. Moreover, the sum of the reference weights approaches the unknown in a series of successive approximations. Finally, the last or least significant bit weight is used to test the unknown. Assuming the unknown weight slightly exceeds 45 units, but is less than 46, the balance will have been approximated with a resolution of one unit. The weight is determined by observing the sum of the reference weights. Because these weights make up a binary sequence, their sum may be represented as a binary sequence of 1s and 0s determined by whether the representative test weight does or does not remain in the pan after the final approximation.

Clearly, the 6 bit resolution of this measurement can be extended by providing ½ unit, ¼ unit, ⅛ unit, etc., reference weights. Each additional weight would be tested once, and the error in the approximation halved by the test.

The electrical analog of this scheme shares the same properties, with two important consequences. The first of these consequences is that the addition of a bit of resolution to an n bit converter will increase the conversion time by little more than a factor of $(n + 1)/n$, rather than by a factor of 2 as in the integrating converter. This means that, although an n bit successive approximation converter requires at least n times as long to convert as does a flash converter of equal resolution, it is much faster than the corresponding integrating converter.

For a more concrete example of an electronic SA converter, refer to Figure 7.7. This figure shows only the analog portion of a 3 bit converter; the digital section is a straightforward collection of gates. The digital portion implements a successive approximation algorithm, to be described below, and operates the switches by means of three pairs of control lines, A, B and C. The final state of these control lines will correspond to the reference weights left in the pan during the weighing experiment, and will be the same as the digital output signal.

The resistor (R) ladder in Figure 7.7 is similar to that of the flash converter. That is, it is powered by a reference voltage, V_{REF}, equal to the converter's full scale input voltage, and develops at its taps the voltages which correspond to the code switching points, as in Figure 7.1. For each combination of the switch control parameters A, B

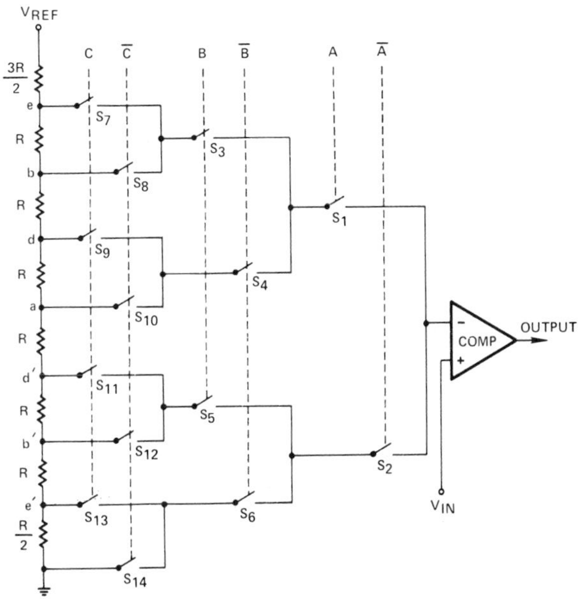

Figure 7.7. Analog portion of a 3 bit converter. (Courtesy of Adib R. Hamade. From A. R. Hamade, "A Single Chip All-MOS A/D Converter," *Journal of Solid State Circuits*, Vol. 13, No. 6 (Dec. 1978), pp. 785–91)

and C, a tap unique to that combination will be connected to the comparator input.

Now, imagine that a voltage somewhat larger than ⅝ full scale, but less than 6/8 full scale, is applied as V_{IN}, in Figure 7.7. The first test consists of the combination A, $\overline{B}$ and $\overline{C}$ representing the 100 code and corresponding to ½ full scale. With the A signal applied, S_1 is closed and S_2 is open. The $\overline{B}$ signal closes S_4 (and incidently S_6 in the unused lower path) and leaves S_3 open. Finally, the $\overline{C}$ signal closes S_{10} and completes a path from the half scale voltage tap to the comparator.

The output of the comparator now indicates that the analog input voltage exceeds half scale. The SA logic retains A, the MSB weight, to test the analog input voltage against the upper half of the scale. The code 110, or A, B, $\overline{C}$, closes switches 1, 3 and 8 by applying the ¾ scale voltage to the comparator. The comparator indicates that the analog input is less than ¾ full scale. The SA logic switches the second bit back to 0 and tests the third bit with A, $\overline{B}$ and C. Switches 1, 4 and 9 close and the comparator indicates that the analog input is greater than ⅝ full scale. The resulting digital output, 101, indicates that the analog input is between ⅝ and ¾ of full scale.

The successive approximation converges much more rapidly than the integrating conversion process. And, the configuration of Figure 7.7 is much less complex than the flash converter. A single comparator is required for converters of any resolution, and the switches can be simply implemented in MOS technology.

Because this configuration minimizes the accuracy required of the individual resistors, it is well suited to MOS integrated circuit (IC) fabrication processes. The microphotograph of Figure 7.8 shows a monolithic 8 bit A/D converter based on this principle. The resistor divider and switch network shown in Figure 7.7 makes up a DAC. The output of the DAC's circuit, to the comparator, is an analog voltage proportional to the digital control signal on the A, B and C lines. It should be apparent from the description that this D/A converter fits the functional requirement of Figure 7.5. The shift register, control logic and output register of Figure 7.5 perform the successive approximation algorithm, and the waveform shown in the figure indicates the DAC output during the first three tests in the conversion.

Despite their simplicity relative to the flash converter,

converters of the type shown in Figure 7.7 share a basic weakness of the flash converter. That is, their complexity doubles with each added bit of resolution. The large central region of Figure 7.8 shows the resistor divider and switch network. This area would double in a 9 bit converter made with the same technology. Nevertheless, because of the ease with which circuits of this type can be implemented as MOS ICs, this scheme is quite practical for intermediate resolution converters.

Notice that it is the DAC portion of Figure 7.7 that grows rapidly with increasing resolution. Alternative implementation of the DAC function can be used to minimize the complexity problem of SA converters. A binary weighted collection of n switchable electrical signals can be summed to approximate an unknown signal, just as the weights are summed to approximate an unknown weight in Figure 7.6. The resolution of such a DAC and the associated A/D converter can be increased 1 bit by adding another of the switchable signals which continues the existing sequence of binary weightings.

Figure 7.9 shows how this may be done. The circuit contains an input resistor, R_{IN}, a voltage comparator, SA

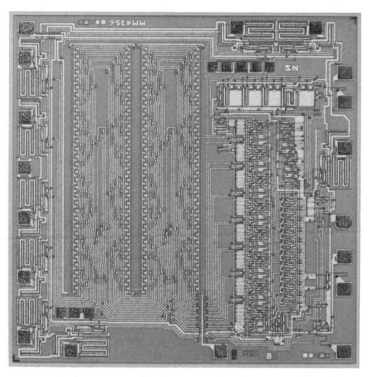

Figure 7.8. Microphotograph of a monolithic 8 bit ADC. (Courtesy of Adib R. Hamade. From A. R. Hamade, "A Single Chip All-MOS A/D Converter," *Journal of Solid State Circuits,* Vol. 13, No. 6 (Dec. 1978), pp. 785–91)

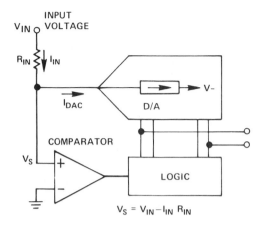

Figure 7.9. Current comparison in a successive approximation conversion. (Courtesy Analog Devices Inc.)

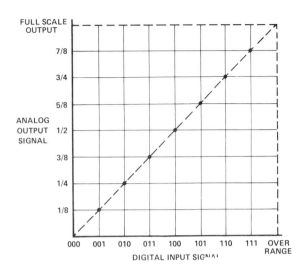

Figure 7.10. Input/output relationship of an ideal 3 bit DAC. (Courtesy Analog Devices Inc.)

logic, and a current output D/A converter. The DAC consists of a binary weighted collection of independent current sources, which may be switched on or off by the control logic. The total of those currents, which are switched on, makes up the DAC output that flows in the input resistor.

The unknown input voltage, V_{IN}, is applied between the input resistor and one comparator input, which is usually grounded. The output current of the DAC develops a voltage across the input resistor. The comparator signals whether the voltage developed across the resistor exceeds the unknown input voltage. The largest of the switchable currents in the DAC develops a half scale voltage across the input resistor. The next develops quarter scale, and so forth, so that the unknown voltage can be approximated in the same way that the unknown weight was approximated in Figure 7.6. The logic implements the successive approximation algorithm, and when the approximation is complete, the digital signals driving the DAC can be used to make up the digital output of the converter.

The current output DAC will be treated as an independently useful component in the next section. One of its special uses is as the core of high speed, high resolution and high accuracy A/D converters.

7.5 DIGITAL TO ANALOG CONVERSION

As mentioned in the previous section, a DAC produces an analog output in response to a digital input signal. The DAC function is illustrated graphically in Figure 7.10. The horizontal axis is the binary input. For this illustration a 3 bit DAC is represented. The eight possible combinations of 3 bits make up the possible input values. Each value of the input signal is mapped into an analog output signal. The vertical axis represents the analog output signal level. In this illustration, the 3 bit combinations are arrayed in the normal binary counting sequence and are mapped into a linearly ascending sequence of output levels. The DAC function is defined only for a finite number of input levels and is a one to one mapping. The function is represented by the dots and the dashed diagonal is a trend line showing the linear relationship between input and output.

Special applications, such as pulse code voice telecommunications (PCM), use nonlinear DACs wherein the trend line is a nonlinear function of the digital inputs. These converters are usually specially designed for this application. The most flexible DACs, which are most often interfaced with computers, generally have an output which increases linearly with the input code, although the digital code sequence may take on other forms such as complementary, offset binary, or Gray code (see Chapter 1).

Before going on with the description of the digital to analog conversion process, I want to emphasize the difference in kind between the input and output signals. The input signal is essentially dimensionless. Although digital signals are generally characterized in terms of a voltage, it is the condition of the signal (1 or 0) rather than the exact voltage that carries the information. The other important characteristic of the input signal is the positional information. The codes 100 and 001 each contain a 1 and two 0s, but the relative position carries the information which makes them different. The condition and position information is all that is required to characterize the DAC input signal.

The output signal of a DAC is one dimensional and its magnitude is the property of interest. The full scale range of the analog output signal is divided into 2^n subintervals in a converter with n bit resolution. Each subinterval has a magnitude or weight called the *least significant bit weight* (LSB).

In a "straight binary" linear converter, the magnitude of the analog output signal is given by the product of one LSB, including its dimension of volts or amps or whatever unit is appropriate, and the integer represented by the input binary number. The analog output, which corresponds to an all 1s code (111 in Figure 7.10), is less by one LSB than a level called "full scale." The result of this full scale convention is that the magnitude of the most significant bit corresponds to half scale. That is, the output of the DAC will be one-half of full scale in response to the code which is a 1 followed by all 0s (100 in Figure 7.10). The analog output which corresponds to the second most significant bit alone (010) will be ¼ of full scale; that corresponding to the next bit, ⅛ of full scale; and in higher resolution DACs, that to the next bit, 1/16 of full scale, and so on.

One conceptually simple way to construct a DAC is illustrated as part of the ADC of Figure 7.7. If the output of the switching tree is connected to a voltage follower, instead of to the comparator, a loadable voltage output can be obtained. This output voltage can be controlled by the switch tree to correspond approximately to the relationship in Figure 7.10. The half bit offset, included in Figure 7.7, can be eliminated by minor adjustment of the resistor values.

In Figure 7.7, voltages corresponding to all possible output values are present on the divider at all times. The switch tree selects as the output one of these values in response to the state of the 3 bit input controlling switches A, B, C and their complements.

Because the DAC output is single valued, it may not be necessary to make all possible output values simultaneously available. It is, in fact, possible to construct any output "on demand" from a relatively small number of additive signals. To see how this might work, consider how a binary counting sequence proceeds. In the binary sequence 1, 10, 11, 100, 101, 110, 111, 1000, . . . , a combination of the 1 and 10 weights, 1 and 2, gives the result 11 or 3. A combination of 100, or 4, with 10, or 2, yields 110, or 6. There is associated with each binary digit a

weight determined by its position in the written number. The value, or equivalent of a binary number, is simply the sum of the weights of those bits which are 1 and exclusion of the weights of those bits which are 0. This idea is illustrated in Figure 7.11.

Figure 7.11 is similar to Figure 7.10, in that it shows the mapping from digital inputs to analog outputs. It also shows how each of the possible outputs is made up of combinations of the three weights 1, 2 and 4. The weights are illustrated by the arrow lengths associated with the codes 001, 010 and 100. Any of the other 3 bit binary numbers can be represented by the sum of a selection from these three. The corresponding output is the sum of the associated weights.

This idea can be used to produce a current output DAC (Figure 7.12). The DAC consists of six currents which are weighted in a binary sequence, and six switches which can direct the currents to an output line or divert them to ground. The switches operate in response to a 1 or 0 state of individual bits of the binary input word.

Each bit of the binary input controls a switch which depends on its condition. In response to a 1 input, a switch directs its associated current to the output bus. In response to a 0, the switch diverts the current to ground. Each switch controls a current of different magnitude. The switches are arranged to associate each input bit with a current weighted in relation to full scale so that it matches the weight implied by the "position" of the bit.

The implementation shown in Figure 7.12 has an ad-

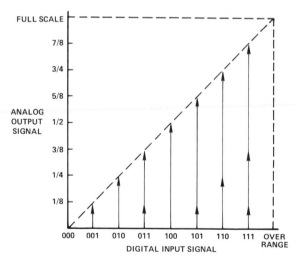

Figure 7.11. DAC function by summation of individual bit weightings. (Courtesy Analog Devices Inc.)

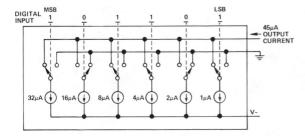

Figure 7.12. Functional schematic of a 6 bit current summation DAC. (Courtesy Analog Devices Inc.)

vantage over DACs of the type shown in Figure 7.7. A single switch and current source combination is associated with each bit of the digital input signal. As a result, the complexity of current output DACs, which use linear current summation, grows only as n, the resolution. For intermediate to high resolution converters, this difference is extremely important.

Because it is the exact magnitude of the output which is important in applications of a DAC, there seems to be no way to escape the conclusion that each bit of additional resolution is twice as "difficult" to add as the last. That is, to expand the DAC of Figure 7.12 to 7 bits would require the addition of a 64 microampere current source and switch combination which has the same absolute stability as the rest of the DAC. Because this current is twice as large as the 6 bit MSB, the relative accuracy requirement is doubled. Nevertheless, only one section need be added to obtain the bit of resolution, and it can be done so that the additional accuracy requirement applies mainly to the added circuitry.

The two most common circuits for current output DACs are illustrated in Figures 7.13 and 7.15. Figure 7.13 is a simplified schematic of a DAC made with bipolar transistors. The bottom part of the figure shows an **R-2R ladder** used to produce a sequence of binary currents. When a voltage is applied across this network, the currents in the 2R legs decrease in a binary sequence from left to right. In order to obtain this result, the legs must all be terminated at the same voltage.

The common base connected transistors provide this voltage at their respective emitters. The transistors convey the binary weighted currents to the differentially connected switch transistors at their respective collectors. Level translator circuitry, which is interfaced with the digital input signal, controls the differential transistors so that one remains off while the other conducts.[1] When the bit input associated with a given differential switch is 1, the righthand transistor switches on to direct its associated binary weighted current to the output bus. Alternatively, a 0 at the same bit switches on the lefthand transistor which directs the associated current into the ground or common bus (occasionally used as a complementary output) and away from the output.

Notice that, in the lower left of the schematic, a reference transistor and a resistance 2R parallels the input to the ladder without an intervening resistance R. The reference transistor and its resistor are matched to these of the MSB so that it produces a current equal to that of the MSB. This current is used to develop a voltage across

[1]Protected by U.S. Patent 3,961,326 assigned to Analog Devices Inc.

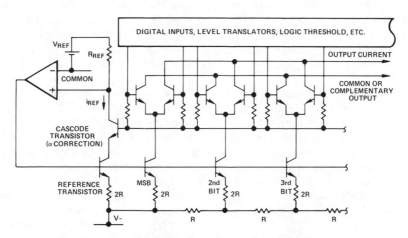

Figure 7.13. A switched current DAC. (Courtesy Analog Devices Inc.)

the resistor, R_{REF}, and the voltage is compared to V_{REF} at the amplifier input. Any difference between the reference voltage and the voltage developed by the reference current is amplified and used to adjust the base voltage of the reference transistor. This negative feedback control loop adjusts the reference current to a value predetermined by the selection of the reference voltage and resistor.[2] Because the MSB current equals the reference current, the feedback loop has the effect of stabilizing the full scale output current of the DAC at twice the value of V_{REF}/R_{REF}.

Although the whole scheme can be inverted in polarity, DACs of the kind shown in Figure 7.13 are generally operated from a negative supply voltage (and often require a positive supply as well). Those weighted currents which are rejected when their associated bit is 0 go to ground by way of the collector of the lefthand switch transistor. The current output terminal, which consists of the collectors of all the righthand switch transistors, must be constrained at some voltage more positive than the base voltage of the switches. This constraint is to prevent voltage saturation of the switch transistors.

One way to provide this constaint is to terminate the output in a resistor connected to ground, or some positive voltage. The maximum voltage that will appear across the resistor is limited to the full scale current times its resistance. By properly choosing the resistance and the voltage to which it connects, the switch collector voltage can be maintained above the saturation level. This level is usually specified by DAC manufacturers as the **compliance voltage,** and is referenced to ground.

The most common applications of the current output DAC involve driving the virtual ground created by an amplifier. Before the other major technique used to build current output DACs is outlined, some representative applications shown in Figure 7.14 will be described.

At the upper left of Figure 7.14a, a semidiagrammatical block represents a current output DAC. The 10 bit digital input is applied between pins 4 and 13 at the bottom. The current output of the DAC connects to pin 15 at the pointed tip of the DAC symbol. Also connected to the current output is a so-called "application resistor," the function of which will become apparent. The end of the application resistor, at pin 16, is connected to the output of the op amp. The inverting input of the amplifier is driven by the DAC output. When the DAC output is zero, the resistor connected between the amplifier input and output "closes the loop" and causes the amplifier output voltage to be zero.

[2]Protected by U.S. Patents 3,803,590 and 3,978,473 assigned to Analog Devices Inc.

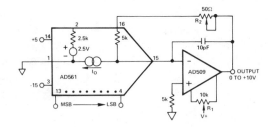

0 TO +10V UNIPOLAR VOLTAGE OUTPUT

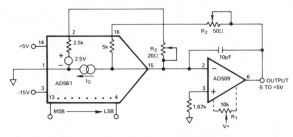

±5V BUFFERED BIPOLAR VOLTAGE OUTPUT

Figure 7.14. Current output DAC. (top) Block diagram. (bottom) Obtaining a biopolar output. (Courtesy Analog Devices Inc.)

put voltage to be zero. When a nonzero code is applied to the DAC, the resulting current will tend to drive the amplifier input negative. Even a small change at the amplifier input, however, will be greatly amplified and cause the amplifier output voltage to swing positive.

The amplifier output voltage becomes sufficiently positive to carry off the DAC output current, I_o, with only the most minute change in the amplifier input voltage. This creates the so-called "virtual ground" at the input of the amplifier. The result is to maintain the DAC output at 0, preventing saturation of the switches, and to produce at the amplifier output a voltage proportional to the value of the application resistor and the current output, which is proportional to the digital input of the DAC. By incorporating the application resistor within the DAC, the full scale output voltage from the amplifier can be accurately scaled to be four times the 2.5 volt reference contained within the DAC. The current output of the DAC has been converted to a unipolar 0 to 10 volt output by the addition of an amplifier.

Because the output current of a DAC is unidirectional, the output voltage which results is unipolar. Figure 7.14b shows how a bipolar output can be obtained. We can take advantage of the virtual ground provided by the amplifier to add a fixed offset current to the DAC output. The bipolar offset resistor at pin 2 is connected between the

DAC output and the internal voltage reference. Because the voltage across the resistor is fixed, a 1.0 milliampere current is forced into the DAC output circuit. When the basic DAC output current, I_o, is 0, the amplifier output goes to -5 volts to maintain the virtual ground. An input code of 1000000000 (the MSB alone) results in a half scale output $I_o = 1.0$ mA. This current cancels the offset and the amplifier output becomes 0. Finally, an all 1s input code causes I_o to approach 2 mA (less one LSB weight) and the voltage output to approach $+5$ V. This simple addition of the offset resistor has transformed the output to a bipolar voltage which responds to an offset binary code.

With the foregoing applications in mind, consider one more type of current output DAC, illustrated in Figure 7.15. This circuit consists of little more than an R-2R ladder and some digitally operated switches. The switches connect each of the 2R branches to one of the output lines, either I_{out1} or I_{out2}. If both these lines are grounded, the 2R branches are terminated at ground regardless of the switch conditions. As a consequence, the branch currents which result from a voltage applied to the V_{REF} input are binary weighted. Current in the leftmost resistor is $V_{REF}/2R$, in the next resistor $V_{REF}/2 \cdot 2R$, in the third resistor $V_{REF}/4 \cdot 2R$, and so on. The switches operate under control of the individual bits of the digital input word. Each switch controls one of the binary weighted currents in the resistors and can send it to either of the grounded outputs.

If current I_{out1} is measured and current I_{out2} is discarded, the measured current can represent any combination of the binary weighted currents, as dictated by the digital input. The current can be measured while the voltage is maintained at zero by connecting I_{out1} to a virtual ground, as in Figure 7.16. While I_{out2} is actually

grounded, I_{out1} drives the amplifier inverting input. An application resistor, $R_{FEEDBACK}$ in Figure 7.15, connects the amplifier input and output. This connection permits the amplifier to create a virtual ground at its input, and in so doing it develops an output voltage given by the product of I_{out1} and $R_{FEEDBACK}$. Because I_{out1} is a function of the digital input, the amplifier output reflects the value of the digital input.

Multiplying DAC

In this converter, as in others, the magnitude of the output depends upon the applied reference voltage, as well as the digital input. Generally, the DAC output is proportional to the product of the digital input and reference voltage input. Converters of many different types are occasionally used in the multiplying mode; however, the inverted ladder shown in Figures 7.15 and 7.16 is most often employed as a **multiplying DAC,** or simply an M-DAC. The reason is the simplicity with which the multiplying function is achieved.

Arrangements like the one shown in Figure 7.13 restrict the voltage reference to a single polarity, and also have deficiencies at low reference voltage levels. On the other hand, the arrangement shown in Figure 7.15 is extremely flexible in the constraints it places on the reference. In practice, the switches are MOS devices which are fashioned so that they are bilateral. That is, when they are "on" they present a low resistance which is largely independent of the direction of current flow. When they are "off," they are effectively open to small applied voltages of either polarity. As a result, once the switches have been operated by more or less conventional gating circuits, the network is effectively resistive and can respond to inputs of either polarity.

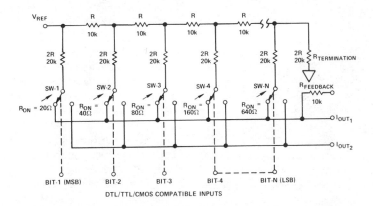

Figure 7.15. An R-2R ladder network with switches. (Courtesy Analog Devices Inc.)

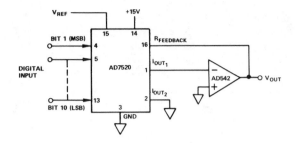

DIGITAL INPUT	ANALOG OUTPUT
1111111111	$-V_{REF}(1 - 2^{-10})$
1000000001	$-V_{REF}(\frac{1}{2} + 2^{-10})$
1000000000	$-V_{REF}/2$
0111111111	$-V_{REF}(\frac{1}{2} - 2^{-10})$
0000000001	$-V_{REF}(2^{-10})$
0000000000	0

NOTE: 1 LSB = $2^{-10} V_{REF}$

Figure 7.16. Unipolar binary operation (two quadrant multiplication). Circuit and code table. (Courtesy Analog Devices Inc.)

An extension of Figure 7.16, which employs I_{out2} by means of another amplifier, can be used as a M-DAC in four quadrants. That is, the reference input can accommodate both signal polarities and the digital input can be represented as a signed number. The resulting output has the correct sign in four quadrants (Figure 7.17).

The circuit of Figure 7.15 can be used in another mode. If the two normal outputs ($I_{out1,2}$) are connected across a reference voltage, the V_{REF} terminal can be used as a voltage output. This configuration was once widely used

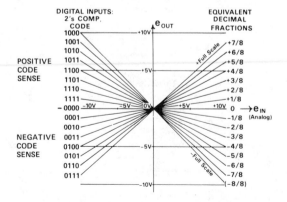

Figure 7.17. D/A converter as four quadrant multiplier. (Courtesy Analog Devices Inc.)

with bipolar transistors as switches. With the availability of easy to use and easy to integrate MOS switches, however, most modern designs use them. Because these switches work best when they are all operated near the same voltage, the circuit of Figure 7.15 is generally applied as in Figure 7.16. This arrangement is called the **inverted ladder** configuration, owing to its historical antecedent.

A number of other and basically different circuit principles have been used to implement the DAC function. Perhaps the simplest method is to provide a binary, or two valued, signal of variable duty cycle. When such a signal is low pass filtered, the result is a steady voltage proportional to the binary signal amplitude and the duty cycle. By controlling the duty cycle, the output amplitude can be readily adjusted. These DACs are, in some ways, analogous to integrating A/D converters. They both rely on time division to subdivide a reference voltage, and each conversion necessarily takes a relatively long time. Duty cycle DACs are most often implemented, at least partially, in software. This factor, combined with their low speed, limits their use to specialized applications, though not necessarily low volume ones.

7.6 COMPUTER INTERFACES

The converters most often selected for computer interface have a parallel interface. Although the parallel word is compatible with computer data format, the simple converters described up to this point cannot be operated directly from the data bus. The digital input to a DAC must not change so long as a given output is desired. A set of data storage latches is generally interposed between the DAC and the computer data bus. These latches are enabled by a system **WRITE** to the address associated with the DAC. The data on the bus goes to the DAC input by way of the latches and is captured by the latches at the end of the write cycle. This basic scheme is illustrated in Figure 7.18, which shows individual transistor transistor logic (TTL) latches.

Often the resolution desired from the converter exceeds the number of bits on the data bus. In this case, additional latches operated from a second address allow the DAC input signal to be broken into two data words, as shown in Figure 7.19. The tactic, which is similar to double precision arithmetic, can result in a skew problem. The digital input applied to the DAC changes from the "old" data to the "new" data by way of an interim value that is a mix of the old and new data. In applications in which this glitch cannot be tolerated, a second rank of

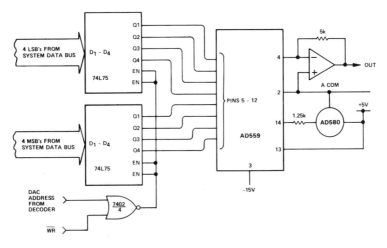

Figure 7.18. Microprocessor control for an 8 bit DAC. (Courtesy Analog Devices Inc.)

latches can be used to hold the old data at the DAC input until both words of the new data have been loaded into the first rank of latches. Then the complete information is transferred to the second set and to the DAC at one time.

The individual TTL gates can be replaced by systems components such as the programmable peripheral interface (PPI) of Figure 7.20 for a microprocessor interface. This component, as well as the extra latches required to

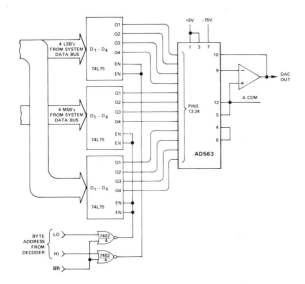

Figure 7.19. A simple logic interface for a standard 12 bit DAC. (Courtesy Analog Devices Inc.)

eliminate skew, can be incorporated in the DAC itself (Figure 7.21). The DAC shown in this figure includes a double rank of 10 bit buffers into which the data can be loaded in 2 bytes. Figure 7.22 shows an 8 bit DAC which includes not only a set of latches but also the chip select gating, the voltage reference, and the output amplifier.

The interface with an A/D converter is usually more complex. The converter output must be gated onto the data bus, generally by means of three-state buffers which are activated by a READ signal. In addition, the converter must be signaled to start conversion and the end of conversion signal must be read back to the computer. Figure 7.23 shows how an interface can be arranged for a 12 bit A/D, while Figure 7.24 an application of a 12 bit A/D which includes its own digital interface hardware.

The status, or end of convert, signal is gated onto the data bus with the least significant bits so that it can be tested. Because the maximum convert time is usually short and well defined, with a successive approximation converter, it is not always necessary to make provision to test the end of convert signal. In some systems, particularly those in which the conversion is initiated directly in response to an event outside the system, the status or end of convert signal is used to signal an interrupt. The interrupt service routine which is called causes the computer to read the results of the conversion.

7.7 ANALOG INTERFACE

An important aspect of the data conversion process is associated with an analog interface to a converter. A major

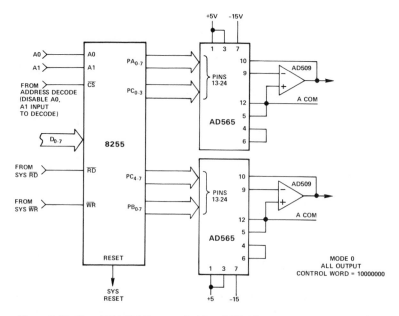

Figure 7.20. Two 12 bit DACs controlled by a PPI. (Courtesy Analog Devices Inc.)

distinction between digital and analog signals concerns the effect of noise, defined as some unwanted addition to the basic signal. Digital signals convey their information by means of their condition with respect to threshold levels. Digital signal sources can transmit with noise immunity by providing outputs which are overdriven with respect to the thresholds. The system will then be unaf-

fected by additive noise signals that are smaller than the differences between the threshold levels and the overdrive levels.

In contrast, however, analog signals are characterized by their exact magnitude, and *any* additive noise constitutes an error. In practice, the uncertainty caused by quantization of the analog signals is also treated as a

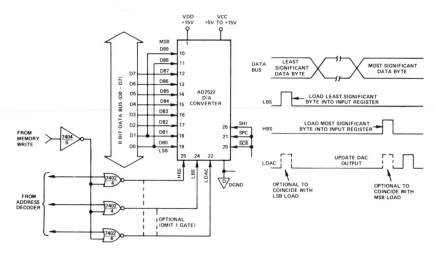

Figure 7.21. A self-contained DAC. (Courtesy Analog Devices Inc.)

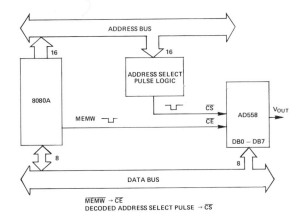

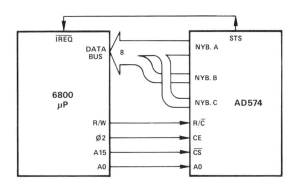

Figure 7.24. Interfacing an AD574 ADC to a 6800 microprocessor. (Courtesy Analog Devices Inc.)

Figure 7.22. An 8 bit DAC containing a set of latches, chip select gating, voltage reference, and output amplifier. (Courtesy Analog Devices Inc.)

noise (quantization noise). "Real" noise, which is substantially below the resolution of the converter, is usually neglected on the grounds that it falls below the error which was determined to be tolerable when the converter resolution was selected. However, this "negligible" noise level (on the order of ½ LSB or less) is generally at least an order of magnitude smaller than the digital noise immunity of a system.

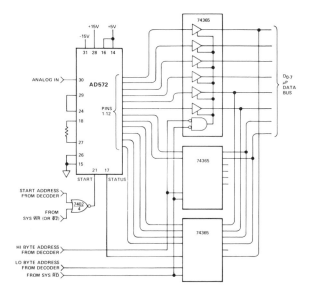

Figure 7.23. Interfacing an AD572 ADC to an 8 bit bus. (Courtesy Analog Devices Inc.)

Analog signal conditioning which may be needed to properly match an available signal level to the input range of an ADC, or to convert the output of a DAC to an appropriate level or parameter, is beyond the scope of this chapter. Nevertheless, it seems important to emphasize a few ideas which become important when treating the analog interface of a converter.

Ideally, the signals in any electronic system are conveyed between output and input ports with no deterioration. Actually, of course, the signals are conveyed by conductors with finite resistance, inductance, and capacitance. As a result, the signal path must be treated as part of the signal shaping circuit. This factor becomes increasingly important when part of a signal path is shared by more than one signal. The common or "ground" connection in most systems is a network of interconnections across which are developed voltage drops related to the various signals in the system. These voltages are prevalent in digital systems in which the ground network carries not only signals but power currents, as well. The effect of these voltages on digital systems is diminished by the noise immunity of the logic. Sometimes even the 400 mV of immunity in TTL systems is insufficient to overcome the "ground noise," and special grounding and differential signal routing must be arranged.

Clearly, these sorts of noise levels are intolerable even in an 8 bit analog system in which, with 10 V full scale, 20 mV is ½ LSB of noise. As illustrated in Figure 7.25, simple grounding errors are one of the most common causes of data converter noise problems. This figure shows an analog system, a logic network, a power supply for the logic, and a converter which is intended to provide

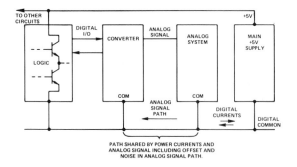

Figure 7.25. An example of poor ground current management. (Courtesy Analog Devices Inc.)

the interface between the analog and digital systems. The power supplies for the analog system and the converter are not shown. The converter connects to the analog portion of the system through an analog signal path. It also communicates with the digital circuits by means of a number of lines which may be inputs or outputs (depending in part upon whether the converter is A/D or D/A). The problem stems from the common connection which joins the systems. The analog signal return path is shared with the logic power currents. The voltage developed along the shared path is effectively in series with the analog signal.

A remedy for the problem of Figure 7.25 is shown in Figure 7.26. A separate return connection is provided between the converter and the analog system. A second path is provided as a return for the digital signals.

Most real systems are more difficult than this simple illustration. For example, it may be necessary to power the converter by way of the analog return; this, however,

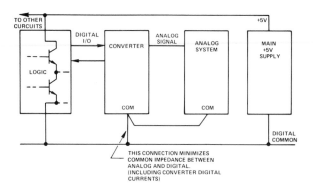

Figure 7.26. Connecting analog system directly to converter common. (Courtesy Analog Devices Inc.)

should be avoided if possible. The basic principle illustrated here applies to systems of all complexity. The analog signal path should not be shared with any other signal or power current. Some converters have separate analog and digital "ground" terminals. Generally, these terminals separate most of the internal analog and digital currents. The converter will tolerate small (usually on the order of digital noise immunity levels) voltage differences between these terminals. This tolerance greatly simplifies ground current management in digital and analog systems.

Usually, the digital and analog portions of a converter are not completely isolated. Small foreign currents pass between them, and it is important for the two ground terminals to be constrained to a small difference in voltage. The general consequence is that analog and digital grounds (there may be several of each in some systems) must join at some point. Through this point passes all the currents that must be interchanged by the various portions of the system. To minimize this current, the system should be divided into subsections which have a minimum of signal current conveyed to or from the remaining sections of the system.

7.8 PRACTICAL LIMITS OF PERFORMANCE

The concepts of A/D and D/A conversion have been described here in ideal terms in order to promote an understanding of the principles involved. In practical situations there are, of course, departures from the ideal which must be dealt with. Figures 7.1 and 7.10 show idealized transfer characteristics for data converters. In addition to the fundamental "errors" or "noise" owing to quantization, practical systems exhibit other errors which stem from the failure of real converters to conform to the idealized performance.

These departures from nominal behavior are as varied in detail as are the types of converters that manifest them. For most purposes, however, a few simple concepts will serve to classify these errors and to estimate their effect on the systems which use converters.

The simplest errors are offset and gain errors, as illustrated in Figure 7.27. In a DAC, an **offset error** appears as a vertical translation of the characteristic of Figure 7.10. When an input of 0 is applied to a DAC with an offset error, the output will not be 0. The output which results from any given input will be translated by the same amount as is the 0 output. Offset error is generally measured at 0 input, in order to separate its effects from gain error.

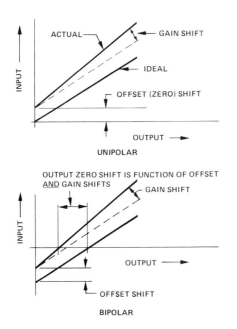

ACTUAL — GAIN SHIFT

IDEAL

OFFSET (ZERO) SHIFT

UNIPOLAR

OUTPUT ZERO SHIFT IS FUNCTION OF OFFSET
AND GAIN SHIFTS — GAIN SHIFT

OFFSET SHIFT

BIPOLAR

Figure 7.27. Illustration of offset and gain errors. (Courtesy Analog Devices Inc.)

Gain error is a proportional change in the value of each output level. It is, in effect, a change in the slope of the output ramp so that although it has the proper form, it fails to pass through full scale (though a gain error does not contribute to offset). Gain error can be quantified by determining the offset error and subtracting it from the full scale error of the maximum DAC output.

Although the effects which produce offset and gain errors differ with the type of converter employed, their effects can often be eliminated. For example, a fixed voltage can be summed with the output of the DAC to correct the effect of an output offset. To achieve this simply, a fixed current can be injected into the summing node of the amplifier, which transforms a current output DAC to a voltage output DAC. Similarly, a gain error can be corrected by an adjustment of the value of the feedback or application resistor in a current to the voltage converter.

Limits on offset and gain error are generally specified by converter manufacturers. Although the effect of both errors can usually be reduced to zero, their magnitude is still of some importance as an indicator of subsequent performance. After these errors have been set to zero, they may reappear owing to the effects of temperature, supply voltage variations, and aging. Generally, coeffi-

cients of the change in zero and gain error with respect to important environmental factors are specified so that errors can be evaluated under anticipated worst case conditions.

A problem more difficult to deal with is called **linearity error.** This error is related to the form, or shape, of the converter transfer function. It cannot be corrected easily with one or two adjustments. Two aspects of linearity error are shown in Figure 7.28. In those two illustrations, the idealized output of a DAC is represented by a diagonal "trend line" passing through the nominal DAC output points. The curved line passes through the actual outputs of the DAC. Notice that offset and gain errors have been eliminated. The straight line which gives the best fit to the actual DAC characteristic, in the sense that the maximum difference between them is minimized, is shown in Figure 7.28a. In Figure 7.28b, the linearity error is specified in terms of the end points and the actual difference between real and ideal characteristics.

Specification limits on linearity in terms of the end points are generally easier to use. Offset and gain errors can be compensated after a few simple measurements, and the maximum departure from the ideal can be estimated from the linearity specification. To obtain the best fit performance, the entire DAC characteristic must first be measured and then computed nonzero offset and gain errors must be introduced. This procedure may be followed to minimize overall error however linearity is specified. If the best linearity fit alone is specified, it *must* be followed to ensure accurate error limit estimates. Otherwise, the maximum errors indicated by best fit specifications must be doubled.

Monotonicity is an additional parameter of a DAC that is important in most applications. Monotonicity means, simply, that the output of the converter is a nondecreasing function of the input. In practical terms, it means that if the magnitude of the DAC input increases, the output must increase by at least a small amount. A one LSB end point linearity specification does not necessarily guarantee monotonicity. For example, just below half scale, 011 in the case of the 3 bit DAC, an output error of $+\frac{3}{4}$ LSB would not violate the linearity specification. If the output produced by the next larger code, 100, has an error of $-\frac{3}{4}$ LSB, the linearity specification will be satisfied; however, in changing to the higher code, the output of the DAC is actually reduced.

To avoid problems of this type, some converters are tested and guaranteed monotonic. An alternative specification, which is more general and can be used to assure monotonicity, is differential linearity.

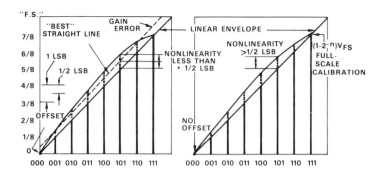

Figure 7.28. Illustration of linearity error. Best straight line fit (left). End points specification (right). (Courtesy Analog Devices Inc.)

Differential linearity errors are a measure of the failure of the DAC output to increase exactly 1 LSB weight when the digital input is increased by 1 LSB. Differential linearity is concerned with the transitions between adjacent bits, as shown in Figure 7.29. To distinguish this specification, the "other" linearity error shown in Figure 7.28 is sometimes called an "integral" linearity error.

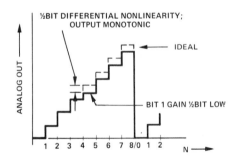

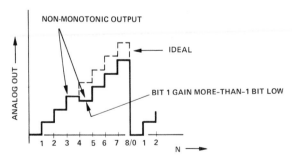

Figure 7.29. Differential nonlinearity. (Courtesy Analog Devices Inc.)

Figure 7.29 shows how a differential linearity specification of less than 1 LSB guarantees monotonicity.

Up to this point, the discussion has been illustrated with digital to analog converter characteristics. Most of the ideas involved are directly and simply applicable to analog to digital conversion. For example, an offset is an additive error which simply adds or subtracts a fixed amount to each output code. The effect is the same as if a fixed amplitude signal were added to the actual input signal. The offset can be determined by searching for the input voltage which causes a transition between zero and one indications at the output. The difference between this level and the "proper" level closely approximates the offset. Similarly, comparison of actual output code indications with the nominal values associated with a given input signal allows determination of gain and integral linearity errors. Specification limits on these errors allow estimates of maximum measurement errors which may occur in applications.

A/D converters also exhibit a form of differential linearity error. In this case, the error manifests as an input signal difference other than 1 LSB between the center of two adjacent transitions. The result is wide and narrow code widths. Wide codes correspond to a large (larger than 1 LSB weight) change in input signal without a change in output code. Narrow codes correspond to changes in output code without a correspondingly large change in input signal. Sometimes code widths become so narrow that they vanish altogether. That is, as the input signal is increased the output code resulting from repeated conversions also increases, but some codes may be skipped over and do not appear in the output sequence. This situation and one of its causes are illustrated in Fig-

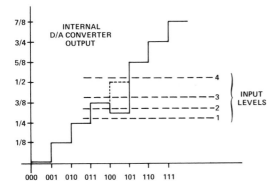

SUCCESSIVE APPROXIMATIONS
(Accept Code If Lower Than Input Level)

SIGNAL

CODE	1	2	3	4
100	NO	YES	YES	YES
010	YES	–	–	–
011	NO	–	–	–
110	–	NO	NO	NO
101	–	NO	NO	NO
ANSWER CORRECT	010	100	100	100
ANSWER	010	010	011	100
ERROR	NONE	2 BITS	1 BIT	NONE

MISSED CODE = 011

TRACKING A/D OSCILLATES

Figure 7.30. Skipping of codes. (Courtesy Analog Devices Inc.)

ure 7.30. A successive approximation converter which employs a DAC that is not monotonic will usually have missing codes. In general, the problems of missing codes

in an ADC and a monotonicity failure in a DAC are analogous. For the user, the remedy is the same: obtain a converter that does not have this problem.

One last error, most often associated with A/D converters, is **hysteresis.** A converter with hysteresis may appear to "stick" at certain codes, so that the output which results from a given input may depend not only on the input level, but also on the result of previous conversions. This problem can have a number of causes, but the most common is interaction between the control logic and the analog signal. The most practical approach to hysteresis problems is to avoid converters which have the problem.

One final word of caution is in order, however. Even error-free converters may exhibit symptoms of hysteresis, missing codes, and similar errors in situations in which analog and digital signals are allowed to mix, such as the condition illustrated by Figure 7.25.

REFERENCES

Adib, R. H., "A Single Chip All-MOS 8-Bit A/D Converter," *Journal of Solid State Circuits,* Vol. 13, No. 6 (Dec. 1978), pp. 785–791.

Analog Digital Conversion Handbook. Norwood, MA: Analog Devices Inc., 1972.

Analog Digital Conversion Notes. Norwood, MA: Analog Devices Inc., 1977.

Integrated Circuit Converters, Data Acquisition Systems and Analog Signal Conditioning Components. Norwood, MA: Analog Devices Inc., 1979.

8
Displays

David R. Baldauf

IBM Corporation

8.1 INTRODUCTION

Displays are the primary output medium through which
users interact with computing systems. They are becoming far more ubiquitous than printers, which used to be
the only output device. A display is characterized by
rapid writing and erasure of non-apriori information on a
viewing screen when a permanent record is not required.

The purpose of this chapter is to provide some insight
into the important characteristics of displays and to provide a basis for the selection of display specifications and/
or technologies for computer output. It is assumed that
users today are concerned not only with legibility, but
also with ease of use, response time, image quality, and
readability.

8.2 DISPLAY ROLE IN COMPUTER
SYSTEMS

Relation to Printers

Computing systems originally provided batch output to
printers, but then grew to include personal interactive
modes using typewriter-like terminals. These terminals
were slow and consumed a lot of paper, most of which
was not retained. Display terminals then appeared which
solved those problems. However, they generated two
other problems: no hardcopy record was available and the
quality of the image was poor compared with typewriter
printing. The evolution of reliable on-line random access

files somewhat eased the problem of no hard copy, since
the data was always readily available for display.

The need for fast writing and erasure prevailed over
image quality and, as a result, today the use of displays
predominate over printers in interactive computer operation. Thus the most important characteristic of computer displays is write and erase speed; image quality is
second. Table 8.1 shows typical values for write time and
image quality factors for the CRT (cathode ray tube)
versus several printing technologies. The dominant technology in computer displays is the CRT, which inherently
satisfies the fast write and erase requirement; it, however,
requires careful design to provide good image quality.

Displays Versus Printers

Terminal printers began with the teletype machines
which, even though they used engraved type, produced
poor quality print. The typewriter based terminal produced good image quality but lacked reliability. Both
were too slow for interactive use, which drove printer development toward the wire matrix, thermal matrix, ink
jet, and daisy wheel. These new technologies, however,
were still slow relative to displays.

TV Technology for Computer Display

The TV technology allowed rapid write and erase with
new pictures being written in $\frac{1}{30}$ second and erased in a
similar time, far faster than required for computer inter-

Table 8.1. Display Printer Comparisons

	CRT Displays	Pel Printers		
		Wire Matrix	Laser Electro-Photographic	Ink Jet
Pel* size (mil)	15	15	6	6
Addressable pels/in.	100	100	240	240
Page response time (s)	1/60	>1	>1	>1

*Picture element.

action. This technology was used initially for the display of still frames of computer generated alphanumeric information. The use of TV sets directly was limited by receiver bandwidth (4 MHz) to the display of only several hundred characters. TV monitors, however, could easily provide a much broader video bandwidth to extend the range of the display to 2,000 characters.

While TV technology sufficed in the initial applications, its deficiencies soon became apparent because applications in computer systems are different from TV, as illustrated:

Computer Application		TV
Viewing distance of 1½ ft	vs.	8 ft
Letters, numbers and words	vs.	Pictures
Detail identification	vs.	Gross interpretation
Work pressure	vs.	Entertainment
Still frames	vs.	Dynamic movement

TV application can tolerate fuzziness at the edges of the screen; TV interlace (wherein a field consisting of every other line of a picture is presented 60 times per second, providing a full picture 30 times per second) obscures flicker at ³⁰⁄₆₀ hertz on picture information viewed at 6 to 8 feet whereas for alphanumeric (AN) characters, it does not; and home living rooms use subdued lighting compared to bright office environments.

For these reasons, the direct use of TV equipment as computer displays is not desirable, although TV technology can be customized for computer displays. When customized, however, computer displays are still sufficiently similar so that cost advantages are derived from the TV manufacturing base. In low content applications, best typified by the use of TV receiver displays on personal computers, the TV display is used directly. Even in that application, options usually are provided to permit the attachment of a higher quality display.

Application Range

Displays span the application range from single digit indicators to full page displays and graphics.

Indicators. These are used usually to indicate output status and while they are displays, their requirements are not stringent and are of minimum concern in computer systems. Technology that is available from digital clocks, home appliances, and hand calculators suffices for these applications. Nothing more will be discussed in this chapter relative to this application class.

Small screen AN. These displays of alphanumeric information range from 10 to 500 characters and generally display message or transaction information. Typical applications include supermarket checkout displays, single line typewriter character displays, bank teller terminals, reservation agent terminals, personal computer displays, and Viewdata displays. The usage of these displays is characterized by high interactivity and relatively short messages. Figure 8.1 shows a typical bank teller terminal using gas panel technology.

Two thousand character AN. This is a popular product; it is low cost, yet provides an adequate amount of information for many general purpose applications. Figure 8.2 is a typical general purpose CRT based terminal. As a result, much computer software assumes the 80 character row by 24 row format, which therefore forces the continuation of this format as a popular design point even when other display technologies and formats may be available. The requirement is for fast write and erase, and good legibility. These displays are often used intensively by operators; thus, increased attention to human factors is required.

Full page displays. These displays are nominally in the 6,000 character range and most often used in text applications. Upper and lower case characters, multiple fonts, rapid updating, and excellent human factors are required. The tasks are generally reading intensive, and consequently, the displays require many of the attributes of printed text.

Facsimile or image displays. These displays will grow in quantity as electronic mail and general purpose file retrieval is handled by computers. The source data is assumed to be scanned, digitized, transmitted or stored (or both), and then distributed to a display device. Data

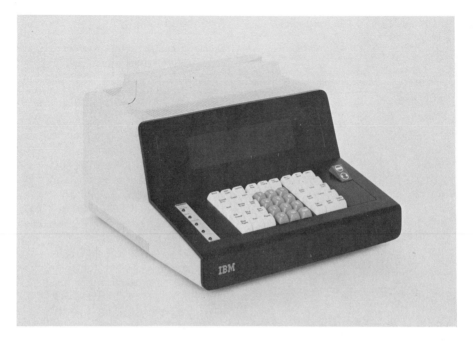

Figure 8.1. The IBM 3604 Bank Teller Terminal, typical of a transaction oriented computer display. (Courtesy IBM Corporation)

handled thus are sometimes called **NCI,** for **Noncoded information;** the displayed image can be anything from text to scenes. The display requirements are similar to those for very high resolution TV.

Additional problems are encountered because the source scanning raster is not in registration with the image information. For example, if an image of facsimile text is being displayed, more scanning lines are required than would be required for coded text to provide the same degree of legibility.

Frequently, both NCI data and coded data will be merged on the display screen. A desirable multimode capability in the future may be combining images from a video disk combined with alphanumerics from a computer. In such applications, displays are replacing printed material and must have pleasing aesthetics in addition to readability and legibility.

Graphics. This application area is treated in detail in Chapter 41. Suffice it to say here that graphic displays are characterized by good line drawing capability, that is, good resolution and little observable stair stepping. Some applications can tolerate slow update times while others require very rapid interactivity.

8.3 DISCUSSION OF TERMS

Computer displays are electro-optical transducers for which traditionally, the electrical properties are well specified but the optical 85 characteristics have been ambiguous. There is no agreement on definitions nor on measurement techniques. What is presented here is the author's view of definitions that are useful for computer displays and a discussion of some pertinent aspects of each.

Resolution is the number of distinctly discernable elements on a display, and frequently is expressed as lines per inch. In optics, resolution is measured as line pairs, that is, a black and a white line pair. In displays, a variety of definitions prevail, as indicated in Table 8.2. One of the most popular is the **shrinking raster** definition, in which raster lines on a display are moved closer and closer together until the eye cannot detect any variation in intensity orthogonal to the raster lines. The number of raster lines per inch at this merge point is called **resolution.**

Another definition, similar in concept to the optical one, is a count of the number of bright points per inch

Figure 8.2. The IBM 3278 Terminal, typical of a 2000 character, CRT based, general purpose computer display. (Courtesy IBM Corporation)

Table 8.2. Converting Measures of Display Resolution

To Convert from ↓	To → Multiply by ↘	TV Limit-ing	10% MTF	TV$_{50}$	Shrink-ing Raster	50% Ampli-tude	50% MTF	Optical	Equiva-lent Pass-band	10% Ampli-tude
TV limiting	1.18σ		0.80	0.71	0.59	0.50	0.44	0.42	0.33	.27
10% MTF	1.47σ	1.25		0.88	0.74	0.62	0.55	0.52	0.42	.34
TV$_{50}$ (3db)	1.67σ	1.4	1.14		0.84	0.71	0.63	0.59	0.47	.38
Shrinking raster	2.00σ	1.7	1.36	1.2		0.85	0.75	0.71	0.56	.47
50% amplitude	2.35σ	2.0	1.6	1.4	1.17		0.88	0.83	0.66	.56
50% MTF	2.67σ	2.26	1.82	1.6	1.33	1.14		0.94	0.75	.62
Optical (1/e)	2.83σ	2.4	1.94	1.7	1.4	1.2	1.06		0.80	.67
Equivalent passband (Ne)	3.54σ	3.0	2.4	2.1	1.77	1.5	1.33	1.25		.83
10% amplitude	4.3 σ	3.6	2.9	2.6	2.15	1.8	1.6	1.5	1.2	

when a 5:1 contrast ratio is maintained between points. This is a useful definition when it is desired to see each point as distinct from the next point. In a CRT, assuming a Gaussian shape, the 5:1 contrast is achieved if the spots overlap at the 10 percent amplitude point. Resolution on a CRT and in some other display technologies is a function of luminance.

Spot size is a useful parameter because, in most display technologies, the image is painted by spots of light. The spot which paints the image is sometimes referred to as the **printing function.** In a conventional CRT, the spot shape approximates a Gaussian curve; in a matrix gas panel it is a double-humped spot, while in a DVST (direct view storage tube) it approximates a rectangular shape (Figures 8.3, 8.4, and 8.5). To be meaningful, spot size or diameter must be specified at a given amplitude of the luminance curve. For a Gaussian CRT spot, the diameter at the 60 percent amplitude point (identified as the 2σ point in Table 8.2) corresponds to the raster pitch in the shrinking raster resolution measurement.

Addressability defines the number of points that the center of a spot can be positioned over the surface of the screen. For example, a CRT spot size may be 15 mils at the 60 percent point, but the digital information that drives the deflection system may be able to place its center on a 1 mil grid. In this example, the shrinking raster resolution is 66 lines per inch, but its addressability is 1,000 lines per inch. Often in the trade literature, *ad-*

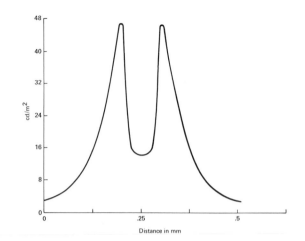

Figure 8.4. Typical spot profile for a large content ac gas plasma panel. (Courtesy L. Jansen, IBM Corporation)

dressability is called *resolution,* causing a great deal of uncertainty in what is meant. Fine addressability provides symbol line smoothness.

The Pel (picture element), or **pixel,** is the smallest displayable element comprising a display screen. Each dot of a dot matrix character is a pel. The information content capability of a display screen oftentimes is expressed in total number of pels. The term pel is used in many

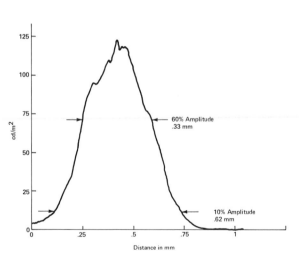

Figure 8.3. Typical spot profile for a CRT used in computer terminals. (Courtesy L. Jansen, IBM Corporation)

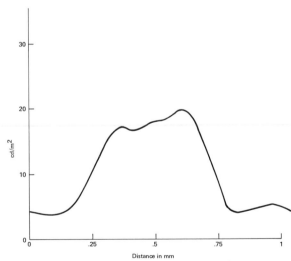

Figure 8.5. Typical spot profile for the DVST. (Courtesy L. Jansen, IBM Corporation)

ways: (1) sometimes to mean discernable picture elements as defined by one of the resolution definitions, (2) sometimes to mean the number of addressable points; (3) while at other times, it is a definition unique to the technology under discussion. In any event, when the word "pel" is used, its meaning should be defined.

Luminance is sometimes referred to as *brightness,* although brightness is a perceived property, while luminance is a physically measured quantity. Luminance is measured for a light emitting display in candellas per square meter (cd/m^2), or, in English units, foot lamberts. The common optical units and conversion factors among systems are provided in Table 8.3. For a reflective display (e.g., liquid crystals), luminance is not an appropriate quantity to specify; in this case, the reflectance of the light areas and contrast ratio are the controlling characteristics.

Luminance can be specified for a single pel using a microphotometer (Figures 8.3, 8.4, 8.5), but more commonly it is specified over a large area where all picture elements are lit. These two measurement conditions lead to large differences in values. For instance, in ac gas panel technology, the peak pel luminance (Figure 8.4)

may be 48 cd/m^2 whereas the luminance integrated over a large area may only be half that because of the distinct separation of pels. Furthermore, under actual alphanumeric operating conditions, all pels will not be lit so that large area luminance may only be 10 to 20 percent of that which would obtain with all pels lit. Thus, the conditions under which luminance is measured must be known. Luminances of familiar objects, for reference, are given in Table 8.4.

Contrast, or **modulation contrast,** is most commonly defined by the ratio

$$\frac{L_s - L_B}{L_s + L_B}$$

where L_s is the symbol luminance and L_B is the background luminance. In this case, the symbol is brighter than the background, as is typical for a CRT or LED display. If the background is brighter, as is the case for printed paper, liquid crystal displays, or reverse image CRTs, the expression is

$$\frac{L_B - L_s}{L_B + L_s}$$

Table 8.3. Conversion Table for Luminance Units*

To obtain ↓		cd/cm²	cd/in.²	cd/ft²	cd/m²	L	mL	ft-L (equiv. ft candle)	m-L
Candela/cm² (stilb)		1	0.1550	0.0010764	10^{-4}	0.3183	0.0003183	0.0003426	0.00003183
Candela/in.²		6.452	1	0.006944	6.452×10^{-4}	2.054	0.002054	0.00221	0.0002054
Candela/ft²		929	144	1	0.0929	295.7	0.2957	0.3183	0.02957
Candela/m²		10,000	1.550	10.764	1	3,183	3.183	3.426	0.3183
Lambert (cm-L)		3.142	0.4869	3.382×10^{-3}	3.142×10^{-4}	1	0.001	0.001076	10^{-4}
Millilambert		3.142	486.9	3.382	0.3142	1,000	1	1.0764	0.1
Foot-lambert		2.919	452.4	3.142	0.2919	929	0.929	1	0.0929
Meter-lambert		31,420	4869	33.282	3.142	10^4	10	10.76	1

To obtain ↓			Lux	Multiply Number of		
				Foot-candle	Phot	Milliphot
Lumen/m²	lux		1.0	10.76	10,000	10.0
Lumen/ft²	foot-candle		0.0929	1.0	929	0.929
Lumen/cm²	phot		0.0001	0.001076	1	0.001
	milliphot		0.1	1.076	1,000	1.0

*After Pender and McIlwain by permission. *Electrical Engineers Handbook: Communication-Electronics,* 4th Ed., Wiley, 1950, and as appearing in Sherr, *Electronic Displays,* Wiley, 1979.

Table 8.4. Typical Luminances (in Foot Lamberts)

Surface of sun	4.8×10^8
Surface of a 60 W frosted incandescent bulb ("hot spot")	36,000
Brightest white cumulus cloud	12,000
Surface of a 60 W "white" incandescent bulb	9,000
White paper in direct sunlight—high sun	9,000
Surface of a 15 W fluorescent tube	3,000
Clear sky	2,000
Surface of moon, bright area	2,000
White paper on office desk	25
Pulsed electroluminescent mosaic panel	20
Television raster	20
Light valve, 10×10 ft diffusing screen, 2 KW lamp	20
Theater screen open gate	16
White paper in full moonlight	10^{-2}

Thus, the result is always a number between 0 and 1. Frequently, luminance ratio or contrast ratio is specified by

$$\frac{L_s}{L_B} \quad \text{or} \quad \frac{L_B}{L_s},$$

using whichever term is brighter as the numerator to obtain a result larger than one.

The results, however, are very sensitive to the way the measurements are made. The background luminance depends primarily on room lighting, reflectivity of the display screen, and degree of stray illumination from lit symbols. The discussion here assumes symbols have higher liminance than background.

Typical room lighting should be in the range of 500 lux (or higher for certain tasks) with the measurement made of the luminance reflected from an unlit area of the display screen. Symbol luminance is more difficult to define. It could be the peak luminance of a small area within a pel dimension, the average over the area of a pel, or the average over a large group of adjacent pels. The last is easier to measure and is practical for displays where the spot size overlaps from pel to pel, as in a CRT.

In matrix technologies such as the gas panel, the large area measurement includes a lot of dark space and results in numbers which may seem low compared to other more familiar displays. The eye is responsive to peak symbol luminance; thus peak luminance within a pel dimension also provides a meaningful contrast ratio value. Typical contrast ratios are printed paper, 20:1; CRT 12:1; ac gas panel, 20:1.

Polarity determines whether the display has bright characters on a dark background, or vice versa. The term *positive image* corresponds to printed pages, that is, dark characters on a bright background. A *negative image* is bright characters on a dark background.

Glare is ambient light reflected from the display surface, which decreases contrast in areas of the screen where it occurs. Glass surfaces typically reflect about 4 percent of the light striking the surface. Typical office lighting produces luminances on the surface of fluorescent lighting fixtures in the range of 5,000 to 8,000 cd/m² which can produce a reflected image of 200 to 300 cd/m². Because this is the same order of magnitude as display screen luminance, the effect can be very disturbing. Some techniques to combat these effects follow:

1. An etched or roughened glass surface will diffuse the light of the glare image and, while the total amount of reflected light remains the same, less light enters the eye and is therefore less disturbing. However, this technique also diffuses the light from the displayed symbols, making them fuzzy.

2. A layer of absorbing micromesh can be placed over the glass surface. This essentially forms an array of holes through which the displayed symbols are seen when one looks on-axis at the display. Off-axis ambient light is absorbed and diffused, reducing reflected glare. The disadvantage of micromesh is that it restricts the operator to on-axis viewing and reduces symbol luminance.

3. A quarter wave thin film layer (or layers) may be deposited on the glass surface. This technique provides an interference filter to reflected light and greatly reduces it. Its effectiveness in reducing glare luminance is around 10:1, yet it does not reduce the symbol res-

olution or luminance. The film layer is, however, susceptible to fingerprinting and must be cleaned frequently.

Flicker is of concern in any display where the luminance is pulsed, rather than continuous. Cathode ray tubes, gas panels, electroluminescent panels, LEDs, vacuum fluorescent displays, and others may have flicker. The eye has a **critical flicker frequency (CFF)** above which pulsed light appears to be continuous (Figure 8.6). The CFF increases as brightness increases and is about 10 Hz higher for peripheral vision than for foveal vision at the luminances of interest. Second order variations of CFF are induced by screen content, room ambient light, display font design, interlace techniques, and screen background light. In addition, a person from day to day may experience a several-hertz variation in sensitivity.

Flicker is most noticeable by young persons; the CFF generally decreases with age. With so many variables, the best way to tell whether flicker is occurring is to have the display used in typical operating conditions by a large number of people. Flicker is observable by some people on almost all CRT display products under some combinations of conditions. A method for comparing the amount of flicker among displays is to determine the ratio of the first harmonic content of the luminance waveform to the average (dc) component. The lower the ratio, the less will be the perceived flicker.

Persistence / storage mitigates flicker as an element disturbing to viewing. CRT phosphors have a luminance decay that lasts long after being excited by the electron beam. Typical curves for long persistence P-4 and P-39 phosphors are given in Figure 8.7. Phosphor decay characteristics are subject to wide variations among manufacturers and from lot to lot. LEDs and gas plasma luminances fall to zero very quickly. Long persistence tends to reduce flicker perception. Thus a CRT may be operated at a lower refreshed rate than a LED. Persistence is usually specified as the time required for luminance to decay to 10 percent of its peak value.

Some technologies have self-storage capability, for example, the DVST or the ac gas panel. The DVST can be thought of as a CRT with an extremely long persistence. Useful storage times should be sufficient to allow the reading of a full screen of information. Technologies such as the DVST have storage times on the order of 15 minutes. Others, such as the ac gas panel, store as long as power is on. Thermally addressed liquid crystals continue to store even with power off. High storage capability is very useful in that it provides flicker-free images, and information content is not limited as is the case for refreshed displays.

Jitter is a small movement of the image which frequently occurs owing to design oversights. Jitter in a CRT may come from extraneous 60 Hz electrical power fields or from other sources of ac fields and transients. In some gas panels, small spatial jitter occurs as a result of a gas ion-

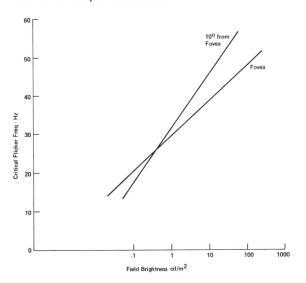

Figure 8.6. Relationship between critical fusion frequency and luminance: the Ferry-Porter law. (Based on A. Cakir et al., *VDT Manual*. Darmstadt: IFRA, 1979)

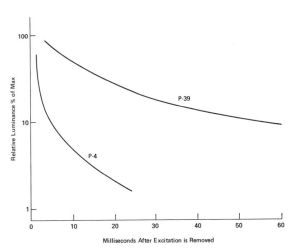

Figure 8.7. Phosphor decay curves for two frequently used phosphors in computer displays.

ization discharge point moving from one edge of an electrode to another edge. Jitter is not generally specified in display terminals and usually must be evaluated in its operating environment. In CRT displays, it tends to make characters fuzzy if it is high frequency jitter; at lower frequency, it shows up as undulations or squirming of the image.

Gray shades is defined as a ratio of 1.41 between two luminance levels. Thus, if a display has a luminance of 100 cd/m^2, the next shade above would be 141 cd/m^2 and the next shade below would be 70.7 cd/m^2. Frequently, a characteristic of importance is how many shades of gray can be displayed from the off condition (background luminance) to the full intensity condition. A common value for CRT displays is approximately seven shades of gray.

In displays which do not have an ability to control the luminance of a picture element, as in some gas panel or electroluminescent terminals, the effect of gray shades may be obtained by half toning at a loss in resolution. Half toning is typified by a newspaper photograph which, when viewed sufficiently far away, appears to have gray shades even though only black dots were used in the printing process.

Color is used in two different senses: the first is the color of a monochrome display; the second is a range of colors available on the same screen at the same time. In the case of monochrome computer displays using a CRT, popular colors are green, white, and orange, and are usually chosen on the basis of the persistence desired for a particular design feature. Green has been popular because phosphors with long persistences, which minimize flicker, are readily available. White phosphors typically have shorter persistence and require higher refresh rates.

The issue of which color is most desirable from the human point of view has not been definitively established, although it is clear that saturated colors at the extremes of the photopic response of the eye, that is red and blue, should be avoided. Gas panel displays are typically orange, LEDs are red, but other colors are available and are preferred. Electrochromics are typically purple, electroluminescent displays are yellow, and liquid crystals are usually black and white, although other colors are becoming available.

Color in the second sense is typified by color TV, with a range of colors available on the screen. Color computer displays almost universally use color CRT technology. The most popular is the shadow mask technology wherein

a pel is comprised of amounts of red, green, and blue luminous components to provide the color desired. Typical structures are shown in Figure 8.8. Three electron beams are modulated and pass through a shadow mask and land on their respective color phosphor, either dot or stripe, as the case may be. The specification for the color is usually expressed in terms of the CIE color coordinate chart, Figure 8.9. This chart describes the three color coordinates on a two coordinate graph. (Refer to the *Raster Graphics Handbook* (Comrac Corporation, 1980) for a detailed derivation and interpretation.) Suffice it to say here that a color is specified in terms of its **hue,** which corresponds to its dominant wavelength, and of **saturation,** which defines the degree to which the color is undiluted with white light.

Alphanumeric display terminals frequently provide four to seven colors whereas graphic terminals may implement hundreds of colors to provide intricate shading effects. **Convergence** is a term of importance in shadow mask color CRTs. It means the degree to which the intersection of the three beams remain at the shadow mask surface as they are scanned across the tube. Misconverg-

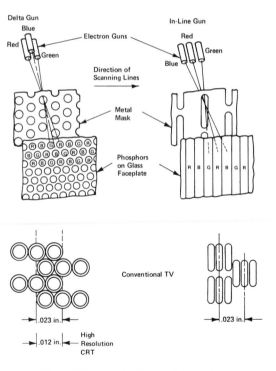

Figure 8.8. CRT shadow mask technology.

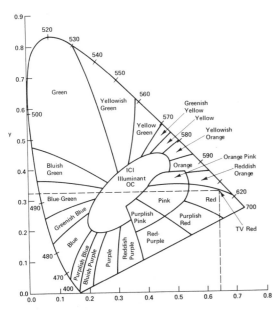

Figure 8.9. Location of colors in the chromaticity diagram. (After Pender and McIlwain. From S. Sherr, *Electronic Displays,* John Wiley & Sons, 1979)

of 60 ms to the 10 percent luminance point and 1 s to the 1 percent residual level. Incomplete erasure is most noticeable in scrolling operations where a smear remains as the text is moved. In refreshed dc gas panels or LEDs, there is no persistence; hence, erase time is not limited by the display technology. In storage technologies, the ac gas panel screen erase is much faster than full screen write and is generally of little concern. In the DVST, erase time is less than 1 s.

8.4 HUMAN VISUAL FACTORS

It is obvious that the computer display must provide an interface compatible with the human eye (Figure 8.10). The brain takes the information from the optic nerve and passes it through several levels of processing. One current model of visual processing is that of a series of narrow band filters wherein the spatial frequency components of an image are sorted out, processed, and finally recognized as a familiar image. Nothing further will be said about how vision is handled by the brain, except to note that the process is very complex, involving many subtleties of the

ence results in color fringing depending on screen position.

Write time, an important characteristic of a display, usually falls within a fraction of a second. It is the time required by the display device and its associated drivers to write a new image on the screen. In a CRT, write time is typically in the range of 15 to 33 milliseconds (ms), as it is for most other refreshed technologies such as dc gas panels, EL panels, or LEDs. For storage technologies, ac gas panel write times run from 25 to 250 ms, whereas those for the DVST may be 1 second or greater, depending on content. Except for the case of the DVST, write time is usually limited by computer response time, the logic circuitry used in the interface, or the communication line speeds, rather than the display technology. These other delays typically can be 1 to 3 seconds in alphanumeric applications.

Erase time is the interval required to clear the screen and prepare it for a new image. In refresh technologies, erasure is automatic. For the CRT, erase time is dependent on the phosphor persistence and may be in the order

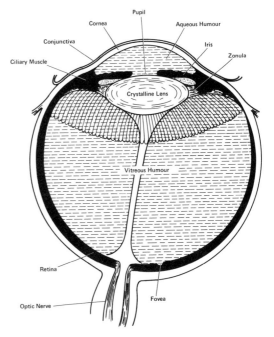

Figure 8.10. The primary components of the human eye.

image, and the mind can partially conpensate (usually at the cost of fatigue) for deficiencies in display equipment.

The functioning of the eye itself is much better understood than is brain processing. The resolution of the eye is approximately 1 minute of arc which, at a traditional terminal viewing distance of 500 mm (20 inches), translates into 0.14 mm (6 mils i). However, even smaller vernier differences can be detected; hence, while two pels spaced 6 mils apart may look like one, a *line* with an offset much less than 6 mils is seen as having an offset.

There are more than 75 million **receptors** on the retina. In a very small (2 degrees) spot called the **fovea**, the cone receptors are more densely packed than they are in other areas of the retina. Reading is achieved by focusing the image to be read on the fovea and its adjacent area, the **para-fovea**. As everyone is aware, the eye moves, or more accurately, jumps, along a line of characters as fast as the meaning is assimilated. These saccadic movements generally embrace several words in each jump. In most typed and printed matter, line-following is enhanced by font design with serifs, which help to guide the eye as it moves along lines of type; but well laid out sans serif fonts, as found on most CRTs, are quite adequate in this respect (serifs require very high resolution). Jumping from the end of one line to the beginning of the next is facilitated either by short lines, as are found in newspaper columns, or by large spaces between lines.

The receptors beyond the fovea contribute to overall image awareness and perception. Receptors (and associated neural processes) near the edge of the field of view, beyond 20 degrees off axis, are supersensitive to movement and flicker. Hence, flicker in a refreshed display always appears worse at the edges. Although one does not ordinarily read at or near the edge of the field of view, flicker nevertheless is distracting.

There are two types of receptors: rods and cones. **Rods** work mainly in dim light to detect shades of gray; **Cones** work in bright light and detect color as well as react to intensity. Because different cones are dominant for the primary colors, the eye's capability for color resolution is less than it is for merely detecting differences in luminance. For example, the resolution limit for red and green is 2 minutes of arc and for blue and yellow it is 7 minutes of arc. Thus, in color computer displays, the maximum content of a given size display screen should be less than that for a monochrome display. This characteristic of the eye is reflected in the NTSC TV standards, which allocates a much greater bandwidth to luminance than to color. This color structure of the eye is fortunate for the

engineer, because in display technology, one usually must give up resolution to achieve color.

The eye is sensitive to colors over the frequency range shown in Figure 8.11, but the extremes of the curve should be avoided. Thus, in color displays, the blues or reds used should be highly unsaturated. In computer CRT displays, for example, phosphors different from those used in TV may be desirable.

The resolution capability of the eye assuming optimal refractive correction does not decrease much before 60 years of age. What does change radically, however, is accomodation. Thus, most people in their forties and beyond wear glasses to provide focus correction for reading print on paper, nominally at 325 mm, and usually for distant viewing as well. Frequently, bifocal lenses are prescribed, neither of which is right for 500 mm display viewing. Display users should therefore be fitted with appropriate glasses. A good compromise is glasses with the reading lens on the bottom for seeing the keyboard or referring to notes, but with the top half either clear or with 500 mm correction. Another solution is to break with tradition and design displays for viewing at the same distance as copy on paper.

The eye has a luminance dynamic range greater than 10^6, most of which is accomplished by retinal adaptation.

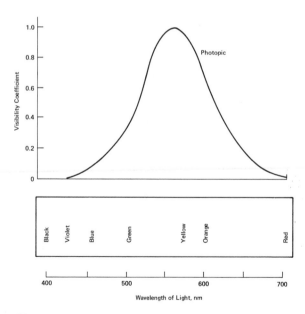

Figure 8.11. The spectral sensitivity of the light adapted eye.

While the eye can adapt, most authorities prefer that display luminance differs by less than a factor of 10 from the environment to minimize the amount of adaptation. Average display luminance levels of 20 to 200 cd/m² are typical. For reference, white paper in an office environment has a luminance in the range of 85 to 200 cd/m². The eye recognizes images by changes in luminance (or color); this is called **contrast**. A reasonable minimum would be 5:1, with 10:1 to 20:1 preferred. Some authorities feel the higher the contrast, the better; others feel extremely high contrast is not pleasing.

Display Environment

Typical office lighting is the environment assumed for computer displays. The lighting environment has been optimized for reading paper with a reflective surface, whereas most computer displays use self-generated light. Typical lighting may be in the range of 500 to 1000 lux. Such lighting reflecting from the phosphor of a CRT could typically produce a background in the range of 10 to 20 cd/m². Assuming a desirable contrast of 10:1, a symbol luminance of 100 to 200 cd/m² is indicated. Typical range of luminance of familiar objects is given in Table 8.4. For reference, the contrast of printed paper in the typical office is 20:1.

The preferred polarity of a display has not been conclusively shown. Some authorities believe black characters on a white background is preferred because there is a better luminance match to the surrounding environment.

Computer display terminals have evolved mostly as CRTs and keyboards, and certain dimensional relationships have been established. Because a comfortable keyboard position is about 300 to 400 mm in front of the body (determined from length of forearm) and the display screen is typically placed behind the keyboard, the traditional viewing distance is 500 mm. This distance has also provided a better match to CRT spot size limitations than attempts to achieve adequate character sharpness at the "normal" reading distance of 325 mm.

Typical typewritten characters are 3.12 mm high and at the normal reading distance of 325 mm subtend an angle of approximately 35 minutes. Studies have been performed on dot matrix computer display characters and show acceptable legibility at 16 minutes (Figure 8.12) if contrast ratios are greater than 10:1. Other contributing factors to readability are continuous strokes versus separated dots and lack of blur or fuzziness of the

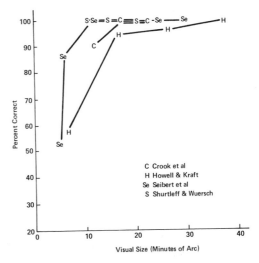

Figure 8.12. The functional relationships for visual size subtended by symbol height and identification accuracy. (Adapted from the data of Crook et al., Howell and Kraft, Siebert et al., and Shurtleff and Wuersch; from D. Shurtleff, *How to Make Displays Legible,* Human Interface Design, [La Mirada, CA], 1980)

character edges. A minimum character height of 2.6 mm, or 18 minutes of arc, which ever is larger, is a good rule to follow for legibility. For some tasks, like browsing, smaller characters would suffice.

Image Quality

In spite of all the specifications and detailed characteristics, the net object of interest is image quality; unfortunately, it is elusive to measure. People can make choices concerning one display or another. But few will dispute that the best computer displays are still not as good as the typewritten page. Some key factors continuing to give the advantage to typed copy are character edge sharpness, edge smoothness, solid strokes, adequate contrast, lack of noise, lack of flicker, and lack of glare.

Several measures of overall image quality have been postulated, none of which is completely satisfactory. Good ones include MTFA (Modulation Transfer Function Area) and the psychophysical JND (Just Noticeable Difference) approach. Figure 8.13 is a MTFA plot of two CRT terminals. The visual threshold of the eye is the lower curve. The MTFA metric is the area bounded by these curves. Thus, one of the CRT terminals defines a

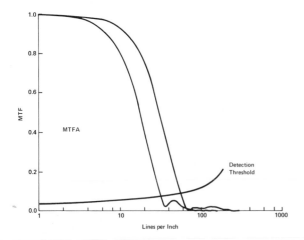

Figure 8.13. Modulation transfer function (MTF) curves for two different CRT display terminals. (Courtesy L. Jansen, IBM Corporation)

larger area and, hence, better quality than the other terminal. Figure 8.14 is a composite photograph of display screens illustrating image quality subjectively.

8.5 CATEGORIES OF DISPLAY TECHNOLOGY

Transducers

The **transducer** converts electrical signals into effects detectable by the eye. A discussion of transducer categories follows.

Passive transducers are those that do not emit light, but operate via modulation of the reflection or transmission characteristics of the display device. Paper is passive because it is reflective in nature. Also in this category are most liquid crystals, electrochromics, electrophoretics, and electromechanical displays.

Active transducers emit light. Examples of this type of display include CRT, LED, gas plasma, electroluminescent, and vacuum fluorescent. These generally require more power than do the passive displays because they generate their own light. Passive displays maintain a relatively constant contrast as ambient light varies, whereas in active displays contrast decreases as ambient light increases unless a corresponding increase in brightness is made in the emitted light.

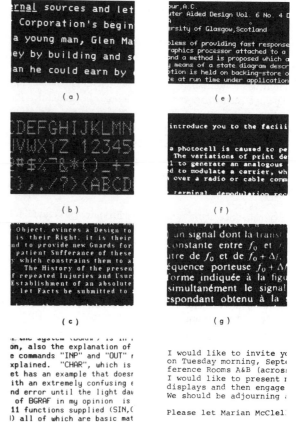

Figure 8.14. Photographs of various display screens: (a) Typical 2000 character CRT. (b) Characters on a high resolution color CRT. (c) Experimental full page CRT display. (d) Typical positive image CRT. (e) Ac gas panel with 768 × 960 addressability. (f) Scanned facsimile displayed on a CRT at 100 lpi. (g) DVST scanned facsimile with 3000 × 4000 addressability. (h) Typewritten paper for reference. The scale factor is approximately the same for all the images, (a) through (h); each image width reproduced here equals approximately 2.5 inches of actual size.

Storage transducers are those which retain the image after it is written on the display; the storage mechanism is an integral part of the transducer. Storage is important in computer displays where generally it is desirable to retain a frame of information while the operator reads, inputs, or thinks. This is in contrast to TV application where, owing to the dynamic movement of the images, storage is undesirable. Storage transducers include the DVST, ac gas plasma, and phase change liquid crystal displays. As noted previously, cathode ray, gas plasma, and liquid crystal devices can be designed with or without storage.

Addressing refers to writing the selected information on the display. In computer displays, the screen is defined as having so many addressable points, and each point is defined in turn by a unique digital code called the **address.** This address is translated into electrical signals to the transducer which activates the display.

Beam addressing is used in cathode ray tubes in which the electron beam is deflected via magnetic fields to a given point on the screen. In vector graphic displays, these points can be addressed in a random sequence. In raster addressing, the beam sequentially scans a line across the screen then indexes down one address unit and scans another line across the screen. This process continues until the entire screen has been painted; that is, the beam addresses every point on the screen whether or not information is to be written at all the points. In the raster scheme, turning the beam on and off to generate the image must be precisely timed to coincide with apriori knowledge of the beam's location. Beam addressing also applies to laser beams, which might activate a liquid crystal material, as is found in the Singer/Librascope laser display.

Matrix addressing involves a structure, or array, in which at least two elements control the write operation and an AND condition must be satisfied to write. The other three conditions of the two element system do not write (Figure 8.15). (Higher element systems are also possible.) One emboidment typical of LED and vacuum fluorescent displays is two sets of drivers. One set drives a given segment (Figure 8.16) of each character position

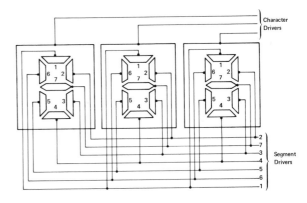

Figure 8.16. Seven segment characters with multiplexing connections illustrated.

while the other set drives an electrode for the selected character position. Thus the AND condition of a given segment and character position leads to writing, while the given segments of all other character positions are not written.

Another embodiment is $X - Y$ **matrix addressing** in which two sets of metal lines orthogonal to each other cause a selected picture element to write, as in Figure 8.17. Gas plasma technology or liquid crystals are ex-

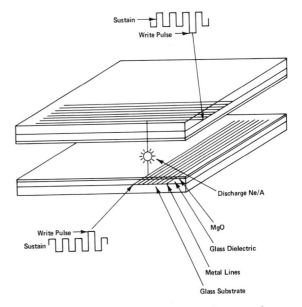

Figure 8.17. Construction of an ac gas plasma panel.

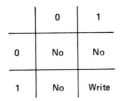

	0	1
0	No	No
1	No	Write

Figure 8.15. Matrix addressing logic table.

amples. Gas plasma has a characteristic curve (Figure 8.18) that prevents light from being emitted until breakdown is exceeded. Thus, one-half the voltage required is applied to the X line and one-half the Y line to light the point at the intersection, with all other points along those lines remaining off.

The liquid crystal curve (Figure 8.19) on the other hand, does not have a steep threshold, and the liquid crystal responds to the rms voltage. How many points may be addressed in an $X - Y$ configuration operating in a refreshed alignment mode depends upon what contrast is acceptable. Liquid crystals operating in the phase change mode (usually via the application of heat) do exhibit storage and hence an indefinite number of points can be $X - Y$ addressed. In this case, heat, which is proportional to current, is applied to one axis and voltage is applied to the other.

Still another embodiment of matrix addressing is an array of circuits in one to one correspondence to the picture elements. Thus if the circuit is on, the pel is on, and vice versa. This opens up the whole gamut of circuit addressing techniques. In high content displays, this array is operated in much the same way as a computer memory (Figure 8.20). In its simplest form, there usually is one drive circuit for every segment of a digital watch for a total of 7 segments $\times$ 4 digits, or 28 circuits. In high content displays, comprised of several hundred thousand pels, integrated circuit fabrication techniques are utilized. With this type of addressing, many transducer

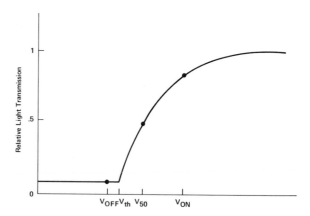

Figure 8.19. Light transmission vs. applied voltage for a standard T.N. LCD between parallel polarizers. (Based on G. Labrunie, *Proceedings of Eurodisplay '81* [Berlin: VDE-Verlag GMBH, 1981], p. 12.

technologies can be used because the AND logic is in the circuitry. Moreover, the circuit could also be given storage attributes.

Multiplexing refers to the time sequence, or duty cycle, over which addressing is done. It is the degree to which a

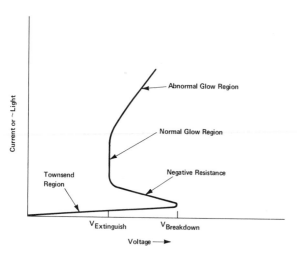

Figure 8.18. Gas plasma V-I curve. Light output is approximately proportional to current.

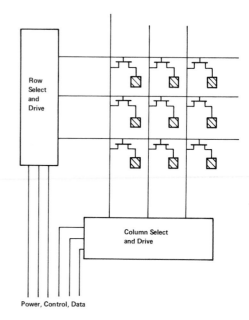

Figure 8.20. Organization of a large area array of circuits.

given resource can be time shared. In other words, how fast can a point(s) be written and then move on to the next point(s) using some of the same device components? The raster CRT is a good example of a high degree of multiplexing. A typical high content display may have 500K pels, all of which are written in $\frac{1}{30}$ second by a single beam for a dwell time per pel of 60 nanoseconds. The degree to which further multiplexing can be done is limited by brightness and bandwidth. In the gas panel, write multiplexing can be done at the pel level with a writing time at each site on the order of a microsecond. In the ac gas panel, owing to other constraints of sustain and circuit switching, writing a matrix one line at a time is practical, such that in a 720 × 400 panel, writing 400 lines may require on the order of 40 to 100 ms.

In technologies which have slow responses, such as electrochromics and liquid crystals, the dwell time required per pel is in the tens of milliseconds range. Therefore, to achieve reasonable full screen write times, one cannot employ much multiplexing (refer to Table 8.5).

The foregoing discussion refers to write times, but erase and storage also may be multiplexed operations.

Refresh operation is frequently associated with multiplexing because refresh requires continuous rewrites.

Mapping Technologies to Categories

Categorizing display devices is difficult because there are so many variations, and continuing technical announcements bring even further variations. Thus any set of categories is not all-inclusive; nevertheless, the six types of characteristics suggested in Figure 8.21 indicate how the display functions; it does not show *how well* it performs any of the functions, which will be discussed in the next section.

Any display device being considered here can be mapped against the six items with one choice per item. Examples shown in Figure 8.21 by linking lines to display characteristics are a CRT typical of most computer displays, an ac gas panel typified by the IBM device used in bank teller terminals, the thermal matrix liquid crystal display typified by a Kylex product, a developmental electrochromic display, and an electroluminescent dis-

Table 8.5. Duty Factor (Multiplex Ratios) for Various Technologies (These Are Approximate Values and Do Not Represent Firm Limits.)

Technology	Duty Factor or Multiplex Ratio	Limiting Factors
Refresh		
CRT	$>10^6$	Brightness, bandwidth
LED	≈ 200	Brightness
Vacuum fluorescent	≈ 200	Brightness
Liquid crystal TNFE	<10	Electro-optic response curve
Electroluminescence	≈ 400	Brightness
Dc scan gas panel	≈ 200	Brightness
*Storage**		
Ac memory gas panel	$\approx 10,000$	Compatibility with sustain frequency
Liquid crystal thermal matrix phase change	≈ 200	Limited by thermal decay curve and drive power
Electrochromics	<5	ELectro-optic response curve
Electrophoretics	<5	Electro-optic response curve

*Assumes write time of 1 sec for 2,000 character display. In *X–Y* matrix panels, the multiplex ratio is the number of horizontal lines across which one set of time shared vertical drivers can be used.

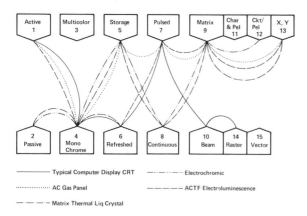

Figure 8.21. Categories of operational display modes.

play, typified by a Sharp product. Figure 8.22 illustrates the variation just within the liquid crystal transducer group.

8.6 DISPLAY TECHNOLOGIES

The primary technologies treated here are those for products which are available for sale and in use. Future variations now in development or research are mentioned only as enhancements to presently available technologies.

CRT

Basics. The cathode ray tube utilizes an electron beam striking a phosphor which in turn emits light (Figure 8.23). The beam is formed in the gun structure via

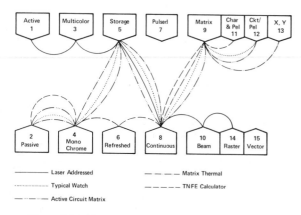

Figure 8.22. Variety of liquid crystal modes of operation.

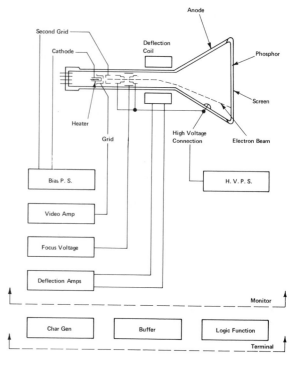

Figure 8.23. Cross-sectional view of cathode ray tube and its associated circuits.

electric potentials which form a lens, analogous to a glass lens in optics. The beam is accelerated to the faceplate by a high voltage, in the order of 20,000 V. The high velocity electrons in the beam strike the phosphor with sufficient energy to cause it to emit light of a characteristic color.

Typically, a beam current of 100 microamps would produce a luminance of about 75 cd/m^2 in a monochrome tube. Deflection of the beam to any point on the screen is usually accomplished by a deflection yoke, which is a set of orthogonal coils of wire through which current is passed to establish a magnetic field in the neck of the tube. Interaction of a moving electron with a magnetic field causes deflection of the beam.

The major types of CRTs and their categorization shown in Figure 8.21.

Type	Category Profile
Raster	1, 4, 6, 7, 10, 14
Vector	1, 4, 6, 7, 10, 15
Color	1, 3, 6, 7, 10, 14
Penetron	1, 3, 6, 7, 10, 15
DVST	1, 4, 5, 8, 10, 15

The *raster* type is by far the most popular computer display and will be discussed further in subsequent paragraphs, after the other types are summarized.

Vector CRTs are used primarily in graphics applications, where they paint vector lines directly from vector lists in the CPUs. This is convenient for light pen identification and ease of making changes in the computer data base. Vector mode is occasionally used in alphanumeric displays where stroked, rather than dot matrix, characters are preferred. Vector displays are more expensive than raster because severe demands are placed on the deflection circuits.

Color CRT terminals use the shadow mask technology, similar to that used in color TV tubes (Figure 8.8). Three beams at slightly different angles converge at the shadow mask aperature and diverge on the other side to strike their respective colored phosphor. Convergence accuracy and long term stability are unique problems to color tubes. Color tubes require larger beam sizes than monochrome for two reasons:

1. To cover enough triads, (typically beam diameter is two to three times the triad pitch) so that an equal number of phosphor dots are illuminated regardless of the beam to mask registration.
2. To provide sufficient luminance to the screen because about 80 percent of the electrons are intercepted by the shadow mask.

Thus, the maximum content of a color tube is intrinsically less than that of a monochrome tube. Higher resolution shadow masks are limited by the need for tight mechanical tolerances and an ability to dissipate a large amount of power without thermal coefficients and gradients exceeding mechanical tolerances.

Penetron CRTs are color tubes which use layered phosphors. By modulating the velocity of the electrons, this system concentrates its energy in a particular colored layer. Because it is difficult to modulate kilovolts of high voltage at rapid rates, a field color sequence is usually followed. The Penetron tube approach is limited by costly electronics and a narrow choice of colors.

Direct View Storage Tubes (DVSTs) are storage CRTs in which a charge pattern can be written on the screen with an electron beam; the screen is then illuminated via a flood gun for continued observation of the pattern. Storage times of 15 minutes or longer are possible; write times in the order of several seconds are typical. The deflection electronics usually have high addressability, for example, $3,000 \times 4,000$ points. The spot size is rectangular in cross-section. With the addressing increment on a typical 19-inch tube of about 0.1 mm, staircasing is not noticeable and the rectangular spot gives sharp edge transitions.

Typically, the screens have low contrast, in the order of 5 to 1, and operators prefer subdued room lighting. The cost for a DVST is much higher than for a raster refresh CRT. Hence, the DVST is primarily used in graphics or for high content text, where moderate or low interactivity is acceptable.

Raster Refresh CRTs are the most popular type and are characterized by operation similar to TV monitors. As the beam scans across the screen, the control grid is modulated to turn on the beam in synchronism with the deflection position to form characters or images via the use of dots or horizontal line segments.

The raster refresh CRT is very versatile in function. It can present up to 6,000 or more legible characters on a monochrome screen or it can use a color tube to present characters in color (albeit fewer in number for the same degree of legibility). The performance is excellent with write and erase times of $\frac{1}{30}$ second or faster.

Brightness, contrast, and efficiency are also good. Coupling these virtues with relatively low cost makes the raster refresh CRT difficult to replace with other technologies. The cost can be expressed at many levels, and for the purpose of clarification, some of these are listed below. The dollar numbers are not intended to be precise since they vary among suppliers and with time, but are merely orders of magnitude to illustrate the price range of progressively comprehensive levels of display function.

Cathode ray tube	$ 20	—	$	50
Monitor subassembly	$ 100	—	$	200
Monitor fully powered and interfaced to computer system	$ 200	—	$	400
With KB and ASCII communication interface	$ 500	—	$	1500
Full terminal with some local logic function	$1000	—	$	3000
Stand-alone display/computer workstation	$1000	—	$10,000

Limitations. The refreshed raster CRT, in spite of its versatility, has two primary limitations: (1) high content, and (2) unwieldly physical size.

The upper content limit, as suggested before, is around 6,000 characters. Everyone can argue that they have seen more, even up to 30,000 characters, on a 15 inch tube. The limit is set by what one considers acceptable image quality. The assumption made in this chapter is that quality is of foremost importance in computer displays. Raising content increases the video drive bandwidth to the CRT grid. The voltage drive required is in the order of 50 volts. For 6,000 9 $\times$ 16 characters; the pel times are in the order of 15 nanoseconds requiring rise and fall times in the order of 4 ns, which converts into an equivalent 3 dB bandwidth of the order of 100 MHz. This assumes a refresh frequency sufficient to avoid the perception of flicker, which for most P-39 green phosphors may be in the range of 50 Hz. For typical white phosphors, refresh should exceed 60 Hz, forcing even higher bandwidths. Because cathode ray tubes have Gaussian spots, the characters will appear to be fuzzy.

Typical beam widths (Figure 8.3) are 0.35 mm at the 60 percent point spreading to 0.6 mm at the 10 percent point, at which the beams are still visible as the edge of the fuzz. Technology can improve spot size somewhat, but if brightness is maintained, practical limits are in the range of 0.25 mm at the 10 percent point.

The physical size of cathode ray tubes has spurred considerable research in alternative flat panel technologies. The CRT itself has evolved to 110 degree deflection systems, which for a 15 inch diagonal tube still requires a depth of about 350 mm. Higher deflection angles are limited by character quality, that is, the ability of the yoke to control spot size, the effectiveness of dynamic focus, and by deflection power consumption (Figure 8.24). Figure 8.25 shows spot growth as a function of displacement for a typical 110 degree tube. The effect is to cause the character strokes to be fatter and fuzzier at the screen edges. A compromise focus is oftentimes used at the cost of degrading the center focus to improve the edge focus. In full page displays, both dynamic focus and correction for astigmatism are necessary.

Flat CRTs have been discussed in the literature for many years. Large sizes have not been of commercial significance owing to very complex structures and control systems. Small sizes, that is, below 500 characters, are being developed. Here the gun is moved to the side, thereby increasing faceprint dimensions. The control of spot size over the full active screen dimensions is difficult.

Gas Panel

Basics. If an electric potential of suitable magnitude is placed across a noble gas, ionization breakdown occurs,

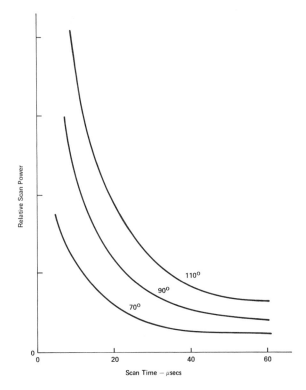

Figure 8.24. Deflection power relationship to scan time. (Courtesy L. Childress, IBM Corporation)

causing the emission of a characteristic color. The most commonly used gas is neon, which emits an orange color and which is mixed with small amounts of argon or xenon (less than 1 percent) to lower the breakdown voltages to the range of 200 to 300 V (Figure 8.17). After breakdown, a lower voltage can maintain the glow.

Types of gas panels. The major types of gas panels used as computer displays and their profile related to Figure 8.21 are as follows:

Brief Name	Category Profile
Starburst	1, 4, 6, 7, 9, 11
Self Scan[R]	1, 4, 6, 7, 9, 13
Self Scan[R] with memory	1, 4, 5, 7, 9, 13
Ac memory	1, 4, 5, 7, 9, 13

Starburst gas panels consist of a glass panel where a starburst pattern (or any other pattern) of a transparent conductor is deposited on the glass surface and a discharge is created under the selected segments; the other electrode is character block size. Multiplexing occurs on a segment and character basis. These are bright displays where the shape of the orange glow is controlled by the

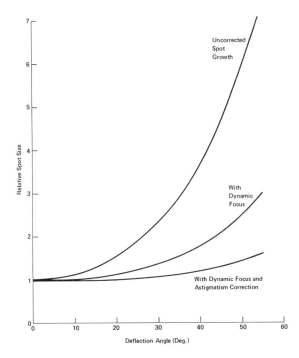

Figure 8.25. CRT spot growth versus deflection angle. The largest dimension of the spot cross-section is used as the spot deviates from circular. (Courtesy J. Hevesi, IBM Corporation)

pattern of the conductor. It is limited in character content by the brightness obtainable in refresh mode.

Self-Scan[R] (a trademark of Burroughs Corporation) is characterized by refreshed dot matrix characters formed in the structure of Figure 8.26. A three-phase signal on the scan anodes automatically drags the ionization formed at one edge across the screen in the scan cavity and along each of the horizontal matrix lines (cathodes). Another set of wires (display anodes) is used to pull the

ionized glow through the hole corresponding to a pel to be written and into the upper chamber, where it becomes visible. Thus dot matrix characters can be formed via a time sequence of the voltage on the upper electrodes using the position of the scanned glow spot. This self-scan approach minimizes driver electronics. Display is limited by brightness, however, to about 40 characters per row. Larger content is achieved by replicating a 40 character row.

Self-Scan with memory is a recent development by Burroughs which uses a similar structure as that just described, except that this new development employs a sustain voltage to keep a cell lit once it is switched on. This removes the limitations on content due to scanning.

Memory Gas Panels, invented at the University of Illinois, are the most important type of gas panel for computer displays. This technology has seen use in the Plato education system and in several hundred thousand bank teller terminals. It uses an $X - Y$ matrix of metal lines which are covered with a dielectric glass (Figure 8.17).

The gas cell at the intersection is ignited by ac coupling. As the current flows through the cell, it charges the capacitance and extinguishes the glow. The next time the opposite polarity transition occurs, the voltage of the charged capacitance aids the breakdown of the cell. Thus once a cell is lit, it continues to reignite each time an alternating transition occurs. Unlit cells do not ignite because they lack the aid of a charged capacitance.

Because the ac gas panel has memory, it is not limited in character content, as are the refreshed approaches. Since writing times, as mentioned before, in the order of 100 milliseconds per screen are practical, the content can be very high, i.e., several million pels, limited primarily by manufacturing yields. Typical write and erase waveforms are shown in Figure 8.27.

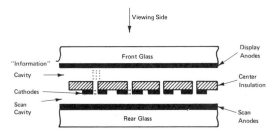

Figure 8.26. Cross sectional view of the dc Self-Scan gas plasma panel.

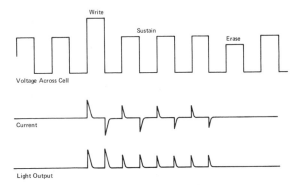

Figure 8.27. Typical waveforms for an ac gas plasma panel.

The memory gas panel solves two of the problems cited previously for the raster refreshed CRT:

1. It is flicker-free even at high content. Typically, the storage mechanism is refreshed at 20 to 40 KHz producing pulses of light at twice that frequency.
2. It has panel dimensions requiring a depth of only several inches.

In addition, this technology produces a very high contrast, of the order of 20 to 1. Such contrast is achieved by painting the surface of the rear glass plate black to absorb reflections. The high contrast and sharply defined dots produce good legibility which some observers feel may be better than that of the CRT. The technology in the bank teller product was first delivered in 1974 and to date has established an excellent reliability record with an MTBF in excess of 30,000 hours.

Limitations. The cost of memory gas panel technology versus the CRT is one of the former's primary limitations. Some of this cost differential stems from the high volume and mature technological position that the CRT enjoys owing to the TV industry. Intrinsically, however, matrix technologies cost more than beam technologies because more components are required to address the screen.

In a CRT of a nominal 288K pel content, one beam addresses all pels using only a horizontal and a vertical deflection circuit. For a corresponding $720 \times 400\ X - Y$ matrix panel, 1,120 drive circuits are required. This would not be a severe limitation if the circuits could be highly integrated; however, the gas panel requires high voltage (300 V) and relatively high current ($\approx$ 50 microamps peak per pel). Thus the gas panel's primary disadvantage is the cost of the drive circuit, not the cost of gas and glass.

The basic light producing mechanism is one of the least efficient, being in the range of 0.1 to 0.5 lumens per watt, while a CRT is more than an order of magnitude better. Nevertheless, efficiency is still within the range of practicality, with approximately 30 to 50 watts being sufficient for a large gas panel screen. Peak luminance is proportional to peak current and while the contrast is exceptionally good, large area luminance (typically 20 cd/m^2) is not. Increasing brightness only exacerbates further cirucit integration owing to the power dissipation in the drivers.

Because of the nature of the $X - Y$ addressing technique, the size of each cell glow must not spread to the next cell or it will alter its firing voltage characteristics.

Thus, each spot size must not overlap the next pel. Although in CRT displays pel overlap is desirable to improve the smoothness of character formation, it is not possible in gas plasma technology. This becomes less of a limitation as gas panel resolution increases and the resolution limit of the eye (6 mils at normal viewing distance) is approached. Resolution itself continues to be limited by the panel fabrication tolerances achievable and difficulty of maintaining desired brightness. To date, only monochrome gas panels are commercially available, although considerable research is underway on full color panels.

Electroluminescent Displays

Basics.   If an electric field is placed across zinc sulphide (ZnS) material suitably doped with impurities, a luminous output is produced. Early uses of this material were in night lights in which 60 Hz line voltage caused a layer of ZnS powder to glow. More recent interest has centered in thin film devices. Figure 8.28 shows basic lu-

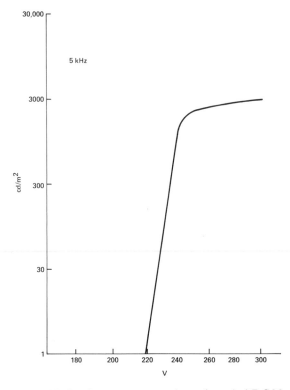

Figure 8.28. Luminance output vs. voltage of a typical ZnS:Mn electroluminescence device. (Based on W. Howard, *Proceedings of the SID,* Vol. 22/1, 1981.)

minance versus voltage for a typical ac driven thin film device. Historically, the problem with these devices has been reliability. How light is produced is not well understood, but is known to be dependent on impurity interactions. Manganese is the most popular activator for thin films and produces a pleasing yellow light.

Types. The most important type commercially available (from Sharp Corporation) is the ac thin film electroluminescent panel. This has a profile in Figure 8.21 of 1, 4, 6, 7, 9, 13. It is a refreshed $X - Y$ addressed panel. Other types include dc EL powders, which are short lived and ac powders. Research is continuing on ac thin film EL with memory, but controlling this pnehomenon well enough to make a product has been elusive.

AC Thin Film ELs are driven by ac voltage, typically in the range of 200 to 300 V, through a capacitor formed by the dielectric layer over the zinc sulphide. (The structure is given in Figure 8.29.) The $X - Y$ matrix drive lines can select a given intersection point by addition of select half voltages. Operation is analogous to that of the ac gas panel.

The efficiency of light production is good (in the range of 3 to 5 lumens per watt) and peak luminances over 4000 cd/m^2 are typical. Characters are formed from dot matrix patterns. One of the present Sharp products is a panel of 128 $\times$ 512 matrix lines refreshed at 70 Hz. The maximum content of EL in the refresh mode can be larger than a refreshed gas panel because EL has greater light output. Contrast is excellent because the back plate can be painted black. EL also has desirable panel dimensions, with packaged depths of 25 to 50 mm being practical.

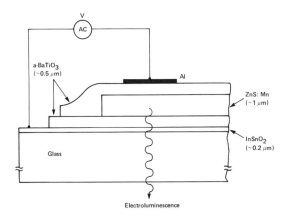

Figure 8.29. Cross-sectional view of the ac thin film EL device.

Limitations. The EL's content is limited owing to refresh/brightness constraints. As the number of pels and peak brightness increases, current also increases and exceeds the limits of the transparent conductors. A 720 $\times$ 400 refreshed matrix is close to the upper limit for content. While it can display more characters than the refreshed gas panel, it cannot show as many as the CRT or ac memory gas panel. As the memory phenomena is brought under control, though, content can increase. EL is a high voltage matrix technology and the cost handicap for the gas panel holds for EL as well. EL technology, while more efficient in producing light than gas panel technology, possesses a higher cell capacitance which adds to its power dissipation.

Liquid Crystal

Basics. Liquid crystals change their reflective or transmissive characteristics via the application of an electric field or heat. The basic contrast curve is shown in Figure 8.19. Liquid crystals operate at relatively low voltages and currents. Molecular alignment, typical of the **twisted nematic field effect** (**TNFE**) mode, requires the use of polarizers. Phase change LCs require greater power and depend on a transition from the isotropic to a liquid crystal phase, freezing in a random disorientation causing scattered incident light. Each of these modes may be combined with suitable dye molecules to impart a characteristic color or to enhance contrast.

Types. The primary types of liquid crystal displays using the same charting method is shown in Figure 8.22:

Brief Name	Category Profile
Watch segment alignment mode	2, 4, 5, 8, 9, 12
Matrix alignment mode	2, 4, 6, 8, 9, 11
Laser thermal	1, 3, 5, 8, 10, 14
Matrix thermal	2, 4, 5, 8, 9, 13
Circuit memory matrix	2, 4, 5, 8, 9, 12

Matrix Alignment This type is a multiplexed drive typically found in hand calculator displays. Owing to the lack of a steep threshold characteristic, only 3 to 10 lines are multiplexed and character content is usually less than 10. Steeper threshold materials are being developed leading to 16, 32, and 64 level multiplexing and higher content. However, because of limitations of contrast, narrow viewing angle, and circuit complexity, matrix alignment displays are not well suited for use at the popular 2000 character computer display design point.

Laser Thermal. At the other end of the spectrum, the laser thermal approach uses the rapid freezing of disoriented molecules to provide self-storage and display very high content images. Each pel of a homogenous LC panel is selectively elevated in temperature into the isotropic state and then cooled rapidly, freezing in the disorientation. The LC panel is small, on the order of several inches, and projection is needed to magnify the image to appropriate size. The spot sizes may be in the order of 12 microns. Such a high content display could show several pages of text, complex graphics, or color via optical superposition. The laser and deflection system are costly. Thus, this display will only appear at the very high end of the market, in limited numbers.

Thermal Matrix, or thermally addressed matrix liquid crystals, are a variation of the laser liquid crystal approach, with heat applied via a resistive matrix wire instead of a laser. This technique, combined with an appropriate voltage on the orthogonal matrix wire, causes the phase change at the intersection either to be preserved or not preserved. Such phase changes may also be accomplished with voltage only, in certain LC mixtures.

The thermal matrix panel typified by the Kylex or Thompson CSF models is a storage panel and hence can have high content limited only by fabrication tolerances, speed, and power. The heat required is in the order of 0.2 joules per cm^2 of screen surface. The tradeoff is power versus writing time. Practical values are 0.3 milliwatt per pel and 7 microseconds dwell time per pel. For a 2,000 character panel, the full screen write time may be in the order of two seconds. The panel has good visual characteristics offering a black and white image with a contrast as high as 10:1. Panel depths of 25 mm are typical.

Limitations. The thermal matrix requires high writing power, on the order of 80 watts if scaled to a 720×400 size with a 2 second full screen write. High peak currents at modest voltage are used. Average power consumption is low if one considers a computer application requiring reading and thinking between entries of new pages. However, for browsing, page flipping, scrolling, and high interactivity, average power use could be excessive. The tradeoff to lower power requires longer write times. Thus, this technology must be used in applications for which it matches the requirements; it is not universally applicable in computer display application.

Circuit arrays are typified by the Seiko and Panelvision liquid crystal displays, which are fabricated on circuit chips or substrates. The display consists of a circuit per picture element directly under the pel, where addressing is performed at the circuit array level. The liquid crystal material merely "sees" a potential across itself, from a circuit pad to a large-area transparent conductive layer on the viewer's side. The LC operates on an alignment principle rather than on phase change, and requires very low power and low voltages, which are compatible with large scale integrated circuits. It has a circuit per picture element, and is capable of good contrast, good viewing angle, and fast write and erase.

Limitations. The major limitations of the circuit per pel approach are the difficulties of achieving good circuit yield and a screen big enough to read. Considering the 720×400 pel array again for comparison, the underlying semiconductor must contain 288,000 circuits, with each circuit composed of several devices. This is stretching the semiconductor art, which presently is producing 64K bit memory chips. Nevertheless, 288,000 circuits per chip will come in time. The other problem, size, is being solved in current research models by the use of projection optics. However, to avoid the size constraints of optics, it would be desirable to build a page size array of circuits for direct viewing. Research on this is underway using thin film transistor technology.

When a page size is achieved, the ultimate in computer display attributes could result: convenient size, light weight, portability, low power, high resolution, high content, potential for color, good contrast, storage, and fast write. In net, it is the technology that may come as close as any to approaching the attributes of the printed page, yet with the desirable write and erase display characteristics.

Light Emitting Diodes (LEDs)

LEDs are semiconductor devices that produce light when current is applied. They are low voltage diodes which usually are red in color, but can be green or yellow, depending on the material used. They are available as single pels, seven segment numerics, 5×7 character matrices, or occasionally in larger matrices. In the context of computer displays, LEDs are of little interest because they provide limited content owing to the high power required. While the power in an 8 digit hand calculator is low, the power for a 720×400 array typical of computer applications would be over 100 watts and prohibitive because the power is dissipated at the screen. The semiconductor material, gallium arsenide, is expensive and does not lend itself to large scale integration.

Vacuum Fluorescent

This device is an array of low voltage cathode ray tubes fabricated in panel dimensions (Figure 8.30). In seven segment form, it is multiplexed via segment and character blocks by application of voltage to the grid and anode. In 5 × 7 dot matrix form, a similar technique is used. The largest size currently available is 480 5 × 7 characters. The display is refreshed, bright, and can be highly multiplexed. Because it requires a complex internal structure, it is not likely to become a high resolution, high content, computer display.

Other Technologies

The following technologies have not yet emerged as products and are mentioned only because of their potential interest to computer displays.

Electrochromics change color upon the application of a potential. They are low voltage, low power devices, are slow, and do not have a desirable matrix addressing threshold. Most likely they will appear with circuit per

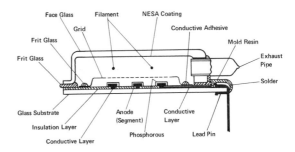

Figure 8.30. Cross-sectional view of the vacuum fluorescent display. (From K. Kasano and T. Nakamura, *Proceedings of Eurodisplay '81* [Berlin: VDE-Verlag GmbH, 1981], p. 159)

pel addressing, and because ECs are self-storing, they can use a simpler circuit than would be required in the circuit per pel liquid crystal.

Electrophoretics are based upon the movement of a suspended colloidal pigment through a liquid under the influence of an electric field. They have similar characteristics to ECs, i.e., they are slow, self-storing, and lack a threshold.

Table 8.6. Comparison of Leading Technologies for a 2,000 Character High Quality Direct View Display

	Raster Refresh CRT	Ac Memory Gas Panel	Refreshed Electro-Luminescence	Thermal Matrix Liquid Crystal	Circuit per Pel Liquid Crystal
Active display screen area (in.)	10.8 × 6	10.8 × 6	10.8 × 6	10.8 × 6	10.8 × 6*
Addressable pels	720 × 400	720 × 400	720 × 400	720 × 400	720 × 400
Pel pitch hor	15 mil	15 mil	15 mil	15 mil	15 mil
vert	15 mil	15 mil	15 mil	15 mil	15 mil
Spot size at 60% of maximum contrast luminance	15 mil	7 mil	10	15 mil	15 mil
Liminance—large area average, all pels on	200 cd/m²	40 cd/m²	40 cd/m²	—	—
Best contrast ratio at 500 lux ambient	12:1	20:1	20:1	10:1	10:1
Write time	16 ms	40 ms	16 ms	2000 ms	40 ms
Erase time	16 ms	0.04 ms	1 ms	Performed during write	40 ms
Power consumption for monitor function (watts)					
1 screen every 2 sec.	35 W	45 W	35 W	80 W	3 W
1 screen per min	35 W	45 W	35 W	3 W	3 W

*Not yet realizable.

(Table based on work by G. Reible, P. Alt, and A. Onton, IBM Corporation)

8.7 COMPARISON OF TECHNOLOGIES

Throughout this chapter many comparisons have been drawn which should help in choosing technologies, new design features, and new products. Because the CRT dominates computer display products and the 1,920 character (or 2,000 character) content is the most popular format, this system is the basis against which other display technologies should be compared.

Table 8.6 compares some of the technologies which are or will be significant in computer displays. A direct view display of 2,000 characters is assumed, with a 720×400 array of addressable points for a total of 288,000 pels. Some of the entries are estimates extrapolated from existing data because actual models of the given size have not been built.

REFERENCES

Bieberman, L. M., *Perception of Displayed Information*. New York: Plenum, 1973.

Cakir, A., D. J. Hart and T. F. M. Stewart, *The VDT Manual*. Darmstadt: IFRA (Inca-Fiej Research Assn.), 1979.

Criscimagna, T. N., and P. Pleshko "AC Plasma Displays," Ch. 3, in J. I. Pankove, ed., *Topics in Applied Physics, Display Devices*. New York: Springer-Verlag, 1980.

Delange, H., "Relationship Between Critical Flicker Frequency and a Set of Low Frequency Characteristics of the Eye," *Journal of the Optical Society of America.*, Vol. 44, pp. 380–89 (1954).

Farrell, R. J., J. M. Booth, *Design Handbook for Imagery Interpretation Equipment*. Seattle: Boeing Aerospace Co., 1975.

Howard, W. E., "Electroluminescent Display Technologies and Their Characteristics," *Proceedings of SID*, Vol. 22, No. 1, pp. 47–55 (1981).

Information Display, May 1981, Jan. 1982.

Kasahara, K., T. Yanagisawa, K. Sakai, T. Adachi, K. Inoue, T. Tsutsumi, and H. Hori, "A Liquid Crystal Display Panel Using an MOS Array with Gate-Bus Drivers," *Proceedings of SID*, Vol. 22, No. 4, p. 318 (1981).

Labrunie, G., *Proceedings of First SID European Display Research Conference*, Sept. 1981

Miller, D., J. Ogle, R. Cola, B. Caras, and T. Maloney, "An Improved Performance Self-Scan® I Panel Design," *Proceedings of SID*, Vol. 22, No. 3, p. 159 (1981).

Pleshko, P., G. W. Smith, D. R. Thompson, N. Vecchiarelli, "The Characteristics and Performance of an Experimental AC Plasma 960 × 768 Line Panel and Electronics Assembly," *International Electron Device Meeting of IEEE*, Dec. 1981, p. 229.

Raster Graphics Handbook Covina, CA: Conrac Corp., 1980.

Sherr, S., *Electronic Displays*. New York: John Wiley and Sons, 1979.

Snyder, H. L., and M. E. Maddox, "On the Image Quality of Dot Matrix Displays," *Proceedings of SID*, Vol. 21, No. 1, 1980.

Uede, H., Y. Kanatani, H. Kishishita, A. Fujimori, and K. Okano, "Thin Film Electroluminescent Display Units," *SID Symposium Digest*, Vol. 12, (1981) p. 28.

9
Modems

Christopher Terry

Microsystems

9.1 INTRODUCTION

Computers can communicate with each other over any distance using serial transmission techniques. Character codes are transmitted bit by bit to the remote station, where the bit stream is reassembled into complete characters in parallel format. When the distance is very short (a few tens of feet), the communication link may consist merely of a two-conductor cable directly connected to the serial interfacing circuitry of each computer. This type of connection is common in small business systems in which each workstation is a complete microcomputer equipped with keyboard, display, main memory, and sometimes minifloppy disk drives for limited secondary storage. A central minicomputer, connected to all the workstations, handles requests for shared resources, such as printers and hard disk storage, which contain data bases beyond the capacity of the local minifloppies. For communication over longer distances, the transmission media might include overland microwave radio links or links via orbiting satellites; or even long distance fiber optics (see Chapter 37).

The first link in any such chain is a telephone line, and it is the connection of a computer or terminal to a telephone line that is the function of a **modem** (MODulator-DEModulator). The modem translates the dc digital bit stream generated by computers into audio signals that conform to the restrictions of frequency and amplitude imposed by the telephone company's equipment. This equipment includes **repeaters** (audio amplifiers) in the lines every few miles to maintain signal strength. In addition, lines pass through switching equipment.

When connection of computer equipment to telephone lines first became commonplace, the Electronic Industries Association (EIA) developed a standard interface between computers and modems (which at that time were supplied solely by the telephone companies). This standard was designated RS-232, and the last revision ($-$C) is still in widespread use although it has been superseded by a new standard, RS-449. Conformance to an industry-wide standard has become all the more vital since telephone companies no longer have a monopoly on the manufacture and installation of modems.

The RS-232 and RS-449 standards specify the number and types of signal and control lines running between the computer and the modem, their electrical characteristics, connector types, and the pin numbers to which the lines are to be connected; interfacing a modem to a computer is discussed later in more detail. For the moment, it is enough to say that the EIA interface converts unipolar digital signals used within the computer (nominally 0 and $+5$ V) to bipolar signals in the range $+3$ to $+18$ V (control lines ON, data lines in the logic 0 state) and -3 to -18 V (control lines OFF, data lines in the logic 1 state). These voltages allow the use of a variety of techniques in guarding against electrical noise that could corrupt the data being transmitted.

9.2 DEFINITION OF TERMS

Half-Duplex, Full Duplex, and Echoplex Modes

Half Duplex. Although computer hardware and software treat the keyboard and the display of a terminal as two separate and independent devices, some terminals (such as those using the IBM I/O Selectric typewriter as the display) have a built-in mechanical or electrical connection between the keyboard and the printer. When a key is struck, the character is printed, regardless of whether it is sent to the computer.

A terminal of this kind, using a two wire data link, can send to the computer or receive from it, but cannot do both at the same time. The interface at each end switches the line between the transmit circuits and the receive circuits (Figure 9.1). Switching is governed by a **line protocol.** The half duplex mode must be used whenever any equipment item in the communications link is incapable of passing data in both directions simultaneously. It is also sometimes employed when these restrictions do not prevail.

Full Duplex. This mode is used primarily for communication between two computers when the data being transferred need not be displayed immediately. The protocol usually calls for the receiving computer to acknowledge each error-free block. The ability to do this, without switching the line equipment from receive to transmit and vice versa, can appreciably reduce transmission time for large messages.

Echoplex is more often used between a terminal and a computer. In dumb terminals, the keyboard and display device are independent. As a key is struck, the corresponding code is sent to the computer, but not to the display. Instead, the computer echoes to the terminal each character it receives. Hence, the operator knows not only

what is typed, but also what the computer receives. Echoplex does not compromise the ability to send in both directions simultaneously. For example, when the computer is sending text to the terminal, the operator can abort the operation by pressing the BREAK key or sending a control character. This signal is transmitted to the computer and is acted on, but not echoed.

9.3 SYNCHRONOUS AND ASYNCHRONOUS TRANSMISSION

At speeds up to 9600 bps (direct connection), or 1200 bps (over a telephone line), each character is usually sent as a separate entity and consists of

1. A start bit (SPACE signal, equivalent to logic 0, for one bit time).
2. Seven data bits (least significant first).
3. A parity check bit.
4. One stop bit for 300–1200 bps, or two stop bits below 300 bps. Each stop bit consists of a MARK signal (equivalent to logic 1) for one bit time.

During an IDLE condition, in which no characters are sent, a continuous MARK signal is transmitted. Because each character contains a built-in indication of the start and end of the character, the interval between any pair of characters may vary considerably. This is the case when the sending device is a manually operated keyboard. Transmissions of this kind, in which the individual bits of a character are strictly timed (synchronized), but there is variable time between characters, are termed synchronous by bit, asynchronous by character, or simply ASYNCHRONOUS.

When large quantities of data are regularly transmitted, a higher transmission rate reduces connect time charges. Connect time is saved and more stringent error detection and correction methods are available when blocks of 256 or more characters are transmitted in SYNCHRONOUS mode. No start or stop bits are transmitted. In the idle condition, the transmitter sends a continuous series of SYNC characters. When initially establishing the link, and after each block, or when multiple errors make it evident that synchronization has been lost, the receiving logic searches the bit stream for this unique SYNC bit pattern.

When two successive SYNC characters have been found, the receiver logic resets the receiver clock and bit counter to match the state at the transmitting end. Thereafter, even though there may be minor differences be-

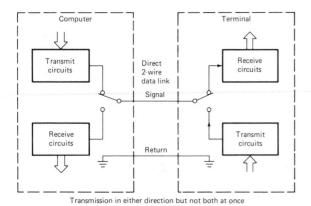

Transmission in either direction but not both at once

Figure 9.1. Local connection, half duplex mode (From *Microcomputer Systems* by Ivan Flores and Christopher Terry. Copyright © 1982 by Van Nostrand Reinhold Company Inc. Reprinted by permission of the Publisher.)

tween the clocks at each end, the start and end of each 8 bit character is positively identified by the state of a modulo 8 counter, without the need for start and stop bits. This reduces the number of bits transmitted for a given message by about twenty percent.

Transmission Rate

In telecommunications, the unit of transmission speed is the **baud.** This unit refers to the number of state changes per second that the link will support, and is referred to the shortest signal element in the code. Thus, on a Morse code telegraphy circuit, where the dash is three times the length of the dot, a transmission rate of 900 baud would allow 900 dots or 300 dashes to be sent in one second. In digital transmissions, the bit is the only signal element and has a fixed length.

As long as there is a one to one correspondence between bits and state changes, the terms *baud* and *bits per second (bps)* are interchangeable. This is generally true for transmission speeds up to 600 bits per second. However, to send data at higher bit rates, while remaining within bandwidth and other restrictions imposed by the telephone equipment, may require encoding methods in which this correspondence no longer holds. Modem transmission speed is, for reasons of tradition rather than accuracy, specified in baud. Thus, a 4800 baud modem is capable of sending or receiving 4800 bits per second, although the real baud rate (meaning changes of state on the line) may be four or even eight times less because each state change represents not one, but four or eight bits.

9.4 MODEM PRINCIPLES

FSK Encoding

Digital data transmission over the public telephone network must meet two restrictions:

1. Only two conductors are provided.
2. Bipolar dc signals are prohibited.

To comply with the latter restriction, a modem changes the bipolar digital bit stream into audio signals within the telephone passband.

A modem might turn on a single tone to indicate a logic 1 and turn the tone off to indicate a logic 0. However, telephone lines are vulnerable to noise from such sources as motors, welding, radiotherapy equipment, power

transmission lines, and other telephone lines running in the same conduit. This one tone scheme is error prone during the off (or 0) operation.

Instead, two tones are used. The frequencies chosen are just far enough apart to allow sharp filters to separate them at the receiving end without difficulty. They are close enough to each other that many pairs of tones can be transmitted over the same pair of wires without mutual interference. In any pair of tones, the upper frequency is the **Mark** frequency, in telecommunications jargon, and indicates a logic 1; the lower frequency is the **Space** frequency and indicates a logic 0. This is shown in Figure 9.2, where the higher tone appears as more waves per unit horizontal length. This method, called **frequency shift keying** (FSK), is used by modems operating at rates up to 1200 bps.

Most low speed modems used on time sharing systems or with microcomputers normally operate at 300 bps in full duplex mode; they also can be switched to half duplex operation. For full duplex operation using only two wires, four different tones are required. One pair is assigned to the "sender" who is in **originate** mode; the other pair is for the "receiver," who is in **answer** mode. However, once the mode of each participant is established, each may send or receive when his or her turn arrives, as we now discuss.

Answer/Originate Modes

For 300-bps transmission, the two MARK/SPACE frequency pairs are standard throughout the U.S. One modem operates in originate mode, transmitting 1270 Hz for mark and 1070 Hz for space, and receiving 2225 Hz for mark and 2025 Hz for space. The other modem operates in answer mode, transmitting 2225 and 2025 Hz and receiving 1270 and 1070 Hz.

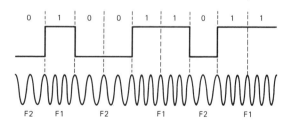

Figure 9.2. Bit stream converted to two frequencies in frequency shift keying (FSK). (From *Microcomputer Systems* by Ivan Flores and Christopher Terry. Copyright © 1982 by Van Nostrand Reinhold Company Inc. Reprinted by permission of the Publisher.)

Modems designed specifically for use with remote terminals (including most acoustic couplers) operate only in originate mode. Some modems, designed for use only at the computer end, operate in answer mode only. Other modems can be switched to either originate or answer mode. When there is a computer at both ends of the link, the master station uses originate mode and may operate automatic dialing equipment to establish communication with a satellite station which is switched to the answer mode.

A modem is specified as *originate only, answer only,* or *originate/answer,* depending upon the frequencies it uses for transmission and reception. However, an answer modem for use with a computer has features not included in originate modems. One of these is the ability to detect a 17-Hz telephone ringing signal and generate an associated digital output signal. Other options also may be available.

Restrictions on FSK Data Rates

The frequency spectrum of telephone links is shown in Figure 9.3, with the two bands used at 300 bps for originate and answer tones. Data transmission at 1200 bps requires a greater bandwidth. To obtain satisfactory separation, the MARK frequency is 2200 Hz and the SPACE frequency is 1200 Hz. Because there is considerable attenuation of frequencies lower than 1000 Hz, and because the region above 2400 Hz is reserved for signalling tones, a second pair of tones cannot be accomodated. Thus, on a two-wire circuit, such as a dial-up line, 1200 bps FSK transmissions are restricted to half-duplex operation.

With leased lines, full-duplex operation becomes possible through the use of a second line to form a 4-wire circuit. Some 1200 bps modems (such as the Bell 202 Series) work only in half duplex mode, and contain within them send/receive switching. This series is somewhat outdated, however, and newer modems (such as the Bell 212 series) use encoding methods that allow full duplex operation over a two wire circuit. Care must be taken in choosing a 1200 baud modem; the encoding method used by Racal-Vadic and other manufacturers is not compatible with that of the Bell 212.

Encoding Methods for Higher Transmission Speeds

As with magnetic tape or disk recording, one way to increase the data density while remaining within the restrictions imposed by the medium is to use more efficient coding methods. Then a signalling element no longer conveys exactly one bit; each element conveys more. Three such coding methods are **amplitude modulation (AM)**, **phase modulation (PM)**, or **quadrature amplitude modulation (QAM)**. Sometimes two of these methods are combined for improved efficiency.

AM represents the possible values of a bit pattern by transmitting a fixed frequency carrier tone at any one of several different amplitude levels, each of which represents a different bit pattern. This method is seldom used by itself since variation in line characteristics cause difficulties in establishing a stable reference level. More often, a few widely different amplitude levels are used in conjunction with PM to increase the number of firmly identifiable line states.

PM represents the four possible values of a 2 bit pattern (**DIBIT**) by transmitting a fixed frequency, fixed am-

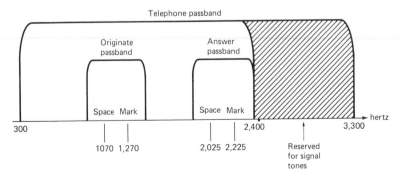

Figure 9.3. Frequency spectrum for 300 bps operation. (From *Microcomputer Systems* by Ivan Flores and Christopher Terry. Copyright © 1982 by Van Nostrand Reinhold Company Inc. Reprinted by permission of the Publisher.)

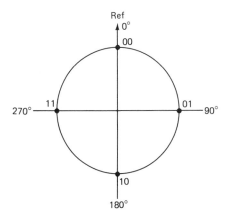

Figure 9.4. Phase modulation giving four 2 bit patterns (one for each 90 degrees of phase shift). The references are the current state, not any fixed phase angle.

plitude carrier tone and shifting its phase angle by 90, 180, or 270 degrees with respect to a reference (Figure 9.4). Each phase angle represents one 2 bit pattern. A data rate of 2400 bps requires transmission of only 1200 phase angles per second. Thus, a two wire circuit can use full duplex mode at 1200 bps (600 baud) or half duplex mode at 2400 bps (1200 baud) within the bandwidth restrictions.

QAM transmits a continuous sine wave and a continuous cosine wave of the same frequency. The amplitude of each wave can be varied in discrete steps that represent multiples of its idle state amplitude. If each wave has two amplitude values (apart from the idle value), their combined states can represent 4 bit patterns. If each wave has five amplitude values of states, it can represent 16 bit patterns, as shown in Figure 9.5. In this case, a simultaneous change of sine amplitude from 0.25 to 4 and of cosine amplitude from 4 to 0.25 might represent a change from binary 1000 to binary 1100, but is still only one signal element. If more than four amplitude steps can be distinguished, 5 bit or 6 bit digital numbers can be conveyed by the relative amplitudes of the sine and cosine waves.

There is no standard for carrier frequencies or for the manner in which bit patterns are assigned to relative amplitudes. But all the modems on a network must use the same system and frequencies, and the computers must follow the same protocol. The pattern shown in Figure 9.5 represents the European CCITT standard V.29 for 9600 bps transmissions, and is compatible neither with AT&T's series 209 modem, nor with Racal-Vadic modems.

Timing Considerations

A low speed interface (bit rates up to 1200 bps) accepts serial data clocked locally into a *deserializer,* which converts a serial bit stream to parallel bytes. Synchronism is derived from the computer master clock, or from a separate crystal controlled oscillator. Because the clock rate is usually 16 times the data bit rate, and incoming bits are sampled at the 8th count of a modulo-16 counter driven by the clock (i.e., at the nominal midpoint of the bit time), some variation between the send and receive clocks is permissible (Figure 9.6). Although errors are cumulative, resynchronization takes place at the start of each character; thus a discrepancy in clock rates of up to 2 percent still allows 10 consecutive bits to be sampled accurately.

At 2400 to 9600 bps, however, the margin for error is small, and synchronous transmissions may consist of 256 or more bytes (2,048 bits) between resynchronizing points. Evidently, independent clocks at the sending and receiving ends would not be satisfactory. Instead, high speed modems transmit clock pulses down the line with the data.

At the transmitting end, clock pulses generated in the modem are passed to the interface circuitry on a separate conductor. They shift data out of the serializer; the modem also combines them with the data. The analog signal placed on the telephone line is a composite of data and clock signals.

At the receiving end, clock pulses recovered by the modem from the analog signal are passed on a separate line to the interface circuitry. They time the shifting of

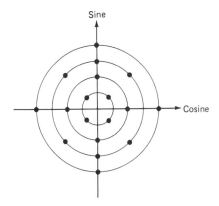

Figure 9.5. Quadrature amplitude modulation (QAM), each combination of phase angle and amplitude representing one out of sixteen 4 bit patterns (0000 through 1111).

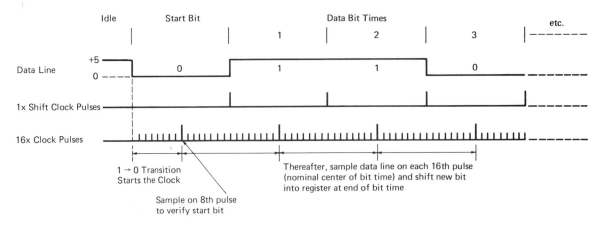

Figure 9.6. Asynchronous transmission showing data line, sampling clock pulses, and shift clock pulses (derived from sampling clock).

data bits into the deserializer. Thus, the same clock is used at both ends of the link. The expense of including in the modem an accurate clock generator and its combining circuits is offset by the ability to maintain synchronism at high transmission rates and by the elimination of the need for the interface circuitry at each end to include a precise (and therefore expensive) clock generator.

9.5 TYPES OF TELECOMMUNICATION EQUIPMENT

Data Access Arrangements

Until recently, it was necessary to use a **data access arrangement** (DAA), supplied by the telephone company, for connecting the modem analog circuits to the telephone line (Figure 9.7). The DAA consists of an isolating transformer and surge limiters to isolate the modem from the line. The DAA passes only audio signals between 300 and 3000 Hz, and limits the amplitude of the outgoing audio. This protects the telephone equipment from any surges that might be generated by a malfunction of the modem or computer. It likewise protects the modem and computer equipment against the 40 V dc always present on the telephone line, surges induced on the telephone line, and overload or damage from the 17 Hz ringing signal (which can sometimes reach 60–100 V).

It is illegal to connect a modem directly to the telephone line. The connection must be made either through a DAA supplied by the telephone company, or through an equivalent device of FCC-approved type supplied by the modem manufacturer. Modems supplied for use with

microcomputers nowadays include an FCC-approved coupler to which the telephone line may be directly connected.

Acoustic Couplers

The acoustic coupler indirectly couples the modem to the line. As shown in Figure 9.8, it consists of a microphone and speaker equipped with rubber cups and mounted at an angle to the upper surface of the coupler casing. The handset of a standard telephone is placed into the coupler so that the earpiece is over the coupler microphone, and the microphone over the speaker. The rubber cups hold it in place and exclude room noise. The acoustic coupler deals only with sound, and hence provides complete electrical isolation.

At transmission rates up to 450 bps, FSK modulation, the acoustic coupler works well. It obviates the expense of DAA installation and the need for a special switch on the telephone to silence it during data transmission. There is no compatibility problem at 300 bps or less; all modems with built-in or external acoustic couplers for rates up to 300 bps are completely compatible with the Bell Series 103 modems and with each other. A few 103-compatible couplers operate up to 450 bps.

If an acoustic coupler is used at 1200 bps, the modem at the computer should be compatible. Some commercial 1200 bps modems have a built-in acoustic coupler or can be used with an external one. Not all of these modems, however, are compatible with Bell modems in the 212 series, and 1200 bps modems of different makes are not necessarily compatible with each other.

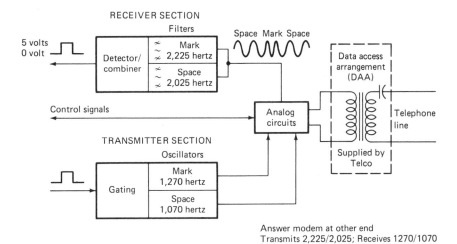

RECEIVER SECTION
Filters
Space Mark Space

5 volts
0 volt

Detector/combiner

~ Mark
~ 2,225 hertz
~ Space
~ 2,025 hertz

Data access arrangement (DAA)

Control signals

Analog circuits

Telephone line

TRANSMITTER SECTION
Oscillators

Gating

Mark
1,270 hertz
Space
1,070 hertz

Supplied by Telco

Answer modem at other end
Transmits 2,225/2,025; Receives 1270/1070

Figure 9.7. Block diagram of modem and DAA. (From *Microcomputer Systems* by Ivan Flores and Christopher Terry. Copyright © 1982 by Van Nostrand Reinhold Company Inc. Reprinted by permission of the Publisher.)

Figure 9.8. Typical accoustic coupler (modem by Anderson Jacobson). (From *Microcomputer Systems* by Ivan Flores and Christopher Terry. Copyright © 1982 by Van Nostrand Reinhold Company Inc. Reprinted by permission of the Publisher.)

Multispeed Modems

The speed range of most modems is quite limited. Many are designed to operate extremely efficiently at one transmission speed only. Others, especially high speed modems, may have only two or three switch-selected rates (e.g., 1800, 2400, or 4800 bps). Until the introduction of the Bell 212 series, it was impossible to find a combination of 103A-compatibility (100–600 bps) with a higher speed. The Bell 212 modems, however, operate in either a low speed mode (300 bps only) or a high speed mode (1200 bps).

Other manufacturers have since marketed similar dual or even triple modems, some following the Bell conventions and others the Racal-Vadic conventions. Dual mode acoustic couplers also are available now.

Programmable Modems

All of the modems so far discussed have been external modems using an EIA interface between the computer and the modem. Software can manipulate the control and status lines for establishing connection, dialing, detecting loss of carrier, and automatic answering of incoming calls. Transmission rate, however, is fixed or manually selected by a switch.

The growth of small business systems and microprocessor based personal computers has stimulated development of a new breed of modems that is completely software controllable and does not require a full set of EIA control and status lines. Hayes Microcomputer Products' Smartmodem (Figure 9.9) is the first of these. Furthermore, where 1200 bps modems and acoustic couplers formerly ranged in price from $850 to $1,250 or more, the Smartmodem is priced at $695. It requires only a three conductor data connection (at EIA signal levels) to the computer. All of its functions are initiated by special sequences of ASCII characters, and it returns a single ASCII character as a completion code indicating success of the requested operation or the nature of the failure. This considerably eases the problem of providing telecommunication facilities for a personal computer lacking a full set of EIA control/status drivers and receivers. A comparison of some modems is provided in Table 9.1.

Multiplexers

When user terminals are grouped within a short distance of each other at a site relatively remote from the host computer, it may not be economically desirable to provide a separate cable, with a modem at each end, for each terminal. In such cases, it is more usual to install a multiplexer that is centrally located with regard to the terminals, and another at the host computer.

The multiplexer at the terminal site provides hardwired communication links to the terminals with a transmission speed of 300 to 1200 bps, and combines these into a single bit stream that is sent to the host site over a single 9600 bps link. The multiplexer at the host site then sep-

Figure 9.9. An example of a smart modem. (Courtesy Hayes Microcomputer Products, Inc.)

Table 9.1 A Comparison of Some Modems

Mfr	Model	Modulation	Data Rate (bps)	Timing	Bell Compatibility	Duplex Modes	Comments
Novation	4202	FSK	1200	Async	202	Half or Full	Optional auto-dial, auto-answer
	Cat	FSK	0–300	Async	103	Half or Full	Originate/answer
Hayes	Smartmodem	FSK	300	Async	103	Full	Auto-dial auto-answer, programmable
	Smartmodem 1200	FSK	300, 1200	Async	212A	Full	Auto-dial, auto-answer programmable
Intertel	M2400	DPSK	2400	Sync	201	Full	Originate/answer
Gandalf	RM3309	—	1800–18.2K	Sync	309	Half or Full	Private lines only
Anderson-Jacobson		FSK	0–450	Async	103	Half or Full	Acoustic coupled
		FSK	0–300, 1200	Async	103 (300), none (1200)	Half or Full	Acoustic coupled
Potomac Micro-Magic	M-103	FSK	0–600	Async	103	Half or Full	Fully programmable, auto-answer, auto-dial, plugs into S-100 bus

arates the high speed bit stream into lower speed bit streams (one for each terminal) that enter the computer via appropriate I/O ports. Multiplexers come in various sizes, from small units (by Codex and Timeplex, among others) capable of handling from 8 to 16 terminals, up to large front end computers capable of handling one hundred or more simultaneous users.

Multiplexers may use either frequency division or time division to combine several data streams at one end of a two or four wire communications link, and to separate them again at the other end. *Frequency division* is the older technique; at the sending end, a high frequency carrier is modulated by low frequency signals, each of which carries one data stream. The number of data streams that can be accomodated on one channel is limited by the bandwidth of the line, which in turn determines the upper limit of carrier center frequency and sidebands.

A *time division* multiplexer generates a continuous bit stream at the highest rate that the line and modem allow. The bit stream is divided into groups in which each bit position in the group is assigned to one of the data channels. Thus, if the multiplexer handles 16 terminals, the output bit stream is divided into groups of 16 bits, each

position in the group being assigned to one terminal. Obviously, the combined data rates of the terminals may not exceed the output data rate to the modem. If the system is fully loaded and drives a 4800 bps modem, the data rate of individual terminals is limited to $4800/16 = 300$ bps, which is a standard rate for typewriter terminals. If CRT terminals running at 1200 bps are to be used, either the number of terminals is limited to $4800/1200 = 4$, or a modem with a higher data rate (9600 or 19,200 bps) must be used to accommodate more terminals.

9.6 THE EIA INTERFACE

A modem or acoustic coupler can be connected to any serial interface equipped to handle RS-232-C bipolar signals. For transmissions up to 1200 bps, nine connections are made to the modem, though not all of these need be used by the interface circuitry and software. A standard 25 pin "D"-type connector is used on all telecommunications equipment; pin numbers in the following descriptions refer to this connector. A terminal or computer which connects to the modem is called a **data terminal** and is normally equipped with a male connector. The

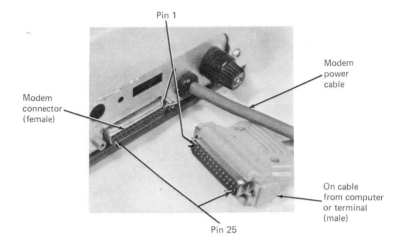

Figure 9.10. Standard 25 pin connectors. (From *Microcomputer Systems* by Ivan Flores and Christopher Terry. Copyright © 1982 by Van Nostrand Reinhold Company Inc. Reprinted by permission of the Publisher.)

modem or acoustic coupler is called the **data set** and is equipped with a female connector. This is shown in Figure 9.10 and wiring connections are provided in Figure 9.11.

Grounds. Two ground connections are provided: the *protective ground, AA/1,* * which connects the frame of the data set to the frame of the data terminal; and the *signal ground, AB/7,* is the common return for data and control signals.

Data lines. *Transmitted data, BA/2,* carries serial data from the data terminal to the data set and thence to the line. *Received data, BB/3,* carries serial data received over the line from the data set to the data terminal. These lines are held in the mark condition (negative) during intervals between data words and at all times when no data are being transmitted.

Ready lines. The *data set ready* line, *CC/6,* is ON (positive) when the data set is ready to send and receive data. This does not mean that a communications link has been established, but does indicate

- Data set power on.
- OFF HOOK condition.

*The letters are the circuit designation and the number is the pin number.

- Automatic dialing completed.
- Data set has sent any answering tone that is under its sole control.

The date terminal raises the data terminal ready line to the on (positive) state to prepare the data set to establish and maintain communication. If the data set has ring

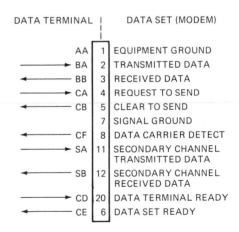

Figure 9.11. RS-232 pin connections of most commonly used lines. (From *Microcomputer Systems* by Ivan Flores and Christopher Terry. Copyright © 1982 by Van Nostrand Reinhold Company Inc. Reprinted by permission of the Publisher.)

detection and automatic answer features, turning the data terminal ready line on puts the data set into the OFF HOOK condition (equivalent to lifting the telephone handset) to answer the detected ring. Turning this line OFF returns the data set to the ON HOOK condition (equivalent to replacing the handset).

Received line signal detector. This line, CF/8, is sometimes called the *carrier detect* line. The data set turns this line ON when a communication link is established and a signal suitable for demodulation is being received. If the line connection is broken, or if the received signal is too distorted to allow demodulation, the data set turns this line OFF, thereby clamping the received data line (BB) to the mark condition.

Request to send. This line, CA/4, is normally used only on half duplex circuits to switch the data link from receive to send. On full duplex circuits, the data terminal holds this line ON to maintain the send condition.

Clear to send. This line, CB/5, is turned ON by the data set to indicate that serial data presented on the BA line will be transmitted. On half duplex circuits, it is the response to a request to send. On full duplex circuits, this line remains ON for as long as the data terminal holds the request to send line (CA) ON.

When the telephone link is dialed up manually and monitored by the operator, control lines are seldom used. However, when the computer system automatically answers incoming calls, or dials to remote stations, all of the control and status lines are used by the (software) modem driver.

Secondary channel lines. Some modems, such as the Bell 201 and 202 series for the range 1200–2400 bps half duplex, provide a secondary channel to transmit control information at 4 bps in the opposite direction to the main channel. This channel can be used, for example, to interrupt transmission on the main channel by sending a break signal, or to convey status information from a remote site. The secondary channel was seldom used, however, even when the 201 and 202 modems were in their heyday. The advent of better encoding methods has allowed large installations to use a high speed channel for such purposes. It is difficult to imagine what use a personal computer installation would find for a secondary channel.

9.7 SOFTWARE CONSIDERATIONS

Telecommunications software, discussed fully in Chapter 37, can range in complexity from a simple hardware driver which, telephone communication having been manually established, allows a personal computer system to link into a time sharing system, up to vast operating systems such as TCAM (Telecommunications access Method) and CICS (Customer Information Control System) which handle hundreds of users in a large mainframe installation. Even at the personal computer level, however, software is at two distinct levels: (1) peripheral drivers that handle the modem itself, establishing communication, passing data, and monitoring the status of the link; and (2) message handling software, including protocols that define the structure of a message and obtain outgoing messages from their source, or route incoming messages to an appropriate destination in the system.

REFERENCES

Bennet, W. R., and J. R. Davey, *Data Transmission.* New York: McGraw-Hill Book Co., 1965.

Doll, D., *Data Communications.* New York: John Wiley and Sons, 1978.

Flores, I., and C. Terry, *Microcomputer Systems.* New York: Van Nostrand Reinhold, 1982.

Held, G., *Data Communications Components.* Rochelle Park, N.J.: Hayden Book Co., 1979.

Martin, J., *Systems Analysis for Data Transmission.* Englewood Cliffs, N.J.: Prentice-Hall, 1972.

10
Computer Recognition of Speech

Harry H. Poole

Poole Associates

10.1 INTRODUCTION

Computers are now in use in almost all kinds of businesses. To make a computer effective, most applications require the entry of data in vast amounts. In addition, computers are now used quite often in a real time, or interactive mode. For these reasons, communicating with the computer is often the most severely limiting factor in trying to extend current applications, or obtaining output data upon demand.

Almost all present day systems have a typewriter based keyboard as the primary data input device, and thus require operators with at least fundamental typing skills. In addition, because physical contact with a keyboard is required, the operator must generally remain stationary, usually seated at a console. It is also difficult and often impractical for the operator to perform any other tasks, such as sorting parcels or inspecting material. In many present applications, therefore, two individuals are required, one for counting or sorting material and the second to enter data into the computer; the operators themselves communicate mainly by voice.

Voice has always been the most important medium in human communication, and the electronic transmission of voice has been essential to business since the invention of the telephone. With the advent of the computer age, it is only natural that research into voice communications with a computer be undertaken.

Some voice recognition research dates back into the early 1950s, paralleling the early introduction of computers to the business world. Only in the last few years, however, have important breakthroughs been made allowing the computer to converse directly with operators via a natural, verbal language.

Voice communication with a computer can go either way. That is, the computer can speak to us, or we can speak to the computer. However, computer speech recognition has lagged behind speech synthesis (the artificial production of speech). There are many reasons for this. One is the difference in our basic understanding about the nature of speech *comprehension,* compared with that of speech *production.* Scientists readily understand most principles involved in the production of speech, using the vocal tract. Their understanding of speech recognition processes within the ear and the brain, however, is much more limited.

A second reason lies in the limitations of computer vocabulary. With the present state of the art, a human listener's vocabulary (which averages 5,000 words) is 50 to 100 times as large as a computer's. Thus, humans can easily use words that computers cannot recognize, but it is unlikely that a computer would produce words that a human cannot understand. Other inhibiting factors include the longer time, and greater costs associated with the development of computer voice recognition, as compared with voice synthesis, and the limited ability of computers to act on the words that they do recognize. For these and other reasons, such as the needs of the market place, and advances in technology, voice techniques in such areas as speech synthesis, speech bandwidth reduction, voice store and forward (voice mail) and even speaker recognition are further advanced than speech recognition.

Some of the major problems researchers face today include the difficulty in recognizing words from multiple speakers, especially those with different accents; recognizing words spoken in a normal conversational mode (connected speech); responding with a minimum of delay (under 2 seconds); and recognizing large vocabularies (greater than 200 words). This chapter addresses this newest area of human-machine interface, and surveys the present state of the art, the principles employed, and the problems which remain to be solved in voice recognition systems.

10.2 HISTORICAL REVIEW

Speech synthesis experiments date from the nineteenth century (with mechanical speech devices), and from the extensive work done by Homer Dudley in the 1930s, culminating in public demonstrations provided by Bell Laboratories during the 1939 World's Fair. In speech recognition, the earliest machines that could *respond* to the human voice were built during the 1950s, although related work in the development of the sound spectragraph was accomplished in the 1940s. All of the early research used analog circuits to perform the necessary accoustical analysis. In the 1960s, digital computers and digital techniques became available, and since 1970, almost all serious speech recognition has relied on primarily digital techniques. This may be unfortunate, because the human ear is basically an analog device.

In the late 1960s, **linear prediction of speech** was introduced as a concept to reduce the vast amount of data requiring analysis (in addition to its capability of producing more realistic and articulate speech synthesis). In this approach, past characteristics of speech patterns are used to predict characteristics of new speech patterns.

In 1971, the Department of Defense initiated a major five year research program in speech recognition (the ARPA project), which has been the most ambitious single undertaking in this field to date. This program funded four companies to develop speech recognition equipment able to meet a number of aspiring (for the times) speech recognition goals. The program culminated in the demonstration of four different systems in the fall of 1976, with the Harpy system (developed at Carnegie-Mellon University) generally considered as providing the best performance. Incidently, all goals were met or exceeded in the Harpy system.

In the commercial area, the first firm devoted exclusively to voice recognition was founded in 1970 (Threshold Technology) and the first commercial system installed in late 1972. By the end of 1981, a total of approximately 2,000 voice recognition systems had been sold, and the list of companies offering commercial products had increased to 18. In addition, almost all major computer firms and many universities have research underway in this field.

Without doubt, practical speech recognition, once fully realized, will have, to say the least, major impact on both the computer industry and many business areas in general.

10.3 SYSTEM CONSIDERATIONS

In any high technology, such as voice recognition, specialized terms and techniques may not be immediately understood by individuals outside the field. This section discusses six major topics related to voice recognition, and provides an overview of their status.

1. **Speaker recognition** (voice identification)—the ability of the system to determine *who* is talking, rather than understanding what has been said. In this category of application, for example, access control, the conputer matches a phrase spoken by the individual to a stored template of that phrase in the authorized speaker's own voice. A more general case is determining who the speaker is from a large pool of known speakers, without his or her specific cooperation (without requiring a predefined set of words to be spoken).

   A third approach, a multi speaker voice recognition system, classifies each speaker into a group of like-sounding speakers via the individual's speaking characteristics. This approach allows word recognition to be performed using the entire groups common set of stored voice templates, rather than requiring a separate set for each speaker in the group.

2. **Speech digitization**—the conversion of conventional speech waveforms (analog) into a digital signal to allow computer processing of the signal, or to provide improvements in communication reliability or security. This approach often requires a higher bandwidth than the original analog signal, depending upon the fidelity desired.

   A number of methods have been developed for this function. Perhaps the most straightforward is *pulse code modulation (PCM),* in which the speech waveform is sampled at a sufficiently high rate to include all of the speech frequencies of interest. Sample rates are typically 8000 to 10,000 Hz. Speech amplitude is preserved by encoding the amplitude of each sample into 8 to 12 bits of digital data, depending upon required accuracy. Thus a data rate of 64 kilobits per second would be required in systems with a sampling rate of 8 kHz and an 8 bit amplitude conversion.

Another approach is *delta modulation,* in which only the changes between adjacent speech samples are encoded. Because speech changes only slightly between successive samples, this method can lower the bandwidth required to 9600 Hz, or somewhat higher, depending upon desired system fidelity. Delta modulation systems do add some complexity to the system design.

Further reductions in data rates have been accomplished through a different approach to digitization. Using Vocoders (a contraction of *voice encoders*), systems have been built based upon a model of the human vocal tract. These devices divide speech into 40 to perhaps 60 segments a second, each speech segment being examined to evaluate the individual parameters in a set representing all of the more important properties of speech.

A technique based on this approach is *linear predictive coding (LPC).* A typical system will have information on 12 parameters of 3 to 6 bits each. Energy, pitch, and 10 reflection coefficients combine to convey voice information, although often a voiced/unvoiced bit or a repeat bit may be added. LPC systems typically utilize 50 bits per frame, and with 50 segments per second, they require a data rate of only 2.5 kilobits per second.

3. **Speech synthesis**—the artificial production of speech through digital techniques. Current methods are based upon one of four major approaches:

- *Formant synthesis,* electronic modeling of the human voice.
- *Phoneme synthesis,* utilizing speech parameters derived from the phoneme, perhaps the fundamental unit of human speech (Table 10.1)
- *Linear predictive coding,* or other types of parameter coding. Known characteristics of speech allow selected parameters to generate recognizable speech.
- *Waveform synthesis,* based upon storing the digitized amplitude characteristics of speech waveforms.

Techniques grounded on phonemes are the most natural sounding, but do not provide the easiest understood (most articulate). Parameter coding provides a higher level of articulation, but sounds more artificial. Waveform synthesis generally requires too much memory storage for most applications, unless the vocabulary is very small.

4. **Single speaker systems**—voice recognition systems in which templates for recognizing words are stored for each potential speaker. This approach requires both training in the system by each potential user, and a large computer memory if a sizable number of speakers are authorized to access the system. This is also the approach followed by most commercial systems providing a practical limit of perhaps 10 speakers.

Although multiple speaker systems can also take this approach with a limited number of potential speakers, the general approach is to store separate templates for separate groups of speakers. This offers the complementary advantages of enabling the system to handle an almost unlimited number of speakers, and eliminating a need for individual training in the system, the latter an important aspect of any system used by the public. However, in multiple speaker systems, exact template matching is more difficult; and decisions must be made on a range of possible matches, thus restricting the available vocabulary even further.

5. **Isolated speech versus continuous speech**—in most normal speech, one word often runs into the next with only a limited break between words. Words which have the same ending sound as the next word's beginning sound (for example, *run now*) often cause the blurring, or merging, of the two separate sounds (two *n* sounds in the example). Further, slurring often affects speech, so that a phrase such as "give the cat your" may easily come out as "give the catcher." These and similar factors greatly complicate the recognition of continuous speech.

In isolated speech, on the other hand, exaggerated pauses (100 to 200 milliseconds) are placed between words by the speaker to assist in defining word boundaries, and to reduce the possibility of slurring. This is an artificial manner of speaking, and must be learned if communicating with computers is the object. It probably cannot be used by the general public for most applications, and in any case it significantly reduces the speed of data entry by voice. It is the easiest system to implement, however, and therefore most current commercial systems require the speaker to pause between words (or at least between phrases on which the system is "trained").

6. **Phonemes**—perhaps the basic unit of human speech:

Table 10.1 Phonetic Symbols

Symbol	Key Word	Symbol	Key Word
Consonants			
/p/	*p*ill	/ʃ/	*sh*all
/b/	*b*et	/ʒ/	trea*s*ure
/t/	*t*old	/tʃ/	*ch*ill
/d/	*d*ee*d*	/dʒ/	*j*am
/k/	*c*all	/m/	*m*an
/g/	*g*one	/n/	*n*ow
/f/	*f*un	/ŋ/	ri*ng*
/v/	*v*ote	/l/	*l*unch
/θ/	*th*in	/r/	*r*at
/ð/	*th*at	/j/	*y*es
/s/	*s*oon	/h/	*h*ope
/z/	*z*oo	/w/	*w*itch
		/ʍ/ or /hw/	*wh*ich
Vowels			
/i/	s*ee*	/ɔ/	*a*ll
/ʌ/	p*i*ll	/o/	h*o*pe
/e/	c*a*ke	/ʊ/	c*ou*ld
/ɛ/	m*e*t	/**u**/	r*u*le
/æ/	f*a*t	/ʌ/	tr*u*ck
/a/	broad, as New Englanders pronounce a*u*nt[1]	/ə/	*a*bove[3]
/ɑ/	f*a*ther	/ɚ/	moth*er*[4]
/ɒ/	a sound somewhere between /ɑ/ as in c*a*lm and /ɔ/ as in s*aw*[2]	/ɜ/ or /ɝ/	th*ir*d[5]
Diphthongs			
/aɪ/	b*y*	/eɪ/	d*ay*[6]
/ɔɪ/	b*oy*	/oɪ/	g*o*[6]
/aʊ/ or /ɑʊ/	c*ow*	/ju/	*you*
		/ɪu/	f*ew*

[1]This vowel is not common.
[2]This vowel is not common.
[3]Used only in unstressed syllables.
[4]Used only in unstressed syllables. Those who do not habitually pronounce their *r* will use /ə/.
[5]Used only in stressed syllables. Those who do not habitually pronounce their *r* will use /ɜ/.
[6]These diphthongs are not considered phonemic but are non-distinctive variants of /e/, /o/, and /ɪ/.
(Table from *Effective Speaking,* by A. N. Kruger. Copyright © 1970 by Van Nostrand Rienhold Company Inc. Reprinted by permission of the Publisher.)

the separate sounds made by the vocal tract while saying a word (Table 10.1). Words are often composed of several syllables, and syllables are composed of one to as many as five phonemes. For example, the word *see* is composed of the phonemes *s* and *i*, and the word *thin* is composed of the phonemes θ (th), ɪ, and *n*. In statistical terms, the average word is made up of 1.7 syllables, and the average syllable has 2.5 phonemes.

Although a lot of research has gone into phoneme recognition, transitions between phonemes and similarities between certain phonemes (such as *n* and *m*) have made this approach less successful than approaches based upon complete word recognition. On the other hand, because there are fewer than 50 phonemes in the English language, only through phoneme recognition can very large vocabularies (1,000 to 5,000 words) be recognized without a call on large amounts of memory for each word template. Even more significant, an inordinate amount of time to search every stored template for a potential match would not be required.

10.4 SPEECH PRODUCTION AND UNDERSTANDING

No discussion on computer recognition of speech can be complete without consideration of the techniques with which humans produce and comprehend speech. Human speech results from the separate acts of respiration, phonation, and articulation, all controlled through the brain, and guided by both acoustical (hearing) and kinesthetic (feeling) feedback to the brain. During speech, the act of controlling the release of breath through the vocal cords generates a pulse of air. This air pulse is converted to a sound pulse by actions of the *glottis* (the aperature in the vocal cords) producing a characteristic buzzing or rasping sound. This glottal sound pulse is further acted upon by the tongue, lips, teeth, and palate within a controlled cavity (the mouth and throat) to produce the individual phoneme sounds; in sequence, these sounds result in words (Figure 10.1).

Some sounds are produced without vocal cord vibration, such as *s* and *f*, and are referred to as *unvoiced speech* because the vocal cords are not used. Sounds are also produced by diversion of some, or all, of the resultant sound pulse to the nose, producing the nasal consonants *n* and ŋ (ng).

Consonant and vowel differentiation is provided by actions of the tongue, palate, and so on. Depending upon the placement of these articulators, we produce sounds which, although often similar in their waveforms, are sufficiently different to allow the brain, in conjunction with the ear, to recognize and comprehend speech.

Vowel differentiation is accomplished primarily by a combination of arching the tongue and selecting the area within the mouth that produces the sound (Figure 10.2). For example, the principal differences between the words *bead, baud* and *bud* are that they are pronounced at the front, back and center of the mouth, respectively.

The opening and closing movements of the vocal cords modulate the air flow at a rate f_o, called the **voice fundamental frequency,** and provide the basic pitch of the voice. This value is typically 100 to 125 Hz for adult males and twice that for adult females. As the sound wave is further acted upon, the multiresonant filter action of the mouth, throat, and nasal cavities impress upon it a characteristic formant structure. The frequencies of the three lowest formants serve as the main speech charac-

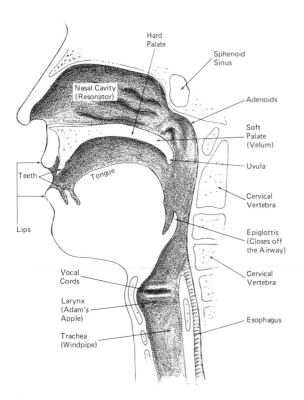

Figure 10.1. Principal articulators. (Adapted from John M. Palmer, *Anatomy of Speech and Hearing,* Harper & Row, Publishers, Inc., 1983. Copyright © 1983 by John M. Palmer.)

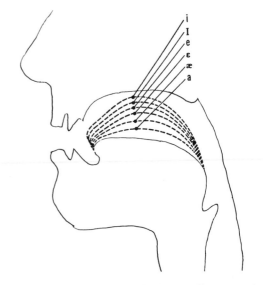

Figure 10.2. Forming front vowels. (From *Effective Speaking: A Complete Course* by Arthur N. Kruger. Copyright © 1970 by Van Nostrand Reinhold Company Inc. Reprinted by permission of the Publisher.)

teristics of the overall voice sound wave. The average spacing of these frequencies is about 1 KHz, but varies with the phoneme being produced.

In addition to producing sounds, the speaker adds stops, pauses, pitch changes, and syllable or word stress to indicate meaning. The resultant sound wave is very complex, and conveys a lot of information to the listener, much of which is redundant. This redundant information is of particular assistance to human recognition during periods of competing noises or voices which add to the total information received.

Unfortunately, as noted earlier, much less is known about the processes involved in understanding speech, as compared with what is known about producing it. It has been determined what effect various factors (such as frequency range and competing noise) have on the correct understanding of speech, and which basic sounds (such as *m* and *n*) are the easiest to confuse. It has also been determined that the ear is extremely sensitive to frequency discrimination, and that different locations within the ear react to different frequencies, thus assisting the hearer with pitch tracking and pitch discrimination, both of fundamental importance in word recognition.

The physical features of the ear have been investigated, and their action on the receipt of sounds, especially tones, analyzed. The ear is basically divided into three separate parts (Figure 10.3) each having a function in speech recognition. The **outer ear** is primarily a funnel (the ear canal) which ends at the eardrum. Because it is open at one end, the region of the outer ear resonates at frequencies determined by the length of the canal. In the average adult male, this length is 2.7 cm, and results in a primary resonance of approximately 3100 Hz. This factor adds enhancement to frequencies near this value by as much as 10 decibels.

The **middle ear** connects the eardrum to the *cochlea,* where actual hearing sensation is located. It is composed of three bones, known as the ossicles. Motion of the eardrum is transmitted to the cochlea through the motions of these three bones. Because the area of the eardrum is larger than the area of the window entering the cochlea, an increase in pressure is produced on the cochlea, thus improving the ear's sensitivity. Characteristics of the middle ear, primarily in the mass of the ossicles, contribute to a reduction in the ear's response to higher frequencies.

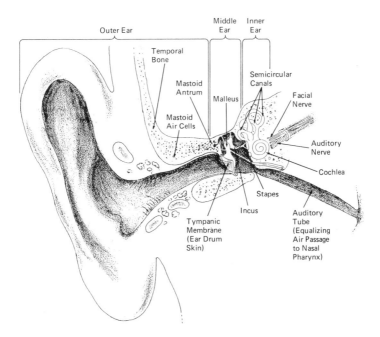

Figure 10.3a. The ear. (Adapted from John M. Palmer, *Anatomy of Speech and Hearing,* Harper & Row, Publishers, Inc., 1983. Copyright © 1983 by John M. Palmer.)

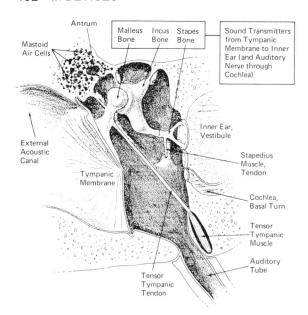

Figure 10.3b. The inner ear—detail. (Adapted from John M. Palmer, *Anatomy of Speech and Hearing,* Harper & Row, Publishers, Inc., 1983. Copyright © 1983 by John M. Palmer.)

The **inner ear** receives the vibrations transmitted through the middle ear on approximately 25,000 hair cells of the organ of Conti, located on the *basilar membrane*. This membrane runs through the middle of the cochlea, a snail shaped structure with a circular path length of about 3.8 cm. The basilar membrane is displaced in a vibratory manner in response to the incoming sound wave. With a pure tone, the motion of the basilar membrane resembles a travelling wave.

We are able to distinguish numerous frequencies because the exact position along the basilar membrane most affected by this motion depends upon the frequency of the received sound wave. Higher frequencies produce their strongest reaction near the base of the cochlea, with lower frequencies peaking farther out on the membrane. Through this reception of frequency according to location, and thus the excitation of different nerve cells, the brain is able to discriminate among various sounds, in sequence or together. But how the brain converts this pitch data into intelligible speech, even in the presence of competing noise, is what is not completely understood.

Complicating this subject further is the vast amount of redundancy in speech. For example, removing a significant portion of amplitude information (as through peak clipping) reduces intelligibility of the resultant waveform very little* Also, the mid frequency of articulation is 1900 Hz, and either the higher or the lower frequencies may be removed with a minimal effect on intelligibility. Although this redundancy is a great help to humans in understanding speech, we have yet to learn *which* pieces of speech information are redundant to other pieces to enable computer analysis.

10.5 CRITERIA IN SPEECH RECOGNITION

Computer recognition of speech is yet further complicated by the need to consider five different types of information conveyed in speech: *accoustical, syntactic, semantic, pragmatic,* and *prosodic.* Literal translation of word meaning, even if possible by a computer, would be insufficient to distinguish numerous words (homonyms), or even phrases which sould alike, without additional types of speech information.

Acoustical clues are those based upon frequency discrimination, and are the primary means by which humans distinguish words which do not sound alike. In fact, when we listen to a series of isolated, unconnected words, they are the only clues available.

Syntax helps us to sort out the meaning of words through their grammatical use. Next to the acoustical, syntax is the most widely used means of telling words apart. It also alerts the listener to possible misunderstandings if the word is not correct grammatically. Syntax would be used, for example, to tell the difference between the homonyms pail and pale. The first *(pail)* is used primarily as a noun, while the second *(pale)* is primarily an adjective.

Semantics relates words to our understanding of reality. For example, the homonyms *steak* and *stake* are both nouns, thus cannot be distinguished accoustically or syntactically. Through semantics, however, we know that we do not serve stakes for dinner, or put up a tent with steaks.

Pragmatics is the use of context to determine the meaning of a word, especially when words have more than one meaning. For example, to respond to the statement "This won't wash" one would require contextual information (or knowledge of the speaker) to determine whether the reference is to being cleaned, or to withstanding examination. Pragmatics also applies to "The program crashed" as contrasted with "The market

*More specifically, 24 dB of peak clipping degrades articulation scores by only 5 percent in isolated words. (Stevens, p. 1058.)

crashed," or "Take a joint" (roast or marijuana), and so on.

Prosodic features include stress, transitions, pitch and related factors. These clues help towards understanding as, for example, syllable stress to distinguish between such words as *deSERT* and *DESert,* or rising pitch to denote a question.

The only way that the need for most or all of the above types of clues can be avoided in speech recognition systems is by keeping the vocabulary artifically small, and by selecting words none of which sound alike. This is the approach taken by almost all current commercial speech recognition systems. If the system must recognize the 10 digits, for example, sound-alike words such as *won, to, fore,* and *ate* must be eliminated, as well as similar-sounding words (*run, hate,* etc.).

10.6 RECOGNITION APPROACHES

Most voice recognition systems follow one of three different sets of assumptions. In the *signal processing* approach, it is assumed that the speech waveform is no different from any other type of waveform, and that standard signal processing techniques, such as Fourier frequency analysis, can be used. The Filter approach toward speech recognition is an example of this method.

In the *speech modeling* approach, the signal parameters to be extracted are those connected with the production of speech, such as vocal tract resonance frequencies and sound energy. Use of the linear predicting chip (LPC) is an example of this method.

In the *speech reception* approach, the signal parameters of importance are those extracted by the ear and the brain. This approach has not been fully implemented, although experimental speech recognizing equipment was developed during the mid 1960s as an analog of the human ear.

Of these three methods, only the first two produce practical results at the present time. Both methods utilize pattern matching techniques to compare the extracted features to those of a stored reference set. In most systems available, these stored patterns are complete words, although in some cases short phrases (of less than 2 seconds) can be stored. Phoneme template matching has not proved as successful, and is not used in isolated word recognition systems.

Pattern matching is illustrated in Figure 10.4. The incoming speech signal is processed, and various parameters measured, such as formant frequencies, sound energy, zero crossing rates, and short term spectrum. These parameters are measured during time "windows" typically of 10 to 50 seconds. The resultant set of time-varying parameters is usually further modified by dynamic or static programming techniques to normalize the pattern length, thus adjusting the received patterns for variations in speaking rates.

The modified pattern is then compared to a set of stored patterns (word or phrase templates). A best-fit decision is made, often based upon weighted difference calculations. In the more complex systems, several candidate words are chosen, and the final decision is based upon language constraints, such as syntax or semantics.

One step implicit in the foregoing process is the detection of the start and endpoints of the incoming word *(word framing).* This step is relatively easy to accomplish in a controlled (quiet) environment, but becomes increas-

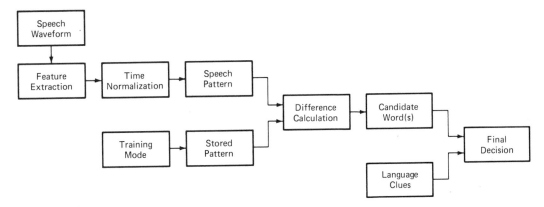

Figure 10.4. Block diagram of a typical speech recognizer.

ingly difficult as the background noise increases. It is also one of the most difficult steps in continuous speech systems, in which syllable segmentation must be made without the assistance of the 100 millisecond pause inserted in isolated speech. For these reasons, most continuous word systems rely on contextual information and/or verbal feedback to the operator to catch errors.

The specific parameters selected for measurement in the first stage of voice recognition depends upon many different factors, such as the type of words contained in the vocabulary, allowable computation time, cost considerations, response time requirements, storage limitations, and the experience of the system designer. In operation, most isolated word recognizers require a training mode, in which each eventual user (speaker) repeats the desired vocabulary from 1 to 10 times. From this information, the system extracts the necessary reference patterns and stores them as templates for matching against future speech data. If the system is to be used over the telephone, these reference patterns are made via a telephone link.

When semantics or syntax is utilized in the final decision process, choices between candidate words may be made on a statistical basis, although this alternative suffers a subtle but serious drawback. If statistics is used to make the final decision, it would be right more often than not. However, this guarantees wrong results whenever the alternate meaning was desired by the speaker, and perhaps more important, it can be shown that the less common meaning, when utilized, is usually more significant than the more common meaning.

Another means of categorizing speech recognition systems is via the basic word unit that they choose to recognize. Systems have been developed that distinguish speech on the basis of word phrases, single words, syllables, phonemes, and even subphoneme matching. Each method of template matching has its advantages and drawbacks; each works better with certain types of words, and less well with others. Although cost, computational time and storage requirements would be extremely severe, a system that uses more than one method of recognition would be the most accurate. There is a strong indication that the brain follows this approach, and makes a final decision on the incoming word on the basis of several differing sets of criteria.

Word matching is the approach of choice in current systems. However, phoneme matching, because there are only 47 phonemes in use in the English language (32 consonants and 15 vowels), at least potentially offers the lowest level of complexity, and therefore the lowest cost and

highest speed. Current problems with phoneme matching primarily concern the effect that adjacent phonemes have on the phoneme being considered.

10.7 PROBLEM AREAS

As noted in the last several sections, recognition of speech by computers has a number of implementation problems which currently limit their usefulness. This is especially true for multispeaker and continuous speech systems. Even so, a number of fundamental problems are present in the more limited single-speaker, isolated word cases.

No individual pronounces a given word in the same way under all circumstances. Differences in timing occur, both in word length and in the internal ratio of syllable lengths. Changes in stress affect recognition. Unless the speaker takes care, slurring or mispronunciation is likely to result. Pronunciation often varies with the context of the words. As the speaker ages, or if the speaker develops a sore throat or a cold, the basic sound pattern also will change.

When electronic distortion is added, for example, the telephone, we find that frequency limitations, phase distortions and line noise all contribute to the problem, thus further distorting the sound pattern. In fact, it may be necessary to have two sets of templates stored for the same speaker—for voice input through a telephone as well as direct (via a microphone). Variations in volume may also affect the system. This is usually a secondary effect, unless the speaker is whispering.

As mentioned earlier, computers have difficulty in determining when a given word (or syllable) stops and another starts. For this reason, isolated word recognizers require the deliberate introduction of a 100 to 200 millisecond pause to assist in word framing. However, this requirement adds other problems. It makes it more difficult for the average individual to use. It slows up data entry rates. It also affects the way the speaker pronounces words, especially through the addition of stress to normally unstressed words.

When more than one speaker must use the system, the problems increase because of inherent differences in accent, pronunciation, pitch, and talking rates. Females and children prove particularly difficult for a computer to understand, primarily owing to the higher pitch of their voices and the resultant upward movement of formants, until some fall outside the bandwidth cutoffs employed by the system.

The approach taken by most commercial systems, storing separate templates for each speaker, is obviously only satisfactory for a limited number of speakers, those whom you can train in the system. For applications involving the general public, a different approach, using templates which represent a *class* of speakers must be used. However, because template matching is now even more difficult, small vocabularies (10 to 40 words) usually result.

Homonyms, or similar-sounding words or phrases, cannot be recognized by acoustical techniques alone. Most current systems bypass this problem by restricting the choice of vocabulary to reduce or eliminate all similar-sounding words. When this is not practical, secondary clues (such as syntax or semantics) must be employed by the computer. This further increases computational and storage problems, as well as system costs. Problems are also present with competing noise, with competing conversations, or even with random words spoken by the operator into a live microphone when not meant as input for the system.

Although each of these problems, and others, are found in current systems, approaches to minimize them through restricted vocabularies, time normalization, feedback from the computer to the operator and other techniques have been developed, allowing commercial systems to perform quite well in many applications. However, indications are that the present state of the art needs a number of improvements before voice input can be utilized to full advantage.

10.8 PRODUCTS AND VENDORS

Commercial voice recognition systems are now available at many levels of complexity and with a wide extent of vocabularies. Vocabulary sizes range from as low as 8 words to as high as 150 words, with 70 to 100 words typical. Systems are available that can handle 1 to as many as 10 speakers, and in the case of quite limited vocabularies (such as the 10 digits), systems are available for general public input (unlimited number of speakers). Recognition time, which is heavily dependent on whether the system handles continuous speech, on how many speakers are to be recognized, and on the size of the vocabulary, ranges from as fast as 25 milliseconds to a more typical 2 seconds to several minutes for some of the most complex systems.

Several firms sell voice recognition chips, and at least one sells voice recognition modules. Also available are standalone boards, and boards built to interface directly into other products, such as the Lear Seigler ADM 3A CRT terminal, the Apple computer, and the Digital Equipment Corporation's Q bus. There are terminals available with voice recognition features. Finally, in addition to all of the above products, many firms sell complete computer systems for voice recognition.

Typical prices, depending upon quantity, vocabulary size, recognition accuracy and other factors are $30 to $200 per chip, $200 to $2,000 per board or module, $3,000 to $15,000 per terminal and $10,000 to $125,000 per complete system.

Although the complete systems provide all necessary software for voice recognition, many of the smaller units are supplied without the necessary software for interfacing to a computer. However, at least one of the major computer hardware suppliers is now offering a software interface package for their equipment for $7,000.

The first commercial system was installed in 1972. Over the past 10 years, perhaps 2,000 systems have been sold, approximately half to the hobbiest or experimental market. Many vendors have entered this field. Some are no longer offering voice recognition products, however, and others have changed their name.

A partial listing of vendors currently offering products in the voice recognition area includes Centigram, E-Systems, Excalibur Technologies, Heuristics, Interstate Electronics, Scott, Threshold Technology, Verbex; NEC and Sun are among the Japanese suppliers.

Although there have been many sets of statistics published by researchers in the speech recognition field, predicting the performance of commercial products is difficult, partially because experimental models, not commercial models, are usually those tested. Other reasons include the laboratory-like conditions typically employed, differences in vocabularies, and differences in performance goals set for the system. Only recently have some organizations attempted to compare the performances of commercially available units under realistic conditions.

It should be emphasized that recognition performance is sensitive to vocabulary size and vocabulary composition, background noise, speaker training, methods employed, number and type of speakers, and the definition of accuracy used. (Some published figures do not include computer mistakes which do not affect the task performance; others do not count times the computer must ask the individual to repeat the input.)

As one example, the difference between recognizing letters of the alphabet, which have many similar-sounding items, and recognizing words from a vocabulary chosen to emphasize distinctness is instructive. The chosen vocabulary had a correct recognition rate of 91.6 percent versus a 79.5 percent correct response for the alphabet. Both of these studies used systems on which 10 speakers had trained. When only a single trained speaker was used, performance on the letters of the alphabet improved to 88.6 percent, and this particular test also included the 10 digits.

It has been shown that systems requiring a very high recognition rate (approaching 98 percent) generally require a single speaker system, and vocabulary of fewer than 100 carefully selected words. If multiple speakers from the general public are desired, the limitation on vocabulary is around 20 words for systems with a high recognition accuracy. Applications in which the system can request repeats of questionable words, or in which the computer always repeats the input to the operator for confirmation (either by voice or by visual display), can operate with lower degrees of accuracy.

10.9 APPLICATIONS

Most current applications have been local, that is, they have not used a telephone input. However, it is just this area that offers the greatest immediate growth potential, for example, the use of voice recognition principles to allow directory assistance without requiring operators, similarly to provide an airline reservation system, and to facilitate banking. One such system currently in use is a stock quotation system, which a subscriber can telephone to determine the status of certain issues.

Other applications include control over material and parcel handling, data entry by quality control inspectors, input of map coordinate data, security access control, voice activation of wheelchairs, job cost entry, robot control, receiving inspection, hospital room environmental control, and elevator control, to name just a few.

10.10 CONCLUSIONS

Besides the obvious general advantages associated with allowing humans to converse with computers in a natural language, speech recognition promises many specific advantages, including

- Permitting the operator to move about during data entry.
- Freeing the operator's hands for other tasks.
- Allowing the handicapped to interface easily with a computer.
- Allowing those with minimal typing skills to access systems with some facility.

- Providing for telephone input of questions from the general public, without requiring a human operator.
- Allowing traveling employees access the central computer through any telephone.
- Opening up more potential areas of computer applications through a different type of human interaction.
- Allowing higher data rates and greater accuracy than now available in data entry.

To exploit these advantages, further advances in the field will be required. In particular, costs must be reduced, speed increased, and accuracy improved. Then voice input should be significantly faster and as accurate as typed entries, and potentially even better.

Environmental considerations need better addressing. We can understand our dinner companion's speech, even if nearby tables are also carrying on many different conversations. Currently, however, the computer ability to interact with the voice is quite limited in noisy environments; close mounted microphones with a highly directional pickup pattern are employed to reduce the effects.

The need for increase in vocabulary size has been alluded to many times, and is probably the major limitation to the widespread utilization of recognition systems today, perhaps more important than cost. Certainly applications possibilities are greatly limited if the computer only has a 20 to 40 word vocabulary. The ideal vocabulary size is probably 2,000 to 5,000 words for electronic office functions. This compares with a vocabulary of about 3000 words normal for telephone conversations. Continuous speech and multiple speaker techniques must also be improved, or operators will find it faster to type in the information than to voice it to the computer.

But all of these current limitations are only natural growing pains in a relatively young technology area. Within the next five years, major cost reductions in complex voice recognition systems will occur, and vocabularies of at least 1,000 words will become available as newer concepts in voice recognition are developed and brought to market.

REFERENCES

Atal, B. S., and S. L. Hanauer, "Speech Analysis and Synthesis by Linear Prediction of the Speech Wave," *Journal of the Acoustical Society of America,* Vol. 50, Aug. 1971.

Alter, R., "Utilization of Contextual Constraints in Automatic Speech Recognition," *IEEE Transactions on Audio and Electroacoustics,* Vol. AU-16, No. 1 (Mar. 1968).

Broad, D. J., and J. E. Shoup, "Concepts for Acoustical Phonetic

Recognition," in D. Raj Reddy, ed., *Speech Recognition.* New York: Academic Press, 1978.

Campanella, S. J., and D. Phyfe, "Application of a Model of the Analog Ear to Speech Signal Analysis," *IEEE Transactions on Audio and Electroacoustics,* Vol. AU-16, No. 1 (Mar. 1968).

Flanagan, J. L., "Voices of Men and Machines," *Journal of the Accoustical Society of America,* Vol. 50, Aug. 1971.

Klatt, D. H., "Results of the ARPA Speech Understanding Project," *Journal of the Accoustical Society of America,* Vol. 62, Dec. 1977.

Licklider, J. C., and G. A. Miller, "The Perception of Speech," in S. S. Stevens, ed., *Handbook of Experimental Psychology.* New York: John Wiley & Sons, 1962.

Lea, W. A., "Speech Recognition: Past, Present and Future," in W. A. Lea, ed., *Lectures on Communication Systems Theory.* Englewood Cliffs, N.J.: Prentice-Hall, 1980.

Markel, J. P., and A. H. Gray, Jr., *Linear Prediction of Speech.* New York: Springer-Verlag, 1976.

Meeker, W., "Speech Characteristics and Acoustical Effects." in J. W. Hamsher, ed., *Communication System Engineering Handbook.* New York: McGraw-Hill Book Co., 1967.

Pollack, I., "Performance Criteria of Speech Systems," in E. J. Baghdady, ed., *Lectures on Communication System Theory.*

Rabiner, L., and S. E. Levinson, "Isolated and Connected Word Recognition—Theory and Selected Applications," *IEEE Transactions on Communications,* Vol. COM-29, No. 5 (May 1981).

Schafer, R. W., and L. R. Rabiner, "Digital Representations of Speech Signals," *Proceedings of the IEEE,* Vol. 63, Apr. 1965.

Simmons, E. J., Jr., "Speech Recognition Technology," *Computer Design,* June 1979.

White, G. M., "Speech Recognition: A Tutorial Overview," *Computer,* Vol. 9, No. 5 (1976).

III
HARDWARE SYSTEMS

11
Desktop and Personal Computers

Lloyd Kusak

Hewlett-Packard

11.1 INTRODUCTION

Desktop computers have existed since the early 1970s as an outgrowth of the sophisticated desktop calculator. The early calculators possessed the capability to perform a number of assembly-language-like instructions in sequence. When the microprocessor chip was developed by the Intel Corporation in 1972, it seemed almost natural that a desktop machine, preprogrammed in a computer language, would appear. Making such an appearance was the IBM 5100, which was preprogrammed in BASIC and APL; another early machine was the Hewlett-Packard 9830, which was preprogrammed in BASIC only. The objective of these computers was that they would be easy to use (hence the implementation of a conversational version of BASIC) and that their cost would be low enough to justify the needs of a single user.

In addition to the generally recognizable "desktop" computers, a wide range of units called "personal computers" has also appeared. The primary means of delineating one type from the other seems to be price. In fact, there are a few large pocket-sized computers, such as the Timex Sinclair 1000 or the TRS-80 (Figure 11.1), which are also programmed in a reasonable version of BASIC. From computers of this size, on up to very large desktops, there is an extremely wide range in computational power and price.

The desktop computer has always been aimed at the single user (as contrasted to multiple users in a time sharing system). The most common language has been BASIC, which is automatically available when the computer is turned on. The language is implemented in an interpretive, conversational mode so that program development is made as convenient as possible. This sacrifices execution speed, which is generally not a factor in desktop applications. Later and larger models of desktop computers implement BASIC in compiler as well as interpreter mode, and they support other languages such as FORTRAN, PASCAL and RPG.

When first introduced, desktop computers were aimed both at business and scientific applications. The majority of the larger desktops are now used in scientific applications and, in a great many cases, in controlling instruments. Many vendors of the smaller desktops or personal computers have accumulated or developed large software libraries particularly for business applications (see Chapter 16). In fact, the choice among computers may hinge not so much upon hardware differences, but upon the software available for a given system.

11.2 INTERNAL ARCHITECTURE

A characteristic of desktop computers is that they are a self-contained device, containing all the components necessary for a practical, useable system. By contrast, the typical mainframe computer is built up of separate components—CPU, terminals, disks, memories, and so on, to make it a working system. The block diagram in Figure 11.2 illustrates a commercially available desktop machine that contains most of the components available in a medium-to-large class of desktop computers. Similar attributes will be found in other systems depending on the capabilities offered, and these, of course, will be reflected in the cost of the device.

Figure 11.1. The Radio Shack PC-1 Pocket Computer is one of the smallest units programmable in BASIC. Two 4 bit CMOS microprocessors (one for arithmetic operation and the other for BASIC) supply the computation power. Memory is divided into 7K bytes for the BASIC interpreter, 4K for the monitor, and 1.9K for user programs. Attachable devices are a cassette tape recorder for program storage and a 16 column 5×7 dot matrix paper tape printer that runs at one line per second. (Courtesy The Tandy Corporation)

The Hewlett-Packard 9826 (as well as the 9836) is based on a Motorola 68000 microprocessor. This microprocessor uses a 16 bit external (16 line data bus) and a 32 bit internal architecture (32 bit program counter), contains a 16 megabyte linear address space (23 line address bus) and operates at an 8 MHz clock rate. This pro-

vides the computational power of a medium size minicomputer. Capabilities of other desktops vary in proportion to the microprocessor selected for its CPU. Many personal and business computers have architecture based on an 8 bit processor. The IBM PC, which became so successful in 1983, is a modified 16-bit structure. At

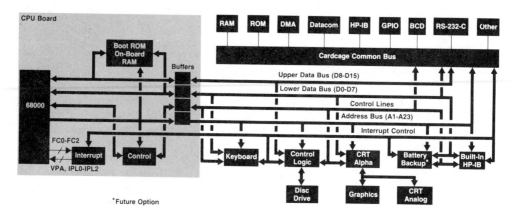

Figure 11.2. Internal architecture of the Hewlett-Packard 9826 Desktop Computer. The CPU is a 16 bit microprocessor (Motorola 68000). The system uses a 16 line data bus, a 23 line address bus, and a 32 bit program counter. RAM memory can be expanded to two megabytes. (© Copyright 1982 Hewlett-Packard Company. Reproduced with permission.)

the upper end, there is a commercially available desktop which utilizes a 32-bit processor.

As noted, most desktops use BASIC on an interpretive, conversational basis. In some cases, the interpreter is stored in ROM, which is addressed as a part of the overall memory structure; i.e., ROM and RAM memory may be addressed as separate portions of the same continguous memory block. In other cases, a ROM block may be provided from which the interpreter is downloaded into RAM memory. The computer, then, does not have the ability to address the ROM portion. With multilingual computers, several language ROMs may be provided for selection by the user. Still, the majority, including the important S-100 bus computers and the IBM PC, bring the BASIC interpreter in from the system disk.

Interfacing

Several types of interfaces are in common use, and they are each represented in the upper right portion of the diagram in Figure 11.2. The most common is **RS-232-C,** which is commonly used for printers, teletypewriters, and in communicating with modems. In its simplest form, it is a 3 wire serial interface utilizing the 8 bit ASCII code. Because so many devices adhere to this standard, this interface is available in the great majority of desktops.

The next most common interface is the **IEE-488,** which is used very frequently in the electronic testing laboratory. In the diagram this is referred to as HP-IB. It uses a 16 line protocol, of which 8 lines are used for sending data and the other 8 are used for control and status information. Because many desktops are used in control applications in which they control other electronic devices, handle automatic tests, and are even used in process control functions, they are frequently found with this interface.

Two other interfaces not so commonly used are GPIO and BCD. The GPIO interface is usually a 16 bit parallel input to the computer and may be used with high-speed devices, such as disks and magnetic tape drives. The BCD interface is, like the IEE-488 interface, used mostly to connect to electronic instruments which have this form of readout. BCD devices utilize 4 lines per digit and may use up to 12 positions when transmitting a sign, a decimal point, and up to 10 digits of data. The interface at the computer will accept the 12 items of data on the buffer at the interface. The data may then need to be converted into a floating point number by a software routine, so that the standard programming language can handle it.

As is indicated in Figure 11.2, data travels from the interfaces into a buffer before it is finally transmitted to the CPU. Control lines are used to signal the CPU when the transmission of a character is completed (i.e., all 8 data bits on an RS-232 line have been accumulated to 1 character). The CPU can then store the sequence of characters into computer memory until the entire message is received.

The **DMA (direct memory access) interface** is used to buffer data directly into or from computer memory. The interface usually is combined with the GPIO interface for high speed transfers from fast peripherals, such as disk and tape drives, and very high speed analog to digital converters (Chapter 7).

The **CPU board,** in addition to containing the computational logic of the computer, may contain a boot-up ROM as well as some dynamic RAM memory. The boot-up ROM is programmed to set all I/O and memory registers to a known start-up state; in addition, it can be programmed to go into an auto-test routine each time the computer is turned on. Other functions of the CPU are interrupt and control. As in larger computers, the interrupt logic can respond to external events to change the course of an internal program. This is obviously a useful function in control computers; it may not always be a feature available in smaller desktops or those used primarily for business applications.

Clocks

An **internal clock** is frequently implemented in a desktop system. For example, in the model shown in Figure 11.3 it is implemented internally by a Model 8041A microprocessor. The clock keeps time to a 10 millisecond resolution and can also be programmed to cause an interrupt to the computer. A very useful feature implemented in this system is that a *clock interrupt* can be used to break the computer out of endless loops that may be caused by less than perfect programming.

11.3 KEYBOARD DESIGN

Desktop computers, because they are self-contained, are almost always provided with a keyboard and a CRT display. In a few instances, these components are purchased separately, and optional devices of differing degrees of quality may be offered.

The arrangement of the keys on the keyboard is almost always identical to that of an office typewriter. Occasionally, some characters, such as the * and / keys may be

Figure 11.3. The Hewlett-Packard Model 9836 Desktop Computer includes an extensive keyboard, two flexible disk drives (5.25-inch diameter), 264K bytes each), a 310 mm diagonal CRT, and up to two megabytes of solid state memory. Graphics resolution on the CRT is 512 × 390 pixels and alphanumeric text is displayed in 25 lines of 80 characters each. For process control applications, an internal clock is provided and IEEE-488, RS-232 BCD, and 8 line parallel interfaces are available. (© Copyright 1982 Hewlett-Packard Company. Reproduced with permission.)

located differently. The keyboard is designed to transmit the ASCII character set so that control and escape keys are also included as they might be on an ASR-33 teletypewriter. Functions such as ETX (end of text) or FF (form feed) are generated while the operator holds down the control key and types D or L, respectively.

As the cost, and capability of the desktop computer increases, so usually does the quality of the keyboard. This is reflected in an improved "touch" or feel, similar to that for a high quality electric typewriter. The keycaps may also be curved to fit the contour of a finger tip.

The simpler systems contain only the keys found on a typewriter plus a few keys to generate the complete ASCII set. More extensive key arrangements may include an additional numeric keypad and a number of special functions keys. The special keys may call in an edit, insert line, display, or delete line function. In addition, if a graphics capability is available, a special group of keys is necessary for cursor control. One desktop manufacturer offers a keyset with many of the BASIC commands

available on a single keystroke (Figure 11.4). Therefore, the commands GO TO, GOSUB, IF, DIM, FOR, and so on, may be printed with a single stroke. Other manufacturers offer a **"soft key" capability.** With this feature, a complete one line command may be programmed as a key function and printed when the key is struck.

An even more useful feature, available on the larger control computers (Figure 11.5), is the capability to interrupt a running program with a given keystroke. The soft key function is programmed to go to a particular subroutine whenever the key is struck. This would happen regardless of what part of the program was executing. Upon completion of the subroutine, program control would return to the next statement in the original program as though no external event had taken place. Several levels of interrupt can be programmed in this manner. A program user, in a process control application, can find this a very useful attribute when it is necessary to examine the status of some data as they are being accumulated in a machine.

When desktops are sold abroad, the manufacturer usually modifies the keyboard to correspond to keyboards in common use in a particular location, country, or region. Even though the majority of European countries use the Latin alphabet, the arrangement of keys may differ. In such cases, modification may be accomplished by means of rewiring the keyboard to generate a different letter from a particular position as contrasted with a U.S. keyboard, or in microprocessor controlled keyboard systems, modification may mean using a differently programmed ROM. In the micro-controlled keyboard, the processor senses the *position* which generates a character and translates it to the correct bit pattern to correspond to the keyboard setup.

11.4 CATHODE RAY TUBE DISPLAYS*

An integral part of a desktop computer is a display device which permits the user to observe results of a program. Although a printer could serve this purpose about as well as an electronic display device, the latter is by far the most popular. With the lower cost "personal" computers, an LED or liquid crystal display may be used, which usually displays approximately 24 characters on a single line (for an example, see Figure 11.1). Right or left scrolling is provided to permit the entire line to be displayed. Frequently, when only this display is available, an output is

*For a detailed discussion of displays, see Chapter 8.

Figure 11.4. The Timex Sinclair 1000 Personal Computer contains a multipurpose keyboard featuring single stroke entry of many BASIC commands as well as many graphics symbols. The minimum system includes 2K bytes of user available memory which can be xpanded to 16K (expansion unit shown attached at rear). For display, a conventional TV receiver is necessary. (Courtesy Timex Computer Corporation).

provided to display more lines on a commercial home television screen.

The most commonly used CRT display consists of a screen which can display a given number of rows and columns of characters. A full size "standard" screen consists of 24 rows containing 80 character positions. The characters are actually stored in RAM memory and are "refreshed" continually on the screen.

There is some variation among manufacturers regarding the refresh rate. Some choose to use a longer lasting phosphor on the display tube, which may be refreshed at a lower cycle rate. When a higher-decay rate phosphor is used, the refresh cycle must be faster, but a quicker display of new information is possible. The CRTs that use a higher refresh rate may use a separate microprocessor for this function.

Alphanumeric characters are formed from a series of dots which are stored as bits in the CRT memory (Figure 11.6). The quality of the character displayed varies substantially among manufacturers. It depends on the number of bits allocated for a character cell and whether an allowance is made for a dot shift in the cell. Character quality ranges from a minimum as formed by a 5 × 7

cell to an almost typewriter quality display formed in a 9 × 15 cell which also allows for a half dot shift.

Screen areas vary from a very modest 190 mm diagonal display to a standard 300 + mm diagonal display. The dot positions are referred to as pixels. If a screen were divided into a 400 × 300 area, for example, and if a character cell occupied 8 × 12 pixels, the display would have a capacity of 25 lines of 50 characters each (i.e., 50 characters, each 8 pixels wide, occupy a screen width of 400 pixels).

Screen size displays range from a low of about 20 × 32 characters to a standard of 80 × 24 characters. In addition, the RAM memory driven display system may store several pages of displays in memory and these may be scrolled by the user. Such display systems are very useful in word processing systems (Chapter 40). Additional features found with some CRTs are blinking, half bright, and underline. These are set up as a special function for an item to be displayed.

Graphics memories are implemented in a manner similar to a dot matrix display for alphanumerics. For a graphics system, each dot in the matrix is addressable under computer control and can be turned on or off by a

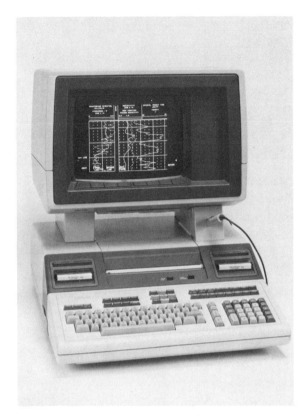

Figure 11.5. The Hewlett-Packard 9845C Desktop Computer is an integrated system containing a high resolution color graphics display, thermal printer, two tape drives, and up to 14 channels for I/O devices. The keyboard includes the standard typewriter key set, a numeric keypad on the lower right, 16 soft keys on the upper right, and special edit and scrolling keys along the upper left. (© Copyright 1980 Hewlett-Packard Company. Reproduced with permission.)

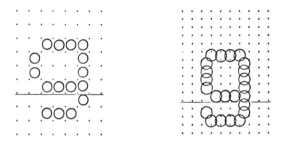

Figure 11.6. Dot matrix character representation showing the differences in character quality between two dot matrix techniques.

modified separately from the other, or that both may be displayed on the screen simultaneously.

Color graphics screens function in the same manner as monochromatic screens, with the exception that *three* memories are used to store images for the three primary colors (normally red, blue and green). For a 560×455 (commercially available) pixel display, this will require a minimum of three memories, with each containing at least 254,800 bits of storage. Color hues are generated by means of varying color intensities for each pixel. In a 17 level color generation pattern, (i.e., 16 intensities + no color) a total of 3^{17} hues can be generated for any point on the screen.

The ultimate capability to interact with a screen is provided by a *light pen* (see Chapter 4). With the proper programs, a light pen can be used to make or modify drawings, and to move or locate printed information. This is a very useful feature in the development of drawings, particularly in machine tool applications.

The key to the light pen's usefulness is the ability of the computer to detect the location of the pixel to which it is pointing. This is accomplished by causing a light dot to traverse the screen and to be sensed by the photo-sensing diode in the pen. The computer then issues the commands necessary to draw a crosshair on the screen which indicates to the user the exact pixel location to which the pen is pointing. From that point on, the user is in command of the program that guides the application.

11.5 FLEXIBLE DISK DRIVES*

Flexible disks are used to increase the storage capacity available to the desktop computer operator. Disks have an advantage over a tape cassette recording in that pro-

graphics programming language. A combination of hardware and preprogrammed ROM functions turns on the dots required to generate the closest possible representation of a desired figure. For example, owing to the limitations of resolution on the screen, a diagonal line may appear as a series of very small steps.

A BASIC language command may be used to draw from one coordinate position to another; the internal subroutines will select the proper pixels that should be turned on. They will remain in this state (i.e., set up in CRT memory and presented to the screen at refresh rates up to 60 Hz) until an erase command is issued. Usually alpha screen memories are stored separately from graphics memories. This means that either can be displayed or

*For a detailed discussion of peripheral devices, see Chapter 6.

grams can be selected directly rather than by a sequential reading process. Flexible disks do not have the speed of conventional or "hard" disks, but they are substantially less expensive. In most cases, the files stored on the disk are used in a single access mode (i.e., one user at a time) rather than in a multiprogrammed mode as might be found with larger computer systems. The general software implementation is to generate a program directory on a set of predetermined tracks; the computer's seek operation goes to the directory, which relates the program or data file name to a track and sector number, and then goes to that location to manage the desired information.

Flexible disk drives are available in 5-¼ inch and 8 inch diameter sizes. The disk medium is a circular sheet of mylar plastic (Figure 11.7), coated with a magnetic iron oxide layer. The medium is always kept in a paper envelope and the entire package is mounted inside the disk drive. In operation, the medium spins inside the envelope while the read/write head moves across an axial opening. The read/write head actually contacts the surface of the disk, with wear the result. For this reason, many manufacturers who supply turnkey software packages instruct users to copy their software before running it in applications. The new copy then becomes the software in use, while the original is saved as a master, or backup, copy.

The more sophisticated drives use a mechanism to lift the head off the surface whenever a read or write function is not required. Furthermore, manufacturers go to substantial efforts to get a good combination of iron oxide and adhesive properties to minimize wear and to reduce

static electricity and residual magnetism. Jacket liners may also be a source of wear and friction: plastic liners and special attention to the lubrication properties of the oxide coatings serve to combat this problem.

Flexible disks are formatted into **tracks** and **sectors;** the minimal addressable unit is the sector (Figure 11.8). It is possible, under direct access methods, to address each sector directly. However, most software systems address programs and files by name and allow the software operating system to use the directory to determine their actual locations.

A typical operating speed of a flexible drive is 360 rpm as contrasted with the 3600 rpm of a hard disk. A 5¼ disk may store from 80K bytes to 1M bytes of information and transfer it at a rate of 16K bytes per second. The transfer rate, of course, depends on the density of the data on the disk and its rotational speed. An average seek time of 300 milliseconds is also typical, so that by the time a complete program is transferred, as much as 2 seconds may elapse.

A typical 8 inch disk drive can store 600K bytes and if it is set up on a double sided basis, it can store 1.2 megabytes. Typical track density is 96 tracks per inch. Average access time and transfer rate again depend on data storage density and rotating speed. Transfers to and from the disk with almost all but the most powerful desktops require that all other activity stops. With the more powerful machines, computational activity can take place asynchronously while data is being transferred through a direct memory access (DMA) channel.

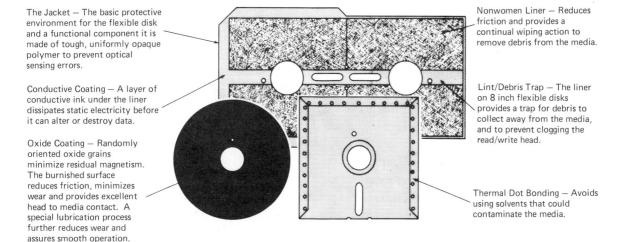

The Jacket — The basic protective environment for the flexible disk and a functional component it is made of tough, uniformly opaque polymer to prevent optical sensing errors.

Conductive Coating — A layer of conductive ink under the liner dissipates static electricity before it can alter or destroy data.

Oxide Coating — Randomly oriented oxide grains minimize residual magnetism. The burnished surface reduces friction, minimizes wear and provides excellent head to media contact. A special lubrication process further reduces wear and assures smooth operation.

Nonwomen Liner — Reduces friction and provides a continual wiping action to remove debris from the media.

Lint/Debris Trap — The liner on 8 inch flexible disks provides a trap for debris to collect away from the media, and to prevent clogging the read/write head.

Thermal Dot Bonding — Avoids using solvents that could contaminate the media.

Figure 11.7. Construction of a flexible disk pack. (Courtesy IBM Corporation)

Figure 11.8. Disk data format. The data is subdivided into concentric tracks which are, in turn, subdivided into sectors. Individual sectors are separated by a gap. Sector addresses are stored within the header.

Also available are multiunit flexible disk drive systems similar to hard disk drives. A single I/O channel can control a master drive which in turn can control up to four drives. Each drive, of course, needs a unique address, or subchannel number. A four drive system, at 1.2 megabytes per drive, would have the capacity of single hard disks. However, the hard disk has the advantage of higher speed and greater convenience.

11.6 WINCHESTER DRIVES

The larger desktops can be connected to standard hard disk drives to gain a storage capacity equal to most minicomputer systems. Hard single disks very commonly have capacities in the range of 50 to 100 megabytes. Although this kind of capacity is very convenient, it is often difficult to justify the cost for a single user system. As an alternate, a small size Winchester drive has been introduced to fulfill the need for reasonable capacity at a modest cost (Figure 11.9).

The key difference between the Winchester drive and

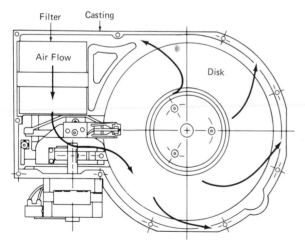

Figure 11.9. The mini-Winchester disk drive (Courtesy Seagate Technology).

a conventional hard disk is that the read/write heads of the Winchester are hermetically sealed inside the same module that contains the disk media. The drives must be manufactured in very clean rooms to avoide contamination. The disk platters are made of polished aluminum and coated with magnetic iron oxide. The read/write heads do not touch the surface, but instead "fly" about 20 microinches above the surface. This allows a much greater storage density and tracks can be formatted up to 250 per inch.

The most common mini-Winchester design uses 2 platters spinning on the same axis at 3600 rpm. Current technology permits the storage of 5 to 10 megabytes on such a drive, but intense research is seeking to increase this capacity substantially. Current data transfer rates from mini-Winchester drives range up to about 600K bytes per second. The cost for a "mini-Wini" is about three to four times the cost for a flexible disc drive, sufficiently low so that some of the larger desktop computers have a "mini-Wini" built right into their cabinets. Although this drive does not have a long operating history owing to its recent commercial introduction, it is expected to have a much better reliability record than either the flexible or hard disk.

11.7 PRINTING DEVICES

Major innovations in printer design have brought down the cost of printers to consistency with the cost of desktop computers. The smaller versions operate with a small number of characters per line (16 for the TRS-80 of Figure 11.1). Also, numerous manufacturers provide a thermal as well as an impact printer in their product lines. Each character is formed by a dot matrix printhead (both in thermal and impact printers). Character quality varies substantially among printers (from 5×7 to 9×15 character cells) as does the number of characters printed per line (from 16 to 132). When a graphics capability is available, drawings can be generated by means of controlling the dot settings or, if the printer's logic is interfaced to the CRT memory, by a "graphics dump" of the CRT image to the printer. An advantage of dot matrix printers (Figure 11.10) is that they can be designed to print characters via keyboard commands of varying sizes and of varying types; i.e., Gothic or Old English.

Discrete printers rely upon three interface types for linking to computers. The most common is the serial interface, or RS-232C, followed by the IEEE-488, and an 8 line parallel interface. In the great majority of desktop

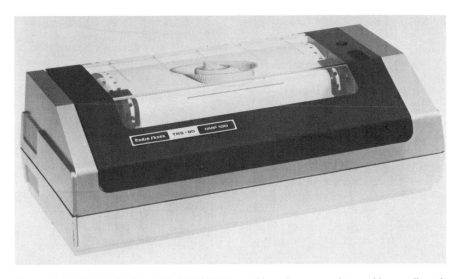

Figure 11.10. The Radio Shack Model DMP100 graphics printer can print graphic as well as alphanumeric information. Graphic images are printed on an 8 inch line from a 480 byte dot buffer. Alpha characters are made up from a 5×7 dot matrix and print at a speed of 50 cps. The printer is an example of a peripheral device designed for personal computer applications. (Courtesy The Tandy Corporation)

units, computation halts to allow printing to take place. With larger computers, both functions can take place simultaneously.

11.8 SPEECH SYNTHESIZER

Several desktop computer manufacturers offer a speech synthesizer. This device can be programmed in BASIC to generate words from a vocabulary stored in ROM chips. Each word is generated by electronic circuitry to form its identifiable sound through a loudspeaker; to accomplish such, each word is represented by a unique pattern of bits in the ROM chip.

The synethesizer can be used to issue commands and to simulate voice communication with the user. Quite obviously, it is especially useful in educational applications and in computer games.

11.9 SYSTEM SOFTWARE

The universal language used with all desktop and personal computers is BASIC. There are many variations of the language; these variations limit the transportability of programs from one computer to another. Furthermore, there is also a variation on interpretation of the data among desktops, which will cause a more subtle variation in the computed results by these programs.

The earlier versions of desktop and personal computers were usually based on an 8 bit microprocessor, whereas the newer ones are based on 16 bit machines, such as the Motorola 68000 and the Intel 8088. To the user, there appears to be no difference because the variations in architecture are concealed in the software. In interpreter mode, a BASIC statement typically takes about a millisecond to execute; consequently the difference of a few microseconds between an 8 bit and a 16 bit machine to execute the same statement may not be noticeable.

Because of their earlier appearance, 8 bit processors have much more software available for them. This is particularly true of Apple II and the TRS-80 Model II. Where possible, manufacturers will build larger versions to operate in a compatibility mode, either by retaining the instruction set of the smaller processor, as a subset of the larger computer, or by including two processors which can operate in either mode.*

---

*For 1982 Digital Equipment Corp. (DEC) introduced its Rainbow model, which contains an 8 bit (Z80) and a 16 bit (8088) microprocessor.

One of the considerations in obtaining a desktop computer is the amount and kinds of software available for it. Because of the rapid application of these machines into many areas, hardware manufacturers have been unable to keep pace with the needs for software. Consequently, many "third party" sources have appeared. These are small organizations of programmers, often former employees of the original manufacturer, who independently supply applications programs for machines built by their former employers. The hardware manufacturers encourage this form of support by advertising the "third party" programs in their hardware catalogs. In other instances, the "third party" may develop a particular software package for a number of desktop machines. An example of such a package is the VisiCalc program developed and registered by VisiCorp. This program permits users to set up business models in their computers and estimate the results from changes in interest rates, plant sizes, cost of labor, etc.

Although BASIC, set up in interpretive, conversational mode is by far the most common language with desktop computers FORTRAN, assembly language, COBOL, and PASCAL also can be used with many models. With a compiler version of BASIC, programs may execute instructions 10 to as much as 100 times faster than in the interpretive mode. A computer with both versions of BASIC enables a user to develop and debug the program in the interpreter mode and when it is correct, compile and execute it in machine language mode for greater execution speed.

Among the differences one sees in the BASIC interpreter is the number of symbols used to identify a variable, a matrix, a string, and a subroutine. The minimum for variables is usually a letter and a number, for a string it is a letter and a $ sign, and for an array, a single letter. Subroutines may not be identified by letter; their starting point may be identified only by the starting statement number.

When desktop computers are supplied with a flexible or hard disk, the commands to access the drive are similar. A file directory is supplied on the disk to locate the actual address of the file. This is not apparent to the user (except by noticing more than one disk access). The FILES, PRINT # and READ # commands are almost universally implemented. However, the user should be wary of different methods of implementing the directories on the disk as well as differences in disk densities when considering swapping data between disk media or between computers from differing manufacturers.

11.10 OPERATING SYSTEMS

An **operating system,** or **executive,** in a computer system is used to perform a number of utility tasks which are not directly related to developing a program, but aid the user in performing useful work with a computer system. Larger computer systems, including the larger desktops, control access among a number of users and schedule the use of peripheral devices so that new jobs are presented to them whenever they are available. Operating systems for the smaller desktops are limited to providing convenient commands for accessing disk files, listing directories, saving and deleting programs, and interpreting keyboard functions.

CP/M Operating System

CP/M (Control Program for Microcomputers)*has evolved as a quasi-standard operating system for desktop computers. It is compatible with any desktop which is based on the Intel 8080, 8085 or Zilog Z-80A microprocessor. It requires a minimum of one disk drive for most functions; for others, such as for copying files, two or more drives are required. The object of the operating system is to provide a uniform set of commands to a user which, in turn, translate to hardware commands that are specific to a given configuration.

The CP/M system is a disk-resident operating system and must first be loaded into the computer. A common procedure is to turn off the computer, turn on the disk drive, install the disk cartridge into the drive, then turn on the computer. The auto-load feature of many desktops gives control to a special program on the disk to load and begin execution of the operating system. If this feature is not present, the user is required to type in the individual commands necessary to load it.

The CP/M software performs the following tasks:

- Loading programs into computer memory.
- Saving programs on the disk.
- Manipulating files on the disk.
- Listing directories.
- Controlling CRT displays.
- Interpreting keyboard functions.
- Operating a peripheral printer.

After the CP/M system is loaded into the computer, it gives a prompt to the user to indicate that it is ready for

*CP/M is a registered trademark of Digital Research Inc.

a command. A typical prompt is A>; this implies that the current address of the disk drive being accessed is A so that all disk-access commands will default to that device. In typical CP/M systems, individual disk drives are addressed by single letters; the manufacturer's software translates this to the particular physical channel or subchannel number where the disk is actually located.

The following are a few examples of typical disk access commands:

A>DIR   Provides a directory listing of the currently accessed disk drive.

A>DIR B: Provides a directory listing for the contents of disk B.

A>DIR WORD?.BAS   Provides a directory listing for all files on disk A whose title contains the word WORD in their first four letters, and any other letter in the fifth position.

A>B:STAT   Loads the program STAT from disk B and starts execution.

A>ERA B:CURFIT.BAS   Erase the file called CURFIT on disk B.

A>ERA*.*   Erases all files on the current disk. Before this command is executed, the system allows the user to reconsider by issuing the following command: ALL (Y/N)?

A>REN   B:NEWNAM.TXT = B:OLDNAM.TXT   Renames the file OLDNAM on disk B to NEWNAM.

A>B: Changes the currently accessed drive from A to B. The system prompt now becomes B > :.

A>B:PIP   Loads a special program (Peripheral Interchange Program) which is used to copy files from one disk to another to verify the files, and to list them to nondisk devices.

A>FORMAT   Loads a special program to restructure the track and sector locations on the disk.

Multiuser Operating Systems

At least two manufacturers have announced multiuser operating systems on their desktop computers. The Hewlett-Packard 9000 is based on a proprietary microprocessor that can execute about a million instructions per second and directly access over 2.5 megabytes of memory. This capability existed until very recently only in medium sized general purpose computers. As a result, such a desktop can readily serve the needs of several users simultaneously.

The HP 9000 can operate in a conventional desktop mode using BASIC as its programming language, or under the control of an operating system called HP-UX, a version of the System III UNIX.* The operating system provides simultaneous access to several users (and up to 59 simultaneous user processes), multitasking, virtual memory for both programs and data, and access to the manufacturer's standard software, such as data base management, various engineering, statistics and communications programs. Available programming languages include PASCAL, FORTRAN 77 assembly language, and a set of graphics utilities. In addition to supporting many users simultaneously, the desktop computers can be linked together in a communications network so that they can interchange programs and data, and share a common disk. Because this "desktop" has all the attributes of a medium-sized computer, the choice as to which computer to obtain for a user becomes one that is very difficult.

The TRS-80 Model 16 employs a 16 bit CPU, and 8.4 megabytes of hard disk memory to establish an operating system that serves 3 users simultaneously. One user is served by the CRT and keyboard of the computer; the remaining two are served by standard CRT terminals. Each user can simultaneously invoke a different program so the system functions in a manner similar to a true multiprogrammed system. In their promotional literature, they illustrate this by showing 3 users simultaneously accessing a payroll program, a inventory program, and an accounting program. As in the case of the Hewlett-Packard system, the software is based on UNIX software. A version of the UNIX software, called XENIX, was developed by the Microsoft Corporation.

A similar software capability has been announced for the TRS-80 Model II, operating as the Model 16, except that the particular software package has not been named. In the Model 16 mode, the Model II contains its original process or the Z-80†, plus the Motorola MC6800 processor. Input/output functions rest with the smaller, 8 bit processor (the Z-80) while the computational functions are given to the larger machine. Up to 256K of memory can be supported.

11.11 APPLICATION SOFTWARE

Desktop computers have been designed and programmed to be "friendly" to their users; i.e., easily learned and easy

*UNIX is a registered trademark of Bell Laboratories, Inc.
†A registered trademark of Zilog Corp.

to use. Consequently, high speed computation and throughput is set aside in favor of elaborate menu displays, instructions, and error codes to enable the noncomputer expert to become familiar with the system very readily. Because the value of the desktop is based very much on the combined hardware and software system, a potential user needs to review both very thoroughly, rather than place undue emphasis on the hardware characteristics. The following paragraphs list a few of the many software packages currently available with desktop machines.

Business Accounting*

This package usually consists of 5 subsets: accounts receivable, accounts payable, general ledger, payroll, and inventory control. The software requires between 32K and 64K of memory and a disk system. Because of the hardware limitations (usually the capacity of the disk), the programs are suitable only for small businesses or small departments which may function as profit centers. Typical limitations may allow for 100 to 300 accounts (vendors or customers), 200 to 1,000 entries per month, 100 to 500 checks per month and quantity limitation based on the arithmetic function of the computer; i.e., 32 bit arithmetic allowing for a resolution of 1 part in 8,388,608 would permit carrying accurately amounts owed only up to $83,886.08. With a 12 digit BCD system, a resolution of 1 part in 999,999,999,999 is possible. With some turnkey software, the resolution can be upgraded with double precision arithmetic.

Payroll packages are rather abundant and, of course, may be limited by the requirements for tax withholding, and for workmen's compensation by each state. The larger computer vendors may have an advantage here in that they may be able to provide software tailored for each state, or, a single package with options. A typical payroll system may provide for up to 100 employees a maximum of 15 entries each for various earnings and deducted amounts.

Inventory packages may be provided as an accessory to a data base system or as separate and independent entity. Desirable functions include notification to reorder, price-break quantities, order dates, reorder requirements, and on-order items. A typical desktop inventory package may contain formation for 1,000 items.

*For further discussion of business systems, see Chapter 16.

Data Base Management

The function of a **data base system** is to provide the user selected items in a large file on a very prompt basis. Data base systems naturally require substantial disk capacity and are usually provided with only the larger desktop systems. Data are stored by **record,** which may be as much as 1,000 characters in length and divided into as many as 100 **fields.** *Indexes* are set up to search records for a particular characteristic in a given field; the search may be based on several record characteristics so that a set of records can be identified according to a collection of simultaneous characteristics. Usually a simplified report generation procedure is provided so that the retrieved reports may be presented in an orderly fashion.

Data base systems may be best used with multiterminal systems because they are not computer-bound. A typical setup combines a data entry station with a number of other stations available for inquiries.

Graphics

Graphics software systems are designed to display business data, mechanical drawings, and mathematical and statistical functions to give the user the image portrayed by the data. Graphics languages provide easy-to-use commands to generate axes, set titles, and generate bar and pie charts. Colors or shadings may also be added. Either with cursor control, or with a light pen, a portion of the image can be modified; i.e., enlarged, deleted, or corrected. A complete graphics package includes some means of transferring the image to a hard copy device; this may be a plotter or a dot matrix printer.

Spread Sheets

Spread sheet programs have been developed and implemented on a very large number of desktop, mini- and even standard computers. Their primary function is to create a model of a business and present answers to what would happen to the business when particular events take place, such as, changes in the cost of raw materials, interest rates, labor rates, and capacity. The program is also applicable in setting up financial, real estate, and general purpose business models.

Word Processing

Word processing systems appear with varying levels of capability, from simple editions to very complex functions. In a true word processing system, the computer checks spelling from a built-in dictionary; and implements shifting of text to allow for changes in margin alignment, movement of text from one location to another, replacement of old text with new text and setting up headers and footnotes. Other features may include automatic hyphenation, centering, and page numbering. Such systems are also available on larger computers, but the portability of the desktop makes it a very suitable vehicle for word processing.

Mailing List

Mailing list programs allow the user to enter, delete, and modify customers' or vendors' names, addresses, telephone numbers, and areas of interest. Usually these programs will generate mailing labels based on areas of interest, buying records, and zip codes. Mailing lists may be set up in conjunction with a data-base system a general business package or a word processor.

CAD-CAM Processing

Computer aided design and computer aided manufacturing programs have also been very successfully implemented on desktop systems. These programs require large amounts of memory as well as a graphics display capability that permits the engineer to see a part as it is designed. Numerical machine tool manufacturers can then program the steps required to produce the part and generate a control tape for the shop floor. Computers for CAD/CAM are larger and require special displays (see Chapter 41).

Games

One cannot even begin to list all the games available with desktop computers. There can be games against the computer, or two or multiple player games with the computer keeping track of each participants actions. Games of chance, such as poker or dice, can readily be simulated by a random number generator available with many systems. Games tend to lessen an individual's inhibitions about making errors, encourage familiarity with the keyboard and, in general, make the desktop computer a more friendly device. Games also offer challenges to programmers, and possibly for that reason, they seem to appear very readily for new computers as the latter are released by manufacturers.

Other Programs

The growth in applications for the desktop or personal computer has been and continues to be one of the most spectacular phenomena in the computer industry. A major contributor to this growth has been the continuous drop in the cost of hardware, particularly microprocessor chips, solid state memories, and disk drives and printers.

The sale of desktops in large volumes has encouraged developers other than the original equipment manufacturers to create programs for sale on the likely supposition that they will be amortized over large numbers of computers. Therefore, there many excellent programs are available, certainly beyond the capability of a single chapter's description. The user of a desktop computer is encouraged to enlist the aid of hardware manufacturers, various computer magazines and user groups to seek the availability of programs and to ascertain their quality.

REFERENCES

Bell, D. H., *The VisiCalc Book*. Reston, Va: Reston Publishing Co., 19.

Boillot, M., *Understanding Fortran*. St. Paul: West Publishing Co., 1981.

Cortesi, D. E., *Inside CP/M*. New York: Holt, Rinehart & Winston, 19.

Curtice, R. M., and P. E. Jones, *Logical Data Base Design*. New York: Van Nostrand Reinhold, 1982.

Date, C. J., *An Introduction to Database Systems*. Reading, MA: Addison-Wesley, 1981.

Dennon, R. C., *CP/M Revealed*. Rochelle Park, NJ: Hayden Book Co., 1982.

Flores, I., *Data Base Architecture*. New York: Van Nostrand Reinhold, 1982.

Flores, I., *Word Processing Handbook*. New York: Van Nostrand Reinhold, 1982.

Flores, I., and Christopher Terry, *Microcomputer System*. New York: Van Nostrand Reinhold, 1982.

Gauthier, R., *Using the UNIX System*. Reston, Va: Reaston Publishing Co., 1981.

Graham, N., *Introduction to Pascal*. St. Paul: West Publishing Co., 1980.

Harrington, S., *Computer Graphics*. New York: McGraw-Hill Book Co., 1983.

Miller, A. R., *Basic Programs for Scientists and Engineers*. Berkeley, CA: Sybex, 1981.

Thomas, R., and J. Yates. *A User Guide to the UNIX System*. Berkeley, CA: Osborne/McGraw-Hill, 1982.

12
Computer Organization

S. G. Zaky
Z. G. Vranesic
V. C. Hamacher

University of Toronto

12.1 INTRODUCTION

Digital computers, whether small (microcomputers) or large (mainframes), consist of five functionally independent main parts: input, memory, arithmetic and logic, output, and control, as shown in Figure 12.1. The input and output units, grouped into the **input/output (I/O)** subsystem, enable communication with the external world, whether human operators or electronic or electromechanical devices. The **main memory,** also called the **primary memory,** stores programs and the data on which they operate. Program instructions are executed in the arithmetic and logic section of the **central processing unit (CPU)** subsystem. The control circuits of the CPU are responsible for fetching instructions and operands (data) from the main memory into the CPU for execution, and for storing results back into the main memory. Control is also responsible, either directly or indirectly, for the sequence of actions needed to move programs and data between the I/O subsystem and the main memory or the CPU.

I/O subsystem

The I/O subsystem contains the circuits which comprise the interface between a wide range of peripheral devices and the main memory of the computer. Typical input devices are CRT terminal keyboards, teletypewriter keyboards, graphical input devices, and analog to digital signal converters. Output devices include CRT terminal displays for characters and graphics, character printers, line printers, and digital to analog signal converters.

A major class of peripheral devices is used for **secondary storage** of program and data files. Magnetic disks, diskettes, tapes, cassettes, and drums all function as both input and output storage devices. They are able to store large amounts of data—billions of bytes (characters) in large hard disks, for example—and have access mechanisms that support data flow rates in the range of 100K to 1M bytes per second in hard disks, drums and tapes. A large part of the cost of a complete computer system, across the full price/performance range, is associated with these peripheral devices.

Main Memory

The size of the main memory can range from 64K or less (1K = 1,024) bytes in small computers to tens of millions of bytes in large systems. The basic building blocks of the main memory are VLSI semiconductor chips that typically contain at least 16K bits each. The read/write access times of these circuits are of the order of a fraction of a microsecond.

The memory access control (see Figure 12.1) is arranged to transfer data in and out of the main memory in bit-parallel units (called **memory words**) ranging from 8 bits in some microcomputers to 64 bits in some large mainframes. The cost per bit of the main memory subsystem has steadily decreased with increasing levels of chip bit-storage density and capacity.

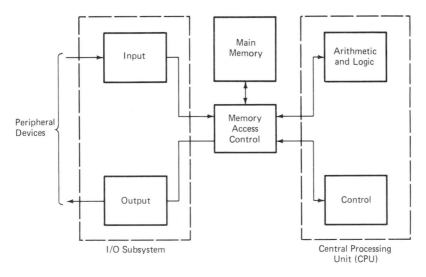

Figure 12.1. Basic functional units of a computer.

Memory access control is implemented in a variety of ways, depending upon performance requirements. The simplest way uses a set of wires, called a **bus,** to link the I/O, memory, and CPU subsystems. Data transfers among these units are individually controlled at the word level by instructions executed by the CPU. In high performance systems, physically separate I/O and memory busses may be used. Memory access control can become quite complicated, with direct memory access (DMA) controllers and I/O processors used to control transfers of large blocks of words, as will be discussed.

CPU

The CPU executes instructions that either process data or cause the transfer of data among different functional units in the computer system. The rate of executing instructions ranges from several hundred thousand instructions per second in small machines to several million instructions per second (called **MIPs**) in some large mainframes. Most CPUs contain a number of registers, typically 8 to 64, that hold temporary data or addresses and are accessible to the programmer. Machine instructions perform arithmetic and logic operations, instruction sequencing control, and input/output transfers.

12.2 INSTRUCTION SETS

To perform a given processing task, the computer's CPU executes an ordered sequence of operations, called **ma-chine instructions,** that constitutes a program. The instructions of the program are stored in consecutive locations in the main memory, and are usually executed in the order in which they appear. Operand data associated with the task may also be stored in the main memory.

A typical instruction begins with a specification of an operation to be performed, followed by addressing information that is used to locate the operands. For example, an instruction might read a number from the main memory and add it to a number stored in a general purpose CPU register, leaving the result in the register. The complete set of operations that can be performed by the CPU of a computer is called its **instruction set.**

This section disscusses some basic and some more complex instructions that are representative of those found in many computers. The control steps that must be performed by the CPU to fetch an instruction from the main memory and execute it is outlined. The ways in which an instruction can specify the location of an operand are called the **addressing modes.** Common addressing modes and their use are given in some detail.

Accessing the Main Memory

The main memory consists of thousands or even millions of words. Each word consists, as observed above, of a fixed number of bits, ranging from 8 bits in some microcomputers to 64 bits in some large mainframes. For the CPU to access the main memory to store or retrieve a single word of information, it must specify the **address** (location) of that word in the memory. Addresses are chosen to be the numbers 0 through M-1 for an M word memory. Figure 12.2 shows how a program consisting of a set of instructions and associated data may be stored in word locations i through k.

An instruction may occupy more than one word. To execute a multiword instruction, the CPU control circuits transfer the individual words comprising the instruction, one at a time, from the main memory into the CPU. It is also necessary to move operands and results between the main memory and the CPU. These steps are accomplished with the basic operations **read** (or **fetch**) and **write** (or **store**). To cause either operation, the CPU sends the address of the required word over the address lines of the bus connecting the CPU to the main memory. A signal to distinguish read from write is also sent over the control lines of the bus. On a read operation, a single word is fetched from the addressed location in the main

memory and transferred over the data lines of the bus into the CPU, leaving the main memory location unchanged. On a write operation, a word is transferred from the CPU into the addressed location, replacing its previous contents.

The CPU keeps track of the location of the next instruction to be executed by maintaining its address in a CPU register called the **program counter** (**PC**). The PC is updated as each word of each instruction is read into the CPU. The detailed control steps, and a discussion of the address, data, and instruction buffer registers required in the CPU to facilitate these word transfers are given in a later section on CPU organization.

Instruction Classes

The tasks performed by programs involve a number of functionally different operations. A typical machine instruction set can be subdivided into three general classes:

- internal data transfers and operations;
- program sequencing control;
- I/O transfers.

The first two classes are discussed in this subsection. Input/Output transfers are treated in a subsequent section on I/O organization.

Data transfers and operations. It is helpful to discuss machine instructions with the aid of a simple task. Suppose we wish to add the contents of main memory locations A and B, placing the sum in location C, without altering the content in locations A or B. A convenient self-explanatory shorthand notation for this task is

$$C \leftarrow [A] + [B] \qquad (12.1)$$

where [A] indicates that the contents of location A are involved in the operation. A single three-address instruction, represented symbolically as

$$\text{Add A,B,C} \qquad (12.2)$$

can be used to accomplish the task. This type of instruction might occupy four main memory words: one for the operation code (opcode) for add, and one for each of the main memory addresses A, B, and C. A total of seven main memory accesses needs to be performed by the CPU to fetch and execute this instruction. These are four reads to fetch the instruction, followed by two reads to fetch the operands at A and B, and a final write to store the sum at C. Note that no general purpose CPU registers are involved in this operation.

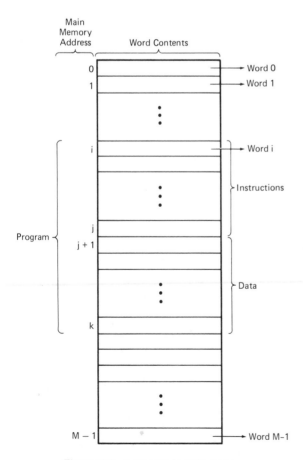

Figure 12.2. A program in main memory.

Another possibility for performing (12.1) is to use a sequence of two instructions

$$\text{Move B,C}$$
$$\text{Add A,C} \qquad (12.3)$$

Each of these instructions contains only two memory addresses. The first instruction reads the contents of main memory location B and writes them into location C, while the second adds the contents of A to the contents of C, writing the sum into location C.

Assuming that each instruction occupies three main memory words, a total of six memory locations are required to store the instructions. A total of 11 main memory accesses (9 reads and 2 writes) are required to fetch and execute the two instructions. Note that more memory space and fetch/execute time is needed for the complete task when the simpler two address instruction format is used. However, the CPU circuits and controls for stepping through the shorter instructions are simpler.

The use of general purpose CPU registers in facilitating program execution is illustrated next. Suppose there are k registers contained in the CPU, addressed as R_0 through R_{k-1}. Each register can hold a word of data. Our running example of $C \leftarrow [A] + [B]$ can be executed by the three-instruction sequence

$$\text{Move A,}R_i$$
$$\text{Add B,}R_i \qquad (12.4)$$
$$\text{Move }R_i\text{,C}$$

Since there are only a few registers, only a few bits are needed to specify one of them.

If we assume that the register involved in each instruction is named in the instruction word, then each of the above three instruction can be represented in two memory words. It is easy to see that the above instruction sequence occupies a total of six words and requires nine memory accesses for its execution. This is slightly more efficient than the second option (12.3), and uses simpler instructions.

In many small computers, when a CPU register is involved in an instruction, often the particular register to be used is implicitly indicated by the opcode. For example, the instruction sequence

$$\text{Load accum } A$$
$$\text{Add accum } B \qquad (12.5)$$
$$\text{Store accum } C$$

implements the operation $C \leftarrow [A] + [B]$. The register involved, called an accumulator, is always implied in the opcode and hence does not take up valuable instruction space.

Let us summarize our discussion about the first class of instructions. We have seen possibilities for referencing three, two, or only one memory operand in a single instruction. As instructions become shorter and simpler, more of them are required to perform a given task. It has also been shown that CPU registeres can be used to increase processing speed.

Program sequencing control. Until now, we have assumed that successive instructions of a program are fetched from consecutive main memory locations. The program counter in the CPU keeps track of the address of the next instruction as execution proceeds. This is accomplished simply by incrementing the contents of PC as successive instruction words are fetched.

This mode of program sequencing is not sufficient for many common computational tasks. Consider the case in which one of two alternative computation paths must be chosen, based on the sign (or some other condition) of an intermediate result. This may be done with a conditional branch instruction, branch on condition C to L.

When this instruction is executed, the condition, C, is tested. If it is *true,* the next instruction is fetched from main memory location L (the beginning of one of the two paths). Otherwise, if C is *false,* execution continues at the instruction immediately following the branch instruction, which is the beginning of the other path.

An example of the use of such an instruction is shown in the program of Figure 12.3. This program adds n numbers stored in memory (beginning at location NUMLIST) and places the sum in memory location SUM. The partial sum is kept in CPU register R_0. Register R_1 keeps track of how many numbers are still to be added. At this point, we explain only how the *decrement* and *branch* instructions operate in order to illustrate the notion of conditional branching. The way in which the remainder of the program operates is discussed after addressing modes are described.

The program is arranged so that each time a number is added to the partial sum in R_0, the count of the remaining numbers, which is kept in R_1, is reduced by 1 by the *decrement* instruction. The result of this operation is tested by the *branch* instruction. If the count is greater than 0 (if some numbers remain to be added), the branch instruction causes execution control to be transferred to the instruction stored at memory location LOOPSTART. To do this, the CPU loads the address value, LOOP-

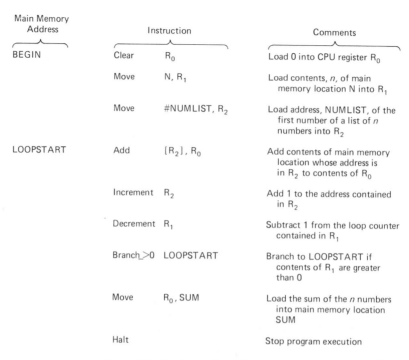

Main Memory Address	Instruction		Comments
BEGIN	Clear	R_0	Load 0 into CPU register R_0
	Move	N, R_1	Load contents, n, of main memory location N into R_1
	Move	#NUMLIST, R_2	Load address, NUMLIST, of the first number of a list of n numbers into R_2
LOOPSTART	Add	$[R_2]$, R_0	Add contents of main memory location whose address is in R_2 to contents of R_0
	Increment	R_2	Add 1 to the address contained in R_2
	Decrement	R_1	Subtract 1 from the loop counter contained in R_1
	Branch_>0	LOOPSTART	Branch to LOOPSTART if contents of R_1 are greater than 0
	Move	R_0, SUM	Load the sum of the n numbers into main memory location SUM
	Halt		Stop program execution

Figure 12.3. A program for adding n numbers.

START, into the PC. Otherwise, when the count reaches 0, execution control continues at the instruction immediately following the branch instruction, by simply proceeding with the instruction pointed at by the incremented address in the PC.

In general, the condition tested by a branch instruction applies to the result of the most recent operation. In the foregoing case, this operation is a decrement instruction, and the result is the value left in R_1. Conditions that can be tested include zero, positive, negative, arithmetic overflow and the results of comparison instructions. Typically each of these attributes is represented by a bit in a CPU register called the *condition code register*.

Addressing Modes

Until now, we have only used the implicit and absolute addressing modes for specifying the location of an operand. Their usage was easy to understand. Next, we consider addressing modes in general.

Implicit mode —the location of the operand is implied by the opcode of the instruction. An example of this was seen in the instruction Load accum A, which moves the contents of main memory location A into the CPU accumulator.

Absolute mode —the address of the location of the operand is given explicitly in the instruction. Two versions of this mode have been used in the earlier examples: *memory absolute mode*, where the operand is in a main memory location, and *register mode*, where the operand is in one of the CPU registers. Both versions are used in the instruction Move A,R_i.

Three other important addressing modes are frequently used:

Immediate mode —the operand itself is contained in the instruction. An example of this mode can be seen in the third instruction in Figure 12.3, where the address value **NUMLIST** (the operand) is moved into register R_2. The symbolic name **NUMLIST** is used to represent the actual numeric value of the address. Note that # is used to indicate the immediate mode; in the instruction word a single bit may convey this.

Indirect mode —the address of the operand is in the location (main memory or CPU register) whose address is given in the instruction. The indirect mode of accessing the first operand in the add instruction in Figure 12.3 uses register R_2 as the location for the address of the operand. This is indicated by the square brackets. In our example program, R_2 has its contents incremented (by the increment instruction) immediately after each execution of the add instruction. This places in R_2 the successive addresses of the locations of the numbers to be added, beginning from the address NUMLIST. It is usual terminology to say that the operands are accessed indirectly through the pointer register R_2.

Index mode —the address of the operand is generated by adding the address contained in the instruction to a value contained in a CPU register. If a CPU register is dedicated solely for this purpose, it is called an **index register.** Many computers permit the general purpose registers to be used as index registers. An example of the use of indexed addressing is

$$ADD \ NUMLIST \ (R_2), \ R_0$$

The first operand in this instruction is in the index mode (specified by the parentheses about R_2). Its address is calculated as NUMLIST $+ \ [R_2]$. The operand at this location is added to the contents of R_0, and the sum is stored into R_0. Suppose R_2 initially contains 0 and is incremented after each execution of the above ADD instruction. Then, it is easy to see that after n executions of the ADD and INCREMENT sequence, the sum of the n numbers beginning at main memory location NUMLIST accumulates in R_0 (assuming that R_0 initially contained 0).

This method of accessing the operands for addition in the program in Figure 11.3 can be achieved by replacing the third and fourth instructions with the instruction pair

$$LOOPSTART \quad CLEAR \quad R_2 \quad\quad (12.7)$$
$$ADD \quad NUMLIST(R_2),R_0$$

This discussion of addressing modes, along with the comments in Figure 12.3, should make clear how the complete program operates. The sequence of four instructions beginning at LOOPSTART is usually called a **program loop,** and register R_1 is referred to as the **loop counter.** To begin execution of the program, the address value, BEGIN is loaded into the PC. Execution stops when the HALT instruction is encountered. It is assumed that the loop count, $n,$ (number of values to be added) has been loaded into memory location N before program execution begins.

Commercially available computers implement variations and combinations of the five basic addressing modes defined above; while details vary, the main concepts remain the same.

Subroutines and Stacks

In many computer programs there is a need to compute some standard function, such as the sine or cosine of an angle or carry out a common operation on a list of operands, for example, sorting by increasing or decreasing order. It is useful to write general routines, called **subroutines,** for such frequently needed tasks, place them in main memory at a known address, and branch to them with specific operands whenever they are required in a program. This results in a saving in memory space because the subroutines do not need to be included in the program at every position where their execution is required. All that is needed at these positions is a branch instruction, which transfers execution control to the beginning of the desired subroutine.

The branch instruction used to access subroutines is referred to as a **subroutine call instruction.** The instruction

$$Subroutine \ call \ LOC \quad\quad (12.8)$$

in the calling program causes a branch to the subroutine whose first instruction is at main memory location LOC. When execution of the subroutine is finished, its last instruction should be

$$Subroutine \ return \quad\quad (12.9)$$

This instruction causes a branch to the calling program at the instruction immediately following the subroutine call instruction.

Suppose the call instruction is in main memory location i, and the next instruction is in location $i + 1$. The address $i + 1$ must be saved so that the subroutine return instruction can load it into the PC to effect a branch back to the proper location. A common way to save the return address $i + 1$ is to place it on a stack structure maintained in the memory.

A stack is a list of words with the accessing rule that elements can be entered or removed at one end of the list only. This end is called the **top of the stack.** The last item placed on the stack is always the first one to be removed when retrieval begins. The terms *push* and *pop* are often used to describe the operations of placing a new item on a stack, and removing the top item from a stack, respectively.

A stack can be conveniently used to store the subroutine return address $i + 1$, the updated value in the PC. The subroutine call instruction pushes the return address $i + 1$ onto a stack, and the subroutine return instruction pops i + 1 off the stack into the PC.

A stack can be kept in the computer memory with successive elements of the stack occupying consecutive locations. It is convenient to dedicate a CPU register, called the **stack pointer (SP)**, to hold the address of the current top item on the stack. If the stack grows in the direction of decreasing addresses, then the SP is decremented when performing a push operation and incremented when performing a pop.

The last-in, first-out (LIFO) nature of stack accessing is particularly appropriate for storing return addresses in nested subroutine calls. Subroutine calls are said to be **nested** when the main program calls subroutine A, which calls subroutine B, and so forth. The return address pushed onto the stack by the call to the last subroutine of the nested call sequence is the first address to be popped when that subroutine executes a return to the second last subroutine. Successive returns pop appropriate return addresses until subroutine A finally pops the first address pushed, effecting return to the main calling program.

Calling programs usually need to pass parameters to the subroutines that they call. Three techniques for passing parameters are commonly used. The simplest technique passes parameters through CPU registers. The second approach is to list the parameters in the calling program, immediately following the subroutine call instruction. In the third technique, parameters are pushed onto a stack.

Complex Instructions

The simple move, add, branch, increment, decrement, (and so forth) instructions described so far constitute the bulk of machine instruction types found in commercial computers. However, more complex instructions are also used. A single instruction may perform a block move of a number of memory words to or from a set of CPU registers or between two areas in memory. Another instruction may perform a matching operation in which a search is made for each occurrence of a given substring of characters in a longer string. Yet other instructions may be provided for polynomial evaluation and floating point numerical operations. Of course, these operations can be implemented by executing a sequence of simpler machine instructions. However, for many applications, both in

business and scientific computing, supporting such operations with single machine instructions is very attractive.

The design of efficient machine instruction sets is a difficult task. Many successful and very different instruction sets are in use in modern digital computers. Our discussion has only raised a few of the issues involved. An important aspect of instruction set design is its suitability for the execution of programs translated automatically from a higher level language by a compiler. However, an appreciation of the factors involved is beyond the scope of this chapter.

12.3 CPU ORGANIZATION

As its name implies, the central processing unit contains most of the processing capability in a computer system. It also provides the control necessary to coordinate the activities of other components in the system. In what follows, we examine in some detail the steps involved in executing individual instructions stored in the main memory. We also present a representative organization of internal data paths in the CPU needed to support these operations.

Instruction Execution

As described earlier, a program is comprised of a sequence of instructions stored in successive locations in memory. During program execution, the CPU fetches and executes one instruction at a time. It keeps track of the location of the instruction to be executed next by storing its address in an internal register known as the program counter (PC).

The process of executing one instruction may be divided into four steps:

1. Fetch the instruction;
2. Update the program counter;
3. Decode the instruction;
4. Perform the operations specified in the instruction.

Step 1 consists of a read operation at the memory location pointed at by the PC. The instruction fetched from memory is stored in an internal CPU register referred to as the **instruction register (IR).** In step 2, the CPU updates the PC to point to the next instruction. For example, if instructions are stored at locations 0, 1, 2, and so on, the PC is incremented by 1. In the case of a byte-addressable machine that uses 16 bit instructions, the PC is incremented by 2. In machines with other instruction lengths, the PC is incremented accordingly.

In step 3, the CPU circuitry decodes the instruction stored in the IR to determine the operations to be performed. These operations, which may or may not involve further references to the main memory, are carried out in step 4.

Internal Data Paths

A simple example illustrating internal data paths in the CPU is given in Figure 12.4. In addition to the program counter and the instruction register, there are n general purpose registers R_0 to R_{n-1}, and a temporary register TEMP. Communication with the memory takes place via the memory address register (MAR) and the memory

data register (MDR). These registers and the arithmetic and logic unit (ALU) are interconnected using two buses, BUS_1 and BUS_0. The ALU consists of circuits for performing various operations on the operands applied at its two inputs A and B. The result is produced at output Y. Typically, the ALU is capable of carrying out operations such as $Y = B$, $Y = A + B$, $Y = B - A$, $Y = A \lor B$, (A OR B), $Y = B + 1$, etc. The function $Y = B$ makes it possible to transfer data from BUS_0 to BUS_1.

Let us now consider in some detail the steps involved in fetching and executing an instruction. The address of the memory location from which the instruction is to be read is in the PC. For transmission on the memory address bus, this address should be transferred to the MAR register. This transfer is accomplished by enabling the output of the PC on BUS_0, setting the ALU function to $Y = B$ and enabling the input for register MAR. The control circuitry of the CPU should also transmit a read request on the control lines of the memory bus. We will use the following abbreviated format to describe the operations which implement step 1:

$$1.\ PC_{out},\ Y = B,\ MAR_{in},\ Read \qquad (12.10)$$

Reading data from memory usually involves some delay. While waiting for the results of the read operation to become available, the CPU may proceed with step 2, since it does not depend upon the data requested from the memory. Assuming that the program counter is to be incremented by 1, step 2 may be stated as:

$$2.\ PC_{out},\ Y = B + 1,\ PC_{in} \qquad (12.11)$$

When the read from memory is completed, the contents of the location specified by the address bus are transmitted on the data bus to the MDR. At the same time, a control signal, which we will call Data-Ready, is sent by the memory to the CPU, indicating that the data is now available in MDR. The CPU must wait for this signal before proceeding further. Hence, step 3 may take the form:

$$3.\ Wait\ for\ Data\text{-}Ready,\ MDR_{out},\ Y = B,\ IR_{in}$$
$$(12.12)$$

Following step 3, an instruction (or the first word of a multiple word instruction) is available in IR. The instruction decoding circuit connected to the IR determines the actions which take place in step 4 and any subsequent steps which may be needed to complete execution of that instruction.

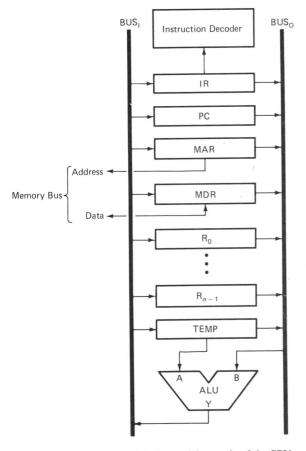

Figure 12.4. An example of the internal data paths of the CPU.

1. PC_{out}, $Y = B$, MAR_{in}, Read
2. PC_{out}, $Y = B + 1$, PC_{in}
3. Wait for data ready, MDR_{out}, $Y = B$, IR_{in}
4. PC_{out}, $Y = B$, MAR_{in}, Read
5. PC_{out}, $Y = B + 1$, PC_{in}
6. Wait for data ready, MDR_{out}, $Y = B$, MAR_{in}, Read
7. $R1_{out}$, $Y = B$, $TEMP_{in}$
8. Wait for data ready, MDR_{out}, $Y = A + B$, $R1_{in}$

Figure 12.5. Sequence of steps involved in fetching and executing the instruction Add VAR, R1.

Figure 12.5 contains a complete sequence of steps for fetching and executing this instruction:

$$\text{Add} \quad \text{VAR}, R_1 \quad\quad (12.13)$$

which adds the source operand at location VAR to register R_1 and stores the result in R_1. Operand VAR is assumed to be stored in memory at the address given in the second word of the instruction. The reader should verify that the sequence in the figure will, in fact, perform the required operations. Note that after fetching the address of the operand, the program counter is incremented so that it points at the first word of the following instruction. Also, observe that internal operations in the CPU, such as incrementing the PC and moving the contents of R_1 to TEMP, are carried out whenever possible, while waiting for the memory to respond.

Control of CPU Operations

The operations referred to in the previous subsection, such as PC_{out} or MAR_{in}, are carried out in response to control signals sent to the registers involved. It can be readily appreciated that there are many such signals transmitted about within the CPU of a computer. The control section of the CPU is responsible for generating these signals in the correct sequence so as to fetch and execute instructions.

The control unit is a sequential machine whose outputs are the control signals that actuate register inputs and outputs, set ALU function, and so on. Its input information consists of the output of the instruction decoder as well as signals from other parts of the computer. This sequential machine may be either a **hardwired** electronic circuit or a **microprogrammed** (see Chapter 13) unit. A hardwired unit is implemented using logic circuitry such that machine behavior is completely specified by the interconnections between individual components. Once the

machine is constructed, the functions performed by the CPU cannot be altered. In a microprogrammed control unit, on the other hand, the required sequence of control signals is stored in a high speed memory in the CPU; the information itself stored in this memory is known as the *microprogram*.

A microprogrammed control unit offers considerable flexibility to the computer designer. Once the design is completed, the microprogram may be stored in a read-only memory (ROM). It becomes essentially a part of the hardware of the CPU. In some cases, all or part of the microprogram is stored in RAM. This makes it possible for the computer user to change the microprogram, and hence the instruction set of that computer. The microprogramming approach is used almost exclusively in modern general purpose computers. For further details, consult Chapter 13.

12.4 MEMORY ORGANIZATION

The devices used for storing programs and data in a computer system may be divided into three functional categories: main memory, (or simply memory) on-line mass storage and off-line mass storage. The memory is that part of the computer from which information can be accessed directly by the CPU at any time during program execution and at speeds commensurate with the operating speed of the CPU. In modern computers, the memory consists almost exclusively of high density intergrated circuit (IC) chips.

On-line mass storage devices typically provide several orders of magnitude more storage capacity than the memory but at proportionately lower speed. To make the information stored on these devices accessible to the CPU, this information must first be copied into the main memory. Typically, several milliseconds are needed for such transfers. The rotating magnetic disk is widely used as an on-line mass storage device.

Off-line storage refers to the storage of information for archival purposes, away from the computer system. Magnetic tapes and removable disk packs are common examples of storage media which can be removed from their respective drives and stored for safe keeping, freeing the drive for other use. The delay involved in accessing information stored on these media may be several minutes to several hours, depending on the amount of human intervention needed for mounting tapes or disk packs.

Mass storage devices are one kind of computer peripheral. Their physical characteristics as well as those of other computer peripherals are described in Chapter 6.

In this section we present some examples of physical implementation of memory, followed by a discussion of memory management.

Physical Organization of the Memory

The characteristics and internal organization of memory ICs are presented in Chapter 3. The following paragraphs briefly discuss how these ICs may be used to construct the main memory of a computer. In particular, we consider a 64K $\times$ 8 bit memory module, having 65,536 (2^{16}) locations of 8 bits each, implemented using 16K $\times$ 1 dynamic memory chips. One such module may constitute the entire memory of an 8 bit microprocessor system. In larger systems, several modules may be combined to provide a large number of words and/or a longer word length.

A schematic of the design of a 64K $\times$ 8 memory module is given in Figure 12.6. It accepts 16 bits of address,

8 bits of data and 3 control signals: read/write, ready, and accept. The first of these control signals indicates the type of operation being requested, while the latter two are timing signals whose role is discussed in the next section.

The module consists of 32 memory chips organized in an array as shown. During a memory access, the least significant 14 bits of an address are strobed into each memory chip. This process takes place 7 bits at a time, via two timing signals, row address strobe (RAS) and column address strobe (CAS). The two most significant address bits, $A_{15,14}$ cause one of four groups of chips to be selected, using the chip-select (CS) inputs.

We assume that dynamic memory chips are being used. This type of memory stores information reliably only for a period of a few milliseconds. To retain information for longer periods, the content of each memory cell is refreshed periodically. Typically, when a read operation is performed at a given address, the contents of all memory cells that have the same row address are re-

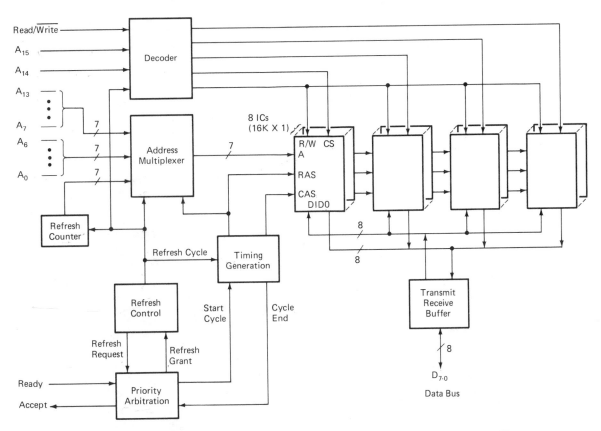

Figure 12.6. Typical organization of a 64K $\times$ 8 dynamic memory using 16K $\times$ 1 memory ICs.

freshed. Thus, the entire memory can be refreshed by successive read operations at all possible row addresses.

In the circuit (Figure 12.6) refresh requests are generated periodically by the refresh control circuit. The priority arbitration circuit gives priority to the refresh request if it happens to arrive at the same time as an access request on the memory bus. During a refresh cycle, the decoder circuit ensures that the memory is in the read mode, independent of the state of the read/write line of the bus. The row address used during that cycle is obtained from a 7 bit refresh counter, which is incremented at the end of the cycle.

Memory cycle time is defined as the minimum time allowed between two successive requests for access. This is an important parameter in determining the performance of a computer system. Faster memories can be achieved not only by using faster circuits but also through organizational techniques. We now describe briefly two such techniques in high performance systems.

Memory interleaving.   A large memory may be organized in several modules, each covering a portion of the addressable space. The effective speed of this memory can be increased if memory access cycles in different modules are overlapped. In such a system, the CPU requests a read or a write operation in one module. Then, it proceeds to request other memory operations in other modules before the result from the first module becomes available. Because program instructions are usually fetched from successive locations in the main memory, overlapped operation may be achieved by arranging memory addresses such that successive addresses refer to different memory modules. For example, if there are 4 modules, the first module should contain words 0, 4, 8, . . . etc.; the second module, words 1, 5, 9, . . . etc.; and so on. The increase in speed with memory interleaving is achieved at the expense of increased complexity in the CPU and memory control circuitry.

Cache memory.   The second technique for increasing the effective speed of the main memory involves a **cache memory.** Conceptually, this technique is simple. A small, high speed memory is introduced between the CPU and the main memory. When a memory location read is requested by the CPU, contents are copied into the cache and appropriately labelled. If the CPU issues a read request at the same location a short while later, the required data is fetched from the high speed cache instead of from the relatively slow main memory. Because computer programs often involve loops, many memory loca-

tions are likely to be accessed repeatedly during program execution. Whenever the content of these locations is available in the cache memory, the speed of execution increases substantially.

Once all available cache locations have been used, the contents of new main memory addresses being accessed by the CPU must replace those already in the cache. There are several replacement algorithms to select the entries that should be discarded. The aim of such algorithms is to maximize the probability that subsequent memory references by the CPU can be serviced directly from the cache. Replacement algorithms range from a simple random selection to the replacement of cache locations which have been least recently used. The latter approach requires the cache controller to keep track of the usage history for every cache location.

Memory Management

In many computer systems, the memory address generated by the CPU is sent directly to the memory. Thus, the memory address space seen by the CPU, and hence by the programmer, is identical to the physical address space of memory. Consider, for example, a CPU which generates a 24 bit address for each memory reference. This represents 2^{24} or 16M locations. Assume that the main memory connected to this CPU has only 256K locations which occupy the addresses 0 to $2^{18} - 1$. Programs executed on this computer must be restricted to the 256K region for which physical memory is available. Thus only a small part of the full 24 bit address capability of the CPU can be used. A large program must be subdivided into sections, such that each section represents a program which can be executed separately within the limits of the physical memory.

Another difficulty is encountered in a computer system which operates in a time shared mode. Such a system has several programs running at the same time. More precisely, the CPU switches on a regular basis among these programs. This means that several programs have to reside simultaneously in the main memory. The object code of a program is usually prepared on the assumption that it is loaded into the main memory starting at some fixed location. Hence, if two programs reside simultaneously in memory, at least one of them has to be relocated—its object code has to be modified so that it will be executed properly in a different area of the main memory. In a time shared system, a program may have to be moved from an on-line mass storage device to the main memory and back several times during the course of its execution.

Hence, its code may have to be relocated during each one of these transfers. A computer intended for use in a time shared environment should provide some means to facilitate the relocation process.

The difficulties mentioned above can be remedied by separating the address space used by the programmer, which we will call the **virtual address space,** from that used to describe locations in the physical memory, which is the **physical address space.** A computer system using this approach is said to have a **virtual memory** organization. The correspondence, or mapping, between the two address spaces is maintained by means transparent to the programmer.

In a virtual memory system, programs are stored in an on-line mass storage device—typically a disk. When a program is to begin execution, only a small part of it is brought into the memory. As execution progresses, other parts of the program are transferred as needed. Since the size of the main memory may not suffice to accommodate the entire program, some portion of the program resident in the main memory may have to be removed to make room for new transfers. To simplify the management of this process, both address spaces are divided into **pages** of fixed size. A table, referred to as the **page table,** is maintained by the system. For each page in the virtual address space, the page table contains an entry which gives the address on the mass storage device where this page is to be found. When a page is copied into the main memory, its starting address in the main memory is also entered into the page table.

In addition to storing address pointers, each entry in the page table includes a few **status bits.** These indicate whether a copy of the corresponding page is in the main memory, whether the contents of that page have been updated during program execution, and so on.

In order to illustrate the concept and some of the details of virtual memory we describe briefly the memory management system of the VAX-11/780 computer. During program execution, the CPU generates a 32 bit virtual address. This is translated into a 30 bit physical address. The low order half of the physical address space refers to main memory locations, while the high order half is used for input and output devices. The physical memory address can accommodate 0.5 gigabytes (2^{29} bytes). However, only a small portion of this space is actually physical memory in practical computer systems.

The page table is stored in the main memory. Each table entry has the format shown in Figure 12.7. The status bit indicates whether the page has been loaded into the main memory. If so, bits 0 to 20 give its starting phys-

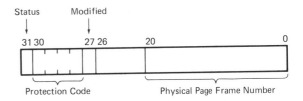

Figure 12.7. Format of a page table entry.

ical address, and bit 26 indicates whether its contents have been modified. Otherwise, bits 0 to 26 provide information to the memory management software to locate that page on disk. Bits 27 to 30 contain a protection code. This determines which programs are allowed to read or write into that page.

Figure 12.8 illustrates the process of translating a virtual address into a physical address. Because pages are 512 bytes long, the least significant 9 bits, which specify a byte location within the page, are moved directly from the virtual to the physical address. The high order 23 bits of the virtual address represent a page number which, in turn, is a pointer into the page table. This number is added to the starting address of the table, and the result is the physical address of the corresponding page table entry in the main memory.

The memory management hardware reads the 32 bit table entry (one word) and checks the status bit. If this bit is equal to 1, if the page is resident in the memory, its page frame number—a **frame** is a block in main memory which can accommodate one page—is retrieved and prefixed to the byte location to complete the physical address, as shown in the figure. This physical address can now access the required word in the memory. Before allowing this access to proceed, however, the hardware ensures that the program which initiated the memory access request has privileges consistent with the protection code of the page in question. In the case of a write operation, the memory management hardware also sets the *modified bit* in the page table entry.

If the status bit indicates that the page is not in the memory, a **page fault** is said to have occurred. That page must be copied into the main memory before the requested memory access can proceed. Hence, the memory management *software* is signalled to carry out the transfer. It searches for a free page frame in the main memory. If none is available, one must be created by forcing a resident page out of the memory. The situation is analogous to the replacement of words in a cache memory, as discussed earlier, and similar replacement algorithms are

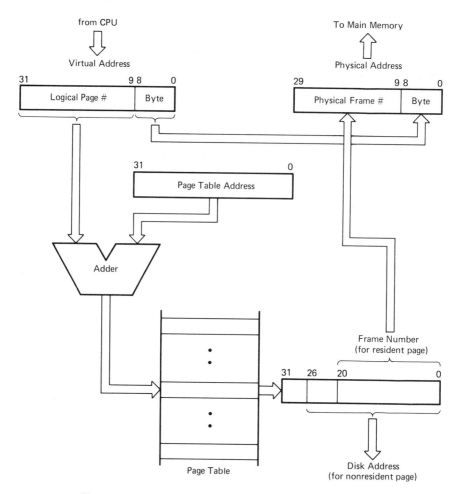

Figure 12.8. A conceptual view of the address translation process.

used. In the VAX computer, the page selected for replacement is the one that has been resident in the main memory the longest. (Note that this is *not* the same as least recently used.) Once a page has been selected, its modified bit is checked. A page which has been modified must be copied back to the disk. Otherwise, since a duplicate exists on disk, its status bit is cleared and the page frame is simply declared free. After the requested page has been transferred to the memory, its frame number is recorded in the page table, its status bit is set, and its modified bit is cleared.

The design of a virtual memory operating system is aimed at minimizing the number of page faults. If this number is large, the computer may spend most of its time transferring pages back and forth between the main

memory and mass storage, with little useful processing being performed—a situation known as **thrashing.** In this regard, parameters such as page size, replacement algorithm, and mimimum size of the main memory must be carefully evaluated at the design stage.

Special techniques may be devised to enhance the performance of virtual memory systems. This includes coordination of the activities of the memory management software with other parts of the operating system of the computer or the use of cache memories to reduce the delay introduced during the address translation process. For example, in the VAX computer, pages to be written back to disk are placed on a queue which serves as a software cache. Also, the VAX software handles pages to be transferred in groups referred to as clusters. This reduces the effective disk access delay. In some machines page tables are maintained in special high speed memory.

Multiuser environment.

Before concluding this discussion of virtual memory organization we comment briefly on the multiuser environment. We have pointed out that it should be possible for user programs to be loaded in the main memory without the need for relocation. A virtual memory organization provides a convenient means for realizing this goal. When a program executes in a virtual address space which is mapped onto the physical address space by the hardware, we can simply provide each user with his or her own virtual address space. Each user, or more precisely, each process, can be given a separate page table. Thus a virtual address is translated into different physical addresses, which depend upon the program generating the virtual address.

12.5 INPUT/OUTPUT ORGANIZATION

An essential computer system requirement is communication with input/output (I/O) devices. It should be easy to transfer data between an I/O device and either the CPU or the main memory. Moreover, any useful scheme must handle a large variety of devices.

Input/Output Interface

In a simple I/O scheme, the CPU handles all I/O transfers by executing one or more instructions for each word of information transferred. Figure 12.9 shows an arrangement in which an I/O device is connected to the computer bus. The CPU can access this device by placing appropriate addressing information on the bus. The addressing information uniquely identifies the device and possibly several addressable locations within the device. Thus an addressable location in an I/O device might be treated as a memory location in the computer, a technique known as **memory mapped I/O.** This enables the CPU to transfer data to and from the I/O device in the manner of main memory transfers.

An I/O device may be a keyboard, printer or CRT terminal. Circuitry to interpret the address and control information from both the bus and the device connects the device to the computer bus and enables proper interchange of data. This circuitry is called the **I/O interface.** Typically it contains

1. Data registers for buffering the data that is transferred between relatively slow devices and a much faster CPU.
2. Status registers for holding information that indicates the state of the device.

The interface includes control registers and circuits which govern the operation of the I/O process. It also contains an address decoder which recognizes when the interface, or, more explicitly, some register within the interface, is being addressed.

Polled I/O

As an example of a simple I/O process, consider an input, or read, operation from a device such as a keyboard. As-

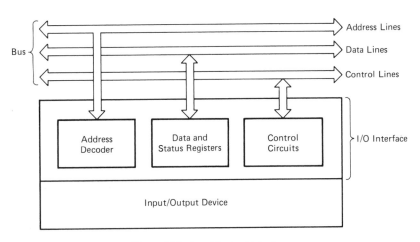

Figure 12.9. Input/output interface.

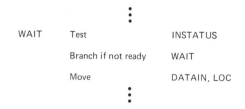

Figure 12.10. Read operation with polled I/O.

sume that the CPU is to read 8 bit encoded characters as they are typed on the keyboard. Characters are entered slowly compared to the CPU's ability to process them. The dedicated CPU has to wait until the next character is entered. A *wait loop* in the I/O segment of the program synchronizes the fast CPU and the slow I/O device.

For the read operation shown in Figure 12.10, a data register, DATAIN, in the keyboard interface, receives the character data from the keyboard and holds it until read by the CPU; a status register, INSTATUS, indicates whether there is a new character in the DATAIN register. The CPU continuously tests the contents of IN-STATUS until it finds that new data is ready. Then the data is transferred from DATAIN to the desired location in the computer. This mode of operation is called **polled I/O.**

The same scheme can handle output, or write, operations. Figure 12.11 indicates the necessary action. In this case, the data is moved from a computer location LOC to the DATAOUT buffer of the output device.

Interrupt Driven I/O

Polled I/O involves the CPU throughout the I/O process. In addition to transferring data, the CPU performs the wait function by executing the two instructions in the wait loop. This is clearly wasteful: the CPU is able to perform much useful work in this time. The I/O device interface should be modified to inform the CPU directly when the device status changes.

Figure 12.11. Write operation with polled I/O.

In the case of a keyboard, the interface signals the CPU when a valid character is available in its DATAIN buffer. The CPU is performing some computational task when the I/O device signal arrives. To ensure a fast response, the I/O signal interrupts the CPU, which carries out the desired I/O function. This method of dealing with I/O functions is called **interrupt dirven I/O.** The **interrput request** sent by the device interface initiates an interrrput.

The interrupt mechanism can be used with a large variety of devices. The I/O task may involve a number of steps, which are performed by executing a small program called an *interrupt service routine.* Upon the arrival of an interrupt request, the CPU leaves the current task and executes the appropriate interrupt service routine. Upon completion of interrupt service routine, the CPU returns to its previous task. Thus the interrupt service routine can be viewed as a special subroutine, which is automatically called when the CPU receives the interrupt request signal.

An interrupt request can be raised at any time. In response, the CPU leaves its current task, processes the interrupt, then returns to the interrupted task. To facilitate this return, information that defines the state of the CPU at the time of interruption is usually stored on a stack in the main memory.

Sometimes it is useful for the CPU to prevent interrupt requests. For example, suppose that a line printer is arranged to raise an interrupt when it completes printing the current line and is ready to accept a new line. If the CPU has no further data to be printed, it should be possible to prevent the printer from generating further interrupts. A simple mechanism is to arrange I/O interfaces to allow the CPU to selectively enable and disable interrupts from various devices. Then an interrupt request is raised only if it is enabled.

Direct Memory Access

In previous subsections, we have considered I/O operations which involve the CPU in all data transfers. For each data transfer the CPU executes one or more machine instructions. Such techniques can be used with many different I/O devices, as long as the relative speed of the device does not pose a problem.

Some high speed devices, such as magnetic disks, can transmit or receive large blocks of data at high speeds. It is desirable to transfer data without involving the CPU in the transfer of each item. A special control circuit enables the transfer of a block of data from a device directly

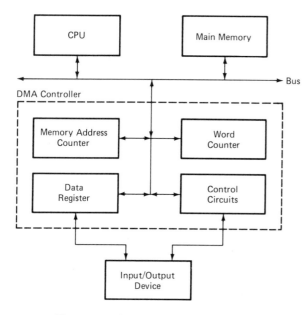

Figure 12.12. Direct memory access scheme.

to the main memory. The control circuit transfers data, one word at a time, at a speed compatible with that of the I/O device. This method of transfer is called **direct memory access (DMA)**.

Figure 12.12 shows a DMA controller interposed between the I/O device and the computer bus. The controller consists of several functional parts. There are two counter registers. One generates the next main memory addresses from which data is read or into which it is stored. This counter register is incremented by successive data transfers. The second counter keeps track of the number of data words that are left to be transferred. A data register serves as the buffer between the main memory and the device. Other registers are provided for more complex devices.

To start a DMA transfer, the CPU sets the contents of the registers in the DMA controller to initial values. Then the DMA controller independently carries out the I/O transfers. When done, the controller thus informs the CPU by raising an interrupt.

While a DMA task is in progress, the CPU executes other program segments. However, a conflict arises when both the DMA controller and the CPU try to access the main memory at the same time. A bus control circuit gives priority to DMA transfers. DMA transfers require a small number of memory access cycles, which may be interwoven with the CPU originated accesses. It is pos-

sible to view the DMA controller as "stealing" memory cycles from the CPU, hence, the name **cycle stealing**.

I/O Processors

In large computer systems, which include numerous I/O devices, it is important to optimize CPU time. Here involving the CPU directly in I/O transfers is highly undesirable. Thus DMA is employed for I/O operations. It is unlikely that a separate DMA controller can be economically provided for each device. A preferred solution shares a DMA controller among several devices. Such a controller becomes a special purpose processor called an **I/O processor** or alternatively an **I/O channel.**

Figure 12.13 indicates how an I/O processor is connected. The I/O processor deals with different data formats and varying speeds dictated by the needs of the devices connected to it. Flexibility is achieved when the I/O processor performs its functions by executing specialized instructions. These instructions are fetched from the main memory and executed in the same way as the CPU executes its instructions. Thus an I/O processor is a computer in its own right, but its instruction set is limited to I/O related operations.

Bus Transfers

Just as essential as an I/O processor is providing adequate means for controlling transfers along the bus. An I/O device communicating with the CPU must know exactly when to receive or send information. The two types of control mechanisms for this purpose are called **synchronous** and **asynchronous.**

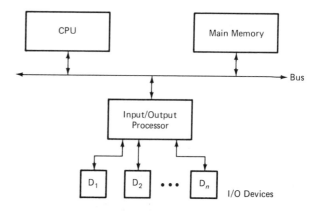

Figure 12.13. Use of an I/O processor in a computer system.

A control signal called the **clock** can force all signalling to occur at well defined time intervals; this is **synchronous** control. Figure 12.14 depicts a typical timing diagram for input. A clock cycle consists of the time interval t_0 to t_3 between positive going edges of the square wave clock signal. At the start of a clock cycle, t_0, the CPU sends the address of the input device and asserts a read/write control line to request a read operation. After a delay, dependent upon the time needed for the device interface address decoder to recognize the address, the device is selected at t_1. Now the device waits for the falling edge of the clock and places the input data on the bus at t_2. The operation is completed at t_3, which is the end of the clock cycle.

The diagram in Figure 12.14 is simplified; it does not take into account propagation delays along the wires of the bus and all circuits in the interface. Nevertheless, it provides a correct representation of the sequence of events that take place.

Arrowheads in the timing waveforms denote the cause and effect relationship between events. For example, address and read/write signals cause a device to be selected, while the device-selected and the falling edge of the clock signal cause input data to be placed on the bus.

Effective control of information transfers on the bus can also be achieved without a clock; this is **asynchronous control.** Figure 12.15 depicts such an input operation. The CPU places the device address on the bus and asserts the read/write line at time t_0. At t_1, after a delay long enough for the address to be decoded by the device interface, the CPU sends a signal, "ready" in the figure, to tell the device that a valid address is to be acted upon. The

ready signal activates the device; it places the input data on the bus at t_2. It also signifies that valid data is on the bus by sending an accept signal. When the CPU receives the accept signal it removes the ready signal at t_3 and gates the input data from the bus into one of its internal registers. A short time later, at t_4, the CPU removes the address and the read/write signal from the bus. At t_5, having observed the fall of the ready signal, the device removes the data and the accept signal from the bus. This terminates the input operation.

A key point in the above operation is the exchange of control signals, ready and accept. The receipt of ready is acknowledged by the device with accept. The CPU tells the device that it has received accept, along with any other information, such as data in this case, by dropping ready. This in turn is acknowledged by the device by removing accept. This operation is called **handshake control**, which obviates the need for a synchronizing clock control signal.

The main advantage of asynchronous control is that the speed of exchange of signals is determined by the speed of the device involved. No time is wasted in waiting for synchronizing clock pulses. On the other hand, synchronous control is often easier to implement in practice. Its chief drawback is that slow devices dictate the speed of operation if synchronization of all devices is done uniformly.

Bus Access Control

The computer bus is a central resource shared by many units, In basic operations in which the CPU dictates the

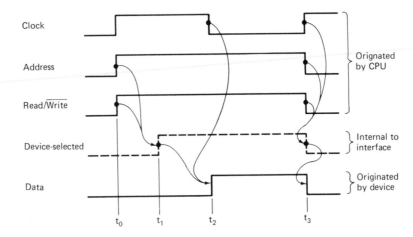

Figure 12.14. Simplified timing diagram for asynchronous input operation.

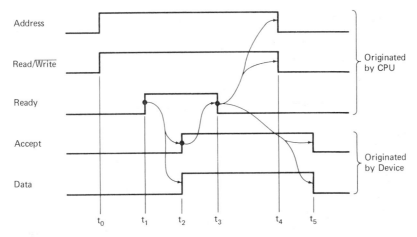

Figure 12.15. Handshake control for an input operation.

use of the bus, there is no difficulty in deciding which functional units will have access to the bus at any given time. But, in more complex situations, such as DMA transfers, simultaneous requests for the bus may be made by two or more devices. Then an arbitration scheme decides the order in which the devices can use the bus.

Consider the scheme depicted in Figure 12.16. Each box labelled D_i corresponds to the control circuit in a device interface. A centralized controller arbitrates the requests. When a deivce requires the bus, it signals the controller by activating a common *bus request (BR)* line, to which connections are ORed. The controller grants the use of the bus by activating the *bus grant (BG)* line. The BG signal propagates through the device chain until it reaches the device that requires the bus. This device stops further propagation of the BG signal and then accesses the bus. The arrangement shown in Figure 12.16 is known as a **daisy chain.**

When two or more devices in a daisy chain request use of the bus, the device closest to the controller receives the BG signal first and inhibits its farther propagation. Thus, the order of connection on the daisy chain establishes the priority in which devices are given access to the bus: the closer device has the higher priority.

The daisy chain is simple, the reason for its wide use. Its drawbacks are the time needed to arbitrate among bus requests (dependent upon chain length.); and the fixed priority determined by the physical wiring (difficult to change).

A faster and more flexible scheme for arbitration of bus requests, shown in Figure 12.17, has separate bus request and bus grant lines for each device, and is known as **independent request control.** The controller assigns priority to each device, which can be fixed or programmable. The obvious disadvantage of this approach is the higher cost of implementation when a large number of devices are involved. In practice, it is often desirable to use a combination of daisy chain and independent request control.

These schemes can be used wherever arbitration of simultaneous requests is needed. For example, it is likely that simultaneous interrupts will occur in interrupt-driven I/O. When signalled on a common interrupt re-

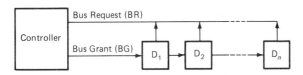

Figure 12.16. Daisy chain control.

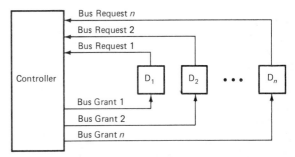

Figure 12.17. Independent request control.

quest line, the CPU can poll all devices in a *predetermined order* to discover which device needs to be serviced. This is a purely software approach. The hardware arbitration schemes described result in better time response. The use of independent requests is straightforward, but expensive. A daisy chain is more cost-effective. When, in addition, an interrupting device identifies itself (by placing its name code on the bus), the scheme is referred to as **vectored interrupts.**

Standard Interfaces

Many will benefit if computer I/O structures and peripheral devices are designed in some standard way, so that different devices from a variety of manufactuers can be readily included in a computer system. Several useful standards have emerged defining interface requirements for the computer and devices connected to it.

The RS-232-C specification for serial interfaces between the CPU and data communication devices (such as modems) or data terminal equipment (such as computers or CRT terminals) is a widely used standard.

The IEEE 488 standard defines a bus for connection of instrumentation equipment. It is used where instruments (signal sources, measuring devices), are digitally controlled but is also suitable for connection of other computer peripherals.

The S-100 bus, used extensively in microprocessor systems, defines a structure for the main bus of a computer.

Computer systems which support stnadard interfaces allow users considerable freedom in selecting peripheral equipment from manufacturers whose devices meet the standards. This freedom of choice, coupled with cost-effectiveness of wider availability, is a compelling attraction.

REFERENCES

Baer, J. L., *Computer Systems Architecture.* Computer Science Press, Potomac,: 1980.

Hamacher, V. C., Z. G. Vranesic, and S. G. Zaky, Computer Organization, McGraw-Hill Book Co., New York: 1978.

Hayes, J. P., *Computer Architecture and Organization* Mc-Graw-Hill Book Co., New York: 1978.

Hill, F. J., and G. R. Peterson, *Digital Systems: Hardware Organization and Design.* New York: John Wiley and Sons, 1973.

IEEE Standard Digital Interface for Programmable Instrumentation. ANSI/IEEE Standard 488-1978.

Interface Between Data Terminal Equipment and Data Communication Equipment Employing Serial Binary Data Interchange. Electronic Industries Association (EIA) Standard RS-232-C, Aug. 1969.

Kells, A. E., H. Fullmer, D. B. Gustavson and G. Morrow, "Standard Specification for S-100 Bus Interface Devices," *Computer,* Vol. 12, No. 7 (July 1979), pp. 28–52.

Khambata, A. J., *Microprocessors/Microcomputers: Architecture, Software and Systems,* New York: John Wiley and Sons, 1982.

Levy, H. M., and P. H. Lipman, "Virtual Memory Management in the VAX/VMS Operating System," *Computer,* March. 1982, pp. 35–41.

Mano,, M. M., *Computer System Architecture,* Prentice-Hall, *Englewood Cliffs, N.J.: 1976.*

Siewiorek, D. P., C. G. Bell, and A. Newell, *Computer Structures: Principles and Examples.* New York: McGraw-Hill Book Co., 1982.

Stone, H. S., *Introduction to Computer Architecture,* 2nd ed. Chicago: Science Research Associates, 1980.

Tanenbaum, A., S. *Structured Computer Organization.* Prentice-Hall, Englewood Cliffs, N.J.: 1976.

Wakerly, J., *Microcomputer Architecture and Programming.* New York: John Wiley and Sons, 1981.

Satyanaraynan, M., and D. Bhandarkar, "Design Trade-Offs in VAX-11 Translation Buffer Organization," *Computer,* Dec. 1981, pp. 103–111.

13
Microprogramming

Ashok K. Agrawala
Nam S. Woo
University of Maryland

13.1 INTRODUCTION

From a user's perspective, a computer is a machine capable of executing programs written in any of a number of programming languages, and carrying out various data manipulation tasks. Before execution, each program has to be converted to **machine language** in which it is expressed as a sequence of machine instructions (or **macroinstructions**). While the structure of machine instructions differs from machine to machine, some common aspects of these instructions can be recognized. Each machine instruction contains an *opcode* and 1 or 2 *operands*. The opcode specifies the operations to be carried out on the specified operands (data). Even though programs are rarely written directly in machine language, machine instructions are usually designed to provide flexible ways of specifying operands through a variety of addressing techniques.

When considering how a computer may execute a machine language program, a user may start from the simple structure shown in Figure 13.1 The computer has to have a **memory** where operands are stored and an **arithmetic and logic unit** (ALU) which carries out the operation specified in the opcode of an instruction. In addition, the machine has to be capable of executing a sequence of machine instructions automatically. Before an instruction stored in the main memory can be executed, the instruction must be *fetched,* i.e., moved to some register for decoding to determine the identity of the opcode and the operands. The operand locations must be determined and the operands themselves accessed and provided to the

ALU. Finally the ALU must be instructed to carry out the desired operation on the operands. After all this is done as part of the execution of an instruction, or an instruction cycle, the next instruction must be fetched and a new instruction cycle started. Clearly, a similar sequence of steps must be carried out for each instruction cycle.

13.2 CONTROL UNIT

In a simplified structure of a computer system, the responsibility of providing the necessary control signals to carry out the sequence of steps is assigned to the **control unit.** This unit generates all the necessary control signals at the appropriate times to ensure the proper execution of each instruction in the programs. If the programs call for any input or output, such operations must also be carried out under the control of the control unit.

The signals generated by the control unit are used to control some primitive operations, such as enabling a component, activating a data path, or selecting a component such as a register. Because the instruction cycle requires that many such operations be carried out in proper sequence, the control unit not only generates the control signals, but does it in proper sequence.

For an example of the control signals and their use, consider Figure 13.2, which shows some of the components of a computer system. In Figure 13.2a, a control signal enables the tri-state buffers. If the enable control signal has a value of 1 (or high), the input data shown as

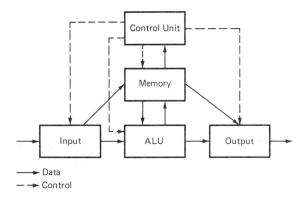

Figure 13.1. A simplified block diagram of a computer system.

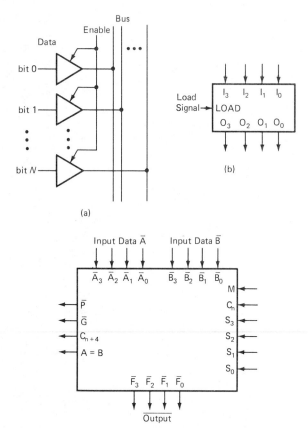

Figure 13.2. Examples of components and control signals in a computer system. (a) Tri-state buffers. (b) A 4 bit latch. (c) Block diagram and a function table of an ALU. (Table courtesy National Semiconductor Corporation)

bit 0 . . . bit N pass through the buffer and are loaded on the bus. If the enable control signal has a value of 0 (or low), the input data are disconnected from the bus.

Figure 13.2b shows another control signal, the LOAD signal, to a latch. In general, there are some registers in a processor which can be implemented as the latches shown in Figure 13.2b.* For each latch, there is a control signal which allows input data to be loaded (or stored) onto the latch.

Figure 13.2c includes a block diagram and a function table for a typical ALU device (74LS181) in a computer system. There are six control signals: S_3, S_2, S_1, S_0, M, and C_n. Control signal M determines the **operation mode** (arithmetic/logic). The four control signals S_3, S_2, S_1, S_0 are used to select a function out of many available functions. The C_n signal is a *carry input*, which may also be considered as a *data input*.

A way of designing a control unit is to treat it as a large sequential circuit, and design and implement it as such. Even for a relatively simple computer, however, the control unit requires a rather complex (as well as large) sequential circuit. Recognizing the the sequence of steps necessary for the execution of an instruction may be treated as the outcome of the execution of a sequence of **microinstructions,** we may organize the control unit in a different way to simplify it. In such a design, the control unit has to be able to generate the control signals by executing a sequence of microinstructions, or a **microprogram.** Microprogramming has been proposed and used as an alternative to the complex sequential circuit implementation of the control unit. In this chapter, we present the basic notions of microprogramming.

13.3 MICROOPERATION, MICROINSTRUCTION AND MICROPROGRAM

An **opcode field** of a machine instruction specifies an operation. Such an operation will be called an *opcode level operation* (or *macrooperation*). Examples of opcode level operation may include ADD, LOAD and STORE. An opcode level operation is a basic operation which allows a user to program in machine languages. However, an opcode level operation usually consists of multiple hardware level operations (or primitive operations, called *microoperations*). A microoperation is an operation which occurs

---

*In practice, a set of general purpose registers is implemented as a *register file*. An example of the register file is shown later in this chapter.

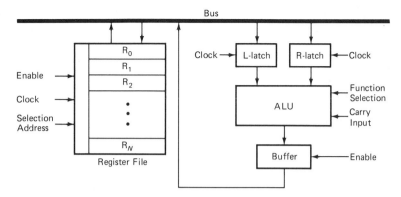

Figure 13.3. A register file and an ALU.

in the hardware unit of a machine. As an example, some of the microoperations for the simple configuration of Figure 13.3 are the following:

- Select a register in the register file (i.e., send the selection address to the register file).
- Enable output of the register file (this microoperation is used to send the content of the register, which is selected by the selection address, to the bus).
- Send clock to the register file (this microoperation may be used to put the contents of the bus into a register which is selected by the selection address).
- Send clock signal, which is the same as the LOAD signal in Figure 13.2b, to the L-latch.
- Send clock signal to the R-latch.
- Select function of the ALU. (i.e., send function selection input (M, S_3, S_2, S_1, and S_0 in Figure 13.2c) to the ALU.)
- Send carry input (C_n in Figure 13.2c), which is 0 or 1, to the ALU.
- Enable the output of the ALU (i.e., send enable signal to the buffer gate at the output of the ALU). If the ALU includes a buffered output, the (tri-state) buffer at the ALU output is not necessary. In this case, the enable signal is one of the control signal inputs to the ALU.

The microoperations may vary depending upon the kinds of hardware units and their interconnection scheme in a machine. For example, consider machine instruction

ADD   R1, R2

where R1 and R2 are register names in the register file of Figure 13.3. The meaning of the machine instruction

is to add the contents of registers R1 and R2, and store the result in register R1. The opcode level operation, **ADD**, of the machine instruction may be performed as a sequence of microoperations (where some microoperations may be performed concurrently):

- Select register R1 from the reigster file (by using the selection address).
- Send enable signal to the register file.
- Send clock to the L-latch.
- Select register R2 from the register file (by using the selection address).
- Send enable signal to the register file.
- Send clock to the R-latch.
- Select add function of the ALU (by using function selection).
- Set carry input properly (0 or 1).
- Send enable signal to the ALU buffer gate.
- Select register R1 from the register file.
- Send clock to the register file.

Clearly, there is no requirement that only one microoperation can proceed at a time. In fact, many nonconflicting microoperations may be executed concurrently. The microoperations are organized in **microinstructions** and usually only one microinstruction is executed at any instant. A microinstruction contains information of one or more microoperations; it may also contain sequencing information.

A **microprogram** is a finite, ordered set of microinstructions. A microprogram may consist of multiple routines, called **microroutines.** A microroutine may contain microinstructions to execute an opcode level operation. The microprogram may reside in a special fast storage, which is called **control storage.**

13.4 MICROINSTRUCTION DESIGN AND IMPLEMENTATION

As has been noted, a microinstruction represents one or more microoperations. The design of microinstructions for a computer includes gathering the information required to control the hardware resources, and deciding how to arrange the information in a microinstruction. Let us consider some design characteristics of the microinstructions.

If a microinstruction represents one microoperation, it is called a *vertical microinstruction*. On the other hand, if a microinstruction represents all microoperations that can be executed concurrently, it is called a *horizontal microinstruction*. (In the middle of the two extremes, vertical and horizontal microinstruction, there is the *diagonal* microinstruction, a compromise of the two extremes.) In general, the horizontal microinstruction has greater length than the vertical type. Because of the concurrency of the execution of multiple microoperations, implementations using horizontal microinstructions usually result in faster executions.

A microinstruction may consist of several *fields;* each field may be encoded. To what level the fields are encoded represents the *degree of encoding* of the microinstruction. Figure 13.4 contains three examples of encoded microinstruction. In general, the greater the degree of encoding, the shorter the length of microinstruction, and the longer the time delay to decode the encoded information. Thus, there is a space-time tradeoff.

The content of a microinstruction is interpreted, or, the microinstruction is executed, by hardware logic, which is known as **MIL (microinstruction interpretation logic)**; refer to Figures 13.7 and 13.8. This hardware logic is much simpler than the hardwired machine, which does not use microprogramming in its control unit.

One of the important characteristics of microinstruction implementation is the *monophase-polyphase* characteristic. In the monophase implementation, the MIL uses only a single clock cycle to generate control signals. Although it is simple in realization, it is seldom used because of the lack of flexibility associated with the use of a single phase clock. In the *polyphase implementation,* there are several distinct clock phases that the MIL can use.

Microoperations in a microinstruction are associated with proper clock phase. An example of the polyphase clock and its use in the register transfer operation occurs in Figure 13.5.

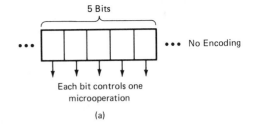

(a)

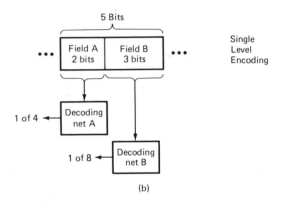

(b)

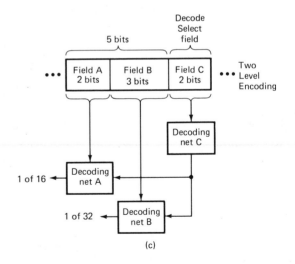

(c)

Figure 13.4. Examples of encoded microinstructions. (From A. Agrawala and T. Rauscher, *Foundations of Microprogramming,* Academic Press, 1976)

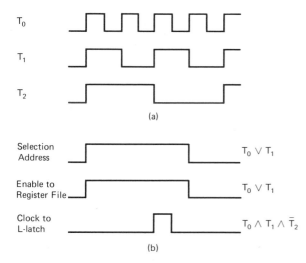

T_0

T_1

T_2

(a)

Selection
Address $T_0 \lor T_1$

Enable to
Register File $T_0 \lor T_1$

Clock to
L-latch $T_0 \land T_1 \land \bar{T_2}$

(b)

Figure 13.5. An example of a polyphase clock and its application. (a) A 3 phase clock at a given instant. (b) Timing signals for a register operation (L LATCH ← R1 in Figure 13.3). It is assumed that the microinstruction cycle time is equal to the T_2 period.

13.5 WILKES MODEL OF A MICROCONTROL UNIT

The concept of microprogramming has been in the literature for many years. It was first proposed by M. Wilkes (see chapter reference) who observed:

It is in the control section of the electronic computer that the greatest degree of complexity generally arises. This is particularly so if the machine has a comprehensive order code* designed to make it simple and fast in operations.

Microprogramming was proposed to provide a systematic alternative to the usual somewhat ad hoc procedure used for designing the control system of a digital computer. Wilkes also gives a basic model of the microcontrol unit as follows.

A control section of a machine may be partitioned into two units: the *control register* and the *microcontrol units*. The control register unit may consist of several registers, such as a program counter and an instruction register; the microcontrol unit sequences microinstructions and gen-

*The order code is the same as the operation code, or opcode.

erates control signals which control the operations in the machine.

The Wilkes model consists of a decoding tree, two matrices, and several registers, as shown in Figure 13.6. A horizontal line of matrices A and B is a microinstruction. Each microinstruction has a unique address; a microinstruction is selected when its address is in register I. Each vertical line in matrix A represents a control signal for a microoperation. A dot in the *i*th horizontal line and the *j*th vertical line in matrix A indicates that the *i*th microinstruction generates a control signal for the *j*th microoperation. The format of the control signal which comes out of the *j*th vertical line in matrix A is the same as the control pulse given to the decoding tree.

Matrix B contains the next microinstruction address. A conditional branch of the microinstruction can occur when the conditional flipflop output is used. A microinstruction to be executed is determined either by the matrix B part of the previous microinstruction executed, or by the opcode of a machine instruction; this is represented as two input paths to Register II. The address of

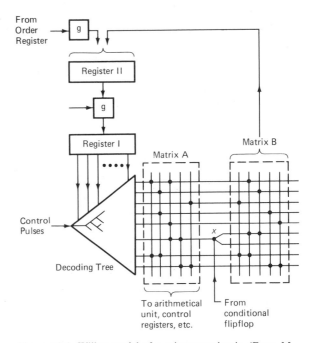

Figure 13.6. Wilkes model of a microcontrol unit. (From M. Wilkes and J. Stringer, "Microprogramming and the Design of the Control Circuits in an Electronic Digital Computer," *Proc. of the Cambridge Philosophical Society*, Vol. 1, No. 3)

the next microinstruction *to be* executed resides in Register II. while the address of the microinstruction *being* executed is in Register I.

13.6 EVOLUTION OF MICROPROGRAMMING

Microprogramming has evolved to become a major technological approach today. Let us consider its evolution: The microprogrammability of a machine represents the degree of difficulty in microprogramming a machine, once the design and implementation of its microinstructions are understood. Microprogrammability is characterized by the following two factors:

1. The hardware facilities for changing the contents of a store which contains the microprogram.
2. The software facilities for writing, translating and debugging a microprogram.

In terms of hardware, a machine may be classified into one of four categories: hardwired machine, microprogrammed machine, statically microprogrammable machine and dynamically microprogrammable machine. If a machine provides the software facilities that help users generate microprograms, it is called *user* microprogrammable. At one extreme of the microprogrammability spectrum is the hardwired machine, and the other extreme of the spectrum is the dynamically user microprogrammable machine. Let us consider the hardware and software aspects of microprogrammability.

Hardware Microprogrammability of a Machine

As it affects microprogramming, the hardware of a machine has developed from the hardwired machine to the dynamically microprogrammable machine. Two assumptions are made for the following discussion. First, a microprogram is used for interpreting machine instructions. (Other applications of microprogramming will be discussed later in this chapter.) Second, the microprogram is accessed from a separate control store. *

A **hardwired machine** does not use microprogramming in its control unit. Its control unit is hardwired and consists of the hardware implementation of the sequential circuits.

A **microprogrammed machine** uses microprogramming in its control unit. A block diagram of a microprogrammed machine is shown in Figure 13.7. The micro-

*The microprogram may also reside in a main memory and be accessed from the main memory. As a consequence, the microinstruction execution time becomes as large as the main memory cycle time. While this approach may result in an inexpensive implementation, the machine is usually significantly slower.

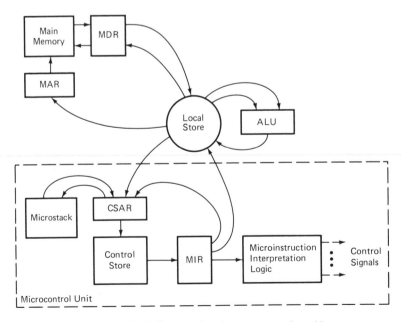

Figure 13.7. Block diagram of a microprogrammed machine.

program is stored in the control store. The contents of a control store cannot be modified in the microprogrammed machine; usually, the microprogram is written and put into the control store by the manufacturer of the microprogrammed machine. The microprogram is "invisible" to a user.

In general, the control store is a fast read-only memory (ROM). The *CSAR (control store address register)* holds the address of the microinstruction that will be executed next. The *MIR (microinstruction register)* holds the microinstruction which is being executed. The content of the MIR is executed by the *MIL (microinstruction interpretation logic)* and, as a result, control signal(s) is(are) generated from the MIL.

The *microstack* stores control store addresses when a microprogram subroutine is invoked. The control store address is restored to the CSAR when a "return from a subroutine" is performed by the microprogram. The CSAR, control store, MIR, MIL, and microstack constitute a microcontrol unit. It may be observed that the microcontrol unit of the microprogrammed machine is similar to that of the Wilkes mode. For example, CSAR in Figure 13.7 corresponds to register I in Figure 13.6.

In a **dynamically microprogrammable machine,** the content of the control store (i.e., the microprogram) may be modified dynamically. A block diagram of a dynami-

cally microprogrammable machine is shown in Figure 13.8. There are at least two differences between the Figures 13.7 and 13.8.

First, the control store in Figure 13.8 is a read/write memory (RAM). The control store in the dynamically microprogrammable machine, therefore, is called a *WCS (writable control store),* while the control store in Figure 13.7 may be a read-only memory. Second, there is an additional register, *CSDR (control store data register),* in the microcontrol unit of Figure 13.8. The CSDR holds information that will be written into the control store.

The microprogram is stored in the control store, whose content may be modified during operation. The new microprogram may be accessed from the main memory and then written into the control store during operation. When a microprogram is written into the control store, the CSDR contains information that is to be written and the CSAR contains the location into which the information in the CSDR is to be written. The mechanism of fetching a microinstruction from the control store and executing it is similar to the mechanism of the microprogrammed machine described above.

Between the microprogrammed and the dynamically microprogrammable machines, is a class of machines in which a microprogram may be modified slowly. The machines in this class are called **statically microprogramm-**

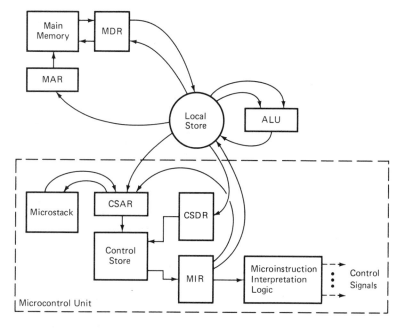

Figure 13.8. Block diagram of a dynamically microprogrammable machine.

able machines. The statically microprogrammable machine may use PROM (programmable read-only memory) or EPROM (erasable programmable read-only memory) as a control store. The content of the control store may not be modified on-line, i.e., at operation speed, but may be modified off-line. The block diagram of a statically microprogrammable machine is similar to that of the microprogrammed machine shown in Figure 13.7.

Software Support for User Microprogramming

Machines which make the supporting software available to the user may be called **user-microprogrammable machines.** In order to prepare the microprograms, a user requires a variety of support software such as language processors, simulators and debuggers.

Microprogramming languages. There are various kinds of microprogramming languages. As indicated in Figure 13.9, the micro, assembly, flowchart, and the register transfer microprogramming languages are low level microprogramming languages. The high level microprogramming languages are classified as machine dependent and machine independent. While the one to one relationship between language statements and microinstructions holds with the low level microprogramming languages, it does not hold with the high level ones.

The **micro languages** correspond to the lowest level of programming languages—machine languages. Micro language programs are a sequence of instructions, each of which is represented as a series of bits. In the *flowchart microprogramming languages,* a microprogram is represented as a network of boxes. Each box represents one microinstruction. The *assembly microprogramming languages* give users the capability to express microinstructions in a mnemonic and symbolic form, similar to that

of traditional assembly languages. In the *register transfer microprogramming languages,* machine register and other resources may be given mnemonic names. Also, move operations may use the format of assignment statements; unary and binary operations may be written in algebraic notation; and conditional execution may be represented by simple IF statements. For example, A = RSH(B + C) would indicate that registers B and C are ALU inputs, the ALU operation is addition, the shift operation is right shift of the ALU result, and the destination of the shifted result is register A. The register transfer microprogramming languages, which include macro facility, are also called *macro register transfer microprogramming languages.*

As the use of microprogramming increases, it becomes expensive and inconvenient to write microprograms in the primitive, low level languages. The need for easy-to-learn and easy-to-use high level microprogramming languages has grown. As a consequence, many machine dependent as well as machine independent high level microprogramming languages have been proposed.

Machine dependent, high level microprogramming languages usually have high level language constructs such as control flow primitives (IF-THEN-ELSE, loops, etc.), compound arithmetic and logical expressions, and data structures (e.g., array). As an example of a machine dependent high level microprogramming language, let us consider **STRUM** for the Burroughs D machine. STRUM has a Pascal-like syntax and is block structured. The data objects defined in STRUM correspond to the registers and memories of the Burroughs D machine. The statements of STRUM include control constructs such as WHILE, REPEAT, and FOR. STRUM also includes statements for proving programs such as ASSERT, ASSUME, and CONCLUDE.

An example of a STRUM program is shown in Figure 13.10. The program is a multiplication program using an add and shift algorithm. Input arguments of the procedure have mnemonic names and are associated with specific registers (line 3). The program makes use of the macro. A macro is defined in line 18 and used in line 31. This program also shows input assertion (lines 6-8) and output assertion (lines 11-15) of the procedure, and a loop assertion (lines 23-28) of a loop. These assertions are used to verify correct operation of the program by the microprogram verifier, which is described below.

A microprogram written in a machine dependent, high level microprogramming language cannot be used in different kinds of machines. For portability, **machine inde-**

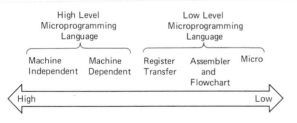

Figure 13.9. A spectrum of microprogramming languages. (From A. Agrawala and T. Rauscher, *Foundations of Microprogramming,* Academic Press, 1976)

```
 1 |
 2 |proc    MULTIPLY
 3 |        ( PARTIAL_PRODUCT = B, MULTIPLICAND = A1, MULTIPLIER = A2;)
 4 |
 5 |                   / WE WANT THE RESULT TO BE LESS THEN 2**15 /
 6 |        assume
 7 |              0 <= MULTIPLICAND.O <= 181 ,
 8 |              0 <= MULTIPLIER.O <= 181 ;
 9 |                      /        181*181 < 2**15 /
10 |
11 |        conclude
12 |              PARTIAL_PRODUCT = MULTIPLICAND.O mul MULTIPLIER.O ,
13 |              0 <= PARTIAL_PRODUCT <= 2 exp 15 ,
14 |              MULTIPLICAND = MULTIPLICAND.O ,
15 |              MULTIPLIER = 0;
16 |
17 |        PARTIAL_PRODUCT := 0;
18 |        begin   MAC 'LSB OF MULTIPLIER = 1' = 1st(MULTIPLIER) CAM;
19 |
20 |              decaler I = DUMMY;
21 |
22 |        for I := 0 to 7
23 |              assert  MULTIPLICAND.O mul MULTIPLIER.O
24 |                      = PARTIAL_PRODUCT + MULTIPLICAND mul MULTIPLIER ,
25 |                      MULTIPLIER = MULTIPLIER.O shr I ,
26 |                      MULTIPLICAND = MULTIPLICAND.O shl I ,
27 |                      0 <= MULTIPLICAND.O <= 181 ,
28 |                      0 <= MULTIPLIER.O <= 181
29 |
30 |              do
31 |                      if 'LSB OF MULTIPLIER = 1'
32 |                      then PARTIAL_PRODUCT := MULTIPLICAND + PARTIAL_PRODUCT
33 |                      fi;
34 |
35 |                      MULTIPLICAND := MULTIPLICAND shl 1;
36 |                      MULTIPLIER := MULTIPLIER shr 1
37 |
38 |        rof
39 |
40 |        end;
41 |
42 |        MULTIPLICAND := MULTIPLICAND shr 8
43 |
44 |
45 |
46 |corp;
47 |
```

Figure 13.10. An example of a STRUM program. (From D. Patterson, "STRUM: Structured Microprogram Development System for Correct Firmware" *CACM*, Vol. 24, No. 10)

pendent, **high level microprogramming languages** are needed. An example of such a language is **EMPL (Extensible Microprogramming Language)**. Variables in EMPL are not machine registers. The basic data type is interger, but a user can define new data types by using an *extension statement*. Such statements in the EMPL include assignment, **PROCEDURE** call, **IF-THEN-ELSE**, **WHILE-DO**, and **GOTO**. A small set of basic operators (such as addition, subtraction, unary minus, multiplication, division, logical **AND**, exclusive **OR**, shift, rotate, and standard relational operators) is included in EMPL. But the user can declare additional operators.

A sample EMPL program is shown in Figure 13.11. This program shows the declaration of a new type (i.e., **TYPE STACK**), and stack operations. Two stack operations, **PUSH** and **POP**, are defined in the program. At the bottom of the program a variable **ADDRESS-STK** is declared to have a type of stack defined above.

In addition to the languages described above, there are many other high level microprogramming languages.

```
TYPE STACK
   DECLARE STK(16) FIXED;
      /* an array of 16 integers */
   DECLARE STKPTR FIXED;
   DECLARE VALUE FIXED;

   INITIALLY DO; STKPTR = 0; END;

   PUSH:  OPERATION ACCEPTS(VALUE)
          MICROOP:  PUSH 3 0;
             /* indicates to the compiler   */
             /* that a PUSH microoperation  */
             /* is available                */
          IF STKPTR = 16
          THEN ERROR;    /* overflow */
          ELSE DO;
                STKPTR = STKPTR + 1;
                STK(STKPTR) = VALUE;
             END
          END;
   END;


   POP:   OPERATION RETURNS(VALUE)
          MICROOP: ' POP 3 0;
          IF STKPTR = 0
          THEN ERROR;       /* underflow */
          ELSE DO;
                VALUE = STK(STKPTR);
                STKPTR = STKPTR - 1;
             END
          END;
      END,
ENDTYPE:

DECLARE ADDRESS_STK STACK;
```

Figure 13.11. An example of an EMPL program. (From M. Sint, "A Survey of High Level Microprogramming Languages," *Simicro Newsletter,* Vol. 11, No. 3, 4.)

Some of them are MPL, SIMPL, S*, YALLL, MPGL, and CHAMIL. For details of these languages, refer to the relevant papers cited at the end of the chapter.

Microprogramming support tools.

Along with the microprogramming languages, microprogramming tools also are important for the user. The lack of proper software tools to support microcode generation results in high cost and poor reliability, especially when the volume of the microcode increases. The application of software tools to microprogramming is called **firmware engineering.** The microprogramming tools may include an assembler, compiler, text editor, simulator, debugger, and microprogram verifier.

The *text editor* is a software tool that allows users to edit their microprograms easily. The *assembler* translates assembly microprogramming languages into microcode. Because each statement in assembly language corresponds to a microinstruction, the translation is straight-forward. The *simulator* executes a microprogram and yields the result of a microprogram execution. Users may employ the simulator to develop microprograms before a machine which will execute the microprograms is built. Users may use a *debugger* to debug microprograms. The debugger may be interactive, and may allow users to set up or retrieve values of some variables (or registers, storage location) during execution. A *microprogram verifier* is a software tool which verifies that the microprogram works correctly as specified. Inputs to the microprogram verifier are microprograms and assertions about the microprograms. (The program of Figure 13.10 contains assertions.) The microprogram verifier checks whether or not the input microprogram matches the input assertions. One example of the microprogram verifier is the STRUM verification system.

The *compiler* (or *microcompiler*) translates a high level microprogramming language into microinstructions. (Because the vertical microinstruction is similar to the machine instruction, a compiler for the *vertical* microinstruction object code may be similar to the conventional compiler). Let us consider the problems associated with the *horizontal* microinstructions in more detail. Since the object code of a microcompiler is hardware oriented and timing is critical, input to the microcompiler has to include a description of the target machine (a machine whose microinstructions are generated) as well as the microprogram. This is one of the differences between the compiler (for high level programming languages) and the microcompiler.

An example of the general structure of a microcompiler is shown in Figure 13.12. There are two inputs to the microcompiler: one is a microprogram written in a high level microprogramming language, and the other is a description of the target machine. The target machine may be described by defining microoperations and rules of operation. For example, in the *MPG* system, a target machine is described by the way control signals and microoperations are issued.

The input microprogram is translated into a machine independent intermediate form by a partial compiler. Based on the machine description input, a *macro table* is constructed. An entry of the macro table is a *macro name,* which is a command of the machine-independent intermediate form (IML), and a *macro definition,* which consists of machine-dependent micro instructions.

Pass 1 maps the IML representation of the input microprogram onto a machine dependent intermediate language (MDIL) code by using the macro table. Each IML statement is bound to a particular machine by means of

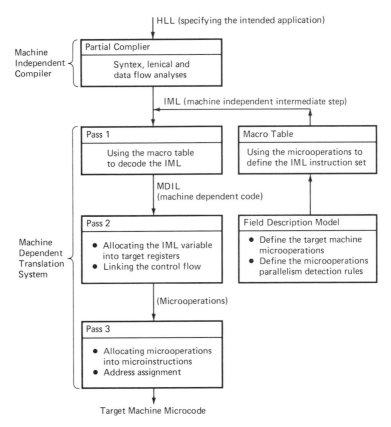

HLL (specifying the intended application)

Machine Independent Compiler

Partial Complier

Syntex, lenical and data flow analyses

IML (machine independent intermediate step)

Pass 1

Using the macro table to decode the IML

Macro Table

Using the microoperations to define the IML instruction set

MDIL (machine dependent code)

Machine Dependent Translation System

Pass 2

- Allocating the IML variable into target registers
- Linking the control flow

Field Description Model

- Define the target machine microoperations
- Define the microoperations parallelism detection rules

(Microoperations)

Pass 3

- Allocating microoperations into microinstructions
- Address assignment

Target Machine Microcode

Figure 13.12. General structure of a microcompiler. (From P. Ma and T. Lewis, "On the Design of a Microcode Compiler for a Machine-Independent High-Level Language," *IEEE Transactions on Software Engineering,* Vol. C-25, No. 10)

the macro expansion. Pass 2 allocates registers of the target machine to each symbolic operand, and assigns the binary code to each statement of MDIL. An efficient register allocation scheme should be used if the number of variables is greater than the number of registers in the target machine. The output of pass 2 is *microoperations.* Pass 3 uses a set of rules to detect the concurrency of microoperations and may combine sequences of microoperations into a *microinstruction.* The compiler may attempt to optimize the microcode generated.

13.7 A MICROPROGRAMMABLE COMPUTER SYSTEM—COMET

The COMET is a microprogrammable computer which is designed specifically to emulate the VAX-11 architecture. It is dynamically microprogrammable (providing up to 8K words of WCS) and user microprogrammable. The

system structure of the COMET is illustrated in Figure 13.13. There are three major internal buses: the WBUS, the MBUS and the RBUS. Each bus is 32 bits wide. There are three major units in the system. The first unit is a microcontrol unit, which consists of a microsequencer, control store, and MIR. The second unit is a data path unit, which includes two sets of scratch pad registers, a bit manipulation combinational logic (called a *super rotator*), an ALU, and some registers (i.e., LON-LIT, D, and Q registers). The third unit includes the VAX memory access and control registers, and the VAX status and control registers. We will describe the first two units in more detail later.

The COMET has a horizontal microinstruction, and the microinstruction is encoded. Each microinstruction is 80 bits long. The microinstruction format of the COMET is shown in Figure 13.14a. Functions of some fields of the microinstruction are briefly described in Figure 13.14b.

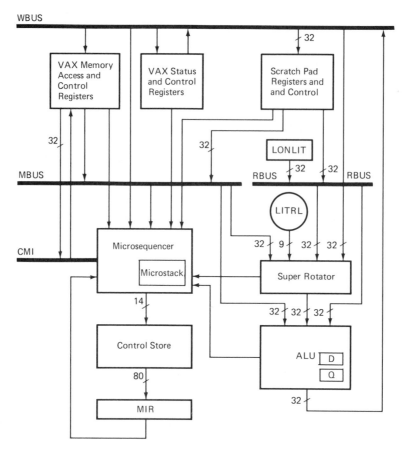

Figure 13.13. A simplified block diagram of a COMET system structure.

The scratch pad registers, along with other registers (e.g., **LONLIT, D,** and **Q** registers), are examples of the local store in our model of a microprogrammable machine (see Figure 13.8). In the COMET there are 56 *scratch pad registers*. They are divided into two sets: MSPs and RSPs. All the scratch pad registers get their input from the WBUS. The MSPs send their output on to the MBUS, and the RSPs on to the RBUS. Eight of the 56 scratch pad registers send their output on to both the MBUS and the RBUS. (We call these registers MSP/RSPs.)

A block diagram of the scratch pad registers is shown in Figure 13.15. A register is selected based on the contents of the **RSRC** and **MSRC** fields of a current microinstruction, and a 4 bit **RNUM** register. Writing input data into a scratch pad register is controlled by the **SPW** field

of a microinstruction. There also exists a register backup stack in this unit, although it is not shown in the figure. The stack has a depth of six. It is used to store or restore the contents of the VAX general purpose registers when the COMET emulates the VAX architecture.

The super rotator consists of combinational circuits to render an efficient bit manipulation capability. As shown in Figure 13.13, the inputs to the super rotator include three buses (MBUS, RBUS, and WBUS) and a **LITRL** field of a microinstruction. Outputs of the super rotator are a 32 bit result and 2 bit status flags. The result is used in the ALU, and the status flags are used in the microsequencer. The super rotator performs 64 different functions. One example of a function is to convert numeric data type to a packed data type.

The ALU of the COMET performs arithmetic and log-

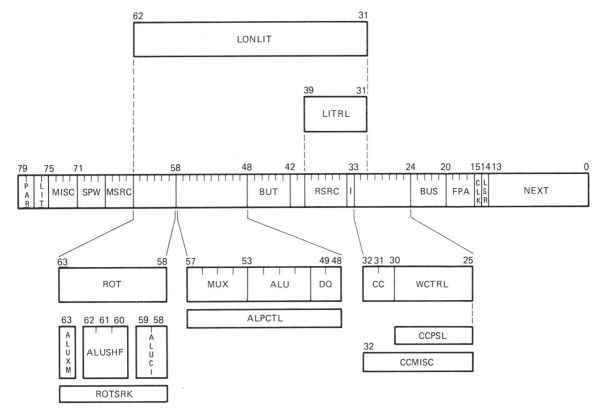

Figure 13.14a. The COMET system. Microinstruction format (from Y. Patt, *Introduction to the COMET Microarchitecture,* Digital Equipment Corp., 1980).

ical functions. Inputs to the ALU come from the RBUS, the MBUS, the super rotator, the D register, the Q register, and a constant 0. A pair of inputs is selected by the MUX field of a microinstruction.* If an input from the MBUS is short (i.e., length is less than 32 bits), it is extended with a sign bit or zero bit, based on the content of the ALUXM field of a microinstruction. A carry input of the ALU is chosen based on the ALUCI field of a microinstruction.†

The ALU can perform 2s complement arithmetic, BCD arithmetic, and logical operations. An ALU oper-

ation is selected by the ALU field of a microinstruction. The output of the ALU can be shifted or rotated. The type of shift is determined by the ALUSHF field and the DQ field of a microinstruction. The result of the shift operation may go on to the WBUS. It also may be stored in the D register or the Q register. The destination of the result is specified by the MUX and DQ fields of a microinstruction.

In addition to the normal ALU operations described above, the ALU can perform 50 special functions. In this case, the ALPCTL field of a microinstruction controls the ALU operation.*

---

*If a special function (described later) is to be executed, the ALPCTL field of a microinstruction controls the ALU operation.

†A carry input may be one of the following: 0, 1, a carry flag (ALKC), or PSL⟨0⟩.

*The MUX field, ALU field, and DQ field of a microinstruction is valid only if the ALPCTL field does not specify a special function. Note that there are 50 special functions while the ALPCTL field is able to specify 1,024 different functions.

Field Name	Bit Range	Length	Function of the Field
LIT	77-76	2	Represents the meaning of a microinstruction field <62:31>
LONLIT	62-31	32	32 bit immediate data may be loaded to the LONLIT register
LITRL	39-31	9	9 bit immediate data may be used as input to the Super Rotator
MSRC	67-64	4	Address of a MSP register
RSRC	39-34	6	Address of a RSP register
SPW	70-68	3	Controls writing into the RSP and MSP registers
ROT	63-58	6	Specify the Super Rotator function
ALPCTL	57-48	10	Specify one of the 50 special functions
MUX	57-54	4	Select inputs to the ALU and destination of the ALU output
ALU	53-50	4	Select an ALU function
DQ	49-48	2	Select a destination of the ALU output associated with the MUX field
ALUCI	59-58	2	Select a carry input to the ALU
ALUSHF	62-60	3	Specify the bits to be shifted when the ALU field specifies shift
ALUXM	63	1	Specify a sign extend or zero extend for a short input to the ALU
ROTSRK	63-58	6	Specify how to set up the two status flags SRKSTA <1:0>
BUT	47-42	6	Specify microinstruction sequencing
CLK	15	1	If this field is '1', the basic microcycle of 320 ns is extended to 480 ns
BUS	24-20	5	Control memory READ/WRITE
JSR	14	1	If this field is '1', push the current control store address into the microstack
NEXT	13-0	14	Contains the next microinstruction address

Figure 13.14b. Functional description of each field in the microinstruction.

A block diagram of the microcontrol unit of the COMET is shown in Figure 13.16. The MIR is an 80 bit long register which holds the microinstruction being executed. The control store may have up to 16K words, each word being 80 bits long. The first 6K words of control store are for the VAX emulation microprogram.

The next 2K words are for the remote diagnostic module (RDM) microprogram. There may be up to 8K words of WCS.

An address of a microinstruction in the control store is determined by multiplexors (CSMUX and ROMMUX in Figure 13.16). The selection is based on the contents of the BUT field of a microinstruction. The multiplexors choose one out of the following five control store addresses:

1. A NEXT field of a current microinstruction. By the current microinstruction, we mean a microinstruction which is in the MIR (or which is being executed).
2. A (possibly) modified NEXT field of a current microinstruction. In this case, the lower six bits of the contents of the NEXT field are logically ORed with information chosen by the BUT field of a current microinstruction. By this ORing, a conditional branch can be achieved.
3. An address from the microstack. A control store address popped from the microstack may be a next microinstruction address. (This is the case when there is a "return from a microprogram subroutine.") In this case, the popped control store address is added to the lower 6 bits of the contents of the NEXT field of a current microinstruction (i.e., a return microinstruction).
4. A starting address of a microcode which is to emulate a VAX instruction (i.e., OPcode). This address is calculated using the output of IRD1 ROM, which is a 1K word, 8 bit wide ROM.
5. A starting address of a microcode which is to evaluate the next operand. This address is calculated from the output of the IRDX ROM, which is 2K words, 15 bits wide.

The microstack, (USTK) can store up to 16 control store addresses. There is an associated stack pointer (USTKP) which points to the first available word in the microstack. A control store address is pushed into the microstack when the JSR field of a current microinstruction is 1. The microstack is popped by a command from the BUT field of a microinstruction.

In this section, we have presented the minimal description of the microprogram level details of the COMET machine with the aim of illustrating the ideas described earlier. Before a user can actually start writing microprograms for the WCS, a more detailed understanding of all components and functions is essential.

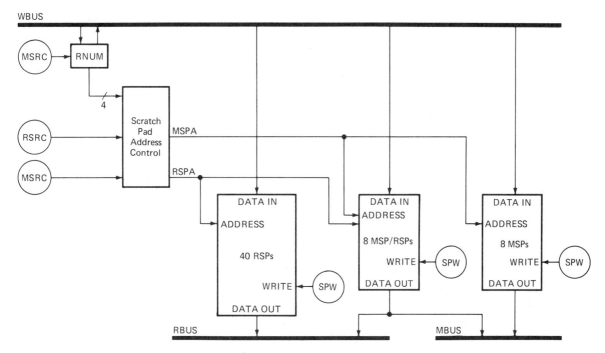

Figure 13.15. A simplified block diagram of the scratch pad registers in the COMET system. (Field name of microinstruction is enclosed in a circle.)

13.8 APPLICATIONS OF MICROPROGRAMMING

Since it was proposed in 1951, microprogramming has been used mainly to implement the control unit of a machine. Nearly all mini- and larger computers (except extremely fast computers such as CRAY-1*are micropro- grammed. Many of them support a writable control store, also. However, there are many other applications in which microprogramming has been used. Some of the applications are described in this section.

When one computer is replaced by another, it is highly desirable that the software developed in the old machine be run on the new machine. But, unless the new computer has the same characteristics (e.g., machine instruction

repertoire) as the old machine, the conversion is not trivial.

Emulation is one of the techniques used to solve the conversion problem. Emulation makes use of micripro- grams (with proper hardware support) in a machine (called a *host machine*) to interpret machine language of another machine (called a *target machine*). Emulation was used in the IBM System 360/model 65 to interpret machine languages of the IBM 7090, 7070, and 7080 familes. Today, a number of host machines support the emulation of other machines. For example, in compati- bility mode a VAX 11/780 can execute a PDP-11 in- struction set.

Microprogramming also may be used to reduce pro- gram execution time by implementing frequently exe- cuted machine language routines directly by micropro- grams. As a consequence, at the very least, the overhead of fetching and decoding the individual machine instruc- tion of a routine can be saved in the microprogram im- plementation. The routines that may be implemented as microprograms include square root, matrix manipulation,

---

*Several microinstructions are fetched and executed for a ma- chine instruction. For extremely fast computer systems, the amount of time for fetching microinstructions from the control store may be intolerable. Hence they use hardwired logic in the control unit.

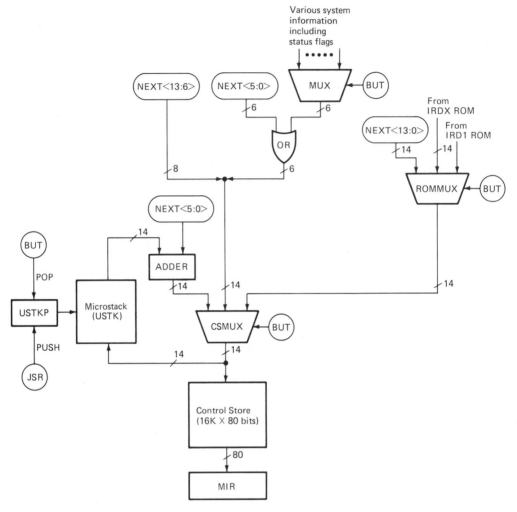

Figure 13.16. A simplified block diagram of the microcontrol unit in the COMET system. (Field name of microinstruction is enclosed in circle.)

searching and sorting, as well as functions carried out frequently by the operating system, such as context switching and queue manipulation.

The user may use microprograms to tune a machine for a given application. Machine instructions not provided by manufacturers can be created for particular applications. For example, a microprogram is used in the Venus operating system to support a number of nonstandard architecture features to assist in the implementation of the operating system. Some Venus operating system features supported by microprograms include segmentation and demand paging.

In addition to those described above, microprograms may be used in many other applications, such as executing high level language programs and processing signals. For more detailed description of such applications, refer to Chapter 8 of Agrawala and Rauscher, *Foundation of Microprogramming* (see this chapter's References).

13.9 Concluding Remarks

Since the early days of computing, the concepts of micro-programming has played a significant role in the development of computer technology. Microprogramming became a dominant theme during late 1960s and early 1970s to the extent that a user was frequently made aware of the capability of a machine at the micro-programming level. Many of the machines designed during this period contained writable control stores, which made the system dynamically microprogrammable. Vendors made an effort to support user microprogramming by making various language processors and other support software available.

The concept of machine instructions has also been with us since the very early days of computing. In most micro-programmed machines, microprogramming is used to interpret machine instructions. An approach taken by some researchers is to use microprograms to interpret high level language programs. This has been the dominant approach in the work on high level language architecture. Another approach has been to translate high level language programs directly into microcode. An interesting recent development is a peripheral array processor, the AP164, made by Floating Point Systems. In this processor, 10 functions are controlled in every machine cycle using a 64 bit microinstruction, and all programs are translated into the microcode. The commonly used high level language on this machine is extended FORTRAN.

The original goal of microprogramming, namely supporting the design of CPUs, continues to be realized by the use of microprogramming. Many new and innovative applications for microprogramming are being devised today by hardware designers of systems, varying in complexity from video games to signal processors. As microprogramming is made easier through the development of appropriate high level microprogramming languages, we can expect the use of these techniques to grow rapidly.

REFERENCES

Agrawala, A., Microprogram Optimization: A Survey, *IEEE Transactions on Computers,* Oct. 1976, pp. 962–73.

Agrawala, A., and T. Rauscher, *Foundation of Microprogramming,* New York: Academic Press, 1976.

Agrawala, A., and T. Rauscher, "Microprogramming: Perspective and Status," *IEEE Transactions on Computers,* Vol. C-23, No. 8, pp. 817–837.

Baba, T., and N. Hagiwara, "The MPG System: A Machine-Independent Efficient Microprogram Generator," *IEEE Transactions on Computers,* Vol. C-30, No. 6, pp. 373–95.

Dasgupta, S., "Some Aspects of High-Level Microprogramming," *Computing Surveys,* Vol. 12, No. 3, pp. 295–323.

Husson, S., *Microprogramming Principles and Practices.* Englewood Cliffs, NJ: Prentice-Hall, 1970.

Ma, P., and T. Lewis, "On the Design of a Microcode Compiler for a Machine-Independent High-Level Language," *IEEE Transactions on Software Engineering,* Vol. SE-7, No. 3, pp. 261–73.

Patt, Y., *Introduction to the COMET Microarchitecture.* Maynard, MA: Digital Equipment Corp., 1980.

Patterson, D., "An Experiment in High Level Language Microprogramming and Verification," *CACM,* Vol. 24, No. 10, pp. 699–709.

Patterson, D., "STRUM: Structured Microprogram Development System for Correct Firmware," *IEEE Transactions on Computers,* Vol. C-25, No. 10, pp. 974–85.

Sint, M., "A Survey of High Level Microprogramming Languages," Procedures of 13th Microprogramming Workshop, *Simicro Newsletter,* Vol. 11, No. 3, 4, pp. 141–53.

Tucker, S., "Emulation of Large Systems," *CACM,* Vol. 8, No. 12, pp. 753–61.

Wilkes, M., "The Best Way to Design an Automatic Calculating Machine," Manchester University Computer Inaugural Conference, Ferranti, Ltd., London, 1951, pp. 16–21.

Wilkes , M., "The Growth of Interest in Microprogramming: A Literature Survey," *Computing Surveys,* Vol. 1, No. 3, pp. 139–45.

Wilkes, M., and J. Stringer, "Microprogramming and design of the control circuits in an electronic digital computer," *Proc. of the Cambridge Philosophical Society,* Part 2, Vol. 49, Apr. 1953, pp. 230–38.

(Reprinted in Bell, C., and A. Newell, *Computer Sturctures: Readings and Examples.* New York: McGraw-Hill Book Co., 1971. Pp. 335–40.)

14
Analog and Hybrid Computers

George Hannauer

Electronic Associates, Inc.

14.1 INTRODUCTION

In many fields of science and engineering, the behavior of a physical system is most conveniently studied by observing a different, but analogous, system. Thus oceanographers study wave motion by inducing waves in specially constructed tanks; such a tank is a *model* or **analog** of a harbor or a bay. Before constructing a large and expensive chemical plant, an engineer may evaluate its behavior by constructing and operating a scale model, or pilot plant. Model airplanes and maps are additional examples. In every case, we have two systems: the "real" one and the model. Although the "real" system is the one of interest, it is often much simpler, cheaper, and safer to experiment with the model instead.

The validity of such experiments is dependent on the closeness between the behavior of the model and that of the original system. It should always be remembered that the model is not *identical* with the original system, but merely *analogous* to it; if it were identical, there would be no purpose in using the model—one might as well experiment with the system itself. Because the relation between a model and the original system is never an exact identity, the basis for the analogy should always be carefully investigated before the model is used. In some cases, this is straightforward; the relation between a map and the corresponding terrain is obvious. In other cases, there is little, if any, physical resemblance, and the validity of the analogy rests on demonstrating that the system and the model obey the same mathematical laws. In such a case, we refer to a *mathematical* model, or an *indirect*

analog, in contrast to a *physical model* or *direct analog,* such as the oceanographer's tank.

As an example of a mathematical model, consider the differential equation

$$dX/dt = KX \qquad (14.1)$$

which states that some quantity X varies at a rate proportional to its present value. This equation is simple enough to be solved explicitly; the solution is

$$X(t) = X_0 e^{Kt} \qquad (14.2)$$

where X_0 is the value of X at time $t = 0$ (the initial condition). Simple as this equation is, it represents a large number of apparently very different phenomena. If K is negative, we have *exponential decay;* the value of X decreases with time, and approaches zero. This situation describes the voltage on a capacitor discharging through a resistive load, the concentration in a simple first order chemical reaction, the flushing of a dissolved substance from a well stirred tank, and the decay of a radioactive isotope. If K is positive, then the solution represents *exponential growth;* typical examples include growth of bacteria in a laboratory culture, and compound interest.

Because all these systems are described by the same equation, all exhibit analogous behavior (the most obvious difference being the sign of the constant K, which distinguishes between growth and decay). It is unfortunate that differences in terminology among distinct fields tend to obscure the basic similarities.

We have thus seen that systems described by the same equations exhibit analogous behavior; any such system may be taken as a model, or analog, of any other. Another term used in this context is **simulation;** one such system is said to **simulate** the other.

Some analogs are *special purpose;* they are designed to model a particular system, or a small set of closely related systems. Other analogs are programmable; they are designed to solve the underlying equations, and may be programmed to simulate any system describable in terms of the basic mathematical operations they can perform. Such **general purpose analog computers** are the subject of this chapter.

Models also may be classified as **discrete** or **continuous.** Models of card games, customers queueing up in a bank, and telephone traffic are essentially *discrete;* each system changes state by finite amounts at discrete times. Such discrete changes in the state of a system are called **events;** typical events include the playing of a card, the arrival of a customer at the bank, the completion of a transaction, and the dialing of a call.

On the other hand, ocean waves, airplane motion, chemical reactions and electronic circuits are generally treated as *continuous* phenomena and described by differential equations. The state of such a system is changing all the time; changes are not confined to discrete instants. In practice, there is a considerable overlap between continuous and discrete models; on the microscopic level, chemical reactions can be described in terms of discrete events—the reaction of individual molecules—and the same may be said for the electrons in a circuit.

Computer Implementation

Not all models are implemented on computers, of course. Direct analogs, like the oceanographer's tank, need no computers; neither do the simpler mathematical models, such as a first order differential equation, which is easy to solve explicitly. However, as systems become more complex, and design constraints more severe, designers turn increasingly to more sophisticated models, which require computers for efficient analysis.

Discrete models are generally best solved on a digital computer, which is a discrete-state machine. Analog computers are used primarily for continuous models—especially those that can be described in terms of differential equations and/or transfer functions. Many models combine both continuous and discrete elements. For example, a chemical plant with its inherently continuous processes is often regulated by a digital controller. An aircraft or space vehicle may have one or more on-board digital computers for monitoring and control. Such "hybrid" systems are best simulated by **hybrid computers,** which combine a digital computer and an analog computer in a single system.

14.2 BASIC ANALOG COMPUTER COMPONENTS

A general purpose analog computer is a collection of processing elements, each of which performs a specific mathematical function, such as addition and subtraction. The inputs and outputs of these components are not discrete numbers, but continuously varying signals. These signals might be mechanical (displacements and shaft rotations), hydraulic (pressures and flow rates) or electronic (voltages and currents). Although the early analogs were mechanical, the speed, reliability and flexibility of electronic components largely has supplanted mechanical methods; modern analog computers are based on electronic signals.

On any given computer, the processing elements are designed to operate over a particular range. This range, normally either $\pm$ 10 V or $\pm$ 100 V, is called the computer's **reference voltage.** Thus, on any machine, signals normally range between minus reference and plus reference. Such signals are usually expressed as a fraction of the reference voltage; i.e., the reference voltage is used as the unit of measurement, and is called one **machine unit.** This convention is analogous to the use of 0 and 1 to describe the logic levels in a digital computer regardless of the actual voltage level. Thus, on any machine the range of a variable is $\pm$ 1 machine unit.

Most computers are equipped with a digital voltmeter (DVM) which is capable of displaying the output of any component directly in machine units. Typical DVMs have four digit resolution; a display of $+0.7500$ corresponds to a voltage of 7.5 V on a 10 volt machine and 75 V on a 100 volt machine. In either case, the display would be interpreted as 0.7500 machine units.

An analog computer is a *parallel* machine; each operation is performed continuously on its own dedicated processing unit. Thus, an analog computer is a multiprocessing system; it may contain anywhere from a few dozen to a few hundred processors, each operating simultaneously. Inputs and outputs of these processing elements are terminated on a *program panel,* or *patch panel* and the machine is programmed by the appropriate interconnecting (patching) of these inputs and outputs.

Summer

A typical summer is shown in Figure 14.1. The pie shaped sector is the conventional symbol for a high gain amplifier. Such an amplifier, as its name implies, has a very high gain—typically 100 million or more. It also produces a net sign reversal; the output is opposite to the input in polarity. Thus, if J represents the summing junction voltage and Z the amplifier output, then

$$Z = -AJ \qquad (14.3)$$

where A is very large (about 10^8). The electronics engineer expresses this same fact by saying that the amplifier has 160 dB of gain and a phase shift of 180 degrees.

The amplifier is also designed to have a very high input impedance (it draws very little input current in relation to the signal currents), and a very low output impedance (its output voltage is essentially independent of the load it drives). Under these assumptions, we may write, using Kirchoff's current law:

$$(X - J)/R_X + (Y - J)/R_Y$$
$$+ (Z - J)/R_F = 0 \qquad (14.4)$$

where R_F is called the *feedback resistor*. Note that the load resistor, R_L, does not appear in this equation. Solving Eq. 14.3 and 14.4 for Z gives

$$Z = -\frac{(R_F/R_X) + (R_F/R_Y)}{1 + R_F/(AR)} \qquad (14.5)$$

where R is the parallel combination of R_X, R_Y, and R_F.

Because the gain A is very large, the second term in the denominator is negligible, and the equation simplifies to

$$Z = -[(R_F/R_X)X + (R_F/R_Y)Y] \qquad (14.6)$$

This equation can be derived more directly by rewriting Eq. 14.3 in the form

$$J = -Z/A \qquad (14.7)$$

and noting that, since A is very large, J must be very small, and may be ignored in comparison with X, Y and Z. This fact is usually expressed by saying that the summing junction J is a *virtual ground;* it is so close to 0 that it may be replaced with 0 in any voltage drop calculation. Thus, the voltage drop $(X - J)$ is essentially X, and similarly for $(Y - J)$ and $(Z - J)$. With this assumption, Eq. 14.4 simplifies to

$$X/R_X + Y/R_Y + Z/R_F = 0 \qquad (14.8)$$

which can be solved directly for Z, yielding Eq. 14.6.

Note that the gains are simply resistor ratios, and can be made equal to, or even greater than, unity. In practice, it is customary to avoid complicating the circuit diagram by drawing resistors; instead, one simply writes the gain as a number at the input to the summer. Figure 14.2 illustrates the usual programmer's symbol for a two input summer with equal input and feedback resistors (gains of 1). A summer with only one input and equal resistors (gain of 1) is an *inverter;* if the input is X, the output is $-X$. Figure 14.3 shows how an inverter and a summer may be combined for subtraction. Note in every case, the output is *minus* the sum of the inputs. There is no reason to limit the number of inputs to two. Summers with three or more inputs are quite common.

Role of Amplifier

Although it is common to talk of "summing amplifiers," it is worth noting that the amplifier itself does not perform summation. The actual summation is a current summation at the junction of the resistors, and takes place whether or not an amplifier is present. The true function of the summer is more subtle; it acts as a buffer, or isolation device, preventing the following circuit from "loading down" the output.

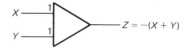

Figure 14.2. Programmer's symbol for a two input summer.

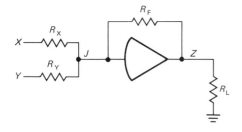

Figure 14.1. A two input summing amplifier.

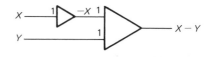

Figure 14.3. Using a summer and inverter for subtractor.

Incidentally, the reason for the minus sign in Eq. 14.6 is *not* the sign inversion in the amplifier itself. If $-A$ were replaced by $+A$ in Eq. 14.3, the result would be a minus sign instead of a plus sign in the denominator of Equation 14.5. Because this term is negligible, it follows that the final result is unaltered. The real reason for building the amplifier with a sign inversion is that the current-balance equation (Eq. 14.4) must be one of stable equilibrium so that any error in Z produces a signal at the summing junction to counteract the error. Without this built-in sign inversion, the equilibrium would be unstable. Any error, however small, would tend to grow rapidly, until the amplifier is driven to the limit of its operating range.

Coefficient Units

A coefficient unit multiplies a time varying signal by a constant coefficient. Two versions are available on modern analog computers: the potentiometer and the digitally controlled attenuator.

The **potentiometer** (*pot,* for short) is essentially an adjustable voltage divider. It consists of a resistive element with one end connected to the input signal, and the other grounded (Figure 14.4). At one end of this resistive element, the voltage is the input signal X; at the other end, it is 0 (ground). The voltage along the resistive element varies continuously between these two extremes. An adjustable contact, or "wiper," can be positioned anywhere along this length, thus producing an adjustable fraction of the input. Thus, for an input X, the output is KX, where $0 < K < 1$.

Pots on modern computers can be set typically to four significant figures, i.e., the value of K can be anywhere from 0.0000 to 1.0000 (physical limitations generally reduce the achievable maximum to about 0.9999). Pots may be either handset or servoset. Handset pots are adjusted with a dial; the operator rotates the dial while observing the four digit setting on the **digital voltmeter** (**DVM**). Servoset pots may be set by entering the four digits of the setting on the keyboard, and pressing a SET button. In a hybrid system (see Section 14.8), servoset pots may be set under program control by the digital computer at the rate of one to three pots per second.

The **digitally controlled attenuator** (**DCA**) is a form of digital to analog converter (see Chapter 7). A set of weighted input resistors is used as the input element for a high gain amplifier with fixed feedback. The resistors are switched on and off under control of a digital register (Figure 14.5). The result is a coefficient whose magnitude lies between 0 and 1, but with a sign inversion owing to the amplifier.

Four-quadrant units, each containing two amplifiers, are also available; they allow any coefficient between -1 and $+1$. DCAs are set, like servopots, either by keyboard input, or from the digital computer in a hybrid system. In the latter case, the setup is very fast; a full system of 120 DCAs can be set in less than 500 microseconds.

The Integrator

Most of the systems simulated on analog computers are dynamic systems; they are modeled with differential equations containing derivatives with respect to time. To solve such equations requires a component performing the inverse of differentiation—an integrator.

The basic analog integrator consists of a high gain amplifier with an input resistor and a feedback capacitor (Figure 14.6a and Figure 14.6b). A capacitor satisfies the basic relation

$$Q = CV \qquad (14.9)$$

where Q is the charge on the capacitor, V is the voltage across it, and C is the capacitance. Differentiating this

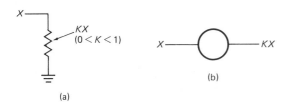

(a)

(b)

Figure 14.4. The potentiometer (pot). (a) Circuit schematic. (b) Programmer's symbol.

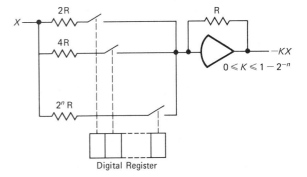

Figure 14.5. A digitally controlled attenuator (DCA).

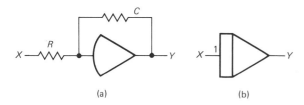

Figure 14.6. An integrator. (a) Circuit schematic. (b) Programmer's symbol.

relation gives

$$I = \dot{Q} = C \, dV/dt \qquad (14.10)$$

which says that the current through a capacitor is proportional to the rate of change of the voltage across it. Applying this result to the circuit in Figure 14.6a yields

$$X/R + C \, dY/dt = 0 \qquad (14.11)$$

This equation is obtained by adding the currents at the summing junction, under the assumption that the amplifier itself draws negligible current and that the summing junction voltage is close to zero at all times. Solving this equation for Y gives

$$dY/dt = -(1/RC)X \quad \text{or} \qquad (14.12)$$

$$Y = -(1/RC) \int X \, dt$$

so that the output is, as desired, proportional to the integral of the input. The gain of the integrator is $1/RC$, which has the units of 1/time. Typical values are $R = 1$ MΩ (megohm) and $C = 1$ μF (microfarad), or R = 100 KΩ and C = 10 μF; both combinations give a time constant of 1 second, or a gain of unity. Integrators on most modern machines offer a range of resistor and capacitor values, selectable by programming, so that the time constant can be varied in decade steps from 1 second (gain = 1) to 10 microseconds (gain = 100,000), accommodating a wide range of solution speeds. The programmer's symbol for an integrator is given in Figure 14.6b.

Mode control.   The integrator is the only dynamic element discussed so far; it integrates with respect to time. This suggests the need for some control signals to synchronize the integrators.

All integrators are provided with programmable initial conditions; the initial output of an integrator can be chosen arbitrarily by the programmer. Mathematically, this reflects that the integral of a function is defined only up

to an additive constant; thus one may specify the initial value arbitrarily. Electrically, this is accomplished by switching circuitry which establishes an initial charge on the feedback capacitor; the details are omitted. Of course, the chosen initial value should correspond to the initial value of the physical variable in the system being simulated.

At the beginning of a computation, all integrators are in the *initial condition* mode; their outputs are the preprogrammed initial conditions. To start a run, the computer is switched to the *operate* mode; all integrators then receive their rate inputs and start to integrate them. At the end of the run, the system may be put into the *hold* mode, which "freezes" all integrator outputs (and hence all variables in the simulation) to whatever values they have reached in the course of the run. These values may then be read out or recorded, and the computer returned to the initial condition mode to initiate another run. Alternative names for the initial condition and operate modes are *reset* and *compute,* respectively. Mode control may be achieved either manually or under program control.

Typical Analog Computing Systems

Figure 14.7 shows a typical medium size (30 integrators) analog computing system—the EAI 681. The major components of the system are as follows:

- The *patch panel* has over 4,000 input and output terminals for interconnection of the individual processing elements. It is removable, so that the program connections may be stored off-line.
- Every major computing component has an *overload indicator,* which is illuminated when that component is driven beyond its nominal operating range (± 1 machine unit).
- The *logic readout panel* provides a parallel display of the states of the various logic elements (Section 14.7).
- The 681 has provision for 132 coefficient units. Most of these (120) are either *servoset pots* or *DCAs,* allowing for rapid problem setup under program control. Twelve *handset pots* are also provided, to allow for manual adjustment of frequently changed parameters.
- The *analog readout panel* contains the display for the DVM, the comparators, and other analog controls and displays.
- The *control keyboard* contains the controls for mode selection, coefficient setting, readout of computing com-

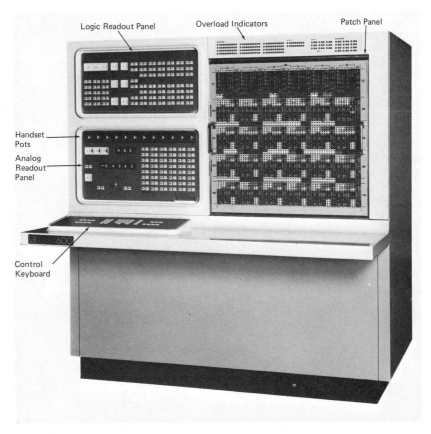

Figure 14.7. Typical medium size analog computer. (Courtesy Electronic Associates, Inc.)

ponents, integrator gain selection, and other manual operations.

The EAI 2000 (Figure 14.8) illustrates a different organization for these functions. Except for the patch panel and handset pots, the setup, control, and monitoring functions are centralized in a microprocessor based *monitoring and control system (MACS)*, which allows any analog or logic signal or overload state to be displayed on a CRT. All manual control is accomplished by commands entered through the MACS keyboard. This arrangement allows for flexible and powerful control in a minimum of space.

14.3 APPLICATION EXAMPLE: RADIOACTIVE DECAY

Consider the first order equation (Eq. 14.1) described in Section 14.1. When the coefficient is negative, it is customary to write the equation in the form

$$dX/dt = -KX \qquad (K > 0) \qquad (14.13)$$

which displays the sign explicitly. Although the solution is well known, so that no computer is necessary, the exercise of programming this equation gives valuable insight into the physical and mathematical basis behind the operation of an analog computer.

The programming process can be summarized in three steps:

1. Assume all derivatives in the equations are available as analog signals.
2. Integrate these derivatives to obtain the state variables.
3. Use these variables to evaluate the derivatives which were assumed available in step 1, thus "closing the loop."

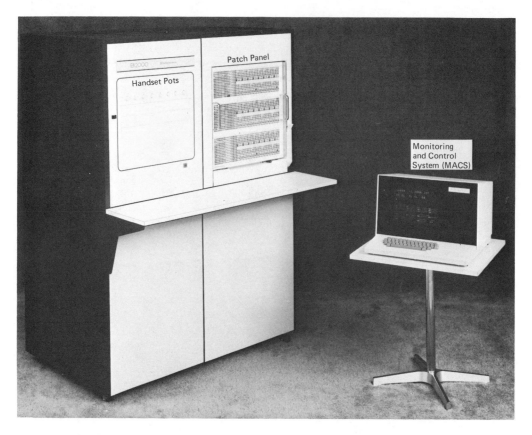

Figure 14.8. The EAI 2000 analog computer. (Courtesy Electronic Associates, Inc.)

Figure 14.9 illustrates the process. Assuming the derivative (dX/dt) is available, integration produces $-X$ (note the sign inversion in the integrator), and multiplying this signal by K produces the signal $-KX$, which is the original derivative. Connecting this output $(-KX)$ to the integrator input (dX/dt) closes the loop; the resultant circuit satisfies Eq. 14.13

Figure 14.9c shows a more usual form of the circuit where the integrator produces X, rather than $-X$, and its input is $-dX/dt = -KX$. Note that the component in-

terconnections are the same in Figures 14.9b and c. The only difference is the sign on of the initial condition. If a negative initial condition is imposed on the circuit, we have Figure 14.9b; a positive initial condition leads to Figure 14.9c.

To visualize the functioning of the circuit, assume an initial condition of 1.0 machine unit on the integrator, and assume $K = 0.5$. Then the input to the integrator is initially 0.5 machine units, and it will integrate downward (because of the sign inversion) at an initial rate of

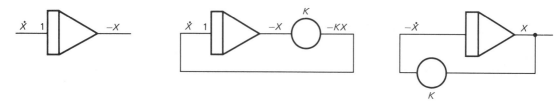

Figure 14.9. Steps in solving the decay equation $dX/dt = -KX$.

0.5 machine units per second. As X approaches zero, so does dX/dt; thus, the signal approaches zero asymptotically as it should. At all times, the integrator output satisfies the equation $dX/dt = -KX$, so that it generates the desired solution to the equation.

Analog programming is the inverse of the usual process of mathematical modeling. Instead of starting with a physical system and deriving a differential equation to describe it, we start with an equation, and develop a physical system (that is, a computer circuit) which satisfies the equation.

14.4 NONLINEAR ANALOG COMPONENTS

The components discussed so far are capable of adding, subtracting, and integrating analog signals, and multiplying them by constants. Such components are called **linear;** they are capable of solving any set of linear equations with constant coefficients. This section describes **nonlinear** components: *function generators* and *multipliers*.

Function Generators

Analog function generators are based on the fact that any continuous function may be approximated arbitrarily closely by a piecewise linear function, i.e., one whose graph consists of straight-line segments. Although such segment functions may be generated in several ways, the most common is to use a network of resistors and diodes, as shown in Figure 14.10.

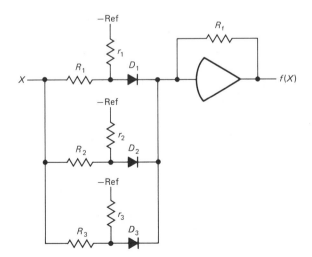

Figure 14.10. Circuit schematic for a diode function generator.

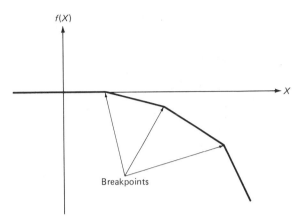

Figure 14.11. Output waveform obtained from the function generator of Figure 14.10.

A diode can pass current in one direction only; it is analogous to a one way valve in a hydraulic system. Thus, in Figure 14.10, diode D_1 prevents any current from flowing into the summing junction until input X becomes large enough to overcome the negative bias (-1 machine unit) on resistor r_1. This happens when $X > R_1/r_1$. For smaller values of X, the output is zero; for larger values, the output changes with a slope of R_F/R_1. The value of X for which the diode just begins to conduct is called the *breakpoint* for that segment; appropriate choice of resistor values allows the breakpoint to be placed at will.

Because the currents flowing into the summing junction are additive, the three segment circuit shown in Figure 14.10 produces an output function like that in Figure 14.11. With proper choice of resistor values and diode arrangements, any segment function can be generated; thus, any continuous function can be approximated as closely as desired. Packaged units are available for all functions commonly encountered in applied mathematics, such as sine, cosine, log, exponential, square, and square root.

Adjustable function generators are also available for empirically defined functions. Such function generators are set up simply by entering a data table, i.e., a set of values of X and $F(X)$. These values may be manually entered via a keyboard or set up from a programmed array by a FORTRAN call in a hybrid system.

Multiplication

Multiplication of two input variables X and Y can be accomplished using the identity

$$XY = \frac{(X + Y)^2 - (X - Y)^2}{4} \qquad (14.14)$$

Resistors and amplifiers are employed to generate the sum and difference, and diode function generators are used to produce the square function. Such *quarter-square multipliers* are available as packaged units; most of them can be reconfigured to perform division as well. Further details for a particular machine are provided in the manufacturer's documentation.

14.5 APPLICATION EXAMPLE: HYDRAULIC TRANSIENT

This problem demonstrates the use of analog computers in a practical application. It also provides a brief introduction to the process of analog programming and scaling. Finally, it illustrates the importance of *on-line interaction* between the programmer and the computer. Once the simulation is programmed and debugged, the user may experiment with it, much as he or she would with the actual physical system.

Problem Statement

A surge tank must accommodate the fluctuations in the flow of effluent from a plant. The tank is currently in service, and is operating with two pumps feeding into it. The plant capacity is to be expanded, necessitating the addition of a third pump (Figure 14.12). The problem is to determine whether the tank can accommodate the extra load without overflowing. (The tank is 9 feet high.) The system equations and necessary problem data are as follows:

$$dH_T/dt = (PQ_A - Q_L)/A_T \qquad (14.15)$$

$$dQ_L/dt = (gA_L/L)(H_T - H_P) \qquad (14.16)$$

$$H_P = MQ_L + NQ_L^2 \qquad (14.17)$$

Variable definitions:

Q_L = outflow from line, ft³/s

H_T = height of liquid in tank, ft

H_P = friction head loss in pipe, ft

t = time, s

Constant and parameter definitions:

Q_A = 90 ft³/s = inflow to tank per pump

A_T = 470 ft² = cross-sectional area of tank

A_L = 12.6 ft² = cross-sectional area of line

L = 665 ft = length of line

g = 32.2 ft/s² = gravitational constant

M = 0.0185; N = 3.60 × 10⁻⁵ empirical constants

P = number of pumps turned on

H_{TMAX} = 9 ft = height of tank

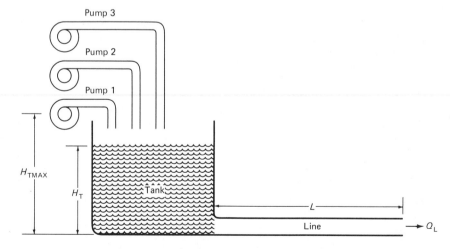

Figure 14.12. Definition of variables in the surge tank problem.

Eq. 14.15 is a statement of mass conservation; it simply says that the rate of change of the tank volume is the difference between the inflow and the outflow. Eq. 14.16 is Newton's third law; it describes the acceleration of the mass of fluid in the pipe owing to the pressure exerted by the fluid in the tank. Term H_P is a friction term, representing energy losses in the line. It is expressed most conveniently in terms of equivalent head loss. It may be determined empirically by observing the steady-state value of H_T for different known inflows, because we must have $H_P = H_T$ and $Q_L = PQ_A$ in steady state. A quadratic polynomial has been found to fit the empirical data adequately, giving Eq. 14.17.

Analysis

As mentioned, under steady state conditions the system must satisfy the relations $H_P = H_T$ and $Q_L = PQ_A$. This provides an easy way to calculate the steady state fluid level as a function of the number of pumps. For one pump, $P = 1$, $Q_L = Q_A$, and

$$H_T = H_P = 0.0185 \times 90$$
$$+ 3.6 \times 10^{-5} \times (90)^2 = 1.9566 \text{ ft}$$

Similar calculations give, for two pumps, $H_T = 4.4964$ feet and, for three pumps, $H_T = 7.6194$ feet.

Because the three pump steady state is less than tank height (9 ft), we may conclude that the system is capable of handling the extra pump, at least under steady state conditions. But this fact is no guarantee against transient overflow. For example, when the system is operating in steady state with one pump, and the second is turned on, the height of fluid in the tank exhibits an initial transient that goes far above the final steady state value of 4.5 feet. This suggests that if the system is operating with two pumps on and a third is added, the initial transient might well go above 9 feet. Thus, it is not clear that the third pump can be safely added to the system without causing the tank to spill over. A computer solution of the system equations is therefore recommended.

Program Flexibility

But much more is required of a simulation than a simple yes or no answer. If the answer is "Yes, the new pump can be added with no danger of spillage," then little else needs to be done. But if the answer is "No, the third pump can cause transient overflows," then we are faced with the question "What can we do about it?"

Several solutions suggest themselves. We can enlarge

the tank, either vertically (making it high enough to withstand the worst-case surge) or horizontally (increasing its cross-sectional area, and hence its capacity). We could enlarge the line, which would change the cross-sectional area A_L, and also the friction coefficients M and N. Any or all of these solutions might be prohibitively expensive, and they may not be necessary. The main point is to keep the simulation flexible, so that the effect of any of these design changes can be easily determined by appropriate parameter changes. It is much easier to experiment with the simulation model (by changing a few coefficients) than to make the corresponding changes in the actual system.

Computer Program

Generating an analog computer program from Eq. 14.15–14.17 is relatively straightforward. As in the previous example, we start by assuming the derivatives available, and integrate them to produce the state variables H_T and Q_L. These variables, in turn, are used as input to the appropriate components to generate the derivatives, thus closing the loops. Naturally, there is a bit more to programming than the above description indicates.

Figure 14.13 illustrates one possible program for this

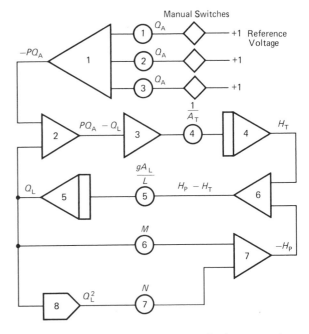

Figure 14.13. Analog computer program for the surge tank.

system. In analyzing this program, one should remember that every summer or integrator has a sign inversion. Thus, when H_T and $-H_P$ are combined in summer 6, the output of the summer is *minus* the sum of the inputs, i.e. $H_P - H_T$. When this is multiplied by pot 5 (gA_L/L), the result is the *negative* of the derivative of Q_L, as given by Equation 14.16. Therefore, the output of integrator 5 is Q_L (not $-Q_L$, because the integrator inverts, too).

The generation of input term PQ_A requires some further explanation. The flow rate Q_A for one pump is constant, but the number of pumps, P, is variable, changing each time a pump is turned on or off. In line with the discussion in the previous section, the simulation should be as flexible as possible, so that the user may experiment with it just as one would with the actual tank. Accordingly, the three pumps are simulated by three pots, each set for Q_A, the flow rate for a single pump. Manual switches allow the user to turn the pumps on and off while the simulation is running, much as an operator would in the actual plant. The switches are connected to the machine's reference voltage (referred to as $+1$, i.e., one machine unit, in the diagram). This signal, multiplied by the pot setting Q_A, gives Q_A as the pot output. The output of summer 1 is therefore $-PQ_A$.

Magnitude Scaling

Up to now, no mention has been made of the *ranges* of the variables or parameters in a simulation. These must be considered before the simulation is actually run. For example, a pot setting of Q_A, as shown in Figure 14.13, is obviously impossible as it stands, because the value of Q_A is 90 ft^3/s, and pot settings must be less than unity. Furthermore, because pots can be set to four significant figures on most machines, the allowable range is from 0.0000 to 1.0000. Since parameter N has the value 3.6×10^{-5}, the setting of N on pot 7 is also impossible; the best four digit approximation to this number is zero!

Similarly, the output flow rate, Q_L, can be as large as 400 or 500 ft^3/s, as we shall see below. Because the output of a computing component cannot go much above the reference voltage of the machine (typically ± 10 V or ± 100 V, depending on the design), there is no way integrator 5 can be made to produce signal Q_L as it stands.

The solution lies in *scaling*. Amplifier outputs and potentiometer settings need not necessarily be numerically *equal* to the corresponding physical variables, but merely *proportional* to them. Appropriate scale factors must be introduced so that the range of the *machine variables* (amplifier outputs) and *machine coefficients* (roughly, pot settings) fit comfortably within the range available on the machine. The process is very similar to plotting a graph on graph paper of fixed size. One must decide, by investigating the maximum values of the data to be plotted, how many physical units to use per inch of graph paper.

Similarly, scaling an analog simulation starts with an estimation of the maximum values assumed by the variables in the program, so that appropriate scale factors may be chosen. Here, the analog programmer has less information to go on than the draftsperson, who usually has the entire data table available before starting. The programmer does not know *exactly* how large the variables will be until after actually running the simulation. In fact, in the present case, the entire point of the simulation is to find the maximum value of variable H_T. Thus, it would appear that we must solve the problem first, before we can put it on the computer!

Fortunately, exact maxima are not needed; all that is required is a good estimate. In many problems, good estimates are readily available from one's knowledge of the physical system, from analysis of the equations, from trial and error, or any combination of these.

For example, consider first the output flow rate, Q_L. In steady state, as we have seen, this equals PQ_A, which, for three pumps, is $3 \times 90 = 270$ ft^3/s. Because overshoots are expected, the maximum value should be somewhat higher than this—say 400 or 500. To be conservative, we will take 500 as the maximum value. (It is common practice to use round numbers for maximum values. Even if the maximum were known to be exactly 432.71, it is easier to read a graph on which 5 inches represents 500 ft^3/s than one in which 5 inches represents 432.71 ft^3/s.) From Eq. 14.8 we may now calculate the maximum value of H_P, which obviously occurs when Q_L is at *its* maximum. Direct substitution yields 18.25 feet; rounding upward, we take 20 feet for the maximum of H_P.

As for H_T, the actual height in the tank, it never can get above 9 feet without running over, so 10 feet would seem like a good bet. However, as mentioned above, one of the possible solutions, should overflow occur, is to increase the height of the tank. In the interest of flexibility, we would like to be able to investigate this possibility. If, then, we want to determine how much extra height is necessary, we had better allow for a larger tank in the simulation. Hence, a maximum value of 20 feet is preferable.

Notice that this happens to be the same as the maximum value for H_P—not entirely coincidence. Because the two are equal in steady state, it seems reasonable that their maximum values should be close. Similar considerations lead to the decision to scale summers 1 and 2 for

500 ft^3/s. Output Q_L^2 virtually "scales itself." A maximum of 500 for Q_L implies a maximum of 250,000 for Q_L^2.

Once the maximum values are estimated, one must use these estimates to adjust the equations so they "fit" on the machine; that is, they must be transformed into equivalent equations involving the machine variables rather than the problem variables. Regardless of the range of a given problem variable, the corresponding machine variable (amplifier output) must not exceed the computer's reference voltage. Thus, on any machine, all properly scaled analog signals have maximum values of one machine unit or less.

With this convention, all properly scaled computer variables will have maximum magnitudes of (at most) unity; computer variables are *normalized* variables. If a given problem variable is, say, X, with an estimated maximum $XMAX$, than the corresponding computer variable is simply $[X/XMAX]$; *every computer variable is the ratio of the corresponding problem variable to its maximum value.*

In the present case, the problem variables H_T, H_P, and Q_L correspond to the computer variables $[H_T/20]$, $[H_P/20]$, and $[Q_L/500]$. The problem variable Q_L^2 will be represented on the machine by the computer variable $[Q_L^2/250,000]$. Square brackets are generally written around computer variables to indicate that they represent scaled quantities.

The task of scaling thus reduces to transforming the original problem equations into equivalent equations connecting the corresponding computer variables. To illustrate the process, recall Equation 14.17: $H_P = MQ_L + NQ_L^2$. This must be transformed into an equation involving only scaled computer variables. We can do this by replacing each variable with an equivalent expression in terms of computer variables. Obviously, H_P is equivalent to $20[H_P/20]$, and similarly for the other variables. This leads to the equation:

$$(20[H_P/20] = 500M[Q_L/500]$$
$$+ 250,000N[Q_L^2/250,000] \quad (14.18)$$

Solving for $[H_P/20]$, the desired computer variable, gives

$$[H_P/20] = (500M/20)[Q_L/500]$$
$$+ (250,000N/20)[Q_L^2/250,000] \quad (14.19)$$

Because the quantities in square brackets are computer variables (amplifier outputs), the quantities in parentheses must be the corresponding settings on the pots con-

necting these amplifiers. This means, for example, that pot 6 in Figure 14.13 should be set to $500M/20 = 25M = 0.4625$ (from the value of M given in the original problem statement). Similarly, pot 7 should be set to $12500N = 0.4500$.

At the beginning of this section, it was stated that the value of N (3.6×10^{-5}) was too small to set accurately on a pot; we now see that with proper scaling, this "problem" has disappeared. The setting is now large enough to set accurately on a pot, to four significant digits. Examination of the other apparently "troublesome" pots yields a similar story. Pots 1, 2, and 3 have unscaled settings of $Q_A = 90$, which is clearly impossible. But if the summer output is actually $[-PQ_A/500]$, then the pot settings become $Q_A/500 = 0.1800$. Once again, proper scaling has yielded "reasonable" pot settings. Similarly, pot 5 (labeled "gA_L/L") should actually be set to $gA_L/(25L) = 0.02440$, and pot 4 (labeled I/A_T) should actually be $25/A_T = 0.05319$.

Time Scaling

The problem, as programmed in the previous section, may now be patched and run on the computer; all variables cover a reasonable range and the corresponding amplifiers will not overload. The solution, however, will be quite slow. This is because the physical system itself is quite slow.

The fluctuations in the tank have a natural period of about three minutes. If one wants to observe several cycles of oscillation, ten minutes or more of computer time are required, since the simulation, as programmed above, runs in "real time"; that is, each second on the computer represents one second in the system. There is no reason the simulation needs to be limited to real time. Depending on the speed of the original system, it might prove desirable to run the simulation either faster or slower. This can be done by making an appropriate scaling transformation on the *independent* variable—time.

It is customary to distinguish between time in the original problem and time on the computer by using the letters t and τ, respectively. Derivatives in the original equations are with respect to t, but intergrators on the machine integrate with respect to τ. The two variables are related by the scaling relation $\tau = \beta t$, which defines the *time scale factor* β. If $\beta < 1$, the simulation runs faster than real time; 1 second of computer time represents more than 1 second of problem time. If $\beta > 1$, the reverse is true. And, of course, if $\beta = 1$, the system runs in real time. In the program of the previous section, the distinction between t and τ was ignored; thus the solution ran in real time by default.

What must be done to implement a time scale factor on the computer? A little reflection will show that, of all the computer components described so far, the only one that has time in its input/output relation is the integrator. The integrator integrates with respect to τ, while the original problem derivatives are expressed with respect to t; if the two times are to be different, this disparity must be reconciled.

From the definition of the time scale factor β, it can easily be seen that, for any variable X,

$$dX/d\tau = (dX/dt)/\beta \qquad (14.20)$$

To produce X as output, the integrator needs $dX/d\tau$ as input; if the available input is dX/dt, it must be divided by β. Thus the general rule: *to time-scale a simulation, divide every integrator input by the time scale factor.*

This rule may also be justified informally on intuitive grounds by observing that if, for example, $\beta < 1$, all integrator inputs are to be *increased* by the same factor. Since the magnitude of an integrator input determines how fast its output will change, increasing them all in the same proportion will make the problem run faster. Similarly, $\beta > 1$ requires that the integrator gains (or pot settings before the integrators) be proportionally *reduced;* the integrators will then integrate more slowly.

In the present example, the computer response is undesirably slow; hence a speedup ($\beta < 1$) is required. How great a speedup? In a *batch* operation, in which efficiency and throughput are prime considerations, the solution should be run as fast as the speed of the equipment will allow, to get the job done as quickly as possible. However, analog computers are generally operated *interactively,* which adds the additional constraint that the solution should not be too fast for the human user to follow. If the solution is too slow, the user gets bored waiting for something to happen; if it is too fast, the user cannot absorb and respond to the information quickly enough. In the present simulation, one should be able to observe the fluid level in the tank and respond to it by turning pumps on and off. Experience with the simulation indicates that a 10 to 1 speedup is about right. Thus, we select a time scale factor of 1/10; all pots feeding integrators are to be divided by this factor, which will make them 10 times bigger.

Of course, this time scale factor should be applied *in addition* to all other scale factors previously introduced. For example, we saw that pot 5 should be set for $gA_L/(25L) = 0.02440$ to take the magnitude scale factors into account; adding time scaling changes, $gA_L/(25L\beta) =$

0.2440. Similarly, pot 4 becomes $25/(A_T\beta) = 0.5319$, since $\beta = 0.1$.

Note an additional side benefit: before time scaling, these pot settings were a bit on the small side (the values were 0.02440 and 0.05319). Although these values are settable, they are small enough to cause some loss of resolution, because the leading digits are zero. In general, it is a good rule to avoid, wherever possible, pot settings much less than 0.1000. Pots can be set only to four digit *absolute* accuracy; the *relative* accuracy of a very small pot setting is poor. Time scaling increases these values so that both are greater than 0.1, while remaining less than unity; they can therefore be set with greater accuracy. This leads to a general principle: very small (or very large) pot settings at the inputs to integrators indicate a very slow (or very fast) system, and hence suggest the need for time scaling.

Earlier, it was stated that "experience with the present simulation indicates that a 10–1 speedup is about right." This fact is not of much use to a programmer who is preparing a *new* simulation, which is, after all, the typical case. In such a case, the best thing to do is to examine the coefficients at the integrator inputs after maximum values have been estimated and appropriate magnitude scale factors introduced. If most of them are "reasonable," that is, between 0.1 and 1.0, then the problem should probably be run in real time. If most of them are excessively small or large, then time scaling is called for. An experienced programmer could infer the need for a 10 to 1 speedup as soon as the integrator pot settings were calculated and observed to be less than 0.1.

With experience, one can gain a lot of insight into the behavior of a system merely by examining the range of gains on a properly scaled analog program. While the computer is capable of generating numbers (and solution curves) in great profusion, the insight gained from the discipline of programming the problem on the computer is often equally valuable.

Results

Figure 14.14 provides computer generated plots illustrating the effects of a single run. The tank is initially empty, and the first pump is turned on at the beginning of the run ($t = 0$). Each pump is allowed to reach steady state before the next is added. As expected, no difficulty is experienced with the first two pumps, but, as feared, adding the third causes a large transient overflow. The value of this peak indicates the additional height needed to prevent overflow.

Further options, such as increasing the cross-sectional

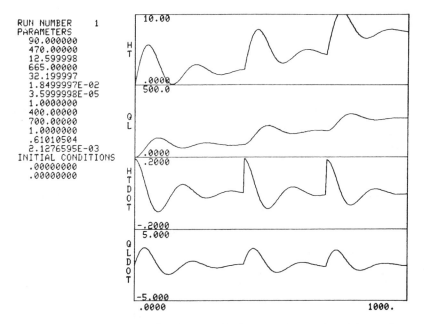

RUN NUMBER   1
PARAMETERS
  90.000000
  470.00000
  12.599998
  665.00000
  32.199997
  1.8499997E-02
  3.5999998E-05
  1.0000000
  400.00000
  700.00000
  1.0000000
  .61010504
  2.1276595E-03
INITIAL CONDITIONS
  .00000000
  .00000000

Figure 14.14. Transient response for 1000 seconds of surge tank operation, with second pump cut in after 400 seconds, and third one at 700 seconds.

area of the tank, can easily be investigated by changing pot settings and repeating the run. For example, the cross-sectional area A_T is controlled by the setting on pot 4; decreasing this pot setting is therefore equivalent to enlarging the tank. The effects of enlarging the line may be investigated by changing pots 5, 6, and 7, which are the line-dependent parameters. An additional solution, which avoids modifications to the tank entirely, is discussed in the next section.

14.6 PHASE PLANE ANALYSIS

Most commonly, analog computer output is observed or recorded in the form of *time histories* (plots of one or more variables versus time). Occasionally, however, a *crossplot* (one variable versus another) can provide a much clearer picture of system behavior. This is especially true if the system is second order, as in the case of the hydraulic transient. In this case, a plot of one state variable (integrator output) versus the other gives a complete description of the state of the system. Such a plot is called a *phase plane plot*.

Figure 14.15 shows a phase plane plot (H_T versus Q_L) for the hydraulic transient problem. A typical trajectory

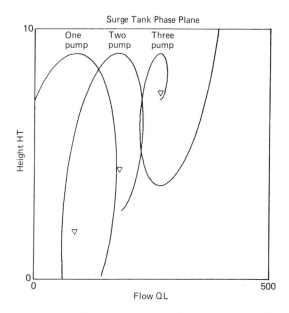

Figure 14.15. Phase plane plot for the surge tank problem, showing critical trajectories. Triangles indicate steady state points.

can be generated by setting arbitrary initial conditions on the state variables and putting the computer into "operate." All trajectories spiral clockwise, and approach one of three steady states, depending on the number of pumps.

Three trajectories of special interest are shown in Figure 14.15. These are the *critical trajectories*—those that just "graze" the top of the tank. Initial conditions for these trajectories can be easily found by trial and error. Since each run takes only a matter of seconds, determining the correct initial conditions is straightforward, and takes only a minute or two. An easier and more elegant method is to observe that each critical trajectory passes through the point ($H_T = 9$ and $\dot{H}_T = 0$). Using the condition on H_T in the original equation, we find that $Q_L = PQ_A$.

Using these values as initial conditions, the computer will generate the "right half" of the critical trajectory—the part that starts at the 9 foot peak value—and spirals in toward steady state. The left half may then be generated starting at the same initial conditions and rerunning the simulation with an additional inverter (not shown in Figure 14.13) between each integrator and the amplifier which drives it. This causes the spiral to "unwind," i.e., to spiral counterclockwise. In effect, this is equivalent to

making the time-scale factor *negative;* computer time literally "runs backwards" with respect to problem time, and the system traces (in reverse) the part of the critical trajectory prior to the peak.

However they are generated, the critical trajectories reveal a lot of information about the possibility of overshoots. This is because *no two trajectories with the same number of pumps can intersect.* (If they did, then taking the point of intersection as an initial state, we would have two different solutions to the same set of equations with the same initial conditions.) Hence, we can predict whether or not it is safe to turn on a pump by observing where the system state is relative to the appropriate critical trajectory.

For example, the one pump steady state lies inside the two pump critical trajectory. This implies that if the second pump is turned on after the first pump has reached steady state conditions, the system will follow a two-pump trajectory that lies *underneath* the critical trajectory, and the peak height will be less than the critical value. The initial part of this trajectory is shown in Figure 14.16a; as expected, the peak is below nine feet. Similar reasoning shows that it is *not* safe to turn on the third pump after the second has reached steady state. Because the two pump steady state is outside the three pump crit-

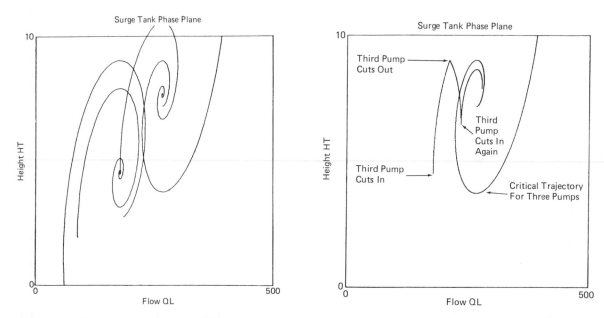

Figure 14.16. Surge tank phase plane. (a, left) Disturbing a steady state by turning on a pump. (b, right) Using the critical trajectory to cycle in the third pump.

ical trajectory, turning on the third pump will overflow the tank.

Further examination indicates that it is possible to switch the third pump in without overflow if it is turned on, then off, and then on again at the appropriate times. Starting, as before, with two pumps operating, the operator should cut in the third pump, observe the height in the tank, and cut the pump out again just before the 9 foot mark is reached. The system will then follow a two pump trajectory, as shown in Figure 14.16b. This trajectory is farther to the right than the critical two pump trajectory, and it will take the system briefly inside the safe region for the third pump. The third pump may then be cut back in. For reasons of safety, this should be done when the system has penetrated most deeply into the safe region; inspection shows that this occurs when the flow rate is at its maximum. Hence, if the operator is provided with a flow meter and positioned so that the fluid level is observed, the procedure can be reduced to a few simple rules: cut in the third pump when the second one has settled out; cut it out again when the level approaches nine feet and then cut it in again when the flow rate reaches its peak. Similar reasoning leads to the conclusion that it is always possible to move the system from any steady state to any other steady state without overflow, by appropriate cycling of the pumps.

The phase plane plots can tell us even more. Suppose the system is intended to be operated at full capacity (all three pumps on) but will be shut down at night. The problem then becomes one of startup. Instead of adding a third pump to a running system, we are faced with the problem of getting the entire system operational, starting each morning with an empty tank.

To be sure, this could be done by waiting for each pump to settle out to steady state before cutting in the next, and using the off-again on-again scenario described above for the third pump. But this would be time consuming, and it may be desirable to avoid the extra switching of the third pump, to minimize wear and tear on the equipment. Is it possible to start with an empty tank ($H_T = Q_L = 0$) and bring the system to its operating point swiftly and safely by turning on each pump *only once*?

Inspection of Figure 14.16a shows that the two pump critical trajectory intersects the three pump critical trajectory, which suggests the following approach: starting with an empty tank, turn on the first pump. Because the origin is well within the critical trajectory, the height will peak safely under the 9 foot limit. After it passes the peak, as soon as it intersects the two pump critical trajectory (which can be determined by monitoring either H_T or Q_L), cut in the second pump. The system will then fol-

low the two-pump trajectory, peaking at 9 feet. As before, the third pump should be cut in when the flow rate reaches its peak. This point will be inside the safe area, and the third pump can be cut in without overflow.

14.7 LOGIC COMPONENTS

Many physical systems contain both discrete and continuous variables. Jets turn on and off; valves open and close; mechanical parts collide and rebound; and so on. To simulate such discontinuities, modern analog computers come equipped with logic elements (gates, flipflops, etc.). The inputs and outputs of such devices are binary signals; they can take on two values. These values are conventionally referred to as 0 and 1 regardless of the actual voltage levels; such signals are called **logic levels** (see Chapter 1).

All logic devices terminate on the patch panel, and may be manually interconnected to satisfy the requirements of the problem, just like analog signals. Some systems terminate both analog signals and logic levels on the same panel; others use separate panels.

Comparators

The basic device for converting analog signals into logic levels is the **comparator.** A typical comparator (Figure 14.17) has two analog inputs and a logic output. The logic level is 1 when the first input is greater than the second and 0 otherwise; it is labeled $X > Y$. Note there is no output to indicate when $X = Y$; testing continuous signals for *exact* equality is generally pointless, because of inevitable errors and limited resolution in the computation.

The comparator, Figure 14.17, is a *differential* comparator; it determines the sign of the difference $X - Y$. Hence the $+$ sign is necessary to distinguish between the two analog inputs. Some comparators generate the sign of the *sum*, rather than the difference; for such comparators, the inputs are identical and interchangeable. To generate the logic level $X > Y$ with such a comparator, the inputs must be X and $-Y$. With either type of comparator, if only one input is shown, the other is assumed to be 0.

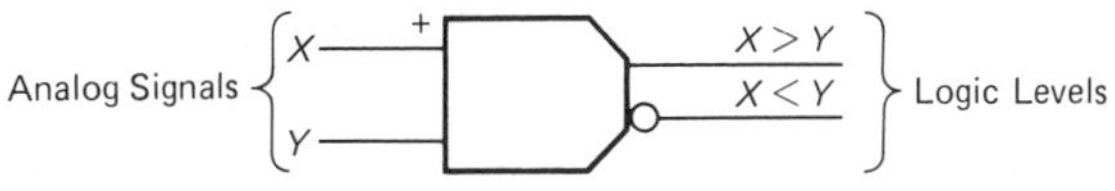

Figure 14.17. The comparator.

Switches

The device for controlling analog signals from logic levels is the **switch.** Switches come in several forms; the most flexible allows a selection between two analog signals under control of a logic level, as in Figure 14.18. The output is one of the two analog inputs; which one is determined by the logic level. If only one analog input is indicated on the diagram, the other is assumed to be 0. On some machines, relays are used for the switching function. More recent designs, however, emphasize electronic switching, because of the faster response (typical switching time is on the order of one microsecond).

Gates

AND gates and OR gates are also provided for performing the basic logical operations. The operation of these devices is covered in more detail in Chapter 1. Figure 14.19 illustrates a typical use of gates to build up a complex Boolean expression from basic logic signals.

Flipflops

The **flipflop** is a basic 1 bit memory device. The typical flipflop has two inputs: "SET" and "RESET." When

both inputs are 0, the flipflop remains in its present state. When both inputs are 1, the flipflop's behavior depends on the design details of the individual unit. On some units, this occurrence causes the flipflop to trigger (change state); on others, the output is erratic.

Counters, Timers and Registers

A variety of other logic devices (counters, timers, shift registers, etc.) are also made available on typical computers. The detailed behavior of these devices is strongly machine-dependent; for specific details, consult the manufacturer's documentation.

14.8 HYBRID COMPUTERS

A **hybrid computer** combines the speed, continuity, and flexibility of an analog computer with the accuracy and stored program capability of a digital computer. Details of the interface between these two subsystems vary widely from one system to another. This section outlines the elements generally available on most hybrid systems.

Control and Monitoring Functions

Most of the manual control functions described in Section 14.2 can also be performed under program control in a hybrid system. This includes the selection of analog modes, integrator gains, the setting of coefficients, and the readout of variables. These facilities provide two major benefits:

1. The *setup* of an analog simulation may require setting several hundred coefficients. If done manually, this is

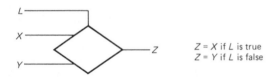

$Z = X$ if L is true
$Z = Y$ if L is false

Figure 14.18. A digital to analog switch.

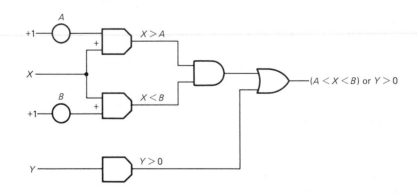

Figure 14.19. Using comparators and gates to realize a complex Boolean function.

an extremely tedious and error prone process. With a stored program, it can be done much more easily, rapidly, and accurately. This consideration also extends to the simulation checkout, which typically requires measuring the output of each component and comparing it with a precalculated value, to verify the correctness of the programming and the proper functioning of the hardware. Manual setup and checkout of a typical simulation can take from several minutes to an hour; performing the same tasks under stored program control can reduce this time to a matter of seconds.

2. The *operation* of the simulation can similarly be automated. System throughput may be greatly enhanced by preprogramming a series of runs. Each run may then be made in a matter of milliseconds, with the digital computer controlling the overall algorithm and changing parameters between runs. An example of this type of operation is given in Section 14.9.

High Speed Data Transfer

In some simulations, it is desirable to simulate part of the model on the analog computer and part on the digital. The example of a continuous plant with a digital controller was mentioned in Section 14.1. Such hybrid systems lend themselves naturally to hybrid simulation. Unlike the control and monitoring functions, mentioned above, these hybrid simulations are time critical. The digital computer must send appropriate signals to the analog and receive signals from it periodically throughout the run. For such applications, the following devices are provided:

Digital to analog converters (DACs) allow variables calculated digitally to be transmitted to the analog patch panel, where they may be patched to the inputs of the analog components as needed. In modern systems, data may be transmitted at a rate of 100,000 samples per second or faster; i.e., 10 microseconds or less per transmitted value.

Analog to digital converters (ADCs) convert signals from the analog computer into digital words, which may be stored in memory and used for digital calculations; speeds are comparable to those for digital to analog transmission. The operation details of these converters are covered in Chapter 7.

Sense lines allow logic levels generated on the analog computer to be read as logic variables to the digital computer. **Control lines** allow logical variables on the digital computer to control logic levels on the analog.

Some systems provide *interrupt lines* from the analog

to the digital. These allow a logic level on the analog to interrupt the digital program and transfer control to an interrupt servicing subroutine. Software is provided to save and restore the status of the interrupted program so that it may complete execution after the interrupt has been serviced.

Graphic Terminals

Because analog computers are generally used interactively, some form of user terminal is a requirement in any hybrid system. In a single-user system, this terminal may be the same as the console device normally used for job control. In a multiuser system, each user normally has his or her own terminal. Whether one or more users, the utility of the terminal is greatly enhanced if it is provided with a graphics capability.

Because analog variables are continuous, a graph is often the natural output medium. Terminals are available which are capable of plotting both digital and analog signals. In fact, the two types of plots may be superimposed on a single graph. In addition, the alphanumeric capability of such terminals allows automatic annotation of the graphs.

Software

The digital computer in a hybrid system is generally furnished with the usual software provided with any scientific digital computer: an operating system, a compiler, an assembler, an editor, and various libraries and utilities. In addition, special software unique to the requirements of hybrid simulation is provided. While the detailed offerings are system dependent, the following list is typical of modern hybrid systems.

The **hybrid library** is a library of FORTRAN callable subroutines which perform the tasks necessary to communicate with the analog. The control, monitoring, and high speed data interface functions are all supported. Depending on system size and sophistication, this library may contain from 60 to over 100 routines.

In view of the interactive nature of most analog and hybrid simulations, some systems provide a **control interpreter** to allow on-line operation of the simulation in response to commands entered at the terminal. Such commands may be executed as soon as they are entered or they may be entered as a stored program, allowing online development of sophisticated control algorithms.

Some systems provide an **analog compiler,** which accepts input in the form of differential equations and performs many of the tasks of component assignment and calculation of pot settings and check values.

To support the **graphics terminal,** a package of FORTRAN callable routines is provided, allowing for program control of such operations as plotting of either digital or analog data; erasing, annotating, drawing, and labeling axes.

14.9. APPLICATION EXAMPLE: LAUNCH WINDOW STUDY

In Section 14.5, it was pointed out that the solution speed of an analog computer is limited principally by the human operator. Analog computers are typically capable of generating solutions much faster than the operator can observe and respond to them. However, in some applications, it is necessary to make a large number of simulation runs (corresponding to experiments with the original system) in order to study the system's behavior for many different combinations of parameter values.

In such problems, the number of runs increases exponentially with the number of parameters, if an "exhaustive" search of the parameter space is required. Consider, for example, a system with 5 adjustable parameters, and suppose its response is to be studied for 10 possible values of each parameter. An exhaustive study of such a system would require 10^5 (100,000) simulation runs. Adding a sixth parameter with 10 possible values increases the number of runs to a million.

Clearly, such systems require careful analysis to limit the number of parameter combinations to a reasonable value. The better the user's understanding of the system, the easier it is to decide which areas of parameter space deserve investigation, and which may be safely omitted. But, even with the best of analysis, it is occasionally necessary to generate large numbers of runs in a "batch" or "production" mode. In such cases, the computer should be operated as fast as possible, for the sake of efficiency. Clearly, it is neither necessary nor desirable for the user to observe and react to each variable in every run.

For example, Stricker and Miessner describe a satellite launching study in which the goal is to determine the combination of parameters which will result in a successful launch (defined, for this study, as one for which the satellite remains in its desired orbit for at least one year). A number of parameters must be varied, such as launch angle and payload, and for each such combination, it is desired to determine the dates and times for which the launch will be successful.

The desired form of output is a graph showing date of launch on the horizontal axis and time of day on the vertical axis. For each combination, a computer run may be made, simulating one year of satellite operation, which will determine the success or failure of the launch. Areas of the plot corresponding to unsuccessful launches are to be shaded; successful areas are to be left unshaded. Such a graph is called a **launch window.**

To obtain the desired resolution, four day increments were used on the horizontal axis, so that 92 values were necessary to generate a launch window for a one year period. The vertical parameter (time of day) was incremented in six-minute steps, so that 240 values of this parameter were plotted. This means that a single launch window requires $240 \times 92 = 22{,}080$ computer runs, each representing one year of satellite operation. Furthermore, since many other parameters besides these two must be varied, an entire *family* of launch windows is called for, each window requiring more than 22,000 runs. For such a study, high speed operation is essential.

The amount of time required for a particular simulation run depends, of course, on the complexity of the problem and the speed of the computer. In the present case, it was found that a year of satellite operation could be simulated in 100 milliseconds on the analog computer. (This means, incidentally, that the computer is operating about 316 million times faster than real time.) At such speeds, manual recording or plotting of data is out of the question; some form of automatic plotting is necessary.

Stricker and Miessner solved the problem by controlling the parameters digitally. For a fixed value of the horizontal parameter, a series of 240 runs was made, with the vertical parameter incremented between runs. The parameters were used to drive the axes of a plotter. A comparator sensed success or failure at the end of each run, and controlled the plotter pen lift. Thus, after each run, the plotter stepped from one parameter value to the next, with the pen down in case of failure and up in case of success. As a result the areas of failure were shaded, while the areas of success were left blank.

The program described in this section is an adaptation of the method of Stricker and Miessner, illustrating the use of a graphics terminal, which is not only faster than a plotter, but allows the plot to be annotated automatically. It provides a good example of the power of combining the stored program capability of a digital computer with the high speed solution capability of the analog. It was run on an EAI PACER 600 Hybrid system, using a 4010 graphics terminal with a hard copy unit.

Figure 14.20 shows the listing for the main program. The program is modular; the main program controls only the parameter sweeping and the calls to the plotting routine. It knows nothing about the nature of the system

```
C   MAIN PROGRAM FOR PARAMETER CROSSPLOTTING
C   GEORGE HANNAUER, OCT. 1, 1982

        COMMON/PLOT2/HP, HPMIN, HPMAX, NH, NAMEH(10),
      $              VP, VPMIN, VPMAX, NV, NAMEV(10), JOBNAM(20)

        LOGICAL FAIL

C   INITIALIZE THE SYSTEM--BOTH THE TERMINAL AND THE ANALOG
        CALL BEGIN(9600, 1)
        CALL QSHYIN(IERROR, 681)
        IF(IERROR.NE.1) STOP

C   REPEAT FOREVER (UNTIL MANUAL TERMINATION).
1       CONTINUE

C       GET NEW PARAMETER VALUES.
        CALL PARAMS

C       LABEL THE NEW PLOT.
        CALL LABEL

C       CALCULATE HORIZONTAL AND VERTICAL PARAMETER INCREMENTS.
        DELH = (HPMAX-HPMIN)/FLOAT(NH-1)
        DELV = (VPMAX-VPMIN)/FLOAT(NV-1)

        DO 200 I = 1, NH
C           CALCULATE HORIZONTAL PARAMETER.
            HP = HPMIN + FLOAT(I-1)*DELH

C           MOVE TO BOTTOM OF PLOTTING AREA.
            CALL TPLOT(HP, VPMIN, 0, 0)

            DO 100 J = 1, NV
C               UPDATE VERTICAL PARAMETER AND MAKE A RUN.
                VP = VPMIN + FLOAT(J-1)*DELV
                CALL RUN(HP, VP, FAIL)

C               PLOT WITH PEN UP FOR SUCCESS, DOWN FOR FAILURE.
                IPEN = 0
                IF(FAIL) IPEN = 1
                CALL TPLOT(HP, VP, IPEN, 0)
100         CONTINUE
200     CONTINUE

        GO TO 1
C   END OF "REPEAT FOREVER" LOOP.

        END
```

Figure 14.20a. Parameter crossplotting: main program.

being simulated; it merely assumes the existence of a subroutine RUN, such that the statement,

CALL RUN (HP, VP, FAIL)   (14.21)

will accept as inputs a horizontal parameter HP and a vertical parameter VP, and return a logical value FAIL, which tells whether the run was a success or a failure.

Thus, it is not restricted to plotting launch windows; it is capable of making a shaded plot for *any* system with two adjustable parameters and a single logical decision as outcome. Thus, it could be used equally well to plot the areas of stability of a servomechanism or the safety areas of a system such as the hydraulic transient described in Section 14.5.

```
      SUBROUTINE RUN(P1, P2, FAIL)
C  GEORGE HANNAUER, OCT. 1, 1982

      LOGICAL DONE, FAIL

C  SELECT IC MODE AND NORMAL MILLISECONDS TIME SCALE
      CALL QSIC(IERROR)
      CALL QSMSN(IERROR)

C  READ SENSE LINES TO RESET THEM.
      CALL QRSLL(0, DONE, IERROR)
      CALL QRSLL(1, FAIL, IERROR)

C  SET ANALOG CO-EFFICIENTS AS FUNCTIONS OF PARAMETERS P1 AND P2.
      CALL QWJDAR(P1/10.0, 0, IERROR)
      CALL QWJDAR(P2/10.0, 1, IERROR)

C  START THE RUN BY PUTTING THE ANALOG INTO THE OPERATE MODE
      CALL QSOP(IERROR)

C  WAIT FOR COMPLETION OF THE RUN
10    CALL QRSLL(0, DONE, IERROR)
      IF(.NOT.DONE) GO TO 10

C  WAS THE RUN A FAILURE OR A SUCCESS?
      CALL QRSLL(1, FAIL, IERROR)
      RETURN
      END
```

Figure 14.20b. Parameter crossplotting: Subroutine.

The **COMMON** block contains essential information for parameter sweeping and plotting. The horizontal parameter HP is to be swept between a minimum value HPMIN and a maximum value HPMAX. NH is the number of values to be used in the sweep. All these parameters are determined by a call to the subroutine **PARAMS**, which allows the user to enter values for a new sweep at will. The corresponding values for the vertical parameter are VP, VPMIN, VPMAX, and NV.

To annotate the graph, a label of up to 20 characters (also input in the **PARAMS** routine) is allowed for in the **COMMON** block. In A2 format (two characters per word) this occupies an array of integers **NAMEH**. There is also a similar array **NAMEV** for annotating the vertical axis, and provision is made for a 40 character job name, which is sorted in A2 format in the array **JOBNAM**.

The first two executable statements are initialization calls to standard system routines. The call to **BEGIN** initializes the terminal to operate at 9600 baud as device number 1. The call to **QSHYIN** initializes the hybrid interface, and defines the type of analog (in this case, a 681). The routine returns an error flag, IERROR, which is 1 if no error occurs. In case the attempt to establish communication with the analog is unsuccessful (if, for ex-

ample, the analog is off-line), then the following statement will cause the program to terminate.

The next statement (**CONTINUE**) is the target for the **GO TO** statement at the end of the program. This is essentially a **REPEAT FOREVER** loop—after making one plot, it returns to the beginning, asking for more input to make another. Thus, the user may make as many plots as are wanted, with a new set of parameters for each one, and terminate the job manually when finished. Of course, a programmed **STOP** could also have been used, terminating the process after a fixed number of runs, but it is usually preferable to allow the user to make this decision at run-time. Thus, although the individual runs are under program control, the plotting remains interactive.

The program then calls **PARAMS** to read in the appropriate parameter values, and **LABEL** to draw the axes and label the graph. These routines communicate via the **COMMON** block **PLOT2**. **LABEL** uses the ranges of the parameters (HPMIN, HPMAX, etc.) and the parameter names and job name for annotation purposes. Neither of these routines needs any knowledge of the nature of the system being simulated. In fact, except for the single initialization call in the main program, no routine except subroutine **RUN** need even know that an analog computer is being used to determine success or failure. Because the subroutines **PARAMS** and **LABEL** have nothing to do with hybrid computation per se, their listings are not included.

After defining parameter values and labeling the plot, the program calculates the increments **DELH** and **DELV**—the amount to be added to the horizontal and vertical parameters between runs. The horizontal parameter is incremented in the outer loop; the vertical parameter in the inner loop. Thus, the plot is shaded by vertical lines. It is easy to verify that the formula for **HP** assigns it the value **HPMIN** on the first sweep (I = 1) and **HPMAX** on the last sweep (I = NH).

TPLOT is a standard system library routine. The first call moves the beam on the CRT to the bottom of the sweep (the horizontal parameter has its current value **HP** and the vertical parameter has the value **VPMIN**). The third argument in the call is for "pen control." A value of 0 for this argument indicates that the "pen is up" (the beam is blanked) so that no line is drawn. The fourth argument is unused in this example.

The inner loop steps the vertical parameter through a range of values. After each step, a call is made to the **RUN** routine to make one run and determine whether the result was success or failure. After the call to **RUN**, the next two statements determine the pen control integer **IPEN**, which should be nonzero to make a visible trace. This value is used in the following call to **TPLOT**. After both **DO** loops are satisfied, the plot is finished, and the system goes back to the beginning to accept another set of parameter values and make another plot.

The PACER 600 does not have enough analog equipment to solve the complete satellite equations. Hence, the analog model was replaced with a simpler one. Because the program design is modular, this is easy to do; most of the routines are "unaware" of the details of the simulation. The example selected for plotting is the Mathieu equation:

$$d^2y/dt^2 = -(A + Q \cos \omega t)y \qquad (14.22)$$

whose solution depends on three parameters—A, Q and ω. It may be thought of as describing an oscillator whose frequency is itself oscillating, with frequency ω, amplitude Q, and offset A. For some combinations of parameter values, the solution is stable; for others it is unstable. Complicated stability plots result from holding one parameter (say, the frequency ω) constant and sweeping the other two parameters.

Determination of stability requires a definition. Mathematically, stability is defined in terms of the behavior of

the solution as $t \to \infty$. Since we don't want to wait that long, we must observe the system's behavior over some finite running time. It seems reasonable to relate this to the frequency of the time-varying coefficient. If we decide to investigate the system behavior for N cycles of this coefficient, then the running time is $t = 2\pi N/\omega$.

The system is thus defined to be stable, for computational purposes, if the magnitude of the solution y remains less than an upper bound K for $0 \leq t \leq 2\pi N/\omega$. Because K and N are arbitrary, they may be taken as additional parameters so that, in addition to A and Q, the vertical and horizontal parameters, we have ω, K, and N to vary to create a family of curves.

The analog program to solve the equation is straightforward, and will not be discussed here. The logic diagram, however, is worth examining (Figure 14.21). The solution $y(t)$ drives a pair of comparators, which determine whether the solution $y(t)$ exceeds K in magnitude. Note the OR gate to detect when $y(t)$ has exceeded the bound K in either the positive or the negative directions. If this happens, the output of the gate becomes true, signaling a failure (instability) for that run. This condition sets sense line 1, which will be tested by the digital computer at the end of the run. It should be noted that the sense lines in the PACER 600 contain flipflops, so that once set, they remain set until read. This guarantees that should the **FAIL** signal become true momentarily during the run, the run will be recorded as a failure (unstable) even though the value of $y(t)$ might have moved back within bounds by the time the sense line is read.

The determination of the stopping condition is performed by an integrator that integrates the constant $\omega/2\pi N$, which drives the comparator output true after N

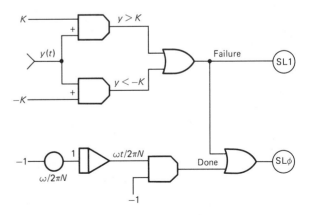

Figure 14.21. Logic program for parameter crossplot.

cycles. This signal is used to drive sense line 0, which is used by the digital computer as an end-of-run condition. Because there is no point in running for the full period of time once a failure has been detected, the **FAIL** signal is ORed with the comparator. Thus, sense line 0 becomes true after N cycle of operation *or* when a failure is detected, which ever happens first.

Subroutine **RUN**, as mentioned before is, except for initialization, the only routine that needs to communicate with the analog. The routine assumes that two logic variables, **DONE** and **FAIL**, will be generated on the analog, and transferred to the digital computer on sense lines numbered 0 and 1, respectively. The signal called **DONE** becomes true when the run is done; at that time, the signal called **FAIL** tells whether the run was a success or failure.

Note that, in line with the principle of modular design, this routine knows nothing about the details of plotting. Its task is to accept two parameters, scale them appropriately for the analog simulation, transmit them to the analog, wait for the analog to finish a run, and return one bit of information. The use to be made of this information is of no concern to the routine.

The routine is basically little more than a series of calls to standard routines in the hybrid system library to set up and control the analog. In the PACER 600 system, all such routines have names beginning with the letter **Q** so that they may be easily distinguished from the user's own routines.

The calls to **QSIC** and **QSMSN** put the computer in the initial condition mode and select the appropriate time scale for high speed operations. The following calls to **QRSLL** read sense lines 0 and 1, which determine respectively the **DONE** and **FAIL** conditions. As mentioned above, these sense lines contain flipflops; once set by an event on the analog, they remain set until they are read. Thus, reading them before the run assures that they will be reset initially.

The calls to **QWJDAR** scale the parameters appropriately and transmit them to the analog. This is the only problem dependent part of the **RUN** program; it must know which analog parameters to set and how they are related to the input parameters.

The call to **QSOP** selects the operate mode; i.e., it initiates the run. The program then goes into a waiting loop, repeatedly testing the **DONE** line until it is found to be **TRUE**, indicating the end of the run. On a multiuser system, this loop could be replaced by a call to a system routine relinquishing control of the computer; the CPU time spent waiting for the analog to complete the run could

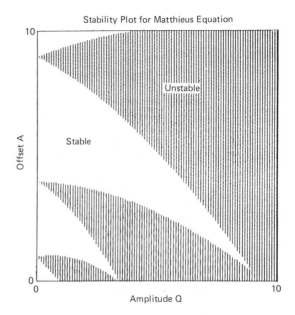

Figure 14.22. Stability plot for Matthieu's equation.

then be devoted to servicing another user. In this case, an interrupt, rather than a sense line, would be used to detect the end of the run, and return control to the program.

After the run terminates, the second sense line is read, and its value returned to the calling program as the value of the argument **FAIL**. Figure 14.22 shows a typical stability plot produced by this program. This plot was run with 100 values on the horizontal scale and 250 values on the vertical scale: a total of 25,000 runs. At 10 seconds per run, such a plot would have required about 70 hours; at 10 milliseconds per run, the entire plot was generated in less than 5 minutes.

REFERENCES

Agnew, R. P., *Differential Equations*. New York: McGraw-Hill Book Co., 1960.

Carlson, A., G. Hannauer, T. Carey and P. Holsberg, *Handbook of Analog Computation,* 2nd ed. West Long Branch, NJ: Electronic Associates, 1965.

Hannauer, G., *Basics of Parallel Hybrid Computers*. West Long Branch, NJ; Electronic Associates, Inc., 1968.

Hausner, A., *Analog and Analog-Hybrid Computer Programming*. Englewood Cliffs, NJ: Prentice-Hall, 1971.

Rogers, A. E., and T. W. Connolly, *Analog Computation in Engineering Design*. New York: McGraw-Hill Book Co., 1960.

Stricker, J., and W. Miessner, "Launch Window Program," *Simulation,* May 1965.

15
Automatic Test Equipment

Gordon C. Padwick

Teradyne, Inc.

15.1 INTRODUCTION

Automatic test equipment (ATE) includes systems that perform computer controlled sequences of tests on electronic components and assemblies. The manufacture of electronic systems begins and ends with testing. ATE is an integral part of the process of designing and manufacturing electronics components, interconnecting components on printed circuit boards and assembling boards into reliable systems. ATE is also an integral part of the process of making tomorrow's products better than today's. As one leader of the industry has said, "If you can't measure it, you can't improve it!" For electronic component and system manufactures, ATE is a matter of survival: "If you can't improve it, you won't stay in the game!"

Need

The ATE business had small beginnings in the mid 1960s. By 1982, worldwide ATE sales had grown to in excess of $1 billion.

ATE tests the following:

- Discrete components, diodes and transistors.
- Small scale integrated (SSI) circuits such as gates, flip-flops, operational amplifiers, comparators.
- Medium scale integrated (MSI) circuits—registers, counters, chroma demodulators, digital to analog converters, and analog to digital converters.
- Large scale integrated (LSI) circuits—large memory devices and microprocessors.
- Very large scale integrated (VLSI) circuits—large memory devices and microprocessors.

At the *assembly level,* ATE systems test printed circuit boards before components are loaded onto them; in-circuit testers test components loaded onto printed circuit boards; and functional testers test the performance of fully loaded printed circuit boards. Interconnection testers test backplane wiring and cables.

At the *system level,* ATE systems verify the performance of complete operational systems.

Components and assemblies are complex and many tests are necessary to verify their performance. ATE systems are automatic and computer controlled. Manual testing is too expensive and prone to error and sufficient skilled labor is not available.

Originally, every ATE system was separately controlled by its own computer and each system tested components of assemblies after a particular stage of the manufacturing process. Now ATE systems are integrated into design and manufacture. Some ATEs control specific parts of the manufacturing process; others generate data fed back to control earlier stages of manufacturing and fed forward as part of the marketing data base.

In a semiconductor manufacturing plant, ATE data modify processes to enhance the yield of prime devices. The results of printed circuit board testing are analyzed to detect faults, to modify assembly processes and to eliminate detected problems.

Whereas in the past data produced by a test system were locally printed, manually analyzed and passed on to

Figure 15.1. The memory test system shown here is typical of today's ATE systems. The system consists of a programmer and operator console (extreme right), a test station (second from the right) which interfaces to a wafer prober or automatic handler, a mainframe (center) that houses the instrumentation, and a computer (left of center). In this photograph, the video display terminal at the left displays color bit maps. (Courtesy Teradyne, Inc.)

other departments, now many systems are linked to a mainframe, part of the factory data network.

Some ATEs control the manufacturing process. In the manufacture of large RAMs that have **redundancy,** nonfunctional rows or columns of cells to be replaced by redundant rows or columns are tested at the wafer stage. If a bad row or column is detected, the test system directly controls the replacement process. In some cases this is done by applying voltage or current to device pads; in other cases, by removing a conductor with a laser beam.

Lasers under control of an ATE system also adjust values of thick and thin film resistors in precision analog circuits and replace defective cells in RAMs having redundancy.

In the manufacture of printed circuit boards, ATE systems are integrated into rework stations. The system guides a technician who replaces faulty components, finds manufacturing problems such as open circuits or short circuits, or adds components that modify a board's performance so that it meets specifications.

ATE systems are not limited to testing components or small assemblies. One example of a more recent application of ATE is in the telephone industry. ATE systems monitor the performance of telephone lines, helping service personnel to locate and correct faults before they create problems for the telephone companies' customers.

15.2 TYPICAL ATE SYSTEM

A typical ATE system (Figure 15.3) provides for

- Stimuli to the device or assembly under test.
- Output of measurements from a device or assembly or comparison of the output response with an expected response.
- Fixtures that connect to the device or assembly.

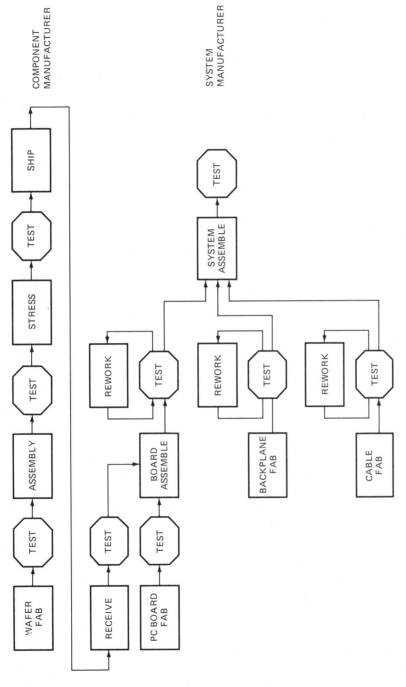

Figure 15.2. ATE systems are used at many stages of manufacture. At each stage, a component or assembly is repaired or discarded before being passed to the next manufacturing step.

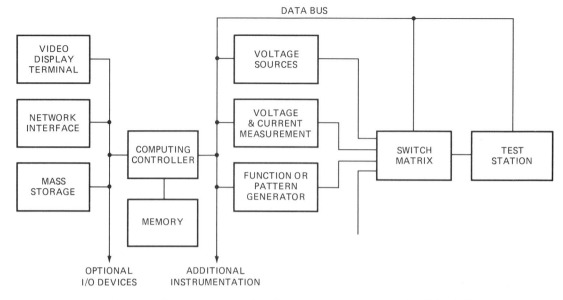

Figure 15.3. Most ATE systems consist of the functional components shown in this block diagram.

- Control of instrumentation and device connections.
- Response interpretation and direction of the sequence of tests.
- Operator interaction.
- Recording of information.
- Transmission of information to a mainframe.
- Preparation of device test programs.

The need for ATE systems arises from the batch processing methods by which devices are manufactured in quantity; each stage of the process progressively adds cost. The success of batch processing depends on eliminating or correcting at the earliest possible stage a component or assembly that does not perform satisfactorily.

An example is the manufacture of a memory board that contains 128 64K dynamic RAMs. While most of the following description can apply to the manufacture of almost any type of printed circuit board, some boards (particularly those that perform digital and analog functions) present additional problems.

Dynamic RAM Memory Board

A memory board containing dynamic RAMs is the largest volume electronic assembly to be manufactured.

In a **dynamic RAM,** data is stored as a charge on re-

verse biased PN junction capacitors. These capacitors gradually discharge. To maintain the data, every capacitor is read and recharged peridically, or **refreshed.**

Static RAMs store data in circuits that have two stable states. Once data are written into the cells of a static RAM, the data remain unchanged as long as power is applied to the device. Unlike dynamic RAMs, static RAMs do not require refresh.

Dynamic RAMs have the advantage of fewer components. They have many more cells and a lower cost per cell than static RAMs. Dynamic RAMs have become the standard for most memory applications.

15.3 THE NECESSITY FOR TESTING

At every stage in the manufacture of an electronic system, testing verifies the performance of semiconductor materials, components, assemblies and complete systems. The reason for so much testing is the complexity of manufacturing and assembly.

Consider a computer memory system consisting of many printed circuit boards. Each 64K dynamic RAM on the board contains address decoders, sense amplifiers, timing and control circuits and 65,536 memory cells. Every cell must be addressable. A 0 or a 1 stored on any cell must not be disturbed by data written into or read from other cells or by noise on the power and ground lines.

When integrated circuits and printed circuit boards were much simpler, component users accepted a 1 to 2 percent reject rate. Testing by device manufacturers was planned to achieve this level. Now purchasers of memory expect reject rates 100 times better; 0.02 percent is the industry standard. Clearly, testing extremely complex components to this level places stringent demands on test equipment and on test engineers.

The reason for such a high quality requirement for components is the densely packaged printed circuit board. If 1 percent of the components are bad on a board with 100 components, on the average 64 percent of assembled boards are rejected. Through a reduction of the component reject rate to 0.1 percent, the board reject rate becomes 10 percent. As the number of components on a board increases, the adverse effect of a few bad components on the board reject rate rapidly becomes very large. Clearly, a high level of component quality is necessary to reduce the cost of board testing and reworking to an acceptable level.

High quality can be achieved economically only by integrating testing into the manufacturing process.

Device Characterization

Characterization is the process by which device manufacturers optimize and specify their products and by which device users assess the suitability of components. In the early development stages of a semiconductor device (RAM in this example), relatively small quantities are fabricated. These are exhaustively tested under various combinations of voltage, timing and temperature to ascertain specifications required for high yield while still meeting the needs of board designers. Characterization at this stage results in modifications to the design and fabrication processes. Eventually a manufacturer has sufficient data to produce a formal device specification.

Continued characterization throughout the life of the product is the basis of performance and specification improvements and allows the manufacturer to make accurate assessments of its ability to supply the devices.

Although device manufacturers provide detailed data sheets, this is rarely sufficient. For this reason, memory board designers perform their own characterization tests on sample devices. The results enable the designer to select optimum devices and to formulate design rules that maximize the board performance. Characterization is also the process by which component engineers qualify a component for use in a project.

Wafer Probe Testing

The fabrication of semiconductor memory devices starts with wafers of silicon, typically four inches in diameter. Wafers are progressively masked, etched, and diffused to form active and passive components. After each diffusion stage, test sites are measured to verify such parameters as the resistivity and breakdown voltage of PN junctions. Only those wafers that pass these tests proceed to the next stage. (A wafer produces several hundred chips.)

Components are connected by low resistance polysilicon and evaporated aluminum to form functional devices. The same materials connect the inputs and outputs of the device to pads around the periphery of each chip. The pads make connection to the device while testing and, during subsequent assembly, to the package pins. Most dynamic RAMs have 16 pads; additional pads are used

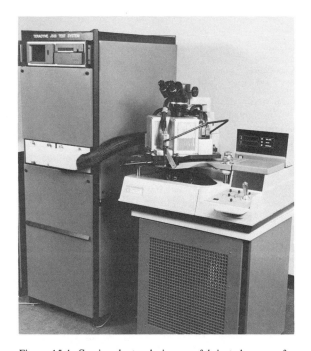

Figure 15.4. Semiconductor devices are fabricated on a wafer that contains hundreds, or even thousands, of individual components. A wafer prober, such as the one shown here, makes contact with pads around the periphery of each device so that it can be tested. (Courtesy Teradyne, Inc.)

for testing at the wafer probe and for replacing cells in devices that have redundancy. After fabrication, every chip is individually tested; only those that pass these tests are assembled into packages.

A component test system with a *wafer prober* tests each chip in a wafer. The wafer is held in the chuck of the wafer prober. Accurately aligned probes make contact with the pads around the periphery of one chip. Tests determine whether a chip is good or bad and, in some cases, sort good chips into performance categories. After the test sequence, the prober marks the surface of each chip with colored ink to indicate its performance category. The probes are then raised and the chuck indexes so that the next chip on the wafer is under the probes. The probes are lowered and that chip is tested. This continues for every chip on the wafer.

Multiplexing two probers to a test system allows testing of a chip in one prober while the second prober is indexing. At the wafer probe stage, testing occupies less than 100 milliseconds for gates and flipflops, 1 to 10 seconds for RAMs, and up to a minute for microprocessors and devices of comparable complexity.

Kinds of Tests

Continuity tests verify that there is continuity between the probe and the chip and also detect any short circuits between pads. If a continuity test fails, this may indicate a poor connection between a probe and a device pad or it may be caused by an open circuit within the chip.

Functional tests verify that every cell in the device can be accessed and that it can store a 0 and a 1. Voltage and current measurements, often referred to as *parametric tests,* check such parameters as the power supply current, input leakage current, input breakdown voltage and output voltage levels.

The data accumulated by wafer tests monitor and control the fabrication processes. If a change in device parameters occurs, the fabrication processes are modified to correct the change.

The yield of devices to each performance specification is used by the marketing staff to anticipate the quantities available for shipment after the remaining stages of manufacturing.

Package Device Testing

Processed wafers are cut into chips and good chips are assembled into packages. Packaged devices are again tested, usually much more stringently than at wafer

Figure 15.5. After being assembled, semiconductor devices are again tested, often at their maximum specified operational temperature. The automatic handler shown here heats devices and then a contactor makes contact with the device pins. Similar handlers can cool devices to allow testing at the minimum specified temperature. (Courtesy Teradyne, Inc.)

probe. Depending on device complexity, package test time may take as much as 10 times longer than wafer probe.

For dynamic RAMs, testing occurs at maximum operating temperatures to ensure that capacitor leakage is not excessive.

After assembly, devices are loaded into plastic tubes, usually known as **sticks.** The sticks are mounted on an automatic handler that feeds them into a heated chamber where they remain until they reach test temperature. The devices then move to a contactor that connects the device pins and the test system.

Basic continuity tests verify the integrity of the connections between the package pins and the pads on the chip. Functional tests sort devices into performance categories.

Performance of RAMs is largely determined by cycle and access time. Testing requires accurate placement of address, data input and clock waveform edges, and accurate timing of data output.

The greater part of the time to test packaged RAMs is required for functional testing. The cost of testing, highly dependent on test time, is minimized by reducing the average functional test time; one method is **parallel testing.**

In a parallel test system, two or four devices are handled in parallel on separate tracks or handlers. Devices are indexed into the contactor positions and continuity, voltage and current measurements are made. If a device fails any of these tests, it is immediately ejected from the contactor and replaced. The same tests are made on the new device. This continues until all contactor positions contain acceptable devices. Then functional tests are done.

When devices are functionally tested in parallel, average test time is substantially reduced. The reduction obtained depends on:

1. The yield of devices from continuity, voltage and current test stage;
2. The number of performance categories into which the devices are sorted;
3. The yield to each performance category.

Parallel testing provides the greatest benefit when device yield is high; benefits are substantially less when yields are low.

After testing, packaged devices are subjected to environmental stress and are then tested a third time prior to shipment to the customer.

Component Qualification and Incoming Inspection

Companies which purchase integrated circuits often test them before loading them onto printed circuit boards. But integrated circuit users differ widely in the extent to which they (1) evaluate vendors, (2) test components before designing their products and (3) test components before loading them onto printed boards.

Many small as well as large manufacturers buy components through distributors, do little formal component evaluation, and have no incoming inspection. They rely entirely on testing by component manufacturers and on their own testing of the end product.

Other manufacturers have extensive component and vendor qualification programs. Components are qualified before they are designed into a system. Components are

rigorously tested at incoming inspection, subjected to environmental stress and then retested before being loaded onto boards. Data are continuously monitored to detect trends in performance that may affect the end product.

Most manufacturers fall between these extremes, doing some component and vendor qualification and some incoming inspection. While some component users have their own component and test engineering departments, others use independent test laboratories.

Visual inspection, electrical tests and other tests are performed by device users and test laboratories using ATE. Visual inspection involves microscopic examination. Many tests also use burn-in equipment, X-ray radiographic systems, destructible physical analysis (DPA) equipment, particle impact noise detection (PIND) equipment, shock and vibration equipment.

Incoming inspection finds gross problems such as incorrectly marked, bad or damaged devices. These tests can be tailored toward the final device application and have a higher probability of detecting devices which would adversely affect end product performance. In some cases a device user selects devices for specific applications instead of paying a premium for selection by the component manufacturer.

Printed Circuit Board Testing

The same principles of finding and correcting problems early in the manufacturing cycle apply as much to printed circuit boards themselves as they do to integrated circuit components. Economics dictates how much testing is done and at which stages in the manufacturing process testing occurs.

There are three distinct types of printed circuit board (**PCB**) test systems (although some systems combine the separate functions):

- A *bare board* test system examines printed circuit boards before components are mounted on it.
- An *in-circuit* test system tests a board after components are loaded, verifying that components are loaded and soldered, and that interconnections exist between components.
- A *functional* test system tests performance and simulates system operating conditions.

In practice, these systems usually work in tandem as follows:

The PCB manufacturer starts with an insulating sub-

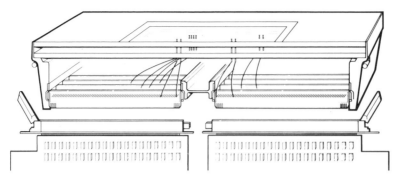

Figure 15.6. A printed circuit board test system makes contact to boards by edge connectors, by a bed of nails, or by both. The bed of nails (see Section 15.11) allows contact with individual devices and conductors on the board, a technique that simplifies identification of faults. (Courtesy Teradyne, Inc.)

strate, one or both sides of which is coated with copper. The copper is etched to leave a pattern of conductors. Holes are drilled. The insides of the holes of two sided PCBs are plated to provide a conducting path. This completes the manufacture of single layer PCBs; a bare board tester verifies continuity and insulation between points as prescribed.

Complex electronic equipment uses multilayer PCBs. These consist of several thin boards which, after etching, are bonded together under pressure. The assembly is drilled and the holes plated to interconnect the layers and a bare board tester verifies the connections.

After passing the bare board test, the board is loaded, the components are soldered into position and the assembly is ready for test. For simple boards, in-circuit testing may be omitted. In-circuit testing identifies component and interconnection problems faster, more accurately and less expensively than functional testing.

Boards are next tested by a functional tester that includes diagnostic capability to give likely reasons for detected failures. Functional testing verifies the overall performance of the board. In some cases a single tester has both in-circuit and functional testing capability.

Interconnections

A system consists of components interconnected by conducting paths on printed circuit boards, and of backpanel wiring and cables to connect PCBs. A functional interconnection test system verifies continuity and insulation. Testers can manually develop a program based on a typical system to learn the interconnections from a known good assembly, or they can use a program automatically derived from a computer aided design system.

System Testing: Special Problems

At the *component* level, test equipment is designed to process many millions of identical or very similar components. *Systems,* on the other hand, are manufactured in much smaller quantities. In general, the sophisticated systems which require specialized tests are manufactured in the smallest quantities. Also, the input stimuli and output responses of systems are more difficult to reproduce than those of components. Systems interact with other systems, including human beings, whereas the interaction of components can be specified purely in terms of voltage, current and time.

There is, however, a growing trend to supplement and replace the skill and experience of test engineers with ATE systems. A major instance of the expansion of ATE is the testing of communication networks; in this case the IEEE 488 communications interface and the ATLAS programming language make it possible to assemble widely different test systems without an inordinate investment in specialized hardware and software design.

15.4 SYSTEM ARCHITECTURE

ATE system architecture varies to some extent according to system type and manufacturer but has many consistent aspects. A typical system consists of a computer, memory, a communications bus, I/O devices, a mainframe, one or more test stations and software.

Computer

The computer may be a single unit or may consist of distributed processors. Some ATE systems are OEM minicomputers; others are controlled by computers specifically designed as test system controllers.

The computer has five principal functions, which are to

1. Generate component or assembly test programs.
2. Assist the programmer to produce and debug test programs.
3. Run calibration and diagnostic routines.
4. Control instrumentation of the component or assembly under test.
5. Analyze and accumulate data produced by the tests.

Input/Output

With few exceptions, ATE systems have a CRT display and keyboard. Software is normally supplied on magnetic tape or floppy disks.

Most systems have a printer, anything from an inexpensive unit for summary test data to a high speed line printer. ATE systems for device characterization sometimes have a graphics printer for bit maps, wafer maps, distribution plots and similar diagrams. They may also have a color CRT display to provide a third dimension for test data. One example, color bit maps for memory devices, is described later.

Most ATE systems have a communications port to connect to a mainframe. Software and test programs can be downloaded from the computer, eliminating the need for separate copies of programs at each test system and avoiding the possibility of the wrong programs being used.

Results condensed by the ATE may be transmitted to the mainframe to be analyzed and formatted. This relieves the local computer of data analysis.

Instrumentation

Test systems include a combination of instrumentation ranging from high speed digital to precision analog circuits. Instrumentation provides power and input stimuli to the unit under test and detects its output. In some systems, instrumentation is in the test station, close to the pins of the tested component or assembly.

All systems have one or more programmable voltage sources that provide power to the unit under test. Most have one or more programmable analog measurement units that can **force voltage** (keep it at one of several fixed levels) while measuring current and force current while measuring voltage and convert the measured analog value into digital form.

Other instrumentation is a function of the unit under test. A memory device test system, for example, has a pattern generator that generates sequences of addresses, input data and clock pulses to the input pins of the memory under test along with criteria to compare the output from the memory. An analog test system may contain precision low voltage sources, programmable oscillators and special purpose signal generators for testing audio, television and communications components.

The test station connects an ATE system to the device and provides convenient and reliable connections. It maintains the integrity of signals at the input pins and provides proper loading. It may be a simple socket or connector attached directly to the ATE or a highly complex electromechanical assembly containing instrumentation.

Software

Software provides an interface between people and the computer and between the computer and system instrumentation. Software provided with an ATE system typically includes

- Utility programs that assist in writing and debugging test programs.
- Operating programs that interpret test programs, control instrumentation and analyze results.
- Applications programs used in conjunction with test programs.
- Data reduction programs that provide distribution analyses and correlation plots.
- Calibration programs to adjust system parameters to specified accuracy.
- Maintenance and diagnostic programs that confirm operation of the system and isolate malfunctions.

15.5 THE EARLY DAYS OF THE ATE INDUSTRY

The ATE industry started in the 1950s, when semiconductor devices were first manufactured in significant quantities. Diodes and transistors were fabricated by alloy and grown (crystal) junction processes that were difficult to control. Parameters such as breakdown voltages, forward voltage drops, and diode leakage currents varied from device to device. Device manufacturers therefore sorted products into performance categories and asked higher prices for premium devices.

In the early days, semiconductor devices were tested by manually passing them from one custom test jig to another. This process was simplified by combining several tests in one instrument. But all testing required operators to insert devices into sockets, turn knobs and press buttons, read meters or judge waveform on oscilloscopes and then take devices out of the socket and drop them into the correct bins.

This slow and tedious work resulted in many devices being placed in the wrong bins. Device manufacturers became concerned about high labor costs and inaccurate sorting. Good devices placed in "bad" bins cost them money. Bad devices in "good" bins brought complaints from customers.

Fairchild designed one of the first ATE systems, the Model 300 transistor tester. It used instruments wired on plug-in cards selected by an automatic sequencer to run a series of tests. Fairchild was only one device manufacturer that designed its own test instrumentation. Among others were Motorola, Philco, Signetics, Sylvania, Texas Instruments and Transitron. While all semiconductor manufacturers today retain instrumentation departments that design and build special purpose test equipment, in 1982 Fairchild is the only semiconductor company that continues to build and sell ATE systems to other companies.

In the late 1950s, Nicholas DeWolf, director of test engineering for Transitron, realized the commercial potential for automatic test equipment. In 1960, DeWolf left Transitron and formed Teradyne, an event that is generally recognized as the beginning of today's ATE industry. Teradyne's first product was a diode tester designed for high reliability and throughput in a production environment.

In 1961 Teradyne, Fairchild, and Texas Instruments were offering diode and transistor testers and Texas Instruments exhibited its TACT Model 520 transistor and component tester. The same year Fairchild's Model 300 transistor tester punched the results of up to 16 tests on IBM cards with 3 digits per test at 1.5 seconds per test.

Teradyne's introduction of the J259 computer controlled integrated circuit test system in 1968 changed the nature of the ATE industry. This was the first time a computer had been used to control a commercial test system. The J259 was designed to test the integrated circuits of its time, primarily gates, half adders, flipflops—the Fairchild Micrologic and Texas Instruments Series 51 product lines; the Teradyne system could be expanded to test operational amplifiers and comparators.

As ATE developed into big business, acquisitions started. Fairchild bought Xincom; Cutler Hammer bought Macrodata and Lorlin; Eaton bought Cutler Hammer.

Fairchild expanded its coverage of the ATE market by

purchasing Testline and Faultfinders. GenRad, previously concentrating on board testers, moved into the component tester business. Teradyne, not neglecting its established position in component tests, invested heavily in board and interconnection test systems.

Following the example of their semiconductor device manufacturer customers, the leading ATE suppliers spawned offshoots. Many of today's well known ATE names are headed by people from the early industry leders. Xincom, now a division of Fairchild, was formed by Redcor and Decade Computer executives. LTX is led by ex-Teradyne people. Accutest came out of Microdyne. The present GenRad system organization sprang out of Fairchild.

The advent of the microprocessor and the explosive growth of semiconductor memory chips in 1978 provided opportunities in the ATE business. Fairchild could sell every Sentry system it could make and Megatest and Adar staked their position as low cost production tester manufacturers.

Linear integrated circuits, operational amplifiers and comparators had been served by Teradyne's J273 tester. But business was growing. In 1976 LTX was formed, just a year before the coder/decoder (codec) device hit the market. LTX focused on testing not just linear amplifiers, but the full range of devices that were not digital. Among these were the coder/decoder devices for the communications industry.

In 1979, GenRad set up its tester business. Several stalwarts from Fairchild left to form this enterprise. GenRad expanded its business from board testing into the memory and VLSI testing business.

By 1981, the ATE industry had grown from Nick DeWolf's few $5000 diode testers to a $1 billion industry. A single system, Teradyne's J941 new VLSI tester, is selling for $1 million.

15.6 COST OF TESTING

The cost of a test system includes *initial cost* and *operating cost* (programming, maintenance, and supervision). In the early days, operating costs were a small fraction of total cost; but as devices have become more complex and testing more sophisticated, operating costs, particularly programming, have become proportionally much greater.

Even ownership cost may be high; still, if a large number of devices are tested, the cost *per device* is low. Throughput, therefore, has become an important issue.

Throughput is the number of devices accurately tested in a specific period and depends on several factors: test time, indexing time, system up time and the amount of retesting that is necessary.

Reducing Average Test Time

The time taken to execute a test program consists of

- Computer time to execute instructions, transmit data to the system instrumentation, receive data from the instrumentation, the process data;
- Switching time to switch instrumentation components to and from the device under test pins;
- Measurement time to establish accurate voltage and current at device pins, to measure the resulting current and voltage and to measure propagation delay, transition time, access time, and so on;
- Functional test time.

Among the ways these times have been reduced in modern systems are the following:

Computer time is minimized with a computer optimized as an instrumentation controller, with an efficient operating system and distributed processing. In modern installations, a network connects individual test systems to a mainframe. The ATE is primarily an instrumentation controller; data processing tasks are assigned to the mainframe.

Computer decision making minimizes test time by eliminating unnecessary tests; the computer can abort tests as soon as a device is known to fall into a particular bin. Tests are aborted, for example, if any continuity test fails. Classifying tests stop as soon as a device is assigned a category.

At least one ATE manufacturer provides a program that continuously evaluates the results of testing. If a particular test passes all devices, that test is eliminated when testing subsequent devices. This reduces average test times significantly.

In older systems, reed relay switching consumed considerable time. In newer systems, solid state switches, switching in nanoseconds, have replaced reeds. Where power or leakage current requirements make solid state switching impractical, reed switches with 1 or 2 millisecond switching times are used.

For most test system applications, measurement time is a small proportion of the overall test time; it has been reduced by making measurements on two or more pins simultaneously.

Early methods of measuring time parameters used a slow sampling technique requiring up to 1,000 repetitive pulses to make one measurement. In the early 1970s, this technique was replaced by a single shot technique that makes the same measurement with only one pulse. As device complexity grows, functional tests occupy a major part of the overall test time. Functional test time depends on the cycle time, the number of cycles in each test, the time required to load patterns and the number of functional tests.

Cycle *time* is limited either by the device being tested or the test system itself. Very complex devices, large RAMs and microprocessors require long test patterns with cycle times usually longer than are available from these early test systems. High speed devices on the other hand, ECL RAMs for example, have cycle times of only a few nanoseconds and test cycle times at the lower end are also limited by the ATE. High speed pattern generators have been designed for testing short cycle devices.

The *number* of cycles in each test is a matter of testing needs and philosophy. Greater device complexity has increased the number of cycles required for thorough testing. But test engineers have also developed efficient test patterns that use fewer cycles to obtain equally reliable test results. Consequently, the number of cycles has remained steady despite device complexity.

Pattern Generation

Pattern time loading differs for algorithmic and nonalgorithmic patterns. **Algorithimic patterns** for RAM testing are generated during the test according to an algorithm. The time needed to transfer the algorithm from the computer memory to the pattern generator is usually small compared with test time.

Nonalgorithmic patterns for testing ROMs, microprocessors and other complex logic devices are part of the device test program. They are transferred from the mainframe into ATE memory before and during the test. A typical early VLSI test system had a 4K memory for every device pin. A typical test requires 100,000 to a million cycles. Pattern data were transferred to the local memory many times during a test, making test times long and adding complexity.

Newer VLSI test systems have reduced test times and simplified programming with larger local memories. One system uses interleaved high speed dynamic RAMs with 264K of pattern storage for each pin.

The number of different functional tests required can be reduced by system capabilities. Testing RAMs, for example, verifies the output data (1) at the beginning and (2) end of the data valid interval, (3) the absence of glitches during the entire interval and (4) the RAM's output after the interval. Functional test times are significantly reduced when all four conditions can be verified during one test.

The biggest fraction of test time for complex devices is taken up by functional testing. Consequently the greatest benefit derives from reducing functional test time. One way is to execute parallel functional tests on several devices. In a typical parallel testing configuration, an automatic handler indexes several devices to the contractors which test them one at a time for continuity, voltage and current. If a device fails, it is discarded into a reject bin and another device indexes to the contactor. When passed devices are in all contactors, functional tests are performed on all in parallel.

Indexing time is required for the test system to make contact with device and to place the device into a bin. *Test time* of 100 milliseconds for gates and flipflops is small compared with times of 250 to 500 milliseconds for *indexing*. Index time for high complexity devices such as large RAMs, microprocessors, and printed circuit boards, on the other hand, is small compared with test times of several seconds or even several minutes.

When indexing times are significant, **multiplexing** reduces the total test time. In a multiplexed system, the system tests devices at one test station while indexing occurs at other test stations, overlapping otherwise unproductive indexing time.

Uptime

Uptime is the proportion of time that the system is available. Time spent for calibration, preventive maintenance, fault finding and correction, programming and program debugging is **downtime** as far as testing is concerned.

Accuracy in testing voltages is stated in millivolts, currents are specified to 1 percent and times are specified to fractions of a nanosecond. But good test system design can only partly meet the requirements for test system accuracy, particularly so far as timing is concerned. Even if the test system has accurate internal timing, delays in cables that connect the system to device under test pins cause errors that must be corrected. Test systems, therefore, have provision for calibration.

Maintenance.   A maintenance technician calibrated earlier systems using external instruments and making manual adjustments. This was tedious and subject to human error. A complete calibration procedure could take several hours. Even after calibration, the possibility of human error caused doubt about the accuracy of the system.

Automatic calibration methods, such as automatic edge lock (to be described further on), replaced manual calibration in most modern systems and substantially reduced system downtime. Instead of the hours, automatic calibration typically takes a minute or two.

Despite the growing complexity of ATE, preventive maintenance has improved. Apart from mechanical components that require periodic adjustment, preventative maintenance consists of loading a program into memory, replacing the device under test with a test fixture and pressing a button. The program exercises all system components in less than one minute and tells whether they are all functioning correctly. If any are not, the maintenance technician uses diagnostic programs to trace the source of the problem.

High reliability is demanded of today's ATE. When a system does fail, users expect the fault to be corrected and the system recalibrated and back on line quickly. If a component test system that tests a device in 10 seconds is out of service for one hour, testing time for 3,600 devices is lost. At a price of $5 per test, the manufacturer looses $18,000 in revenue. It is not surprising, therefore, that system owners want failures to be rare and quickly corrected.

ATE system manufacturers meet this requirement by careful design, developing diagnostic test programs, training their customers' maintenance technicians and making spare parts kits available to their customers.

Interconnecting test systems into data networks, an increasing trend, provides additional opportunities for quickly identifying system malfunctions and correcting them. A suspect system can be connected to a diagnostic terminal at a remote location where an experienced engineer can diagnose the problem.

Programming

Programming ATEs is time consuming. With increasingly complex components and assemblies, this has become a problem. The industry has responded with better programming languages and sophisticated debugging aids. The test programmer thus needs a detailed knowledge of the device being tested and its applications, the programming language, and the test system's structure and capabilities.

Linking CAD (computer aided design) to the test system helps produce a test program automatically. Another approach is automatic learning. A ROM test system, for example can read a good ROM and subsequently test other ROMs against this data. An interconnection test system reads the wiring of a backpanel, recording every pin interconnection; the system subsequently tests other backpanels against this data.

Pascal-T allows a programmer to control system instrumentation and program flow with English-like statements. This results in fast program preparation with few errors. The program is largely **self-documenting**—it can be understood without the need for many comments, thus simplifying maintenance.

Computer programs that automatically generate test programs are becoming increasingly available. Teradyne's Lasar program, for example, requires only a description of a printed circuit board to generate a program for testing that board in a functional test system. The same program can generate programs to test a wide range of digital integrated circuits. Program writing and translation themselves take little, if any, time away from test-ing because they are usually time-shared with testing or done on an off-line computer.

But program debugging and verification require test system time. A comprehensive and effective debugging capability, however, is important. Most test systems have debugging aids, as part of the operating system or as a separate program. These allow a program to be executed one test at a time or one instruction at a time, then displaying test system conditions and results; and they allow errors to be corrected from the keyboard.

Retesting

Retesting is necessary whenever devices are suspected to have been incorrectly tested. This happens if the test system drifts out of calibration, if the wrong test program is used, or if a sorting mechanism malfunctions. Retesting, of course, reduces a test system's throughput. Since a change in system accuracy is one of the most frequent causes of retesting, a major remedy is automatic calibration which, when executed periodically, can detect such a flaw before retesting is required.

Figure 15.7. The programmer and operator terminal shown here contains an integral computer, data cartridge tape transports, a real-time clock, and an RS232 interface for connection to a data network. (Courtesy Teradyne, Inc.)

15.7 DIGITAL INTEGRATED CIRCUIT TEST SYSTEMS

The digital integrated circuit test system is a descendent of earlier systems, differing mainly in speed, accuracy and the ability to test devices having more pins. Software is also greatly improved.

The data sheet for a digital integrated circuit consists of a truth table that defines the logical operation of the device, specifications for voltage and current measurement (parametric tests), and time parameters. The truth table is verified by functional tests in which a sequence of high and low logic levels are delivered to input pins while the states of the output pins are compared with expected levels. Specified loads are applied to the output pins during functional tests.

Voltage and current tests apply power and bias levels to pins that are not being tested and force a voltage while measuring current or force a current while measuring voltage at one or more pins. This measurement is digitized and transmitted to the controller where it is compared with programmed limits.

Time measurements are made only on devices for high speed applications. Propagation delay measurements check the interval between a voltage transition at an input pin and the resulting transition at an output pin.

Tests for setup and release times of sequential devices are made similarly.

Typical System

The typical digital integrated circuit test system consists of a computing controller with memory and peripheral devices, a CPU that contains system instrumentation and one or more test stations. The system makes voltage and current measurements on device pins and performs functional test at approximately 100 kilohertz. With a dynamic test option, the system makes subnanosecond time measurements.

The typical controller is an 18 bit processor with memory expandable to 256K and a CRT terminal. System software and device test programs are on magnetic cartridges, also used to record test results. A line printer and reel to reel magnetic tape transport can also be supported.

The ATE has a programmable voltage source, an analog measurement unit and digital to analog converters that provide test and comparison voltages. Each unit of the systems instrumentation receives data from and transmits data to the controller by a data bus. Data from the controller establishes voltage and current levels, connects the instrumentation to the device pins and selects high or low logic states. Data from functional tests and values of measured voltage and current are transmitted to the controller.

During operation the controller sends data from its memory onto the bus. An address identifies the instrumentation unit for which the data are intended; it responds to its address on the bus and subsequent data are routed into its registers.

Test stations are optimized for *high level* or *low level* testing. A system can have up to four test stations of intermixed types. The high level test station tests CMOS and static MOS devices; voltage drivers provide up to 20 volts with 10 millivolt resolution. The station can rapidly measure the extremely low currents encountered when testing CMOS devices. The low level station is optimized for ECL and TTL testing; it can drive devices at up to 7.5 volts and has a one millivolt resolution range. It has solid state switching for fast testing of ECL and TTL devices.

Subnanosecond Time Measurements

The low level test station can be expanded with a subnanosecond time measurement capability using single shot instrumentation. The single shot technique makes a time measurement with just one pulse.

Time measurement instrumentation in a typical system consists of two programmable pulse generators, two level detectors, a dynamic measurement system and a high frequency switching matrix.

Sources generate pulses with programmable high and

Figure 15.8. This system tests digital integrated circuits. In addition to functional tests and voltage and current measurements, the system can make subnanosecond time measurements. (Courtesy Teradyne, Inc.)

low levels, involving transition times and widths transmitted through a switching matrix to pins of the device under test. Level detectors connected to device pins by the switching matrix detect input or output transitions. When the transition occurs, a level detector generates a voltage transition transmitted to the system which measures the time between the two pulses.

Time parameters are critical for integrated circuits because of propagation delays in the subnanosecond region. Measuring such small intervals presents significant problems. A difference of one inch in lines connecting pulse generators or level detectors to device pins causes an error of 125 picoseconds. For a device with a 1 nanosecond propagation delay, this represents 12.5 percent error.

Calibration

Manual calibration is limited by calibration equipment and the patience and tenacity of the maintenance technician. The system is accurate only at the time it is calibrated. The calibration procedure is time consuming and, with the pressing need for device throughput, can only be repeated occasionally.

Built in automatic calibration takes only a few seconds and can be repeated whenever necessary. One method uses NBS traceable delay lines to verify accuracy and computer controlled time domain reflectometry to adjust delays.

The device under test is replaced with a delay line and a pulse is applied at one end. Level detectors are connected through the switch matrix to both ends of the line. The system measures the interval between the transition and confirms or denies the accuracy of the system.

Production Testing and Device Characterization

Digital integrated circuit test systems are used for production testing at the wafer probe and packaged device stages of manufacture and for incoming inspection. They are also used for characterization.

Production testing sorts devices into performance categories and produces summarized data from large quantities of devices. Only in particular circumstances is it necessary to accumulate data on individual devices. In contrast, **characterization** accumulates a mass of data from relatively few devices.

The results of tests can be accumulated as pass/fail decisions or as numerical data. Subsequently the computer can produce a summary report that shows the number of devices tested, the number allocated to each category,

Figure 15.9. Test results can be displayed on a CRT terminal, printed, or recorded. The results shown here are propagation delays measured on an ECL device. (Courtesy Teradyne, Inc.)

and the number of times each test in the program has deleted failures.

A *summary report* produced at wafer probes provides immediate information about any shift in yield. This information can be used to control fabrication processes before the yield change causes a significant problem. A summary report at incoming inspection gives a device user an early warning of changes in devices that might

```
MX   2.07   64K 3 SORT LOT£    2  MAR  4 1982 08:06:02
UNITS    25
MX
  2.07      25     100.00  %

BIN
    3       11      44.00  %
    8       14      56.00  %


TEST
    1       13
   20       12
  151       12
  251       12
  337        1
```

Figure 15.10. A summary report shows the number of devices that have been tested, the number and percentage in each pass and fail category, and the number of times each test has failed. (Courtesy, Teradyne, Inc.)

have an effect on end product performance. A *wafer map* locates every circuit on a wafer and identifies its category.

While summary reports and maps are used primarily in production testing, more comprehensive data is required for device characterization. The system can provide numerical data with results of all tests. It also accumulates distribution data automatically while devices are tested.

15.8 TYPICAL MEMORY DEVICE TEST SYSTEM

A typical memory device test system is controlled by an 18 bit computer with a memory that can expand from 64K to 256K. The computer is built into a mobile console that has a CRT display, keyboard and two data cartridge transports. A real-time clock allows test results produced by the system to be identified by date and time. An RS232/422 interface permits communication with main-

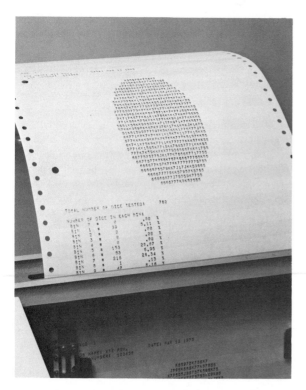

Figure 15.11. A wafer map shows the pass or fail category of every device on a wafer. Wafer maps provide information that can be used to identify and, therefore, correct process problems to enhance yield. (Courtesy Teradyne, Inc.)

frames. Additional I/O devices such as printers, reel to reel rape transports and a color CRT display may be added.

The system contains a pattern generator, an analog measurement unit, timing circuits, voltage sources and address, data input, clock drivers and data output detectors. Automatic calibration is integrated.

Voltage Levels

Programmable voltage sources provide power for the bias voltages. Current drain is often large and Kelvin feedback corrects for voltage drop in the cables and connectors. One millivolt resolution provides for testing ECL devices; 10 millivolt resolution provides for other types of devices.

Programmable waveforms have both high and low levels. Separate levels are provided for address, data input, and two groups of clock drivers. Alternative pairs of levels can replace normal levels for threshold testing at specific pins. A pair of programmable high and low levels is a reference for output levels. An alternative pair allows threshold testing.

Pattern Generator

The **pattern generator** generates address sequences, data input and expected output for the memory under test. It also controls cycle time selection, edge delay sets and waveform format sets.

Pattern generator operation is controlled by 48 bit microinstructions (see Chapter 13) stored in a 64 word pattern control RAM, one for each cycle. Every microinstruction identifies the next microinstruction. When a functional test involves scanning memory under test addresses in sequence, a single microinstruction is executed repetitively. More complex address sequences require several microinstructions.

The address generator section of the pattern generator has separate X and Y address sections, each of these sections containing a main counter and a reference counter, and incremented or decremented under microprogram control. The microinstruction defines one of these counters, or alternatively, certain registers, as the source of the memory under test address.

RAM designers often minimize chip size by using *address scrambling*: the physical location of a cell on the chip does not correspond to the cell address. While this is of little concern to the device user, it is important for the test engineer.

Figure 15.12. This memory test system is widely used to test fast, ECL RAMs as well as slower dynamic RAMs. The systems pattern generator and waveform generator can produce complex waveforms needed with subnanosecond accuracy. (Courtesy Teradyne, Inc.)

Many tests made on RAMs address cells in a specific topological relationship. A checkerboard pattern, for example, writes 0s and 1s into the memory under test so that cells containing a 0 are surrounded by cells containing 1s and vice versa. A memory test system usually contains an address descramble RAM that converts address information from the pattern generator into the equivalent memory under test addresses.

Refresh.   Refresh must be considered when testing dynamic RAMs. It is accomplished by periodically addressing every column of the device. When refresh is written into the test program, the test engineer knows precisely when refresh occurs. The disadvantage is that a change in cycle time results in a change interval between refresh and, therefore, requires a change in the program.

Some memory test systems have automatic refresh capability. Refresh occurs at specific intervals during a test. This simplifies programming but then the test engineer no longer knows when test refresh occurs. If a refresh related failure occurs during a test, the uncertainty of when refresh occurs may make it difficult, or even impossible, to duplicate the failure.

The data generator section produces input data written into the memory cells and provides data with which device output is compared. Data comes from one or more registers or from function generators that perform logical operations on address bits. The checkerboard pattern, for example, is produced by an exclusive or on the least significant X and Y address bits.

Waveform Generation

Accurate timing and versatile waveform generation are among the most important characteristics of a memory test system because RAMs are specified primarily by cycle time and access time. Manufacturers sort their product into speed categories. Users verify device speed at incoming inspection.

A glance at any dynamic RAM data sheet reveals the importance of waveform generation versatility. Every cycle requires accurately placed address, data input and clock waveforms. These are different for read cycles, write cycles and read/write cycles. Page mode and nibble mode add additional waveform requirements.

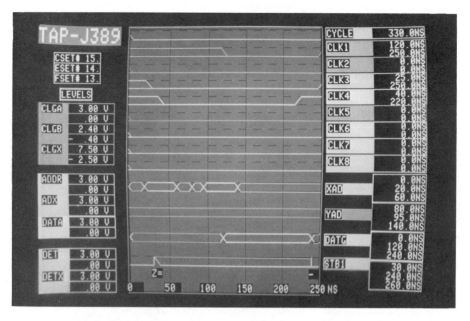

Figure 15.13. Verifying the accuracy of device test programs and debugging them is simplified by computer generated waveform displays. This display, produced by a memory test waveforms, shows waveforms and the times at which transitions are programmed to occur. (Courtesy Teradyne, Inc.)

In many RAMs, pin functions are multiplexed to reduce the number of pins on the packages. Dynamic RAMs are usually **address multiplexed:** the pins carry the X address during the early part of a cycle and the Y address later in the cycle. In other devices, input data and address information are multiplexed on the same set of pins. In yet others, input data and output data are multiplexed; a pin is used for input data while writing and for output data when reading. Whenever devices with pin multiplexing are tested, the test system has to switch pin functions at precise times.

Skew (see below) is particularly important when testing byte-wide devices—RAMs that store more than one bit at each address. A 1024×4 device, for example has 1,024 addresses, each of which stores 4 bits of data.

Input data transitions must occur at precise times within a memory cycle and they should ideally be coincident. In a practical test system, data transitions are not perfectly coincident; **skew** is the interval between the first and last transitions of a set. The skew of input data transitions and the skew of data output detection must be small if precision is to be maintained.

Device specifications define an interval within a read cycle during which valid output data may be read. Com-

prehensive testing requires that the system verify output data at the beginning and end of this data valid interval and that the data is present without glitches throughout the interval. The high impedance output state that occurs a specific time after the data valid interval in many RAMs must also be verified.

During each test cycle there may be many times at which a waveform transition can occur, pin functions can switch or output data can be compared with expected data. These actions must be precisely timed.

Any timing error must be small compared with device access time. Fast RAMs with access times of a few nanoseconds require timing accuracy of 100 picoseconds or less, because errors are cumulative within a cycle. One nanosecond error in timing can lead to several nanoseconds uncertainty toward the end of a cycle. This, in turn, leads to excessive guardbands and loss of yield in prime categories.

Functional tests consist of a sequence of memory cycles. Read cycles, write cycles, and read/write cycles are intermixed. Since each cycle has different timing requirements, the test system must produce adjacent cycles with different timing and waveform conditions; cycles must be generated without interruption. Thus the system must be able to generate one accurately timed cycle after another without delay between cycles.

Waveform Generator

The waveform generator in a typical memory test system consists of

- A timing generator.
- A format generator that controls waveform transitions, output data detection modes, and I/O and load switching.

Output of the format generator controls drivers that produce waveform transitions and have an output impedance matched to the cables.

Cycle times and delays are derived from a crystal controlled oscillator. The oscillator (in the system described) works at 125 MHz, giving a basic period of 8 nanoseconds. Dividers provide multiples of this period. Precision delay lines add 0.5 ns increments. The cycle time generator produces periods of up to 32 microseconds with 0.5 ns resolution.

Up to 16 different cycle times programmed for functional tests are stored in a 16 word RAM selected by a microinstruction.

Every timed function is controlled by a separate edge delay circuit derived from the crystal oscillator. Sixteen sets of edge delays may be programmed and stored in an edge delay RAM selected by microinstructions.

Edge delays are times in a cycle at which waveform transition, output data detection or switching may occur. The activity that occurs at each time is defined by waveform format sets.

A **format set** defines whether the driver output remains unchanged, switches to high, switches to low, or switches to the complement of its previous state for

- Each clock driver;
- The X and Y address drivers;
- The data input drivers.

For testing devices with multiplexed pin functions, a format statement allows X address, Y address, or data input information from the pattern generator. The Y address and data input drivers have similar flexibility.

A **format statement** at three different edge delays controls whether the data output detectors

- Ignore data output from the memory under test.
- Compare data outputs with expected data or the com-

plement of the expected data from the pattern generator.
- Compare data outputs with programmed high or low levels.
- Verify a high impedance data output condition.

A format statement also controls I/O and load switching at three different edge delays:

- All open, disconnecting data drivers from I/O data pins and disconnecting output loads;
- I/O switch closed, connecting data drivers to I/O data pins and load switches open, disconnecting output loads;
- I/O switch open, disconnecting data drivers from I/O pins, and second load switch closed, connecting loads on device interface board to data output pins.

Up to 16 format sets are stored in a format set RAM and selected on a cycle basis by microinstructions.

The combination of 16 cycle times, 16 edge delay sets, and 16 waveform format sets gives the flexibility necessary to test dynamic and static RAMs.

Automatic Edge Delay Calibration

It is essential that the waveform transitions at the device pads be accurately timed. In the first memory test systems, a maintenance technician made adjustments until timing was within specification. As RAMs became more complex, manual calibration techniques became impractical. Today's memory test systems incorporate automatic calibration techniques, such as **automatic edge lock (AEL)**.

Every timed function in the system has a computer controlled variable delay circuit. AEL uses time domain reflectometry to measure the instant at which waveform transitions occur as contact is made with device pins. The computer varies delays until the timing of all waveform transitions, output data detection and I/O and load switching is within specification. The entire calibration process takes less than one minute and may be repeated whenever there is doubt about the system's accuracy.

When the system is first turned on, or after any change that could affect timing, the AEL procedure calibrates the complete system. A technique such as AEL has many advantages. It is fast, taking only a few milliseconds to calibrate each waveform. It is automatic, using the system's internal crystal oscillator as a reference; as a result, it almost completely eliminates the possibility of human error. It requires no special test fixture. It provides the ability to confirm accuracy by reference to delay lines verified by the National Bureau of Standards. If any change is made that could affect the system's timing, such as changing a prober or handler configuration, the complete system can be recalibrated in only a few seconds.

Production Testing and Device Characterization

In addition to the types of data described, shmoo plots and bit maps are frequently used to characterize memory devices.

A **shmoo plot** resembles the cartoon character and shows how two or more parameters affect device performance, for example, how access time is affected by supply voltage. A shmoo plot is produced by executing functional tests with many different values both of voltage and of strobe time. The plot is displayed on the CRT screen or it can be printed.

One point on the plot corresponds to each combination of voltage and access time. If a functional test fails at a specific voltage and access time, the corresponding point on the plot is left blank; if the test passes, an asterisk appears. Individual devices are tested in this manner and the results stored in memory or on magnetic tape. After a number of devices have been tested, the computer creates a cumulative plot that shows the area of operation for all the devices.

In one version of a cumulative shmoo plot, the asterisks are replaced by digits. The digit 9 in a position indicates that between 90 and 100 percent of devices have passed the test at the corresponding voltage and time values; the digit 8 indicates that between 80 and 90 percent have passed, and so on.

Shmoo plots give a pictorial representation of the performance of an enter device. When a memory device fails, the device design engineer needs to know which cells are bad to correct the design. This is revealed by a **bit map.** The test system uses a chunk of its memory as an image of the memory under test; each bit of this memory (known as **catch RAM**) corresponds to a cell of the memory under test. At the beginning all bits of catch RAM are cleared to 0. During the functional test, catch RAM bits are accessed in parallel with memory under test cells. Whenever a memory cell fails, the corresponding catch RAM bit is set to 1.

One version of bit mapping uses a color CRT display to display failed cells. Colors show the conditions under which each cell fails.

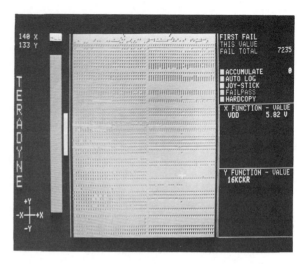

Figure 15.14. A bit map, shown on a color CRT terminal, shows each bit of a RAM that fails during functional testing. Color identifies the test conditions under which each failure has occurred. (Courtesy Teradyne, Inc.)

Interactive bit mapping allows an engineer to vary voltages and times with a joy stick; performance can be explored without changing values in the device test program.

Catch RAM has other applications for manufacturers of very large RAMs. The larger a RAM (physical size and number of cells) the more difficult it is to obtain a good yield. Two techniques increase yields: partials and redundancy.

A **partial** is a partially functional RAM. If even one cell is nonfunctional, the RAM cannot be sold. But there is no reason a 64K RAM cannot be used as a 16K or 32K device if that is physically possible. The catch RAM allows a manufacturer to identify the good parts of a RAM and package it as a smaller operational RAM.

For **redundancy,** larger RAMs are designed with spare rows or columns or individual spare cells. The device is tested at the wafer probe. If a few cells fail, the rows or columns containing these cells can be replaced. The catch RAM locates failing cells and these are replaced by removing a conducting path with a laser beam or opening a conductor with a relatively high current.

15.9 VLSI TEST SYSTEM

The 1980s have seen an explosive growth of **very large scale integrated** circuits (**VLSI**), both in terms of individual device complexity and number of devices manufactured and used. Technology for VLSI testers has developed from memory testers.

The prime requirements for a VLSI test system are timing accuracy, waveform fidelity and waveform formatting.

Whereas memory devices generally have a limited number of pins (even 64K and 256K RAMs are built with only 16 pins) VLSI devices tend to have large numbers of pins (in excess of 100). This makes VLSI testers large and expensive.

The assignment of memory device pins is well defined. In contrast, pin functions of VLSI devices vary considerably. Some devices have many inputs and few outputs and vice versa. A VLSI test has a more generalized pin structure, adding to complexity and cost.

Pattern generation for a VLSI test system is more complex. Data patterns are nonalgorithmic. The data has to be stored in the test system memory and transferred to fast, local storage to control input pin drivers and output pin detectors at the test rate.

Early VLSI test systems had limited local storage and operated at low speed. A typical system had a 4K bit storage at each pin and operated at up to 10 megahertz. Since many VLSI devices require a pattern depth extending to one million or more, the limitation of 4K bit storage made programming difficult and needed repeated reload of the local memories.

A recent VLSI test system provides local storage of 264 kilobits per pin, made economically possible by interweaving very high speed ECL RAMs with lower speed dynamic RAMs. This system tests devices with up to 96 pins at cycle rates up to 40 megahertz. Another version tests devices with over 200 pins at the same speed. Sixteen separately programmable timing edges in each cycle generate waveform edges. Local memory in the timing generator contains 256 sets of times allowing adjacent cycles to have different timing and waveform formats without interrupting a test.

15.10 ANALOG TEST SYSTEMS

Early analog test systems were digital, modified to test operational amplifiers and comparators. A modern analog test system can test a large variety of simple and complex devices such as analog to digital and digital to analog converters, codecs, and radio, hifi, television and automotive devices. Some analog test systems can also test digital devices and be interfaced to lasers cutting thin and thick film circuit components.

Some analog test systems test a specific class of de-

Figure 15.15. The A351 is one of a family of ATE systems that tests analog devices. This system is optimized for testing linear devices. (Courtesy Teradyne, Inc.)

vices; others can test many kinds of devices. A typical system may be configured to test a specific class of devices. The system may be modified to enhance its capabilities.

The basic system consists of a computing controller, programmable voltage and current sources, an analog measurement unit and a guarded Kelvin matrix that connects instrumentation to device pins. The system tests devices with custom designed test fixtures. The system manufacturer can supply test fixtures or the user can design its own.

The system can be expanded by the addition of digital modules that provide up to 84 channels of drivers and detectors, each with storage for a 4K data pattern to accommodate digital to analog and analog to digital converters, or other devices that combine both analog and digital functions, which are to be tested.

Instrumentation modules that can be added to suit specific device types include

- Digital multimeter.
- An audio source and voltmeter.
- A time measurement unit.
- A television signal module.
- A VHF synthesizer.

An IEEE488 interface allows the addition of compatible instruments from other manufacturers. Laser trim stations are also available for thick or thin film trimming.

15.11 PRINTED CIRCUIT BOARDS

Printed circuit boards are tested by three different types of systems:

- Bare board test systems, which check for continuity and the absence of short circuits,
- Circuit test systems, which verify that the correct components have been inserted and are functional,
- Functional test systems, which check the overall board function, simulating the range of operating conditions.

Not many years ago the majority of printed in circuit boards were single sided. The $\frac{1}{10}$ inch spacing between pins of the dual in line integrated circuit package (DIP) became common because conducting paths were spaced on $\frac{1}{10}$ inch centers. Boards were visually inspected for defects before components were inserted into them.

Now multilayer PCPBs are common and line width and spacing are measured in units of $\frac{1}{100}$ inch. Visual inspection can no longer be relied on to find faults. A manufacturer, though, cannot afford to assemble components on a board that is defective.

A multilayer printed circuit board starts with the fabrication of individual layers. In many cases, a bare board test system tests each layer for opens and shorts: layers with rejects are either repaired or discarded; repaired layers are retested.

Layers are bonded and drilled, the holes are plated and the assembly is again tested by a bare board tester. Bonded boards that have problems are repaired and retested if possible; if repair is impractical, the boards are discarded.

Bonded boards are assembled and tested in an in-circuit test system. This verifies that components have been inserted into correct positions, are correctly oriented, are functional and that no shorts or opens have been created during assembly and soldering. Again, boards that fail are repaired if possible and retested.

Assembled boards pass to a functional board test system where performance is verified. The test system may be integrated into a rework station where problems are corrected or where components are added or substituted to bring boards into specification.

Bare Board Test Systems

Testing for opens and shorts on any printed circuit board or layer is straightforward. The test system makes contact by a test fixture known as a **bed of nails,** an array of pins that make contact with the board.

One widely used system can apply voltages of 0 to 10 volts at up to 65,000 points on a board up to 20 by 24 inches. Continuity between one point and any others, and isolation between one point and any other, can be verified. The system measures continuity and isolation at the rate of 2,000 points per second. It can be configured with four test stations to maximize productivity by testing at one station while boards are being changed at the other three, and each station can test a different type of board.

The system can be programmed manually or it can self-program by reference to a known good board or to a computer aided design system (CAD). In the latter case, the system would "learn" the connections from a good board. For a typical 4,000 point board, learning takes about 15 seconds. A communications interface also allows the bare board being tested to be programmed directly from a CAD system.

In-Circuit Board Test System

A typical in-circuit test system is microprocessor controlled and has memory for storing board test programs. The system is programmed from a keyboard and CRT display and supplemented with self-learning. Programs are stored on data cartridges. A printer lists faults after each board is tested.

A system can test boards up to 14 × 17.5 inches and can make contact to a board with up to 700 bed of nails probes. The test fixture is normally assembled by the user with a kit supplied by the test system manufacturer and with two unloaded boards of the type to be tested to hold the probes.

A board to be tested is placed into the test fixture by an operator. When the start test button or foot switch is pressed, the system automatically moves the board into the test position and rubber tipped pressure rods force the

Figure 15.16. A typical printed circuit board test system contacts boards with edge connectors and a bed of nails (also see Figure 15.6). The operator can also use a probe to make contact with individual points on the board. (Courtesy Teradyne, Inc.)

board firmly into contact with the probes. Alternative contacting systems use a vacuum to ensure contact between the board and the probes.

The system verifies continuity between nodes by applying 0.2 volts to one node of a group that should be interconnected. This application's current is limited to 25 milliamperes to preclude damage to components and turning on active components. With voltage applied to one node of a group, the other nodes are individually grounded and, after a delay for capacitors to charge, the current is measured. Nodes with less than 15 ohms resistance between them are reported as connected; those separated by more than 15 ohms resistance are reported as open.

Resistance values are measured by a *guarded component technique*. A forcing voltage of 0.2 volts is applied to all components that are connected to the two ends of the component being measured so that no current flows internally. None of the current flowing *into* the component being measured is diverted into other components, thus allowing accurate resistance measurements.

A similar guarded measurement technique for reactive components employs a 0.2 volt rms sine wave at 1, 3, or 30 kilohertz. By measuring out of phase current, the system checks values of capacitors and inductors, even when they are in parallel with resistive components.

The correct orientation of semiconductor devices is verified by forcing +2.5 volts or −2.5 volts, limited to 25 milliamperes, into a node. This voltage is sufficient *to forward bias* three PN junctions in series; the current does not damage the devices.

Programming. The system is programmed in two stages. First the operator describes the board. Second, the system analyzes a sample of good boards to learn testing limits. The operator supplies labels for all components on the board and lists the components connected to each node. The labels correspond to designations in the documentation and classify the components as resistive, reactive, integrated circuit, transistor, diode or linear integrated circuit. Tests are automatically selected according to the class of components connected to a mode.

After initial programming, 8 to 10 good boards are sampled to determine measurement limits and tolerance. Test limits can be set manually by the operator.

A board that passes all tests lights a green light. If any test fails, the system prints out a list of failures. Each item identifies component names and node numbers for the failure to simplify repair.

15.12 FUNCTIONAL TEST SYSTEMS

Various types of functional testers are available to test:

- Specific types of boards (for example, memory boards).
- Digital boards (or analog boards).
- Both functionally and in circuit.

Functional testers make contact with a board at its connectors as when it is installed in a system. According to the test fixture used, the board may be attached to the system with plug-in connectors or with a bed of nails that contacts the board close to its connectors.

Since a functional tester reproduces the conditions under which a board operates, the requirements are stringent. The tester must reproduce voltage and timing conditions accurately. When testing digital integrated circuits, the system tests a board over the full range of operating frequencies.

Typical Combined In-Circuit and Functional Test System

A combined in-circuit and functional system containing digital and analog functions is the most complex ATE system available. A typical system consists of a supervisory processor with peripheral input/output devices, instrumentation, a test station and a fixture for making contact with the board being tested.

The supervisory processor, for example, a Digital Equipment Corporation PDP 11/44, is in control. Board test programs are stored in a 1 Mbyte main memory, with dual 10 Mbyte removable cartridge disks as primary storage.

During production testing, data is transmitted to and from the processor and instrumentation. Time sharing enables the CPU to process test data and to be used for programming while testing is in progress. The CPU can also be connected to a data network to link to a factory control and reporting system.

Many different combinations of instrumentation are possible. An analog instrumentation processor communicates with its board via an analog control bus. Instrumentation includes programmable voltage and current

supplies, a digital multimeter, a timer/counter and a function generator. An IEEE-488 bus is compatible with instruments from many sources. Instrumentation in the mainframe is connected by a Kelvin matrix. Additional analog instrumentation provides capability for passive and active devices.

The test station contains the digital processor that controls analog and digital channel cards; the digital pattern controller; the data acquisition controller and the timing controller. During digital testing, patterns are transferred from the supervisory processor to memory in the channel cards; this transfer which delivers the patterns to the board input pins and compares the board's response with an ideal response in order to make a pass or fail decision.

Patterns can be applied to board pins at speeds up to 10 MHz. The timing generator provides eight opportunities within each cycle for input voltage transitions to occur and eight windows during which output data can be detected, all programmable with no resolution. An optional algorithmic pattern generator expands the system's capabilities to test RAMs and ROMs.

When a failure is detected, software automatically pinpoints the problem nodes and directs further testing to them. If the system has a bed of nails fixture, similar additional testing is performed.

Messages guide the operator to use a hand probe to contact nodes. The system's electronic knife, comparing internal and external impedance at device pins, can isolate the fault to specific dual in-line devices.

Programming

Programming the test system is a significant part of cost. Test system manufacturers have concentrated effort in automated and semiautomated methods of program generation.

The Teradyne Lasar software package is an off-line system that has a library of digital test functions ranging from gates through microprocessors. Lasar can generate a complete functional test program from a printed circuit board description. This package can be purchased or is available on time sharing. Lasar generated programs for specific boards may be purchased as well.

The functional test system described here is supplied with general purpose program generation software including a library of test data for many common components. The user can add test data for other components. To generate a program for a particular device, the user defines a list of nodes and a list of components to be connected to each. The software produces an optimized program for testing and diagnosing a board. Subsequent editing allows the user to modify the program to suit specific requirements.

REFERENCES

Books

Electronics Test Staff, *ATE Reference Handbook*. Morgan Grampian, 1983.

Healy, J. T., *Automatic Testing and Evaluation of Digital Integrated Circuits*. Reston, VA: Reston Publishing Co., 1981.

Proceedings of International Test Conference. Long Beach, CA: IEEE Computer Society. Published yearly.

Magazines

The following is a representative list of periodicals that frequently contain ATE-related articles.

Digital Design, 1050 Commonwealth Avenue, Boston, MA 02215

Evaluation Engineering, A. Verner Nelson Associates, 1282 Old Skokie Road, Highland Park, IL 60035. See annual ATE issue for names and addresses of manufacturers of ATE and related equipment.

EDN, Cahners Publishing Company, 221 Columbus Avenue, Boston, MA 02116. See particularly Silver Anniversary Issue, October 14, 1981.

Electronic Business, Cahners Publishing Company, 221 Columbus Avenue, Boston, MA 02116

Electronic Engineering Times, CMP Publications, Inc., 333 East Shore Road, Manhasset, NY 11030

Electronics, McGraw-Hill Inc., 1221 Ave. of the Americas, New York, NY 10020. See particularly Special Commemorative Issue, April 17, 1980.

Electronics Test, 1050 Commonwealth Avenue, Boston, MA 02215

Test, Network, Printers Mews, Market Hill, Buckingham MK18.1JX, England

Test and Measurement World, 215 Brighton Avenue, Boston, MA 02134

Test Technology Newsletter, IEEE Computer Society, 10662 Los Vaqueros Circle, Los Alamitos, CA 90720

ATE Manufacturers

The following is a representative selection of ATE manufacturers from whom brochures, applications reports, and other literature are available.

Accutest Corporation, 25 Industrial Avenue, Chemlmsford, MA 01824

Adar/Scientific-Atlanta, 154 Middlesex Turnpike, Burlington, MA 01803

Computer Automation, Inc., 2181 Dupont Drive, Irvine, CA. 92713

Datatron, Inc., 2942 Cow Avenue, Tustin, CA 92680

Daymarc, 301 Second Avenue, Waltham, MA 02154

Delta Design, Inc., 5775 Kearny Villa Road, San Diego, CA 92123

DIT-MCO International, 5612 Brighton Terrace, Kansas City, MO 64130

Eaton Test Systems, 21135 Erwin Street, Woodland Hills, CA 91365

E-H International Inc., 7303 Edgewater Drive, Oakland, CA 94621

Everett/Charles Test Equipment, Inc., 2887 North Towne Avenue, Pomona, CA 91767

Fairchild Test Systems, 299 Old Hiskayuna Road, Latham, NY 12110

Fairchild Test Systems, 1400 White Drive, Titusville, FL 32780

Fairchild Test Systems, Middlesex Technology Center, 3 Suburban Park Drive, Billerica, MA 01821

Fairchild Test Systems, 1725 Technology Drive, San Jose, CA 95115

Fluke Automated Systems, 630 Clyde Avenue, Mountain View, CA 94043

GenRad, Inc., 300 Baker Avenue, Concord, MA 01742

GenRad, Inc., 510 Cottonwood Drive, Milpitas, CA 95035

Hewlett-Packard Company, 1820 Embarcadero Road, Palo Alto, CA 94303

LTX Corporation, 145 University Avenue, Westwood, MA 02090

Megatest Corporation, 3940 Freedom Circle, Santa Clara, CA 95050

Takeda Riken Company Limited, 1-32-1 Asai-Cho Nerima-Ku, Tokyo, Japan

Tektronix, Inc., Beaverton, OR 97077

Teradyne, Inc., 183 Essex Street, Boston, Massachusetts 02111

Teradyne, Inc., 21255 Califa Street, Woodland Hills, CA 91367

Zehntel, 2625 Shadelands Drive, Walnut Creek, CA 94598

16
Small Business Systems

Donald R. Shaw

Business Counselors, Inc.

16.1 INTRODUCTION

Even a cursory glance at Figure 16.1 depicts the explosive growth in small business systems. This deluge of small business microcomputer systems started from virtually nowhere in the late 1970s. However, the automation of small business systems goes back as far as, or beyond, the automation of similar functions in larger businesses. In the early days of electric accounting machines, or tabulators as they were often called, in the 1940s and 1950s, a growing number of small businesses were braving the high cost, extremely limited capacity and flexibility, low speeds, and the necessity for skillful wiring of control program plug boards to mechanize certain routine calculations, storage, and printing functions such as customer billing, inventory reporting, accounts receivable, and sales analysis.

It is probably a fair statement to say that the electric accounting machine in those days was competitive in cost with manual and bookkeeping machine alternatives; it also provided a higher degree of calculation and transcription accuracy, and a much neater and more business-like end product in the form of invoices, documents, and reports. The electric accounting machine probably would have prevailed totally over other means of handling data were it not for the fact that this system required the small businessman to give up the ever precious, much desired, and indispensible ledger card. It was then, and still is, extremely difficult to re-enter a printed document into an automated system, post a line representing current activity, bring the balances up to date, and reinsert the document in a readily accessible file for immediate visual reference.

Nevertheless, by the dawn of the small business computer, in the late 1960s, there were thousands of small companies using tabulating equipment and compact scientific computers for the purpose of performing, in most cases, routine clerical posting and accounting functions. IBM made a strong effort to encourage this trend in the mid-1960s by offering repossessed tabulating equipment to small businesses at greatly reduced prices. This equipment was refurbished, and modified to *reduce* its basic cycle speeds from the usual 100–150 items per minute down to 50, yielding the designation "Series 50." Users and competitors alike dubbed the product line the "Nifty 50." The Nifty 50 and comparable equipment of its time brought the cost of automation down to $1,000–$2,000 per month for a typical small business. But it still lacked the capacity to store business information internally for immediate retrieval as a substitute for the ledger card, thus forcing the business person to rely on printed reports, reference documents and the like to answer inquiries, analyze information and trace and track activities.

The real explosion in small business data processing awaited the introduction of small computers with sufficient randomly accessible on-line storage capacity to effectively substitute for the convenience and visibility of ledger card information at a price the small business could reasonably afford. The boom began when minicomputers appeared with several megabytes of on-line storage at a price of $30,000 to $50,000, yielding a monthly ownership cost of around $1,500 or less. It began with the

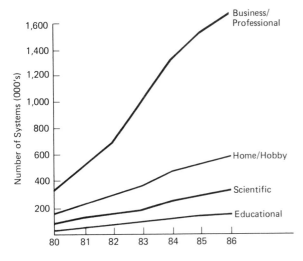

Figure 16.1. Growth of small business systems. (Courtesy International Data Corp.)

At the very same time, the micro revolution was brewing. Hobby computers, beginning with the MITS Altair, the IMSAI, and similar machines, using at first Intel 4 bit microprocessor and later the Intel 8080 8 bit chip, spawned a whole new generation of hobbyists and experimenters. With BASIC borrowed as a programming language from the time sharing world, they began performing exciting and useful work on tiny machines the size of a suitcase, costing a few hundred dollars. In 1977 the famous Apple computer made its appearance, accelerating the process and spawning a rapid proliferation of corner computer stores offering a widening range of small microprocessor-based hobbyist machines, together with a growing array of peripheral devices.

The entry of Tandy Corporation with the TRS-80 line in 1978, offered through a growing number of its owned and franchised Radio Shack outlets, greatly accelerated the process. As can be seen from Figure 16.2, these two early entrants now—Apple and Radio Shack—dominate the field. Having soon run out of hobbyists and educators interested in tinkering with computers, microprocessor and peripheral manufacturers turned their attention rapidly to the business and professional realm with more powerful machines, faster printers, larger disks and, most important, credible although not always competently crafted and fully supported, business software. As Figure 16.1 suggests, the vast majority of microcomputers are now, and will continue to be, sold for business purposes. The exact number of these small machines that are employed for legitimate business purposes will probably

Digital Equipment Corporation PDP-8 and the early PDP-11 models, the Data General Nova line, and was followed in the mid-1970s by a number of high performance, low cost minicomputers, which were sold to the end user primarily by third parties rather than the manufacturers themselves. IBM stayed primarily on the sidelines during this era, preferring to concentrate on selling larger equipment to *Fortune* 1000-type accounts. Companies, such as Burroughs and NCR, which were small-business oriented, continued to develop and market increasingly sophisticated electronic bookkeeping machines. Because they were designed around the ledger card, these machines continued in much favor although they were much less flexible and cost-effective than the blossoming minicomputer.

By 1977, a business doing perhaps $1–$15 million in sales in the wholesaling trades could purchase a "turnkey" computer system. Typically such a system would consist of a PDP11-34 or a Data General Nova IV with 64,000 positions of main memory, 5 or 10 megabytes of disk storage—part removable—and a dot matrix character printer capable of printing the equivalent of 60 lines per minute. In addition, custom tailored software packages to perform functions like order entry, billing, inventory control, accounts receivable, commission accounting, sales analysis, accounts payable, payroll, general ledger accounting and financial statement preparation, all reasonably well integrated, brought the total price to around $30,000–$60,000.

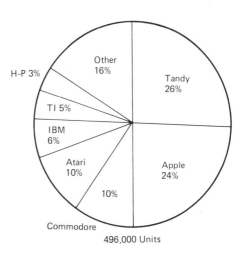

Figure 16.2. Share (1982) of desktop computer market. (Courtesy International Data Corp.)

never be precisely known because so many of them were bought at retail with the hope of successfully employing the little machines in the business or professional office sooner or later. In many cases "sooner or later" became "never," and these machines are still at home either playing video games or gathering dust.

However, in tens of thousands of cases, the microcomputers have been productive to an extent undreamed of a few years ago and at a cost so astoundingly low, when compared to past standards, as to boggle the imagination. For example, many desktop computers today contain as much internal memory, have the same or better internal processing speed, and can support as much (and much faster) random access disk storage as the mainstay of major corporate computing of 15 years ago, the IBM System 360 Model 40. The Model 40 in those days cost its *Fortune* 1000 users $8,000–$12,000 per month, yet today's little machines cost $6,000 outright! They are hardly larger than an office typewriter, sit on the user's desk, and respond to their masters instantaneously.

16.2 CURRENT STATUS

There were perhaps 400,000 small business computers, including micros, installed in 1982 in the United States[1] performing legitimate business functions in support of small companies and professional offices. There are about 600,000–700,000 other small businesses which employ outside computing services* to perform all or some of the same functions. The archetypical small business computer is a 48K or 64K microprocessor-based system with, perhaps, two 600KB disk drives and a 120 cps matrix printer, all costing about $6,000 at a retail store. To this, perhaps five or six prepackaged software application systems costing $400 to $600 each have been added. Our archetypical small business user has spent something in the vicinity of $200–$300 for an annual extended warranty contract, giving the user the right to return the computer to the computer store for remedial maintenance if a problem should arise, at no cost or a reduced cost.

If a clearly ascertainable and documented "bug" appears in the software, the user-purchaser may be able to get the author (original vendor, customizer, or in some cases, the retail point of purchase) to fix it through mail and telephone entreaties. In many cases, the purchaser

*From various sources including Creative Strategies International: *Microcomputer Software Strategies,* 1981, and Focus Research Systems: *Small Business Computing and Data Processing,* 1980.

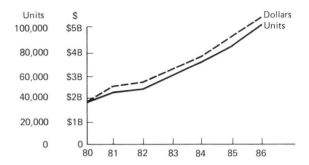

Figure 16.3. Shipment of small business computers. (Courtesy International Data Corp.)

has already modified the software packages, conveniently written in BASIC to begin with, to facilitate modification, in order to fit these programs to a particular business or profession. Having done so, any software warranty service which might have otherwise been available, has probably been voided. This hypothetical but typical user is confined to a single workstation with a 12 inch CRT and a typewriter keyboard possibly supplemented with a 10-key adding machine-like numeric pad, and does some judicious scheduling in order to give the machine over to one application at a time as needed. If, as business and professional activities always do, changes occur, then the user must likely go back to the original authors of the programs for modification.

The typical small company that has not yet taken the plunge into computer ownership in all probability has a manual or semimechanized posting or bookkeeping ma-

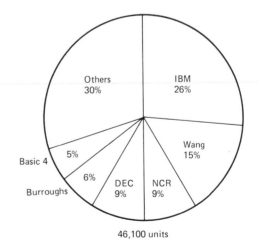

Figure 16.4. Market share (1982) of small business computers. (Courtesy International Data Corp.)

chine system, supplemented by outside services from such companies as Automatic Data Processing or the Service Bureau Corporation. Specific applications in "batch" mode are performed wherein the source information is picked up, keyed into the service bureau's computer system along with similar work from other customers, and processed. Reports and documents are returned in typically a 1–4 day interval. The most popular application for the service is payroll.

This user is likely to be spending, perhaps, $40–$50 per week for payroll services, $300 per month additional for accounts receivable processing, perhaps $200 or $300 per month for general accounting, and $200 or $300 per month for accounts payable or some other miscellaneous function. The advantage of freedom from worry and concern about the process is enjoyed, but is also accompanied by the inconvenience of several-day turnaround of results. These reports reflect status as of the date on which the information was originally prepared for pickup by the service bureau but omit all of the ensuing activities up to the moment. Today, the elements of cost, convenience, and utility clearly favor the microcomputer.

But the microcomputer is not without problems. First and foremost is software, followed by service and on-going support, and the problems of expansibility. One has only to visit the nearest computer store to be astounded and confused by the dizzying array of diskette based application software packages hanging in heat-shrink packs in supermarket-type racks. Which ones do what? Which authors will be in business six months from now? Which ones employ sound technical and accounting principles? Which ones are easy to modify? If a particular procedure, or if the system as a whole, fails, what can one do about it? Will someone come to the office and quickly diagnose and remedy the problem? If not, what other recourse is there?

What happens if the number of new accounts grows beyond the capacity of hardware and software? Can more components be added as the business grows in size and complexity? What about the potential bottleneck of a single operator work station? Can processing two or more functions simultaneously be arranged? What hardware, system software, and application software complications lie ahead if capacity must be doubled, or simultaneous multiple access to important processes and data files allowed?

In short, how do we fill in the technical "pot holes" that we are likely to encounter, and how do we ensure an orderly path of growth in volume and complexity? These are questions that have been adequately addressed for the larger accounts, where the price tags involved provide at-

tractive inducement and sufficient margins to encourage and permit the vendors' provision of extensive training, consultation, and "hand holding."* At today's microcomputer price levels, neither the incentive nor the profit margin exist to provide such services.

16.3 APPLICATIONS

A well established pattern for applying small computers to business operations is clearly evident in the numerous studies and surveys that have been conducted among users. First and foremost are accounting applications, substituting for the use of manual, one-write ledger cards, posting machines, and batch service bureaus. Among the small business computers already installed, accounts receivable leads the pack by a wide margin in frequent— almost universal—application. Following accounts receivable in popularity are accounts payable, payroll, general ledger and financial statement preparation, inventory, billing, purchasing, order entry and, finally, cost accounting, in that order. Accounts receivable at the top of the list is found typically in 70–80 percent of the installations, whereas the last three or four applications, billing through costing, are encountered in the 10–15 percent range.

On the other hand, user groups surveyed with respect to *intentions* indicate that inventory, purchasing, order entry, accounts payable, general ledger, payroll, accounts receivable and billing, in that order of frequency of mention, are the applications which will be installed on small business computers either already in place or intended for purchase in the near future.† In the author's recent experience as a consultant to small businesses, the main interests in applications for automation appeared to be order processing, inventory control and, in the case of small manufacturers, materials requirements planning and production scheduling and control. These applications were, and continue to be, the real "payoff" for automation in many small businesses. On the other hand, they are the most difficult to implement, and the ones for which fewer well accepted packaged programs exist. As a result, many businesses whose long range intentions and priorities are focused on operational applications will gravitate in the short run to the more mundane and eas-

*Figure 16.3 depicts shipments of genuine "small business computers" as distinct from personal, tabletop micros. Although numerically about one-tenth as numerous as their microcomputer counterparts, they average approximately $50,000 apiece in cost. Figure 16.4 shows that a different set of vendors dominate this end of the market.

†Main source: Focus Research Systems (see previous footnote).

ier-to-install functions, such as accounts receivable, accounts payable, and general accounting.

There appears to be little question that the properly employed small business computer can substitute for a good deal of manual labor and expense in accounting functions, materially improve the timeliness of month-end closings, statements, checks and bills, and, in many cases, improve the appearance and accuracy of such outputs. It is also generally accepted that very little in the way of net cost will be saved. Because most small businesses do not have departments with large groups of clerks dedicated to various accounting functions, people are very seldom displaced when these functions are automated. The typical employee in a small business is a jack-of-all-trades, performing many varied and useful jobs in addition to merely posting or processing business transactions. The real payoff for computerization in most small businesses is *the optimum deployment of assets and resources as exemplified by better inventory management, improved production scheduling, faster customer service, and the like.* It is in these applications that the small computer can materially impact on the success of a business, its revenue growth, and its profitability.

By long tradition in the computer industry, one can expect that a properly designed inventory control application on a computer will, by keeping constant surveillance over inventory balances and employing various reorder formulas, consistently reduce inventories on the order of 20–25 percent without a reduction in customer service. In fact, inventory reduction is frequently accompanied by an *increase* in service levels through the retention of high demand items in sufficient amounts, and reduction of balances for those items in little demand—the converse of what happens when inventory is controlled manually or by rule of thumb.

In the same vein, the improved availability of management and decision making information can have a startling impact on the success of a business or institutional organization. By and large, the posting of information into an automated accounting system is as costly and time consuming using a computer as it was using a manual, mechanical, or semiautomated procedure. The reasons are obvious: information must be keyed into the computer in much the same way it was keyed into a posting machine or recorded in pen and ink in a ledger. It is still a wholly manual process. However, once the data is recorded in the computer's database, the opportunity for extracting important information from that data and displaying it for management purposes is virtually infinite and represents a very small incremental cost, far less than the cost of original capture.

The classic example of this phenomenon can be found in managing a sales force. By capturing unit and dollar sales by salesperson, customer, product, and other categories, management is able to keep track of what particular activities are fruitful or nonproductive, with respect to profitable sales. Looking at such reports may tell management that in a particular territory, or set of territories, a certain product or product line is selling very well to a specific class of customers, say, plumbers, dairies, apartment owners, and so forth. Then, in looking at the results from other, less successful territories, management may discover that a similar pattern is absent. The conclusion is to direct the selling effort in the nonproductive territories toward the particular class of clientele, stressing the particular product lines that have been successful elsewhere. The payoff for doing this is obvious. Through such methods, one will likely find many opportunities for obtaining "leverage" through the use of more comprehensive and readily digestible information about what is happening and not happening within an enterprise.

A very important, fast moving new frontier for the small computer realm, having received a tremendous impetus from the introduction of VisiCalc in the late 1970s, is *modeling*. Although mathematical and financial modeling has been a fixture in the large computer scene for two generations, it made its real impact in small computers only when systems designers and programmers were able to facilitate the construction of simple "spreadsheet" calculation models with packaged programs such as VisiCalc and its successors. Simply stated, the user interacts, or carries on a dialog, with the program package expressing the arithmetical relationships among the various determinants and factors measurable in a business.

For example, when expressing sales dollars as a function of the number of experienced salesmen on board in a given month, one might also express the relationship of revenue to an inexperienced salesman as a series of percentages of full productivity based on months of service, for example, 0% effectivity in month 1, 20% in month 2, 50% in month 3, 80% in month 4, and 100% thereafter. Likewise, expenses in maintaining such a sales force—salaries, sales commissions as a percent of projected revenues, travel and entertainment, and so on—can easily be related to the headcount. Having once expressed these arithmetical relationships based on past experience, one has then "built a model" of revenue production versus sales expense based on the number of people in the sales force and their job longevity.

The user could then use the model as a method of projecting future results based on some anticipated manpower levels, including new-hire additions to the sales force, spread over, say, the next twelve months. One specifies the parameters for the model, runs the program, and then looks at the result. If the results are not satisfactory, it is a simple matter to go back and alter any, or all, of the original inputs, or even the formulas which make up the model, and rerun it in a matter of a few minutes. In this way, one may play "what if" games of a business forecasting nature using even the smallest microcomputer to forecast and adjust physical, economic, and manpower parameters which will have an enormous impact, measured perhaps in millions of dollars, on the effectiveness of an enterprise.

Another of the techniques that formerly was the province of large computers and their *Fortune* 1000 owners is computer graphics. As prices have come down, the power of small computers has risen, and the resourcefulness of systems designers and programmers multiplied, it has become possible to reduce volumes of numerical information to simple graphic presentations in the form of line charts, bar graphs, pie charts and other pictorial presentations, which, unlike long columns of figures in dry reports, convey important trends and patterns to the viewer immediately (Figure 16.5). Not only are the smallest

computers able to transform data automatically into monochrome or polychrome graphs, but they also require no special knowledge or programming effort with today's well human-engineered graphics program packages.

Far beyond merely charting financial and statistical data, even complex and three dimensional graphic presentations are now easy to develop and store on small computers using today's **computer aided design (CAD)** programs. Once stored, these complex drawings with related descriptions and specifications can be recalled to the screen of a CRT and instantly modified by the designer, with the changes automatically integrated into the original for instant or future "replay." In effect, the designer is creating an electronic blueprint which can be retrieved and modified instantaneously on call. As specifications are altered, all of the related positional, dimensional, and performance characteristics can be updated automatically with the change so that the entire design and its documentation constantly reflects the latest revision. It is not uncommon to find the productivity of designers, architects, and engineers multiplied by several hundred percent through the use of such systems, and even more startling is their affordability as compared to even a handful

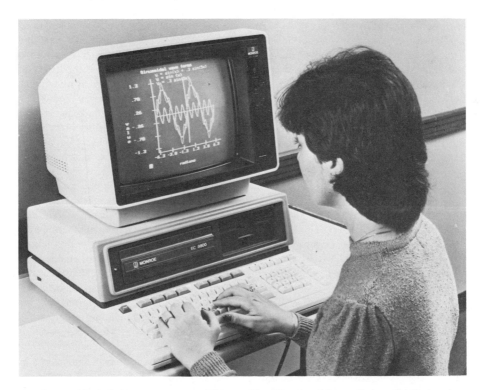

Figure 16.5. A desktop computer providing graphics. (Courtesy Monroe Systems For Business)

of years ago. Such systems, costing $50,000 and up, often pay back acquisition costs in their first few months of effective employment.

In education—primary, secondary, and postsecondary—and in the training departments of corporate and government organizations, one finds small computers tutoring students with interactive computer aided instruction packages. These programs facilitate the development of tutorial routines which not only complement normal classroom training, but often replace it in certain disciplines. For example, it is possible to teach sentence diagramming, or algebraic or geometric concepts, through a tutorial program that not only depicts the material on a computer screen, but tests the student's progressive understanding of the material. Such programming provides a totally self-paced and tailored progression through the course based on the student's own individual learning process.

Small computers in the several hundred to several thousand dollar class are being employed by the tens of thousands in such applications. In many cases, they are directly connected to other audio-visual devices such as video tape players, slide projectors and the like, so that the course materials can be vividly supplemented by animated presentations integrated with the programmed instruction material. At the same time, the teacher is often able to communicate with each student workstation via a direct wire communication link between the "master" computer and the student "slave" units. Many who went through school with the suspicion that "slave" applied to students was not wholly inappropriate will readily identify with this methodology. The effect of it, however, is that the teacher can keep informed of each student's progress and directly initiate remedial coursework for those not making adequate headway.

16.4 DATA COMMUNICATIONS IN SMALL BUSINESS SYSTEMS

A common method of applying the larger microcomputers and their elder and larger brethren, the mini's, to small business, because of the multiple functions required of a small business, has been to host multiple CRT and printer terminals on a common system, using what is often referred to as the "shared logic" technique. With a large enough computer, sufficient memory and an operating system capable of multiprogramming or time sharing, it is not unusual to see several operators transacting business into the same computer system, updating appropriate segments of the computer database simultaneously.

In a wholesale establishment one sees several operators sitting at CRT terminals wearing telephone headsets, receiving orders over the telephone from customers or salespeople, typing the requested items into the computer workstation, receiving instantaneous response regarding stock availability, prices, warehouse locations, and what not. At the same time, in another part of the office, another clerk is inputting accounts payable transactions, journal entries, or the like, while the printer attached to the computer is steadily outputting a large stack of invoices, customer statements, or an accounts receivable aged trial balance. Hardware systems capable of performing in this mode are available for well under $50,000.

In most cases it is possible to locate some of these workstations several hundred or a thousand feet away from the central processing unit; but, there is a limit in every case beyond which it is necessary to employ the public telephone network. With the use of modems to translate computer language into analog signals for interconnection to dedicated or dial-up telephone lines, the activities just depicted can be extended to virtually anywhere on the globe. However, if the interaction required of the computer demands very high speed transfer of information to and from the workstation and/or if the distances are very great, the expense of operating in a data communications mode mounts precipitously. To exactly duplicate the speed with which the screen fills when directly connected to the computer, when the computer itself is hooked up across the telephone system at a long distance, it might easily cost hundreds or even thousands of dollars per month. Nevertheless, one finds numerous businesses and institutions of all sizes using either dedicated or occasional dial-up data communications among terminals and computers at long distance as a matter of course.

To reduce the cost of communications, provide relatively instantaneous response at remote locations, and give the responsible managers at remote sites a greater degree of latitude and control over the processes performed, users in increasing numbers are resorting to what has become known as **DDP**, or **distributed data processing.** In this mode, very small computers, including "intelligent" terminals, are employed in each locality to carry on quick response local dialogue with the operator to capture, edit and store information.

An example is the microcomputer based loan transaction system offered by Monroe Systems For Business for use by loan officers and managers in branch banks, savings and loans, insurance companies, and automobile dealerships. The parameters of a consumer loan, including payment schedules, creditor insurance provisions, and other details are set up locally in a three way interaction between the customer, the loaning authority, and the computer. Then after the details are settled upon, the deal struck, and the forms produced and signed, the computer is able to pass along a record of the finalized loan and all its financial and statistical detail to the parent company's central computer for billing, accounting, and management information purposes (Figure 16.6). This represents distributed data processing in a clear-cut division of labor between the point of activity and the home office.

An optional feature of this system is the ability to dial automatically a credit rating service at the appropriate stage of a transaction to exchange an authorizing message between the loan transaction system and the computer at the credit rating service as to whether the applicant is creditworthy. Negative results from that brief exchange could very well truncate the entire process near its inception.

Such an automated query is a specialized, though very clear, example of access to a public database: namely, the consumer credit rating files at the retail credit bureau. Access to such specialized services is usually limited to subscribers only, and carries relatively high initiation fees plus a per transaction charge to the authorized user. On the other hand, time sharing services companies offer virtually unlimited computer access to all manner of data, programs, and information services for business and consumer alike, accessible from desktop microcomputers up through larger systems. They frequently employ slow, but simple, teletype asynchronous communications protocols, characteristic of commonly used "dumb" terminals, to access such services.

In this mode, a microcomputer user may access, for ex-

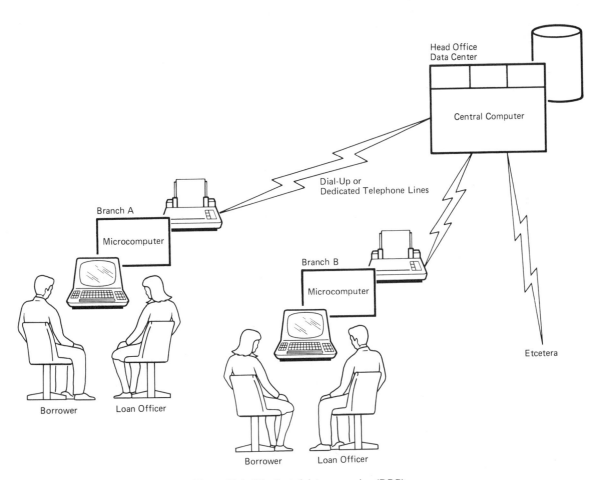

Figure 16.6. Distributed data processing (DDP).

ample, an information service which will provide a display or printed listing of weather forecasts, crop prices, movie reviews, theater schedules and prices, physical and chemical properties of materials, potential adverse drug interactions, stock and bond prices, and so on. It is completely safe to forecast that businesses, institutions, and even individuals will increasingly depend upon such public database services for their daily ration of vital information, and be willing to pay for such information on a subscription or "as used" basis. The "electronic library" is already a permanent fixture in the medical and legal fraternities, for example.

The interconnectivity among terminals and computers through a public access mechanism facilitates the advent of what could be termed the "electronic marketplace." Not only can users of small computers access information through time sharing networks, but they can *act* on it by making reservations, bids, commitments, and the like. Thus, we see the phenomenon of institutional investors trading stocks computer to computer, real estate brokers accessing lists of available homes in local or distant areas meeting buyers' specific desires and circumstances, speculators bidding and trading agricultural commodities over the wires via computer, agents committing airline reservations, hotel accommodations, and theater seats directly to consumers or to other agents employing intelligent terminals or small computers. To repeat, one can safely extrapolate current technical and economic trends to forecast more and more such activities in which small computers, in even modest sized businesses and professional practices, will conduct business with each other over dial-up or dedicated networks.

Marketing departments will be selling by means of electronic bidding among a number of similar buyers interconnected via a common network; at the same time, purchasing departments will be replenishing stock using similar interconnections with wholesalers or manufacturers. Planners and managers will, still at the same time, be interacting with vast libraries of statistical, demographic, and performance data to forecast economic trends, consumer tastes, commodity prices, and other important factors upon which to base major business decisions. Physicians, clinics, and hospitals will be transmitting treatment data for reimbursement to insurance companies and other third party intermediaries through *their* small business computers. Payroll data will be transmitted directly to local, state, and federal agencies for periodic reporting. In all probability, the total energy use of enterprises and institutions, including air conditioners, heating systems, production machinery, and all other energy consuming and dissipating appurtenances, will be monitored and controlled by a small computer, perhaps the same one employed for routine bookkeeping and other such tasks.

One can certainly expect to see in a small retail establishment, for example, a cash register which not only checks consumer credit automatically through public database access, but which also registers the sale, posts it automatically to the customer's credit card account or debits his or her bank account. Through scanning merchandise labels optically, or the use of a handheld optical "wand," the system will relieve inventory of the items purchased, record costs of sale, and eventually result in the reorder and replenishment of the stock which has been sold. The computer "intelligence" required to accomplish all these tasks will reside partly in the cash register (or point of sale device) at the counter and, perhaps, partly in a computer system in the "back office" to which the register is connected and which is performing other posting and accounting tasks.

16.5 SOURCES OF HARDWARE AND SOFTWARE

The channels through which all of these present and future miracles can be obtained consist first of the equipment manufacturers themselves. They range from multibillion dollar *Fortune* 100 corporations such as IBM, NCR, Burroughs, Honeywell, Univac, which have been in the business of supplying office equipment to businesses for many years, down to recent start-up (in some cases astounding upstart) companies such as Apple, Tandy, North Star, Ohio Scientific, Cromenco and literally hundreds of others. For the most part, the traditional equipment suppliers aforementioned are still selling directly to users, even in the smaller equipment lines. A new and, to some, startling trend began with IBM's 1981 introduction of its Personal Computer and Xerox's introduction of its Model 820 microcomputer the same year. In a radical departure from the past, both these companies are offering their new under-$10,000 microcomputers through independent computer stores (or store chains) and dealerships, while, in the case of IBM, refusing to sell direct to end users except when the quantities purchased exceed a significant number, thus precluding the sale of these systems directly to small businesses. Indeed, nearly all minicomputers sold up to this point to small businesses and to professional practices were channeled through intermediaries such as software houses, systems integrators and, to a lesser extent, computer stores. Thus the manufacturer has abdicated the responsibility of educating, consulting with, and supporting the small business user or the professional. The office equipment dealers and computer store owners who have taken on this responsibility have fulfilled it with varying degrees of skill and success.

Traditional office equipment dealers, those who sell typewriters, dictating equipment, adding machines, bookkeeping machines and the like, have quickly adopted small computers as part of their standard repertoire as well. Some have emulated the computer store, providing a display of hardware and packaged software through which the user can simply browse and make a selection. In some cases, these dealers provide expert, and not so expert, consulting services and systems designs bordering on the custom "turnkey" systems available in the minicomputer realm from systems integrators and software houses.

The computer store phenomenon is one of the most startling in the short history of the computer industry. Up from a few hobby shops in the middle 1970s has sprung an enormous array of computer stores, including some large and successful chains like Byte Shop and Computerland, the latter with over 300 franchised outlets. Many are doing a million dollars a year or more in business, and more recently include mass merchandisers and traditional retailers such as the Radio Shack chain of Tandy Corporation, Sears Roebuck, and classical department stores. There are at this point approximately 2,000 such outlets in the United States, with new ones opening almost daily, although the permanence of some of the stores has been less than absolute. A number of individual stores already have exited from the scene, and one or two of the major chains have sought protection under Chapter 11 of the bankruptcy code.

Based on the volume of business done by these stores and their growth in numbers, one can plausibly assume that the trend is a continuous and accelerating one. Many of the stores will eventually evolve into full service outlets which can provide consultation, training, maintenance, and software support of the type required by small businesses to make sensible initial decisions, to install their systems successfully, and to keep them not only operable but continually evolving and growing to meet changing business conditions. It is perhaps in this last regard that the computer store revolution may meet its greatest challenge.

Many of the batch and time share service bureaus, numbering perhaps 2,000 or so firms in the United States, have seen the growing power and steadily declining prices of microcomputers and small minis as a serious threat. Consequently, many of these have adopted the "let's join 'em" philosophy rather than assuming a fighting posture. To the extent that service bureaus offer installed on-site hardware and related software, they are assuming the coloration of traditional systems integrators and software houses. There is also the added virtue of being able to offer a gradual approach to automation for the first time user, beginning with simple batch services, moving upward to perhaps compatible time sharing services, and ultimately culminating in the installation of an in-house mini or microcomputer. While continuing to provide the original batch and time shared services, this process adds still more comprehensive and integrated data processing functions and affords the user relatively complete control over operations and, in many cases, places an absolute cap on what those services can cost. The latter may come as a relief to the beleaguered small business user who having started with a simple $40 per week payroll service, now has experienced an upward graduation in the number of services and transaction volume to the point these services are costing many hundreds or even thousands of dollars per month.

Supplementary channels through which mini and microcomputers are distributed are many and varied, including major banks to their correspondents, insurance companies to their agents, trade associations to their members, and so forth. There appears to be no end in sight to this groundswell in business, the professions, and government.

16.6 KEY CONCERNS

The main problems in the burgeoning small computer field can be summarized in two words: *professionalism* and *support*. Much of the selling activity and a great deal of the systems design and programming going on at present are simply not up to reasonable professional standards and lack architectural soundness, accounting integrity, and ease of future maintenance and modification. Today's user can, if unlucky or misguided, be the owner of a computer hardware and software complement which (a) won't work, (b) is subject to serious and unpredictable error, or (c) cannot be properly modified or expanded as business conditions change.

Much of the software available today over the retail counter, from mail order distributors, and even directly from manufacturers and systems houses, is also of questionable quality. The authors of such materials float into and out of business and are frequently far gone from the scene a few months after purchase, thus forcing the buyer to fall back on his or her own devices if, as is almost always the case, changes are required to meet changing regulatory and business conditions. For this reason, many users have been obliged to take on the responsibility of maintaining and modifying programs by themselves or with the help of friends, neighbors, relatives or part-time "moonlighters." Sometimes this activity can be a thoroughly pleasurable and satisfying experience for the do-it-yourself systems designer/programmer. On the other hand, it is not without its frustrations and risks:

1. The structure of the system and the quality and quantity of documentation may not facilitate changes, which indeed often yield strange and virtually untraceable errors and unexpected consequences, whether modifications are large or small.
2. Whatever warranty or supporting thread back to the originator remains may be obviated immediately upon any alteration of any sort to the system.
3. Systems design and programming can be addictive, and in some cases may become so engrossing and preoccupying as to inhibit the small business person or the professional from properly conducting normal business activities, and thus impact adversely on their success.

Clearly, the antidote for all of this is to deal in the first place with a supplier of hardware and software whose references and reputation are impeccable.

16.7 PROMISING NEW SOFTWARE TECHNOLOGIES

Some of today's grave difficulties in the software area are certain to be alleviated in the future through systems software techniques and packaged programs which will make the process of applications system design and programming much simpler, better, and in some cases even substitute altogether for the process. For example, there are generative systems available for virtually all types of business micro and minicomputers which obviate the need for programming screen formats for input and report formats for output. These master programs, interactive structures into which the user places data to be processed and output, automatically generate the internal program code to receive, edit and validate the incoming data in the one case, and to extract, format, and report the output from the computer's database in the other.

In many cases, the generative screen formatting and

report systems are also accompanied by, or based upon, **data base management software,** or **DBMS**s. DBMSs take total responsibility for managing and maintaining all the information in the computer, relieving the user and the applications programs from the housekeeping details of building and maintaining files, adding and deleting information, and dealing with the physical location of such information in the computer and its peripherals.

For example, an accounts receivable program might make reference to files and data by name: to wit, "customer file" and "account balance" without reference to the physical location of the file and its particular size and format. Thus, as the file moves or changes in format, size, or location, the program remains viable. It is able to continue to access data through the intermediation of the DBMS, avoiding any adjustment or reprogramming whatever.

Another important emerging trend in small business computing is the development of standard operating systems and universally transportable applications programs. Unlike the case in larger machines, a single operating system has taken dominion over the 8 bit microcomputer realm including machines of all sizes, types, descriptions, and manufacture. That operating system, called CP/M, is a product of Digital Research, Inc. going back to 1975 when it was originated for the first and simplest hobby machines. Over the years, CP/M has proliferated with regard to the number of machines for which a usable version of the operating system exists and, perhaps to a lesser extent, in the features and functions of CP/M itself, which, like other operating systems, has continued to evolve. Language processors have been written to run under various versions of CP/M and bear a strong family resemblance to one another. Programs written for one manufacturer's machine tend to run, if not unmodified, at least with a minimum amount of "tweaking" and "tuning" on equipment of other manufacturers, so long as there is a version of CP/M available on each machine.

The result has been the blossoming of an enormous software industry producing thousands of applications packages written in BASIC, COBOL, PASCAL and other fairly standard programming languages, which come in either a generic form or in various "flavors" ready to run on a wide variety of microcomputers. The user may buy a license, for example, to use an array of accounting packages ranging from accounts receivable through order processing, inventory control, general ledger, and payroll, preferably from a reputable software house or software distributor which counts among its audience tens of thousands of users on a great variety of equipment. This assures the buyer that the package is stable and viable and that, should he or she decide to migrate to another CP/M based machine, a minimum of translation and probably little or no retraining will be required.

The dark side of the evolving standardization of CP/M, though it has maintained a strong thread of compatibility throughout the microcomputer evolution, more or less a "least common denominator" kind of system, is that CP/M was written for the earliest, smallest and most primitive of the microcomputers and is severely limited in the size of memory addressed. It lacks many human-engineered features which would enhance or ease the burden of operator interaction, and also lacks in one very important capability otherwise easily supportable on today's small machines: multiprogramming, or multitasking. As will be noted in the next section, Hardware Trends, developers of more comprehensive operating systems must keep a very sharp eye on the huge and evolving standardization of software at the CP/M level. A maximum effort is necessary to make their more advanced systems somehow or another compatible with, or capable of coexisting with, the CP/M operating system.

16.8 HARDWARE TRENDS

The original microcomputers used 4 bit microprocessor chips, but by the time the trend had flowered in full, production had shifted to 8 bit chips. The Intel 8080, Zilog Z-80, Mostek 6502, and Motorola 800 are now almost universal in hundreds of thousands of machines. With a data path width of only 8 bits, these processors have distinct limits in the speed with which they can conduct certain processes, particularly heavy computation or large amounts of data transfer to and from memory. The practicalities of addressing and memory mapping schemes and the limitations of their operating systems confine 8 bit processors to 48 or 64Kb of main memory.

Therefore, a new trend is to 16 bit processors like the Intel 8086, the Zilog Z-8000, and the Motorola 68000, thus joining the large array of 16 bit systems in the minicomputer realm. These larger micros, like minis, can address very large data spaces, measured in hundreds of thousands or even millions of characters, and possess more than double—in some cases up to six to eight times—the speed of their 8 bit predecessors. This superiority stems from not only the increased data width, but also from a much greater "clock" or cycle speed as well as more efficient and comprehensive operating systems

and greater program language capabilities. By 1982, several vendors had released and were actively selling and installing 16 bit microcomputers only slightly more expensive than comparable 8 bit systems. And, while the 16 bit trend had hardly set in, the same and other manufacturers were beginning to experiment with 32 bit microprocessors, which will have a similar multiplier effect on addressing space and throughput potential as compared with their 16 bit predecessors.

One of the big questions with respect to the new 16 bit machines and the 32 bit machines to come is standardization of operating systems and applications software. Digital Research Corporation, the originators of CP/M, have announced CP/M-86, an upward compatible, multitasking, and more sophisticated version of CP/M. It runs on 16 bit processors and enables those processors to continue to run CP/M based applications in a compatible, but "degraded," mode with respect to the advanced features of the 16 bit machine. Meanwhile, other much more advanced operating systems have emerged and are gaining momentum in the 16 and 32 bit atmosphere, chief of which is UNIX, a product of Bell Laboratories now being licensed to manufacturers and users by Western Electric.

UNIX and its many imitators or look-alike operating systems, embody all the virtues of large scale computer operating systems, including multitasking, dynamic resources allocation, improved operator interface, and extremely useful and refined systems development tools to greatly ease the jobs of programming and testing new applications. Many industry pundits are predicting that, despite the pressure for CP/M compatibility, the 16 bit world will go UNIX as a standard because of the virtues of the operating system and its superior fit with the power and sophistication of the larger processors. Two of the main inhibiting factors to date with respect to UNIX have been Western Electric Corporation's reluctance to lower the price to within reasonable competitive range of CP/M and its unwillingness to get heavily involved in the marketing and support of the software directly. For these reasons, the UNIX look-alikes have been spawned, including XENIX from Microsoft, which has more than a passing resemblance to UNIX not only in concept but also in every detail. Western Electric, however, appears at this writing to be having a change of heart by lowering the license fee, showing signs of a willingness to promote UNIX in the broad marketplace.

Another entrant in the operating system standardization "derby" is MS-DOS from Microsoft. It is the single user CP/M competitor provided free with the IBM Personal Computer (and it imitators). The sale of the IBM product and the number of software developers now writing programs for it have been overwhelming. MS-DOS has become another standard OS, perhaps eclipsing both CP/M and UNIX.

Another emerging clear cut trend in the small computer arena has been the installation of hard disks in sizable quantities, as opposed to the almost exclusive reliance in the earlier era on floppy disks for data storage. Every minicomputer maker offers a variety of fixed and removable hard disk storage, some upgradable from 2.5 to 5 megabytes on up into the hundreds of megabytes should the user need and be willing to pay for such large quantities of disk storage. However, until recently, such capabilities for microcomputers have been lacking.

One of the pioneers in breaking through the microcomputer disk barrier in 1979 was Corvus with a 5 megabyte Winchester hard disk with an intelligent controller now expanded to include multiple ports, permitting the clustering of up to 64 independent microcomputers into a common disk data base. The Corvus product line has also expanded to include still larger capacity Winchester disks. This trend shows no signs of diminishing; Nestar is another pioneer in this field, with multiported cluster controllers supporting a common hard disk, having specialized initially in Apple computers and more lately offering similar facilities for a variety of small machines. There is no question now that all of the major microcomputer manufacturers are, or will soon be, offering compact, inexpensive hard disk storage systems with their computers. Most systems are in the 5 or 10 megabyte range but are sure to step up from there into much larger capacities. Given the limitations of a single workstation on most micros, large disk capacity almost certainly militates in favor of networking or clustering of multiple micros into a common shared resource pool of storage, and adding other shared facilities such as printing and data communications.

Thus one can readily foresee a profusion of offerings from computer manufacturers and independents alike of multiported disk and communications controllers and low, medium, and high speed hard-wired networking facilities similar to what has long been available from Datapoint Corporation on their minicomputers under the name "ARC." Systems are already beginning to emerge which allocate most of the local formatting, editing, and response responsibilities to individual microcomputer workstations. They interconnect, however, through cluster networks to a common hub to permit interchange of information and access to a common pool of information, and in the most advanced cases, to a single gateway into a larger processor (Figure 16.7).

One hungers for and waits for the emergence of a standard to which the burgeoning networking systems will adhere so that systems purchased at different times from the same or different manufacturers with various application sets will be able to interface within a common framework and talk to each other compatibly. Unfortunately, no such standard has yet evolved, and it is not clear that one will. One portentous straw in the wind might be the fact that Apple Computer and Radio Shack both now offer a compatible interface to Datapoint's ARC System, but other manufacturers have not followed suit.

16.9 THE OFFICE OF THE FUTURE—SMALL BUSINESS STYLE

Today there is hardly a microcomputer, or at least one version of every popular minicomputer, which does not offer a word processing capability. Among the micros, MicroPro's WordStar package has taken an enormous lead as the de facto standard. Although functionally rich, and capable of doing a large percentage of the work associated with the larger, more expensive dedicated word processing stations, WordStar and similar systems are not particularly easy to understand and use, and definitely suffer from lack of clerical/secretarial orientation. Also, the machines on which they run are typically designed for hobbyists, experimenters, and to a lesser extent small business data processing, and are not optimized in any way for secretarial functions. Therefore, what are quite likely to evolve are specialized microcomputers with improved word processing software, optimal screen size and format, special keytops and keyboard layout, and with teaching and reference aids aimed at and optimally fitting the functions of a secretary or document preparer. Beneath the skin, of course, these systems will be standard 8 or 16 bit microprocessors, and thus have at least the potential of being shared by people also doing other work, such as data processing. They will also have a capability of interfacing, via cluster controllers, hard wired networks, and data communications to similar machines, with common resource and data pools, and to other, more senior data processing networks.

One can not only (Figure 16.7) visualize, but now find in operation, combination systems with specialized workstations in small businesses. The operator at one station may be performing text or word processing functions, while others are working within the province of classical

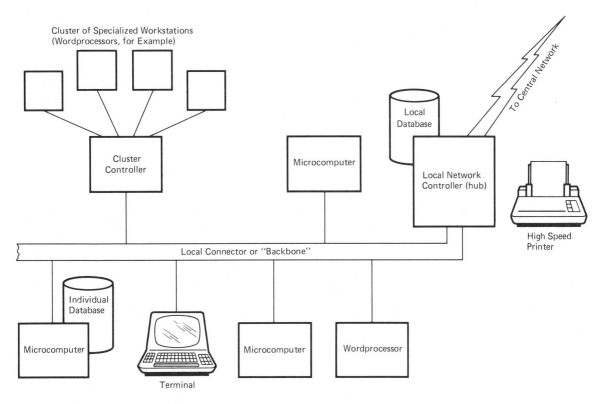

Figure 16.7. Local area networking.

data processing. Projecting ahead just a bit, one can see another class of analytical workstations, utilizing financial planning software which extracts data from a common resource pool of operational and accounting data reflecting day to day transactions, and then transforms, analyzes, and extrapolates from this information into the future. Let us call this latter hardware vehicle the "professional workstation," in the hands of a financial manager, budget analyst, or similar specialist. Looking a bit even beyond that, we can visualize similar but further tailored versions of the same processors making appearances as data collection workstations on loading docks, in the warehouse, on plant floors, in laboratories; in short, everywhere throughout the business, small or large, where work is being done. All these tailored workstations will, too, in some way or another be interconnected so they can cooperate and share data to whatever extent is desirable.

It is almost certain that these local network aggregations in small businesses or in departmental units of larger businesses will, in addition, have specialized hubs or controllers capable not only of aggregating information, but also of interacting with external networks connected to the outside world or to more senior elements of the corporate hierarchy, or to both. Thus we can visualize a small computer in a pharmacy, in daily contact with a wholesaler, placing automatic replenishment orders for drugs and other merchandise which have fallen to predetermined quantities in inventory; at another moment, the same computer would be in contact with the area's Medicaid/Medicare intermediary transmitting reimbursement claims for prescription drugs dispensed to authorized participants. This would, of course, be an automatic byproduct of the normal work a day activities which make up prescription processing. In this context, then, through interconnected networks, a single computer could participate in three totally different processing and communications environments fulfilling a perfectly rational scheme tied directly to the basic conduct of the business.

We may reach the point soon at which businesses will begin to exchange basic ordering, accounts receivable, and accounts payable data through common public computer networks, which would perhaps overlay the existing public communications facilities provided by the telephone company, or as an alternative, make the exchange by value added carriers specializing in public data communications, such as Telenet, Tymnet, or Southern Pacific Communications Corporation, or many others to come. This interaction could easily transpire via the "mailbox" method currently being pioneered and promoted by The Source, a micro oriented time sharing service. Using this service, one subscriber leaves messages addressed in storage for other subscribers, who then later dial in and check their "in baskets" in memory to see what resides there. Replies can then be instituted using the same method in reverse. And with a bank or other fiduciary institution serving as an intermediary somewhere in this process, it will be an easy matter for businesses to settle accounts with one another electronically, small computer to small computer, employing virtually the same technique. Obviously, sensitive and difficult questions involving security and privacy arise in such a context, and must be dealt with firmly before such systems become prevalent.

16.10 GETTING RESULTS

The strongest causes of disappointment and outright failure in small business automation lie in the user's lack of diligence to assess correctly what applications to automate and the features and functions reasonable to demand of those applications, and in insufficient planning and preparation for installing the automated system. Business and professional people who ordinarily perform a very careful, competent analysis to determine the acquisition of a piece of productive machinery for the mainline conduct of their business, in the way a printer evaluates a printing press or a trucker a piece of rolling stock, often unhesitatingly plunge into the installation of a computerized system on the bare recommendation of a vendor or another user, or simply on a hunch.

Surveys show that the average computer buyer does not conduct a cost/benefit analysis prior to making a commitment, and that many buyers—almost a majority—consider only a single vendor in making their decision. It is no wonder, then, that many such enterprises have come to grief on the rocks and shoals of automation. In the author's experience, and that of numerous other professionals in the field, *fully half* of the computers installed in small businesses end up as disappointments to greater or lesser extent. In the most flagrant cases, the

computer installation may create more work than it absorbs and may also be so inflexible as to prevent the user from meeting legitimate business requirements because "the computer can't handle it."

Vendors traditionally make a significant contribution to this high disappointment quotient. Under enormous pressure to maintain market share and to keep up with the spectacular growth of the business itself, vendors find themselves impelled to overcommit. In order to get orders, they characteristically promise more than they can possibly deliver in hopes that when the time comes, they will be able to "muddle through." Unfortunately, the vendor who is scrupulously honest about what can be done for the user often ends up out in the cold when the procurement decision is made, because other vendors are "promising the moon" and the user is too naive to recognize the insincerity and unsoundness of their claims.

The remedy, obviously, for these unfortunate practices is for the user to acquire the necessary knowledge to make an intelligent and discriminating decision among the various competing claimants, and to perform a methodical, objective analysis of (a) real needs and (b) the worthiness of each particular seller's solution to those needs. Buyers would do well to borrow a rather formal and ritualistic technique employed by large companies and government agencies in procuring major equipment; namely, the formal **request for proposal**, or **RFP**. By clearly stating all needs in writing, the user gains a much greater assurance of evoking a proposal from vendors which is responsive to those needs, rather than merely representative of what the vendors wish to sell. Because the RFP demands uniform responses to the same questions and issues from all vendors, the buyer is able to compare point by point one vendor's offering to another's rather than having to view a jumble of dissimilar approaches to the problem.

Under the RFP approach, many prospective bidders will eliminate themselves immediately through failing to make the required response, preferring to depend upon the more familiar selling techniques of verbalizing and demonstrating to convince users to buy the vendor's solution to the problem as opposed to what the buyer really needs. Also, some vendors simply make a gesture in the direction of a response without truly addressing the requirements or major issues embodied in the RFP. Still others may be totally out of range in terms of cost, delivery time, or some other parameter.

Among the survivors there may be one or two or a handful of worthy offerings which then have to be analyzed at a much greater depth; perhaps this process would involve a breakdown of offerings into a series of factors, each of which could be rated on a scale of, say, 1 to 5 or 1 to 10 in terms of merit, and then weighted according to a preestablished priority. For example, price may weigh in as 25 percent of the total decision, whereas a group of factors making up an overall assessment of "ease of use" may weigh in as 30 percent. Then the rating of a particular offering in terms of price competitiveness would be multiplied by 0.25 while the rating for ease of use factors would be multiplied by 0.30 and the results summed with all other rated and weighted factors into an overall figure. This "figure of merit," though by no means deciding the issued by itself, would be an acceptably objective guide to the overall worthiness of various proposals.

Having once selected a winner, the user is well advised to engage in a rather protracted contract negotiation which would include a business and legal review of the vendor's proffered standard document by the buyer and the buyer's consultant and attorney. Various important changes and additions should be negotiated which afford the buyer as much protection as the vendor has carefully provided for himself in the standard contract. One of the most common failures in this regard is for the buyer to sign a contract in which acceptance of and payment for a computer system, typically with systems and applications software, is not at all contingent upon performance. This exposure, of course, is not acceptable in the purchase of any other business or professional equipment, and there is no reason it should be the norm in procuring computer hardware and software. Concrete specifications and acceptance criteria related to actual performance should definitely be a part of every computer contract and used as an incentive to force the vendor to deliver on proposed features and benefits.

Even after deciding to automate based on real need, soliciting bids, selecting the right equipment and software, and negotiating a favorable arrangement with the vendor or vendors, there still remains an important obligation on the part of the buyer: to plan and manage the process of installing the new system and converting operations to it. Most buyers, particularly small business people, are surprised at the complexity and number of activities, and the importance of their timely execution, which remain in going from the signing of a contract to the final installation and successful day to day operation of an automated system. Each phase of this "realization" process—systems design, forms design, documentation, training, programming, data conversion, installation, parallel execution, acceptance testing, and final cut-over procedures—must be thought out carefully in advance and planned.

Planning itself, of course, means identifying the resources required to accomplish the various phases, including the people who are going to be responsible for their execution: the time in the installation calendar that each event must begin; and the time by which it must be completed. The most important, critical step in the whole process is, then, to ensure by careful management, control, and follow-up that the activities contemplated actually do occur in conformity with the schedule, and if not, to take remedial action. In the majority of businesses this requires periodic meetings, perhaps biweekly, with vendor and user personnel alike to ascertain status and progress in accordance with the plan.

REFERENCES

Atkinson, C., *Inventory Management for Small Computers*. Beaverton, OR.: dilithium Press, 1981.

Barden, Jr., W., *Microcomputers for Business Applications*. Indianapolis: Howard W. Sams, 1979.

Rosa, N., and S. Rosa, *Small Computers for the Small Business*. Beaverton, OR.: dilithium Press, 1980.

Shaw, D. R., *Your Small Business Computer*. New York: Van Nostrand Reinhold, 1982.

Zaks, R., *An Introduction to Personal and Business Computing*. Berkeley, CA.: Sybex, 1979.

17
Robotics

Ronald D. Potter

Robot Systems Inc.

17.1 INTRODUCTION

During the past two decades, the concept of a flexible, programmable automation device, which has come to be known as an "industrial robot," has become a reality. Automation modules in considerable variety have been developed, varying in size, shape, sophistication, and cost, and offering a wide range of capabilities and application possibilities to almost every manufacturing industry in the world. Robots currently weld, cast, form, transfer, inspect, and load and unload parts into and out of a multiplicity of machines and processes.

The industrial robot that has evolved to its present state is better termed a "robot arm" than a "mechanical man." It is essentially a mechanical arm that is bolted to the floor (or the ceiling, or wall in some cases), fitted with a special set of fingers or a special tool, and taught to go through a series of repetitive motions to perform a particular task. It possesses neither the ability to move from one plant location to another, nor the ability to see or feel the part it is working on, except in some models with equipment features and software provided for sensory feedback. However, even with these limitations, robots make outstanding contributions towards the improvement of manufacturing operations.

More specifically, an **industrial robot**, as defined by The Robot Institute of America, is "a reprogrammable, multifunctional manipulator designed to move material, parts, tools, or specialized devices through variable programmed motions for the performance of a variety of tasks." The terms *reprogrammable, multifunctional, variable programmed,* and *variety of tasks* are the key words which differentiate robots from other forms of special purpose, or fixed, automation. As "flexible automation," a robot must be adaptable to many kinds of jobs in numerous industries and perform these jobs with some degree of dexterity and flexibility in its motions. In contrast, fixed or special purpose automation is less universal and includes machines designed to do one particular job in one specific industry.

A robot is a mechanical arm down to a wrist which may be moved and oriented to any point in space within its reach (Figure 17.1). It is an assembly of various axes of motion which can be "taught" to move the end of the arm within a three dimensional volume to points in space called its **work envelope.** At the end of the arm's outermost radius of motion is a flat plate, or shaft, for attaching specialized devices which pick up parts or hold tools to work on parts. The end-of-arm tooling, or **end effector,** is not part of the robot, but must be designed and built specifically for a particular application.

Essentially, purchasing an industrial robot is purchasing the ability to move a flat tool-mounting plate to a given number of points in space in a teachable sequence of motions. The number of points the robot can move to, the distance between these points, how the robot moves from one point to the next, the speeds of these movements, and the adaptability of the sequence to external conditions constitute the functional differences between the various types and makes of robots. (At the end of this chapter is a listing of major manufacturers and distributors of robots in the U.S.)

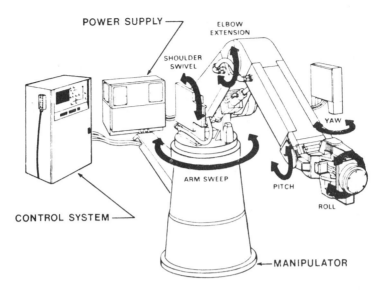

Figure 17.1. Basic structure of a robot. (Courtesy Cincinnati Milacron)

17.2 ROBOT STRUCTURE

Although industrial robots vary widely in size, configuration, and capabilities, they share a family structure: three basic components which may come assembled in one integral unit or separated into individual components connected by pneumatic, hydraulic, or electrical "umbilical cords."

As shown in Figure 17.1, the mechanical portion, or **manipulator** component, is the assembly of axes capable of motion in various directions which carries the part pickup device or tool at the end of its outermost axis. The manipulator performs the actual work of the robot, and is made up of parts such as bearings, joints, linkages, actuators, control valves, and feedback devices which form the muscles, skeleton, and nervous system of the robot.

Actuators, such as hydraulic or pneumatic cylinders or rotary actuators, and electric or hydraulic motors, power the various axes of motion, either directly or indirectly through gears, sprockets, chains, or ball screws. *Control valves* mounted on the manipulator control the flow of fluid to the actuators. Directional control valves are used in simpler types of hydraulic and pneumatic robots, while servo valves control the motions of more sophisticated hydraulic robots. Electric dc servo motors power the motions of electrically driven robots.

Also attached to the manipulator are *feedback devices* which sense and measure the position and, in some cases, the velocity of each axis of motion. This information is

then sent to the control system for use in coordinating the motions of the robot. These feedback devices provide either analog or digital feedback signals, depending on type or make of robot. Simpler robots use devices such as electric limit or proximity switches for digital position feedback of the end points of motion for each axis. More sophisticated robots use devices such as optical or magnetic encoders for digital feedback of axis position, or resolvers and potentiometers for analog position feedback. Robots may also use tachometers as feedback devices to measure the velocity of the axes of motion.

The second component of a robot is the **power supply,** which provides and regulates the energy that is converted to motion by the robot's actuators. An air compressor, usually present in most production facilities, provides the compressed air used to power pneumatically actuated robots. A conventional industrial hydraulic power supply unit, consisting of an electric-motor driven pump, filter, reservoir, and an air or water cooled heat exchanger, supplies energy to hydraulically actuated robots. This power supply can either be built into the manipulator as an integral part or supplied as a separate unit. Hydraulic operating pressures of from 500 to 2500 psi are current in commercially available robots. Petroleum based fluids are normally used, although fire retardant fluids are also available. Electronic voltage supplies regulate the incoming electrical voltage and current for electrically actuated robots.

The third component of a robot is the **control system,**

the "brains" of the robot. The control system sequences and coordinates the motions of the various axes of the robot, and provides interlocking communication with external devices and machines. Reacting to feedback signals from the position and velocity sensing devices, the robot initiates and terminates motions in a programmed sequence by actuating the control valves at the appropriate time.

Robot control systems vary greatly in complexity and determine the functional capabilities of a robot to perform a particular task. Control systems vary from simple stepping drum sequencers, air logic sequencers, and programmable controllers in simpler robots to solid state electronic sequencers, diode matrix board sequencers, microprocessor (see Chapter 4) and minicomputer based control systems in sophisticated robots. The latter control system gives the robot the ability to perform mathematical computations in going through its program, and significantly increases its capabilities in many applications.

Various types of memory devices in robot control systems store data, including electronic counters, magnetic tape, magnetic disks, plated wire, solid state RAM, ROM, and core memory (see Chapter 3). Robot control systems can either be attached as an integral part of the robot or mounted in a separate control cabinet. The latter is advantageous when the robot operates in a hostile environment.

17.3 STRUCTURAL DIFFERENCES

Robots can be classified structurally according to their work envelopes. The **work envelope** of a robot is most precisely defined as all of the points in space that can be touched by the end of the robot's arm or tool mounting plate. The work envelope, then, is a three dimensional space whose structure depends on how the axes of motion are assembled.

A robot has three major axes of motion which provide the largest portion of its work envelope. Up to three additional axes of motion can be provided at the end of the last major axis to provide added degrees of freedom to the robot motions.

Robot Mechanical Structures

Robots can be classified structurally according to the coordinate system of their three major axes of motion. The three major axes of motion provide a vertical lift stroke, an in-and-out reach stroke of the arm, and a rotational motion about the vertical lift axis of the robot, or a linear traverse motion of the robot arm.

A *cylindrical coordinate* robot (Figure 17.2) is configured with a horizontal arm assembled to a vertical column, which is mounted on a rotating base. The horizontal arm can move in and out (this movement is termed a *reach stroke*), and move up and down on the vertical axis. In addition, this arm assembly can rotate left and right about the vertical axis; thus, the motions of the three major axes describe a portion of a *cylinder* as the work envelope of the robot. Assemblies such as the ASEA MHU, Copperweld, GMFanuc, Prab servo, Seiko, and Sterling are typical examples of cylindrical coordinate robots.

Embodying the second work envelope structure is the *spherical coordinate*, or *polar*, robot (Figure 17.3). This configuration consists of an arm which moves in and out

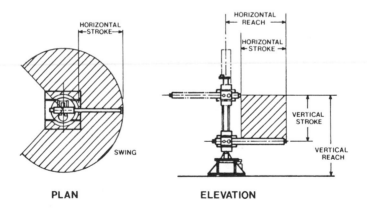

PLAN   **ELEVATION**

Figure 17.2. Cylindrical coordinate work envelope.

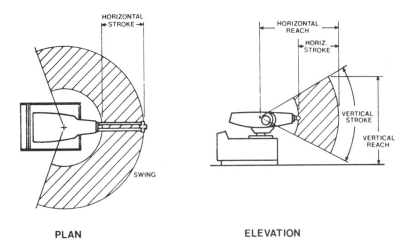

PLAN   ELEVATION

Figure 17.3. Spherical coordinate work envelope.

in a reach stroke, but utilizes a *pivoting* vertical motion instead of a true vertical stroke. In addition, the arm can rotate left and right about the vertical pivot axis. Thus, the motions of the major axes form a portion of a sphere as a work envelope. The Prab nonservo and Unimate hydraulic models are examples of spherical coordinate robots.

The *jointed arm,* or *revolute,* robot constitutes the third work envelope structure (Figure 17.4). This type of robot contains rotary joints (called a *shoulder and elbow*) which are mounted on a rotating base to provide the three major axes of motion. This allows the robot arm to fold up very close to the rotating base, minimizes floor space requirements, and extends the robot's work envelope. Models by ASEA, Cincinnati Milacron, Unimate Puma, DeVilbiss Trallfa, and Nordson are typical examples of jointed arm robots.

A fourth work envelope structure is defined by the *rectangular coordinate,* or *Cartesian* robot (Figure 17.5). This configuration consists of a horizontal arm mounted to a vertical column, which in turn is mounted on a linear-traversing base. Thus, straightline X-Y-Z axes of motion

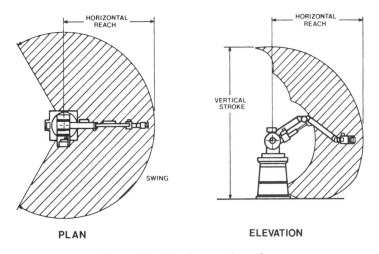

PLAN   ELEVATION

Figure 17.4. Jointed arm work envelope.

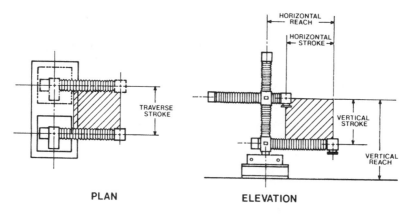

Figure 17.5. Rectangular coordinate work envelope.

are produced. The Advanced Robotics Cyro and General Electric Allegro are examples of rectangular coordinate robots. Gantry mounted rectangular coordinate robots, such as the IBM 7565 and Westinghouse 5000, are also available.

Minor Axes of Motion

The minor axes of motion of a robot are contained in an assembly called a *wrist* mounted to the end of the robot's arm. From one to three axes of motion can be provided, depending on the particular robot model or make. There is no standard terminology in the industry, but these axes may be termed the *pitch, yaw,* and *roll* axes, or the *bend, yaw,* and *swivel* axes (Figure 17.6). Additional axes of motions can be provided by mounting the robot on a traverse track on the floor, or overhead. Also, many robot models can be mounted upside down or sideways on walls to change the orientation of their work envelopes.

Many of the robots commercially available are modular in design, and users may select as few as two or as many as seven degrees of freedom, depending upon their needs. As previously noted, mounting surface in the form of a flat plate or round shaft is provided on the last axis of the wrist for installation of the tool or gripper with

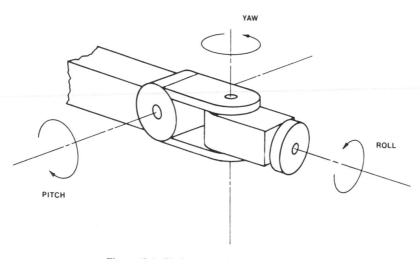

Figure 17.6. Pitch, yaw and roll axes of a wrist.

which the robot performs its intended task. These devices are usually unique to the robot application and are thus provided by the user. However, several robot manufacturers offer a selection of devices for grasping parts which may be directly applicable or adaptable to the particular work to be performed.

17.4 ROBOT FUNCTIONAL CLASSIFICATION

Industrial robots can be separated into three functional classifications. These classifications are important in applying the right kind of robot to a particular job.

Nonservo Point to Point Robots

The simplest class of robots is called *nonservo* controlled *point to point,* also, perhaps more commonly, "pick and place" (Figure 17.7). Actuators for the various axes of motion consist of pneumatic or hydraulic cylinders or motors connected to a directional control valve. When the control valve is shifted by an input signal, it allows fluid to flow into one port of the actuator while the other port vents or returns fluid to a supply tank. Flow control valves mounted on the actuators are adjustable for speed control of the axes of motion. The stroke of each axis of motion is determined by two adjustable mechanical endstops.

Sensors, normally limit switches, are mounted on each axis of motion and are adjustable to sense the two end points of each axis stroke. Only the endpoints of motion

for each axis are sensed, and not any other points in between.

Sequencing of motions is accomplished by coordinating the inputs to the control valves with the outputs from the axis-stroke endpoint sensors. This requires a fairly simple sequencing control system, such as a stepping drum programmer, air logic sequencer, or programmable controller. Programming for a particular application is done *mechanically,* by setting up the desired sequence of axis motions and adjusting the mechanical endstops on each axis to their desired position. Programs normally involve a limited number of sequencial steps, with from 15 to 100 steps typical in commercially available units.

Among the nonservo robots commercially available in the U.S. are models from ASEA MHU, Copperweld, Prab, Seiko, and Sterling. These robots vary in cost from $8000 to $35,000 and can handle parts weighing from a few ounces to 125 pounds. Nonservo robots are used almost exclusively for part handling tasks.

Servocontrolled Robots

These robots (Figure 17.8) offer more capabilities to end users; they allow the use of tools to work on parts, but also perform more sophisticated part handling tasks. Instead of using mechanical stops at the endpoints of each axis, these robots utilize servovalves or motors which are capable of stopping the robot at any point along each axis of motion. Feedback devices, such as encoders, resolvers, potentiometers, and tachometers, mounted on each axis

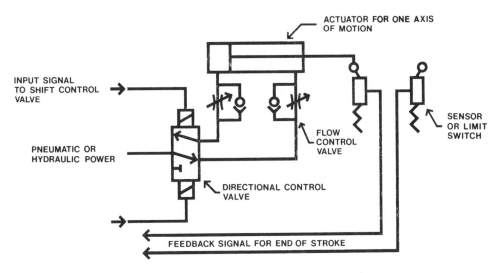

Figure 17.7. Typical nonservo robot control schematic.

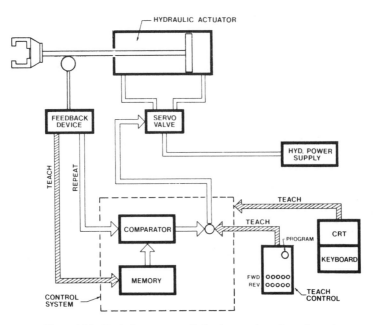

Figure 17.8. Typical servo controlled point to point robot schematic.

constantly monitor the position and/or velocity of each axis and provide a feedback signal to the robot control system.

The control system compares the actual position of each axis to a preprogrammed point in space and, through an electrical signal, causes a proportional flow of oil or electrical current to the actuators to drive the axes to the preprogrammed point. As the axes approach this point, the control system decelerates the robot and eventually closes the servo valve or stops the servomotor, bringing the axes to a stop at the point. Control systems for servo controlled robots provide many more points in memory than nonservo robot controls, varying from 32 to 33,000 steps.

In commercially available point to point servocontrolled robots, teaching of programs is done via a handheld *teach pendant,* which contains buttons for each axis of motion. In the teach mode, when an axis button is depressed, the axis begins to move until the button is released. In this way, the programmer walks the robot to various points in space via the teach pendant; and when the hand or tool reaches a desired position, the programmer depresses a record button, putting that point in space in the robot's memory. The robot is sequentially lead through an entire sequence of motions in this manner.

On most microprocessor or minicomputer based robots, the programmer also uses a keyboard with CRT to enter

functional data at each step, such as velocity desired, input or output signals to or from external devices, and any logical statement that the robot is capable of performing (search, branch to another program, track a moving line, and so on). The robot then repeats the programmed sequence of motions in the automatic mode, with qualifying inputs from external sensors programmed into the robot.

Point to Point and Continuous Path Servorobots

Servocontrolled robots can be separated into two functional classifications according to the type of work they perform.

Point to point servocontrolled robots store a finite number of points in space in their memories and proceed point to point carrying out their programmed sequences of motions. Base costs for servocontrolled point to point robots vary from $30,000 to $150,000, with payloads ranging from 5 to 2,000 pounds. Such robots are available in the U.S. from, among others, ASEA, Bendix, Cincinnati Milacron, Cybotech, General Electric, GMFanuc, Prab Servo, Thermwood, Unimation, and Yaskawa.

Continuous path servocontrolled robots function in much the same manner as point to point servocontrolled robots, except in the ways they are taught a program and store data in their memories. Utilizing the same type feedback devices on each axis of motion as the point to point servo robots, continuous path robots store data on a time basis rather than on the basis of discrete points in space. Teaching of programs is accomplished by the operator actually grasping the end of the robot's arm and physically *leading* it through a pattern of motions while the control system is sampling and recording feedback data for the axes position sensors.

Sampling rates of typically 80 points per second are employed in commercially available robots. Continuous path robots are applied specifically to paint-spraying and other coating operations: they vary in cost from $50,000 to $150,000.

Some continuous path servocontrolled robots available in the U.S. are models from Binks, Cybotech (P-15), DeVilbiss Trallfa, Graco, Nordson, and Thermwood.

17.5 SELECTING A ROBOT

Many different sizes and mechanical structures make up the machines that comprise the "family" of commercially available robots, as do differing "IQ's" for robot control

systems. Much like a person, a given robot may be best suited for a particular industrial task.

Table 17.1 matches robots by type—nonservo, servo point to point, servo continuous path—with job types in industry: the robot types are in accordance with those established by the Robot Institute of America. Note that servocontrolled point to point robots are the general purpose robots, with capabilities of performing almost all tasks allotted to present day robots, while the other two types are more limited in their applications. To date, approximately 70 percent of the robots available in the U.S. are of the servocontrolled point to point type.

17.6 CURRENT AND FUTURE TRENDS IN ROBOTICS

The first industrial robot used in the U.S. was made in 1961. Since that time, the robot has undergone several stages of development, including increased sophistication of its control system and specialization in handling more difficult tasks. However, the robot of today essentially remains, when compared with its human counterpart, a "blind, deaf and dumb, one armed machine, with its hand cut off, novacaine running through its veins, rigormortis

Table 17.1. Selection Guidelines for a Robot

TYPE OF ROBOT	TYPE OF JOB									
	PART HANDLING	MATERIAL HANDLING	TOOL HANDLING	SPECIAL DEVICE HANDLING	PALLETIZING	INSPECTION	ASSEMBLY	PACKAGING	MOVING LINE OPERATIONS	
NON-SERVO POINT-TO-POINT	✓ LIMITED PAYLOAD CAPACITY	✓ LIMITED PAYLOAD CAPACITY				✓ LIMITED TO SIMPLE PARTS HANDLING TASKS	✓ LIMITED TO SIMPLE PARTS HANDLING TASKS	✓ LIMITED TO SIMPLE PARTS HANDLING TASKS		
SERVO POINT-TO-POINT	✓	✓ PAYLOAD CAPACITY UP TO 2000 LBS	✓ GENERAL PURPOSE	✓	✓	✓ PARTS OR INSPECTION DEVICE HANDLING	✓ PARTS OR ASSEMBLY TOOL HANDLING	✓	✓ LINE TRACKING	
SERVO CONTINUOUS PATH				✓ SPECIAL PURPOSE DEVICES					✓	

in its joints, and a relatively low IQ." Current developments in paralleling control and sensor technology, most notably vision and tactile sensing, are now being integrated into robot systems, giving robots increased abilities to perform more dexterous and difficult jobs. Among the current trends in robotics are

1. *Specialized sensors for particular processes and applications integrated into the robot controls.* As one example, the parameters of the arc welding process (arc voltage, wire feed speed, adaptive control for seam tracking, etc.) are now being controlled by the robot controller. This makes the general purpose robot a specialized robot for performing arc welding applications. Another example involves the assembly process, in which specialized robots are equipped with tactile sensing strain gauges, remote center compliance devices, and video cameras to perform the assembly process more efficiently. Many of their sensors are commercially available now, integrated into the robot, while ongoing developments in sensor and control technology are being implemented as they become available.

2. *Electric versus hydraulic drive.* The current trend in robots being introduced to the market is the use of electric drive in place of hydraulic drives. Although hydraulic actuators are more powerful than electric actuators of equivilent size, offering more "muscle" or load carrying capability to hydraulic robots, several application advantages of electric robots make them more attractive:
   a. Electric robots run quieter than hydraulic robots.
   b. Electric robots are not subject to hydraulic leaks, which can contaminate the work place or parts being manipulated.
   c. Electric robots use less energy. A hydraulic robot has its power supply running even when the robot is not moving, thereby consuming extra electrical power. An electric robot uses very little energy when it is not moving.
   d. Hydraulic robots normally require a warmup period (15 to 30 minutes) to get the oil up to operating temperature for repeatability and smooth motions. An electric robot does not require this warmup period.
   e. Electric robots tend to function with higher accuracy and greater repeatability than hydraulic robots.

3. *Off-line programming capabilities.* As previously described, today's servo controlled robots are "taught" by walking or leading them through a sequence of mo-

tions between various points and recording this sequence in the robot's memory. This must be "on-line" teaching, with the robot available for the walk-through process. Current developments in robot control systems are allowing the robot to be taught off-line by a programmer, the program generated being input into the robot's memory without need of the walk-through process. In many batch manufacturing operations involving robots, this is a necessary requirement for the robots' programming.

4. *CAD/CAM system integration* The integration of CAD/CAM (computed aided design/computer aided manufacture) systems into robotics is currently ongoing, with the desired result being off-line programming, ease of workplace layout, work envelope analysis, and workflow into and out of the manufacturing cell. Several robotic CAD/CAM systems are now available.

Major Manufacturers and Distributors of Robots in the U.S.

Advanced Robotics Corporation
Building 8, Route 79
Hebron, OH 43025
614-929-1065

ASEA, Inc./Industrial Robot Division
1176 East Big Beaver Road
Troy, MI 48084
313-528-3630

Automatix Inc.
217 Middlesex Turnpike
Burlington, MA 01803
617-273-4340

Bendix Robotics Division
21238 Bridge Street
Southfield, MI 48034
313-352-7700

Binks Manufacturing Co. (Thermwood)
9201 West Belmont Avenue
Franklin Park, IL 60131
312-671-3300

Cincinnati Milacron Inc.
Industrial Robot Division
215 South West Street
Lebanon, OH 45036
513-932-4400

Copperweld Robotics
1401 East Fourteen Mile Road
Troy, MI 48084
313-585-5972

Prab Robots, Inc.
5944 East Kilgore Road
Kalamazoo, MI 49003
616-349-8761

Robot Systems Inc.
110 Technology Parkway
Norcross, GA 30092
404-448-6700

Seiko Instruments USA, Inc.
Torrance, CA 90505
213-530-3400

Thermwood Machinery Mfg. Co.
P.O. Box 436
Dale, IN 47523
812-937-4476

Unimation, Inc.
(Headquarters)
Shelter Rock Lane
Danbury, CT 06810
203-744-1800

United States Robots Inc.
1000 Conshohocken Road
Conshohocken, P A 19428
215-825-8550

Westinghouse Electric Corp.
Industry Automation Division
400 Media Drive
Pittsbury, PA 15205
412-778-4300

Yaskawa Electric America, Inc.
Motoman Division
305 Era Drive
Northbrook, IL 60062
312-564-0070

Cybotech, Inc.
P.O. Box 88514
Indianapolis, IN 46208
317-298-5000

DeVilbiss Company
300 Phillips Avenue
Toledo, OH 43692
419-470-2081

General Electric
Automation Systems
1285 Boston Avenue
Bridgeport, CT 06602
203-382-2876

GM Fanuc Robotics Corp.
Northfield Hills Corp. Center
5600 New King Street
Troy, MI 48098
313-575-8311

Graco Robotics, Inc.
12898 Westmore Avenue
Livonia, MI 48150
313-261-3270

Hitachi America, Ltd.
6 Pearl Court
Allendale, NJ 07401
201-825-8000

International Business Machines Corp.
Advanced Manufacturing Systems
1000 N.W. 51st Street
Boca Raton, FL 33432
305-998-4191

Nordson Corporation
555 Jackson Street
P.O. Box 151
Amherst, OH 44001
216-988-9411

References

Books

Engelberger, Joseph F., *Robotics in Practice,* New York: Amacom, 1980.
Tanner, William R., ed., *Industrial Robots,* Dearborn, MI: Society of Manufacturing Engineers, 1979.

Reports

Society of Manufacturing Engineers, *SME Technical Reports and Papers* (papers and reports abstracted and indexed quarterly in *Technical Digest*) Dearborn, MI: Society of Manufacturing Engineers. Numerous specialized reports on robotics are published.

Proceedings of Symposia and Conferences

First National Symposium on Industrial Robots, Chicago, Apr 2 and 3, 1970. Chicago: IIT Research Institute, 1970.
Second International Symposium on Industrial Robots, Chicago, May 16, 17 and 18, 1972. Chicago: IIT Research Institute, 1972.
First Conference on Industrial Robot Technology, University of Nottingham (UK), Mar. 27, 28 and 29, 1973. Bedford, England: International Fluidics Services, 1973.
Second Conference on Industrial Robot Technology, University of Birmingham (UK), Mar. 27, 28 and 29, 1974. Bedford, England: International Fluidics Services, 1974.
Fourth International Symposium on Industrial Robots, Tokyo, Nov. 19, 20 and 21, 1974. Tokyo: Japan Industrial Robot Association, 1974.

Fifth International Symposium on Industrial Robots, Chicago, Sept. 22, 23 and 24, 1975. Chicago: IIT Research Institute, 1975.

Third Conference on Industrial Robot Technology and Sixth International Symposium on Industrial Robots, University of Nottingham (UK), Mar. 24, 25 and 26, 1976. Bedford, England: International Fluidics Services, 1976.

Seventh International Symposium on Industrial Robots, Tokyo, Oct. 19, 20 and 21, 1977. Tokyo: Japan Industrial Robot Association, 1977.

Eighth International Symposium on Industrial Robots and Fourth International Conference on Industrial Robot Technology, Stuttgart, May 30, 31 and June 1, 1978. Bedford, England.: International Fluidics Services, 1978.

Ninth International Symposium on Industrial Robots, Washington, D.C., Mar. 13, 14 and 15, 1979. Dearborn, MI: Society of Manufacturing Engineers, 1979.

Tenth International Symposium on Industrial Robots and Fifth International Conference on Industrial Robot Technology, Milan, Mar. 5, 6 and 7, 1980. Bedford, England.: International Fluidics Services, 1980.

Eleventh International Symposium on Industrial Robots, Tokyo, Oct. 7, 8 and 9, 1981. Tokyo: Japan Industrial Robot Association, 1981.

Twelfth International Symposium on Industrial Robots, Paris, June 9, 10 and 11, 1982. Paris: French Industrial Robot Association, 1981.

IV
LANGUAGES

18
An Overview of Programming Languages

Paul W. Abrahams

18.1 INTRODUCTION

Higher level programming languages have been in common use since the late 1950s; they were in limited use several years before that. The design of programming languages is now better understood than it was in those early days. Although designers still do not agree on what a programming language ought to be, they do seem to agree on the inadequacies of the early languages. The purpose of this article is to discuss several central issues in programming language design, showing how our understanding of those issues has improved and how they are treated in various programming languages. The issues are strong, representational, and weak typing; level of discourse; control structures; and program structure and representation. Examples based on current programming languages illustrate different views on these issues.

The ultimate shape of a programming language is influenced both by the designer's earlier experience and by the intended audience for the language. Most, but by no means all, programming languages, are clearly and explicitly based on an earlier language. Recently, PASCAL has been a popular takeoff point for language designers; PASCAL, in turn, has derived many of its ideas from ALGOL 60. In turn, ALGOL 60, the progenitor of many languages, adopted ideas from several sources, notably LISP, FORTRAN, and IAL (International Algebraic Language). The earliest languages had their roots in assembly language, which in turn was an improvement over coding in absolute octal notation. A notable exception is APL, whose roots (at least according to its author) lie almost entirely in mathematics.

Programming languages are usually designed with an application area in mind, and with some notation of the level of sophistication of the typical user. BASIC is an example of a language designed explicitly for unsophisticated users. COBOL was intended as a language to be read, and possibly written, by managers with not much knowledge of programming; that accounts for many of its English-like aspects. On the other hand, languages such as ADA* and C are clearly intended for users whose primary occupation is programming. Languages for systems programming are, almost by definition, designed to be used by professional programmers.

18.1 STRONG, REPRESENTATIONAL, AND WEAK TYPING

A **strongly typed language** is one in which the computational objects have descriptive information attached to them as part of their explicit definition in the program. The description of an object is known as its **type.** A strongly typed language must provide some way of defining new types. If an object is used in a context where its type is not appropriate, an error is generated, preferably when the program is translated but otherwise when the program is executed. The most strongly typed languages are those in which almost all type mismatches are detected during translation; i.e., they are determined by examining the program without actually executing it.

Representational typing is common among older programming languages. In a representationally typed lan-

*The Department of Defense, which has trademarked this language, prefers the usage "Ada."

guage the available types correspond closely to the available machine representations. A representationally typed language resembles a strongly typed language in that the type of every variable is known when the program is translated from its source form. The type may be determined either explicitly by declaration or implicitly by the form of the variable. However, in a representationally typed language the only available types are those of the machine representations; there is no facility for defining new types.

In a **weakly typed language** there is no way of specifying the type of a variable; a variable has the type of whatever object is currently assigned to it. As a program is executing, the type of a variable can change. Moreover, implicit conversions are usually defined between types, so that most assignments from one variable to another are legal no matter what the types involved.

ADA is an example of a very strongly typed language. In ADA, one can write:

$$
\begin{aligned}
&\text{type Apples is new integer;}\\
&\text{type Oranges is new integer;} \qquad (18.1)\\
&\text{Macs: Apples;}\\
&\text{Valencias: Oranges;}
\end{aligned}
$$

However, the expression,

$$\text{Macs + Valencias} \qquad (18.2)$$

is illegal, i.e., apples cannot be added to oranges. Although both Macs and Valencias have the same underlying representation (as defined in the type definitions), they are nonetheless regarded as having different and incompatible types. The fact that Apples and Oranges are defined types is essential; the incompatibility arises only because there is a way of defining such incompatible types.

Two other properties of ADA illustrate its strong typing. In ADA pointers to data objects can be defined, e.g.,

$$\text{type Book\_name is access Book;} \qquad (18.3)$$

Objects of type Book_name can be used only to reference Books; they cannot be used to reference other objects, even those whose representation is the same as that of a Book. In ADA, as in many other languages, one can define record types, which describe objects that in turn contain other objects of various types. A particular component of a record may be a variant part, i.e., its type may vary according to what is stored there at the moment. In ADA a variant part has a discriminant associated with it that specifies just what the actual type currently is, e.g.,

```
type vehicle_type is (car, truck);

type Vehicle(class: vehicle_type) is
  record
    cost: integer range 1 . . 10000:
    case class is
      when truck = >
        load_capacity: integer range 2000 . . 20000;
      when car = >
        passengers: integer range 2 . . 9;
    end case;
  end record;
```

$$(18.4)$$

In this illustration, the rules of ADA insure that the value of **passengers** will be accessed or changed only when **class** has the value car. Moreover, the only way to change the value of **class** for a particular object of type **Vehicle** is to assign a whole record to the object, thus insuring that the components are consistently described.

PASCAL is also considered a strongly typed language, but its constraints are far weaker than those of ADA. In PASCAL the following might be written:

$$
\begin{aligned}
&\text{type Apples = integer;} \qquad (18.5)\\
&\text{type Oranges = integer;}
\end{aligned}
$$

but in fact the two types, Apples and Oranges, are considered to be identical, and they can be used interchangeably with each other and with **integer**. In effect, PASCAL considers type names to be synonyms for the underlying representation type (integer, real, Boolean, etc.). It is still illegal in PASCAL to use an object of one representation type in a context where a different representation type is expected, that is, to use an integer where a Boolean is expected.

PASCAL, like ADA, does treat pointers to different types as distinct types themselves; there is no such thing in PASCAL as a pointer that can point to *anything*. In PASCAL a record with a variant part is known as a *variant record;* the particular type currently associated with the variant part is indicated by a *tag,* and the alternatives within the part are known as the *variants.* It is an error to misuse a variant record, i.e., to reference a variant that is not currently selected by the tag.

For example, one can write

$$\text{type vehicletype = (car, truck);}$$

```
type Vehicle = record
    cost: integer;
    case class: vehicletype of          (18.6)
        truck: (loadcapacity: 2000. .20000);
        car: (passengers: 2. .9)
end;
```

The setting of **class** determines which component is valid. If **class** is set to **truck** then it is an error to assign a value to **car**; nonetheless, PASCAL provides no way of detecting that the error has been made. In that sense its typing is weaker than that of ADA. Moreover, PASCAL also allows variants in records that have no tag at all; it is assumed that the context determines which variant is correct.

C, although not generally not considered a strongly typed language, comes close to being one, particularly if the UNIX TM program LINT, which checks for type violations, is employed. C, like PASCAL, starts with a set of representation types and then provides a facility for defining new types. C has typed pointers too, but variant records do not have tags associated with them at all. It is up to the C programmer to track the current type of a component of a variant record (called a **union** in C).

Most C compilers allow a variety of assignments among elements of different types, e.g., assigning a pointer to an integer, even though the official definition of the language considers such assignments illegal. For instance, if in C you write

```
int n: /* n is an integer */
char *cp; /* cp is a pointer to a character */   (18.7)
cp = n;
```

the value stored in n is simply moved to the variable cp, without any change at all. (Note that comments are found between /* and */.) This behavior is often useful in systems programming, but it is a clear violation of strong typing. In C the same effect can also be achieved by writing

$$cp = (char *) n;   (18.8)$$

which indicates explicitly that **n** is to be taken as a pointer to a character; conservative programming practice uses the second method. The C notation, known as *coercion,* is derived from ALGOL 68. ADA has a similar facility (unchecked_conversion) for changing type without changing representation, but indicating exactly what is going on.

FORTRAN is a good example of a representationally typed language. In FORTRAN 77 the available types are INTEGER, LOGICAL (for truth values), REAL, DOUBLE PRECISION, COMPLEX, and CHARACTER. These correspond quite obviously and directly with machine representations, although many possible representations exist for logical quantities. Arrays of elements of these types are provided, but records and pointers are not; if you want them you must simulate them using the available types. Officially, as in C, assignments between different types are illegal except in those cases, such as INTEGER to REAL, in which an implicit conversion takes place. Often compilers do not enforce the restrictions.

PL/I is also a representationally typed language, although a more powerful one than FORTRAN. PL/I provides a far larger variety of types, including a generalized POINTER which can point to anything. PL/I also provides for defining records, but not for defining record types. Thus in PL/I one can write

```
DECLARE
    1 PERSON,
        2 ID_NUMBER CHAR(9),
        2 AGE FIXED DECIMAL(3),
        2 NAME,
            3 (FIRST, LAST) CHAR(20) VARYING,
            3 INITIAL CHAR(1);
```
$$(18.9)$$

This declaration in effect associates two levels of record types with the variable PERSON: a PERSON contains an ID_NUMBER, an AGE, and a NAME, while the NAME in turn contains a FIRST name, a LAST name, and an INITIAL. One might also write

```
DECLARE PEOPLE(100) LIKE PERSON;    (18.10)
```

which establishes PEOPLE as an array of 100 PERSONs, each having the same structure as PERSON. The LIKE attribute thus provides a form of type definition for records, but this attribute has too many limitations to be considered as a true type definition facility.

PL/I provides implicit conversion from almost every type to another, and thus has virtually no provision for type checking. If a character string is added to a number, PL/I will convert the string to a number and then add the two numbers; if a scalar is added to an array, PL/I will promote the scalar to an array of the same dimensionality and then add the two arrays. Since so many different combinations are meaningful, forms that would be erroneous in PASCAL, say, are perfectly acceptable in PL/I.

COBOL is an extreme example of a representationally typed language; in COBOL, character strings are used as an almost universal type. A record might be defined (in the **DATA DIVISION**) as

```
01 ACTION-RECORD.
      02 ITEM-CODE PICTURE A(8).           (18.11)
      02 NUMBER-IN-STOCK PICTURE 99.
      02 UNIT-PRICE PICTURE $$$$.99.
```

The second two components are both sequences of characters that represent numerical values: in the case of UNIT-PRICE the declaration indicates how that value is to be formatted for input or output. Later one might write

$$\text{77 ACTION-INPUT PICTURE X(17).} \quad (18.12)$$

indicating that an **ACTION-INPUT** consists of 17 arbitrary characters. Now suppose that the **PROCEDURE DIVISION** contains the statement

```
MOVE ACTION-RECORD TO ACTION-INPUT.
```
$$(18.13)$$

The characters in **ACTION-RECORD** are simply moved en bloc to **ACTION-INPUT**. Only the representation (as a sequence of characters) is significant here; the actual type structures (a record of three components versus a single string) are entirely ignored. Thus not only is COBOL representationally typed; there is only one representation! (However, numerical items can be declared COMPUTATIONAL, indicating that they are to be stored in a format that will yield greater efficiency in arithmetic operations.)

APL is a good example of a weakly typed language. In APL there are no declarations at all, so that the type of a variable is determined solely by what is assigned to it at the moment. That might be a number, a string, or an array. Whether a number is real or an integer is determined by its value; if the number is within some "fuzz" of an integer, then it is treated as an integer (a heuristic that works remarkably well).

SNOBOL4 is like APL in that it has no declarations of variables, but it goes even further: the set of variables itself can change dynamically. For example, in SNOBOL4 you might write

$$\text{SEAT = ROW POSITION} \quad (18.14)$$
$$\text{\$SEAT = 'WILSON'}$$

The first assignment indicates that **SEAT** is a character string obtained by concatenating **ROW** and **POSITION**. (Assuming that **ROW** and **POSITION** are non-null, then the concatenation necessarily yields a character string.) If **POSITION** happens to be a number, it will be implicitly converted to the character string that represents it, e.g., 24 will be converted to a string consisting of 2 followed by 4. The second assignment indicates that the string **WILSON** is assigned to the variable whose name is the current value of **SEAT**. Thus if **SEAT** has the value "K24," then **WILSON** is assigned to the variable K24. That variable might or might not exist prior to the first assignment. This example also shows that SNOBOL, like PL/I, provides an implicit conversion in just about every context where it would be meaningful.

LISP, also a weakly typed language, has *lists* and *atoms* as the usual objects. Lists are recursively defined in terms of atoms, which are elementary objects of different kinds. LISP has no declarations, so that the type of object assigned to a variable is unconstrained.

BASIC is an interesting case; it is essentially a representationally typed language, but its treatment of numbers is similar to that of APL. In BASIC the name of a variable determines its type. If the name ends with $ it is a string; otherwise it is a number. No aggregates other than arrays are provided. However, whether a number is or is not an integer is determined by its value, as in APL, so that the same variable might contain a real at one time and an integer at another time (but never a string).

The major advantage of *strong typing* is safety in programming; it allows the compiler to intercept errors caused by the use of an object in the wrong context. Furthermore, many errors that the compiler cannot catch can still be detected during execution. In addition, strong typing encourages a programming style that employs abstract data types. An **abstract data type** is a data type for which the actual representation is deliberately made inaccessible. You can change the representation of an abstract data type without having to modify all of the places it is used. Furthermore, abstract data types discourage programming techniques based on representational accidents; such techniques are prone to errors when the representation is modified. But strong typing has two major disadvantages: it makes programming more laborious, and the language is harder to compile.

Weak typing has complementary attributes. A weakly typed language is easier to use, particularly for the novice writing small programs. All the syntactic overhead associated with declarations and types simply disappears; most of the work is done for the programmer. At the same time, a program written in a weakly typed language is vulnerable to errors that could be detected in a strongly typed language. If a number is assigned to a variable intended only for strings, the implementation will probably never reveal such.

Representational typing has little except inertia to recommend it; it has neither the advantages of weak typing nor of strong typing. Representationally typed languages have survived mainly because they became established very early, so that many programmers know them and there are large libraries of programs in these languages. Also, representational languages may have other advantages unrelated to their type structure that convince programmers to use them. Nonetheless, designers of programming languages, who rarely agree on anything, do seem to agree that representational typing is obsolete.

18.2 LEVEL OF DISCOURSE

The **level of discourse** of a programming language is its distance from the underlying properties of the machine on which it is implemented. A **low level language** is close to the machine, and hence provides access to its facilities almost directly; a **high level language** is far from the machine, and hence insulated from the machine's peculiarities. A language may provide both low level and high level constructs. Weakly typed languages are usually high level, but often provide some way of calling low level subroutines. Strongly typed languages are more likely to be low level, but are not necessarily so.

The level of a language may be difficult to define because of the role of user-defined and library functions and procedures. FORTRAN is a low level language; yet it can be made to function as a high level langauge by the provision of an appropriate set of subroutines designed for the application. A program then may consist of little more than subroutine calls, and the actual structure of FORTRAN is only marginally relevant.

APL, SNOBOL, and SETL (a set-theoretic language) are all high level languages. Each of them has a fundamental data type that pervades the language. In APL it is the array; in SNOBOL it is the string; and in SETL it is the set. Each of these languages provides other data types, but the tone of each language is established by its fundamental type.

In all three of these languages, high level operators are provided for the fundamental types, while the actual representation of the types is invisible and inaccessible to the user. Indeed, the actual representation may even vary from one implementation to another, but programs using these representations will still be valid in all the implementations.

The power of **APL** is illustrated by the following sequence of operations:

$$A \leftarrow 2\ 5\ 3\ 10\ 5\ 8\ 7$$
$$(\iota\rho A \neq A)/A \qquad (18.15)$$
$$2\ 5\ 10\ 8$$

The first statement assigns a vector of 7 elements to A. The following statement produces a value, which is then printed (the third line). The printed value is a vector of those elements x of A such that $x(i)$ is not equal to i, i.e., the value is not equal to its index. It is computed by taking the shape (dimensionality) of A, using the ρ operator; the result is 7. Next the ι operator is applied to yield a vector of the integers from 1 to 7. This vector is compared to A itself, and the result of the comparison is a vector of 0s and 1s:

$$1\ 1\ 0\ 1\ 0\ 1\ 0 \qquad (18.16)$$

The vector contains a 1 in those positions where $x(i)$ differs from i. Finally the compression operator / extracts from A just those elements for which the left operand of / contains a 1. The final result is the vector indicated; note that its length depends on the original value of A. APL has a large collection of powerful operators such as those shown in this example; one can imagine what the equivalent program in a lower level language would look like.

Similarly, in **SNOBOL4** one could write

```
       TEXT = 'THE LAST OF THE MOHICANS'
LISP: TEXT 'S' = 'TH' :S(LISP)
       OUTPUT = TEXT
```
$$(18.17)$$

and

        THE LATHT OF THE MOHICANTH   (18.18)

would print out. The second statement does most of the work: it searches **TEXT** for an occurrence of S and replaces it by TH. As long as the replacement succeeds, the statement is reexecuted. When it fails, control moves to the next statement and the current value of **TEXT** is printed.

In the **SETL** language, sets are the primary data structure. A sample SETL sequence is

```
n := 3;
primes := n1;
```

```
(while n ≤ 101)
    if not ( ∃y in primes | n // y = 0)     (18.19)
        primes : = primes + n;
    n := n + 2;
end while;
```

This program fragment sets n to 3 and primes to the null set. It then iterates through odd values of n from 3 to 101, searching for primes. For each candidate value n, it checks whether there exists a number y already in the set such that y evenly divides n. If no such y exists, n is added to the set. The resulting value of primes is a set of the primes from 3 to 101.

In all three of these languages, we see operations requested that have no obvious relationship to particular primitive machine operations. In fact, it is not even obvious how the data involved is actually stored. High level languages such as these require an elaborate storage allocation system, including the storage recovery technique known as "garbage collection." Since the implementation needs to maintain close control over data objects, their representations and where they are stored, the programmer cannot be allowed to manipulate these objects to any significant degree. However, in the case of SNOBOL4 at least, there is a facility for calling FORTRAN programs to carry out computations that are inefficient or inconvenient in SNOBOL4 or are already available in prewritten programs.

PASCAL, FORTRAN, COBOL, C, and PL/I are all relatively low level languages, in which the correspondence between a program and the computations it causes to be executed is fairly obvious. However, in some cases a program action may correspond to a call on an elaborate subroutine, e.g., an output formatter or a sort program. None of these languages have the storage management systems found in the foregoing high level languages, and in most cases it is possible to manipulate actual machine locations; FORTRAN and C are particularly adept at that. For all of these low level languages, how data is stored is quite clear, and in fact programs written in these languages often rely on particular properties of the arrangement of stored data. A good example is the use of the FORTRAN EQUIVALENCE statement to reference the same storage location under two different names, and often with two different sets of attributes.

ADA is an interesting example of a language with both low level and high level properties. ADA provides quite explicit mechanisms for specifying the layout of data structures in storage, for accessing particular machine lo-

cations and even for communicating with machine interrupt routines. Yet its type definitional facilities promote an abstract style of programming in which objects are manipulated without regard to their actual representation. Moreover, ADA has another property in common with high level languages: automatic storage allocation. In ADA you can write

$$b := \text{new buffer}(100); \qquad (18.20)$$

thus causing storage for a new object of type buffer, with size 100, to be assigned to b. When this newly created buffer is no longer accessible, the storage for it is reclaimed using the garbage collection techniques mentioned earlier. Thus ADA, too, has a storage allocation system that is not accessible to the programmer and that must not be interfered with.

High level languages have far more expressive power than low level languages and the modes of expression are well integrated into the language. One can write quite short programs which accomplish very complex operations. Yet these languages are not suited for applications, such as systems programming, which require close control over machine details. Moreover, despite a great deal of effort devoted to optimization, particularly in the case of SETL, high level languages are relatively inefficient. It is faster to write a program in a high level language, but the program will probably take much longer to run. Despite its naturalness for expressing numerical algorithms, APL has not made major inroads into the domain of number-crunching programs, where FORTRAN is still the dominant language by far.

Control Structures

The control structures of a programming language determine the sequence of computation. Traditional machines have a limited repertoire of control structures (sequential execution, conditional and unconditional transfer, and possibly subroutine calls). This limited repertoire is reflected in the control structures of traditional programming languages. Recent developments in programming languages have led rather than followed machine design; data flow languages (not discussed here) and their relation to data flow machines are good examples.

BASIC is a good language to examine since its control structures are elementary. In BASIC, statements have line numbers associated with them (though there can be more than one statement on a line). A conditional transfer takes the form

$$\text{IF condition THEN line number} \qquad (18.21)$$

in which control is transferred to the specified line number if the condition is true. The condition takes the form of a relation (equal, less than, etc.) between two expressions. The GOTO statement transfers control to a given line number

$$\text{GOTO line number} \qquad (18.22)$$

unconditionally. One can also obtain iteration in BASIC using the FOR-NEXT construct:

```
FOR N = 1 TO 10
    PRINT N; N*N
NEXT N                        (18.23)
```

This loop will print values of N and N*N for N ranging from 1 to 10.

The GOSUB statement in BASIC transfers control to a subroutine,

$$\text{GOSUB line number} \qquad (18.24)$$

while RETURN returns control. However, BASIC subroutines have no explicit boundaries. The effect of the GOSUB is merely to store the location in the program where the GOSUB was executed: control returns to that place when the corresponding RETURN is executed.

Oddly enough, some very high level languages have some very low level control constructs. In SNOBOL4, for instance, subroutines resemble those of BASIC in that they do not have fixed boundaries; a subroutine consists of whatever statements happen to be executed in response to a subroutine call. Moreover, the only other way to transfer control in a SNOBOL program is with a GOTO (expressed as part of a statement), although the GOTO can be triggered by an ingenious success-failure mechanism, discussed below. There are no looping constructs in SNOBOL, nor are there conditional statements; these effects are achieved by combining GOTOs with the success-failure mechanism. Similarly, APL has just the GO TO and the function call as its control mechanisms, though again one can achieve quite sophisticated effects by constructing functions that select an appropriate target for a GO TO.

FORTRAN has control structures much like those of BASIC, although a FORTRAN subroutine call is more powerful. A FORTRAN program may consist of a sequence of independent subroutines and functions (a function is a subroutine that returns a value). Functions may be called by function references in expressions: subroutines are called by CALL statements. A function or subroutine may have arguments passed to it. Also, in FORTRAN 77, an IF statement may have an ELSE part associated with it; the ELSE part specifies actions to be taken if the condition in the IF part is false.

$$\text{IF condition THEN statement 1 ELSE statement 2}$$
$$(18.25)$$

COBOL's control structures are about at the same level as those of FORTRAN, although COBOL does have an interesting variant on the subroutine call: the PERFORM verb. The COBOL statement

```
PERFORM FIND-TOWN THRU COMPLETE-TOWN
    VARYING TOWN-NUMBER FROM 1 BY 1
    UNTIL TOWN-NUMBER = 100
```
$$(18.26)$$

causes control to be transferred to the paragraph (or section) named FIND-TOWN. When control reaches the end of the paragraph (or section) COMPLETE-TOWN, then control returns to PERFORM. Each time control is at the PERFORM, TOWN-NUMBER is incremented by 1. Thus the paragraph is executed for successive values of TOWN-NUMBER from 1 to 100. After the last such execution, control passes to the statement after the PERFORM.

An interesting property of the PERFORM verb is that the iterated section of the program is off somewhere else, rather like a subroutine. In fact, a variant on the PERFORM verb allows a section of text to be PERFORMed without any iteration control at all. In addition to PERFORM, COBOL also has a CALL verb which allows a subroutine to be called with parameters.

Although BASIC, FORTRAN, and COBOL all have subroutine calls, none of them allow **recursive subroutines,** that is, subroutines that call themselves. In contrast, LISP not only allows recursion but uses recursion as one of its principal control mechanisms. For instance, in LISP one can write a function to search a list for a particular element. By using a variation on the standard LISP built-in names, such a function might be defined as

```
(SEARCH (LAMBDA(ELT LIST) (COND
    ((NULL LIST) FALSE)
    ((EQUAL (FIRST LIST) ELT) TRUE)
    (T (SEARCH ELT (REST LIST)))))))    (18.24)
```

If we overlook LISP's rather odd syntax, it is easy to follow how this function works. LAMBDA defines the parameters to the function, which are ELT, the element we seek, and LIST, the list in which we seek ELT. COND specifies two conditions that we test. If LIST is empty (null) then clearly ELT cannot be contained in it, so we return FALSE. If the first element of LIST is equal to ELT, then we have found it, so we return TRUE. Otherwise—and here is the interesting case—we search the rest of the list for ELT. But this task is precisely what SEARCH does, so we invoke SEARCH in order to accomplish it. In other words, we define the function using its own definition in a simpler case. The validity of the method depends on the fact that the recursive call on SEARCH applies to a shorter list than the original one, so that eventually we either find ELT or run out of list elements.

PL/I includes control structures similar to those of FORTRAN, and also has a facility for handling exception conditions, as will be discussed shortly. The DO statement in PL/I, which controls iterations, is more elaborate than the FORTRAN DO statement. A typical PL/I DO group is

```
DO N = 1 TO M BY 5 WHILE (X(N) > 0);
    Y(N) = X(N) + 1;
    Z(N) = X(N) − 1:
END;
```
(18.28)

This loop can terminate either because N reaches its limit of M, or because, for this N, X(N) is not greater than 0. PL/I also allows a DO with a WHILE only, as in

$$DO\ WHILE\ (X(N) <= X(N + 1));\quad (18.29)$$

DO loops can have negative as well as positive increments, the former causing a loop to run backwards. PL/I also allows recursive procedure calls, although a recursive procedure must be labelled as such.

PL/I provides for handling exceptional conditions such as a subscript out of range, arithmetic overflow or end of file on an input file. Conditions may be either enabled or disabled: when a condition is **enabled,** the compiler checks for it: when the condition is **disabled,** the compiler need not check for it. (If the test for the condition is relatively cheap, the compiler may check for it anyway.) The intent is that conditions are disabled only when there is good reason to expect that they will not arise. For example, if the following is written,

```
(SUBSCRIPTRANGE): A(I)
         = A(I − 1) + A(I + 1);   (18.30)
```

then the compiler will check the value of I to make sure that it is within the bounds of the array A. One can control the action taken in response to a SUBSCRIPTRANGE error by writing, for instance

```
ON SUBSCRIPTRANGE CALL SUBR__ERROR;
```
(18.31)

When a SUBSCRIPTRANGE error is detected the SUBR __ERROR routine is called. PL/I also allows the programmer to define on-conditions, e.g.,

```
IF DATVAL > MAXVAL THEN
    SIGNAL CONDITION(VALUE__ERROR);   (18.32)
```

with the accompanying statement

```
ON CONDITION(VALUE__ERROR)
        GO TO NEXT__CASE;   (18.33)
```

Executing the ON statement associates an action with a condition (which may be overridden by a subsequent ON statement); the action is actually carried out when the tested condition arises, either because it is signalled or because it is a predefined condition and the executing code detects that condition.

The advocates of structured programming recommend a programming style in which GO TO statements are not used and the only control structures allowed are DO WHILE, IF-THEN-ELSE, subroutine calls, and sequential execution. However, an exception is usually made for case statements. Case statements appear in PASCAL, a language usually recommended for structured programming. The control structures of PASCAL are like those we have seen. A typical PASCAL case statement is

```
case i of
    0: x := ln(x);
    1: x := sin(x);
    2: x := cos(x);
    3: x := exp(x);
    4: x := ln(x)
end                   (18.34)
```

The expression following **case** is evaluated and to select one of the cases, which has a statement associated with it. For example, if i has the label 2, then the statement x := cos(x) is executed. Case labels must be constants, but more than one label can be associated with a particular case, thus

$$6, 7, 8:\ x := cos(x);\quad (18.35)$$

The C language has control structures similar to the ones we have seen, though it has no exception-handling mechanism. It does have two statements useful for terminating loops: **break** and **continue**. The **break** statement, when executed, causes termination of the innermost loop containing the break. The **continue** statement, when executed, causes termination of the current iteration of the loop, so that execution resumes with the next iteration.

ADA has almost all of the control structures mentioned so far: recursive procedure calls, iteration statements, case selection, conditional and unconditional GO TOs, exception handling, and breaking out of loops. In addition, it has facilities for **multitasking,** allowing two portions of a program to execute simultaneously. The major design problem in multitasking languages is finding an effective means for parallel tasks to communicate and to synchronize their activities. ADA's mechanism to achieve this is the **rendezvous.** Two tasks are involved: the *calling task* and the *called task*. The called task must explicitly be created as a task; the calling task need not be.

The **called task** is specified using the keyword **task** and an entry declaration in turn specifying parameters that might be passed to the task. To initiate a called task, one executes a program unit in which that task is declared. Execution of the calling task proceeds until control reaches a call on an entry of the called task. Meanwhile, execution of the called task proceeds until control reaches an accept statement. If the call is reached first, the called task waits: if the accept statement is reached first, the calling task waits. The **rendezvous** is the point at which the calling task has reached its call statement and the called task has reached its accept statement. Parameters of the call are transmitted to the called task and both tasks resume execution. A task may be called by more than one task; when that happens, callers wait in a queue and are serviced one by one as the called task repeatedly executes accept statements.

SNOBOL4 has a control structure based on the notion of success and failure. Evaluation of an expression may fail in a number of different ways, e.g., not finding a particular pattern in a string, or not satisfying a particular test. Failure is not generally considered an error; it is simply a negative test outcome. For example, if you write

$$\text{GE(X, 2) :S(BIG)F(SMALL)} \qquad (18.36)$$

the predicate **GE** tests whether **X** is greater than 2; for x $\geq$ 2, the predicate succeeds and control goes to the statement labelled **BIG**; for x < 2 the predicate fails and con-

trol goes to the statement labelled **SMALL**. Success and failure are primitive notions in the **ICON** language, a successor to SNOBOL4 developed by Griswold and Hanson. In ICON, these notions are used in a far more general and powerful way than in SNOBOL4. For instance, in ICON the expression

repeat e

repeatedly evaluates **e** until a condition described earlier fails.

ICON also provides **backtracking,** implicit in the pattern matching mechanisms of SNOBOL4. Using backtracking, one can generate a sequence of values that are used in an outer context. If evaluation succeeds in the outer context, then no new values are used; if evaluation fails, then a new value is taken from the sequence and the evaluation is attempted with the new value. Backtracking is used extensively in artificial intelligence programming, beyond the scope of this article.

SETL is another high level language with unusual control structures. In SETL, iterations can be specified over sets, e.g., the set of primes in the example given earlier. The two iterators are the two set quantifiers, $\forall$ (for all) and $\exists$ (there exists). The $\forall$ quantifier applies an operation to all elements of a set; the $\exists$ quantifier searches a set for an element with a given property. In addition, a set can be created using a set former. A **set former** specifies an expression, $e(x1, x2, \ldots, xn)$, a collection of sets, $\{e1, e2, \ldots, en\}$, and a predicate, $C(x1, x2, \ldots, \times n)$. The set formed by the set former contains all values obtainable by applying e to elements of the sets $e1$ through en that satisfy the predicate C.

Program Structure and Representation

Early programming languages, of which FORTRAN is a good example, were oriented in terms of punched cards and batch processing. In FORTRAN, for instance, a statement occupies a single *line image,* in specified columns. The statement proper occupies columns 7–72; columns 1–5 contain the statement number, while column 6 is reserved to indicate statement continuations. A FORTRAN program consists of a sequence of separately compiled subprograms; communication among the subprograms is accomplished either by passing parameters or by placing data in **COMMON,** a storage area reserved for such communication. The FORTRAN character set is limited to the characters available on early keypunches. In particular, comparison operators are indicated by notations such as .GT. rather than by >.

The structure and representation of COBOL have a similar flavor to that of FORTRAN. A line of a COBOL program is divided into *zones* and there are restrictions on what can go into each zone. The original version of COBOL required a program written as a single unit; the 1974 COBOL standard allows, as an option, programs consisting of several independent parts which can be compiled separately.

A COBOL program unit consists of four divisions: the IDENTIFICATION DIVISION (really just heading information): the ENVIRONMENT DIVISION, which contains machine dependent specifications: the DATA DIVISION, describing the data structures of the program; and the PROCEDURE DIVISION, which gives the program itself. These divisions are divided in turn into *sections* and *paragraphs,* each labelled with a section name or a paragraph name. In the first three divisions, at least, particular sections are used for particular purposes, e.g., the WORKING-STORAGE SECTION in the DATA DIVISION. In the PROCEDURE DIVISION, the sections and paragraphs are selected by the programmer to represent the structure of the computations to be carried out.

Block structure, with or without modifications, is common to many of the programming languages discussed in this article. Block structure originated with Algol 60. In a block structured language, program units such as procedures and code segments may be *nested* one within another. A unit typically starts with a *header statement* and ends with an *end statement.* Examples of fully or partially block structured languages are PL/I, PASCAL, C and ADA. Of these, all but PASCAL allow a program to be divided into separately compiled units. (Some implementations of Pascal allow separate compilation also.) Block structured languages generally have **free form syntax:** line boundaries are ignored, and statements are either delimited or terminated by semicolons. PASCAL uses the semicolon as a statement delimiter; the others use it as a statement terminator. The distinction shows up in the last statement of a unit; in PASCAL, the last statement does not have a semicolon, but in the other languages it does.

In PL/I, a program consists of a sequence of external procedures, each of which in turn may contain internal procedures. The procedures communicate with each other through passed parameters and through external storage.

In C, a program exists in a sequence of files, each containing some data declarations and some procedures. The data declarations can be either external, and thus communicated among the files, or static, and thus internal to a single file. Procedures are external by default. Proce-

dures cannot be nested within each other, but other program units can be. Files are compiled independently and then linked together.

ADA provides several kinds of program units which can be nested, notably the **package,** which contains a set of definitions, both of procedures and of data. Typically a package implements an abstract data type, providing both the necessary data structures and the operators which apply to the data type. ADA has **private types** that localize the implementation of an abstract data type within a package, while still providing for a declaration of the same data type and name outside the package (so the data type can actually be used). ADA also provides a mechanism, the **use clause,** for making names available to some program units but not others. In effect, a unit gains access to a name and what it denotes by specifying that name in a use clause. This contrasts with the rules for sharing data in, say, PL/I, where two nonnested procedures that want to share data must do so through *externally* declared names which are universally visible.

ADA allows separate compilation not only of program units at the outermost level, but also of nested program units. Since the compiled code for an embedded unit needs to reference information in its containing unit, linking of separately compiled units is far more complicated than it is in any of the other languages considered here.

LISP has a program structure which differs from other languages. A program is written as a sequence of *actions,* which can be, among other things, the definition of a LISP function. Each action is written as a LISP expression using the LISP notation for lists. Thus LISP programs (an example was given earlier) look like LISP data.

PL/I, C, PASCAL, and ADA all are defined in terms of moderate size general purpose character sets—EBCDIC, ASCII, or (for the original version of PASCAL) CDC display code. APL, on the other hand, has a character set unique to itself, causing some difficulty for the language's implementors, since the APL character set is often not available on the hardware at hand. The APL operator symbols are mathematical in nature; some of them are double characters formed by the overstriking of two single characters. When APL was first implemented, a typeball was produced with the APL character set (for Selectric-compatible printing devices), so that the tradition was established early of using these special characters rather than making some ad hoc substitution. SETL also has an unusual character set, but the existing implementation of SETL makes do with substitutions from ASCII.

Almost any programming language can be used interactively with a terminal as an input/output device. However, APL and BASIC have interactive operation as part of their philosophy. In both languages, an user at a terminal can type expressions as well as programs. When an expression is typed, it is evaluated and the result displayed. In BASIC, when a line with a line number is typed, the line is inserted into the program rather than executed. In APL, when the user types an assignment, it is executed but nothing is printed. However, one can also operate in function definition mode, in which the typed-in statements are added to a function definition.

Concluding Remarks

This overview has concentrated on some of the central properties of programming languages, with examples provided from popular languages. Many aspects of languages have been omitted or treated only tangentially, such as the types of data available and facilities for input and output. The reader should also be aware that new programming languages are continually being devised and that existing languages do not reflect current development in research. Nonetheless, one who understands the significant questions to ask about a programming language is in a good position to understand a new language and how it relates to existing ones.

REFERENCES

American National Standard Programming Language COBOL, Document X3.23—1974. New York: American National Standards Institute, 1974.

American National Standard Programming Language PL/I, Document X3.53—1976. New York: American National Standards Institute, 1976.

American National Standard Programming Language FORTRAN, Document X3.9—1978. New York: American National Standards Institute, 1978.

Dewar, Robert B. K., Arthur Grand, Ssu-Cheng Liu, and Jacob T. Schwartz, "Programming by Refinement, as exemplified by the SETL Representation Sublanguage," *ACM Transactions Programming Languages and Systems,* Vol. 1, No. 1 (July 1979), pp. 27–49.

Gilman, Leonard, and Allen J. Rose, *APL: An Interactive Approach,* 2nd Ed. New York: John Wiley & Sons, 1976.

Griswold, R. E., J. F. Poage, and I. P. Polonsky, *The SNOBOL4 Programming Language.* Englewood Cliffs, N.J.: Prentice-Hall, 1970.

Griswold, R., "The ICON Programming Language: a New Approach to High-Level String Processing." *Proceedings 1979 Annual Conference* (Detroit, Oct. 29–31, 1979), New York: Association for Computing Machinery, pp. 8–13.

Jensen, Kathleen, and Niklaus Wirth, *Pascal User Manual and Report,* 2nd Ed. New York: Springer-Verlag, 1976.

Kemeny, J. G., and T. E. Kurtz, *BASIC Programming.* New York: John Wiley & Sons, 1967.

Kernighan, Brian W., and Dennis M. Ritchie, *The C Programming Language.* Englewood Cliffs, N.J.: Prentice-Hall, 1978.

McCarthy, J., P. W. Abrahams, D. J. Edwards, T. P. Hart, and M. I. Levin, *LISP 1.5 Programmer's Manual.* Cambridge, MA: MIT Press, 1966.

United States Department of Defence, *Reference Manual for the Ada Programming Language,* July 1980.

19
FORTRAN

Walter S. Brainerd

UNICOMP
University of New Mexico

19.1 INTRODUCTION

FORTRAN was developed by a small group at IBM under the leadership of John Backus. It is difficult to appreciate what a radical idea it was in the middle 1950s to propose a high level language as the tool that would be needed most by a programmer interested in development of efficient programs for science and engineering applications. The first FORTRAN compiler was delivered for use on the IBM 704 in 1957. The quality of the object code produced by this compiler is amazing, even in the context of current optimization techniques.

It was not long before other computer manufacturers, mainly in the United States, developed FORTRAN compilers for their own machines. However, during the same time, ALGOL was developed and adopted by many programmers in Europe. It certainly can be argued that ALGOL was superior to Fortran in several respects. But Fortran was available on a large number of machines in the U.S., it was efficient, and it had reasonable facilities for input and output, a property not shared by ALGOL. Thus FORTRAN soon became the most popular programming language for applications involving numerical computations.

19.2 STANDARDIZATION

The basic strategy of IBM's competitors was to provide a compiler with the functionality of IBM FORTRAN, but with some features added as a competitive inducement. While these new features contributed to the development of the language, they also had the effect of creating a myriad of incompatible dialects.

At that time, the predecessor organizations of ANSI (the American National Standards Institute) and CBEMA (the Computer and Business Equipment Manufacturing Association) undertook a massive standardization effort in a variety of data processing areas. Someone had the daring idea of including programming languages, and FORTRAN, ALGOL, and COBOL were selected as candidates. In October 1964, the proposed draft FORTRAN standard was published. In 1966 the standard was adopted in the United States, and shortly thereafter it was also adopted as an international standard. Thus Fortran became the first programming language to be standardized.

Even before 1966, many extensions beyond the 1966 standard had already appeared in FORTRAN implementations. After investigating how these extensions could be standardized, the ANSI committee voted in 1968 to revise the standard. The revised standard was produced in 1977 and soon thereafter officially adopted both as the U.S. and the international standard. It is this current standard version, informally called **FORTRAN 77,** which is discussed in the remainder of this chapter.

19.3 THE STRENGTHS AND WEAKNESSES OF FORTRAN

FORTRAN was developed in what is now regarded as the initial period of development of computer science. Why, after all these years, with the development of many new langauges, is an old timer like FORTRAN still one of the more popular languages? Some of the reasons have already been mentioned; however, there are others. It has been widely used for many years. There is a tremendous economic investment in FORTRAN programs; an organization does not shift languages unless there is a very big advantage in doing so. A large number of programmers are trained in FORTRAN. Retraining people is also expensive and most people tend to resist change.

Pure inertia, of course, is not the main cause of the continued popularity of FORTRAN. The language is still fairly easy to learn. As a complement to its large scale virtues, it is easy to write simple small FORTRAN programs to perform simple tasks. FORTRAN is widely available, and it is efficient.

Areas of Application

FORTRAN continues to be most widely used in applications requiring heavy amounts of numerical computation. FORTRAN may still be the best language available for programming tasks of this kind. On many of the largest and fastest machines designed primarily for large numerical computational problems, FORTRAN may be the only choice. In addition, language development for large scientific programs involving the introduction of array processing and numerical precision usually occurs in the FORTRAN environment.

Efficiency

As already noted, FORTRAN continues to have the property that made it competitive in the first place. Although the language has become more complicated in the last 25 years, the compilers for it still generate efficient code. Excellent optimizing compilers have been the hallmark of FORTRAN implementations from the first one produced in 1957.

Portability

Another important reason for the continued popularity of FORTRAN is its availability on a wide variety of computers. COBOL is probably the only language that is as widely available as FORTRAN, but COBOL is designed for applications requiring sophisticated data manipulations, whereas FORTRAN is designed for scientific and engineering applications.

Virtually every implementation of FORTRAN includes features not described in the standard. In fact, the standard explicitly permits such extensions; they stimulate development of the language. However, the programmer who wants to write a portable program must be aware of nonstandard features.

Portability takes many guises sometimes ignored by programmers and managers. Even when programs are not used on more than one machine at a time, it is likely that a useful program will need to run on the *next machine* acquired by the organization. The next machine and its FORTRAN compiler may be provided by a different vendor. Any nonstandard features used in this program may have to be removed, possibly at great cost.

A programmer who is careful to stick to standard FORTRAN can get a program running on many different kinds of computers with a reasonabe amount of effort. It is essential that the programmer refers to a manual that indicates nonstandard features (e.g., by shading on the pages). Equally valuable is a compiler option that flags nonstandard features. With these two tools, it is possible to decide when a particular nonstandard language feature is beneficial.

In general, there are few reasons to select one FORTRAN compiler over another based on language features, most of which are relatively unimportant and usually best not used anyway. However, for certain types of programming applications, a few extensions are quite beneficial.

Array processing features are very convenient at times and on some machines provide substantial improvements in execution performance. Additional array features probably will be included in the next standard version of FORTRAN in a form slightly different from anything available now. Some programs require manipulation of the bits that make up a single word; such features may never be in standard FORTRAN because they tend to be nonportable.

Separate Compilation

A very important feature of FORTRAN is the capability to compile parts of the program separately and then *link* or *load* the separately compiled parts together to form a running program. One advantage to this feature is that it is easy to use a general procedure (e.g., for solving an equation) in many different programs without having to rewrite the procedure or take any special steps to make sure it is part of the program.

Another advantage is that the programmer may make a small change to one part of the program and revise the entire program by compiling only the changed part and then linking it in to replace the old portion. For large programs, this can save a considerable amount of compilation time.

Weaknesses

FORTRAN has some definite weaknesses; at the current stage of language development, no language excels in all possible application areas. FORTRAN's weakest area is data structures, both large and small. For example, it is not possible to have a data object that consists of three components: a person's name which is a character string, the person's hourly wage which is a real number, and the person's identification number which is an integer. In other languages, such as COBOL, PL/I, and PASCAL, this is possible. Also large data structures that must be accessed in complex ways, such as bulky data bases, are not easy to implement in FORTRAN.

FORTRAN, like any language, has many minor faults. Compared to some more modern languages, the syntax is not elegant. This makes it hard to remember how to write some things. Modern control structures are lacking, but probably will be added in the next revision of the standard. Other features which are lacking are not considered important by some programmers, but are very helpful when needed, for example, recursion.

19.4 LANGUAGE FEATURES

Some of the main features of FORTRAN are described here as a sampling of what is available.

Evaluating Mathematical Formulas

The name FORTRAN comes from the words *FOR*mula *TRAN*slation, so the ease of expressing mathematical formulas in the language is not surprising. It correspondingly easy to write a complete FORTRAN program to evaluate a mathematical expression. For example

$$\text{PRINT} *, \text{SIN}(2.7) + 2*\text{COS}(2.7) \quad (19.1)$$
$$\text{END}$$

is a complete FORTRAN program that evaluates sin (2.7) + 2 cos (2.7) and prints the result. This may not seem like such an important feature, since it is possible to get the same result by pushing a few buttons on a handheld calculator. However, suppose the task at hand is to evaluate this same expression for the numbers 2.1, 2.2, 2.3, . . . , 2.9? This becomes quite tedious with a calculator, but can be done by a FORTRAN program with

just one more line:

$$\text{DO} \quad 8 \text{ X} = 2.1, 2.9, 0.1$$
$$8 \qquad \text{PRINT} *, \text{SIN}(X) + 2*\text{COS}(X) \quad (19.2)$$
$$\text{END}$$

The DO statement says to repeat the PRINT statement once for each value of x from 2.1 to 2.9 in increments of 0.1. Of course, it is possible to have a whole block of statements executed once for each value of X. This makes the DO statement a powerful FORTRAN feature.

Even though writing this program is easy, getting it to run on a particular computer may be easy or difficult. In the simplest case, a text editor is needed to create a file called, say, CALCULATION and then a command such as RUN CALCULATION is typed. Whether running this program on a particular computer is difficult or hard, the task is comparable to getting a program in any other language to run on the same computer.

The IF Statement

A second basic feature of FORTRAN that allows the programmer to specify which statements are executed is the IF-THEN-ELSE construct. A simple example follows:

$$\text{IF (X .LT. 0) THEN}$$
$$\quad \text{Y1} = \text{SIN}(X + 2)$$
$$\quad \text{Y2} = \text{COS}(X + 2)$$
$$\text{ELSE} \qquad\qquad\qquad (19.3)$$
$$\quad \text{Y1} = \text{COS}(X - 2)$$
$$\quad \text{Y2} = \text{SIN}(X - 2)$$
$$\text{END IF}$$

If the value of the variable X is less than 0, then Y1 and Y2 are assigned values as specified by the first two assignment statements. If the value of X is greater than or equal to 0, then Y1 and Y2 are assigned values according to the last two assignment statements.

ELSE IF statements can be incorporated into an IF-THEN-ELSE construct to give the effect of selecting from one of several possible cases. For example

$$\text{IF (N .LE. 0) THEN}$$
$$\quad \text{Y} = \text{F0}(X)$$
$$\text{ELSE IF (N .EQ. 1) THEN}$$
$$\quad \text{Y} = \text{F1}(X0)$$
$$\text{ELSE IF (N .EQ. 2) THEN} \qquad (19.4)$$
$$\quad \text{Y} = \text{F2}(X)$$
$$\text{ELSE}$$
$$\quad \text{PRINT} *, \text{'ERROR'}$$
$$\text{END IF}$$

DO statements and IF statements may be combined and nested to specify an arbitrarily complex algorithm. To illustrate this, the following statements determine whether the value of the integer N is a prime number (divisible only by 1 and itself) and set the logical variable PRIME accordingly:

```
      IF (N .LE 1) THEN
         PRIME = .FALSE.
      ELSE IF (N .EQ. 2) THEN
         PRIME = .TRUE.
      ELSE IF (MOD (N,2) .EQ. 0) THEN
         PRIME = .FALSE.
      ELSE
         DO 8 DIVISR = 3,INT(SQRT(REAL(N))),2
         IF (MOD (N,DIVISR) .EQ. 0) THEN
                  PRIME = .FALSE.
                  GO TO 9
                END IF
8               CONTINUE                        (19.5)
                PRIME = .TRUE.
             END IF
9         CONTINUE
```

Arrays

In scientific and engineering applications, *arrays* of numbers are used frequently. These may represent objects to be treated as mathematical vectors and matrices or simply may be tables of statistical data. In FORTRAN, a table of real numbers with 9 rows and 5 columns is declared as

$$REAL\ TABLE(9,5) \qquad (19.6)$$

The DO statement is useful for processing data in arrays. A simple example is this sequence of statements to sum up the numbers in the sixth row of the table declared above.

```
      SUM = 0
      DO 18 J = 1,5                    (19.7)
   18    SUM = SUM + TABLE(6,J)
```

Character Data

Because of the intended areas of application, FORTRAN always has had excellent facilities for numerical calculations. However, most programs also involve manipulation of characters, e.g., names, addresses, or symbolic formulas. FORTRAN 77 includes a reasonable facility for manipulating character strings. For example,

$$CHARACTER\ TEXT\ *100,\ WORD\ *4 \qquad (19.8)$$

declares TEXT to be a string of 100 characters and declares WORD to be a string of 4 characters.

$$WORD = \text{'LOVE'} \qquad (19.9)$$
$$TEXT = \text{'FORTRAN 77 IS OK!'}$$

assign the four letter word LOVE as the value of the variable WORD. The variable TEXT is assigned the value which is a string whose first 17 characters are FORTRAN 77 IS OK! (the count of 17 includes the space characters). These characters are followed by 83 more spaces. One can change the value of TEXT to FORTRAN 77 IS TERRIFIC! by executing the statement

$$TEXT\ (15:23) = \text{'TERRIFIC!'} \qquad (19.10)$$

which replaces characters 15 through 23 of the string.

The main advantage of the new character string operations in FORTRAN is that they are portable, i.e., they will work the same way on all computers. This was not true of the very nonportable Hollerith feature of the previous standard FORTRAN.

Procedures

In addition to the DO and IF statement, there is a third way that the FORTRAN programmer can control the order in which statements of a program are executed. Procedures that may be executed more than once or may be used by more than one program can be written and kept separate from other parts of programs. Such procedures can be compiled separately and incorporated into only those programs that need them. If a procedure itself needs to be changed, the alterations need be made in only one place, the single copy of the procedure in the library, thus minimizing the effort involved and reducing the chance for errors.

Example. Let us suppose that matrix multiplication is needed by several programs. This procedure can be written once as follows:

```
      SUBROUTINE MATMUL (A,B,C,N)
      REAL A(N,N),B(N,N),C(N,N)
      DO 8 I = 1,N
        DO 8 J = 1,N
          C (I,J) = 0
          DO 8 K = 1,N
8          C(I,J) = C (I,J) + A (I,K) * B (K,J)
      END                                        (19.11)
```

This subroutine may be used by any program to compute the matrix produce of any two square matrices of the same size. For example, if three arrays P1, P2, and Q are declared by

$$\text{REAL P1(10,10),P2(10,10),Q(10,10)} \quad (19.12)$$

then, at any point in the program, the product of P1 and P2 can be computed and assigned to Q by the statement

$$\text{CALL MATMUL (P1,P2,Q,10)} \quad (19.13)$$

File Handling

Traditionally, FORTRAN has provided facilities only for the sequential access of data files. Still this allowed the programmer to provide fairly elaborate specifications for formatting the data in the file. Many new file handling capabilities have been added to FORTRAN 77.

A simple version of the READ and WRITE statements invokes a default format as in the statements

$$\text{READ *, X,Y}$$
$$\text{PRINT *, (A(I),I = 1,9)} \quad (19.14)$$

The OPEN, CLOSE, and INQUIRE statements permit the programmer to indicate actions related to files used within the FORTRAN program, so that system-dependent operating system commands are not required.

Files may be accessed directly by record number as well as in sequence. Direct file access models more closely the type of access required for disk files. Sequential access fits better for magnetic tapes.

For example, the following statements open and read the 47th record of a payroll file:

$$\text{OPEN (NAME = 'PAYROLL',}$$
$$\text{+ \quad ACCESS = 'DIRECT',}$$
$$\text{+ \quad UNIT = 10)}$$
$$\text{READ (10,REC = 47) RECORD} \quad (19.15)$$

19.5 THE FUTURE OF FORTRAN

When selecting a programming language, there are many things to consider. Some requirements are obvious, such as the appropriateness of the language for the particular application. For a short term project availability of a language processor and familiarity with the available languages are important considerations.

However, if one is making a long range decision, specifically, which language to use for a large project or to adopt for continued use by a large group of programmers,

one must consider other things. Is it possible to pick one language that will serve all (or most) of the needs of the group? Which languages will be widely available for the next several years? What programmer training will be needed to utilize the chosen language(s)?

A lot of information about many programming languages is needed to answer these questions, but perhaps some of the information relevant to the future of FORTRAN can be provided here.

For many years, it has been popular to predict that FORTRAN soon will be a dead language, to be replaced by a "better" language. Despite the undeniable fact that there are more eloquent, rich and powerful languages available, FORTRAN continues to be used widely and, indeed, is still the most popular programming language for scientific and engineering applications. One indication of the continued interest in FORTRAN is the 2,500 pages of responses received from the public when the proposal for the FORTRAN 77 standard was put out for comment. As soon as FORTRAN 77 was adopted as a standard, work began on the next revision, and the number of participants on the standardization committee nearly doubled.

Some of the changes proposed for the next version of the FORTRAN standard probably will not be available widely until the late 1980s, but they may help determine whether FORTRAN will remain a popular language. This, in turn, influences any decision that involves selecting a language for a long term project.

Some of the more important features being considered are central to the use of the language for numerical computations. These features involve the manipulation of arrays. As a simple example of such considerations, suppose A, B, C, D, and V are declared arrays by the statements

$$\text{REAL A(90,10),B(10,10),C(10,10)}$$
$$\text{REAL V(100)} \quad (19.16)$$

then the following statements

$$\text{A = 0}$$
$$\text{B = C + D}$$
$$\text{V (1:99) = V (2:100)} \quad (19.17)$$

would respectively set all of the elements of A to zero, add corresponding elements of C and D, place the sum in the corresponding element of the array B, and shift the elements of V one place to the left. Such extensions of the language seem to be in the FORTRAN spirit. The formulas could then express array manipulations in the same way as those for scalar values.

A second major extension being considered would permit the programmer to name a data structure consisting of components with different data types. For example, a single variable could be assigned values that record all the information pertinent to one core sample from the ocean floor. This data might contain the date of collection, location, oceanographic ship used, name of the scientist and values describing the composition of the sample core.

This capability has long been available in languages such as COBOL, PL/I and PASCAL, and will enhance FORTRAN for use as a general purpose language. It would be a significant aid to scientific programmers who frequently write programs that process nonnumerical as well as numerical data.

Other enhancements are being considered. These include:

- A much less restrictive form for writing programs.
- Other control structures, such as an EXIT statement to jump out of a loop.

- Portable means of specifying the precision requirements for real variables.

If features are added as reasonably efficient implementations of the whole language, it is likely that FORTRAN will remain the most popular choice for a programming language in science and engineering well into the next millenium.

REFERENCES

American National Standard Programming Language FORTRAN. New York: American National Standards Institute, 1978.

Brainerd, Walt (ed.), "Fortran 77," *Communications of the ACM,* Vol. 21, No. 10 (Oct. 1978), pp. 806–20.

Brainerd, Walt, and Jeanne Adams, "Fortran for the 1980s," *Information Processing 80*. Amsterdam: North-Holland, 1980.

20
COBOL

William J. Harrison

Fireman's Fund Insurance Companies

20.1 INTRODUCTION

COBOL is the world's most popular and widely used computer programming language. Uncounted thousands of programs have been written in COBOL; many large corporations and government agencies are dependent upon their COBOL programs for day to day operations. There are many other computer programming languages around, some older, some newer, and some better. Why is it COBOL has had such an outstanding success as a language?

The answer can be summed up in several words: *standardization; maintainability; orientation* towrds business problems. Computer programming languages describe solutions to specific problems. If the problem is to determine the orbit of a space station, then COBOL is of little value. But, if the problem is to calculate and write paychecks for the engineers who are working on the orbit problem, then COBOL is likely to be the language used. The first of these problems is not a business problem (it is in the engineering arena), but the second problem is a classic business situation. COBOL *could* be used to calculate the orbit, and the engineering language *could* handle the payroll job, but is very unlikey that the two would ever switch roles in practice. In this chapter, we look at and get a feeling for the *COmmon Business Oriented Language*, COBOL.

20.2 STANDARDIZATION

For years, commercial data processing problems had been handled by punchcard and mechanical tabulator methods. With the advent of computers, analysts began converting these older applications and developed many early languages to simplify the process. Since any natural language is quite complex and often ambiguous, stylized programming languages were developed. These were translated into computer machine code by means of other new programs called *compilers*. In the late 1950s, the U.S. Department of Defense and several other groups formed the CODASYL committe to develop one standard commercial programming language. The result was the 1959 COBOL document. This served as the basis for a series of standards approved by the American National Standards Association (ANS, or USASI) and other international standards organizations. Any computer manufacturer or software developer wishing to use the name COBOL for their product must assure that it agrees with the ANS Standard.

20.3 MAINTAINABILITY

The primary need for maintainability is ensuring that a statement means the same thing in all versions of the language. Thus COBOL is standardized, both in the U.S. and other parts of the world. A key to standardization is **upwards compatibility,** regardless of new features or changes incorporated into the language; a program written under the old standard when recompiled under the new must continue to perform as before.

In the "198x" level of the ANS COBOL standard, quite a ruckus was raised when several non-upward-compatible features were proposed for standardization; the outcome is still undecided as of this writing.

The value of a standardized language is obvious, considering the inventory of old programs which must keep running even though recompiled for relatively minor changes under new versions of the standard.

COBOL is an English-like language. It separates the four major areas of any program written in the language (see Section 20.4) and describes the problem solution in a detailed, step by step manner. It is easy for a new programmer to look at an existing program, determine what it is doing and then modify it to handle some new aspect of the problem area.

Maintenance is a way of life with most commercial installations, so maintainability becomes a highly prized feature for any computer programming language. Large inventories of older programs must continue to work in the future, even if there are major changes in the environment of the data processing "shop."

Since it is (compared with other programming languages) easy to read by programmers, COBOL is said to be *self-documenting*. COBOL allows 30 character names for data elements, procedures and program entry points, which enhance documentation when properly used. Many computer "shops" (the computer departments of most large companies) have their own in-house or purchased set of standards which defines how COBOL is to be used locally. Procedure name and data name formation is often a major part of such a standard.

One need of business is a language which enables one or two employees to develop a proposed solution to a data processing problem over a period of time (often 30, or more, employees are required for larger projects), allowing for a fair amount of employee turnover during the development process. Turnover means that a partially written program segment will have to be transferred from one person to another for completion. A language should be flexible and commonly understood to allow both a simultaneous and sequential division of the work over time while producing an effective product. Moreover, this product should also lend itself to simple maintenance.

In most data processing shops, hundreds, even thousands of "old" programs constitute the life blood of the corporation as they grind on, day after day.

A program represents a solution to a business problem. But business problems do not remain static. A new product line may be added, discount rates may change, commission calculation rules altered, a new contract for factory employees negotiatiated; and(or) the state legislature may impose a new tax or change a regulatory law. Any number of events may cause procedures and the programs which implement them to change. A corporation might even change computer vendors and install a whole new computer system with a new operating system.

In the face of such events, maintenance for a single program may go on for years.

It is not unusual to find business programs dating back to the 1960s or even 1950s in large installations. Most of these old programs (and the inventory of them is growing daily) must be kept working and updated to meet changing business needs for an indefinite time. This is the primary thrust behind the philosophy of COBOL—it was there in the 60s; it is here now. There is no way of getting rid of COBOL without bringing the business of the world to a near halt.

20.4 ORGANIZATION

A COBOL program is organized into four major divisions: *identification; environment; data; procedure.* Each program must have a name if we are to maintain any order or control over the huge inventory of programs usually available in an installation. The first division, identification, records the principal writer(s) of the program and often carries text about what the program does, the history of maintenance or other information of interest.

The environment division names the files or other external data associations of the program. The data division describes all of the data formats and types available to the program, both incoming and outgoing (with trivial exceptions). Special data-related areas, such as telecommunications control and report formats, are also covered here. The procedure division details all of the operations performed on the data; it constitutes the work performed by the program. Thus the divisions interact while separating the major portions of the program.

Logic

COBOL is not usually thought of as a tool for the formal logician but its logical structures are powerful. These include the **IF** statement and the concept of condition. Logical capabilities are also provided in various other places such as the **UNTIL** clause of the **PERFORM** statement. Based upon **AND** and the inclusive **OR**, with the added capabilities of **NOT**, COBOL supports essentially unlimited nesting by means of parentheses. The power of COBOL logic is illustrated by the number of decision table preprocessors and related higher level logic packages which have been implemented for COBOL and which convert higher level logical structure to the COBOL language level.

Although arithmetic is designated in terms of real numbers, it is actually executed (with the exception of the now defunct "floating point" mode) with integers in the computer (packed number for IBM system 370). The compiler keeps track of the fractional point and, when printing is requested, issues procedure commands to properly position it within the number. By contrast, statistical and scientific computations generally use floating point arithmetic. Integer arithmetic is more business oriented and saves conversion time as compared to scientific notation used by some other languages. (Some of the latter are sold as business languages! This is not so much to downgrade scientific languages as to note their misuse; we would never get a rocket to Venus without them.)

COBOL arithmetic provides the choice between the **COMPUTE** statement (the programmer writes an equation but all decimal places and data conversion are handled automatically) and the individual arithmetic statements **ADD**, **SUBTRACT**, **MULTIPLY**, and **DIVIDE**. Although exponentiation is allowed in the **COMPUTE** statement, the developers of COBOL did not define a separate verb for it. While it is needed by the engineer or the scientist, the accountant rarely uses exponentiation.

Input/Output

COBOL handles data to and from the external data storage media using the concept of the record. A **record** is a collection of data about one subject, say, an employee or a stock item. Records consist of **fields,** which can be numeric or in characters as defined by the COBOL data description. All the data associated with an entity is in the record. Or sets of records may be coordinated with an **identifying key. Files** (collections) of records may be sorted upon those keys. Files containing different types of information about the same entity can be *matched* or *merged*, and include the traditional master/transaction approach to file updating. Files may also be updated on a direct access storage medium, though usually not tape, by means of the **REWRITE** statement. In COBOL, files are always explicitly opened and closed (except in sorting) so that full control of file access can be maintained.

A very powerful nonrecord data base facility has been designed for COBOL, but it is *not* yet accepted as part of the language standard. Several excellent techniques based on procedure calls *are* available, however, to access *data bases*.

20.5 EXAMPLE PROGRAM

For a better idea of how COBOL really works, let us look at a sample simplified COBOL program which reads a

single input file and produces two output files, one to be printed as paychecks and the other to be printed as a check register. In practice, this application would probably involve several separate programs and many more functins that the two simple output functions shown in Figure 20.1a and 20.1b.

First, notice that the program is 80 characters wide, a holdover from the days of punchcards. Columns 1–6 may contain a *sequence number* (in punchcard days, if the deck of cards were dropped, it could be put back into order by these numbers). Columns 73–80 is for an *alternate sequence* field or may be used for any other prupose.

The important columns are 7 through 72. Column 7 is an indicator. An asterisk (*) marks the line as a comment. Other indicators could appear here also. Columns 8 through 11 compose a field called the *A area,* and 9–72 from a field called the *B area*. Certain COBOL statements are required to start in the A area, others in the B area; otherwise COBOL statements are not tied to columns or areas. (Some styles of programming, such as "structured" techniques, or in-house standards, may introduce column dependencies.)

Input File

Let us see how the input file is handled. The data consists of employee name, employee number (perhaps the Social Security number) and gross pay. They are recorded on some external medium, such as a magnetic disk. How they got there is not important; probably they were the output of some other program.

The file is a collection of records, one per employee, which exists in the program's environment. The ENVIRONMENT DIVISION assigns a name by which that file is known in the program, here PAYROLL-FILE. A SELECT statement in FILE-CONTROL associates that name with a DD name *(data definition)* PYRGROSS, by which the file is known in the JCL. The DD name PYRGROSS identifies the JCL statement which names the file to the *job manager,* part of the operating system. In this way file independence is achieved whereby the program is not locked into a file; the file for this job run is named at runtime in the JCL.

The COBOL name and external name are associated by a COBOL statement, which starts with the verb SELECT and ends with a period (or with another COBOL verb, or by several other means). That COBOL sentence (collection of one or more statements ending with a period) is in a COBOL paragraph called FILE-CONTROL which in turn is in the COBOL section called INPUT-OUTPUT.

```
          1         2         3         4         5         6         7         8
1234567890123456789012345678901234567890123456789012345678901234567890
          IDENTIFICATION DIVISION.
          PROGRAM-ID.  PYRSAMPL.
      *              * IN COL. 7 = COMMENT LINE
      *AAAA      --- A AREA IS 8-11      B AREA IS 12-72
      *   BBBBBBBBBBBBBBBBBBBBBBBBBBBBBBBBBBBBBBBBBBBBBBBBBBBBBBBBBBB
      *                                         73-80=COMMENTS ----XXXXXXXX
          ENVIRONMENT DIVISION.
          INPUT-OUTPUT SECTION.
          FILE-CONTROL.
              SELECT PAYROLL-FILE              ASSIGN TO PYRGROSS
              SELECT CHECK-FILE                ASSIGN TO PYRCHECK
              SELECT REGISTER-FILE             ASSIGN TO PYRREGIS.
          DATA DIVISION.
          FILE SECTION.
          FD  PAYROLL-FILE, DATA RECORDS ARE PAYROLL-RECORD.
          01  PAYROLL-RECORD.
              05 EMPL-NUM                  PICTURE 9(9).
              05 EMPL-NAME                 PIC X(20).
              05 EMPL-DEPT                 PIC XXXX.
              05 EMPL-GROSS                PIC S9(7)V99.
              05 TAX-INFO.
                 10   STATE-TAX            PIC S9(6)V99.
                 10   FED-TAX              PIC S9(6)V99.
                 10   OTHER-DED            PIC S9(7)V99.
              05 FILLER                    PIC X(13).
          FD  CHECK-FILE DATA RECORD IS CHECK-RECORD.
          01  CHECK-RECORD.
              02 FILLER PIC X.
              02 CHK-NAME PIC X(20).
              02 FILLER PIC X.
              02 CHK-DEPT PIC X(4).
              02 FILLER PIC X(25).
              02 CHK-NET              PIC $*,***,***.99.
          FD  REGISTER-FILE DATA RECORD IS REGISTER-RECORD.
              01 REGISTER-RECORD.
              02 FILLER                    PIC XX.
              02 REG-NAME                  PIC X(20).
              02 FILLER                    PIC X.
              02 REG-DEPT                  PIC XXXX.
              02 FILLER                    PIC X.
              02 REG-TOTAL-DED             PIC $$,$$$,$$$.99DB.
              02 REG-NET                   PIC $$,$$$,$$$.99DB.
          WORKING-STORAGE SECTION.
          01  EOF-SW  PIC S9  VALUE +0  USAGE IS COMPUTATIONAL.
          01  TEMP    PIC S9(8)V99 COMP.
```

Figure 20.1a. Simplified payroll program in COBOL.

Data Division

In the **DATA DIVISION**, we see **PAYROLL-FILE** used again, this time in a section called **FILE SECTION** and preceeded by the letters **FD**. This constitutes the *file description* entry. Various aspects of the file are described here and the **FD** entry is immediately followed by the record description.

This record description is an example of how data is described in COBOL. In this case, the record is shown as it looks on the external storage medium. The **01** level names the record for any employee. The **05** level describes the various parts, or fields, of that record. The last of these **05** levels is further subdivided into level **10** items.

The **PICTURE** (or **PIC**) describes each field of the re-

```
           1             2             3             4             5             6             7             8
  12345678901234567890123456789012345678901234567890123456789012345678901234567890
           PROCEDURE DIVISION.
           MAIN-PGM SECTION.
           M-1-PARAGRAPH.
               OPEN INPUT PAYROLL-FILE, OUTPUT CHECK-FILE REGISTER-FILE.
               PERFORM CHECK-WRITE UNTIL EOF-SW = 1.
               CLOSE PAYROLL-FILE, CHECK-FILE, REGISTER-FILE.
               STOP RUN.
       *
       * THE SECTION BELOW IS EXECUTED ONCE PER INPUT REC. BY THE PERFORM

           CHECK-WRITE SECTION.
           GET-INPUT-RECORD.
               READ PAYROLL-FILE
                   AT END MOVE 1 TO EOF-SW, GO TO CHECK-END.
           BUILD-CHECK.
               MOVE SPACES TO CHECK-RECORD REGISTER-RECORD.
               MOVE EMPL-NAME TO CHK-NAME REG-NAME.
               MOVE EMPL-DEPT TO CHK-DEPT REG-DEPT.
               ADD STATE-TAX FED-TAX OTHER-DED
                   GIVING REG-TOTAL-DED ROUNDED, TEMP.
               COMPUTE CHK-NET  ROUNDED   REG-NET ROUNDED =
                   EMPL-GROSS - TEMP.
           WRITE-OUTPUT-FILES.
               WRITE CHECK-RECORD.
               WRITE REGISTER-RECORD.
           CHECK-END.  EXIT.
       *         --- END OF SAMPLE PROGRAM ***
```

Figure 20.1b. Simplified payroll program in COBOL (cont.).

cord data: X is text; 9 is numeric only. In the picture, S indicates that the numeric field may have a sign. Those levels, when further subdivided, are called "group" data items and have no picture clause.

Procedure Division

In the PROCEDURE DIVISION, reading from top to bottom, we first see a section name, MAIN-PGM. In the first three divisions, all of the section and paragraph names are specified by COBOL and must appear exactly as specified. But in the procedure division, all (with one exception) section and procedure names are chosen by the programmer. These names must avoid a long list of COBOL reserved words, but otherwise may be any combination of letters, numbers and dashes up to 30 characters. Section names must be unique, and paragraph names must be unique within any one section.

The first statement of this program starts with the COBOL verb OPEN. Any file must be opened before it is used in COBOL, showing the type of use (INPUT here).

Notice that two more files are opened with one OPEN statement. OUTPUT is specified for them.

The next statement is PERFORM. This COBOL verb causes the statements at the indicated section (CHECK-WRITE) to be executed as if they were actually located where PERFORM is found. In fact, in this case the perform statement contains the clause UNTIL. This requests that the section named CHECK-WRITE is performed repeatedly *until* the test indicated in the until clause is true. Here this is done until the end of file switch is set (EOF-SW = 1) because the file is exhausted. After this, the next statement after the PERFORM statement is executed.

Now look at the section indicated CHECK-WRITE. In paragraph GET-INPUT-RECORD, there is a READ statement referencing our input file, along with a special clause, AT END. Each time the flow of control passes through that read statement, a new record from the input file appears in the area created by the data description for PAYROLL-RECORD.

After all input records have been read from the input file, the next attempt to read causes a branch to the AT

END clause. Since no further data is forthcoming, the statements in this **AT END** clause are executed.

The data item EOF-SW is not part of the input record or of any output record. Data items are fully described in the **WORKING-STORAGE** section of the **DATA** division, where they may have their initial values indicated by **VALUE** clauses. Once the data item switch is set to 1, the flow of control is directed to the end of the section. **PER-FORM** then does the **UNTIL** check, finds the data item switch equal to 1 and lets the flow of control go on to the next instruction. Thus the CHECK-WRITE section is performed once for each record in the input file, and no more.

The next instruction is **CLOSE**, which terminates activity on all three files. Following this, **STOP RUN** terminates the action of the program.

Output Files

The two remaining files are output files intended to be printed rather than to be used as input to some other program.

There is a major difference in the picture in the data description of an output record. PICTURE $$,$$$.99 is an example of a **report picture,** which consists of insertion and replacement characters. The dollar sign floats with the check amount. It is placed next to the leftmost non-zero digit. The amounts $1,105.20, or $23.11, or $.05, are examples of formatted contents for this field. The leftmost unused characters are set to *blanks*. On the check, $**,***.99 gives the same values: $1,105.20, or $**,*23.11, or $**,***.05 respectively. This use of asterisks in unused positions rather than blanks is sometimes called *check protection*.

Some Further Notes

DB in a picture clause causes the letters DB (for debit) to print *after* the field *when it is negative*. For instance, if *other deductions* is used to pay a bonus, it would be negative, perhaps exceeding the deductions, to produce an overall negative total deduction.

The data name FILLER is a special COBOL reserved word used in place of any data name and need not be unique. Data may not be moved to any FILLER field. It is used here to provide spacing on the check and register output. Normally other techniques would be used, but in the interest of simplicity less ideal methods appear in this example.

20.6 OTHER AREAS OF INTEREST IN COBOL

Tables

Adding **OCCURS** to the description of any data item (with some reservations as detailed in the COBOL manuals) causes that item to be repeated to form a table. Any single occurance of data in that table may be referenced by giving its occurence number in parentheses after its name when used in the procedure division. Both subscripting and indexing may be used. For indexing, **IN-DEXED BY** is added after **OCCURS** in the data division. **SET** is used to do arithmetic on indexes.

Sort and Merge

One common operation in solving business data processing problems is changing the *sequence* of records within a file, called **sorting.** Another frequent operation is matching one file against another based upon some key (if both files are in order by that key), called **merging.** COBOL provides verbs and statement formats for both of these functions. The sequence of records in the file is determined by the contents of some data field(s) common to all of the records in the file, or key(s). In addition, **SORT** provides access to the unsorted records as they enter the sorting process, and both **SORT** and **MERGE** provide access to each record as it leaves the specified process. These are called **INPUT PROCEDURE** and **OUT-PUT PROCEDURE** respectively.

If such access is not required in the program, the **USING** clause may name all of the files to be sorted or merged and the **GIVING** clause may be used to name the resulting file. Sort and merge operations usually make use of a separate sort/merge program.

Reporting

One of COBOL's greatest strengths lies in its ability to develop elaborate reports. Three main methods are available:

1. Raw COBOL statements, which may include report pictures of data fields, standard I/O, logic and computational facilities.
2. The relatively new **LINAGE** feature combined with page spacing controls in standard I/O.
3. The very powerful (but sadly little used and often attacked) report writer facility.

COBOL offers the most complete report preparation facility of any language by any of these three means. Some other languages offer lesser reporting facilities but provide them more automatically.

The **report writer facility** (**RPW**) permits automatic heading, footing, total rolling, crossfooting, and further preparation facilities in a nonprocedural way, all sufficiently different from COBOL's main procedural approach to set them apart.

Report writer.   The special report writer language of COBOL (not to be confused with report *pictures* mentioned earlier) describes the printed report layout and associates data with the report format symbolically.

Another section of the DATA DIVISION, the REPORT SECTION, contains RD entries (like FD entries) followed by descriptions. In the PROCEDURE DIVISION, INITIATE and TERMINATE for reports are like OPEN and CLOSE for files, while the GENERATE statement causes a specified line type of the report to be prepared automatically. Each report is named and associated with some output file, which in turn is intended to be printed.

Interprogram Communication

The COBOL verb CALL allows one program to call another program by name, passing along data the called program needs. A called COBOL program in turn has provisions for using that data in part of its DATA DIVISION.

The Linkage Section

Structures of programs can be built using linkage conventions.

Other Features

COBOL has still more featues which should be touched upon:

- The teleprocessing feature permits networks of remote terminals to be controlled by, and communicate with the program.
- String processing permits using and building strings of data from smaller parts.
- SEARCH permits binary or serial searches or indexed tables.
- The FIPS flagger provides details on the makeup of programs.
- Powerful debugging aids help get programs working.

- Segmentation permits programs to be broken into separate parts in order to make better use of machine resources.

20.7 SUPPLEMENTARY SYSTEMS

Other systems may be used with COBOL programs. These can be roughly classified into pre-, post-, and coprocessors.

Preprocessors

Preprocessors convert nonCOBOL language information embedded in programs into COBOL statements suitable for compilation. Preprocessors include program generators, macro systems, shorthand processors (abbreviations for verbs), and so on. The **decision table preprocessor** is one important example. It allows the specification of complex logic in the form of a decision table which is treated by the programmer as if it were part of the COBOL language itself. Since it is *not* part of the language, the table is converted by the preporcessor to structures consisting of IF statements in pure COBOL.

Another example is the **language conversion program** (**LCP**), which exists because the COBOL language *does* change. The input to an LCP is the old COBOL dialect program and the output is in the new dialect. LCPs greatly ease one of COBOL's greatest problem areas, the "not always perfect" upwards compatibility in the occasional revisions to the ANS (and that of other bodies) official COBOL language.

Postprocessors

Postprocessors take the output of the COBOL compiler and change it in various ways, usually for improved efficiency or to introduce debugging or accounting code.

Coprocessors

There are two kinds of coprocessors. Those which run at the same time as the COBOL compiler are usually restricted to control systems to organize compilation or to enhance efficiency of the final COBOL program execution.

The others include sort/merge packages, utility functions which the COBOL program can call, and subroutine libraries. One very important class of coprocessor is the **DBMS** (**data base management system**) which, among other things, replaces the concept of *file* with a much more sophisticated concept of *data base*. A teleprocessing capability separate from COBOL's own TP language may also be a coprocessor.

Nonprocedural Languages

COBOL does almost everything (except in RPW) step by step with great detail. A few languages, such as the proprietary MARK IV, stress the description of input and output (or reports). The package decides how to get from one to the other. This is an excellent and efficient approach to programming and maintaining business programs. The major problem may be the lack of industry standardization and vendor support. Procedural or step by step operations start to creep into these nonprocedural programs to handle special cases, thus reducing their benefits.

20.8 COMPARISON OF COBOL WITH OTHER LANGUAGES

Some programming languages have tried to *add* business capabilities over the years, since business for languages in general is the major market. But most languages are excellent for one purpose or another or they would not have survived, particularly in special areas for which COBOL may not be well suited. Here is a sampling.

FORTRAN

The traditional scientific language, FORTRAN is strongly based upon floating point arithmetic. An integer capability is available, but automatic handling of decimal places is not provided. FORTRAN's file number approach to input/output is far less flexible than is COBOL's SELECT . . . ASSIGN approach. The former's approach is based upon mulitfile tape use prevalent in the early days of computer development. FORTRAN boasts a wide variety of built-in functions which are of great use to the engineer but of little use to the accountant.

BASIC

Meant as a beginner's language, BASIC does not have the richness of COBOL. Some dialects are limited in symbolic addressing capability. Input/output is often oriented to streams of data.

PL/I

This is perhaps the most successful competitor for COBOL. PL/I has powerful logical constructions, a structured approach and data description capability. This makes it useful as a combination of COBOL and FORTRAN. Sadly, PL/I has fallen prey to multivendors and a proliferation of dialects, although the latter is just now coming under control. In business, PL/I is still considered somewhat an esoteric language by some.

APL

An extremely powerful means of expressing programs, APL is gaining in popularity. But, although sometimes touted as an end-user language, it is too esoteric for almost all end users without advanced degrees in mathematics. A few actual payrolls programmed in APL probably exist somewhere, but thousands do exist in COBOL.

ALGOL, JOVIAL, and so on, are too lacking in business orientation, perhaps more important, in vendor support and in applications at least in the U.S., for consideration here.

REFERENCES

To learn more about COBOL, the books listed below offer offer a good beginning. If you have access to a particular COBOL compiler, obtain its language manual programmer's guide and related documentation.

American National Standard Programming Language— COBOL, Document X3.23, 1974. Available from the American National Standards Institute, 1430 Broadway, New York, NY 10018.

Diebold Group, ed. *Automatic Data Processing Handbook.* New York: McGraw-Hill Book Co., 1977. Refer particularly to William Harrison, "Programming Basics" and "Programming Techniques."

Harrison, William, *A Programmer's Guide to COBOL.* New York: Van Nostrand Reinhold, 1980.

McClure, Carma, *Reducing COBOL Complexity Through Structured Programming.* New York: Van Nostrand Reinhold, 1978.

McCracken, D. D., *A Simplified Guide to Structured COBOL Programming,* New York: John Wiley & Sons, 1976.

Pollack, Hicks, and Harrison, *Decision Tables, Theory and Practice.* New York: John Wiley & Sons, 1971.

Sammet, Jean, "The Early History of COBOL," *ACM SIGPLAN Notices,* Vol. 13, No. 8 (Aug. 1978).

Weinberg, Gerald, Wright, Kaufman and Goetz, *High Level COBOL Programming.* Boston: Winthrop, 1971.

Yourdon, Edward, Cane and Sarson, *Learning to Program in Structured COBOL,* Part I; Edward Yourdon, Lister and Timothy, *Learning to Program in Structured COBOL,* Part II. New York: Yourdon Press, 1976, 1978.

21
PL/I

Seymour V. Pollack

Washington University, St. Louis

21.1 INTRODUCTION AND BACKGROUND

PL/I stands for **P**rogramming **L**anguage **1**. The likelihood of a PL/II in the foreseeable future is rather small and keeps shrinking as time goes by. The initial version of the language, developed by IBM for its System/360 line of computers, appeared in 1965. Since that time, implementations have been produced for a wide range of machines, including microcomputers, from a variety of manufacturers throughout the world.

Basic Motivations for PL/I's Development

Examination of the major factors contributing to the introduction of PL/I helps provide a useful perspective for exploring the language's overall orientation. Certainly the complete picture is much more complex than one can hope to portray in a brief sketch. Accordingly, discussion is limited to the more prominent motivations:

1. Computing systems available and under development at the time of PL/I's inception embodied technological and conceptual advances beyond the inherent capabilities of the major contemporary programming languages. These advances included more extensive input/output capabilities, multitasking improved manipulative power at the byte and bit levels, and a wider variety of data types and organizations.
2. During the decade or so following the introduction of the initial high level languages (i.e., FORTRAN and

COBOL) there had been tremendous growth both in the use of computers and the variety of endeavors to which they were applied. With this expansion came new algorithms and programming techniques whose effective exploitation was restricted (and often thwarted) by the existing languages.
3. While growing in volume and diversity, computer use also began to mature. Computer applications were being approached with a new understanding which tended to move away from the simplistic characterizations that molded earlier languages. For example, the fundamental distinctions drawn between "business" and "scientific" computing, mostly mythical to begin with, were seen to be more impediments than aids. A *general purpose language* transcends these largely artificial boundaries.

An additional factor, perhaps as strong as the others, was IBM's interest in supplanting FORTRAN and COBOL, each of which required considerable support, with a single language richer and more powerful than either or both combined. For a variety of reasons, the desired replacement did not occur. Instead, PL/I occupies a distinct but relatively minor position among computer users.

General Characteristics of PL/I

PL/I is a **block structured language;** its features are designed to encourage the construction of programs as a series of distinct procedural modules. These may be implemented as separately compiled subprograms or as unified groups of statements. In any case, the intent is to facilitate the use of blocks of code, with each block representing a procedural activity whose nature is governed by its significance in the application, rather than by the properties of the language. For example, when a particular operation is inexpressible as a single language statement, it is a simple matter in PL/I to represent it as an arbitrarily long sequence of statements, with the entire group still being organized and treated as a "single" activity.

The language is designed to deal with a great variety of data types. Numerical values can be represented in many ways and the programmer has direct control over precision. In addition, definition and processing of non-arithmetic data such as character strings and logical switches are intrinsic parts of the language.

A variety of language features enable the programmer to pay serious attention to the organization of data. In addition to the arrays and hierarchical records supported in earlier languages, PL/I makes it relatively straightforward to define and use such data structures as lists, trees, stacks, and queues, as well as other types prompted by the requirements of a particular application.

The importance of program testing and monitoring is reflected in features intended specifically to support such activities. When used (temporarily) during program development, these features facilitate detailed tracing of events to provide interim information that reveals the state of the processing. When installed as part of an operating program during routine use, the features provide automatic means for detecting error conditions and activating mechanisms for subsequent recovery.

21.2 SYNTACTIC FEATURES

In general terms, a PL/I source program consists of *a string of characters* (letters, numbers, special symbols and blanks). This reflects the language designers' objective of not tying PL/I programs to any particular input medium. Thus, although many PL/I programs are submitted on punched cards, there is nothing in the language to give it a bias in favor of that particular form. As in other high level languages, the unit of expression (and the unit analyzed and processed by the compiler) is the statement; however, the beginning or end of a statement need not coincide with the beginning or end of a punched card. Instead, the string of characters that comprises a PL/I source program is divided into statements by explicit punctuation symbols interspersed throughout the string (this is examined in the next section).

Construction of PL/I Statements and Programs

The basic processing unit in PL/I is the **procedure,** the smallest block of code that may be compiled and executed independently. A PL/I program consists of a **main procedure** and zero or more additional procedures. The main procedure always is the first one in the program.

The boundaries of a PL/I procedure are defined explicitly by special statements: Each procedure begins with a PROCEDURE statement and concludes with an END statement. The main procedure is earmarked as such and its overall construction appears as in Figure 21.1. The label preceding the colon in the PROCEDURE statement is assigned by the programmer and constitutes the **program name,** thereby providing a means for gaining access to the entire program. The program name also appears in the main procedure's END statement.

Programs consisting of several procedures may be organized in a variety of ways, each with its own properties and advantages. Because there is only one main procedure in a program, the OPTIONS(MAIN) part of the PROCEDURE statement does not appear in any of the other PROCEDURE statements. Procedures may be added to a main procedure simply by attaching them at the end. The program layout exemplified in Figure 21.2 can be said to consist of a main procedure and two **external procedures.** Alternatively, it is possible to incorporate a procedure completely within another one; this process is called **nesting.** The program organization shown in Figure 21.3 can be described as a main procedure (PMAIN) containing two **internal procedures,** P1 and P2. PL/I programs can be constructed using arbitrarily complex combinations of internal and external procedures, with the "best choice" depending on the individual situation. Discussion in this chapter is limited to internal procedures.

The individual PL/I statement follows the general form

label: body of statement;

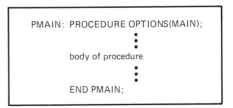

Figure 21.1. Main PL/I procedure.

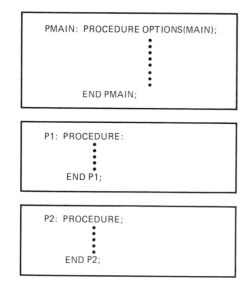

Figure 21.2. External procedures in PL/I.

Labels are optional for most statements. When used, the label should provide a unique name for that statement, so that reference can be made to it from other parts of the procedure. A label generally consists of 1–31 characters (some compilers restrict the length to six or eight characters) in which the initial character is one of the 26 upper case letters, or $, #, or @. These, as well as the

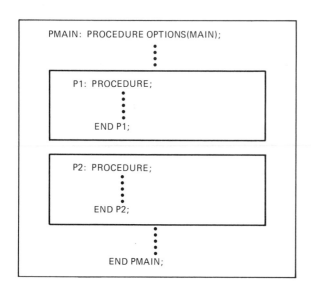

Figure 21.3. Internal, or nested, procedures in PL/I.

ten numerical digits (0–9) and the break character (_), may be used as subsequent characters in a label. The colon, which appears when there is a label, separates the label from the body of the statement. All PL/I statements end with a semicolon, so that, except for the **PRO-CEDURE** statement, each PL/I statement consists of a string of characters between two semicolons.

Descriptions, explanations and other remarks about a program may be included in the form of **comments.** A comment begins with the two characters /* and, after an arbitrary length, concludes with */. Comments may appear anywhere in a program.

Major Data Types

The forms of data used most commonly in PL/I programs may be characterized as follows:

1. *Numerical data*—numbers may be expressed in traditional or scientific notation, and in decimal or binary form. For example, the assignment of -17.25 to a variable Y could be specified in a wide variety of ways including the following:

$$Y = -17.25; \qquad Y = -0.1725E+2;$$
$$Y = -1.725*10**1; \qquad Y = -10001.01B;$$

$$(21.1)$$

In addition, it is possible to specify and manipulate complex numbers.

2. *Character data*—PL/I allows the use of strings of any length containing arbitrary combinations of characters (i.e., letters, number, blanks, special symbols). For instance, the statement

$$X = \text{'THEY'}; \qquad (21.2)$$

places the four-character **THEY** in a variable named **X**.

3. *Bit strings*—individual bits can be strung together to form banks of logical switches, each of which may be manipulated independently. For example, the assignment

$$S = \text{'1001'B}; \qquad (21.3)$$

sets the four switches in variable S to respective values of "true," "false," "false," and "true."

Major Statement Types

A very wide variety of computational and bookkeeping operations can be specified by means of five basic statement types whose discussion follows. Additional structural facilities allow these statements to be combined for more intricate directives.

Specification of variables.

Variables in PL/I are defined by means of the DECLARE statement:

DECLARE name attributes, name attributes, . . . ;

$$(21.4)$$

Each programmer-defined name (whose construction rules are the same as for a label) reserves storage to accommodate a value having the properties specified by the attributes following that name. For example,

DECLARE HEIGHT FIXED BINARY(15);   (21.5)

reserves storage under the name HEIGHT to contain a signed binary integer 15 bits long.

Assignment statements.

Values are generated and stored by means of the assignment statement:

destination = expression;   (21.6)

the "=" indicates a replacement operation. Accordingly, the expression to the right of that operation is evaluated by performing the operations indicated. Then the result (which may be a number, character string or bit string) is stored in the location indicated by the name specified as the destination, thereby replacing the previous contents of that location. Thus, the statement

B = 2*A**2−C/(SQRT(A+C));   (21.7)

specifies that the expression

$$2A^2 - \frac{C}{\sqrt{A + C}} \qquad (21.8)$$

be evaluated, with the result to be stored in location B.

Input/output statements.

Data to be transmitted to or from the processor are treated as **files.** These are either **stream oriented** or **record oriented.** In the former type of organization, we deal with an input or output stream consisting of individual data items, each of which may be transmitted independently. The alternative organization collects a predefined set of individual data items into **records,** and each record constitutes a unit of transmission.

Stream input/output is handled by the GET and PUT statements, respectively. To illustrate,

GET FILE (FILEB) LIST (X,Y,X);   (21.9)

takes the next three items out of the input data stream named FILEB and places them in the respective locations associated with the variable names X, Y, and Z. Similarly, the statement

PUT FILE (FILEC) LIST (W,T,E,D);   (21.10)

copies the contents of locations W, T, E and D into the output stream named FILEC in the order specified.

Record transmission is handled with the READ and WRITE statements. For instance,

READ FILE (TRX) INTO (RBUF);   (21.11)

brings the next record into the processor from input file TRX. It is stored in a variable named RBUF, at which point it is ready for subsequent dissection into individual data items comprising that record. Using the same general mechanism,

WRITE FILE (WBY) FROM (OTREC);   (21.12)

uses the contents of the variable OTREC as the next record to be transmitted to the output file WBY. (Presumably, a particular grouping of individual data items was assembled earlier to form the record in WBY). Subsequent discussion will concentrate on stream input/output.

Decision and control statements.

PL/I's extensive facilities for implementing decision rules stem from a single statement type which serves as a building block. The IF statement provides a convenient vehicle for implementing simple yes-or-no decisions based on an arbitrarily complex test that the programmer devises. For example, in the statement

IF X >= Y*(Z−17.2) THEN W = W−X;
ELSE W = W+X/2;

$$(21.13)$$

the specified activity is almost self-explanatory: if the indicated comparison is true (i.e., the current value in X is greater than or equal to the value obtained by subtracting 17.2 from the current value of Z and multiplying the result by Y), then W's value is to be decreased by an amount corresponding to X. On the other hand, if the test fails, W's value is to be increased by an amount corresponding to half the value in X. Note that the actions motivated by the tests are mutually exclusive; one or the other will be performed for any test, but not both. These consequent actions may be as simple or as complex as the situation demands.

An important facility in any programming language

provides the ability to specify some operation that is repeated in a controlled manner. PL/I handles such **program loops** as single conceptual activities regardless of their extent or complexity. This is emphasized by bounding the loop with special statements; each loop begins with a **DO** statement that describes the mechanism controlling the loop, and it concludes with an **END** statement (as with a procedure).

Two basic mechanisms control cyclic operations through a loop. The decision to repeat the operations within the loop can be based on the number of times the loop has been repeated. Alternatively, some arbitrary condition can be specified, with the loop being repeated as long as the condition is in effect. In the latter situation, the number of repetitions may be of no significance. This construction can be illustrated as follows:

$$\text{LP1: DO WHILE } (S=0);$$

.

.

statements;

.

.

$$\text{END LP1;} \qquad (21.14)$$

The activity to be repeated in the foregoing example consists of the statements between the **DO** and **END** statements. The label (LP1 in this example) is repeated in both statements to enhance clarity. Presumably there is something in the processing that (sooner or later) will affect the value of variable S so that it will no longer be 0. Then, when the program attempts another repetition of the loop and tests prior to embarking on *that* repetition, the stated condition is violated and the loop bypassed.

Statements for monitoring execution. Today's computing systems include elaborate hardware and software mechanisms for detecting and reacting to a variety of extraordinary conditions. PL/I provides the programmer with access to these mechanisms through the **ON** statement. One such feature, for example, automatically detects attempts to divide by zero and gives the programmer the opportunity to intercept and circumvent the attempt. Each type of **ON** statement enables the programmer to describe an action that will be taken whenever a particular situation arises. As an illustration, consider the following statement:

$$\text{ON ENDFILE (IPR) } S=1; \qquad (21.15)$$

IPR is the name of some input file. This statement activates a mechanism that automatically sets a variable S to a value of 1 when the program seeks to obtain input from IPR and there are no more data. The attempt precipitating the action may appear anywhere in the program following the placement of the ON statement. Any effect on the program would have to be specified by the programmer. (For instance, to make use of the **ON END-FILE** statement given above, the program tests S and does something special when it finds its value to be 1).

A sample program. To establish the "flavor" of a PL/I program by using what has been discussed up to now, an example would be helpful; Figure 21.4 serves that purpose. Note that the **ON** statement applies over the extent of the program subsequent to its physical placement: Every time a new value for X is read successfully in statement 15, the value of S remains unchanged. Once an attempt fails (i.e., the input is exhausted), the **ENDFILE** mechanism triggers automatically. When the program tries another iteration of the loop starting in statement 7, S's value has changed and the loop is bypassed. Hence, statement 17 is executed next. Note also that the action specified in response to a "successful" sum is easily perceived as a single conceptual action because of the **DO** and **END** statements which bracket expressed in statements 12 and 13.

21.3 SPECIFICATION OF VARIABLES

As indicated earlier, all variables are specified explicitly with the **DECLARE** statement. For clarity, all declarations are usually placed together at the beginning of a procedure.

Numerical Variables

Storage for accommodating numerical values is described in terms of three distinct attributes:

- **Base**—either **BINARY** or **DECIMAL**.
- **Scale**—either **FIXED** or **FLOAT**.
- **Precision**—the size of the numerical variable, i.e., the number of digits required to represent the variable.

A fourth attribute (**mode**) indicates whether a numerical variable is **REAL** or **COMPLEX**. Mode is not considered further in this chapter; accordingly PL/I's assumption of REAL is used implicitly hereafter.

Numerical variables used for arbitrarily complicated computations usually are declared as **FLOAT DECI-**

```
                XMPL:   PROCEDURE OPTIONS (MAIN);

   STMT LEVEL NEST
     1                  XMPL: PROCEDURE OPTIONS (MAIN);

                        /*****************************************************************/
                        /*      THIS PROGRAM READS AN INTEGER Y, FOLLOWED BY A SUCCESSION OF  */
                        /*      INTEGER VALUES FOR X. A CUMULATIVE SUM OF THE X'S IS     */
                        /*      MAINTAINED, THE GOAL BEING TO REACH OR EXCEED THE VALUE  */
                        /*      SPECIFIED BY Y. IF THIS HAPPENS BEFORE WE RUN OUT OF X'S, */
                        /*      THE PROGRAM WILL PRINT Y, THE CUMULATIVE SUM (WHICH WE SHALL */
                        /*      CALL TOTAL), AND N, THE NUMBER OF X VALUES USED TO ATTAIN */
                        /*      THAT SUM; THEN IT WILL STOP. IF WE RUN OUT OF DATA BEFORE */
                        /*      TOTAL REACHES Y, THE PROGRAM PRINTS A MESSAGE TO THAT EFFECT, */
                        /*      FOLLOWED BY Y, AND THEN IT STOPS.                        */
                        /*      S IS A VARIABLE THAT WE SHALL USE AS A FLAG TO SIGNAL WHEN WE */
                        /*      RUN OUT OF DATA.  FOR THIS PURPOSE, S WILL BE INITIALIZED TO */
                        /*      ZERO AT THE BEGINNING OF THE PROGRAM. AFTER THAT, THE ON */
                        /*      STATEMENT WILL CONTROL ITS VALUE.                        */
                        /*****************************************************************/

     2    1            DECLARE (X,Y,TOTAL,N,S) FIXED BINARY;

     3    1            N,TOTAL,S = 0;
     4    1            ON ENDFILE (SYSIN) S=1;
     6    1            GET FILE (SYSIN) LIST (Y,X);

                        /*****************************************************************/
                        /*      INITIAL VALUES HAVE BEEN PROVIDED FOR THE PERTINENT VARIABLES */
                        /*      SO THAT OUR PROCESSING LOOP CAN BE STRAIGHTFORWARD. NOTE */
                        /*      THAT AS PART OF THE INITIALIZATION PROCESS, WE HAVE READ IN */
                        /*      THE FIRST VALUE FOR X AS WELL AS Y, THE VALUE AGAINST WHICH */
                        /*      WE SHALL BE COMPARING.                                   */
                        /*****************************************************************/

     7    1            CL:DO WHILE (S=0);
     8    1    1           N = N+1;      TOTAL = TOTAL+X;
    10    1    1           IF TOTAL >= Y THEN DO;
    12    1    2                   PUT FILE (SYSPRINT) LIST (Y,TOTAL,N);
    13    1    2                   STOP;
    14    1    2                END;
    15    1    1              ELSE GET FILE (SYSIN) LIST (X);
    16    1    1           END CL;

                        /*****************************************************************/
                        /*      THE ONLY WAY WE CAN REACH THIS PART OF THE PROGRAM IS FOR US */
                        /*      TO RUN OUT OF X'S BEFORE TOTAL REACHES Y. WHEN THAT HAPPENS, */
                        /*      THE ON ENDFILE STATEMENT WILL (AUTOMATICALLY) SET S TO 1 AND */
                        /*      THE PROGRAM WILL BYPASS THE LOOP AND CONTINUE AT THIS POINT. */
                        /*****************************************************************/

    17    1            PUT FILE (SYSPRINT) LIST ('NOT ENOUGH X VALUES TO REACH Y OF: ',Y);
    18    1            STOP;
    19    1            END XMPL;
```

Figure 21.4. A sample program in PL/I.

MAL(6). The precision of 6 indicates that the number stored in the variable is available with six digits of precision. For example, a value of -342 would be expressed as -0.342000×10^3. Note that **FLOAT DECIMAL** is a convenience provided by the compiler so that binary places need not be counted. For instance, declarations of **FLOAT DECIMAL(6)** and **FLOAT BINARY(24)** produce the same numerical representation inside the machine. Maximum allowable precision varies with the implementation.

A scale of **FIXED** normally is used for integers (e.g., variables serving as counters). Because of the way many machines are organized internally, integers declared as **FIXED BINARY(15)** or **FIXED BINARY(31)** are commonly used. **FIXED DECIMAL** also is possible, but its internal representation differs from that produced by **FIXED BINARY** and there are potential processing difficulties which make it a good thing to avoid.

To illustrate, the statement

> DECLARE (VELOC,MASS) FLOAT DECIMAL(6),
>   NUMX FIXED BINARY(31),   (21.16)
>   (COUNTZ,COUNTW) FIXED BINARY(15):

reserves storage for five numerical variables with the indicated names and attributes.

Character String Variables

Character strings are described in terms of their lengths:

> DECLARE NAME__T CHARACTER(10),
>   (PART,WORD)CHARACTER(8);   (21.17)

reserves storage for three character strings: **NAME_T** with a capacity of ten characters; and two strings, **PART** and **WORD**, each with a capacity of eight characters.

These lengths are fixed in the sense that a reference to a particular character variable implies the length that was declared for it.

Character string variables which "grow" and "shrink" in length can be set up by attaching the VARYING attribute when they are declared.

DECLARE VOCAB CHARACTER(20) VARYING;

(21.18)

reserves storage for a variable named VOCAB whose length may not exceed 20 characters but can fall below that maximum depending on the string to be stored at any given time. Thus, a reference to this type of variable will imply a length depending on the string currently stored there.

Bit String Variables

Variables declared with the BIT attribute contain individual logical switches, each of which can be set independently to a value of "true" ('1'B) or "false" ('0'B). Declaration of bit string variables is similar to that of character string variables.

DECLARE(SWMAIN,SWBIG)
      BIT(8) VARYING, CONTROL BIT(4);   (21.19)

reserves storage for the variables as indicated. The parenthesized length specifies the number of bits in the string and the VARYING attribute has the same meaning as has been described for character strings.

Declaration and Organization of Collective Variables

For many applications convenience dictates organizing a group of values with the same attributes into a collection such that they can be addressed collectively by a single name, yet isolated independently when desired. Such groupings are called **arrays** and may be declared within the general mechanism described. The **dimensionality** of an array indicates the manner in which it is organized, i.e., the number of criteria that have to be specified in order to isolate a single member (**element**) of an array. A one dimensional array is simply a linear vector in which a single identifier, or **subscript,** is sufficient to distinguish any of its elements. To illustrate, the statement

DECLARE PRICE(12) FLOAT DECIMAL(6);   (21.20)

reserves storage for 12 floating point decimal values with 6 places of precision known collectively as PRICE. The first element in PRICE is identified by PRICE(1), the second by PRICE(2), and so on. This is seen in Figure 21.5a.

Each element in a two dimensional array requires two subscripts to isolate it. The implied organization is a rectangular arrangement of **rows** and **columns.** Thus, the

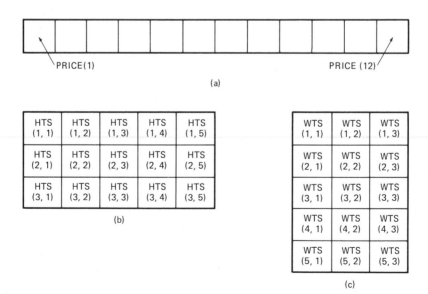

Figure 21.5. (a) A one dimensional array. (b) A 3×5 array. (c) A 5×3 array.

statement

DECLARE (HTS(3,5),WTS(5,3))FIXED BINARY(15);
                                              (21.21)

defines two 15 element arrays of fixed binary integers: the
first of these, named HTS, is organized into three rows
and five columns (Figure 5b), while the second (WTS) is
organized as five rows and three columns (Figure 5c). Internally elements in a two dimensional array are stored
in **row major order:** All the elements in a given row are
stored consecutively. Thus the elements in the array WTS
are stored in the sequence WTS(1,1), WTS(1,2),
WTS(1,3), WTS(2,1), ... , WTS(5,1),... ,
WTS(5,3).

Higher dimensional arrays may be specified following
the same organizational rules. Row major order is used
for internal storage regardless of the number of dimensions. Another way of describing row major order is to
say that the elements are sequenced such that the rightmost subscript varies the fastest, followed by the next
rightmost subscript, and so on.

Declarations: General Remarks

There is no limit with regard to the number of variables
that may be declared in a single statement except that
imposed by the compiler and the available memory. It is
possible (using parentheses) to group variables with a
common set of attributes to form a **factored declaration.**
This holds true for arrays as well as single-valued variables. Thus, the statement

DECLARE (SPGRAV(2,5), MASS,DIST(80))
                       FLOAT DECIMAL(6),
     TRADE(8) CHARACTER(10) VARYING;   (21.22)

is valid. Any number of DECLARE statements may appear in a procedure.

21.4 THE ASSIGNMENT STATEMENT

Numerical Computations

The arithmetic expression provides the basic vehicle for
describing numerical computations. PL/I recognizes six
operations, each of which must always be indicated explicitly: addition($+$), subtraction($-$), multiplication ($*$),
division($/$), exponentiation($**$), and negation ($-$ as in
$Y = -B**2;$).

The evaluation of arithmetic expressions follows a set
of priority rules in which negation is handled prior to ex-

ponentiation, which is followed by multiplication and division; addition and subtraction are the lowest priority
operations. Thus, the expression $A + B/C - D$ is equivalent to $a + (b/c) - d$ and not $a + b/(c - d)$. Parentheses override normal priorities, so that the programmer
may express the computational intent explicitly. There is
no doubt about the operations intended in the expression
$3.8*((A+B)/(2*C-D))**2$. Superfluous parentheses are legal as long as they are specified in matching
pairs.

The terms in a numerical expression may or may not
have similar attributes. If there are differences in scale
and/or base, PL/I automatically makes the necessary
conversions to perform the indicated arithmetic. The
presence of at least one component with the FLOAT attribute will force conversion of every number in an
expression to FLOAT so that floating point arithmetic can
be performed. If all the components are integers, PL/I
will use integer (rather than floating point) arithmetic,
thereby producing results with fractional values trun-
cated. For example, if variable Y is declared with the
FLOAT attribute, the assignment statement $Y = 9/5;$
produces a result of 1. Then, after the integer division has
been performed, the result will be converted to floating
point form (to match the attributes declared for the variable in which the result is to be stored), and the floating
point equivalent of the integer 1 will be placed in location
Y. Sometimes this is a good thing; other times it is not.
$Y = 9.0/5.0;$ will produce 1.8.

Arithmetic expressions also may include **function references.** A function is a procedure which can be activated
automatically (**invoked**) by referring to it in an expression.
When invoked, the function processes the information
supplied to it (**arguments**), thereby allowing its users to
treat that processing as a single operation. For example,
even though the computation of a square root involves
several individual operations, they are hidden beneath a
simple invocation of the square root function. Thus,

$$Z = X*SQRT(Y-X);   \quad (21.23)$$

supplies the square root function with an argument (the
number obtained by evaluating the subexpression $Y-X$).
The function produces the square root of this number and
that result is used as indicated (i.e., multiplied by X in
the example) to develop the final rsult which ultimately
replaces the value in Z.

SQRT is one of a library of **built-in functions** with
which PL/I is equipped. Therefore, a reference to one of
these function names (implicitly) instructs the compiler
to incorporate that function into the program. User-de-

veloped functions may be added to this library but are not considered here.

Character String Assignments

Simple replacement (e.g., A = B;) is governed by the lengths of the strings involved. The length of the destination (i.e., the string named on the left side of the assignment statement) determines the number of characters transferred to that string. Thus, if string B is declared as CHARACTER(10), a statement such as B = C; (where C is assumed to be a character string) places 10 characters in B regardless of C's length. If C is longer than 10, its leftmost 10 characters owe transferred. If it is shorter than 10 (say 7), it fills the leftmost seven characters in B, with the remainder being filled with blanks. In any event, all 10 characters in B are replaced.

When a destination variable is declared with the VARYING attribute, its apparent size will change to accommodate the string assigned to it. For instance, if W3 is declared as CHARACTER(15) VARYING and T is declared as CHARACTER(4), the statement W3 = T; will place T's four characters in W3 and W3's "new" length will be 4 regardless of what it was previously.

The formation of character string expressions involves a relatively limited number of basic manipulations. The only explicit operation is **concatenation,** indicated by || which builds a larger character string from two smaller ones. For example, assuming string G contains the four characters MARK, string H contains the five characters PLACE, and all variables have been appropriately declared, the assignment

$$S = G \, || \, 'ET' \, || \, H; \qquad (21.24)$$

replaces the current contents of string S with the 11 character string MARKETPLACE.

Additional facilities for constructing character expressions are provided through built-in functions. The most powerful of these is the substring function, SUBSTR, which identifies and manipulates portions of strings independent of their respective string content. SUBSTR requires three arguments as exemplified below:

$$SUBSTR(s,p,n); \qquad (21.25)$$

The first argument, s, names the string from which the substring will be subtracted; p indicates the starting position of the desired substring (the leftmost position in s is 1); n indicates the length of the desired substring. Using the value PLACE of string H as defined above, the expression SUBSTR(H,2,4) identifies a string four char-

acters long taken from string H and starting in the second position of H. Accordingly, the value of that string is LACE. Still assuming the values given above, the statement

$$S = SUBSTR(H,1,1) \, || \, SUBSTR(G,2,3); \qquad (21.26)$$

places the four characters PARK in character string S. Another function, LENGTH(s), allows the programmer to determine the current length of a designated character string declared with the VARYING attribute. The resulting integer may be used in any arithmetic expression.

Bit String Manipulations

PL/I has facilities for performing *logical operations* on bit strings, with the result being expressed as a bit string. Three basic logical operations may be performed on bit strings. Their properties are summarized in Figure 21.6. When a logical expression is evaluated, each indicated operation is performed in turn on the bits in corresponding positions of the operands. Assume, for example, that a procedure has the following statements:

$$DECLARE(ST1,ST2,ST3)BIT(4);$$
$$ST1 = '1001'B; ST2 = '0101'B; \qquad (21.27)$$

The assignment statement ST3 = ST1 & ST2; performs four separate "AND" operations on the corresponding bits in ST1 and ST2. The result, '0001'B, is then placed in ST3 as the replacement operation indicates.

NOT is the highest priority logical operation with OR being the lowest. Parentheses may override the priorities and clarify the programmer's intent.

Because each bit in a string is manipulated independently, the operations described for character string manipulations (see "Character String Manipulation," immediately preceding) apply to bit strings as well. Thus a shorter bit string will be stored in the leftmost positions

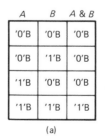
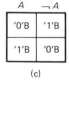

Figure 21.6. Basic logical operations, bit strings.

of a longer one, with the excess positions being padded with logical 0.

Logical Expressions with Single Bit Strings

When all the components of a bit string expression are restricted to a length of 1, the result is a **logical expression** whose outcome is either true ('1'B) or false ('0'B). When this restriction is met, it is possible to expand the versatility of such expressions by including another type of component, the *relational expression,* which consists of two arithmetic expressions connected by one of six *relational operators*. This produces a comparison between the two numbers represented by the arithmetic expression. For instance, the expression

$$X+Y < 17.2-Z \qquad (21.28)$$

fits this construction. Accordingly, the overall value of the resulting logical expression is "true" if the number obtained by evaluating $X + Y$ is algebraically less than that obtained by evaluating $17.2 - Z$. Thus, if TEST were to be declared as a bit string with length 1, we could write an assignment statement such as

$$TEST = X+Y < 17.2-Z; \qquad (24.29)$$

and it would have its expected meaning. The other five relational operators are greater than ($>$), greater than or equal to ($> =$), less than or equal to ($< =$), not equal to ($\neg =$), and equal to ($=$). The dual purpose served by the equals sign is unfortunate but not ambiguous since the compiler can determine its intended meaning based on context.

Since relational expressions evaluate to "true" or "false," they can be combined with logical operators to form more complex logical expressions. The example

$$TEST = (X+Y < 17.2-Z) \ \&$$
$$(Z-2*7 > = 26.7); \quad (21.30)$$

requires both relational expressions to be "true" in order for a value of "true" to be assigned to TEST. The parentheses are not required but may be included for clarity.

Manipulation of Arrays

The assignmnt statement described in the previous discussions apply to entire arrays as well as single-valued variables. For example, the sequence

```
DECLARE (AR1(12),AR2,(12))FLOAT DECIMAL(6);
AR1 = 14.8; AR2 = 1.05*AR1;         (21.31)
```

sets all of AR1's elements to the value indicated in the first assignment statement. Then, the program multiplies the value in each element of AR1 by 1.05 and places the results in the corresponding element of AR2. In both assignment statements the multiple activities are performed in the expected sequence, i.e., AR(1) is processed first, followed by AR1(2), and so on. In order for multiple assignments to work, the arrays involved must have the same number of dimensions, and corresponding dimensions must be the same size. If array X is 5×4 and Y is 4×5, the assignment X = Y; would not be valid.

21.5 INPUT/OUTPUT STATEMENTS

Declaration of Files

Before a file can be used as a source or destination for transmitted data, it must be identified (defined) for the program in which it is to be used. This is done in a normal declaration statement:

```
DECLARE SRFILE FILE STREAM INPUT,
        DTFILE FILE STREAM OUTPUT;      (21.32)
```

Each file is explicitly named (like any PL/I variable) and is declared with the FILE attribute, along with its intended usage. This establishes the fact that SRFILE may be used with a GET statement and DTFILE may be used with a PUT statement. The appearance of the data in those files is not defined here; rather, it is established by the type of GET/PUT statement used with the file.

Certain files are available in PL/I itself as standard data streams. Two of these, used for input and output respectively, are SYSIN and SYSPRINT. Associations between these names and physical devices are predefined so that PL/I can assume these associations in the absence of explicit specifications. For instance, the two statements

```
GET FILE (SYSIN) LIST(A,MASS,WORD1);

GET LIST(A,MASS,WORD1);              (21.33)
```

will produce identical results, i.e., the next three data items will be read from the standard input data stream and placed in respective locations A,MASS, and WORD1. Here we assume SYSIN and SYSPRINT refer to a card reader and line printer respectively.

List-Directed Input/Output

A list-directed input stream consists of a sequence of data items with a comma or an arbitrary number of blanks separating successive values. Data are expressed as *constants* (described in Section 21.2). Thus the statement

$$\text{GET LIST(VMAX,N3,SYM,NUM);} \qquad (21.34)$$

will read four input values regardless of whether they are on the same card or distributed over several cards. Before being stored in its specified destination, each value is converted (if possible) to match the attributes declared for it as a variable. Thus, a value headed for a variable declared as **FIXED BINARY(15)** need not be presented that way in the input stream.

Because of its simplicity, list-directed output offers little opportunity for control over the form of the resulting output stream. A statement like

$$\text{PUT LIST(V1,V2,V3);} \qquad (21.35)$$

places the three named variables in the output stream according to predefined rules. Assuming a line printer as the output destination, a typical format is five variables on each line of print regardless of the number of different **PUT** statements used to print them. For example, the statements

$$\text{PUT LIST(A); PUT LIST(B);}$$
$$\text{PUT LIST(C): PUT LIST(D);} \quad (21.36a)$$

will produce exactly the same result as the single statement

$$\text{PUT LIST(A,B,C,D);} \qquad (21.36b)$$

Limited control over output format can be exercised by including either or both of the following modifiers:

- **PUT PAGE LIST(** variable names **)**; forces the output to begin at the top of a new page.
- **PUT SKIP(** n **)LIST(** variable names **)**; forces the output to begin on a new line regardless of the position of the last item to be printed. Here, n is an integer indicating that $n-1$ blank lines are to be left between the last printed line and the one about to be printed.

For instance,

$$\text{PUT PAGE SKIP(3)LIST(VAR1,TEMP);} \quad (21.37)$$

will print the values for **VAR1** and **TEMP** after going to the top of a new page and skipping the first two lines.

Edit-Directed Input/Output

This form of data stream requires complete specification in that it allows detailed control of its format. There are no explicit punctuation or separation symbols; interpretation of the data stream is supplied as part of the associated **GET** or **PUT** statement. This information appears in the form of a specification list in which each data item is explicitly described and each position in the data stream accounted for. The most common types follow.

- $X(n)$—when this specification is part of an input stream description, the next n spaces (positions) in that stream are to be ignored regardless of their contents. When this specification refers to output, the next n positions of the output stream are to be filled with blanks.
- $F(w,d)$—when this specification describes part of an input stream, the information in the next w positions is to be treated as a decimal value with the d rightmost digits being decimal places. (If a decimal point actually appears as part of the information, it occupies a position and therefore is included in w). When this specification is applied to output, the next w positions in the output stream are to be filled with a decimal value having d decimal digits. The count for w is assumed to include positions for a decimal point and a sign. Simplification to $F(w)$—describes a w-digit decimal integer.
- $A(n)$—describes a character string w positions (characters) in length. Contrary to list-directed streams, apostrophes in this case count as part of the character string.
- $COLUMN(n)$—when part of an input description, this specification directs the next input value to be taken from column n of the card. Thus, a specification of $COLUMN(1)$ forces the input process to begin at the first column of the next card. For output, this forces the next item to be printed starting in column n of the line.

To see how this last works, suppose we have a card containing data as shown in Table 21.1.

The parenthesized periods in the table indicate the position of an assumed decimal point; none are actually punched. A suitable input statement describing these data would appear as follows:

$$\text{GET EDIT(V1,IDENTI,WTG,GPR)}$$
$$\text{(COLUMN(1),F(3,1),X(5),A(12),}$$
$$\text{F(6,3),X(14),F(3));} \quad (21.38)$$

Now, having read this information, suppose we wanted to print it on a new line starting in column 5, complete with minus sign and decimal points. Moreover, each of the items would be separated by five spaces. The **PUT** statement would look as follows:

Table 21.1 Data for Edit-Directed I/O

Column Numbers	Name	Declared as	Input Value
1–3	V1	FLOAT DECIMAL(6)	32(.)7
4–8	—	—	NOT INTERESTED
9–20	IDENTI	CHARACTER(12)	CARDWELL INC
21–26	WTG	FLOAT DECIMAL(6)	−22(.)017
27–40	—	—	NOT INTERESTED
41–43	GPR	FIXED BINARY(15)	614

```
PUT SKIP EDIT(V1,IDENTI,WTG,GPR);
(COLUMN(5),F(4,1),X(5),A(12),X(5),
          F(7,3),X(5),F(3));   (21.39)
```

Input/Output of Arrays

The GET and PUT statements may be used to transmit an entire array simply by specifying the array name in the statement. The underlying assumptions are that the entire array will be transmitted, and that the order of transmission will correspond to that implied by the declaration. For example, if PR is declared as a 5×4 array of FLOAT DECIMAL(6) numbers, the statement GET LIST(PR); will read the next 20 values from the input stream and place them, respectively, in PR(1,1), PR(1.2) and so on.

21.6 DECISION AND CONTROL FACILITIES

The IF Statement

The basic decision statement exemplified in Section 2.3 generalizes as follows:

```
IF logical condition THEN action;
          ELSE alternative action;   (21.40)
```

The "logical condition" motivating the selection of one of the two alternative actions can be any expression whose resulting value is '1'B or '0'B (see Section 21.4). For example, assuming S to be declared as BIT(1) and X to be a numerical variable, we can use S in a decision, e.g.,

```
IF S = '1'B THEN X = 3;
            ELSE X = 2;   (21.41)
```

or, more simply,

```
IF S THEN X = 3;
     ELSE X = 2;   (21.42)
```

A more elaborate example hints at the possibilities: assuming Y and X are numerical variables, the logical condition in the statement

```
IF Y < 3 | Y > 17 THEN X = 3;
               ELSE X = 2;   (21.43)
```

still meets the structural requirements. In the example X will be set to a value of 3 only when Y is outside the indicated range (3–17); otherwise X will be set to 2.

More Complicated Actions

The action after THEN or ELSE may be as simple as the single statement in the previous example. When an action's expression extends beyond one statement, a DO **group** is used to form compound statements. For instance, in the decision structure

```
IF X > Y+7 THEN DO;
          X = 3;
          Y = Y+4;
          END;
       ELSE X = 2;   (21.44)
```

the action taken when X exceeds Y + 7 consists of two assignments. The entire group is ignored when X does not exceed Y + 7, and X is set at 2.

More Complicated Decisions

Extensive structures of decision rules can be formed by specifying an IF statement as an action stemming from another **IF** statement. The general structure is as follows:

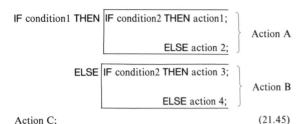

IF condition1 THEN IF condition2 THEN action1;

ELSE action 2;   } Action A

ELSE IF condition2 THEN action 3;

ELSE action 4;   } Action B

Action C;   (21.45)

Action A, performed only if condition1 is true, consists of action1 *or* action2, depending on condition2. Action B, performed only if condition1 is false, consits either of action3 *or* action4, depending on condition3. Thus, condition3 is not tested unless condition1 was found to be false. Action C is performed in any event. Of course, it is not necessary for the structure to be symmetrical: a THEN IF does not force the presence of an ELSE IF. If desired, this *nesting* of IF statements can be carried well beyond the limits of reason.

Repetitive Operations

A group of statements can be repeated under automatic control by setting up a **DO loop.** One mechanism (Section 21.3) enables the activity to be repeated as long as a specified condition is true:

DO WHILE (condition);

.
.
.

statements;

.
.
.

END;   (21.46)

The controlling condition is the same type as that tested in an **IF** statement.

Another form of **DO** loop regulates a cyclic process based on the number of repetitions. The control information is concentrated in the **DO** statement at the head of the loop:

DO index = starting **TO** limit **BY** increment;

(21.47)

The **index** names a variable to be used for counting the number of iterations. After setting the index to the specified starting value, the loop's actions are performed repeatedly, with the index being modified by the increment

each time through the loop until the limiting value is reached or exceeded. For instance, the following sequence

```
            X = 0:
ADLOOP: DO I = 5 TO 13 BY 2;
            X = X + 2.3*I
            END ADLOOP;
```
                                                 (21.48)

produces the value $2.3(5+7+9+11+13)$ in X. The increment may be negative, in which case the starting value must exceed the limiting value.

Either type of loop may be placed entirely inside another loop (nested). The inner loop then will go through a complete set of cycles for each iteration of the outer loop. If Y is declared as a 6x10 array of numbers (see Section 21.3), the displayed sequence

```
         GET LIST (Y);
LPOUT:DO I = TO 5 BY 2;
     LPIN:DO J = 1 TO 10 BY 1;
         IF J < 6 THEN DO;
             Y(I,J) = 2*Y(I,J);
             Y(I+1,J) = 1.8*Y(I+1,J);
             END;

         ELSE DO;
             Y(I,J) = 0.5*Y(I,J);
             Y(I+1,J) = 0.9*Y(I+1,J);
             END;
         END LPIN:
END LPOUT;
```
                                                 (41.49)

will double the values in the first 5 columns and, in odd-numbered rows, increase by 80 percent those elements in the first 5 columns; and in even-numbered rows, halve the remaining values in odd-numbered rows, and reduce by 10 percent those values in columns 6–10 and rows 2, 4 and 6.

Since a loop is a single conceptual activity, it may be specified as a choice in an **IF** statement.

The GO TO Statement

Explicit changes in the executing sequence are specified by means of the statement **GO TO** label; the designated label matches one attached to a statement elsewhere in the procedure.

21.7 PROGRAM MONITORING

Certain events ordinarily curtailing execution can be intercepted, thereby enabling the program to continue. The mechanism permitting such intervention is called an **in-**

terrupt. The ON statement gives the PL/I programmer access to a variety of such interrupts:

$$\text{ON interrupt action ;} \qquad (21.50)$$

The following are commonly encountered interrupt types;

- ENDFILE(filename)—an attempt to read input data from an already "emptied" file.
- OVERFLOW—an attempt to produce a floating point number larger than the maximum value that can be expressed by the machine.
- UNDERFLOW—an attempt to produce a floating point number greater than zero but less than the smallest expressible floating point number.
- FIXEDOVERFLOW—an attempt to store an integer larger than the maximum expressible value.
- ZERODIVIDE—an attempt to divide by zero.
- CONVERSION—an attempt (typically) to use non-numeric characters as numbers.

If a program does not include an ON statement for a particular type of interrupt, occurrence of that interrupt will force the system to halt the program. Thus, inclusion of the ON statement gives the programmer the opportunity to substitute some other action. As in the case of the IF statement, the action may be a single statement or a compound statement. Unlike the IF statement, however, the compound statement cannot be a DO group. Instead, the BEGIN **block** is used in this situation:

$$\text{ON interrupt BEGIN;}$$
$$\vdots$$
$$\text{END;} \qquad (21.51)$$

Placement of an ON statement in a program makes the programmer-defined action automatically available anywhere after that statement. Then, when the specified interrupt occurs, the program performs the action indicated by the appropriate ON statement and resumes processing (if it can) where it left off.

21.8 CONSTRUCTION OF PROGRAMS FROM PROCEDURES

A main procedure may contain any number of internal procedures. Each procedure is executed when needed by being **invoked** explicitly from the main program.

Organization of Internal Procedures

The overall structure for procedures is as follows:

$$\text{procname: PROCEDURE(p1,p2, . . .);}$$
$$\cdot$$
$$\text{statements;}$$
$$\cdot$$
$$\cdot$$
$$\text{RETURN;}$$
$$\text{END procname;} \qquad (21.52)$$

The procedure is invoked by referring to its *entry point,* indicated by "procname." (Procedure names follow the same structural rules as variable names). The *parameter list* (p1, p2, etc.), which defines the way in which the procedure is used, indicates the number of data items to be supplied to the procedure (i.e., *arguments*) when invoked. Declarations inside the procedure establish the attributes associated with each parameter and, therefore, determine the attributes expected for the corresponding arguments. The body of the procedure shows the role of each parameter in the processing. By implication, then, the first argument will be used the way the first parameter is used, and so on.

The following example

```
PCOMP: PROCEDURE(A,B,C,D);
        DECLARE(A,B,C,D) FLOAT DECIMAL(6);
        C = A**2 + B**2
        D = A**3 − B**3;
        RETURN;
END PCOMP:
```

shows a procedure named PCOMP which, when invoked, is to be supplied with four FLOAT DECIMAL(6) arguments. PCOMP will compute the sum of the squares of the first two arguments, placing the result in the third argument. In addition, it will compute the difference between the cubed values of the first and second arguments, placing the result in the fourth argu
ters are only for bookkeeping pu
spond to actual locations or valu~~.~~   (21.53)

Invocation of Procedures

Procedures are used by explicit reference made through a CALL statement:

$$\text{CALL procname(a1,a2, . . .);} \qquad (21.54)$$

```
              BOWL: PROCEDURE OPTIONS(MAIN);

STMT LEVEL NEST
   1                      BOWL: PROCEDURE OPTIONS(MAIN);
                          /****************************************************************/
                          /*      THIS PROGRAM COMPUTES INDIVIDUAL BOWLING SCORES FOR ANY  */
                          /*      NUMBER OF GAMES. EACH GAME IS ON A CARD SHOWING:         */
                          /*          GAME NO.                            COLS  4-5        */
                          /*          PINS DOWNED BY 1ST BALL             COLS  7-8        8/
                          /*          PINS DOWNED BY 2ND BALL             COLS  7-8        */
                          /*          PINS DOWNED BY 3RD BALL             COLS 10-11       */
                          /*                             ETC.                              */
                          /*          PINS DOWNED BY 21ST BALL           COLS 64-65        */
                          /*                                                              */
                          /*      SINCE A GAME MAY NOT REQUIRE THE MAXIMUM NUMBER OF 21 BALLS */
                          /*      (E.G., A PERFECT GAME NEEDS ONLY 12), VALUES OF 99 WILL BE */
                          /*      USED TO FILL OUT 21 ENTRIES FOR EACH GAME. TO KEEP IT     */
                          /*      SIMPLE WE SHALL ASSUME ONLY ACCURATE INPUT.              */
                          /*      THE MAIN PROCEDURE CONTAINS THREE PROCEDURES:            */
                          /*          PREAD: GETS THE INPUT FOR ONE GAME                   */
                          /*          PGAME: COMPUTES A GAME SCORE                         */
                          /*          PPRT: PRINTS THE GAME SCORE                          */
                          /*      THE FOLLOWING VARIABLES ARE USED BY THE MAIN PROCEDURE:  */
                          /*      GMNO: -- THE GAME NUMBER                                 */
                          /*      PINS: -- AN ARRAY CONTAINING THE 21 INPUT ENTRIES        */
                          /*      SCORE: -- THE 10 FRAME SCORES (SCORE(10) 8 GAME SCORE)   */
                          /****************************************************************/

                          /****************************************************************/
                          /*                        PREAD                                 */
                          /*      THE 21 (X(1),F(2)) SAVES WRITING X(1),F(2) 21 TIMES      */
                          /****************************************************************/
   2    1                 PREAD: PROCEDURE(GAME,BALL);
   3    2                     DECLARE (GAME,BALL(21)) FIXED BINARY (15);
   4    2                     GET EDIT (GAME,BALL)(COLUMN(1),F(2),21 (X(1),F(2)));
   5    2                     PUT SKIP(2) EDIT('GAME NO. ',GAME,BALL)
                                   (X(5),A(9),X(2),F(2),X(5), 21 (F(2),X(2)));
   6    2                     RETURN
   7    2                     END PREAD;

                          /****************************************************************/
                          /*                        PGAME                                 */
                          /*      THIS PROCEDURE USES BLNO, A COUNTER TO KEEP TRACK OF WHICH */
                          /*      BALL WE ARE WORKING ON. SINCE IT IS NOT NEEDED ANYWHERE  */
                          /*      ELSE, IT IS SET UP AND USED AS A LOCAL VARIABLE: IT DOES */
                          /*      NOT APPEAR IN THE PARAMETER LIST AND IS UNKNOWN EVERYWHERE */
                          /*      IN THE PROGRAM EXCEPT IN PGAME.                          */
                          /****************************************************************/
   8    1                 PGAME: PROCEDURE (ROLL,SC);
   9    2                     DECLARE (ROLL(21),SC(10)) FIXED BINARY (15),
                                   BLNO FIXED BINARY(15);
  10    2                 SC = 0;    BLNO = 1;
  12    2                 FRLP: DO NFRM = 1 TO 10;
  13    2    1               IF ROLL(BLNO)=10 THEN DO;
  15    2    2                       SC(NFRM)=10+ROLL(BLNO+1)+ROLL(BLNO+2);
  16    2    2                       BLNO=BLNO+1;
  17    2    2                       END;
  18    2    1               ELSE IF ROLL(BLNO)+ROLL(BLNO+1)=10
  19    2    1                   THEN DO;
  20    2    2                       SC(NFRM)=10+ROLL(BLNO+2);
  21    2    2                       BLNO=BLNO+2;
  22    2    2                       END;
  23    2    1               ELSE DO;
  24    2    2                       SC(NFRM)=ROLL(BLNO)+ROLL(BLNO+1);
  25    2    2                       BLNO=BLNO+2;
  26    2    2                       END;
  27    2    1               IF NFRM > 1 THEN SC(NFRM)=SC(NFRM)+SC(NFRM-1);
  29    2    1               END FRLP;
  30    2                 RETURN;
  31    2                 END PGAME;

                          /****************************************************************/
                          /*                        PPRT                                  */
                          /****************************************************************/
  32    1                 PPRT: PROCEDURE (NGM,NPN);
  33    2                     DECLARE (NGM,NPN(10)) FIXED BINARY(15);
  34    2                     PUT SKIP EDIT('SCORE FOR GAME ',NGM,' : ',NPN)
                                   (X(5),A(15),F(2),A(3), 10(F(3),X(2)));
  35    2                 RETURN;
  36    2                 END PPRT;
```

Figure 21.7a. Main procedure with procedures in PL/I. (Continued)

```
              BOWL: PROCEDURE OPTIONS(MAIN);
STMT LEVEL NEST
                   /******************************************************************/
                   /*                        THE MAIN PROCEDURE                      */
                   /******************************************************************/
 37    1                DECLARE (GMNO,PINS(21),SCORE(10)) FIXED BINARY,
                             FLAG BIT(1);
 38    1                FLAG = '1'B;
 39    1                PUT PAGE;
 40    1                CALL PREAD (GMNO,PINS);
 41    1                ON ENDFILE (SYSIN) BEGIN:
 43    2                               PUT SKIP(3) LIST('--END OF RUN--');
 44    2                               STOP;
 45    2                               END;

 46    1          BGLP: DO WHILE (FLAG);        /*  AN ENDLESS LOOP BROKEN BY ENDFILE  */
 47    1    1               CALL PGAME (PINS,SCORE);
 48    1    1               CALL PPRT(GMNO,SCORE);
 49    1    1               CALL PREAD(GMNO,PINS);
 50    1    1               END BGLP;

 51    1                END BOWL;

GAME NO.   21    10 10  10  10  10  10  10  10  10  10  10  10  99  99  99  99  99  99  99  99  99
SCORE FOR GAME 21 :  30  60  90 120 150 180 210 240 270 300

GAME NO.   22    10  9   1  10  10   8   2  10   7   2   9   1   9   1   9   1  10  99  99  99  99
SCORE FOR GAME 22 :  20  40  68  88 108 127 136 155 174 194

GAME NO.   23     9  1   9   1   9   1   9   1   9   1   9   1   9   1   9   1   9   1   7   3   9
SCORE FOR GAME 23 :  19  38  57  76  95 114 133 152 169 188

--END OF RUN--
```

Figure 21.7b. Main procedure with procedures in PL/I. (Conclusion)

the *argument list* (a1, a2, etc.) must match the parameter list in number. attributes, and order. Thus, if we invoke the procedure PCOMP with the statement

$$\text{CALL PCOMP(U,V,W,X);} \qquad (21.55)$$

(assuming all four variables are declared as FLOAT DECIMAL(6) in the invoking procedure), PCOMP will place the value $U^2 + V^2$ in W, and $U^3 - V^3$ in X.

A CALL statement may appear anywhere in a procedure, including such places as the middle of a DO group, and an IF or ON statement. Conceptually, it is easiest to think of the CALL together with the activity invoked by it as a single statement.

A FINAL EXAMPLE

The example in Figure 27.7 shows the use of several procedures in a main procedure.

REFERENCES

American National Standard Programming Language PL/I. Document X3.53-1976, American National Standards Institute.

PL/I Optimizing Compiler. Documents GC33-0001 through GC33-0006, **IBM** Corporation.

Pollack, S. V., and T. D. Sterling, *A Guide to Structured Programming and PL/I,* 3rd Ed. New York: Holt, Rinehart & Winston, 1979.

22
APL

Michael Montalbano

IBM Corporation

22.1 INTRODUCTION

The name **APL** derives from the initials of the title of *A Programming Language,* by Kenneth Iverson, the first book in which this language was described.

The notation used in the book could not conveniently be entered from a terminal; for example, elements, rows and columns of an array were selected by means of superscripts and subscripts, a matter of some awkwardness for most terminals, particularly since more than two indices are required for multidimensional arrays.

In the early 1960s, the development of an APL interpreter resulted in modifications to the notation that made it suitable for keyboard entry. This notation is now in common use in a variety of time sharing APL systems. Thus *APL* now means

- A notation, or *language,* for describing algorithms;
- A *time sharing system* built on an interpreter for the language.

Though the two meanings are closely related, it is important to distinguish between them. In this chapter, this is done in two major sections: "APL: The Language," and "APL: The Time Sharing System."

However, before starting a detailed discussion of either of these topics, it will be helpful to take a preliminary look at APL as a whole. A great many interconnected ideas are required to describe APL. If these ideas were to be defined one after another, they would make very heavy reading for most people: the early definitions would be hard to understand because they would require familiarity with terms not yet defined; the later ones would be hard to understand because, by the time they were reached, the early ones would be forgotten.

When an APL terminal is available, the best way to avoid this kind of difficulty is to run through a carefully designed series of exercises and explain each result as it is produced, introducing terminology, ideas and explanations as they are required. Section 22.2 is an attempt to do this with a series of figures that are annotated copies of an actual APL terminal session.

Figures 22.1 and 22.2 show a series of terminal entries and APL system responses which introduce us at once to many of the interconnected ideas that make up APL as a whole. These ideas are introduced in the following section and discussed in greater detail in sections that follow.

22.2 PRELIMINARIES: APL IN ACTION

Figures 22.1 and 22.2 contain an annotated copy of an APL terminal session. They show

- Illustrative terminal entries;
- APL system responses to those entries;
- Five topic headings (I–V);
- Numbers at the right (in parentheses) that provide a key to comments in the text.

Entries made by the terminal user are indented six positions from the left margin. This is the normal position for the cursor or type ball when the APL system expects *user* response. Entries that are flush left are *system* responses.

For example, the intended user entry 3+4 (Figure 22.1 (1)) results in the system response 7 flush left on the line below.

Execution (I)

APL's fundamental mode of operation is called **execution** mode. In this mode the APL action is to evaluate an expression. That is, except for expressions preceded by a), (the prefix for **system commands**) or a ▽, (which puts the system in **function definition** mode), *any entry from an APL keyboard is assumed to be an expression to be evaluated.*

The entries in (I) introduce several key ideas:

- **Scalars** (1): the numbers 3 and 4 added.
- **Vector notation** (2): the entry 4 5 6 reprsents an ordered sequence of three numbers. Blanks separate the components. (The entry 456, on the other hand, is a single number.)
- Addition of a **single number** to a **set** of numbers (2): 3 + 4 5 6 to give 7 8 9.
- Addition of **two sets** of numbers that have the same number of elements (3): 1 2 3 + 4 5 6.
- An **error message** for a request to add two sets of numbers that do not have the same number of elements (5): 2 3 + 4 5 6. In this case the message is *LENGTH ERROR* followed by a copy of the expression in which the error occurred. This, in turn, is followed by a line (7) in which the symbol ∧ is placed under the position in the expression at which the error was detected.

Name Conventions (II)

This section introduces:

- Variable names;
- The specification symbol, ←;
- Data types: character, numeric;
- Two APL functions with the same symbol, ρ;
- Indexing.

APL variable and function **names** are constructed in the same way. A name must start with a nonnumeric character, $A \ldots Z$, $\triangle$, and possibly others, depending on the system. The name may be followed by a sequence of characters (up to 77 in many systems) that may include the numerals 0 . . . 9 in addition to the original set. The **specification symbol** ←, associates a name with a value. A named value is called a **variable** and can either be a single character or number or a set of characters or numbers.

APL data is **structured:** it consists of sets of numbers or characters ordered along *axes*. Names chosen for variables in the example of Figure 22.1 describe both type and structure:

$CV1$—a character vector (8).
$NV1$—a numeric vector (9).
$NM1$—a numeric matrix (10).

Vectors are sets of elements ordered from left to right along one axis. **Matrices** are sets of elements ordered from left to right and from top to bottom along two axes.

We define a matrix (12) by shaping a sequence of numbers into an array of 3 rows and 5 columns. The symbol ρ, in this case, denotes the **reshape function.** It reshapes the value on its right as specified by the value on its left. Values used as inputs to functions are called **arguments** in APL.

In (13), ρ is used with only one argument; this use is called **monadic**. Used this way, it denotes the *shape of* function, which returns as a value the shape of its argument. Note that a name by itself is an expression to be evaluated (14). Entering the name, $NM1$, results in a display of its value immediately below. Expressions enclosed within brackets select elements or subarrays from an APL variable (10, 15). Thus $CV1$, (8), is a character vector; $NV1$ is a numerical vector (9). It selects characters by their ordinal position within the character vector $CV1$ (8) for the **selection** request $CV1[NV1]$ (10) to produce and display a new character vector (11). When the indexing variable is a matrix (15), the value returned is an array of the same shape.

System Commands (III)

Here are several system commands and associated responses as found in Figure 22.2:

-)*WSID* (16) asks for the name of the current active workspace.
-)*WSID EXAMPLES* (17) changes the workspace name from *CLEAR* to *EXAMPLES*.
-)*SAVE* (18) stores a copy of the active workspace in auxiliary storage.
-)*FNS* (19) requests a list of names of defined functions in the active workspace. Since none are defined, no names appear on the line below.
-)*VARS* (20) requests a list of names of variables in the

```
        I. Evaluation.  Length Compatibility Requirements.
           Vector Notation.  Error Messages

            3+4                          (1)
    7
            3+4 5 6                      (2)
    7 8 9
            1 2 3+4 5 6                  (3)
    5 7 9
            123+456                      (4)
    579
            2 3+4 5 6                    (5)
    LENGTH ERROR                         (6)
            2 3 + 4 5 6
                ^                        (7)


        II.  Name Conventions.  Data Types.  Indexing.
             Shaping.  Determining Shape.

            CV1←'ABCDEFGHIJKLMNOPQRSTUVWXYZ 01234567ΔΔ'     (8)

            NV1←2 5 4 1 26 26 12 5 4                        (9)

            CV1[NV1]                        (10)
    BEDAZZLED                               (11)

            NM1←3 5ρ18 15 15 13 27 2 5 4 27 27 2 15 1 18 4     (12)

            ρNM1                            (13)
    3 5

            NM1                             (14)
    18 15 15 13 27
     2  5  4 27 27
     2 15  1 18  4

            CV1[NM1]                        (15)
    ROOM
    BED
    BOARD
```

Figure 22.1. An introduction to APL characteristics.

active workspace. The response shows those variables defined in Figure 22.1.

System Variables (IV)

This section introduces two system variables, $\square IO$ and $\square AI$, and illustrates the influence of $\square IO$ on indexing.

The index of the first of a set of elements can be defined as either 0 or 1 in APL by setting the **index origin system variable,** $\square IO$. One may request a display of the current setting of $\square IO$ in the active workspace (22) and then change it from 1 to 0 (23) (or vice versa). The results of the change when $NV1$ (24) and $NM1$ (25) are used to index $CV1$ can be compared against the previous results in Figure 22.1 (10,15).

$\square AI$ (26) is a system variable. It is introduced here primarily to illustrate how an APL program can access system dependent information. The four elements provided by $\square AI$ give

1. The account number of the current terminal user;
2. The computer time consumed, in milliseconds;
3. Terminal connect time;
4. Keying time expended since the beginning of the current APL session.

Operators and Relational Functions (V)

This section provides a preliminary look at two important features:

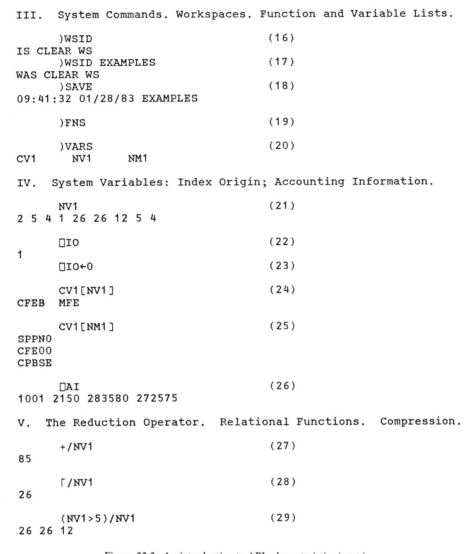

III.   System Commands. Workspaces. Function and Variable Lists.

```
      )WSID                    (16)
IS CLEAR WS
      )WSID EXAMPLES           (17)
WAS CLEAR WS
      )SAVE                    (18)
09:41:32 01/28/83 EXAMPLES

      )FNS                     (19)

      )VARS                    (20)
CV1    NV1    NM1
```

IV.   System Variables: Index Origin; Accounting Information.

```
      NV1                      (21)
2 5 4 1 26 26 12 5 4

      □IO                      (22)
1
      □IO←0                    (23)

      CV1[NV1]                 (24)
CFEB   MFE

      CV1[NM1]                 (25)
SPPNO
CFE0O
CPBSE

      □AI                      (26)
1001 2150 283580 272575
```

V.   The Reduction Operator. Relational Functions. Compression.

```
      +/NV1                    (27)
85

      ⌈/NV1                    (28)
26

      (NV1>5)/NV1              (29)
26 26 12
```

Figure 22.2. An introduction to APL characteristics (cont.).

- Operators.
- Selection by vectors generated by relational functions.

Operators.   To add together all the elements of the vector $NV1$, place $+/$ in front of the letters $NV1$ (27). Used this way, $/$ is called the **reduction operator.** (We justify the name "reduction" later.) Preceded by a **function symbol** ($+$ in this case), $/$ creates a new function called a **derived function.** Here, the derived function is the "add them all up" function, called SUM in other programming languages.

The effect of the slash is as a reduction operator is described thus:

Take the function symbol to the left of the slash, insert it between successive elements of the variable to the right of the slash, and evaluate the resulting expression.

If the function symbol is $+$, the result is the *SUM* function.

Inserted between two numbers, the **maximum** function returns the larger of the two. Thus $5\lceil 12$ returns a 12. The

derived function produced by the combination ⌈/ is called MAX in some programming languages. It is used in (28) to return the value of the largest number in *NV*1.

What do the results (27, 28) have in common? In both cases, a vector of nine elements, *NV*1, is subjected to an action that returns a single value: the sum of the elements in *NV*1 (27); the biggest element in *NV*1 (28).

It is the **reduction** of a vector to a scalar (and a matrix to a vector, and so on for arrays of more than two dimensions) that gives the operator its name.

Compression and relational selection. The next example (29) illustrates several things:

1. We use the symbol / as a function rather than as an operator.
2. We generate a Boolean vector (consisting solely of 0s and 1s) with a relational function.
3. We use this vector to select from the array the elements that satisfy the relation.

When used as a reduction operator, / was preceded by a function symbol, + or ⌈. In (29), it is preceded by the

```
      )LOAD EXAMPLES
   SAVED 10:13:19 01/28/83

      )FNS

      )VARS
   CV1     NM1      NV1

   I.  APL Data.  Shape and Rank.

      ρNV1              (30)  Shape
   9
      ρρNV1             (31)  Rank
   1
      ρρρNV1            (32)  Identically 1 for any variable
   1

      ρNM1              (33)  Shape
   3 5
      ρρNM1             (34)  Rank
   2
      ρρρNM1            (35)  1
   1


      NS1←7

      ρNS1              (36)  Shape
                        (37)  Empty vector.  No visible output
                              except line feed.
      ρρNS1             (38)  Rank
   0
      ρρρNS1            (39)  1
   1

   II.  Converting Data to Vector Form.  The Ravel Function.

      NS1
   7
      ρNS1              (40)  Shape of scalar is
                        (41)  null vector.

      TEMP←,NS1         (42)  Ravel scalar and name result TEMP.
      ρTEMP             (43)  TEMP is vector.
   1                    (44)  Shape is 1.
```

Figure 22.3. APL data.

III.   Converting Arrays into Scalars.

```
       NV1                       (45)   Value
2  5  4  1 26 26 12 5 4
       ρNV1                      (46)   Shape
9

       TEMP←''ρNV1               (47)   Reshape into scalar and name
       TEMP                             result TEMP.
2                                (48)   Value is first item in NV1.
       ρTEMP                     (49)   Shape is null or
                                          "empty" vector.
       ρρTEMP                    (50)   Rank is 0.
0
```

IV. Null or "Empty" Vectors.   Data Types.   "Take" Function: ↑

```
       NULLC←''                  (51)   Empty character vector
       NULLN←ι0                  (52)   Empty numeric vector

       NULLC                     (53)   Value

       ρNULLC                    (54)   Rank
0

       NULLN                     (55)   Value

       ρNULLN                    (56)   Rank
0

       1↑NULLC                   (57)   1↑ of empty character vector
                                          gives blank character.
       1↑NULLN                   (58)   1↑ of empty numeric vector
0                                        gives zero.
       ' '=1↑NULLC               (59)   Test for blank character.
1                                (60)   True.  Result of 1↑ is blank.
       ' '=1↑NULLN               (61)   Test for blank character.
0                                (62)   False.  Result not blank.
       0=1↑NULLN                 (63)   Test for 0 result
1                                (64)   True.  Result is 0.
```

Figure 22.4. APL data (cont.).

expression *(NV1>5)*. *NV1*>5 is what generates the 0s and 1s. The/uses the result as an argument which generates 0 or a 1 for each element of *NV1*. It generates 0s for elements not greater than 5; it generates 1s for those greater than 5. The result is a **logical,** or **Boolean, vector.**

A logical vector followed by / and then a compatible array, **compresses** the array by selecting the elements that correspond in position to 1s in the logical vector. In the example, this chooses the elements 26 26 12 from *NV1*, those that are greater than 5.

The / function (29) is called **compression.**

Note: Newcomers to APL are apt to be confused by use of the symbol / for the two different purposes. Take the time *now* to understand the difference between / used as a function (compression) and as an operator (reduction).

This care will save considerable grief in APL programming.

Summary. We have looked at terminal interactions that illustrate many APL features. The next sections discuss these features in more detail.

22.3 APL: THE LANGUAGE—DATA

Three key ideas are fundamental to an understanding of the APL language; these are discussed in this and the next three sections:

• Data
• Functions
• Operators

Data in APL refers to ordered sets of numbers or characters. *All* APL data are ordered. Keep in mind this fact and its implications when writing APL programs.

The most puzzling aspects of APL data structure are apt to be those concerned with

- Empty or null arrays.
- Multidimensional arrays containing a single element.

Figures 22.3 through 22.5 contain annotated terminal entries that illustrate and describe key facts about APL data, with particular emphasis on these points.

Figure 22.3 starts with the user entry

$$)LOAD\ EXAMPLES \qquad (22.1)$$

This loads the workspace defined and saved in the first two figures. Note that the responses to)*FNS* and)*VARS* are as in Figure 22.2 (19, 20).

The remainder of the figure is divided into two sections.

Shape and Rank (I)

The **shape** of a vector is the number of elements it contains. The shape of a matrix is the number of its rows followed by the number of its columns. The **monadic function**, ρ, determines the shape of $NV1$ (30) and $NM1$ (33).

Monadic ρ, the *shape of* function, always returns a vector result. The shape of this result, i.e., the shape of the

```
     V. APL Data.  Indexing.  Selecting Subarrays.
                   Index-origin Dependencies.
                   ι, the index-generating function

        ⎕IO                    (65)
1
        NM1[2;]                (66)   Select second row of NM1
   2 5 4 27 27
        NM1[;5]                (67)   Select fifth column of NM1
   27 27 4
        NM1[2;5]               (68)   Select item in second row and
   27                                 fifth column of NM1

        ⎕IO←0                  (69)   Change index origin to 0

        NM1[;5]                (70)   Error.  Index of rightmost
INDEX ERROR                           column is 4 in 0-origin.
        NM1[;5]
           ∧

        ι5                     (71)   Generate first five indices.
   0 1 2 3 4

        ⎕IO←1                  (72)   Change index origin to 1.

        ι5                     (73)   Generate first five indices.
   1 2 3 4 5

        NM1                    (74)   Display NM1
   18 15 15 13 27
    2  5  4 27 27
    2 15  1 18  4

        NM1[1;]←5ρ1            (75)   Specify first row of NM1 as 1 1 1 1

        NM1                    (76)   Display NM1
    1  1  1  1  1
    2  5  4 27 27
    2 15  1 18  4
```

Figure 22.5. APL data (cont.).

shape vector, tells us the **rank** of the original array. The rank of a vector is 1; the rank of a matrix is 2.

The idea of rank generalizes in an obvious way to arrays ordered along 3, 4, 5, . . . axes. However, what is the shape of a single element? What is its rank? When we request the shape of *NS*1, defined in the previous entry as the single number 7, the answer is invisible, as the comment (37) points out. The shape of a single number entered from the keyboard is an *empty* or *null* vector—a vector that contains no elements. The only visible effect of printing out a null vector is an extra line feed. However, a null vector does have a shape; application of ρ twice, to *NS*1 tells us that its rank is 0.of variable NS1 is 0 (38).

To summarize:

- The rank of a matrix is 2, since it is ordered along two axes (34).
- The rank of a vector is 1, since it is ordered along one axis (31).
- The rank of a *scalar* is 0 since it is ordered along zero axes (38).

Ravel (II)

While a single element entered from the keyboard is assumed to be a scalar, as in the case of *NS*1, a single element generated as the result of other operations need not be a scalar. It can be of any rank, *as long as its shape vector consists exclusively of 1s.*

- A vector with one element;
- A matrix with one row and one column;
- An array of rank 3 with one row, one column and one plane;
—and so on.

The conversion of the scalar *NS*1 to vector *TEMP* by means of the **ravel** function (symbolized by a comma) is illustrated and described in Figure 22.3, (42)-(44).

Unravel (III)

It is sometimes necessary to reshape a single-element vector or array of higher rank into a scalar. This can be done by using the **reshape** function with an *empty* or *null* vector as its left argument. The most convenient way to generate a null vector is '' (two single-quote marks with no intervening space). The expressions $\iota 0$, $0\rho 0$ and 0ρ' ' also generate empty vectors but they are not as convenient

since they have to be set off from the remainder of the expression by parentheses.

Empty Vectors and Data Types (IV)

NULLC is generated as an **empty character vector** (51); *NULLN* as an **empty numeric vector** (52). Their value and rank are easily verified (53–56). The **take function,** $\uparrow$, takes one element from each of these vectors (57, 58). When more elements are *taken* from a vector than it contains, the extra elements are blanks if the vector is a character vector and 0s if it is numeric. The **equals function,** = (59, 64), can determine whether an invisible output is really a blank or an empty vector.

Indexing (V)

Above we saw the generality of APL indexing which contributes to simplifying APL programs. Figure 22.5 provides further illustrations and also introduces the **index generating function,**

It is possible to index a variable on the left of a specification arrow (74, 75). The effect is to specify only that part of the variable selected by the index. *The only calculations permitted to the left of a specification arrow are those that calculate indices for an existing variable.*

Summary

The simplicity and generality of the rules governing APL data structure contribute greatly to simplifying programs that deal with arrays and subarrays. Only a hint of the power of these APL characteristics is given here.

2.4 APL: THE LANGUAGE—FUNCTIONS

APL functions are the active elements of the language. They take none, one, or two *arguments* and produce *values.* They are of three kinds:

- Primitive.
- Defined.
- System.

Primitive functions are an intrinsic part of the APL language. **Defined functions** are the APL equivalent of *programs, subroutines, procedures,* or *functions* in other languages.

System functions help manage the resources of the APL time sharing system. They will be discussed in Section 22.6, the time sharing system.

Primitive Functions

The primitive APL functions are presented in five tables, Figures 22.6 through 22.10.

Monadic and dyadic function symbols. The function symbols in the first table, Figure 22.6, denote one of two functions, depending on whether they are executed with one or two arguments; these uses are called, respectively, **monadic** and **dyadic.** All function symbols in Figure 22.6 have both monadic and dyadic forms.

What determines which of the two possible uses is intended in a particular expression? The answer is simple. The use is *monadic* if:

- Nothing appears to the left of the symbol;
- A function that requires an argument (a *monadic* or *dyadic* function) appears to the left.

If the term at the left of the function symbol produces a *value*, the use is *dyadic*.

The following examples illustrate monadic and dyadic uses of a representative function, *:

$$*2 \qquad e^2 \text{ (monadic use)}$$
$$7.389056099 \qquad\qquad (22.2)$$
$$10*2 \qquad 10^2 \text{ (dyadic use)}$$
$$100 \qquad\qquad (22.3)$$

Scalar functions. The functions in Figure 22.6 are called **scalar functions** and merit some discussion here. Figure 22.1 (1–6) introduced some of the key ideas that characterize scalar functions:

- If given scalar arguments, they return scalar results.
- If the two arguments of a dyadic scalar function are arrays of the same shape, the result has that shape.

- If one of the arguments of a dyadic scalar function is a single element and the other is an array, the single element is replicated into an array of matching shape.
- Action is performed on corresponding elements of the two arrays to produce a result element of a third array. Consequently, the result array has the same shape as the original argument.
- The shape of the result of a monadic scalar function is the shape of its argument.

Figure 22.7 illustrates these properties of scalar functions. It also sets the system variable $\Box PP$ to specify printing of 6 significant digits rather than 10 (the default value in a *CLEAR* workspace).

The first statement in Figure 22.7 contains a monadic scalar function called **roll,** a name suggested by its behavior: ?6 6, for example, returns two randomly selected numbers, each between 1 and 6, such as 6 1 (Natural,) or, perhaps, 2 2 (Little Joe).

In general, ?n, where n is a positive integer, generates a random number from 1 to n when $\Box IO$ is 1 and from 0 to n − 1 when $\Box IO$ is 0. The figure shows it applied to 5 5ρ10, a five row, five column array, all of whose elements are 10. The ? produces a 5 by 5 array of random numbers from 0 to 9 or 1 to 10, depending on index origin.

Consult manuals describing APL in detail to learn the precise meaning of the primitive functions discussed briefly here. The references at the end of the chapter list sources of information.

The names of the functions given in the figures tell what they do. It is hard to convey the degree of generality behind the name. The *factorial* function, for example, is defined for all arguments except negative integers; in other words, !n is evaluated as the Gamma function of n + 1. This generalization is not immediately obvious from the function name alone.

	MONADIC USE	DYADIC USE
+	Conjugate	Plus
−	Negative	Minus
×	Signum	Times
÷	Reciprocal	Divide
|	Magnitude	Residue
⌊	Floor	Minimum
⌈	Ceiling	Maximum
*	Exponential	Power
⊛	Natural logarithm	General logarithm
!	Factorial	Binomial

Figure 22.6. Arithmetic scalar functions.

```
        RANDOM←?5 5ρ10

        RANDOM
 2  8  5  6  3
 1  7  7 10  4
 6  9  1  1  6
 7  1  4  1  5
 7  6 10  9  6

        ÷RANDOM
0.5            0.125       0.2          0.1666666667 0.3333333333
1              0.1428571429 0.1428571429 0.1          0.25
0.1666666667   0.1111111111 1            1            0.1666666667
0.1428571429   1           0.25          1            0.2
0.1428571429   0.1666666667 0.1          0.1111111111 0.1666666667

        □PP←6

        ÷RANDOM
0.5      0.125    0.2      0.166667 0.333333
1        0.142857 0.142857 0.1      0.25
0.166667 0.111111 1        1        0.166667
0.142857 1        0.25     1        0.2
0.142857 0.166667 0.1      0.111111 0.166667

        10÷RANDOM
 5        1.25     2        1.66667  3.33333
10        1.42857  1.42857  1        2.5
 1.66667  1.11111 10       10        1.66667
 1.42857 10        2.5     10        2
 1.42857  1.66667  1        1.11111  1.66667

        RANDOM+RANDOM
 4 16 10 12  6
 2 14 14 20  8
12 18  2  2 12
14  2  8  2 10
14 12 20 18 12
```

Figure 22.7. Properties of scalar functions. System variable □ *PP*.

Trigonometric functions. The symbol ○ denotes two families of functions. Monadically, the ○ function can be verbalized as "Pi times . . .". That is,

- ○ 1 is π
- ○ is 2π
- ○ is $\pi/2$.

When ○ is used dyadically, the left argument specifies one of 15 circular, hyperbolic and Pythagorean functions. These are shown in Figure 22.8.

Logical and relational functions. Figure 22.9 presents the Boolean and relational functions. Of these, *not*, ~, is monadic only. The others are dyadic only. The Boolean functions require Boolean arguments and produce Boolean (0,1) results. The relational functions require arguments for which the relations are defined; they give a Boolean result. Figure 22.2 (29) gives an example of the use of a relational function.

All of the relational functions take numerical arguments. The function = and ≠ take character arguments as well. (These can also take one numeric and one alphabetic argument; in this instance, = returns a 0 result and ≠ returns 1.)

Mixed functions. The functions shown in Figure 22.10 are called **mixed functions.** The arguments do not have the same shape compatibility requirements as the scalar functions. The shape of the result can, for some functions, be different from the shape of *either* argument.

(-A) ○ B	A	A ○ B
(1-B*2)*0.5	0	(1-B*2)*0.5
Arcsin B	1	Sine B
Arccos B	2	Cosine B
Arctan B	3	Tangent B
(⁻1+B*2)*0.5	4	(1+B*2)*0.5
Arcsinh B	5	Sinh B
Arccosh B	6	Cosh B
Arctanh B	7	Tanh B

Figure 22.8. Scalar functions: trigonometric and Pythagorean.

These functions have individual properties rather than a class of characteristic general properties.

Space does not permit a discussion of all the mixed functions in the figure. Consult the sources in the References. Some of the functions have been used in earlier exercises. A brief discussion of one or two other functions may help give a feel for what they can do.

The **compress** function, /, is illustrated in Figure 22.2 (29). The **expand** function is its inverse. As with most mixed functions, *compress* and *expand* are described better by examples than by definitions; see Figure 22.11.

Expand uses a Boolean vector for the left argument. The number of 1s in the left argument must be the same as the number of elements in the right argument. The result is evaluated as follows:

Proceeding from left to right along the left argument, copy an element from the right argument when a 1 is encountered; insert a **pad** element when a 0 is encountered. (The *pad* element is a blank for a character right argument and a 0 for a numeric right argument.)

The *expand* example in Figure 22.11 should be convincing evidence that a picture is worth a thousand words.

The ⊟ symbol is used monadically for matrix inverse and dyadically to solve simultaneous linear equations (called "Matrix division" in Figure 22.10). It is defined more generally than the names *inverse* and *matrix division* imply.

For example, consider the matrix of coefficients, *HILB*4, in Figure 22.12. In Figure 22.13, ⊟ *HILB*4

	COMMENTS
	Boolean Functions. Domain (0,1). Range (0,1)
~	Not. Monadic only. No dyadic version.
∧	And Dyadic only. No monadic version.
∨	Or " "
⍲	Nand " "
⍱	Nor " "
	Relational Functions. Domain: Real numbers or characters. Range (0,1).
<	Less than
≤	Less than or equal (or not greater)
=	Equal
≥	Greater than or equal (or not less)
>	Greater than
≠	Not equal

Figure 22.9. Scalar functions: logical and relational.

	MONADIC	DYADIC
I	Monadic	Dyadic
ρ	Shape	Reshape
,	Ravel	Catenate, Laminate
φ	Reverse	Rotate
⍉	Transpose	Generalized Transpose
II		
↑		Take
↓		Drop
/		Compress
\		Expand
III		
ι	Index generator	Index of
∈		Membership
⍋	Grade up	
⍒	Grade down	
?	Roll (scalar function)	Deal
IV		
⌹	Matrix inverse	Matrix division
⊥		Decode (base value)
⊤		Encode (representation)
V		
⍎	Execute	See system function ⎕EA
⍕	Format	Format

Figure 22.10. Mixed functions.

```
      COMP←1 0 1 1 0 1 1 1/'ABCDEFGH'

      COMP
ACDFGH

      EXPD←1 0 1 1 0 1 1 1\COMP

      EXPD
A CD FGH
```

Figure 22.11. Expand and compress.

```
      HILB4
1         0.5        0.333333 0.25
0.5       0.333333   0.25     0.2
0.333333  0.25       0.2      0.166667
0.25      0.2        0.166667 0.142857
```

Figure 22.12. A matrix, *HILB4*.

yields its inverse and $(\iota 4)\boxplus HILB4$ solves four simultaneous equations as displayed in Figure 22.14.

However, consider an **overdetermined matrix** with more rows than columns in Figure 22.15. Both the matrix inverse and matrix division function are also defined. They produce what is sometimes called a **pseudoinverse** in the first case and a least squares approximation to solution values in the second.

Typical calculations are shown in Figure 22.16. ($\square PW$ is a system variable that controls how many characters

```
      ⌹HILB4
  16   ⁻120    240   ⁻140
⁻120   1200  ⁻2700   1680
 240  ⁻2700   6480  ⁻4200
⁻140   1680  ⁻4200   2800
```

Figure 22.13. ⌹ *HILB4*.

```
   w+        0.5x+0.333333y+      0.25z = 1
  0.5w+0.333333x      +0.25y+       0.2z = 2
0.333333w+     0.25x+      0.2y+0.166667z = 3
  0.25w+      0.2x+0.166667y+0.142857z = 4

    (ι4)⊞HILB4
⁻64 900 ⁻2520 1820
```

Figure 22.14. (ι4)⊞*HILB4*.

```
      HILB4I
1         0.5        0.333333 0.25
0.5       0.333333   0.25     0.2
0.333333  0.25       0.2      0.166667
0.25      0.2        0.166667 0.142857
1         0          0        0
0         1          0        0
0         0          1        0
0         0          0        1
```

Figure 22.15. An overdetermined matrix.

are to print or display on a line. It is set to 60 to ensure that the results will fit on the printed page.)

As the results show, least squares curve fitting is virtually built-in for APL. So is the solution of sets of simultaneous equations that differ only in their right hand sides. The left argument to ⊞ can be either a vector or a matrix:

- In the first case, one set of simultaneous equations is solved;
- In the second, as many sets are solved as there are columns in the left argument.

Defined Functions

Figure 22.17 lists a monadic function, *FRAME*. It defines some terminology and shows an example of execution. *FRAME* puts a box around a variable value, as shown at the bottom of the figure. The first line in the figure shows how to request a function listing.

The **function header** appears first in the listing and consists of two parts. The second part starts with a semicolon and consists of the names of local variables separated by semicolons. Local variables can have values that are independent of the values of variables with the same names in other functions or in the active workspace.

The first part of the header conains A, the local name of the result produced by the function, a **specification arrow**, the name of the function, *FRAME*, and the local name of its argument, *B*.

The arrow indicates that this function produces an explicit result. Functions need not produce explicit results; they can, for example work only with global variables. Application programs are apt to be defined as functions that do not produce explicit results. They merely update global variables or files. However, the *FRAME* function *does* produce a result which has the local name *A*.

```
    □PW←60

    ⊞HILB4I
0.345865   0.128954   0.0692887  0.0438075   0.55561
   ⁻0.242001  ⁻0.168686  ⁻0.130063
0.128954   0.120549   0.0977654  0.0807364  ⁻0.242001
   0.854752  ⁻0.106131  ⁻0.0841762
0.0692887  0.0977654  0.090803   0.080987   ⁻0.168686
   ⁻0.106131   0.920804  ⁻0.0635787
0.0438075  0.0807364  0.080987   0.0755678 ⁻0.130063
   ⁻0.0841762 ⁻0.0635787  0.948608

    (ι8)⊞HILB4I
0.0916059 3.48847 5.31796 6.73895
```

Figure 22.16. Operations on *HILB4I*.

```
        ∇FRAME[◻]∇       (Request for function listing)

        ∇ A←FRAME B;C;D;◻IO
[1]     ⍝ B is a character array.  A is B enclosed
[2]     ⍝ in a "frame" of lines and corners.
[3]     ⍝
[4]     ◻IO←0
[5]     C←1↑ρB←(¯2↑ 1 1 ,ρB)ρB
[6]     D←1↓ρB
[7]     A←HLINE,[0] B,[0] HLINE
[8]     A←VLINE,A,VLINE
[9]     A[0;0,D+1]←NWCOR,NECOR
[10]    A[C+1;0,D+1]←SWCOR,SECOR
        ∇
```

A←FRAME B;C;D;◻IO is a <u>function header</u>. It contains

        the name of the function (FRAME)
        the local name of its one argument (B)
        the local name of its result (A)
        the names of two local variables (C, D)
        the name of a localized system variable (◻IO)

Lines 1, 2 and 3 of the function (the ones that start with the
character "⍝") are comment lines. They are used to explain what
the function does.

Example of Execution of FRAME Defined Function

        FRAME CV1[NM1]

```
┌─────┐
│ROOM │
│BED  │
│BOARD│
└─────┘
```

Figure 22.17. Defined function listing and comments.

The arrow is followed by two names: the first is the name of the function and the second is the local name of its argument. If, as in Figure 22.19, the arrow is followed by three names, the middle one is the function name and the other two are its arguments. As Figure 22.18 shows, a **niladic function,** one with *no* arguments, has only the function name after the arrow.

Figure 22.18 lists the niladic functions used in the *FRAME* function to provide the sides and corners of the *frame* for the character matrix argument of *FRAME*.

These niladic functions serve two purposes. First, they make it possible to use characters that cannot be entered directly from the keyboard. These can be selected from ◻AV, the "atomic vector," a 256 element character vector that gives all the possible combinations of bits in a byte, that is, the character assignment combinations from hexadecimal 00 through FF. The listing of a representative function, *HLINE*, which generates the horizontal line character, shows that the hexadecimal code EC (decimal 236) is assigned to this print configuration.

When code assignments for print characters are needed, it is a good idea to use functions like those illustrated in Figure 22.18 rather than to index ◻AV directly. This simplifies the task of modifying the workspace if it is ever transferred to another APL system in which the order of characters in ◻AV is different. If, for example, the functions in a given workspace use *HLINE* whenever they need a horizontal line character, the only thing necessary to redefine if ◻AV changes is the *HLINE* function. On the other hand, if

```
Niladic Functions:

The names HLINE, VLINE, NWCOR, NECOR, SECOR and SWCOR are the
names of defined functions that produce the following characters:

        HLINE —
        VLINE |
        NWCOR ⌐
        NECOR ┐
        SWCOR └
        SECOR ┘


        ⎕NC 'HLINE'
3

        ∇HLINE[⎕]∇
        ∇ A←HLINE
[1]       A←⎕AV[⎕IO+236]
        ∇
```

Figure 22.18. Niladic functions and the system function ⎕NC.

$\Box AV[\sqcup IO+236]$ is used to get a horizontal line, then all function definitions must be searched to find where this occurs and change it.

Niladic functions, like those in Figure 22.18, serve a second purpose. They act as APL reserved words. If a niladic function called PI should be defined to give the value of π, any attempt to specify another value for it will result in the error message: *SYNTAX ERROR.*

NC, the **name class function,** is a system function to determine if a name is in use in the workspace and what kind of entity it names. The digit returned, *3*, tells us that *HLINE* is the name of a defined function in the workspace.

Function headers determine whether a function is niladic, monadic or dyadic. Figure 22.19 gives an example of a dyadic function. It defines the defined function *PLUS* to be equivalent to the primitive function $+$.

SUM.

SUM. Figure 22.20 lists and uses a function, *SUM*, that illustrates

- Branching statements.
- Labels.
- Identity elements.

As can be seen from the sample executions that follow the function listing, the function is not needed since it merely does what $+/$ did for us in Figure 22.2. It illustrates the kind of looping that is unnecessary in APL because of its data structure, its specialized functions and its operators.

```
        ∇ A←B  PLUS  C
[1]       A←B+C
        ∇

        3+4
7

        3 PLUS 4
7

        3+NM1
    21 18 18 16 30
     5  8  7 30 30
     5 18  4 21  7

        3 PLUS NM1
    21 18 18 16 30
     5  8  7 30 30
     5 18  4 21  7
```

Figure 22.19. Dyadic function *PLUS*. Replacing symbols with names.

Branching. APL has two *statement types:*

- ←, specification.
- →, branching.

We have seen many examples of specification statements in the preceding figures.

The right pointing arrow must be the first symbol in the **branching statement,** except that it may be preceded by a label. As illustrated in statement 4 of the *SUM* function (Figure 22.20), a label must appear as the first entry on the line it labels and must be separated from the re-

```
        ∇SUM[□]∇

        ∇ A←SUM B;□IO;N;I
[1]     □IO←1
[2]     N←ρB←,B
[3]     A←I←0
[4]     L1:→(N<I←I+1)/0
[5]     A←A+B[I]
[6]     →L1
        ∇


    RND←?4ρ100

    RND
14 76 46 54

    SUM RND
190

    +/RND
190

    NULL←0ρ0

    SUM NULL
0

    +/NULL
0
```

Figure 22.20. Defined function *SUM*. Identity element: 0.

mainder of the line by a colon. A **label name** is local to the function in which it appears; its value is the number of the line it labels.

The expression to the right of the branch arrow must produce a value that is one of the following:

1. An integer that is the number of a statement (in brackets in the display) in the function (or a vector whose first value is such an integer).
2. An integer that is *not* the number of a statement in the function (or a vector whose first value is such an integer).
3. An empty vector.

These three possibilities correspond respectively to:

1. A branch to the indicated statement.
2. A *RETURN* from the current function to the function or state from which it was invoked.
3. A branch to the next statement in sequence (a *fall through*).

Statement 4 in the *SUM* function updates the *loop variable*, I, and compares it with N, the number of elements to be summed. As long as N is greater than or equal to I, this comparison produces the value 0. This value is used to *compress* the value to the right of the /, as in Figure 22.2 (29). Compression by 0 produces a null vector so the next statement to be executed is 5. This is followed by statement 6, which branches back to statement 4.

As soon as N is less than the newly updated I, the selection expression becomes 1/0, which has the value 0, a statement number *not* valid for this (or any other) function. The function terminates at this point and *RETURNs* to the condition from which it was invoked, producing a value that can be given a name, used in an APL expression or displayed.

The *SUM* function adds up all the items in a vector. What value should it return when the vector (perhaps as the result of a selection process) *has* no values? This is the same as asking how we should initialize the variable (local variable A, in this case) that will contain the sum. Clearly, we initialize it as 0, and this is the value the sum will have if there are no numbers to be added.

The number 0 is the proper initial value for a variable that will contain a sum because it is the *identity element* for addition; adding anything to it will give you the value of what was added. For a function called *PRODUCT*, say, which multiplies all the numbers in a vector, we clearly cannot initialize the product variable at 0; if we did, the cumulative product produced as a result would always have the value 0. The initial value for a product variable—the identity element for multiplication—must be 1.

In APL, whenever reduction is performed on an empty vector, the result is the identity element of the function used in the reduction. This is illustrated in Figure 22.20 for plus reduction; the expressions *SUM NULL* and *+/NULL* both return 0, the identity element for addition.

What would the identity element for ⌈ be? (See Figure 22.2 (28).) The answer is left as an exercise.

22.5 APL: THE LANGUAGE—OPERATORS

Earlier examples introduced the *reduction* operator. Operators are an important concept. This section discusses all of them briefly.

Again, the most effective discussion technique is "show and tell." The showing is done in four figures. Figure 22.21 displays the values of the variables used for the examples in the other figures. Figure 22.22 illustrates the

```
        NV1
2  5  4  1 26 26 12  5  4
```

```
       NM1
 18 15 15 13 27
  2  5  4 27 27
  2 15  1 18  4
```

```
    QUANTITIES←4 12 3
```

```
    PRICES←1.52 3 4.5
```

```
    NV2←3 9 2 14
```

```
    NV3←5 6 2 17
```

```
    BOOLMAT←¯1+?5 5 ρ2
```

```
    BOOLMAT
0 1 0 1 0
0 1 1 1 0
1 1 0 0 1
1 0 0 0 0
1 1 1 1 1
```

```
    NAMES←3 6ρ'MIKE   JOE     EDWARD'
```

```
    NAMES
MIKE
JOE
EDWARD
```

Figure 22.21. Variables used in examples illustrating APL operators.

`    +/NV2`		Reduce
`28`		
`    +\NV2`		Scan
`3 12 14 28`		
`    -/NV2`		Reduce
`¯18`		
`    -\NV2`		Scan
`3 ¯6 ¯4 ¯18`		
`    ⌈/NV2`		Reduce
`14`		
`    ⌈\NV2`		Scan
`3 9 9 14`		
`    +/NM1`		Row-reduce
`88 65 40`		
`    +\NM1`		Row-scan
`18 33 48 61 88`		
`2  7 11 38 65`		
`2 17 18 36 40`		
`    +/[1]NM1`		Column-reduce
`22 35 20 58 58`		
`    +\[1]NM1`		Column-scan
`18 15 15 13 27`		
`20 20 19 40 54`		
`22 35 20 58 58`		

Figure 22.22. Reduction, scan and axis operator examples.

reduction, scan and axis operators. Figure 22.23 illustrates the inner product. Figure 22.24 illustrates the outer product.

Reduction, Scan and Axis

The **scan** operator, symbolized by a \, is related to the reduction operator in the same way a yearly sales total is related to the cumulative monthly sales figures for the same year. In other words, a *plus scan* of a vector with +\ produces a vector of the same size whose elements are, successively, the sum of the first, the first two, the first three, . . . , the first *n* elements of the vector. Figure 22.22 shows the relationship between reduction and scan by using them in pairs.

The illustrations of minus reduction are puzzling to people unfamiliar with APL's order of evaluation of an expression. Unlike most programming languages, APL functions have no hierarchy or relative priorities. Functions are evaluated in the order in which they appear, *and*

the right argument of a function is the value of the entire expression to its right.

This gives rise to the **right to left rule** for evaluating APL expressions. Consider

$$1 - 2 - 3 \qquad (22.4)$$

Reading (22.4) from the left, the first minus sign has as its arguments 1 on the left and the expression $2 - 3$ on the right. The result of substracting 3 from 2 is ¯1 so that the expression becomes

$1 - {}^{-}1$ (verbalized as "one minus negative one").

Thus the value of the expression is 2, not the ¯4 the new APL user probably expects.

Note that APL distinguishes between the *substract* function symbol and the *negative* symbol used as part of the representation of a negative number or a negative exponent. The latter symbol is as much a part of a number's representation as a decimal digit or a decimal point or a letter E used to identify the exponent in a number in exponential notation.

Minus reduction provides a convenient way to evaluate an alternating series once the rule of formation of its components is known. For example, consider the result $^-18$ for $-/NV2$ in Figure 22.22. Putting in the value for $NV2$, we get

$$3 - 9 - 2 - 14.$$

In APL, this evaluates as

$$\begin{aligned} 3 - 9 - {}^-12 \\ 3 - 21 \\ {}^-18 \end{aligned} \qquad (22.6)$$

Which is the same result as the alternating sum of NV2:

$$3 - 9 + 2 - 14$$

in a left-to-right evaluation.

When reduction or scan is applied to a matrix or array of higher rank, there must be a way to specify the axis or dimension along which the action takes place. If none is specified, the last axis is assumed. Otherwise, the axis number must be placed in brackets immediately after the reduction symbol. The bottom two examples in Figure 22.22 illustrates this.

Inner product   Figure 22.23 illustrates one of APL's most useful and versatile operators, the **inner product**. The first two entries show the equivalence, for vector arguments, of

$$+/QUANTITIES \times PRICES$$

```
        +/QUANTITIES×PRICES      + reduction of product of
55.58                              two vectors

        QUANTITIES+.×PRICES      Equivalent calculation in
55.58                              inner-product form

        1 2 3+.×NM1              Vector-matrix multiplication
28 70 26 121 93

        NM1+.×ι5                Matrix-vector multiplication
280 267 127

        NM1+.×⌽NM1              Matrix-matrix multiplication
 1672 1251  618
 1251 1503  677
  618  677  570

        NAMES∧.=6↑'MIKE'        ∧.= inner product
1 0 0
        NAMES∧.='EDWARD'         "    "        "
0 0 1

        BOOLMAT∨.∧BOOLMAT       ∨.∧ inner product
 1 1 1 1 0                        (useful in tracing circuits
 1 1 1 1 1                          among interconnected elements)
 1 1 1 1 1
 0 1 0 1 0
 1 1 1 1 1

        BOOLMAT+.∧BOOLMAT       +.∧ inner product
 1 1 1 1 0                        (useful in counting
 2 2 1 1 1                          interconnections)
 1 3 2 3 1
 0 1 0 1 0
 3 4 2 3 2
```

Figure 22.23. Inner product examples.

and

$$QUANTITIES + . \times PRICES \qquad (22.7)$$

so that the first expression can be considered a definition of the second and both can be remembered as the sequence of operations performed in calculating the total amount of a bill: multiply quantities by prices and add up the results.

The inner product of two vectors gives a scalar result. For arrays of higher rank, the fundamental operation is that described for vectors, *but it is performed for all combinations of row vectors from the left argument with column vectors from the right argument*. For the $+ . \times$ inner product, this describes matrix multiplication (linear algebra) whenever a matrix is one of the arguments. Examples in Figure 22.23 using *NM*1 illustrate this.

However, as for all APL operators, the inner product operator is defined more generally, not just for $+$ and $\times$. The general operation is symbolized as

$$\alpha . \omega \qquad (22.8)$$

where α and ω represent any dyadic scalar functions. The function to the right of . is applied component by component (like $\times$ in the example already discussed). The function to the left of . reduces, in the APL sense, the

vector resulting from the component by component operation.

The remaining examples, illustrating the $\wedge . =$, $\vee . \wedge$ and $+ . \wedge$ inner products, show just a few of the many useful function combinations.

Outer product.   Anyone who has learned the multiplication table has seen the outer product. The generalized outer product is a table generator for which any function can serve in the place of multiply. It takes the form

$$A \circ . \alpha B \qquad (22.9)$$

in which α is a function and A and B are variables.

The first example in Figure 22.24 is a 12 by 12 multiplication table of the kind printed on the back cover of elementary school notebooks.

The second example is not a times table but a "maximum" table.

The third (which also gives an example of the format function, $\overline{\Phi}$), is a table of the sine, cosine, arcsine and arccosine of

$$\frac{\pi}{8}, \frac{\pi}{4}, \ldots, \frac{7\pi}{8}, \pi \qquad (22.10)$$

generated by monadic and dyadic uses of the $\circ$ function.

```
      (ι12)∘.×ι12
 1     2    3    4    5    6    7    8    9   10   11   12
 2     4    6    8   10   12   14   16   18   20   22   24
 3     6    9   12   15   18   21   24   27   30   33   36
 4     8   12   16   20   24   28   32   36   40   44   48
 5    10   15   20   25   30   35   40   45   50   55   60
 6    12   18   24   30   36   42   48   54   60   66   72
 7    14   21   28   35   42   49   56   63   70   77   84
 8    16   24   32   40   48   56   64   72   80   88   96
 9    18   27   36   45   54   63   72   81   90   99  108
10    20   30   40   50   60   70   80   90  100  110  120
11    22   33   44   55   66   77   88   99  110  121  132
12    24   36   48   60   72   84   96  108  120  132  144

      NV2∘.⌈NV3
 5     6    3   17
 9     9    9   17
 5     6    2   17
14    14   14   17

      8 4⍕1 2 5 6∘.○(ο18)÷8
 .3827     .7071     .9239   1.0000     .9239     .7071     .3827      .0000
 .9239     .7071     .3827    .0000    ¯.3827    ¯.7071    ¯.9239   ¯1.0000
 .4029     .8687    1.4702   2.3013    3.4919    5.2280    7.7807   11.5487
1.0781    1.3246    1.7780   2.5092    3.6323    5.3228    7.8447   11.5920
```

Figure 22.24. Outer product examples.

22.6 APL: THE TIME SHARING SYSTEM

The figures in this paper are copies of terminal sessions. That is, they are printouts of the input to and output from an APL time sharing system, (here, VS APL Release 4 under CMS). The copies were made using the *COPY* facility of the **session manager,** the part of the APL system that controls graphic terminal input, output, display, recording, scrolling and other features.

The emphasis of the preceding sections is, of course, on the APL language, but features of a particular time sharing system have also been introduced as part of the language discussion: Figure 22.2 shows how to save a workspace, Figure 22.3 shows how to load a previously saved workspace. These actions rely on a file system which in turn depends on the "environment" in which APL is embedded.

The IBM product, VS APL Release 4, works in four environments: CMS, TSO, CICS, VSPC. In each, the way workspaces is saved on auxiliary storage is unique to the particular environment. APL vendors other than IBM have their own file systems or provide modifications of IBM file systems.

This situation applies to other aspects of the computing environment within which APL is embedded. Thus anyone interested in using APL will find that the language, at least at the level discussed in this paper, is the same in any system, but services provided as part of the computing environment differ.

It is beyond the scope of this paper to describe all the APL services currently available. Two important APL vendors are listed in the References as sources of information about their systems. There is no intention to slight other vendors; the main limitation is that of of space and personal knowledge.

We now examine the general principles used by APL systems in communicating between the APL workspace and the environment in which it is embedded.

An illustration of workspace/environment interaction is the system variable $\Box AI$ as illustrated in Figure 22.2 (26). It requests accounting information that cannot be calculated without access to the host computer clock. $\Box$ as the first character indicates a system name, either of a function or a variable. An example of a system function is $\Box NC$, Figure 22.12. Given one or more names, $\Box NC$ returns a number for each, telling if the name is in use and if so, whether it names a variable, a function, a group or, conceivably, some other type of APL entity.

Thus one extralinguistic aspect of APL is the set of system functions and system variables that characterizes a particular APL implementation. Another is the general mechanism, characteristic of all APL systems, for accessing devices outside of APL:

- Data access methods such as BDAM, QSAM or VSAM.
- Devices such as color terminals.
- Commands of the host system within which APL is embedded.
- "Stack" or "alternate input" services to allow the generation of answers to questions asked by application programs.

Again, these vary from system to system, but all systems use a general mechanism with two elements:

1. Shared variables.
2. Auxiliary processors.

To suggest what auxiliary processors do, those provided for VS APL Release 4 are shown in Figure 22.25. Numbers in the table identify the auxiliary processors. Thus, the alternate input processor is numbered 101 in CMS, TSO and VSPC, and 139 in CICS. Figure 22.25 is from IBM publication SG22-9263, *A Guide to the VS APL Workspace Library.* This guide describes the workspaces that are part of the VS APL program product. It also has an extensive discussion of shared variables, auxiliary processors and related topics.

Shared Variables and Auxiliary Processors

There is one conspicuous omission in the discussion of defined functions presented earlier: input/output under program control, postponed to this point because it illustrates the original, primitive form generalized into the concept of a shared variable.

$\Box$ and $\Box$ within a program request input from a terminal. When they are encountered, the program unlocks the keyboard and waits until the terminal user indicates that typing is complete by sending an end-of-transmission signal (usually by pressing a carriage-return or a new-line key).

$\Box$ requests **evaluated input**. The symbols $\Box$: appear at the left of the line; any APL expression that produces a value may be typed in response.

For example, statement 10 of a program might be:

$$[10] \ DATA \leftarrow \Box \qquad (22.11)$$

| Processor | Environment | | | |
Name	CMS	TSO	CICS	VSPC
Command	100	100	100	100
Alternate Input	101	101	139	101
Direct-Access	110	210		
Queued Access	111	111		
Session Manager	120	120	120	120
APL Data Format	121	121	121	121
EBCDIC Format				122
VSAM	123	123	123	123
Full-screen Manager	*	*	124	124
DL/I			125	
Full-screen Manager	126	126	126	126
Transient Data			132	

* Available (as AP 124X) as part of <u>VS APL Extended Editor and Full Screen Manager</u>, Program Number 5796-PLY

Figure 22.25. Auxiliary processors, VS APL Release 4.

After (22.11) is executed, the variable *DATA* will have the value of whatever expression the user typed.

▢ requests "literal" input. Nothing is displayed when the keyboard unlocks and input is treated as a literal character string.

This process is called **evaluated input;** the user may type in any APL expression that produces a value or is a value. The variable called *DATA* is then given that value.

The expression

$$[nn] \ \Box \leftarrow DATA \qquad (22.12)$$

as one might expect, is one way to output the value of *DATA*. Normally, though, this expression is not used since the name *DATA* in the program on a line has the same effect. To request **literal input**—input treated as a string of characters—the symbol ▢ is used.

Now what does ▢ represent? In effect, it is the name of a variable that can be set by one of two cooperating partners or processes (in this case APL and the terminal user) and read by the other. In other words, it is *shared* by two *processors*.

This sharing provides a model for all APL interactions with the external world. One or more variables are shared with an independently operating processor, including even another APL user in some systems. Communication between the two processors takes place by alternate specification and use of these variables.

The protocol governing specification and use is established differently for different systems. Data going to a printer, for example, is *specified* by the APL partner and *used* by the printer partner; (clearly no data can go from the printer to the APL user).

Control information, however, can return from any device. For example, if a tape runs out, a control code is returned indicating what has happened. To accommodate both control and data transmissions, at least two variables are usually shared, one to transmit and receive data and the other to transmit and receive control codes. The shared variable mechanism is thus a formal, general "interface" that governs any interaction between APL and its environment. It is managed by four system functions:

▢*SVO* As a dyadic function, this provides one or more variable names to an auxiliary processor for sharing. (Auxiliary processors are specified by number. Thus *100* identifies the auxiliary processor that, in all four IBM environments, makes it possible to issue environment commands.) As a monadic function, ▢*SVO* checks the share status of one or more variables.

▢*SVC* As a dyadic function, this sets the transmit/receive protocol desired by the requester. As a monadic function, it checks to see what protocol is in effect.

▢*SVR* This retracts one or more shared variables, terminating communication with the processor(s) with which they were shared.

▢*SVQ* This is used to determine what processors are currently offering to share variables or what variable names a particular processor is offering.

The mechanism described above requires many detailed actions onerous to program. Therefore it is customary to write general purpose APL functions such as *OPEN* and *CLOSE* to take care of the details of establishing and managing shares.

Once the shares have been established, reading and writing records is done by means of simple APL specification statements. For example, if a sequential file has been opened for input and the shared variable used to access it is named *SEQ*, then

$$REC \leftarrow SEQ \qquad (22.13)$$

reads a record from the file and gives it the name *REC*. If the same file is opened for output, then

$$SEQ \leftarrow REC \qquad (22.14)$$

writes the contents of the variable called *REC* to this file. In other words, once the data variable is shared, reading and writing from the file is done by simple APL specification statements.

22.7 FUTURE DIRECTIONS

APL is still developing. Systems in existence or under development transcend some of the limitations described here. New developments include these features:

- Arrays can have other arrays as elements.
- Arrays can combine character and numeric elements.
- Operators can be defined in much the same way as functions.
- Defined functions can be used with operators to form new derived functions. (In most current APLs, this can be done only with primitive functions.)
- More useful format and sort functions are available.
- Arithmetic functions can take complex as well as real arguments.
- More powerful character manipulation functions are available.
- The right argument function in an inner product is not restricted to being a dyadic scalar function.

More could be listed, but the point is made. APL, despite its superficial appearance of complexity, is, in practice, one of the simplest, most productive time sharing languages. Its appearance suggests that only mathematicians would be attracted to it or able to master it. In practice, the reverse has been true. Its widest area of current use is in the day-to-day tasks of business and industry: management reporting, data base interrogation, production planning, financial planning, data base devel-

opment and maintenance, and so on. Current and future developments should make it even more productive in applications of this kind.

REFERENCES

Books

Polivka, R., and S. Pakin, *APL: The Language and Its Usage.* Englewood Cliffs, NJ: Prentice-Hall, 1975.

Gilman, L., and A. S. Rose, *APL—An Interactive Approach*, 2nd Ed. New York: John Wiley & Sons, 1974.

IBM Publications

The *APL Language* manual, Form No. GC26-3847, describes the language of the VS APL Release 4 Program Product. This description is independent of the host system within which APL is embedded.

The *Terminal User's Guides* describe, for CMS, TSO, CICS and VSPC, the system dependent portions of APL (the auxiliary processors, logon procedures, libraries, and so on).

A Guide to the VS APL Workspace Library, Form No. SG22-9263, describes the workspaces that come with the VS APL Release 4 Program Product. It also includes a general discussion of many APL topics and ideas.

Extended APL: the most advanced form of APL provided by IBM is, at the time of writing, APL2. This is described in several manuals, of which two are most useful if the reader's primary interest is in APL rather than particular APL systems:

APL2 Introduction Manual, Form No. SB21-3039.
APL2 Language Manual, Form No. SB21-3015.

APL2 contains many extensions to the language discussed in the body of this paper. A few of these are mentioned in the last section.

APL Services

Several companies provide APL services. Each of these has manuals describing the APL language and extensions characteristic of their systems. Two of the major APL vendors are

I. P. Sharp Associates Limited,
2 First Canadian Place, Suite 1900,
Toronto, Ontario, M5X 1E3

STSC, Inc.,
7316 Wisconsin Avenue,
Bethesda, MD 20014

23
BASIC

Bill Burton

Teratek Company

23.1 INTRODUCTION

This chapter is about **BASIC,** a computer language whose name derives from the acronym for **B**eginner's **A**ll-purpose **S**ymbolic **I**nstruction **C**ode. The names of the following computer languages are also derived from acronyms and are capitalized accordingly:

FORTRAN— *FOR*mula *TRAN*slation [language]

COBOL   — *CO*mmon *B*usiness *O*riented *L*anguage

ALGOL   — *ALGO*rithmic *L*anguage

PL/I   — *P*rogramming *L*anguage One

APL   — *A P*rogramming *L*anguage

Any discussion of computer languages which suggests their probable use must be general in nature. Exceptions are inevitable because many programmers use only the language or languages in which they are most fluent even if other languages might be better suited to a particular project.

Historically, the architecture of computer systems has dictated the choice of available languages. For many years, COBOL, a business oriented language, has been the "lingua franca" of mainframe systems because it was established early, works well to process data on a large scale, and is known by the majority of business programmers.

Any useful business language must overcome a major limitation of computer arithmetic. Fractional values such as 1/3 cannot be expressed precisely by binary numbers.

Approximations of such values introduce small roundoff errors whose cumulative effect may cause computed totals to become inaccurate in terms of their purpose. For a business language to be considered reliable for monetary transactions, it should include a capability for adjusting roundoff errors to produce totals accurate to within one-half of 1 percent.

A business oriented language such as COBOL must also be able to generate a wide variety of reports and summaries efficiently. These requirements do not necessarily oblige the use of a mainframe system; rather the use of mainframes by large businesses is dictated by the enormity of their data bases and the need to have this information accessed and updated by many different terminals. COBOL was the first "universal" business language to provide these capabilities and it has endured despite its cumbersome nature.

Today COBOL remains a viable choice for implementing very large and complex business systems as required by banks, credit card companies and the like. This is probably due to tradition and to the training of most programmers.

FORTRAN was designed as a language tool for the scientific and engineering communities and has become a standard of sorts on many minicomputer systems. This wide use reflects the lesser system and I/O requirements of scientific data processing. Few implementations of FORTRAN provide time sharing capability or report generation but FORTRAN is especially well suited for applications which require fast, high precision calculation or machine process control.

BASIC is a *general purpose language* which has been

used successfully on both mainframe and minicomputer systems. However, the evolution of BASIC as a microcomputer language provides the principal focus of this chapter.

23.2 THE ORIGINS OF BASIC

BASIC was developed at Dartmouth College during the early 1960s by Professors John G. Kemeny and Thomas E. Kurtz, whose research was aided by a grant from the National Science Foundation.

The first version of BASIC (often called Dartmouth BASIC) was formally introduced in 1966. Prior to this time, the procedure oriented languages in widest use were FORTRAN, COBOL and ALGOL (in Europe). BASIC was originally conceived as a tutorial procedure oriented language, making it easier to learn and use than any of these. Dartmouth BASIC was essentially a derivative of FORTRAN, but since 1966 many extended versions of BASIC have been introduced with convenience and structuring features borrowed from COBOL and, to a lesser degree, ALGOL.

23.3 PROCEDURE ORIENTED LANGUAGES

A few words about procedure oriented languages are in order. Before a computer can do anything, it must be given instructions that it understands. Computers process nothing other than fixed length streams of binary information, called *machine language.* The most modern and sophisticated computers differ from their ancestors only insomuch as they offer improved performance and higher reliability for less money. They are still bound to machine language. The drawback of machine language is that the programmer must keep track of and refer to the exact locations of all data in memory as well as the numeric codes which correspond to specific commands in a machine's instruction set. The number of details which a programmer must keep track of can make creation of a successful machine language program inefficient in terms of cost and development time. This is especially true when the program in question is long or complex.

Symbolic or mnemonic languages, most notably assembler, have improved the programmer's lot considerably in this regard, but still leave much to be desired. Even the best symbolic assembly language is somewhat difficult to learn and is specific to the instruction set of a single processor. In most cases, this means that one cannot install a new computer system without discarding an entire existing software base.

Procedure oriented languages, also called *high level languages,* have risen from the common need to transport programs from one machine to another. These languages make the limitations of computer architecture transparent to the programmer and minimize the time and expense involved in transporting programs to a new machine. Procedure oriented languages offer the additional advantage of being comparatively easy to learn.

23.4 BATCH PROCESSING LANGUAGES

When BASIC was under development, FORTRAN, COBOL and ALGOL were primarily batch processing languages. Programs written in these languages were submitted to the computer as source statements in the form of punched cards or paper tape. Typically, several programs would be pending at one time and the computer would assign each a position in a queue. When the computer determined that a certain program's "turn" had arrived, the source statements would be compiled, calculations performed and printed answers made available (often at a remote site, several hours later).

23.5 BASIC: A TIME SHARING LANGUAGE

BASIC was developed in an academic environment, which undoubtedly influenced its design. Kemeny and Kurtz offer this explanation in the second edition of their definitive book, *BASIC Programming:*

Time sharing involves submitting the program by typing it on a typewriter-like console, having the computer system "share" its resources by giving each program a small amount of attention when it needs it, and then providing the answers almost immediately on the same typewriter-like console....

The distinction between batch processing and time-sharing is necessarily oversimplified, as most computer systems today operate in a mode that has a combination of the properties of the two processes. Furthermore, certain types of applications are well handled in one type of computer environment and poorly handled in the other. One type of application that time-sharing does well is the training of inexperienced users. This is because the results of a student's program come back to him almost immediately—if his program works, he is 'rewarded' immediately; if there are errors, he is told at once and can correct them before he forgets what he is doing.

Most of BASIC is as much at home in batch processing as it is in time-sharing. However, BASIC does have the capability to be used in interactive programs, that is, programs that require the user's participation in order to achieve the desired results.

Several of the large data processing firms immediately recognized the potential of BASIC as a time sharing language, most notably General Electric whose time shared BASIC was offered nationwide. Still, old habits die hard, and, except for educational applications, the potential of BASIC was never truly exploited on large mainframe systems.

BASIC achieved great popularity as a minicomputer language during the early 1970s. The BASIC Four Corporation introduced a line of time sharing minicomputers whose main system language was a powerful business oriented BASIC (also called **BASIC Four**). BASIC Four systems (the hardware and the language) continue to prove themselves in business applications.

Over the years, Hewlett-Packard has offered versions of HP BASIC for their minicomputer systems. HP BASIC is more suited to scientific needs than most BASICs, possibly reflecting the design philosophy and traditional end use of Hewlett-Packard products.

Some of the most successful and powerful minicomputer BASICs are offered by Digital Equipment Corporation. They include BASIC Plus, BASIC+2 and VAX BASIC. BASIC Plus is the oldest and least powerful of the DEC BASICs, but its influence on many popular microcomputer BASICs (especially those written by Microsoft) is testament to the excellence its design.

23.6 COMPILED AND INTERPRETED LANGUAGES

FORTRAN, COBOL and ALGOL are *compiled* languages, in which a human-readable source program is submitted to the computer and a special program, called a **compiler,** produces a machine-readable object program. All lines of code in the source program are compiled at one time. This process is analogous to batch processing. There are two major categories of compilers, those which produce native machine code and those which produce *pseudocode* (also called *P-code*). In the latter case, another step is required to translate P-code into executable machine code, but P-code offers the advantage of being transportable to any machine for which a suitable P-code interpreter exists.

A completely different approach is presented by *interpreted* languages (often called "true interpreters" to distinguish them from P-code interpreters). Unlike compilers, interpreters scan the source program a single line at a time.

Compilers generally produce physically smaller object programs which execute faster than the same program running under control of an interpreter. Compiled object programs cannot be read by the user and they do not lend themselves to meaningful disassembly. On the other hand, interpreters are easier for beginners to use, and they make debugging a far simpler undertaking.

23.7 ABOUT BASIC

BASIC was originally designed as an interpreted language. Today, interpreted versions remain the most common despite the success of true compiler and P code implementations.

The American National Standards Institute (ANSI) has proposed formal standards for minimal BASIC. Although most BASICs are supersets of these standards, the ANSI standard provides a reasonable starting point for a description of the language.

BASIC programs consist of consecutively numbered lines. Each line may contain one or more valid statements. The lines are interpreted in order from top to bottom, unless program flow is redirected by **GOTO**, **GOSUB**, **THEN [GOTO]** or **RETURN** statements. Program execution halts at the physical end of a program, when an error is detected or when a **STOP** or **END** statement is encountered.*

BASIC supports character (string), integer and real variables. Any variable may be assigned during program execution, read from **DATA** statements within the program or accessed from an external input device (typically magnetic tape). Variables may be discrete or they may be elements of an array set. A variable whose value remains unchanged during program execution is called a *constant.*

$X = X + 1$	X is a discrete variable.	(23.1)*
$A(X) = 3*Y$	A(X) is a member of an array.	(23.2)
$P = 3.14159$	P is a constant (Pi).	(23.3)

BASIC console I/O is accomplished with the **INPUT** and **PRINT** statements. For example

INPUT X	User is prompted to assign a value to X.	(23.4)
PRINT X	The value of X is displayed on the CRT.	(23.5)

*In the following displayed examples, line numbers have been omitted for clarity.

The **PRINT** statement allows quoted literals, computed results or the result of any string operation to be displayed.

```
PRINT "HELLO"
PRINT 3+2
A$ = "HELLO "
B$ = "THERE"
PRINT A$ + B$                        (23.6)
```

If these statements are executed in order, the following will be displayed:

```
HELLO
 5
HELLO THERE                          (23.7)
```

Note that the computed numeric result shown in the second line is displayed with a leading space. This idiosyncracy of BASIC is intentional and it assures that computed numeric results will be separated by at least one space from any preceding literal message appearing on the same line. For example

```
X = 2
Y = 3
Z = 4
PRINT "2*3*4"; X*Y*Z                 (23.8)
```
displays:
```
2*3*4 24                             (23.9)
```
not:
```
2*3*424                              (23.10)
```

Values may be read from system ports with the **INP** command and sent to ports with the **OUT** command. In these examples, assume that the console is implemented at port 1:

X = INP(1)	Returns ASCII code of last character typed.	(23.11)
OUT 1,65	Equivalent to typing upper case 'A'.	(23.12)

Iteration (loops) may be specified by the **FOR-NEXT** construct. The optional **STEP** statement may be used with **FOR-NEXT** to specify a *decrementing* loop or to override the default loop increment.

```
FOR X = 1 TO 10
PRINT X
NEXT X                               (23.13)
```

The values 1–10 will be printed in order.

```
FOR X = 10 TO 1 STEP −1
PRINT X
NEXT X                               (23.14)
```

The values 10–1 are printed in [reverse] order.

```
FOR X = 0 TO 10 STEP 2
PRINT X
NEXT X                               (23.15)
```

This will print 0,2,4,6,8 and 10, skipping the even values.

Conditions may be tested in BASIC and one of several possible program continuations selected according to the result. This is called *branching*. The BASIC statements which branch on condition are signaled by **IF-THEN-ELSE**.

IF X = 2 THEN 210   (23.16)

IF X = 2 THEN PRINT X ELSE PRINT "X NOT EQUAL TO 2"   (23.17)

IF X AND Y THEN PRINT "X AND Y ARE BOTH NON-ZERO"   (23.18)

Program flow in BASIC may continue along one of several different paths according to the current value of a variable. This capability is referred to as "computed GOTO" and "computed GOSUB." The **SGN** (signum) command may precede either of these to test whether a variable is negative, zero or positive:

ON X GOTO 300,400,500,600   (23.19)

ON X GOSUB 1000,1010,1020,1030,1040   (23.20)

ON SGN(X) +2 GOTO 100,200,300   (23.21)

Here SGN(X) yields −1, 0 or +1 for negative, zero or positive X.

Type conversion between character and numeric variables can be forced with the **VAL** and **STR$** statements. The **ASC** and **CHR$** statements offer a similar convenience for ASCII coded data:

```
A$ = "3.14159"
P = VAL(A$)                          (23.22)

P = 3.14159
A$ = STR$(P)                         (23.23)

PRINT ASC("A")                       (23.24)
PRINT CHR$(65)                       (23.25)
```

BASIC prohibits mathematical operations involving string variables. However, testing and validating string input is easier and far more efficient. When required, type conversion may be forced in either direction.

In the first of the preceding examples (23.22), a value for the constant pi has been expressed as the character string A\$. P = VAL(A\$) assigns an equivalent numeric value to the real variable P, which may then (unlike A\$) be used whenever pi is needed in subsequent calculations. Conversion from numeric to string is shown in the second example, (23.23). In the third example (23.24), ASC("A") is used to display the decimal value corresponding to the ASCII code for the upper case letter A, (it is 65). The inverse is shown in the last example, (23.25).

Earlier in this chapter, interpreted BASIC was categorized as a very good introductory (learning) language. There are several reasons this is so, but one deserves special mention. Interpreted BASIC may be used in either **program** (indirect) or **nonprogram** (direct) mode. In program mode, one or more numbered lines in memory execute under control of the BASIC interpreter when the RUN command is issued. In nonprogram or direct mode, one or more BASIC statements are entered without line numbers. Each line is interpreted as soon as the carriage return key is pressed. The choice of mode is determined by the task at hand *and* how the statements are keyed in. For example, if one wishes to compute the sum of 1 to 100, there are two ways to proceed:

Program mode:
```
10 FOR X = 1 TO 100
20 Y = Y + X
30 NEXT X
40 PRINT Y
RUN
   5050 (Displayed result)          (23.26)
```

Non program mode:
```
X = 100
PRINT X*(X+1)/2
   5050 (Displayed result)          (23.27)
```

The correct sum, 5050, is easily determined by either method but users familiar with the formula in the second example will find that the direct mode offers a more concise solution.

23.8 BASIC: ADVANTAGES AND DISADVANTAGES

At present, there are many computer languages in wide use; in the opinion of many computer professionals, BASIC is far from the best. Indeed, BASIC is a very good choice for some tasks and an equally unsuitable choice for others. Of course, this is by no means unique to BASIC. No computer language provides special benefits without offsetting disadvantages.

Prior to any discussion of BASIC's strengths and weaknesses, a more important insight should not be overlooked. Before 1975, there was no practical way for one to learn much about computers without formal training and access to a mainframe. With the advent of inexpensive computers and a user-friendly BASIC, computing power has been brought to millions.

One of BASIC's best qualities is its ability to perform the equivalent of many machine instructions with compact and readable commands. Consider the following example:

$$\text{PRINT INT(RND*6)} + 1 \qquad (23.28)$$

This BASIC statement produces a random integer from 1 to 6 (the roll of a single die perhaps) and displays its value. A machine language routine to accomplish the same result would fill several pages and require hours to program and test. (Equivalent routines in FORTRAN or COBOL would fall somewhere between these two extremes). Other languages, most notably APL, can instruct the computer to perform more machine instructions with even more compact commands, but they are not easy to learn and some require unusual character sets.

Unlike many other languages, BASIC is suited to general purpose programming. This flexibility offers the programmer the advantage of having to learn only a single language for assorted tasks. Other languages, such as PL/I, are even more universal, but they are more difficult to learn. In fact, PL/I is such a vast language that most PL/I programmers only remember and use a subset dictated by the nature of their projects.

As a drawback, compiled BASIC programs tend to be physically larger than those produced by other compiled languages and their execution time is only average by comparison. Interpreted BASIC is rather slow and, since the interpreter must be in memory at all times, even the smallest programs are effectively quite large.

The most frequently voiced complaint about BASIC concerns its unstructured nature (a complaint even more applicable to FORTRAN). BASIC programs, especially those written by beginners, make liberal use of GOTO statements. When BASIC programs become large, it can be all but impossible to follow execution flow and program logic. Large BASIC programs are difficult to maintain. Often the intent of complex, unstructured programs cannot be deduced by anyone other than the original programmer.

A related problem concerns the variable-naming conventions of standard BASIC. Label length is limited to two characters; when more than two are used by the programmer, the interpreter ignores the last few characters. This limitation does not allow variables to be identified meaningfully. Considerable confusion can be caused by assigning names such as P3, A1, DD and Y to variables in large BASIC programs. Recently some versions of BASIC have been enhanced by support of long variable names and structure oriented constructs, improving the usefulness of BASIC to a great degree.

One of the reasons BASIC remains popular despite its drawbacks is that programmers of all skill levels can produce working programs in less time than would be possible using other languages. Admittedly, when speed and program size are critical factors, as might be the case when writing operating systems, language translators, system utilities, real time games, sorting programs or diagnostics, BASIC is not a viable choice. Conversely, BASIC is ideal for many other types of applications, including complex business and accounting systems, computer aided instruction and a wide variety of games and recreations.

23.9 THE INFLUENCE OF MICROCOMPUTERS

The first microcomputers were manufactured by firms which had no real idea of their potential. These machines were marketed primarily to electronic hobbyists and, initially, no useful language options existed. Programs had to be loaded into memory with front panel switches or hexadecimal keypads, an unbelievably tedious process. Needless to say, Altair BASIC represented a quantum jump in improvement. The early versions allowed programs to be stored on cassette tape and later versions supported disk file I/O. The latter enhancement meant that microcomputer BASIC had finally become a useful language for business applications and that, as a result, microcomputers had proven themselves capable of servicing the needs of smaller businesses.

By the late 1970s, it had become quite apparent that no microcomputer system could survive in the marketplace unless a respectable implementation of BASIC was offered. It was a case of the tail wagging the dog in which the eventual choice of many small systems was influenced more by the quality of the available BASICs than by the

systems themselves. A substantial competitive advantage was realized by the manufacturers who offered bigger and better BASICs than their rivals and, as a result, many of the most innovative enhancements to BASIC were first seen in microprocessor based versions.

The unprecedented (and somewhat unexpected) growth of the microcomputer field began in the late 1970's. What had started as a cottage industry, catering to electronic tinkerers, became a multibillion dollar business within five years. In retrospect, the reasons are obvious: microcomputers were affordable machines whose wide acceptance was due in large measure to the fact that they offered BASIC.

23.10 MICROCOMPUTER BASIC: THE EARLY PIONEERS

In 1974, Bill Gates, Paul Allen and Monty Davidoff wrote an 8080 BASIC interpreter. (Gates and Allen later founded Microsoft.) Shortly thereafter, an enhanced version of this BASIC appeared as a language option for the Altair computers, manufactured by MITS, Inc., of Albuquerque, New Mexico. MITS is no longer in business, but they shall be remembered as the first to offer an affordable microcomputer system and also as the originators of the S-100 bus. Microsoft has since become a successful software concern whose offerings include many OEM versions of BASIC and other major languages, operating systems, editors and assemblers, for many different hardware configurations.

An event of considerable significance occurred in 1976, when Gordon Eubanks developed a BASIC pseudo-compiler as a thesis project at the Naval Postgraduate School in Monterey, California. Interestingly, the director of this thesis project was Gary Kildall, the creator of the CP/M operating system and founder of Digital Research, Inc. The compiler developed by Eubanks was called BASIC-E and it was the first disk BASIC to run under CP/M. Today, CP/M has become the defacto standard for disk based microcomputer systems and its early success was undoubtedly influenced by the existence of BASIC-E in the public domain.

Eubanks joined with Keith Parsons and Alan Cooper of the Structured Systems Group to develop a business oriented language similar to BASIC-E. In 1977, Eubanks founded Compiler Systems, Inc. whose first product was **CBASIC**. These two companies continued to work together to refine CBASIC and a third generation product, called CBASIC2, was introduced in January of 1979.

This product proved itself a capable performer for business applications and, within a year, Compiler Systems had signed more than 200 OEM and dealer agreements.

23.11 MICROSOFT BASICS

The majority of current microcomputer BASICs have been written by Microsoft. At present, interpreted versions exist which will run on the 8080, 8085, Z80, 6800, 6502, 8088 and 8086 processors. In addition, a number of different operating systems, including CP/M, are explicitly supported by Microsoft BASIC. A partial list of Microsoft's special OEM versions would include BASICs offered by Apple, Radio Shack, Texas Instruments, NCR, Intel, NEC, Mostek and IBM.

Microsoft's BASIC interpreters differ from each other somewhat in the OEM versions but all are useful for serious applications and all are especially well suited as a first language for beginners.

Microsoft offers true compiler versions for CP/M and the TRS-80 model II. Those fortunate enough to have both interpreted and compiled versions will be able to develop and test their program using the interpreter and then compile the finished product. The compiled versions are more compact and execute much faster. Another benefit exists in that the source code of a compiled program is not available to the end user. (The interpreter option which prevents programs from being listed is easily defeated.)

It is hard to fault any BASIC written by Microsoft, but there are some rough edges. All arithmetic operations are done in binary (as opposed to BCD—binary coded decimal). In applications where cumulative rounding error would be unacceptable, the programmer must include rather intricate routines to circumvent this problem. Random file I/O requires that all data elements in a random record be explicitly "fielded" as fixed length strings with type conversion forced when necessary. This, too, can prove somewhat awkward.

The compiled versions of Microsoft BASIC differ very slightly in capability from the interpreted versions. However, one of these differences can be quite limiting in some applications: in the interpreted versions, arrays may be dimensioned dynamically; the compiled versions require that arrays be dimensioned explicitly. This restriction means that array dimensions in compiled programs must reflect the largest possible number of array elements, which can pose problems for small users using

commercially written programs which also allow for larger jobs.

Finally, all versions of Microsoft BASIC which support random data files write those files in binary (as opposed to ASCII). This allows faster file I/O but exacts a penalty in that the contents of the files are often unreadable (by the user) and that the files may not be repaired or concatenated with text editing programs. Still, the flaws of Microsoft's BASIC products are few (and arguable perhaps). The good points far outweigh the bad as might be assumed by the number of OEM versions written for so many demanding manufacturers.

23.11 CBASIC AND CB-80*

CBASIC is compatible with the 8080, 8085, Z80, 8088 and 8086 processors. CP/M, CP/M-86 and TRSDOS are presently supported. CBASIC programs are prepared with a text editor and the finished program is then compiled into P-code (called an INT file), which is subsequently interpreted at run time. P-code object programs may be moved unmodified to any processor or operating system for which an appropriate P-code interpreter exists. For example, any 8 bit computer using CP/M could be used to develop and test application packages for 8086 based machines running CP/M-86.

CBASIC was the first widely used BASIC to incorporate useful solutions to BASIC's traditional deficiencies for business applications. The more standard BASICs which existed at the time all suffered from excessive rounding error and the maintenance problems dictated by the language. Much of what was first introduced by CBASIC has been adopted by other BASICs. The most important features are listed below.

1. Line numbers are no longer required except as "targets" of **GOTO, GOSUB, THEN** or **ELSE** statements.
2. Long and significant variable names are supported.
3. **WHILE-WEND** improves program structure.
4. Individual program lines can be continued, or wrapped, over any number of physical lines.
5. Tabs, spaces, remarks and blank lines can be used freely in CBASIC source programs without increasing the size of the compiled object program.

---

*To ease confusion, the generic family of languages which include BASIC-E, CBASIC, CBASIC2 and CBASIC-86 will be referred to as CBASIC. Necessary distinctions among them become apparent in context.

6. BCD arithmetic, accurate to 14 places, is used throughout, except when integers are explicitly declared.
7. Record length of random files may be declared dynamically.
8. There is no way for a user to reconstruct the source code from a working application package.
9. CBASIC is the first of the microcomputer BASICs to implement the **CHAIN** command with **COMMON** variables. This feature allows you to create programs whose size is limited by available disk storage rather than free system memory.

The value of these features is obvious to any programmer who has worked around the deficiencies of a typical BASIC interpreter in order to create any complex business oriented application.

Indeed, CBASIC was never intended to be a general purpose programming language. It was expressly designed for business applications. In that capacity, CBASIC is unexcelled. A frequent (and unfair) complaint about CBASIC relates to slow execution. This complaint is seldom (if ever) voiced by competent programmers who write the kind of programs for which CBASIC was originally designed.

CBASIC is not a beginner's language: errors which may occur during compilation or run time demand further editing, recompiling and rerunning the resulting object program. These steps soon frustrate a neophyte programmer whose programs usually contain multiple errors.

When speed or program size becomes a valid concern, **CB-80** affords an excellent solution. CB-80 is a native code compiler (producing executable machine language) which accepts a superset of the CBASIC language while imposing few noticeable restrictions. Most CBASIC programs can be compiled without modification.

Programs compiled by CB-80 are compact and they are very fast. Initially, the widest use may be expected from those wishing to improve the performance of existing CBASIC programs. In time, new programs, written explicitly for CB-80, will be able to take full advantage of its many enhancements. One merits special mention: CB-80 programs may include relocatable, user-developed procedures. These are essentially relocatable library routines which may be used locally or externally by a CB-80 program. Once they are developed, the programmer may use relocatable procedures freely, concerned only as to which formal parameters (if any) are required.

Whereas CBASIC is mainly a business language, CB-80 may be considered more universal. The remarkable execution speed of many programs compiled by CB-80 suggests its applicability for a wide field of nonbusiness applications.

23.13 SOME OTHER MICROCOMPUTER BASICS

During the past few years, North Star Computers, Inc., has offered several superbly designed BASIC interpreters whose performance in almost all published benchmark testing has been singularly impressive. This is especially remarkable since North Star BASICs use BCD arithmetic (the slower and more accurate system). The commercial potential of North Star BASIC remains largely unrealized because North Star has tied their software products to their proprietary operating system. Recently, CP/M-compatible versions of North Star BASIC have become available but have not yet have been picked up by many users.

SBASIC, a product of Topaz Programming, is an 8080-compatible native code compiler. SBASIC compiles most interpreted source programs while offering many structure-oriented extensions. Valid SBASIC programs might look like normal BASIC or they might look more like PASCAL. As in the case of CBASIC, some SBASIC programs bear only a superficial resemblance to textbook BASIC. But SBASIC can be quite valuable for helping BASIC programmers learn about the structured languages. The value of SBASIC as a serious application language has yet to be established.

XYBASIC, from the Mark Williams Company, is the generic name given to another specialized family of BASIC interpreters. Their performance is comparable to Microsoft's products, but most features of the Microsoft BASICs which serve engineering or business needs are matched in the case of the XYBASIC family with enhancements geared to machine and process control.

23.14 THE FUTURE OF BASIC

Versions of BASIC designed for increasingly specialized use abound, but the commercial potential remains uncertain. Two unusual and disparate BASICs were introduced during the first quarter of 1982. One of these, **Precision BASIC,** is a Z80 interpreter, virtually devoid of string functions and disk I/O, which performs numeric calculations to 63 significant places with no discernable delay. The other, **BASIC-Z,** is a native code compiler which offers more options than any other BASIC and more than almost any other language (with the possible exception of PL/I).

BASIC was initially intended to be a somewhat standardized language, but attempts in this direction have obviously failed. If there ever was a real standard, it has been exceeded so often, in so many different ways, that it no longer effectively exists.

Whenever structured language compilers such as C, PASCAL or PL/I are first implemented on microcomputer systems, experts (who should know better) proclaim the imminent demise of BASIC. As of publication of this book, it has not happened. Nonetheless, ADA is heralded by many as the [next] language which will finally render BASIC obsolete. ADA is not likely to re-place BASIC, nor is any other language in the forseeable future.

REFERENCES

D. K. Carver, *Introduction to Data Processing.* New York: John Wiley & Sons, 1974.

Kemeny John G., and Thomas E. Kurtz, *BASIC Programming,* 2nd Ed. New York: John Wiley & Sons, 1971.

Acknowledgements

The author wishes to thank the following individuals for their assistance in the preparation of this chapter:

Gordon Eubanks, Digital Research, Inc.
Edward H. Currie, Lifeboat Associates
Marilyn J. Narcisi, Bank Hapaolim B.M.

24
PASCAL

John M. Cameron
Avrum E. Itzkowitz
Data General Corporation
Steven W. Weingart
Language Processors, Inc.

24.1 INTRODUCTION

The programming language PASCAL was designed by Professor Niklaus Wirth in the late 1960s and early 1970s. The initial report on the language appeared in the literature in 1971 [A-1]. Revised descriptions appeared in 1972 [A-2] and in subsequent years [A-3].

Wirth developed PASCAL to provide features then lacking in other languages. The principal objectives of PASCAL are to

- Be efficient to implement and run;
- Allow the development of well structured and well organized programs;
- Serve as a vehicle for the teaching of the important concepts of computer programming.

To achieve these objectives, PASCAL has several characteristics that distinguish it from its predecessors.

PASCAL offers a wide repertoire of control constructs and a rich set of mechanisms for loop control and conditional execution. Although this set of control constructs has been found to be incomplete, it does offer more variety than other languages in widespread use. Further, PASCAL facilitates the writing of programs so as to exhibit well structured flow of control.

PASCAL also offers a very rich set of data types and structures. Built-in data types include integer, real, character, and Boolean. Additionally, the programmer can define his or her own scalar types as well as subranges of those data types. Among the data structures provided by PASCAL are arrays, records, files and sets. These data types and data structures provide the programmer with a flexible set of tools for writing well structured programs.

Another important attribute of PASCAL is its strong data typing, and the compile time and execution time diagnostics that are typically provided when these data typing rules are violated. For example, PASCAL compilers diagnose an incompatible assignment of data of one type to a variable of another type. Additionally, at execution time, diagnostics can be issued if array bounds are exceeded or if an assignment is made to an undefined variant field of a record structure.

The extensive set of control constructs, the rich and varied data structures and data types, and the enforcement of rules of data type conformance at both compile time and execution time encourage the PASCAL programmer to code in a manner that is natural for a given application area and also consistent with modern principles of good programming practice.

24.2 PASCAL'S HISTORY

As we have seen, PASCAL was designed during the late 1960s and early 1970s. As the language caught on, especially in colleges and universities in the mid 1970s, some of its inadequacies became apparent. (In Section 24.6 we discuss some of the more serious problems with the language.) This fundamental popularity led to numerous implementations of the language (some are discussed in Section 24.7); at the same time, the inadequacies of the language led many compiler developers to make extensions to the language. As a result, program portability began to suffer. This led to a groundswell of support for an official PASCAL language standard.

In the early stages of PASCAL standardization activity, there was intense interest within IEEE as well as within the ANSI technical committees, which had been the traditional forum for developing language standards for FORTRAN, PL/I, COBOL, and BASIC. A joint technical committee was set up in 1978, operating under the auspices of both IEEE and ANSI.

A bit earlier in mid 1977, the British Standards Institute initiated work on a PASCAL language standard within the scope of the international standards organization. This activity quickly provoked two very different schools of thought. A number of individuals felt that PASCAL as was then defined (in *Pascal User Manual and Report* [A-3]) had some serious problems and therefore the standard-developing process should seek to modify and enhance the language to alleviate these problems. Another group, equally vocal, felt that the definition that already existed was good enough on which to base a standard, and given the many different opinions about which extensions to the language were appropriate, the better course of action would be to standardize PASCAL as quickly as possible, based on Jensen and Wirth's *User Manual and Report,* and then consider extensions in due course.

After considerable discussion, the second approach was taken and a draft standard was prepared, based on the *User Manual and Report.* This draft international standard went through several revisions. An especially noteworthy item appeared in one of these drafts in late 1979: a feature that came to be known as "conformant arrays." This was an attempt to alleviate a serious PASCAL shortcoming—that arrays of different sizes cannot be substituted for a formal array parameter in procedure and function calls. Although there was general agreement that this was a serious problem in the language, there was considerable disagreement about the merits of the proposed solution.

Against this backdrop of international standardization activity on PASCAL, the United States standardization efforts began. Again, two schools of thought emerged: fix the problems in the language, or standardize as quickly as possible and consider "fixes" and extensions later. The conformant array feature continued to be a particular area of contention and disagreement.

Eventually a draft international standard was issued for public comment. This document reflected the view that the traditional PASCAL language was fundamentally suitable for standardization, and significant extensions should be added later. However, the conformant array feature was included in the draft international standard that was opened to public comment. Because everyone recognized the importance of having an American national standard that would be fully consistent with an international standard for PASCAL, the international standard was depicted as having two levels: level 1 consists of the entire PASCAL language, essentially as defined in the *User Manual and Report,* with one change and several clarifications, plus the conformant array feature, while level 0 excludes the conformant array feature. The American standardization group then used level 0 of the draft international standard in preparing the draft American national standard.

These two draft standards have been subjected to a round of public comments. These comments were considered by the standards groups and they lead to slight changes in the draft standards. The American standard was formally adopted in December 1982 [A-4]. As of mid 1983 the draft international standard [A-4] is proceeding through the 150 standardization process. In the meantime, extensive discussion and analysis are taking place with respect to future standardization of several extensions to the PASCAL language.

The Pascal Users Group [B-1] (sometimes referred to as PUG) publishes *Pascal News* several times a year, containing significant information of interest to the Pascal user community. The Pascal Users Group came into existence in the mid 1970s as interest in PASCAL grew rapidly. Within a few years it had several thousand members.

24.3 SIGNIFICANCE AND IMPACT OF PASCAL

Since PASCAL was designed specifically as a vehicle to teach programming concepts, it should be no suprise that PASCAL has had its greatest acceptance in the academic community. Many universities that have routinely taught FORTRAN in their introductory computer programming courses now use PASCAL. Experience has shown that programming courses using PASCAL have been better able to focus on programming concepts and methodology, while courses using other languages often become bogged down in the details of using the language.

PASCAL has also been used extensively as a research

vehicle within the academic community. It has become common to express algorithms in technical papers using PASCAL. It has also been used as a host language for experiments in language extensions, both syntactic and semantic. The cleanliness of the language coupled with its nonproprietary origins has made PASCAL very hospitable for experimentation. Most of the initial implementations of the language were done in academic environments, and the source code for these compilers is widely available.

Not all of strengths PASCAL'S for the academic enviroments lend themselves to the commercial environment. One of the strengths of the language for academic work has been the easy modification of existing compilers. This is a decided weakness in the commercial environment, which places a premium on consistency, reliability and support. Even so, PASCAL has had an impact in the commercial market place, and continues to gain acceptance as more and more vendors offer supported PASCAL products.

It is natural for there to be an increased demand for PASCAL within industry. Most of today's college students in technical disciplines have been exposed to PASCAL, and prefer it to other computer languages. As these students graduate and enter industry, they carry this preference with them. In addition, PASCAL offers the programmer the expressibility, self documentation and program diagnostic capability that can reduce program development time and maintenance cost, and improve reliability.

PASCAL has been used most successfully in commercial environments for general and system applications. Such applications as document preparation and programming tools have been successfully developed using PASCAL. Also, PASCAL has been popular for commercial applications implemented on microcomputers.

Possibly the strongest impact of Pascal is the influence that it has had on ADA development. ADA is a new high level language being developed for the United States Department of Defense for embedded systems software (Chapter 20). ADA is a richer and more complex language than PASCAL, but its roots are undeniably based on the PASCAL experience.

24.4 LANGUAGE SUMMARY

This section is an overview of the structure of the PASCAL language. The intent here is to provide a feel for the language, rather than a detailed description. A more complete description of PASCAL can be found in a number of different PASCAL texts, several of which are noted in the References.

PASCAL is statement oriented; the statements are separated by semicolons. The language is free form, with no column sensitivity (in contrast to FORTRAN, for example). A PASCAL program consists of three principal parts:

1. Program heading.
2. Declaration.
3. Statement.

The program heading typically consists of

$$\text{PROGRAM name (input, output);} \qquad (24.1)$$

PASCAL implementations that support separate compilation of modules typically use a variation of the program heading syntax to identify separate modules.

The **declaration** part of a PASCAL program may include declarations for any of these items:

• Labels.
• Named constants.
• User defined types.
• Variables.
• Procedures and/or functions.

These portions must be in the order of the above listing, but not all need be present in a given program.

Although PASCAL does provide a GOTO statement, in an effort to limit its use and improve readability, the language requires the programmer to declare every label in a program. The intention is that the programmer be required to think ahead and use GOTOs only under more controlled circumstances than is the case in some other programming languages. The PASCAL programmer is encouraged to make extensive use of the more structured mechanisms for controlling program flow, and to use the GOTO statement sparingly.

The **statement** part consists of one or more PASCAL statements, surrounded by the reserved words BEGIN and END:

```
BEGIN
    statement_1; statement_2;
    . . . ;
    statement_n
END                                    (24.2)
```

This structure shows the general form of a compound statement, which permits any number of individual statements to be grouped together, surrounded by a BEGIN . . . END bracket, and used anywhere a statement is permitted in the language.

Commentary can be freely added to a PASCAL program by surrounding the comment text with { and }. (PASCAL also allows the use of (* and *) as substitutes for { and } where character sets are of limited size.) A PASCAL comment can extend for as many lines as necessary and can appear anywhere a space can appear in a PASCAL program.

PASCAL offers the typical set of arithmetic operators and includes a DIV operator for integer division and a MOD operator for the modulus, the remainder after integer division.

All six relational operators are provided: $<, <=, >,$ $>=, =, <>$. The Boolean operators AND, OR, and NOT are provided, as well as seven operators that relate to operations on sets (intersection, difference, union, membership, inclusion, inequality, and equality).

PASCAL includes the traditional assignment, procedure call, and GOTO statements; several loop control mechanisms (WHILE, REPEAT, and FOR statements); and two statements that deal with conditional execution, CASE and IF–THEN–ELSE.

PASCAL offers the programmer a considerable amount of flexibility with respect to data types. Enumerated scalar data types can be defined by the programmer to suit the nature of the application. Any number of variables can then be declared to be instances of a programmer-defined data type. Additionally, subranges can be defined so that the PASCAL compiler and execution time system can enforce constraints on the values that a particular variable might assume.

Consistent with the "strongly typed" nature of PASCAL, pointers in PASCAL are associated with a data type. The data type with which a particular pointer is associated is specified as part of the pointer's declaration. This helps ensure that pointers are used in a reasonably disciplined manner in PASCAL. In contrast, the PL/I language provides pointers which are not typed, and this frequently leads to programming errors that cannot occur in PASCAL. Additionally, PASCAL does not allow pointers to point to declared variables. This helps eliminate a source of bugs, and allows compilers to produce more efficient code.

Here (Figure 24.1) is an example of a PASCAL program. Although this program uses only a few features of the language, it provides a feel for the syntactic structure of PASCAL:

```
PROGRAM area (input, output);
{read radius; compute area of circle}

CONST   pi = 3.14159;      {pi is a named constant}

VAR   radius, area: REAL; {declares two real variables}

FUNCTION get_radius:REAL; {a function of no
                            arguments that returns a
                            real value}
VAR r: REAL;              {a declaration local to the
                            function}
BEGIN        {get_radius}
  write ('Enter value for radius (0.0 to halt):   );
readln(r);
get_radius: = r
END;         {get_radius}

BEGIN     {main program 'area'}
radius: = get_radius;
WHILE radius <> 0.0 DO {test is done at top of loop}
  BEGIN
  area: = pi * radius * radius;
  writeln ('Radius = ', radius, ' Area =', area);
  radius: = get_radius
  END         {while}
END.
```

Figure 24.1. Elemental PASCAL Program.

24.5 STRENGTHS OF PASCAL

PASCAL is a teaching tool. It is a small, clean language that is easy to learn, yet it contains many features found in modern high level languages. The language contains the necessary control structures: if-then-else, various loop controls, and a case statement using constants as labels. It contains data structures such as arrays and user defined logical collections of elements called records. It provides dynamic allocation and pointers that have become necessities in modern languages. PASCAL also contains features not found in some other popular languages: strong typing, mathematical sets and an enumerated scaler type which is an extension of typing to parameterized names.

As we have seen, PASCAL is a strongly typed language. There are rules which govern the legality of an operation, based on the operands which are the object of the operation. With the exception of real and integer values, and set expressions, there is no implied coercion: if the types do not match, such is listed as an error at compilation time. That is an especially desirable feature in a learning situation. A beginning programmer can easily grasp the idea of moving objects, but has a hard time understanding a coercion that may depend on internal representation. Strong typing can catch those unintended coercions at compile time; they are otherwise difficult to find and can require large amounts of debugging time even for the experienced programmer.

Types can be extended to include range information. Runtime tests are thus made in the object code to insure that assignments to variables are within the specified range. A type is created which is a subrange of an existing type, by way of a range declaration as follows:

```
type   eggcount = 0. .12;
       lowercase = 'a'. .'z';
var    myeggs: eggcount;
       small: lowercase;          (24.3)
```

If myeggs assumes a value outside the range of 0 to 12 or if small is assigned a character value outside the range 'a' to 'z', a runtime error occurs. This feature is a developmental aid which may be disabled to improve program execution efficiency when there is sufficient confidence in the program. Other runtime validity checks are furnished, all of which appear to be of significant help in program debugging and development.

The control structures in PASCAL include those found in most higher level languages: an incremental loop, two loops with logical tests, one with the test at the beginning (while), one with the test at the end (until), an if-then-else statement, a case statement, and a goto statement to cover anything which may have been overlooked. In practice the only missing element seems to be a structured means to escape from an arbitrary point in a loop.

One truly elegant feature of PASCAL is the **enumerated type.** It is a part of the language allowing a programmer to use uniquely named constants which are collected together as one type. The user creates a new type by simply writing down a list of names, which can then be used interchangeably with other names in the list. Variables may thus be created which may assume a value that is a name from a particular list, and only from that list. For example, to keep track of the state of a fuel tank the following declarations may be used:

```
type state = (empty, full, filling, draining);   (24.4)
var tank1: state;
```

This creates a variable, tank1, which may assume one of the values empty, full, filling or draining. Since these names are constants, they may be used as the labels of a case statement; the variable value then controls the evaluation of the case statement, as follows:

```
begin . . .
    case tank1 of
        empty: fillit;
        full: useit;
        filling, draining: {do nothing}
    end;

        . . .
end.                                            (24.5)
```

PASCAL contains a data structure called a **set,** similar to a mathematical set, but which may only contain an implementation-defined range of scalar elements. Sets are permitted to contain elements of only one type; this type determines the compatibility of the set operations. Set elements may include the following types: char (character), boolean, user defined enumerated types, and subranges of these and of the integers. The implementation range of the set is normally from zero to some finite limit; the range usually handles at least the printable elements of the "char" type. The standard set operations of intersection and union are available, as well as a set difference operation which gives those elements in the first set which are not in the second set. An operation in tests whether a given element is within a named set.

Sets work well with enumerated types. For example, a work schedule can be described using a set which contains the days a person is at work. First, a type **days** is created using letters representing the days of the week. Now a type **schedule** can be created which is a set of **days.** A simple set assignment then describes a person's work schedule:

```
type   days = (sun, mon, tue, wed, thur, fri, sat);
       schedule = set of days;
var    fredjones: schedule;
       begin
       fredjones: = [mon..thur, sat];
       etc                                      (24.6)
```

Note the two dots (. .) used as an ellipsis.

Set operations perform tests in parallel in an efficient manner. There is a one to one mapping of Boolean arrays onto sets: and and or correspond to set *intersection* and *union*. Therefore sets are usually implemented by the compiler as aligned bit strings. Since set operations may be performed a word at a time, this yields a quasi-parallel Boolean operation.

24.6 WEAKNESSES OF PASCAL

Some of PASCAL's strengths also seem to be its weaknesses. As a small, easy to learn, teaching language, it does not have the tools necessary to develop large production systems. The problems are in the areas of I/O, parameter passing, and missing functionality, such as data initialization and separate compilation.

PASCAL files seem to have been added as an afterthought. An attempt was made to make them like any other data object in the language. Restrictions were then added to prevent any misuse by neophyte programmers. The primary restriction is that no file assignment is allowed. Treating files as data structures implies that file assignment is actually a file copy. Traditionally, PASCAL files have been implemented as pointers to existing files and file assignment has allowed two objects to reference the same file. Any program that requires file reference manipulation, such as a sort/merge package, cannot be written in a straightforward manner in PASCAL.

The PASCAL I/O system works best with sequential files running in a batch environment. Except by extensions, it does not support the notions of variable length records, direct access files or interactive consoles. Reset, a built-in file *open* function, is required to fill an input buffer according to the traditional language specification. This leads to timing problems in an interactive system, where no data yet exists. This problem can be circumvented by constant testing, but it leads to inefficiency.

A further interactive problem occurs when it is necessary to assure that all output reaches the I/O device. Interactively, all output to the console must be flushed from the buffer to assure proper interaction between the program and the user. Since there are no character strings in PASCAL, output is character by character. In some implementations, this is a terribly inefficient process—a flush for each character.

Strong typing may be a mild inconvenience in some cases; for passing an array as a parameter, PASCAL's strong typing becomes a very serious problem. It is not possible to write general array handling routines because parameter types must match exactly. If the parameter type is an array, the procedure can handle only the type of array specified, complete with its constant dimensions. A programmer writing a matrix multiplication routine must either use the maximum space for every array, or write separate routines for each class of matrix expected

to be encountered. If the different matrices are close in size, it is best to use the same space for each, but if there is a large difference it may be best to have multiple routines.

The inability of PASCAL to initialize variables or to create constants of structured types makes it difficult to write certain kinds of programs efficiently.

The language as traditionally defined has no facilities for separate compilation. Pascal procedures and functions cannot be compiled independently of a main program. This lack of a separate compilation facility can lead to increased development costs for large systems.

Many PASCAL dialects have arisen to handle the shortcomings of the language. It is a testimonial to the basic structure of the language that these dialects are still called PASCAL. The most popular changes to the language seem to be the addition of separate compilation and string handling.

All too often alterations to the PASCAL language are used so extensively that there are few truly portable PASCAL programs of any significance. Those that are portable usually pay a tremendous price in efficiency. Standardization activities now underway are seeking to alleviate these problems.

24.7 IMPLEMENTATIONS

Many implementations of PASCAL are available over the whole range of computer systems, from microcomputers to supercomputers. They implement dialects of PASCAL ranging from restricted subsets to large supersets of the standard. Some have extensions specifically aimed at particular application domains. Many are available from the academic community, some from software suppliers, and some from computer system vendors. Implementations of PASCAL can be divided into three categories, based upon their developmental history: descendents of Wirth's PASCAL-6000 compiler, descendents of the Sequential Pascal compiler, and other independent implementations.

Wirth's PASCAL compiler for the Control Data 6000 and Cyber series machines was the first generally available PASCAL implementation [A-3]. The compiler itself is written in PASCAL, and is a single pass recursive descent design. This compiler was later modified to produce code for a simplified virtual machine [B-3]. Support for several features was dropped to simplify the implementation. This allowed the rehosting of the compiler onto different systems by means of implementing an interpreter for the virtual machine. That compiler (and its descendants) is called the **P-code** compiler, and the virtual machine intermediate form produced by the compiler is called P-code. There have been several versions of P-code used, the most common of which is known as P4.

A large number of PASCAL implementations have been derived from the P-code compilers, from the UCSD PASCAL system to IBM's PASCAL/VS.

The **UCSD** (University of California, San Diego) **PASCAL** system [B-2] is designed to run on microcomputer systems. The P-code compiler was modified and enhanced, and the form of the P-code itself was changed to be more space-efficient. The UCSD PASCAL system is fully interpreted at runtime; versions of it are available for most current microcomputer systems.

IBM's **PASCAL/VS** [B-3] runs on the IBM 370, 303x, and 43xx systems. The P4 compiler was extensively modified, both to extend the language and to retarget the P-code output of the compiler to **U-code**, which is an enhanced intermediate form. Instead of interpreting the intermediate code, as does the UCSD PASCAL system, a second pass has been added to the compiler, which generates object code and performs several forms of optimizations. This yields a compiler which is fast and produces good quality runtime code.

As single pass recursive descent compilers, the P-code compilers are somewhat limited in memory constrained systems. They may be heavily overlaid, with a resulting compile speed degradation, and they may limit the size of a program that can be compiled. The **Sequential PASCAL** compiler [B-4] is designed specifically to deal with the memory constrained environment. It is a multiple pass compiler that produces code for a virtual machine, which is interpreted at runtime.

Data General's **MP/PASCAL** [B-6] is an example of a PASCAL implementation derived from the Sequential PASCAL compiler. MP/PASCAL runs on Data General's Nova and Eclipse processors. The compiler is extensively modified to enhance the language and to improve its environment. Interpretive implementations tend to produce compact code, but there is a large overhead penalty paid in the runtime interpretation process. Interpretive implementations also usually do not provide the programmer with access to routines written in assembly language. MP/PASCAL uses threaded code instead of the interpretive approach. While the code is not as compact as interpretive code can be, this approach yields an implementation that runs efficiently and allows calling procedures and functions written in assembly language.

Other PASCAL implementations have been developed to meet a variety of needs. For example, Data General's SP/PASCAL [B-7] is a dialect of PASCAL oriented for system programming, with a compile and runtime orientation for memory constrained real time environments. It is a multiple pass compiler which produces object code for the Data General 16 bit Eclipse family of processors.

Data General's AOS/VS PASCAL [B-8, B-9] is a full ANSI standard compatible PASCAL product for Eclipse MV/family 32 bit processors. It is a multipass compiler which shares a common environment, including a high level language debugger, with the other Data General 32 bit languages. The SP/PASCAL and AOS/VS PASCAL compilers incorporate modern compiler techniques and component technology in their design.

24.8 PRACTICAL ASPECTS

There are several factors to be considered when deciding whether PASCAL should be used for a particular application. The first is how well PASCAL *supports* the application. If the application requires specific domain support, such as decimal arithmetic or data base management, PASCAL may offer no advantage over other language processors which have such support. Where very little specific application domain support is required, PASCAL could be an attractive choice.

Another consideration is the *availability* of a PASCAL product for an intended hardware configuration. PASCAL compilers are currently available for most computer systems, but their characteristics vary widely. A key question is whether the size and speed constraints of the candidate PASCAL system meet the application's needs. Consider that some PASCAL products are subsets or dialects of "standard" PASCAL. One should evaluate the PASCAL implementation to ensure that the language features required by the application are present. Especially at the microcomputer level, packed structures, labels, gotos, file buffer variables, and parametric procedures and functions may not be implemented.

Portability is another factor. If the application may be rehosted to another system, it may be necessary to restrict the use of features which may not be implemented on other systems. Even commonly supported features can suffer from differing implementation limits, that is, the maximum length of identifiers, literal strings and input lines. Some implementations restrict the maximum nesting level of procedures and functions. The available range of sets may be limited. Other differences include the range of integer numbers and the precision of real numbers.

Language *extensions* differ from system to system. For example, many implementations support separate compilation, but few support it in the same way. The same is true for interactive console support. Some implementations allow the user to call external procedures written in other languages and to request system services not available through PASCAL. These features can simplify application development. Indeed, their use can make it possible to use PASCAL for applications that would otherwise require assembly language, but this does adversely impact program portability.

The development of a *support environment* is another consideration. How well does the system diagnose compile time and runtime errors? Is there support for a PASCAL source level debugger or must debugging be done at the assembly language level? Are utilities, such as text editors and cross-referencers, available to aid development? The quality of the development environment can have a large impact, positive or negative, on the cost and quality of the application program.

24.9 CONCLUSION

PASCAL has much to offer. The syntactic structure itself is one of its selling points and has served as a template for other languages. *PASCAL-like* has become a buzz word to describe some sort of desirable language structure. It has the tools to do most of the sophisticated things required of modern languages, particularly in the area of information structures.

PASCAL has extremely sophisticated capabilities which may be used effectively in developing small systems and as a test bed for ideas. Although it is often not a good language to use for systems in production environments, especially those heavy in I/O, the I/O system works well to create simple displays with little user knowledge required. Above all, PASCAL is an excellent computer science teaching tool and provides source programs which are easy to understand.

REFERENCES

For a comprehensive PASCAL bibliography (303 entries), compiled in June 1980 by David V. Moffat, see *Pascal News*, No. 19 (Sept. 1980).

A. Language Definitions and Standards

[1] Wirth, N., "The Programming Language Pascal," *Acta Informatica*, Vol. 1, No. 1 (1971), pp. 34–65.
[2] Wirth, N., *The Programming Language Pascal (Revised Report)*. Zurich: ETH Technical Report 5, 1972.
[3] Jensen K., and Niklaus Wirth, *Pascal User Manual and Report*. New York: Springer-Verlag, 1975; 2nd Ed., 1978.
[4] American National Standards Institute, ANSI/IEEE 77OX 3.97–1983, *Programming Lanugauge Pascal*.
[5] Internationals Standards Organization, ISO/DIS 7185, *Draft International Standard Programming Language Pascal*.

B. Implementation Notes and References

[1] Pascal Users Group, 2903 Huntington Road, Cleveland, OH 44120.
[2] Bowles, K., "Status of UCSD Project," *Pascal News*, No. 11, (Feb. 1978), pp. 36–40.
[3] Nori, K.V., U. Amman, K. Jensen, H.H. Nageli, and C. Jacobi, "The Pascal <P> Compiler: Implementation Notes," Technical Report, Eidgenossische Technische Hochschule, July 1976.
[4] Brinch Hansen, P. and A. C. Hartman, "Sequential Pascal Report," Technical Report, Information Science, California Institute of Technology, 1975.
[5] "IBM Pascal/VS," *Pascal News*, No. 19 (Sept. 1980), pp. 117–319.
[6] Data General Corporation, *MP/Pascal Reference Manual*.
[7] Data General Corporation, *SP/Pascal Reference Manual*.
[8] Data General Corporation, *AOS/VS Pascal Reference Manual*.
[9] Data General Corporation, *AOS/VS Pascal Reference Card* (069-000037-00).

C. Textbooks

[1] Findlay, W., and D. Watt, *Pascal—An Introduction to Methodical Programming*, 2nd Ed. Rockville, MD: Computer Science Press, 1981.
[2] Grogono, P., *Programming in Pascal*, 2nd ed. Reading MA: Addison-Wesley, 1981.
[3] Kieburtz, R., *Structured Programming and Problem Solving With Pascal*. Englewood Cliffs, NJ: Prentice-Hall, 1979.
[4] Schneider, G., S. Weingart, and D. Perlman, *An Introduction to Programming and Problem Solving With Pascal*, 2nd Ed. New York: John Wiley & Sons, 1982.

25
RPG

D. S. Owings

Pratt Institute

25.1 INTRODUCTION

Today **RPG** is more than the simple **G**enerator of **R**eport **P**rograms that the acronym implies; it is, in fact, a full feature programming language for data processing use. In its first form, RPG was one of the multitude of compilers and near compilers which were designed to produce programs that would print listings of card files and which could be used by those without extensive training in programming. The need for such aids was clearly apparent when wired panel data processing installations were installing their first computers. Simple account ing machine listings, once the product of a few hours work, now had to be produced by a machine or assembly language program. However, it could take days to write code to do this. Then it might require several time consuming passes to assemble, as well as the services of an expensive and perhaps temperamental programmer.

From this simple beginning, RPG has evolved into its present state—that of a language which

- Allows quick and easy preparation of programs to print reports.
- Provides for accessing, updating and creating files.
- Permits not only sequential or indexed sequential files but also direct or random access and, in the versions of some vendors, even a data base.
- Many convenient on-line and remote terminal capabilities, now common in the language.

Despite growth in their capabilities, RPGII and RPGIII in their current forms remain easy to learn and use. Although those with a minimum of training in pro-

gramming can use the language, experienced programmers find the terse language, with its inherent discipline and its file handling features, to be of the greatest value.

Three characteristics of RPG set it off from other current languages:

- An implicit program cycle.
- A fixed format for source statements.
- Built-in switches known as *indicators*.

Individually and collectively, these characteristics contribute to the power of the language, the ease with which it may be used and the brevity with which a programming problem can be solved. Since these features are not often found in other languages, they also tend to inhibit the use of RPG by programmers whose previous experience has been with other languages. A further obstacle to the use of RPG is that it is regarded as a language used by lower level programmers on small machines. While this may be true, it does not reduce the capabilities of RPG nor the speed with which an effective program or system can be completed.

25.2 RPG PROGRAM CYCLE

All RPG programs use a common flow of processing— the RPG program cycle. The cycle is customized for each program by the parameters chosen and entered by the programmer as part of the source statements. The cycle consists of the following in the listed order:

1. Initialization;
2. Input file handling. The appropriate record of the ap-

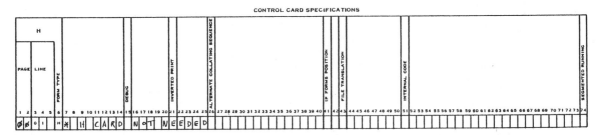

Figure 25.1. Simple program to read a disk file and print a list: control card specifications. (Header boxes for Programmer, Date, and Program Identification omitted from this and the following forms.)

propriate file is made available to the program. In the case of sequential access (either of sequential files or indexed files), the programmer need enter no specific read commands. Code generated by the cycle chooses the appropriate file in multifile programs and, if various record types are defined, identifies and selects the appropriate record. Records may be tested for type and for control level breaks;

3. Requested calculations and outputs, if control level breaks on a given field or group of fields are called for.

4. Calculations called for by specific records or types of records (which include testing, mathematical actions, and various types of moves or other data manipulations);

5. Outputs called for by specific records, such as detail lines on listings;

6. Return of control to the input phase;

7. Appropriate calculations, written outputs, and closing of all files at the end of processing (normally at the end of one or more files).

Although the cycle is predetermined by the chosen parameters, the programmer can override any phase where this is desirable. One can both read and write records and perform groups of calculations as needed. While the novice RPG programmer should become familiar with the power to override or ignore the RPG cycle, it should be maintained as much as practical. Using the cycle reduces both coding and mistakes.

To illustrate the simplicity of the language, two sample RPG programs are now examined. Both of them rely upon the RPG cycle to accomplish their ends. The first is presented in Figures 25.1 through 25.4. It reads all records of a sequential disk file and produces a single-spaced report showing the contents of four fields from the records in the file. The two numeric fields are properly edited; each page has a heading line which includes the date of the run and the page number. Notice how few lines of code are required and how little actual coding is needed.

The second program is shown in Figures 25.5 through 25.8. It is an elaboration of the first. It assumes a sorted

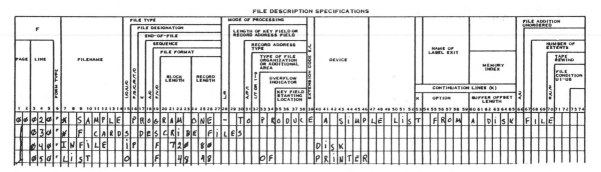

Figure 25.2. Continuation of Figure 25.1: file description specifications.

RPG II INPUT SPECIFICATIONS

PAGE	LINE		FILENAME												FROM	TO		FIELD NAME					
Ø1	Ø1Ø	*	I CARD DESCRIBES FIELDS AND RECORDS TO BE USED																				
	Ø2Ø	INFILE	NS	Ø1																			
	Ø3Ø														6	35	NAME						
	Ø4Ø	*	NAME is AN ALPHA-NUMERIC FIELD																				
	Ø5Ø														36	44Ø	SSNO						
	Ø6Ø	*	SSNO is A NUMERIC FIELD - AS SHOWN BY DECIMAL POSITION ENTRY																				
	Ø7Ø														45	46	DEPT						
	Ø8Ø															5Ø	CREDIT						
	Ø9Ø	*	FIELDS DO NOT HAVE TO BE LISTED IN ACTUAL SEQUENCE																				

Figure 25.3. Continuation of Figure 25.1: input specifications.

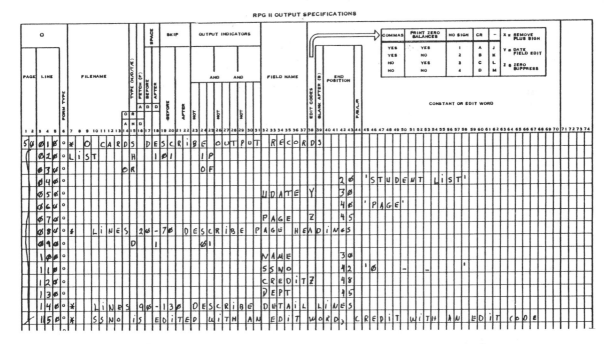

RPG II OUTPUT SPECIFICATIONS

PAGE	LINE		FILENAME					FIELD NAME		END POSITION		CONSTANT OR EDIT WORD
5Ø	Ø1Ø	*	O CARDS DESCRIBE OUTPUT RECORDS									
	Ø2Ø	LIST	H	1Ø1		1P						
	Ø3Ø		OR			OF						
	Ø4Ø									2Ø		'STUDENT LIST'
	Ø5Ø							UDATE Y		3Ø		
	Ø6Ø									4Ø		'PAGE'
	Ø7Ø							PAGE Z		45		
	Ø8Ø	*	LINES 2Ø-7Ø DESCRIBE PAGE HEADINGS									
	Ø9Ø		D	1		Ø1						
	1ØØ							NAME		3Ø		
	11Ø							SSNO		42		'Ø - '
	12Ø							CREDITZ		48		
	13Ø							DEPT		45		
	14Ø	*	LINES 9Ø-13Ø DESCRIBE DETAIL LINES									
	15Ø	*	SSNO is EDITED WITH AN EDIT WORD, CREDIT WITH AN EDIT CODE									

Figure 25.4. Continuation of Figure 25.1: output specifications.

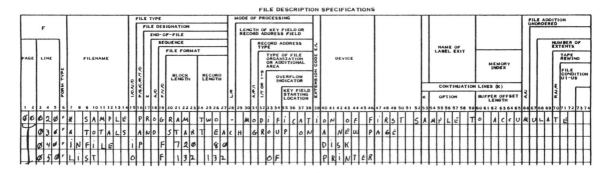

Figure 25.5. Elaboration of the first sample program (Figures 25.1–25.4), accumulating totals and starting each group on a new page: file description specifications.

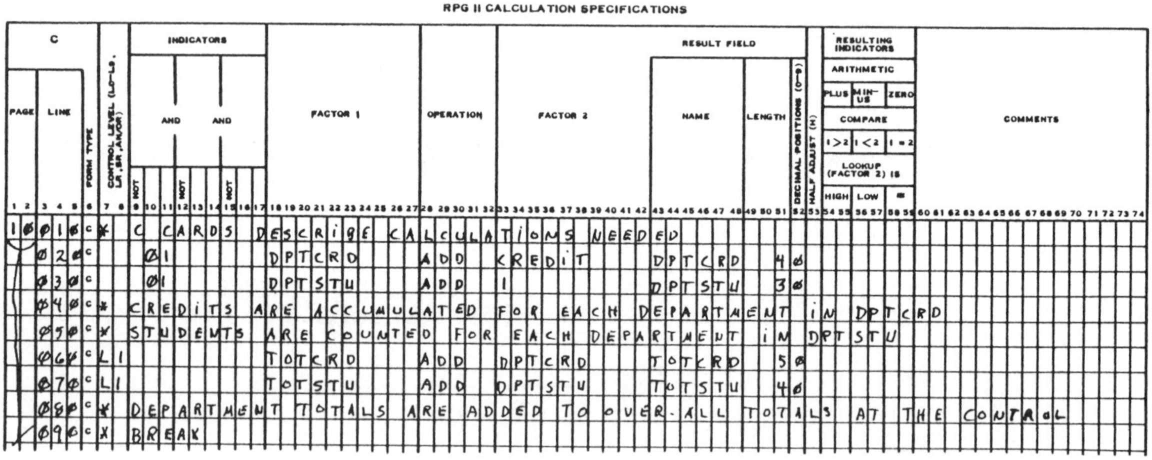

Figure 25.6. Continuation of Figure 25.5: calculation specifications.

file and starts each group on a new page. A count of the individuals whose records are contained in the file is made and the contents of one data field are summed. These two totals are accumulated and printed by group and overall. Notice how little coding is needed to provide the elaboration.

25.3 FIXED FORMAT

Source statements must be entered in a *fixed format* with regard to both the layout of the statements and their sequence within the source program. To programmers trained in other languages, fixed format may seem a drawback. In point of fact, all languages require some discipline in writing. Furthermore, good programmers have always chosen to develop their own conventions of indentation and arrangement, which effectively override the free format capabilities. The fixed format of RPG simplifies coding and materially aids debugging. The field name appears in a limited number of columns on the compile listing; consequently it can be found and examined quickly.

The only real disadvantage of fixed format is that labels are restricted to six characters. In practice, however, using label conventions and comments, this disadvantage can be overcome. Thus terseness is enforced.

RPG II OUTPUT SPECIFICATIONS

Page	Line	Form Type	Filename	Type (H/D/T/E)	Space Before/After	Skip	Output Indicators	Field Name	Edit Codes / Blank After (B)	End Position	Constant or Edit Word
50	010	O	LIST	H	2	61	L1				
	020	O		OR			OFNL1				
	030	O*	NEW PAGE EITHER AT START OF A NEW GROUP OR AT OVERFLOW								
	040	O								20	'STUDENT LIST'
	050	O						UDATE	Y	30	
	060	O								40	'PAGE'
	070	O						PAGE	Z	45	
	080	O		D	1		01				
	090	O						NAME		36	
	100	O						SSNO		42	'0 - - '
	110	O						CREDITZ		48	
	120	O					L1	DEPT		45	
	130	O*	DEPT WILL ONLY PRINT FOR FIRST PERSON IN EACH DEPARTMENT								
	140	O		T	11		L1				
	150	O								3	'IN'
	160	O						DEPT		6	
	170	O						DPTSTUZB		16	
	180	O								30	'STUDENTS ARE TAKING'
	190	O						DPTCRDIB		36	
	200	O								44	'CREDITS'
	210	O		T	11		LR				
	220	O								6	'IN ALL'
	230	O						TOTSTUZB		11	
	240	O								31	'STUDENTS ARE TAKING'
	250	O						TOTCRDIB		38	
	260	O								46	'CREDITS'
	270	O*	LINES 140-200 PRODUCE DEPARTMENT TOTAL LINES								
	280	O*	LINES 210-260 PRODUCE FINAL TOTAL LINE								

Figure 25.7. Continuation of Figure 25.5: output specifications.

RPG II INPUT SPECIFICATIONS

Page	Line	Form Type	Filename	Sequence	Number (1-N)	Record Identifying Indicator	From	To	Decimal Positions	Field Name	Control Level (L1-L9)	Field Indicators
61	010	I	INFILE	NS		01						
	020	I					6	35		NAME		
	030	I					36	44	0	SSNO		
	040	I					45	46		DEPT	L1	
	050	I*	A CONTROL BREAK IS CALLED FOR WHEN CONTENTS OF DEPT CHANGE									
	060	I					4	50		CREDIT		

Figure 25.8. Continuation of Figure 25.5: input specifications.

411

25.4 SOURCE STATEMENTS—INDICATORS AND TYPES

Indicators in RPG are a series of program switches which may be set and tested both by the RPG cycle and by the programmer. They are identified by two character labels and are either **specific** or **general.** A specific use indicator is LR or last record, which is set when one or more input files (at the programmer's discretion) has reached an end of file condition. This indicator triggers the end of job calculations and outputs.

General use indicators are numbered from 01 to **99.** These may be directly set by the programmer or, under the programmer's control, set through the RPG cycle by actions such as

- Reading a specific type of record.
- Determining that a numeric is positive, negative or zero.

Testing the indicators, in effect, generates an IF statement. Like any switch, an indicator which is not turned off at the right time gives trouble, but it is a powerful tool when used carefully.

Coding sheets for the each type of source statement are available from the computer vendors who support the language and from firms selling computer supplies. Since the forms are standardized, price and availability are the practical criteria in chosing a source. On cardless systems which support RPG, CRT screens for the various source statements are usually available even if only on a local or informal basis. While the programmer who does the source statement keying may at first find the fixed format somewhat annoying, the logical arrangement of the various source formats assists unconscious memorization of basic field locations. The source statement has fixed common field locations. Source statements are numbered in positions 1 through 5 for sequencing (generally broken into a 2 digit page and 3 digit line number). Position 6 always contains the source statement type. An asterisk in position 7 of any source statement indicates a comment. Positions 75 through 80 may contain the program identifier, a revision date, a subroutine name or other identification the programmer needs.

The major types of source statements, in the order in which they must appear within the source program, are

- H for control specification.
- F for file description.
- E for vector specification.
- L for line count specification.
- I for input file description.

- C for calculation instruction.
- O for output file description.

Implementations of RPG by various vendors may require additional types of source statements to handle data base or terminal applications. In any given program, not all types of statements may be required (see earlier Figures), but those which are needed must be in the proper order. Though separate vendors may require slightly different data or a slightly different arrangement of data in some types of source statements, there is complete agreement on the commonly used types. Differences are minor and easily learned.

The H (control specification) statement is perhaps the one with the greatest variety of vendor differences. Indeed, some vendors, such as Burroughs, do not even require this entry unless unusual conditions are to be handled, for example, the debugging mode, inverted dates, or European punctuation.

All files used by a program are described in the F (file description) statements. Internal file name, record size, blocking factor, type of file (input, output, etc.) and device type are consistently required. The *sequence* in which the RPG program cycle will access files is determined by this attribute. Primary file records are read first and then the records of the secondary files within the F specifications sequence.

25.5 INPUT, UPDATE FILES

A standard characteristic of RPG is that a primary input or update file is required. Under some circumstances when the input files are to be read using programmer supplied commands, as opposed to those generated by the RPG Program cycle, a primary or update file would not be needed. There are at least two ways around this restriction. Often runtime options need to be set; a logical way to do so is to use a load or header record which would comprise the primary input file. Should that approach not be valid, a disk file which is always present, perhaps part of the operating system, can be defined as the primary file. In this case the LR (last record) indicator is set on by a programmer command; and that file would not actually be used. Again, variations between vendors are found on the F specifications but they are minor.

25.6 VECTORS AND ARRAYS

Vectors and arrays were later major enhancements to RPG and have greatly simplified programming. They are described in the E (extension specification) statement.

Vectors can be loaded at compile time, when the program execution begins, or during execution. RPG arrays are one dimensional, but proper computation and manipulation of subscripts can give the appearance of multidimensional ones. A point to remember when naming an RPG vector which is to be accessed through subscripts is that a label is restricted to 6 characters and must include a comma as well as the vector name and the subscript. A useful convention is to use a 3 character vector name and a 2 character subscript name. The E specifications also allow for the description of two alternating vectors which normally are used in a look-up situation in which one vector contains identifying keys and the other some characteristic, such as customer number and discount rate respectively. A special command, LOKUP, in the calculation specifications provides easily coded vector searches.

Line counting to control vertical spacing on the printer is defined in the L (line count) specification. These specifications allow for forms of different sizes to be handled, for a variation in the number of lines to be printed per inch, and for the relationship between the carriage control tape and the printer lines to be established. If no L entries are given, a page of 66 lines is assumed and handled automatically.

25.7 FIELDS

The I (input description) specifications describe the *fields* of records used by the program. Each type of record, identified by the presence or absence of characters in specific positions, is assigned an indicator. When a record is read, code generated by the RPG cycle tests the record and turns on the appropriate record type indicator. Unwanted types of records are automatically bypassed.

If a control level break is called for, the related calculations are done and outputs produced. The defined data is then released and indicators related to field contents are set on. Defined data is moved from the input buffer to storage areas identified by the field names assigned in the specifications. These storage areas and not the input buffer are accessed by the program.

Consequently, data in these areas remains unchanged until another record of the same type is released to the program, or until changed by a programmer command. Therefore, data read from a record at the start of a program's execution can remain unchanged and available throughout the program, even though other records are read from the file. However, redefinition in the form provided by some other languages does not occur. For example, if positions 1 through 6 of a record are called

Date, positions 1 and 2, *Month,* positions 3 and 4, *Day,* and 5 and 6, *Year,* these four storage areas are established and filled. A subsequent change to the contents of *Date* does not change the contents of *Month, Day* or *Year.*

Individual field descriptions can also include indicators set on or off depending upon the occurrence of control level breaks or the value of the field. These field descriptions can also indicate matching keys to establish the relationships between files.

25.8 RELATING FILES

Figure 25.9 illustrates the combination of coding in the F and I specifications to cause two files to be read in step. On the F sheet FILE1 is described as input primary (ip) and FILE2 as input secondary (is); both are in ascending sequence. On the I sheet positions 1 through 5 are defined as a matching field for FILE1 and positions 6 through 10 are the matching field for FILE2. The RPG cycle compares the key fields of the next available record in each file and releases the one with the lowest value to be processed. Where the two key fields have equal values, the record from the primary file is released first.

With the C, or calculation, specifications, the programmer specifies data manipulations and file accesses. Normal arithmetic operations are available as well as are some unusual ones. RPG has an operation which zeroes a field before adding or subtracting a value to it, and it has a single instruction to obtain the value of a remainder in division. Move operations include right to left and left to right, zone moves and moves involving arrays.

Testing can go down to the bit level. Calculation commands operate on either a single element or all elements of an array; and there is a command to sum all of the elements of one. Branching between the calculation specifications is allowed. A subroutine capability added to RPGII allows single entry, single exit blocks of code to be executed similar to COBOL's PERFORM or FORTRAN's CALL. Unlike FORTRAN, labels and definitions are global in RPG. Programmer controlled inputs and outputs provide access to nonsequential files.

The general format of the C specifications allows testing of indicators to provide the equivalent of IF statements, setting indicators either conditionally or unconditionally and commands in the form of a verb and up to three operands. Fields not described in the I specifications can be defined in the C specifications and rounding can be automatic. The sequential arrangement of (1) detail time calculations—those which occur when a record is released to the program, (2) total time calculations—those

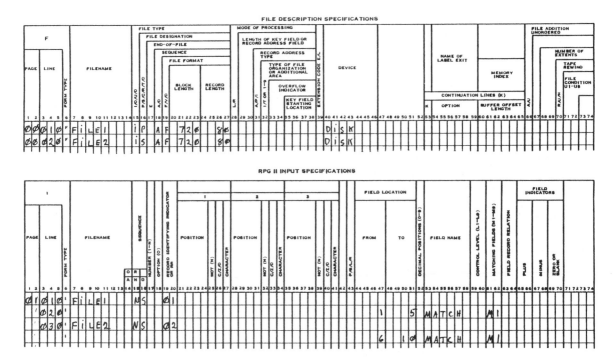

Figure 25.9. Controlling the reading of two files in step.

which occur when there is a control break, and (3) sub-routine calculations must appear in sequence in the calculation specifications. Furthermore, branching between detail time and total time calculations is not allowed, although a subroutine can be called from both and subroutines can call subroutines.

Alphanumeric literals are limited to 8 characters and numeric literals to 10 digits by the size of the fixed operand fields in the C specification format. These limitations can be surmounted by such techniques as using a combination of left to right and right to left moves with work fields.

The records of the output file are described in the O (output) specifications. Output fields are moved to output record buffers in the sequence that they are defined in the O specifications. Consequently, if a field is located so as to overlap a previously described one, the data described first is overlaid. In Figure 25.10 an output record consists of an input record with only field changed by the program. The I specifications define the entire input record as one field (RECORD) and also mention the field to be changed (DOLLAR). The O specifications first move the complete record to the output buffer and then overlay the changed field in its proper location.

The writing of both fields and records is controlled by indicators and fields can automatically be set to blanks or zeroes once the output record has been written. Areas in output records which are not described are set to blanks automatically. Editing is possible either through the use of edit words or single character edit codes. These edit codes are single character entries which replace several commonly used edit words.

As may be expected, there is a required sequence of O specifications: heading records, detail records, total records, and exception records—in that order. Exception records can be written at any point in the RPG cycle under programmer control. Records called for by the same indicators are written in the sequence listed in the O specifications. Therefore the automatic blanking feature must be used only on the last occurrence of a field if at all. Page headings and numbering are easily controlled by the O specifications.

25.9 THE PROPER USE OF RPG

Like any other programming language, RPG is a tool; specifically it is a tool to be used in data processing applications as opposed to scientific or engineering ones.

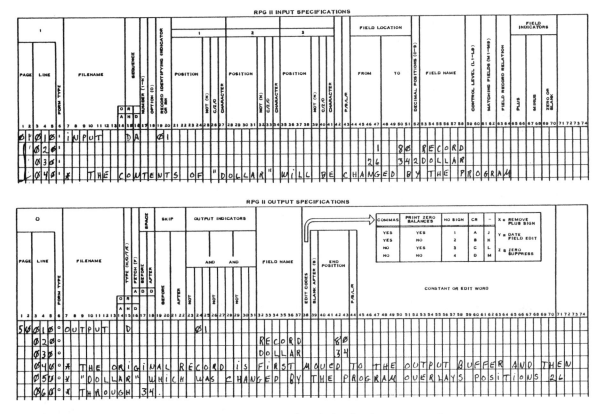

Figure 25.10. Demonstration of overlaying data in output records.

Like any good tool, RPG deserves to be used in a craft-like manner. A craftsperson uses tools in the way they are designed to be used, only after planning a task and in the most economical way practical. Such use of good tools will produce an effective, efficient, and aesthetically pleasing product.

In RPG, planning includes a general approach to the task, the development of an adherence to programming conventions, and the detailed planning of each module of each program. Proper utilization of the language includes not only knowing and using the proper commands but also understanding and exploiting the inherent facilities of the RPG program cycle. Programs written in RPG should not be mere paraphrases of BAL (Basic Assembly Language) or COBOL coding. Instead, the unique features of the language should be called upon to produce terse and effective answers to data processing problems.

Style, which includes the approach to coding and the conventions which a programmer uses, should be the result of conscious thought, and not merely haphazardly acquired habits. It is far easier to develop a good style initially than to improve a poor one later on. Outside forces such as installation standards can influence a programmer's style only to a limited extent. There can be no doubt that programs which maintain a good, consistent style are written faster, more accurately, more easily, and are easier to debug or modify than those written without style.

The general approach to programming in RPG, if this choice of language is to be effective, includes a knowledge of and a willingness to work within the RPG program cycle. The cycle can be overridden and to a large extent ignored; unfortunately there is a tendency on the part of programmers with experience in other languages to do this excessively. Such a basic violation of technique increases the amount of programmer code written and the chance of error. Certainly any report which accesses large portions of a file should use its cycle. For example, data base files are often better accessed along one of the defined access paths, even though programmer coded read commands could be used. Also, when a direct access file is updated by records submitted in random sequence, the RPG cycle can be useful in identifying the beginning and end of each set of input.

Use should be made of the hold area capabilities of the input specifications instead of user programmed hold areas and the overlaying capabilities of the output specifications. It is best to avoid substituting programmer coding for some aspect of the RPG cycle. RPG instructions should be used for the purposes for which they have been designed, without shortcuts to save memory or increase execution speed. Adherence to this standard reduces coding time and improves RPG program readability. For example, MVR (move remainder) provides the remainder in a division. On at least one machine, a multiplication and a subtraction get the value with less machine code. But any such saving is offset by the time spent by the programmer in writing the original code and debugging the program.

Basic Programming Conventions

Programming **conventions,** the consistent use of programming elements, are important, whether there are many programmers or only one in the installation. Conventions may be as elementary as how page numbers are assigned or as complex as program modularization. The purpose of conventions is to reduce the amount of effort and thought necessary for minor and repetitive actions and to facilitate reading a program for maintenance.

Some examples of RPG programming conventions follow. With page numbers, a practical approach is to use page 00 for H and F specifications, page 01 for vector descriptions, pages 02 through 09 for input specifications, pages 10 through 49 for the calculation specifications, and pages 50 through 99 for outputs. Some suggested conventional indicator assignments follow:

01–29	Input related—record types and field contents (positive, negative, or zero).
30–39	Reusable general purpose—indicators which are both set and tested within the same module or small block of code.
40–49	Intermodule communication or parameter passing.
50–89	As needed.
90–99	Identification of options set in a multiuse program by the header or parameter record.

The possibilities are numerous and subject to individual tastes. The important thing is to be consistent within an installation. Figure 25.11 and 25.12 show examples of conventional indicator use.

Label Conventions

Ideally labels should be meaningful; this may become difficult with the use of the 6 characters allowed by RPG. A helpful approach is to make the labels of work fields descriptive of the field, not its use. For example, a 6 digit numeric field with 2 decimal places could be called WORK62, or a field of blanks 22 characters long, BLAN22. Within any application, data element labels should be kept consistent.

One way to ensure this is to use the library feature supplied by many vendors. At the least, the normal input file descriptions can be entered in the library and copied into individual programs; this ensures consistency and reduces errors. File names lend themselves to name conventions in view of the number of short programs that are often required. Again the names should be indicative of function and not of content. Conventions such as INCARD and OUTCARD or LIST1 and LIST2 have obvious meaning; and IN1 and IN2 for primary and secondary disk files soon become second nature. The use of conventional labels in connection with subroutines used in program modularization is discussed later.

Conventions also apply to the order of operands in commands in C (calculation specifications). Where the name of a result field is the same as that of one of the other two fields, the duplicated name should be in Factor One. Where a literal is involved in a command it should be placed in Factor Two. RPGII allows the linking of calculation specification lines to provide for the use of more than three indicators or to describe an AND or OR relationship. This linkage through AN/OR codes should provide clarity. One operation may be triggered by two different conditions represented by two sets of indicators. Although the operation could be coded twice, the use of the AN/OR option shows the intent of the program more clearly.

Conventions concerning comments or remarks are highly desirable; they are too seldom used. A minimum

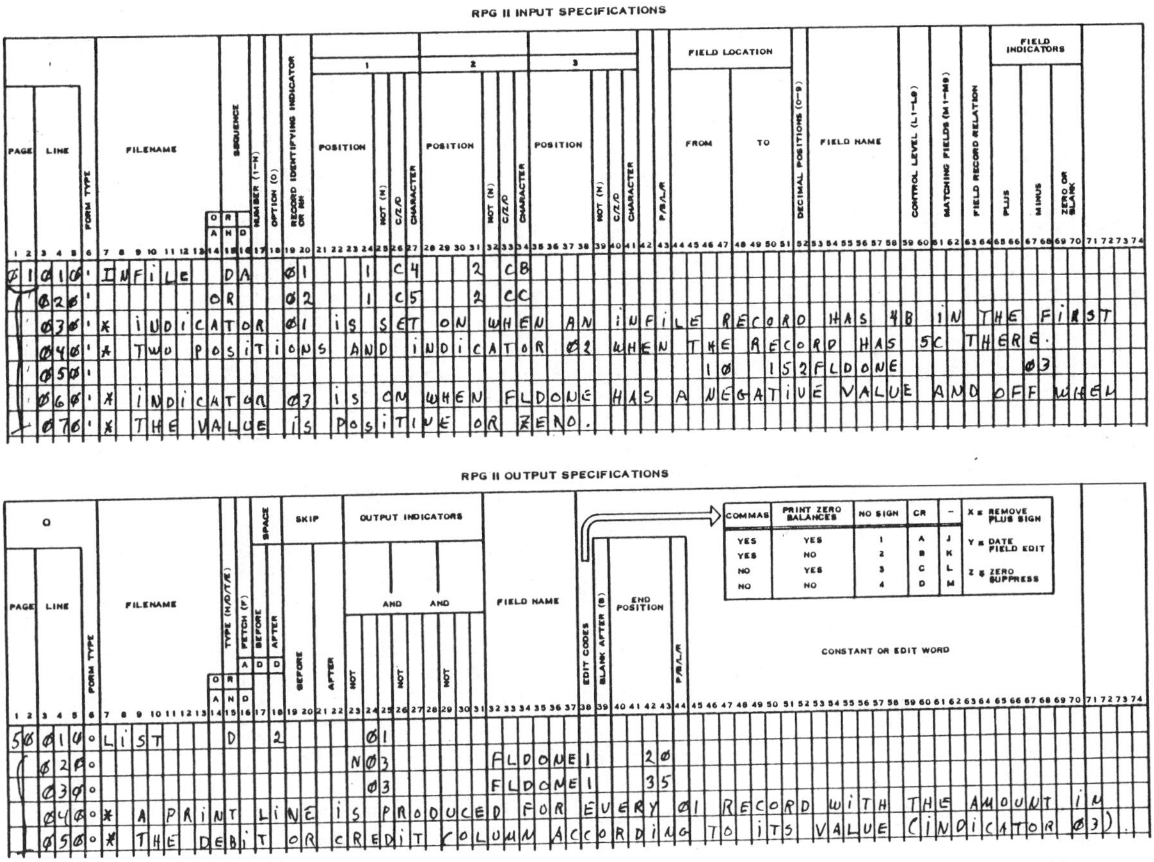

RPG II INPUT SPECIFICATIONS

```
01 010  INFILE   DA  01      1 C4  2 CB
   020           OR  02      1 C5  2 CC
   030 * INDICATOR 01 IS SET ON WHEN AN INFILE RECORD HAS 4B IN THE FIRST
   040 * TWO POSITIONS AND INDICATOR 02 WHEN THE RECORD HAS 5C THERE.
   050                                    10 152FLDONE            03
   060 * INDICATOR 03 IS ON WHEN FLDONE HAS A NEGATIVE VALUE AND OFF WHEN
   070 * THE VALUE IS POSITIVE OR ZERO.
```

RPG II OUTPUT SPECIFICATIONS

COMMAS	PRINT ZERO BALANCES	NO SIGN	CR	−	X = REMOVE PLUS SIGN
YES	YES	1	A	J	Y = DATE FIELD EDIT
YES	NO	2	B	K	
NO	YES	3	C	L	Z = ZERO SUPPRESS
NO	NO	4	D	M	

```
50 010  LIST     D  2      01
   020                     N03    FLDONE1       20
   030                      03    FLDONE1       35
   040 * A PRINT LINE IS PRODUCED FOR EVERY 01 RECORD WITH THE AMOUNT IN
   050 * THE DEBIT OR CREDIT COLUMN ACCORDING TO ITS VALUE (INDICATOR 03).
```

Figure 25.11. Using indicators according to convention: input and output specifications.

requirement is at least one comment line at the start of each program and subroutine, briefly describing it. A string of periods in the remarks field of the first statement of a subroutine serves as a visual flag.

Conventions described so far may seem minor. Their value is substantial. Programming consists of much simple repetitious activity and only a little creative activity. Whatever reduces the repetitious (and boring) part is worthwhile; it allows the programmer to concentrate on the creative part.

Modules

One important facilitation is modularization. Structured programming has value that is generally accepted. **DO WHILE** and **DO UNTIL** constructs *are* currently implemented but only in RPGIII (which is available from just one vendor); most RPG programs use GOTOs. There is,

however, no reason programs should not be written as modules especially in the calculation specification portion of the program.

Any RPG program which contains more than fifteen calculation specifications should be modular. The choice of 15 specifications is arbitrary. Programs of even fewer specifications may lend themselves to this style. A **module** is a block of code with one entry point and one exit point that is designed to accomplish one clearly defined function. It should not exceed 30 lines of code; and, except for the main line module which drives the program, treated as a subroutine. The function which the module accomplishes may be general or it may be specific (such as computing a single payroll decuction). In the latter case it may not need other modules. Without exception, if the module requires more than 30 lines of RPG calculations, either the programmer has not divided the program into modules properly, or has written poor code. Improper

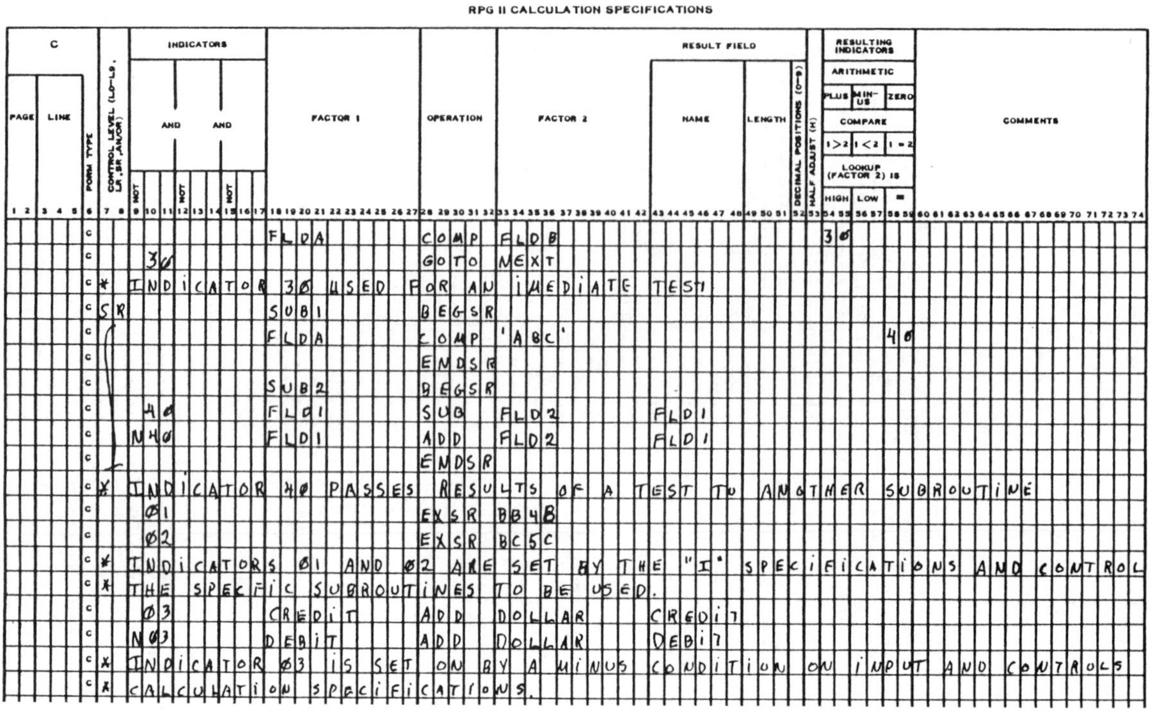

RPG II CALCULATION SPECIFICATIONS

Indicators	Factor 1	Operation	Factor 2	Result Field Name	Resulting Indicators / Comments
	FLDA	COMP	FLDB		30
30		GOTO	NEXT		
C* INDICATOR 30 USED FOR AN IMEDIATE TEST.					
CSR	SUB1	BEGSR			
	FLDA	COMP	'ABC'		40
		ENDSR			
	SUB2	BEGSR			
40	FLD1	SUB	FLD2	FLD1	
N40	FLD1	ADD	FLD2	FLD1	
		ENDSR			
C* INDICATOR 40 PASSES RESULTS OF A TEST TO ANOTHER SUBROUTINE					
01		EXSR	BB4B		
02		EXSR	BC5C		
C* INDICATORS 01 AND 02 ARE SET BY THE "I" SPECIFICATIONS AND CONTROL					
C* THE SPECIFIC SUBROUTINES TO BE USED.					
03	CREDIT	ADD	DOLLAR	CREDIT	
N03	DEBIT	ADD	DOLLAR	DEBIT	
C* INDICATOR 03 IS SET ON BY A MINUS CONDITION ON INPUT AND CONTROLS					
C* CALCULATION SPECIFICATIONS.					

Figure 25.12. Continuation of Figure 25.11: calculation specifications.

modularization usually is the result of combining logically separate functions through insufficient analysis.

Hierarchical Structuring

The structure of the program as represented by its modules should be hierarchical. That is, the program should be designed as a series of levels with the modules on one level calling or using only modules on lower levels. In a typical arrangement, the main or driver module calls an initialization module, perhaps a start of set or end of set module, a general processing module, and an end of job module. The general processing module in turn calls others to handle particular types of input or other specific conditions. These third level modules may themselves use even lower level modules to perform either specific or common functions. In the latter case, a common function module would be called from two or more of the higher levels or more than once by the same module.

The hierarchical levels should show in the names of the modules. Since RPG labels must begin with an alphabetical character, it is practical to use the first character to represent the level and the second character to show the sequence of the module within the level. Typically AAxxxx would call BAxxxx, BBxxxx, and BCxxxx; BAxxxx would call CAxxxx, CBxxxx; and so on. Within any module, any label used for branching should have the same two first characters as the module name. A further refinement is to skip to the middle third of the alphabet to name common use modules which are called by two or more modules on different levels. Finally, modules used in several programs such as a Julian date conversion should be named from the last third of the alphabet. A master list of these modules used by several programs should be centrally maintained in the installation to avoid duplicate names.

Modules would generally appear sequentially in the program in alphabetical order by name. Maintaining a module naming convention by mentioning module names in the remarks portion of the first entry of each module simplifies finding a given module while debugging or making changes.

Straight Line Vs. Modular

Figures 25.13 and 25.14 along with Figures 25.15 and 25.16 show two sets of calculation specifications for the same problem; the former uses a straight line approach;

RPG II CALCULATION SPECIFICATIONS

Page/Line	Form Type	Control Level	Indicators	Factor 1	Operation	Factor 2	Result Field Name	Length	Dec/H	Resulting Indicators	Comments
01 010	C	X		STRAIGHT LINE CODING							
020	C			MANNO	CHAIN	MASTER				40	40=NOT FOUND
030	C		40		GOTO	EOP					
040	C			TOTHRS	SUB	35	OTHOUR	42		30	30=WORKED FEWER
050	C		30		Z-ADD	0	OTHOUR				THAN 35 HOURS
060	C			TOTHRS	SUB	OTHOUR	REGHRS	42			
070	C			REGHRS	MULT	REGRTE	REGSAL	62H			H=HALF ADJUST
080	C			REGRTE	MULT	1.5	OTRATE	42H			
090	C			OTHOUR	MULT	OTRATE	OTSAL	62H			
100	C			REGSAL	ADD	OTSAL	GROSS	62			
110	C	X		COMPUTE 3 LEVELS OF TAXES							INITIALIZES
120	C				Z-ADD	1	SC	10			< SUBSCRIPT
130	C				Z-ADD	GROSS	NETPAY	62			< NET PAY AMT
140	C			TXLOOP	TAG						
150	C			GROSS	MULT	RTE,SC	TAX,SC		H		
160	C			NETPAY	SUB	TAX,SC	WORK72	72		30	30=TOO MANY
170	C		30		Z-ADD	NETPAY	TAX,SC				DEDUCTIONS
180	C			NETPAY	SUB	TAX,SC	NETPAY				
190	C			SC	ADD	1	SC				
200	C		N30	SC	COMP	3				30	30=TAXES DONE
210	C		N30 '		GOTO	TXLOOP					OR NO PAY LEFT

Figure 25.13. A simple program coded in the straight line manner, without subroutines.

RPG II CALCULATION SPECIFICATIONS

Page/Line	Form Type	Control Level	Indicators	Factor 1	Operation	Factor 2	Result Field Name	Length	Dec/H	Resulting Indicators	Comments
1 010	C	X		COMPUTE FICA							
020	C			GROSS	MULT	FICRTE	TWFICA	62H			
030	C			YTDFIC	ADD	TWFICA	WORK72				
040	C			WORK72	COMP	FICLIM				30	30=OVER LIMIT
050	C		30	FICLIM	SUB	YTDFIC	TWFICA				
060	C			TWFICA	COMP	NETPAY				30	30=DEDUCTIONS
070	C		30		Z-ADD	NETPAY	TWFICA				GT PAY
080	C			YTDFIC	ADD	TWFICA	YTDFIC				
090	C			NETPAY	SUB	TWFICA	NETPAY				
100	C			EOP	TAG						

Figure 25.14. Continuation of Figure 25.13.

RPG II CALCULATION SPECIFICATIONS

Page	Line	Form Type	Control Level	NOT	Ind AND	Ind AND	Factor 1	Operation	Factor 2	Result Name	Length	Dec/H	Resulting Ind	Comments
01	01 0	C	*				MODULAR CODING							. . . . MAIN LINE
	02 0	C					MANNO	CHAIN	MASTER		40			40=NOT FOUND
	03 0	C		40				GOTO	AAEXIT					
	04 0	C						EXSR	BASALC					
	05 0	C		N40				EXSR	BBTAX					
	06 0	C		N40				EXSR	BCFICA					
	07 0	C					AAEXIT	TAG						
	08 0	C	*				BA-SALARY COMPUTATION							. . . . BA
	09 0	C	SR				BASALC	BEGSR						
	10 0	C	SR				TOTHRS	SUB	35	OTHOUR	42		30	30=WORKED FEWER
	11 0	C	SR	30				Z-ADD0		OTHOUR				THAN 35 HOURS
	12 0	C	SR				TOTHRS	SUB	OTHOUR	REGHRS	42			
	13 0	C	SR				REGHRS	MULT	REGRTE	REGSAL	62H			
	14 0	C	SR				REGRTE	MULT	1.5	OTRATE	42H			
	15 0	C	SR				OTHOUR	MULT	OTRATE	OTSAL	62H			
	16 0	C	SR				REGSAL	ADD	OTSAL	GROSS	62			
	17 0	C	SR					ENDSR						
	18 0	C	*				BB-TAX CALCULATION (THREE LEVELS)							. . . . BB
	19 0	C	SR				BBTAX	BEGSR						INITIALIZE
	20 0	C	SR					Z-ADD1		SC	10			← SUBSCRIPT
	21 0	C	SR					Z-ADDGROSS		NETPAY	62			← NET PAY AMNT.
	22 0	C	SR				BBLOOP	TAG						
	23 0	C	SR				GROSS	MULT	RTE,SC	TAX,SC	H			
	24 0	C	SR				NETPAY	SUB	TAX,SC	WORK72			40	40=TOO MANY
	25 0	C	SR	40				Z-ADDNETPAY		TAX,SC				DEDUCTIONS
	26 0	C	SR				NETPAY	SUB	TAX,SC	NETPAY				

Figure 25.15. The same program as Figures 25.13–25.14, coded in the modular manner with subroutines.

the latter, a modular one. The common problem is simple enough. An input record with employee number and number of hours worked is read using the RPG cycle. The employee number is used as a relative record number to find a payroll master record which contains wage rate, three tax table lines, and year to date amounts. If the employee's record is not found, an error message is triggered and no further processing for the employee is done. Otherwise, gross salary is computed with overtime hours paid at time and a half, three tax amounts are calculated and deducted, FICA is computed and deducted, and the RPG cycle updates the master record and produces an output list.

Actual coding is the same in both examples. While the modular example takes more lines of code, it is obviously easier to read, and to change, and, particularly in the case of complex programs, it also makes planning and coding easier.

Figures 25.17 and 25.18 show computer produced diagrams which list the subroutines used. Names follow the conventions just described. They demonstrate hierarchical design. This useful form of documentation is produced directly from RPG source code by a program, itself written in RPG.

Planning

Program planning should always be done. A short report program can be planned mentally; a complex program requires a written plan of some form. Planning should consist of the problem statement, input and output record layouts, and the calculation specifications. Input record

RPG II CALCULATION SPECIFICATIONS

	C			INDICATORS				FACTOR 1	OPERATION	FACTOR 2	RESULT FIELD			RESULTING INDICATORS			COMMENTS
PAGE	LINE	FORM TYPE	CONTROL LEVEL	AND	AND			FACTOR 1	OPERATION	FACTOR 2	NAME	LENGTH	DECIMAL POSITIONS	ARITHMETIC PLUS/MINUS/ZERO	COMPARE / LOOKUP		COMMENTS

01	0	C	SR				SC	ADD	1	SC			IF FEWER THAN 3
02	0	C	SRN1Ø				SC	COMP	3			1Ø	TAXES COMPUTED
03	0	C	SRNH1					GOTO	BALØØF				AND ANY NET PAY
04	0	C	SR					ENDSR					LEFT DO NEXT TAX
05	0	C	*				BC-FICA COMPUTATION						. . . . BC
06	0	C	SR				BCFICA	BEGSR					
07	0	C	SR				GROSS	MULT	FICRTE	TWFICA	62	H	
08	0	C	SR				YTDFIC	ADD	TWFICA	WORK72			
09	0	C	SR				WORK72	COMP	FICLIM			4Ø	4Ø = OVER LIMIT
10	0	C	SR	4Ø			FICLIM	SUB	YTDFIC	TWFICA			
11	0	C	SR				TWFICA	COMP	NETPAY			4Ø	4Ø = DEDUCTIONS
12	0	C	SR	4Ø				Z-ADD	NETPAY	TWFICA			GT PAY
13	0	C	SR				YTDFIC	ADD	TWFICA	YTDFIC			
14	0	C	SR				NETPAY	SUB	TWFICA	NETPAY			
15	0	C	SR					ENDSR					

Figure 25.16. Continuation of Figure 25.15.

layouts can become the I specifications established at the beginning of work on a system and made available through the vendor's library capabilities. The plan for the calculation specifications can be a flowchart or in pseudocode. Input and output operations which are part of the RPG cycle can be assumed and not specifically shown. With either a flowchart or pseudocode, the initial plan should be general and refer to concepts, not to specific indicators or commands.

Specifics can be inserted before the coding is done; but

```
            CR802   CONTROL FLOW    7/23/83   LISTS CASH RECEIPTS AND MAKES OFFSETS

     AAMAIN

         BALOAD   LOAD-CARD

         BBCOM    COMMON-TESTS

         BCGLED   GENERAL-LEDGER

              DAGLAC   GENERAL-LEDGER-ACCUMULATIONS

         BDSUBL   SUB-LEDGERS(INCOME/EXPENSE)

         BEBEGS   START-OF-SSNC-SET

         BFSTUD   STUDENT-OR-AUXILIARY

              CAAUX    AUXILIARY-ENTRY

                   DAGLAC   DUP CALL

              CBSTUN   STUDENT-NAME-SEEK

                   DBSSKY   BUILD-KEY-FROM-STUDENT-SS

                   DCSEEK   SEEK-STUDENT-IN-SA-MASTER

         BGNAME   STORE-NAME

         BHENCB   END-BATCH
```

Figure 25.17. Computer produced diagram showing the modularization of a proof listing program.

```
              AC815    CONTROL FLOW    7/23/83    CHANGE ACCOUNT NUMBERS

      AAMAIN                              (This program generates the appropriate accounting offset
         BADET    DETAIL-PROCESS          entries when an account number is changed.)

            CAANAL  ANALYZE-OLD/NEW-ACCOUNT-NUMBERS

               DAFDSW  FUND-SWITCH

                  EAOUTP  OUT-PUT-CHANGED-AND-ADDED-RECORDS

                  EAOUTP  DUP CALL    (A common output routine is frequently used.)

                  EAOUTP  DUP CALL

                  EAOUTP  DUP CALL

               DBSBGL  SUB-LEDGER-BECOMES-GENERAL-LEDGER

                  EAOUTP  DUP CALL

                  EAOUTP  DUP CALL

                  EAOUTP  DUP CALL

               DCGLSB  GENERAL-LEDGER-TO-A-SUB-LEDGER

                  EAOUTP  DUP CALL

                  EAOUTP  DUP CALL

                  EAOUTP  DUP CALL

               DDSLSW  SUE-LEDGER-SWITCH

                  EAOUTP  DUP CALL

                  EAOUTP  DUP CALL
```

(The use of four separate routines for the four basic types of changes facilitated both coding and de-bugging.)

Figure 25.18. Computer produced diagram showing the modularization of a program to change account numbers and handle offset entries.

they obscure the issues if they appear too soon. A useful coding technique attacks one level at a time and puts only one module on a page. This enforces top down planning and restricts modules to a single function. One module to a page also makes the programmer more willing to discard an incorrect idea completely instead of trying to salvage it.

Pessimistic anticipation allows for easy debugging. Most **RPG** compilers include debugging aids, such as the **DEBUG** command, which displays literals and data during program execution. The programmer, when trying an algorithm for the first time or using a particularly involved approach, may put **DEBUG** into the program initially. It is removed easily when its usefulness is over.

Another helpful technique controls implanted debugging aids by external program switches available from most vendors. This can reduce the length and complexity of test printouts, and it overcomes the tendency to remove debugging aids when the program is thought to be correct instead of when it actually is correct.

For nearly 20 years RPG has been growing and evolving, from a limited way of quickly preparing programs to produce simple reports into a powerful practical data processing language. Automatic file handling gets programs written with a minimum of user coding. RPG's terseness and fixed format make it easy to learn and use, and reduce chances for error. While there are no official standards for RPG, the de facto ones followed by the major vendors make possible migration between its dialects, and between vendors themselves.

25.10 AN RPG SYNTACTICAL SUMMARY

A brief syntactical guide and some suggestions for further study follow.

1. RPG source statements follow certain categories with fixed roles.
   a. The sequence of the various types of statements.
   b. The order in which the statements of each type must be arranged.
   c. The location of the data in each statement.

2. The categories of source statements, their function and sequence are the following:

H (control) sets options for the program. H itself may be optional.

F (file description) describes all files accessed by the object program.

E (vector description) describes arrays used by the object program.

L (line count) describes vertical spacing used by printer files.

I (input description) describes both records and fields within records of all input and update files.

C (calculation) describes data manipulation, logic tests, and programmer controlled input and output operations.

O (output description) describes both records and fields within records of all output and update files.

3. The required arrangement of source statements within a category may vary among vendors. Generally acceptable rules follow.

a. *File description.* Files should be listed in the following sequence:

Primary input or update files.

Secondary input or update files.

Chained input or update files.

Table input or update files.

Output files.

b. *Input descriptions.* Files should be listed in the same sequence as they are in the file description. While no requirement for records within file sequences exists, defining the most common record type first may increase efficiency. If some other arrangement is more logical, one should use it. Some compilers require that fields defined as matching fields appear in the same sequence within each record type in which they are used.

c. *Calculation specifications.* Calculations must be grouped by type in the following sequence:

Detail calculations.

Total calculations (preferably by level).

Subroutine calculations.

d. *Output descriptions.* Records should be described by type as shown below. The arrangement of files within type is unrestricted but watch for the automatic blanking of fields.

Heading outputs.

Detail outputs.

Total outputs (preferably by level).

Exception outputs.

4. Data input.

a. *Sequential files.* If matching fields are defined in the file specifications, files are read in step based on the values in the matching fields, with primary records of a specific key value being processed before secondary file records with the same key values. If matching fields are not defined, the primary file is read first and then each secondary file in turn.

b. *Direct files.* The CHAIN command used in the calculation specifications handles these reads. **Note:** a primary input or update file is always required.

5. Data output.

a. *Sequential files.* Heading, detail, and total time outputs are normal products of the RPG cycle. More specific control is provided by indicators. Exception outputs directed to files implicitly defined as sequential produce a variable number of output records.

b. *Direct files.* Exception outputs, appropriately controlled by indicators, are used to update or create records of direct files; but must be preceded by CHAIN command to locate the record to be added or changed.

6. Indicators (switches).

a. *General purpose* (01 through 99). These are set on by the RPG cycle as chosen by the programmer, by tests in the calculation specifications, or by direct programmer commands. They are tested by the RPG cycle or in calculation specifications to control outputs or data manipulations.

b) *Special purpose* (see below). These are normally set by the RPG cycle testing. Programmer manipulation may be done with caution.

Level breaks (L1 through L9).

Indicate breaks in programmer defined control fields. When one of these is set on by the RPG cycle, all lower level breaks are also set to facilitate handling multiple levels of totals.

Matching record (M1 through M9 and MR)

Input fields defined as M1 through M9. If a match among files is obtained on all defined matching fields, MR is turned on.

Provides for processing multiple sequential files in step.

Overflow (OA through OG and OV)

Detection of end of page condition on up to eight printer files.

Provides convenient page ejection, page numbering and heading line outputs.

First page (1P)
Set on by the RPG cycle at the beginning of execution. Used to trigger headings on the first page of reports.

Last record (LR)
Set by end of file condition in one or more of the input files. Note that this is one of the few special purpose indicators which might be set directly by a programmer command; it causes a program to end gracefully.

7. Format of calculation specifications (see Figure 25.19).
   a. The general order is (1) first operand, (2) operator, (3) second operand, (4) result. On line 010 of Figure 25.19, A is added to B, giving C; on line 020, B is subtracted from A, giving C; and on line 030, A is multiplied by .52, giving B rounded.
   b. Execution of a calculation is controlled by both the level (detail, total or subroutine) and the combination of indicators. The calculation on line 040 is performed at detail time (shown by the blanks in positions 7 and 8) when indicators 04 and 05 are on. The calculation on line 050 is performed when a level 1 control break has occurred and indicator 20 is off. Line 070 shows a calculation performed only when subroutine CAEXAM has been called. Indicators can be combined in "and" and "or" relationships as in lines 090 and 100 where the subroutine DACALC will be called either if indicator 01 is on and 02 is not, or if indicator 02 is on and 03 is not. Lines 110 and 120 show a part of a subroutine in which indicators 01, 02, 03, and 04 must be on for A to be added to B to give C.
   c. Indicators may be set on and off by calculations. On line 130 indicator 10 will be set on if A is greater than B, 20 if A is less than B, and 30 if they are equal. On line 140, 10 will be set on if A is greater than 25, 20 if it is less, and 30 if A equals 25. The indicator settings are mutually exclusive. Lines 150 and 160 show indicators 98 and 75 set on and off unconditionally (respectively).
   d. Fields which are not part of input records may be defined in the calculation specifications. Line 170 of Figure 25.19 shows the creation of a new 6 digit field with 2 decimal positions called GROSS. On line 180 a 45 position field of blanks, WORK45,

RPG II CALCULATION SPECIFICATIONS

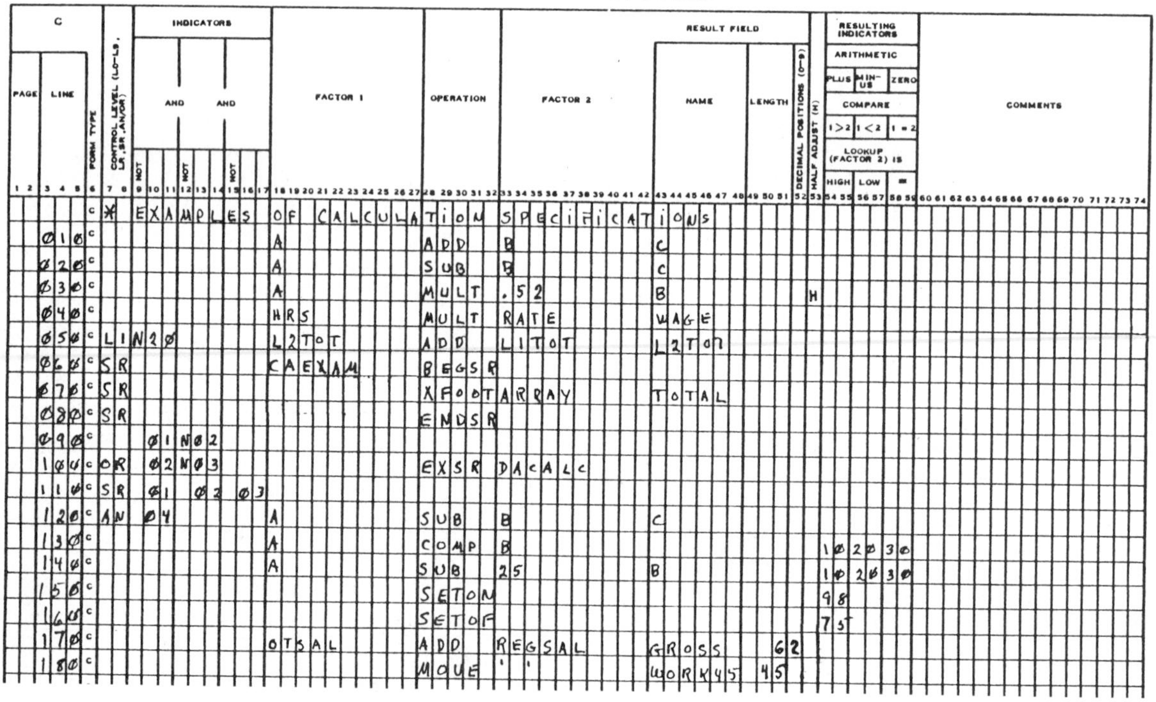

Line	Form Type	Control Level	Indicators	Factor 1	Operation	Factor 2	Result Name	Length	Dec. Pos.	Half Adjust	Resulting Ind. Plus/>/High	Minus/</Low	Zero/=/=	Comments
	C	* EXAMPLES OF CALCULATION SPECIFICATIONS												
Ø1Ø	C			A	ADD	B	C							
Ø2Ø	C			A	SUB	B	C							
Ø3Ø	C			A	MULT	.52	B			H				
Ø4Ø	C			HRS	MULT	RATE	WAGE							
Ø5Ø	C	L1	N2Ø	L2TOT	ADD	L1TOT	L2TOT							
Ø6Ø	C	SR		CAEXAM	BEGSR									
Ø7Ø	C	SR			XFOOT	ARRAY	TOTAL							
Ø8Ø	C	SR			ENDSR									
Ø9Ø	C		Ø1 NØ2											
1ØØ	C	OR	Ø2 NØ3		EXSR	DACALC								
11Ø	C	SR	Ø1 Ø2 Ø3											
12Ø	C	AN	Ø4	A	SUB	B	C							
13Ø	C			A	COMP	B					1Ø	2Ø	3Ø	
14Ø	C			A	SUB	25	B				1Ø	2Ø	3Ø	
15Ø	C				SETON						98			
16Ø	C				SETOF						75			
17Ø	C			OTSAL	ADD	REGSAL	GROSS	6	2					
18Ø	C				MOVE	' '	WORK45	45						

Figure 25.19. Sample calculation specifications.

is created. RPG initializes a new field to blanks (character) or zeroes (numeric) and then performs a calculation specified on that line.

8. Remarks and comments. Two RPG source statement types each have a field dedicated to remarks: vector descriptions and calculation specifications. Since vector names are limited to three characters, this comment field should elaborate on the symbol's use. Calculations are most variable in their meaning and comment can clarify the intent. An asterisk (*) in position 7 of any source statement converts matter at that point into a comment line. This allows for detailed explanation of succeeding lines.

25.11 SUGGESTIONS FOR FURTHER READING AND STUDY

Its very simplicity and ease of use have given RPG the reputation of being an elementary language for programmers of limited scope. Unfortunately, this view has been both accepted and perpetuated by the publishing and educational communities. Consequently, the bulk of the literature about RPG and most of the courses offered in it are of little value and less interest to capable data processing craftspersons. It is left to such individuals to discover the value and charm of the language, overcome prejudice against it, and develop sound and sophisticated techniques on their own.

RPG manuals provided by vendors are necessary aids; all programmers should have one. These are reference manuals, however, designed to answer specific questions and not to teach the language. They treat each form of source specification in detail and in the sequence the specification is included in the program. Appendices cover characteristics unique to the vendor and the RPG cycle. The better vendor manuals include examples and avoid gross mistakes. But users should make sure that their manuals are the most recent editions and include all currently released inserts.

The textbooks listed below assume no previous data processing, programming knowledge nor experience. Consequently, they may only interest a beginner. With any, diligent effort provides a sound knowledge of the language; few inspire enthusiasm for RPG. They are best used as adjuncts to formal courses. Typically, subroutines will be mentioned once (perhaps in an appendix) and never used in subsequent coding examples. Be warned that there are probably still texts available in major bookstores which have no reference to RPGII and its major enhancements to the language.

Like the available textbooks, most courses given are elementary. Obviously there is a need for courses at this level; however, the concept of RPG as a tool for crafting data processing is usually not in the university syllabus. Experience with and appreciation of RPG are rare among the upper levels of instructors. Community colleges offer better coverage of RPG. But the best courses are given by vendors.

A programmed instruction course using tape cassettes and workbooks is also listed below.

The periodical *Small Systems World* treats RPG as a valid language. An article by Dick Eagleson in the March and April 1980 issues remains one of the very few published references which treats RPG style. This magazine has frequently published the specific coding of various data processing problems which were sophisticated and aesthetically pleasing.

REFERENCES

Vendor Manuals

Available from all vendors who support RPG. Form numbers and order procedures seem to be in a continual state of flux, but the sales representatives should be willing to help.

Textbooks

Bux, William E., and Edward C. Cunningham, *RPG and RPGII Programming: Applied Fundamentals*. Englewood Cliffs, NJ: Prentice-Hall, 1980.

Lewis, Thomas S., *RPGII Programming*. Dubuque, IA: Wm. C. Brown, 1977.

Seeds, Harice L., *Programming RPG, RPGII*. New York: John Wiley & Sons, 1971.

Shelly, Gary B., and Thomas J. Cashman, *Computer Programming RPGII*. Fullerton, CA: Anaheim Publishing Co., 1976.

Programmed Instruction Course

INFO III RPG II
Automated Training and Software
21250 Califa Street
Woodland Hills, CA 91367

Periodical

Small Systems World
53 West Jackson Blvd.
Chicago, IL 60604

26
ADA

Thomas J. Wheeler

U.S. Army Communications Electronics Command

26.1 INTRODUCTION

ADA is a computer language which provides for structured programming, data constructs, modularization, separate compilation and parallel programming facilities. ADA both facilitates and enforces design and programming techniques which are shown by software engineering research to facilitate the development of reliable, maintainable data processing and embedded computer systems.

ADA was developed by the United States Department of Defense in response to the exponential growth of the cost of computer software which occurred in the mid 1970s. Since the majority of the software costs were incurred in embedded computer systems, DOD's efforts focused on the problems involved in development and maintenance.

An analysis of these systems showed almost as many languages extant as systems: many were assembly level languages. As a result, the DOD High Order Language (HOL) project was set up. The HOL project took as its goal standardization upon a single HOL for use in most embedded systems.

To converge on a single HOL, the first step was to limit the number of languages to be considered for the development of computer systems. The second step attempted to standardize one existing language and develop a set of language requirements. When none of the existing languages proved suitable, a third step was undertaken: evolving a state-of-the-art language for developing and maintaining embedded computer systems. This language development effort, known as DOD-1, resulted in the development of ADA and its programming environment [1]. (Also see footnote on p. 327.)

26.2 EMBEDDED COMPUTER SYSTEMS

Computers have become less expensive over the years. Not only are traditional computer based systems being drastically reduced in price and therefore invading new markets, but also new systems which include the computer as a component are becoming feasible. These latter systems, termed **embedded computer systems,** include functions which existed previously only as hardware now provided as software. In these systems, whether a computer itself provides some of the functions within a system is relatively unimportant to the systems user.

Embedded computer systems have a number of characteristics which influence the design method and choice of programming language:

1. The computer interface is defined by system requirements, with ease of developing software being a relatively minor consideration in the design of the hardware in the system.
2. The characteristics of the interface change often during the development of the system, again with little thought to the effects of the changes on the software.
3. The life time of embedded computer systems is relatively long, so that the maintainers of the system are not usually the ones who develop it.

426

4. The function of the system evolves over its lifetime, so that major features of the design often change.
5. These systems are often large, at least insofar as they are developed and maintained by a group rather than an individual.
6. The software controls every system activity unit without a general purpose operating system.

These characteristics cause significant problems in development and maintenance of these systems. The development of new systems was being curtailed due to the projected lifetime cost of the software in the systems, a problem was not confined, of course, to embedded computer systems.

In response to this explosive growth in the cost of development and maintenance of embedded systems, computer science researchers have developed a large number of design principles and techniques for new software, including structured programming, top-down design and implementation, structured analysis and design, stepwise refinement, information hiding and programming teams and walkthroughs. The central aim is to provide control of design by systematic decomposition and abstraction of the problem into component modules and synthesis of these into the system.

While most of these techniques have produced impressive results, their use with embedded systems until recently was limited; the crucial reason was the lack of a suitable high level language and the compiler to go with it.

This barrier to the use of modern theories and techniques was overcome with the introduction of languages and techniques specifically designed for embedded computer applications. This chapter addresses the effect of the Department of Defense's ADA language on the development process for embedded systems.

ADA has a lot in common with the other major programming languages existing today, but it is also substantially different. The major differences can be traced to one notion. ADA is meant to be applicable at the *design* level of systems as well as the *implementation* or programming level. ADA provides structure to allow it to be used as a system design language as well as a programming language by

1. Providing the means for describing the components of a system;
2. Separating the specification of components from the implementation;

3. Allowing interconnection of components only by those means documented in their specification.

This allows the system architecture to be documented by the interconnection of the module interfaces without reference to the implementations of the modules.

These rules are constraints on the system structure imposed by the use of ADA for documenting the system's design. However, these constraints help make the system design and implementation easier, once the designer is used to them and the resulting system is hence more easily maintainable. Additionally, the use of ADA as both the design and implementation language helps control system documentation since the major part of the documentation, even at the design level, is found in the source program itself.

26.3 THE ADA LANGUAGE

ADA was designed with three specific goals:

1. Reliability and maintainability;
2. Recognition of programming as a human activity;
3. Efficiency.

The first two of these determine the structure of the language and its intended use, while the last filters out potentially inefficient structures from the language.

ADA is designed to encourage modularization and the accompanying ability to factor a system and compose it from separately built parts. In ADA, a program is composed of **program units, subprograms, packages** (which define collections of entities) and **tasks** (which define concurrent or parallel computations).

Each of these program units is made up of two parts:

- A *specification* which contains entities visible to other program units, thus defining its external characteristics;
- A *body* which implements these entities and is not visible to other units.

Units and their parts are separately compilable.

This separation of specification and implementation, along with separate compilation capability, allows and encourages both the construction of systems from separately built parts and the construction and use of libraries of generally available modules.

Program Units

As noted, the program units from which ADA programs are constructed are packages, subprograms and tasks. **Packages,** the main structuring mechanism in ADA, are the units for encapsulating collections of logically related objects. Packages define sets of related types, data and operations (subprograms). Only those entities which are defined in the visible or definition part of the package may be used by other units. The *implementation* of the visible entities is hidden in the body of the package.

The **subprogram** is the basic unit for expressing algorithms and naming definable actions. The two kinds of subprograms are procedures and functions. A **procedure** provides the series of actions defined in its body whenever it is invoked. It may have parameters to accept information or pass information back to the invoker. A **function** is a named activity which computes a value. It is similar to a procedure but returns exactly one value as the result of its invocation.

Tasks define operations or procedures which may execute *in parallel* with other tasks. The language allows the tasks to be implemented on multiprocessors, multicomputers or interleaved on a single processor. Task *types* define entities which can have multiple instances.

Program Unit Bodies

Program unit bodies consist of a declarative part, which embodies the definition of all entities which are to be contained in the unit, and a sequence of statements, which define the actions. In packages, the declarative part is usually more substantial than the sequence of statements, while in subprograms and tasks the opposite is usually true.

The **declarative part** defines the named entities which are contained within the unit and can only be used within the unit. These include types, objects, exception and other nested program units.

The **sequence of statements** describes the actions of the unit. Statements may be the assignment of values to variables, procedure calls or structuring constructs. Structuring constructs include **if** and **case** for selection, **while** and **for** loops for interation and **blocks** for temporary declarations and actions.

Tasks are constructed with action statements supplemented with real time and synchronization statements. These include **delay** or **entry** to provide services to other tasks, and **select** and **accept** for controlling the rendez-

vous which synchronizes one task with another. In a **rendezvous,** either the requester or the provider of the action, whichever arrives at the rendezvous point first, waits for the other. When the other arrives, the action stated there is performed and they both proceed to their next statements.

Exceptional conditions, which make continuing with normal program execution impossible, are handled by sequences of statements inclosed in exception handlers in the program. An *exception handler* is invoked to replace the remainder of the unit when an exception occurs. Exceptions can also be raised explicitly in the program.

Types

Every object and value in the program must have a type associated with it. A **type** consists of a range of values and a set of applicable operations. The four classes of types are scalar, composite, access and user defined.

The **scalar type** includes:

- Numeric;
- Integer;
- Fixed point;
- Floating point; and
- Enumeration.

These allow the programmer to define ordered sets of distinct enumeration literals to be used to hold values in the program.

Composite types are the means of defining structured objects formed from related components. Two kinds of composite types are *arrays,* which have indexed components of the same type, and *records,* which have named components of possibly different types.

Access types are set up and used for the construction of dynamic data structures through the definition of a mechanism for accessing unnamed objects created by allocators. Both the contents of the objects and the access values to the objects may be changed by the program.

User defined types are defined in packages but only their names are made visible in the definition part of the package. All operations on values of variables of this grouping of types are defined in the package specification and the structure of the data used to define the type, and accompanied by the algorithms which implement the operations and are hidden in the body of the package. Such algorithms are called *hidden* because they are not visible to the caller.

Other Features

ADA provides a number of other facilities to give the program designer complete control of the computer when necessary. These include representation control of entities, interrupt control and machine code insertion. Input/output is provided as a library feature rather than as an integral part of the language. ADA provides for generic program units to encapsulate general sets of algorithms applicable to types in certain classes.

Additional information about ADA and its use is found in the ADA reference manual [1] and textbooks [b1, b2, b3].

26.3 THE DESIGN PROCESS USING ADA

Modularization and Abstraction

Mechanical and electronic system designers are familiar with the concept of modularization. There are well developed methods of documenting designs in terms of their component modules, viz. blueprints and schematic drawings. ADA provides the means of documenting software designs and communicating the design to others when the design is supplemented with its equivalent graphic drawing.

In ADA a design is represented as an interconnection of interface characteristics of either system or program components. The overall interconnection is a model for understanding the system. The interface characteristics define the behavior of the components, which is needed to use or to design the components.

The view of modularization embodied in ADA has evolved over the past decade. The two means of modularization are decomposition and abstraction. **Decomposition** is viewed as the proper method of modularization, whereas **abstraction** is seen as a mental tool rather than as a language supportable mechanism. In systems in FORTRAN, COBOL and ALGOL, the interconnection of the major subtasks of the system, such as linkage editing and system generation, is viewed as the responsibility of the operating system.

Modularization by abstraction has its roots in the *virtual machine concept* [3] also described in Chapter 36 and has been influenced by most of the major advances produced by software engineering research, e.g. the data typing mechanism of PASCAL [15], information hiding [19,20] abstract data types [8,9] and module interconnection languages [5].

The consensus of the researchers on the ADA project is that a software system can and should be constructed as an interconnected network of software objects known as **abstract data types.** Each of these objects is constructed from a set of values, which may be a complex composite of simpler values, and a set of operations applicable to the values, with no other operations allowed. Each object represents a logical entity such as a design decision or a related set of properties.

A graphical representation of a sample system modularized in this way is shown in Figure 26.1. This system prints reports from local files. If the file is not available locally, the report manager requests it from remote files and prints the report after the file has been copied locally.

The *generic diagramming method* is represented in Figure 26.2, which shows a single generic module. The abstract type or object is indicated by the named box; the resources—types, functions, etc., provided by the module and those required by the module are indicated respectively by the incoming and outgoing arrows.

ADA accommodates this style of design by employing

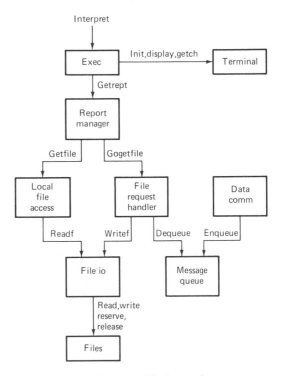

Figure 26.1. Program with abstract data types.

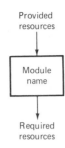

Figure 26.2. A generic module.

packages of data and procedures as its large scale structuring mechanism. In the system diagrammed in Figure 26.1, each module becomes a package in ADA. For example, the files module (at base of system) which provides access to the local file system, can be specified in ADA as

```
package FILES is
    type FILE is STRING (32);
    type LINE is STRING (80);
    procedure READ (F:in FILE;L:out LINE);
    procedure WRITE (F:in FILE;L: in LINE);
    procedure RESERVE(F:in FILE);
    procedure RELEASE(F:in FILE);
end FILES;                              (26.10)
```

Since a programming language influences the way that people think about systems, the use of ADA over a period of time leads designers to use abstract data types in a natural way to visualize a system design.

Design of System Architecture

System quality is dependent on the design and construction of the language. The criteria are the ease with which the user's requirement can be mapped into the design and the design in turn can be mapped into implementation. An ideal language allows both design and implementation to have a structure which records accurately the solution to the problem.

Few current high level languages encourage this sort of mapping solution. Their sole concern is the expression of data and algorithms of single tasks. This is fine for small programs but inadequate for large systems. These languages have been referred to as "programming in the small" [5]. A *system design* language [25] which provides for interconnection information (the essence of system structuring) is a language for programming in the large. ADA is the integration of both classes of language.

26.4 DESIGN METHODOLOGIES

This section presents three methods of structuring systems and shows how ADA documents the resulting designs: functional decomposition, information hiding and abstract data types. These techniques are complementary; they may be used together for refining and enhancing design during system development.

Functional Decomposition

Functional decomposition (the data transformation method of design) is illustrated as an example of structured analysis (discussed in detail in Chapters 33–35). This method may use graphs, that is, data flow diagrams in conjunction with logical data descriptions stored in data dictionaries to model the behavioral structure of the system. This structural description of system behavior permits a modularization of the system requirements to guide the designer in the first phase of the design process, the allocation of function to components.

A data flow diagram documents system behavior by the logical flow of data items through the system, shown as labeled arrows, and the transformations which happen to these data flows, shown as labeled circles or boxes. The structure of each data item is accompanied by a definition which names and describes its components.

Logical data flow is accomplished in three steps. First, if there is an existing physical system, its data flow is diagramed to develop an abstract model. Otherwise, an abstract model is intuitively developed. In the second phase, the abstract model guides the development of a detailed logical model composed of logical data flow and transforms. Finally, the resulting logical data flow model guides the design process to structure implementation.

An example of this process is the design of a stoplight control system. The abstract model is diagrammed in Figure 26.3. The presence or absence of a vehicle in a lane is observed by a detector. The state of the approach is entered into the system. The change in state causes the light to be set to red on green in the appropriate direction according to the current state of the intersection. This method seeks to discover and name the logical types of data which arrive at the system and then activate activities which manipulate these types.

When these data types (arrows), their transformations (boxes) and storage (horizontal lines) are named and connected, the **data flow diagram** shown in Figure 26.3 results. This diagram is then the basis for designing the structure of the system in ADA.

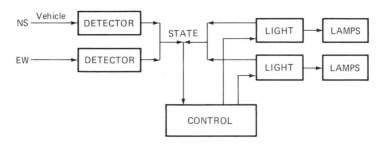

Figure 26.3. Data flow diagram.

This data flow diagram guides the design documented as the visible part of an ADA program in Figure 26.4. In the design there is one detector and approach module for each direction. The complete system is in the appendix.

The transformation from data flow diagram to program structure (the visible part of ADA program) makes use of information hiding data abstraction, discussed below. Modularization is guided by the data flow diagram.

Structured analysis is one of a number of functional decomposition methodologies which derive the logical data types in a system from the other logical data types in the system. Similar methodologies which produce equivalent system structures are SADT[22] and data directed decomposition [17].

Information hiding. Information hiding [19] is a method which hides currently irrelevant information about entities inside the module while showing only the information required about the internal interaction. Thus the module interface provides an abstract view [20] of the module. The entities which are enclosed in the modules comprise the decisions made during the design process.

The rationale for this methodology describes why the design decisions are the entities in the module:

Conventional design methods produce systems which are expensive to maintain because the resulting systems are difficult to change. Changing a system means altering some design decision: to be easy to change (maintain), each design decision should af-

```
STOPLIGHT_CONTROL_SYSTEM is
    type DIRECTION is (NS,EW);
    type LANE_STATUS is (EMPTY,OCCUPIED);
  package DETECTOR(NS,EW) is end DETECTOR;  — hardware
  package APPROACH(NS,EW) is
        procedure APPROACH_OCCUPIED;  — interrupt.
        procedure APPROACH_EMPTY;     — interrupt.
    end APPROACH;
  package INTERSECTION_MODEL is
        procedure SET(DIRECTION;TO=>STATUS);
        procedure GET(STATE);
        procedure GREEN_IN(DIRECTION);
    end INTERSECTION;
  package INTERSECTION_CONTROLLER is
        -- control light
    end INTERSECTION_CONTROLLER;
  package SIGNAL_CONTROLLER is
        procedure TURN_GREEN(DIRECTION);
    end SIGNAL_CONTROLLER;
  package LIGHT_PKG is
        type COLOR is RED,AMBER,GREEN);
        LIGHT:ARRAY(DIRECTION) of COLOR;
    end LIGHT_PKG;
end STOPLIGHT_CONTROL_SYSTEM;
```

Figure 26.4. Visible part of ADA program.

fect as little of the system as possible; there should be little coupling between design decisions.

This last phrase is the rationale for information hiding. Restated, for a maintainable system, each module hides the result of *one* design decision by presenting an abstract view of the entity to other modules.

Some guidelines for making design decisions about decomposition of the system are:

1. Make an informal list of all the "things" in the system for which change cannot be ruled out and derive a list of design decisions from it.
2. Each design decision becomes *one* module; all data and procedures involved in this decision, and only those, comprise the module.
3. Design the abstract interface so the users need only refer to it without knowing how the entity is implemented.

Using those rules, components can be independently designed and later modified if need be.

As an example, for a text editor, how text is stored is a design decision. The data may be stored in memory, on a disk file, or in virtual memory; they may be stored as an array or a linked list. The entity, the contents of a module called DOCUMENT-HOLDER, is shown in Figure 26.5 as an ADA package specification.

The ADA package specification is just the abstract interface; it specifies DOCUMENT-HOLDER as a sequence of lines. They can be operated on with procedures and functions implemented in any so long as the specified types, procedures and functions are consistent.

Abstract data types.

The system designer's approach to the design is influenced by the language used. The data abstraction facilities in ADA let the designer modularize the system into the logical entities (abstract objects) most appropriate to the problem being solved.

Data abstraction reduces the complexity in statements describing the system design. Reduction of complexity is accomplished by concentrating on defining only the essential logical characteristics of the system and ignoring for the time being, the nonessential implementation details of the system. This concentration upon logical properties leads to the specification of the system as a collection of objects of abstract data types. This translates the system into package specifications consisting of the type name declarations and sets of operations (procedures or functions) applicable to objects of that type.

Once the system is specified[20] in terms of abstract type(s), additional types and operations to implement the system are conceived and specified in terms of abstract data types. Successive refinement is iterative: the abstract data types needed at one level are represented with less abstract (more concrete) data types; these are in turn implemented with less abstract data types, and so on. This process continues until all the specified data types are available directly in the programming language.

As an example, a *one pass assembler* may be described at the most abstract level as an assembly procedure which gets symbols from a source file and, using a symbol table for guidance, puts data and instructions in an object file as shown in Figure 26.6. Each named box is an abstract data type.

The specification of the abstract data type symbol table as an ADA package is shown in Figure 26.7. The symbol table is not the set of memory locations and storage pat-

```
package DOCUMENT_HOLDER is
      type LINE is STRING(LINE_LENGTH);
      type LINE_NUMBER is private;
   procedure CLEAR;
   function EMPTY return BOOLEAN;
   function NEXT_LINE return LINE_NUMBER;
   function PREVIOUS_LINE return LINE_NUMBER;
   function FIRST_LINE return LINE_NUMBER;
   function LAST_LINE return LINE_NUMBER;
   procedure INSERT(LINE_NUM:in LINE_NUMBER;BEFORE:in LINE);
   procedure APPEND(LINE_NUM:in LINE_NUMBER;AFTER:in LINE);
   procedure GET_LINE(LINE_NUM:in LINE_NUMBER;CURRENT:out LINE);
end DOCUMENT_HOLDER;
```

Figure 26.5. Package specification.

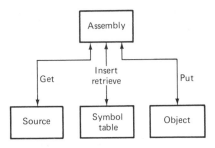

Figure 26.6. One pass assembler.

```
package SYMBOL_TABLE is
 type SYM_TYPE is (INT,FLOAT)
 type ITEM is
   record
     NAME:STRING(20);
     TYPE:SYM_TYPE;
     LOCATION:INTEGER;
   end record;
 procedure INSERT(SYMBOL:in ITEM);
 procedure RETRIEVE(SYM_NAME:NAME;
                    SYMBOL:out ITEM);
 NOT_FOUND:exception;
         --raised by retrieve
end SYMBOL_TABLE;
```

Figure 26.7. Abstract data type symbol table.

terns that is classically thought of as describing a table; it is a set of logical operations applicable to the *type* symbol table. A significant advantage of decomposing systems into abstract data types is that some may be generally useful in other system points or for other systems. The abstract data type interface is simple and minimum information is needed to use it; hence the abstract data type is an ideal basis for building libraries. An example of another useful data type is the character buffer in Figure 26.8.

26.5 DOCUMENTATION

A significant advantage of using ADA as the means of documenting the structure of the system is that it is main-

```
task type BUFFER is
 entry READ(C:out CHARACTER);
 entry WRITE(C:in CHARACTER);
end BUFFER;
```

Figure 26.8. Character buffer.

tainable using the same methods and tools as with computer programs. In the case where ADA is also the implementation language, the maintenance of the design documentation becomes more automatic, since it is an integral part of the implementation.

The documentation of system structure is in the visible part of each package which constitutes the specification of the system. Viewed in this light, the syntax of ADA at the design level is just that of ADA restricted to the specification parts of compilation units.

Since package specification must be textually nested as required by the language processor and provides only the syntax of the abstract data types, it is wise to supplement the ADA specification in a number of ways. First, it might be supplemented with its equivalent graphical rendition as in Figure 26.1.

Second, since the ADA text provides only the syntax of the provided types and operations, that text might be supplemented with descriptive semantic information with a list of the required types and operations included as comments.

Third, since embedded systems usually deal with cooperating concurrent and real time activities, the design of those systems must express the necessary timing and sequence information without referencing the implementation. This can be accomplished by including path expressions [3] as comments in the specifications of system modules.

For example, the specification of the buffer module in the previous section should include the comment line:

—Path ([notfull] Write | [notempty] Read) *   (26.2)

Path expressions describe the ordering (path) of a set of operations which follow. For instance, (26.2) expresses the order of operations in this fashion:

- * says that any number of repetitions may be required from 0 to any positive integer;
- [notfull] Write says that the operation to be done is Write if the buffer is notfull;
- [notempty] Read says that the operation to be done is Read if the buffer is notempty;
- | stands for *or*.

If # appears instead of *, this means 1 or more times.

A complete system description includes a requirements specification [13] integrated into the design specification and a design rationale. The requirements specification is a modularized formal description of the behavior of the system and the constraints imposed on the software by the hardware. The design rationale includes the simple abstract model(s) necessary to convey to the reader the intuitive understanding of system structure. A complete system description of the stoplight control system shown in Figures 26.3 and 26.4 is included in this chapter's appendix as an example of system documentation using ADA.

Programming in ADA

Programming for the three types of program units is basically similar. This process is based on the small scale structuring mechanisms of the ADA language: strong data typing, user definable data types, structured control constructs and procedure or function invocation. ADA requires that every object have a declared type and conversion between objects of different types is disallowed. (This latter demand is sometimes inconvenient.) But during the compilation this restriction may catch design errors which might occur in nontyped languages.

ADA provides built in numeric types, enumeration types (the programmer defines by name the values of the type) and built in enumeration types such as Boolean and character. Additionally, ADA provides user defined composite types whereby the programmer can define arrays with elements of the same type and record with elements of different types. ADA also provides the ability to create dynamic objects of any type by defining access types to those objects. Finally, ADA lets the programmer use abstract data types as needed.

The control constructs consist of statement sequencing, an alternative choice mechanism, an interaction construct and procedure or function invocation. The choice mechanic is **if then else, case,** and **select** in the case of tasks. Iteration uses **loop** with a number of termination methods. The basic loop is nonterminating. However it can be modified by either a **for** statement to loop a designated number of times, or a **while** statement to test for a designated condition before each loop. Procedure invocation occurs as a statement and the function invocation occurs in an expression, thereby calling needed operations defined elsewhere.

There are a few fundamental differences between these types of units. At the logical level, a procedure or function defines a single abstract event, whereas a package defines an abstract object or data type which is passive and performs operations on a permanent object of the type when requested. A task also defines an abstract object or data type but it is an active entity which operates in parallel with other tasks, either providing or asking for operations with other tasks.

A *procedure implementation* such as shown in Figure 26.9 may declare some local types, objects, procedures, functions, packages or tasks. These declared entities are only visible within the procedure and have a lifetime limited to the current invocation of the procedure.

A *package implementation,* for instance Figure 26.10, may also declare some local types, objects, procedures, functions, packages or tasks. These declared entities are, again, only visible within the procedure. But they now have a lifetime which is not limited by invocation of one of the procedures in the package's visible part, but rather

```
procedure SORT (A:in INTEGER_ARRAY) is
       -- bubble sort
     procedure EXCHANGE(LEFT,RIGHT:in out INTEGER) is
       TEMP:INTEGER;
       begin
         TEMP:=LEFT;
         LEFT:=RIGHT;
         RIGHT:=TEMP;
     end EXCHANGE;
   begin
     for LAST in reverse A'RANGE loop
       for CURRENT in A'FIRST..LAST loop
         if A(CURRENT) > A(CURRENT+1) then
           EXCHANGE (A(CURRENT),A(CURRENT+1));
           end if;
         end loop;
       end loop;
   end SORT;
```

Figure 26.9. Procedure implementation.

```
package body SYMBOL_TABLE is
    subtype INDEX is INTEGER range 1..200;
    TABLE: array(INDEX) of ITEM;
    function FIRST_FREE return INDEX is ... end;
    procedure INSERT(SYMBOL:in ITEM) is
        begin
            TABLE(FIRST_FREE):=SYMBOL;
        end INSERT;
    procedure RETRIEVE(SYM_NAME:in NAME;
                       SYMBOL:out ITEM) is
        begin
            for I in INDEX loop
                if SYM_NAME = TABLE(I).NAME then
                    SYMBOL := TABLE(I);
                    return;
                    end if;
                end loop;
                raise NOT_FOUND;
        end RETRIEVE;
begin
    -- initialize table
end SYMBOL_TABLE;
```

Figure 26.10. Implementation of Figure 26.7.

lasts as long as the package lasts. The package specifications provide all of the operations which are allowed to be applied to the enclosed entities by other program units.

A *task implementation* may, like a package, declare local types, objects, procedures, functions, packages and tasks, but can export only entries. Local entities have a lifetime equal to that of the task. Additionally, the order

in which entries may be called in synchronization with other tasks is represented. Sequential parts of tasks may, of course, use the normal control structures.

Control structure is based on entry selection acceptable in its current state. Normally the main part of the task body is in an infinite loop. (Tasks normally run until explicitly terminated.) An example task body is shown in Figure 26.11 and a complete system using tasks is shown in the chapter's Appendix.

The small scale structuring mechanisms in the ADA language are component constraints. Their purpose is not only to assist in the development of algorithms but also to force the implementor to display clearly the logic of the algorithm. In addition, these mechanisms keep local the information used by the algorithm. Thus, by constraining structure ADA enhances maintainability of system components as well as of the system itself. Here the system (or program) clearly displays the logic of the solution to the problem and the information necessary to understand any part of the system.

26.7 THE SYSTEM DEVELOPMENT ENVIRONMENT

Embedded computer systems are usually large and complex. They are developed by a team of people with responsibilities for different facets of the system. A typical system might involve the following: system manager, sys-

```
task body BUFFER is
    SIZE:constant INTEGER:=10;
    BUFF:array(1..SIZE) of CHARACTER;
    SLOTS_FULL:INTEGER range 0..SIZE:=0;
    WRITE_INDEX,READ_INDEX:INTEGER range 1..SIZE:=1;
begin
    loop
        select
            when SLOTS_FULL < SIZE =>
                accept WRITE(C:in CHARACTER) do
                    BUFF(WRITE_INDEX):=C;
                    end;
                WRITE_INDEX:= WRITE_INDEX mod SIZE +1;
                SLOTS_FULL:=SLOTS_FULL+1;
            or when SLOTS_FULL > 0 =>
                accept READ(C:out CHARACTER) do
                    C:=BUFF(READ_INDEX);
                    end;
                READ_INDEX:=READ_INDEX mod SIZE+1;
                SLOTS_FULL:=SLOTS_FULL-1;
            end select;
        end loop;
    end BUFFER;
```

Figure 26.11. Implementation of Figure 26.8.

tem designer, programmers, a configuration manager, testers and documenters. Traditionally, the development environment is the host computer's operating system with facilities only for assisting the programmers. Some more advanced environments might contain a few isolated tools for administration.

ADA takes an integrated approach to the development process. ADA contains features which are not just for programming but aimed at system design. Built upon these, the ADA environment provides facilities which integrate and coordinate the entire development and maintenance process.

The key to the integrated approach taken by ADA is the realization that a software system can be contained entirely within the developmental computer [24]. In addition, the software system's operation is totally independent of the way in which the system's source language representation is structured within the developmental computer. Thus the source language representation may be structured in a way that facilitates the management of the system's development and maintenance.

ADA provides facilities for structuring a system composed of subsystems consisting of packages of modules. The embedded system is the interconnection of these subsystems. ADA adds facilities for describing, controlling and constructing multiple versions of systems and subsystems needed by the developers, maintainers and users over the system's lifetime.

The (sub)system version description, control and construction facilities of ADA may be used for nontraditional purposes. *Traditional* use includes generation and control of fielded versions of the embedded system, system versions for validation, including test modules and data, and system versions for experimentation and doctrine development. These users view versions exclusively as different programs.

Examples of *nontraditional* system versions are operator's and user's manuals maintained as structured English text versions of the system. These versions include documentation external to the program text such as design decisions and formal specifications.

Management Project

Each member of the system development team views and interacts with the development process. One way to do this uses **GANDALF** [12], a system development environment which is now examined.

The manager of the development of an embedded computer system may view it as a collection of system ver-

sions, each of which is a set of modules. The manager also has individuals to be assigned to module development. He or she supervises the development process by controlling the assignment of individuals to different module versions via the version access list and by monitoring their progress via tasking and status history facilities associated with the module by the development environment.

The designer of the embedded computer system views the system as an interconnection of a collection of modules. The collection exists in a number of versions and it is the designer's responsibility to construct the interface specification of these modules and to configure the modules into systems. The designer constructs the interfaces and their interconnection via a system description language which provides for module version names, their interface specifications and for collecting and interconnecting modules into (sub)systems. The interface specifications list the resources (types, objects and operations) which each module provides and those it uses.

The programmer is concerned with an individual module version specified by the module interface specification. He or she constructs the module and validates it with a testing version of the system.

The testing versions of the system are the responsibility of the testers and are constructed in a similar manner. The tester, however, produces from the module's specification a (sub)system version which accepts the implementation of the module produced by the programmer and validates its behavior.

Building the system field versions is done by the configuration manager. The description of each version of the system is named and contains sufficient information to allow the environment to (re)generate it whenever needed.

The documenters of the system develop and maintain documentation versions of system and modules in versions external to the computer programs—user and operator manuals and requirement specifications. These versions are usually in some form of structured text and are entered by editors provided by the environment.

The ADA system development environment integrates the efforts of these individuals by using the knowledge it has of the system development process to structure the system and the interactions with it.

REFERENCES

[1] *Ada Reference Manual*, July 1980.
[2] Caine, S., and E. Gordon, "PDL-A Tool for Software Design," *Proceedings, National Computer Conference, 1975.*

[3] Campbell, R. H., and A. N. Habermann, "The Specification of Process Synchronization by Path Expressions," in *Lecture Notes in Computer Science,* Vol. 16. New York: Springer-Verlag.

[4] Demarco, T., *Structured Analysis and System Specification.* Englewood Cliffs, NJ: Prentice-Hall, 1979.

[5] DeRemer, F., and H. Kron, "Programming in the Large Versus Programming in the Small," *IEEE Transactions on Software Engineering,* June 1976.

[6] "Design and Implementation of Programming Languages," in *Lecture Notes in Computer Science,* Vol. 54. New York: Springer-Verlag.

[7] Dijkstra, E.W., "The Structure of 'THE' Multiprogramming System," *Communications of the ACM,* Vol. 11, No. 5 (May 1968), pp. 341–46.

[8] Guttag, J., "Abstract Data Types and the Development of Data Structures," *Communications of the ACM,* Vol. 20, No. 6 (June 1977), pp. 396–404.

[9] Guttag, J., "Notes on Type Abstraction," *Proceedings, Specification of Reliable Software,* IEEE Computer Society, 1979; and *IEEE Transactions on Software Engineering,* Jan. 1980.

[10] Habermann, A. N., L. Flon and L. Cooprider, "Modularization and Hierarchy in a Family of Operating Systems," *Communications of the ACM,* Vol. 19, No. 5 (May 1976), pp. 266–72.

[11] Habermann, A. N., and D. Perry, "Well Formed System Compositions," *Computer Science Report,* Mar. 1980.

[12] Habermann, A. N., "An Overview of the GANDALF Project," in *Computer Science Review 1978–1979.* Pittsburgh: Carnegie-Mellon University.

[13] Heninger, K., "Specifying Software Requirements for Complex Systems: New Techniques and Their Application," *Proceedings, Specification of Reliable Software,* IEEE Computer Society, 1979; and *IEEE Transactions on Software Engineering,* Jan. 1980.

[14] Jackson, K., "Parallel Processing and Modular Software Construction," in *Design and Implementation of Programming Languages. Lecture Notes in Computer Science,* Vol. 54, New York: Springer-Verlag.

[15] Jensen, K., and N. Wirth, *Pascal User Manual and Report,* 2nd Ed. New York: Springer-Verlag, 1976.

[16] Jones, C., "A Survey of Programming Design and Specification Techniques," *Proceedings, Specification of Reliable Software,* IEEE Computer Society, 1979.

[17] Morris, J. B., "Programming by Successive Refinement of Data Abstractions," *Software Practice and Experience,* Apr. 1980.

[18] Pager, D., "On the Problem of Communicating Complex Information," *Communications of the ACM,* Vol. 16, No. 5 (May 1973), pp. 275–81.

[19] Parnas, D., "On the Criteria to be Used in Decomposing Systems into Modules," *Communications of the ACM,* Vol. 15, No. 12 (Dec. 1972), pp. 1053–58.

[20] Parnas, D., "Use of Abstract Interfaces in the Development of Software for Embedded Systems," *NRL Report 8047,* 1977.

[21] "Rationale for the Design of the Ada Programming Language," *ACM SIGPLAN Notices,* Vol. 14, No. 6 (June 1979), Part B.

[22] Ross, D. T., "Structured Analysis (SA): A Language for Communicating Ideas," *IEEE Transactions on Software Engineering,* Jan. 1977.

[23] Steelman, J., *DOD HOL Requirements,* June 1977.

[24] Wheeler, T. J., "Data Engineering," 1977 NSWSES-NPS Engineering Data Symposium.

[25] Wheeler, T. J., "Embedded System Design with Ada as the System Design Language," *Journal of Systems and Software,* Vol. 2, No. 1 (1981), pp. 11–21.

[26] Wirth, N., "Program Development by Stepwise Refinement," *Communications of the ACM,* Vol. 14, No. 4 (April 1971), pp. 221–27.

[27] Youdon, E., *Structured Walkthroughs,* 2nd Ed. Englewood Cliffs, NJ: Prentice-Hall, 1980.

[b1] Pyle, I. C., *The Ada Programming Language.* Englewood Cliffs, NJ: Prentice-Hall International, 1981.

[b2] Barnes, J. B. G., *Programming in Ada.* Reading, MA: Addison-Wesley, 1982.

[b3] Hibbard, P., A. Hisgen, J. Rosenberg, M. Shaw and M. Sherman, *Studies in Ada Style.* New York: Springer-Verlag, 1982.

APPENDIX

```
--              STOPLIGHT_CONTROL_SYSTEM SPECIFICATION



--1. INTRODUCTION.
--     This system specification describes a stoplight control system
--and its components. It controls the stoplight at a four way inter-
--section based on the detection of vehicles in the approaching lanes
--(FIG 1).

-- NOTE: This specification is written in the Ada Language, with the
--text (sections 1-4) being Ada comments, the design description
```

--(section 5,6) being Ada package specifications, and the implementa-
--tion (section 7) being Ada package bodies.

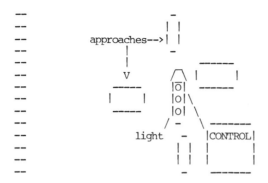

FIG 1.   INTERSECTION DIAGRAM

--   The specification first gives the underlying abstract model on
--which the design of the system is based, and then gives a set of
--module descriptions to describe the system itself and each of the
--hardware and software components, followed by the implementation
--of the system. The module descriptions give only the external
--behavior (interface characteristics) of the system or component.
--These interface characteristics are just the visible behavior of
--the module and are described independent of other modules which
--this module may be connected to. This means that, for instance,
--hardware modules descriptions refrain from describing the system
--effects which the module causes or displays. Software modules
--likewise refrain from describing their effect on either the
--hardware or other software modules but merely the functions that
--each provides.

--2. STOPLIGHT_CONTROL_SYSTEM BEHAVIOR SPECIFICATION.

--   MODULE NAME: STOPLIGHT_CONTROL_SYSTEM

--   BEHAVIOR: The stoplight system controls a signal at a fourway
--intersection. It detects vehicles in an approach area of each
--approaching lane of the intersection and provides a green light to
--occupied lanes.
--   When a lane is occupied the light in its direction is made
--green, if the other lane is empty.
--   As long as the lane remains occupied the light in its direction
--remains green. If however, a lane in the opposite direction becomes
--occupied then, after 10 seconds, the light in the current direction
--goes through amber to red and the light in the opposite direction
--becomes green.

--3. ABSTRACT SYSTEM MODEL.

--   The underlying model for the stoplight control system is the
--generic control system model (FIG 2). In a generic control system,

--certain observable characteristics of the "external world" are
--monitored by sensor subsystem which "understands" the meaning of
--those characteristics. Values of those characteristics are
--translated by the sensor subsystem into internal values which are
--stored in the system's internal model of the outside world. An
--effector subsystem monitors the internal model with respect to
--reference values and adjusts the values of certain characteristics
--in the external world so as to maintain equilibrium, as defined by
--the system, in the external world.

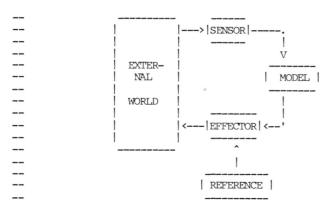

FIG 2. CONTROL SYSTEM MODEL

--4. DESIGN RATIONALE.
--   The stoplight control system structure, which is based on the
--underlying abstract control system model, was derived by performing
--a structured system analysis of information flow within the system.
--The resulting data flow diagram is shown in fig 3 and depicts the
--logical data flow and transformations in a stoplight control system.

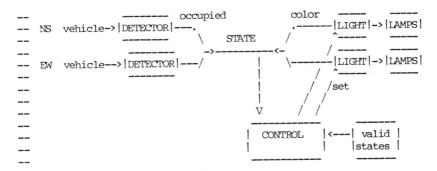

FIG 3. DATA FLOW DIAGRAM

--   The results of this analysis were used in the design process to guide
--the modularization of the system based on encapsulation of functions or
--design decisions,ie. Information Hiding. (FIG 4 as an access diagram and
--sections 5 & 6 as design in Ada, section 7 is implementation in Ada.)

```
--      --------occupied --------  set  ----------   -----    -----
--NS |DETECTOR|----->|APPROACH|----->|INTERSEC- |green |SIG- |->|LIGHT|
--      --------  empty  --------  empty |  TION  |in(dir) NAL |  | PKG |
--      --------           -------- occupied     |<-----|CONTR|  |     |
--EW |DETECTOR|----->|APPROACH|----->|  MODEL   |  .->|OLLER|->|     |
--      --------           --------           ----------   -----    -----
--          inter-                  get ^        | turn green
--          rupts                  state|        |  (lane)
--                                        ------------
--                                       |INTERSECTION|
--                                       |  CONTROL   |
--                                        ------------
--
--              FIG 4.STOPLIGHT_CONTROL_SYSTEM DESIGN DIAGRAM
```

    --   In this design the detector is a hardware transformation module
    --which detects the presence or absence of vehicles and transforms this
    --information into hardware (interrupt) signals. The approach is a
    --transform module. The intersection model is an abstract data type
    --which models the internal state of the intersection. Intersection
    --control is a process which monitors the state and effects the behavior
    --of the signal as defined by rules for consistency of the system. The
    --signal controller and light pkg are abstract data types which abstract
    --(hide the details of) the actual signal and its lamps.

    -- STOPLIGHT_CONTROL_SYSTEM design specification is

    -- 5. HARDWARE MODULES.

    -- 5.1 MODULE NAME: DETECTOR
----
        with NS_APPROACH;
    package NS_DETECTOR is   end NS_DETECTOR ;-- hardware
----
        with EW_APPROACH;
    package EW_DETECTOR is   end EW_DETECTOR ;-- hardware

    --   BEHAVIOR: Detects when a lane approach becomes occupied
    --and signals that its lane is occupied (ie. generates an
    --occupied interrupt). Detects when a lane becomes empty and
    --signals that its lane is empty (ie. generates an empty
    --interrupt).
    --   There are two detectors, one which responds to lanes
    --in the north-south direction (the north detector is ORed
    --with the south detector), and one of which responds to the
    --east-west direction.
    --
    --   CHARACTERISTIC VALUES:
    --   N-S OCCUPIED => INTERRUPT AT LOCATION 8
    --   N-S EMPTY => INTERRUPT AT LOCATION 12
    --   E-W OCCUPIED => INTERRUPT AT LOCATION 16
    --   E-W EMPTY => INTERRUPT AT LOCATION 20

    -- 5.2 MODULE NAME: LIGHT
    --   PROVIDES:
----
      with TYPE_DEFS ; use TYPE_DEFS ;
    package LIGHT_PKG is
      type COLOR is (RED,AMBER,GREEN) ;
      type LIGHT is array(DIRECTION) of COLOR;

```
     SIGNAL : LIGHT := (NS=>GREEN ,EW=>RED) ;
     private
       for COLOR'SIZE use 8 ;
       for COLOR use (RED=>2#001#,AMBER=>2#010#,GREEN=>2#100#);
       for LIGHT'SIZE use 16 ;
       for SIGNAL use at 76 ;
     end LIGHT_PKG ;
----------------------------------------------------------------
--   BEHAVIOR: LIGHT = Two dimension array of three lamps with red,
--                     amber and green filters.
--                     Each lamp can be on or off
--
--   CHARACTERISTIC VALUES:
--         LIGHT = LOCATIONS 76,77
--         RED = b 001
--         YELLOW = b 010
--         GREEN = b 100
----------------------------------------------------------------
-- 6. SOFTWARE MODULES.
----------------------------------------------------------------
-- 6.1 MODULE NAME: TYPE DEFINITIONS
--      PROVIDES:
----------------------------------------------------------------
package TYPE_DEFS is
  type DIRECTION is (NS,EW) ;
  type LANE_STATUS is (EMPTY,OCCUPIED) ;
  end TYPE_DEFS ;
----------------------------------------------------------------
--
-- 6.2 MODULE NAME: APPROACH (NS,EW)
--      PROVIDES:
----------------------------------------------------------------
  with INTERSECTION_MODEL ,TYPE_DEFS ; use TYPE_DEFS ;
package NS_APPROACH is --handles signals from the ns detector
  procedure OCCUPIED ;
  procedure EMPTY ;
  end NS_APPROACH ;
----------------------------------------------------------------
  with INTERSECTION_MODEL ,TYPE_DEFS ; use TYPE_DEFS ;
package EW_APPROACH is --handles signals from the ew detector
  procedure OCCUPIED ;
  procedure EMPTY ;
  end EW_APPROACH ;
----------------------------------------------------------------
--   REQUIRES: SET(DIRECTION,TO_STATUS)
--
--   BEHAVIOR: OCCUPIED causes SET(DIRECTION,TO=>OCCUPIED).
--             EMPTY causes SET(DIRECTION,TO=>EMPTY).
----------------------------------------------------------------
--
-- 6.3 MODULE NAME: INTERSECTION_MODEL.
--      PROVIDES:
----------------------------------------------------------------
  with TYPE_DEFS ; use TYPE_DEFS ;
package INTERSECTION_MODEL is
  type LANE_ARRAY is array(DIRECTION) of LANE_STATUS ;
  type STATUS is
    record
      GREEN_IN : DIRECTION ;
      LANE     : LANE_ARRAY ;
    end record ;
```

```
      procedure SET(LN:DIRECTION ; TO:LANE_STATUS) ;
      procedure GET(STATE:out STATUS);
      procedure GREEN_IN(LN:DIRECTION);
   --Path (SET* GET{(SET+ GREEN_IN) | GREEN_IN (SET+ | [LANE=(occ,occ)]DELAY1Ø)})*
      end INTERSECTION_MODEL ;
   -----------------------------------------------------------------------------
   --    BEHAVIOR: Models state of approach lanes and lights. Changes status on
   --              receipt of SET and GREEN_IN commands. GET command is accepted
   --              only when lane state is different from the state that existed
   --              at the time of the previous GET.
   -----------------------------------------------------------------------------
   -- 6.4 MODULE NAME: INTERSECTION_CONTROLLER
   --      PROVIDES:
   -----------------------------------------------------------------------------
      with SIGNAL_CONTROLLER,INTERSECTION_MODEL,TYPE_DEFS ; use TYPE_DEFS ;
   package INTERSECTION_CONTROLLER is
      procedure OPERATE ;
      end INTERSECTION_CONTROLLER ;
   -----------------------------------------------------------------------------
   --    REQUIRES: GET(STATE); TURN_GREEN(LANE);
   --
   --    BEHAVIOR: When return from GET(STATE) occurs changes signal in
   --              appropriate direction to green.
   -----------------------------------------------------------------------------
   -- 6.5 MODULE NAME: SIGNAL_CONTROLLER
   --      PROVIDES:
   -----------------------------------------------------------------------------
      with INTERNAL_MODEL,LIGHT_PKG,TYPE_DEFS ; use TYPE_DEFS ;
   package SIGNAL_CONTROLLER is
      procedure TURN_GREEN(LN:DIRECTION) ;
      end SIGNAL_CONTROLLER ;
   -----------------------------------------------------------------------------
   --    REQUIRES: LIGHT(DIR)(COLOR(ON,OFF)); GREEN_IN(DIR);
   --
   --    BEHAVIOR: Set direction to the color requested and inform model,
   --    while making sure light is always in a consistent state.
   -----------------------------------------------------------------------------


   -- end STOPLIGHT_CONTROL_SYSTEM design specification

   -- 7.  STOPLIGHT_CONTROL_SYSTEM implementation
   -----------------------------------------------------------------------------
   package body NS_APPROACH is
      task CONTROL is
        entry OCCUPIED ;
        entry EMPTY ;
          for OCCUPIED use at  8 ;
          for EMPTY     use at 12 ;
      end CONTROL ;

      procedure OCCUPIED renames CONTROL.OCCUPIED ;
      procedure EMPTY     renames CONTROL.EMPTY ;

      task body CONTROL is
        begin
          loop
            select
              accept OCCUPIED ;
                INTERSECTION_MODEL.SET(NS,TO=>OCCUPIED) ;
              or accept EMPTY ;
                INTERSECTION_MODEL.SET(NS,TO=>EMPTY) ;
```

```
          end select ;
        end loop ;
      end CONTROL ;

   begin -- initialize NS_APPROACH
      EMPTY ;
   end NS_APPROACH ;
```

```
package body EW_APPROACH is
   task CONTROL is
      entry OCCUPIED ;
      entry EMPTY ;
        for OCCUPIED use at 16 ;
        for EMPTY    use at 20 ;
   end CONTROL ;

   procedure OCCUPIED renames CONTROL.OCCUPIED ;
   procedure EMPTY     renames CONTROL.EMPTY ;

   task body CONTROL is
     begin
       loop
         select
           accept OCCUPIED ;
             INTERSECTION_MODEL.SET(EW,TO=>OCCUPIED) ;
           or accept EMPTY ;
             INTERSECTION_MODEL.SET(EW,TO=>EMPTY) ;
         end select ;
       end loop ;
     end CONTROL ;

   begin -- initialize EW_APPROACH
      EMPTY ;
   end EW_APPROACH ;
```

```
package body INTERSECTION_MODEL is
      task CONTROL is
        entry SET(LN:DIRECTION; TO:LANE_STATUS) ;
        entry GET(STATE:out STATUS) ;
        entry GREEN_IN(LN:DIRECTION) ;
        end CONTROL ;
   procedure SET(LN:DIRECTION; TO:LANE_STATUS) renames CONTROL.SET ;
   procedure GET(STATE:out STATUS) renames CONTROL.GET ;
   procedure GREEN_IN(LN:DIRECTION) renames CONTROL.GREEN_IN ;
   task body CONTROL is
-- This task must handle asynchronous invocations of SET, GET and GREEN_IN with
--the constraint that GET can only be accepted when (a) the state has changed
--since the previous GET or (b) both lanes are occupied and 10 seconds have
--elapsed. SET may occur at any time(1). After a GET(2)there must be at least
--one SET(3), or a delay(4) (if both lanes are occupied), either before(5) or
--after(6) GREEN_IN before another GET.
     INTERNAL_STATE:STATUS:=(GREEN_IN=>NS,LANE=>(NS=>EMPTY,EW=>EMPTY));
     begin
       loop                    -- numbers in text above correspond to |
         select              --                                       v
           accept SET(LN:DIRECTION; TO:LANE_STATUS) do          --(1)
             INTERNAL_STATE.LANE(LN) := TO ;
             end SET ;
```

```
            or accept GET(STATE: in out STATUS) do            --(2)
              STATE := INTERNAL_STATE ;
              end GET ;
            select
               accept SET(LN:DIRECTION;TO:LANE_STATUS) do      --(3)
                 INTERNAL_STATE.LANE(LN) := TO ;
                 end SET ;
                 loop
                   select
                      accept SET(LN:DIRECTION;TO:LANE_STATUS) do --(3)
                        INTERNAL_STATE.LANE(LN) := TO ;
                        end SET ;
                      or accept GREEN_IN (LN:DIRECTION) do      --(5)
                        INTERNAL_STATE.GREEN_IN(LN) ;
                        end GREEN_IN ;     exit ; --to main loop
                   end select ;
                 end loop ;
               or accept GREEN_IN (LN:DIRECTION) do             --(6)
                 INTERNAL_STATE.GREEN_IN(LN) ;
                 end GREEN_IN ;
                 select
                   accept SET(LN:DIRECTION;TO:LANE_STATUS) do    --(3)
                     INTERNAL_STATE.LANE(LN) := TO ;
                     end SET ;
                   or when INTERNAL_STATE.LANE=(OCCUPIED,OCCUPIED)=>delay(10.0);
                 end select ;--after GREEN_IN                    --(4)^
            end select ;--after GET
          end select ;--main
        end loop ;
     end CONTROL ;
  end INTERSECTION_MODEL ;
```

```
package body SIGNAL_CONTROLLER is

    function OTHER(DIR:DIRECTION) return DIRECTION is
      begin
        if DIR = EW then return NS ;
        else              return EW ;
        end if ;
      end OTHER ;

    procedure TURN_GREEN(LN:DIRECTION) is
      begin
        if LIGHT_PKG.SIGNAL(LN) /= GREEN then --only change if necessary
          LIGHT_PKG.SIGNAL(OTHER(LN)) := AMBER ;
          delay(3*SECONDS) ;
          LIGHT_PKG.SIGNAL(OTHER(LN)) := RED ;
          LIGHT_PKG.SIGNAL(LN) := GREEN ;
          INTERNAL_MODEL.GREEN_IN(LN);
          end if ;
        end TURN_GREEN ;

    end SIGNAL_CONTROLLER ;
```

```
package body INTERSECTION_CONTROLLER is
```

```
procedure OPERATE is
  pragma MAIN ;
  STATE : INTERSECTION_MODEL.STATUS ;
  begin
    loop
      GET(STATE) ;
      if STATE.LANE = (OCCUPIED,OCCUPIED) then
          if STATE.GREEN_IN = NS then
            SIGNAL_CONTROLLER.TURN_GREEN(EW) ;
          else -- GREEN_IN = EW
            SIGNAL_CONTROLLER.TURN_GREEN(NS) ;
          end if ;
      elsif STATE.LANE(EW) = OCCUPIED then
          SIGNAL_CONTROLLER.TURN_GREEN(EW) ;
      elsif STATE.LANE(NS) = OCCUPIED then
          SIGNAL_CONTROLLER.TURN_GREEN(NS) ;
      -- else everything empty leave alone
      end if ;
    end loop ;
  end OPERATE ;

end INTERSECTION_CONTROLLER ;
```

```
-- end STOPLIGHT_CONTROL_SYSTEM implementation
```

27
Assembly Language

Peter Abel

*British Columbia Institute
of Technology*

27.1 INTRODUCTION

Largely because of microcomputers, interest is being revived for **assembly language.** *B*asic *A*ssembler *L*anguage (**BAL**) is the lowest level programming language; one assembly instruction generates one machine language instruction. Consequently, writing a program in assembly language gives a programmer complete control over the content of the program. Further, an assembly program when translated into machine language is more efficient in terms of small size and fast execution. Indeed, this is often important to realize the processing of a large production program; for example, a COBOL program could link to an assembly subprogram which can execute a commonly used routine more efficiently.

Today, because programming in assembly language involves careful, exacting skills, most programmers code in high level languages. But a knowledge of assembly language provides

- An understanding of the architecture of the machine;
- Better in-depth understanding of the foundation of high level languages (for example, COBOL and PL/I, to name two high level languages) when compiled translate into assembler code);
- Improved debugging skills;
- A useful and often necessary skill for the systems programmer and the data communications specialist.

Assembly languages vary according to the architecture of the CPU. But since the basic principles remain the same, a knowledge of one version facilitates learning another. Technical details vary, for example, for the 6502 CPU (Apple II, Commodore CBM), the Z80A (North Star Horizon, TRS-80 II and III), and the 8088 (IBM Personal Computer). This chapter covers the assembly language for the large mainframe IBM 370 series computers and its various clones such as the IBM 3000 and 4300 series.

Because a full text devoted exclusively to the topic of assembly language is really required, this chapter covers only important features. Included is sufficient material to give the reader some background and understanding of basic concepts and enough detail for an appreciation of the subject. Learning BAL is rigorous and challenging—expect to have to reread parts and to work through examples carefully. But the results should amply reward the efforts.

27.2 DATA REPRESENTATION

As the title indicates, this section covers the representation of different types of data; a later section covers the representation of machine language instructions.

A programmer writes **symbolic assembly** instructions and defines data areas that machine language instructions reference. As the next step, the programmer submits the program to the **assembler** (translator) program, which converts the symbolic instructions and defines data into machine code, the **object module**. Figure 27.1 illustrates a theoretical layout of a machine language program in main storage.

Instructions	Contains instructions such as read a record, move data, add, multiply data, and print a record
Input area	Reads records into this area
Output area	Prints or displays data from this area
Data and workareas	Various constants and work fields used in computations.

Figure 27.1. General layout of a program in main storage.

Internally, a byte consists of 8 bits (plus 1 bit for odd parity). One or more adjacent bytes are combined to form either instructions or data. Basically, when a machine language program is running, the instructions cause the computer to process the data; for example, one instruction can move data from one data area to another, and another instruction can add data from one data area into another.

We can view a byte as consisting of two 4 bit portions or **nibbles,** and any bit can be 0 (off) or 1 (on). Table 27.1 shows all the possible 4-bit combinations of a nibble (Binary columns).

A binary value of 0000 (all bits off) has a decimal value of 0. A binary value of 0001 has a decimal value of 1. A binary value of 1010 has a decimal value of 10 (8 plus 2), and a binary value of 1111 (all bits on) has a decimal value of 15—the largest value that a 4-bit number can represent.

Hexadecimal Representation

The binary numbers 1010 through 1111 each require two digits (10 through 15) for representation as decimal values. As a shorthand notation, each of these values is expressed as one character—10 as the letter A, 11 as B, 12 as C, 13 as D, 14 as E, and 15 as F. With this notation, we can now represent the binary values 0000 through 1111 with a *single* character 0 through F. Since there are 16 such characters, the resulting number system is *base 16* and is called **hexadecimal** or **hex** format—see Figure 27.2.

Hex representation is an important concept in use on many computers. Although at first a bit tricky for decimal oriented users, most soon become familiar, and fairly comfortable, with it.

Since a byte consists of two nibbles, we can represent the contents of a byte with two hexadecimal (**hex**) digits, as follows:

Binary	Hexadecimal
0000 0000	00
0100 0000	40
0101 0110	56
1011 1000	B8

With hex notation, we can depict the contents of any byte or group of bytes, and consequently the contents of any instruction or data area in main storage. Table 27.2 contains some of the most common representations of characters in binary and hex formats.

There are two main applications for hex representation:

• After assembling a source program, the assembler

Table 27.1. Representation of Decimal, Binary, and Hexadecimal Values.

Decimal	Binary	Hexa-decimal	Decimal	Binary	Hexa-decimal
0	0000	0	8	1000	8
1	0001	1	9	1001	9
2	0010	2	10	1010	A
3	0011	3	11	1011	B
4	0100	4	12	1100	C
5	0101	5	13	1101	D
6	0110	6	14	1110	E
7	0111	7	15	1111	F

Table 27.2 Representation of Common Characters in Hexadecimal and Binary

Character	Hexadecimal	Binary
(blank)	40	0100 0000
$ (dollar)	5B	0101 1011
. (period)	5C	0101 1100
− (minus)	60	0110 0000
, (comma)	6B	0110 1011
A–I	C1–C9	1100 0001–1100 1001
J–R	D1–D9	1101 0001–1101 1001
S–Z	E2–E9	1110 0001–1110 1001
0–9	F0–F9	1111 0000–1111 1001

prints the original symbolic instructions as well as the generated machine *object code* in hex format.

- In the event of a program "crashing," the system may print the contents of main storage (called a **storage dump**) in hex format at the end of the crash.

Data Definition

A **field** consists of related adjacent bytes of data, such as customer name, customer address, or amount owing. A **record** consists of a collection of related fields. A **file** (or **data set**) consists of all the related records, such as a customer file that contains all the records for a company's customers. Each record in a file usually contains fields in the same relative positions.

Consider a program that contains a definition of a customer record: name, address, and amount owing. The name consists of alphabetic characters, and the address is a mixture of alphabetic characters and numbers. The amount owing is a signed numeric value (plus or minus) and has an implied decimal point, such as 157ᶺ25+ (the caret indicates this decimal point). This value is subject to regular change and will have sales amounts added to it and payments subtracted from it.

At the simplest level, then, the data is either descriptive (such as name and address) or arithmetic (such as amount owing). A programmer defines descriptive data as *character format* and defines arithmetic data as *packed format,* or in special cases as *binary format.* Each type of data has its own set of processing instructions.

One may use the assembler DS instruction to define data fields (declaratives) without initial values and use the DC instruction to define them with initial values, as the following subsections explain.

Define Storage (DS)

The define storage (DS) instruction defines one or more related bytes of main storage. Typically, the field may receive data from another field (for example, to store a dividend prior to dividing), or it may accept an input record. The general format of DS is

column 1   10   16

[optional name]   DS   fLn   (27.1)

The field may have a name beginning in column 1. The name, if any, may be one to eight characters long. The first character must be a *letter* A through Z, $, #, or @. Remaining characters may be letters or digits.

In the foregoing example, the instruction DS begins in column 10. The operand for DS begins in position 16. The *format (f)* designates the type of data that one will expect the field to contain, such as C for "character" or P for "packed." However, since DS generates no data, the contents of the field is unpredictable at the beginning of program execution. The *length (Ln)* provides the length of the field in bytes.

Three examples of valid DS definitions follow:

1	10	16	
CUSTNAME	DS	CL25	(27.2)
FACTOR3	DS	CL3	(27.3)
$QUOT	DS	PL5	(27.4)

Here (27.2) defines a 25 byte field named CUSTNAME to contain character data for a customer name; (27.3) defines a 3 byte field named FACTOR3; and (27.4) defines a 5 byte field named $QUOT for packed (arithmetic) data, a quotient generated by a divide operation. Note that none of these fields as yet contain defined values. During execution, the program can move values into these fields.

The DS instruction is also commonly used to define records and their contained fields. The following example defines a 100 byte disk record named CUSTREC. The zero in the operand of CUSTREC (0CL100) means that the following defined 100 bytes are contained within a field bearing the name CUSTREC:

CUSTREC	DS	0CL100	Defines a record.	
CUSTNAME	DS	CL20	Redefines	
CUSTADDR	DS	CL40	fields	
CUSTAMT	DS	PL05	within	
	DS	CL35	the record.	(27.5)

CUSTNAME, CUSTADDR, and CUSTAMT are all defined within CUSTREC. Since these fields comprise only 65 positions of storage, another 35 byte definition is required to complete the disk record length. This latter unnamed field could be used for future expansion of the customer record, for example, for a credit rating field. This last DS could have a name, but if the program that reads records into main storage never references this field, it may remain unnamed.

Define Constant (DC)

The assembler instruction that defines a data field and fills it with a constant is DC (define constant). Its general format is

column 1   10   16

     [optional name] DC   fLn 'constant'   (27.6)

The DC consists of three parts: an optional name of the defined field, the assembler instruction DC, and an operand that describes the data being defined. These three parts, like DS, begin respectively in columns 1, 10 and 16. The operand is comprised of format (f) to signify the type of data and length (Ln) to define the length of the data area. The entry 'constant' expresses the value that the field is initially to contain. The next section contains examples.

27.3 CHARACTER DATA

Data defined as character (C) format may contain letters (A–Z), numbers, or special characters such as @, #, $, %, &, or +. Typical use for this format is for descriptive information such as names, addresses, and report headings.

The following two examples define fields that are 8 bytes long. HDGSAVE contains the constant value 'ACE CORP'. Note the hex representation of each of the 8 characters including the blank (hex '40'). HDGOUT contains all blank characters.

Hex representation
of contents: 1   10   16

C1C3C540C3D6D9D7   HDGSAVE   DC   CL8 'ACE CORP'
4040404040404040   HDGOUT   DC   CL8 ' '

                                        (27.7)

The contents of one field can be moved to another field. The instruction to move data defined as character (C) format is MVC (move character). The following example moves the contents of HDGSAVE to HDGOUT:

     1   10   16

          MVC   HDGOUT,HDGSAVE   (27.8)

The net effect is to copy the contents of HDGSAVE into HDGOUT such that the blanks in HDGOUT are replaced by ACE CORP, and HDGSAVE is unchanged.

One may want to use an instruction like the one just preceding to move a heading to an output area prior to printing. The instruction begins with the leftmost byte of HDGSAVE and moves 1 byte at a time from left to right. The normal practice is to move a field into another field which is defined as the same length.

27.4 PACKED DATA

Data defined as packed (P) may contain only the digits 0 through 9 and a sign (plus or minus). For efficiency, a packed field contains two decimal digits in each byte, except for the rightmost byte which contains one digit and the sign. Valid signs include hex 'C' and 'F' for plus and hex 'D' for minus. A packed field always contains an odd number (1, 3, 5, etc.) of digits. The following illustrate packed fields defined with DC, with the hexadecimal contents shown to the left. Note that you can define a decimal point in the constant but since it acts only as documentation, the assembler ignores it.

Hex representation
of contents: 1   10   16

02 50 0C   AMTA   DC   PL3'02500'
01 00 0C   AMTB   DC   PL3'010.00'
00 00 15 0D   AMTC   DC   PL4'0000150—'

                                        (27.9)

One can "move" the contents of one packed field to another packed field using the ZAP (zero add packed) instruction. The following ZAP example in effect clears AMTB to zero and copies the contents of AMTA into AMTB:

            ZAP   AMTB,AMTA   (27.10)

Both AMTA and AMTB now contain hex '02500C'. The receiving field (AMTB) should normally be defined as at least the length of the sending field (AMTA). If the receiving field is longer, ZAP initializes the leftmost bytes with 0.

You can also add the contents of two packed fields using the AP (add packed) instruction. The following AP example adds the contents of AMTA to AMTC,

            AP   AMTC,AMTA   (27.11)

After the AP operation, AMTC contains hex '002350C' (2500+ plus 150−), and AMTA still contains hex '02500C'. The receiving field (AMTC) in most cases should be defined as longer than the sending field (AMTA) to allow space to accumulate large values.

In the case of ZAP, the sending field (operand 2) must contain valid packed data (0-9 plus sign), and in the case of AP, both the sending field (operand 2) and the receiving field (operand 1) must contain valid packed data. The following example attempts to add the contents of AMTA to HDGOUT, the latter defined as a (C) format field in the preceding section.

$$AP \qquad HDGOUT,AMTA \qquad (27.12)$$

Since **HDGOUT** does not contain valid packed data, an attempt by the computer to execute this **AP** instruction will cause the very common "data exception"—the system supervisor interrupts execution to print an error message, and, unless there is a recovery procedure, the supervisor terminates the program. **AP** can also cause a "decimal overflow" error if the length of the receiving field is too short for the generated sum.

Conversion

Other arithmetic packed operations include **SP** (subtract packed), **MP** (multiply packed), and **DP** (divide packed). These are all true algebraic operations; for example, multiplying a positive value by a negative value yields a negative product, and so on.

It is often necessary to convert character data into packed data and vice versa. Character data that is to be converted to packed should contain only the numbers 0–9. The following defines a character field, **CHARFLD**, containing the numbers 12345 and a packed field, **PACKFLD**, containing packed 0s:

Hex contents:	1		10	16
F1F2F3F4F5	CHARFLD	DC		CL5'12345'
00000C	PACKFLD	DC		PL3'0'

$$(27.13)$$

CHARFLD for example could contain a numeric value entered from a terminal and necessary to use for arithmetic. Note that numeric values entered from terminals or cards require 1 byte for each number and are therefore characters.

The following **PACK** instruction converts character data into packed format:

$$PACK \qquad PACKFLD,CHARFLD \qquad (27.14)$$

The **PACK** operation works from right to left in both specified fields as follows:

1. Extract the rightmost byte of **CHARFLD** (hex 'F5'), reverse the two 4-bit portions, and store the result (hex '5F') in the rightmost byte of **PACKFLD**.
2. Extract the next byte to the left from **CHARFLD** (hex 'F4') and extract and save the numeric portion (4).

Extract the next byte to the left from **CHARFLD** (hex 'F3') and extract the numeric portion (3).
3. Store the combined result (hex '34') into the next byte to the left in **PACKFLD**:

CHARFLD   F1 F2 F3 F4 F5

PACKFLD   12 34 5F   (27.15)

4. Perform a similar operation with the next 2 left bytes of **CHARFLD** (hex 'F1F2'): extract the numeric portions ('12') and store in the next byte to the left in **PACKFLD**. The operation terminates at this point.

The **PACK** operation has selected a plus sign (hex 'F') and each numeric portion of **CHARFLD**. The net effect is compression of a 5 byte field into a 3 byte field containing valid packed data. The **PACK** operation leaves **CHARFLD**, the sending field, unchanged.

Since a packed field such as hex '12345F' contains nonprintable characters, it is necessary when printing or displaying the field to convert the packed field into character format. The instruction for this is **UNPK** (unpack), used as follows:

$$UNPK \qquad CHARFLD,PACKFLD \qquad (27.16)$$

Basically, **UNPK** reverses the steps of the **PACK** operation and works from right to left in both specified fields, as follows:

1. Extract the right byte of **PACKFLD** (hex '5F'), reverse the two 4 bit portions, and store the result (hex 'F5') in the rightmost byte of **CHARFLD**.
2. Extract the next byte to the left in **PACKFLD** (hex '34'), store the 4 as F4 in the next byte to the left in **CHARFLD** and the 3 as F3 in the next byte to the left in **CHARFLD**.
3. Continue in this fashion with hex '12' from **PACKFLD**:

PACKFLD: 12 34 5F

CHARFLD: F1 F2 F3 F4 F5   (27.17)

As can be seen, **CHARFLD** now contains the numeric characters 12345, which are printable in this format. However, if **CHARFLD** contained a negative value such as 12345−, it would appear as **F1F2F3F4D5**. This value would print or display as **1234N**. The instruction that is normally used to convert packed data into printable character data is ED (edit) that provides for suppression of leftmost 0, insertion of commas and decimal point, and proper handling of minus or CR sign.

27.5 LOGIC

The preceding section described the movement of data (MVC and ZAP) and simple arithmetic (AP). Another important processing function is logic: the comparison of two character data fields in main storage to check whether one (and which) should come first alphabetically or whether they are equal, or to determine for a single numeric field its arithmetic sign—minus, zero or plus. For example, one may want to check whether a customer's balance exceeds the credit limit, or an input field contains all blank characters (hex '40's).

The effect of executing a command which compares two fields sets the computer's condition code, which can be tested subsequently by means of a conditional branch instruction.

A comparison of fields defined in character (C) format is logical. That is, the compared fields are considered to be unsigned, for example, names or addresses. The instruction for this purpose is SS (compare logical character). Suppose, for example, a field named SALECODE designates whether a salesman works in the East, North, West, or South (E, N, W, S) regions. A program has to determine if the given sales were for the West (W) region. You could use the following declaratives and CLC instruction:

```
SALECODE    DS     CL1 (unknown contents)
WESTREG     DC     C'W'
            . . .
            CLC    SALECODE,WESTREG
```
                                        (27.18)

The computer's condition code is set as follows:

Equal—the content of SALECODE is 'W'.
Not equal (high or low)—the content is not 'W'.

CLC can also compare for high or low; for example, the name ADAM is "lower" than the name JOHN.

A comparison of fields defined as packed (P) format is algebraic, that is, one which considers the signs of the compared fields. Regardless of the absolute values in the compared fields, a positive value is always higher than a negative value. The instruction for such a comparison is CP (compare packed). Suppose, for example, a customer's balance owing is stored in CUSTBAL and the credit limit is in CREDLIM. A program has to determine if the balance in CUSTBAL is greater than the credit limit:

```
CUSTBAL     DS     PL4
CREDLIM     DC     PL4'01000.00'
            . . .
            CP     CUSTBAL,CREDLIM
```
                                        (27.19)

The condition code is set depending on the contents of CUSTBAL:

CUSTBAL	CREDLIM	Condition Code
00025.00	01000.00	low
01000.00	01000.00	equal
01520.00	01000.00	high

Technically, CLC compares any type of data, but if one uses CLC to compare packed fields, the operation does not treat the fields as signed. Consequently, CLC treats $04123-$ as higher than $00575+$. CP compares only fields containing valid packed data (0 through 9 plus a sign); comparison of invalid packed data causes a data exception.

Conditional Branching

A program can compare values using CP and CLC, and then test the results to determine the action to take. The following CP example compares a customer's balance with the credit limit. The next instruction, BL (branch low), uses a conditional branch: if the condition code set by the CP is "low," then there is a branch to get the next command at the instruction labelled D20. Otherwise, the condition is "equal" or "high": a warning message is printed (assembler code for printing is not shown):

```
            CP     CUSTBAL,CREDLIM
            BL     D20
            . . .  (print warning message) . . .
D20         . . .  (continue processing)
```
                                        (27.21)

Conditional branch instructions used after compares are

BE (branch equal)   BNE (branch not equal)
BL (branch low)   BNL (branch not low)
BH (branch high)   BNH (branch not high)   (27.22)

A program can also test the results of arithmetic operations such as ZAP, AP and SP, and then test the resulting condition. Suppose AMTA is a divisor. Since dividing by a zero divisor will cause a zero divide error, the program ZAPs the divisor into itself. This action sets the condition code. The next instruction, BZ, tests: If the condition code is set to zero, then branch to the instruction labelled D50. Otherwise, the condition is nonzero; divide using AMTA as a divisor.

```
        ZAP    AMTA,AMTA
        BZ     D50
        . . .    (divide using AMTA as divisor)
D50     . . .    (continue processing)
```

$$(27.23)$$

Conditional branch instructions used after arithmetic operations are

BZ (branch zero)   BNZ (branch not zero)
BM (branch minus)   BNM (branch not minus)
BP (branch plus)   BNP (branch not positive)

$$(27.24)$$

27.6 THE GENERAL PURPOSE REGISTERS

The IBM 370 series computers have 16 general purpose registers numbered 0 through 15 (or hex '0' through hex 'F'). The general registers each contain 32 bits and have two main purposes:

- *Addressing*—All instructions that reference fields in main storage use an address that is contained in a register. Typically, the rightmost 24 bits in the register contain the address, providing a maximum of 2^{24} (16,777,216) addressable locations. More recent computer models provide an extension to this addressing scheme.
- *Binary arithmetic*—The general registers can hold operands which might be used to perform binary arithmetic. For binary values, the leftmost bit is the sign (0 = plus and 1 = minus), while the remaining 31 bits convey the magnitude of binary data.

The programmer designates the specific use of registers—for addressing or for binary arithmetic—and typically reserves registers so designated for the full execution of the program.

27.7 BASE/DISPLACEMENT ADDRESSING

All instructions that reference data in main storage use a **base address** that is contained in a register. Technically, a register used to contain a base address is called a **base register,** and contains the starting point for a 4K area of main storage. The registers normally available as base registers are 3 through 12.

The data field addressed is at a specified number of bytes from the base address starting point; this distance is its **displacement.** The combination of base address plus displacement provides a unique address in main storage for data fields.

This feature facilitates relocating programs. Since a base address can theoretically contain almost any value, a program can be located almost anywhere in main storage. All data in the program is described *relative* to this starting point of the program regardless of the actual address of the starting point.

For simplicity, assume that the assembled program shown in Figure 27.2 resides in main storage beginning at location 10000. (Since supervisor programs are large, a program would normally begin at a higher address.) Within the program, every location is relative to the starting byte. Thus, a byte that has a displacement of 56 bytes from 10000 is at location 10056, and a byte with a displacement of 1525 bytes from 10000 is at location 11525.

All addressing of main storage locations is by means of the starting position (base address) and the distance from

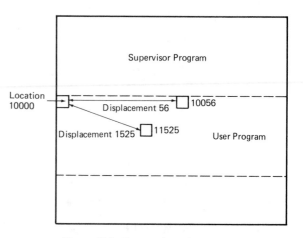

Figure 27.2. Program in main storage.

that position (displacement). When the assembled program is loaded in main storage for execution, a special instruction, **BALR**, loads the starting address into a designated register. As stated above, regardless of the actual starting address, all locations within the program are described relative to this address in the *base* register.

Here are some likely questions:

1. What determines where the program is to load in main storage?

   When one submits the job control statement to execute (the statement varies by operating system, but will resemble // **EXEC**), the supervisor loads the assembled program into main storage. The program may have been just assembled and is waiting on disk for execution, or it may be permanently catalogued on disk in object code. Either way, the supervisor loads the program into an available area (partition) in main storage.

2. How does the program know the starting address?

   The supervisor keeps track of where it loads a program, and inserts the starting address ("load point") in a special piece of hardware named the *program status word (PSW)*. The program automatically begins execution at the address designated in the PSW, and the system always automatically stores in the PSW the address of the next instruction to be executed.

   In an assembly language program, one of the first executable instructions is always **BALR**, as shown:

10	16	
BALR	3,0	(27.25)

   The instruction reads as follows: load the address of the next instruction (stored in the PSW) into register 3. In this case, we want register 3 to be a base register. The zero in the operand is unused by the operation.

3. How does the program know the displacement for the data in the program?

   The assembler has translated the original symbolic statements into object code, and since the assembler determines the length of each instruction and data field, it knows their relative position in the program. For each instruction that requires data in main storage, the assembler inserts this displacement as part of the object code instruction.

Example of an Assembled Program

Figure 27.3 illustrates a skeleton disk operating system (DOS) assembly program consisting of seven statements. The program contains two fields defined as **HDGSAVE** and **HDGOUT**, and has instructions to initialize a base register and to move the contents of **HDGSAVE** to **HDGOUT**. The heading across the top means the following:

LOC (for location) indicates the relative location of an instruction or declarative from the start of the listing.

LOC	OBJECT CODE	ADDR1	ADDR2	STMT	SOURCE STATEMENT		
				1		PRINT	ON,NOGEN
000000				3	PROG01	START	
000000	0530			4		BALR	3,0
			00002	5		USING	*,3
000002	D207 300E 3006	00010	00008	7		MVC	HDGOUT,HDGSAVE
				8	*	.	
				9	*	.	
				10	*	.	
000008	C1C3C540C3D6D9D7			11	HDGSAVE	DC	CL8'ACE CORP'
000010	4040404040404040			12	HDGOUT	DC	CL8' '
			00000	14		END	PROG01

Figure 27.3. Example of an assembled program.

The hex number refers to the leftmost byte. This value is not the displacement, although it has a relationship.

OBJECT CODE shows the actual object code that the assembler generates for instructions and for the hex contents of a DC.

ADDR1 and ADDR2 are only documentation and show the programmer the location (under LOC) of the operands for instructions.

STMT provides the statement number that the assembler has generated for each instruction and declarative. Lines 6 and 13 do not show (i.e., print) numbers or statements because they contained commands that told the assembler to space a line (a SPACE statement beginning in column 10 of the source program).

SOURCE STATEMENT lists the source program that the programmer wrote and submitted for assembly.

A detailed explanation of each statement by number follows:

1 PRINT instructs the assembler what print functions to perform during assembly. ON specifies that a listing is required, and NOGEN tells the assembler to omit showing the generated code for macro instructions (this program contains no macros). (For macros themselves, see Section 27.9.)

3 The START statement tells the assembler that this is the start of a program named PROG01. Like PRINT, START generates no object code.

4 BALR is the instruction that, when assembled and executed, loads register 3 with the base address for the program. As shown to the left on the illustrated printout, the machine object code for this instruction (05 30) is 2 bytes in length. (There is 1 hex digit for each nibble of machine code produced.)

5 USING is a message to the assembler that the program is to use register 3 as a base register. One may have expected the assembler to deduce this fact from the BALR instruction preceding, but BALR can be used in a program in other places and for other reasons. The BALR/USING combination found here is the common beginning instruction of an assembler program. They both must specify the same register, although not necessarily register 3. The asterisk (*) in the USING statement tells the assembler to begin assigning register 3 as a base register from this point on. USING, like START, generates no object code; both are called pseudos.

7 The purpose of the MVC is to move (copy) the contents of HDGSAVE into HDGOUT. Note that the

MVC instruction begins at location 000002, since the BALR object code is 2 bytes long. The object code for MVC consists of 6 bytes.

8, 9, and 10 contain an asterisk in column 1 to indicate that the line is a comment only. An actual program would contain more instructions here.

11 HDGSAVE begins at location 000008 with its contents shown to the left.

12 HDGOUT begins at location 000010 with its contents shown to the left.

14 END PROG01 tells the assembler that this is the last statement of the program named PROG01. The operand PROG01 also serves notice that when the assembled program begins execution, it is to start at the location named PROG01. Since START at that location generates no object code, the first executable instruction is BALR.

Assembly Steps

During assembly, the assembler converts the instruction BALR 3,0 to 2 byte object code as 05 30. USING tells the assembler: from this point (0002) during assembly, use register 3 as a base register. The assembler knows that MVC generates a 6 byte object code instruction. The next statement is DC at 008 for SS and at 0010 for HDGOUT (note that hex 8 plus hex 8 = hex 10). The displacement of HDGSAVE from the USING statement (0002) is 6 bytes, and the displacement of HDGOUT is 14 (hex 'E') bytes.

The object code for the MVC follows:

D207 300E 3006 (the blank spaces are inserted for readabili

- D2 is the machine code for MVC.
- 07 represents the length of operand 1 (HDGOUT), which is actually 8 bytes—the assembler deducts 1 and stores the "length" as 7. For MVC, the length of operand 1 governs the number of bytes moved.
- 300E represents operand 1 (HDGOUT) and consists of base register 3 and displacement 00E.
- 3006 represents operand 2 (HDGSAVE) and consists of base register 3 and displacement 006.

Execution Steps

For execution, only the object code (shown under OBJECT CODE) loads into main storage. Let's say that the program loads beginning at location 10000. The BALR instruction (0530) occupies bytes 10000 and 10001, the

MVC (D2) begins at 10002, HDGSAVE at 10008, and HDGOUT at 10010.:

```
0530D2073006300EC1C3C540C3D6D9D74040404040404040
  |     |        |           |
10000 10002    10008       10010
```

(27.26)

On execution, beginning at 10000, BALR loads the address of the next instruction (10002) into register 3. The computer then executes the MVC (D2) instruction by first combining the base and displacement for each operand (contents of register 3 plus displacement):

	Operand 1	Operand 2
Base register 3	10002	10002
Displacement	006	00E
Effective address	10008	10010

Consequently, the instruction moves the contents beginning at 10010 to 10008. The computer adds 1 to the length (07) (it was deducted during assembly) and moves 8 bytes in total. Note that the program is incomplete. Although BALR and MVC would execute, there is no executable instruction following MVC; such a program would "bomb." Note also that a program that exceeds more than 4K bytes in size would have to define and load more than one base register.

27.8 INSTRUCTION FORMATS

Instructions have specific purposes and are classified according to how they process data. There are five main instruction formats:

1. *Register to register (RR) format.* RR format processes data only in registers. Although the instruction itself will reside in main storage, its operands reference data in registers. The BALR illustrated earlier is an RR format instruction. Other examples are the following:

```
1          10        16
           LR        6,8
           AR        9,5
```

The LR (load register) instruction loads (or copies) the contents of register 8 into register 6; register 8 is unchanged. The AR (add register) instruction adds the contents of register 5 to register 9; this addition is performed as binary arithmetic in terms of data con-

tent and sign. Register 5 is unchanged by the operation.

2. and 3. *Register to storage (RS)* and *Register to indexed-storage (RX) formats.* The RS and RX formats are used to process data between registers and main storage. In the following example of RX format instructions, CVB converts packed data into binary format in register 12, and CVD converts binary data in register 10 into packed format in main storage:

```
1                10              16
                 CVB             12,PACKFLD
                 LR              10,12
                 CVD             10,PACKFLD
                 . . .
PACKFLD          DC              PL8 '12345'
```

(27.28)

Both CVB and CVD require that the packed field be 8 bytes in length.

4. *Storage-to-storage (SS) format.* SS format processes data only in main storage. Keep in mind that although the instruction and the referenced data are in main storage, the base address is in a register. Examples of SS format instructions used earlier are MVC, CLC, ZAP, AP, and SP.

5. *Storage-immediate (SI) format.* SI format consists of one reference to an address in main storage and a 1 byte "immediate" constant. The following example moves a dollar sign to a field named DOLLARPR:

```
1                10              16
                 MVI             DOLLARPR,C '$'
                 ...
DOLLARPR         DS              CL1
```

(28.29)

Since immediate operands are restricted to 1 byte, SI format is of somewhat limited use.

27.9 INPUT/OUTPUT AND I/O MACROS

All input/output is controlled by the supervisor program. To perform an I/O operation, a user program has to deliver information to the supervisor as to the kind of operation and data that is to be transmitted. High level languages such as COBOL and PL/I handle most of the complexity behind the scenes. But assembly, being closer to machine language, requires more concise coding to define and perform I/O operations. Since these operations are quite complex, assembly language comes supplied with a number of powerful macroinstructions.

A **macroinstruction** (or **macro**) is a high level statement that causes the assembler to generate one or more assembly instructions. There are two types of macros for assembler input/output operations:

- *File definition macros*—define the file (or data set) that is to be processed. The definition may include, for example, the name of the file, the length of records, the actual device used, and for input files being read sequentially, the end of file address for the exit routine. Under OS the file definition macro is a DCB, and under DOS it is a DTF. Examples follow:

OS:

```
     1       1 0   16
     filename  DCB   . . . (entries)
```

DOS:

```
     1           10      16
     filename    DTFSD   . . . (entries)
```

(27.30)

Any valid descriptive name, such as FILEIN, is suitable for the name of a file.

- *Imperative macros*—initiate I/O operations and include OPEN, CLOSE, GET, and PUT. OPEN makes a file available to a program. CLOSE terminates use of a file and makes it available to other programs in the system. Examples for OS and DOS are:

OS:

```
10    16

OPEN   (FILEIN,(INPUT),FILEPR,(OUTPUT)

CLOSE (FILEIN,,FILEPR)
```

DOS:

```
        10      16
        OPEN    FILEIN,FILEPR
        CLOSE   FILEIN,FILEPR       (27.31)
```

Note that OS OPEN includes a parameter to indicate whether the file is to be used for INPUTor OUTPUT. OS CLOSE does not require a repetition of the parameter, but the two commas indicate that the INPUT parameter is omitted.

The GET macro causes the supervisor to read a record from an input device into a designated area in the program. The PUT macro causes the supervisor to write a record from an area in the program onto an output device. Examples for both OS and DOS follow:

```
1            10        16

RECORDIN   DS     CL80   (input area)
RECORDPR   DS     CL133  (print area)

   . . .

           GET    FILEIN,RECORDIN
           PUT    FILEPR,RECORDPR
```

(27.32)

The GET operation reads a record into RECORDIN and the PUT operation prints a record from RECORDPR.

The following section describes a program using OS to read input records, to move employee name and address to a print area, and to print records. The program continues processing until all input has been processed.

Example OS Program

OS assembler requires a special macro at the beginning of program execution (see statement 2 in Figure 27.4):

$$\text{SAVE} \quad (14,12) \qquad (27.33)$$

SAVE stores the contents of registers 14 through 12 for the supervisor (the operation wraps around register 15 then 0). Register 13 serves a special purpose for linking between programs—in this case between the supervisor program and this program. Statement 5 stores the contents of register 13 in SAVEAREA+4. Statement 33 shows SAVEAREA defined as 18 fullwords (a fullword is a 4 byte field), and the 4 byte contents of register 13 is stored beginning at the fourth byte:

```
SAVEAREA: |  |  |  |  |x|x|x|x|  |  |  |  |  | . . .
          0  1  2  3  4  5  6  7 etc . . .
```

(27.34)

Statement 6 loads the *address* of SAVEAREA in register 13. Various I/O macros will use register 13 for linking back to the supervisor for input/output processing.

For termination of program execution and return to the supervisor, statement 15 loads the four bytes from SAVEAREA+4 back into register 13 (this is the saved address that was in register 13 on entry to the program). The RETURN macro in statement 16 then restores the other values from SAVEAREA back into the registers as they were on entry to the program. In this way, the pro-

```
 1 EXOS      START

 2           SAVE   (14,12)                SAVE REGS FOR SUPERVISOR

 3           BALR   3,0                    INITIALIZE BASE REGISTER
 4           USING  *,3

 5           ST     13,SAVEAREA+4          SAVE ADDRESSES FOR RETURN
 6           LA     13,SAVEAREA            *   TO SUPERVISOR

 7           OPEN   (FILEIN,(INPUT),FILEPR,(OUTPUT))

 8 A10READ   GET    FILEIN,RECORDIN        READ
 9           MVC    EMPNOPR,EMPNOIN        MOVE INPUT FIELDS
10           MVC    EMPNAMPR,EMPNAMIN      *   TO OUTPUT
11           MVC    EMPADRPR,EMPADRIN      *   AREA
12           PUT    FILEPR,RECORDPR        PRINT LINE
13           B      A10READ                READ NEXT RECORD

14 B10END    CLOSE  (FILEIN,,FILEPR)
15           L      13,SAVEAREA+4          END-OF-JOB,  RETURN
16           RETURN (14,12)                *   TO SUPERVISOR

17 FILEIN    DCB    BLKSIZE=80,            DEFINE                    +
                    DDNAME=SYSIN,          *   INPUT                 +
                    DEVD=DA,               *   FILE                  +
                    DSORG=PS,                                        +
                    EODAD=B10END,                                    +
                    MACRF=(GM)

18 RECORDIN  DS     0CL80                  INPUT RECORD:
19 EMPNOIN   DS     CL05                   *   EMP NUMBER
20 EMPNAMIN  DS     CL20                   *   EMP NAME
21 EMPADRIN  DS     CL40                   *   EMP ADDRESS
22           DS     CL15                   *   UNUSED

23 FILEPR    DCB    BLKSIZE=133,           DEFINE                    +
                    DDNAME=SYSPRINT,       *   PRINT                 +
                    DEVD=DA,               *   FILE                  +
                    DSORG=PS,                                        +
                    MACRF=(PM),                                      +
                    RECFM=FM

24 RECORDPR  DS     0CL133                 PRINT AREA :
25           DC     XL01'09'               *   CONTROL CHAR
26           DC     CL05' '                *
27 EMPNOPR   DS     CL05                   *   EMP NUMBER
28           DC     CL05' '                *
29 EMPNAMPR  DS     CL20                   *   EMP NAME
30           DC     CL05' '                *
31 EMPADRPR  DS     CL40                   *   EMP ADDRESS
32           DC     CL52' '                *

33 SAVEAREA  DS     18F                    REGISTER SAVE AREA

34           END    EXOS
```

Figure 27.4. Sample OS program.

gram has saved the contents of the supervisor's registers, used the registers for its own purposes, and on termination restored the supervisor's registers and returned control to the supervisor.

The DCB macros (statements 17 and 23) define the data sets for input and output. Each parameter for a DCB data set provides special information about the data set. Note that except for the last one, a comma follows each parameter, and a continuation character (in this case a +) in column 72 signifies continuation onto the next line.

The DCB for the input data set, FILEIN, contains the following entries:

BLKSIZE = 80 means that each input data block is 80 bytes.
DDNAME = SYSIN says that the "data definition name" is the system address SYSIN.
DEVD = DA signifies that the input device is "direct access," or disk.
DSORG = PS means that input organization is "physical sequential" that is, a sequential file.
EODAD = B10END assigns the program address where the system is to link when it encounters the end of the input data set (see statement 14).
MACRF = (GM) means that the GET is to use "get and move" to read an input record into a workarea (in this case, RECORDIN defined in statement 18).

The DCB for the output printer data set, FILEPR, contains the following entries:

BLKSIZE, DEVD, and DSORG serve the same purpose as the definitions for the input data set.
DDNAME = SYSPRINT says that the system printer is the device for the data set.
MACRF = (PM) means that the PUT is to use "put and move" to write from a work area (in this case, RECORDPR defined in statement 24).
RECFM = FM describes the records. F means "fixed length" and M stands for "machine code," the code for the normal IBM 370 print control character to handle printer spacing.

Concerning the last parameter, statement 25 defines the print control character (hex '09') as the first byte in the print area. This character (which does not itself print) causes the printer to print and space one line. Other hex characters perform such operations as to eject to a new page or space without printing.

27.10 BINARY OPERATIONS

All binary arithmetic is performed in the general registers. For this purpose, there is a special instruction set to convert packed data to binary (CVB) and to convert binary to packed (CVD), to process binary data in registers, and to transfer binary data between registers and main storage. Binary arithmetic is particularly efficient on a computer and there are times when an operation is better done in binary or can only be done in binary.

Definition of Binary Data

Binary data can be defined as either halfword (H) or as fullword (F). *Halfword* format consists of 2 bytes (16 bits) with a maximum value of 32,767. *Fullword* format consists of 4 bytes (32 bits) with a maximum value of 2,147,483,647. For efficiency, the assembler aligns halfword format on a storage address evenly divisible by 2 and fullword on an address divisible by 4. This alignment was more important on earlier IBM 360 series computer models. Examples:

1	10	16	
HALFCTR	DC	H'25'	(defines halfword)
FULLCTR	DC	F'25'	(defines fullword)

(27.35)

The operand field contains a decimal value, in this case '25', which the assembler converts to binary 11001. Representation of the binary and hex contents is as follows:

Binary:

HALFCTR: 0000 0000 0001 1001

FULLCTR: 0000 0000 0000 0000 0000 0000 0001 1001

Hexadecimal:

	HALFCTR:	0019	
	FULLCTR:	00000019	(27.36)

Binary Operations

Character data and packed data both have their own set of instructions. For example, MVC and CLC process character data, and ZAP and AP process packed data. Binary data requires its own special instructions as shown in the incomplete list below. Transfer instructions are especially useful for saving the contents of a register, using the register for another purpose, and reloading the register with the original value.

10   16   Format:

Transfer of Binary Data:

LR	reg-a,reg-b	RR	Load content of reg-b into reg-a.
L	reg,fullword	RX	Load binary fullword into register.
LH	reg,halfword	RX	Load binary halfword into register.
ST	reg,fullword	RX	Store register into fullword.
STH	reg,halfword	RX	Store rightmost 2 bytes of register in halfword.

Comparison of Binary Data:

CR	reg-a,reg-b	RR	Compare contents of reg-a to reg-b.
C	reg,fullword	RX	Compare register to fullword.
CH	reg,halfword	RX	Compare rightmost 2 bytes of register to halfword.

Binary Arithmetic:

AR	reg-a,reg-b	RR	Add contents of reg-b to reg-a.
A	reg,fullword	RX	Add fullword to register.
AH	reg,halfword	RX	Add halfword to register.

Other operations include subtract, multiply, divide, and shifting bits in registers left and right.

Example of Binary Operations

The example shown below adds the sum of the digits from 1 through 10, as $1+2+3+ \ldots +10$. The program uses a loop that executes ten times—it adds 1 to register 7 repetitively until reaching 10.

1	10	16	
	SR	7,7	Clear reg. 7 to zero.
	SR	8,8	Clear reg. 8 to zero.

LOOP	AH	7,HALFONE	Add 1 to reg. 7.
	AR	8,7	Add content of reg. 7 to reg. 8.
	CH	7,HALFTEN	Reg. 7 contains '10'?
	BNE	LOOP	* No—continue loop.
	STH	8,HALFSUM	* Yes—store sum of digits.

HALFONE	DC	H'1'
HALFTEN	DC	H'10'
HALFSUM	DC	H'0'

In the loop, the AR instruction accumulates the sum of the digits $1+2+3 \ldots$. On termination of the loop, the STH instruction stores the contents of register 8 (which is 55) into HALFSUM. Actually, these values are in binary format, so that decimal 10 is binary 1010, and 55 is binary 110111.

Other instructions that process binary data (either algebraic or logical) include Boolean operations (AND, OR, EXCLUSIVE OR); translating (TR); scanning for unique characters (TRT); and decrementing the contents of registers (BCT, BCTR, BXLE and BXH), often used in table handling.

REFERENCES

Abel, Peter, *Programming Assembler Language*. Reston, VA: Reston Publishing Co., 1979.

Burian, Barbara J., *A Simplified Approach to S/370 Assembly Language Programming*. Englewood Cliffs, NJ: Prentice-Hall, 1977.

Chapin, Ned, *360/370 Programming in Assembly Language*. New York: McGraw-Hill Book Co., 1973.

Tuggle, Sharon K., *Assembly Language Programming; System/360 and 370*. Chicago: Science Research Associates, 1975.

Yarmish, R., and J. Yarmish, *Assembly Language Fundamentals*. Reading, MA: Addison-Wesley, 1975.

28
Job Control Language

Wayne Clary

Data Systems Associates

28.1 INTRODUCTION

Job Control Language, **JCL,** is not a programming language; it is a language to direct the operating system in general and the job manager in particular about what programs to run for one and in what sequence they are to run. It describes the devices to be used, the volumes mounted on the devices and the file to be processed. It gives all the particulars about a job.

In the mid 1960s, a new concept developed that would forever change the way we view computers. That concept is the **operating system (OS).** Briefly, an operating system is a collection of computer programs to control the computer's resources. Application programs are both read into the system and are executed under the direct control of the operating system. Job Control Language is our means of communicating with the OS. Through a series of control statements in 80 column card format, JCL tells the OS of job requirements. There are as many job control languages as there are operating systems. Some use simple one line commands to run a particular program or scratch (delete) a certain file, while others are complex and require extensive study and experience to master. This chapter deals primarily with one of the more complex of the current job control languages, that for the IBM 360-370 series of computers (330X and 4300 also) operating under the IBM full operating system. Its abbreviated name is **OS JCL,** or simply **JCL** in this chapter.

28.2 OS JCL: A BASIC SUBSET

This sections examines a few of the more important JCL statements, a "subset" of the overall language.

With experience in a programming language such as COBOL, FORTRAN, PL/I, or assembly, one can read and write data records, manipulate data fields, and control the flow of programs by coding certain instructions in the language. But JCL is a different kind of language: it doesn't allow input or output, manipulation of data, or control of program flow. Instead, it is *a collection of job specifications given to the operating system.* Through JCL, the user tells the OS what a job requires in terms of computer resources and OS services. The information given to the OS is classified into information about

1. The job as a whole and its relationship to other jobs currently in the system;
2. Each program (step) which comprises the job;
3. Each file that each program in the job will read and write.

To the OS, a job is a collection of one or more related **job steps;** a job step is the execution of one program. Each job step may access several files. In later sections in this chapter, we will see that the **JOB** statement provides job information, the **EXEC** statement provides job step information, and the **DD** (data definition) statement provides information about the input and output files.

28.3 CONTROL STATEMENT FORMAT

Job control language statements are read into the system as 80 character records. This length allows JCL statements to be read as punchcard input, although they may be read from any type of input device including magnetic tape, disk, and keyboard terminals.

The first two positions of a JCL statement must be // (slash-slash). This identifies the statement to the reader/interpreter program of the OS as a JCL statement and distinguishes it from data that may be in the input stream. The **delimiter statement** (to be described later) is the only exception to this rule. To enter this statement, /* (slash-asterisk) is coded in the first two positions. Positions 3 through 71 contain the name, operation, operand, and comments fields. These four fields are discussed individually just below. Position 72 can be a continuation indicator if a single control statement continues from one line to the next. Finally, positions 73 through 80 can be identification or sequence numbers. In practice, these last eight columns are usually left blank with two exceptions: (1) when the JCL is a deck of cards that may be dropped (so that the cards may be put back into sequence manually); and (2) when the JCL is cataloged in a procedure library—then sequence numbers enable the user to update individual statements. In both of these cases, sequence numbers are keyed into positions 73 through 80.

The **name** field identifies the name of a job, job step, or file. It is optional on most statement formats, but if coded, it must be placed immediately after the slash-slash with no intervening spaces. If coded, the name field must contain from one to eight letters, numerals, or the special characters #, @, and $ (known as **national characters**). The first character of the name field must be an alphabetic or national character. Figure 28.1 shows some valid and invalid name field examples.

The **operation** field of a control statement specifies the type of operation. For example, JOB is the operation of a job statement, EXEC is the operation of an execute statement, and DD is the operation of a data definition statement. It must follow the name field with at least one separating space. If the name field is omitted, the operation field must be the first field after the slash-slash, with at lease one separating space.

Valid name fields:

//PAYFILE
//EDITPROG
//UPDATE
//$NUMCALC

Invalid name fields:

//107RPT	Name begins with a numeric character
//UDATERPTS	More than eight characters
//DATA/IN	Illegal character: /
// RPT1	Space between the // and the name

Figure 28.1. Valid and invalid name fields.

The **operand** field is the one to which most of this chapter refers. It is within this field that the job, step and file specifications are made by means of parameters coded in free form, separated by commas. Some of the parameters are *keyword* parameters. That is, the parameter name and its value are furnished in that order, separated by = as, for example,

$$UNIT = SYSDA \qquad (28.1)$$

where the reader/interpreter recognizes the key name UNIT and associates the value SYSDA with that parameter. Other parameters or subparameters are *positional* and the values must be listed in a fixed order as with

$$DISP = (OLD, CATLG, DELETE) \qquad (28.2)$$

In this case, the position of the value within the parentheses is significant to its meaning. If one of the values is to default to a system defined value, it is coded like this:

$$DISP = (OLD,, DELETE) \qquad (28.3)$$

The two commas togther indicate the absence of the second value. If only the first value is to be included, the boundaries and commas are not required, as in this example:

$$DISP = OLD \qquad (28.4)$$

In this case, the reader/interpreter assumes that OLD is the first value, and since there are no commas following, it assumes default values for the remaining parameters.

The *comments* field is optional and may contain any information which will help to document that statement. Later, the *comment statement* will be introduced; it documents larger areas of JCL coding, while the comments field on each statement is useful for documenting one or two lines of JCL coding.

Continuing Job Control Statements

If a complete JCL statement does not fit in columns 3 through 71, or if it is desirable to divide the parameters onto more than one line for readability, the statement can continue on the next card or line. To ensure such a transition, one should first find a convenient, logical place to break off between two parameters or subparameters; then, second, code a comma to indicate that another parameter or subparameter follows; and, finally, continue the statement on the next line.

Figure 28.2 contains examples of continuation lines. The first example shows how to continue operand parameters, and the second example shows how to continue statements with a comments field. Notice that a nonblank

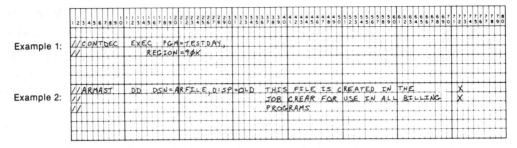

Figure 28.2. Continuing job control statements.

character *must* be coded in position 72 to continue a comments field legally; this continuation character is optional when continuing operand fileds. A JCL continuation statement with parameters must begin before position 17 or the statement is treated as a comment.

28.4 THE SYNTAX OF THE LANGUAGE

This section introduces the JCL elements that make up the basis subset of the language—the elementary parameters of the **JOB**, **EXEC**, and **DD** statements, and the comment, delimiter, and null statements will also be surveyed. Together, these elements represent the core content of the language, and they comprise about 90 percent of the JCL needed to process any job on the IBM System/360-370 computers.

The Job Statement

The **JOB** statement identifies the beginning of a job to the reader/interpreter and gives a name to that job. This **job name** is used by the OS to communicate with the operator concerning the job. For example, if one of the steps in a job calls for a magnetic tape, the OS will instruct the operator to mount that tape on a drive and tell him or her that the tape is for the given job.

The **JOB** statement also relates a computer run to an accounting charge out number. Then the computer time for the job can be charged to the department or company responsible for the job by an accounting procedure invoked by the OS. In this regard, a job run for the engineering department of a company will usually have a different account number than a job run for the personnel department. In this chapter's examples, I have used the *accounting information* required by the system on which the examples were tested. If the reader wishes to copy the examples to run on a particular system, it may be necessary to modify the accounting information to conform to the system's installation standards.

Figure 28.3 shows the composite statement structure (or skeleton) of the **JOB** statement. The examples in Figure 28.4 illustrate how acceptable values are coded in the **JOB** statement.

Accounting Information and Programmer-Name Parameters

The first two parameters after the word **JOB** are accounting information and programmer name. They are positional parameters and must be coded in this order. In the examples in Figure 28.4, the accounting information is **HE66YFNH**. This identifies my account on the System/370 I used for testing all of the JCL examples.

Following the accounting information is programmer name. Notice in example 1 of Figure 28.4 that the programmer name is 'MMA-LOWE'. If the name contains special characters, such as the dash, apostrophes are required. If the name contains no special characters except for the period, no apostrophes are required, as shown in example 2. To code embedded spaces in the name as shown in example 3, the apostrophes are required. In addition, if the programmer name contains an apostrophe as part of the name, like O'Reilly, it is necessary to code two consecutive apostrophes as shown in example 4. In a

```
//jobname   JOB   accounting-information,
                  programmer-name,
                  CLASS=job-class,
                  PRTY=priority-number,
                  MSGCLASS=message-class,
                  MSGLEVEL=(statements,messages),
                  REGION=region-sizeK
```

Figure 28.3. **JOB** statement skeleton.

Example 1

```
//PROJECT1 JOB  HE66YFNH,
//               'MMA-LOWE',
//               CLASS=N,
//               MSGLEVEL=1
```

Example 2

```
//PROJECT2 JOB  HE66YFNH,
//               A.D.CLARY,
//               CLASS=D,
//               PRTY=5,
//               MSGCLASS=E,
//               MSGLEVEL=(0,0),
//               REGION=150K
```

Example 3

```
//PROJECT3 JOB  HE66YFNH,
//               'PAT MARTIN',
//               REGION=90K
```

Example 4

```
//PROJECT4 JOB  HE66YFNH,
//               (0''REILLY),
//               CLASS=D
```

Figure 28.4. JOB statement examples.

case like this, the name can be enclosed in parentheses as shown, or apostrophes can be used as in the other examples.

The CLASS and PRTY Parameters

One of the main purposes of an operating system is to apply available central processing unit (CPU) cycles to programs in such a way as to make use of as many cycles as possible. (Briefly, a **CPU cycle** is the amount of time devoted to the execution of one program while another program is waiting for an input/output request to be completed.) Part of this time management by the operating system includes distributing the cycles to the most important jobs first and to the least important jobs last. It is the class (CLASS) and priority (PRTY) parameters of the JOB statement that tell OS into which category a particular program falls.

These two parameters are examples of *installation-dependent* requirements. Technically, CLASS can be any letter from A to O for MFT and MVT operating systems, and any letter from A to Z or the numerals 0 to 9 for VS1 and VS2 operating systems. However, in actual practice, the installation sets certain CLASS codes for the execution of certain types of jobs. For example, an installation could have a standard that says one may only use CLASS=A if a job uses no magnetic tape, writes less than 10,000 lines of printed output, and uses no more than 20 seconds of CPU time.

Similarly, PRTY may be any number from 1 to 13, but in actual practice the use of PRTY is established by the policy of the installation. In many cases, PRTY is omitted and the distribution of CPU cycles is determined by job class only. As a result, jobs in similar classes get equal priority scheduling.

The MSGCLASS Parameter

As a job is executing, the OS puts out **system messages** to tell what is happening in each step. For example, it tells whether a file was kept or deleted after a job step was finished, how long the step took to execute, whether the step was abnormally terminated, and other information that will help to analyze the results of the computer run. Figure 28.5 contains an example of system messages.

```
IEF236I ALLOC. FOR MMASRAT  COB
IEF237I 375   ALLOCATED TO SYSUT1
IEF237I 37A   ALLOCATED TO SYSUT2
IEF237I 37B   ALLOCATED TO SYSUT3
IEF237I 375   ALLOCATED TO SYSUT4
IEF237I 37A   ALLOCATED TO SYSLIN
IEF142I - STEP WAS EXECUTED - COND CODE 0004
IEF285I   SYS80100.T132743.RF108.MMASRAT.SYSUT1      DELETED
IEF285I   VOL SER NOS= VSAM006.
IEF285I   SYS80100.T132743.RF108.MMASRAT.SYSUT2      DELETED
IEF285I   VOL SER NOS= PUB001.
IEF285I   SYS80100.T132743.RF108.MMASRAT.SYSUT3      DELETED
IEF285I   VOL SER NOS= PUB002.
IEF285I   SYS80100.T132743.RF108.MMASRAT.SYSUT4      DELETED
IEF285I   VOL SER NOS= VSAM06.
IEF285I   SYS80100.T132743.RF108.MMASRAT.LOADSET     PASSED
IEF285I   VOL SER NOS= PUB001.
IEF373I STEP /COB    /START 80100.1327
IEF374I STEP /COB    /STOP  80100.1328 CPU   0MIN 03.25SEC STOR VIRT 64K
```

Figure 28.5. OS system messages.

```
MSGLEVEL=(statements,messages)
```

statements   0 = Print only the JOB statement
               1 = Print all JCL statements including statements from
                     cataloged procedures
               2 = Print only the input JCL (excluding cataloged procedures)

messages   0 = Print system messages only if the job abnormally
                     terminates
               1 = Print all system messages every time

Figure 28.6. Valid MSGLEVEL values and their meanings.

The message class parameter (MSGCLASS) is associated with an output writer, a software writing component which, in turn, is associated with a specific output device. Specifying a message class enables routing system messages to a specific printer or other output device. If you omit MSGCLASS, the installation default will apply. Some installations use MSGCLASS to separate system messages from the output of the application programs, while others let the default values take effect so system messages come out before the applications output.

The MSGLEVEL Parameter

This parameter tells the OS which messages to print. The format of the parameter is

$$MSGLEVEL = (statements,messages) \qquad (28.5)$$

where statements refers to coded JCL statements and messages refers to the system output messages generated by the OS. Since the user may not want either the JCL or the messages or neither printed every time the job is run (especially after the system goes into production), you can tell the OS not to print them. Figure 28.6 shows the valid values and their meanings.

If you don't code the MSGLEVEL parameter, the installation default will apply. On the system I am using, the default for MSGLEVEL is (1,1). This means that if I want to see all of the JCL and all of the system messages each time the job is run, I just omit the parameter as shown in examples 3 and 4 of Figure 28.4. If I want to see the system messages, but not the JCL, I will code MSGLEVEL = 0. Since there is no comma, I don't need the parentheses and the OS knows I am referring to the first value in a positional string; for the second value, the system will default to 1. In example 2 of Figure 28.4, I use MSGLEVEL = (0,0) to tell the OS that I want to see (1) only the JOB statement and (2) the system messages only if the job abnormally terminates.

The REGION Parameter

If a system operates under MVT, the user can specify the amount of main storage to be allocated to a job by coding the REGION parameter. In other words, one can override default values regarding the maximum amount of main storage allocated to a program, as in this example:

```
//ACCTJOB JOB HE66YFNH,
          'WAYNE CLARY',
          REGION = 180K      (28.6)
```

Note that the amount of storage is specified in kilobytes (K = 1,024 bytes). The number coded in should be an even number, not to exceed 16383. However, if an odd number is coded, the OS will assume the next higher even number.

If the REGION parameter is coded into the JOB statement, that size can be set for the entire job. If coded into the EXEC statement, the REGION parameter sets the size for that job step only.

28.5 THE EXEC STATEMENT

The execute statement (EXEC) is the operational statement of each job step. An EXEC statement can put precoded JCL statements known as **procedures** into the job stream or it can cause the execution of one program. Since the concept of cataloged procedures is beyond the scope of this introductory treatment, this discussion focuses on the EXEC statement as it causes the execution of one program.

Figure 28.7 shows the statement skeleton for the EXEC

```
//stepname    EXEC  PGM=program-name,
                    PARM=program-parameters,
                    REGION=region-sizeK
```

Figure 28.7. EXEC statement skeleton.

Example 1

```
//REDCTR    EXEC  PGM=EDITPAY,
//                PARM=MOD
```

Example 2

```
//SORTTRAN EXEC  PGM=ADCOST,
//                PARM=(JANUARY 12, 1980),
//                REGION=100K
```

Example 3

```
//UPDATE    EXEC  PGM=PAYUPDT,
//                PARM=(017,019,'+022'),
//                REGION=90K
```

Example 4

```
//PRODRSL   EXEC  PGM=ENG001,
//                REGION=100K
```

Example 5

```
//ACCTSTP   EXEC  PGM=PRODCOST
```

Figure 28.8. EXEC statement examples.

statement. As with the JOB skeleton, the reader will want to refer to it while learning to code the EXEC statement. Figure 28.8 gives coding examples for the EXEC statement.

The PGM Parameter

The EXEC statement identifies the program to be executed in each step. Example 1 of Figure 28.8 causes the execution of a program named EDITPAY; example 2 causes the execution of a program named ADCOST; example 3 causes the execution of a program named PAYUPDT; example 4 causes the execution of a program named ENG001; and example 5 causes the execution of a program named PRODCOST. These programs must be in *load module form*. That is, they must be object programs that have been link edited and are now ready to be executed by the computer.

The PARM Parameter

If a program requires data that can only be obtained at run time, the user can send it that data by coding a PARM parameter in the EXEC statement. If, for example, a program requires a date, that date can go into the PARM parameter and the program will receive it. Of course, the program must be expecting the data and have provisions for receiving it. In COBOL, this is accomplished by coding a linkage section where the data is defined and coding the USING option in the procedure division header. When the program is executed, the information is transferred to the definition area of the linkage section. The same facility is available in PL/I and assembly language.

Example 1 of Figure 28.8 shows a PARM of MOD being sent to the program. Example 2 shows a PARM of JANUARY 12, 1980. Since this PARM contains a special character (the comma), and embedded spaces, it is enclosed in parentheses. Example 3 shows some numbers being sent to the program. In this case, one of the values contains a special character (the plus sign) as a significant part of its value. As a result, it is enclosed in apostrophes. Then, since there are commas in the PARM as separators, parentheses are coded around the entire field.

The REGION Parameter

If a system operates under MVT, the user can specify the amount of main storage to be allocated to the job step. By coding the REGION parameter, one overrides default values regarding the maximum amount of main storage allocated to a program, as in this example:

```
//PROJCOST EXEC PGM=PROJ001,
//                  REGION=150K    (28.7)
```

Here again, as in the REGION parameter of the JOB statement, the amount of storage requested is in kilobytes (1,024 bytes), and the number coded should be even, not to exceed 16383. Again, if you code an odd number, the OS uses the next higher even number. Examples 2, 3, and 4 of Figure 28.8 use the REGION parameter.

28.6 THE DD STATEMENT

Every program usually requires some form of input and output data. After each EXEC statement, it is necessary to define the characteristics of the data required by the program. This is done with the **data definition** (DD) statement. One DD statement is coded for each file which might be used by the program. The DD statement tells the OS the name, status, disposition, location, space requirements and characteristics of the file.

Figure 28.9 illustrates the DD statement skeleton to code the parameters. Presented in this section are the basic parameters and subparameters needed to process jobs with sequential files. Section 28.9 on advanced concepts presents still further DD statement parameters and how to use them.

Format 1:

```
//ddname   DD   DSN=data-set-name,
                DISP=(status,normal-disposition,abnormal-disposition),
                UNIT=device-name or group-name,
                VOL=SER=volume-serial-number,
                SPACE=(unit-of-measure(primary, secondary),RLSE),
                DCB=(LRECL=logical-record-length,BLKSIZE=block-size,
                 RECFM=record-format)
```

Format 2:

```
//ddname   DD   *
```

or

```
//ddname   DD   DATA
```

Format 3:

```
//ddname   DD   SYSOUT=sysout-class
```

Figure 28.9. DD statement skeleton.

Naming a File

In IBM terminology, a file is called a **data set** and each data set must have a unique **data set name.** It may be coded DSN = name or DSNAME = name in the DD statement. The name given to a data set must be unique for a particular volume (a complete disk, tape, reel or other storage unit). In other words, there may be identically named files on two separate volumes, but not on the *same* volume. The name consists of from 1 to 8 alphabetic, numeric, or national characters, and the first character must be alphabetic or national. The OS uses the data set name for all references to the file.

The DD statement that refers to the data set has a name also, *ddname*. In a processing program, one assigns a file to a ddname that is associated with a data set name. In Figure 28.10, the first example contains a portion of a COBOL program—the SELECT statement for a file called PARTFILE. It is assigned to a DD statement named PARTS. This DD statement defines the data set named PTABLE. So the file the OS knows as PTABLE will be processed by the COBOL program as PARTFILE.

The second example shows the relationship between a FORTRAN program and its data set. In FORTRAN the assignment is implied by the coding of a device code in an input/output statement. The third example shows the assignment of a file in PL/I. Finally, the fourth example shows this relationship between an assembler program and a file defined in a DD statement.

A *temporary file* can be identified (meaning the user does not intend to save it when the job is completed) through the coding of two ampersands (**&&**) preceding the data set name, as follows:

$$DSN = \&\&TEMPFILE \qquad (28.8)$$

To illustrate the use of temporary data set names, consider a job that reads input data in one job step, sorts it in the next, and prints it in the last step. In this case, one could use a temporary file to pass the input data to the sort step and another temporary file to pass the sorted data to the print step. Further examples of temporary files will occur later in this chapter.

Status and Disposition of the File (DISP)

The **disposition parameter** (DISP) is composed of three positional subparameters: status, normal disposition, abnormal disposition. The first subparameter, *status,* tells the OS whether the file is (1) a new file being created in this job step (NEW); an existing file to which exclusive access (OLD) is desired; an existing file one wants to access while others may also access it (SHR); or an existing file to which to add records (MOD).

The second subparameter is *normal disposition.* It tells the OS what to do with the file if the job step completes normally. The values this file will accept as code are KEEP, CATLG, DELETE, UNCATLG, and PASS.

Example 1: COBOL

    Source code: `SELECT PARTFILE   ASSIGN TO UT-S-PARTS.`

    JCL: `//PARTS    DD  DSN=PTABLE,`

Example 2: FORTRAN

    Source code: `READ   (5,100) X,Y,Z`

    JCL: `//FT05F001 DD  DSN=PTABLE,`

Example 3: PL/I

    Source code: `OPEN FILE(PARTS) INPUT;`

    JCL: `//PARTS    DD  DSN=PTABLE,`

Example 4: Assembler

    Source code: `PARTFILE   DCB  DDNAME=PARTS,...file description...`

    JCL: `//PARTS    DD  DSN=PTABLE,`

Figure 28.10. The relationship between the source program and the DD statement.

The third subparameter, *abnormal disposition,* tells the OS what to do with the file if the job step abnormally terminates. The values one may code are identical to the values of normal disposition except that PASS is not a valid value.

Figure 28.11 presents a table of valid DISP parameter values. Note the default values. If status is coded as OLD, SHR, or MOD, the default value for normal disposition is KEEP. If status is NEW, the second subparameter (normal disposition) must be coded since there is no default value. The third subparameter (abnormal disposition) will always default to the value one codes for normal disposition. If status is not coded, it will default to NEW. For example, if DISP = (,PASS) is coded, the status is NEW.

Now we will discuss the meaning of each of the DISP parameter values in detail.

Status values.   Coding NEW in the first subparameter of the DISP parameter tells the OS that a new file on the volume specified is being created. As a result, if the OS finds a file on that volume with the same name as the one given the file, it will issue an error message to the effect that there is a duplicate file on the volume.

When OLD is coded in the first subparameter of the DISP parameter, this tells the OS that there is a file on the volume with the name specified in the data set name field. If the OS can't find a file by that name, it will issue a JCL error message that says the file was not found. If the user specifies only data set name and disposition for a file (no VOLUME parameter), thinking that the file was cataloged when it really was not, this same error message will be issued. A disposition status of OLD also tells the OS that exclusive control over the file is required; if another job tries to access the same file, it will have to wait until the current job finishes.

When SHR is coded as the first subparameter, the OS is being told that the file exists on the volume, but one does *not* need exclusive control over it (SHR means "share," so more than one program can have access to the

Status	Normal disposition	Abnormal disposition
NEW	KEEP	KEEP
	CATLG	CATLG
	PASS	DELETE
	DELETE	
OLD	KEEP	KEEP
SHR	CATLG	CATLG
MOD	PASS	DELETE
	DELETE	UNCATLG
	UNCATLG	

Note: Default values are underlined. The abnormal disposition defaults to the value coded for the normal disposition.

Figure 28.11. Valid DISP parameter values and default values.

file concurrently). If the OS can't find the file, it will send a JCL error message. One should code **SHR** when accessing a file of general interest, such as a program library, unless updating that file.

When **MOD** is coded, the OS is being told that the user wants to write on an existing file. If the OS can't find the file on the volume specified, a data-set-not-found message will be issued. If the OS does find the file on the volume, it will pass over all the records of the file and prepare the file for processing at the end of the previous data. Then, when the user performs an output operation in the program, the new records will be added at the end of the existing records.

Disposition values. KEEP tells the OS to save the file and make it available for later retrieval, but not to keep track of where the file is kept. As a result, a request to retrieve a file that has been kept in this manner must provide the OS with the data set name, the type of hardware unit, and the volume serial number of the volume where the file resides. In other words, the programmer keeps track of the unit and volume information concerning the file. This type of disposition is required for **ISAM** files that are created via the use of more than one **DD** statement (discussed in a later section). In addition, if several files are to have the same name, each residing on a different volume, one must code **KEEP** as the disposition.

CATLG tells the OS to save the file and enter its name into a **catalog** for future requests. In the catalog, the OS keeps the name, the type of hardware unit, the volume serial number, and the characteristics of the file. As a result, when a subsequent request is made for the file, only the data set name and disposition are required. The OS finds the data set name in the catalog that refers it to the correct volume where the file resides. The difference between **KEEP** and **CATLG** is that a "kept" file is merely preserved for later access, while a "cataloged" file is not only preserved but its name is added to a catalog for easy retrieval without the JCL programmer having to specify the location of the file.

DELETE tells the OS to remove all references to the file and make it unavailable for future requests. This includes removing its name from the catalog if it was previously cataloged. A request to retrieve a file that has been deleted will result in a JCL error stating that the file was not found.

UNCATLG tells the OS that the file had been previously cataloged and now its name is to be removed from the catalog, but the file itself is to be kept. As a result,

future requests for the file must specify the data set name, type of hardware unit, and volume serial number, since it has been kept while not cataloged. The difference between **DELETE** and **UNCATLG** is that when a file is uncataloged, its name is removed from the catalog but not deleted; but when a file is deleted, it is also uncataloged.

PASS tells the OS to hold the file temporarily until a subsequent job step uses the file and gives it a final disposition. If no final disposition is given, or if no subsequent job step requests the file, it will be deleted at the completion of the job. To access a passed file in a later job step, one only need to code the data set name and the disposition status of **OLD**. Note in Figure 28.11 that **PASS** can be coded only for the normal disposition subparameter; it is not valid for abnormal disposition.

The Location of the File (UNIT and VOLUME)

If an output file is being created, the OS must be told where to put it; if an existing file that has not been cataloged is being accessed, the OS must be told where it resides. The **UNIT** parameter tells the OS what kind of hardware device the volume containing the file requires for mounting. The **VOLUME** parameter tells the OS the serial number of the volume in which the file is to be placed, or from which it is to be retrieved.

The UNIT parameter. The unit can be specified in one of three ways. First, one may code a unit address identifying a particular input/output device. However, this method is not recommended since it can interfere with the automatic functions of the OS, so it is not covered here.

Second, one can specify the unit number of the device—for instance, 3330, 2314, 3350, 3380, and so forth. Although examples are presented in this manner here, it is necessary to note that many installations do not allow the user to specify actual device types. Each installation should be checked to determine its standards in this respect.

Third (and most common), the user can code a **group name** that includes all devices of a particular kind. Group names are given to categories of devices at system generation time by the installation system programming. Usually, names such as **DISKA**, **TAPE**, **DRUM**, **SYSDA**, and **MICR** are used to indicate such groups of associated devices. Here again, each installation should be checked to determine the group names it will accept for the devices to be used.

The VOLUME parameter. The VOLUME parameter has several subparameters, but in this introductory treatment only one will be covered—the most common one, the SER subparameter. It may be coded VOLUME = SER = serial number or VOL = SER = serial number; in either case, the serial number identifies the storage volume. This subparameter assigns an output file to a specific storage volume or tells the OS the volume serial number of the storage volume in which an uncataloged input file resides. This storage volume may be a disk pack, a tape reel, a drum or some other unique storage entity.

Allocating Space to a File (SPACE)

When a job requests a direct access device on which to place a new file, the OS must be told how much direct access space is to be allocated to that file by means of the SPACE parameter on the DD statement. There are four basic subparameters of the SPACE parameter: unit of measure, primary quantity, secondary quantity, and the release (RLSE) option. These are *positional* subparameters, so they do not need key word identifiers.

Unit of measure. You may allocate space for a file in cylinders, tracks, or blocks of data. Figure 28.12 shows examples of each unit of measure. Examples 1 and 4 show the allocation in cylinders. Examples 2 and 5 show the allocation in tracks. Examples 3 and 6 show the al-

Example 1
```
    //                  SPACE=(CYL,(1,1),RLSE)
```
Example 2
```
    //                  SPACE=(TRK,(5,2),RLSE)
```
Example 3
```
    //                  SPACE=(960,(3,3),RLSE)
```
Example 4
```
    //                  SPACE=(CYL,(10,2))
```
Example 5
```
    //                  SPACE=(TRK,5,RLSE)
```
Example 6
```
    //                  SPACE=(1400,10)
```

Figure 28.12. Examples of the SPACE parameter.

location in blocks of data: 960 byte blocks in example 3 and 1,400 byte blocks in example 6.

Primary and secondary allocations. As a general rule, the second subparameter (primary allocation) should be the user estimated amount of space the file will require. In example 1 of Figure 28.12, the file should take one cylinder; in example 2, the file should take five tracks; in example 3, the file should take three blocks of 960 bytes; and so on.

However, estimates can be wrong and file sizes do change. As a result, the *secondary allocation* allows for extensions or *extents* to the primary allocation. Then, if the primary allocation of space is not large enough for the file, the OS makes the secondary allocation. If this still is not enough space for the file, the secondary allocation is repeated until 16 total extents have been allocated. After that, if there still is not enough space for the file, the job will terminate abnormally.

In example 1, if one cylinder cannot hold the file, another cylinder will be allocated. If that is not enough space for the entire file, another cylinder will be allocated, and so on until 15 such secondary allocations of one cylinder have been made. So the total possible allocation for the file in example 1 is 16 cylinders.

Similarly, in example 2, if the file cannot be stored in the primary allocation of five tracks, additional tracks will be allocated (two at a time), until a total of 15 two track areas have been added to the primary amount. So the total possible allocation for this file is 36 tracks.

The same holds true when the allocation is made in blocks of data. Example 3 shows a primary allocation of three blocks of 960 bytes. If the file is larger than this area, space to hold three more blocks of data is allocated until a total of 15 secondary extents are allocated. So the total capacity of the file illustrated in example 3 is 48 blocks of 960 bytes.

Notice that if both the primary and secondary allocations are coded, they must be enclosed in parentheses. If the secondary allocation is omitted, as in examples 5 and 6, this set of parentheses is not required.

RLSE option. Direct access space is a system resource, just as CPU time is. As a result, the amount of disk or drum space the files use is a factor in calculating the cost of an application. It is therefore wise to use any available means to reduce the amount of unused direct access space. The RLSE option tells the OS to free unused space in the allocated area, making it available for use by other jobs. In other words, after the completion of a job step that has allocated and used direct access space, the OS deallocates any space that has not been used by the records in the file. For instance, example 2 in Figure 28.12 shows a space request for five tracks of primary storage, and up to 15 additional extents of two tracks. Suppose, then, that after a job step is completed, the actual number of tracks required by the file is only two. The RLSE option tells the OS to release the extra three tracks of primary storage back to the system resource pool.

If RLSE is not coded, the unused space at the end of a file will remain with that file, unavailable for other jobs. As a result, the cost of that additional space is added to the cost of storing the file. Notice in examples 4 and 6 that the RLSE option is not coded. In this case, you close the parentheses directly behind the primary and secondary allocation.

Describing the Characteristics of a File (DCB)

The **data control block** (DCB) parameter provides the information used by the OS to perform some of its data management services. Certain subparameters of the DCB are required for almost every file; others are optional depending on the access method and the application. In this section, the discussion concerns the three basic subparameters required for all files: logical record length (LRECL), block size (BLKSIZE), and record format (RECFM).

The data control block represents a table of information about the file you are using in your program. The entries in this table come from three sources: (1) a program, (2) the JCL, and (3) OS default values. As a result, although I said that LRECL, BLKSIZE, and RECFM must be entered for all files, they do not necessarily have to be coded in the JCL each time.

RECFM tells the OS the record format of the file. Figure 28.13 lists the acceptable values for this subparameter. Most of these values probably will not be used because they refer to special types of data. The codes likely to be used are F, FB, V, and VB.

LRECL is the logical record length of the records in the file. If the records are variable length, blocked or unblocked, the record length is the largest record size in the file. Variable records are identified by a 4 byte control field before each record, so the logical record length is the longest record length plus four bytes.

The BLKSIZE subparameter tells the OS the size of a block of records in the file and, for fixed records

A	Records with ASA control characters
B	Blocked records
D	Variable length ASCII records
F	Fixed length records
G	Teleprocessing message data
M	Records with machine code control characters
R	Teleprocessing message data
S	Standard blocks of fixed length records or records that may span blocks of variable length records
T	Records that may be written on overflow tracks
U	Undefined length records
V	Variable length records

The most common record formats are: F, FB, V, and VB

Figure 28.13. Values which may be coded for record format (RECFM).

(RECFM = F) is a multiple of the record length. For variable length records, 4 should be added to include the 4 bytes which precede each block and tell the OS the number of records in the block.

Figure 28.14 shows examples of the DCB parameter and its three subparameters.

Other DD Statement Formats

Refer back to Figure 28.9 for two alternate formats for the DD statement. Format 2 is used for data which is part of the input stream; that is, a file that is coded right along with the JCL. For example, if both the JCL and a source program file is on punchcards, the input file is placed immediately after the format 2 DD statement in the JCL deck. The DD * is used for files that do not include any JCL statements; the DD DATA statement is used for input files that also contain JCL or control statements.

The DD statement in format 3 of Figure 28.9 directs an output file to a printing or punching device. The SYSOUT class determines *which* device. In many installations, SYSOUT = A is the standard print class and SYSOUT = B is the standard punch class. Other· values coded for SYSOUT data sets can request off-line printers, printers with special paper forms, plotters, magnetic character printers, and other devices not assumed to be the installation's standard output device.

28.7 THE COMMENT STATEMENT

When comments need inclusion in JCL coding, a **comment statement** is the means. Comments can clarify ab-

Example 1
```
//                    DCB=(LRECL=80,BLKSIZE=960,RECFM=FB)
```

Example 2
```
//                    DCB=(LRECL=144,BLKSIZE=1444,RECFM=VB)
```

Example 3
```
//                    DCB=BLKSIZE=133
```

Figure 28.14. Examples of the DCB parameter.

struse procedures, and even serve as "blank" areas between job steps or DD statements; in short, they can make a JCL listing easier to read. The comments *field* in a JCL statement can clarify the single statement, while a comment *statement* can explain a larger section of JCL coding.

To code the comment statement, the user places //* in the first three positions of the statement and puts a comment in positions 4 through 71. There is no need to continue a comment statement; if more space for a comment is required, a second comment statement continues the narrative, as shown:

```
//* THIS JOB STEP SORTS ACCOUNTS RECEIVABLE RECORDS
//* FOR INPUT TO THE MONTHLY BILLING PROGRAM.
```
(28.9)

28.8 THE DELIMITER STATEMENT

The *delimiter statement* marks the end of data in the input stream. When there is a file on punchcards or in the input stream with the JCL, DD * or DD DATA indicates that data follows. After the data, a delimiter statement, /*, is placed in the input stream to mark the end of the data.

When DD * is being used to read data, the delimiter is optional; the OS assumes end-of-data when it encounters the next JCL statement (// in positions 1 and 2). However, when using DD DATA, one must code the delimiter statement since then the OS treats everything in the input stream, including JCL statements, as data. If a delimiter statement is not used, all of the JCL following the DD DATA statement, including other jobs in the input stream, will be treated as data.

Here is how to use the delimiter statement:

```
//SSICARD DD DATA
      data
/*                                    (28.10)
```

28.9 ADVANCED JCL PARAMETERS

This group of parameters and subparameters serve specific applications and/or provide optional or alternate ways to accomplish previous functions.

The JOB Statement

Additional JOB statement parameters provide more control over jobs. If an error is detected by a program in one of the job steps, the user can tell the OS to bypass the rest of the steps in the job; he or she can set a time limit for a job, and also tell OS to hold (not execute) a job until instructed to release it. Figure 28.15 shows the expanded JOB statement skeleton.

The COND parameter. Sometimes a job step executes to normal completion, but the program discovers a condition (such as invalid data) which may adversely affect subsequent job steps. In such cases, the condition (COND) parameter can be used to tell the OS to bypass subsequent job steps when a code of a certain value, called the *return code*, is passed from the program.

There are two types of return codes: operating system return codes and user return codes. *Operating system return codes* are generated by the OS and its service programs to give an indication of the success or failure of a job step. For example, language translators such as those for COBOL, PL/I, and FORTRAN send a return code of 0000 if no errors are detected in the source code and if the contrary, a return code of 0004 through 0016 according to the severity of the errors detected.

User return codes are passed from one application program to communicate to other application programs. For example, if a job edits and validates data in one step and updates a master file in the next step, the edit program can pass a return code of 0000 if the data is valid, or 0004 if the data is invalid. Then, one can code a COND parameter in the JOB statement that says, in effect, "If 4 is less than or equal to the return code issued by any

```
//jobname   JOB   accounting-information,
                  programmer-name,
                  CLASS=job-class,
                  PRTY=priority-number,
                  MSGCLASS=message-class,
                  MSGLEVEL=(statements,messages),
                  REGION=region-sizeK,
                  COND=(number,relational-operator),
                  TIME=(minutes,seconds),
                  TYPRUN=HOLD
```

Figure 28.15. Expanded **JOB** statement skeleton.

step in the job, do not execute subsequent job steps." In other words, if the condition described in a **COND** parameter is true, all subsequent job steps are bypassed.

Figure 28.16 shows the JCL for this edit-update job using the **COND** parameter. **COND = (4,LE)** means that if 4 is less than or equal to any return code, the remaining steps should be bypassed. In our example, this means that if all the data were good, the return code of **0000** passed by the edit program would not satisfy the condition. As a result, the update step *would* be executed (not bypassed). If some of the input records were invalid, a return code of **0004** would be issued, thus satisfying the condition and the update step would be bypassed.

The relational operators for the **COND** parameter and their meanings are as follows:

GT Greater than
GE Greater than or equal to
LT Less than
LE Less than or equal to
EQ Equal to
NE Not equal to

```
//EDUP    JOB   HE66YFNH,
//              'W. CLARY',
//              COND=(4,LE)
//EDIT    EXEC  PGM=EDPGM
  .
  .
  .
//UPDATE  EXEC  PGM=UPPGM
  .
  .
  .
//
```

Figure 28.16. Using the **COND** parameter in the **JOB** statement.

Figure 28-17 shows examples of some of these how to use operators. Example 1 says: If 8 is greater than any return code, bypass all subsequent job steps. Examples 2 and 3 illustrate that more than one condition can be combined in the parameter—in fact, up to eight conditions in one **COND** parameter. Example 2 says: If 16 is less than any return code, or if 4 is greater than or equal to any return code, bypass all subsequent job steps. Example 3 shows three conditions. It says: If 0 is equal to, 37 is less than or equal to, or 8 is less than or equal to any return code, bypass all subsequent job steps.

As with other **JOB** statement parameters, **COND** can also be coded on the **EXEC** statement. If it is coded in the **JOB** statement and the condition is true, all job steps following the one issuing the return code will be bypassed. If it is coded on the **EXEC** statement and the condition is true, only the step executed by that **EXEC** statement will be bypassed.

The TIME parameter. Each installation has a predefined time limit for CPU usage. When a job exceeds the time limit, it is terminated. To extend or reduce the installation time limit, the **TIME** parameter is coded. (The OS may be altered by the installation to reject a **TIME** subparameter unless the user's account number says that he or she is authorized to run such long jobs)

The format of the **TIME** parameter is

$$\text{TIME} = (\text{minutes,seconds}) \qquad (28.12)$$

This tells the OS the number of minutes and seconds the job is allowed to run.

Figure 28.18 contains examples of the **TIME** parameter. Example 1 illustrates a time limit of 3 minutes 30 seconds. Example 2 shows a time limit of 17 minutes. Example 3 shows a time limit of 25 seconds. Example 4 il-

Example no.	JCL code	Meaning
		Bypass subsequent job steps if...
1	`//    COND=(8,GT)`	8 is greater than the return code
2	`//    COND=((16,LT),(4,GE))`	16 is less than the return code or 4 is greater than or equal to the return code
3	`//    COND=((0,EQ),(37,LE),(8,LE))`	(1) 0 is equal to the return code, (2) 37 is less than or equal to the return code, or (3) 8 is less than or equal to the return code

Figure 28.17. Examples of the COND parameter of the JOB statement.

lustrates the **TIME** parameter to eliminate timing (there are 1,440 minutes in 24 hours).

A time limit can also be specified for each job step by coding it on the **EXEC** statement. If coded in both the **JOB** statement and the **EXEC** statement, the time limit specified on the **JOB** statement takes precedence. In other words, if 10 minutes is specified on the **EXEC** statement, but the execution of previous job steps has left only 5 minutes remaining of the time limit specified on the **JOB** statement, then the step can only use those 5 minutes. If it takes more, the job will be abnormally terminated.

The TYPRUN parameter.   A job can be placed in a hold status by coding **TYPRUN = HOLD** on the **JOB** statement. Then the job will not be initiated until the operator (or in some cases a special release program) releases it. The purpose of this is to allow the submission of a job before it is ready for execution. Of course, the operator must know what conditions must be met for the job to be released.

To illustrate, suppose that a program is to be compiled in one job and then executed in another job. To do this, one submits both jobs at the same time with **TYPRUN = HOLD** on the second **JOB** statement like this:

```
//UPJOB   JOB HE66YFNH,
//            'WAYNE CLARY',
//            TYPRUN=HOLD      (28.13)
```

Then, the operator can be told to release the held job when the compile job is finished.

The EXEC Statement

The two new parameters of the **EXEC** statement are **COND** and **TIME**. They are similar to the **COND** and **TIME** parameters just presented for the **JOB** statement. Figure 28.19 shows the expanded skeleton for the **EXEC** statement.

The COND parameter.   Although the COND parameter of the EXEC statement is similar to the COND parameter of the **JOB** statement, it has additional capabilities: the operator can not only specify the conditions

Example no.	JCL code		Meaning

1	`//PRJOB   JOB   HE66YFNH,`
	`//            'W. CLARY',`
	`//            TIME=(3,30)`
			3 minutes, 30 seconds

2	`//            TIME=17`		17 minutes
3	`//            TIME=(,25)`		25 seconds
4	`//            TIME=1440`		Unlimited (24 hours)

Figure 28.18. Examples of the **TIME** parameter of the **JOB** statement.

```
//stepname EXEC  PGM=program-name,
                 PARM=program-parameters,
                 REGION=region-sizeK,
                 COND=(number,relational-operator),
                     =(number,relational-operator,stepname),
                     =(number,relational-operator,stepname.procstepname),
                     =EVEN,
                     =ONLY,
                 TIME=(minutes,seconds)
```

Figure 28.19. Expanded **EXEC** statement skeleton.

under which the job step may *not* be executed, but also special cases when the step should be executed. The **COND** parameter in the **EXEC** statement can cause a step to be executed even if a previous job step abnormally terminates. (Usually, when a step fails, all subsequent steps are bypassed.) One can also set a special condition to cause a step to be executed *only* if a previous step fails.

Figure 28.20 shows examples of the **EXEC** statement with **COND** parameters. The **EXEC** statement in example 1 causes the step to be bypassed if any preceding step is-

sues a return code greater than 0007. Example 2 shows a **COND** parameter that causes this step to be bypassed if EDSTEP issues a return code of 0004 or less. Example 3 causes the step to be bypassed if the return code generated by a step in a cataloged procedure (RPGEN) called by a previous job step (UPSTEP) is greater than 0020.

Up to eight conditions may be coded in a **COND** parameter. Example 4 shows two conditions that cause the step to be bypassed: if 16 is less than the return code is-

Example no.	JCL code	Meaning Bypass this step if...
1	`//PAYSTEP EXEC  PGM=PAYPROG,` `//            COND=(7,LT)`	7 is less than any return code
2	`//       COND=(4,GE,EDSTEP)`	4 is greater than or equal to the return code from EDSTEP
3	`//       COND=(20,LT,UPSTEP.RPGEN)`	20 is less than the return code from the procedure step RPGEN called by UPSTEP
4	`//       COND=((16,LT,INSTEP),(8,GE,PROJ1))`	16 is less than the return code from INSTEP or 8 is greater than or equal to the return code from PROJ1
5	`//       COND=((16,LE),(6,EQ,ACCTUP.UPPROG))`	16 is less than or equal to any return code or 6 is equal to the return code from the procedure step UPPROG called by ACCTUP
6	`//       COND=((9,LT),EVEN)`	9 is less than any return code; otherwise, execute the step even if a previous step was abnormally terminated
7	`//       COND=((8,LE,PROD1),ONLY)`	8 is less than or equal to the return code from PROD1; otherwise, execute the program only if a previous step was abnormally terminated
8	`//       COND=EVEN`	Execute this step regardless of the outcome of other steps
9	`//       COND=ONLY`	Execute this step only if a previous step was abnormally terminated

Figure 28.20. Examples of the **COND** parameter of the **EXEC** statement.

sued by the step named INSTEP, or if 8 is greater than or equal to the return code issued by the step named PROJ1. The conditions may be mixed as in example 5; it shows a step that is to be bypassed if *any* previous job step issues a return code of 0016 or greater, or if the procedure step named UPPROG when executed by a job step named ACCTUP issues a return code of 0006.

Example 6 uses the EVEN option: the step is bypassed if 9 is less than any return code; otherwise it is to be executed. *Even* if one of the other steps abnormally terminates, as long as no return code greater than 9 is issued, the step will be executed. Example 7 illustrates ONLY: it is to be executed *only* if a previous job step abnormally terminates. However, if 8 is less than or equal to the return code issued by the step named PROD1, even though a previous job step abnormally terminates, the step will be bypassed. In other words, when EVEN or ONLY is coded with other conditions, those other conditions have priority.

In example 8 the step is executed no matter what happens in previous steps. It executes if all job steps run normally; and because EVEN is coded, it runs if one or more preceding steps are abnormally terminated. In contrast, example 9 shows a step that will be executed *only* if one of the preceding steps abnormally terminates.

EVEN and ONLY are mutually exclusive, so they must not be coded in the same COND parameter. They are counted when the number of conditions is limited to eight. In other words, one can code seven conditions *plus* an EVEN or ONLY, or eight conditions *without* an EVEN or ONLY.

The TIME parameter. The TIME parameter on the EXEC statement works like the TIME parameter on the JOB statement. However, it causes the installation of the standard time limit to be increased or decreased at the job step level rather than the job level. Remember, the sum of the time limits for the job steps cannot exceed the time limit set by the TIME parameter coded on the JOB statement.

The DD Statement

The (DD) statement is the most flexible of all JCL statements. It allows the operator to define a file in any format that can be stored within the IBM 360-370 series computer systems. There are more than 20 parameters that may be coded for the DD statement. Some have many subparameters; others have more than one format. A "professional subset" of the language is illustrated with the parameters shown in the statement skeleton of Figure 28.21, all one needs to solve normal data processing problems.

```
Format 1:
//ddname    DD   DUMMY,
                 DSN=filename,
                    =NULLFILE,
                 DISP=(status,normal-disposition,abnormal-disposition),
                 UNIT=(device,unit-count),
                 VOL=SER/REF=serial-number/ddname/dsname,
                 SPACE=(unit-of-measure,
                        (primary,secondary, directory/index),
                        RLSE,
                        CONTIG,
                        ROUND),


                 DCB=(LRECL=logical-record-length,
                      BLKSIZE=blocksize,
                      RECFM=record-format)


Format 2:
//ddname    DD   *        or      //ddname   DD    DATA
Format 3:
//ddname    DD   SYSOUT=(sysout-class,program-name,form-id)
```

Figure 28.21. Expanded DD statement skeleton.

Example 1

```
//PAYIN     DD   DUMMY
```

Example 2

```
//PROJDATA DD   DUMMY,
//              DCB=BLKSIZE=190
```

Example 3

```
//OVERREC  DD   DUMMY,
//              DSN=OVERHIST,
//              DISP=(NEW,CATLG,KEEP),
//              UNIT=SYSDA,
//              VOL=SER=D00102,
//              SPACE=(95,(6,3),RLSE),
//              DCB=(LRECL=95,BLKSIZE=95,RECFM=F)
```

Example 4

```
//ALTFILE  DD   DSN=NULLFILE,
//              DISP=OLD,
//              DCB=BLKSIZE=4000
```

Figure 28.22. Examples of the DUMMY parameter and NULLFILE option to simulate the presence of a file.

The DUMMY parameter and DSN = NULLFILE option. The OS can simulate the presence of a file, whether or not that file is actually available to the system when DUMMY or DSN = NULLFILE is coded on the DD statement. Thus, one can test portions of a program that read or write the file without actually affecting the file. When a program reads a file associated with DUMMY or DSN = NULLFILE, the OS passes an end-of-file indicator to the program. When a program write to a file associated with one of these options, no data is transferred.

Other parameters can be coded on the DD statement along with DUMMY or DSN = NULLFILE, and edited for JCL syntax. Suppose the user has written a program that requires several input and output files and is ready to test it module by module. The operator codes DUMMY or

DSN = NULLFILE on the DD statements associated with the input and output modules and this JCL is tested without affecting the real data files. If a program specifies zero records per block, the DCB parameter must be coded with the BLKSIZE parameter. When ready to use real data for your testing, simply remove the DUMMY or DSN = NULLFILE, replacing with DSN = (the real file name) and execute the job, reading and writing the real file (see the examples presented in Figure 28.22).

The UNIT parameter. This parameter tells the OS what kind of device to make available for reading or writing a file. If that file requires more than one volume, the operator requests accessibility to more than one device by coding the unit count subparameter, shown in Figure

$$\text{UNIT} = (\begin{Bmatrix} \text{unit-address} \\ \text{device-type} \\ \text{group-name} \end{Bmatrix} \begin{Bmatrix} \text{,unit-count} \\ \text{,P} \end{Bmatrix})$$

unit-address	The channel, control unit, and unit number of a particular device. This method of assigning devices is not covered in this book.
device-type	The name of a type of device such as 2400, 3330, 1403.
group-name	A name assigned to a group of device types logically relating them. For example, SYSDA (system direct access) for disk and drum devices.
unit-count	The number of devices to be assigned to this data set.
P	Parallel mounting: use one device for each volume serial number coded in the VOLUME parameter.

Figure 28.23. Format of the UNIT parameter.

Example 1

```
//              UNIT=(2400,3),
//              VOL=SER=(0123,9074,0972)
```

Example 2

```
//              UNIT=(2400,P),
//              VOL=SER=(0123,9074,0972)
```

Example 3

```
//              UNIT=(2400,2),
//              VOL=SER=(0123,9074,0972)
```

Example 4

```
//              UNIT=2400,
//              VOL=SER=(0123,9074,0972)
```

Example 5

```
//              UNIT=DISKA,
//              VOL=REF=*.OUT1
```

Example 6

```
//              UNIT=DISKA,
//              VOL=REF=PAYDATA
```

Figure 28.24. Examples of the UNIT and VOLUME parameters.

28.23. There are two ways to code this value. First, a number causes the OS to assign that number of units to the file (the number of volumes may be greater than the number of units assigned). For example,

$$UNIT = (SYSDA,3) \qquad (28.14)$$

causes three disk devices to be assigned.

Or second, one can code a P for *parallel mounting,* this cause the OS to assign one device for each volume serial number in the VOLUME parameter. Thus for

$$UNIT = (SYSDA,P) \qquad (28.15)$$

the number of disk devices assigned to the file depends on how many volumes are mentioned in the VOLUME parameter.

If the unit count subparameter is omitted and more than one volume serial number coded in the VOLUME parameter, all of the volumes must be processed sequentially on the one device assigned. The operator is required to mount and demount the volumes when the program requests them.

The VOLUME parameter. With the VOLUME parameter, a volume serial number identifies a specific volume of media. With the expanded format (Figure 28.24) the user can request more than one volume or refer to a previous volume. Figure 28.24 shows examples of both types of VOLUME parameters, one type in examples 1–4 and the other in examples 5–6.

The SPACE parameter. Figure 28.25 gives a more complete format for the SPACE parameter. The unit of

$$SPACE=(\begin{Bmatrix} TRK \\ CYL \\ block\text{-}length \end{Bmatrix},(primary,secondary\begin{Bmatrix} ,directory \\ ,index \end{Bmatrix}),RLSE,CONTIG,ROUND)$$

TRK	Allocate space in tracks
CYL	Allocate space in cylinders
block-length	Allocate space in blocks of data
primary	Number of tracks, cylinders, or blocks to allocate to the file as a primary allocation
secondary	Number of tracks, cylinders, or blocks to allocate to the file as a secondary allocation; up to 16 extents will be added to the amount specified in primary
directory	Number of 256-character records to be contained in the partitioned data set directory
index	Number of cylinders to be allocated for the index of an indexed sequential file
RLSE	Tells OS to release unused space back to the system after the file has been closed
CONTIG	Allocate space in contiguous area
ROUND	Allocation in number of blocks should be rounded to whole cylinders

Figure 28.25. Format of the SPACE parameter.

Example 1
```
//              SPACE=(TRK,(5,2,1),,CONTIG)
```
Example 2
```
//              SPACE=(CYL,(20,,2),RLSE)
```
Example 3
```
//              SPACE=(960,5,,,ROUND)
```

Figure 28.26. Examples of the SPACE parameter.

measure, primary and secondary allocation, and the RLSE option have already been discussed. Now, we will look at (1) the directory/index allocation, (2) the CONTIG option for formatting the allocated area, and (3) a method of allocating whole cylinders when the unit of measure is blocks of data.

The third feature of the SPACE parameter is a method of allocating whole cylinders to the file even though the allocation is requested in blocks of data. This method allows for file expansion within the same cylinders. Here again, the benefit is efficiency—if the data is wholly contained on a definite group of cylinders, the movement of the access mechanism is reduced, resulting in a faster I/O rate. To allocate space in this manner, one codes the ROUND option in the SPACE parameter. Figure 28.26 provides examples of the SPACE parameter with the extended features.

The **directory** or **index allocation** subparameter tells the OS how much space is to be allocated to a directory or index. A directory keeps track of files in a collection of files called a *partitioned data set*. An *index* accesses records randomly by means of the *indexed sequential access method,* or *ISAM.* If a file is partitioned, it must have a directory; if it is indexed, it must have an index.

If the file is partitioned, the number coded after the secondary allocation subparameter reserves that number of 256 byte records for containment in the directory. For an ISAM file, the number coded indicates the number of cylinders to allocate to the index. Secondary allocation is not allowed for indexed sequential files, so one codes the primary allocation with two commas following, then the index allocation.

The CONTIG subparameter allocates a file in a contiguous (continuous) block. For a three cylinder file, for instance, this means that instead of one cylinder being made available in one area of the disk, another cylinder in another area, and the third cylinder in still another area, an area of three adjacent cylinders must be assigned. The advantage of having a file in this format is that the read/write access mechanism does not have to move as far to access records in the file, so input/output speeds are faster. If the system cannot find enough contiguous space for the file, the job is terminated.

REFERENCES

This chapter has exposed the reader to a "professional subset" of OS job-control language. For those who feel somewhat confused about the purpose or application of some of the information presented in this chapter, my book, *OS JCL* (from which this chapter's illustrations are derived) is available from Mike Murach and Associates, 4222 W. Alamos, Fresno, California 93705. It demonstrates how each parameter of JCL helps to establish a complete set of characteristics about a job, a job step, or a file. The following readings are also recommended:

Brown, Gary, *System/360 Job Control Language.* New York: John Wiley & Sons, 1970.

Carroll, Harry, *OS Data Processing with a Review of OS/VS.* New York: John Wiley & Sons, 1974.

Cadow, Harry, *OS/360 Job Control Language.* Englewood Cliffs, NJ: Prentice-Hall, 1970.

Clary, Wayne, *OS JCL.* Fresno, CA: Mike Murach and Associates, 1980.

Flores, Ivan, *Job Control Language and File Definition.* Englewood Cliffs, NJ: Prentice-Hall, 1971.

OS/VS2 JCL. Form GC28-0692, IBM Corp.

OS/VS JCL Reference. Form GC28-0618, IBM Corp.

OS/VS JCL Services. Form GC28-0617, IBM Corp.

29
Compiler Construction

James B. Maginnis

Drexel University

29.1 OVERVIEW

The goal of programmers in writing a computer program is to have some computing machine execute their desires. It is best to do this in a language with a high degree of abstraction and not at the level of great detail required by machines. A **compiler** provides the link between the programmer and the machine, translating abstract desires into a precise and detailed machine executable structure. In addition, the programmer wants help in writing the source program so that the resulting execution will be correct.

A compiler, therefore, should

1. Translate a source language program into a machine executable form;
2. Produce an efficient runtime performance;
3. Provide diagnostics and error reporting to help prevent programmer mistakes or misuse of the source language;
4. Do this quickly, using as little machine resource as possible;
5. Be portable and extensible;
6. Be a model of good programming.

Program translation and execution is shown in Figure 29.1, separated into two major parts: compile time translation and runtime execution. Runtime execution may be performed by an interpreter or pseudomachine execution program.

Interpretation usually produces a runtime execution that is slower by one or two orders of magnitude than complete translation into a specific machine language and subsequent loading and execution. Subsequent loading when done on a different machine is called **cross-compiling** and is occasionally done for microcomputers, utilizing the power and storage capacity of a large computer to produce an "optimized" program for the smaller system.

Different languages are associated with compilation. The **source language,** the language to be compiled, is a high level language, such as FORTRAN or PL/I, which specifies operations and the types and structures of operands available. A **source program** consists of declarative and imperative statements and represents one solution by one programmer for a problem. The **target program** is a representation of that intent in some **target language,** such as a standard assembly language or a binary machine code or an input to an interpreter for immediate execution. The format of the target program is different from the source program with respect to organization, the operations executed and the data formats. But hopefully the intent of the programmer to transform external data to new values is not modified during the translation—the prime requirement a compiler should satisfy.

Compilation from the source program to the target program usually takes place in a series of phases and the output of each phase is in a different "language." These intermediate forms may be in tabular representation, strings of special characters, a tree or list structure or in commands of two or three data addressed called *triples*

479

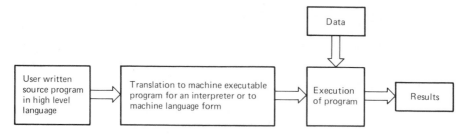

Figure 29.1. Source program translation and execution.

and *quadruples*. A particular form is chosen to suit each phase; the output of one phase is input to the next.

The compiler, itself a program, is written in some **implementation language** chosen for ease in executing recursive calls, handling strings, walking trees, doing tree searches and all the other nonarithmetic operations associated with translation. A widely accepted high level language, say PASCAL, for implementation enhances the portability and extensibility of the compiler. Remember though, the compiler program must be translated into machine language and loaded into some computer to be used.

This brings to mind the vision of a series of translators, each translating a compiler to some other language, like fleas on the back of fleas ad infinitum. For simplicity, we can ignore the secondary compilations or pretend that the compiler program is written directly into machine language, a method used in the early days of computing. Figure 29.2 shows the language relations during compile time and runtime.

The source language should be designed for easy use by a human, permitting mnemonic identifiers for variables and procedure calls, simplistic writing of constants, and structured control statements. A great deal of flexibility is desired to cover a range of applications. At the same time, the language is intended for eventual computer execution and should be easy to compile and be subject to precise interpretation.

The specification of the source language requires considerable thought and clarity of definition. This is achieved indirectly by describing the **grammar.** A grammar provides rules for selecting, from all possible combinations of symbols in an alphabet, those programs that are legal for the language being defined. The grammar also specifies the results desired for each of the possible legal programs. There are many approaches to grammar specification, but most of them formally define a grammar that specifies most of the permissable **syntax** (rules of construction) and then adds restrictions and restraints. The formal grammar, for example, specifies that a statement label consists of a letter followed by either letters or digits. A syntactical constraint would be that only one in-

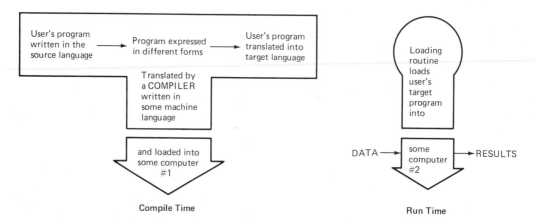

Figure 29.2. Languages and machines used in translating programs.

stance of a given combination is permitted per program. The meaning, or runtime results desired, is specified by semantics which, for syntax driven translation, are appended to the formal rules of syntax.

A formal grammar has four parts:

1. A finite set of symbols, called **terminals.** These are the characters permitted in the source language, such as C or * or compound symbols such as begin or identifier. The latter are regarded as single, indivisible symbols.
2. A finite set of symbols, called **nonterminals.** These are names of aggregates of symbols (either terminals or nonterminals) and the set is disjoint from the terminal set. An example is that the mark 9 might have the name of ⟨digit⟩. These nonterminals are the syntactical groupings of the grammar.
3. A single **start symbol.** A head of language nonterminal that is never used to define any other terminal, but is defined by the other nonterminals and terminals. An example is ⟨program⟩.
4. A finite set of **production rules.** Each rule is composed of a lefthand part and a righthand part. The lefthand part is syntactically or structurally defined by the concatenation of terminals or nonterminals on the righthand side. A production rule is written $\alpha \to \beta$ where α and β each are sequences of nonterminals and terminals.

In mathematical usage, capital letters denote nonterminals, lower case letters for terminals and Greek letters for a sequence of either. Historically, production rules are written either as they appear in the source language or in boldface to denote a special symbol. The nonterminals are enclosed in right-corner braces; the metasymbol ::= stands for "is defined by" and a vertical bar means "or," which avoids writing the left hand part again and again. For example,

$$\langle digit \rangle ::= 0|1|2|3|4|5|6|7|8|9 \qquad (29.1)$$

specifies that a syntactic unit named ⟨digit⟩ could be written as 0 or as 1 or as 2 and so on. There are 10 different production rules on that one line, with the lefthand part written only once. Recursive production rules are permitted, such as

$$\langle number \rangle ::= \langle digit \rangle | \langle digit \rangle \langle number \rangle \qquad (29.2)$$

which states that the nonterminal ⟨number⟩ is either a single ⟨digit⟩ or it is any number of digits preceded by a ⟨digit⟩. Thus those two rules could be used in conjunction

with the first 10 production rules to produce the symbol string 23 as a ⟨number⟩, or 423, or 6423; all are examples of legal ⟨number⟩ strings. Production rules define legal strings; they are used in the compiler to recognize and parse strings of the source program. Defined in this context, a *grammar* is a set of production rules which can be used in any order, commencing with the start symbol, to produce all possible legal combinations of terminal symbols. Each expansion of a lefthand part to a righthand part creates a **sentential form.** Eventually this process, called a *derivation,* produces strings composed only of terminal symbols; these strings are called **sentences.**

The choice of the production rules determines the characteristics of the grammar. For a **context-free grammar** the lefthand part of every production rule is only one nonterminal. There may be more than one production rule with the same lefthand nonterminal but the production (replacement of the lefthand part by the righthand part) may occur in any context. Thus, if a rule such as $\alpha A\beta \to \alpha\lambda\beta$ were permitted, the nonterminal A could be replaced by λ only when it is preceded by α and followed by β. Context-free grammars permit formal analysis of their properties and easier understanding of parsing their strings. Context-free grammars are capable of describing most, but not all, of the syntax of any useful programming language.

This syntax definition, along with semantical definitions that determine the output desired for each possible input string, provide the basis for the compiler to recognize, parse, and translate the source program into intermediate form. Compilers are organized into several phases which complete the translation in steps. The first phase is the **lexical scanner,** which converts the original source statement in its raw form into a formal string suitable for parsing. The **syntax analyzer** accepts that string and produces a parse tree describing the appropriate grouping into syntactical units. The syntactical tree is processed, in turn, by the **semantical evaluator** to create an intermediate program, frequently a series of quadruples. The **optimizer** scans the intermediate form and rearranges it to improve the runtime performance.

For some compilers, the optimized form is used directly by the host computer for interpretive execution. In fact, there are interpretive compilers that skip the generation of intermediate form and optimization altogether and retranslate and execute each source statement as the flow of control designates; thus, the statements in a loop would consume considerable runtime.

The compiler-interpreter is a useful approach for interactive languages which permit runtime changes in the source program. Should the ability to process itself be necessary, the source program string would have to be kept and treated as data for other source statements. Any change would require the creation of new quadruples. Thus the memory requirement for the interactive compiler-interpreter is large: the original source program, the compiler, the interpretive mechanism, data storage.

There is a continuum of possibilities from the simple interpretive compiler to the full compiler. In the latter case, the optimized intermediate form is input to a code generator that produces either binary code or assembly language output.

Assembly language output requires still another pass to produce final output. The final program may be left directly in the memory of the host computer for immediate execution or it may be stored externally for later loading.

The program finally created is designed to interact with the target computer operating system. External storage can thus provide subroutine library support and make available parameterized application programs such as

sorting algorithms, statistical packages, and data base manipulation systems.

The relation between modules is shown in Figure 29.3. In actual implementation the phases may be blocked together. Rather than converting the entire source program in a separate pass, the lexical scanner might be called whenever the syntax analyzer requires a new symbol. The syntax and semantic phases might be combined, particularly in the one pass compiler. During all of this, errors should be detected and reported. The final target language might be another high level language rather than a machine level code and require further compilation.

29.2 LEXICAL SCANNING

Lexical scanning converts the source program into a sequence of terminal symbols and also creates reference data describing the symbols. The input character string is composed of substrings called words, punctuation marks, operators, comments, and sequences of spaces. Words can be keywords, procedure calls, labels, variable

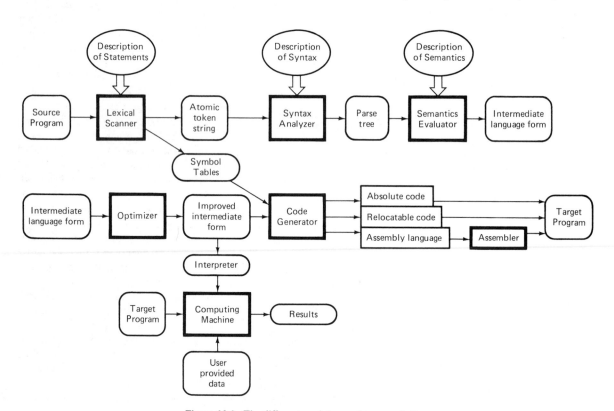

Figure 29.3. The different modules used in compilation.

names, subscript names, literals, and verbal punctuation or operator symbols. The lexical scanner must recognize such substrings, isolate them, compute data describing them, and produce a compact string of terminal symbols suitable for efficient parsing.

Some of the substrings are single characters, as * for a multiplication operator, others are longer and in a different form from parser expectation. The parser may expect **if** as a single character but it might have to be represented as   _IF_   in the character mode of an input device which can only delimit the **if** symbol with underscores. Also, overstruck symbols, as $\not/$, will be entered as three characters, either / ← — or as — ← /, and each sequence will be converted to the same terminal symbol. Some strings are complete in themselves, others have names, types, and other attributes associated with them. These attributes or properties could be determined in the syntax analyzer but many times it is more convenient to do it in the scanner. In some languages, the same character may be used for different purposes, such as a period or as a decimal point, and this context sensitivity must be determined. FORTRAN and PL/I, with the absence of delimited or reserved words, require considerable context examination.

The scanner must do all that, and more. An example of the process is, given this FORTRAN statement:

$$\text{IF (ABLE(K) .GT. 25.6) GO TO 300} \quad (29.3)$$

the scanner would convert that string of characters to what are frequently referred to as *atomic* tokens (terminal symbols with associated attributes):

if

(

identifier-1; function name, real, double precision:
ABLE

(

identifier-2; variable name, integer, single precision: K

)

)

identifier-3; numeric literal, real, single precision: 25.6

)

goto

identifier-4; label: 300

The lexical scanner would recognize the type of **identifier-1** from the absence of a **DIMENSION** statement and the mode from a declaration. The context affecting the type or mode could be after the statement being scanned and this might require two passes before a token's properties could be determined. The initial letter in the name K and the presence of the decimal point in 25.6 would give the modes of those identifiers. And what could 300 be in that location but a label for the GO TO? The terminal string would be

$$\textbf{if} (\ \textbf{id}_1 (\ \textbf{id}_2 \ ) > \textbf{id}_3 \ ) \ \textbf{goto} \ \textbf{id}_4 \qquad (29.5)$$

where $\textbf{id}_n$ could be different terminals, reflecting their status, if the context-free grammar expected such differentiation. The other attributes would be stored in tables, referenced by pointers from the string. Subsequent phases of the compiler would eventually use those attributes. Reference could be made to the original spellings, should error routines need to use them in diagnostic messages.

The conversion of 25.6 to a double precision representation to match the results of ABLE is best left to the code generation phase to isolate the specific target machine requirements from the scanner module.

Identifier attributes may change as they are defined in an outer block and redefined in an inner block, as in ALGOL or PL/I. In simple cases, when the inner block terminates, the attribute values return to those defined in the outer block. The attributes may be used to indicate whether the identifier has been ever referenced or properly initialized, but this might be better left to the syntax phase which could better handle complicated flow of control situations that might be found in the source program.

Recognition by the scanner of a substring is based on its description. One description might be: words start with a letter and are followed only by letters or digits. Another could be nonnumeric literals are enclosed in quotation marks. A restricted form of context-free grammar, called *regular grammar,* may be used to describe much of the simple syntax of words and literals within statements. A regular grammar has the restriction that the production rules must be written such that no derivation will produce an embedded nonterminal.

A **derivation** is a sequential application of production rules to expand the right hand part of a rule by replacement of nonterminals with their righthand parts. Given a grammar with a, b, c as terminals, A, B as nonterminals, S as the start symbol and the production rules

$$
\begin{aligned}
S &\rightarrow a \ A \\
A &\rightarrow b \ B \\
B &\rightarrow c
\end{aligned}
\qquad (29.6)
$$

then a derivation would be

$$S \Rightarrow a\ A$$
$$\Rightarrow a\ b\ B$$
$$\Rightarrow a\ b\ c \qquad (29.7)$$

The sentence a b c (composed of all terminals) is derived from S, via the intermediate sentential forms a A and a b B. A regular grammar must not have any derivation $S \Rightarrow \alpha A \beta$ unless either α or β is the empty string; otherwise A is embedded. These production rules would produce such a derivation:

$$S \rightarrow a\ A$$
$$A \rightarrow B\ b \qquad (29.8)$$

which could derive:

$$S \Rightarrow a\ A$$
$$\Rightarrow a\ B\ b. \qquad (29.9)$$

A single rule of the form $A \rightarrow a\ B\ b$ would directly embed B. Regular grammars can be written by ensuring that all production rules are of the form:

$$A \rightarrow a$$
$$A \rightarrow B\ a \qquad \text{(left linear grammar)} \qquad (29.10)$$

or are of the form:

$$A \rightarrow a$$
$$A \rightarrow a\ B \qquad \text{(right linear grammar)} \qquad (29.11)$$

For Eq. 29.10 we have that the lefthand part of every rule must be a single nonterminal only (the context-free restriction) and the righthand part must be either a single terminal or a single nonterminal followed by a terminal and nothing more. An alternate regular grammar is to use the right recursive form (Eq. 29.11), but only one or the other, not both.

The advantage of a regular grammar is that it can be parsed with a **finite state parser**—a mechanism that, given the current state and the next input character, changes to the next state that matches one of the allowable productions. Such parsers or recognizers can be described through a **transition table**.

Let **digit** stand for any digit in the input string, and **sign** stand for + or −; then Figure 29.4 shows a regular grammar for a real constant and gives a transition table with seven states. Starting at the initial state of row 1, the transition table entry at (nonterminal, terminal) shows the next state (row) to use for continued scanning of the input string. EXIT implies successful recognition of a real constant. The transition table would be augmented

Syntax of a Real Constant

\<real constant\>	::=	digit \<integer part\>
		|. \<fraction\>
\<integer part\>	::=	digit \<integer part\>
		|. \<fraction part\>
\<fraction\>	::=	digit \<fraction part\>
\<fraction part\>	::=	digit \<fraction part\>
		|E \<exponent\>
		|empty-string
\<exponent\>	::=	digit \<last of exponent\>
		|sign \<rest of exponent\>
\<rest of exponent\>	::=	digit \<last of exponent\>
\<last of exponent\>	::=	digit \<last of exponent\>
		|empty-string

Transition Table

State	State Name	digit	.	E	sign	empty-string
1	\<real constant\>	2	3			
2	\<integer part\>	2	4			
3	\<fraction\>	4				
4	\<fraction part\>	4		5		EXIT
5	\<exponent\>	7			6	
6	\<rest of exponent\>	7				
7	\<last of exponent\>	7				EXIT

Figure 29.4. Syntax and transition table for a real constant.

in execution by routines to isolate the input characters from the input string and make them available upon EXIT.

The blank entries in the transition table imply an ERROR condition. Error conditions have three parts: the detection of an error, recovery from the error to permit continued scanning, and possible error corrections to repair the mistake and continue. Error detection is based on the fact that the lexical scanner has accepted some part of the input string (such as the initial quote of a nonnumeric literal) that must be followed by some specific context to the right. Should an impossible combination occur, say the end of line prior to a terminal quote, then an error is detected.

The simplest recovery is to skip to the next input statement. For long statements this might leave a large amount of input unscanned. Some attempt at error correction is usually made, with a message to the user announcing that fact. The recovery action might cause subsequent errors or distort the meaning of what follows. Here are examples of recovery techniques:

1. Change one character: **PROCIDURE** to **PROCEDURE**, for example, when an identifier is not appropriate in that context.
2. Insert one character: (a + b)(c + d) to (a + b) * (c

+ d), or add a parenthesis to an unbalanced expression.

3. Delete one character: (a + b)) to (a + b).
4. Remove what appears to be a stutter input (extra ;;;).

Typically the user might view this correction procedure with dual emotion: delight when the scanner helps overcome a "stupid" mistake; anger when the kindly attempts of the scanner go astray.

Additional tasks for the scanner exist. Generally, the source statements are free format for convenience of entry. The scanner converts them into a compact format for the parser while, at the same time, printing the source program for user verification. The principles of structured programming state that the printed format of a source program should be indented and structured for easy reading. This can be done by the scanner so that an input of:

while a < b **do; if** x = y **then do;**
               a = a + 1; get (y); **end; end;**   (29.12)

displays as

       while a < b **do;**
          if x = y **then do;**
             a = a + 1;
             get (y);
          end;
       end;   (29.13)

Comments and excessive spaces are allowed in most source languages with the rule that a comment may appear anywhere a space is permitted. Also, anywhere a space is permitted, any number of spaces are allowed. Comments are delimited by a special combination of characters, such as /* to commence a comment and */ to end it. The end of a statement may be the end of the input record; or it may continue on to marked continuation records; or (most convenient) it may continue in free format until a semicolon.

Any of these situations can be handled by the scanner: eliding spaces, stripping out the comment, concatenating continuation lines. And always looking for context-sensitive situations: separating procedure argument lists from array subscript expressions, determining array bounds, looking ahead to resolve ambiguity. The classical case of look ahead is the FORTRAN DO statement where

$$DO\ K = I, J \qquad (29.14)$$

could be an assignment statement up to the comma.

The lexical scanner serves as an interface between the compiler and the external world as follows:

1. It provides for a free format oriented for human use and converts that to a nearly context-free language so that the syntactical analysis is simplified.
2. It determines attributes of the terminal symbols for further processing control.
3. It performs editing and simple error detection and correction.
4. A separate scanning phase provides simplicity and easy conversion, should the input device change or new definitions of words be desired.

29.3 SYNTACTICAL ANALYSIS

The syntax analyzer accepts the string of terminal symbols and associated attributes from the lexical scanner and attempts to create a parse tree as output. The **parse tree** is a structured list of the derivation steps needed to connect the start symbol to the program string. Should the analyzer fail, the source program is considered grammatically illegal and error messages are printed.

There are a number of parsing algorithms; the grammar selected to describe the source language determines the choice. More than one grammar can describe a given language so, although the choices are not infinite, it is often possible to decide on a parsing technique and then define a suitable grammar. The parsing algorithms have implementation tradeoffs of simplicity in programming, time of execution, storage consumption, ease of modification, convenience for code generation, ability to identify and correct errors, and so on. Often a context-free grammar is selected because of the relative simplicity of context-free grammar (CFG) parsers, particularly if the lexical scanner can handle most of the context sensitive constraints. One approach uses different grammars for different parts of the language and calls up different parsers as appropriate.

With rare exception, all parsers scan the input string from left to right. The difference between parsers is in how they attempt to build the parse tree. Recall that a grammar defines a language by expanding the start symbol, through repeated applications of all possible production rules, to derive an infinite number of sentences. The intermediate sentential forms may be derived systematically in two major ways.

One system replaces the leftmost nonterminals of the righthand part of a rule until a terminal is reached, and then the next nonterminal is expanded, and so forth, working left to right until a sentence is finally derived. This is called a *leftmost derivation sequence.* The second major system for deriving sentences is a *rightmost sequence,* starting with the rightmost nonterminal and expanding it in steps to a terminal and gradually working to the left. For example, given the grammar G_1

(1)	$S \rightarrow E$	
(1)	$E \rightarrow E + T$	
(2)	$E \rightarrow T$	
(3)	$T \rightarrow a$	
(4)	$T \rightarrow b$	(29.15)

a derivation could be done in the leftmost or the rightmost fashion:

Leftmost	**Rightmost**
$S \Rightarrow E$	$S \Rightarrow E$
$\Rightarrow E + T$	$\Rightarrow E + T$
$\Rightarrow T + T$	$\Rightarrow E + b$
$\Rightarrow a + T$	$\Rightarrow T + b$
$\Rightarrow a + b$ (29.16)	$\Rightarrow a + b$ (29.17)

The final sentence (the string of terminals: a + b) is the same in both derivations. The partially constructed trees by the two approaches is shown in Figure 29.5. The tree structure connecting S with a + b is the same; only the way it is constructed differs.

Derivation is a way to generate a sentence. The reverse is *parsing;* that is, given a sentence, find the derivation that leads up to the start symbol. If the grammar is unambiguous, there is only one parse tree that fits.

Two major parsing schemes try to construct the parse tree by discovering a derivation sequence in a leftmost fashion or in a rightmost fashion. Given the sentence a + b, a rightmost parser attempts to reduce it to the sentential form T + b (which is going *up* the rightmost sequence in Fig. 29.5): and in turn, E + b; E + T, and E. As it trys to reduce the last sentential to the start symbol S, success is recognized and the sentence a + b is accpeted as legal. The sequence of sententials is from the input sentence up to the start symbol; rightmost parsers are often called *bottom up parsers.*

A leftmost parser still scans the input sentence from left to right; since that does not change, it does not attempt to reduce the b to a T. It's approach is top down. Starting with the start symbol (because all parse trees

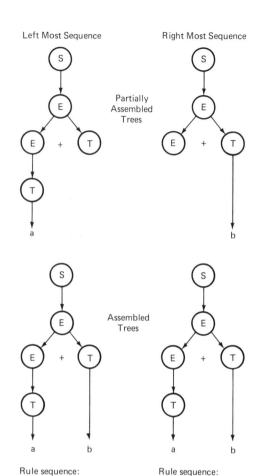

Left Most Sequence   Right Most Sequence

Partially Assembled Trees

Assembled Trees

Rule sequence: Rule sequence:
(0), (1), (2), (3), (4)   (0), (1), (4), (2), (3)

Figure 29.5. Two derivations for the tree of a + b.

terminate with S, there is no question of it being first), the leftmost parser replaces S with its righthand part E. In turn, the sentential E is replaced by E + T; T + T; a + T; and eventually a + b. With all terminals of the string accounted for, the parse ends successfully.

The question is: how did each parser know which production rule to use next in producing the reverse sequence? One technique is *trial and error.* A legal sentence from an unambiguous grammar will have only one parse tree; by trial and error the proper selection of the production rules could be determined. Such a random approach is not reliable and parsing algorithms use different strategies. Many permit a form of trial and error involving backtracking, in which a partially assembled tree must be torn down when a cul-de-sac is reached and reassembled with a different choice of a production rule. This is like a robot working through a maze with the instruction: always take the left choice until failure, then backtrack to the previous choice and try the next path.

The best parsing algorithms are *deterministic*. At each point where one or more productions could be selected, the parser knows exactly which one to choose. Without backtracking, a deterministic parser can complete the scan from left to right in one pass. Perhaps even more important, illegal strings are detected as soon as the appropriate production does not fit. The exact determination of the next production rule to use is based on a combination of the grammar and a selection algorithm. Perhaps a precedence rule exists as to the choice among alternate rules or perhaps the parser could look ahead into the string. The next symbol might settle the indecision.

In any event, there are deterministic parsers. An example of one class is the LR parsing algorithm: L stands for the standard left to right scan and R for the rightmost derivation sequence. The LR method shifts terminal symbols from the input sentence onto a stack (a push-down pop-up memory) and examines the stack until the top n symbols are the righthand part of a production rule. Then those symbols are "reduced" to the corresponding lefthand part of that production rule; that is, they are popped off the top of the stack and replaced by the appropriate nonterminal. If the stack is

$$E \quad \text{(top of stack)}$$
$$+$$
$$T \qquad\qquad (29.18)$$

these three symbols are reduced, by rule (1) of grammar G_1 (Eq. 29.15) to just E. If possible, the top n symbols of the stack are again reduced. When the stack is not reducible, the next terminal is shifted from the input sentence to the top of the stack and reduction again attempted. Using the grammar G_1 for S and the sentence a + b, the procedure appears in Table 29.1. There **null** is the empty string and **EOL** is an end of line symbol not in the grammar's alphabet but appended to the sentence by the lexical scanner. The stack grows to the right. The number after "reduce" specifies which production rule is used to reduce the top of the stack (the right as printed).

On line 4 and on line 8, the stack contains E but the action is different in the two cases; the history and the current symbol are different. A second stack, not shown, contains a *state symbol,* representing the progress so far. For LR parsing, only a finite number of "states" need be

Table 29.1. Reduction Procedure

Line	Reference Stack	Action	Input String
1	**null**		a + b
		shift	
2	a		+ b
		reduce 3	
3	T		+ b
		reduce 2	
4	E		+ b
		shift	
5	E +		b
		shift	
6	E + b		**EOL**
		reduce 4	
7	E + T		**EOL**
		reduce 1	
8	E		**EOL**
		success	
9	S		**EOL**

described and all transitions between states may be tabulated in advance. That state symbol represents instructions as to whether to "shift" or "reduce n" for all possible legal current symbols. The state symbol also helps specify which state symbol to place next on the state stack for the new parse situation.

The algorithm for LR parsing is straightforward. It uses two tables, the *action table* and the *new state table.* The entries in the action table, specify by row by the symbol on the top of the state symbol stack and by column by the current symbol, tell whether to shift or to reduce n, and also whether to indicate success (reduce to the start symbol) or error (next current symbol illegal).

The entries in the new state table, specified by row by the state symbol and by column by the symbol on the top of the reference stack, indicate what new state to place on the state symbol stack. The algorithm is:

(1) Initialize state stack to 0, reference stack to **null;**
(2) **until** "success" or "error"**do**
    (2a) action = action table (state stack, current symbol);

(2b) **if** action = "shift" **then**

shift current symbol to reference stack

orif action = "reduce n" **then** reduce reference stack

to rule n nonterminal;

popoff equal number of state stack symbols

fi; {distinguishes end of **if** statement}

(2c) place on state stack symbol from

new state table (state stack, reference stack)

od; {end of **until** statement}   (29.19)

Figure 29.6 shows the action table and the new state table for the example grammar G_1. The parsing steps and behavior of the stacks is also shown with the intermediate values on the state stack in brackets.

The algorithm is straightforward; for LR parsing, it is the creation of the two tables which is difficult. The tables are literally impossible to make by hand for any real language and require the use of a parser constructor. If one is not available to generate the tables for the BNF (Bachus Normal Form) description of the grammar, then LR is not a viable technique. Storage of the tables in computer memory could be a problem; but they are sparse

LR Drive Tables

ACTION TABLE
Current Symbol Value

State Stack Value	a	b	+	EOL
0	S	S		
1			S	EXIT
2			R2	R2
3			R3	R3
4			R4	R4
5	S	S		
6			R1	R1

NEW STATE TABLE
Reference Stack Value

State Stack Value	a	b	+	E	T
0	3	4		1	2
1			5		
2					
3					
4					
5	3	4			6
6					

Example Parse of a + b

State Stack	Reference Stack	Input String	
0	null	a + b	
			Action: (0, a) : shift New state: (0, a) : 3
0 3	a	+ b	
			Action: (3, +) : reduce 3 New state: (0, T) : 2
0 2	T	+ b	
			Action: (2, +) :reduce 2 New state: (0, E) : 1
0 1	E	+ b	
			Action: (1, +) : shift New state: (1, +) : 5
0 1 5	E +	b	
			Action: (5, b) : shift New state: (5, b) : 4
0 1 5 4	E + b	EOL	
			Action: (4, EOL) : reduce 4 New state: (5, T) : 6
0 1 5 6	E + T	EOL	
			Action: (6, EOL) : reduce 1 New state: (0, E) : 1
0 1	E	EOL	
			Action: (1, EOL) : EXIT Successful parse
0	S		

Figure 29.6. LR parsing tables and example parse.

tables being that many of the entries are empty because these alternatives are either impossible or they are error combinations that can be omitted.

A different approach is the LL parser. The first L for left to right scan and the second L for leftmost derivation construction. In these approaches, there is a single reference stack which is initialized to the start symbol, S. Starting at the top of the grammar, the LL parser attempts to expand nonterminal symbols on the reference stack until they become matching terminals to those on the input string. Matching symbols are popped off the stack and the current symbol pointer moved to the right. When all input symbols are scanned and the reference stack is empty, the parse is successful.

Not all grammars can be parsed by LL parsers, just as the LR parser is useful only for certain grammars. Eligible LL grammars have no left recursion in their definitions. Left recursion is exemplified by rule (1) in grammar G_1: $E \rightarrow E + T$, where the nonterminal is defined in terms of itself on the right hand part. Right recursion is defined by $E \rightarrow T + E$, where the nonterminal is on the righthand side of the righthand part. This is *direct recursion*. *Indirect* left recursion is also forbidden in LL grammars. For example,

$$A \rightarrow B \ \alpha$$

$$B \rightarrow A \ \beta \qquad (29.20)$$

is an indirect form of left recursion because $A \Rightarrow A \ \beta \ \alpha$. Further, there must be no two righthand parts in an LL grammar that start in the same way; such common prefixes must be factored out. That is,

$$A \rightarrow \alpha B \mid \alpha \ \alpha \qquad (29.21)$$

must be replaced by

$$A \rightarrow \alpha \beta$$

$$B \rightarrow \beta \mid \alpha \qquad (29.22)$$

where β or α may be the empty string. Rewriting the example grammar G_1 gives grammar G_2:

$$(0) \qquad S \rightarrow E$$
$$(1) \qquad E \rightarrow T \ E'$$
$$(2) \qquad E' \rightarrow + T E$$
$$(3) \qquad E' \rightarrow \epsilon$$
$$(4) \qquad T \rightarrow a$$
$$(5) \qquad T \rightarrow b \qquad (29.23)$$

where ϵ is the empty string. Now two grammars, G_1 and G_2, create sentences for the same language.

The algorithm for an LL parser follows:

(1) Initialize current symbol pointer;
(2) Place start symbol on reference-stack;
(3) **Until SUCCESS do**
    (3a) **if** top of reference stack is nonterminal **then** replace by righthand part of production rule specified by parse table (stack, current symbol)
    (3b) **orif** top of reference stack is terminal **then**
        if current symbol is not EOL **then** pop off symbol
        and advance pointer
        orif current symbol is **EOL then** SUCCESS **fi od**   (29.24)

The algorithm does not have any provision for error conditions. Errors mean an illegal string, such as a terminal symbol on the top of the stack that does not match the current symbol on the input string. If the parse table contains no entry for the intersection of the row specified by the nonterminal on the stack and the column for the current symbol value, this is another error.

The parse table, prepared from the production rules of the grammar, is the heart of this table driven parser just as the two tables of Figure 29.6 are for the LR parser. The LL parse table is slightly easier to prepare but still a parser constructor should be available for any useful grammar. The parse sequence for a + b is shown in Figure 29.7 along with the parse table for grammar G_2. Note that the righthand part of any rule is stacked such that the leftmost symbol is on top, to correspond with the left to right scan of the input string.

There are many parsing algorithms other than the table driven approaches described. Some could be used on any context-free grammar. Usually a restricted form of a grammar can be found which specifies all the syntax features described in the source language and which may be parsed deterministically and efficiently. Syntactical analysis must not only reject all illegal input strings but must produce a tree as output. A tree structure, such as that in Figure 29.5, is a two dimensional graph. It can only be stored in a computer memory in some linearized form. The list of production rules numbers given in a leftmost or a rightmost derivation may be used to represent a linearized tree if the degree of branching is the number of nonterminals in the righthand part. For example,

Typical Production Rule	Degree of Branching	
T → a	0	
E → T	1	
E → E + T	2	(29.25)

where the terminals do not count in the tree assembly because only nonterminals are allowed in the lefthand part of context-free grammars. The leftmost derivation sequence from Figure 29.5 follows:

	Production Rule	Degree of Branching	
(0)	S → E	1	
(1)	E → E + T	2	
(2)	E → T	1	
(3)	T → a	0	
(4)	T → b	0	(29.26)

The degree of branching shows that the tree starting with S will proceed directly from rule (0) to the next one following. Rule (1) has two branches, each that will eventually terminate in 0 degree rules, which do not have subordinate trees. In this case, one branch goes to the subtree rule (2) and rule (3); the second branch is found by skipping down to rule (4). Of course, many types of linearization are possible for tree representation.

29.4 SEMANTIC EVALUATION

Each phase described so far has processed the structure of its input and has interpreted that structure to add meaning to the output. The lexical scanner not only isolates words, but associates with them the meanings of variable names, procedure calls, array identifiers, and so on. The syntactical analyzer not only screens illegal strings but groups the terminal symbols according to production rules. Different grammars give different meanings to the same sequence of symbols, as in the hierarchial grouping of a/b*c into (a/b)*c or a/(b*c). The semantic evaluation phase continues this process, adding the meaning of machine execution to the parse tree.

"Meaning" in this phase is closely tied to the ultimate effect the intermediate form has on a computer when executed. The user often does not see this aspect of the meaning of a program. High level languages should remove the user from such consideration. The user is interested in the results obtained but not in the details of the machine language coding. The intermediate form output of the **semantic evaluator** is not yet machine coding but

Parse Table for Grammar G_2

Terminal Symbols

		a	b	+	EOL
Non Terminal Symbols	S	S → E	S → E		
	E	E → T E'	E → T E'		
	E'			E' → + T E	E' → ∈
	T	T → a	T → b		

Parse Steps for a + b

Step	Reference Stack	Input String Remaining	Action to Take
1	S	a + b	Replace S by E
2	E	a + b	Replace E by T E'
3	T E'	a + b	Replace T by a
4	a E'	a + b	Pop off a; move pointer
5	E'	+ b	Replace E' by + TE
6	+ T E	+ b	Pop off a; move pointer
7	T E	b	Replace T by b
8	b E	b	Pop off b; move pointer
9	E	EOL	Replace E by ∈
10	∈	EOL	SUCCESS

Figure 29.7. IL parsing table and example parse.

it is getting close to it with regard to permissible operations and structure.

The output of the evaluator may take different forms. It may be interpretive oriented phrases which can immediately be executed by an abstract machine. Generally such an approach has slower execution time but better interactive possibility then complete compiling. Another intermediate form is postfix notation, which is familiar to anyone using a Hewlett-Packard hand calculator. Frequently called **reverse Polish notation,** operators are written *after* their operands and are applied working left to right across the string. Each operation replaces itself and the associated operands with a temporary value and the scan continues. Thus y = a + b ∗ c becomes y a b c ∗ + =, where the order of the operands is unchanged; only the operators move to new positions. The scan produces,

$$y \, a \, b \, c \, * \, + \, =$$

$$y \, a \, t_1 \, + \, =$$

$$y \, t_2 \, =$$

$$y \qquad\qquad (29.27)$$

Here b c ∗ becomes t_1 and a t_1 + becomes t_2. The postfix notation is useful for representing expressions but is awkward for handling control structures and label references.

The intermediate form might be in machine-like commands with one, two, or three operands. Each command has a single operator, but the repertoire is much greater than that of a normal computer; the similarity is more to the macros of assembly language than the opcodes of the target computer. Single operand output is frequently in some standard assembly language and looks like this:

$$
\begin{array}{ll}
\text{LOAD} & \text{b} \\
\text{FMPY} & \text{c} \\
\text{FADD} & \text{a} \\
\text{STORE} & \text{y} \qquad\qquad (29.28)
\end{array}
$$

The final output of the code generation phase is frequently of this form.

At this phase, assembly language doesn't allow for easy optimization. A multiple address form is more appropriate. Two operand commands, or *triples*, are sometimes used. The triples (an operator and two operands) do not specify intermediate storage. The value computed is associated with the triple itself and the value can be subsequently referenced by name. Such indirect use of triples might look like this, with the triples' number shown in parentheses:

$$
\begin{array}{lll}
(1) & \text{FMPY} & \text{b, c} \\
(2) & \text{FADD} & \text{a, (1)} \\
(3) & \text{STORE} & \text{y, (2)} \qquad (29.29)
\end{array}
$$

A *quadruple* has four parts, an operator and three operands. This form is the easiest for optimization but creates a large number of temporary names. The equation y = a + b ∗ c now becomes

$$
\begin{array}{ll}
\text{FMPY} & t_1, \text{b, c} \\
\text{FADD} & \text{y, a, } t_1 \qquad (29.30)
\end{array}
$$

The creation of the intermediate form in syntax directed translation, associates a semantic action with every production rule. This provides the connection between structure and meaning. The syntax tree of Figure 29.5 for the G_1 parse of a + b could have each node containing a rule number, as shown in (29.31):

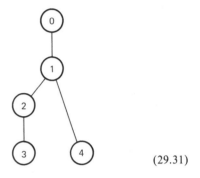

$$(29.31)$$

Letting each node value now stand for a semantic action turns the parse tree into a semantic tree. The tree structure is necessary because the result produced by the individual semantic actions depends on the relationships shown by the tree structure.

A compiler routine called the **evaluator** starts at the root of the parse tree and executes the semantic actions there. The evaluator examines one branch to the next node of a subtree. This tree walk can be controlled by the semantic actions themselves. A special control language uses *metasymbols*. For example, |j| means go down branch j: that is, visit progeny node j, execute the action there and return. Another metasymbol, the apostrophe, requests emitting text until the next apostrophe encountered and is useful for generating output. Still another is S_n, which means to emit a temporary name modified by the current value of *n*. If *n* were 1 then S_n would output t_1. Two more metasymbols are **CR** (for carriage return), a simple format control to separate emitted quadruples; and **\$**, an end of action symbol to indicate the finish of the current node's action and signal a return to the ancestor node to finish executing that action. For example, for rule (3) for grammar G_1

$$
\begin{array}{lll}
\text{Rule (3):} & & T \to a \\
\text{Semantic action:} & \text{'a' \$} & (29.32)
\end{array}
$$

means emit the terminal symbol a, return to the ancestor node and continue executing. We have

Rule (4): T → b

Semantic action: 'b' $ (29.33)

and:

Rule (2): T → t

Semantic action: **CR** 'STORE' S_n ',' |1| $ (29.34)

This means: (a) start another quadruple; (b) emit STORE t_n,; (c) go down branch one, to execute an action there; and (d) return to the previous rule. Thus a sequence of nodes would be

Rule (2) E → T   Action: **CR** 'STORE' S_n ',' |1| $

Rule (3) T → a   Action: 'a' $

                                           (29.35)

This produces the complete quadruple, STORE t_n, a.

The semantic action of rule (1) is,

|1| **CR** 'FADD' S_{n+1} ',' S_n ',' |2|

Compute $n = n + 1$ $ (29.36)

The evaluator goes down branch |1| and emits part of a new output, FADD t_{n+1}, t_n. The rest of the output comes from action occurring at the subtree in branch |2|. Grammar G_1, (Eq. 29.15), augmented with the semantic actions, might now look like this:

Production Rules	Semantic Actions
(0) S → E	**Compute** $n = 0$ |1| $
(1) E → E + T	|1| **CR** 'FADD' S_{n+1} ',' |2|
	Compute $n = n + 1$ $
(2) E → T	**CR** 'STORE' S_n ',' |1| $
(3) T → a	'a' $
(4) T → b	'b' $ (29.37)

An expression a + b, producing the parse tree of Figure 29.5, now has the semantic evaluator walk that tree, starting at the root, and carrying out the instructions at each node as shown in Table 29.2.

A more efficient set of actions might produce only a single quadruple instead of placing a into a temporary location before addition, but that improvement may be left for the optimization phase.

Each nonterminal has attributes associated with it which may change during the action. These attributes are many and varied. One attribute for the start symbol might be "program" whose value would be all the quadruples produced in the translation. Another start symbol

Table 29.2. Walking the Tree

	Actions	Output Generated
1. Node (0)	Compute n = 0. Go down |1|.	
2. Node (1)	Go down |2|.	
3. Node (2)	Emit partial quadruple Go down 1.	STORE t_0,
4. Node (3)	Emit an added 'a'. Return to ancestor.	STORE t_0, a
5. Node (2)	Return to ancestor.	
6. Node (1)	Emit partial quadruple. Go down 2.	FADD t_1, t_0,
7. Node (4)	Emit an added 'b'. Return to ancestor.	FADD t_1, t_0, b
8. Node (1)	Return to ancestor.	
9. Node (0)	Find last $ and terminate tree walk with output of:	STORE t_0, a FADD t_1, t_0, b

attribute might be "program length" to detect programs that are too long.

An attribute for an arithmetic term or an expression (T or E of G_1) could be "mode" with the values of "real," "integer" or "complex." Assignment is by semantic action or is passed up and down the tree by a semantic evaluator. The meaning of a source program is thus defined as the value of an attribute of a nonterminal. The values of each nonterminal's attributes are determined by the semantic evaluator, a compiler routine which performs a tree walk by visiting every node, executing semantic actions and passing values up and down the tree. Values passed *up* the tree, from progeny nodes to ancestor nodes, are called *synthesized values* while those passed *down*, from ancestor to progeny, are called *inherited values*. Different compilers use different tree walk strategies with typical tradeoffs in time and storage efficiencies.

Selection of attributes, whether inherited or synthesized, and writing the semantic actions require more skill than writing the syntax production rules. The legality of a program is easier to define than its meaning. Ambiguity may be permitted in syntax specifications but there must be none in meaning.

A semantic action relates to nonterminals in production rules. When the same nonterminal is in both the left and right part of a rule, they are differentiated by a subscript, perhaps L or R. The attribute is associated with the nonterminal by a dot, as "E_L.mode." An arrow may indicate whether the value is inherited from above (↓) or synthesized from below (↑), but they will be omitted in examples here for clarity. The production Rule (3) in G_1 (Eq. 29.37) might act thus,

Rule (3)   T → a

Semantic action: T.identifier = 'a';

                   T.mode = 'real';   (29.38)

The attribute "identifier" has the value of 'a' associated with the nonterminal T when the evaluator visits the node of the tree containing Rule 3. In a like fashion, T.mode is evaluated (assigned a value in this case). Other attributes may have quadruples as their value, as

Rule (1)   E → E + T
Semantic action:
E_L.quadruple = 'FADD t_1,' E_R.identifier ','
T.identifier;   (29.39)

where the apostrophe indicates that a literal value is assigned.

The E_L.quadruple could be, after execution of the action, something like 'FADD t_1, a, b'. The semantic actions for each node are all small procedures in which assignment and selective statements may be executed. The language in which these procedures are written depends on the compiler implementation. Selective statements in the semantic actions may be used to make compile time decisions, as in the selection of either **FADD** or **ADD** operators for real or integer operands.

Rule (1)   E → E + T
Semantic action:
   if E_R.mode = T.mode = 'integer' **then**
      E_L.quad = 'ADD T_1,' E_R.id ',' T.id;
   if E_R.mode = T.mode = 'real' **then**
      E_L.quad = 'FADD t_1' E_R.id ',' T.id;
   if E_R mode ≠ T.mode **then**
      E_L.quad = 'MSG MIXED MODE';
                                           (29.40)

In an actual implementation, the **MIXED MODE** message might be replaced with **CVIR** (convert integer to real) for the appropriate identifier.

The quadruples created by the actions are straightforward for arithmetic and logical operators. They have the meaning of combining the value of the second and third operand according to the operator, and placing the result in the location specified by the first. Thus y = a + b is represented by **FADD** y, a, b. Some operators need fewer operand positions. Thus, **MOVE** a, b copies the value of b

into the location of a. Unary operators replace the value of the single operand as, **NEG** a.

Quadruples are not labeled; a special operator provides a reference point for selective or repetitive statements. **LABEL** a creates a point named 'a' as the object of a **BRANCH** in the program. Conditional branches, such as **BHI** a, b, c branch to the label point 'a' if b is higher than c. Otherwise, the next quadruple is executed.

For array elements, the subscript names are enclosed in brackets following the array name. Thus

ADD a[i, j], a[i, j], 5   (29.41)

means "add the value of the literal 5 to the (i,j)th element of the array a." Because multidimensional arrays are stored as vectors, a calculation is required to convert the row and column values to a single index. That is, a[i, j] is expressed as

$$a[(j - 1) * I + i]   \quad (29.42)$$

where I is the row dimension of the array. This requires semantic actions something like

SUB t_1, j, 1

MPY t_2, t_1, I

ADD t_3, t_2, i

ADD   a[t_3], a[t_3], 5   (29.43)

The quadruples issued for procedure calls depends on whether the source language uses *call by name, call by reference,* or *call by value*. In *call by name,* the computation of the parameter is transformed into a closed subroutine and the parameters of that subroutine made available to the called procedure. In *call by reference,* quadruples compute parameter values and make their identifiers available by **PARAM** operators. A call of P(a + b, c) produces

FADD t_1, a, b

PARAM t_1

PARAM   c

CALL   P

LABEL t_2 (29.44)

where the reference point, t_2, is a return from the procedure P. In *call by value,* the parameter values are copied into local variables by the called procedure. The choice could be made in the procedure heading. There is need at compile time for communication between procedure declarations and procedure calls.

29.5 PROGRAM ENHANCEMENT

A source language may be specified by many grammars, each with aspects permitting different parsing efficiencies. Similarly a source program may be compiled into a target program even for different computers. Program enhancement is the creation of one of these alternate possibilities with desirable run time characteristics. Individual compiler designs select different characteristics as desireable. At the machine language level, efficiency is better than modifiability or understandability, characteristics better left for the source language. The target program should be short and execute fast, should utilize the target machine's capabilities appropriately, and should fit into the machine environment, such as operating system or library files.

Execution time reduction is the major goal of program enhancement, with some consideration given to space requirements. Little attention is paid to compiler execution time, becuase the source program is compiled once and executed many times. A compromise uses more than one compiler: one, for source program preparation, is designed to assist the programmer with diagnostics and debugging aids; a second "optimizing" compiler performs the final translation into a production program.

Program enhancement really begins in the semantic evaluation phase, where good choice of actions produces a better sequence of quadruples. The optimization phase concentrates on altering quadruples for faster execution and better use of memory. The major gain in speed is made by moving commands out of inner loops.

The next step of program enhancement is at the level of machine coding. Assemblers do not optimize; the code generation is the ultimate compiler product. Code generation selects machine codes from the repertoire of the target machine, makes final data storage assignment and selects registers for efficient utilization.

The improvement in execution time of a compiled program can be considerable. Wortman, Khaiat and Lasker in 1976, in a study of six PL/I compilers, reported average execution ranging from 878 microseconds per statement to a low of 24.5 microseconds. The worst case was for a teaching environment; production compilers showed factors of 2 to 5 improvement in running time. The results are summarized in Table 29.3.

Final enhancement, often called **program refinement** or **tune up,** is done in production usage. According to runtime statistics and experience, there is "10 percent of the program where 90 percent of the time is spent." The programmer can locate this area, concentrate on modifications of its basic algorithm, and then recompile for improved performance.

Optimization achieves increased running speed by eliminating some quadruples or changing them to ones that execute faster. The greatest improvement comes from modifying the sequence inside of loops: each saving is multiplied by the number of run time repetitions of the loop. Loops are recognized from source language statements like DO, FOR and UNTIL. The header region of

Table 29.3. Six PL/I Compilers*

Compiler	Average Statement Execution Time (μ sec)
1. OS PL/I Optimizing Compiler (a production compiler)	24.5
2. PL/I-F (a production compiler)	46.1
3. PL/C (a diagnostic compiler)	139.8
4. CHECKOUT OS PL/I (a diagnostic and optimizing compiler)	377.8
5. SP/K (a university subset of PL/I)	333.1
6. PLUTO (a teaching compiler)	878.2

*After David B. Wortman, Philly J. Khaiat, and David M. Lasker, in *Software Procedure and Experience,* vol 6, 3 (July–Sept. 1976), pp. 411–422. Runs were made on an IBM 370/165.

such source commands is a safe area into which to move quadruples from the loop. If the source language requires all loops to have a single entry, then loop invariant actions can be placed at this entry point. Well structured source languages are not only desirable for good programming practice but are a direct aid to improving the runtime performance of target programs. Here is a simple example of moving a loop invariant action out of a loop.

Before	After
DO I = 1 TO 100;	T = B * C;
A(I) = B * C;	DO I = 1 TO 100;
END;	A(I) = T;
	END; (29.45)

The simple computation of T outside the loop saves the repetitive execution of B * C. It is better done by the optimizing phase of the compiler and not in the source program. It is not as natural to write that way and interferes, however slightly, in this example, with programming simplicity, understandability and modifiability.

A more complex analysis of overall program flow is required for languages permitting conditional transfers to GO TO commands. The intermediate program form is divided into basic blocks (not the same as a block in ALGOL or PL/I). A **basic block** is a sequence of quadruples executed in sequence with no branches and only one entrance and one exit. A program flow graph, using basic blocks as nodes, permits identification of loops other than those from control statements. Optimization done within a basic block is **local;** that involving more than one block is **global.** Global optimization offers the opportunity for more sophisticated improvements but must be limited to program modules to allow for uncoupled recompilation of individual parts of a large program as problem specifications change.

Within a block it is possible to perform strength reduction, constant folding, and to eliminate redundancy. Strength reduction replaces a slow operation, such as divide, by a faster one, such as add. For example, one can replace 2 * a by a + a; replace a**2 by a * a. This should be done for integer variables only because of numerical differences in replacing floating point multiplication with addition.

Constant folding is doing calculations at compiler time to eliminate runtime calculation. Folding combines constants in an expression, for example, a = j + 3.0 into a = j + 3 (or, sometimes, j into real, to avoid another conversion). Redundancy elimination removes common subexpressions. Of course, care must be taken that the values of the variables are unchanged between occurrences.

Sorting the operands of the operators, multiply and divide, can detect commutative identities such as a * b and b * a. Repeated passes pick up nested redundancies exemplified by

$$x = a + c * b$$

$$y = e + d + b * c$$

$$z = b * c + d \qquad (29.46)$$

Redundancy also may enter into the calculations of subscripts in a less obvious manner. The assignment

$$a[i,j + 1] = a[i,j] \qquad (29.47)$$

because of vector storage of arrays becomes

$$a[(j + 1 - 1) * I + i]$$
$$= a[(j - 1) * I + i] \qquad (29.48)$$

or

$$a[(j * I + i)] = a[(j * I + i) - I] \qquad (29.49)$$

Optimizations for loops are unrolling, merging loops, and moving out invariant operations. Unrolling always saves time. Initialization, modification and test for exit are eliminated and runtime subscript calculation may be reduced to compile fixed values. Unrolling loop exchanges space for time. Merging loops may save both, as the following example shows, where two loops have similar spans of control:

Before	After
DO I = 1 to 3;	DO I = 1 to 3;
A(I) = A(I) + 5.0;	A(I) = A(I) + 5.0;
END;	B(I) = I;
DO K = 1 TO 3;	END;
B(K) = K;	
END;	(29.50)

For simple invariant operations, try to move them, one at a time, upwards in the program until one of the operands changes. The goal is achieved if a quadruple rises out of the loop. The unused subscript of multidimensional arrays in an inner loop is a good candidate for such invariant moves:

$$DO\ J = 1\ TO\ 100;$$

$$DO\ I = 1\ TO\ 50;$$

$$A(I, J) = 0.0;$$

$$END;\ END: \qquad (29.51)$$

Calculate $t_1 = (j - 1) * I$, where I is the dimension of i, above the inner loop and only A $[t_1 + i]$ for the remaining inner 50 steps.

Statements such as **if** and **do** that involve logical expressions for deciding on the flow of control, for example,

if ⟨logical-expression⟩ **then** ⟨any-statement⟩ **fi**   (29.52)

do not need to calculate the entire ⟨logical-expression⟩ if the decision can be made early in the expression. The expression $a \wedge (b \vee c)$ does not require any further test beyond a if a is false, nor any test beyond b if b is true.

Before			**After**		
OR	t_1, b, c		BNE	t_2, a, 'true'
AND	t_2, t_1, a		BEQ	t_1, b, 'true'
BNE	t_3, t_2, 'true'		BNE	t_2, c, 'true'
(⟨any statement⟩)			LABEL	t_1
LABEL t_3			(⟨any-statement⟩)	
			LABEL	t_2 (29.53)

Any saving depends on the availability of logical operations in the target machine and the relative speed of **compare** and **branch.**

The final phase, code generation, translates the optimized quadruples into a specific machine language code or an assembly language. Runtime improvement can result from efficient use of high speed registers, good storage allocation and the selection of appropriate machine codes. Source text literal strings are converted to machine language and a number base is chosen. Fixed value subscripts convert to specific addresses. Procedure calling sequences are generated with transfer of control and data specification protocols. For assembly language, macro calls and in-line open subroutines may be generated.

Interaction with the target machine's operating system must be anticipated. The input/output control system requires file descriptors, control blocks and files in a compatible format. Generic names for subroutine calls requires a match of data type specifications.

Simple nonrecursive languages with fixed data allocation, such as FORTRAN, assign the number and length of operands at compile time. Modern languages require dynamic, or runtime data allocation. High speed register assignment is usually done during generation. Registers store subroutine links, base addresses, temporary arithmetic values, stack pointers, and subscript displacements. As requirements for registers occur, the optimizing question is: which of the previous allocations must be abandoned? Certainly a frequently used variable should be kept in a register to avoid generation of store and fetch commands. One algorithm stores the register whose reference is oldest. Optimization of the quadruples has already reduced the need for temporary storage.

Each target computer has a different command repertoire. Some machines move data from one main memory location to another with a single command. Immediate commands incorporate small integer data values. Reverse divide or subtract saves intermediate storage when the sequence of operations is not compatible with the usual divide and subtract. Indirect addressing can save much internal data movement. Stack computers facilitate memory referencing in blocked source languages.

The code generation phase is linked directly to specific machine architecture; and isolating this phase is necessary for efficient run time performance.

29.6 CONSTRUCTING COMPILERS

A compiler is a large program. There are two approaches, frequently combined, in writing a compiler. One approach is to write it in a high level language, for which a compiler already exists as sketched in Figure 29.8. A COBOL compiler for machine A is desired. Step 1 shows the compiler, written in PASCAL and translated to machine A language. Step 2 shows the use of the new compiler on machine A and, finally in step 3, the user's machine language program produces results.

The high level language approach eliminates the numerous details of low level coding and provides aids for string processing, stack manipulation and recursive procedure calls. The compiler writer can concentrate on the logic of translation. The completed program has portability in proportion to the number of compilers that exist for the implementation language. Portability is weakened, however, by the need to modify the lexical scanner for different character classes that exist on different machines; changes definitely would be required in code generation and register allocation for a different machine.

The second approach uses the support of a translator writing system. Its input is

1. A description of the lexical and syntactical structure of the source language, and
2. A description of the target computer.

The output of the translator system is a generated lexical scanner, a generated parser, and code generation routines. The output might be in a higher level language, as would be produced by a human programmer using the first approach. The support offered varies; sometimes the user must write separate semantic routines to create the desired target language program.

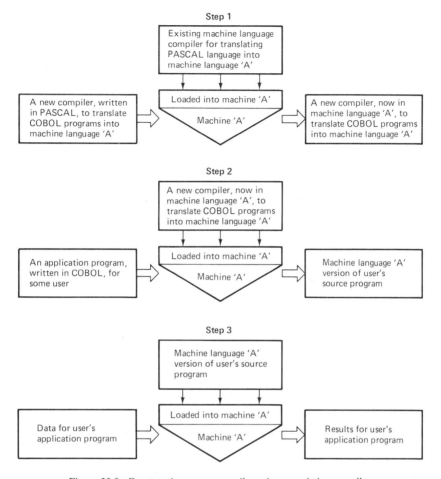

Figure 29.8. Constructing a new compiler using an existing compiler.

The portability of the translator writing system itself is also a desirable feature. Portable and easily used systems have been available since 1974. Descriptions for the lexical constructors includes a list of reserved words or delimiters, a list of legal input characters and the structure of lexical units, usually limited to those that can be processed by a finite state analyzer. Comment conventions, maximum lengths of words and statements, end of line symbols, and program termination values are also needed. The syntax of the language is given to the translator system in a set of BNF-like production rules. Along with each rule there should be static semantics (constraints on the context-free grammar) or attribute specifications. Semantic actions may be given to the translator system in a specialized language or written as separate routines in a standard high level language, as FORTRAN or PASCAL.

There is often an automatic transformation of the grammar described into one that will fit the parsing mechanism. In some systems the user may have a choice between different parsing strategies put into the generated compiler.

Translator writing systems are useful when several compilers are to be written or the source language changes frequently. It provides simplification and helps enforce standardization. A drawback is that the user must learn a special notation or another high level language. Some systems suffer from poor error recovery or optimization procedures in the generated compiler.

There seems to be little doubt, though, that the writing

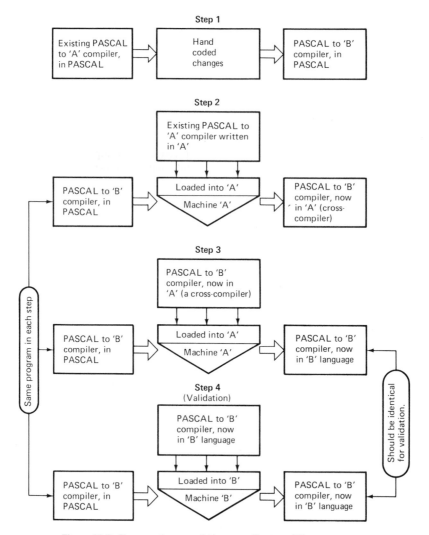

Figure 29.9. Transporting an existing compiler to a different computer.

of a compiler requires assistance, if not in the generation of a complete one pass deterministic translator, then at least in the creation of tables or in handling static and dynamic semantic definitions.

As computer architecture changes, new compilers have to be written, even for the same source language. Achieving portability from machine A to machine B is not the same as cross-compiling but is a rewriting of the compiler that used to run on machine A to now execute on machine B. Many compilers designed to be portable are **selfcompiling,** i.e., they are written in the language they compile.

But always, the code generation portion must be rewritten to generate target code for the new machine and the programmer must create new runtime support routines. Then an existing compiler on machine A can be used to create a compiler for the new machine. Done properly, this effort will be less than writing a complete compiler from scratch. It may not be less effort than using a translator writing system if one were available on machine B. Also, machine B or a simulation of it should be available at the same time as A for final validation.

Figure 29.9 shows the steps to follow to transport an

existing PASCAL compiler, written earlier in machine A language, to one for machine B; this illustration assumes that a PASCAL to 'A' compiler written in PASCAL also exists. Step 2 shows relatively simple changes to create a PASCAL to 'B' compiler, written in PASCAL. From now on, the process is mechanical. Step 2 uses the existing compiler on machine A to produce a machine A version of the PASCAL to the 'B' compiler. This is a cross-compiler and it is used in step 3 to translate the same PASCAL to 'B' compiler into 'B' language. The output of step 3 is the desired new PASCAL compiler for machine B. Validation is carried out in step 4, when this compiler is used on machine B to translate the PASCAL to 'B' compiler into 'B' language. The output should be identical to the output of step 3 run on the A machine.

There are going to be portability problems for any machine change, no matter how well planned the transition. Hand coding of some type is always involved. The implementor for the new version may interpret the language specifications differently from before or make a mistake in making the transition. A frequent difference between versions is that a source program that violates the rules of the language may have that error detected on one version and not on another. The creation of new compilers should be thought of as a test for the specifications.

In the process of fitting the compiler into the second machine, weaknesses in the source language may be uncovered. Finally, machine B not only has an architecture that differs from A but also has a different system environment, i.e., a different operating system, random access devices instead of sequential ones, time sharing, a different type of parallelism, and so forth. In any programming, compilers included, system independence is much more difficult to attain than machine independence.

The completed compiler, however written, should provide the user with more than a simple translation. It should provide error detection and, if possible, error correction. User errors may be syntax errors such as unbalanced parentheses, touching operators, and omitted delimiters and should be detected in the lexical scan or parsing phase. There may be logical errors such as undefined variables, divide by zero, or closed loops. Semantic evaluation, particularly when using a program flow graph, could detect them.

Inserted in the target program, in addition to the programmer's logic, should be routines to provide support at runtime to detect, for example, when a program exceeds the bounds of array declarations. It should record, as time passes, the execution frequency of each statement or block to maintain an audit trail of procedure calls, para-graph sequencing, and file opening and closing, along with the number of records processed.

The development of an application program can be likened to the development of a new product passing through stages: laboratory testing; final pilot plant experiments; semi-works evaluation; final production with operational evolution. A program should successfully pass through many compilations in its life cycle. A compiler with a standards enforcing pass not only detects mistakes but refuses to compile language violations. Unfortunately, individual installations and even published standards encourage extensions of such violations to languages.

Some means should be used to test that the output program does do what the programmer intended. This is particularly important when optimization changes the quadruple sequences considerably. There are three possibilities: program proving, decompilation techniques, and program testing. The first involves making assertions about the intent of the program and the proving that the assertions hold for the target program. Decompilation is a reversal from the target program back to the original source language. It is similar in concept to having a second programmer draw a flow chart from the final code for comparison with the initial flow chart. Program testing tries to find faults or bugs by running a program against different kinds of test data.

The compiler itself should be tested. When the compiler survives an exhaustive series of well-designed tests, one can assume that any translation is correct and does not violate the programmer's desires. Such tests might well take longer than the writing itself of the compiler!

REFERENCES

Aho, A. V., and S. C. Johnson, "LR Parsing," *Computing Surveys,* Vol. 6, No. 2 (June 1974), pp. 99–124.

Aho, Alfred V., and Jeffrey D. Ullman, *Principles of Compiler Design.* Reading, MA: Addison-Wesley, 1977.

Baer, Jean-Loup, "Model, Design, and Evaluation of a Compiler for a Parallel Processing Environment," *IEEE Transactions on Software Engineering,* Vol. SE-3, No. 6 (Nov. 1977), pp. 394–405.

Barrett, William A., and John D. Couch, *Compiler Construction: Theory and Practice.* Chicago: Science Research Associates, 1978.

Bochman, G. V., and P. Ward, "Compiler Writing System for Attribute Grammars," *The Computer Journal,* Vol. 21, No. 2 (Feb. 1977), pp. 144–48.

Bochmann, Gregor V., "Compile Time Memory Allocation for Parallel Processes," *IEEE Transactions on Software Engineering,* Vol. SE-4, No. 6 (Nov. 1978), pp. 517–20.

Calinhaert, Peter, *Assemblers, Compilers and Program Translations.* Rockville, MD: Computer Science Press, 1978.

Feyock, Stefan, and Paul Lazarus, "Syntax-directed Correction of Syntax Errors," *Software-Practice and Experience,* Vol. 6 (1976), pp. 207–19.

Gries, David, *Compiler Construction for Digital Computers.* New York: John Wiley & Sons, Inc. 1971.

Ginsburg, Seymour, "Dynamic Syntax Specification Using Grammar Forms," *IEEE Transactions on Software Engineering,* Vol. SE-4, No. 1 (Jan. 1978), pp. 44–45.

Heindel, Lee E., and Jerry T. Roberto, *LANG-PAK: An Interactive Language Design System.* New York: American Elsevier, 1975.

Henderson, D. S., and M. R. Levy, "An Extended Operator Procedure Parsing Algorithm," *The Computer Journal,* Vol. 19, No. 3 (Mar. 1975), pp. 229–33.

LeCarme, O., and M. Peyrolle-Thomas, "Self-compiling Compilers: An Appraisal of Their Implementation and Portability," *Software—Practice and Experience,* Vol. 8 (1978), pp. 149–70.

Ledgard, Henry F., "Production Systems: A Notation for Defining Syntax and Translation," *IEEE Transactions on Software Engineering,* Vol. SE-3, No. 2 (Mar. 1977), pp. 105–24.

Marcotty, M., H. F. Ledgard, and G. V. Bochmann, "A Sampler of Formal Definitions," *Computing Surveys,* Vol. 8, No. 2 (June 1976), pp. 192–276.

Pyster, Arthur, and Amitava Dutta, "Error-checking Compilers and Portability," *Software—Practice and Experience,* Vol. 8 (1978), pp. 99–108.

Samet, Hanan, "A Machine Description Facility for Compiler Testing," *IEEE Transactions on Software Engineering,* Vol. SE-3, No. 5 (Sept. 1977), pp. 348–51.

V
SOFTWARE SYSTEMS

30
Operating Systems

Harold Lorin
IBM Corporation

30.1 INTRODUCTION

The concept of an **operating system (OS)** is now over 25 years old and numerous examples of operating systems of different types are available. A substantial literature includes a number of books that provide introductory and overview material. Despite the apparent maturity of this topic, however, there is a renewed interest in some rather basic questions of what an operating system is, what functions it should perform, how it should relate to other software elements, how it should look to a user, and how reliable, correct and secure systems can be organized.

The recent activity in this area is a result of some fundamental changes in hardware economics and capability that provide the basis for new types of computing devices and new types of computer uses. Thus a considerably expanded range of specialized capabilities, from small personal computers to very large intensively shared on-line data base management systems, are becoming available. The role of an operating system in a context of flux in hardware, concepts of usage, and dramatically changing economics assumptions is being reinvestigated. In addition, new concepts in software engineering and programming methodology are affecting some basic ideas of how operating systems should be constructed and how they should look to users.

30.2 CHARACTERIZATION OF FUNCTIONS OF AN OPERATING SYSTEM

There has always been some diversity of opinion about what the fundamental functions of an operating system are. This diversity has existed because operating systems of different types find a different set of fundamental functions appropriate for the environment in which they operate. Thus, some functions considered fundamental for an on-line real time operating system supporting a rocket tracking application may not include functions necessary for an operating system supporting a community of professional programmers.

In addition to variations as a result of system type, differences of opinion have occurred over time as new developments in hardware and perceptions of the user community develop arguments both for extending operating systems functions and reducing them.

Various influences on the design of an operating system, beyond the nature of the hardware on which it runs, include the kinds of workload brought to the system, the level of professionals who install and maintain the system, and the nature of the people who use the system for applications. In general, the basic functions of an operating system are the following:

1. To define an abstract machine composed of logical resources more conveniently manipulated than the physical set of resources.
2. To protect the use of logical and physical resources to assure coherence and correctness in an environment of sharing.
3. To interpret and enforce policies of allocating computer resources as regards intensity of resource loading, rate of response to users, and resolution of contention for resources among users.

Clearly, this broad characterization of function provides for considerable diversity as regards what specific functions are available, what level of support is provided for a specific function, and the manner in which functions are related to each other. A full range of systems types and organization exist that attempt to manage the resources of large machines efficiently. In addition, they furnish service to numerous diverse users of operating systems that provide program development tools for single user small systems.

30.3 TYPES OF OPERATING SYSTEMS

No formal classification scheme really exists as the basis for a taxomony of operating systems. Operating systems seem to be classified by some intersecting and overlapping criteria such as the nature of the interfaces presented to users, and the generality of function provided. Changes in usage and hardware types have resulted in a continuing change in the population of operating systems types. A rough characterization of contemporary systems might include the following types.

Large General Purpose Operating Systems

This class includes those systems primarily intended for use with the largest machines. Such systems attempt to manage a large population of machine resources in an environment of many different uses. An operating system may provide service to application programs being run on-line or in a batch mode, or may provide support for a subsystem that in turn creates an environment for support of applications programs. The types of subsystems that a contemporary large operating system may service are data base management, programming development, and even personal computing systems. Examples of this kind of large operating system include IBM's MVS (Multiple Virtual Storage System), UNIVAC's OS 1100, and Honeywell's HECOS and MULTICS.

The outstanding characteristics of these large operating systems are their size, the richness of functions they provide, and the general requirement that a staff of trained professional systems programmers be available for installation, parameterization, extension, and so forth. They attempt to provide truly general purpose service—local and remote, on-line and batch—to balance policies of efficiency with response time requirements and to provide suitable hosts for a wide diversity of application types. Inherent in their design are concepts of multiprogramming and time sharing permitting alternation of periods of service among diverse users sharing the system.

Real Time Operating Systems

Large general purpose operating systems frequently are inappropriate for use in an environment in which a single application must be run within rigorous time constraints. Real time operating systems generally have fewer functions and rather different structures as contrasted with general purpose operating systems. They offer only those services that will furnish computer response to a set of monitored events in minimum time and within certain set periods. For example, the classical real time operating system is one that is used to monitor the position of rockets.

Real time operating systems are sometimes specially written for the application that they are intended to support. They include only functions necessary for the application and are less aggressive in monitoring the efficient use of hardware. Their response time is so critically important that machine efficiency may have to be sacrificed to ensure on-time performance of functions.

There are a number of specialized operating systems in the military and space research programs. Also existing, however, are a number of real time operating systems that have been written as an appropriate base for a variety of real time applications. These may be intended for small or large machines.

Perhaps the earliest example of a generalized real time oriented operating system was the Omega system for the UNIVAC 490. Other systems include IBM's Airline Control Program (used now in banking as well as for reservations systems in the airlines industry) and, for smaller systems, Data General's RDOS, and various operating systems for Digital Equipment's PDP-11 architecture.

The design approaches used in real time operating systems have been used frequently in the design of operating systems for "mini" and "micro" computers. Minimization of function and overhead is sometimes appropriate not only for real time, but for other on-line environments as well. This is particularly true when applications development activity is performed by competent programmers who desire a basic operating system on which to build an application for which a smaller machine will be dedicated. Intel's RMX-80 is an example of such a microprocessor operating system.

Single User Operating Systems

Computer economics have progressed to the point of often providing a computer for a personal use, or for use by only one person at a time. The goal of such systems is maximum ease of use and minimum professional support. In such environments, the operating system functions associated with effective utilization tend to disappear completely. Even the awareness of the existence of an operating system, as such, tends to disappear for the user. Personal computing systems provide a language for the user to enter data and programs, a set of basic data processing functions such as copying a file, altering a file, or sorting a file. The operating system is delivered in such a way that it is easy to talk to and no professional tending is required.

Program Development Systems

The general purpose system provides services both for program development and for production; the real time system tends to provide services only for a production environment. There is also a class of operating systems that primarily support the development of programs which are more substantial and complex than programs being developed in a personal computing environment.

Program development tools include compiler services, program module management, editing, testing, and debugging, all at very high language level. Programming systems may, as mentioned above, be subsystems of large general purpose operating systems. They may also be provided as stand-alone operating systems for machines that will be dedicated to the programming function. The UNIX operating system lays great stress on its usability in a development environment. IBM's VM operating system, running with the CMS monitor, is another widely used program development system.

Microcomputer manufacturers frequently provide program development systems for use in creating production programs that fit microcomputer architecture. A program development system is a packaged version of the microcomputer delivered with an operating system, a debugging system, a file manager, an editor, and similar functions in a single integrated package. Examples abound: one is the INTELLEC development system for the Intel 80X0 line of single board computers.

Smaller General Purpose Operating Systems

Essential differences between operating systems of the same general type may occur because of the varying sizes of machines for which the operating systems are designed. There are general purpose operating systems for smaller machines, including the IBM DOS/VSE (Disk

Operating System/Virtual Storage Extended), VAX/VMS, the operating system for the VAX-11 architecture. They provide both production and development environments for general purpose use. These systems are confined to situations in which the size of the machine make very aggressive resource management strategies less necessary because of an anticipated lower level of diversity of use or sharing.

In smaller machines, very elaborate attempts to determine the level of use of I/O, memory, and the processor may consume more systems power and time than the amount of unused resource brought into play. In addition, systems programmers, and operators or programmers using the system, may be called upon to provide more complete descriptions of the resources they use, for example, specifying exact devices rather than just naming a class of device for a file, because of the modest design of resource management features.

30.4 OPERATING SYSTEMS FUNCTIONS

We have discussed, in general, the diversity of operating systems types. This section will detail some specific operating system functions.

Processor Management

Processor management, as its name states, provides a set of programs for the management of processors. These include interrupt handlers that enable a program to be interrupted, then correctly resumed as a result of some system event such as the completion of an I/O request; a dispatcher program that switches the attention of the processor from one program to another in a mix of programs sharing the system; and a programmed mechanism that prohibits two programs from using the same resource when such concurrent use might lead to a systems error.

Processor management details depend on the specific architecture of the processor on which the operating system is running. Interrupt handling and task switching commonly involve the saving of program data, such as register contents, in a designated area of memory so that a program that is being suspended may be correctly resumed. A task switch involves a storage of program status, the bringing of the status of a successor program to the registers of the processor and, perhaps, an initial memory load of some kind for the new program. The new program is selected from a dispatch list that represents programs to use on the computer. Programs in a time sharing or multiprogramming environment commonly experience intervals of running and suspension while they are being processed on a terminal, or within a batched program mix.

Memory Management

Memory management provides a set of programs that manages the memory content of a system. Such management includes the assignment of programs to memory locations, and the movement of program segments and data to and from memory and storage devices. The management of memory may be rather static, with a complete program assigned to memory locations throughout its running time. Or it may be dynamic, with each segment of a program brought to memory on reference with the possibility of occupying a different memory location each time it is used.

Program Management

Program management is concerned with programs that manage the set of application programs running in the system. Each program that has been allocated some resources of the system and is a contender for system use is represented by a structure that can be generically called a *process control block*. This process control block is a software defined structure that identifies the code to be executed and the data to be used for execution. The registers saved for a suspended program during a task switch are stored in the process control block representing that program. The dispatch list of programs that can use the system is a list of process control blocks.

Task switch is the act of a dispatcher alternating a processor between contending processes. In addition to task switch, an operating system must have facilities to create processes (process control blocks), to provide for processes to send messages to each other, to delete process control blocks, and to mark process control blocks as runnable or not runnable. A not runnable (blocked) process control block is one which represents a program that cannot run because it is waiting for a resource to become available or for some event to be completed.

An important part of an operating systems function is the provision of mechanisms by which running programs may communicate with each other. This feature is commonly called *interprocess communication* and is intended to let programs that do not have a CALL/RETURN relationship communicate with each other. Two basic approaches for program communication exist: memory sharing and message based.

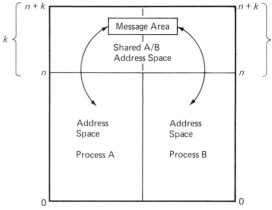

Notes: Addresses 0 to *n* unique to A, B; *n* + 1 to *n* + *k* address identical locations

Figure 30.1. Shared memory communications.

Programs that wish to communicate may do so through a shared memory (Figure 30.1) area defined by the operating system. More recently, under the influence of networking concepts, to be discussed below, there has been a tendency to design message based procedures for communication (Figure 30.2) between programs that do not share memory. A fundamental mechanism of the operating system is the interprocess communication mechanism (IPC) that defines the protocols for the transmission and receipt of messages. A common form for the sending

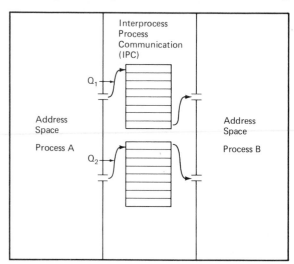

Notes: A/B interact through messages passed through IPC.
A/B share no space. IPC receives and transmits messages through queuing structure.

Figure 30.2. Message based communications.

of a message is the SEND macro; the common form for receiving or requesting a message is the RECEIVE macro. The IPC design determines how SENDing programs may be informed that the system has the message and that the intended receiver has the message, the queuing and pathfinding details of message delivery, the manner of notification of a RECEIVE that a message exists for it, and so forth.

Data Management

Data management includes facilities for controlling devices, providing buffer space, providing record advance on behalf of an application program making input/output requests, and reporting on the status of I/O requests. In addition, functions to control the allocation of space on disk devices, to maintain catalogs of on-line data, and to provide backup and version control of files are generally provided. More extensive data management, such as dictionaries and complex logical relationships between data elements, is more commonly provided in a data base management subsystem.

Resource Management

Resource management involves a set of programs that use concepts of priority, urgency, deadline, etc., to enforce policies about the use of a machine and its responsiveness to users. A set of workload and utilization management facilities are common to most operating systems, especially those intended for larger, multiuse, multiusers systems.

The dispatch list of an operating system is commonly ordered to reflect the goals of the system as regards service to particular users and efficient use of resources. In addition, a large operating system, of the IBM/MVS type, may have a set of distinct queues and lists to control resource use and program progress. Thus, in addition to selecting a next program to run on the basis of order in the dispatch list, an operating system scheduling function may determine which programs of a set of programs may contend for service over a scheduling interval, change the population of programs using resources on the basis of overall systems load, or load on a particular resource, and so forth.

In large multiuser general purpose operating systems, the resource management functions may be very extensive. Data on the load placed on various resources, and the utilization of channels, memory, and the processing unit, is constantly collected. In addition, goals about the

level of service to a user are kept by the system, as well as data that tells whether a user is being served at the rate that his or her priority requires.

A high level resource manager, like the Systems Resource Manager of MVS, or the Dyanamic Allocator of OS 1100, constantly reviews machine status in an attempt to achieve the stated policy of the installation as regards tradeoffs between service, utilization, and contention between users. Allocation of memory, lengths of continuous time allowed on the processor, frequency of activation on the processor, and so on, of a mix of contending programs are constantly modified by heuristic techniques that undertake to project systems performance on the basis of recent systems history.

The justification for large amounts of computer time and memory to control the status of a machine is that the resources effectively used as a result of intensive management may exceed resources spent on management. Smaller systems, with fewer resources to manage and consequently less exposure to under-utilization, universally use less ambitious resource management strategies. The expected level of resource recapture is less than what must be spent to determine that resources are being optimally used.

Explicit and Implicit Functions

Some operating system functions are explicitly called for by a program while it is running (in the runtime environment). Thus operating system calls may be made for such functions as READ, WRITE, GET STORAGE, GET BUFFER SPACE, WAIT (for some event), and CREATE PROCESS. These callable services may be thought of as extensions to the instruction set of a machine, providing complex services as if they were instructions. It is this aspect of an operating system that provides a set of abstract resources more easily manipulatable than raw hardware resources.

An operating system also provides a set of functions that may be thought of as extensions to the control mechanisms of hardware. These functions are performed at the discretion of the system rather than on call from a particular program. Imposing locks to protect shared resources, handling interrupts, dispatching, and assigning memory locations dynamically may be examples of implicit functions.

One difference between operating systems involves the concept of who is master and who is slave. A general purpose operating system frequently takes the position that an application program runs at the convenience of the operating system. Many smaller systems, with a real time orientation, view the application program as master and the operating system as a provider of services. The difference between these views may be demonstrated by the question, "What happens if a program requests a record from an input file and a record is not there?" When the operating system is clearly master, it suspends the program and replaces it with another. When the application is clearly master, the operating system simply reports the condition to the program.

In addition to functions performed in the runtime environment, an operating system offers certain services that are performed before or after a program is running on a computer. These services are invoked through the use of a control language that describes the resources required to run the program and dispose of its results.

30.5 FUNDAMENTAL CONCEPTS OF STRUCTURE

There is as wide a variation in the sizes of operating systems, in terms of instructions required to represent all functions provided, as there is in functional capability. A small operating system, with modest functional goals, may occupy in the order of 8K bytes; a large, ambitious general purpose operating system for larger processors may occupy in the order of 8 megabytes.

The organization of such programs in terms of module count, the relationship between modules, and the flow of data between modules is attracting much interest. Reliable, easily modifiable, easily installed, provably secure systems must be built within the framework of some programming methodology. A great amount of work has been involved in the attempt to increase the structural coherence of operating systems employing emerging ideas of software engineering, composite design, structured programming, and so forth.

Object/Operator Mappings

An operating system is a collection of objects and operators. In such a collection it is possible to undertake various mappings involving object and operator. One mapping is the operator to object. Here, a set of generic operators are defined, among them READ, WRITE, DESTROY, CREATE, which may be performed on all objects of various types in the system. For example, the READ operator takes some semantically meaningful action upon any object of the system it is asked to READ.

As can be expected, an alternative is the object to operator mapping. In such an organization, procedures are defined that apply all of the functions which can be implemented to a specific object type. CREATE, READ, WRITE, DESTROY Object of Type A means that any function on object A is performed by the generalized operator of that object. These generalized operators are called *monitors*. The idea of a monitor is to use principles of information-hiding and wrap a specific program around a specific resource or class of resources. This allows changing the details of a resource's organization while impacting the programming only of its monitor. For example, because all programs reference a table or list through the monitor, any changes in the structure of the table or list affect only the monitor.

Real operating systems tend to be combinations of both these mappings. One of the problems in contemporary operating system design is that it is yet to be demonstrated that particular structural approaches, which seem to give good coherence to smaller operating systems, can be effectively used with very large operating systems. Generalizations concerning the mappings between objects and operators necessary in a system with an enormous population of resources and variety may lead to systems lacking the crisp structural characteristics of the small models in which the structural concepts have been seen to apply.

Hierarchic Structure

One notion that has been applied to operating systems is *hierarchy*. In a hierarchic system, various functions are structured into well defined layers of programs (Figure 30.3). Each program at a particular layer can be called

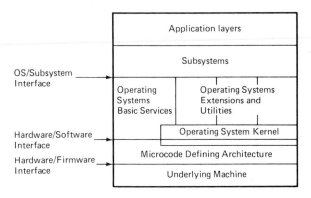

Figure 30.3. Operating system viewed as a set of layers.

only by a program at a higher layer and may return control to the higher layer when it is completed.

One use of the hierarchic principle is to associate increasing levels of privilege with each layer. The right to manipulate a certain file or inspect a certain table is reserved to a program running at a certain level. A program wishing to perform an operation on a resource associated with a program at a lower level must call downward into the structure for the program at the appropriate level to perform the function.

Very rigid computational structures may be imposed on operating system components in search of hierarchic purity. Some workers are interested in the degree to which rigid hierarchic structure may be relaxed, but the advantages of protection and debugability may be preserved.

30.6 TRENDS AND INFLUENCES ON DESIGN

Operating systems originated in a period when work was brought to a computer in the form of batched jobs that ran close to the user of the system. The function of the operating system was to smooth the transition from one job to another by automating the process of job initiation.

As computer systems matured, the job of the operating system was extended to provide multiprogramming so that a number of unrelated jobs could share the machine. The fundamental goal of multiprogramming was to alternate between programs in such a way that one program would use the processor while input/output for another program was accomplished. Thus the time a processor might wait for input/output operations to complete one job could be productively used in the service of another job. In addition, more effective use might be made of memory by holding more than one job, or parts of more than one job, in the memory at the same time.

Because hardware was expensive, a major concern of operating systems was the effective use of hardware resources. The expense of hardware also provided motivation for putting as little function as permissible into hardware circuitry. The cost of providing complex functions in hardware with rather sophisticated instructions was considered to be greater than the cost of providing enhancements to a system through delivered service programs.

A major hardware influence on operating system design was the development of large on-line disk storage that provided the possibility of holding large populations

of programs and data in media permanently accessible to the processor. This provided the essential hardware basis for on-line operations, real time control, and time sharing of various types.

But the existence of on-line storage is not the only important hardware development influencing operating systems design. Recent hardware trends indicate that the cost of delivering systems functions through software media may be, or shortly become, less economic than providing functions in various hardware forms. Thus, many of the functions commonly furnished in operating systems may be provided through hardwiring in a computer or through microcode in control memories. There is wide interest in how much operating systems function may effectively be provided in hardware.

Hardware and Operating Systems: Mutual Influences

The relationship between operating system and hardware design has been to a large extent bidirectional. As operating systems concepts matured, attention was directed to the hardware/software interface, the line between functions provided by hardware, and those by operating systems.

By the early 1960s, machine architecture and design began to reflect a general acceptance of the fact that applications programs would run in the presence of an operating system and that machines would be shared in some fashion. The earliest machine reflections of these notions came in the form of memory protection mechanisms, concepts of privileged state, and enhanced mechanisms for the dynamic allocation of memory locations to programs (i.e., relocation mechanisms). Memory protection and relocation mechanisms may be complementary: the fundamental mechanism for providing addressability to a particular set of memory locations protects other memory locations from reference.

In a *virtual memory architecture,* the addresses represented in a running program do not indicate actual hardware memory locations. The goal is to provide an addressing space for a program that is larger than the physical memory of an object machine.

In an architecture that supports a virtual memory operating system, a table is maintained by the operating system that translates the addresses used by a compiled program into real memory locations. Each memory reference is applied to the table to find a corresponding real memory location. Memory is allocated in structures,

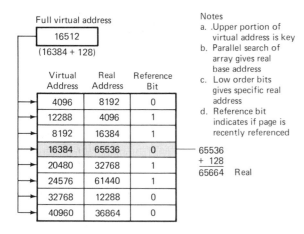

Full virtual address

16512

(16384 + 128)

Virtual Address	Real Address	Reference Bit
4096	8192	0
12288	4096	1
8192	16384	1
16384	65536	0
20480	32768	1
24576	61440	1
32768	12288	0
40960	36864	0

Notes
a. .Upper portion of virtual address is key
b. Parallel search of array gives real base address
c. Low order bits gives specific real address
d. Reference bit indicates if page is recently referenced

65536
+ 128
65664   Real

Figure 30.4. Translation lookaside buffer.

commonly called *pages,* and a program memory address is treated as a reference to a basic page plus an offset in the page.

When a memory address used by the program is not represented by the memory translation table, a signal is developed that causes the operating system to find the location on disk or drum of the page containing the program address. Then the system locates an area in memory that is free to receive the page, brings the page into that block of memory, and represents the allocation of the page in memory in the memory table.

In order to speed the process of determining whether a particular page is in memory, many contemporary computers use a hardware mechanism called a *translation lookaside buffer* (Figure 30.4). This buffer is built from a content-addressable memory and permits an address search and translation at processor logic rather than memory logic speeds. The memory locations of some set of most recently referenced pages are represented in the buffer. Reference to the operating-system-maintained software table is only necessary when a page is not found in the translation lookaside buffer. Thus considerable hardware support is provided to an operating system that is managing a set of programs whose total demand for memory exceeds the physical size of the memory.

The *privileged state,* also called *control state* or *master mode* in various sytems, constricts both the addressing possibilities of a program and the instructions that a program can use. The hardware architecture is extended to reflect the fact that the machine will be shared and that

certain functions must be coordinated in order to guarantee the correct execution of a mix of programs. Many hardware architectures do not allow, for example, the issuance of an I/O instruction by a program that is not in the control state.

Because programs may share devices, and since many programs that share devices may not know of each other's existence on the system, it is necessary for the operating system to act as a coordinating mechanism between program references to the device population. The operating system runs in control state and provides queuing, signalling and coordinating functions.

Control state, relocation and memory protect mechanisms are three early examples of movement in computer architecture that enable more aggressive resource sharing and more eaborate resource management strategies on the part of an operating system.

There is recent interest in extending the hardware/software interface still further toward providing increased hardware support for operating system functions. A number of architectures now furnish hardware support for the operating system concept of a process control block. They also contain instructions that facilitate more efficient manipulation of fundamental data structures which associate with operating systems. Thus queue management, stack management, space acquisition, and linkage functions may be performed by the use of fewer instructions in an operating system.

The concept of program hierarchy and layering is supported in some hardware by multiple control states that represent operating system functions hierarchically structured in layers. Thus, in place of control and noncontrol states, there may be many levels of control. Each control level corresponds to a level of privilege and authority associated with a layer of the operating system.

Microcode Support

In addition to bringing some software structure concepts into hardware, the refinement of control structure concepts, and the provision of more powerful structure manipulating instructions, there is also a movement toward the representation of operating system function in microcode. *Microcode* is a rather informal notion, but it essentially represents the idea that the architecture of a computer system can be represented by programming an underlying less complex computer in such a way as to emulate the features of a target machine. In effect, a simulation program is written that runs on one computer to simulate another. The simulation may be efficient and price/performance effective because of the speed of the underlying machine.

Given the ability to simulate a target machine, it is also possible to represent operating system functions in microcode, in addition to the basic instructions of the target machine. Thus the fundamental control functions of an operating system—interrupt handling, memory allocation and dispatching—may be represented in microcode.

An area of interest is how to identify operating system mechanisms most profitably represented in microcode. Two considerations in selecting functions to put into microcode are: the generality and constancy of use of the function, and the stability of the function. Clearly, the greatest benefit to a system is achieved by microcoding those operating system functions that are most frequently used by the majority of systems users. These tend to be the underlying control functions and the services most frequently called for by a running program. It is important, however, to be sure that the microcoded functions are stable, and that they are not subject to frequent change or modification over the life of an operating system.

It is usual that different target machines are supported by different underlying processors appropriate for the price/performance goals of various models of the target architecture. Thus, encoding of operating systems functions must be accomplished for each model of a target machine because the functions in each instance are actually performed by a unique underlying machine. If a function is provided in software, then software can be written one time for the target architecture to run independently of the details of the design of the underlying machine. It is important to minimize the additional work involved in supplying a model dependent function by selecting those operating systems functions that have a minimum probability of change. Any change that is made must be reflected in the dependent code of *each* model of the target architecture.

A concept that is becoming prevalent in this regard is the distinction between policy and mechanism. The concept was promulgated at Carnegie-Mellon University by workers developing an experimental hardware/software system called C.mmp (Carnegie-Mellon multiprocessor) with the associated operating system HYDRA. It has since been used as a basic concept for other operating systems, including the operating system for the Intel 432. Only mechanisms should be placed in microcode.

Relations between Operating Systems and Subsystems

Early general purpose operating systems made a fundamental assumption that they would provide interfaces to applications programs. They further assumed that there would be a large diversity of uses requiring a rather extensive assortment of functions in different versions. Designers tended to be concerned about accommodating a wide variety of input/output options for recording formats, to minimize resource usage constraints and offer very flexible methods for describing the resources required to do a job. As a consequence, operating systems tended to be inclusive and rich in function. This was consistent with a rather short span of experience concerning how machines would be used.

As operating systems have matured, much has been learned about the different patterns of machine use. That is, our ability to assign a set of operational characteristics to a system in an on-line data base environment, as distinguished from a program development environment, has improved.

As a result of growing specialization in computer use, some questions have been raised about identifying the proper specific functions of an operating system. In particular, questions are put to the split of work between an operating system and subsystems. By implication, the question arises as to whether an operating system should be viewed as a support mechanism for users and user programs, or as a support mechanism for subsystems that in turn interface with users and user applications programs.

There are various views on this issue. One view is that the operating system is only a mechanism to support subsystems. Only those functions that are commonly used by subsystems should be put into the operating system. Those functions that are used only by applications running in the context of a subsystem should be placed in the subsystem so that the underlying operating system is smaller and more efficient. Thus a search for the minimum operating system, the kernel functions, is underway in much design work and in the literature.

As an example, consider the functions associated with I/O in a layered structure. At the lowest layer, there is device support that handles device characteristics. At the next layer, there is blocking and buffering support, and at the top layer there is record advance support that presents records to a program or receives records from a program. An underlying operating system is commonly thought to be responsible for the device handling layer because all potential users of a system are users of device level services. Whether the other two layers are considered part of an operating system or properly part of a subsystem, depends on the degree of similarity of buffering, blocking, and the different kinds of record presentation services offered to applications running in the context of various subsystems.

The goal of an orderly design of an operating system/subsystem interface is to minimize the amount of interpretive coding and the path length required to provide a service on behalf of an application program. The danger of elaborate functional richness in the underlying operating system is that applications programs that want simple functions may have to go through a lot of code to determine exactly what to do, because of the diversity of option that is allowed.

An additional pathology at the operating system/subsystem interface is that there is some duplication of effort. In order to meet some specific interface requirements, a subsystem must use some of its own record advance and buffer management techniques, some of its own scheduling and dispatching techniques, and some of its own interpretive algorithms, even though these functions may be substantially performed in the operating system. Pathologies of this type exist in many older systems because of their assumption that they would be the application interface.

Two main streams of development seem to be occurring in operating systems. In older systems, there is a considerable extension to the concept of a specialized subsystem interface that permits authorized subsystems to perform certain functions without the overhead or constraint associated with applications programs. Examples of this may be found in IBM's MVS, which provides a set of service calls that may be made only by an authorized subsystem. In newer systems, special attention is paid to the interfaces and structure of the operating system so that enhanced subsystem functions may be added without disturbing an applications program interface.

As an example, DPPX (Distributed Processing Programming Executive) for the IBM 8100 is a carefully layered system that has a well defined interface layer to applications programs. The basic operating system contains a series of functional layers for various levels of service for resource management, storage, I/O devices, and communications I/O devices. An application program running on the basic DPPX operating system must perform functions of advanced data management in its own coding. As an option, however, it is possible to acquire a data base management system to run as a subsystem with

DPPX. The data base management functional layers are added to the system by splicing them into the structure at various points beneath the applications program interface layer. Applications programs using data base management functions are served by the enhanced layered structure.

Thus the industry has tried to accommodate the need for increased capability in older systems by enhancing the subsystem interface with the operating system, giving up some of its global prerogatives and functions to subsystems. With newer systems, there has been an attempt to define operating systems structure so that new functions may be spliced into the system.

Yet a third approach has been taken. The above two approaches still reveal the concept of an operating and a subsystem. The third approach minimizes the concept of multiple software packages and reveals to the user a single software structure that appears to be specialized and integrated. In place of being aware of various levels of interface, the user is aware of only one integrated package containing a subsystem and an operating system combined to reflect the nature of the expected use of the system. The operating system is in effect hidden from the user, who sees only the subsystem. Structurally, subsystem and operating system functions may also be integrated in a way to blur the interface between them. An example of this kind of approach, of course, is in almost all personal computers. Among larger computers, the IBM System/38 is a system with many of these characteristics.

Across the set of existing operating systems, there is a good deal of diversity as regards the specific functional split between operating systems and the subsystems that they support. The tendency is to move function into subsystems, but there is also a suspicion that there are new functions, particularly in the communications area, that should be placed into the basic operating systems. Sometimes the historical influences on an older operating system make it difficult to add new functions that might be thought basic, and the functions are added instead at a subsystem level.

Usability Characteristics

Closely connected with issues of the split of work between operating and subsystems is the view of a system as seen by different people with different roles in a user enterprise. An operating system may be shielded from an application program or a terminal user by interfaces provided by a subsystem. For systems programmers, however, the operating system is still very much there because a programmer must generate, parameterize, and configure it, and perhaps talk to it. One aspect of concern to users is the amount of professional talent that is required to live with an operating system and its attendant subsystems and utilities. There are costs of tuning, installation, and evolution.

In addition, there are concerns about the degree to which applications programmers are affected by characteristics of an operating system in terms of how much additional work is required to get a program to run on the system.

As regards professional tending of an operating system and its subsystems, there have been efforts to reduce the amount of work involved in installing and configuring software complexes by the use of preconfigured options that deliver a system largely configured and parameterized beforehand. At the cost of some performance and functional optimization, the time and cost involved in achieving a running, installed system are considerably reduced. In addition, supplementary work in the area of remote problem determination, programmed operator functions, and so on, reduces the amount of professional work required with a large software system.

From the point of view of a programmer or casual user of a machine, the extended functions available through subsystems have reduced programming efforts. The provision of canned control language statements have relieved programmers from much of the burden of defining resource and configuration requirements. There is, however, despite progress in this area, a considerable way to go before the achievement of operatorless, programmerless operating and subsystem environments for most general purpose systems. The problem is not restricted to the large general purpose system. Many small operating systems also require a high level of professional talent.

Influences of Distributed Processing and Networking

Among the major influences on contemporary operating systems design is the development of computing environments in which a number of terminals access a computer from a location requiring either telecommunications or local networking support (see Chapter 37). Even more dramatic is the definition of distributed systems or computer networks in which computing systems communicate with each other to acquire remote data or perform functions remotely.

The issues to be faced involve the specific functions that a software environment must provide for these activities and the structure in which the functions are provided. The solutions are diverse and not yet completely realized.

One type of solution is represented by the software elements developed by IBM and associated with the MVS, DOS, and other operating systems. The fundamental approach is to provide a telecommunications access method, VTAM (Virtual Telecommunications Access Method), that is operating system independent. A set of message and control protocols are defined so that different operating systems can communicate with each other over the commonality provided by versions of VTAM running with different operating systems. The major subsystems running on various operating systems use VTAM to communicate with each other. For the most part, the interfaces and service calls used for node to node communication are packaged in the subsystems as part of a set of high level communications protocols called the ISC (Inter-systems Communication), an extension of the SNA (Systems Network Architecture).

The IBM approach undertakes to provide communication across systems composed of heterogeneous operating systems by providing special communications packaging and a set of interfaces defined at the subsystem level. An alternate approach is to integrate the communications functions into the basic operating system. The fundamental issue in the emergence of operating system in networking environments is the determination of where to place new functions and what kinds of structural modifications may be necessary.

30.7 EMERGING CONCEPTUAL MODELS OF OPERATING SYSTEMS

In the face of changing functional requirements, changing concepts of hardware economics, and increased user demands for good interfaces, there has been a lot of activity in exploring operating systems definitions and designs that provide easy to use, reliable, secure, portable, extendable software systems. In the early days of operating systems, the bulk of attention was paid to efficient resource usage and the literature was dominated by various algorithmic approaches to processor, I/O, and memory management.

Lately, resource management issues preoccupied with machine efficiency have been receiving less attention. More attention is being paid to how systems should be structured and how resources should be managed at a conceptual level. A large number of projects in universities are addressing issues of this kind and some of the work is beginning to influence commercially available operating systems.

One of the most important projects is the HYDRA operating system developed at Carnegie Mellon University. It, and its successors, STAROS and MEDUSA, are aimed at discovering the nature of an operating system that runs on a processing system containing a large number of processing units. However, many contemporary notions of operating systems independent of the multiprocessor basis for operating systems have come out of the work. Similar concepts at MIT and other places seem to indicate that there is a mainstream of research connected with the notion of the object model operating system. Contemporary operating systems that have been influenced by the object model include the operating system for the Intel 432, MULTICS, UNIX, Plessey 250, and IBM's System/38.

Fundamental to the notion of an object model operating system is the existence of a set of defined objects of various types. Each object has a system wide, unchanging, universal name. Possession of the name of an object is what makes it possible to refer to, modify, or manipulate the object. Systems differ in the details of the object types they may define and in the attributes associated with an object. All object model operating systems share a notion of object addressability called *capability addressing.*

Capabilities

A *capability* is a name of an object and a statement of rights over the object. *Rights* are the ability to change the object, destroy the object, or control the rights of others to the object.

Capabilities are represented as tokens within a system. The system-wide name is translated to a conceptual address when a program acquires a capability. In a capability based object system, the collection of capabilities held by a program constitute the name space of referenceable objects external to a program.

In this context, a view of the organization of virtual memory emerges different than the view of virtual memory that exists in many contemporary systems. Current contemporary systems create an image of a very large linear address space associated with a particular program cluster. For example, an addressing range of 16 megabytes may be supported. The action of the operating system supported by relocation hardware dynamically maps the allocation of virtual address spaces onto a physical address space in accordance with the reference pattern of a running program.

In an object management system, a virtual name space is a collection of objects for which a program has a capability. Therefore, the program view of memory is not as a single dimensional linear address space, but as a two dimensional space consisting of a set of uniquely named objects and offsets into the objects. An address is a unique pointer and an offset. The total amount of linear address space represented by the set of uniquely named objects in a name space may not be clearly visible to a user.

Object Types

Object management systems have various populations of objects of different types. Here the discussion will focus three basic types of objects: data, procedure, and process.

A *data object* contains data. It is approximated by the general notion of a file or a data set. A data object contains no computer programming. In HYDRA, but not in all systems, a data object may have capabilities that relate it to other objects. An important point about a data ojbect in an object model system is that it is referenced by its unique name in the same manner whether the object resides in main memory or it is on a storage device.

A *procedure object* is an operator of the system. A procedure object contains a code portion, a private space, and a representation of the capabilities that it has to other objects. A procedure object code portion may address freely within the private space of an object. To encourage modularization of programs, the directly addressable space of a procedure object is generally held to be small; this discourages the development of large, unstructured modules that are difficult to modify and debug.

Addressing outside of the private space of a procedure is accomplished through capabilities to access other objects. Commonly, a procedure object has capabilities both to access other procedure objects, which it may CALL, to which it may send messages, and so on; and to data objects. The capabilities may or may not be formed on a capabilities list. A *capabilities list* is a formal part of a procedure object that lists all of the objects that a procedure may reference. When capabilities lists are not used, as in SWARD, capabilities are then placed in the private space of the procedure. There is some difference of opinion about the performance and resource management benefits of capabilities lists versus placing capabilities in a procedure's private space.

A *process object* is a named structure that represents

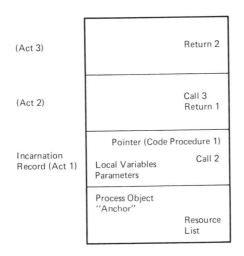

Notes
a. Process anchor owns resources
b. Each incarnation record contains pointer to executable code, local variables, etc.
c. Each record may CALL another routine, placing incarnation record on process stock
d. Return removes record

Figure 30.5. Process as a LIFO stack.

an instance of a procedure or of a set of procedures that invoke each other and which form a LIFO stack. There is quite a wide diversity of specific meaning applied to the word *process* in the literature of operating systems. Some use the word to refer to the incarnation (see below) of a procedure. Others use the word to describe a formal structure of the operating system that may be the holder and user of various resources. One operational concept of a process is as an anchor upon which incarnation records may be stacked in a LIFO fashion (Figure 30.5) to represent the activity of CALLs and RETURNs associated with a particular named user. A running process always contains an incarnation record at the top of the stack, and a set of incarnation records representing programs that have CALLed programs running above them in the stack. On a RETURN, an incarnation record is taken from the stack.

An *incarnation record* represents the invocation of a particular procedure. Each time a program is called, it requires a work space into which to place parameters and to develop private values. An incarnation record contains a pointer to the procedure being run and a pointer to a list of values. In addition, if there is a formal capabilities list, an incarnation record contains the capabilities associated with a particular invocation of the procedure.

The notion of a process with a capabilities list unique in each incarnation record brings up some notions of protection and security; these are very important to the object model school of operating systems design. Sometimes rigid hierarchic structures are not efficient. A goal, for

example, of HYDRA design, is to investigate whether features of debugability, security, and integrity may be preserved without a rigid hierarchic structure.

Protection

A fundamental function of an operating system is to protect the resources of the system from illegitimate reference or accidental distortion. The capabilities concept provides a formal way to state the rights that operators have over objects. An important part of a capability design is to ensure that the rights of a program are not illegitimately enlarged as a result of calling another program or as a result of the extended rights of a calling program. Hierarchy associated with levels of privilege is one way of approaching this problem.

Another approach is to design an underlying operating system function that is responsible for dynamically developing the capabilities of an incarnation whenever it is called. The goal of a design in this area is to show that security may be maintained without a rigid hierarchic structure. One approach is to do a rights merger. The operating system uses the rights of the calling incarnation, the residual rights of a called procedure, and a statement of rights passing limitations, to create a capabilities list for the incarnation record that will run on the calling process.

In HYDRA, this incarnation record is called a *local name space*. The design undertakes to find an intersection of capabilities and rights levels such that, regardless of the residual rights of the called procedure, no enlargement of rights may occur for a calling program that is not legitimate. Only a proper intersection of rights are copied over into the incarnation record and all other capabilities of the called procedure are irrelevant for a particular incarnation.

Structure

The structure of an object model operating system contains a population of basic kernel functions, the operating system itelf, that include a protection mechanism of the type just described: a basic dispatcher, an interrupt handler and a locking mechanism. Care is taken to ensure that only mechanisms are included in the basic kernel. Beyond this a set of services and fundamental tools that run on process stacks are provided. These features not only provide the service, but also serve as building blocks for the creation of subsystems and extended operating systems services, such as long term scheduling.

An interesting change in the relationship between operating systems and application program elements may occur in an object model system. In effect, the operating system, beyond the kernel functions, is just a set of procedures that may be invoked by applications programs in the same manner that an application program procedure may be invoked. Thus, the master/slave relationship is tilted toward the application program set. A particular set of operating systems functions may or may not be made available to an application program process in terms of the capabilities the applications program is given. Beyond this, different versions of operating systems, or actually different operating systems, may be defined for an application in terms of the specific operating system data objects and procedure objects to which an application program is given capability.

We are in a period in which the technology and economic bases for operating systems are shifting rapidly and causing a basic rethinking of what an operating system is and what it should do. The literature of operating systems reflects this; there is a deemphasis of interest in hardware resource management algorithms and a new emphasis on structure and usability.

REFERENCES

Agoston, D. H., et al., "An Operating System for the Intel MDS System," *SIGMini Newsletter*, Vol. 3, No. 2 (Apr. 1977).

Auslander, M. A., and J. F. Jaffe, "Influences of Dynamic Address Translation on Operating System Technology," *IBM Systems Journal*, Vol. 12, No. 4 (1973), p. 368.

Brinch-Hansen, P., *Operating Systems Principles*. Englewood Cliffs, NJ: Prentice-Hall, 1973.

Brinch-Hansen, P., *The Architecture of Concurrent Programs*. Englewood Cliffs, NJ: Prentice-Hall, 1977.

Cutler, D. N., et al., "The Nucleus of a Real-time Operating System," *ACM Conference Proceedings*, 1976, p. 241.

Dijkstra, E. W., "The Structure of T.H.E. Multiprogramming System," *Communications of the ACM*, Vol. 11, No. 5 (May 1968), p. 341.

Fabry, R. S., "Capability-Based Addressing," *Communications of the ACM*, Vol. 17, No. 7 (July 1974), p. 403.

Flink, C. W. II., "Easy—An Operating System for QM-1," *SIGMicro Newsletter*, Vol. 8, No. 3 (Sept. 1977).

Habermann, A. N., et al., "Modularization and Hierarchy in a Family of Operating Systems," *Communications of the ACM*, Vol. 19, No. 5 (May 1976), p. 266.

Heistand, R., "ACP System, Concepts and Facilities," IBM Corporation, GH20-1473.

Holt, R. C., et al., *Structured Concurrent Programming with Operating Systems Applications*. Reading, MA: Addison-Wesley, 1978.

Jones, A. K., "The Object Model: A Conceptual Tool for Structuring Software," in R. Bayer, R. M. Graham, G. Seegmuller, eds., *Operating Systems: An Advanced Course*, New York: Springer-Verlag, 1979, p. 7.

Jones, A. K., et al., "StarOS, a Multiprocessor Operating System for the Support of Task Forces," *Ninth Annual Symposium on Operating Systems Principles*, 1979.

Lampson, B., and H. E. Sturgis, "Reflections on an Operating System Design," *Communications of ACM*, Vol. 19, No. 5 (May 1976), p. 251.

Lans, M. G., "The Subsystem Approach to Enhancing Small Processor Operating Systems," *SIGMini Newsletter*, Vol. 4, No. 4 (Aug. 1978).

Lister, A. M., and P. J. Sayer, "Hierarchical Monitors," *Software—Practice and Experience*, Vol. 7, No. 5 (1977), p. 613.

Lorin, H. and H. Dietel, *Operating Systems*. Reading, MA: Addison-Wesley, 1980.

Mohan, G., "Survey of Recent Operating Systems Research," *Operating Systems Review*, Vol. 12, No. 1 (Jan. 1978).

Madnick, S., and J. Donovan, *Operating Systems*. New York: McGraw-Hill Book Co., 1974.

Parnas, D. L., "On a Buzzword: Hierarchical Structure," *Proceedings IFIP Congress*, 1974, p. 336.

Parnas, D. L., G. Handzel and H. Wurges, "Design and Specification of the Minimal Subset of an Operating System," *Software Systems Engineering*, 1976, p. 23.

Ritchie, D. M., and K. Thompson, "The UNIX Time-Sharing System," *Communications of the ACM*, Vol. 17, No. 7 (July 1974), p. 365.

Schroeder, M. D., D. Clark and J. Saltzer, "MULTICS Kernel Design Project," *Proceedings 6th Annual Symposium on Op-*

erating Systems Principles, Operating Systems Review, Vol. 11, No. 5 (Nov. 1977).

Shaw, A., *Logical Design of Operating Systems.* Englewood Cliffs, NJ: Prentice-Hall, 1974.

Wettstein, H., "Implementation of Synchronizing Operations in Various Environments," *Software Practice and Experience,* Vol. 4 (1977), p. 215.

Wulf, W., et al., "HYDRA: The Kernel of a Multiprocessor Operating System," *Communications of the ACM,* Vol. 17, No. 6 (June 1974), p. 337.

31
Data Structures and Management

Ned Chapin

InfoSci Inc.

31.1 INTRODUCTION

From the user's point of view, the most fundamental aspect of computers is that they process data. That is, people supply data as input to the computers and the computers produce some corresponding data as output. In a fundamental sense, there is nothing else that a computer can do.

The implications of that opportunity, which masquerades as a restriction, are enormous. Every piece of work that a user wants a computer to do must be expressed in terms of some data the user is to provide to the computer, and some data the computer is, in turn, to provide in response. Until the user can define precisely and exactly what are the data available as input and what are the corresponding data expected as output, the user is not able to get the computer to do the work satisfactorily.

The need for the user to define and describe data, however, does not stop just with the data going into and the data coming out from the computer. Because the preparation of output data by the computer starts with the input data, but may go through a large number of intermediate stages, the user must also be concerned with data inside the computer. Each of these intermediate stages in turn are represented as data. Their selection, organization, and effective utilization constitute a significant management problem for the user of a computer.

The way people think about the data is usually referred to as **data structure.** In this chapter, we will focus only upon what are technically known as **operand data structures**—that is, structures for the data which are worked on or produced by the computer. They are the data which the computer will accept as input, produce as output, or

produce and utilize as intermediate results. These data are the most numerous, the most dynamic, and offer the most significant management problems.

The problem of data mangement, given that a choice of data structure has been made, consists of obtaining the most economic, reliable, and accurate performance of the computer as it produces the output from the available input data. These involve important questions of the ordering or sequencing of data, the identification of the parts of the data, and access to the parts so identified, as well as the preservation of data integrity and data security. Some of these data management problems occur in an even more severe form for data bases. Nearly all of the material on data base management is also applicable to data management generally, and will not be repeated in this chapter, except occasionally for emphasis.

Over the history of computers a number of different varieties of data structure and data management have been developed. Only a few, however, have received the bulk of attention and use. These will be the ones considered in this chapter. The fact that other forms of data structure and other data management issues are not addressed or referenced does not mean they are not of value or significance in some situations. It only indicates that they are relatively rare, and hence suitable for coverage in more specialized publications.

31.2 SOME DISTINCTIONS AND DEFINITIONS

As we embark upon this examination of data structures and management, the introduction of several distinctions and definitions is important for a clear understanding of concepts and practices. The first distinction is the one between data structures and storage structures. A **data structure** is how people visualize, conceptualize, or think about data. A **storage structure** is the pattern or arrangement of data in some physical storage device or medium such as magnetic tape, magnetic disk, magnetic cores, thin films, ROMs, RAMs, CCDs, or the like. As the chapter title specifies, the coverage here is on data structures, not on storage structures.

Storage structures, however, are nonetheless important. For any practical implementation to be made of any particular data structure, a corresponding storage structure must be chosen that provides some mapping, or direct correspondence between the features or characteristics of the storage and data structures. This mapping may be a physical mapping of corresponding component parts, or it may be a functional mapping which relies upon computer hardware or computer software to make the storage structure perform in a way that corresponds with the data structure.

Our focus here, however, is on data structure. We shall look at the way that people think about data from a syntactic, not a semantic, point of view. That is, our concern is with organization, pattern, arrangement, and relationship. We are generally not concerned with the specific values items of data may take, the particular coding of the data, the source of the values of the data, the reliability or integrity or security of the data, nor the timeliness or utility of the data. An analogy may help clarify this point. Data structures are like house structures. They provide particular capabilities and features such as a kitchen, garage, bedrooms, living room, basement, plumbing, heating, stairs, lights, and so on. The experience of living (semantics) in the house does not alter the number of bathrooms nor where the stairways are located.

The second significant distinction involves the concept of component. An item of data is said to be a **component** of another item if two or more of the first item may combine, or be taken together, as an equivalent to the second item. That does not mean that the combination is not something greater than the sum of its parts. It only argues that if a part is missing or significantly impaired, the overall structure does not perform as expected. Thus by analogy, three of the major components of a book are the table of contents, the text, and the index. It is possible to have a book without all three components, but a book is more useful (especially if it is a technical book) when all three components are present and consistent with each other. And as the analogy reminds us, the individual com-

Table 31.1. A Hierarchy of Data and Storage Structure Components

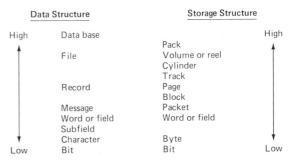

Data Structure		Storage Structure	
High	Data base		High
		Pack	
	File	Volume or reel	
		Cylinder	
		Track	
	Record	Page	
		Block	
	Message	Packet	
	Word or field	Word or field	
	Subfield		
	Character	Byte	
Low	Bit	Bit	Low

ponents that comprise a larger unit need not be identical in character. They may be identical—or nearly so—for instance, the text may have as its components the chapter, and may have from one to many chapters.

The data structure components that are most relevant here are summarized in Table 31.1. Our primary focus is on the center portion of the hierarchy, where we shall deal primarily with ways of organizing and establishing patterns and relationships among fields, words and records. *Fields* or *words* participate in forming data structures in two special ways, based upon two particular concepts. One of these concepts is of the address. An **address** is the place or location of specific data in some data structure or in some storage structure. This place, or location, is itself represented by identifying data, data which usually can be expressed as words or fields. When the value of the data in the field or word serves as an identification of data location, then the field or word serves as an expression of an address.

Three varieties of address are used with data structures. One is a *symbolic address*. This, the most common, is an aribtrarily chosen name to serve as an address. An example is PAY-HISTORY-RECORD to designate where the data about an employee payroll history may be located. A second variety of address is an *absolute address*. This names a location in terms directly useable by the computer without further translation. Hence, it is common in storage structures but rare in data structures. A third variety of address is a *relative address*. This describes a location in terms of a count from some base or reference location. These are roughly equivalent to "third door on your left." Figure 31.1 summarizes these three varieties of addresses.

The second concept is the concept of key. A **key** can usually be represented as the value of some particular field or word which serves in either of two ways:

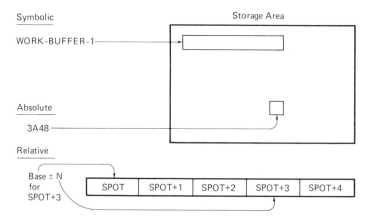

Figure 31.1. Examples of three varieties of addresses.

1. It may serve as the basis for ordering the larger items of data in which it is included as a component. For example, if we have some data about each number of a group of people, we can sort the data by the person's name.
2. The key may serve as the basis for a search. For example, as shown in Figure 31.2, we could search the data addressed as **RECORDS** for the name **GHEN-SON**. Note that a search does not always succeed in finding a match to the key field or work.

In the material that follows, the more common data structures are clustered into two main groups: (1) *regular structures* which have a consistent or symmetrical character to their patterns, and (2) *irregular structures*, which may have some internal symmetry or regularity to their patterns, but also have significant irregularities present. The regular structures are less numerous and less diverse than the irregular structures. For that reason, and because they are simpler to understand, the regular structures are considered first.

31.3 REGULAR STRUCTURES

The three common regular structures are the *scalar*, the *vector*, and the *array*. Typically, the regular structures are implemented in storage structures by computer words or by fields of uniform length. This length may vary from situation to situation, but given the situation, is normally the same for all.

The **scalar** structure is often used for representing a single item of data, because scalars are thought of as being isolated. They have no fixed or established relation-

ships with other scalars unless they are used for addresses as noted below. Figure 31.3 gives three examples of scalars. A common use for scalars is as the operands in numeric computations. Typically, scalars are themselves assigned symbolic addresses. Scalars are easily implemented in most programing languages such as COBOL, FORTRAN, APL, and PL/1.

Sometimes scalars have an address-like relationship to some other structure, such as a vector, an array, a table, or a file. Four terms are used to describe scalars which have these relationships: pointer, link, index, and subscript.

A *pointer* is a scalar which has as its value an address of some part of another data structure. The data structure pointed to normally is of fairly large or complex type, such as a string, record, or array; Figure 31.4 provides an example of a pointer. Pointers are not convenient to use in COBOL and FORTRAN, but are convenient in many other languages.

A *link* is a scalar incorporated within a larger structure and serving as a pointer to another such structure. An example is a link indicating the next record in sequence in a group of records. Figure 31.5 shows an example of a

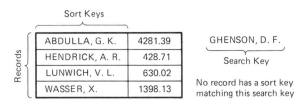

Figure 31.2. Examples of a key.

Numeric

Integers   487

Real Numbers   + 2.71828

Nonnumeric   CLEVELAND

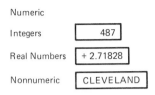

Figure 31.3. Three examples of scalars.

circular use of links in two directions. Links are easily implemented in list processing languages, such as IPL-V.

An *index* is a scalar that has as its value the count part of a relative address pointing to some particular part of one or more larger data structures, such as tables or arrays. The index is independent of the larger structures to which it may be used as a pointer (Figure 31.6). Indexes can also be used as subscripts, and are easily implemented in languages such as COBOL, FORTRAN, and PL/1.

A *subscript* is a scalar serving as a pointer, but tied to a specific part of a particular data structure; it is not itself a part of the larger structure. The subscript normally identifies specific components from a larger structure such as a table or an array. Subscripts are conveniently available in all of the major programming languages. Figure 31.6 gives an example of two subscripts used to identify the row and column respectively in an array. Note that a subscript is in effect a relative address, in which the base point is implied and not explicitly stated.

A **vector** is a data structure which may consist of any number of similar data elements. The data elements almost always are themselves numeric scalars and the elements are assumed to be in a fixed sequence relative to each other. A vector, therefore, is commonly thought of as having either up or down, or left or right elements. Typically, the position of an element in the vector is determined by the count from the left or top portion of the vector, and can be indicated by a subscript. Figure 31.7 provides an example of a vector. At the extreme, a null or empty vector is possible—that is, a vector which exists as a structure but which happens at the moment to con-

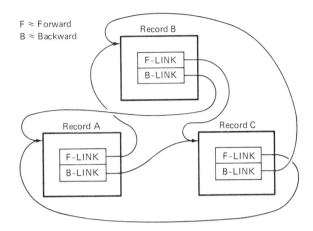

F ≈ Forward
B ≈ Backward

Figure 31.5. Example of circular bidirectional links between records.

tain no elements. An example of a non-null vector is the amount of stock withdrawn each day, day by day, during the month for one item in an inventory. Vectors are commonly implemented in numeric computational work in such languages as FORTRAN, APL, and PL/1.

An **array** represents a generalization of the vector structure to vectors going in more than one direction simultaneously. That is, any one element in the array participates simultaneously in two or more vectors. Thus in Figure 31.8 the element whose value is 7 participates in the third column, the second row, and the first plane of the three-dimensional array shown. The addresses of arrays are commonly used with subscripts when it is desirable to identify particular positions in an array. Null or empty arrays are possible.

Arrays are commonly used in computational work and can easily be implemeneted in major programming languages. Usually, particular meanings are assigned to the columns, rows, and planes, and higher dimensions in the array. Thus in a payroll application, the columns in an array might represent the day of the week, the rows

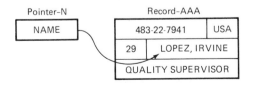

Figure 31.4. Example of a pointer using a symbolic address **NAME**.

Subscripts	Array–HH				Index
ARRAY–HH(2 3) Points to the boxed element in the second row in the third column in ARRAY–HH	4	5	6	7	INDEX–A could point to any row or any column in the array
	9	1	2	3	
	5	6	7	8	

Figure 31.6. Example of subscripts to the rows and columns of an array.

Represented vertically	Represented horizontally
4	4 5 6 7 8 9
5	
6	If the vector has the
7	symbolic address VEC,
8	then the element with
9	the value 7 is VEC(4)

Figure 31.7. Example of a vector.

might represent the weeks in the pay period, and the planes might represent the person. Then the array elements individually represent the number of hours worked each day by each person during the week of the pay period. Some mathematical operations are defined in terms of arrays, for example, matrix multiplication and inversion.

The *dimension* of an array is the number of vectors in which each element of the array participates. One subscript is used for each dimension. Thus a two dimensional array is one in which the vectors can be thought of as arranged in columns and rows, and requires two subscripts. Such a two dimensional array is commonly referred to as a *matrix*. The subscripts that are associated with an array have a specific ordering in relation to the dimension of the array; this ordering varies from one programing language to another.

A common practice is for the "fastest moving index" to be represented by the rightmost subscript, which usually represents the columns. The next subscript to the left is used to represent the next highest dimension, the rows. Thus a subscript of (3 2) indicates the element in the third row and the second column of a matrix. The index at the far right is said to "move faster" because if a per-

son traverses the vectors in an array in a regular pattern, such as beginning with the row starting at the upper left, the right-most index runs through all of its values while the other indices remain unchanged. Then the next index to the left increases by 1, and the rightmost index starts again at 1 and again runs through all its values. This process continues until every array element has been touched just once.

In review, regular data structures are characterized by uniformity of their component elements and by simple positional relationships among components. The simple positional relationships are commonly summarized in terms of indices or subscripts to express the complexity of the structures as dimensions. Thus a regular structure with zero dimensions is a scalar, with one dimension is a vector, and with two dimensions is a matrix. The size of the structure is expressed as the number of components that comprise each dimension, as for example, a 5×8 matrix.

31.4 IRREGULAR STRUCTURES

The most basic of the irregular data structures is the string. The **string** is a sequence, of any size, of data items, in a fixed order. The elements or components in a string commonly are individual characters, names, numbers, or addresses, but are not limited to any of these.

The string is similar to the vector but differs from it in three significant ways. First, a string is not limited to numeric items of data; second, a string relaxes the strict positional relationships among the components; and third, structures composed of strings are themselves strings unless added restrictions are imposed. Hence, the elements in a string may be numbered and a subscript used to in-

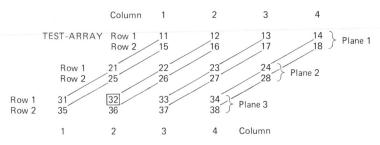

The boxed element is TEST-ARRAY(3 1 2)

Figure 31.8. Example of a three dimensional array, where the lines indicate the plane to plane vectors.

SAMPLE(8) is the space between "is" and "a",
and is marked by the pointer

Figure 31.9. Example of a string of characters, called **SAMPLE**, showing the start or head, the end or tail, a pointer, and a subscript.

dicate its position in the string. The concept of dimension, however, does not apply to strings because of their irregularity.

Strings may have a start, usually visualized as at the left, and an end, usually visualized as at the right, as diagramed in Figure 31.9. A null string is possible.

In terms of storage structures, strings are commonly implemented by contiguous successive fields or words. Some languages handle strings with difficulty, such as COBOL and FORTRAN; some with ease, such as APL and PL/1; and a few exist primarily for string handling, such as SNOBOL.

Stack and Queue

In spite of the inherent difficulties in handling strings with a computer, two varieties of strings find fair use in computers, and some generalizations and disciplining of strings find common use. Let us look at the two varieties first. One of these is the queue and the other is the stack.

A **queue** is a string in which additions of components to the string are made at the tail, and the deletions of components from the string are made at the head. An analogy for a queue is the checkout line at a grocery store (Figure 31.10). The queue provides effectively a first-in, first-out (FIFO) inventory of string elements. A queue is commonly used in computer operating systems to keep track of tasks waiting for assignment, requests for storage

Figure 31.10. Example of a queue.

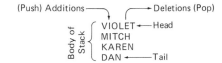

Figure 31.11. Example of a stack.

utilization, customers waiting to be served, and so forth. A set of queues may be used, with a different queue for each priority of work.

A **stack** is another useful variety of a string. A stack accepts all additions and deletions at the head. Hence, it is a last-in, first-out (LIFO) inventory of string elements (Figure 31.11). Because all additions and deletions are from the head of a stack, special terminology is used to describe them. To put a new component on a stack is *pushing the stack,* and removing a component from a stack is *popping the stack.* Thus a push lengthens the stack by increasing the number of components in it, and a pop decreases the length of the stack.

In spite of the difficulties of working with stacks, because of their string based character, they nonetheless play a useful role in computer programs. A stack is a convenient way of representing the sequence of work needed when the performance of the work may be interrupted by the occurence of some condition. For instance, suppose that a program is executing and an interrupt occurs to admit a new program (or data). The resume address in the program that has been interrupted is pushed onto the stack. Then the execution of the new program is begun. If for some reason that program also is interrupted, then its resume address, too, is pushed onto the stack. When this last interruption has been carried to completion, the program most recently interrupted, that is, the one at the top of the stack, is resumed by popping the stack. When that program, in turn, is completed, the stack is again popped and execution resumed on the first program.

Tables

When strings can be repeated and are composed of the same components in the same sequence, then the strings can be arranged into a string of strings. For convenience, such strings of strings are arranged in a pattern termed a **table.** An example of a table is given in Figure 31.12.

The components that comprise the table need not all be of like character (unlike an array), but those at any given position in the table must be like kinds of compo-

428-A	DIODE	EACH	1.22
495-G	CLAMP	PAIR	1.89
537-D	SOLDER	LB	6.87
721-A	CLIP	EACH	3.41

Figure 31.12. Example of a table, called **TAB** composed of four strings.

nents. Thus, as shown in Figure 31.12, the fourth component in each component string is a price, the first component is a stock number, and the second is a stock name. For convenience in table reference, we use subscripts in the same way we use them for arrays. Thus, in Figure 30.12 the unit of measure **PAIR** is **TAB(2 3)**.

Tables as data structures have a diverse representation in storage structures. The strings may be physically contiguous; or they may be noncontiguous, as when separated by known address gaps in storage. Sometimes the table is formed from strings for the columns, not the rows, and these, too, are not always contiguous. In some implementations, the storage structures use pointers or links for the equivalent of rows or columns.

Some special terminology applies to tables because of the way they are commonly used to show relationships among data values. To facilitate the use of tables, the position in the table that is looked at is referred to as the *argument,* and the datum which is found there and is associated with the argument is referred to as the *function.* An argument-function pair is called a *table entry.* What in the table serves as the argument need not be the first component along a row—that is, the first column in a table, but commonly is some column. It can be any column, just as the function may be any column. The correspondence is along the row between the argument and the function.

Tables occur so frequently that special procedures have been developed for finding the function desired when the argument is known but its location in the table is not known. For this purpose, a search key is identified and used to search the arguments in the table until a matching argument is found, or no match is found, and the arguments available in the table are exhausted. Sometimes the closest higher or lower argument is acceptable when an extract match cannot be found for a search key. A brief review of some of the more popular methods of table search follows.

If the arguments in the table are unordered from row to row, that is, the sequence of values in the column shows no regular pattern of variations, then the usual search technique is *sequential.* Taking this approach, we begin at the top of the table and compare the search key with the argument (Figure 31.13). If we find a match, we are finished with the search. If not, we advance to the next row. We repeat the process until encountering the end of the table or finding an acceptable match. For example, we could search **TAB** in Figure 31.12 for **CLAMP** (because that table is unordered by name) and find it in the second row, or for **TUBE**, and encounter a search failure. In large tables, a sequential search can become lengthy.

Two major ways to reduce lengthy sequential searches are to order the arguments by frequency of search, or to sort them by treating the arguments as sort keys. In the first method, the most frequently searched-for entries are placed first in the table, and the rarely searched-for entries are placed last in the table. In the second method, the entries are sorted by their arguments, for example, by putting them in alphabetic order.

When the arguments are in a sorted order, additional search strategies become reasonable to use. If the table is short, usually of fewer than 10 to 12 rows, then the straight sequential search is generally the preferred choice. If the table is more extensive and has few or no duplicate arguments, then a binary search is usually the most economic (Figure 31.14). The *binary search* proceeds by dividing the table in half, and comparing the boundary argument between the halves against the search key. If the search key is equal to the boundary argument, then the item sought has been found. If the search key is larger than the boundary argument, then the first half is ignored, and the search continues only in the other half. If, by contrast, the search key is smaller than the boundary item between the halves, then the sec-

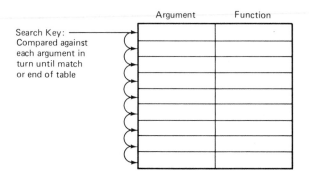

Figure 31.13. Diagram of sequential search of a table.

Function   Argument

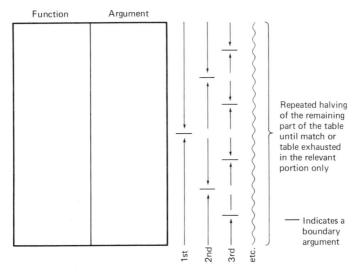

Repeated halving
of the remaining
part of the table
until match or
table exhausted
in the relevant
portion only

—— Indicates a
    boundary
    argument

1st 2nd 3rd etc.

Figure 31.14. Diagram of binary search of a table.

ond half is ignored and the search is conducted in the first half. Whichever half is chosen is then treated in the same manner as before, and the selected portion of the table is successively divided in half until the table is exhausted or the entry found.

Another search method useful for sorted arguments is the *interval search*. This procedes in a manner somewhat similar to the sequential search (Figure 31.15). Instead of checking every item in the table, this scheme checks every *n*th item, where *n* is usually chosen as some fraction of the table, such as 10'th, 50'th, or 100'th. If the sort is an ascending sort, then once an argument is found that is equal to or greater than the search key, the interval search is ended. Then the located interval is searched sequentially. If duplicate arguments are in the table, several contiguous intervals may have to be sequentially searched. The interval search works well on small to medium size tables, but is not as efficient as the next method for large tables.

The last of the four search methods is the *calculated*, or *computed*, or *hash search*. This method also requires the table arguments to be ordered. In this search (Figure 31.16), a conversion operation is applied to the search key to calculate an address in the table. A sequential search is then begun at the address calculated. If duplicate keys occur in the table, or if the keys are not well randomized in value, a sequential search of as much as 5 percent of the table may be necessary. To enable the use of the calculated search, the data must first be placed in the table

with some known relationship between the row position of the argument and the argument value. To achieve this may require vacant or dummy entries in the table. Where data are relatively static or changing but slowly in the table, such a relationship can be derived and work reasonably well. When arguments in the table change radically and frequently, other search methods generally work more effectively.

Because of its convenience for showing arbitrary rela-

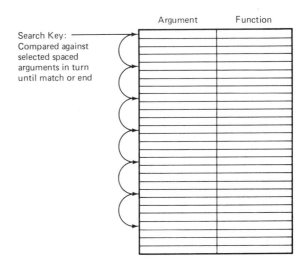

Search Key:
Compared against
selected spaced
arguments in turn
until match or end

Argument   Function

Figure 31.15. Diagram of interval search of a table.

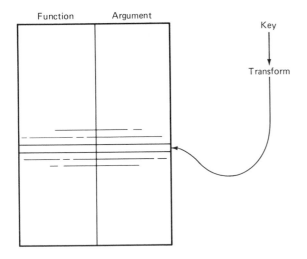

Figure 31.16. Diagram of computed search of a table.

tionships among data, the table is one of the most widely used of data structures. COBOL, PL/1, and RPG work conveniently with tables. FORTRAN and APL can work with them, but less conveniently. Some common applications of tables are to indicate to the computer which items of peripheral equipment are in a working condition, the charge numbers associated with customers' accounts, the prices to be charged for merchandise, the warehouse locations of stock items, and the wage rates of employees.

The contrast, however much exists, between "scientific computation" and "business data processing" is probably best exemplified by the use of data structures. "Scientific computation" typically uses the array, whereas business data processing typically uses the table. This reflects the general rule that data being worked with in business lacks the mathematical elegance and symmetry found in science and engineering work.

31.5 RECORDS

Basic to an understanding of data structures and management is a concept of the record and the place of the record in the file. A **file** is effectively a string in which the string elements are records (Figure 31.17). The string components may be fixed or variable in length. If the records are fixed or uniform in length, then effectively the file becomes a table. If the records are variable, or non-uniform in length, then the table view does not fit. But whereas the usual string consists of relatively small elements, such as characters or fields, the records that com-

prise a file are typically considerably larger. It is rare to find records of fewer than about 20 characters in length; conversely, it is not uncommon to find records of more than 5,000 characters in length. Also, files may be composed of millions or more records, and a null or empty file is possible.

The **record**, the basic component of the file, is typically defined to be a group of data all on a single topic, for example, data about an employee, a customer, or a product. The specific items of data about the subject are then often placed in the record in a fixed sequence (because the record is itself a string). If an item of data is to serve as the key, then that item is often, but not always, placed first in the record.

Record Size

Records themselves may be of fixed or uniform length—that is, always have the same number of characters—and always have the same sequence of fields. This is a common situation for personnel records, stock records, sales records, accounting records, and the like. Each fixed length record may be regarded as a string and the elements within the string from record to record are expected to occur in the same sequence with the same significance or expected meaning. Thus, each inventory record might begin with the stock number, followed by the stock name, followed by the stock location, then the unit of measure, the quantity on hand, and so on.

But the data being recorded may be inherently variable in quantity and character. For instance, records holding patients' medical histories show great variety. While the patient always has a name and a billing address, not all patients have lung trouble, nor does every patient have a broken leg or diabetes. Some see their physicians frequently, some rarely; some have extensive laboratory work done and some hardly ever need or use the services of a medical laboratory. Hence data will likely vary drastically from patient to patient in quantity and content. The result is that the records that represent that data not

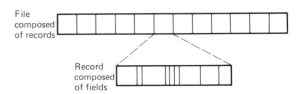

Figure 31.17. A file is composed of records, and is effectively a string of records, where each record is itself a string.

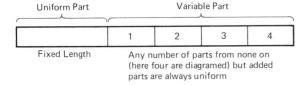

Figure 31.18. Variable records formed by incremental use of a repeated part.

only vary in length from record to record, but also what is found within any given record may vary as time passes.

When records are nonuniform, one needs to make the components within each record identifiable or the situation is unmanageable. Two alternatives are commonly used. One involves concentrating the variation of the records in only a portion of each and forcing the remaining data to fit a repetitive pattern. The second involves putting pointers in the records individually to define the internal character of each record.

The more common alternative is the first because it is easier to manage. This involves composing the string of fields within the record to concentrate the uniform part in the left end or first part of the record. For example, in an inventory file, the basic identifying and descriptive information about the stock items, its balance on hand, its location, and the like, can be consistent from one record to the next. But what is not consistent might be the history of receipts and issue; yet each has a basic amount of data. Active stock items might in a year's time accumulate a large number of such transactions, whereas relatively inactive items might have only a few such transactions during a year. This alternative is diagrammed in Figure 31.18.

The second, and less popular, alternative is to add pointers to the record defining the record organization (layout) and content. This involves placing at fixed or known locations in the record some data that can direct the identification of other data in the record. This attributed string involves a special use of pointers that now point to addresses within the record in which they themselves occur, rather than to other records (see Figure 31.19).

The potential for an extremely large file size means that the storage structures needed to implement file data structures look quite different from those appropriate for ordinary strings. The economics of the various alternative storage devices has a strong influence. Currently, disk storage is the most popular for files. Yet the attempt to use this means of storage well has in turn led to modifi-

cations of the data structure for files. One example is in length of the string. Some lengths, depending upon the hardware, make a more efficient use of the storage space.

Records on disk, whether fixed or variable, may be grouped together or broken into parts to create file blocks of nearly ideal length. When records are grouped together, a distinction is made between the logical record (a data structure, one record), and a physical record (a storage structure, one group of logical records). Then in the storage structure, the individual record becomes inaccessible except as a part of a block. This causes the handling of unwanted data and requires identifying the location in the block of records. From a management point of view, blocking fixed length records causes only minor difficulties. But blocking variable length records creates major difficulties for record modification or update, and for record insertion.

31.6 FILE STRUCTURES

The file, as has been pointed out, is a string composed of records. Because of the sheer size a file can assume, data management becomes difficult. The primary management problems involve record access; record updating, changing or modification; record insertion; and record deletion. Many different ways have been attempted to make these operations more manageable. Most of them use particular data structures to facilitate file access and file maintenance, most commonly sequential or serial structure, the direct or random structure, and the indexed sequential structure. Some variations of these structures are encountered, and are discussed briefly.

From the viewpoint of data management, the primary situations that arise in working with file structures are creation of the file, access to a particular record, updating data within a record, inserting a new record, and deleting

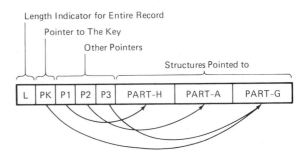

Figure 31.19. Variable records formed by the use of pointers to yield an attributed string.

Figure 31.20. Diagram of the structure of a sequential file. The data records are in a sorted order based upon a key.

an existing record. Now here is a brief look at each of these situations.

By far the most common, and historically the dominant, file structure is the *sequential* or *serial structure.* In this structure, each record comprising the file must contain an identifying key. Normally the key is at the same fixed position in each record, even if the records are of variable length.

The file building process consists of identifying the file by means of a *header label.* The formats for both header and trailer labels may vary from user to user, but standard labels have been prescribed and are commonly used. After the header label, which is the first record in the file, the data records appear one by one in the file until the last record has been provided. A *trailer record* may be written at the end of the file, depending upon local practices. The trailer record, if present, provides a count of the number of records that composed the file when it was last written, as well as providing again an identification of the file. The data records are usually placed in the file in an ascending sequence. The record with the lowest or smallest key goes first, and the record with the largest or greatest key last. The intervening records are placed in sorted order based upon their keys. Figure 31.20 provides a diagram of a sequential file. (Headers and trailers are associated with tape files and are not necessary with disk files.)

The reasons for having a sequentially ordered file structure are the following:

1. There is the matter of logical convenience. People working not with computers but with paper, pencil, file cabinets and file folders are used to sorting things and storing them in a sorted order. It seems natural to people who have had that experience to expect the computer to follow a similar practice, whether or not it be a good use of computer capability.
2. The early computers typically had relatively small storage devices and their capabilities for external storage of information for random access was quite limited. The early media used were punched cards, paper

tape, and magnetic tape. The latter two were used often in a "unit record" manner, much like a series of punched cards. A card was a "unit record" in which one card held a unit amount of data about one topic, as for example, one stock item, one employee, one customer, or one transaction. For convenience in data management, the data were often retained in a punched-card-like manner. Data integrity was preserved by the card; file integrity was dependent upon people's care in handling decks of cards.
3. When nonhuman-readable low cost media were introduced to hold data for computers, the earliest forms happened to be convenient for physically sequential data. Magnetic tape and paper tape are serial media. The access to any item of data can be achieved only by first accessing all of the prior data.

Access to the file takes two forms when the file is sequential. One form is simply to read the next record in the file regardless of its key and to process the record read. This processing of the next record is common practice when every, or nearly every, record in the file must have something done to it each time the file is read, for example, accessing a payroll file when preparing paychecks.

When a significant number of the records in the file can be skipped, access by key is used. This can be done by a sequential search. If less than half of the file needs to be accessed, then the sequential structure is probably a poor choice.

For access by key, it is sometimes convenient to use not a *single* but a *compound key,* having what was referred to as major, intermediate, and minor parts. The major part is the overall sort order to the entire file. For a personnel file, for instance, it might be by department number. The intermediate sort might be by mail stop, and the detailed or minor sort might be by employee number. Such a file is described as being sorted by an employee number within mail stop within department number.

Once a record has been accessed, the data in it may then be updated. The update may be either "in place" or it may involve writing new copy. If the update is to be made "in place," then the record read from the file is modified in internal storage and returned to the same place in the file. To fit there, the record must remain the same length, or be shorter than it was originally.

If the entire file is to be rewritten (copied to another file), this restriction on length can be lifted. Each record, as it is accessed to obtain the record desired, is written (copied) to create in effect a new copy of the whole file. When the desired record itself is accessed, it is modified and then is written to the next available place in the new copy of the file. Thus this new copy becomes the modified, or updated, version of the file.

Creating a new copy of a file each time it is accessed for record modification is the common practice for sequential files. The new copy is called the "son"; the copy accessed the "father;" and the prior copy, the "grandfather." The usual practice is to save three generations of sequential files as backup in case of hardware or other failures.

Insertions of new records into a sequential file can, in practice, only be accomplished by rewriting the file. The file is copied up to the point of insertion. Then the new record is written onto the new copy of the file at the next available place, and the copying of the old file is resumed.

Deletions of records from a sequential file are accomplished in two ways. One way is to create a new copy of the file by simply omitting from the new copy the records to be deleted. The other way, involving a deletion "in place," consists of marking with a deletion symbol the key area of the record in the file being accessed. A common deletion symbol is the highest character representation permitted in the computer. Then the next time the file is copied (rewritten), all records with this key are deleted physically from the file.

Direct or Random Files

Computers have always had random access storage devices for internal storage. But internal storage has also always been relatively expensive compared to bulk, or external, storage. Yet in the early days whatever external storage was available was primarily sequential devices. The introduction by the late 1950s of random access devices in the form of magnetic disks, which were less expensive than the earlier magnetic drums, was followed by falling prices. This led to greater attention to developing data structures useable with random access devices.

The impetus for such attention came from applications. In many applications, sequential access was incon-

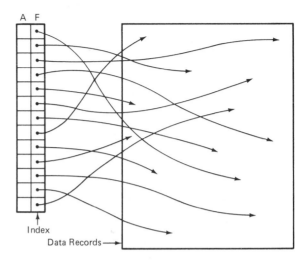

Figure 31.21. Diagram of index-based direct or random file structure.

veniently slow. Furthermore, during the course of a day customers did not present themselves at the sales desks in sorted order by account numbers to have merchandise charged to their accounts.

For the *direct* (or *random*) *access file,* a particular record may be accessed without having to access or pass through any other record in the file. Most important, it makes access of the next record in the file independent of which record was accessed immediately previously. As a practical matter, the time required to access any record, regardless of where it is in the file, becomes close to a constant. In order to achieve direct or random access, two methods have been used.

One is the development of an **index.** To make this possible, a table is established for record addresses and record keys, as diagrammed in Figure 31.21. To permit rapid access, the table is maintained in sorted order so that a binary search or other rapid technique may be used. The function in the table is the record address, in the storage medium, with an argument key matching the search key.

The other technique is the use of a **hashing algorithm** to convert the key into a storage address for the record. A number of different algorithms can be used for this purpose, but conceptually they work to achieve the result described in Figure 31.22. But if insertions or variable length records are to be handled, some vacant space must be included with the data records in the file. It may all be scattered, as indicated in Figure 31.22, or it may be

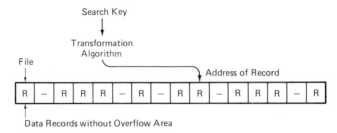

Figure 31.22. Diagram of a hash-based direct or random file organization.

mostly concentrated into "overflow" areas. In the latter case, the entire amount of storage space available is divided into two parts, the "prime" area, which must provide enough storage space to store all of the records in the file; and the "overflow" area, which is described later.

In the selection of the hashing algorithm, the distribution of keys—that is, the numbers of keys of different values—is examined. The frequency of duplicate keys is a critical factor, and the occurrence of certain character or digit combinations in the keys is also critical. Thus, the digits 1, 5 and 0 are common in keys. Where keys have a high degree of redundancy and duplicates are common, different hashing algorithms can be used than would be possible in situations with little redundancy in keys and no duplicates. The numeric values of the absolute addresses available for record storage must also be considered. And the variation in record lengths must be considered, too. The hashing algorithm should give a reasonably even distribution of records throughout the available storage space, with little unused space. Perfectly even distribution in practice is almost never achieved. Some records will be located close to each other and others will be separated by intervening unused space.

Each record, as it is to be entered into the file, has a copy of its key transformed to identify the address at which the record is to be stored. That address is then checked to verify the availability of sufficient space to store the entire record. If sufficient space is available, the record is then stored at the address. If sufficient space is not available at the address, because of an uneven distribution of the keys, then space is made available for the record at that address or at an address immediately following in one of two ways:

1. The record which is in partial or full conflict is moved to the overflow area and a short dummy record indicating the address of the moved record is inserted in the prime area at the desired location. This exchange

clears space in the prime area for the new record to be inserted. Alternatively, both records may be placed in the overflow area and an indication that both are there may be stored in the prime area.
2. The record with the higher key is moved just enough, later, in the prime area—assuming space is available—to make room for the new record to be inserted at its expected address.

The net result of either of these techniques is that a record may not always be stored at exactly the address which would be expected from the direct application of the hashing algorithm.

The access procedure for a direct, or random, file typically consists of transforming a copy of the key to obtain the corresponding address in storage, either through a table or a hashing algorithm. This address is then examined to determine whether it contains the record with that key. The address may contain a pointer to an address in the overflow area, in which case the pointer is followed, and that address examined to see if it contains the record desired. If it does not, or if the first area does not contain a pointer but contains a record with a different key, then records are read sequentially in the area until the desired record is found, or a lower key is encountered.

The update of a record in a random or direct file is usually done in place, that is, the record is read from the file by copying in into internal storage. The changes desired are then made in the record, and the record is returned to its original place in external storage. This is possible, provided that sufficient length is available at the external storage address to accommodate the updated record. If sufficient space is not available, then the situation is handled in the same way as during file building. Notice that a new location completely different from the old location cannot be chosen if a hashing algorithm has been used, but can be chosen if a table is used for finding the address.

Insertions to a random, or direct, file are made in the same way that the file was originally built or created. Deletions from a direct or random file are simple and straightforward. The record area is marked as being vacant or available and that is all that is necessary where a hashing algorithm has been used. If a table has been used to obtain the address, then the function for the argument, or the entire entry, must be deleted from the table. This may mean simply marking the address as being no longer in use and deferring rewriting the table until the file is recreated. If insertions to the file in a table look-up situation are frequent, however, then procedures for changing the length of the table will be well established and deletion will probably be made by directly removing the entire entry from the table for the deleted record.

The inconveniences of the direct or random file are small when the primary access is to fixed length records and when the number of records in the file changes only slowly. When file sizes are more dynamic and record lengths are variable, the idle storage space that is required becomes excessive, or access becomes prolonged and cumbersome through heavy use of the overflow area. Furthermore, if sequential access is occasionally desired to the file, there is no easy way of establishing where a hashing algorithm has been used, or what are the keys of the records actually in the file without reading them all and then sorting them into some sequential order. To minimize the frequency of key clashes and the movement of records arising from inserted records, a random or direct file is periodically recreated with changed amounts of storage space to accommodate the file in a clean form with nearly no overflow. As files grow, the need for these periodical recreations may require an occasional modification to the hashing algorithm, as well as the use of additional storage space.

Indexed Sequential Files

To offset some of these difficulties, combinations have been sought for the good features of the sequential file and the good features of the direct or random file. The middle ground that is most frequently used is the *indexed sequential file;* a number of varieties of this file type exist in practice. The basic character of the indexed sequential file is illustrated in Figure 31.23. This scheme provides a way of obtaining both sequential and random access to a file based upon a key.

The "indexed sequential" file obtains its name because the data structure incorporates a directory to accompany the stored data records. This directory is commonly

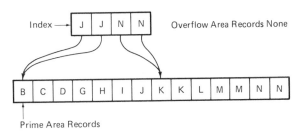

As File Built

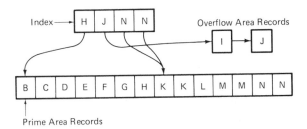

After Insertion of Records with Key F and Then Key E

Figure 31.23. Diagram of an indexed sequential file, showing only a single level of index. The letters in the boxes represent the keys of the respective data records.

called an "index," although properly it is really a directory serving effectively as a table of contents to the stored data. But because the underlying data are in sequence according to key, the directory is also in sequence by the key and hence takes on the characteristics also of an index.

Typical practice is to copy the key from every n'th record and to note with that key the address at which the first record of this n'th group may be found. A string of these keys and associated addresses then effectively serve as a new sequential file containing two kinds of records, the key followed by the address in strict alternation. To facilitate access still further, every nth record pair in this sequential file can in turn be recorded in a new file, also with strict alternationa of key and address. Now, however, the address is of the index or directory portion from which the last key has been copied. This new file could in turn be summarized into a new still higher level directory, and this process continued as far as desired.

A quick review of the process indicates that the number of intervening records to be skipped between keys to be included in the next higher level is crucial in determining the number of levels, given the size of the file. Thus, if every 100th record has its key copied, then each entry in that directory represents 100 records stored. Then if this directory is summarized in the same way, each entry in the second level of the directory will represent 10,000 data records, and each entry in the third level of the directory will represents 1 million data records.

A large *n*, therefore, not only leads to a high degree of summarization in the directory, but also leads to relatively slow access. Once an entry has been located in a directory, as many as *n* items may have to be searched through in each lower directory and eventually in the data itself. Some compromise is therefore needed between few levels of directory to check and the number of items that must be checked in the next lower directory. Common compromises seem to be in the 20 to 50 area.

The creation of an indexed sequential file is quite straightforward. The usual header record begins the file and the records are then placed in the file in sorted, or sequential, order one after another, completely occupying the prime space in the file. As each *n*'th record is written, two entries are made in the directory; as each *n*th pair of entries is made in the directory, two entries are made in the next higher directory, and so on. When the end of the file has been reached, the final entries in the directories are made to correspond. End of directory markers are added, and any final, terminating, or trailer records are added to the file.

Access to the file may therefore occur in either of two ways. *Sequential access* is possible if one ignores the directories and simply goes directly to the data area and reads the records successively, one after another. If contiguous areas of physical storage have been used so that the storage structure can be easily related to a string-like character, this can be rapid and simple process. If, on the other hand, the areas of storage space used in the storage device have been scattered around and are not contiguous, then access even on a sequential basis will have to be made through the directory. Notice that this approach imposes a restriction on the directory: that all of the data records referenced by the lowest level of the directory must be located contiguously in the storage device. For this reason, sometimes the various levels in the directory are given names to reflect physical storage devices used. Thus, we may have a track index, a cylinder index, and a master index because the *n* that is for one level of directory need not be the same for other levels.

Random, or *direct*, access to the file is possible on the same key used for sequencing the file. In this case, the highest level directory is compared against the search key. When a greater condition is encountered, then the

record sought be somewhere earlier in the file. Hence the address shown in the index becomes the starting point for the search in the next level of directory. This directory is searched on the same basis. When all of the directories have been searched, then the data records pointed to by the lowest directory match are searched sequentially. The record is then either found, or is determined to be not in the file. This entire process goes fairly rapidly provided the number of records with duplicate keys is small. Some complications to this search procedure arise because of the use of overflow areas, as described later.

The update of an indexed sequential file normally consists of accessing the record to be updated, copying the data from external storage into internal storage, making the modification, and then returning the record to external storage in place. But the process can be more complex. If variable length records are used and record lengths increase as a result of the update process, then the use of an overflow area is required. The record's actual location in storage is replaced with an indicator that the record will be found in the overflow area. The record is then placed in the overflow area at the first available space.

The insertion of records into an indexed sequential file is shown in Figure 31.23. All the data records fill the available space in the prime area of storage when the file is created. No space is available for the insertion of new records; all must go into the overflow area. The question, therefore, is how is sequence maintained in the overflow area, and what happens to the directory?

Several ways of handling the situation have, in practice, been used. A common one requires that the directory be originally created with repeated entries, as diagramed in Figure 31.23. Then, when insertions are made in the area of storage covered by a particular entry in the lowest level of index, the former highest record in the data area is moved to the overflow area. The second address of the pair shown in the lowest level directory is changed to show the address in the overflow area for this record. The area vacated in the prime area of storage by the movement of the record to the overflow area is then occupied by moving into it the record that was next in sequence. This process continues until a vacant space is available in the correct position for the new record to be inserted. The record is inserted.

Finally, the first of the key pair in the lowest level directory is then modified to show the key of the new last record in that part of the data area. This process of inserting new records may be accomplished any number of times. But each time, a link must be included with the

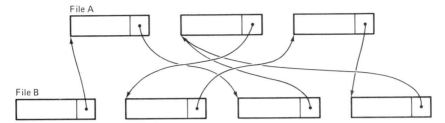

Figure 31.24. Diagram of interfile pointers in chained files, where each box represents a record, and arrows represent pointers.

overflow record to point to the next record in sequence. The last record (the first one pushed out of the specific prime area) is marked with an end marker instead of a link. The address in the directory that points to the overflow records indicates the record pushed off with the lowest key.

The deletion of records from an indexed sequential file is a much simpler process. The typical practice is simply to mark the record in its key field as having been deleted, and to leave the overflow links and directions unchanged. Then when the file is rewritten, as is occasionally done to eliminate the need for the use of overflow areas, the records are copied from the overflow area and inserted at their correct sequence locations. Any deletions are physically concluded by *not* copying the records to be omitted into the new version of the file.

The most significant management matter that arises with indexed sequential files is determining when to reorganize or recopy the file. To make this decision appropriately requires monitoring the performance of the systems using the indexed sequential file. If the system's performance becomes sufficiently degraded to require a larger proportion of disk seeks, or a longer time to process information than before, then there is a need to copy the file. The process of copying the file, however, may take several hours or even overnight. The amount of degradation, therefore, that can be tolerated has to be, as a practical matter, traded off against computer time lost from copying the file to eliminate the need for using overflow areas.

Other File Structures

Additional file structures are in use beyond the three just described, but with comparative infrequency. One of these structures, although it is not commonly encountered, is worthy of some comment because of its tie to some data base practices. A *chained,* or *linked,* file, diagrammed in Figure 31.24, provides a way of linking two or more files by incorporating in one or more of them pointers that point from the record of one file to the record or records of other files. If these files in turn include pointers back to the records (in the first file), that pointed to them, then this linkage is referred to as a two way chain; otherwise, it is a one way chain.

Chained, or linked, files provide a way of representing additional information which may be difficult to represent in direct terms of file content. Chained or linked files can be used to represent hierarchical relationships among data, as for example, in bill of materials processing. The use of linked structures, particularly a ring-like structure, which links back upon itself, also finds some applications. For instance, the linked structure can enable access on more than one key, something not normally possible with hashing-based random or direct files, indexed sequential files, or sequential files. Thus links can be added to each record to give the address of the next record in the different sequence. This complicates additions and deletions, but provides a greater choice of keys by which to access a file. Such linked records are normally treated like records in a sequential file. Two other ways of achieving similar access flexbility are the use of inverted files and table-based random or direct files.

REFERENCES

Amble, O., and D. E. Knuth, "Ordered Hash Tables," *Computer Journal,* vol. 17, No. 2 (May 1974), pp. 135–41.

Behymer, J. A., R. A. Ogilvie, and A. G. Merten, "Analysis of Indexed-sequential and Direct Access File Organizations," in R. Rustin, ed., *Proceedings of ACM SIGMOD Workshop.* New York: Association for Computing Machinery, 1974. Pp. 389–418.

Bradley, James. *File and Data Base Techniques*. New York: Holt, Rinehart and Winston, 1981.

Chapin, N., *Computers: A Systems Approach*. New York: Van Nostrand Reinhold, 1971. Chapter 6.

Flores, I., *Data Structures and Management*. Englewood Cliffs, NJ: Prentice-Hall, 1977.

Gotlieb, C. C., and L. R. Gotlieb, *Data Types and Structures*. Englewood Cliffs, NJ: Prentice-Hall, 1978.

Hanson, Owen. *Design of Computer Data Files*. Rockville, MD: Computer Science Press Inc., 1982.

Loomis, Mary E. S. *Data Management and File Processing*. Englewood Cliffs, NJ.: Prentice-Hall, Inc., 1983.

Madnick, S. E. "String Processing Techniques," *Communications of the ACM,* Vol. 10, No. 7 (July 1967), pp. 420–424.

Pfaltz, J. L., *Computer Data Structures*. New York: McGraw-Hill Book Co., 1977.

32
A Survey of Data Base Technology

Myles Walsh

CBS, Inc.

32.1 DATA BASE CONCEPTS

In the ten years from 1970 to 1980, the technology of data base evolved from some collections of leading edge prototype models to combinations of hardware, software and microcode that make data base and data base management an established and viable electronic data processing and management information service (EDP/ MIS) tool. However, because of its complexity and, in some situations, its magnitude, data base technology is a cause of concern and skepticism. While it is true that data base technology is complex, it is also true that this complexity is compounded by the semantics of data base technology. As with most technologies, that of data base comes complete with acronyms and buzzwords. The objective of this chapter is to explain and clarify data base concepts, to examine the functions and facilities of data base management, to give useful meaning to a number of the acrynoyms and buzzwords and to explore some operational factors that ought to be considered by organizations or individuals contemplating the establishment of a data base environment.

Data and Information

Let's start at the beginning. In most dictionaries, the words data and information are defined as virtually synonymous. For the majority of situations this presents no difficulty. However, when dealing with computer equipment, which is prerequisite to contemporary data bases and data base management systems, one finds a subtle but important difference between data and information.

Computer storage is able to hold information/data in a form void of certain syntax and punctuation required for understanding by human beings. When that information/ data is displayed on the CRT screen of a terminal device or printed on paper, the required syntax and punctuation can be added so that it becomes recognizable.

Figure 32.1 shows a string of information/data as it is stored and as it looks when displayed on a CRT screen. The difference between the two is format. In discussions involving computers, **data** often describes information stored "in the computer", and **information** is data displayed on a CRT screen or printed on paper. Therefore, data can be thought of as unformatted information and information can be thought of as formatted data. The difference is a matter of organization and the addition of a few symbols. The *value* expressed by the information and by the data is exactly the same. The number 2000 in specified computer storage locations and the expression $20.00 on a CRT screen both represent twenty dollars. The human being recognizes its monetary meaning by the presence of the dollar sign and the decimal point, while the computer program recognizes its meaning because a file or data base designer has specified a four position section of computer storage to contain dollar and cents information. The term **data base** begins to take on some meaning—something in computer storage that holds data.

What is a Data Base?

The concept of data base can be discussed apart from the context of computer equipment; many authors do this.

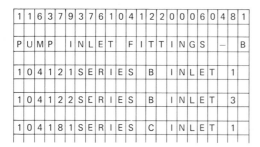

Figure 32.1. Storage and display of information/data.

There is a great variety of data base definitions among the recognized authorities. For example;

- The IBM Data Processing Glossary [1] defines a data base as "a set of data, part of the whole of another set of data, and consisting of at least one file, that is sufficient for a given purpose or for a given data processing system."
- James Martin in *Principles of Data-Base Management*, [2] defines a data base as "a collection of interrelated data stored together with controlled redundancy to serve one or more applications; the data are stored so that they are independent of programs which use the data; a common and controlled approach is used in adding new data and in modifying and retrieving existing data within a data base. A system is said to contain a collection of data bases if they are disjoint in structure." In *Computer Data-Base Organization* [3], Martin is consistent; he uses the same definition.
- C. J. Date [4] another knowledgeable author on the subject of data base offers the following working definition: "A database is a collection of stored operational data used by the application systems of some particular enterprise."
- Ronald Ross [5] offers: "A collection of interrelated, largely unique data items or records, in one or more computer files, which may be processed by multiple application programs."
- Three definitions are given by Leo Cohen [6]: "(a) The aggregate data elements that comprise the set of files and records of a given system or set of systems. (b) A collection of files having logical interrelationships. (c) A nonredundant collection of interrelated data items processable by one or more applications."

The foregoing definitions are merely a sample of what exists. It is apparent that there are a number of subtle differences among the the experts on what constitutes a data base. As the illustrative definitions show, even the spelling differs. Some use one word—database; others use two words—data base (this chapter's usage). Are these two expressions the same or are they different? This question will be analyzed further on.

Data Base Versus Database

Another area of complexity with regard to data base involves the use of data base management software. In an article in the *Journal of Systems Management*, Charles J. Lewis [7] discusses the semantic problems of data base technology. In his article, Lewis explains the difference between (a) adopting a "database" approach to data handling and (b) building a "data base" by using sophisticated software. He defines his terms as follows:

Database is (1) a systematic methodology for the standardization and integration of data resources at an organizational level or (2) all of the data of the organization which is organized or controlled using a database methodology.

A computerized data base is a set of computerized files on which an organization's activities are based and upon which high reliance is placed for availability and accuracy.

He goes on to make the point that using sophisticated software, a "database" management system or an internally developed system can be used to establish a **data base environment**, that is, an environment in which there is an organizational commitment to create and enforce "database" policies and procedures for the collection, storage, retrieval and manipulation of data. However, he also points out that using "database" management software does not constitute creating a "data base" environment. It is quite conceivable that elaborate "database" management system software products can be installed that do not come anywhere near achieving their potential.

The preceeding references represent the thoughts of a couple of theoreticians, Martin and Date, and some management consultants, Cohen, Ross and Lewis on the subject of "database," "data base" and "database" management. Their ideas help to crystallize what follows, as the concepts, languages, functions and operational considerations are discussed. (The high refinement of database vs. data base having been noted, we return to "data base" as useable, in practice, to indicate both methodology and files.)

One can readily see that definitions of data base tend to vary depending upon context. There are straightforward, easy to understand definitions that appear in literature introductory in nature. As one pursues a more detailed knowledge and understanding about the nature of data bases, the definitions become more complicated. Although definitions vary in complexity based on their context, it is easily perceived that all of the definitions are common in a couple of respects. A data base in any context is always a collection of data elements with interrelationships among them. The mechanisms for establishing and maintaining these relationships are many and varied. The use of these mechanisms, such as indexes, tables, inversions and chains, is not restricted to database technology. They are also used in sophisticated file arrangements. The point is this: merely using indexes, inversions, tables or chains in a data management function does not make a database. What distinguishes a collection of files that use some data management mechanisms from a database is interrelationships among data elements *that transcend file boundaries*.

A non-EDP/MIS illustration of this can be seen in the Bible. Figure 32.2 contains a copy of a passage (in Isaiah 53) from a King James version. Figure 32.3 is a copy of the same passage from another format of the Bible, the *Ryrie Study Bible*. Notice, in the latter, the margin notes that refer the reader to other places in the Bible. If one allows that the Bible is made up of 66 files (books), then the King James version is a collection of files, while the Ryrie Study version is a data base, with the margin notes establishing relationships that transcend file (book) boundaries.

32.2 DATA REPRESENTATIONS AND ARRANGEMENTS

Basic Representations and Arrangements

Bibles may be all right as illustrations, but they are books and not computerized files. Information stored in a computer is not the same as that stored in a book. Since, for all practical purposes, data bases require computers, let us talk computers. Information stored in computers takes the form of characters, fields, records, keys and files [in the language of data base there are some other forms but they appear later in the discussion].

- *Characters* are merely letters such as G, L, T, numbers such as 1, 5, 9, or symbols such as commas, periods, and colons.
- *Fields* are values or identifiers made up of one or more characters. An individual's name, a part number, a state code and an amount of total sale are examples of fields.
- A *record* is an orderly arrangement of fields of information making up attributes and characteristics that identify items, entities or individuals. Examples of records are an employee master record identifying and describing an employee; an inventory record identifying a part, describing it and indicating stock and production status on it; or a record containing the sales history of a product.

4 Surely he hath borne our griefs, and carried our sorrows: yet we did esteem him stricken, smitten of God, and afflicted.

5 But he *was* wounded for our transgressions, *he was* bruised for our iniquities: the chastisement of our peace *was* upon him; and with his stripes we are healed.

6 All we like sheep have gone astray; we have turned every one to his own way; and the LORD hath laid on him the iniquity of us all.

7 He was oppressed, and he was afflicted, yet he opened not his mouth: he is brought as a lamb to the slaughter, and as a sheep before her shearers is dumb, so he openeth not his mouth.

8 He was taken from prison and from judgment: and who shall declare his generation? for he was cut off out of the land of the living: for the transgression of my people was he stricken.

9 And he made his grave with the wicked, and with the rich in his death; because he had done no violence, neither *was any* deceit in his mouth.

Figure 32.2. Passage from King James version.

ISAIAH 53:2   1093   ISAIAH 53:10

2 ªIs 11.1
ᵇIs 52.14

2 For He grew up before Him like a ªtender shoot,
And like a root out of parched ground;
He has ᵇno *stately* form or majesty
That we should look upon Him,
Nor appearance that we should be attracted to Him.

But the LORD has caused the iniquity of us all
To fall on Him.

7 He was oppressed and He was afflicted,
Yet He did not ªopen His mouth;
ᵇLike a lamb that is led to slaughter,
And like a sheep that is silent before its shearers,
So He did not open His mouth.

* 7-9

7 ªMatt 26.63 27.12-14. Mark 14.61. 15.5 Luke 23.9 John 19.9 ᵇActs 8.32.33 Rev 5.6

3 ªPs 22.6.
Is 49.7. Luke 18.31-33 ᵇIs 53.10 ᶜMark 10.33.34
ᵈJohn 1.10.11

3 He was ªdespised and forsaken of men,
A man of sorrows, and ᵇacquainted with grief;
And like one from whom men hide their face,
He was ᶜdespised, and we did not ᵈesteem Him.

8 By oppression and judgment He was taken away;
And as for His generation, who considered
That He was cut off out of the land of the living,
*For the transgression of my people to whom the stroke *was* due?

8 ªIs 53.5.12

* 4-6

4 ªMatt 8.17 ᵇJohn 19.7

4 Surely our griefs He Himself ªbore,
And our sorrows He carried;
Yet we ourselves esteemed Him stricken,
Smitten of ᵇGod, and afflicted.

9 His grave was assigned with wicked men,
Yet He was with a ªrich man in His death,
ᵇBecause He had ᶜdone no violence,
Nor was there any deceit in His mouth.

9 ªMatt 27.57-60 ᵇIs 42.1-3 ᶜ1 Pet 2.22

5 ªIs 53.8.
Heb 9.28
ᵇIs 53.10.
Rom 4.25.
1 Cor 15.3
ᶜDeut 11.2.
Heb 5.8
ᵈ1 Pet 2.24.25

5 But He was pierced through for *our transgressions,
He was crushed for ᵇour iniquities;
The ᶜchastening for our well-being *fell* upon Him,
And by ᵈHis scourging we are healed.

6 All of us like sheep have gone astray,
Each of us has turned to his own way;

10 But the LORD was pleased To *crush Him, ᵇputting *Him* to grief;
If He would render Himself *as* a guilt ᶜoffering,
He will see ᵈHis offspring,
He will prolong *His* days,
And the good *pleasure of the LORD will prosper in His hand.

* 10-12

10 ªIs 53.5 ᵇIs 53.3.4 ᶜIs 53.6.12 John 1.29 ᵈPs 22.30 Is 54.3 61.9. 66.22 ᵉIs 46.10

53:4-6 The passion of the Servant. Though men would think that God was causing the Servant to suffer for His own sins, the truth was that He suffered vicariously for theirs. *pierced through* (v. 5) A term appropriate to crucifixion. *chastening for our well-being.* I.e., His punishment which obtained peace or well-being for us.
53:7-9 The passivity of the Servant. *He did not open His mouth* (v. 7). See Matt. 26:63-64; Jesus did affirm His deity when placed under oath. Compare Isa. 53:9 with Matt. 27:57-60.

53:10-12 The portion of the Servant. His whole being, including *His soul* (v. 11), was involved in the *offering* (v. 10) (the word used in Lev. 6-7 of the trespass offering, which required 120% restitution, Lev. 6:5). *His offspring* (Isa. 53:10) are those who would believe on Him. To *prolong His days* after being made an offering would necessitate bodily resurrection. *By His knowledge* (v. 11). I.e., by knowledge of Him (cf. Rom. 3:26). *the great* (Isa. 53:12). Lit., the many, as in Isa. 53:11.

Figure 32.3. Page from a study Bible; Verses 4–9 correspond to the verses shown in Figure 32.2. (From *Ryrie Study Bible—New American Standard Version* [New Testament] by Charles C. Ryrie. Copyright 1976. Moody Press, Moody Bible Institute of Chicago. Used by permission.)

- A *key* is a field or a group of fields that is specified as an identifier. In a payroll record, for instance, the employee number field might be specified as the key. When a group of inventory records are being sorted into sequence by part number within a warehouse, the warehouse and part number fields would be specified as the key.
- A *file* is a collection of records, generally, but not necessarily, of the same type. A grouping of all employee records and a grouping of all inventory records are ex-

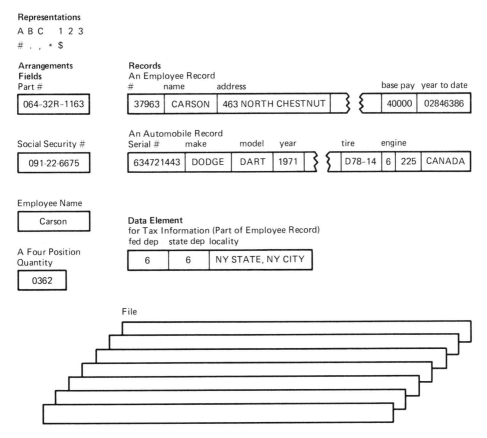

Figure 32.4. Representations and arrangements of records.

amples of files. Representations and arrangements are illustrated in Figure 32.4.

Types of Arrangements

In conventional or traditional computer applications, there are three ways in which records are arranged in files. These arrangements are generally referred to as *sequential, direct access* and *indexed*. Each arrangement lends itself to a particular type of application. Using the term *transaction* to connote individual units of activity against files facilitates understanding the different arrangements and their applications.

A **sorted file** is one in which records are arranged in order according to a key. The records are generally contiguous, that is, they are in sequence both logically and physically. Magnetic tape is a commonly used storage medium. Sequential files lend themselves to sequential processing, in which transactions are batched into groups, sorted into the same sequence as the file they are to be processed against, and processed by being matched to that file. In those situations in which transactions result in additions or deletions of records or changes to records in the file, the entire file is recopied during the process. This type of processing is an efficient way to do file maintenance when the percentage of records changed is high. Sequential processing is also efficient in preparing ordered detailed listings and tabulations of information. The batching of transactions into groups for processing has led to the term **batch processing,** which is sometimes used as a synonym for sequential processing.

A **direct access file** is one in which a record is found at a location determined by an algorithm performed on the key of the record. As a result of the algorithm, a correlation is established between the value contained in the key of the record and a particular storage location address. An additional area may be set aside for duplicates that are generated by the algorithm. Writing transactions into a direct access file is carried out using the same algorithm. An individual transaction has its key transformed into the corresponding storage location address. During direct access processing, the file need not be recopied. Additions are put into available space, and deletions actually remove records and make space available, while changes are made to existing records in place. This type of processing is efficient in situations in which transactions arrive randomly, and in no particular order.

Indexed files get the benefits of both direct and sequential processing. Although there are several variations, the basic idea involves the creation of a two part file. The data is kept in one part and the key is kept in another part called the *index*. A linkage exists between individual keys in the index and the data in the other part of the file. Access to data in the file is through the index. Since the index is kept in sequence, it is possible to do sequential processing. Direct processing is possible through the index rather than by an algorithm. The advantage of indexed files lies in the fact that sequential and direct processing are possible. The disadvantage of indexed files is that they are slower in processing because all operations require more accesses: both the index and the data need to be accessed.

In the early days of computing, computer programmers wrote relatively complex input/output instructions in each program they developed to access data on the various types of files. It quickly became apparent that this was an inefficient use of programmers' time, since the methodology of input/output was mostly redundant. To remedy this inefficiency, generalized input/output programs were developed which programmers could invoke and tailor to their particular need by specifying parameters indicating characteristics such as device type and record length. As time passed and the sophistication of computer configurations increased, so too did these input/output programs. In the process, they became known as access methods. Acronyms such as SAM, BDAM, ISAM* and others are now a common place part of the information systems landscape.

Data storage and retrieval, using the methods and techniques described thus far, operate on groupings of data which we have defined as records. Access methods

*SAM—sequential access method; BDAM—basic direct access method; ISAM—indexed sequential access method.

store and retrieve data as records. If data is required from more than one source, then records from more than one file must be accessed. The logic, required to "match and mix," data from different files, has to be contained in the program that is going to process that data. In some situations the logic to perform such a "match and mix" can be quite complicated.

Data Base Semantics

The Bible has been used to illustrate a data base (Figure 32.2-3). Let's now explain data base using computer language. A data base is a *passive* component in a data base system. The *active* component is made up of mechanisms that make possible the storage and retrieval of data in a data base system environment. These mechanisms, depending upon the computer configuration, are made up of combinations of hardware and software in products that are commonly known as data base management systems. A data base is the data. The structures that hold the data are generated by data base management systems. The structures vary from system to system and so do the terms that are used to define the sturctures and the elements within the structures. This leads to some semantic difficulties, a discussion of which follows.

In our examination of basic representations and arrangements, we have established that fields, records and files are the basic structures that hold data. Keys and indexes and algorithms are the mechanisms that are utilized in the identification, storage and retrieval of information contained in those structures. Data base systems have the capability of complicating those structures. If data base complicates things, why bother? The reasons offered are numerous but they can be reduced to four. Data base systems

1. Reduce data redundancy.
2. Achieve a degree of data independence.
3. Increase productivity.
4. Simplify retrieval of related data from multiple files.

For each of these data base system justifications there is a corresponding trade-off disscussed later. For the present, however, structures and semantics are examined.

In a data base environment, there is an additional data arrangement. Rather than attempting to give it a precise name (it varies from one data base management system product to another), let's just call it a **data element,** and think of it as being an arrangement that is generally

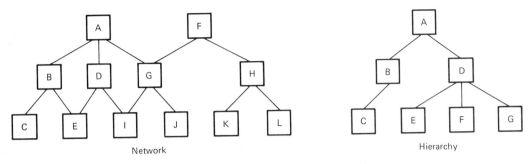

Figure 32.5. Network and hierarchical models.

larger than a field, but smaller than a record. Semantics is a problem here because there are at least four different names given by different products to this arrangement of data. In addition to data element, there are: **segment, tuple** and **record.** Although data element is a legitimate term according to several data base management systems products, its selection for use here is completely arbitrary; there is no subtle endorsement of any particular product. The illustrations in Figure 32.4 show characters, fields, data elements, records and files.

32.3 DATA BASE MODELS

Logical Structures

In contemporary data base circles, there are three basic logical models used to express data base structures; the network, the heirarchical structure and the relational model. Volumes have been written on these models. No effort is made here to rewrite what has been done well and exhaustively elsewhere. This material merely surveys the topics. For readers requiring more detail, the works of James Martin [2,3], C. J. Date [4], E. F. Codd [8] and I. Flores [12] are suggested.

Network and Hierarchical

A **network model** is a logical construct in which some of the data elements have a subordinate relationship to other data elements. Those in a subordinate relationship are called *members* and those having subordinates are called *owners.* In a network data model, subordinate data elements can have more than one owner data element.

A **hierarchical model** is also a logical construct with owner and subordinate relationships. In a hierarchical structure, however, subordinates can have only a single owner and there is one data element that has no owner. These two constructs are depicted in Figure 32.5. A hierarchical model and a network are not totally dissimilar. A network is a more complex structure than a hierarchy, but a hierarchical structure can be thought of as a network with some discipline imposed on it. Furthermore, networks can be expressed in hierarchical form, showing the redundancies of subordinates with multiple owners. Figure 32.6 exhibits an example.

The basic advantage of the network model as opposed to the hierarchical model is its flexibility. In a network, it is possible to relate virtually any data element with any other data element within the structure. This flexibility has to be evaluated against the possibility of creating a

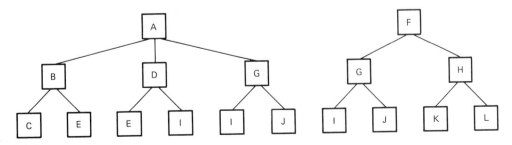

Figure 32.6. A network in hierarchical form.

network consisting of so many interrelationships that it becomes virtually impossible for transactions to navigate its paths due to processing overhead and conflicting needs. Hierarchies impose the discipline of defining a limited number of paths between data elements for transactions to follow as they store and retrieve data. As a result, in hierarchies there is a certain lack of flexibility.

The relative merits of a network or a hierarchical model are often a function of the application to which the construct is put. For instance, a bill of materials application with its finished goods, subassemblies and parts is by its very nature a hierarchical model. On the other hand, an application with which crew members, aircraft, routes and schedules are related is by its nature a network model.

Relational Model

A **relational model** is different in structure from the network and hierarchical models. Besides being different on concept, it is also different in physical structure. Whereas hierarchical and network structures are established and maintained by mechanisms called *pointers* (discussed later), relational structures are tabular with elements physically related. Figures 32.5 and 32.6 have data elements interconnected by lines, with the lines representing pointers. Figure 32.7 depicts relations with related data elements physically adjacent. The obvious advantage to this type of structure is the increased speed at which related data can be retrieved by the avoidance of the processing overhead associated with pointers.

The disadvantage of the relational model is subtle. The designer of a physical data base using the relational model theory is obliged to perform an activity known as *normalization* through which redundancies are eliminated. This activity results in a data base free of redundancies. While theoretically possible, the process of normalization rests on an understanding of all the data elements in a data base and the relationships, both real and potential, that exist among them. In practice, this may be rather elusive.

Physical Structure Mechanisms

In networks and hierarchical structures, the physical relationships among data elements are established and maintained by means of pointers. **Pointers** are nothing more than addresses of storage locations. Within data elements, fields are designated as pointer fields. Quite often these fields take the form of a *prefix* located at the beginning of a data element or a *suffix* located at the end. There is a prefix or a suffix pointer field for each of the relationships specified for a data element. For example, the data element may be related to the data elements logically preceeding it and following it in a file, and/or it may be related to a data element or several data elements in other files. Below are discussed terms used to connote this physical connecting of data elements that are logically related.

Chains and Links

A **chain** is a sequence of data elements or records joined by means of pointers. In the case of data elements, a chain may join all the data elements of a single record. The pointers may point forward to the next data element in the record and or backward to the previous data element in the record. Records within files can be joined in the same fashion, with pointers going forward or backward. Such relationships are also known as **linked lists.** Figure 32.8 illustrates the concepts of chains and links. Chains are also used to make the logical connections among elements in data bases, where the relationships

Emp #	Emp Name	Soc Sec #		Part #	Part Desc.
37963	CARSON	091-30-2614		N47-36-R	RATCHET
39217	SCHULZBERG	074-22-7608		64-1632	SPOKE
44619	NELSON	078-22-3065		R32-6412	CHAIN
47852	ONEILL	064-34-7123		6713921R	PISTON
59042	MCSWEENEY	074-18-4711		3716-R-17	BOLT
64279	EVANS	094-37-3988		66714911	SHAFT
67438	PETERSON	083-77-1817		M73-110-2	MOTOR
74830	OVERTON	082-13-7641		P106-4	SPARK PLUG

Figure 32.7. A relational model.

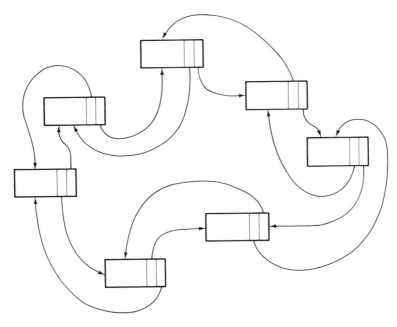

Figure 32.8. A chain, or linked, list.

transend record and file boundaries. Such relationships can be *unidirectional* or *bidirectional,* that is, a pointer in a prefix or suffix of a data element may contain the address of another data element, and the latter may or may not have a pointer back to the former element; the size of prefixes and suffixes can become substantial. In summary there are three possible types of pointers establishing relationships among data elements: forward within a record, backward within a record, and to a data element in another record or file.

Indexes and Tables

An **index** is used primarily to locate a record that is stored in a sequence other than the sequence of the index itself. Think of a textbook. It may contain hundreds of pages of information. You may want to locate information on a particular subject. Using the index enables you to determine the page or pages in the book having information on that subject. The alternative method would have you skim through the entire book, a page at a time, examining all the material in an attempt to locate the information.

Access to records in files stored on computer storage devices can also be facilitated by indexes. Several different indexes can be kept and used, depending upon application needs. For example a payroll file that is arranged in ascending sequence on employee number (00141, 00142 . . . 00262, 00264 . . . 96132, 96137. . . .) can have two indexes, one based on social security number and the other based on employee name, with both indexes referring (pointing) to employee numbers.

As stated earlier, the advantage of indexed files is that they lend themselves to both sequential and direct processing and eliminate the need for sorting. The disadvantage is that both sequential and direct processing are slower with indexed files because the necessary input/output operations are greater in number since accesses of both index records and data records are required.

Indexes are made up of keys and pointers. Within the key there are values that identify the data record. The pointer is the address of the data record. Using the textbook analogy again, the key is the identifier of the information you are seeking and the pointer is the page number on which the information is located.

A **table** is similar to an index. It also contains a key, but rather than a pointer, it contains another value identified by the key. For example, a tax table might contain a number of entries consisting of keys and tax notes. In a sales tax table, the key would be state (Alabama, Alaska, . . . Wyoming); the tax rate would vary depending upon the state. Each entry in the table would contain a state

Location	Name	#	Job CL	State
A	CARSON	37963	WH 4671	CALIFORNIA
B	SCHULZBERG	39217	CL 8117	NEVADA
C	NELSON	44619	SR 9401	CALIFORNIA
D	ONEILL	47852	DI 1214	ARIZONA
E	MCSWEENEY	59042	VP 6710	CALIFORNIA
F	EVANS	64279	SA 2944	CALIFORNIA
G	PETERSON	67438	SW 1184	ARIZONA
H	OVERTON	74830	MA 3176	CALIFORNIA

Conventional File

Location	#	J/C	ST
A	37963	N	I
B	39217	L	K
C	44619	Q	I
D	47852	O	J
E	59042	R	I
F	64279	P	I
G	67438	S	J
H	74830	M	I

Location	State	Table			
I	CALIFORNIA	A	C	E	F	H
J	ARIZONA	D	G			
K	NEVADA	B				

Inverted File

Location	Job CL	Table
L	CL 3117	B
M	MA 3176	H
N	WH 4671	A
O	DI 1214	D
P	SA 2944	F
Q	SR 9401	C
R	VP 6710	E
S	SW 1184	G

Figure 32.9. Conventional versus inverted file.

name and the sales tax rate for that state. When transactions within applications require sales tax rates, the appropriate rate would be accessed by matching the state in the transaction against the key of the table.

Inversion

An **inverted file** is a structure that makes use of tables, indexes and pointers. In an inverted structure, values within the file are listed in table entries together with pointers to positions within the records of the file(s) in which those values apply. The fields themselves contain pointers to the values in the tables. The inversion focuses on the key field of the file being inverted. A simplistic inverted structure is illustrated in Figure 32.9. The advantage of an inverted file lies in its use to respond to queries about the entire contents of the data file, without the necessity of examining every record in the file. The disadvantage of the inverted file structure is that file maintenance incurs high overhead: additions, deletions and changes require pointer maintenance as well as data value maintenance.

Inversion can be full or partial. A *partially* inverted structure is one in which individual table entries consist of a field value and a pointer to a field in one record for which the value applies; the field itself (in that record) contains a pointer to another record for which the field also has that value; and so on. A *fully* inverted structure is one in which individual table entries contain a value and a series of pointers to all records with fields containing that value.

32.4 DATA BASE MANAGEMENT SYSTEMS (DBMS)

Data Base and DBMS

We have noted that a data base is a passive entity; that is, it is acted upon. The DBMS is an active entity that acts upon a data base. A number of commercially available software products are called data base management systems. They are somewhat difficult to categorize. Although all have the capacity to define data bases and to store and retrieve data elements from data bases, each has characteristics, other than terminology, that distinguish it from the others. Many of the data base management system products have either the ability to interface with, or are integrated with, a telecommunications monitor. As such they are frequently referred to as *data base/data communications* (DB/DC) products. Selection of a DBMS or a DB/DC product should be pursued only if there is a demonstrated need. Any attempt to select the "right" DBMS or DB/DC product in the absence of applications that require some specific data base/data communications facilities is an exercise in futility. Two examples of data base/data communications are briefly described.

IMS/VS is a product that is perhaps the most elaborate of all DB/DC products available. On the plus side, it can support a network of terminal devices; it is sensitive to tuning; it can handle significant volumes of on-line and batch transactions without degradation of performance; and it is a stable product complete with recovery, restart and reorganization utilities as well as a host of support products. On the negative side, it is complex, uses significant computer resources, and requires a highly skilled and consequently well compensated technical staff to support and tune it.

FOCUS is a product that, while elaborate and complex in itself, is offered as a "user friendly" data base management system. Its communications capabilities include an availability to the Time Shared Option (TSO) of IBM's operating system. FOCUS accomodates many users concurrently, but each user requires a copy of the entire FOCUS program in his region. On the plus side, users of the product, with a limited amount of training, are able to specify requirements to FOCUS and retrieve information from a predefined database in report form rather quickly. It does not require the support of a highly qualified technical staff. On the negative side, with several concurrent users FOCUS can tie up a significant amount of computer resource; further, it is neither tunable nor on-line transaction oriented.

Schema and Subschema

Common to virtually all data base managment systems are data description language (DDL) and data manipulation language (DML) facilities. Data description language statements define the database, the files, the records, the data elements and the fields to the data base management system. The definition of an entire data base is known as a **schema,** which is simply a global view of some collection of data. A schema contains descriptive information, the characteristics and attributes, one can say, of a database.

A data base is a pool of data from which information can be extracted and into which information can be put. Specific applications are designed and programs written to perform input/output operations on certain data elements of the database. The specific data elements impacted by given transactions and programs represent incomplete or partial views of the data base. These partial views are referred to as **subschemas.** Each program or transaction has its own subschema or view of part of the databse; DDL statements define subschemas also.

A subschema provides both a degree of data independence and a degree of security. Data independence results since modifications to a total schema require corresponding modifications to only those programs whose subschemas are included in the area of the schema being modified. Those programs with subschemas outside of the area being modified are unaffected. Security is partially enhanced since the subschema restricts a program's access to only the data elements defined to it. The remaining data elements in the total schema do not exist as far as that program is concerned.

Problems in Evaluating DBMSs

Most data base management systems support hybrids of both logical and physical structures. As we have seen, there is some overlap of hierarchical and network models. A true relational model as defined by Codd [8] is made up of entities called *tuples, relations* and *domains.* These entities are virtually the same as table entries, records and fields. The physical structures of indexes and inverted files have similar characteristics. Pointers relate data elements to other data elements, values in table entries to fields within records, records to records and key values to records. Chains and links are employed one way or another in virtually every commercially available data base management system.

Promotional literature for database management invariably plays fast and loose with jargon. For instance, there are several products that vendors promote as relational DBMS's. An examination of the kinds of structures that are possible using these products reveals some form of indexing, network or inversion. The relational methodology turns out to be relationships structured with pointers. The semantic license taken by data base management system vendors complicates the evaluation process. True analysis to determine relative merits is possible only for organizations having significant computer resources in which to evaluate them. Promotional and other introductory literature often is misleading. Some basic axioms of DBMS evaluation are found in Walsh [9].

32.5 OPERATIONAL CONSIDERATIONS FOR DATA BASE

A Batch Environment

Primitive data base management systems had the capability of performing input/output operations against complex data structures and producing reports that contained information which had been stored in those structures. File maintenance transactions and inquiries were submitted in batches. The primary benefits were the data independence explained earlier and increased programmer productivity. These primitive DBMS's provided a mechanism that made it possible to store data in and to retrieve data from complex data structures without requiring programmers to develop complicated input/output routines; those routines were included in the DBMS. Then, and today, they make up the data manipulation language (DML) facility, which are the parameter driven routines contained in a program that make possible the storage and retrieval of data elements.

An On-Line Environment

The real potential of a data base management system is realized when the system is combined with a data communications mechanism. Data communications, or *teleprocessing* (see Chapter 38) as it is sometimes called, is a subject beyond the scope of this chapter. Suffice it to say here that the joining of a data communications mechanism with a data base management system introduces the additional enhancement of interactive transaction processing through a network of computer terminal devices. Updating can be done directly to on-line files with single transactions coming from the terminal devices. Inquiries can be made against files or a data base that is on-line and, in turn, responses to those inquiries can be made instantaneously.

Utilities

While on-line data bases, available through communications facilities, offer many advantages, they are also more vulnerable to corruption than files processed in a batch environment. On-line files and data bases are updated in place. Batch files when updated are recopied. In a batch situation there is something to go back to; the old data is still available. Destruction of the updated file can be prevented by merely rerunning the most recent update process. In an on-line situation, the new data overlays the old data. Rerunning is impossible. Damage to the on-line file or data base requires another kind of recovery methodology. A viable data base/data communication product contains utility programs for recovery and restart, for logging and back-out and also for reorganization.

Recovery and restart in an on-line environment requires that the entire data base be periodically copied to a back up file. Logging of transactions that update the data base is also necessary. In the event that damage occurs, it is possible first to restore the data base from the backup file. Updates that have taken place since the backup was created can be reapplied from the log. A backout utility is required to remove partial updates made to a data base when a program making those updates terminates abnormally. In other words, if a program handling a transaction that updates four data elements in a database, malfunctions after only two of those updates have been made, those two must be backed out so that, when the program is fixed and rerun, the first two updates are not applied twice.

Data bases, even those designed properly at first, need to be reorganized periodically. Whether they need to be reorganized frequently or infrequently, any viable data base/data communication product ought to include reorganization utility programs. **Reorganization** of a database reclaims space occupied by data elements that have been logically, but not physically, deleted, and reorganization also reorders remaining data elements so that they can be accessed more efficiently.

Reorganization is necessary because over time data bases tend to become fragmented: as file maintenance takes place, additions and deletions are handled expeditiously but generally at the price of loosened organization. Different structures treat file maintenance in different ways and some require less reorganization than other. Direct access data bases and files, for instance, require less reorganization than do indexed data bases and files. Some structures delete data elements logically, that is, they are "flagged" as deleted but are physically still present. This method is used because it is faster than physically deleting a data element. Reorganization itself gets rid of the data elements physically. In the case of added data elements, they are generally put whenever there is some space available. In large data bases, which are dynamic in nature, performance in terms of access tends to degrade over time as the mechanisms (usually disk storage devices) are kept quite busy accessing these data elements that have been stored rather haphazardly.

Summing up, reorganizations are somewhat like cleaning a garage and basement. Every year or so, a day is set aside for cleaning. Useless items stored periodically in the garage or basement are put in a trash pile to be discarded. Other items, such as screws and bolts, screw drivers, snow tires, rakes, shovels, saws, drills, toy trucks, hammers, and axes, are stored in a more orderly fashion so that retrieving them becomes a relatively simple task. Before cleaning, finding a hammer and 6d nail might have taken half an hour.

32.6 "BELLS AND WHISTLES"

Data Dictionary

In a data base environment, there are a number of support products, frequently called *aids,* that are "nice to have." One is virtually indispensible: a data dictionary, which goes a long way in helping to identify and classify all the data stored in a business's computer. (For a full description of the data dictionary, see Walsh [10,11].)

A data dictionary, like a DBMS, has a passive component consisting of files, records and fields that contain descriptive information about the files, records, data elements and fields in an organization's files and data bases. For example, a data dictionary record describing a field would contain the name of the field; specifications such as its length and the type of data (numeric, packed, alphabetic) found in the field; the values valid for the field; a list of the records in which the field is found; and a list of programs that use the field.

The active component of a data dictionary is the mechanism for getting the descriptive information into and out of the data dictionary files. This mechanism can be a batch facility, an interactive facility, or both. A data dictionary is basically an automated documentation tool. As enhancements continue to be made, data dictionary products will come to include other facilities such as data base design aid and schema and subschema structure generators.

Productivity Aids

Other aids that add to the effectiveness of a data base/data communications environment include the following types of product:

- A batch simulator that permits the testing and debugging (error correction) of on-line transactions without the use of on-line facilities,—an economical alternative. Depending upon program complexity, it is possible that 60 to 80 percent of on-line program development can be done in batch mode.
- A prototype modelling aid that assists data base designers in determining the relative responsiveness of alternate structures. It provides information on how well transactions run against a particular structure. Changes can be made to the structure, transactions run again, and the information from the two runs compared to determine the more effective structure.
- A mapping aid that "draws pictures" and documents the structures which are developed. It is a useful aid in documenting data base structures.
- Design aids, working in conjunction with data dictionaries, that are iterative processes producing data base designs based on parameters specified by the user.
- Report writers, parameter driven products that facilitate the preparation of reports from information extracted from data bases.
- Query packages that facilitate the formulation of inquiries made against data bases to retrieve specific information.
- Products that can be run against a data base to certify structural integrity (no broken pointer relationships).
- Productivity aids that enable users to develop applications and files with little technical support. However, such aids are rather expensive in terms of resources used.

Productivity aids beyond those discussed are also available. New products are constantly being developed. As the trend toward database systems continues, so will the growth in the number of productivity aids and utilities to support them.

Installing a Data Base Management System

Installing a data base management system software varies in complexity depending upon the type of product selected. Some DBMS products are relatively simple to install and use. They are also rigid in specification and capacity of use and their performance cannot be improved by software tuning; "What you see is what you get." But some installations' needs can be totally met by the features of a such a straightforward, simple data base management systems product.

At the other end of the scale elaborate database management systems are much more difficult to install and maintain, but they are also flexible enough to meet the needs of a dynamic data base environment. These products can have adjustments made by software tuning to improve their performance. The features of these elaborate systems are many and varied.

Software products, DBMs and others, are generally delivered to an installation on a reel of magnetic tape. After copying the information from this reel onto an area of a disk storage device, a systems programmer begins a process known as *system definition* or *system generation.* **SYSGEN** or simply **GEN** connotes this process. The GEN is a series of activities performed by the system programmer and a computer configuration, whereby the appropriate features are selected and compiled (generated) into a form executable by the computer configuration. A period of stringent testing should follow in which every attempt is made to validate the selected features to assure that they function according to specifications. Obviously the simpler the product, the simpler is this procedure. Complex products require more effort. Moreover, the environment with elaborate data base management systems have more in the way of productivity aids and utilities. Each of these products should undergo a similar installation process, thereby compounding the overall complexity of supporting an eleborate data base management installation.

A data base environment in which many thousands of transactions are processed daily requires an elaborate DBMS. That same environment in all probability also requires other software support in the form of complex operating systems and telecommunications network software products. Each of these products as well, and their associated productivity aids and utilites, require in turn the same kind of GEN and testing process. Also, they all interact with each other and the main system, thereby kicking off an even further integrated testing process to assure that all the interfaces between the products—as well as the products themselves—are working properly. This entire process is often ignored by DBMS product vendors and in discussions about the finer points of data base found in books, journals and presentations.

Charging Users for DBMS Services

As we have seen, the services supplied by a computer installation with data base management system software, network support software and other facilities can be an expensive proposition. Developing a billing algorithm, so that users of the facilities are equitably charged for the services they receive, is an important function, as any centralized computer installation manager can testify. Charging for the services provided by a DBMS is actually part of a more universal billing scheme. One device is to establish rates for the variables of a computer application. These variables include the number of input/output operations, the amount of processing time, the units of dedicated equipment, the amount of elapsed time an application spends in a computer, and the number of lines printed. An elaborate data base management system with telecommunications capability is likely to be costly since it involves extensive use of a computer processor in handling data bases with interrelated data elements, significant quantities of storage to hold large data bases, and a high degree of technical support.

Performance and Tuning

With a simple to install, easy to use data base management system, performance measurement and tuning generally involves tracking application programs and transactions and either rewriting the programs or restructuring the data base schemas and subschemas. Elaborate DBMS's, offer additional options. There are often buffer pools and queues that can be adjusted in data base/data communications environments. Interactive monitors can "see inside" a DBMS control region while it is running and internal adjustments can be made. The assignment of proper priority and class can help a long running transaction get a single processing leg of the system, isolating it from the rest of the transactions so that it does not create bottleneck. The trade off of sophistication against simplicity ought to be evaluated according to the requirements of the applications that are going to use the DBMS. The additional expense of an elaborate system is necessary in those installations where high volume, quick response time and a multiterminal network are supported.

Application Programming

In a data base/data communications environment, those to execute the application programming function require the least amount of training before becoming productive. Systems programmers and data base administrators (DBAs) require some education and training before they become productive. DBAs need to understand fully the concepts of data base management as well as have experience with file design, file structures and in application programming. System programmers require the same education and training as the DBAs; any experience they possess in file design and structure is an asset. On top of that, systems programmers need to be completely familiar with the internal processing logic of the DBMS they are supporting. They are also the final authority on the utilities and aids that enhance the data base management system software.

Application programmers need to learn data base concepts and then become familiar with the input/ouput operation language (the DML) capabilities of the DBMS they are using. Since application processing logic in a data base environment is virtually the same as in a conventional environment, the application programming skill is transferable; only input/output operations in a the data base environment will differ from system to system. Once the application programmers master these primary skills, they are on their way to being productive. In situations employing simple to install, easy to use DBMSs, an application programmer usually becomes productive in a week or two. On an elaborate data base/data communications system, an application programmer should become productive within two or three months.

Security

Security in a data base management system is somewhat different from that in conventional systems. Some of the characteristics of data bases create an element of security. The subschema, for example, make a portion of a data base inaccessible. Beyond that, other basic security is made possible by the full data base management systems. In the simple to install, easy to use systems, security is left largely for the users to develop. In the more elaborate data base/date communications products, security options are often built into the software. It is not uncommon to find capabilities to apply security by terminal, by transaction and by individual. Where security capabilities do not exist within the product itself, it is possible to interface it with other products that provide security. However implemented, the major data base systems, with their large volumes of data upon which organizations are heavily dependent, make consideration of security of the highest importance.

CONCLUSIONS

Data Base Is Potential

Glossy promotional literature with the neat, orderly data structures and the multicolored view graph presentations portray data base systems in terms of what they are capable when they are completly and correctly installed. In theory, virtually all of the claims made about data base systems are valid. Yet, in practice, it turns out that realization of the potential of a data base is largely the responsibility of the user.

The main difficulties encountered are not with data base technology; by and large, the technology works according to specifications. The difficulties, alluded to earlier in the discussion of installing a DBMS, lie in creating and sustaining an operating environment in which data base/data communications software products can function. Think of a working database environment as something like an airport. On a clear day, provided there are no strikes, no fuel shortages and no major equipment malfunctions, the airport functions beautifully. Flights arrive and depart on schedule; traffic in and out of the airport moves steadily and freely since no bottlenecks are being caused by disruptions.

Now add some rain, a dense fog, a demonstration by some irate taxi drivers or a baggage handlers' strike. To disrupt a smoothly functioning data base/data communications systems, add a failure of a disk storage device that contains some frequently used operating system programs; a malfunction of a major application program; repeated intermittant failures of a communications line; or a somewhat harried computer operator overriding a warning message and causing damage to major data elements within a data base. Potential efficiencies can be offset by human and equipment failures. Granted that these error situations can be recovered from with adequate back up and recovery procedures and software, it is still likely to be a time consuming—and expensive—process.

A great quantity of words has been expended, on the relative merits of one data base model as compared with the others. While this is useful and to some degree necessary, it often is done at the expense of other realities of the world of data base systems. These real world considerations ought to receive more attention.

There are managerial as well as technical considerations involved in implementing a data base system. The managerial aspects receive less than adequate attention; the consequences can be some unpleasant surprises. There are several key areas in which these surprises can occur, but a bit of planning can blunt their impact:

1. When installing a data base management system, estimates should include space for at least two versions: a production version and a test and development version.

2. Time allowance ought to be made for unforseen difficulties that arise as the data base/data communications product is integrated with other software products. A significant portion of the technicians' time is taken up with troubleshooting and support of applications, especially when elaborate DBMS products are used.

3. A significant portion of the total processing time for data base applications should be devoted to backing up data bases. Dynamic data bases that are heavily modified ought to be copied (backed up) on a daily basis. It is not uncommon for this process to take several hours.

4. Reorganization of data bases is required periodically. This process is extremely time consuming, taking from several hours to a full day (the latter in the case of a large data base); reorganization is best scheduled for a weekend.

Again, these considerations are independent of the DBMS product or of the data base model.

Space/Processing Trade-off

Nearly every application and software product, DBMSs included, can be evaluated in terms of the space/processing trade off. Complex structures that eliminate redundancies save space but increase processing complexity. Simple structures require more space because of redundancies, yet do not make great processing demands. This simplistic truism should be kept in mind whenever one encounters claims by DBMS vendors that their products offer reduced redundancies or require less storage.

What's Next

Developments now under way indicate a trend away from data base products that are made up of software exclusively. The term "user friendly" describes computer systems with which individual may interact without being skilled technicians or programmers. This term also applies to computer systems that include database capabilities. One factor that contributes to making interaction with data base/data communication systems difficult is that they are exclusively software.

Technological progress has led to the creation of data base/data communications systems that are a combination of software, circuitry and microcode, the later consisting of fabrications or small programmed routines that reside in a special type of high speed read-only memory. Some manufacturers are now marketing and promoting a "database machine." The concepts and techniques used

in data base—the models, the structures and the mechanisms—are such that technological advances can only improve their potential. Yet realization of that potential remains in the hands of those who use the DBMSs. No matter how great the potential, there is still a requirement that data bases be designed, developed and implemented by skilled individuals who are able to apply the potential of the technology to a carefully planned and logically sound set of data relationships.

Earlier in this chapter, four reasons commonly offered for justifying the use of data base technology were listed. Let us now conclude by examining the trade-offs that are necessary if these justifications are to be accepted.

1. A reduction in redundancy is possible and is facilitated by data base technology. However, it is the user's responsibility to establish the file or data base structures that bring about the reduction in redundant data. A structure that results in reducing data redundancy often leads to more complex processing.

2. Achieving a degree of data independence also increases processing complexity and creates a need for the talents of data base administrators and designers, that is, highly skilled and highly compensated individuals not required in a conventional (non-data base) environment.

3. Increasing application programmer productivity is also possible, because file design is no longer an application programming consideration. However, this gain is offset by the need for highly skilled, highly compensated data base administrators and designers.

4. The simplification of retrieving data from multiple files is a partial truth. Logically, the process is simplified; physically, the process is the same. The task of determining the steps to perform the data retrieval has merely been moved from the jurisdiction of the application programmer to the jurisdiction of the DBMS software.

Data base technology is a sound technology, with strengths and limitations. It provides great potential, but realization of that potential lies in proper application, and that remains the responsibility of the user.

REFERENCES

[1] *Data Processing Glossary, GC20-1699-5,* IBM Data Processing Division, 1133 Westchester Avenue, White Plains, NY 10604. Oct. 1977, p. 63

[2] Martin, James, *Principles of Data-Base Management.* Englewood Cliffs, NJ: Prentice Hall, 1976. P. 329.

[3] Martin, James, *Computer Data-Base Organization,* 2nd Ed. Englewood Cliffs, NJ: Prentice Hall, 1977. P. 686.

[4] Date, C. J., *An Introduction to Database Systems.* Reading, MA: Addison-Wesley, 1976. P. 1.

[5] Ross, Ronald, *Data Base Systems.* AMACOM, a Division of American Management Associations, 135 West 50th Street, New York, NY 10020. P. 207

[6] Cohen, Leo, *Data Base Management Systems.* QED Information Sciences, 141 Linden Street, Wellesley, MA 02181. P. 5–2.

[7] Lewis, Charles, J., "Understanding Database and Data Base," *Journal of Systems Management,* Bagley Road, Cleveland, Ohio. (Sept. 1977)

[8] Codd, E. F., "A Relational Model of Data for Large Shared Data Banks," *Communications of the ACM,* Vol. 13, No. 6 (June 1970).

[9] Walsh, Myles E. *Information Management Systems/Virtual Storage.* Reston, VA: Reston Publishing Co., 1980. (Chapter 10)

[10] Walsh, Myles E., "Update on Data Dictionaries" *Journal of Systems Management,* July 1978.

[11] Walsh, Myles E., *Realizing the Potential of Computerized Information Systems.* New York: Macmillan, 1984. (Chapter 7)

[12] Flores, Ivan, *Data Base Architecture.* New York: Van Nostrand Reinhold, 1981.

33
Software Engineering

Vladimir Zwass

Fairleigh Dickinson University

33.1 INTRODUCTION

Software engineering is an emerging discipline of development and maintenance of computer software systems through the creation and use of methodologies and automated tools. A computer software system includes the code itself, as well as the documentation and the procedures for system operation. The origins of the discipline date back to the late 1960s, when it was recognized that the complexity presented by software systems called for a structured engineering approach.

Currently, the discipline is still in its infancy. The production of software is still largely a craft; with automatic support seemingly within the grasp (or rather on the fingertips), few truly important tools for radically improving programming productivity and product reliability have been developed in the last decade. Customary drastic overruns of time and cost estimates for programming projects are another indicator of the lack of engineering control.

Software engineering in its present form represents a distillation of programming lore, management experience, and application of a limited body of theoretical results, together with certain tooling skills.

33.2 THE "SOFTWARE PROBLEM"

The dimensions of what is often called the "software bottleneck" on the path to more effective automation are best characterized by the following figures. The annual software expenditures in the U.S. are estimated at $20 billion [1], although much higher estimates also exist.

This constitutes approximately two-thirds of the total computerization costs. The cost of the software components is expected to increase further in relation to the hardware costs owing to the economics of the progressive circuit integration (hardware costs have dropped by three orders of magnitude during the last 25 years) on the one hand, and the increasingly more expensive labor intensity of software. The cost per instruction in a programming product of average complexity was estimated in 1975 at $8 [2], although at about that time the costs of highly responsible avionics software were reported to be $75 per instruction in development and $4,000(!) in maintenance [3].

Of the total software expenditure, more is spent by a typical installation on maintenance than on development (48 percent and 46 percent, respectively, according to a recent comprehensive survey [4]). In many installations, maintenance activities absorb 70–75 percent of the software effort. This would have been a heartening state of affairs in a mature industry, with most user needs satisfied by the systems already in existence. Yet, most companies report one to three year backlogs of unimplemented applications, judged economically worthy of development but waiting for the attention of scarce information processing professionals. More than half of the information processing departments are understaffed because of this scarcity.

In very large part, these significant maintenance efforts are caused by the poor maintainability and reliability of existing software. Software engineering is thus called upon to solve the intertwined problems of programming productivity and software product reliability. Increasing pervasiveness of computer systems and the ever larger reliance on them call for more software and for more reliable software. Defense systems and electronic fund transfer systems ought to suffice as examples. In general, besides systems software, two categories of applications software may be identified: **business information systems,** relying on large data bases, and **embedded systems,** which are a part of larger engineering systems and where the stress is on real time response.

Only in recent years the complexity and specificity of software have been recognized through the introduction of software engineering techniques. Software specificity takes into account the following factors:

1. Systemic complexity, reflecting the complexity of the functions realized and interaction with the environment.
2. Very large number of states that can be assumed by an operating software system, which precludes exhaustive testing.
3. Modifiability as a rationale for using software rather than hardware. Software (if not tampered with) does not deteriorate with time, and may be used much longer than the environment for which it was originally intended will last.
4. Ease of uncontrolled corruption if protection measures are not applied.
5. Because software is intangible, the necessity for its development to be explicitly visualized through the use of appropriate tools.
6. The human interface envelope provided by software. This envelope must be adjusted to human psychology to enable the overall system to perform satisfactorily.

33.3 PROPERTIES OF PROPER PROGRAMMING PRODUCTS

These qualities are desired in valid programming products:

Effectiveness

This signifies satisfaction of the user requirement and can be further analyzed as:

- Functional effectiveness;
- Fit into the overall information plan of the company;
- User-friendliness.

Owing to the nature of software, no software can be judged fully effective, however, unless it is maintainable.

Reliability

This quality is defined as a satisfactory probability of effective operation over a sufficiently long time period.

Maintainability

This is achieved through

- Understandability of the system, due to correct design and programming;
- Modifiability, needed to adapt the system to a new environment.

A software system is not maintainable unless its complete and consistent documentation allows the user to establish a trace from its functional specifications to the code.

Efficiency

This characterizes system's performance with economcal use of reserves.

The main objectives in defining the structural properties of the programming product are making the development process manageable and simplifying system modification. Software engineering discipline has identified the following properties of software systems as a necessary means to the end.

Functional Modularity

The system should be built of modules—short code segments, invoked only by specifying their name and, possibly, the data elements needed to communicate with them. A module ought to perform completely a well defined function in the overall system; in doing so, the module may in turn invoke lower level modules.

Hierarchical Structure

The modules of a given program (a system may consist of several programs) ought to be identified and organized hierarchically. That is, starting with the single module which provides the overall control, by a process of decomposition into constituent functions, lower level modules are identified. In this fashion, by gradually decomposing modules level by level, the designer concentrates on the problem at a consistent level of abstraction, without considering as yet unnecessary detail. During the system maintenance, in turn, the system's functioning can be understood by analyzing its modular structure.

Localization and Hiding of Information

Modules should be defined so as to handle completely certain aspects of system's functioning. In doing so, they usually hide a particular design solution or a data structure from the rest of the system. Such selection of modules is reflected in their relative independence from the rest of the system since few data elements have to be communicated to them or by them.

Structured Programming

Modules should be implemented by adherence to the structured programming discipline: the use of single entry/single exit control structures, excluding undisciplined transfer of control (goto's) within a module; these significantly enhance the reliability and readability of a module. **Hierarchical systems,** built of relatively independent functional modules, make it possible to identify and isolate the part of the system affected by a modification procedure.

33.4 SOFTWARE LIFE CYCLE

In organizing the process of development and maintenance of programming products as complex systems, software engineering has tapped established manufacturing practice of a product life cycle. This management strategy structures the process into well defined phases with continuous quality control.

Life cycle management has become the essential par-adigm of software engineering. The sequentiality of the phases needs to be strictly enforced: *no phase is begun unless the deliverables of its predecessor phase have been audited and approved.*

While variations exist in the definition of the life cycle, the essential tasks have been firmly established (Figure 33.1). These are the system requirements analysis, architectural and detailed system design, and system implementation. The methodologies and tools for these phases are discussed further in the chapter.

As the basic technique of software quality assurance, the deliverables of every phase need to be validated before the process continues. Timely correction of errors is of the essence. It has been established that the cost of error correction grows exponentially with the time lapsed between the error and its discovery. Thus, the cost of fixing an error in the requirements specifications during system operation (if the situation is at all retrievable) is about 100-fold that of the cost of a coding error.

The developmental life cycle of a large project lasts for years; user requirements will probably change during this period. A procedure for handling change requests during the life cycle must be established. Some organizations implement a **configuration management** discipline, under which a **baseline** configuration for the software system is established, and all changes to it undergo strict approval procedures. This discipline, applied throughout the life cycle, maintains the integrity of the product.

During the system life cycle, system **documentation** is to be generated. It includes the analysis and design graphics, as well as the logic and data description. Ulti-

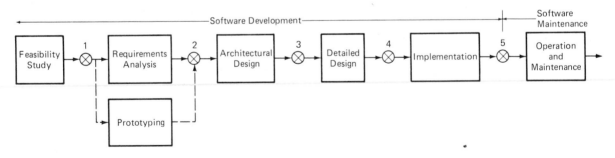

Milestones:
1. Recommendation to proceed; outline of the system and its environment
2. Requirements specifications, possibly including approved prototype
3. Structure chart(s) of the system
4. Specification of the system modules
5. Accepted system

Figure 33.1. Software life cycle.

mately, *commented code* constitutes the most important part of the documentation. Also, user's and operator's manuals are to be provided; in some cases, a maintenance manual is also necessary.

The following is the description of the life cycle phases (Figure 33.1). More detailed discussion of requirements analysis, system design, and implementation is provided subsequently.

Feasibility Study

The objective of this phase is to decide whether the project is justified in the light of the overall information policy of the company. The tasks of the phase are to establish:

1. The area to be automated by the system, and the total user population;
2. Information inputs/outputs of the system (these may be presented as a context diagram, discussed below);
3. Broad alternative solutions to the problem;
4. For each solution identified:
   - Organizational impact, including risks involved.
   - Conformance with long-range company plans.
   - Interfaces with other systems and/or ongoing development projects.
   - Time/budget resource-use estimates.
   - Cost/benefit analysis.
   - Future evolution of the system within the strategic plan of the company.

Final recommendation on the desirability of the project needs to be made in conclusion.

Feasibility study is a management rather than a software oriented phase. Thus, management oriented techniques and tools are employed. Several methodologies are available for establishing the overall information plan of a company, and considering large projects in this perspective. These include most prominently IBM's Business Systems Planning [5].

Requirements Analysis and Prototyping

This phase, also called **system analysis,** entails a complete examination of the problem, and results in the approved requirements specifications. This document states in detail what the software system will accomplish, and constitutes a contract between developers and users.

The essential tools for requirements analysis are dis-cussed below. Requirements specifications, expressed with the use of these tools, should include the following:

- A complete, consistent, and unambiguous representation of the business to be included in the system.
- Hardware, systems software, and communication requirements of the system.

Requirements specifications should conform to the following principles:

1. They should be expressed in terms understood by the users, who in many cases participate in, or even conduct, the analysis.
2. They should be expressed in a fashion helpful in subsequent design phases.
3. Requirements should be measurable whenever possible, for the system to be validated during the acceptance testing.
4. Traceability between the requirements and the code needs to be ensured for maintenance purposes.
5. The specifications have to be maintainable themselves.

Requirements specifications should state only *what* will be accomplished by the software system, rather than make premature commitments as to *how* will the system accomplish it.

When early visualization of the system is desired, its prototype may be built. This can prevent the most dramatic failure of all: a completed system that does not satisfy user requirements. The prototype is an inexpensive model of the system to be developed; it contains only the major functions and outputs, with the particular stress on the user interface. It is best to build a prototype when the preliminary version of the requirements specification is available. Users and developers interact with the prototype, needed modifications are established, and the requirements specifications are completed (see [6] for the discussion of a successful prototype use).

Architectural design. During the architectural (logical) design, the modular structure of the system is established, together with the interfaces between the modules. External specifications of system modules are provided. At the same time, the logical structure of the data base is designed.

Detailed design. During the detailed (physical) design, the logic of individual modules is designed. Physical design of the data base is also performed. Detailed plan for the system implementation, prominently including the module testing sequence, is prepared.

Implementation.   System modules are coded, with the use of structured programming techniques, tested individually, and integrated. The integration sequence has important implications and is further discussed below.

Thus, several stages of subsystem validation (testing) are performed, followed by the complete system test under the workloads expected (possibly including stress testing under surpassing loads). Code "hot spots" (heavily executed segments) may be identified with performance measurement tools, and the system tuned to improve such parameters as transaction response time and memory utilization. Validation process ends with the acceptance testing of the system, procedures, and documentation; the users and the future maintainers participate. Subsequently, gradual or one shot installation of the new system and conversion to it is performed, followed by installation testing (in some cases, installation testing can precede acceptance testing).

Operation and maintenance.   Following its installation and acceptance, the system becomes operational and undergoes maintenance. As part of maintenance, the evaluation phase for the system's performance and for its development process needs to be defined. As the result of this evaluation, the system may be further modified, and the development process itself adjusted.

33.5 REQUIREMENTS ANALYSIS

The requirements analysis stage of the system life cycle results in a complete **requirements specification:** a detailed description of what the system will accomplish. The demands placed on requirements specifications, as already discussed, are stringent. A narrative description does not satisfy any of them. Thus, graphical tools, semiformal description techniques, and automatic aids, ought to be used.

A widespread comprehensive technique is **structured analysis** [7, 8]. Its principal graphical tool is the **data flow diagram,** whose origins lie in office document flow graphics. The data flow diagram uses only four graphical symbols:

1. Data flows, represented by vectors.
2. Processes (data transformers), represented by circles ("bubbles").

3. Data stores, represented by open rectangles.
4. External entities (i.e., other systems, organizational units, customers, etc.) which feed the data into the system and/or receive data from it, shown as boxes.

All these symbols need to be named, with significant attention to semantics.

Data flow diagrams show the flow of data through the system being analyzed, transformation of this data by the processes, and the repositories (data stores) logically necessary to hold it. The use of data flow diagrams is illustrated in Figure 33.2. Such use lends itself to a stepwise refinement process, called *leveling,* whereby the detail can be brought in gradually. During the leveling process, shown in Figure 33.2, balancing rules need to be observed; the inputs and outputs of the higher level bubbles need to match these in its lower level decomposition.

Data flow diagram graphics need to be supported by the description of all the entities represented. The repository of such descriptions is the *data dictionary.* For an extensive system, an automatic data dictionary has to be used. The structure of the data flows and data stores, as well as the physical makeup of all data items, is described using the conventions of the dictionary. The processes are described in a user accessible form of *pseudocode* (called *structured English*), with a recourse to decision tables or decision trees in the case of more complex branching policies.

A rather widely used automatic tool for the analysis of large software systems is PSL/PSA, a product of the ISDOS project at the University of Michigan [9]. It provides the problem statement language (PSL), in which system requirements can be incrementally stated and submitted for analysis to the problem statement analyzer (PSA). The latter checks the consistency and completeness of the specifications. This elaborate software tool produces, and further helps to maintain, a very extensive documentation.

A more modest approach to automatic support of the requirements analysis involves the use of one of the automated data dictionaries such as, for example, the freestanding DATAMANAGER [10]. They enable developers to cope with the vast amount of development data, and further simplify implementation and maintenance.

As alternatives to structured analysis, comprehensive methodologies in practical use include SADT [11], a nonautomatic technique, and SREM [12], a derivative of the PSL/PSA system, thus largely automated, and used predominantly for the development of real time systems.

After the functional requirements of the system under

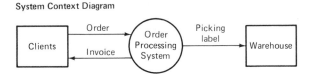

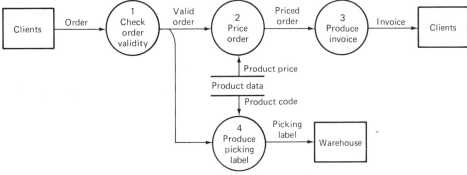

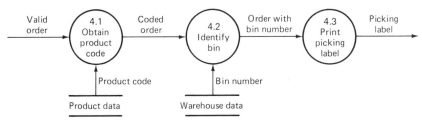

Figure 33.2. Data flow diagrams with leveling.

development have been analyzed, its hardware and systems software environments are established and the specific processes are assigned to ("packaged into") programs which are to be designed. This assignment is based on

1. Mode of operation (on-line/batch/real-time).
2. Geography, in the case of distributed processing.
3. Local hardware constraints.
4. Batch periodicity (business cycle).
5. Security, backup, and recovery considerations.

33.6 ARCHITECTURAL DESIGN

Architectural design of the system's programs consists in factoring them into increasingly more detailed, less ab-

stract, modules. Thus, beginning with the main module, which provides the top level logic of the program, the subfunctions are identified and modules provided to handle them. While the higher level modules determine the logic of the program operation, the lower level ones perform computation, read/write files, and provide screen and report outputs.

Structured design technique, originated by Constantine [13], uses a **structure chart** as its main graphical tool, and provides a set of heuristics for obtaining a modular decomposition of programs and judges the goodness of alternative decompositions [14]. This technique is applied as a sequel to structured analysis. An example of a structure chart, for the system of Figure 33.2, is presented in Figure 33.3; for the sake of clarity the design has not been completed. The comparison of these two fig-

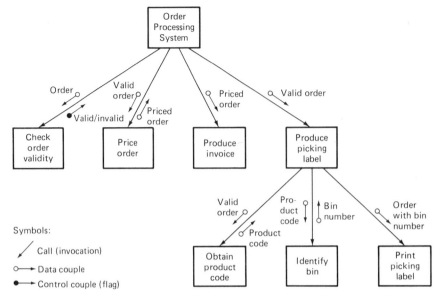

Figure 33.3. A structure chart for Figure 33.2.

ures suggests that a data flow diagram lends itself to a transformation into a structure chart; additional controlling modules and provisions are usually necessary, however.

Structure charts use rectangular boxes to indicate modules, vectors to show invocations (calls), and arrows to show couples (argument transfer). Thus, for example, in Figure 33.3 the order processing system module (the main module of our system) calls the price order module, passing to it "valid order" as an argument, in order to retrieve the "priced order" argument. On further consideration, it may be seen that it is not necessary to pass down the entire order; product identification and quantity alone may be sufficient. The looser the connection between modules, the better the design, because a possible future modification of certain modules is less likely to affect their neighbors.

The structure chart design needs to aim at a proper programming product, with the properties specified in Section 33.3 of the chapter. In particular, a structure chart should represent a good model of the problem itself.

Important criteria for evaluating a structure chart are those of **module cohesion** (Table 33.1), and **coupling** between two modules, the calling and the called one (Table 33.2). The more cohesive is a module, the fewer data it needs from the surrounding modules, and thus the weaker is module coupling. Strong modules with weak coupling are the goal of the modular decomposition, because they

provide for localized modification during system maintenance, avoiding a ripple effect of changes through the entire system.

Alternative, practice proven techniques for decomposing a system into modules are the Jackson methodology [15] and the Warnier-Orr logical construction of programs/systems [16]. Both of these are data centered, that is, they organize the system on the premise that its purpose is to derive the output data structures from the input structures. The HIPO technique, developed by IBM, is also used sometimes [17].

During the architectural design process, the overall data base of the system is specified in logical terms by providing its schema, and if needed, subschemas for various user groups. Architectural design is completed by establishment of external specification of all modules, including the

- Module name.
- Input and output arguments.
- Function.

The logic and internal data of modules are specified during the subsequent detailed design.

Detailed Design

Detailed system design entails the specification of logic for all the system modules. This specification can be ex-

Table 33.1. Module Cohesion (Strength)

Name of Cohesion Level		Reason for Module Creation
Functional ⎤	⎫ excellent	Single, complete function is performed.
Clustered ⎦		Module with multiple-entry points manages completely ("hides") a data structure by performing all functions on it.
Sequential ⎤		Performs a sequence of functions, passing data from one to the next.
Communicational	⎬ acceptable	Performs several functions on the same data, but does not hide it.
Temporal ⎦		Performs a number of actions related by timing, such as initialization or termination.
Procedural ⎤		Module created by algorithmic considerations (for example, by subdividing a flow chart).
Logical	⎬ undesirable	Module performs a general set of functions (e.g. "general edit"), with the action controlled by a flag passed to it.
Coincidental ⎦		No functional meaning.

pressed in pseudocode, in a formal program design language, or via structured flowcharts.

All of these tools help to build a module from a limited set of control structures with single entry and single exit. During the coding stage of system implementation, these specifications are translated into the programming language of choice. Such programming practice, resting on the use of standard single entry/single exit control structures, is **structured programming.** By avoiding undisciplined control transfers, structured programming supports orderly thinking of the programmer, thus resulting in reliable code; it also makes the code readable in a top down fashion, thus simplifying maintenance.

The basic control structures, sufficient to represent any logic, as proven by the famous Böhm and Jacopini theorem of 1966, are sequence, selection, and **while-do** iteration (Figure 33.4). To enrich the expressiveness of the specification language, and thus shorten the specification, additional logic structures are most often used. These include the following (also see Figure 33.5):

- Open (**repeat-until**) iteration, which allows the loop body to be executed once in order to establish the condition.
- **Case** construct, to provide for testing of nonbinary conditions.
- **Exit** to the end of the iteration loop (in order to prevent setting additional flags).

All these control structures control the order of execution of the action statements: assignments, input and output statements, and module invocations.

Pseudocode consists in sequential and/or nested (to a limited degree) use of these constructs to present the logic of the module. Comments may be used freely. The level of description offered by pseudocode ranges from informal to very formal; sometimes several levels, or "cuts," are used by the module designer as the module logic becomes clearer. An example of an informal pseudocode is shown in Table 33.3.

Alternatively, **structured flowcharts** (also called Nassi-Schneiderman charts, for their inventors) may be used to express logic (see Figures 33.4 and 33.5). The basic advantages of these graphics over traditional flowcharts is the absence of unstructured transfer of control (no flow-

Table 33.2. Coupling Between Modules

Coupling	Control Transfer	Argument Type	Argument Complexity	Argument Exclusivity
Loose	To the opening statement via invoking module/ entry point name	Data	Data item	Explicit argument
Tight	To an internal statement	Control flag	Data structure	Global data

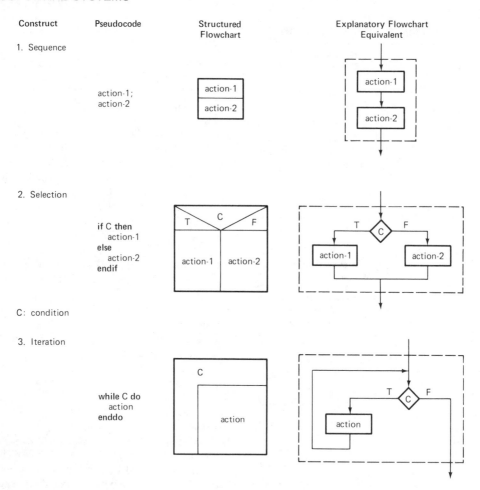

Figure 33.4. Basic logic constructs.

lines!) and of the off-page connectors, limiting the size of the module to a readable one page description (stepwise refinement is possible).

A formal **program design language** [18] imposes a strict syntax, the correctness of which may be checked by automatic processors. Because the use of such a language to a large degree duplicates coding effort and limits descriptional flexibility, it is not widespread.

Before the system implementation is begun, a module integration plan needs to be established. This plan conforms to the integration sequence adapted, as discussed below.

33.7 SYSTEM IMPLEMENTATION

During the system implementation stage of the life cycle, individual modules are coded and tested. They are pro-

gressively integrated into the overall structure, and the resulting subsystems are tested. The process ends in full system and acceptance testing.

Coding

In module coding, structured programming principles should be followed. Disciplined use of the selected programming language is called for, because most languages in common practice were developed before the desirable programming techniques were identified. Installation coding standards, if available, ought to be strictly followed.

Modules are best implemented as closed subroutines, that is, external procedures which communicate with other modules only via explicit arguments. This provides

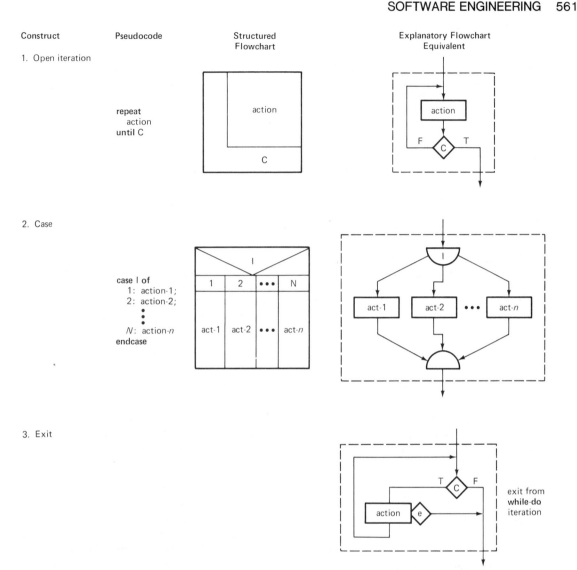

Construct	Pseudocode	Structured Flowchart	Explanatory Flowchart Equivalent
1. Open iteration	repeat action until C		

Figure 33.5. Supplementary logic constructs.

Table 33.3. Pseudocode

* Bubble sort*
Input array;
while exchanges are expected **do**
    start at the bottom of the array;
    while below last exchange limit **do** *single pass*
        compare items pairwise and exchange if out of order;
        move to the next pair
    enddo;
    mark new exchange limit
enddo;
Output sorted array

better module isolation—and thus enhances reliability and modifiability more than alternative module implementations, such as internal procedures, paragraphs, macros, or code segments copied during the compilation. Many programming languages provide for separate compilation of external subroutines. Global data use is to be avoided.

Programming logic should be implemented through the equivalents of the constructs of Figures 33.4 and 33.5, available in the language. The use of unconditional control transfer (**goto**) is permissible to implement missing higher level constructs; otherwise, it is best limited to those exceptional situations for which the structured alternative would be less expressive.

Comments, meaningful in terms of the problem, should be used throughout. Furthermore, the readability of the code should be enhanced by indentation within the control structures (Table 33.3) and by grouping of meaningful code units with the use of blank lines.

Testing

Software quality does not emerge as the result of proper testing of the coded system modules. The process of quality assurance has to be built into the entire development life cycle, with the deliverables of every phase being validated before the next phase is begun. The final sequence of tests is the validation of the system code against the functional requirements of the system. It should be realized, however, that testing cannot prove the *absence* of errors; it can only diagnose their *presence*. Formal proof techniques, called **verification** of software, are not yet ready to be used for larger systems. A proper sequence of tests, if passed, should provide, however, a fair degree of confidence in the product. General principles of code testing follow:

1. A test plan has to be prepared to specify the sequence in which the modules will be integrated.
2. Test cases need to be prepared, together with the results expected from a successful outcome.
3. The aim of a test case should be clearly understood as that of trying to destroy the entity tested, rather than to prove its correctness.
4. All tests should be studied and recorded.
5. Test cases should be prepared for both valid and invalid input conditions.
6. If testing a particular system component or aspect yields many errors, this is an indication of more errors to be found.
7. It is desirable to have a specialized testing group to perform tests beyond module testing.

Testing is a time consuming process, taking up from one-third to one-half of the overall developmental life cycle. Satisfaction of the requirements stated in the functional specifications needs to be ascertained, in particular the following:

1. External system interfaces are to correspond to the specification.
2. Modules are to be interfaced correctly.

3. Module logic has to be correct.
4. System performance is to be satisfactory.
5. System has to be robust: it has to resist erroneous inputs.
6. Documentation has to correspond to the code.

The testing process consists of module, integration, system, and acceptance testing.

Module (unit) testing. These tests are performed by the module coder; however, state analysis (reading) of the code during a walk-through is important. Several guidelines exist. In general, path exercising calls for executing each statement at least once, bringing each decision to each of its outcomes, and testing the limits of every loop.

Integration testing. Modules are brought together to test their interaction and interfaces. Incremental approaches, whereby modules are coded, unit-tested, and added one by one to the overall structure, are preferred to one shot integration. Incremental approaches provide for a better error isolation and establish a more uniform use of computer resources. The order in which incremental integration is performed depends on the objectives pursued. The following test sequences are possible:

1. *Bottom up testing,* a traditional approach, calling for the lowest level modules to be implemented first and tested with the use of dummy *driver* (caller) modules. The advantage is having the "worker" modules which read in the data and produce the outputs available early.
2. *Top down testing,* under which, starting with the top module, progressively lower module layers are implemented; as yet unavailable lower level modules are temporarily replaced by dummy modules called *stubs.* The advantage of this technique is having the system skeleton available early, which provides insight into the overall system operation and confidence in it as well.
3. *Sandwich testing,* designed to garner the advantages of both bottom-up and top-down testing. This method calls for the initial implementation and testing of the top module and the lowest level modules, with the middle modules added subsequently.
4. *Thread testing,* under which the key functional module threads are identified and implemented first; thus complete subsystems may be tested and released to the users as preliminary system versions. This approach is gaining popularity.

System testing. Full functionality of the system, and its performance, are tested against the functional specifications in the environment and under the loads resembling as closely as possible the actual system operation. System tuning may be necessary.

Acceptance testing. This is the final test of the system, testing its satisfaction of the user requirements. As such, it is performed by the users, maintainers and information systems auditors, with the developers participating. The system is subjected to stress loads, and all its procedures and documentation are validated.

A set of tests validating the overall system operation needs to be identified, documented and preserved for maintenance purposes. These *regression tests* are used to revalidate the system following each maintenance procedure.

Implementation Tools

The implementation stage, as opposed to the analysis and design phases, is rather well supported by automatic tools. Their use is mandatory for larger projects. The tools for system implementation include

1. Text editors, which serve to insert, delete, modify or move portions of any text, such as code, data file or documentation; some newer editors also perform syntax validation of code.
2. Automatic library systems, serving to store multiple versions of source and object code of subsystems at various testing stages; these tools may be used to implement a program production library, discussed below.
3. Test generators, generating input files for systems being tested.
4. Test harnesses, which drive modules or partially coded systems by feeding to them required input arguments, and simulating as yet uncoded lower level modules by stubs.
5. Debuggers which are on-line tools enabling the programmer to interact with the program during its execution in order to locate the errors established by testing.

An integrated set of tools is provided by a so-called *programming environment,* of which the most widespread at this time is the Programmer's Workbench, implemented under the UNIX operating system [19]. Such environments offer simplified use of a complement of tools through a single command language interface.

33.8 SYSTEM MAINTENANCE

Maintenance activities include all the efforts needed to keep software operational and adapt it to the changing environment and user requirements. These activities consume from about 50 to 80 percent of systems and programming efforts of computer installations. Such efforts are growing with the increasing inventories of operational systems.

Maintenance activities generally fall into one of the following three categories (from the survey in [4]):

- Corrective: removal of development errors—17.4 percent.
- Adaptive: accomodation to hardware/software/data environment changes—18.2 percent.
- Perfective: modification for higher effectiveness or efficiency—60.3 percent

The techniques and tools of development are applicable during maintenance. Uncontrolled maintenance should be avoided. Rather, a maintenance procedure similar to that shown in Figure 33.6 ought to be implemented. Perfective and adaptive maintenance can be performed on a scheduled basis, with requests for maintenance accumulated over an established period of time. Aside from economy of resources, this enhances software integrity. These maintenance principles should be followed:

1. Change as little as needed to fulfill the purpose of the maintenance work.
2. Strictly follow all the standards for development work, in particular those concerning coding practices.
3. Consistently change the documentation, preferably using automated tools.
4. Document the change in the maintenance journal.

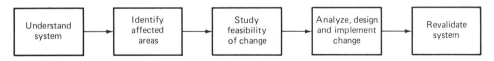

Figure 33.6. A software maintenance procedure.

5. Revalidate the system with the following sequence of tests:
   - Unit tests of modules modified,
   - Integration tests involving the modified areas,
   - System and acceptance tests, with the use of regression test sequences, to establish that the system as a whole has not been damaged.

No changes to the system code or documentation are to be allowed outside of the established procedure.

33.9 ORGANIZATION OF PROGRAMMING EFFORT

Development and maintenance of large software systems are sizable projects which require specialized management techniques. A number of software engineering principles have been established in this regard [20]; the following are the most important organizational aspects.

Strictly Enforced Sequential Life Cycle

Software life cycle is a most important management tool, and should be defined with regard to the specific environment of the company. Each phase of a life cycle ought to terminate in a **milestone**, a demonstrable event with well defined *deliverables*, such as the development documentation or code. No phase should be commenced before the deliverables of the preceding one have been completed and validated; this provides continuous quality assurance.

The final and formal acceptance of the phase deliverables is to be performed by a body constituted of management and user representatives, as well as information systems professionals, often called the *design review committee*.

Teams and Walkthroughs

Software development is best done in small teams of up to 10 people. This removes the overhead of multiple person to person communication and ensures tight control (the span of control is based on the well known 7 ± 2 rule). The small team concept, coupled with the recognition that programmers differ by more than an order of magnitude in their performance, led to the idea of a **chief programmer team** [21]. Such a team is established to support an exceptionally creative and productive individual, the chief programmer. As further elaborated by Brooks [22], the team is to consist of the following:

1. *The chief programmer,* who under the strict definition of the concept (which has found scarce application) defines, designs, codes, tests and documents the entire system, with other members acting as assistants. In practice, the chief programmer usually acts as the technical manager of the team, designs the system (thus providing it with the conceptual integrity of a single ratiocination), and then specifies and implements the crucial (usually higher level) modules.
2. *The backup programmer*—a professional peer to the chief—who provides the critical assistance, and is able to replace the chief programmer.
3. Two or three junior programmers, to whom the following functions may be assigned:
   - The toolsmith, responsible for maintaining and customizing automatic development tools.
   - The tester, devising test cases.
   - The language lawyer, an expert on the intricacies of the programming language used.
4. Programming librarian, who maintains all the team products in their current state in the program production library.
5. Technical writer, responsible for the documentation.
6. Administrator and secretaries, relieving the programming professionals from all nonprogramming duties.

Larger projects require involvement of several teams; it is best if the additional teams are spawned *following* the definition of the system, in order to ensure the conceptual integrity of the product. The work of all teams should be supported by on-line availability of well documented program development tools.

One of the most important aspects of teamwork are **structured walkthroughs**, quality assurance procedures carried out quite frequently during the life cycle. This form of status review assembles four to six team members (possibly including invited experts) for up to two hours, in order to review a specific product of one of the team's members (such as a data flow diagram, a structure chart, or a module code). All participants come fully prepared, having studied the work, and are ready either to approve it or to point out specific failings. No corrections are performed during a walkthrough.

Project Visibility

For maintenance of project control, the current status of the work needs to be made visible. The analysis and design tools described above serve this purpose during the respective developmental stages. Two major visibility tools are also the **project notebook,** reflecting the daily status, and the **program production library.**

The program production library, both a programming and a management tool, contains

1. Individual libraries of the members.
2. Development libraries, holding tested and approved modules.
3. The subsystem library, storing the currently complete version of the system.
4. Test data.
5. JCL (job control language) and procedure files.

The movement of modules from the individual libraries through development libraries to the subsystem library is strictly controlled. The program production library is thus an important tool in configuration management.

Project Control

Automatic project planning and control systems may be used to assist in the life cycle oriented scheduling, monitoring and status reporting. Estimates of resource needs should be obtained at project initiation and continually refined.

The best estimates are developed by gathering experimental data from comparable projects and analyzing them during the evaluation phase of these projects. After being adjusted for the relative functional and environmental complexity, these data can then be used during the requirements analysis of future projects. Certain theoretical results concerning software estimation are now available for practical use [23]. Code length consideration is no longer sufficient for estimating, and software complexity should be probed deeper [24].

Standards

Every installation ought to define and enforce a set of standards for software development and maintenance. These should be introduced with a well selected pilot project and periodically updated to reflect accumulated experience and general advances in software engineering.

33.10 PERSPECTIVE

As one may conclude from the foregoing discussion, software engineering still requires vast research and, espe-

cially, experimentation to become a fully established discipline. The following are the important areas of promise for the near future.

Formal System Specification

By specifying system requirements in a formal fashion, and having them automatically validated, as well as by validating automatically their agreement with the design and implementation products, the developers of a system can ensure its validity. A number of formal specification languages are being designed at present. The PSL/PSA system [9] is a step in this direction.

Adequate Programming Languages

The programming language determines to a large extent the thinking pattern of the programmer. Several influential higher level languages have been designed to express the concepts acquired by software engineering since the 1960s, when the currently most popular languages took their shape. To implement the most important of these new concepts, the new languages

- Support **data abstraction** by allowing programmers to define their own data types as templates, with specified operations defined on them. This makes possible encapsulating certain operations within the data type "manager" modules, thus hiding their detail from the higher level modules, and laying the foundation for hierarchical system design.
- Provide for **concurrent processing,** necessary in the increasingly distributed environment of mini- and microcomputers. This is accomplished with synchronizing abstract data type managers, called *monitors.*
- Provide general module and logic constructs.

An important language providing some of these facilities is PASCAL. A much more general language recently evolved at the behest of the United States Department of Defense, and certain to shape much of the computing environment during the next decade, is ADA [25].

System Verification

Formal verification of system correction needs to be extended to realistic application systems. At this time, only a constrained subset of programs can be verified. Among several techniques of formal correctness proofs, the most widely investigated is the **method of inductive assertions.** It associates with every program branch a predicate (assertion) and requires a proof that the intervening program statements do indeed perform a transformation which derives the output assertion from the input one.

Automatic Program Generation

An automatic program generator accepts the specification of the system to be developed in a nonprocedural language, that is, only *what* is needed, rather than the steps to be taken by the computer to effect it. The generator automatically provides the code of the system by customizing its set of ready routines. Generators provide programs within a specific application domain; programmer modifications of the generated code are necessary.

A large number of automatic program generators are available commercially and their power and use will grow. Also, libraries of documented reusable code will be created.

User Accessible Systems

With the continuing trend to less and less expensive hardware, the end users will be offered more tools which obviate the need for a development cycle in the case of many applications. Systems software will be further extended to the end user's level of interaction.

Systems of this kind already exist. End-user oriented data base systems, such as FOCUS or RAMIS, provide direct access to data bases in a powerful, English-like query language. This trend will be further enhanced with the use of relational data base systems. Thus the necessity for application development will in many cases fade as end users directly employ a tool designed for them.

REFERENCES

[1] Boehm, B. W., "Software Engineering: R & D Trends and Defense Needs," in P. Wegner (ed.), *Research Directions in Software Technology.* Cambridge, MA: MIT Press, 1979, pp. 44–86.

[2] Lecht, C. P., *The Waves of Change.* New York: McGraw-Hill, 1977.

[3] De Roze, B. C., and T. H. Nyman, "The Software Life Cycle—a Management and Technological Challenge in the Department of Defense," *IEEE Transactions on Software Engineering,* July 1978, pp. 309–18.

[4] Lientz, B. P., E. B. Swanson, and G. E. Tompkins, "Characteristics of Application Software Maintenance," *Communications of the ACM,* June 1978, pp. 466–71.

[5] *Business Systems Planning—Information Systems Planning Guide,* Armonk, NY: IBM Corp., Publ. No. GE20-0527.

[6] Gomaa, H., and D. B. H. Scott, "Prototyping as a Tool in the Specification of User Requirements," *Fifth International Conference on Software Engineering,* New York: IEEE Computer Society, 1981, pp. 333–42.

[7] Gane, C., and T. Sarson, *Structured Systems Analysis: Tools and Techniques.* New York: Improved System Technologies, 1977.

[8] DeMarco, T., *Structured Analysis and System Specification.* Englewood Cliffs, NJ: Prentice-Hall, 1979.

[9] Teichroew, D., and E. A. Hershey III, "PSL/PSA: A Computer-Aided Technique for Structured Documentation and Analysis of Information Processing Systems," *IEEE Transactions on Software Engineering,* Jan. 1977, pp. 41–48.

[10] *DATAMANAGER: Implementation Plan and Management Report,* Lexington, MA: MSP, 1979.

[11] Ross, D. T., and K. E. Schoman, Jr., "Structured Analysis for Requirements Definition," *IEEE Transactions on Software Engineering,* Jan. 1977, pp. 6–15.

[12] Alford, M. W., "Software Requirements Methodology, (SREM) at the Age of Two," in M. P. Mariani and D. F. Palmer (ed.) *Tutorial: Distributed System Design,* New York: IEEE Computer Society, pp. 157–64.

[13] Stevens, W., G. Myers, and L. Constantine, "Structured Design," *IBM Systems Journal,* May 1974, pp. 115–39.

[14] Yourdon, E., and L. Constantine, *Structured Design.* Englewood Cliffs, NJ: Prentice-Hall, 1979.

[15] Jackson, M. A., *Principles of Program Design.* New York: Academic Press, 1975.

[16] Orr, K. T., *Structured Systems Development.* New York: Yourdon Press, 1977.

[17] Stay, J. F., "HIPO and Integrated Program Design," *IBM Systems Journal,* May 1976, pp. 143–54.

[18] Caine, S. H., and E. K. Gordon, "PDL—a Tool for Software Design," *Proceedings of AFIPS 1975 NCC,* 1975, pp. 271–76.

[19] Kernighan, B. W., and J. R. Mashey, "The Unix Programming Environment," *Computer,* Apr. 1981, pp. 12–22.

[20] Boehm, B. W., "Seven Basic Principles of Software Engineering," in *Infotech State of the Art Report on Software Engineering Techniques, 1977.* Maidenhead, UK: Infotech International, 1976.

[21] Baker, F. T., "Chief Programmer Team Management of Production Programming," *IBM Systems Journal,* Jan. 1972, pp. 56–73.

[22] Brooks, F. P., Jr., *The Mythical Man-Month.* Reading, MA: Addison-Wesley, 1975.

[23] Putnam, L., and R. Wolverton, *Quantitative Management: Software Cost Estimating.* New York: IEEE Computer Society, 1977.

[24] Halstead, M., *Elements of Software Science.* Amsterdam: Elsevier North Holland, 1977.

[25] Braun, C. L. (ed.), "Ada: Programming in the 80's," *Computer,* June 1981, pp. 11–64.

GENERAL REFERENCES

Jensen, R. W., and C. C. Tonies, *Software Engineering.* Englewood Cliffs, NJ: Prentice-Hall, 1979

McGowan, C. L., and J. R. Kelly, *Top-Down Structured Programming Techniques,* New York: Petrocelli/Charter, 1979

Tausworthe, R. C., *Standardized Development of Computer Software,* Vols. I and II. Englewood Cliffs, NJ: Prentice-Hall, 1977–9

Zelkowitz, M. V., A. C. Shaw, and J. D. Gannon, *Principles of Software Engineering and Design.* Englewood Cliffs, NJ: Prentice-Hall, 1979

34
Systems Synthesis

Salvatore d'Ambra
American International Group

34.1 INTRODUCTION

Chapter 33, on software engineering, surveys the many structured methodologies in use today in the data processing industry; the major thrust of that chapter is defining and critiquing the methodologies. Vladimir Zwass analyses the end product of various subjects subsumed under structure. The operative word here is **analysis,** tearing apart a whole into smaller parts to understand or delineate the whole. This approach assumes that a finished product is available.

Here we examine the *creation* of this finished product, which is **synthesis,** a putting together rather than tearing apart. Another way of putting it is that analysis is deductive (subtractive) whereas synthesis is inductive (additive).

Methodology

A **system** in this chapter refers to a set of interrelated items considered as a unit which further involves the use of computer technology in its exposition. We see two recurring key factors: ambiguity of problems and complexity of solutions; any methodology should address both factors. The methodology itself can be separated into two functions: a way of finding a solution and a way of presenting a solution. Usually these two functions are not clearly separated and a confusion exists. For instance, ways of *presenting* solutions, together with prescriptive standards for evaluation of these presentations, are mistakenly put forward as methods for *finding* solutions.

Notation

A symbolic notation is usually presented, along with the methodology to write out solutions. Again, there is confusion if this symbolic notation is presented as a paradigm for achieving solutions. Felicitious notation is of significance in problem solving because it indicates paths to be followed in solving classes of problems which are, in effect, trivial once properly posed. However, insistence that notation *solves* the problem may inhibit the solution of deeper problems which are not so trivial. That is, notation is good insofar as it sharpens associations and leads naturally to rigorous solutions, and bad when it inhibits the free flow of thought necessary to create new associations which are not apparent.

A good notation enables

- People to communicate with a minimum of circumlocution.
- One to implement the solution, perhaps with further technology, parismonously in a clear, unambiguous manner.
- A solution to be "checked" for effectiveness and rigor.

Structured methodologies employ excellent notations for this purpose.

In systems synthesis we have a further peculiar need which the notation should address, to change a solution easily in response to an incremental change or perturbation in the problem. This need may be brought about either through a change in specifications or, what is more likely, some unforeseen failure in the system. To see that this is not trivial, consider the difficulties with various atomic reactors where the lack of an easily modified initial solution has led to grave consequences. Using this analogy, we call attention to the need for notation which makes apparent the placement of adequate dynamic checks and balances to monitor a system in real time.

Problems

We have been talking about *problems* and we should clarify what we mean. We use the following ideas proposed by Weldon as explicated by Spiegel and Spiegel [1] and here paraphrased:

- A **difficulty** is a situation whose solution is either self-evident or almost so.
- A **puzzle** is a game-like situation with a well defined set of rules. It is clear that a solution exists and can be found using the rules, although any one individual may lack sufficient perspicacity or ingenuity to find a solution.
- A **problem** is a situation that is so ambiguous and possibly irrational, that the most one can do is approach it by finding various puzzle-like points of view which can mirror some of its aspects. Problems abound in the real world. For example, all physics is a series of various puzzle-like pictures of an immensely more complex reality.

Under the rubric of puzzle we obviously include solutions achievable by computer programs.

We consider two viewpoints:

1. Static representation.
   a. Who owns the system?
   b. Who uses the system?
   c. Who creates, implements, runs and maintains the system?
2. Dynamic representation.
   a. Who creates the system, maintains it, and when?
   b. What are the stages in this process?
   c. Who are the players at each stage?

We construct a paradigm for the dynamic viewpoint through a scenario including a set of players. The players are the persons and entities in the static viewpoint. An important factor for the success of the system is a clear realization that players in each viewpoint are physically

the same but that they may have different goals in each viewpoint. For example, the owner may want an inexpensive system (static) but one which is fast with a real time implementation (dynamic). Of necessity, the owner at various times expresses requirements which are dissonant.

This is a condition of paradox or dilemma which requires resolution. One way to do this is by making the player indicate which hat he or she is wearing when enunciating a requirement. Systems synthesis is fraught with instances of individuals having multiple functions. The resolution of conflict arising from this type of condition is at the heart of both the technique of system synthesis in particular, and solution of problems in general.

The Beginning

Let us now proceed to more concrete matters. Assume a project has been given the go-ahead by whatever process an enabling entity has to follow. We shall not look into the dynamics leading up to this point. Keen's article [2] introduces this phase, which is likely to be a matter purely of politics and hence beyond our purview.

Assume that some perceived need is put forth for starting the project. Keep in mind that there may or may not be a *real* need; and if there is a real need, it may only vaguely resemble the enunciated need. This suggests, as an initial phase in a project, a careful inquiry into "the true state of affairs."

The beginning of our scenario is an investigation into the rationale given for the project. The players belong to three categories:

1. The **owner,** the entity paying for and/or approving, the system. The owner may be only a figurehead, never seeing or using the system directly.
2. The **user(s),** the persons or entities directly concerned with the products of the final system.
3. The **creators** and **maintainers** of the system—those persons whose function is to design, create and maintain the system. Their interests range from inquiring into the nature of the problem, to coding and testing of the final computer product and finally to its maintenance.

In addition to the players, the scenario includes documents and other deliverables which should appear at specific times.

34.2 DESCRIPTION OF THE DYNAMIC PARADIGM

We separate the scenario into seven phases, 0 through 6.

Phase 0

Phase 0, which precedes the data processing phase, provides the perceived need, the impetus for all that follows. The players are from the owner and user categories:

- *Upper management* sets company-wide goals, which determine the requirements, for example, for management information services.
- *Middle management* needs, for example, a new system to keep track of various new lines of business or an extention of a current system to capture or analyze information better.
- *Lower level users* need data extracted from corporate files to monitor the daily flow of inventory.

Any of the these categories may include a user and/or an owner. Notice there are no computer personnel involved at this stage.

Assuming the decision of the investigation is to pursue the project, the result of Phase 0 is the translation of the perceived need into written documents. These present the problem to be solved, including a discussion of the perceived need and its resolution. They should also contain management considerations such as a budget and a delivery date and specify a project manager and a staff. However, it is important that all of the above pertain only to Phase 1. This fits into our general principle that the decision as to whether to continue should be made independently at the end of *each* phase. To use a data processing term, we opt for **late binding.**

The process of military procurement with its attendant cost overruns and excessive redesign, which leads to many strange, uncoordinated pieces of ordinance, points to the problems which arise from the attempt at early total design for a project. Sometimes, however, the need for acquisition of staff and hardware requires some commitments due to realistic time considerations. But in general, early major commitments should be seen as an abberation to be avoided insofar as possible, rather than the normal procedure. Industries such as automobile manufacturing seem to be paying the price for not trying to postpone binding.

Phase 1

We enter Phase 1 with a budget, a staff and a problem statement. The players and their functional responsibilities are now examined.

The project manager. The project manager's main duties are:

a. To manage *upward* to upper management to see, among other things, that adequate support is forthcoming. A large part of his or her duties here are political. To get insight into this area see Keen [2]. This aricle is *"must"* reading for the project manager. Politics, in its nonperjorative sense, is the way things get done when people are involved. No amount of data processing expertise can guarantee the successful conclusion of a project in the absence of the proper handling of these interpersonal aspects.
b. To manage *sidewards*. A number of players are at the level of the project manager (e.g., the data base administrator) and their cooperation and good will is necessary. Again, Keen [2] is a source of insight.
c. To manage *downwards*. The project manager is in charge of all other players on the Phase 2 team. Among the better books dealing with managing downwards is Hersy and Blanchard [3].

It is unusual to pay attention to (a) and (b) above. Courses and textbooks rarely discuss these matters in detail. It may be there is simply no way to achieve the requisite skills through training as contrasted with experience. However, as we have noted, it is performance in just these areas that prove to be critical for project success.

The system analyst. The system analyst's functions in Phase 1 are the following:

a. Formulation and investigation of puzzle statements for the problem.
b. Production of documents which relate the results found to proposals in Phase 2:
   (1) Budgets.
   (2) High level systems designs and staffing.

Users. Users are still an intergral part of Phase 1 for the reaons described below.

PROBLEM STATEMENT. Users are a resource for the system analyst in attempting to clarify the intent of the problem document, Phase 0. Because of knowledge and experience, the user may have an intuitive idea of what is needed, but not be able to present these facts and ideas in a manner easily understood by the analyst, who in turn lacks the user's extensive background. It is the analyst's job to find out, in a comprehensive way, what the user's requirements are. This query often causes the user to define the problem better, or to redefine it completely.

In any case, if the changes to the problem are substantial, a return to Phase 0 may be needed. This process of formulation, and *re*formulation, the method of successive approximation, helps any set of players to define successfully and unequivocally the problem and the solution.

UNDERSTANDING. By the same token, when the analyst presents a solution to a problem, at this stage a puzzle to be resolved by data processing methods, the user ideally reverses roles with the analyst and becomes the party who insists upon understanding what the analyst has proposed. Such a user, sometimes called the *intelligent user,* can contribute significantly to the eventual successful solution of the initial problem. The analyst should be eager to encourage such user participation and, if necessary, play the role of instructor, vis-à-vis data processing ideas, to make the user as comfortable as possible in this mutual endeavor.

The analyst should take the role of an inquiring student to the user's teacher. Ultimately, the analyst insists that the user make clear what the analyst does not understand. Similarly, it is the analyst's duty to learn enough of the user's business to be able to have meaningful input into the process of clarifying the problem.

DOCUMENT APPROVAL. The user is responsible for indicating approval of the end documents of Phase 1, which propose Phase 2, indicate that the project should go back to Phase 0, or be aborted. Management may, in Phase 1, play any roles assigned to the user.

The deliverables from Phase 1 are

a. A narrative for each puzzle presented as a potential solution to the posed problem. These narratives restate the problem operationally and provide a high level proposal for data processing to flesh out in Phase 2.
b. A statement of what the users are going to get.
c. Budget and time proposal for Phase 2. There may be more than one for any given puzzle, reflecting, for example, time consideration.

These documents are the joint responsibility of the user, project manager and analyst. This is the end of Phase 1. These deliverables go to whomever makes the decision whether to continue to Phase 2, abort, or perhaps go back to a prior level to restart the whole process.

Phase 2

There are two distinct parts to Phase 2: external design and internal design.

External design. The players for the external design phase are now examined.

Project manager. The project manager has the same duties as in Phase 1.

Analyst. The analyst now creates a design at the systems level for each puzzle selected. We assume that the methodology of data flow diagrams and data dictionaries is used. A test plan is also developed to validate each data flow diagram. These products are presented to user for the input, change or approval.

User. The user continues to function by fusing intuition and knowledge of the business into this stage of the product.

Output. The output of the external design part of Phase 2 is a set of tested data flow diagrams and data dictionaries. It is not usual to test data flow diagrams, but this eliminates trouble further down the road where it is not as easily resolved. Again, return to a previous level may be decided upon.

Internal design. In the internal part of Phase 2, a new player appears for the first time, the **systems designer.** In general, the user is no longer present during the internal part, unless some contretemps calls for drastic reevaluation.

The analyst functions as a manager of the systems designer, supplying explications of the external design wherever necessary. The project manager continues as before.

The systems designer breaks down the data flow diagram into modules and relates them to one another by using structured design, whose primary feature is treelike intermodular structures. The designer also pseudocodes the modules and extends the data dictionary to take these activities into account. Two test plans are created: one for testing the system at the design level; the other eventually to test the coded system.

As part of the extended data dictionary, layouts and access methods for all internal and external fields are included and all reports produced to satisfy user requirements. Report descriptions are made available so that the user can decide intelligently whether the system meets the user's needs.

The systems designer produces, in addition to the foregoing documents, a test of the system using the design level test plan and a clear statement about the expected external environment, such as the chosen computer system.

The user approves the report formats, contents and, the definition of the data stored on the internal files.

A proposal for Phase 3 includes budgeting, and so on. Again, at this point a decision as how and whether to proceed has to be made with the usual choices.

Phase 3

The *project manager* is still with us, functioning as usual.

The analyst

a. Manages the designer and programmers;
b. Designs a test plan at the systems level to validate the entire system;
c. Oversees the test plans for the modules and programs created by the designer;
d. Develops statistics for systems runs;
e. Makes sure that all results are valid.

The designer

a. Manages the programmers who code modules and programs;
b. Designs and implements the code level test plan.

The programmers

a. Code the modules in structural code;
b. Test the modules;
c. Join the modules in programs and test these;
d. Document the code and additions made to the data dictionary.

The deliverables for Phase 3 are

a. Documented code.
b. Tested modules.

c. Tested programs.
d. Tested initial system.
e. Updated data dictionary.
f. Statistics on initial system runs under systems test plan.
g. Budget for Phase 4.

Phase 4

The players are those of Phase 2 together with production personnel. By this time we are fairly certain that the system will function; the primary job is to implement it so that the production group can run it. The only real problem may be that the system is running on a computer other than the one on which it was designed and coded; thus the operative computer would not have been emulated during the design and coding process. It is not clear what the effect of this might be. Therefore no roles can be assigned to the players; each case needs individual consideration.

Many straightforward tasks may have to be accomplished at this time:

- Enter programs into source and program libraries;
- Enter data sets into systems libraries;
- Link external modules;
- Write systems job control language;
- Modify the systems test used in Phase 3 to test the implemented system;
- Run the system under this test plan.

The product of Phase 4 is a set of validated production documents.

Phase 5

This phase is the final validation and verification of the system.

The players are *management, users,* the *project manager* and the *analysts.* They review all pertinent documents and test results, including projected costs and times for production runs. The system is run against live data (parallel, if this is a replacement for an old system). It is verified for the correctness of all new data sets and reports.

Again, management makes the decision: abort, redesign at any previous phase, or put into production. If the decision is to go into production, Phase 6 is entered.

Phase 6

Production and maintainance teams are designated and the system is put into production.

The maintainance team may have permanent members under the direction of a *project leader*. Its function is twofold: find and correct bugs in the system, and respond to any needs for minor system changes. If, instead, **major redesign** is indicated, a full blown new project is called for.

Finally, a mechanism should be set in place to oversee the death of the system. This may be a data processing responsibility or a management function or both. The proliferation of systems which no longer serve the functions for which they were designed, or do so badly but live on, shows the need for this mechanism.

34.3 DISCUSSION OF THE PARADIGM

In any instance, some of the above phases may collapse into one another or become vestigial. One should also be aware of any subsumed or missing phases.

One major feature of the methodology is successive approximation with timely revision. Another is its sequential nature, allowing no early overall decisions with regard to the entire system. Usually such decisions are based on guesses made in response to management pressure. Shortcomings resulting from early budget and design decisions are often projected by management into another data processing function failure. To what extent the persistent report of failure in the data processing area is a result of such unrealistic demands upon the data processing function is a fertile area for further investigation. Indeed, perhaps a frequent near total ascription of blame for inadequate results to the data processing function has harmfully drawn attention away from the contributions of the nonDP areas to the failures.

Note that, in the scenario, players are really *roles* and one person may play several roles. For example, the project manager may play the role of user or owner. This, however, can lead to operational ambiguity, if it is not clear at all times exactly what multicharacter role each player is assaying.

For example, a user wants the rapid resources of an on line system while, as owner, he or she wants to keep expenses down and use batch techinques. It is appropriate for such requests to be made, but the *role under which they are made* should be clearly indicated. Lacking this, confusion and its attendant misunderstanding are likely to have a baleful effect on the project.

We have mentioned problems and puzzles in our paradigm. We have assumed that problems are stated in deliverable documents produced from perceived needs. These problems should be resolved into puzzles also reported in deliverables.

34.4 INQUIRY SYSTEMS

Many techniques have been developed to help. A generic name for them is **inquiry systems.** Now we look at several of the most prevalent and assess their relative merits.

Brainstorming

For brainstorming, a group of people meet (with or without a formal structure) to exchange ideas. The hope is that some synergism might produce a group product, the consolidation of everyone's best ideas.

(Systems have been formalized and packaged under catchy names. Some use what purport to be deep psychological subconscious insights under a trained leader, but all operate under the general assumptions underlying brainstorming.)

Relatively unstructured, brainstorming is susceptible to counterproductive influences:

- Inconsistent quality of leadership, when it exists;
- Overwhelming personalities controlling sessions;
- Participants whose style of processing ideas runs counter to immediate thought and fast reaction.

In general, these problems seem insurmountable and render the technique fallible.

Delphi.   This is a sort of nonconcurrent anonymous brainstorming in which the participants

- Are identified only to a referee who runs the process.
- Work independently.
- Use written communication to the referee.
- Receive reports from the referee on the other participants' viewpoints for further consideration, the problem having been posed to all separately.
- The problem is "solved" by all separately and these solutions are then reorganized by the referee and passed back to the participants for further work.

The solutions process may be repeated several times until no further improvements are made or time runs out. Ideally a consensus occurs or a number of viable puzzles are posed.

This method removes many of the shortcomings of unstructured brainstorming and is far more successful in practice. Although it loses the coruscating effect of real time interaction as in brainstorming, it seems to be an improvement.

Expert Investigation

The previous two methods, from brainstorming, do not specifically nominate experts to the various groups (although Delphi usually assumes a high degree of competence). It is also common to have widely varying viewpoints represented in the brainstorming groups.

In contrast, expert investigation calls upon recognized experts to present solutions without the back and forth interactions of brainstorming and Delphi. These solutions are evaluated and integrated by the project control unit. Among the advantages are

- Unequivocal solutions rather than several perhaps conflicting ones.
- Timeliness (because the indirect communication of Delphi is eliminated).
- The knowledge that decisions to be made by management are now protected by the aura of expertise.

A shortcoming is that only one puzzle may be presented, which, furthermore, may be configured to suit the myopia of the expert (who may be biased against one or more otherwise useable options—or simply not competent).

Think of a surgeon as your expert—the range of opinions from even such a single class of expert is indeed wide and variable. However unfortunate, because this method provides protection by transfering responsibility it is very popular. These experts are usually outside consultants.

Perseveration

This approach is, strictly speaking, not a technique but an *attitude* an individual uses in solving problems. It entails learning everything one can about the problem at hand and then "forgetting about it." The idea is that the subconscius mind now takes over and solves the problem and moreover, when the solution is complete, alerts the conscious mind and passes over the solution. Many of the world's great thinkers claim to have used this method, among them Albert Einstein, Bertrand Russell and Florence Nightingale.

Simpler manifestations of the process are seen when the name or identity of a person one has recognized, but

has not been able too place, pops into the head (seemingly "out of the blue") at some later time; another example is "getting" the punch line of a joke not understood when it was told.

Using the technique requires discipline (put the problem out of mind), belief (the solution will come) and patience (feeling comfortable just doing nothing about the problem, letting it take its own time).

Dialectic (Hegelian)

Dialectic is available to groups or individuals. One starts by considering all the data available and comes up with a solution model which seems to satisfy that data best, using any of the foregoing techniques. The model is called the **thesis.** Next, a model *opposite* to that proposed is put forth—the **antithesis.** Finally a new model is constructed encompassing both thesis and antithesis and therefore, in all likelihood, more representative of reality. This third model is called the **synthesis.** Since this usage of the word *synthesis* is not its common meaning, to eliminate confusion we use **conciliation** in its place.

These definitions are necessarily very vague, representing a major area of contention among professional philosophers. Nevertheless we can employ the generic ideas to help us solve problems.

EXAMPLE. Thesis: Structured methodology is a panacea that solves all software development problems. This statement is usually made by someone who has developed such a methodology. Inevitably, even where the methodology is in use, no such complete abatement of problems seems to come about.

Possible candidates for an antithesis, the opposite of the thesis, are:

1. Structured methodology does not solve *all* software development problems.
2. Structured methodology does not solves *any* software development problems.
3. Another unstated alternative is better.

Neither of the first two seems promising for conciliation.

Let us look more closely at structured methodology—a set of rules to be followed. Implementation of the rules may not be easy or clear. Words which spring to mind are *data flow, modules, cohesion, coupling, afferent, efferent,* and so on (See Chapter 33, on software engineering). People seem to be missing! Where do people, in all their diversity, fit into the solution of problems? Here is a promising beginning for an antithesis.

Consider another thesis: *Structured methodology is a method for the solution of data processing problems.* An antithesis is: *Structured methodology does not present a method of solution but rather a notation for presenting a solution.* An immediate conciliation presents itself: A structured methodology presents a notation. In most structured methodologies, it is good notation that suggests to receptive people a strategy for the forthright solution of a posed problem.

But who is receptive? For one thing, those who think like the inventor of the method. Is this everyone? Obviously not, or there would be no complaints in the literature (G. D. Bergluent [4]). Where a notation flows like its inventor's thought processes (as it usually does), the inventor finds this method natural and purveys it as "the" solution to the software creation problem.

The lack of consensus points to the fundamental difficulty (embodied in the antithesis) of fitting people into the process of software creation.

We now have a basis upon which to build a conciliation which imbeds both thesis and antithesis in a new whole. Systems synthesis has, among its parts, structured methodology and various personal strategies for problem solving as applied to software creation.

Personal Strategy

Personal strategy rarely has been addressed more than superficially in discourses on systems analysis (see [5], pages 67–76). A model presented by Spiegel and Spiegel [2] helps address the problem. It needs a description of behavior, which follows.

In the literature about creative arts, such as poetry and music, antithetical styles of creation and performance are categorized by designating the persons involved as Dionysian or Appolonian. This dichotomy appears in the writings of the philosopher Nietzsche (see Spiegel and Spiegel [1] for citations and exerpts).

For our purposes we define these styles in terms of behavior and attitudes. Some of the following descriptions involve only a matter of style while other have direct bearing on how to solve problems.

Spatial awareness. The dialectic here is losing contact with everything but what is being immediately concentrated on, in other words, intense concentration as opposed to peripheral (constantly scanning over a wide area, including one's current concern). In the latter mode,

one constantly compares, looking for agreements and conflicts between a central problem and potential bypaths.

Locus of interpersonal control. The dialectic is control, on a *feeling level,* by the feelings of others, that is, external control, versus control by internal rational process and agreements on a rational basis with the thought of others.

Trust proneness. The dialectic is high trust of people and ideas in an irrational way versus low trust accompanied by suspicion.

Critical appraisal. The dialectic is suspension of appraisal until all the returns are in, versus the search for immediate validation, including letting no partial development go untested.

Learning style. The dialectic is absorption of new ideas without an awareness of each as being distinct, that is, a tendency to permit systems of ideas to come together in some unconscius way in which one "knows" the result is right, versus assimilation, in which the style is to build *consciously* a new edifice encompassing a series of concepts carefully, brick by brick. Decisions as to validity are not made until the whole structure is available.

Responsibility. The dialectic is a low value placed on what is customarily called "responsibility," an intense involvement with a small area of interest and a disregard of other matters, as contrasted with high values responsibility—keeping of one's word and a maintaining steadfastness of purpose.

Preferred contact mode. The dialectic is a preference for a tactile sensory mode of contact, one which is close, a desire to physically apprehend, versus a visual mode, a desire to see what is under consideration, a stepping back from.

Processing. The dialectic is a proclivity to luxuriate in ideas, to wallow in consideration and reconsideration of new and old ideas and to treat the implementation of ideas only as a byproduct, versus a need to see an idea to fruition through a process of execution, even if only writing out of the idea, and perhaps accompanied even by a denegration of the idea vis-à-vis its execution. In the latter mode, the execution of another's ideas would take precedence over one's own ideas without implementation; it is the implementation itself that counts.

Written communication.
The dialectic is an aversion towards communication in writing and reliance, instead, on oral communication as the prefered mode, versus a need to write out all communications to the extent that none could be properly considered as an idea until in writing.

DISCUSSION. A person who exhibits behavior and attitudes embodied by the first description for each dialectic is charactierized as **Dionysian;** the second describes the **Apollonian.** These are extremes which are, none the less, frequently found in real life, both public and private. Varied mixtures of the extremes are caled **Odyssean.** There are examples of each among the famous thinkers of the world. For example, description of the attitudes and behavior of Descartes, Norbert Weiner and Albert Einstein place them as Dionysian, whereas Pascal, John von Neumann and most successful captains of commerce and government are Apollonian.

Spiegel and Spiegel [1] observe that these categorizations represent a fixed core of behavior and beliefs that are nonnegotiable. They seemingly cannot be changed by any known force and may be innate to one's personality.

If this is true, no amount of insistence upon a specific style of performance which does not coincide with that of the performer will avail. It is our contention that, as the judo expert cooperates with the opponent's own physical behavior to achieve dominance, we can use a person's style to gather with our own to help solve, or dominate, problems if we can only recognize the aspects of each style that works toward that end. Note that all styles are satisfactory; no one is of necessity better than the others. They are just different.

34.5 PEOPLE DESIGN SYSTEMS

So far we have inquired into three different matters:

1. System paradigm.
2. Problem solving.
3. Personal style.

Common to all, of course, are people. In (1) people are referenced by their roles, in (2) by their functions in problem solving and in (3) by their style of behavior. Various cross-references can be made. For example, it is obvious that an Apollonian personality with attention to writing, building solutions by detail, and a strong drive to achieve results, is well suited to group problem solving. Perhaps this person might serve as the group leader in the Delphi method, and be ideal for management positions which require the overview of projects with emphasis on written documents and timely delivery.

A Dionysian personality seems best to deal with problem solving techniques needing introspection such as perseveration. A Dionysian manager should have some Apollonian help to monitor deliverables, for both production time and sufficiency of written documentation.

Each individual on the data processing team should be aware of his or her own style when choosing a suitable problem solving technique. Management should also be aware of the style of the players so as to understand their attitudes (i.e., unwillingness to take written documents seriously) and to get maximal efficiency from the proper meld of styles.

It is customary for successful people in any area to expect it is *their* system of behavior which is crucial to success and to insist, to the extent that they are in control, that all others follow. This can cause severe dissonance. A proper ascription of style to others can ameliorate these situations.

Conciliation

Now we can put the pieces together and achieve the conciliation we have been looking for. **Systems synthesis** is the interaction of people operating in their diverse styles to state problems, find and solve ensuing puzzles, and present their solutions in an acceptable manner (one which can be effectively checked). This last function on the systems level can be accomplished by the project management system presented in this chapter.

Suitable systems to program and implement projects appear in Chapter 35, on structured methodology.

Further Observations

Here are some miscellaneous observations which are useful:

1. Difficult (and perhaps almost all) problems are not solved in a top down fashion but rather through some crucial fact or solution found "deep" in the problem.
2. All data processing personnel, from the systems analyst upwards, should keep in mind the following goals:
   a. To learn and internalize all suitable data processing technology;

b. To do the same for the business concepts of the problem at hand;

c. To present the data processing facts in the language of the user's business, with minimum jargon.

34.6 EXAMPLE: LIABILITY MANAGEMENT

To set these matters into a real life context, we examine a real problem and the steps in its solution.

A prime concern of upper management is the accurate assessment of financial liability. In any financial operation, there are times information is particularly important, namely calendar quarters and year end. Two major contributions to liabilities are

- Monies already paid for active known losses which have yet to be completely settled, called **on account losses.**
- Monies set aside, called **set asides,** which are, to the best knowledge of the operation, needed to reach final settlement for the known losses.

The sum of on account losses and set asides is called **incurred loss.** Any inaccuracy in calculating incurred loss has serious implications for future rates charges for financial instruments, profits on a suitable calendar basis and collections for those instruments which require adjustment of charges, such as variable rated instruments.

There is a strong impetus to put losses on the company's books as soon as possible. Naturally, if error lists of loss payments become large due to some data processing flow, this is a cause for concern. Immediate steps must be taken to remove this flaw.

Phase 0: Problem Detection

Our study starts when upper management, knowledgeable about the expected values of incurred loss, notices values outside normal expected variations for quarterly periods. Bells ring, a problem is born. We are not privy to upper management's considerations; data processing personnel are not yet involved. Signals are sent out to all parts of the enterprise seeking reasons for the purported discrepancies.

Someone is assigned to seek out any out-of-the-ordinary procedures implemented since the beginning of the calendar year. Soon uncovered are special coding procedures designed to relieve the error file of an abnormally large build-up of records representing payments made for known losses. Management does not know what these procedures are, only that they took place. This is enough

to produce a charge to go on to Phase 1, the systems synthesis procedure. Budgetary considerations are of no consequence yet, because of the importance of clearing up this problem.

The only document produced states, "Find out what effect the special coding procedures had on the losses incurred and spend whatever it takes to do so."

Phase 1: Systems Synthesis

We have now reached the stage where our heroes and heroines, the data processing group, starts the first phase of the systems synthesis for a solution of the problem, to wit: how can we calculate the error in incurred loss and then what machinery can we invoke to undo it in the corporate files?

Interviews. The project leader and systems analysts are named. The systems analysts are investigators in the discovery phase of the paradigm. The first interview is with the manager of the loss processing unit, where all loss decisions are made. The manager indicates that the problem has probably arisen from the transformation of all loss payments on the error file into so-called immediate payments. This was done so that these payments, which bypass almost all the edits inherent in the system, could be posted onto the corporate file, eliminating the build-up on the error file. We are presenting the information and nomenclature as it is given to the analyst. Note that many terms are used whose meanings are not yet clear. Part of the further investigation which follows clarifies these points just as they were clarified to the analyst.

Unfortunately, the information collected is devoid of sufficient specifics to permit any data processing interventions. The analysts go to the next step, to interrogate the loss coding people about what they did to make the changes. To understand what really happened, a thorough investigation has to be made concerning the flow of loss processing for the entire company. This leads to a series of data flow diagrams, which enable the systems analysts to make decisions for further investigation. The programs designed to carry out this investigation are examined in Chapter 35.

The analysts now have a clear picture of the method used to correct the error files and of what seems to be the cause of the observed excessive incurred liabilities.

File posting. To appreciate this procedure, one has to understand how payments and set asides get onto the files and how set asides are altered to compensate for the incurred loss in light of the various payments made by the company.

Set asides are directly entered onto the corporate files as stand alone records identified as set asides, with the amount involved and other data to identify the particular loss.

There are essentailly four types of **loss payment:**

1. An **on account payment** is a partial payment against a loss. It is subtracted from the set aside and thereby leaves the incurred loss constant. If these are processed to the corporate file, it has no effect on the incurred loss.
2. A **cancel** indicates that a mistake was made and there is indeed no claim against the company. Therefore, the set aside is reduced to zero. This of course, has a strong effect upon the total incurred loss.
3. An **immediate payment** is made for a case which has no set aside. It is an immediate settlement of losses. It increases the incurred loss, once posted to the file, which should be done.
4. A **terminal payment** is entered for an actual loss which occurs against a set aside. The set aside for this claim is hence reduced to zero. (There is no further obligation against this claim.) This changes the incurred loss by the payment less the set aside. If the payment is *greater* than the set aside, there is an increase in the incurred loss; if the payment is *less* than the set aside, there is a decrease in the incurred loss.

But how does a loss payment get into the file? On account payments, cancels, and terminal payments all require a set aside record which reflects a specific loss to precede them into the corporate file. These loss records have to find an associated set aside record on the corporate file. If there is no set aside record there, or if there is miscoding on the loss record, then this loss payment record ends up on the error file. A set aside record which is miscoded may get into the corporate file. Then even a correctly coded loss payment does not find it; it remains on the error file.

It is important for payments on the error file to get into the corporate file as soon as possible. The original strategem changes all on account and terminal payments to immediate payments which have had no difficulty getting into the corporate file. They do not have to match set aside records. Immediate payment records have no effect on set aside records.

Collection method.

So far, all the information acquired is factual. No interpretation is yet placed upon the effect of these facts on the solution of the problem. The skills required to obtain these facts are the following:

1. Interogatory, i.e., to conduct an interview properly as a source of information.
2. Knowledge of the financial business under consideration, so that the questions for the interview can be properly formulated and the answers evaluated.
3. The ability to analyze the data processing methods used by the company to manipulate the data entering into the problem. A lack of proper documentation requires data flow diagrams, and so forth, to reconstruct these methods.

The picture described would not be put together in the logical way it is presented here, but built from a collection of many diverse facts.

Problem statement.

We have yet to come up with a solution in a puzzle-like form. One thought is to back out false immediate payments and change them. But there was no way to recognize them after the fact. Also, many were posted in a previous quarter and therefore may not be changed.

However, after some perseveration, it is realized that it is not the false immediate payments which count but their effect upon related set asides. For example, if the immediate payment masks an on account record, then the proper subtraction from the set aside record should be made while leaving the immediate payment "as is"; for a terminal payment, just reduce the appropriate set aside record to zero. (Cancels are special terminal payments.)

All changes are made to set asides. To reduce a set aside to zero, merely process the appropriate cancel record. To reduce it by a specific amount, we cannot use an on account payment, as this would also enter the payment into the corporate file causing a misstatement of incurred loss. Another category, the *change in set aside* transaction, is used for this.

Solution type.

The above process may be seen as a dialetic solution. The opposite of operating on the paids is to operate on the set asides. The conciliation is to use some "new" paid record to operate upon the set asides.

To find the erroneous immediate payments, locate a proper set aside to alter. From the facts at hand, the only way such a set aside could exist is for an on account or terminal record to appear in the system when a matching set aside is not present and thus be altered to an immediate payment and entered as such on the master file before the set aside apears. Thus, the solution presented at the end of Phase 1 is the following:

1. To collect all immediate payment records in the corporate file since special processing began. (Note that all good and false immediate payments are captured.)
2. To match their records against all the set asides on the current version of the corporate files.
3. When a hit is obtained, to capture both the immediate records and matching set asides, label them, and produce a print register of all the immediate records.
4. To investigate each record on this immediate record print register and, for those which are in error, have an appropriate record created to properly alter the corresponding set aside using the labels attached.

Instance

An instance is in order. The operation is a multinational conglomerate, which we shall call the **parent**. One of its functions is to guarantee loans to foreign entities which, due to local laws, are not wholly owned, but are subsidiaries of the parent. We may assume that due to local political upheavals in the foreign country local currencies cannot be readily converted to dollars and then used to pay for loans due. Thus the parent is now liable for loans from American banks to the foreign entity. To what extent this situation will obtain in the future is not clear.

So the occurence together with the fact that the situation in the foreign country may change in the future means the best that the parent can do is to estimate the amount that the parent will eventually have to pay out to the lending banks. Say this amount is, in total, $100,000. This means $100,000 should be set aside to cover this future libility. Then a set aside record should be entered onto the parent's file for $100,000.

Assume a loan payment schedule which amortizes the principal while paying the requisite interest of $10,000 each quarter. As each payment is made by the parent, it is entered into the corporate file as an on account payment and properly reduces the set aside by this amount; the first $10,000 reduces the set aside $90,000.

Another possibility is that the foreign government changes its policy and, for the time being, there is no longer a future liability. This leads us to process a cancel which removes the $100,000 set aside from the file. The net effect is a gain of $100,000 in the parent's financial condition.

Another possibility is that we effect a settlement with the lending bank for, say, $70,000. We enter this as a terminal payment and reduce the set aside to zero as no future liability. The net effect is to increase the parent's financial position by $30,000.

It is also possible that the same hope we may have had that the situation would ameliorate lead us to set aside $100,000 and in fact this turns out to be a forelorn hope. The actual settlement is $120,000. This leads to a deterioration of the parent's position by $20,000. So settlements can go both ways.

Of course, the foreign situation could be so clear that there is no question but that our loss is certain. In this case, we would process an immediate payment of $100,000 with no set aside created.

For our situation, we find a payment record on the error file. It can only be a final payment, an on account payment or a cancel record. Immediate payments are processed without any need to find a matching set aside and therefore cannot end up on the error file. We have seen that to remove the payment record from the error file, it is changed to an immediate payment and passed through.

Assume that our $100,000 set aside has entered the flow of processing and ended up on the master file after

1. An on account payment relating to this liability of $10,000 tried to enter the master file and, due to the absence of set aside on the file, was changed to an immediate payment entered onto the file.
2. Same situation, but a cancel payment changed to immediate payment.
3. Same situation, but a terminal payment of $10,000 changed to an immediate payment.

Our solution requires us to keep a file of all immediate payments made up to date. This file is matched with the new set asides at each master file update to find matching set asides (using identifying fields on each record). When a match is found, the set aside and the immediate payment record are written out and examined to determine which case above pertains. For

Case 1: A change in the set aside reduction record of $10,000 is processed to balance the incurred amount.
Case 2: Another cancel record is processed reducing the

set aside to zero, which then correctly states the incurred.

Case 3: Same solution as Case 2, since the $10,000 paid on the file already properly states the incurred loss.

Summary

Our real life example has been handled by a single Dionysian analyst. The analyst has interviewed those concerned to acquire as many facts as possible while withholding judgment concerning these facts. Interviews have been verbal rather than written. Finally, by a combination of preseveration and mental rumination, the analyst has found a solution, which has appeared full blown and entire at one time. Parenthetically, the project manager has exerted extra persuasion to get a written report. Considering the style of the analyst, this had to be done.

The rest of the example (Phases 2–6) appears in Chaper 35 on structured methodologies.

Epilogue

The solution above is in fact faulty. The firm has a number of partners in each of its ventures. While payments are broken out by individual partner, part of the record key, the set asides are lumped into "ours" and "theirs." This means that, when matches between immediate records and set asides are made, no partnership records show up.

This disparity was noted immediately by the users when the print register of immediate records which matched the set asides appeared. At that time, no one could figure out what happened; this anomaly in coding was not documented anywhere. A return to Phase 1, together with some investigations of the corporate files, found the cause.

The solution has adjusted the matching algorithm. The change in the data processing system was simple, due to the use of structured methodology, even though this last problem did not arise until the first live run in Phase 5. Again, this is an example of successive approximation.

As promised, we see the problem itself is ambiguous. Moreover, the solution does not fall into any structured methodology, since it has appeared in the middle of a badly documented system used perversely to achieve corporate rather than data processing needs.

Note that now the solution has been found, it will be recast into structured methodology, which will enable it to be logically studied for validity and, when verification fails, easily fixed to behave properly.

REFERENCES

[1] Spiegel, Herbert, and David Spiegel, *Trance and Treatment*. New York: Basic Books, 1981.
[2] Keen, Peter G. W., "Information Systems and Organizational Change," *Communications of the ACM*, 24(1) (1981).
[3] Hersy, P., and K. H. Blanchard, *Management of Organizational Behavior*. Englewood Cliffs, NJ: Prentice-Hall, 1977.
[4] Berglunet, G. D., "A Guided Tour of Program Design Methodologies," *Computer* 14(10) (1981).
[5] Jensen, Randall W., and Charles C. Tonies, *Software Engineering*. Englewood Cliffs, NJ: Prentice-Hall, 1979.

35
Structured Methodology

Salvatore d'Ambra

American International Group

35.1 SYSTEMS METHODOLOGIES

System methodologies are put forth by their inventors as ways to solve practical data processing problems. Vladimir Zwass (Chapter 33) and his references quantify the cost of system creation and the amelioration of excessive costs in dollars, personnel and time.

Various methodologies, for example, functional decomposition, data flow, top down and data structure, all insist *they* solve the data processing problem. It would be well if we could find some standards to decide which method is most appropriate. This may be a function of other considerations such as the training and capability of personnel and the type of problem to be resolved into puzzles (see Chapter 34 for definitions).

Two major measures of appropriateness are efficiency and effectiveness. **Efficiency** for data processing is usually a question of less: less time for creating a system, fewer computer resources needed, fewer personnel, faster throughput, and so on. **Effectiveness,** more difficult to quantify, includes these qualities:

- *User friendly*—the system works so that it seems that the user's needs are directly and easily achieved with a minimum data processing understanding of the system on the part of the user.
- *Maintenance and update friendly*—the system is constructed so that running and maintaining (fixing bugs and updating it to provide new functions) is easy.
- *Responsiveness*—the system does what is asked quickly.

- *Proper technical level*—the system is apprehensible by the least technically prepared personnel assigned to it in the design, implementation, maintainence and update phases.

Terms which reflect effectiveness relate to personnel directly, whereas those refering to efficiency refer to measures of time or amount of resources and not primarily to the quality of personnel.

We shall see that there is a way (notation) to present systems at all levels of design which is intuitively accepted by the largest class of users, designers and programmers. The key is that the notation be *linear, logical* and *pictoral.*

A prime goal of a system paradigm is to recognize the classes of persons available to use it. For example, a method may depend upon set theory, graph theory or the theory of mappings (functions). However, few are trained in these concepts, especially so as to be able to use them in an inductive problem solving setting. It is not sufficient to recognize these mathematical entities; it is necessary to put them to work at the internal or subconscious level. These are sophisticated ideas which are only properly apprehended after considerable exposure and training. Those who have acquired these disciplines may find them useful and natural to solve problems and to develop methodologies for solutions which are valid and satisfactory. Yet how few current practitioners can be brought to this stage of concept development!

Chaos ensued when the "new math," based on concepts such as mappings and set theory, was used as a basis for instruction in the elementary schools. It is possible that the teachers were not competent, the level of intelligence of the average student was deficient or the concepts were counter-intuitive. It does not matter. What does matter is that any of these shortcomings is sufficient to render the entire process fallible.

The vast majority of data processing personnel and users have not received sufficient mathematical training in these subjects to render them natural. More important, there is no desire to spend the time and effort to acquire training in these matters.

We conclude that the most suitable methodology, if one exists, must have characteristics whose conceptual underpinnings are already part of the intuitive arsenal of the average user or of the creator of data processing systems.

35.2 STRUCTURE ITSELF

The Saphir-Whorf hypothesis states that the content and structure of one's language directly influences one's way of thinking. Hence we start our study with an attempt to recognize what connotations the word *structure* can have. Consulting dictionaries and thesauruses we find that structure appears as a noun, adjective or verb. Various meanings follow:

As a noun:
Complex entity.
Relatively intricate.
Relating to architectural aspects of an entity.
An assembly of discernible parts together with recognizable connections.
An edifice.
A configuration.
As a verb:
To organize.
To arrange.
To shape.
To compose from other parts.
To build.
To fabricate.
To synthesize.
To constitute.
As an adjective:
Highly organized coherent entity

Thus *any complex entity* has structure with recognizable parts and interrelations among them. We talk about constructing an entity by arranging subentities. *Only highly organized entities may be considered structured.*

Of course there are contradictions: any complex entity is a structure regardless of its degree of organization. In varied situations, one is liable subconsciously to use different meanings when thinking about anything involving the word "structure" and thereby characterize one's thoughts with a lack of clarity.

A structure is also applied to mathematical structure:

- *Proof structures* are exemplified by the way one lays out proofs in plane geometry. A series of statements are made sequentially (linearly)—postuates, theorems already proved, the theorem to be proved and definitions already made. Laws of logic, primarily *modus ponens,* are used to prove that the hypothesis is indeed true. The major observation here is that proofs are a sequence of verified or verifiable statements.

- *Algorithmic structures* consists of a number of steps, again in linear order, some of which may be iterated. The algorithm should **converge**—terminate in a finite number of steps and achieve its mission, or signal that it cannot do so. An example is Euclid's method for finding the greatest common divisor of two integers. Algorithms also prove theorems, especially for combinatorial mathematics and graph theory.

- *Recursive structures* are algorithms which refer to themselves repeatedly. Definitions and functions can also appear in recursive guise, as with Peano's definition of the integers. It may seem that there are situations natural for recursion; languages such as PL/I, ALGOL and APL make provision for implementing recursive algorithms. However, since few examples (usually the computation of the factorial is given) are cited and the cost of doing recursive algorithms on a computer is high, recursion is neither prevalent nor important for the majority of current data processing practitioners. For an elementary example of recursion, see Perlis [1].

35.3 DATA STRUCTURES

Business data structures are best approached through the concept of an entity in the real world such as a person or an automobile. An entity can be described through measurement or identification when not completely delineated. For example, we may know a person's name (identification) and his or her age (measurement). We may record these facts, but no matter how many facts we capture, we have not captured the person. There are still unknown or unknowable facts remaining. We are abstracting from the entity to describe it to satisfy our needs, but the entity exists in the real world outside of the facts (data) we collect.

When an instance of an individual abstraction is capturable in a way that can be coded unambiguously in a finite space, we call it a **field**. A field is the smallest datum we consider; it is not further decomposable. We may, of course, use characteristics of a field to do processing, (e.g., use the collation sequence of the alphabet to alphabetize), but we may not ascribe meaning to these characteristics in our entity system.

We gather a collection of facts about an entity which have a natural interrelationship and consider them as a whole. In this case, we talk about a **record.** A collection of records is a **file.**

Record layouts are linear. The file is an ordered set of records, usually utilizing an identifiable set of fields in the record called a **key** as the orienting device.

There is yet another way that data is created. Entities in a system are the focus of *actions*. Let us consider as the entity a person, and the action to receive a salary for work on a job. Here the data are hours worked, salary rate and salary received for the week—attributes in an appropriate file. Looking at entities, actions and derived data emphasizes that data have structure. This structure, together with the development of data as a means of delineating an entity, is an artifact, a product of the mind.

35.4 LINEARITY

The above considerations are concerned with **linearity;** it may be **global,** prevading the entire structure, as in geometric proof; it may be **local** as in some algorithms where sequential groups of operations are performed. Change in conditions may cause other sequential sets to be entered and subsequently performed. What appeals most to our perception of logic is a *linear* sequence of steps.

35.5 LEFT BRAIN, RIGHT BRAIN

Studies in psychology dichotomize thought into linear verbal and nonlinear nonverbal. *Nonverbal thought* seems to be concerned with esthetic matters including the pictorial, while the *verbal thought* is concerned with reasoning. These opposite modalities of thought and perception seem to be the function of different sides of the brain, left for verbal and right for nonverbal, but not always.

The implications of this dichotomy are that effective logic deals with a linear ordered sequence of steps, eschewing disordered random statements or representations. Further, it is possible that pictorial representations may enhance system design by appealing to a nonlogical esthetic sense which also perceives the world in a useful way. From our consideration of structure, we see that mathematical proof appears in linear form and, returning to plane geometry, diagrams do help us realize significant logical interrelations, probably in some nonlinear, nonverbal way. Most structured methodologies use both these aspects of the brain: linearity and the pictorial.

35.6 APPLICATION TO STRUCTURED METHODOLOGY

Whatever methodology we create, it must be psychologically viable. Structure itself is too amorphous to be useful without further specification. Historically and culturally, logic and its ramifications are extremely attractive as a basis of design; logic is a verbal left brain activity. Finally, linearity, global or at least local, is a pervasive concommitant for logical left brain activity. We should therefore seek various *linear* structured methodologies. This permits us to have confidence based on an appreciation of logic in our designs.

However, as noted in Chapter 34, discoveries of solutions to problems (puzzles) are not necessarily or usually achieved in a logical linear fashion but in some sort of intuitive "Aha" or "Eureka" action. Diagrams in geometry are effective in enhancing this activity, both for the discovery of solutions and the comprehension of logical linear arguments already laid out.

Then the final criteria are linear and diagrammatic; systems based on these criteria have become popular, unlike equally intellectually valid systems lacking in one or the other of these criteria.

35.7 FLOW CHARTS

A flow chart conveys the control structure of an algorithm. The initial users of computer technology computed values of mathematical functions and solved mathematical problems using well defined algorithms. Decision to continue computations in the algorithm were based on the number of iterations or the difference between two successive values of an interation. The program had all the decision criteria built into it.

Flow charting enables the program to mirror the algorithms. Boxes represent both decisions and *test and branch* instructions for the computer. Flow charts are locally linear and pictoral and therefore a linear structured methodology. Flow charts were a great success in this early phase of computer development. Even today, programming texts in FORTRAN for scientists and scientific journals still teach and use flow charting as their linear systems methods. Moreover flow charting works effectively in these situations.

As time went on, persons working on computer enhancements (such as operating systems) perceived the inadequacy of flow charting alone. Changes and additions necessary to make flow charting a suitable vehicle for design led to structured programming as a program design method (still relying on flow charts). Then **modularization** emerged: programs are broken into **modules** which are separate and yet, through interconnections, constitute the program.

New programmers in the data processing environment use techniques they learned in school, namely flow charting and pseudocode. The former methodology, especially, leaves much to be desired. Although flow charting shows the flow of control, data processing control functions are not obvious without reference to the dynamic needs of the data system. One may say that it may be necessary for the system to "learn" from the data what decisions are needed.

The lessons learned in the technical area of systems design took some time to filter into data processing. Myers [2] gives an annotated bibliography of articles dealing with the methodology of linear systems. The chronology of the entry of structured methodology into data processing may be found there.

Where does this leave flow charting? In any area where decisions and criteria are clear and are developed externally, flow charting is of considerable value. Usually this is at the module level. An example is a complex decision process depending on the relationship of data fields available when the module is entered.

35.8 FLOW CHART EXAMPLE

In our bank (see the first part of this problem in Chapter 34), it is necessary at one point to "collapse" several old records refering to various aspects of a single loss claim into one new claim record. Each old record which represents a duration of loss has three dates associated with it:

- The date the loss was reported to the bank is designated REPT-DTE. When a new record representing a pay-

ment or set aside is posted to the master file, two date fields on the record receive the current date, machine entered. As each updated entry is made to this record, the second date field receives the date for that update.
- The earliest accounting date on this record refers to is designated ORIG-ACCT-DTE.
- The latest accounting date on this record is designated ENDG-ACCT-DTE.

The only other field in the record which interests us is called **FEATURE**, which may be a 0 or a 1: 0 for direct loss payments; 1 for internal expenses such as legal fees.

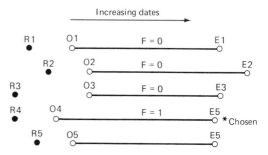

Record 4 is on first, so report date = R4

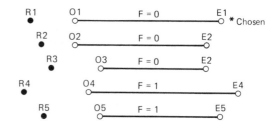

Records 1 and 2 on at same time, but record 1 on longer. Choose R1 = Report date

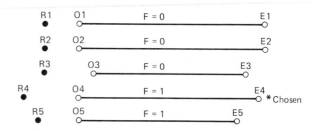

Records 1, 2 and 4 are on at same time and for same length of time, but record 4 has earliest report date. Report date = R4

Figure 35.1. Collapsing several records concerning one loss claim into one new claim record: choosing a report date.

It is necessary to collapse old records into the new ones to represent losses with unique single records. Accounting dates are automatically machine generated and therefore assumed accurate.

All records that refer to the same loss should have the same report date. Unfortunately, this date is not machine generated but entered by keyboard and is not always the same on all records due to keying errors. Ideally, there should be two records for each claim, one with feature 0 and sometimes one with feature 1. Due to the multiplicity of bank partners whose accounts must reflect each gain or loss, there are as many as 15 of each. This was determined by a study of the Master File. Each record may have a different report date.

Which report date should we choose for our collapsed single record? The decision is made as follows:

To straighten this out, the report date is taken from the record which got on first. If several records got on at the same time, the loss report date with the latest entry date is taken, i.e., the one which is on longest. Further, if there are several of these, the one with the earliest report date is taken.

Each of the possible maximum of 30 records has a feature of field with values 0 or 1 and three date fields:

- Original accounting date.
- Ending accounting date.
- Reporting date.

The records are sorted in this order:

1. Feature ascending;
2. Original accounting date ascending;
3. Ending accounting date descending;
4. Reporting date.

To picture this, we show three cases with five records each, three with feature 0 and two with feature 1, in Fig. 35.1. The original accounting dates are indicated by O1 through O5; E1 through E5 indicate the ending accounting dates. F = 0 and F = 1 indicate the feature 0 and feature 1 records respectively. The diagrams show the three possible cases and that it is sufficient to consider the *first* feature 0 and 1 records to obtain the proper report date. A table is constructed and queried only if records with both features exist for a loss. In Figure 35.2, the position of the first 1 feature record on the table is indicated with the subscript **NEW-SYM**. The -T in the data names refers to table.

The code to do this is in Figure 35.2 and the flow chart for this code is Figure 35.3. In Figure 35.3, the decisions are denoted by the circled numbers, which refer to the circled numbers in Figure 35.2. The false actions of the numbered decisions are indicated by square numbers in Figure 35.2. The actions taken in the process boxes in Figure 35.2 are the circled letters in Figure 35.2.

A denial of equality confirms an inequality; failure of 4, 5 or 6 implies that the opposite inequality holds. Here, **ELSE** statements 4, 5 and 6 meet the conditions imposed upon them.

It is not easy to check Figure 35.2 but it is easy to

```
GET-REPORT-DATE.
  ①IF   ORIG-ACCT-DTE-T (1) = ORIG-ACCT-DTE-T (NEW-SYM)
     ②IF   ENDG-ACCT-DTE-T (1) = ENDG-ACCT-DTE-T (NEW-SYM)
        ③IF   REPT-DTE-T (1) = REPT-DTE-T (NEW-SYM)
              MOVE REPT-DTE-T (1) TO REPORT-DATE Ⓐ
        ③ELSE
           ④IF   REPT-DTE-T (1) < REPT-DTE-T (NEW-SYM)
                 MOVE REPT-DTE-T (1) TO REPORT-DATE Ⓑ
           ④ELSE
                 MOVE REPT-DTE-T (NEW-SYM) TO REPORT-DATE Ⓒ
     ②ELSE
        ⑤IF   ENDG-ACCT-DTE-T (1) > ENDG-ACCT-DTE-T (NEW-SYM)
              MOVE REPT-DTE-T (1) TO REPORT-DATE Ⓓ
        ⑤ELSE
              MOVE REPT-DTE-T (NEW-SYM) TO REPORT-DATE Ⓔ
  ①ELSE
     ⑥IF   ORIG-ACCT-DTE-T (1) < ORIG-ACCT-DTE-T (NEW-SYM)
           MOVE REPT-DTE-T (1) TO PEPORT-DATE Ⓕ
     ⑥ELSE
           MOVE REPT-DTE-T (NEW-SYM) TO REPORT-DATE. Ⓖ
```

Figure 35.2. Table of single loss claim record, based on Figure 35.1.

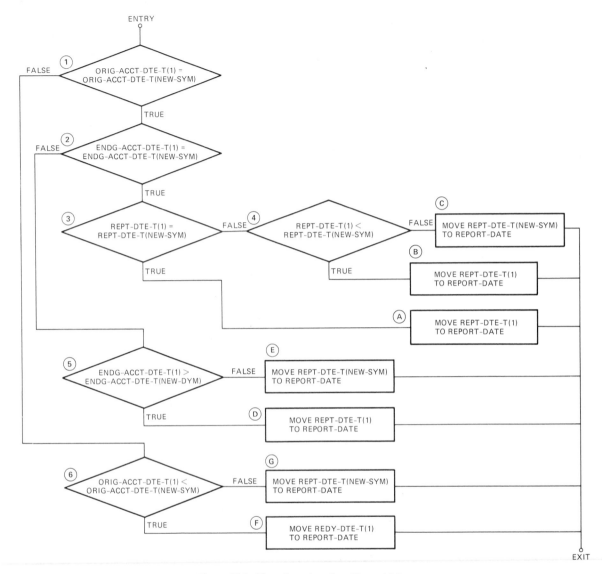

Figure 35.3. Flow chart, based on Figure 35.2.

check Figure 35.3 and also to see that Figure 35.2 and Figure 35.3 call for the same action. Hence the flow chart of Figure 35.3 shows its value as a tool.

The flow chart, Figure 35.3, is created beginning with a decision box for the first query (1) The consequences, true and false, follow with further decision boxes in the correct order.

An alternative is to draw a decision tree and transform it into code. The correspondence between decision trees and code, however, is not as direct as between flow charts and code.

35.9 DATA FLOW DIAGRAM

A data flow diagram is a notation (similar to the flow chart) for modeling the effect of an algorithm where the driving consideration is the flow of data and its *transformation*. A data flow diagram is a directed graph with *arcs* representing *data* and *nodes* (circles) designating *actions* upon them. An **action** either modifies data entering or splits them into one of several possible output streams or both (see Chapter 33, Figure 33.2, and also Figure 35.6 in this chapter).

35.10 PROGRAM STRUCTURE DIAGRAM

The data flow chart and the program flow chart (see Figure 33.3) help in the design of programs. They naturally lead to the next step, which is the construction of a **program design chart** such as that shown in Figure 35.4.

The chart consists of boxes which represent processes. Arrows with hollow tails represent data flowing in the direction shown; arrows with solid tails point to boxes where decisions are made and are labeled with flags describing the decision. By convention, each box can only communicate (pass data and flags) with a box directly above it and also connected to it. Thus boxes 2.1, 2.2, 2.3 and 2.4 communicate only with 2.0 and not with each other or 1.0 or 0.0. This condition is **locally linear**—no circuits between nodes, as the notation displays.

A further (external) level of design is necessary to clarify the diagram because it is not evident how the function of each box is achieved. This level consists of **pseudocode,** statements that are clear and easily transformable to code in a programming language. An example is shown in Figure 35.5. Chapter 33 gives the requisite definitions, notations and structures.

35.11 BANK EXAMPLE

We continue the example of Chapter 34, producing the explication of the solution and the intermediate steps and reasoning which generate it. The discussion puts into place the illogical nonstructured elements involved in creating a solution. These elements make up the human *problem* formulation, to be resolved into a linear logical framework, succeptable to machine translation and easy human validation.

Liability Management

A prime concern of upper management is the accurate assessment of financial liability. In any financial operation, there are times when information is particularly important: calendar quarters and year end. Two major contributions to liabilities are:

- Monies already paid for active known losses which have yet to be completely settled, called **on account losses;**
- Monies set aside, called **set asides,** which are, to the best knowledge of the operation, monies eventually needed to reach final settlement for the known losses.

The sum of on account losses and set asides is called **incurred loss.** Any inaccuracy in calculating incurred loss has serious implications for future charges for financial instruments, profits on a suitable calendar basis and collections for those instruments which require adjustment of charges, such as variable rated instruments.

There is a strong impetus to put losses on the company's books as soon as possible. Naturally, if error lists of loss payments become large due to some data processing flaw, this is cause for the highest concern. Immediate steps must be taken to remove this flaw.

Problem Detection

Our study starts when upper management, knowledgeable about the expected values of incurred loss, notices values outside normal expected variations for quarterly periods. Bells ring, a problem is born. We are not privy to their considerations; data processing personnel are not yet involved; signals are sent out to all parts of the enterprise seeking reasons for the purported discrepancies.

Someone is assigned to seek out any out of the ordinary procedures implemented since the beginning of the calendar year. Lo and behold, special coding procedures had been designed to relieve the error file of an abnormally large build-up of records representing payments which were made for known losses. Management does not know what these procedures are, only that they took place.

Approach

The charge is to calculate the error in the incurred loss due to the initiation of the special coding procedures used to clear the backlog of payments hung up on the error file and then to find some data processing means to correct the ensuing misstatement on the corporate files. The first chore is understanding the data entry system in its largest context, through the creation of the **loss master file.** Figure 35.6 shows the outcome of this investigation, depicted in a data flow diagram. The team carried the diagram only to the point where it seemed adequate for understanding the data entry system (because of time constraints imposed on the study).

Data flow, indicated by arrows, has labels describing data being transported, sometimes omitted if their nature

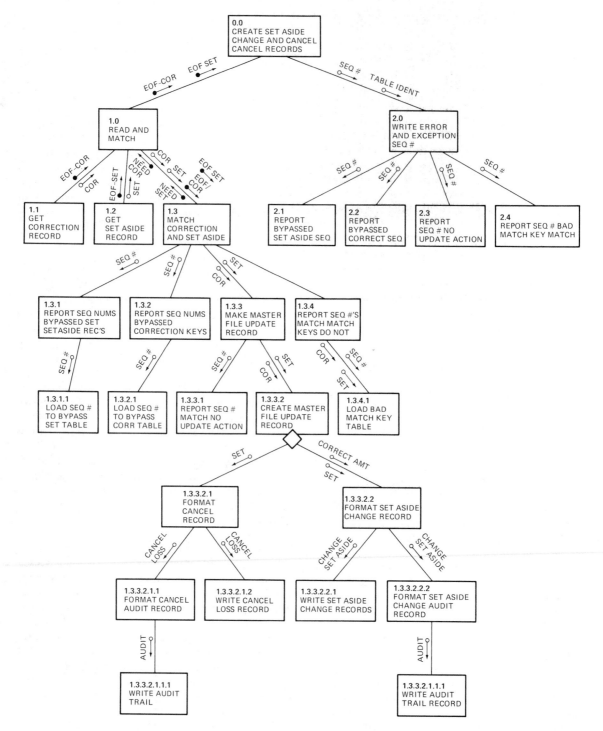

Figure 35.4. Program design chart.

```
INITIAL KEY SETTINGS   NEED-CORR = 'T'   NEED-SET = 'T'
                       MORE-CORR = 'T'   MORE-SET = 'T'
READ AND MATCH ( 1.0)
    IF NEED-CORR AND MORE-CORR CALL GET CORRECTION RECORD
    IF NEED-SET AND MORE-SET CALL GETS SET ASIDE RECORD
    IF MORE-CORR OR MORE-SET CALL MATCH

MATCH CORRECTION SET ASIDE ( 1.3)
    IF CORR SEQ > SET-SEQ
        NET-SET = T
        NEED-CORR = F
        CALL REPORT SEQ NUMS BYPASSED SET ASIDE REC'S
    ELSE
        IF CORR-SEQ < SET-SEQ
        NEED-SET = F
        NEED-CORR = T
    CALL REPORT SEQ NUMS BYPASSED CORRECION KEYS
        ELSE
            NEED-CORR = T 15
            NEED-SET = T
            IF CORR-KEY = SET-KEY
                CALL MAKE MASTER FILE UPDATE RECORD
            ELSE
                CALL REPORT SEQ NUMS MATCH MATCH KEYS DO NOT.
```

Figure 35.5. Clarifying a program design chart (Figure 35.4): pseudocode.

is clear. Data stores are indicated by open boxes. Activities and decisions made about data are indicated by circles. External sources and destinations are shown as square boxes. These conventions are more or less universal. The data flow diagram, when a processing system exists, is a simple restatement of the system in easily understood pictorial notation. It appeals to and reinforces intuition, therefore meeting our requirements for a maximally visable structure notation.

35.12 LOSS MASTER DATA FLOW DIAGRAM

We now examine Figure 35.6 in detail, discussing the forms and levels found there. The explanation is keyed to the figure by boldface letters and numbers.

A notice of loss enters the system from one of four sources (**A**). Each provides a written form called a **loss sheet.** An entry on the sheet identifies a loan and an estimated loss. This estimated loss contains the *amount* of loss expected and a possibility estimate. For example, if there is no question of the loss, the probability indication

would be 1.0. Next, from the loss sheets, coding sheets called **preloss records** are compiled at PRELIM LOSS RECORD CREATE (**1**)*. The loss sheets contain minimal data which must be fleshed out for the preloss records before corporate records can be created. Complete information about loans is in a paper file (**B**) of all loans. This file, for example, lists loan partners, their participation, their responsibility in the case of loss, whether the loan has been insured and the conditions of insurance.

If the estimated amount of loss is small, the preloss record goes directly to LOSS CODING (**2**); if not, it goes to LOSS ANALYSIS AND VERIFICATION (**C**), a group knowledgeable about losses (nondata processing) for further analysis.

The number of special considerations which each loan can engender are manifold (**B**). The team cannot, within the time constraints, achieve a complete definition of the loan file nor a complete catalog of the role for each item in the individual records in the creation of the prelimi-

*The number and letter cross-references to Figure 35.6–35.9 are set in boldface to facilitate reading from text to illustration.

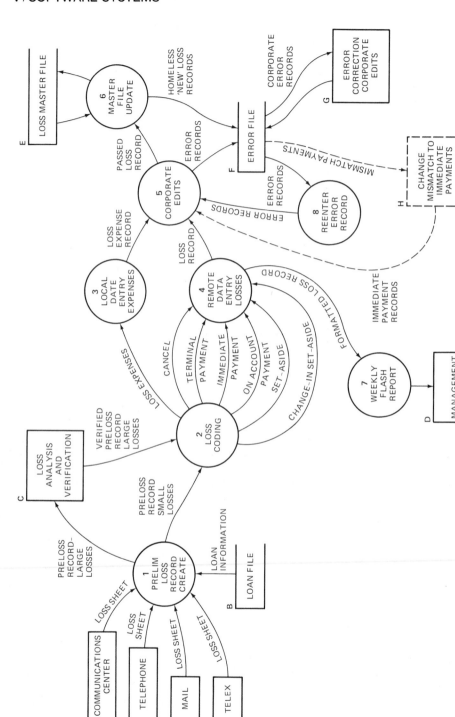

Figure 35.6. Data flow diagram: outcome of investigation.

nary loss record. This lack of completeness causes the team to make an egregious error in their initial solution. Fortunately, it is easy to repair. On the other hand, it is doubtful that, if all the actions were cataloged, the error would not have happened. It came from an action which was completely counter-intuitive, as we shall see in Section 35.13.

In **LOSS ANALYSIS AND VERIFICATION (C)**, the participants consult with experts on international banking and foreign loans and request more data regarding the loss when needed. The outcome produced a verified preloss record, perhaps much altered, or no record at all.

For **LOSS CODING (2)**, paper forms are prepared including coded data ready to be keyed into computer files. Note that

1. Expenses incurred in loss generation, such as fees to expert assessors and legal fees, are split off and separately entered at the home office, while all other records are sent to, and entered at, a remote location.
2. The various species of loss record are differentiated.

One loss may generate several loss records because of a mixture of losses, expenses and/or partnership agreements. Each loss must be apportioned among all the involved partners and an individual record of the proper type created for each partner. In general, a gross record shows the gross amount of loss; a partnership record shows the type of partnership and the amount of loss according to the percentage of the partner's participation. Examples of partnership type are *across the board* (the partner participates in all loans in a given area) and *individual agreement* (a partnership on a loan by loan basis).

Next, handwritten sheets are keyed into a computer terminal to provide formatted input (3) and (4). A subsystem, **WEEKLY FLASH REPORT (7)**, produces a nonexpense weekly flash report for management showing nonexpense losses (**D**). It supplements monthly corporate reports, an amalgamated report.

In the weekly **CORPORATE EDITS (5)**, a system record is rejected to an **ERROR FILE** if an inconsistency in its fields is noted. The **ERROR FILE (F)** is a collection of errors captured but which have not been cleared since the inception of the system. The records are considerably expanded from the passed loss records (those that make it through the corporate edits); error flags indicate the cause of rejection. The error file also contains the mismatch failures defined below.

The passed loss records are accepted by the **MASTER FILE UPDATE (6)**, as follows, to update the loss master file:

1. Immediate payments and loss expenses with year and month of entry are put on the Loss Master File without further action.
2. Set asides (new) are also entered.
3. All other records (cancels, terminal payments, on account payments and change in set asides) must match, using a **match key** with an existing set aside on the Loss Master File.

The actions when a match is achieved are the following:

A. *Cancel*—cancel the set aside record and enter the cancel record into the file.
B. *Final payment*—cancel the set aside and enter the Final Payment record, including the amount of the final payment on the file.
C. *On account payments*—reduce the set aside by the amount of the on account payment leaving it on the file and enter the on account record onto the file.
D. *Change in set aside*—change the set aside in the master file where matched by the amount of the change in set aside record; the change in set aside record hence disappears.
E. *Duplicate of the set aside*—if a set aside on the master file is not matched by a transaction record, create a duplicate, date it to the correct (new) entry date and enter it onto the file.

If a transaction record which requires a key match to a set aside record does not find such a match, reformat this "homeless" loss record as an error record and enter it onto the **ERROR FILE (F)**. A flag shows the origin of this error record as a mismatch and not a corporate edit rejection.

The master file update system is run monthly. The **LOSS MASTER FILE (E)** is actually a transaction history file because each month's entries remain on the file unaltered. It is a year to date file encompassing at its completion one calendar year.

An on-line system, **ERROR CORRECTION CORPORATE EDITS (G)** can access individual **corporate error loss records** from the error file so that an operator can repair them, making alterations in place. This system operates continuously.

At the end of the month, just before the **MASTER FILE UPDATE (6)** system is run, the **REENTER ERROR RECORD (8)** system is run. It takes corporate errors and mismatched records, reformats them as standard loss up-date records and reenters them through the update procedure (**5**).

Here are the contents of the match key:

- *Loan number*—an arbitrarily assigned number indicating a loan.
- *Loss number*—a number which is assigned to separate loss instances under a common loan.
- *Type of loan*—a code which distinguishes a loan so that profits or losses may be assigned by class.
- *Feature*—indicates different loss holders under single loss.
- *Transaction*—the loss type by gross and type of partnership agreement.
- *Kind*—indicates the differences between various classes of record, i.e., expenses of both types, set asides, cancels, and so forth.
- *Partner number.*

There are many other fields; the team found some and ignored many more. In the end, the only other field of concern is the money field. Also the various files have different data fields and hence record lengths. These matters are merely technical details. All data files are sequential, except the error file, which is direct.

35.13   THE ADDITIONAL (PROBLEM) FILE

The CHANGE MISMATCHES TO IMMEDIATE PAY-MENTS system (**H**) extracts three types of mismatch records: terminal payment, on account payment, and cancel payment, all from the mismatch part of the error file. It converts them to immediate payments and reenters them at (**5**) into the LOSS MASTER FILE update process. They have already passed corporate edits (**5**) and will do so again. These loss records are copied to the LOSS MAS-TER FILE (**E**).

This insures that corporate reports derived form the LOSS MASTER FILE include these loss amounts. However, the seeds of a serious problem (our problem) are thereby planted. The reason for a mismatch is the lack of a corresponding set aside on the LOSS MASTER FILE.

To resume our narrative, the team notes two scenarios:

1. The set aside and/or loss record may have an improperly entered key. Thus the set aside may be on the master file and inaccessible to the update procedure because the keys do not match. In this case, the correction procedure is the best that can be done.

2. The loss record appears in the LOSS MASTER FILE before the set aside arrives and some correction may be possible.

The work outlined above takes three days and requires interviewing about 15 people. Timeliness is possible because of management support. In such cases, there are often attempts at obstruction from those responsible for a system and therefore likely to receive the blame. The team's insistence that success in fixing the situation will be shared in reports to management, and support by management, helps get cooperation.

35.14   THE SOLUTION

The first solution proposed is to locate the erroneous immediate payment records, remove them from the file, change them back to their proper form and reenter them into the file.

Problem I

Removing records is all right in an incomplete file (before the year is over) but not permissible in a completed file whose records are already included in a published annual statement. However, we have been assured that this system had not been in operation more than three to four months and this was September. It will be later established that the system had been in use for three years, but at the present this fact is unknown to the manager of the system, who has had responsibility for only the past two months. "Do not trust the user unless absolutely necessary."

Problem II

How can the team find which immediate payment records are to be altered? "No problem," management assured them, "just dump them all and we will match them against the LOAN FILE and LOSS SHEETS" (which are saved). To measure the feasibility of this proposal, the team runs a program which counts the number of immediate payment records. There are 65,000! There is no way the solution can be implemented in two weeks.

Problem III

What happens with records which continue to mismatch after reentry? Upper management still want the monies on the LOSS MASTER FILE.

QUESTION. A new question now arises: If the team *can* fix the file to reflect the proper dollar amounts, as of what date *should* they fix it?

The first suggestion is to back up credit to when it *could* have been fixed if what is now known had been known then. But this is anathema to upper management since a veritable Niagara of reports would have to be altered. The decision was to make the change in incurred loss effective when implemented.

SOLUTION. The solution to be implemented eventually now appears on the horizon. Loss records already on the file are not to be touched. If not losses, then what? Obviously set asides! Which set asides? Those that might be credited at the latest possible moments. This, then, is the solution reached:

1. Credit only immediate payment records identified without exception.
2. To do this, attempt to match the immediate payment records on the **LOSS MASTER FILE** with the latest month's set asides. If no terminal payment or cancel appears to change a set aside, the set aside remains indefinitely, recreated each month, awaiting a reacting transaction record. Further, only one terminal or cancel is coded. This satisfies management's stricture to credit an altered cancel, terminal or partial payment as an immediate payment until it is proved to be otherwise.
3. For a match of payment record and set aside, dump and send both to **LOSS ANALYSIS AND VERIFICATION** for checking and action.
4. If **LOSS ANALYSIS AND VERIFICATION** finds a terminal payment or cancel, enter a cancel record for the corresponding set aside. If it finds an on account payment, enter a change in the set aside record to reduce the set aside by the proper amount.
5. For an *ongoing* system, keep a file of previous immediate payments which do not match and add only the new immediate payments for the current month as they appear.

If this solution can be properly implemented, it ensures that (1) credits are taken as soon as possible, (2) loss records are not touched, and (3) no new payment losses are added to the error file, but are credited on the basis of best possible information.

No structured methodology can be used in this process. In fact J. W. Johnson [3] calls this portion of systems development the "magic" part.

35.15 IMPLEMENTATION OF THE SOLUTION

The suggested solution is in "precise" narrative form. To test the solution and prepare it for computer inplementation, the team uses the data flow notation which appears in Figures 35.7 and 35.8. The LOSS MASTER FILE (**A**) appears in Figure 35.7 as described above for Figure 35.6. EXTRACT AND REFORMAT IMMEDIATE (**1**) finds all immediate payment records for current months in LOSS MASTER FILE. It then reformats these records by

1. Eliminating fields not pertinent to update and writing out the rest in the update format (loss records in Figure 35.6 (**4**)):
2. Extending the loss record by inserting at its front the match key composed of data fields in the loss record, to expedite later sorting.

The CURRENT MONTHS IMMEDIATE PAYMENTS file (**B**) receives reformatted immediate payment for the current month.

EXTRACT AND REFORMAT SET ASIDES (**8**) selects the current set asides and processes them as in (**1**). This creates the file CURRENT MONTHS SET ASIDES (**D**) of reformatted set asides. The first time the system is run, a file of all IMMEDIATE PAYMENT RECORDS (**C**) from nonmatching previous months is preloaded with all immediate payments to date from the master file.

KEY IMMEDIATE PAYMENTS GROSS (**2**) takes all the immediate payments from both the current and the previous months' unmatched files, locates those records which are gross records and copies off the match key in front of each record to write the keys to GROSS IMMEDIATE PAYMENT KEYS (**E**).

KEY SET ASIDE GROSS (**7**) does this for set asides to produce GROSS SET ASIDE KEYS (**F**). This creates a file of keys that appear only on gross records. Management decided it made no sense to consider a partner record without a matching primary lender, which a gross record indicates. A need for this match arises if a gross record comes into the file later than the partner records or is miscoded for match key (with respect to the true gross record). In either case, without the desired change, it is hopeless to try to match partner and lender.

GROSS IMMEDIATE PAYMENT KEYS (**E**) are matched with GROSS SET ASIDE KEYS (**F**). The match key for matches is written out to the MATCH GROSS KEY FILE (**G**). All PREVIOUS IMMEDIATE

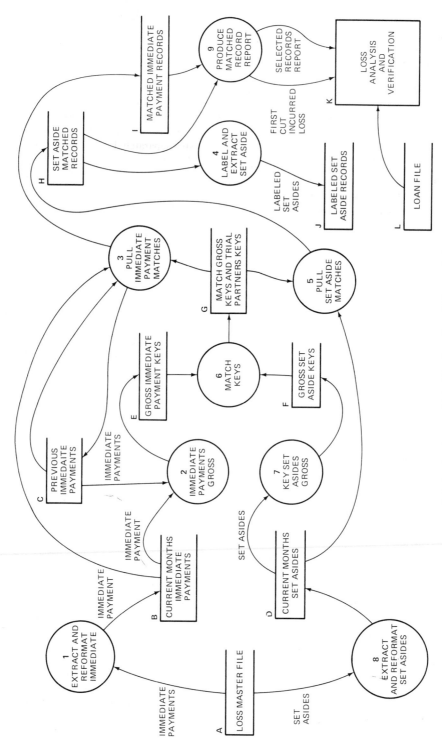

Figure 35.7. Solution implemented (1). (Continuation of Figure 35.6)

PAYMENT RECORDS (C) are matched with the file (G) for both gross and partner records in PULL IMMEDIATE MATCHES (3) and are written to MATCHED IMMEDIATE PAYMENT RECORDS (I). For *no match,* the immediate payment is written to the *new* PREVIOUS IMMEDIATE PAYMENT FILE (C), completely recreated each month.

CURRENT MONTHS SET ASIDES (D) are treated in the same way at PULL SET ASIDE MATCHES (5) to produce the file of MATCHED SET ASIDE RECORDS (H). Set asides (H) and immediate payments (I) are organized by PRODUCE MATCHED RECORD REPORT (9) in an interleaved sequence, set asides followed by immediate payments in match key order (K).

To alter set aside records to correct the LOSS MASTER FILE (A) for incurred loss, set aside records requiring change unambiguously are located. Each set aside matched record is numbered and a report with data from the interleaved file (K) in match key order is produced.

LOSS ANALYSIS AND VERIFICATION (K) can now locate the loan in the LOAN FILE (L). The analysis in LOSS ANALYSIS AND VERIFICATION decide what ac-

tion to take for each set aside to correct the incurred loss. LABELED SET ASIDE RECORDS (J) are made by LABEL AND EXTRACT SET ASIDES (4) by numbering MATCHED SET ASIDES (H).

LOSS ANALYSIS AND VERIFICATION (K) receives two reports. The first contains interleaved set aside correction records. The FIRST CUT INCURRED LOSS report (K) gives the estimated change in incurred loss if all immediate payments were to become cancels. Changes are listed separately by gross and partnership participation. The difference between these totals is the net incurred loss to the company.

Refer now to Figure 35.8. LOSS ANALYSIS AND VERIFICATION (M) investigates the reports using the loan file and the loss sheets to correct the master file by canceling or changing set aside records in the matching sets. They create a correction file from which EDIT CORRECTION RECORDS (10) produces a CORRECTION TO SET ASIDE file (P), checking also for obvious errors in the correction records (such as multiple records with the same sequence numbers) and writes them to an error file (N). The CORRECTION TO SET ASIDE records (P)

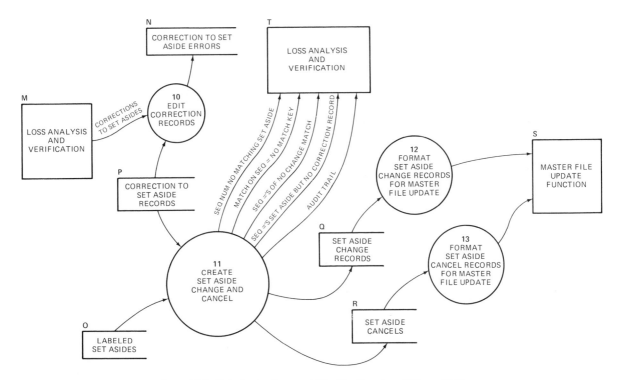

Figure 35.8. Solution implemented (2). (Continuation of Figure 35.7)

contain the corporate match key, the sequence number from the report and the amount of change in the set aside (which equals the amount of the immediate payment record) or 0 for a cancel record.

LABELED SET ASIDES (O), is the file created in Figure 35.7 (3). CREATE SET ASIDE CHANGE AND CANCEL (11) is the key program in the correction procedure. Records from the labeled set aside file (O) have all the fields needed to create either set aside change or set aside cancel records which may be immediately entered into the update system. This is accomplished in CREATE SET ASIDE CHANGE AND CANCEL (11) by referring to the sequence matched correction file (P) and creating the set aside change file (O) and the set aside cancel file (R). Format programs (12, 13) then batch the update records with header, trailer and hash totals to create the master file update.

Many reports (T) on the effect of the updates are also provided by (11) to LOSS ANALYSIS AND VERIFICATION (T), as follows:

1. Sequence numbers, where a correction record with a sequence number appears but with no matching (sequence number) set aside. This file has never been invoked to date since the labeled set aside file should have all sequence numbers listed.
2. Sequence numbers together with a count of the same for records, where a correction record with a particular sequence number does not appear on file [Figure 35.8, (P)]. This report always has output. There are two major reasons: the correction record cannot be formulated by the LOSS ANALYSIS AND VERIFICATION function, or the created record ends up on the error file. Both of these situations occur frequently. The first time the correction record file is prepared by the LOSS ANALYSIS AND VERIFICATION section, this file is replete with error records. No attempt is made to verify the correction file. Again, we see the result of an inexperienced (in the data processing sense) group being trusted to do the right thing. The report enables the team to track down and correct the situation. By means of the introduction verification into the correction file creation process, the errors are reduced to 2 percent.
3. Correction records which indicate no action, since everything is in order, including the sequence numbers for these records.
4. A check of the match key on matching sequence numbers which makes sure all records are properly matched. When the match keys do not match, an ob-

vious error should be reported. The sequence numbers of these records should be listed on a mismatch file.
5. Finally, an audit trail report which shows the type of update record created.

The system is created and tested through (9), Figure 35.7, within seven days. Then—disaster. The FIRST CUT INCURRED LOSS report is passed out to an incredulous management: the report indicates that there are no partner losses in all matched immediate payment set aside matches, a most unlikely result.

The code is correct. Following the scheme of Figure 35.6, the team strike pay dirt when they walk through with a preliminary loss record preparer, checking all the steps in the creation of a partner's loss record. For no reason they can determine, *all* partners' set aside records carry a feature code of 0; loss records carry alphabetic feature codes.

To ensure a correct system, when creating match gross keys (Figure 35.7 (6)), one now checks for the following: If a gross record key match has a feature of 0 (it happens sometimes but rarely), just one key is created. For gross match with an alphabetic feature code, the programmer creates an extra MATCH KEY record with a partnership code *and* a feature of 0, besides the rest of the match key details.

The team runs the system again to produce the FIRST CUT INCURRED LOSS report and it passes the new text with flying colors.

35.16 NEXT LEVEL

The team next "explodes" (11) of Figure 35.8 into a lower level flow diagram which appears as Figure 35.9. Several internal files are created: T1, T2, T3, T4, Q, R and AT. O, the labeled set aside file contains a record for each sequence number read in Figure 35.5. P contains correction records created by LOSS ANALYSIS AND VERIFICATION, edited and presumed to have no duplicate sequence numbers, the last a common error. If this error does occur, all records with a common sequence number are removed and put on an error file for "balancing" purposes. No attempt is made to correct them at this time.

Processes

Now here are the processing steps:

- Read the records from the files P and O into the system, which creates update records (11.1, 11.2).

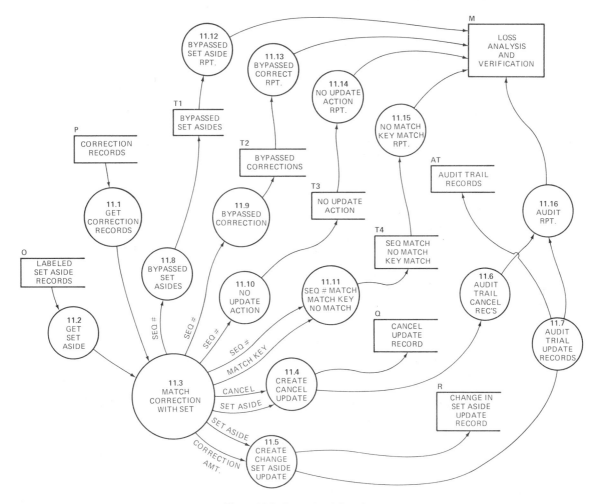

Figure 35.9. Lower level flow diagram.

- Compare sequence numbers and, depending upon circumstances, act upon the correction record, the labeled set aside record, or both (**11.3**).
- Check sequence numbers on the labeled set asides for completeness (**11.8**). If a sequence number is missing (which should not happen), it is captured and reported.
- List all sequence numbers missing from the correction records (**11.9**). This file has never been empty. Among causes of missing sequence numbers are inability to correct the immediate payment record with the sequence number and miscoding of multiple records with this sequence number.
- List all sequence numbers for which no correction is necessary (**11.10**).

- List those sequence numbers for which there is a sequence number match but the match keys do not match, (**11.11**). This does happen due to an incorrectly entered correction record.
- Create update records to update the corporate loss file (**11.4, 11.5**). A cancel record is produced when a final payment or cancel is indicated by the correction file. A change in set aside is created when a partial payment record is indicated by the correction file.
- Take in update records and prepare audit trail records (**11.7, 11.16**). Records entered on file **Q** and **R** are put on the audit trail file with sufficient information to indicate unequivocally the records created.
- Prepare and print reports relating to the files they ac-

cess (**11.12–11.15**). These reports go to LOSS ANALYSIS AND VERIFICATION.

Finally, a program design which we have aready viewed as Figure 35.4 is created from Figure 35.9. Tables 35.1, 35.2 and 35.3 help to translate between the two. Table 35.1 converts data transfer labels (on arrows with open tails) to file names; Table 35.2 describes the flags (arrows with solid tails); and Table 35.3 matches processing steps (circles in Figure 35.9) with routine descriptions (rectangles in Figure 35.9).

35.17 RESULTS

To solve the problem, the team has used:

1. Elements of data flow centered structured methodology;
2. Tree-like structures to design programs;
3. Structured programming.

To what extent did this help or perhaps hinder them? The initial phase, the translation to a puzzle, did not use any structured methodology. However, the act of setting up the conditions of the problem where a system already existed benefited from the use of data flow, which linearized the elements of the underlying system. The process picture appealed to their esthetic sense. It helped everyone—management, the people running the system and the analysts—to agree on what was happening and where. It is very important *to agree on the problem* to be solved.

35.18 DISCUSSION

Any notation which makes agreement possible among those involved in these decisions and who may have minimal training facilitates problem statement and solution for data processing. The difficulty of reaching such agreement is exacerbated by the heterogeneous background of data processing personnel, the high rate of turnover of such personnel, their unwillingness to learn skills which take long to acquire and the unwillingness of the majority of management to concern themselves with technical matters.

It may be that outside of the United States different management and data processing cultures permit the acquisition of more recondite methodologies. It seems that Jackson's [4] methodologies are extensively and success-

Table 35.1. Data Transfer Labels

Label	Meaning
COR =	CORRECTION RECORD
SET =	LABELED SET ASIDE RECORD
ERR =	ERR OR CAUSE ON A ERROR RECORD
SEQ # =	Sequence number.
TABLE INDENT =	Which table we are accessing; the files **T1, T2, T3** and **T4** indicated in Figure 35.8 are tables in storage.
CORRECT AMT =	The dollar value of the change in setaside update record comes from the correction record.
CANCEL LOSS =	Update cancel record properly formatted.
CHANGE SET ASIDE =	Update change in set aside record properly formatted.
AUDIT RECORD =	Either change in set aside or cancel audit record. The only difference is a nonzero dollar amount field in change in set aside audit record versus a 0 dollar amount field in the cancel audit record.

fully used in parts of Europe, more so than in the United States.

Another desirable feature of data flow is flexibility. A prescriptive presentation of structural data flow methodology would find that we have broken some rules in its use. However it works and it is **robust** (relatively impervious to variation in rules and abuse). The extended bank example shows how well it works with a live problem when time for a solution is limited, not an unusual circumstance. Such situations arise frequently: an ill-defined system or one which is incapable of full definition in reasonable time; files in which data have been irretrivably altered.

The precepts of data flow notation such as arrows for data flow and circles for transformations and transactions

Table 35.2. Flag Labels

Label	Meaning
EOF-COR=	End of file correction file.
EOF-SET=	End of file, labeled set aside records.
NEED-COR=	Flag indicating, when on, a correction record is needed.
NEED-SET=	Flag indicating, when on, a labeled set aside record is needed.

Table 35.3. Correspondence Between Circles of Flow Diagram and Boxes of Program Design.

Flow Diagram (Figure 35.9)	Program Design (Figure 35.4)
11.1	1.1
11.2	1.2
11.3	1.3.3, 1.3.3.2, 1.3.3.2.1, 1.3.3.2.2
11.5	1.3.3.2.1.2
11.6	1.3.3.2.1.1
11.7	1.3.3.2.1.2
11.16	1.3.3.2.1.1.1
11.8	1.3.1, 1.3.1.1
11.9	1.3.2, 1.3.2.1
11.10	1.3.3.1
11.11	1.3.4, 1.3.4.1
11.12	2.0 2.1
11.13	2.0 2.2
11.14	2.0 2.3
11.15	2.0 2.4

are intuitive, leading one to believe them, accept them and, in fact, often claim to have been using them all the time, albeit in a less felicitous notation. Moreover, we see various vendors of training in data flow methodology claiming to be able to present it in just 5 to 10 full-day seminars. They can at least present the full facts and several simplistic examples concerning data flow.

As in all intellectual inventions it pays to look at the masters, at least before they begin to ramify their discoveries; again, refer to Myers [2].

In the last analysis data flow proves another exemplification of Gibbons as cited by Feynman [5]: "The power of instruction is seldom of much efficacy, except in those happy dispositions where it is almost superfluous."

There are three mutually independent areas using the word "structure":

- Structured analysis (of problems).
- Structured design (of programs).
- Structured programming (of code).

So far, in this and the preceding chapter, we have only talked about the first in detail. If structured analysis (presentation of a problem and its solution with data flow) is used, it is easy to convert data flow into a structured design. The translation in our banking problem was virtually immediate.

Establishing a program design as a tree structure allows each program block to be identified with a node in the data flow; this provides a two way check. When the program design is presented, cohesion and coupling between modules can be introduced (see Chapter 33). These concepts help to produce changes in program design to achieve more desirable characteristics. Experience in training programmers shows that cohesion and coupling are best introduced after the basics of design. Only as these concepts become internalized, program design tends to reflect higher levels of cohesion and coupling. This is to be expected since they are not particularly intuitive. Good programs written from a tree structure can yet be unsatisfactory in terms of cohesion and coupling. Programmers do not seem to appreciate cohesion and coupling, some even after extensive coaching, although tree structure itself becomes natural very quickly. But complete rejection of cohseion and coupling is rare.

Structured programming also involves a relatively nonintuitive set of concepts. However, the advantages of structurally coded programs—for example, especially, they are much easier to debug than in structured designs—soon leads programmers to structured code.

It is easier to get analysts and programmers to do structured design and programming if one gets them early, preferably without commercial experience. Retraining experienced analysts and programmers under fiat is much more difficult because it is all too easy to convey the suggestion that they are inadequate in some sense. They often see themselves as professionals just as capable of making technical decisions as the trainee is. And their decision is often "My method is just as good as this": this protects their self image. One cannot insist on structure too strongly unless one wants to build up a whole staff by such training. And even then, how to hold onto them? "Stonewalling" by trained personnel can be overcome, but it requires time, effort and a willingness to settle for partial success.

Myers [2] states that structured design is not a science but a set of normative and notational standards whose employment by an experienced user results in superior products (on the average). We have noted here that not all facets of structure are of equal importance.

The key word for Myers is *experience.* It is not enough to just *read;* one must *do.* In this respect linear structured methdologies are conventions for the creation of design products; creation is an esthetic activity just as with the production of mathematical proofs. Comparison of good data processing to engineering with its connotation of precision and mechanistic activity is counterproductive. It would be interesting to study the correlation between training in various fields and exceptional data processing skills.

The author wants to thank Mr. Robert Schaaf for permission to use his program designs, pseudocode and code.

REFERENCES

[1] Perlis, Alan, et al., *Software Metrics.* Cambridge, MA: M.I.T. Press, 1981.

[2] Myers, Glenford J, *Composite/Structured Design.* New York: Van Nostrand Reinhold, 1978.

[3] Johnson, J. W., "Software Design Techniques," *Proceedings of the National Electronics Conference* (1977), Chicago, IL.

[4] Jackson, M. A., *Principles of Program Design.* New York: Academic Press, 1975.

[5] Feynman, R. D., R. B. Leighton and M. Sands. *The Feynman Lectures on Physics.* Reading, MA: Addison-Wesley, 1963.

36
On-Line Systems

Ivan Flores

Baruch College
City University of New York

36.1 INTRODUCTION

This chapter examines the design of on-line computer systems. An **on-line** system is one in which the computer and its program accept data as they are entered, either by a human or from input devices. In the early days, the computer was necessarily on-line because it was

- **Uniprogrammed:** it could execute only one program at a time.
- **Dedicated:** it worked until it finished its program, then stopped.
- and had little, if any, operating system.

Since it executed only one program at a time, that program would often wait for data from the human operator or the devices which ran it.

As computers evolved, the second generation machine became large and expensive. If the computer were idle, much money would be lost in an investment, which was hardly productive. Hence it is almost mandatory to have the computer execute more than one program at once; this is called **multiprogramming.** When several programs are running **concurrently,** the computer is seemingly executing several programs *simultaneously* while actually it is executing only one command from one program at any given instant. When a program reaches an impasse, the computer is switched to another *ready* program for much more efficient use—with little idle time.

As the applications of computers grew and blossomed into the data processing environment that we have today, more and more programmers became involved in writing and debugging programs. In the batch environment, **turnaround time** is the time it takes for a program to be entered, run and returned to the operator. With a large number of users and production jobs in progress, this time increased from minutes to days. While efficient use was made of the computer, the same could not be said of the programmers that worked with it!

Eventually it became feasible, if not necessary, to have the programmer work at a terminal to enter and modify each program and then run it **interactively** (that is, the computer is in a dialog with the user). Hence the interactive computer provides results quickly, thus minimizing turnaround time. The first approach to interaction was to have an operating system manage a dedicated computer and a number of terminals for the programmers. In this way, one computer could support many programmers interacting with it directly. However, it was difficult, if not impossible, to run batch jobs at the same time.

Systems developed in the past decade provide both interactive on-line facilities and let batch jobs run concurrently. We examine several of these operating systems later in the chapter.

36.2 TERMINOLOGY

Early applications of computer technology were designed with inputs and outputs flowing in batches. Inputs were read from decks of punchcards and outputs were printed at some later time. A **batch system** is so-called because prepared inputs from one or more users are batched together in the input stream. It delivers output to a device, such as a printer, when each program has finished processing. The user who submits a program to the computer center receives the printed output by the action of a computer operator who removes it from the printer, separates and distributes it. Batch computer programming cannot properly support computing which is **time dependent,** where the results of calculations control an activity which is constantly changing and with which the computer must *keep up.*

A program for an **on-line computer system** may receive input directly from a keyboard or a data collection device; it may deliver output directly to a terminal or an output transducer. Real time, time sharing and transaction processing systems are classified as on-line systems by this definition. These are defined in turn in the following paragraphs.

A **data terminal** is a device to enter data into an on-line or dedicated system and receive output from the system. Since not all of an on-line system's outputs are required immediately, many such systems can distribute output to a printer in the same manner as with a batch system. In both cases, for multiprogramming the output is **spooled,** that is, sent to a temporary disk file from which it can be printed directly and continuously. The major difference between the batch and on-line system is that on-line systems have physical location and timing constraints for receiving inputs and delivering outputs; this adds complexity to their design.

A **dedicated system,** such as a microcomputer based system, is meant to be used by only one operator at a time and often for only one purpose. All input and output is controlled from its terminal. A **multiuser terminal based system** is multiprogrammed. It generally uses the concept of **time sharing,** in which each user gets a "piece" of computer time. This gives the impression to each user that he or she has exclusive control of the processor.

Response time for both dedicated and time sharing systems is the time between a user's request of the system and its initial response as evidenced by some indication at the terminal.

A **real time system** is an on-line system which receives input data from peripherals integrated into its environment, processes that data, and returns the results fast enough to affect the environment in the desired fashion. The environment is affected by the application of control signals to computer output devices, for example, to control the path of a missile. Clearly response time is critical here, if the missile is to reach its target.

36.3 TIME SHARING CONCEPTS

Today many people use time sharing systems to satisfy their data processing needs. Program development and data entry are typical. Management information system users have time sharing terminals. Any application which doesn't have to respond immediately to actions occurring in its environment can be served by a time shared multiuser system. As more users enter the system, however, the response time seen by each user may degrade.

Time shared on-line systems take advantage of the fact that terminal users spend a large amount of time thinking before they enter data at a terminal. Because data for one user is processed while the others are thinking, each user can seem to have exclusive use of the computer.

Associated with each terminal user is a program, which executes to service the user's needs. Each process takes some of the computer's time and runs concurrently with processes for other users. Again, it *seems* to take place simultaneously with other user processes and keying. Since computer instructions execute in nanoseconds and human thinking takes seconds, the time shared computer system gives the appearance of simultaneous action, even though only one process executes at any given time. These user processes are switched between wait and run states by the time sharing operating system. While one process is running, input/output may be taking place for other processes.

Many time sharing systems use **time slicing.** A time slice is typically a fraction of a second. Each user's process gets the processor for one slice *or* until the process can no longer proceed. For instance, suppose a process requires input or output of data. When a user process gives up the computer, the next waiting process gets it; this is called **round robin.** When the block on a process is removed (e.g. I/O completed), that process again joins the time slice queue to wait for another slice of the computer.

If a maximum number of users were not established, a time shared system would exhibit poor response time. Although time shared systems may work with simultaneous users, response time degrades significantly when an excessive number of users log on. The number of users is controlled by limiting the number of input ports to the system.

36.4 ON-LINE OPERATING SYSTEMS

What Are They?

An **on-line operating system** is one which supports on-line terminal data entry and/or program development. There are at least two ways to design such a system. The first supports on-line operations; and the on-line operating system is, in fact, the operating system for the configuration. The second is, one might say, an operating system within an operating system. That is, the on-line executive reports to an overall operating system. The two function concurrently. The on-line operating system services on-line users, while the overall operating system allows batch operations to go on at the same time.

It is possible to classify on-line operating systems into four classes:

1. The dedicated online operating system.
2. One which works as part of a batch environment.
3. One which is used to activate programs within a batch environment.
4. A combination of the above.

Brief History

The need for an on-line operating system was obvious from the beginning. The question was how easy it would be to achieve such a system with the computers of the time. In the 1950s, expensive computers only had 8K words of memory. Even in the 1960s, 32K or 64K of memory was found only in a large computer.

In the 1960s, a project began at MIT to make a computer time shared system, called CTSS. In the framework of today's computers it was an elementary system, but it was the first one of its kind. It was a uniprogramming system. That is, the operating system and one user program were all that the system supported. Switching from one user to the next was done by means of **swapping,** the system writing out a user's program on tape or disk and reading in another user's program, which was then activated.

It was a tribute to the designers that the system worked, albeit considerably slower than the computer which was dedicated to terminal users. Peripheral devices were considerably slower in those days, so that the system consumed a great deal of overhead to write out one program and read in the next. Still, it did work and it supported a number of users.

The late 1960s saw the emergence of the IBM System 360 as well as a new project for a new computer started by General Electric. The latter computer system was called MULTICS, which stands for MULTiplexed Information and Computer Service. It used the large General Electric Model 635 computer.

Another system, TSS, was in development by IBM, an advancement on their System 360. It used a computer specially built for time sharing, namely, the Model 67.

Both of these computers used virtual storage and paging, so that *parts* of programs belonging to *a number* of users were resident in memory. The hardware was specially designed to support translation of virtual addresses to real addresses.

Meanwhile, the University of California at Berkeley was developing its own time sharing system for the Scientific Data System, Model 940, providing on-line facilities for the entire university.

All of these operating systems were designed mainly for on-line use. Any batch processing that they were able to do was only secondary to their main purpose.

One of the forerunners of on-line systems was Project MAC, which stands for Multiple Access Computer. It was funded by the U.S. Advanced Research Agency of the Department of Defense (ARPA) and was executed by the Massachusetts Institute of Technology. Project MAC used a IBM 7094 computer with two banks of memory, each consisting of 32K words of 32 bits each. Users had teletypewriters to communicate with the system and truly appreciated the opportunity to have a "piece of the computer" for themselves without waiting for batch processing to do their work.

36.5 THE TIME SHARING MONITOR

The **time sharing monitor** (TSM) is an executive, a miniature operating system, which services multiple on-line users:

1. It occupies a region or partition in a multiprogramming environment.
2. It handles data input from terminals and provides messages and screen output to the users.
3. It acquires application programs and utilities for the user and runs them under the user's direction.
4. It allocates time to users and their programs according to a variety of disciplines.

TSO

The initials **TSO** stand for **Time Shared Option.** This is a system developed by IBM to be used with their larger operating systems, such as OS/MFT, OS/MVT; it has persisted and can be used under any of the virtual memory operating system. TSO is an operating system within an operating system.

Figure 36.1 demonstrates what is meant by this. Conventional memory is divided as shown in that figure, where the resident operating system occupies a portion of the bottom of memory (called the **nucleus**) and also another portion at the top of memory. The remainder is available for use by application programs and is called the **dynamic area.** The block of memory assigned to an application program is called a **region.** One region is assigned to TSO as shown in the figure.

But the region occupied by TSO is large and complex. It contains a number of components and interfaces as well as user programs for on-line users. This is conveyed by Figure 36.2.

The users view.   Of immediate impact to the user is the existence of a **command language.** This provides an ability to enter and retrieve data at a terminal as well as to write programs and request their execution, but only within the TSO environment. The command language is distinct from both the **job control language,** which describes the programs to run for a user, and the **programming language,** used for the construction of the user's program. The command language must be learned be-

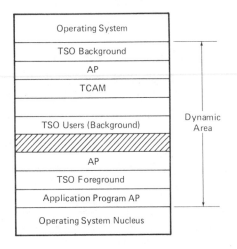

Figure 36.1. A TSO system.

Message Control
Time Shave Control Task
Logon Scheduler
Terminal Monitor
Command Processor
System Driver

Figure 36.2. TSO foreground.

cause it controls the activities of TSO. Still, it is a simple language and not difficult to master.

When the user has a program which is to be executed outside of the TSO system but within the overall computer system, he or she can create a file which contains JCL and is passed over to the external operating system with a **SUBMIT** command. In other words, **SUBMIT** is a way to pass a job from TSO to the batch system.

A complementary method is provided to run a compiler under TSO which would normally run under the parent system. A **CALL** command is issued from the terminal and causes the compiler to run in the TSO region.

Program development.   There are two ways in which a programmer can write and debug a TSO program:

- Alternatively edit and compile.
- Incrementally compile.

Both methods use the **interactive terminal facility (ITF).**

In the first case, alternative editing and compilation, the programmer creates the source statements which comprise the program, using an editor provided by ITF. When sufficient statements accumulate so that determining the correctness and effect of these statements becomes desirable, the programmer can call for a compilation. This can be done in three ways, which we examine shortly.

To implement the second case, ITF provides at least three incremental compilation languages—BASIC, FORTRAN and PL/I. If the programmer chooses to use one of these languages, then incremental syntax checking and compilation is possible.

For **incremental compilation** the programmer invokes the language processor and indicates that syntax checking or compilation is desired on a line by line basis. Then the programmer enters a statement, after which the checking or compilation function is performed and the results are returned. Now it is possible immediately to revise a statement and recheck it as required. Upon completion, a programmer's subprogram which has been checked statement by statement is available for further debugging.

Full compilation.

Once a complete subprogram is available, there are three choices:

1. Execute with the ITF compiler, which is immediately available under TSO;
2. Request through TSO that an existing compiler normally used for batch processing is brought into the TSO environment to compile the program;
3. Request TSO to send this program into the batch environment and schedule it as a batch compilation job through JCL.

These are arranged in order of difficulty. Only an understanding of the TSO command language is required for (1). To run a compiler in the TSO region (2) requires a knowledge of the **ALLOCATE** statements in the TSO command language and also information about various data sets involved and the space required for them. The last alternative (3) employs JCL to get the batch program started and running.

Use of space.

Figure 36.2 shows a map of memory and demonstrates how space is occupied by TSO services. A region is allocated to the main components of TSO. These components are examined shortly below. Then there are a number of regions which contain TSO user programs. The number of such regions is under the control of the installation, which may establish one or possibly several of them.

Each region, called a **background region,** generally services several users. Each user has a terminal by which communication is established with the services. Since several users are assigned to one TSO region, there is usually contention among the users' programs for occupation of this region.

There is a resident control program in each region, shown in Figure 36.3 as the region control program. It determines which user program occupies the region at any given time. The basis for occupancy is the recency of use. When the user becomes idle, a clock begins to tick. If the user does not enter a command or data within a fixed period, usually a few seconds, the use of the region lapses. The space occupied by the program is freed by

| TSO User's Program |
| Region Control Program |

Figure 36.3. TSO background.

swapping, writing it out to an external medium and then reading in another user's program to replace it.

This is one of the biggest complaints that users have of TSO. If a user spends too much time thinking, his or her program lapses and is swapped from the region onto a direct storage device. Swapping entails not only overhead but a time delay. When the user stops thinking and tries to activate the system again there, a response time is incurred which may be as large as 10 to 15 seconds. Some users get around this difficulty by trying to maintain occupancy. This they do by hitting the <u>enter</u> key at their terminals at frequent intervals to keep the region control program on its toes and make it seem as if the program is running.

Components.

The components which comprise TSO are put together in a single TSO region called the **foreground region** as shown in Figure 36.1. These components are shown in more detail in Figure 36.2.

LOGON scheduler.

This scheduler processes messages from terminal users who wish to log on. The user's profile is found in a library and JCL statements are constructed and sent to the basic system, where the profile acquires the resources needed for the user.

Terminal monitor program.

The terminal monitor program services all users. When a command processor is needed, it is activated by TMP, brought into the region and made available for command processing.

Message control program.

The MCP is the mediator between the **telecommunication access method,** shown as **TCAM** in Figure 36.1, and TSO. The telecommunication access method runs in its own region and services all user's terminals: it receives messages and sends them messages directly to terminals. The MCP buffers these messages and activates the main TSO executive to serve them promptly.

Time sharing control task.

The executive which controls and coordinates the TSO is the component called the **TSC.** It obtains memory and establishes regions as required for each group of users, builds control blocks to monitor each region, and provides memory and swapping space used by active terminals to communicate with their regions.

Other processors.   We have mentioned the command processor and the interactive terminal facility. There are also individual interactive incremental compilers. These all have to be managed by the TSC.

Wylbur and Roscoe

Wylbur is another TSM, developed by On-line Systems. **Roscoe**, also a TSM, is a product of Applied Data Research. Together with TSO they comprise the majority of on-line systems of this nature. They have similarities and differences but they essentially provide similar service. A comparison is beyond the scope of this chapter.

36.7 THE VIRTUAL MACHINE

The **virtual machine** concept (or **VM**) was introduced by IBM in the middle of the 1970s. They intended to take the on-line system to its ultimate: provide each user with a *piece* of a computer which seems to be a complete instrument, capable of performing all the functions of even a large machine.

Purpose

The purpose of VM is to provide an assortment of on-line facilities for different classes of users, as follows:

- The student or amateur who wants to enter text or programs interactively;
- The program developer who wants to create complicated programs or subprograms at the console and have them compiled and debugged interactively;
- The system programmer who want to make changes in an operating system and to debug these changes without interfering with production time for other important jobs or with interactive terminal users.

Interactive program development and text entry is provided by a component called the **Conversational Monitor System,** or **CMS,** which can support a large number of users in a simple interactive mode. The full facility supplies a virtual machine to each user as supported by the **control program,** or **CP.** It is reached through CMS as will be described shortly.

A virtual machine consists of

1. A virtual processor: this is similar to the processor resource awarded to a user who is operating in any multiprogramming system; that is, the user's program gets control of the computer according to his or her priority for a period of time based on this priority, while being interspersed with use by other application programs and with an operating system.
2. An operating system which may be an advanced multiprogram operating system and support many application programs.
3. Peripheral devices or portions thereof which appear to the user as complete devices.

It is important to realize that several such virtual machines can run concurrently in the VM operating environment.

Multiple Users

It should now be clear to the reader that at any point in time a VM system supports many interactive terminal users who are busy doing different jobs and starting and stopping programs within the overall system. Further, each may have his or her own virtual machine which itself can be running multiple concurrent programs.

Virtual Resources

Virtual resources are what meet the eye of the beholder. The VM user determines the system configuration and communicates this to the VM system, which allocates the requested resources as long as they do not conflict with the actual resources and their current allocations.

Processor.   First there is the **virtual processor;** it is uniprocessor simulation of some System 370 models. The one restriction is that the virtual processor may not be a **multiprocessor** configuration—one that contains two or more processors. The user describes the amount of **simulated** physical memory. Next there is a virtual system console to communicate with the CP (the control program portion of VM). By means of the console, three main functions are performed:

1. Tell the CP actions that are to be performed as though requested from a real system console; some such actions as IPL, START, STORE, and DISPLAY.

2. Provide the means for dynamically altering specific attributes of this virtual machine, such as storage size, operational control and performance options.
3. Talk with an application program running on the virtual machine, especially necessary if the applications program is interactive.

Devices. Of course a real console *is* the hardware which supplies these virtual console functions as implemented through VM.

Next there are **virtual devices.** Any device that a real system might have support, for the most part, can be simulated by the VM environment. The user describes, for instance, the disk storage required. A chargeback environment prevents the user from demanding more space than might actually be used. The user specifies a **minidisk** which contains a number of cylinders, tracks per cylinder, bytes per track and so forth as the user requests. One real disk can support several minidisks as shown in Figure 36.4. Unit record devices are simulated in a similar fashion; of course, spooling is provided for them so that printer output, for example, goes to a disk instead of to a printer, which is probably occupied with other tasks.

Finally, the users specifies the operating system to be used, which might be any real (OS or DOS) or virtual storage operating system (SVS, MVS, or DOS/VS)

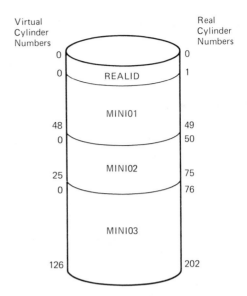

Figure 36.4. Real disk containing minidisks.

which IBM supplies, including VM itself. Together with this is a description of the virtual storage size, how it is used, and so forth. A typical host system supporting several guest systems appears in Figure 36.5

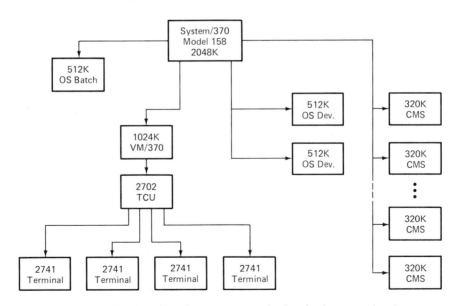

Figure 36.5. Virtual machines for concurrent production, development and testing.

Establishing the Guest System

Not all users are authorized to set up their own guest virtual machine. As is good practice with all multiuser interactive systems, information about each user is entered by the installation operator or manager and authorizes that user for more or less of the virtual machine system's facilities. The user description entered is put into a user table to be available to the VM's CP when the user logs on. (*Note:* to avoid confusion, we call the host virtual machine *VMS* (for the VM system) and the guest's machine simply the *VM*.)

To get the guest system up, the user logs onto a CMS terminal. After authorization is verified, the user gives commands to request communication with the CP. For an existing machine, VMS finds it specification and makes the machine available.

As with any real machine, the operator cannot begin to operate it until he or she IPL's (Initial Program Load) the system to bring in the operating system. Once the operating system comes up, it presents messages on the terminal which the operator should answer.

The VM needs a job stream. If one already exists (on disk, say) the user connects it to the VM, which then begins to execute the jobs described there. If there is no job stream, the user can go back to CMS and create one with its editor. The job stream created with CMS is sent over to a shared disk facility which can then be accessed by the guest VM.

Requests in this job stream are to start programs, presumably accessible to the guest VM's OS. When their turns arrive, they begin to run as tasks under that OS.

CMS

The casual CMS user can do a considerable amount of work at the console. To eliminate the onerous chores of allocating and reserving resources, the neophyte is given a typical configuration such as shown in Figure 36.6. All the facilities are virtual except the system, which belongs to VM.

The user talks to CMS with a special command language unique to the VM system. The language is flexible and can be tailored, either by the installation or by individual users to create additional commands with special meanings. Further, there is a help facility so that the user can find out what commands mean and which ones to use in certain situations. The components which alter commands are called EXEC and EXEC2. They have extensive logical capabilities for defining intricate commands.

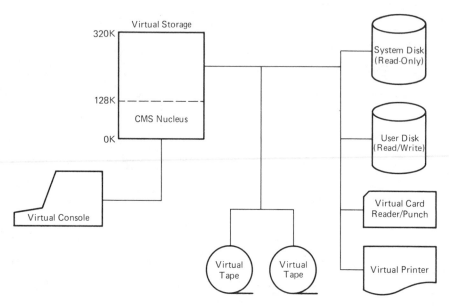

Figure 36.6. Sample CMS configuration.

Here are some of the things one can do with CMS:

- Create and compile source programs.
- Build test files.
- Execute and test programs.
- Debug programs at the terminal.

CMS includes two editors: one comes with CMS and the other is a system product (purchased separately). The latter, which costs extra, is more powerful. Both of them can provide line editing functions. That is, if the lines of the text are numbered, the user can specify to the editor what changes to make in a particular numbered line. The system product editor is a screen editor, which means that the user can go to any place on the screen and make a change directly at the cursor. Also available is a text or word processor, called SCRIPT.

Many language processors are provided, including assembly language, APL, PL/I and FORTRAN. These provide translations which run directly under CMS. Other languages may be programmed in CMS, such as OS COBOL and OS PL/I. These load modules are then sent over to another virtual machine to be compiled and run.

For the compilation facilities which exist under CMS, it is possible to include CMS commands within the source program. These provide a powerful debugging tool.

Supporting multiple VMs.

The VM control program, CP, is the host operating system for all guest VMs. This is illustrated in Figure 36.7. Notice that there is one CMS shown for each logged-on CMS user. Truly, each user has a copy of CMS, but on a demand paged basis. CMS is **reentrant** so that multiple users can execute it concurrently. Each use has his or her own **working set** of pages currently needed for execution. It is easy for two (or more) users to share a resident page in real memory, if they are executing it concurrently.

Figure 36.8 shows how one might make alterations in VM itself where VM is a guest on a VM host. Notice the three level of operating systems:

1. CP at the bottom is the host VM.
2. CP just above it is the guest VM.
3. MVS and CMS are supported by the guest VM.

Efficiency problems

Running two or more nested operating systems as described is bound to create a certain amount of inefficiency, for example, when a guest needs to execute a privileged instruction (one prohibited to application programs). If it could actually do so, it would circumvent its host and all the accounting would get mucked up. Hence the guest OS operates in user mode; privileged commands cause an interrupt which the host OS intercepts. Then it must determine if the command came from the guest OS or its application program (AP):

- If the former, the host provides the service (after interpreting it) and returns to the guest OS
- If the latter, the AP is at fault and the host returns to the guest OS with an error message so that the AP may be chastised.

Another problem is multiple spooling. The job stream enters via a real device operated by the host OS (CP). This is spooled. If it destined for a guest OS, that OS must access that input and spool it into its own file. The complexity is observed from Figure 36.9.

Both of these problems, along with many other considerations, have led to rethinking and subsequent improve-

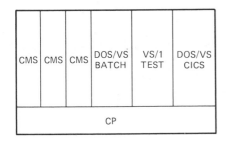

Figure 36.7. A VM/370 environment.

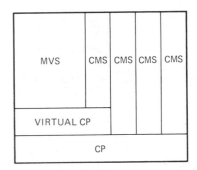

Figure 36.8. VM/370 running in a virtual machine.

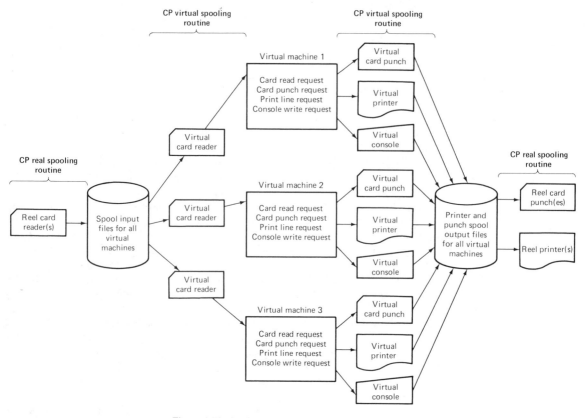

Figure 36.9. Logical flow of local spooling facilities.

ments to VM. The addition of special commands and microprogramming has been especially helpful. VM's current high efficiency is a tribute to its designers.

36.7 REMOTE JOB ENTRY

The title of this feature, **remote job entry,** or **RJE,** explains its operation. Its purpose is to enable users at a remote site to enter jobs and to receive the printout from the running of these jobs. RJE is not strictly an on-line system because it is not interactive in the sense that the user communicates with the running program.

RJE *does* make a combination of peripheral devices seem like a computer and that is the reason this subject is covered here. The RJE hardware configuration is presented in Figure 36.10. A card reader holds the **job stream,** a mixture of job control language cards and input data for each job submitted.

Cards are read by the card reader under the control of

the card reader controller. The card images are converted by the modem and multiplexer and passed over leased or owned lines to be received by the remote host computer. That computer has an operating system which reads the job stream, compresses it and places it onto the computer's job queue.

The host computer is controlled by an operating system such as some version of OS or VS for System 360 or System 370. The operating system contains an optional component, RJE. It is this component that receives the remote job stream and queues it for the job manager, which then schedules jobs to be run in terms of their priority.

Figure 36.11 shows a typical operating system with RJE. One of the regions in the dynamic area of memory holds the **job entry system (JES).** JES is the OS job manager component that runs the local card reader, which contains the local job stream. The jobs read by the JES are compressed and placed onto the job queue, which resides on a resident disk volume.

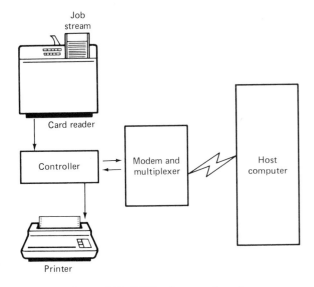

Figure 36.10. RJE hardware configuration.

The RJE component performs the same kind of operation. However, the job stream it receives is provided by a telecommunications access method (shown here as TCAM). This access method activates a multiplexer/modem combination which runs the communication lines. It receives information from the remote job stream and passes it over to RJE.

RJE in turn places the JCL in the job stream provided by the remote station onto the job queue. Here they compete with local jobs according to their class and priority for activation and for running in the host computer. Data in the job stream are spooled by RJE.

Spooling

As application programs are run, they produce output. This output is spooled to temporary files on some direct access volume as shown in the Figure 36.11. Spooling is necessary in a multiprogramming environment. To convert the spooled output, **writers** are necessary. These op-

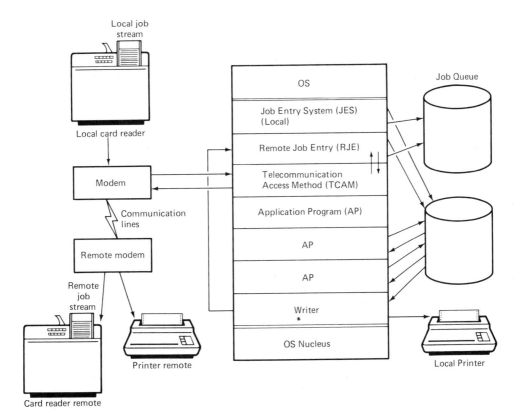

Figure 36.11. Operating system with RJE.

erating system components convert the *print* data into printable output. Output data destined for local printers are converted by a writer which activates those printers; output for the remote terminal is passed by a different writer to TCAM, which in turn activates the communication lines that send this output to the remote printer. There the user can pick up hard copy of the job after it has been run.

36.8 CUSTOMER INFORMATION CONTROL SYSTEM

The Customer Information Control System, or CICS, is truly an on-line system. However, its purpose is quite distinct from the other on-line systems discussed so far. It certainly serves the naive operator and nonprogrammer. It is introduced here but discussed in detail in Chapter 42.

Consider a large data base or conglomeration of facts which is to be accessed by a multitude of operators sitting at terminals. An operator is trained in using the terminal for the purpose for which it is intended—to access this particular conglomeration of facts. The operators are not programmers but simply employ the terminal as a communications device between the system and the general public.

Here are examples of typical CICS terminal applications:

- A public utility service bureau which customers call to make inquiries about their billings and from which operators respond by interrogating the system data base.
- A reservation system, for example, for airlines, hotels or automobile leasing companies, which a customer calls to make a reservation request that is confirmed or denied by the operator using the terminal to interrogate the system and to enter reservations.
- A data entry system to which operators key in information from bills, invoices or other paper documents.

In all these cases, it is up to the system designer to present screens at the operator's terminal which facilitate the terminal's use to acquire information from the data base and to enter information into it.

CICS is particularly useful and unique. It allows programmers to set up a screen to facilitate interrogation and data entry. Still the programmer uses a familiar programming language such as COBOL. Directives to CICS and are imbedded in the language and handled by means of preprocessors.

36.9 THE REAL TIME SYSTEM

A real time system responds to inputs from a changing environment within *sufficient time* to have the desired and calculated effect on the environment. A real time system is characterized by the nature of the environment requiring timely service. Typical applications include controlling an assembly line and collecting experimental data in a scientific environment.

Process Control

A major class of real time systems is **process control,** in which a computer system directly controls an industrial process. The system receives input for transactions and adjusts parameters for the controlled process through output control by devices called **transducers** which are physically integrated into the environment. These systems employ feedback; data consists of observations on the environment takes by **sensors.** The computer makes calculations to determine the departure of the process from its operating norm. It then sends correction signals to the transducers. This causes a correction in the system with the aim of bringing it back to its operating center.

Examples of process control applications include

- Adjusting engine parameters based on sampled emissions.
- Setting up telephone call routing based on customer dialed digits.
- Shutting down a nuclear reactor based on the detection of excessive coolant temperature.

Transaction Processing

On-line transaction processing makes a real time demand since customer satisfaction depends on rapid response. Here a file or data base is modified frequently to service the requests of operators or customers of the organization which owns and maintains the system. Typical on-line users with real time demands are airlines, for seat reservations; public utilities; and bank inquiry systems.

The real time nature arises because the data base must be up to date. For instance, airlines customers at several locations could be vying for the same seats.) Long response times may mean lost sales in some cases. The critical time for transaction systems varies by application.

36.10 POLLED PERIPHERAL DEVICE INTERFACES

This and the next few sections discuss how data from input and output devices get into the system to activate it either on an on-line or real time basis.

Polling is a simple and effective way to receive data from real time peripheral devices. It is excellent for regularly spaced data transfer events (**synchronous**) and its inherent simplicity allows for a design which has reliable and predictable performance.

The basis of polling is simple: the processor periodically examines the status of the attached peripheral devices in a predetermined sequence to determine if any are waiting for service. A device requiring service raises a hardware flag for the processor to check it when scanned in the polling sequence.

If a device does not need service, it is passed over and the flag of the next device in the polling sequence is examined. When service is required, the processor

1. Reads the input data from the device;
2. Processes them;
3. Sends any required output data;
4. Lowers the flag;
5. Moves on to the next device in the sequence.

Device polling is less attractive for servicing requests which occur infrequently or at nondeterministic times. The overhead of regular polling may be excessive; the time to do this may amount to a large fraction of the useful computer time. Therefore some other mechanism such as interrupt processing is preferable.

36.11 INTERRUPT DRIVEN PERIPHERAL INTERFACE

Many peripheral actions do not require service at regular or predictable time intervals. These are **asynchronous.** It is difficult if not impossible to anticipate when an operator might activate a process. An extreme example of an unscheduled event is a device breakdown or a power failure. An interface mechanism which is actively driven by

an event occurrence is superior in these cases. The **interrupt driven interface** provides flexibility and insures that important events get prompt service because this device stops program processing at the earliest possible moment and apply the computer immediately to the problem at hand.

A device needing service from the processor generates an **interrupt request signal.** This signal invokes an **interrupt:** a hardware initiated activity which takes control away from the currently executing program and gives control to the operating system in such a way that the interrupted program *may* be reinstated later as though nothing had happened to it. This capability requires that special interrupt hardware be designed into the processor.

In many computer systems, multiple levels of interrupt are available, permitting interrupts to occur during interrupt service. Once the operating system receives control and does its housekeeping chores, it must identify the device requesting service. In systems having minimal interrupt hardware, the operating system polls the attached peripheral devices to determine the one which has generated the interrupt. This differs from the polling interface discussed above, since this last form of polling occurs only as a result of an interrupt signal.

To identify devices requesting service modern computers have hardware which is activated by the interrupt request. The device interrupt request signals include an identifier (often known as an **interrupt vector**) which the operating system uses to locate a routine previously set up to service the kind of interrupt identified. The operating system

1. Saves the status information from the program that is currently running:
2. Services the request (since the interrupt routine is associated with a particular group of devices):
3. Then *may* return control to the program which was running before the interrupt.

In the section on priorities, we discuss system designs with multiple priorities in which an interrupt routine can, itself, be interrupted by a higher priority request for service.

36.12 PRIORITY SERVICE DISCIPLINES

In real time systems, it often happens that several devices may need service at the same time. Some of these devices may be associated with more important programs or assignments than others. Some mechanism is needed to provide a higher priority to such devices so that the programs receive faster service. **Priority** is a measure of urgency. Service disciplines allocate the processor's time among devices wanting to use the processor according to priority.

In time shared systems, the operating system uses a **dynamic priority** discipline to allocate the processor among the processes. It is *dynamic* because it permits the rating of a task to be changed while the task is running. Dynamic priorities are not under the control of the application program. In real time systems, priority service disciplines are static; this is a crucial part of the design. We restrict our attention to priority service disciplines for real time systems.

Polling

For polled devices, the frequency of polling can be scheduled to satisfy the priority of each device. Devices which require shorter response time are polled more frequently. The time interval from (1) a device raising its flag to (2) the processor accessing that device depends on how frequently the processor polls the device. This priority discipline, like polling in general, is appropriate for regular tasks with known frequencies of occurrence.

For interrupt driven peripheral device interfaces, priorities are implemented by employing multiple levels of interrupt. Multiple interrupt levels must be built into the computer hardware and use software routines to sort out the sequence of action. Great system flexibility results from the judicious use of multilevel interrupts.

Typically each peripheral device is assigned a hardware priority level. Several devices may be assigned the same level with a mechanism to resolve concurrent requests. For instance, in the **daisy chain** approach, the device electrically closest to the processor has first priority. Thus there is a hierarchy of device priorities, both logical and physical, to arbitrate which device receives the service at any time.

Priority interrupt systems can be classified as either preemptive or nonpreemptive. For a **preemptive interrupt,** the currently running process is interrupted as soon as the current instruction is completed, provided the interrupt has a high enough priority. In a **nonpreemptive priority** system, the current process runs to completion. A requesting device causes a control block to be put at a position in a queue of requests according to the interrupt's relative priority. Preemptive interrupts are more common

in on-line systems; the remainder of this section provides examples of how this scheme works.

Two event streams are shown in Figure 36.12. Both have, running at the start, a base level process which executes while no devices request service. Typically the base process does work which has no stringent response time requirements (for example, off-line report generation). Two interrupt requests are shown for each stream. In (a), the second interrupt request has higher priority than the first, in (b), the second request has lower priority then the first.

In (a), service begins immediately for the first interrupt. The base process finishes the current instruction and then waits while the request causes control to go to an interrupt routine to service the device. When the routine has completed, the base process resumes at the instruction following the interrupt. Since the second interrupt has a higher priority than the first, it preempts the service given to the first interrupt. When the second interrupt is fully served, the first interrupt service resumes. The base process gets control after the first interrupt is served.

In (b), the second interrupt request has lower priority than the first and the device waits for service until the

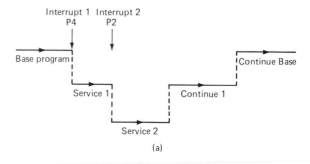

(a)

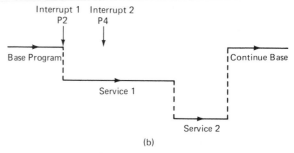

(b)

Figure 36.12. Preemptive priority discipline.

first interrupt is done. After the second interrupt is served, the base process continues.

A poor system design could lead to loss of data or erroneous responses. When priority levels are not carefully assigned, some requesting devices may not receive quick service and may remain idle for excessive periods of time, even though there is work waiting for them. The analysis of priority discipline is difficult because all permutations of alternatives should be explored.

36.13 DESIGN PHASE PERFORMANCE CONSIDERATIONS

A definition of functional requirements for the system precedes the system design phase. This definition includes a description of system features and the inputs which drive each feature, as well as the outputs expected to result from the system processing for each feature. **System load** is an important consideration:

- How many users of each type are expected in the worst case?
- What is the average input volume for each?
- What are the performance objectives in terms of response time?
- What is the variability of demand from peak to off-peak to idle condition?

The design team is responsible for an implementation to meet these requirements. They propose an overall architecture evaluated against expected performance before detailed system design begins.

System features have interactions which are difficult to predict until some of the more detailed aspects of system design are decided upon. Before feature interaction is considered, it is fruitful to carry out an analysis of the system workload. First, arrival distribution functions for each system demand type, with estimated parameters, are developed. Then come estimates of the resources required to process each type of input, processing time per transaction, number of file accesses per transaction, and so forth. The goal is to identify potential system capability and potential bottlenecks before the system is committed to detailed design.

The analysis can employ both mathematics and computer simulation. If a proposed system architecture fails the scrutiny of the review, the inherent weaknesses should be evident; a redesign is in order.

An on-line system is a design and iterative process as described in Chapter 34:

1. Architecture is proposed;
2. Analytic tools determine the suitability of the proposed architecture;
3. Improvements to the architecture are suggested;
4. More iterations follow.

Queuing system analysis helps to evaluate proposed system architectures. Both analytical and simulation studies can be used by the design organization. As system designs get more detailed, simulation studies allow for expression of design details in the modeling effort. Finally, the early system development stages should include assessments of the actual system's performance using simulated input load in a test environment.

36.14 OVERLOAD CONTROL

The random nature of on-line system demand is expected to create overload situations at times. An **overload** results when the system cannot process all input requests within the user's expectation or patience. Sometimes the system actually produces less output during overload then normally; the overloaded computer spends much of its time arbitrating the barrage of requests coming in for its services. A carefully designed overload control scheme insures that the most important system demands are processed.

For the majority of overload schemes, the computer should be kept doing the most critical work first. Overload strategy may simply deny processing to some requests in favor of the more critical ones to insure system health. As an example, since system output ports have limited capacity, care should be taken to give higher output priority to the more important and also to short duration outputs.

In general, a system must recognize an overload situation and have a strategy to eliminate, bypass or postpone some of its work. An example is the VS thrashing monitor. It eliminates, or **quiesces,** one or more tasks in a paging environment when the OS computer is spending undue time in paging activity and application execution time is dwindling.

Overload control should be incorporated *early* in the system design. Historically it has been added as an enhancement after a catastrophic bout with an overload situation. As we come to depend more upon on-line systems, we should insure the integrity of the systems by including overload control strategies to avoid costly system delays and failures.

36.15 SYSTEM LOAD MEASUREMENT TECHNIQUES

Ideally, the system administrator builds good performance measurement provisions into the system when it is designed. During operation, a performance evaluation package records statistics about performance on a sampled basis in a detailed transaction log.

Times to be monitored include

1. System idle time;
2. Operating system overhead;
3. Productive processing for each transaction type;
4. Time waiting for resources;
5. System input/output operations;
6. User entry;
7. Average user idle time (for thinking?).

Measurement collection built into the software helps determine overall performance of an on-line system. Difficulties and degradation can be corrected efficiently later as the designers examine these performance measurements and tune the system accordingly.

Where the system has no measurement technique built into it, benefit is derived from hardware monitoring equipment (see Chapter 49). Hardware monitors count occurrences of selected events at selected access points is in the hardware. The presence of an address on a bus may indicate the occurrence of a key input or output operation. Hardware monitoring opens up many possibilities, but, since the equipment is relatively expensive, it is usually employed only on a sample basis or when poor system response is observed. Information which can be obtained from a hardware monitor is useful for the design organi-

zation in developing enhancements to correct poor system performance.

36.16 SUMMARY

No single development, except perhaps the microcomputer explosion, has had the impact of on-line systems. People want to get information *now;* waiting means expenses and tries patience.

On-line computers mean that users have immediate access to data, as with dedicated personal computers. This access speeds program development, information retrieval and process control—to mention just a few such applications. We have reviewed the hardware and software developments making this possible.

REFERENCES

Chandy, K. Mani, and R. T. Yeh, eds., *Current Trends in Programming Methodology:* Vol. 3, *Software Modeling.* Englewood Cliffs, NJ: Prentice-Hall, 1978.

Ferrari, D., *Computer Systems Performance Evaluation.* Englewood Cliffs, NJ: Prentice-Hall, 1978.

Healey, M., *Minicomputers and Microprocessors.* New York: Crane, Russak, 1976.

Kleinrock, L., *Queueing Systems:* Vol. 2, *Computer Applications.* John Wiley & Sons, 1976.

Lorin, Harold, and Harvey Deitel, *Operating Systems.* Reading, MA: Addison-Wesley, 1981.

MacKinnon, R. A., "The changing Virtual Machine Environment: Interfaces to Real Hardware, Virtual Hardware and Other Virtual Machines," *IBM Systems Journal,* Vol. 8, No. 1 (1979), pp. 18–46.

Martin, J., *Design of Real-Time Computer Systems.* Englewood Cliffs, NJ: Prentice-Hall, 1967.

Scherr, A. A., *An Analysis of Time Shared Computer Systems.* Cambridge, MA: M.I.T. Press, 1967.

Seawright, L. H., and P. A. MacKinnon, "VM/370, A Study of Multiplicity and Usefulness," *IBM Systems Journal,* Vol. 18, No. 1 (1979), pp. 4–17.

Yourdon, E., *Design of On-Line Computer Systems.* Englewood Cliffs, NJ: Prentice-Hall, 1972.

37
Telecommunications and Computers

Mary N. Youssef

IBM Corporation

37.1 INTRODUCTION

Telecommunication science is little over a century old, yet it is considered one of the most advanced fields in technology. It has been influenced by a sequence of technological breakthroughs and inventions that have changed even its most fundamental goal—to provide world-wide telephone communication with least possible cost.

The recent merger of telecommunications and computers is a significant technological event. As a result, we are able to transport the computer's power from special computer rooms to remote locations. This is a mark of a new era, characterized by the information explosion phenomenon we are witnessing today. Systems and services such as the office of the future, teleconferencing, electronic mail, automated newspaper, and home banking and shopping, are modest examples of what will become a new lifestyle.

The technological concepts underlying these systems and services are readily available. It will take some years, however, before they actually become a way of life. What we lack is a far-reaching, economical data network, similar to the telephone network.

The use of the telephone network in data communication exists today, but not without problems. The telephone network was built over the years for *voice* communication. Voice signals are analog and, traditionally, transmitted in analog form. An analog signal is usually distorted by the unavoidable low level noise that always exists in communication lines. Unlike voice, data cannot tolerate distortion (errors) in their transmission.

Moreover, when a telephone call is connected, an idle path through the network is found and assigned to the call during its entire time. In contrast, data are transmitted either in large uninterrupted blocks (as those generated with the speed of computer processing) or in bursts (as those generated from a user's terminal). An uninterrupted flow of data should be transmitted at a much faster rate than a subscriber telephone line can permit. In the transmission of burst data, however, while the speed of the telephone line is adequate, it is uneconomical to keep the connection established between bursts.

Existing data networks are still in their infancy. Many private data networks are owned and used by private corporations. A few public networks also offer limited services, mainly of time sharing capability. Most, if not all, data networks of today are isolated entities. The differences in their architecture and the incompatibilities among their components are the main barriers in internetworking. The dire need for overcoming these barriers has given birth to many organizations whose functions are to issue standards and define protocols. The so-called X.25 recommendation of the CCITT (Comité Consultatif Internationale de Télegraphique et Téléphonique) and the ISO (International Standard Organization) reference model, while still incomplete, give some hope for progress.

Building a data network similar to the telephone network for public use of computers requires a large capital investment. The telephone network has $160 billion invested in devices that range from the obsolete to the most modern. Current technology indicates that the telephone network will continue to evolve to encompass transmission of all kinds of information—voice, data, text and image. Eventually, all transmission in the network will be in digital form. Pulse code modulation (PCM) techniques make possible the transmission of analog signals in a digital form. Digital transmission is more efficient and more reliable than its analog counterpart, even in transmitting analog signals.

37.2 BASIC CONCEPTS IN DATA TRANSMISSION

Analog Versus Digital

An acoustical signal such as voice or music is a rapid change of air pressure which can be decomposed into many oscillations. These oscillations can be described in terms of two quantities: amplitude and frequency. The **amplitude** is the peak value of an oscillation. The instantaneous amplitude at a given point oscillates very rapidly. The number of these oscillations per second, at this point, is the **frequency** of the signal. A signal frequency is measured in cycles per second, or hertz (Hz). The analog voice signal is a superposition of many different frequencies, and can be represented by a set of sine waves spanning the range of these frequencies.

Unlike voice, data, as generated by a computer, is represented by binary digits (bits). The resulting string of 0s and 1s may then be represented by a sequence of on and off pulses. These pulses comprise the **digital signal.** The speed of a digital signal is measured in bits per second (bps). Both analog and digital signals can be transmitted over a communication medium in either form. The transmission form depends on the communication path and the devices attached to the path. Figure 37.1a illustrates an analog signal and Figure 37.1b a digital signal.

Transmission Media

A transmission medium is usually referenced by the term *line,* although it may not be a physical wire. A transmission medium can be, among others, a two wire line, a coaxial cable, a microwave link, a satellite link, a waveguide, or an optical fiber.

A *two wire line* is usually used in a telephone network for local loops to connect a customer phone to the telephone company local switching office (central office).

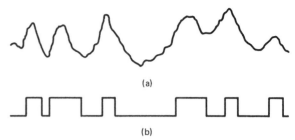

Figure 37.1. (a) An analog signal. (b) A digital signal.

Tens of signals can be packed simultaneously in one line. A two wire line, however, is inadequate for long distance transmission because of the delay distortion problem, whereby higher frequencies travel with higher speed than lower frequencies.

A *coaxial cable* is made of an inner conductor surrounded by a cylindrical conductor. The two conductors are separated from each other by an insulator. A coaxial cable can transmit at much higher frequencies than a two wire line, and it is mostly used for long distance transmission. In a coaxial cable, hundreds of thousands of calls can be transmitted simultaneously. Both two wire lines and coaxial cables are usually made of copper.

A *microwave radio link* can also transmit thousands of calls in one path. With microwave connections, however, transmission is usually limited to line of sight. A microwave path must be clear from any obstruction such as trees, hills or buildings.

Satellite links are very similar to terrestrial microwave links, except that the transmission path goes from a ground station to a satellite from which it is retransmitted to other terminals on the ground. The major drawback in satellite transmission is propagation delay. For a signal to travel from an earth station to the satellite and back takes a quarter of a second. In a two way telephone conversation, a one-half second delay is therefore encountered at each response.

A new transmission medium, called *circular waveguide,* seemed promising a few years ago. It was found that the propagation of waves through metal tubes (circular waveguides) have many distinct characteristics and peculiarities. These characteristics would allow hundreds of thousands of telephone channels to be sent through one waveguide. Recently, however, low loss *optical fibers* have proved to be more economically attractive for broadband communication than circular waveguides. Highly transparent fibers, made of pure glassy materials, are used to guide light waves. The bandwidth of the signal sent over the fibers is many million hertz.

Analog Transmission

Voice and other analog signals are usually transmitted over a communication medium in their analog form. A transmission channel is a path through a communication line which may be described by its bandwidth. A channel's **bandwidth** is defined as the difference between the maximum and minimum frequencies a channel can handle. Usually, a channel allows transmission of a chosen range within the signal range of frequencies. This range must be sufficiently wide for the signal to be recognizable and intelligible.

When an analog signal is transmitted with its original range of frequencies, the transmission is called *baseband signaling*. On most long distance channels, however, a signal is shifted from its baseband level to another level of frequencies in order to pack many other signals into one path.

For example, a voice grade signal may range in frequencies between 100 to 8000 hertz. A telephone line transmits the range between 200 to 3400 hertz. This is equivalent to a bandwidth of 3200 hertz. Most telephone channels have a larger bandwidth to carry many voice signals simultaneously. A 48,000 hertz channel may be divided into 12 channels, each having a 4000 hertz bandwidth. The range of frequencies must be shifted by varying amounts to transmit the 12 separate voice signals without interference. The tenth signal, for instance, could be transmitted using a bandwidth of 36,000 to 40,000 hertz.

The technique of sending signals in different frequency ranges is important in packing (**multiplexing**) many signals into one path without overlapping. Also, out of the 4000 hertz, 3200 hertz is used for transmitting the signal. The remaining bandwidth of 800 hertz serves as a guard band between the channels to prevent interferences of adjacent signals (**crosstalk**).

To transmit a digital signal over an analog telephone line, the discrete binary pulses must first be converted to an analog signal in a band of frequencies that fit into the bandwidth of a voice channel. After transmission, another conversion must take place to restore the digital form of the signal before it is delivered to the receiver. This process is called modulation-demodulation and is performed by a device called a modem (see Chapter 9).

A **modem** consists of two parts: a modulator and a demodulator. In the transmission of data over a telephone line, both parts must be connected between each of the communicating data terminal equipments (DTEs) and the transmission lines. (Throughout the chapter the term **DTE** refers to any device that is attached to the network and is capable of sending or receiving data. Thus, terminals, computers and peripheral devices are DTEs. The term *terminal* will refer to a device that can input data to, and receive data from, the computer.)

At the sending site, the modulator part of the modem provides a modulated sine wave carrier to transmit data generated by the DTE. The modulated waveform is tailored to the characteristics of the channel. At the other end of the channel, the demodulator part intercepts the carrier and sends the digital signal to the receiving DTE. Modems on telephone lines operate at speeds up to 9600 bps. Figure 37.2 shows a connection between two DTEs via a transmission line using modems.

Digital Transmission

Any kind of information (data, voice, text, image) can be transmitted in digital form. Analog signals can be transmitted using a device, called a codec which performs the reverse function of a modem. Recently, codecs have become available as inexpensive integrated circuit chips. The term **codec** stands for coder-decoder. The coding process converts the analog signal into a pulse form by sampling the amplitude of the signal at specific times. The pulse coded signal is represented by the binary code. This process is a form of modulation called *pulse code modulation (PCM)*. At the end of the transmission line, the decoding process transforms the pusle signal to analog form before it delivers the signal to the receiver.

Digital transmission of information is desirable for reasons that will be discussed later. The only reason for transmitting digital data in analog form is to use the ubiquitous telephone network. It is a matter of availability, not adequacy.

Noise in Transmission

Noise is always present in all transmission systems, both analog and digital, and all transmitted signals contain a noise component. It is this component which causes signal

Figure 37.2. Modems connected in an analog line.

distortion. While some sources of noise can be eliminated or reduced, others are unavoidable. For example, thermal noise is caused by any object whose temperature is above $-273°$ Celsius.

The quality of the signal in transmission is not measured by the absolute value of the power of the noise component, but by a measure known as signal to noise ratio. The **signal to noise ratio** is the ratio of the total signal power to the total noise power. Shannon's information theory provides an explanation of the communication process through the relationship of this ratio and the bandwidth of the channel. In this relationship, Shannon showed that the capacity of the channel, C, in bits per second can be expressed by

$$C = B \log_2(1 + S/N) \qquad (37.1)$$

where S/N is the signal to noise ratio and B is the channel bandwidth in hertz.

A reduction of the signal to noise ratio is experienced in the transmission of a signal over a long haul. This loss is caused by signal attenuation as well as other factors. Amplifiers (sometimes called **repeaters**) are usually placed along a communication path to compensate for the attenuation of the signal. In amplifying an analog signal, any noise in the system is amplified along with the signal. The amplified noise accumulates as it passes through several amplifiers. Despite the many innovative ideas in the design of amplifiers, the signal received at the end of a long channel usually differs from the original signal.

On the other hand, a repeater along a digital line regenerates the digital signal by determining the original strings of zeroes and ones and then transmitting a fresh, relatively nonnoisy signal. Thus any noise unless it is ex-

cessive is removed and the new signal is reconstructed perfectly. Unlike in analog signals, distortion does not accumulate because of signal amplification.

Multiplexing

Transmission lines are expensive and for this reason many methods for sharing the line have been invented. Some have been in existence since the early days of the telephone network. Multiplexing is the technique of sending many signals through one path simultaneously while keeping them from interfering with each other. There are two types of multiplexing: frequency division multiplexing (FDM) and time division multiplexing (TDM).

Frequency division multiplexing is generally used on long distance analog telephone lines. The basic idea in FDM is frequency shifting. Many narrowband lines can be multiplexed to a broadband line by means of shifting the baseband signal to new frequency ranges that lie one above the other. *Time division multiplexing* is used on digital lines. Many low speed bit streams from low capacity transmission lines are interleaved to form a single bit stream for transmission over a high speed channel. Figure 37.3 shows the process of frequency division and time division multiplexing.

Multiplexing can provide substantial savings in constructing a network. One long distance broadband (high speed) line can replace many narrow band (low speed) lines with a considerable saving in cost. The process of multiplexing is performed by a **multiplexer.** There are many kinds of multiplexers, some of which (time division) use electronic technology. With the reduction of integrated circuit prices, these multiplexers are making the

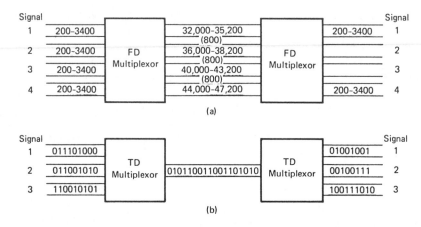

Figure 37.3. Examples of multiplexing. (a) Frequency division. (b) Time division.

multiplexing technique increasingly more economical, even for short distance transmission.

Multiplexers are connected at both ends of a long distance line. The input side of the multiplexer combines the narrowband channels, and at the other end it separates the signals from the broadband channel to recreate the original signals. It should be noted that in multiplexing the capacity of a long distance line must be at least equal to the total capacity of the input lines. Also, the process of multiplexing is transparent in that the transmitted signal is not altered in any way.

Concentrators are electronic devices that provide the same functions as multiplexers in the digital environment, but in a different manner. A concentrator is usually a minicomputer that uses buffer storage to store information from a number of incoming low speed digital lines (as from terminals), and then to transmit it to a high speed line (connected to a computer) which may have much less capacity than the combined capacities of the input lines. The concentrator has combined the data to require less total capacity.

Concentrators usually provide functions in the network besides line sharing. A *front end computer* is a special type of a concentrator. It may be used to provide the interface needed between a computer, transmission lines, terminals, and other connected devices incompatible otherwise. A front end computer usually handles most of the communication processing to relieve the host computer from an unnecessary load. It can also perform code conversion and format conversion of the data to achieve the needed compatibility among devices. In this sense, the effect of its operation on the data is not transparent.

A *cluster controller* is another type of a concentrator that provides the needed interface between terminals and transmission lines. It performs concentration for a group of terminals, allowing multiple terminals to be connected simultaneously to a computer via a single transmission line.

Multipoint, or **multidrop, lines** provide another type of line sharing. A multipoint line is used to connect several terminals to a single line. It allows one terminal to transmit at any given time. Multipoint lines, which take advantage of the sporadic nature of terminal activities, are suited only for buffered terminals.

Codes for Data Transmission

Data communication codes are based on the binary system and they have been in existence since 1874. They were first developed for telegraphy. Transmission codes are similar to computer codes such as BCD and IBM's EBCDIC (Extended Binary Coded Decimal Interchange Code). The two most commonly used transmission codes are the International Alphabet No. 2 for Telex and telegraph, and International Alphabet No. 5 for electronic systems. They are both recommendations of the CCITT.

International Alphabet No. 2 is a 5 bit code. It is a modified version of the Murray code (also known as Baudot) used in telegraphy and Telex transmission. The code can represent 32 characters and it can be extended by using two of the characters for letter shift and figure shift, in the same sense as the shift key of a typewriter.

The **ASCII** (American Standard Code for Information Interchange) is a U.S. version of the International Alphabet No. 5 code; adopted by the American National Standard Institution (ANSI). ASCII is an 8 bit code, 7 bits of which are used to represent 128 characters and the remaining bit for parity checking. Table 37.1 shows the ASCII code chart. Columns 1 and 2 of this chart include 32 control characters, used for various functions, such as message control and its proper framing, message heading and formating, and error detection and corrections. The function of some of these characters are explained in Table 37.2. Internal computer codes are sometimes used in transmission. Such use is discouraged because it adds to the problem of incompatibility among systems.

37.3 SWITCHING

The Basic Concept

The fundamental concept of switching was born in the early days of telephone. The need for switching was probably perceived during the installatin of the third phone. It is switching that makes communication from one phone to another possible.

Without switching, the interconnection of N phones, whereby each phone reaches each other phone, requires $N(N - 1)/2$ transmission links. Thus, the 300 million telephones in the world would require 4.5×10^{16} links. If, on the other hand, the N phones are interconnected via a central switch (Figure 37.4a), the number of needed links is reduced to N. But if these N (where N is a large number) phones are distributed over a wide geographic area, further reduction in the total amount of transmission links and more flexibility in establishing communication are necessary to make such a system feasible. A single central switch entails the obvious risk of a total system failure in the event of an outage of the central switch. Many design ideas that vary in sophistication were developed to provide timely telephone service with a mini-

Table 37.1. American Standards Code for Information Exchange

b7 b6 b5 b4 b3 b2 b1	Row	Column 0	1	2	3	4	5	6	7
0 0 0 0	0	NUL	DLE	SP	0	·	P	@	p
0 0 0 1	1	SOH	DC1	!	1	A	Q	a	q
0 0 1 0	2	STX	DC2	"	2	B	R	b	r
0 0 1 1	3	ETX	DC3	#	3	C	S	c	s
0 1 0 0	4	EOT	DC4	$	4	D	T	d	t
0 1 0 1	5	ENQ	NAK	%	5	E	U	e	u
0 1 1 0	6	ACK	SYN	&	6	F	V	f	v
0 1 1 1	7	BEL	ETB	'	7	G	W	g	w
1 0 0 0	8	BS	CAN	(	8	H	X	h	x
1 0 0 1	9	HT	EM	)	9	I	Y	i	y
1 0 1 0	10	LF	SS	*	:	J	Z	j	z
1 0 1 1	11	VT	ESC	+	;	K	[	k	l
1 1 0 0	12	FF	FS	,	<	L	~	l	⌐
1 1 0 1	13	CR	GS	–	=	M	]	m	}
1 1 1 0	14	SO	RS	.	>	N	^	n		
1 1 1 1	15	SI	US	/	?	O	–	o	DEL

(From William Sinnema, *Digital, Analog and Data Communication,* 1982, p. 39. Reproduced with permission of Reston Publishing Company, Inc., A Prentice-Hall Co., 11480 Sunset Hills Road, Reston, VA 22090.)

Table 37.2 ASCII Control Codes

NUL (null)	All zeros character, used for fill.
SYN (synchronous idle)	Used in synchronous transmission for character synchronization.
SOH (start of header)	Used at the beginning to indicate routing information.
STX (start of text)	Used at the beginning of a sequence of characters which are to be referred to as text.
ETX (end of text)	Used at the end of text.
ETB (end of block)	Indicates end of a block of data.
EOT (end of transmission)	Used at end of transmission or end of call.
ACK,NAK	Sent by receiving station to the transmitting station to indicate successful (ACK) or unsuccessful (NAK) reception of a message.
DLE (data link escape)	Changes the meaning of a limited number of contiguously following characters.
ENQ (enquiry)	Used as a request for a response from a remote station; typical response may be address or status content of station's buffer.
CAN (cancel)	Disregard the accompanied data.

(From William Sinnema, *Digital, Analog and Data Communication,* 1982, p. 39. Reproduced with permission of Reston Publishing Company, Inc., A Prentice-Hall Co., 11480 Sunset Hills Road, Reston, VA 22090.)

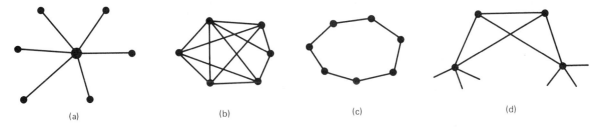

Figure 37.4. Basic network configuration. (a) Star. (b) Mesh. (c) Ring. (d) Hierarchical structure.

mum number of links and to ensure against system failure.

Switching networks are designed for point to point communcation. For instance, television and radio communications are not based on such networks. In the following sections we discuss some basic structures of these networks.

Switching Network Structure

Figure 37.4 illustrates four basic network configurations. These are the star, the mesh, the ring, and the hierarchical structures. The **star structure** (Figure 37.4a) is the most common in connecting subscriber phones to their central offices. It is also suitable for connecting a number of terminals to a central computer. Generally, the purpose of such a connection is to provide communications between the terminals and the computer.

Terminal to terminal communication can also be established via the computer, in which case the computer acts as a switch. A star configuration is dependent on the integrity of the central switch. A duplication of the switch is sometimes necessary to protect service. In a star network, there is exactly one path between any two points that may be connected.

A **mesh structure** (Figure 37.4b) may connect several nodes (switching machines or DTEs) over more than one path. If a path fails owing to a node outage, a second path becomes available to provide connections among other nodes. The number of paths among the nodes is a design parameter that is carefully engineered to provide good service—safeguarding against congestion and link and node failure while requiring the least possible number of links.

A **ring connection** (Figure 37.4c) provides exactly two paths from any node to any other node. A failure of more than one node in the ring splits the ring into disjointed parts that cannot communicate with one another.

A **hierarchical structure** includes a combination of one or more of the previous three configurations in a multi-

level arrangement. Figure 37.4d shows a two level hierarchy whereby the first level connects groups of terminals in various locations to their central site computers. In the second level, computers are connected with one another via a mesh network. In practice, distributed systems are organized as a multilevel hierarchy. The number of levels in the hierarchy is usually a function of the size of the network. As the number of levels increases, the size of the network, as well as its flexibility, increases.

Telephone networks of all nations, other than the U.S., have at most four levels. The U.S. network is a *five level hierarchy* (Figure 37.5). These levels are from lowest to highest: the end office, toll center, primary center, sectional center and regional center. They are also designated as Class 5 to Class 1, in the order of the lowest to the highest level.

At the lowest level, subscriber loops are connected to their end offices (Class 5) in a star configuration. End offices also are connected to toll centers in a star structure. The toll centers are connected to each other, as well as to primary centers via a mixture of star and mesh configurations. Similar structures are used at the higher levels.

The nodes of the telephone network constitute the switching machines. These machines vary from simple step by step to the more elaborate electro-mechanical with common control (crossbar machines) on to the most sophisticated electronic switching systems (ESS). Basically, the electronic switching machines perform the same functions as early systems. The use of stored program control (SPC) in these systems, however, add a new dimension. A change in a system software can alter or modify the functions. This flexibility allows one to incorporate new technology and to delete the old.

Circuit Switching

When a telephone subscriber calls another subscriber, the swtiching machines set up the call by seeking a path through the network to connect the two telephones. The

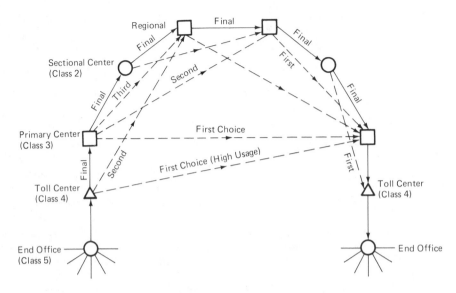

Figure 37.5. Bell System hierarchical network.

elapsed time in setting up a call is usually seconds. The talking path is composed of end to end transmission facilities (links). These facilities are dedicated to the call for its entire duration. The call is terminated when either party hangs up. Upon the termination of the call, the switching machines release the talking connection and free the engaged links.

Circuit switching is suitable for voice communication. Human conversation is usually monotonic with no significant gaps in between. Circuit switching is also suitable for bulk data when a continuous flow exists. In a terminal-computer environment, however, a different type of traffic exists. A terminal user sends data sporadically to a computer. These data are usually transmitted in blocks or messages over the communication links. The intermittent use of the circuit for this type of traffic makes dedicated connections uneconomical. Other methods of switching that are more suitable for data communication have been developed; a discussion of some of these methods follow.

Fast Connect Circuit Switching

This type of switching is the offspring of traditional telephone switching used for voice. It is also referred to as *circuit swtiching*. The concept of fast connect circuit switching assumes a digital environment and a time division network, whereby messages can be sent rapidly and

interleaved with other messages. When a message is ready to be sent, a circuit is established to transmit this message; then it is immediately disconnected. A message may be a digitized voice or data block.

Thus, the circuit is shared with many users simultaneously. Because of the fast connect-disconnect operation, it becomes available very quickly, in which case sharing of the line is transparent to the users. In fast connect circuit switching, the setup of a call is usually in milliseconds. Messages (both digitized voice and data) can be individually reconstructed without any loss owing to the sharing of the line with other messages. This concept in switching is beginning to replace traditional circuit switching.

Message Switching

Message switching has been in use in Telex networks for a long time. It is a type of store-and-forward system, in which data blocks or messages are first stored in the switching node and then sent to the next node through the network when an idle link between the two nodes becomes available. No path is established in the network between the sender and the receiver in advance. Transmission of messages takes place one hop at a time. This type of switching is usually not suitable for computer communication, because messages suffer somewhat long delays in their transmission.

Packet Switching

Packet switching is primarily designed to take advantage of the sporadic nature of interactive computer traffic. The first version of the technique was implemented in the ARPA (Advanced Research Project Agency) network. In packet switching, long data messages are sliced into blocks, called *packets,* before they are sent into the network. The length of these packets is a design parameter which is chosen to optimize delivery time. The packets are then individually enveloped with the necessary information, such as addresses, flow control codes and error checking codes. They are then sent to the next node enroute to their particular destination, one packet at a time.

If errors are made in the transmission of a packet between node A and node B, node A keeps retransmitting this packet until node B sends an acknowledgement to node A. At the final destination, the original message is reassembled and the final confirmation of message reception is transmitted to the source.

Several **routing algorithms** that range from the very simple to the ingenious are in existence today. A routing algorithm is responsible for deciding on which path a given packet should travel. The established route may be determined for each individual packet, for a group of packets in one message, or for all packets generated during a session.

Static routing algorithms are probably the simplest and the most widely used. In *static routing,* each switching node usually maintains a routing table that provides the best route from this node to the packet destination, and another alternate route to be used if the primary route fails.

Adaptive routing algorithms, while numerous, are not commonly used because of the complexity of their techniques and the excessive overhead they incur. In *adaptive routing,* each node usually maintains information on the traffic congestion at various spots. It exchanges this information with neighboring nodes and may estimate the time and distance for each possible path to a destination. When a packet arrives at a specific node, the optimum routing to the destination is determined, and the packet is whisked to the next node of that route.

Hybrid Switching

As indicated above, fast connect circuit switching is more efficient for long messages whereas packet switching is more economical for bursty data. Consequently, a new switching methodology which encompasses both fast con-

nect circuit switching and packet switching has emerged. This new method, hybrid switching is currently under extensive investigation. Hybrid switching technology assumes a digital environment and allows for dynamic sharing of a channel bandwidth between circuit switched and packet switched modes of operation. This new technology has many other advantages. It is likely that this type of switching will be a prospect for future integrated networks of both voice and data. This conjecture, however, disregards the preliminary results on the analysis of hybrid switching which has shown it to be less economical than packet switching.

37.4 COMMUNICATION NETWORKS

Telecommunication Services

In most countries, telecommunication service is provided by the national government. Telecommunication organizations are usually called Post Telegraph and Telephone (PTT) administrations. In the U.S., the telecommunication service is offered by private companies and regulated by the Federal Communication Commission. The FCC must approve private companies services and their tariff structures as well. The term *common carrier* usually refers to any organization, either governmental or private, that provides telephone, telegraph, Telex, or data communication services.

Public networks can only be built by common carriers. The telephone network is the oldest and widest public network existing today. Unlike the telephone network, public data networks are few in number and lack compatibility with one another. Moreover, most existing data networks rely, in major part, on the telephone network for user accessibility. However, a revolution in public data communication is imminent. The evolution of telecommunication networks towards an integrated (voice and data) services digital network (ISDN) is progressing throughout the world. AT&T has already established the Dataphone Digital Service (DDS) network, offering wideband communication up to 56,000 bps. It also has a plan to add the so-called public switched digital capability (PSDC) to the Bell System network in 1983. The PSDC will also provide almost ubiquitous 56,000 bps circuit switched digital communications.

Private networks may be owned by private corporations to connect their distributed devices. If the connection of these devices is to be set up over public properties, or private properties other than their own, only a common carrier can establish the connection. A private organization may then lease or rent these circuits from the common carrier.

Private corporate data networks are growing very rapidly. Multicorporate networks that can handle specific applications are less common. The problem of providing wide general applications for data communication for private or public networks mainly stems from the difficulties in getting organizations to agree on the rules that govern their networks. The need for standardization of these rules has become so essential for further progress that many international, as well as national, organizations have committed themselves to resolving these disagreements.

Organizations for Standardization

The CCITT is one of three main organizations within the International Telecommunication Union (ITU). In 1948, the ITU was organized under the auspices of the United Nations to coordinate international telecommunications service. The CCITT function is to formulate standards and to issue recommendations concerning telephone, telegraph, and data communication services. Its main members are the governing bodies of all nations. The FCC is the representative U.S. member. Recommendations issued by CCITT are usually put into practice worldwide. The X.25 is a CCITT recommendation that will be implemented in most, if not all, public data networks and many private ones. Recommendation X.25 specifies the interface between a DTE and the network.

Another international organization that issues standards for data communication is ISO. It has proposed the so-called Open Systems Interconnection (OSI) model for the international standardization of protocols. The ISO model is a seven layer protocol.

National organizations also provide standards, and approve or modify international recommendations according to their needs. In the U.S., the American National Standards Institute (ANSI), the National Bureau of Standards (NBS) and the Institute of Electrical and Electronic Engineers (IEEE), among others, provide guidelines to resolve differences. These guidelines are most useful particularly to the hardware and software manufacturers.

Examples of Private Computer Networks

The *SITA* (Société Internationale de Télécommunications Aëronatiques) *network* is a worldwide private message switching network that handles airlines traffic. This so-called high level network interlinks airline computers and terminals. The network nodes, also called *high level centers,* include the processing computers. These computers are connected to minicomputers or concentrators through which agents' terminals access the network. The high level centers are interconnected by 4800 voice grade lines. In 1975, the network consisted of 9 nodes and has been expanding since. Present plans shows an expansion up to 15 nodes (Figure 37.6).

The SITA network accepts two types of messages: conversational messages, which have the higher priority, and telegraphic messages. Type B messages are telegraphic and hence have lower priority. Messages are accepted from the airlines terminals and computers, processed by the high level network computers, and then passed to the airlines' computers and terminals. The average response time for a conversational message is about 3 seconds and for a telegraphic message in the order of several minutes. SITA is a cooperative corporation of 241 airline members that serves over 150 countries. It provides high level network service and develops the needed standards.

The *SWIFT* (Society for Worldwide International Finance Transactions) *network* is also a multicorporate message switching private network. It serves the banking industry in the electronic transfer of funds. Like SITA, the network interlinks computers and terminals of the participating banks. The backbone of the network consists of 2 switching centers and 13 concentrators interconnected by voice-grade lines. It can easily expand without redesign. At the switching centers, all transactions are stored for several days after their transmission. During this period, the information can be retrieved if desired.

SWIFT handles about a third of a million financial transactions daily, with an average response time for each transaction of less than a minute. Data security is a fundamental concern of this network, foolproof methods against fraud are continually sought. The network is managed by the SWIFT organization, a nonprofit organization that is owned by several hundred banks.

The *ARPA network* (Figure 37.7) is the first packet switching network ever built. It is the result of a project funded by the Department of Defense Administrative Research Project Agency. It was designed by many research organizations and universities across the U.S. It uses mostly 50,000 bps leased phone lines for transmission. The network nodes are called interface message processors (IMPs). They are connected in a mesh configuration to provide the backbone of the network (called the *subnet*) through which the connected computers *(hosts)* can communicate. An IMP connects one to four hosts.

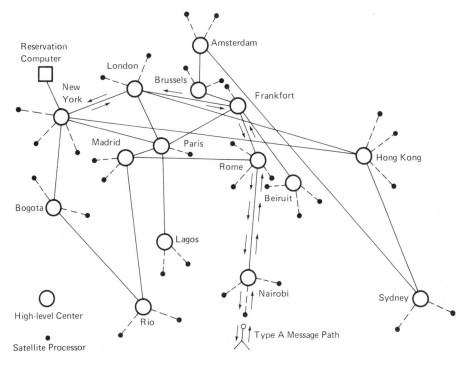

Figure 37.6. SITA high level network.

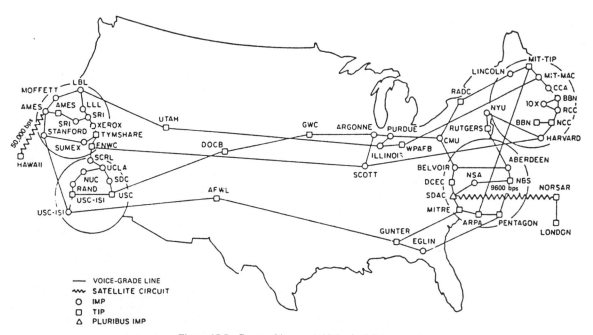

Figure 37.7. Geographic map (1976) of ARPA network.

Newly installed Pluribus IMPs can handle tens of hosts. Terminals can also be connected to the network without going through a host via a second type interface machine, called a terminal interface processor (TIP). A TIP includes a small host in its node. In 1981, the ARPA network contained 55 IMPs and 25 TIPs and served 100 hosts.

The ARPA network was designed to handle general applications. Different hosts provide different services. No data format is required. The experience gained in developing the ARPA network has been valuable in demonstrating the feasibility and the potential use of a wide data network. Most private networks are different from ARPA, the latter being a one time implementation for research purposes.*

Other private networks that are growing at a fast rate are the local area networks. A *local area network* connects computer devices that are located within a few kilometers of each other (typically in a factory or an office building, or on a university campus). Transmission in this type of network usually exceeds 1 million bits per second. Local area networks are essentially the backbone of distributed office systems. The main interest in these networks, however, is in allowing all computers and terminals in an area to communicate with wide area networks or with remote individual computers. Without local area networks, individual connection of each machine to a wide area network would be required.

The most common technology used in local area networks is the broadcast channel and the carrier sense multiple access (CSMA) protocol. The Xerox Ethernet is an example of the latter type. Many other organizations have developed their own local networks. Examples include the Aloha system of the University of Hawaii, the MITERNET of Mitre Corporation, Datakit of Bell Laboratories, and ARC of Datapoint.

Some Public Data Networks

Telenet, owned by GT&E, is the first public packet switching network to be established in the U.S. Telenet's techniques are based on the ARPA network. It offers mainly time sharing services. TYMNET and DATRAN are other examples of public data networks. TYMNET has evolved from a private network. It is very similar to Telenet and provides its customers with data base services. Currently, TYMNET can be accessed from 270 U.S. cities and 34 foreign countries. DATRAN was a

fast connect circuit switching network which used microwave links for transmission. It had three level hierarchy and time division multiplexing. DATRAN was viewed with great expectation during its debut, in 1971. In 1976, however, it ceased operations owing to financial difficulties.

During the 1970s, computer manufacturers were complaining bitterly to the FCC about the shortcomings of the common carriers in providing adequate transmission facilities to connect their products. AT&T, the largest common carrier, was then investigating the idea of a public data network. In 1976, AT&T engaged its researchers in designing what is referred to as the Bell Data Network (BDN). Three years later, the idea was scrapped. In 1980, Advanced Communication Service (ACS) was under investigation once more. At the time of this writing, ACS has changed its name to AIS (Advanced Information System)/NET One. The network is now owned by American Bell, Inc., a nonregulated subsidiary of AT&T.

AIS/NET One will allow most of the computers and terminals in the U.S. to communicate with each other. It emulates the existing terminals and can act as an interface between incompatible machines. It will be able to link with a broad range of other networks and carrier services. Many services including electronic mail will be offered. Processing power and storage capabilities at the nodes will also be provided to its customers. Many new services and ideas are expected to emerge later.

The network uses X.25 packet switching standards. It is built over the existing DDS lines and has a two level hierarchy. The first level constitutes the nodes that house IBM Series/I computers; the second level is called the Packet Transport Network (PTN). Its nodes, called tandems, are equipped with Western Electric 3B20 processors. The tandems will perform the toll function for the system.

By the end of 1984, there will be 100 nodes installed in major cities of the U.S. Customers within a service area will use 56,000 digital transmission access lines; customers outside the service area can use their telephone lines to access the nearest node. Leased wideband lines also will be available for customers with a large number of users located outside the service area. These lines will be connected between customer premises and the closest network node.

37.5 NETWORK ARCHITECTURE

It was only in the 1960s that the idea of accessing a computer from outside the computer room was introduced.

---

*For greater security, in late 1983 this network was subdivided into R&DNET (civilian) and MILNET (military).

Computer networks then were simple star configurations that connected a central computer to a number of terminals at remote locations. Simple access methods were defined and implemented in the computer software to perform the function of moving data over communication lines. An example of this early software is IBM's Basic Telecommunication Access Method (BTAM) used with the 360 computer. As the network grew, data transmission functions of greater complexity were required. Consequently, more elaborate generalized software packages were designed and the task of communication processing became a significant burden on the machines whose prime functions were data processing.

Meanwhile, processing capabilities became available in other parts of the network. Intelligent terminals, cluster controllers, concentrators, and front end computers were used to handle communication processing. Some communication functions also were implemented through hardwired logic. Network complexities led to the idea of a *layered protocol,* by which the communication task is divided into separate functions independent of one another.

A **protocol** is a set of rules that defines some function, such as making a connection, transmitting a message or transferring a file, to solve a specific problem. The layered functions are designed one on top of the other, whereby each layer offers certain services to the higher layers. A layer requesting service supplies this information by adding a header, and sometimes a trailer, to the information accepted from a higher layer, before passing it across the interface presented by the next lower layer (Figure 37.8). As the network grows, more functions would be introduced and the layers grow. With this concept in place, a change in the function or an addition of a new function due to network evolution would not require the redesign of software or hardware, other than those parts involved with the change. The layered protocol concept also makes the transmission task and the complexities of the network transparent to the user.

Most computer manufacturers have devised their own sets of protocols, called *network architecture,* to provide their customers with tools to construct private networks. Different manufacturers use different architectures each with different numbers, functions, and names for the layers. In an effort towards standardization, the ISO developed its *OSI reference model.*

The Open Systems Interconnection (OSI) Reference Model

This model from ISO has seven layers which are called, from the lowest to the highest: physical, data link control, network, transport, session, presentation, and application.

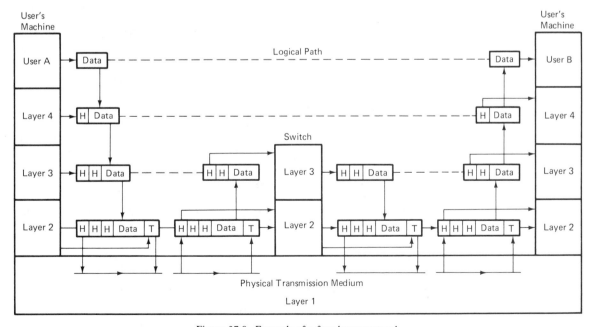

Figure 37.8. Example of a four layer protocol.

1. The *physical layer* is at the hardware level. It is concerned with the physical transmission of bit streams over the communication links. It deals with the function of converting the actual bits of 0s and 1s into a form acceptable to the transmission line. For example, if transmission is to be in analog form, the protocol assigns a modem.

2. The *data link control layer* is concerned with sending a block of data from one end of a data link to the other correctly. It performs functions such as framing the data, detecting transmission errors, processing acknowledgements for delivered frames, and retransmitting corrupt or lost frames. The protocol is specified by a procedure called HDLC (high level data link control). CCITT's X.25 and IBM's SDLC are versions of the HDLC.

   The HDLC frame (Figure 37.9) consists of two flag bytes that mark the beginning and the end of a frame, an address byte (for the next hop), a control byte that indicates the frame function or type, an arbitrary number of bits of information up to a specified limit, and two bytes for error checking. The cyclic redundancy check (CRC) code is used for checking errors in the address, control, and information fields of the frame. The error checking bytes contain the parity bits for this checking.

3. The *network layer's* function is to establish and terminate calls. It accepts messages from the source, slices them into packets, and determines the packet's routes through the network towards their destinations. It creates the so-called virtual circuits. A *virtual circuit* is a permanent logical connection through the network for delivering all packets making up a message to the same destination. The network layer also controls the traffic flow and processes billing information.

4. The *transport layer* is concerned with end to end flow of data from source to destination. Its function is to prevent the loss or double processing of messages. It regulates the flow of information between users' machines.

5. The *session layer* is the actual user's interface into the network. It initiates, manages, and terminates a session. It also regulates the dialog between machines and sets priorities on who is to transmit next.

6. The *presentation layer* may perform various types of services that are frequently requested by users. Such services include data editing, formating, and displaying. Other functions that may also be implemented in this layer are encryption, decryption, and data compression.

7. The *application layer* is concerned with functions such as remote job entry, file transfer, and distributed data base activities.

Layers 1, 2 and 3 are fundamental to all networks. The higher layers, however, are not distinctly defined in many architectural designs. In the following subsections, we discuss two specific manufacturers' protocols, IBM's SNA and DEC's DECNET. We also discuss CCITT's X.25, which has been, and will be, implemented in all future public networks.

System Network Architecture (SNA)

Over the years, IBM did not anticipate the need to link its products of various generations and various topologies together. In 1970, when such a need arose, IBM designed the SNA. SNA services and functions have been evolving over the years.

The nodes of an SNA network comprise four types of devices: terminals, controllers, front end computers, and host computers. Each network node must contain a NAU (Network Addressable Unit), which is a software procedure that allows a node to use the network.

The SNA protocol, as mapped into the ISO layers, includes the following: physical, data link control, path control, transmission control (also called *session*), data flow control, NAU services, and end user.

The data link control procedure is called the Synchronous Data Link Protocol (SDLC). The data flow control layer does not control the flow of data as its name suggests. Its function is to assign priorities for users' dialog. It is also concerned with error recovery problems.

DECNET

DECNET is the Digital Equipment Corporation network. Its architecture was designed to allow customers to

Figure 37.9. Frame format for HDLC.

interconnect DEC's minicomputers. The network is a collection of these computers whereby a given computer may offer data processing or communication processing, or both. DECNET has also evolved over time. Its architecture can be described in five layers: physical, data link, layer called DDCMP (Digital Data Communications Management Protocol), transport, network service protocol (NSP), and the dialog.

Unlike HDLC, DDCMP frames contain a character count in its header which specifies the length of the frame. A transmission error that corrupts the header byte may cause DDCMP's protocol to lose track of the frame boundaries. DECNET's NSP provides a datagram service, whereby messages are limited to a maximum length. A datagram message consists of one packet only. The protocol addresses each packet individually and routes it to its destination independently of all other packets. Delivered packets are usually out of sequence, a situation that causes users many problems.

DECNET has no session layer. Its dialog layer is a mixture of the ISO presentation and application layers.

In general, manufacturers' architectures are usually complex and cumbersome. This to be is expected, however, because the designer is constrained to link existing products that are, in major part, incompatible. Standard organizations' protocols are independent of products and, hence, can provide cleaner and clearer definitions of functions and services.

CCITT's X.25

X.25 defines the interface between a DTE and a DCE (Data Circuit-Terminating Equipment) for packet switched networks. A DCE is a piece of equipment that converts the signal generated by the DTE into a form which can be transmitted over a communication line.

The X.25 interface consists only of three layers, called *levels*. These levels are the physical interface, the link access procedure (LAP and later LAPB), and the packet level. They correspond to ISO layers 1, 2 and 3, respectively.

The physical interface is specified as CCITT Recommendation X.21. It provides a common interface for accessing both packet and circuit switched networks. It requires digital and not analog signaling on the lines. Digital transmissions, however, are not widely available today, which makes it difficult for organizations to support this standard. CCITT provided the RS-232C for the analog interface in the interim. Also, X.25 requires a buffered terminal whereas most existing terminals are the simple unbuffered type. For this, the CCITT specified an interface, called the Packet Assembler Disassembler (PAD), to allow a simple terminal to connect to an X.25 network.

Level 2 LAP is similar to ISO HDLC. It uses the latter's terminology and some of the specified options.

REFERENCES

Atkins, J. "Path Control: the Transport Network of SNA," *IEEE Transactions Communications*, Vol. COM-28, Apr. 1980, pp. 527–38.

Balkovic, M. D., Klancer, H. W., Klare, S. W. and McGruther, W. C., "High Speed Voiceband Data Transmission Performance of the Switched Telecommunications Network," *Bell Systems Technical Journal*, Vol. 50, Apr. 1971, pp. 1349–84.

CCITT Fifth Plenary Assembly, *The CCITT Green Book*, Vol. VII. Geneva: Telegraph Technique, International Telecommunications Union, 1973.

Chretien, G. J., W. M. Konig and J. H. Rech, "The SITA Network, Summary and Description," Computer-Communication Networks Conference, University of Sussex, Brighton, U.K.: Sept. 1973.

Chu. W. W., *Advances in Computer Communications and Networking*. Dedham, Ma.: Artech House, 1979.

Davies, D. W., D. L. A. Barber, W. L. Price and C. M. Solomonides, "Computer Networks and Their Protocols," *IEEE Transactions on Communications*, Vol. COM-28, Apr. 1980, pp. 585–93.

Doll, D. R., *Data Communications*. New York: John Wiley & Sons, 1978.

Donnelley, J. E., "Components of a Network Operating System," *Computer Networks*, Vol. 3, Dec. 1979, pp. 389–99.

Folts, H. C., "Procedures for Circuit-Switched Service in Synchronous Public Data Networks," *IEEE Transactions on Communications* Vol. COM-28, Apr. 1980, pp. 489–96.

Green, P. E., "An Introduction to Network Architectures and Protocols," *IEEE Transactions on Communications*, Vol. COM-28, Apr. 1980, pp. 413–24.

Hoberecht, V. L., "SNA Function Management," *IEEE Transactions on Communications*, Vol. COM-28, Apr. 1980, pp. 594–603.

Martin, J., *Telecommunications and the Computer*. Englewood Cliffs, NJ: Prentice-Hall, 1977.

Martin, J., *Computer Networks and Distributed Processing*. Englewood Cliffs, NJ: Prentice-Hall, 1981.

McQuillan, J., and D. C. Walden, "The ARPA Network Design Decision," *Computer Networks*, Vol. 1, Aug. 1977, pp. 243–89.

Metcalfe, R. M., and D. R. Boggs, "Ethernet: Distributed Packet Switching for Local Computer Networks," *Communications of the ACM*, Vol. 19, July 1976, pp. 395–404.

Pierce, J. R., *Signals: The Telephone and Beyond*. San Francisco: W. H. Freeman, 1981.

Schwartz, M., *Computer-Communication Network Design and Analysis*. Englewood Cliffs, NJ. Prentice-Hall, 1977.

Shannon, C., "A Mathematical Theory of Communication," *Bell Systems Technical Journal,* Vol. 27, July 1948, pp. 379–423 and Oct. 1948, pp. 623–56.

Sinnema, W., *Digital, Analog and Data Communication*. Reston VA: Reston Publishing Co., 1982.

Sloman, M. S., "X.25 Explained," *Computer Communications,* Vol. 1, Dec. 1978.

Tanenbaum, A. S., *Computer Networks*. Englewood Cliffs, NJ: Prentice-Hall, 1981.

Wecker, S., "DNA: the Digital Network Architecture," *IEEE Transactions on Communications,* Vol. COM-28, Apr. 1980, pp. 510–526.

Zimmerman, H., "OSI Reference Model—The ISO Model of Architecture for Open Systems Interconnection," *IEEE Transactions on Communication,* Vol. COM-28, Apr. 1980, pp. 425–32.

38
Teleprocessing Networks

Howard Frank

Contel Information Systems, Inc.

38.1 INTRODUCTION

The trend towards network communications began in the mid 1960s when users started to realize that it was more productive to use computer resources over long distance lines. Unfortunately, while these primitive networks improved the use of computer resources, they did not provide for comparable efficiencies in the use of communications facilities. Costs began to increase rapidly and planners began to search for means to increase network efficiency.

One method that came out of this search was sharing the cost of a single communications line among several terminals. This was practical because the average amount of data sent from a typical low speed terminal is much smaller than the capacity of the line needed to accommodate its peak requirement. However, to share lines effectively, **protocols** had to be constructed to resolve the contention problems that arose when several terminals simultaneously attempted to gain access to the host processor. This increased the complexity of both the planning process and the central processor software. Another result was incompatibility among the various approaches chosen by different terminal and mainframe vendors since their protocols were usually developed ad hoc, with no attempt made at consistency within the industry. In some cases, the situation was so bad that a manufacturer like IBM found itself with terminals developed for one application on a CPU unable to communicate with terminals developed for another application on the same CPU. Protocol incompatibility also blocked different types of terminals from sharing lines, thus reducing opportunities for lowering communications costs.

To redress some of these problems, the **front end processor** was developed. Primarily because of low cost minicomputer technology, this type of device has become a frequently encountered element of the modern teleprocessing network. Its role is to reduce processing overhead in the main CPU by absorbing some of the network control functions, to simplify development and modification to mainframe software, and often to accommodate specialized application processing better done outside the CPU. Some manufacturers have also begun to address the protocol incompatibility problem in the front end by incorporating protocol translation elements. Others, like IBM, have attempted to solve this problem by creating a standard set of protocols and counting on systems evolution over the course of time to standardize access methods for their systems.

Additional network developments resulted in the introduction of **multiplexers** and **concentrators** as a means of cutting communications costs. These devices lower the cost of transmitting data by taking advantage of economies of scale available from the carriers providing communications lines. They permit many low activity terminals to share a much smaller number of long haul communications lines, thus utilizing the lines' transmission capacity with greater efficiency. These devices achieve still further economies of scale when standard communications lines and low activity terminals are combined with high speed modems to lower the average cost per bit of transmitted information.

The present structure of a terminal oriented network (see Figure 38.1) often contains several levels of concentration, which can range from simple multidrop polling to complex multiplexing schemes. Such networks contribute to lower cost because, in most cases, one pays for communications capacity whether it is used or not; tariffs and technology thus offer economies of scale but compel structuring of networks in complex arrangements to achieve these economies.

Today's data communications system is likely to comprise a wide range of devices including terminals (dumb, smart, or intelligent), interfaces, modems, multiplexers (static, dynamic), concentrators, front ends, message processors, and computers (mini-, micro-, mono-, or multi-). Typical devices can be placed into categories as follows:

1. Bandwidth sharing.
   • Multiplexers/lineplexers.
   • Concentrators.
   • MSU/PSU.
   • PBX.
   • Software multiplexing (polling).
2. Distribution of information processing.
   • Front end processors.
   • Message switches.
   • Concentrators.
   • Line controllers.

3. Switching.
   • Circuit or line switches: trunk switch, PBX.
   • Store-and-forward switches: message, packet.
4. Interface.
   • Modems.
   • Terminal/equipment interfaces (DAAs).
5. Testing/diagnostics.
   • Communications quality.
   • Network control.

A decade or so ago, most of the concepts embodied by these devices existed, but few practical, cost-effective components had been built. Major developments include the emergence of low cost statistical (dynamic) multiplexing/concentrating devices, off-loading from hosts of communications functions into special purpose mini- and microprocessors, and the development of network control and diagnostic systems. Accompanying the emergence of network devices were new architectures which allow users to incorporate these devices into a network system with high cost-efficiency.

38.2 PACKET SWITCHING: FROM CONCEPT TO WORLDWIDE ACCEPTANCE

As access to computers and remote data bases became widespread, the need for communicating between com-

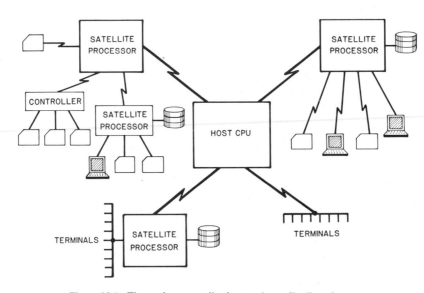

Figure 38.1. The modem centralized network—a distributed system.

puters arose. The first such communication schemes involved the physical transport of a tape from one computer location to another. Conceptually similar, but somewhat faster, means for transferring files involves the use of message-switched systems to connect low speed CPU ports (typically teletype grade) through an on-line computer called a *message switch.*

Most users are familiar with the classical "centralized" teleprocessing system which originally consisted of a processor connected by leased or dial-up lines to terminals. During the past decade, this structure evolved to include front end processors, multiplexers, concentrators, remote satellite processing units, control units, and terminals (possibly intelligent), as illustrated in Figure 38. 1. Such a network, while still generally classified as a centralized system is, in reality, a "distributed" system. However, today the word "distributed," when used in the context of networking, generally evokes the term "packet switching."

Packet switching combines several innovative approaches for handling data with current minicomputer technology to provide significant enhancements to computer networking. Packet switching operates by allowing the breakup of messages into segments called *packets,* attaching headers to the packets, and guiding them along multiple independent paths from origin to destination without centralized control. At the destination point, the packets are reassembled into the original message. This process is virtually transparent to the user.

Packet switching is almost entirely a development of the 1970s. Pioneered by the Advanced Research Projects Agency of the Department of Defense (ARPA), the ARPANET began life in 1969 on the West Coast as a four node network. By 1975, ARPANET interconnected over 100 computers of diverse manufacturers through a network of more than 50 minicomputer-based packet switches. Today, packet switched networks are providing data communications in the U.S., Canada, France, England, and Spain. Moreover, numerous networks are being planned as public or private offerings.

To understand why packet switching is superior in many respects to its **message switching** (store-and-forward) ancestor, it is useful to see how the constraints which shaped message switching have changed in the last few years.

A communications network can be envisioned as a system of channels and nodes. **Nodes** are terminals or relay points, and **channels** are the communications links connecting the nodes. Control procedures for communications networks can be divided into two general classes. *Message control procedures* are those that ensure the proper movement of messages from originator to addressee (between terminal nodes) through the network. *Channel control procedures* are those that ensure the proper movement of messages over a particular channel, which is only one component of the network.

The primary medium for modern long distance communications channels was originally high frequency radio. The primary terminal was an electromechanical teletypewriter device. The channel was characterized by a limited data rate and a high error rate. The terminal had almost no logical capability and was limited to printing, as best it could, whatever data came over the channel. Messages and channel procedures were exclusively oriented towards visual interpretation by a human operator.

The availability of high speed channels, digital logic and advances in adaptive routing techniques have led to new classes of store-and-forward networks with a new message control philosophy. In packet networks, message delivery from originator to addressee occurs in a few seconds instead of hours or days. This quality, among others, makes feasible a superior concept of message control characterized by end-to-end positive acknowledgment, whereby a node receiving a message sends an acknowledgment back to the originator. Intermediate relay nodes are relieved of elaborate accounting and storage requirements for transmitting messages because the end-to-end or addressee-to-originator acknowledgment philosophy is an encompassing and protective message control scheme. It minimizes the role of intermediate relay nodes to that of routing and participation in channel control.

The error control scheme on each channel is so powerful that the possibility of an undetected error is once in several years. Channel control and coordination are sufficiently sophisticated so that there is essentially no lost data. Storage at intermediate nodes is necessary only to provide buffering for short term queueing efforts.

End-to-end message control philosophy means that the storage of messages for retransmission is necessary only at the originating terminal. Storage at intermediate nodes is necessary only to provide buffering for short term queueing conditions.

Each nodal switch in the packet switching network performs all network communications functions for its hosts, and is responsible for routing, monitoring the alive/dead status of its communications links and neighboring packet switches, controlling errors, preventing traffic

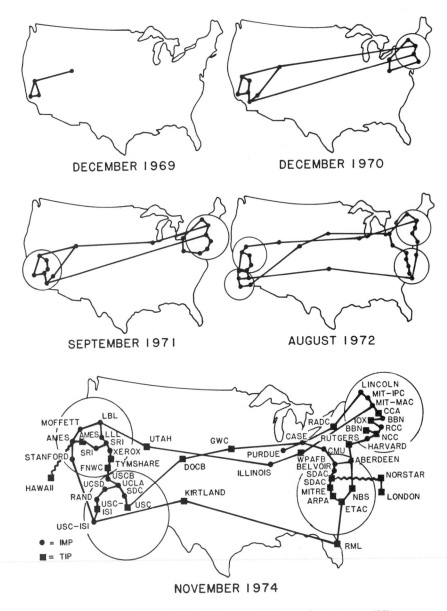

Figure 38.2. Evolution of the ARPA network (also see footnote on p. 628).

congestion and monitoring time delays. Thus the switch functions as a local network manager, deriving its information from the network and deducing the status of other elements within the system.

Because local network management functions are so naturally performed by the network itself, the environment is provided for extremely effective "global" network management. This function is implemented through a Network Control Center (NCC), which is vital to the operation of a reliable network.

The NCC appears to the network as another host. This host automatically collects, on a nearly instantaneous

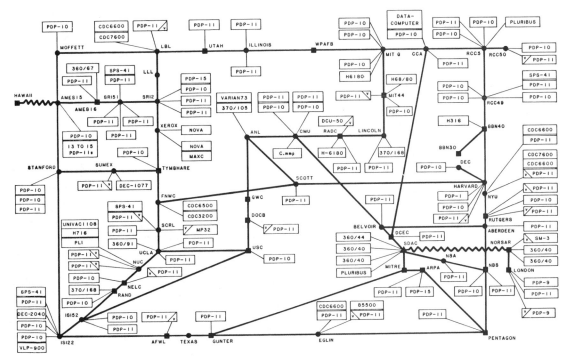

Figure 38.3. ARPA network, logical map, November 1974.

basis, status reports generated by each switch. It is thus able to alert operators rapidly when switches or communications lines fail, or when line errors or other fault conditions appear. The NCC thus helps to minimize the time required to identify and initiate corrective actions and to maximize system reliability and availability. This characteristic of rapid access to vital health and performance data is substantially different from most present networks, in which it is usually extremely difficult to monitor performance and to isolate trouble spots. The use of a NCC in the packet switched network is a management tool superior to that seen in other implemented communications network approaches.

Reliability characteristics of a distributed packet switched network are totally different from those of other available network technologies. Because of adaptive routing capability, the distributed network's performance is not critically dependent on the perfect operation of each element. For example, after a link failure, the network is able to redefine network routes rapidly to adjust for the failure.

Typically, the distributed network design provides several alternate paths for network communications between important points. This allows the network designer to judiciously and economically add links so that the only limitation imposed on network reliability derives from the host and switches. In addition, arbitrarily high network reliability can be easily achieved by using redundant switches and ordinary communications lines.

An important characteristic of a packet network is that its many computers communicate through common network languages and protocols. For example, the network nodes contain a virtual terminal protocol with which a variety of different terminals can find a common base for communications. The switches within the system allow the conversion of the local terminal language to the network virtual language and, at the destination, conversion into the language of the supporting computer. Another major characteristic of packet switched networks is the ability to achieve high utilization of the communications lines via the natural multiplexing ability of packet switches which, in this mode, perform much the same function as a concentrator. These two features, along with packet switching's potential to achieve reliability superior to more classical approaches, are largely responsible for the rapid commercial acceptance of the technology over the past few years.

38.3 THE RISE OF THE VENDOR ARCHITECTURES

During the early 1970s, the large majority of data communications systems were built by the mainframe computer vendors. These networks were generally developed to support application packages running on the vendors' hosts. Obviously, data communications software systems developed by different manufacturers were bound to be incompatible. However, even the software systems developed to support different applications of the same manufacturer were generally incompatible with one another. The result, throughout the industry, was multiple networks of incompatible terminals often connected to the same host and terminal locations. IBM was the first vendor to respond to this problem by announcing in 1974 its Systems Network Architecture (SNA).

Before the introduction of SNA, IBM had more than 200 communications products requiring 35 teleprocessing access methods and 15 different data link control procedures. The goal of SNA was to provide a unified approach to IBM networking by introducing a single standard host access method and link control procedure. The use of these standards would achieve terminal compatibility at the communications line level as well as independence between network devices (e.g., terminals) and host applications. This represented a major step forward: IBM's recognition of networks as a vital element of future computing systems. SNA, as originally proposed and implemented, was a sophisticated architecture, designed primarily for centralized teleprocessing. Since late 1976, SNA announcements have extended the implementation of the architecture to operate in a multihost environment by incorporating in the access method at the host and front end an "Advanced Communication Function" (ACF), and in increasing system networking capabilities.

The advantages of SNA derive primarily from a consistent, unified architecture in place of the ad hoc procedures of the past. Full duplex terminals (based on IBM's Synchronous Data Link Control protocol) allows more efficient utilization of communication lines, yielding fewer lines and lower line costs. Independence of applications and network hardware, including terminals, permits different applications to use the same terminals, reducing the number of terminals needed to perform a set of functions. Furthermore, a somewhat reduced load on the main CPU can be achieved through off-loading to front end processors, controllers and intelligent terminals.

The original disadvantages of SNA related primarily to three factors: the cost of increased memory and processing at the host, the cost of upgrading from more primitive terminals, and the conversion cost incurred by moving to a full SNA implementation. Moreover, IBM began its marketing of SNA by trying to convince its users to adopt SNA on a full scale basis, rather than through an evolutionary approach which would allow both SNA and nonSNA systems to coexist. Development, however, over the last few years have reduced these disadvantages considerably.

First, IBM has backed away from its original "revolutionary" approach by departing from its original intent to support only SDLC terminals in SNA Systems and by extending the range of access methods supported under SNA. Both binary synchronous and start/stop terminals are now accommodated, and it has become considerably easier to chart migration paths to SNA. (Additionally, the costs of new SDLC terminals from IBM are usually comparable to older bisync models.) Second, the recent major reductions in the cost of memory and CPU hardware have helped reduce the penalty of SNA's greater memory and processing requirements.

Additional problems and issues associated with SNA have related to the strong influence and control of the network by the host rather than by a front end or a general purpose communications processor. This latter architecture makes it impossible to effect direct terminal-to-terminal communications without passing through an intermediate host. Other problems which stemmed from the strong host involvement were the complex network definition procedure required when the original system software was generated, the operational difficulty of implementing changes to network structures and software, and the difficulty of using SNA in a multiple host environment. This last problem impacts reliability since recent implementations of SNA did not have automatic alternate routing capabilities; it also inhibited the use of resources across software-defined host "domains". SNA releases beginning in 1980 and 1981 addressed many of these problems and are introducing significant improvements. Thus, the SNA of the 1970s can be viewed as IBM's first step to develop a viable networking approach for the 1980s.

Since the introduction of SNA, many other vendors, including DEC, Burroughs, Univac, Comten, CCI, Raytheon, Prime, and Data General have introduced their own network architectures. Some of these, such as DEC's

DECNET, have already achieved considerable maturity. Others were only announced within the last few years and are just beginning to be implemented. Thus, the last decade can be considered as the period when vendors recognized the problems implied by large scale data communications systems and began the activities required to address them. The fruits of these activities are yet to be fully realized.

38.4 RANDOM ACCESS COMMON CHANNEL SYSTEMS

During the past decade, a sequence of experimental systems have been built to allow many users to share the resources of single broadband channels. For example, the Aloha System was built at the University of Hawaii as an experiment in radio communications via packet switching. It consists of standard data terminals with radio front ends communicating with a central station connected into a satellite ground station and also into ARPANET. Aloha forms the basis of a new technology being applied to both terrestrial and satellite radio data communications: **random access multiplexing.**

In a random access multiplexing scheme, the medium itself is the multiplexer. In its most straightforward implementation, random access is analogous to the situation in which several nearby people speak simultaneously. When conflicts occur, a natural protocol causes a subset of these people to retransmit at a later time. This scheme is similar to that which occurs when several terminals are connected to the same port on a front end or computer without using a multidrop polling discipline. If simultaneous transmissions occur, all become distorted and retransmissions are required.

In a random access multiplexing scheme, simultaneous transmissions are detected by means of requiring a positive acknowledgment for every correctly received packet of data. If packets collide, they are incorrectly received, and no acknowledgments are generated. Thus, the senders must retransmit at later times. If the retransmission schemes are properly handled, it appears from a number of analyses and tests that very high utilization of the channel is possible. The most sophisticated of the random access schemes can yield data throughput of 90 percent or more of the channel capacity. Compared with the utilization of channels under conventional transmission protocols, major improvements in cost and performance are possible.

Random access techniques are currently being studied for both extensive ground and satellite broadcast systems.

One experiment now underway is investigating random access transmission on satellites connecting users in the U.S. and Europe. This experiment is evaluating the validity and efficiency of a variety of different access and retransmission schemes and will, if successful, provide a major input for new satellite and ground station developments.

Another system currently under development by ARPA utilizes random access transmission for mobile ground terminals. Called the Packet Radio System (PRS), it is aimed at providing efficient local access for mobile terminals, terminals in remote or environmentally hostile locations where cables are not feasible, terminals with high ratios of peak-to-average bandwidth requirements and terminals which require small bandwidth so that hardwired connections are uneconomical.

Contel studies have shown that packet radio provides a viable and cost-effective communications technique for local distribution in conventional urban or suburban environments. One reason for PRS efficiency is that only the "active" terminals with information to send or receive impose overhead on the system.

This property is not true for most conventional communications schemes. For example, all terminals on multidropped lines must be polled periodically, whether or not they are active. Thus, a single broadcast channel in a PRS can accommodate many more terminals than an equivalent channel which uses polling. Interestingly, random access techniques are suitable for conventional leased line systems, providing a superior channel protocol for many typical applications. Similar concepts have recently been employed to address the problem of intrafacility communications. Here, the capacity of a single broadband coaxial cable (or optical fiber) is shared among local computers or terminals. Several such systems (e.g., Xerox's Ethernet) have been built and are now in operation.

38.5 NETWORK PROTOCOLS AND STANDARDS

The 1970s saw major advances in the recognition of network protocols as a major area impacting data network performance, compatibility and flexibility, and as an important topic for study and standardization. Over the last few years, various groups have addressed the problem of developing standard levels of protocols and protocol standards within each level. For example, committees working under the auspices of the American National Standards Institute (ANSI) and the International Organization for Standardization (ISO) have defined a working reference model which incorporates seven distinct levels of protocol as illustrated in Table 38.1.

Of interest is that most network architectures conform to concepts similar to those embodied in the Reference Model. However, little agreement among vendors occurs above Levels 2 or 3. For instance, the X.25 standard has been widely adopted for packet switching systems, but this standard addresses only the first three levels. Furthermore, there are today at least six incompatible implementations of X.25. Thus, while standards emerged during the last decade, much work is needed before one even remotely resembling a universal standard is possible.

Table 38.1 ANSI / ISO Protocol Reference Model

Physical Layer (Level 1)

Provides mechanical, electrical, functional and procedural characteristics to establish, maintain and release data-circuits between link-entities.

Link Layer (Level 2)

Provides functional and procedural means to establish, maintain and release one or more data-links between two or more network entities.

Network Layer (Level 3)

Provides functional and procedural means to exchange data between two transport entities, independent of routing and switching considerations.

Transport Layer (Level 4)

Provides reliable, cost-effective, transparent, location-independent transfer of data between session processing entities.

Session Layer (Level 5)

Supports dialog ("session") between cooperating application entities.

Presentation Layer (Level 6)

Provides services to allow application processes to interpret the data exchanged, by managing the entry, exchange, storage, retrieval, display and control of structured data.

Applications Layer (Level 7)

Provides distributed information service for end user, application management or system management.

38.6 THE VALUE ADDED NETWORKS AND NEW CARRIER SERVICES

One of the most exciting developments of the past few years has been the emergence of the Value Added Network (VAN). A VAN can be distinguished from a classical common carrier because it does not build transmission facilities. Instead, it leases conventional common carrier facilities and combines them with specialized message processing services which add "value" to the network.

VANs currently operating within the United States include GTE's Telenet, Tymshare's Tymnet, and ITT's FAXPAK. Both Telenet and Tymnet provide data communications service while FAXPAK currently serves facsimile terminals. ITT's plans include extension of FAXPAK services to data communications.

Until recently, users thought of networks as transparent channels that simply accommodated bit streams from origin to destination, with all special features incorporated at the endpoints of the network. Thus, if the user wished to add an error correction scheme to protect data, it was built into the processors or front ends.

Similarly, a code conversion scheme would be built into the sources and destinations. By using minicomputer switches, a VAN introduces this service into the switching nodes so that the network is no longer a transparent device.

The VAN gives the user a ready-made backbone network (a resource which might be too expensive to be developed independently by the small user). Thus the user's network problem then becomes one of achieving access to the VAN through the appropriate interfaces and his or her own local distribution network.

Distribution of VAN access locations relative to the user's locations determines the size and cost of the local distribution networks; if the VAN has many access locations, the local network may be quite limited. Thus, a VAN's attractiveness varies with its growth in geographical coverage, even though its tariffs do not change.

Today's VANs offer access ports in over 150 cities within the United States. Currently, most data service is for low speed asynchronous terminal (up to 1200 bps). However, synchronous service on a limited basis is now available and, within the next few years, could be widespread. Still, today's VAN represents only a minimum resource compared with the data communications utility which will be required by tomorrow's user.

Another important recent development is the emergence of domestic satellite carriers which, because of technological economics, can offer attractive tariffs, especially for higher volume users. Using current satellite technology, ground stations tend to be somewhat expensive and are usually supplied by the satellite carrier on a shared basis; this serves to limit their role in the local access area. On the other hand, satellites can substantially reduce the cost of backbone communications given sufficient data requirements. In particular, the cost of high data-rate satellite channels is substantially lower than their terrestrial equivalents.

38.7 THE NETWORK OF THE FUTURE

Technology which is now emerging will allow many organizations to implement integrated systems to carry numerous types of traffic. For a large organization, there are significant advantages in integrating voice, message, data and facsimile requirements:

- Voice circuits currently not utilized after business hours will be available for data, message and facsimile traffic during off hours.
- If separate requirements for voice, message and data are combined, the total number of circuits needed can be reduced without degrading service quality.
- The individual requirements of voice, message and data at a given site may not justify a leased circuit but the combined requirements might, thus introducing economies of scale.
- An integrated network will facilitate the use of new digital communication transmission service offerings when these become generally available.

Because of the radical reduction in cost of digital logic, it is now relatively inexpensive to convert voice and facsimile to digital signals and to perform sophisticated digital switching. This, coupled with the facts that digital transmission has more resistance to noise than analog transmission and that switching, compression, encryption and other "added value" services can be more easily implemented digitally, results in a strong motivation for combining all modes of communication onto digital channels.

Sophisticated digital switches are being developed which will be able to switch voice, data, message, and facsimile traffic in any combination. While the specific characteristics of future networks containing these switches are now unknown, a pattern has emerged which allows us to predict the architecture of the future integrated network. This architecture is illustrated in Figure 38.4.

The future integrated network will have a primary digital backbone connecting a set of either public (owned by a carrier) or private (owned by the user) switching nodes. Initially, these switching nodes will be based on circuit switching technology. They will be replaced later by hybrid switches combining the best elements of circuit switching with packet switching. Ultimately, the switching nodes may become pure packet switches serving both voice and data. The nodes will be connected together via common carrier digital lines, either terrestrial or satellite. If via satellite, there may be additional transmission facilities from the site of each switch to the satellite ground station.

Connected to the switching nodes will be local access trunk lines emanating from computerized telephone branch exchanges (CBXs) located on customer premises. For a long time, many trunks will remain analog if routed on terrestrial facilities. Eventually, the link between the CBX and switch might become a radio channel, but this migration will depend on the cost of radios and ground stations, and the tariffs for terrestrial circuits.

Technological innovation during the past decade has focused on the long haul backbone networks for which

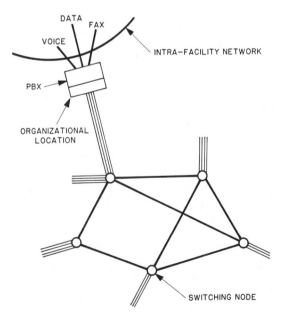

Figure 38.4. The future integrated network.

equipment manufacturers and carriers have provided numerous cost-effective options. Future efforts, however, will center on the local access area, with the CBX as the focus of attention. The future CBX will be the interface between growing intrafacility networks and the outside world. In addition to its most advanced current features and elements, it will contain banks of voice digitizers and dynamic multiplexers and will also be able to interface directly with remote CBXs, packet switches and a variety of other network controllers.

The integrated network of the future is technically feasible now, and many of its necessary components exist as "off the shelf" devices. Within the next five years, the costs of these components will most probably have become low enough to allow large organizations to begin cost-effective implementation. Since the need to transmit combinations of voice, data, message and facsimile requirements is characteristic of the modern organization, strategic planning for these networks will soon become a major area of attention. None of the existing network im-plementations are fully suited for use within integrated networks, and substantial efforts will be needed to incorporate the emerging requirements for electronic mail, facsimile and what has come to be called the "office of the future." Provided that substantial user feedback is maintained, it is likely that these efforts will be made, and will prove successful.

REFERENCES

Frank, H, "What to Do While Waiting for Utopia," *Datamation,* Nov. 25, 1979, pp. 40–44.

Frank, H., "Plan Today for Tomorrow's Data/Voice Nets," *Data Communications,* Sept. 1978, pp. 51–62.

Roberts, L. G., "Packet Switching Economics," *Journal of Telecommunication Networks,* Vol. 1, No. 3 (Fall 1982) pp. 213–218.

Martin, J. *Future Developments in Telecommunications,* Englewood Cliffs, NJ: Prentice Hall, 1979.

39
Sorting

William Jennings

Synesort, Inc.

39.1 INTRODUCTION

What is sorting? It is the rearrangement of data into ascending or descending order. Calling this arrangement *sorting* is really a misnomer. It should more accurately be called **sequencing** or the **ordering** of data. However, the various meanings and connotations of these words, along with the convention that has arisen of using *sorting,* precludes their use.

Sorting is perhaps the single greatest consumer of computer resources. Various estimates of computer usage show that sorting accounts for 15 to 20 percent* of running time and resource utilization at most installations. The sort program is the most frequently executed on computers today. This chapter is devoted to sorting, its theory, sorting techniques in use today, and execution requirements for the most popular sort/merge packages available on IBM System/360 and System/370 computers.

While this discussion deals primarily with sorts for the IBM computers, the capabilities and requirements described apply to most sort packages, including IBM's 5740/SM1, SYNCSORT® for 360/370 OS/VS; CA-SORT R, PISORT 2 for IBM DOS and DOS/VS, OMSI SORT-1-PLUS, ZIPSORT II, and SPEED-SORT for PDP11; CSORT and IBM disk sort for System 3; and SuperSort®, which is available for most microcomputers.

---

*These estimates are a reduction from previous estimates of 20 to 60 percent primarily due to faster machine speeds and the increased use of on-line systems.

39.2 SORT THEORY, PROGRAM ORGANIZATION AND OPERATION

Terms

Let us first define a few terms so that we have a framework upon which to base our discussion. First, the definitions. **Sorting** is the ordering of data records according to a predefined sequence. The field within the record that is used to order the data is called the **key.** The key defined for a particular sort may be a **multifield key,** consisting of more than one field. In the data record in Figure 39.1, we wish to sort on the last name, and if we have two customers with the same last name, then on the first name. The customer's last name is the **major key** and the first name is the **minor key.** Depending on the complexity of the record and the user's needs, there may be a number of minor keys.

A predefined sequence that is referenced to order the records is called a **collating sequence.** It defines the order of occurrence of characters in the (computer) alphabet—which character is *greater* than another. For instance, SMITH precedes SMITHE since the blank is defined as *less* than 'E'. The collating sequence is a function of the code used within the computer to represent data and is different for ASCII (digits before letters) as compared with EBCIDIC. The EBCIDIC collating sequence (employed on IBM systems) for character data is the following: special characters; alphabetic, A–Z; and then numeric, 0–9. The **order** that we use to sequence the data can be **ascending,** which is the order just mentioned; or **descending** which would be the reverse (9–0, Z–A, spe-

1	30	40	75	80	95	110	120	130
Last Name	First	Address	Zip	Account #	Balance	Debits	Credits	

Figure 39.1. A sample data record.

cial characters). User defined orders may also be acceptable to the sort program, but these normally require that the collating sequence be modified.

Need

Now let's explore the need for sorting. We use the illustrated data record, which is kept in a file sorted upon account number. We need, instead, to have the data arranged according to zip code for a mailing to the customers. This is a case in which the file must be sorted. Also the accounting department needs customer files in descending order according to balance due. Time for another sort. Well, one might say, why not keep multiple files for each need? That requires very expensive computer-accessible storage and updating multiple files is much more difficult and time consuming.

Because the majority of sorts involve more data than can fit in the main memory of the computer, much input/output activity is required, besides simply reading the input file and writing the output file. I/O is done most efficiently when the characteristics of the device are given careful consideration. For random access devices, such characteristics are seek time and rotational delay.

Seek time is the time required to move the read/write head assembly across the medium to the desired cylinder and is measured in milliseconds. Seek time is long (tens of milliseconds) compared with the cycle time of the computer, which is in the range of 35 to 300 nanoseconds (1 nanosecond = 10^{-9} seconds). Minimizing the number of seeks and thus keeping small the overall seek time is of importance in increasing I/O efficiency.

Rotational delay, the time required to reach the appropriate read/write location once the head is over the correct track, depends on the speed of rotation for the device. It can vary from zero to the time required for a full rotation.*

Sort programs are large because they execute in many environments and adapt to different sorting requirements. They are commonly overlay structures, which op-

*As an example, IBM 3350 disk drives have an average seek time of 25ms (1 millisecond = 10^{-3} seconds) and an average rotational delay of 8.4ms.

erate in a minimum of memory. For an **overlay,** the program is broken into small load modules to be called as necessary and loaded into memory to replace a module that is no longer needed. With an overlay structure, a sort program can execute in as little as 36K bytes of memory and leave considerable memory for buffers, record storage areas and node tables.

Phases

Sort programs operate in up to four phases: one need not use all four, but must use at least two. The phases are (see Figure 39.2) the following:

1. Phase 0 is the *initialization* or *control* phase. Its functions include reading control cards, determining the amount of main storage available, generating the code to perform the sort with the fields described on the sort control card, and optimizing for and selecting the internal sort technique, merge order, buffer sizes and intermediate storage blocksize.
2. Phase 1 is the internal sort phase. The input data is read, sorted into **strings** (subsets of the input data that are in sorted order); interfaces with user routines (**exits);** and the strings are written either to the sort-work data sets or, if the number of records are few, to the output data set.
3. Phase 2 is an *intermediate* step. If the number of strings generated in phase 1 is more than can be merged at one time, then this phase merges the strings into fewer but longer strings and repeats until there are sufficiently few to enable the next phase to create a single string in one pass.
4. Phase 3 is the *last pass,* or *final merge,* phase. It merges the remaining strings into a single merged file, writes the output and also, if required, interfaces with user exits.

There are four possible combinations of phase execution: the **incore** or **turnaround** sort (phase 0,1), the **conventional** sort (phase 0,1,2,3 or phase 0,1,3), the **high performance** sort (phase 0,1,2–3), and the **merge** (phase 0,3).

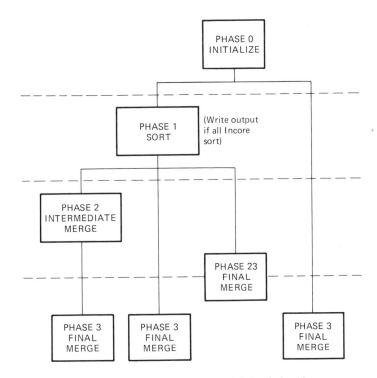

Figure 39.2. Sort porgram phases and their relationships.

The phase 0,1 sort. This sort occurs when the complete input data set fits within the main storage available to the program. The output data set is written directly.

The conventional sort. When all phases (0,1,2,3) are needed or only the intermediate merge is skipped (phase 0,1,3), the conventional sort is performed. The intermediate merge phase may be bypassed, regardless of the input data set size, if the number of strings generated during phase 1 is small enough to be handled by a one pass merge. If not, phase 2 reduces the number of strings by merging them into fewer and longer strings which are written to data sets.

The high performance sort. The phase 0,1,2–3 sort, a new technique called **blockset** is used when applicable. It combines phases 2 and 3 so that blocks from work data sets can be read directly by key sequence and the output written directly, regardless of the number of strings generated, in phase 1. This technique uses index records to access as discussed in the next section.

The merge. The phase 0,3 sort is actually a *merge* to combine multiple data sets in sorted order into one output file. The merge is called for on the sort control card. Theoretically, this is a phase 0,3 sort; most packages use a different code here than provided by the sort's phase 3 to achieve more efficient execution.

39.3 SORTING TECHNIQUES

There are currently five sorting techniques in use today: BLOCKSET, PEER, and the conventional techniques of VALE, BALN, and CRCX. **BLOCKSET** is the latest and most complicated of the techniques, but offers the greatest overall efficiency when it can be employed.

Sorting in phase 1 uses either the binary or quadratic tournament replacement techniques. Both of these methods set up trees through which the records are passed, pushing out the "winner" record among all those in the tree. When a record enters the tree with a key lower than the last winner record sent to the current string, it is slated for the *next* string which is started when this one is complete. This entails flagging the new record so that it is ignored during subsequent scans of the tree. When the tree is full of only flagged records, this halts the addition of any more records to the current string and a new string is started.

The **binary tournament method** groups the records two at a time in the record spaces. Keys of each pair are compared and the "winner" record is moved to the corresponding node, leaving an empty record space. This is done for all pairs in the record space area to create a number of nodes equal to half of the record spaces. Then the records in this first level of nodes (nodes 4, 5, 6, 7 in Figure 39.3) are compared two at a time, creating a second level of nodes (half the number of the first level nodes—nodes 2 and 3 in Figure 39.3). The second level nodes are in turn compared creating third level nodes, again reducing the number to half. This process continues thus until only one node results. In our example of eight records, we now have a "winner" record. This works for any number of records.

The **quadratic tournament method** is similar to the binary, except that it uses groups of four records or nodes, i.e., *quartets*. The quadratic technique sorts records using half the number of node *levels* as compared with the binary method. This decreases record handling and tree complexity. However, the number of comparisons of records is the same for both methods.

The Conventional Techniques of VALE, BALN, and CRCX

These techniques sort data into strings and write them to the sortwork data sets in phase 1 operation. Strings are

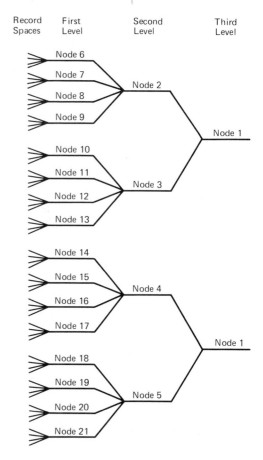

Figure 39.4. Quardratic sorting with 64 records, 21 nodes, and 3 levels.

read into main storage, merged into longer strings and then written to the sortworks. This continues until only one string results, the output data set. The techniques differ only in two respects:

1. The manner in which they handle the destination of the strings among the sortwork data sets;
2. The I/O techniques involved.

VALE.   This is the most powerful conventional method and was designed for random access devices. It uses the lowest possible level to initiate the I/O operation (EXCP or EXCPVR), which eliminates much system overhead. Its other feature is that it assigns priorities to the sortwork data sets according to unit and channel allocation as well as device contention. If, for example, three sort-

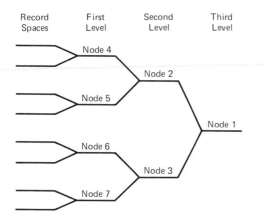

Figure 39.3. Binary sorting with 8 records, 7 nodes, and 3 node levels.

work data sets are allocated, but during the job initialization only two devices are assigned, then one of the devices gets two of the sortwork data sets allocated. Therefore, if one writes to the two data sets on the same volume, time is lost due to arm movement. It is more efficient to use only one of these two data sets, even at the cost of getting secondary space if necessary, until all its space is exhausted. The other data set should be used only if it becomes necessary. This is the design philosophy behind VALE.

BALN (balanced). The balanced technique is old, originally designed for tape. Magnetic tape is a sequential access medium. BALN distributes one string to each in rotation (round robin) as they are generated to all but one (the largest) sortwork area. During the merge phases, sequences of strings are taken from one of the filled sortworks, merged together and written to the empty area. When a filled area becomes exhausted, it is considered empty and receives data from some other sortwork area. This intermediate merge is continued until the merge order is reduced to a number that can be handled by a last pass merge to create the output.

CRCX (crisscross). Crisscross is another tapesort technique that has been applied to random access devices. By distributing string sequences to one less than the number of intermediate storage areas available, it alternates control between the sort and intermediate merge phases. When the intermediate merge phase is entered, all $n - 1$ sequences of strings written so far are merged into one string on the remaining work area. Because the shorter sequences are merged first and handling longer strings is delayed until absolutely necessary, the amount of data passed by each intermediate merge is minimized and efficiency gained.

PEER

The PEER technique was developed by IBM to take advantage of the high probability that (in many applications) the data sorted have a substantial amount of **bias,** that is, not randomly distributed across the possible sort keys. Data in the file have a high degree of prior sequencing. PEER uses index records containing the high and low key of the string segment (or block), along with their disk address. It then redefines strings into fewer, but longer, strings by looking at the high and low keys, and sorting the index records according to low key.

When the string segment is created, it is a ministring of a predetermined size (usually one track). A string segment number is assigned to identify the index record. The redefinition of a number of ministrings into one string is now a matter of sorting the index records by their low key. This sorted ministring list (see Figure 39.5) is used to find segments to combine into strings effectively. When the low key of one string segment is higher than the high key of another, then these two segments are **concatenated** (pasted together) into one string. Note that some segments may be combined naturally to form a string because the string segment is of a predetermined fixed size (Segs. 3, 4; 5, 6 and others in Figure 39.5). For combination, if the next string segment has a low key lower than this segment, either the following segment is checked or a new string started. Figure 39.5 shows how 16 string segments are combined into two strings, one of 12 segments, and the other of 4.

When string redefinition is complete, this reduced population of defined strings is then partitioned into work areas. The first partition contains $m - 1$ strings; all other partitions contain m strings. Each partition is now ordered by use of the indices and replacement selection. This reduces the string population to correspond with the strings defined by the index lists. A merge phase reduces the strings in each partition to one. If, at the completion of this merge, the merge order is not low enough to perform a last pass merge, then the sequence of string redefinition and intrapartition merge is repeated until the last pass merge can be done.

BLOCKSET

The BLOCKSET technique differs from the conventional technique in two ways. First, it uses index records to monitor each string segment (similar to PEER, but the indexes are used differently). Second, a different algorithm is employed when writing the data to the sortworks on the disks. The conventional technique treats the sortworks as a continuum of tracks CYL 0, TRK $0 - n$, CYL 1, TRK $0 - n$, and so forth. BLOCKSET considers the sortwork space in discrete groups (see Figures 39.6 and 39.7).

By creating and analyzing the index records which show the low key of each string block (rather than an entire string of many blocks), BLOCKSET can write the block to an area (cylinder or group of cylinders) on the sortworks that has blocks from other strings with similar keys. Now the phases utilizing the index records are combined, in place of merging strings of data in the intermediate and final merge phases of a sort. Because we

Seg. #	KEY Low	Hi
1	23	29
2	29	34
3	2	4
4	8	11
5	3	7
6	9	16
7	11	17
8	34	39
9	38	43
10	41	45
11	53	60
12	61	68
13	46	49
14	70	74
15	49	57
16	78	93

Original String Segment Indices in Order of Generation

Seg. #	KEY Low	Hi
3	2	4
5	3	7
4	8	11
6	9	16
7	11	17
1	23	29
2	29	34
8	34	39
9	38	43
10	41	45
13	46	49
15	49	57
11	53	60
12	61	68
14	70	74
16	78	93

Original String Segment Indices Sorted by Low Key

Seg. #	KEY Low	Hi
3	2	4
4	8	11
7	11	17
1	23	29
2	29	34
8	34	39
10	41	45
13	46	49
15	49	57
12	61	69
14	70	74
16	78	93

New String 1

Seg. #	KEY Low	Hi
5	3	7
6	9	10
9	38	43
11	53	60

New String 2

Figure 39.5. String redefinition in the peer technique.

know where the blocks with low keys are located on the sortworks, we may now read those blocks. The first block read back has the lowest record in the sort; that record may be eliminated from future consideration by writing it to the output file. Other blocks having low keys are also eligible for elimination to the output file.

When all low key records have been thus eliminated, records remaining in the buffers are combined to form new blocks. This makes buffers available for the next I/O. Since we have written the blocks with low keys in the same range on the same or adjacent cylinders, large number of blocks can be read back with little or no delay due to seek time. Creating, sorting, analyzing and writing indexes obviously requires substantial overhead. However, the result is extremely efficient I/O, and reduces the number of times data are read in or written out. To make a comparison, the conventional technique described ear-

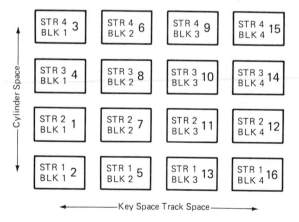

Figure 39.6. Data written and read by string in the same order in which the strings are generated. The large numbers represent the low keys within the blocks.

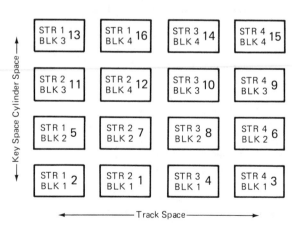

Figure 39.7. Data written and read based upon the low key (large number) within each block.

lier requires four I/Os for 75 percent of the data and two I/Os for the remainder. BLOCKSET requires two I/Os for the entire data set plus the indexes.

39.4 CONTROL CARDS

We now investigate how to tell the program what to sort and what options we want. There are two required control cards, the sort/merge and end cards. Optional (though required in some cases) are the record statement, mods card, and where needed, special control cards. A card containing only END marks the end of the control card set.

The Sort Card

The sort (or merge) card defines the key fields on which to sort: their position, length, whether they are used in ascending or descending order and their format. The sort card can also contain parameters to govern the execution of the program. The format of the sort card is:

SORT FIELDS = $(p_1, l_1, f_1, o_1, \ldots p_n, l_n, f_n, o_n)$,
param1,param2,paramn;

MERGE FIELDS = $(p_1, l_1, o_1, \ldots, p_n, l_n, o_n)$,
FORMAT = f, param1, ... paramn

where, for each of the quartets (SORT) or triplets (MERGE) we have

p = the position of the field within the record;
l = the length of the field (the total of all lengths cannot exceed 4092, 4088 if equal keys are permitted);
o = the desired sequencing or ordering, valid codes are
  A—ascending;
  D—descending;
  E—user modified collating sequence.[*]
f = the format of the field. Available formats and their lengths are:

Format	Length	Description
CH	1–4092	Character, EBCDIC, unsigned
ZD	1–32	Zoned decimal, signed
PD	1–32	Packed decimal, signed
FI	1–256	Fixed-point, signed
BI	1 bit–4092 bytes	Binary, unsigned
FL	1–256	Floating-point, signed
AC	1–256	Character, ASCII

[*]Exit E61 or ALTSEQ parameter required, ascending sequence is implied.

Format	Length	Description
CSL	2–256	Signed numeric, separate leading sign
CST	2–256	Signed numeric, separate trailing sign
CLO	1–256	Signed numeric, leading overpunch sign
CTO	1–256	Signed numeric, trailing overpunch sign
ASL	2–256	Signed numeric, ASCII, leading separate sign
AST	2–256	Signed numeric, ASCII, trailing separate sign
AQ	1–256	Character, EBCDIC, alternate collating sequence

There are five parameters that are optionally specified on the sort control card:

FILSZ = (E) y	The number of records to be sorted. If this number is an estimate, E must precede the number.
SKIPREC = z	Skip the first z records in the input file.
CKPT CHKPT	Take system checkpoints.
EQUALS NO EQUALS	The order of records with equal keys should be/need not be maintained from input to output.
DYNALLOC = (D,N)	For MVS operating systems, to dynamically allocate sortwork files that are needed. A FILSZ should be specified when using DYNALLOC. D represents the device type or generic name of the devices to be used. N is the number of data sets to be allocated.

The Record Card

The record card describes the type and length of records. It is required whenever the input is handled by an exit E15, either in a JCL sort or when the sort is invoked by another program. Its format is:

$$\text{RECORD TYPE} = x, \text{LENGTH} = (l_1, l_2, l_3, l_4, l_5)$$

where x = F for fixed records
V for variable length records
D for variable length ASCII records

l_1 = maximum record length of the input data set.
l_2 = record length after exit E15 processing.
l_3 = maximum record length of the output data set.
l_4 = minimum record length of the input data set. $\left.\begin{array}{l} \text{variable} \\ \text{length} \end{array}\right.$
l_5 = modal or most frequent record length. $\left.\begin{array}{l} \text{records} \end{array}\right\}$

The MODS Card

The MODS card defines **program exits,** user written routines that get control from the sort at various points throughout all phases. (Exits defined to get control at specific points are discussed at length in Section 39.6) The format of the MODS card follows:

MODS exit name

$$= (n_1, s_1, d_1, e_1), \ldots, \text{exit name} = (n_n, s_n, d_n, e_n)$$

where exit name = the name of the exit to be activated. It must be a valid exit name, e.g. E15, E35.

n = the name of the routine, the member name if in a library.

s = the size of the exit routine in bytes, including space for any buffers or getmains, if any.

d = the name of the DD statement that defines the library in which the exit resides.

e = the link editing requirements of the routine:

N—link editing is not required.

S—link editing is required; appropriate DD cards must be in the job stream.

Special Control Cards

This section describes features not available on every sort/merge utility. They often save time by eliminating the need to code exits. The installation programmer's guide gives the availability and specific coding requirements:

1. The include/omit control statement selects records from an input file based on comparisons which test the contents of specified fields in the record. Fields may be compared to a constant or to another field within the same record.
2. The inrec/outrec control card(s) reformat fields within the record or change record lengths by adding or deleting fields. It is possible to repeat portions of the record, insert spaces, realign fields and/or change their order. Reformat capability is the same. The difference between the statements occurs when the processing is done—inrec processing before sorting, outrec after the final merge.
3. The sum control card is for equal keyed records. It specifies the fields to be summarized for all records which have equal sort keys. All values in these fields (for equal keyed records) are added into the summary record. The other records are deleted. Nonsummary fields and records without equal keys remain unchanged.

There are many parameter options available to the user in addition to the control cards and the options described. These alternatives differ from one sort to the next and affect such things as the main memory used by the sort, where and which messages are to be printed, and error termination options (abend or return code). Again, consult the programmer's guide for this product for complete descriptions and coding requirements.

39.5 JCL REQUIREMENTS

This section describes the job control language for the sort execution. The descriptions below are limited to naming the statements, their function and when they are required. Subparameters are not discussed since they vary widely.

JOB and EXEC statements are *always* required to identify the job and the programs to be executed to perform the sort. Other statements and when they are needed are listed below:

Name	Description
//STEPLIB	Needed to identify the library where the sort resides when it is not in LINKLIB.
//SORTLIB	Needed only for tapesorts or techniques that derived from it (**BALN** or **CRCX**).

Name	Description
//SYSOUT	Usually needed to define the output data set for messages.
//SORTIN	Usually required to define the input data set. May not be required if the sort is program invoked or has an exit E15 to supply the records to the sort.
//SORTINnn	Required to define the input data sets for a merge application unless exit E32 supplies the various inputs.
//SORTOUT	Usually required to define the output data set. Not required if the sort is program invoked or an exit E35 is handling the output.
//SORTWORKnn	Usually required to define the work data sets. Under MVS, the DYNALLOC parameter may be used in its place. Not required for merge applications or sorts in which the input data set fits entirely in core.
//DDNAME	Required only if exits are used. Referenced by the MODS control card. It defines the libraries containing user written exits.
//SORTCKPT	Needed only if system checkpoints are taken.
//SYSUDUMP	Occasionally needed to define the dump data set in case of an abend.
//SYSIN	Always required to define the control card data set unless the sort is program-invoked.
//SORTMODS	Required only if SYSIN also contains user exits.
//SYSLIN //SYSLMOD //SYSUT1 //SYSPRINT	Required only if user exits require link editing.
//SORTCNTL*	Overrides parm or control card information.

39.6 EXITS

At designated places in the sort program, control may be passed to user written routines called **exits.** When this is requested, most exit routines take control once for every record processed. This increases the overall sort execution

*The DDNAME for this data set will vary with the sort package.

time and consumes main memory that could otherwise be used by the sort. Wherever possible, control cards should replace exits because they generate inline code that is much more efficient. When circumstances do not allow for the use of control cards, or they are not available, then exits may be used.

Exit naming generally follows the following convention: Exy where

x is the number of the phase in which the exit is called.
y is the ordinal number of the exit within the phase.

The exception is E61, which can be called in either phase 1 or phase 3.

Exits E11, E21, and E31

These exits prepare for other exit routines. They are only entered once, at the beginning of their associated phase. They may open files or perform some other initialization function for exits that are called later in the phase.

Exits E15, E25, and E35

These are the most common exits. They may delete, create and insert or modify records. E15 may be used with or without a sortin data set. It may add, delete or change input records. It may analyze the input data set or create the entire input for the sort.

Exits E25 and E35 are used to delete, insert, modify or summarize records. They are entered when the sort is about to place a record in the output sequence of that phase. E25 has certain restrictions and is not entered if phase 2 is bypassed. Restrictions on E25 include

1. It may not add records.
2. It may not change sort control fields.
3. It may not destroy the contents of its parameter list.

E35 may be used in conjunction with a sortout data set or, if there is none, it is responsible for handling the output processing.

Exit E14

E14 may change the contents of data fields, delete or summarize records. Unlike E15, it is entered when the sort is about to add a record to the phase 1 output sequence and it may not insert records. It may not change the sort control fields.

Exit E32

E32 is available for invoked merges only. It must be part of an invoking program, as it cannot appear on a MODS card. It must supply all the input records and the invoking programs parameter list must supply the number of input files to be merged.

Exits E17, E27, and E37

These exits clean up after other exit routines. They are entered only once, at the end of their associated phase. Their cleanup may include closing data sets, issuing freemains and the like.

Exit E16

E16 is only called when the input data set cannot fit into the intermediate storage available. The exit routine tells the sort whether to terminate or to sort the records presently written to the sortwork data sets.

Exits E18 and E38

These exits, E18 for sorts and E38 for merges, are primarily for I/O error recovery routines. However, they may also do label checking, end of file processing, or provide VSAM exits or passwords. They are entered only once, at the beginning of SORTIN processing.

Exit E39

E39 processes I/O errors also, but for the SORTOUT data set. It is entered once, at the beginning of phase 3.

Exit E61

E61, in conjunction with the sort control card order value of E, modifies the collating sequence of the key field. For example, it might cause numbers to appear before letters. Within the modified collated sequence, only ascending order is used.

39.7 INITIATING THE SORT FROM A PROGRAM

The sort can be invoked by a program written in COBOL, PL/I, or assembly. This provides programming flexibility when performance is not a major consideration.

SORTWORK and SYSOUT (or other DD names specified by an installation) DD cards are required in the JCL for the invoking program. SYSIN, SORTIN, and SORTOUT are required if the program does not pass a parameter list or if the appropriate exit is not included.

COBOL

In COBOL the SORT verb initiates a sort. Its format follows:

$$\text{SORT(sort-file-name) ON} \begin{Bmatrix} \text{ASCENDING} \\ \text{DESCENDING} \end{Bmatrix} \text{KEY data-name-1}$$

$$\left[\begin{Bmatrix} \text{ASCENDING} \\ \text{DESCENDING} \end{Bmatrix} \text{KEY data-name-2} \right] \dots$$

$$\left\{ \begin{array}{l} \text{Using file-name-1 GIVING data-name-2} \\ \text{INPUT PROCEDURE section-name-1} \\ \text{OUTPUT PROCEDURE section-name-2} \end{array} \right.$$

Three major files are used in a sort: the input file, the sort, or work, file and the output file. The *input* file contains the unsorted records. The sorted records go to the *output* file. Both files must be defined by the appropriate FD and select statements in the environment division. The *sort,* or *work,* file is defined by the SD, which is the same as the FD, but without a label records clause. Data names which define the sort key are elementary items within the input file FD.

USING / GIVING statements are used when a file is sorted directly. When record processing is preferred before they are sorted, the INPUT PROCEDURE may be used to build, edit, count and display records. The OUTPUT PROCEDURE processes records after they are sorted. The INPUT and OUTPUT PROCEDURES may be used together or separately, but an INPUT PROCEDURE may not contain a USING statement nor may an OUTPUT PROCEDURE contain a GIVING statement.

PL/I

A PL/I program invokes the sort program via a call to one of the four entry points to the sort interface subroutine:

PLISRTA   Invokes the sort program to sort records in the SORTIN data set and writes them to the SORTOUT data set.

PLISRTB Invokes the sort program and as one of the arguments and defines an exit E15 to supply records to the sort. A SORTOUT dataset is required.

PLISRTC Invokes the sort with an exit E35 procedure defined as one of the arguments. A SORTIN data set is required.

PLISRTD Invokes the sort with both an exit E15 and E35 defined as arguments. Neither SORTIN nor SORTOUT data sets are required.

The general syntax of the CALL statement for each of the four entry points is

CALL PLISRTA(arg1,arg2,arg3,arg4)

CALL PLISRTB(arg1,arg2,arg3,arg4,arg5)

CALL PLISRTC(arg1,arg2,arg3,arg4,arg6)

CALL PLISRTD(arg1,arg2,arg3,arg4,arg5,arg6)

The arguments are

arg1 A character string containing the SORT / MERGE statement. The statement must be preceded and followed by a blank.

arg2 A character string containing the RECORD statement. It also must be preceded and followed by a blank.

arg3 The amount of main storage for the sort program. As explained later, this value should be zeros, representing MAX.

arg4 Name of the variable in the invoking procedure that is to receive the sort return code.

arg5 The entry point name of the PL/1 procedure to be invoked as the exit E15.

arg6 The entry point name of the PL/1 procedure to be invoked as the exit E35.

Assembly

Initiating the sort from an assembly program is accomplished via the ATTACH, LINK or XCTL macro instruc-

tions. The calling program passes a pointer containing the address of a parameter list to the sort program; this parameter list contains the addresses of the control statements to be used by the sort. The choice of macro determines the linkage relationship between the calling program and the sort. With XCTL, care must be taken to ensure that the storage area for the parameter list and other sort control information does not reside in the module issuing the macro; XCTL wipes out the calling module. The procedure follows:

To pass the parameter list, load the address of a full-word pointer into register 1. Code X'80' in the pointer's first byte and the address of the parameter list byte count in its last three bytes. The byte count in the last two bytes of the first full-word entry in the list is the number of bytes remaining in the list. The first seven entries of the parameter list are obligatory and are coded as shown in the example of Section 39.8. Note that whenever the address of an exit routine is supplied (in entry 6 or 7), it is *not* provided in the MODS card.

The remaining entries are optional and may be specified in any order after the first seven entries. If exit E32 is used in a merge, its address must be passed in the parameter list and *not* on a MODS card. A RECORD statement is always required. Its LENGTH parameter is required whenever an inline E15 or E35 exit routine is used. Additionally, the MODS card is not supported for an invoked tape sort. Control statements must begin and end with a blank.

Some suggestions for invoking the sort. Whenever possible, always open files before calling the sort. As a corollary, code either 0 or do not specify a main storage value unless necessary. By making the amount of storage available selectable by the sort and external to the program, the sort executes more efficiently, which reduces the possibility of required program changes if the environment changes.

Be sure to check the return code from the sort in the next instruction following the call to (request for) the sort. While many installations ask the sort to abend if it detects an error or if for any reason it terminates early, just as many do not. For COBOL, the return code is in the sort-return-code special register; for PL/1 it is in the variable specified to receive it; in assembly language it is in register 15. The return code is 0 for normal termination, 16 (sometimes 8 in some PL/I compilers) if the sort is not completed successfully.

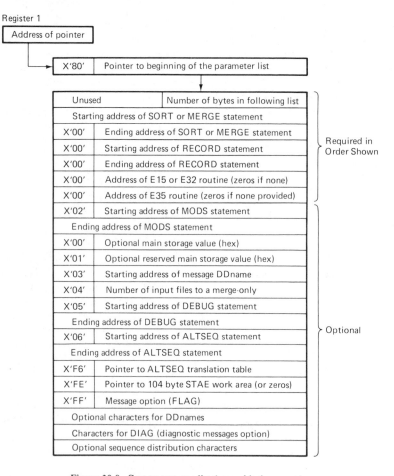

Figure 39.8. Sort parameter list (assembly language).

39.8 EXAMPLES

Here are examples of requesting sorts from a program
(COBOL, PL/I, and Assembler) and with JCL, with and
without exits.

A. JCL sort

```
//stepname     EXEC     PGM=SORT,PARM='options'
//STEPLIB      DD       DSN=library.name,DISP=SHR
//SYSOUT       DD       SYSOUT=A
//SORTIN       DD       DSN=input.for.sort,DISP=(OLD,KEEP)
//SORTWK01     DD       SPACE=(CYL,(10,2)),UNIT=SYSDA
//SORTWK02     DD       SPACE=(CYL,(10,2)),UNIT=SYSDA
//SORTWK03     DD       SPACE=*CYL,(10,2)),UNIT=SYSDA
//SORTOUT      DD       DSN=output.from.sort,DISP=(NEW,KEEP),
//                      UNIT=TAPE,VOL=SER=012345,LABEL=(1,SL)
```

```
//SYSIN        DD      *
  SORT FIELDS=(5,4,CH,A,10,4,ZD,D),EQUALS,FILSZ=E25000
  RECORD TYPE=V,LTNGTH=(200,175,180,50,80)
  END
/*
```

B. JCL sort with exits

```
//stepname     EXEC    PGM=SORT,PARM='options'
//STEPLIB      DD      DSN=sort.library.name,DISP=SHR
//             DD      DSN=exit.library.name,DISP=SHR
//SYSOUT       DD      SYSOUT=A
//SORTWK01     DD      SPACE=(TRK,(5,1)),UNIT=3350
//SORTWK02     DD      SPACE=(TRK,(5,1)),UNIT=3350
//SORTWK03     DD      SPACE=(TRK,(5,1)),UNIT=3350
//EXITLIB      DD      DSN=sort.exits,DISP=(OLD,KEEP)
//SORTCKPT     DD      DSN=check.point,VOL=SER=135790,DISP=(NEW,KEEP),
//                     UNIT=TAPE
//SYSIN        DD      *
  SORT FIELDS=(4,5,A,15,20,D),FORMAT=CH,CKPT
  RECORD TYPE=F,LENGTH=(,,120)
  MODS E15=(EXITIN,1156,EXITLIB,N),E35=(EXITOUT,580,EXITLIB,N)
  END
/*
```

C. COBOL

```
//             EXEC COBUGCLG
//COB.SYSIN    DD      *

  ENVIRONMENT DIVISION.
  SELECT  IN-FILE ASSIGN TO UT-S-INPUT.
  SELECT  OUT-FILE ASSIGN TO UT-S-OUTPUT.
  SELECT  SORT-FILE ASSIGN TO UT-S-DUMMY.

  DATA DIVISION.
  FD  IN-FILE
  .
  .
  FD  OUT-FILE
  .
  .
  SD  SORT-FILE
  .
  .
  01  SORT-REC
      02  SORT-KEY
  .
  .
```

```
            PROCEDURE DIVISION.
                OPEN INPUT IN-FILE.
                OPEN OUTPUT OUT-FILE.
                SORT SORT-FILE ASCENDING KEY SORT-KEY
                    INPUT PROCEDURE GET-RECS
                    GIVING OUT-FILE.
                IF SORT-RETURN-CODE NOT ZERO THEN DISPLAY 'SORT FAILED'
                    GO TO STOP-RUN
                    ELSE NEXT-SECTION.
            NEXT-SECTION.
                .
                .
                .
            GET-RECS.
                READ IN-FILE AT END MOVE 1 TO EOF.
                MOVE IN-REC TO SORT-REC.
                IF EOF NOT 1 THEN RELEASE SORT-REC
                    ELSE CLOSE IN-FILE.
            GET-RECS-EXIT.
                EXIT.
            STOP-RUN.
                STOP RUN.
//GO.SYSOUT   DD    SYSOUT=A
//GO.SORTWK01 DD    UNIT=SYSDA,SPACE=(CYL,(5,1))
//GO.SORTWK02 DD    UNIT=SYSDA,SPACE=(CYL,(5,1))
//GO.SORTWK03 DD    UNIT=SYSDA,SPACE=(CYL,(5,1))
//GO.INPUT    DD    DSN=input.file,DISP=(OLD,KEEP)
//GO.OUTPUT   DD    DSN=output.file,DISP=(NEW,KEEP),UNIT=3350,
//                  SPACE=(CYL,(10,2))
```

D. PL/I

```
//            EXEC PLIXCLG
//PLI.SYSIN   DD    *
 EX108: PROC OPTIONS(MAIN);

        DCL RETURN-CODE FIXED BIN(32.0);

        CALL PLISRTC (' SORT FIELDS=(7,74,CH,A),DYNALLOC=(SYSDA,3) ',
                      ' RECORD TYPE=F,LENGTH=(80) ',
                      200000,
                      RETURN-CODE,
                      E35X);
        IF RETURN-CODE = 16 THEN PUT SKIP EDIT ('SORT FAILED') (A);
        ELSE IF RETURN-CODE = 0 THEN PUT SKIP EDIT ('SORT COMPLETE') (A);
            ELSE PUT SKIP EDIT ('INVALIDE SORT RETURN CODE') (A);

    E35X:  /* THIS PROCEDURE OBTAINS SORTED RECORDS */
        PROC (INREC);
            DCL INREC CHAR (80);
            PUT SKIP EDIT (INREC) (A);
            CALL PLIRETC(4);  /* REQUEST NEXT RECORD FROM SORT */
            END E35X;
```

```
      END EX108;
/*
//GO.SYSOUT   DD   SYSOUT=A
//GO.SORTIN   DD   DSN=input.file,DISP=(OLD,KEEP)
```

E. Assembly

```
//              EXEC ASMFCLG
//ASM.SYSIN  DD   *
         Standard Linkage
         LA    1,PTRWORD              LOAD ADDRESS OF PARAM LIST POINTER
         LINK  EP=SORT                INITIATE SORT
         LTR   15,15                  TEST RETURN CODE
         BNZ   SORTERR                BRANCH ON ERROR CONDITION
         B     SORTOK                 BRANCH TO NORMAL PROCESSING
         CNOP  0,4                    INSURE FULLWORD ALIGNMENT FOR POINTER
PTRWORD  DC    X'80'                  INDICATES POINTER TO PARAM LIST
         DC    AL3(PARMS)             ADDRESS OF PARAMETER LIST
         DS    H                      UNUSED FIRST TWO BYTES OF PARAM LIST
PARMS    DC    AL2(PARMSEND-PARMBEG)  BYTE COUNT OF REMAINING LIST
PARMSBEG DC    A(SORTBEG)             BEGINNING ADDRESS OF SORT STATEMENT
         DC    A(SORTEND)             ENDING ADDRESS OF SORT STATEMENT
         DC    A(RECBEG)              BEGINNING ADDRESS OF RECORD CARD
         DC    A(RECEND)              ENDING ADDRESS OF RECORD CARD IMAGE
         DC    F'0'                   NO E15/E32 EXIT ROUTINE
         DC    A(E35)                 ADDRESS OF E35 EXIT ROUTINE
PARMSEND EQU   *                      ADDRESS OF E35 EXIT ROUTINE
SORTBEG  DC    C' SORT FIELDS=(1,10,CH,A,15,20,CH,D)'  SORT
SORTEND  DC    C' '                                     CARD IMAGE
RECBEG   DC    C' RECORD TYPE'F'          RECORD CARD IMAGE
RECEND   DC    C' '
         CNOP  0,4                    INSURE FULLWORD ALIGNMENT
         USING *,15                   REGISTER 15 WILL BE THE BASE
E35      EQU   *                      E35 EXIT ROUTINE
         .
         .
         BR    14                     RETURN TO SORT
SORTERR  EQU   *                      PROGRAM ERROR ROUTINE
         .
         .
         .
         BR    14                     RETURN TO SYSTEM
SORTOF   EQU   *                      PROGRAM NORMAL PROCESSING
         .
         .
         BR    14                     RETURN TO SYSTEM
```

REFERENCES

Flores, Ivan, *Computer Sorting*. Englewood Cliffs, N.J.: Prentice-Hall, 1969.

Knuth, Donald E., *The Art of Computer Programming, Volume 3: Sorting and Searching*. Reading, MA: Addison-Wesley, 1973.

Lorin, Harold, *Sorting and Sort Systems*. Reading, MA: Addison-Wesley, 1975.

McCullock, C., "A New Approach to Random Access Sorting," unpublished paper, 1976.

OS PL/1 Optimizing Compiler: Programmer's Guide. SC33-0006-2, IBM Corp., 1973.

OS/VS Sort/Merge Logic, 3rd Ed. LY33-8042-2, IBM Corp., 1975.

OS/VS Sort/Merge Logic 7th Ed. LY33-8042-6, IBM Corp., 1979.

OS/VS Sort/Merge Programmer's Guide, 7th Ed. SC33-4035-6, IBM Corp., 1979.

Stern, Nancy, and Robert Stern, *Structured COBOL Programming, 3rd Ed. New York: John Wiley & Sons, 1979.*

SYNCSORT OS Installation Guide. SI-0102-1, Syncsort, Inc., 1981.

SYNCSORT OS Programmer's Guide. SI-0101-1, Syncsort, Inc., 1981.

40
Word Processing

Ivan Flores

Baruch College
City University of New York

40.1 INTRODUCTION

The **word processor** is a system composed of computer hardware driven by one or more computer programs. The ultimate output of the word processor is a **document**—a letter, report, or manual such as would be produced by a typewriter. That same document is initially keyed into the equipment at a keyboard which looks much like a typewriter. However, as information is keyed in, the document is not printed immediately. Instead, it is stored in an electronic form called an **electronic document.**

The biggest advantage of word processing comes after the document is keyed in and before it is finally printed out. During this period one may review and alter the electronic document until it has been perfected to the writer's satisfaction. Even after printing out a copy of the document, as long as it is maintained in electronic form, one can modify and then print it again. This means that the writer can constantly improve and refine his or her product.

To make changes in a typed document and provide good, clean copy, the document has to be retyped. As the document is rekeyed mistakes are bound to occur. The old method was not only time-consuming but error-prone.

During the past decade or so, not only has the word processor sprung into being, but the typewriter has also evolved by providing electronic memory and additional functions. This more powerful typewriter has been dubbed an **intelligent typewriter;** though not our main concern, it is discussed briefly as background in the next section, on the history of word processors.

40.2 HISTORY

The mechanical typewriter had been around since the turn of the century and had become an office fixture by the century's middle. With a careful and vigilant operator and considerable time and effort, it could be used to prepare a neat, clean, and acceptable document for office correspondence. Regardless of the competency of the operator, there were still problems with the typewriter that technology has now overcome. These improvements, implemented in the word processor, provide capability for

- Simple correction—80 per cent of the errors that a typist makes are noted immediately and can be corrected at once when a good mechanism to do this is provided.
- Reasonable changes in the document during creation.
- Major changes in the document without the need for retyping.

The point of reference for these changes is the mechanical typewriter. It was the first popular device with formed letters that produced neat, clean output with a minimum of training and skill.

Separation of Input from Output

The mechanical typewriter takes the force provided by the operator and applies it to mechanical linkages to place an image of the character. The force is transmitted directly to a type bar which flies through the air and hits the ribbon against the paper.

The electrical typewriter provides a "power assist" like power steering or power brakes in an automobile. The operator directs the mechanism, and it applies the force. The force applied is converted by the mechanism into a strong and uniform force. The letter selected by the typist activates an electrical arrangement to send the type bar to hit the ribbon against the paper. However, the force with which the type hits the paper does not depend upon how hard one hits the key. The electrical typewriter is a considerable improvement because the appearance of the document is independent of the force exerted by the operator.

The important feature to note about both the mechanical and electrical typewriter is that the action (printing) happens immediately after the choice is made (hitting the key).

Intermediate Storage

Then the problem was to enter keystroke information, store it on some medium externally, and later have it operate the typewriter. The first technique provided is illustrated in Figure 40.1. What we want to do is

1. Collect stroke information.
2. Convert each key stroke into code.
3. Store the information in memory.
4. Permit the information to be altered.
5. Extract and send the codes from memory over to the printer.
6. Activate the type bars mechanically with the codes and print the document.

Paper Tape

The 1950s saw the beginning of the computer revolution. Computer input rates were (and are) almost limitless. For large installations, the initial solution was punchcards. They speed up the input process considerably.

However, the card reader was fairly expensive. A more economical source for computer input became the Flexowriter. Figure 40.2 illustrates how it is used. This device consists of an electrical typewriter to which a small paper tape punch is attached. As the operator keys information at the keyboard, the electrical typewriter prints it and simultaneously each key stroke is converted into a set of electrical impulses fed to the paper tape punch.

The paper tape produced was primarily to make computer input faster, a hundred times faster then the operator could type it. For office use one could play back the paper tape on the paper tape reader attached to the typewriter.

Immediate corrections.   Suppose, during the course of typing the operator keys "Teh" instead of "The." Here's the correction routine: Stop and back up the paper punch by two characters. Hit the delete key twice to punch a set of all ones to replace each character being deleted. Now continue typing "he" to replace the "eh" which has been deleted.

Cut and paste.   Editing with the Flexowriter is cut and paste. One can create a paper tape insert by simultaneously typing the insert on the typewriter and punching the tape. To alter the original tape, the operator types it back through the tape reader to the insertion point, and pastes in the insert there.

Deletion is done similarly. The procedure is to find the area to be deleted by reading the tape into the typewriter, then to simply snip out the unwanted area and join the tape.

Use.   Direct mail firms and business service bureaus used paper tape to duplicate thousands of form letters with little human effort. A form letter was put onto paper tape with stop codes where distinctive information was to be entered. Thus the name and address were entered at the keyboard, whereas the rest of the letter was produced

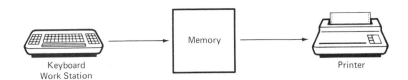

Figure 40.1. A memory typewriter schematic. (From I. Flores, *Word Processing Handbook.* Copyright © 1982 by Van Nostrand Reinhold Company Inc. Reprinted by permission of the publisher.)

Figure 40.2. The Flexiwriter stored keystroke information on punched paper tape. (From I. Flores, *Word Processing Handbook*. Copyright © 1982 by Van Nostrand Reinhold Company Inc. Reprinted by permission of the publisher.)

from the paper tape. Typewriters were operated at maximum speed and human operators were required only to enter the variable information.

Internal Memory

Internal memory provides a means for holding the document so that changes during editing can be done easily and quickly. The word processor now takes the form of the schematic in Figure 40.3. As the document is keyed in, it is placed in memory and also printed on the typewriter. Changes made in the electronic document (ED) are made directly into memory and/or produced in the typewriter. When the ED is assumed to be perfect, it can be played back on the typewriter for verification; when the operator is satisfied, the document can be stored on an external medium, such as a floppy disk, for later editing or playback.

External Medium

The most important desirable feature for an external medium is that it be *reusable,* as the punched tape was not. The medium is reusable when it will store new information where the old information used to be. The three important media for the evolution of word processing are

- The magnetic tape cassette;
- The magnetic card;
- The floppy disk.

Mag tape.   A cassette of magnetic tape, as used in the home recorder, was adapted to store many pages of text, making editing considerably easier. To edit a short document, one simply reads the document from the tape into memory, then rewinds the cassette to receive the new copy of the document. The ED in memory is edited using the help of the program and the keyboard. Once the new document is satisfactory, hard copy can be produced and/or the document can be rerecorded onto the cassette.

Mag card.   A plastic card, coated with a magnetizible material and about the size and shape of a punchcard, was used in early word processing systems. The card holds a single-spaced page of text. It is used like the cassette: read the document back; edit it; return the revised document.

Floppy disk.   In the mid-1970s, IBM developed the floppy disk to hold small operating system programs to be loaded into its computer. The medium was an immediate success and imitations sprang up all over the world. The ability to go to any part of the disk and extract information without reviewing the entire disk makes the medium appealing for word processing use.

Visual Display

Without a display, every time a change, from a small correction to editing of a whole electronic documents, is required, the operator would have to cause the typewriter

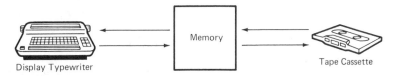

Figure 40.3. Word processor components. (From I. Flores, *Word Processing Handbook*. Copyright © 1982 by Van Nostrand Reinhold Company Inc. Reprinted by permission of the publisher.)

to produce hard copy. The **video display terminal (VDT)**, first available in the 1960s, displayed textual information on the screen of a television tube. The VDT was invaluable to the operator who worked the EDP installation computer. But VDTs of this type cost $2000 to $4000 at the time, considerably more than a typewriter. Offices were loathe to acquire such an expensive piece of equipment when document output was still limited by the attached typewriter to a slightly higher speed than that of the human operator. When the cost came down, the VDT became a natural choice for WP.

Printers

Until the early 1970s, there were only two real choices for hard copy computer printout:

- The low speed, high quality typewriter.
- The high speed, low quality, high priced line printer.

Line printers produce great quantities of output in a hurry, but of poor quality and often only in upper case.

For many years engineers sought a compromise in cost, speed, and attractiveness. In the early 1970s, the **daisy wheel printer** (Figure 40.4) was developed. It was adopted by the word processing field because of its fully

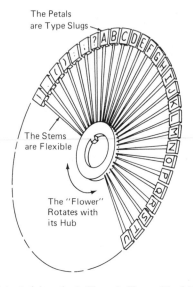

The Petals are Type Slugs

The Stems are Flexible

The "Flower" Rotates with its Hub

Figure 40.4. A daisy wheel. (From I. Flores, *Word Processing Handbook*. Copyright © 1982 by Van Nostrand Reinhold Company Inc. Reprinted by permission of the publisher.)

formed high quality printing. Today speeds of 60 characters per second (cps) provide correspondence quality.

As already noted, in the early 1970s there was no economical way to use the VDT in a WP system. The daisy wheel printer made high quality fast WP possible. A printer working at top speed could handle the output of three efficient operators. Three terminals could share one printer. There were further developments at the end of the 1970s which made possible fast and accurate printing at a higher price. These were the *ink jet printer* and *dot matrix printer* and later the *laser printer*.

Microprocessors and Internal Memory

One further development was necessary: large scale integration (LSI) made available high powered computing capability and considerable amounts of internal memory at a low cost. Now all the necessary components to form an economical word processing system were available; the block diagram of a typical system appears in Figure 40.5.

Intelligent Typewriters

In the middle and late 1970s, word processing separated into two camps: advanced typewriter versus true word processor. The typewriter, sometimes with advanced capability, was available to the office secretary at a modest cost. Millions of intelligent typewriters have been and will be sold. What these devices can do is limited in scope and in speed [1]. However, they serve a useful purpose, especially if they are properly integrated into the office environment.

To keep this chapter to a reasonable size, we direct our attention only to the VDT based word processor outlined in Figure 40.3.

40.3 CONFIGURATIONS

A word processing system consists of components which fall into three general categories: hardware, software and people. All of these are of interest:

- *Hardware* consists of mechanical, electrical and structural components placed in a cabinet. Open up the cabinet and we can see, feel and touch them—they are "hard."
- *Software* consists of the programs, which are sets of instructions that run the computer, the power behind the word processor. The computer cannot operate without a program.

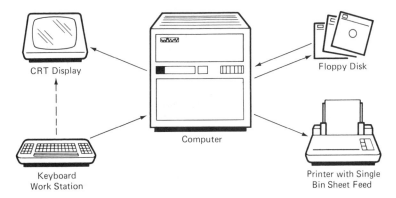

Figure 40.5. The VDT based word processor. (From I. Flores, *Word Processing Handbook.* Copyright © 1982 by Van Nostrand Reinhold Company Inc. Reprinted by permission of the publisher.)

- *People* use the system. Without people, the system sits idle. Both the people that use the system and those who receive their results have to be pleased with the system. Most users are pleased with WP.

The hardware consists of a number of components—printers, terminals, consoles, and so forth. Hardware systems are fabricated through the assembly of different types and quantities of these components to make configurations which differ considerably in both price and capability from existent alternatives.

Minimum Needs

The following are the minimum functions needed to provide word processing capabilities above those of the memory typewriter:

- The keyboard permits the entry of both text and editing commands.
- The display presents the portion of the text being edited.
- A computer manages input, accepts commands and temporarily stores text as the computer is asked to do all the word processing chores that are required.
- Memory in the computer stores the current piece of text that being edited and also programs to serve WP needs.
- External storage accepts text and stores it so that the operator can work with it again at some later point.
- A printer converts the electronic text into a document.

A **configuration** is a number of components tied together to satisfy a need. Configurations differ according to number and type of components and the specifications of each. We now examine some of these configurations, but first we pause a moment to define them:

Stand-alone—A complete word processing machine which is self-contained, independent, and sometimes in its own cabinet, except perhaps for the printer.
Shared resource—Multiple stations which share one or more pieces of common equipment, such as a printer.
Shared logic—Multiple stations which share computing power or other resources.
Mainframe—A large computer to which one or more stations is hooked up by means of wires, a local net, or telephone lines.
Microcomputer—A small, inexpensive, but capable computer from which a word processing machine may be assembled by adding other components.

Stand-alone

The stand-alone WP is independent and "stands alone." If any of the other equipment in the office breaks down, that has no effect on this unit. However, documents prepared and stored on disks in one stand alone unit can be transferred and edited and/or printed in another similar unit of the same vendor, should the first unit fail.

The stand-alone unit consists of two or more cabinets: the printer produces the output documents; the other cabinet contains the computer and the hardware which make the unit function. A single plastic cabinet may house the microcomputer, the keyboard, the display and the disk drives. This makes the unit look like a television set with a keyboard pasted on. Displays vary in length and height; some are wider than they are high, and vice versa. One or two slots with small doors accommodate floppy disks which hold the documents in electronic form or programs to run the computer.

An alternative is to keep the keyboard and display in one unit; the other module holds the computer and the disk drive(s). The entry keyboard resembles a typewriter keyboard but it has additional editing keys. Sometimes the keyboard is independently movable, attached to the display by a cable; one can situate it for the most comfort.

Shared Resource

One printer sometimes serves several stations. What the vendor must do is

1. Determine how to connect several stations to the same printer.
2. Make sure that printing from one station does not interfere with a request from a second. There is a computer-organized waiting line (queue) for the printer. As requests come from different stations to use the printer, they are put on the waiting line and serviced in the order of their arrival. It would not do to intermix text from one station with that of another.

If one resource is shared among a number of stations, it is generally the printer. However, another resource which some larger systems have, the *hard disk,* is like a very large file cabinet full of documents which a number of people might share. It is a fine place to store less active documents to be used by several stations. For the more modest WP installation, occasionally we find floppy disk systems shared among several users.

Shared Logic

The microcomputer in word processors is very fast and adept. It can perform a million operations in a single second. Most of the time text is being entered, the microcomputer is idle and has nothing to do. There are only certain times it can be kept fully occupied, as when repaginating a document or retrieving a document from the disk. Because the computer is so powerful, some vendors provide a single computer to service a number of stations simultaneously. Generally, there is no interaction be-

tween the stations. Occasionally, however, the computer is fully occupied working for one operator and the other stations have to wait a few seconds.

The computer is indispensable to such shared word processing activity. If the computer becomes faulty, all stations connected to it are inhibited, if not disabled. More recently, the cost of the microprocessor chip has become almost inconsequential. It therefore costs little to incorporate a computer into *each* terminal; as a result, shared logic has gone out of vogue.

Microcomputer System

All the hardware required to produce a microcomputer WP system can be purchased as separate modules. But will they match? And how does one put them together? And what if they don't work properly? Who is responsible then? Who is going to maintain and and guarantee the equipment? All the necessary components for a WP system are available from personal computer vendors. Some microcomputer components are of the same quality as WP equipment found in large office systems, but as a rule there is considerable variation in quality.

Very few offices have gone in the direction of mixing components. Consultants who know how to select and purchase separate components and organizations which supply the equipment are not generally known in the small office community, nor do they look for business there.

Mainframes

Many large offices, which were the first to purchase word processing equipment, are part of organizations that use large computers. All of that computing power can be brought to bear in such offices. The problem is that people to make the arrangements and select the equipment are frequently absent or unavailable. Data processing staffs all too often do not want to be bothered with office people, with the result there is little conversation, if any, between the two parts of big organizations.

A computing facility has tremendous power. It also has considerable disk storage and probably a high speed, poor quality printer. What one needs to tie into such a facility is a terminal. A **dumb terminal** relies totally on the intelligence of its host, the central computer. A **smart terminal** provides some editing and format capability within its own box. A terminal can be hooked to the computer by wiring it in, by linking it into a local net, or by means of telephone lines if long distances are involved.

The trouble with using a centralized computing facility is manifold:

1. What if it breaks down? All WPs shut down, and entered data may be lost.
2. During periods of high use, its response slows down. Sometimes there is a considerable wait to connect up with, and use, the computer; then when one keys data or commands at the terminal, it responds sluggishly.
3. The proper advice and help is not available for hooking in.
4. The printer is often at a remote location and it may be of low quality.
5. The printer when hooked to a mainframe may be slowed by the response time of the central computer, if not impeded entirely. (Mainframes are generally overloaded.)

In the not too distant future, it may be possible to take the best of the two worlds: to hook in completely independent word processing stations to the main computer facility and benefit from the power that it can provide, and yet to remain independent of it.

40.4 BASIC INPUT AND EDITING

Word processing is usually done in an office setting and consequently the equipment required must be appropriate for that setting. It consists of a keyboard and a CRT (cathode ray tube) screen, which may be packaged integrally. The keyboard may be attached by a cable to the cabinet which holds the CRT. This provides the operator freedom to move the keyboard for most comfortable positioning. Further, the screen may be tiltable and adjustable so as to produce the least amount of glare and be the most readable for the operator.

Documents are stored on floppy disks. The drives which hold these disks should be in a convenient position because the operator needs access to them. Sometimes the drives are built into the screen console. In other cases, they are in small cabinets in a drawer of the desk or on the top of the desk at its side, usually built into the computer cabinet.

The printer might be the largest component. It often sits on a table of its own. It may have an automatic sheet feeder so that letterhead paper may be fed a sheet at a time, automatically, and not require the presence of an operator. Sometimes continuous stock is provided to the printer. Such stock is excellent for drafts and can be easily burst apart to yield acceptable copy.

The keyboard is designed to look and feel like a typewriter. The only difference is a few additional keys (Figure 40.6). Most of these are specific function keys, each of which bears the label of the action it performs, as explained later in the chapter. For instance, you might find a key labelled delete or insert. (Please note that in the remainder of this chapter the names of keys are underlined to distinguish them.) The keyboard may also have a control or code key which is a multiplier to provide special codes.

Start Up

When approaching the console to use it, one should have the system disk in hand. Here is the procedure: Open the door for the floppy disk drive and insert the system disk, closing the door after the disk is seated properly. Turn on the power. This activates the computer, which loads the word processing program from the floppy into the computer memory, initializing the system. Loading takes a few seconds. During this time, the screen may display some message such as "System loading." A further message, such as "Ready," will appear when the system is ready for use. In some systems, this message signals that one may start to enter a document without further ado.

Needs are communicated to the system in essentially two ways:

Prompt. A prompt is a visual indication to the user to supply information. For the personal computer or mainframe system, the operating system may indicate a prompt with an asterisk (∗) or a "greater than" sign (>). This requires that the user know the range of replies and supply the proper answer in the correct format. For instance, the CP/M (a microcomputer operating system) prompt is >, which is preceded by a drive designator. To request the *copy* utility, the conversation is simply

A> COPY

The second kind of prompt is a question. For example, at start up the word processor might need the date to enter onto electronic documents to record their creation or alteration date; it prompts with **TODAYS DATE?** The operator replies by supplying the date.

The required format of a request is sometimes unfamiliar to the new user, who may enter a formal date such as February 12, 1982, when it might suffice to separate numerics by slashes: 2/12/82. Hence another kind of

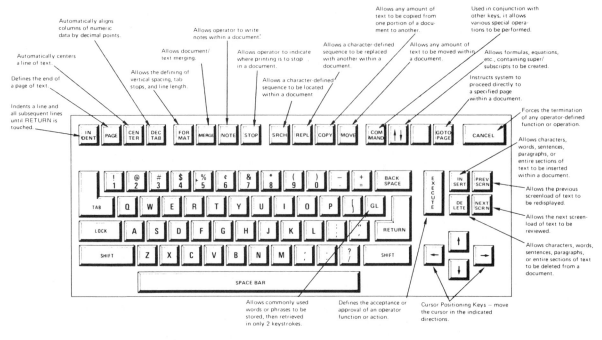

Figure 40.6. An example of a keyboard layout. (Courtesy of Wang Laboratories, Inc.)

prompt supplies a stencil for the format, such as

ENTER DATE AS mm / dd / yy.

The system asks a question which one answers according to the format displayed.

Menu.   The system asks the user to choose from a list it provides, the *menu;* one enters only one keystroke to indicate a choice. A typical menu is presented in Figure 40.7. One replies to the menu by hitting one key.

A complicated activity might require considerable information from the operator, prompted by a sequence of menus. The reply to the main menu chooses one of several activities. The choice ellicits another menu with still more choices. These activities, in turn, have menus associated with them. For example, when starting up the word processor, one may have the choice of creating, editing, repaginating, or printing a document. Suppose the choice is to *create* a document by hitting a designated key. Another menu appears which provides further choices, for formats for the document to be created.

The menu technique is considerably superior for the operator new at the system. It simply and completely delineates the alternatives for the operator, who responds with a single keystroke. A problem may arise after one

has become familiar with the system. Even before the menu appears the operator will probably know what key to hit. One could reply to the first menu with an optional sequence of keystrokes which would take the system through the final menu. A system is properly designed if it accepts the sequence of keystrokes. On the other hand,

Figure 40.7. A typical menu. (Courtesy of NBI)

after a keystroke reply is received, some systems *must* go through the action of presenting the next menu. This consumes time for experienced operators and slows down system response and interaction with the user.

Phases

For the sake of discussion it is well to consider the actions of the word processor as consisting of four phases. Actually these phases can overlap and one or more activity can be performed at a given time. We have

1. Creation.
2. Editing and alteration;
3. Formatting;
4. Printing.

For **creation** one keys in the document. An originator can enter the document directly at the keyboard as the words come to mind. Editing is usually combined with creation; the document is altered and rearranged as it is created.

Few professionals, especially those in the upper age group, find it convenient or acceptable to use a terminal for document origination. Instead, they dictate or write out the document in longhand. This is then transcribed by an operator at a terminal. There is little, if any, editing required during transcription; when editing is done, it is simply the eradication of mistakes or misunderstandings.

Editing is the review of an electronic document to make changes. Editing may be done by the originator who reviews the document at the terminal. More often the originator gets a hard copy document on which to make changes. This is passed back to an operator who makes these changes in the electronic document, printing up a new copy for the originator to review.

Formatting is setting up the hard copy document on the page. It consists of determining the top, bottom, right, and left margins, spacing, and other particulars about the printing process.

To **print** the document is to activate the printer so as to create a hard copy.

There may be a separate module for each phase of the word processing activity. Printing and editing definitely require different program modules. In some systems it is possible to carry on the two actions simultaneously. Printing does not involve the operator; it may go on in the **background**—while the operator is editing a different document. In some cases it is even possible to edit the document which is being printed.

Creation

When one creates a document, a blank screen is generally furnished. At the top of the screen may appear information about the document being created: its name, position on the disk, current size, as well as format.

Creation requires a minimum of additional skill over typing. In just a few minutes a typist can take over a word processing station and produce useful output. The operator uses the keyboard just as though it were a typewriter keyboard. Each key pressed creates a code that goes back to the computer. It is accepted by the program, verified, and retransmitted to appear at the next position on the screen.

The operator types continuously without regard for line makeup. When a line fills up, the WP observes this and performs an action called **word wrap** (Figure 40.8). The WP notes that the operator keys the last word to go on a line. When the length of this word exceeds the remaining capacity of the line, the WP removes that word from the current line and places it at the beginning of the next line, where character entry continues. Word wrap does not interfere in any way with the operator, who keys in continuously without regard for line endings. Only when the paragraph ends need the operator press return.

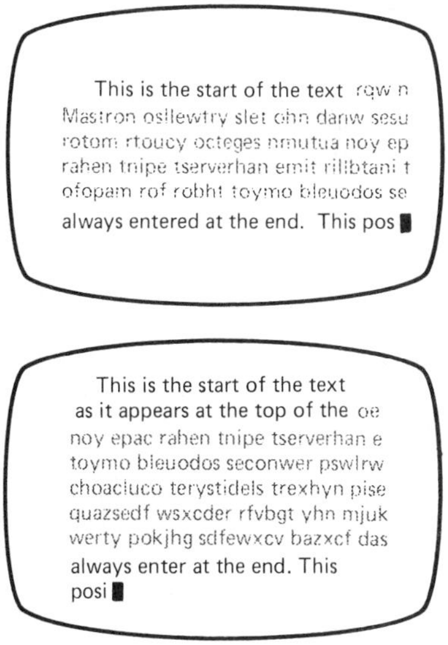

Figure 40.8. Word wrapping. (top) Display just before word wrap. (bottom) Display after word wrap. (From I. Flores, *Word Processing Handbook*. Copyright © 1982 by Van Nostrand Reinhold Company Inc. Reprinted by permission of the publisher.)

The second difference from the typewriter is **backspace correction.** Most entry mistakes are noted as soon as they are made. Correction for a typewriter is messy; the WP operator need only backspace over a few characters by hitting either rub or backspace. Rub produces a code received by the WP program. A character just entered is deleted from the electronic document in memory and from the screen for each rub code received as the current entry point is moved backward.

Now the operator keys the correct characters into successive positions in memory, which the WP program sends to the screen.

Positioning

To *edit* text one must find the place in the text which requires correction. It is impossible to view all of the text simultaneously. The screen presents only a portion of the text. Screen size differs from one WP to another. Some screens present the equivalent of a printed page (66 lines of 80 or more characters); others restrict the amount displayed to 24 lines of 80 characters. Positioning consists of two actions. The first action finds the screenful which contains the text to be worked on. The second finds the character(s) on the screen where a change is to be initiated. These are discussed in reverse order.

The cursor.   The cursor is a mark on the screen which distinguishes a character from which editing may begin. It is important that the operator be able to find the cursor among a mass of text. It should stand out in some way such as one of the following:

- **Underline**—the character of interest has an underline beneath it and other text does not.
- **Reverse video**—if the rest of the characters are presented as white on black, reverse video means that the cursor position appears as black on a small square of white.
- **Blink**—the character at the cursor position blinks on and off, usually at a rate of once per second; this may be combined with underline or reverse video.

The place the cursor is *now* sitting may not be the place at which editing is to start; how does one move it? The WP may have several ways to move the cursor:

- By geometry;
- Express;
- By context.

Geometrical positioning is usually implemented by four keys with arrows which point respectively left, right, up, and down. Touching one of these keys moves the cursor one character position in the designated direction.

Most keyboards have a **repeat key:** touch the key and one code for that letter is sent to the computer; hold the key down and first one code is produced, then a second later repeatedly produced at about 10 per second. This feature is particularly useful in cursor positioning. If right is held down, the cursor moves rightward one character position; a second later it moves to the right at 10 positions per second. The arrow keys and the repeat function will send the cursor to almost any point on the screen in a few seconds.

Express positioning moves the cursor immediately to a particular spot on the screen. This action might be initiated by a home key with an arrow pointing diagonally which might move the cursor to the upper lefthand corner of the screen.

Context positioning moves the cursor through the text in increments corresponding to grammatical quantities. One can move the cursor forward by a character, word, paragraph, or page by touching char, word, para, or page, respectively. This requires one key for each context.

A reverse key, rev, permits a move backwards in the text. Press rev followed by a number of context keys and the cursor moves backwards to the appropriate position.

Content positioning causes the cursor to move to the next occurrence of a particular character. When this feature is activated, pressing f moves the cursor forward to the next occurrence of f. Pressing f three times more moves the cursor to the third f from *this* position. One can use this method to get to the next sentence by pressing the period or to the next word by pressing the space bar.

Scrolling.   Moving the cursor is effective only for text displayed on the screen. If the desired text is absent, we ask the WP to display a screen which shows another part of text. There are two ways to do this:

- Scrolling.
- Paging.

Scrolling causes text to move up or down the screen a line at a time; new text is brought in at the bottom (or top) as old text moves out the top (or bottom) of the screen. Consider the text to be a long continuous stream of document just like a piece of papyrus in ancient times. The papyrus reader would "scroll" the text by rotating the upper cylinder to advance to new material.

In the writer's opinion, continuous scroll with variable speed is the most useful. Once scroll is activated, text moves continuously onto the screen. When the desired chunk of text becomes visible, pressing another key stops the scroll action. **Reverse scroll** moves new text in at the top. Continuous scrolling requires sophisticated file management software in the WP.

Paging alters the screen content by a much larger amount, bringing in the next screenful of information. It is disconcerting to see a new screenful without context. Hence most paging mechanisms provide overlap of one, two or more lines from the previous screen. The operator can either page forward or backwards or can request screen renewal by a particular page number.

Deletion.   To *delete* is to remove some of the text from the electronic document and the screen. WPs provide two techniques for doing this:

- Immediate.
- Discretionary.

For **immediate deletion,** the operator's request is honored as soon as it arrives and the characters are removed. For instance, to remove three words from the text with this technique, the operator positions the cursor to the first of the words and hits delete word word word. The three words following the cursor are removed from the electronic document and disappear from the screen. The cursor is found positioned at the beginning of the fourth word; the intervening gap left by the deleted three words closes up to one regular word space.

For **discretionary deletion,** the operator distinguishes a string of characters on the screen by hitting the appropriate keys. The operator can then decide if the string should be eliminated or kept.

Consider how one WP might implement this method. As the first action, move the cursor to the beginning of the string. Then mark off the characters which comprise the string. Again, using context positioning, hit mark sent word word. To determine which string is marked for deletion, the string may be **highlighted**—set off in some way. For highlighting, a string is

- Put in reverse video;
- Made to blink; or
- Given a special character, such as an up arrow or triangle at each end.

Some WPs allow marking a string backwards.

After the string has been marked, there is time to de-cide whether to delete or keep the string: press delete and the highlighted material disappears and the text closes up to realign the paragraph; press accpt and the screen goes back to normal. Most WPs provide either immediate or discretionary deletion, but few provide both.

Insertion.   To *insert* is to add new data to the text. There are three methods of insertion:

1. *Replace*—characters are keyed in to replace existing characters, starting at the current cursor position.
2. *Open up*—the screen seems to open up at the cursor to make room for new characters to be inserted.
3. *Push aside*—as characters are keyed they enter at the current cursor position, but before the character on which the cursor sits.

For **replacement insertion** (Figure 40.9) the cursor is positioned. As a new character is keyed in, the text editor program replaces the content of the current character position with the code for the keyed character. It updates the cursor position on the screen to show the new character and moves the cursor over one position, keeping track of this movement internally. The next character is typed into that position. Replacement insertion is useful when the old and new material are the same size. Otherwise, a combination method is required.

For **open up insertion** (Figure 40.10) one initiates the action by pressing insert. The text on the screen parts at the cursor, leaving a large blank space on the screen. Some text following the cursor has moved to the bottom of the screen so that insertion can be done in context. Text keyed in appears in the blank space following the break in the old text. The text editor actually puts the characters in an **insertion buffer** but displays them as noted.

After entering new material, one has a choice: if accpt is pressed, the inserted material actually goes into the electronic document; if cancel is pressed, the electronic document is not altered and the screen is restored to its original condition.

```
Products of th█s nature.        Read to replace

Products of tha█ nature.        Replace i with a

Products of that█nature.        Replace s with t
```

Figure 40.9. Insertion by replacement. (From I. Flores, *Word Processing Handbook*. Copyright © 1982 by Van Nostrand Reinhold Company Inc. Reprinted by permission of the publisher.)

```
Let's add to this line.  OK?          1.  Line to add to

Let's add ▮o this line.  OK?          2.  Position cursor

Let's add ▮                           3.  Press open
         to this line.  OK?

Let's add something ▮                 4.  Key in "something".
         to this line.  OK?

Let's add something to this           5.  Press close or halt.
line.  OK?
```

Figure 40.10. Steps for insertion by opening up. (From I. Flores, *Word Processing Handbook*. Copyright © 1982 by Van Nostrand Reinhold Company Inc. Reprinted by permission of the publisher.)

When accpt is pressed, the text editor reorganizes the electronic document in memory. It now separates the document into two parts, a front and back end. It moves the front of the document forward by the size of text in the insertion buffer. It then moves the contents of the insertion buffer into the electronic document. Finally the text editor reforms and displays the text.

For **push aside** insertion (Figure 40.11), the keyed characters immediately enter the electronic document and display. If the characters are inserted into a line which has blanks at the end, the text on the line can expand without affecting succeeding text. When inserted characters cause the line to expand beyond the margin,

then word wrap is invoked. The last word of the current line is pushed onto the next line. If that line can absorb the additional characters, future lines are unaffected. However, it is likely that a word will be wrapped from the next line, too. This may continue to the end of the paragraph. Usually, there are enough blanks at the end of a paragraph to accommodate a few words pushed off from previous lines.

For a large insertion, even the space at the end of a paragraph is insufficient. Insertion intrudes into the next paragraph and it may push down succeeding paragraphs. The effect which looks like a waterfall may cause the final line on the screen to be pushed off entirely.

```
Inserting into text which spans        1.  Text for ensection.
a number of lines.  As each letter
is keyed, text is pushed off one line
and onto the next.

Inserting ▮nto text which spans        2.  Position to cursor.
a number of lines.  As each letter
is keyed, text is pushed off one line
and onto the next.

Inserting t▮nto text which             3.  Press insert and key in "t".
spans a number of lines.  As each
letter is keyed, text is pushed off
one line and onto the next.

Inserting two ▮nto text which          4.  Key in "wo ".
spans a number of lines.  As each
letter is keyed, text is pushed off
one line and onto the next.

Inserting two words ▮nto text          5.  Finish keying "two words ".
which spans a number of lines.  As
each letter is keyed in, text is pushed
off one line and onto the next.
```

Figure 40.11. Steps for insertion by pushing aside. (From I. Flores, *Word Processing Handbook*. Copyright © 1982 by Van Nostrand Reinhold Company Inc. Reprinted by permission of the publisher.)

Push aside insertion is dynamic. Both memory and the screen are updated each time a character is keyed in. Although readjusting memory takes microseconds or at worst milliseconds, readjusting the screen may take a perceptible amount of time. While reforming is going on, one may key in more characters. However, these characters do not appear on the screen until reforming for the previous character is completed. This effect is startling to the new operator, who soon accommodates to it though.

Search

We have seen how the operator moves the cursor to a particular point in the text to make corrections. Often these corrections to be entered into the electronic document are on a marked up draft. When the number of corrections is high, it is simple to spot each new site and move the cursor there. But consider a large document in which the corrections are light. The next correction may be one or two screens away. It is tedious to hunt through the text for the defective word. This is alleviated by a search facility—the WP finds the next correction. The sequence might go as follows:

1. Press search.
2. The WP prompts for the **string,** the set of characters it is to find.
3. Key in the string, using backspace correction should a mistake occur.
4. Press return when the string is correctly displayed.
5. The WP searches the electronic document in its memory to find the string.
6. If found, the WP presents a screen with text which contains the desired string and with the cursor at its beginning.

The WP has a **search buffer** to hold the search string. The WP reviews the text from the current cursor position onward, to match up characters in sequence with those in the search buffer.

Reverse search. Many WPs provide a capability to search from the cursor *backwards.* This requires that the WP examine the search string backwards as well as forward, as normally typed into the text.

Repeat. Once a search string is stored in the buffer, the WP can honor a second request for the same string. It may be desired to alter the text at the same target word in several places. The initial search is requested. Then the operator presses repeat and another search is executed against the same search string.

Ignore case. A search is carried out for an exact match. If a request is made for an occurrence of "text," then only the word written in lower case is found by the WP. Should a sentence begin with "Text," it would not be found. Nor would "TEXT" be found. To catch *all* occurrences of a string, regardless of whether upper or lower case characters are used, one can ask the WP to ignore case.

Whole word. Should the WP be asked to find "less," it could turn up "lesson." A string is identified regardless of context. To avoid the foregoing error, the **whole word option** makes sure that the designated string is surrounded on either side by blanks.

Search and replace. Not only does the WP find strings, but it replaces a string with a second string. It *remedies* a mistake throughout the text. For instance, in dictation one may have used "site" which was transcribed as "sight," a natural mistake. If "sight" appears 15 times in the text, it would be tedious to fix without **search and replace.** To invoke this feature, one presses search and replace and the WP prompts for the *search* string; "sight" is entered and *return* pressed. The WP then prompts for the *replace* string; the operator supplies "site," then again presses *return.* Each and every "sight" in the text subsequently becomes "site."

Discretion. If the text contains a few occurrences of "sight" which *are* correct, **discretionary search and replace** is the answer. Each time the WP finds the search string, it asks whether replacement should take place. According to the operator's response, "yes" or "no," the string is replaced or ignored.

Global search and replace. Most WPs perform this operation for an entire small document. Page oriented WPs may be restricted to one or two pages. In this case one may have to make a search and replace request several times to scan the entire text.

The action takes only a couple of seconds per page for most WPs. However, if the computer is holding a 30 or 40 page document, to save time search and replace can be restricted to the next few pages.

Indeed, the power of search and replace can save considerable trouble. Suppose I am preparing a document which contains the name of my school, "Baruch College,

City University of New York," at a number of places in the text. I save a lot of trouble if, instead of writing each instance out entirely, I only enter "BC." Once the document has been entered, it is a simple task for the WP to start at the beginning and replace each occurrence of "BC" with the desired phrase.

Format

"Format" refers to how the document appears on the printed page. If the document prints as shown on the display, this is a **responsive display.** Features which are not likely to change throughout the course of the document are called **long term format parameters.** Some of these are

- *Paper size*—the length and width of the sheet of paper.
- *Margins*—the space on the right, left, top and bottom which is left blank.
- *Line spacing*—single, double, and so forth.

There are other parameters which can be altered for a short period of time. For instance, one may want, for emphasis, to underline a letter, a word or a sentence; or, also for emphasis, to use boldface. Giving a whole paragraph extra indentation from the left margin or changing its line spacing, say, from double to single, makes it stand out, too; such visual alteration is usually employed to set off a longer quoted passage from the writer's own text.

Describing the format.
All systems allow the operator to set format. To lighten the burden in this respect, many WPs provide a **default format:** if no format is specified, the machine assumes its standard format is wanted. For the menu driven WP, a format menu is presented in the course of creating a new document. One

```
              FORMAT SETTINGS

          Format:              Setting:

      1.  Page length              66
      2.  Text length              54
      3.  Left margin              10
      4.  Right margin             10
      5.  Top margin                5
      6.  Bottom margin             5
      7.  Line spacing              1
      8.  Pitch                    10
      9.  Proportional spacing      0
     10.  Justification             0
     11.  Paragraph indent          5
     12.  Paragraph spacing         1
```

Figure 40.12. A format menu. (From I. Flores, *Word Processing Handboook.* Copyright © 1982 by Van Nostrand Reinhold Company Inc. Reprinted by permission of the publisher.)

keystroke specifies the standard format. To make changes, one simply positions the cursor on each line describing a format feature to be altered. For instance, to change the left margin from 10 to 15, the operator would position the cursor to "left margin" on the menu (as in Figure 40.12) and change the value accordingly.

Some WPs furnish several standard formats: one for correspondence, another for reports, and so forth. When you get such a menu, a single key stroke chooses one of these.

Format line and tabs.   A neat way to show the present vertical margins and the tab stops is the *format line*, as illustrated in Figure 40.13. It is always presented at the top (or bottom) of the screen for some WPs. It extends from one margin to the other; the margin limits are indicated by a character or a graphic symbol.

The **tab key** positions the cursor to the next tab stop in much the same way as on the typewriter. On a number

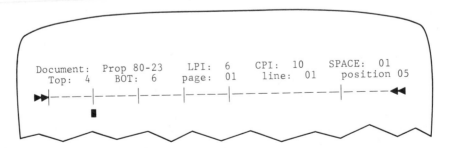

Figure 40.13. An example of a format line. (From I. Flores, *Word Processing Handbook.* Copyright © 1982 by Van Nostrand Reinhold Company Inc. Reprinted by permission of the publisher.)

of WPs, tab stops are automatically set at uniform intervals by default. A **tab clear** key clears the stops either one at a time or all at once. A **tab set** key enables the setting of tabs.

The word processor may provide three kinds of tabs:

- **Normal**—characters entered after tabbing are placed in successive positions along the line.
- **Decimal**—the integers go to the left and, after the decimal point is entered, the fractional part goes to the right of the tab stop.
- **Center**—characters are centered about the center tab position.

Short term. Short term action prevails for a few characters or words. Here are some examples:

1. **Underline**—the printer underlines a set of characters or words.
2. **Boldface**—each character is printed twice, the second impression being offset from the first by a fraction of an inch so that the characters appear emboldened.
3. **Superscript**—characters print slightly higher on the line than the rest, as, for example, footnote references.
4. **Subscript**—characters print slightly lower on the line, as in mathematical formulas.
5. **Different typeface**—the printer is stopped by the WP so that the operator can change the daisy wheel to supply a different typeface.

Each of these features is usually invoked, depending on the WP, by special keys on the keyboard which turn the feature on and off.

Responsive displays. On some WPs, the display indicates each requested change in format. A display might show boldface by using brighter characters for the string of boldface characters. Most WPs are not responsive for *all* format activities, however. For instance, the majority of WPs will show margins and page alignments, but they will not show boldface or type changes.

Printing

The electronic document that the operator creates is written on the disk in page-size chunks. If the electronic document has been subjected to heavy editing, these chunks may contain more or less than a properly formatted page.

Repagination. Some WPs provide a program to *repaginate* the document, that is, divide it up into new chunks of proper page size regardless of the current division of the text.

Head and foot. A **heading** is fixed text for the top of each page; a **footing** goes on the bottom of each page. During either editing or creation, the operator can indicate either or both, and what each should be.

Justifying. To *justify* is to print a document so that it has an even margin on both the left and right side. In practice, this term applies to the right margin, since all word processors automatically (as do typewriters) align on the left. One can indicate at any time that the document is to be justified. Some WPs provide a responsive display which also shows the text justified on the screen. Most WPs provide the capability to print the document with even margins.

Proportional spacing. Some typewriters and WP printers provide *proportional spacing;* i.e., some characters (such as the period) print narrow while others (such as the M) print much wider.

Printing out. When you are ready, a separate program prints a document. For a draft document it is more convenient to print on a continuous form. Most printers come with either a **tractor feed** or a **pin feed;** continuous paper stock can be placed in the bin and the paper is moved continuously past the printer without the need for the operator to monitor the action.

For correspondence and reports, most offices use letterhead stock and require paper which is neatly cut on each side. Each sheet of paper must be fed to the printer separately. An **automatic sheet feeder** feeds single sheets of paper under the control of the computer. Although this device costs between one and two thousand dollars, it is a necessary item in an office environment because it cuts down considerably on operator time and thus enables the printer to perform its mission unattended. For some WPs, editing may go on while printing is taking place.

40.5 PORTIONS OF DOCUMENTS

It is important to be able to divide any electronic document into pieces which can be manipulated as required. We discuss three kinds of document subdivision:

- **Blocks,** which are designated by the operator in the text currently being edited in memory;
- **Phrases,** which are extracted from the text being edited, and set aside elsewhere in memory (*not* in the text

being edited) to be called up and entered into another electronic document at will.

- **Subdocuments,** which are portions of text on external storage that can be called up and entered as needed into the document being edited, or put together in various ways as will be discussed later.

Blocks

Earlier, we discussed how to delineate a block in the electronic document and on the screen for the purpose of deletion. Recall that in the typical WP one might mark off a block by pressing a sequence of keys, such as mark para para sent word. After mark is pressed, each additional key causes additional text to be highlighted. When done, the operator presses mark again to distinguish a continuous block of text which can now be manipulated.

Then the cursor goes where the action is to take place. To move the block to the cursor position, one simply presses move. If, instead, the block is to be left where it is and copied, the operator presses copy. He or she can write the block onto the disk by pressing write and furnishing a name for it.

Block manipulation provides the "cut and paste" that extensive editing requires. Now the operator can mark off pieces of text anyplace in a document and move them to any other place or make copies of them.

Phrase Storage

Some WPs provide *phrase storage* to record a *phrase* in an area in memory set aside for that purpose. One can *recall* a phrase and enter it anyplace in the text. Phrases are usually a few words, such as a salutation in a letter, the title of the executive sending a letter, or a set of words which may be repeated on multiple documents.

Setting up a phrase calls for a name for the operation. On a typical WP one hits phrase-store then the numeral 5 followed by the phrase to be stored; the action is completed by pressing accpt. This sends the phrase into memory, *not* into the text. Whenever this phrase is to be inserted into the text, the operator simply presses phrase-recall 5 for insertion at the cursor position.

Phrases remain in their designated spots even when the text being worked on is completed and stored on disk. These phrases are available for the next and subsequent documents that may be created and edited. However, when the computer is turned off, these phrases disappear from memory.

Subdocuments

A piece of a document on an external medium is a *subdocument*. The WP enables the operator to name the subdocument, put it on a disk, save it indefinitely, and later call it back from the disk into any document being worked on. Each time a portion of text which may be of use later is encountered, one may save it, giving it a name easily remembered.

When creating a new document, the operator may realize that a subdocument saved earlier is of use here, and call it forth by hitting insert and giving the name of the subdocument. The text of the subdocument is inserted at the cursor position without otherwise affecting the text in memory. Once the subdocument is part of the new document, it can be edited, modified, or thrown away as much as the text just entered.

A previously created full document may act as a subdocument if one so chooses. Simply insert it in the text as just described and edit out all the undesirable material.

40.6 EDITING ASSISTANCE

The WP provides invaluable assistance in creating a document by helping with hyphenation, spelling, and do other things as described below.

Hyphenation

The WP provides word wrap which assures that lines only contain whole words. When a large word does not fit at the end of a line, it is wrapped to the next line. Unfortunately, that often contributes to excessively ragged lines. Even when justification is used to provide even margins, short lines in terms of word count will have large spaces between words. When the copy being created is polished and one is ready to produce a final document, it is also desirable to have lines about equal in length and with uniform spaces throughout the text.

Some WPs provide **automatic hyphenation.** Before a large word is wrapped, it is examined and rules applied to place the hyphen. The hyphen is inserted automatically and the word split before it is wrapped. The trouble is that most of these programs are only 80 percent accurate, and mishyphenation often results.

Computer assisted hyphenation helps, but the operator must do some of the work. This is a separate program which is run against the text when one is satisfied that it is almost perfect. The program reviews the text, accepting all lines which are already of a reasonable length. When a line is found that is too long, the word which would ordinarily be wrapped is left on its current line instead and the program stops. It presents the line with the large word at the left and the cursor positioned for optimum separation in terms of even lines. It is unlikely to be positioned for *correct* hyphenation, however. The operator may move the cursor (backwards only) to the appropriate position and press hyphenate. A **soft hyphen** is inserted where designated, and the word is separated with the second part wrapped to the next line. (If the operator declines to hyphenate, the whole word is wrapped.) If a long line follows one that is short, a word, or part of a word, at the beginning of the long line can move back to the *end* of the preceding line, with any needed hyphenation performed as described.

A soft hyphen is so-called because it is printed only when the hyphen comes at the end of the line. Thus if the text as it is now displayed is printed, the hyphen will appear. However, if the text is subjected to further editing and the hyphenated word is moved so that a hyphen is no longer needed at the end of the line, then the soft hyphen will not print.

Spelling

Spelling programs are effective in coping with misspelled words. These programs ferret out misspellings and even provide choices for their correction. Large dictionaries are built into these programs to verify a wide range of words.

Spelling programs may make two kinds of mistakes: (1) they erroneously flag properly spelled words, or (2) they may accept words which are incorrectly spelled. The second class of error is, of course, intolerable. But the first kind of mistake is only natural. There are many disciplines which have their own **jargon**—words unique to a given discipline, not usually coming up in common conversation. We could not expect a spelling program of reasonable size to cope with all such disciplines.

A good spelling program permits the user to send jargon that it marks as incorrect to a supplementary dictionary added by the user. Now, when the program examines the next document, it can refer to this supplementary dictionary and will no longer mark such jargon as incorrect.

Outline Form

Some WPs have an automatic outline form which helps to set up and maintain an outline properly, even during heavy editing. These programs are useful in some situations and almost indispensable in others, such as preparing a proposal for the military. Such proposals often have each paragraph numbered and indented according to a hierarchy.

Tables and Charts

Many business presentations include charts and tables. These are often oversize documents. Some WPs provide features for manipulating rows and columns in tables. They enable the user to move around, delete, alter, and otherwise affect a table's columns and rows.

When the document is wide, its entire width cannot be presented on the screen. It requires **horizontal scrolling**—the ability to move the screen contents to the left or the right to display previously invisible portions of a wide document.

Some WPs provide mathematical capability, sometimes as an option. The WP can put totals and subtotals in tables and perform all the basic arithmetic operations, which can be useful in reducing the operator's time.

Footnotes

Footnotes are important, especially in the law office and in writing involving many references to articles in a professional or displinary body of literature. Some WPs have elaborate footnote programs (including superscripts) which enable the user to edit text heavily without adversely affecting the footnotes. Footnotes move along with the page on which they are cited, regardless of what editing occurs in the text, including large insertions and deletions; that is, a footnote cited in the text will always fall on the page with its text citation.

40.7 AUTOMATIC ASSEMBLY

The WP can help to assemble documents from subdocuments on disk. This assistance is invaluable in reducing the amount of time required to prepare repetitious documents.

Preprinted Forms

Some offices abound with forms which must be filled out: petty cash, travel vouchers, travel requests, passes, etc. These forms are difficult to handle, even with a good typewriter, because they require tediously accurate alignments of the typewriter with often complicated fill-in forms; they require that the operator moves the carriage to just the right position to enter the value to a field, and that the line advance on the form is geared to the typewriter advance.

One can prepare a duplicate of the form on the WP and keep it *as an electronic document on disk.* Then the following procedure applies: Whenever filling in a printed form, simply call up the matching electronic document, then insert the *printed form* into the printer. The operator only need align it once in the upper left hand corner and it is ready to receive the computer's output. Now call up the electronic form to the screen. By tabbing, get to the start of each blank field on the form. Upon finishing, direct the completed form to the printer; only the filled-in fields print on the form in the printer.

Form Letters

When one sends the same letter to a number of people with only certain information changed, the WP can provide extensive help. Three electronic documents are involved:

1. The **stencil,** which is a copy of the letter with names or symbols where individualizing substitutions are to be made;
2. The **variable list,** which consists of a separate set of values to be filled into each letter to be sent; and
3. The **output document,** the copy of each outgoing letter with values filled in.

Stencil.   The stencil looks like the letter except that a variable name or a switch code is entered at places where substitutions are to be made. A **switch code** is a special symbol, often a graphic, which displays on the screen but does not print. It tells the print program that something is to be filled in at a given point. The variable starts with a similar symbol and continues with a name which identifies what is to be substituted at the point.

Having prepared the stencil the operator can print it out for reference. Then it goes on a disk as an electronic document, with a name.

Variable value list.   The *variable value list* is the information which is to be substituted into the form letter to create the output document. The information for one output document is called a **record.** It is divided into **fields,** one for each substitution to be made into the form letter. All the information for each letter is collected and put in the variable list. This becomes a separate electronic document with its own label and is placed on a disk, usually the same disk that holds the stencil.

Output document.   Some WPs create one electronic document for each output document. However this step is often unnecessary. In other WPs the output document is sent directly to the printer. The print program reads in the stencil. It reproduces an output document continuously until it finds a switch code or variable name. Then it looks at the variable list and finds the proper field within the current record which is substituted in place of the switch code, or variable name. Then it switches back to the stencil to find more information to include in the output document. It stops at each switch code or variable name to enter the special information.

After this document is printed, the print program checks to see if there are more records in the variable list. If so, a new document is prepared. The stencil is reviewed again from the beginning and the text is merged with the next value record to print in the next output document.

Document Assembly

The WP is almost indispensable when much of the work in the office consists of putting together documents which resemble each other in many respects, yet are different. If these documents can be composed of standard paragraphs drawn from a library of paragraphs, then the WP document assembly feature can perform this function in a fraction of the time required to type the document. For this action the following documents are associated:

1. A **library** of standard paragraphs in electronic document form.
2. A set of **assembly instructions** for producing the single output document.
3. The output document itself.

Library.   The library of standard paragraphs is fabricated by one or more operators during normal processing of documents. When a paragraph is noted that may be useful in the future, the operator marks it as a block and writes the block onto the library disk.

Assembly instructions.   A hard copy printout of the standard paragraphs together with their names is kept on hand for reference. In a frequent application, a lawyer making up a will looks at the standard paragraphs, or "boiler plate," which apply to wills. Once the paragraphs needed to fabricate this will are found, they are noted in the desired sequence.

When the operator receives the list of paragraphs, or **section,** required, an assembly instruction document is fabricated. It consists of a list of the names of the required subdocuments or paragraphs and a name for the output document. The WP is activated and goes to the library, copying out the paragraphs required in the proper sequence. The WP "pastes" them together to form an electronic document which is used to print up the final hard copy form.

Inserting variables. As described, each section is a complete set of text. This need not be so. There may be variable information inserted into each section. That is, a section is like a single copy of a form letter. It may be a stencil into which one plugs values.

When the operator makes up the assembly instructions, if a section needs variable values, then these values are included. For example, sections assembled to make a will include the names of the beneficiaries, the bequestor, the attorney, dates, and addresses. The WP prints the will by assembling the sections and inserting the variables.

Records Processing

Once there is a set of records in a variable list, it is possible to process this list and extract even further power from the WP. Usually records processing is an option, a program purchased for an additional price with a WP. But it can be added later. Management of records is often considered a data processing function.

It is beyond the scope of this chapter to describe in detail the activities which **records processing (RP)** might perform. For a whiff of the flavor, here is a list:

1. RP can provide simplified data entry of the values for each record.
2. Single records can be found, altered, printed out, and processed in various ways.

3. A group of records can be selected according to some criterion, such as zip code, state, amount of balance, current debit, credit rating, and so forth.
4. Form letters can be sent out from a selected list.
5. The list can be reordered or sorted according to any criterion, for example, alphabetized by name or account number, or put in zip code order.
6. A report can be printed, structured as the user chooses.

40.8 THE FUTURE

Word processing has gained considerable popularity in the last decade; however, its potential has hardly been tapped. Most of those who have WPs have not used all the available features to their fullest extent.

In the next few years, high technology equipment will come to the market. Hard disk storage will become available to hold hundreds of times more documents than the floppy disks currently available. Dot matrix printers with letter quality printout are beginning to become available. Because of their design, they can provide many type faces and special characters under the direct control of the computer, without the need for operator intervention. Dot matrix printers can operate many times faster to produce rough drafts. Within the next five years, they will be the printers in use in the office.

REFERENCES

Chirlian, B., *A Tenderfoot's Guide to Word Processing.* Beaverton, OR: Matrix Publishers, 1982.

Flores, I., *Word Processing Handbook.* New York: Van Nostrand Reinhold, 1982.

Naiman, A., *Word Processing Buyer's Guide.* New York: McGraw-Hill Book Co., 1981.

Van Uchelen, R., *Word Processing.* New York: Van Nostrand Reinhold, 1980.

Waite, M., and J. Arca, *Wordprocessing Primer.* New York: McGraw-Hill Book Co., 1982.

41
Graphics

Ivan Flores

Baruch College
City University of New York

41.1 INTRODUCTION

Pictures have a fascination which goes far beyond what words can convey. Add color and the attraction increases. Add motion and the attraction becomes almost irresistible.

We have seen this dramatically in the development of entertainment. The evolution was not quite parallel. The still photograph came first. Adding motion, no matter how primitive, attracted considerable attention. Almost all cinema today uses color and integrates it into the plot. There is hardly anyone who does not have a color television set. Arcade games came along a few years ago and have become a multibillion dollar operation. Their ups and downs shake the stock market.

Video games sprang up when computer graphics came of age. They pervade Epcot (the newest Disney venture); several movies (for example, *Tron*) are based on computer graphics.

Powerful graphics require a fast computer and sophisticated terminal circuitry, previously beyond the scope of the personal computer. Now components are dropping drastically in cost; in less than a decade these capabilities will be available on the personal computer.

The remainder of this chapter gives an overview of computer graphics: the smallest system such as the small Atari costs $200; the largest for computer aided design and manufacture (CAD/CAM) costs $200,000 to a million dollars. Yet each pays its way. Only with the help of CAD/CAM is VLSI (very large scale integration) possible for a mass market. Chips can now hold 450,000

transistors and perform innumerable functions. How much effort would it take to lay out such a chip without the help of computer aided design, if that were possible?

Before we examine how graphics work, let us see what they can do. Many books have been written about graphics, some devoted to single applications. This section is a brief overview, divided into three parts aimed at low, medium and high resolution graphics. The higher the resolution, the more detail appears in the picture.

Games and Amusements

The biggest application of low resolution graphics is television and arcade games. Many man-months of design on a personal computer or the equivalent creates the presentation. Once the game is perfected, further effort is invested to put the program in ROM (read only memory). In mass production, the ROM chip costs only a few dollars to fabricate.

The chip *is* the program which runs a small, single purpose display computer. This is part of the game set one buys, such as made by Atari or Colleco. The computer contains a section of RAM which holds data given to and altered by the players. The background graphics and the action program is contained on the chip in a cartridge which fits into the game box. During play, data is collected from the input buttons and the joy stick.

Some personal computers provide low resolution graphics as part of the software package. These use a monitor terminal or tie into a television set.

At the next level of cost, personal computers provide a

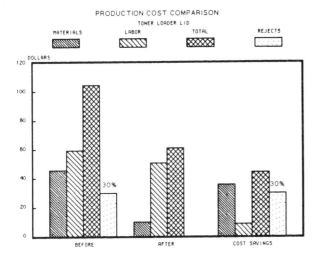

Figure 41.1. Bar chart. (Courtesy Hewlett-Packard)

language interpreter, usually an additional set of BASIC commands. These let you plot points, draw lines and curves and fill in figures. To write a BASIC program to project a graphic image on the screen is a challenge. Adding animation can also be fun.

Software suppliers (such as Stoneware) provide packages for micros (such as the Apple) to permit the *drawing*

of crude images. Even a joy stick or tablet can be attached.

Business

Business applications are best done with medium resolution graphics. No one wants to look at a chart in which the lines look like a flight of steps. Software helps create bar (and pie charts) such as those shown in Figure 41.1. Displaying them is useful but incorporating them in hard output is even more valuable. Figure 41.2 shows a typical business graphics capability with a keyboard for control, a CRT for display and a plotter for hard copy. Software for these activities does the following at your bidding:

1. Creates forms—bars or sectors of circles.
2. Tailors each bar or sector to quantities entered.
3. Determines the overall size of the chart.
4. Positions it properly on the display and printout area.
5. Colors parts to distinguish them.
6. Enters text to label each part.

Graphs. Graph software accepts a number of points specified as sets of two coordinates, plots them, scales the graphs and displays them. Some handle multiple superimposed graphs. If an appropriate display and peripheral device are available, these may be colored.

Figure 41.2. Graphs: terminal with plotter. (Courtesy Hewlett-Packard)

Figure 41.3. Office layout. (Courtesy GTCO)

Advanced business applications. Graphics has a real place in business beyond those mentioned above. Here is a bare outline:

1. *Office layout.* Today the office is in constant flux. People move around readily. Partitions and furniture are pushed about to accommodate them. The careful office manager has to sketch a new office layout at frequent intervals to suit growth and attrition. Graphics, as in Figure 41.3 create a top view of all furniture which may be screen-positioned freely on an office floor plan to see how different arrangements look. Alternatives can be printed out for reference and quick modification. The arrangement in the figure lets the operator create the layout and makes alterations with the mouse and tablet as described later.

2. *Flow charts and PERT charts* are aids to plan and run complex projects. Figure 41.4 provides an example.

3. *Illustrations for reports and texts* help elucidate the reading matter and are easy to absorb by the busy executive. These can be sketched at a good graphics terminal and printed on a dot matrix printer, even integrated with a report. A typical illustration for a report is shown in Figure 41.5.

4. *Data base integration.* Data available in machine readable form are growing exponentially. It is hard to find and digest. If we could apply graphical methods to data, things might be a lot easier.

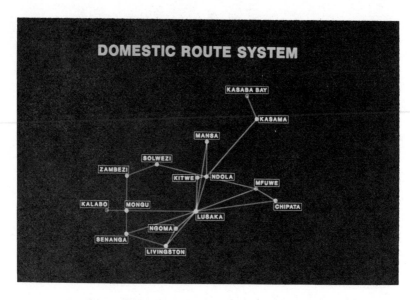

Figure 41.4. PERT chart. (Courtesy Carl Marchover Associates)

The Toner Loader Lid (See Figure 4-2) was previously produced using a vendor casting process plus an in-house machining and painting procedure. A recent production change order changed the process to a 100% numerically controlled vendor machined part. Details of the machined part are shown in drawing D-2682-20182-1.

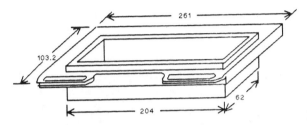

Figure 41.5. Sketch for report (Courtesy Hewlett-Packard)

High Resolution

Architecture and engineering. All engineering and architectural work requires detailed plans and mechanical drawings. Draftspeople still spend many boring hours drawing lines and hand-lettering text on drawings such as those shown in Figure 41.6 (mechanical), 41.7 (electrical) and 41.8 (architectural). Now this tedium has almost become a thing of the past in large manufacturing facilities. It is so simple to make a drawing, no matter how complicated, on a CRT screen with zoom and pan capability.

Parallel and perpendicular lines are common in mechanical drawings. They require an accurate T-square and near-perfect alignment. On the screen, a perfect grid may be superimposed; rough lines drawn are repositioned and aligned automatically.

The final output, an inked, scale drawing, is produced on an elaborate and expensive plotting board. Its cost is more than made up for by the tedium it eliminates and the time it saves.

Medicine. We are just beginning to scratch the surface. Medical illustrators do not appreciate graphics as yet. It is just coming into use in images for sketches and plots for results. Even the laboratory has taken up image analysis and is applying it to diagnoses.

Education. Computer aided instruction (CAI) has been around for several decades. (PLATO is the name of one such teaching system.) Teaching programs involve words and language. However, illustrating principles of physics, mathematics, biology and so forth is aided considerably with graphics. The instructor sets up a lesson with illustrations he or she has created on the screen, possibly including animation.

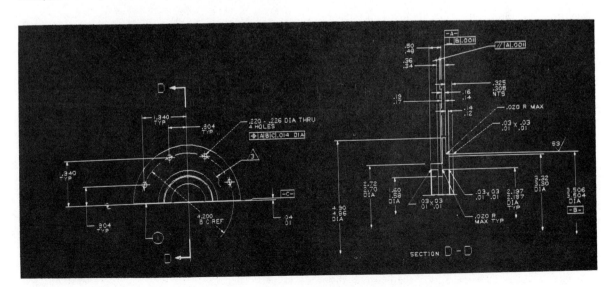

Figure 41.6. Mechanical drawing. (Courtesy Lexidata Corporation)

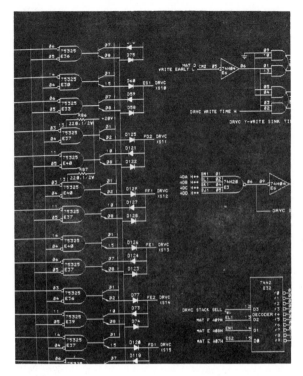

Figure 41.7. Electrical drawing (partial). (Courtesy Lexidata Corporation)

Publishing. Scientific and technical books include a host of illustrations, all hand tailored to the author's sketches. Now, with plotting machines, it is possible for an artist to create illustrations, including labels and captions, at the CRT. Then the plotter produces them accurately and quickly.

Another application is to typography for the creation of new type faces.

Cartography. Application of graphics maps is apparent. A large map can be stored on a small floppy disk. To make changes in a map, one simply brings it to the screen, alters it and on the computer store it on the disk. The map can be printed on a plotting board, and, if needed, show a vertical projection in three dimensions as Figures 41.9 and 41.10.

Statistics. Programs plot one or more graphs and superimpose them. A more complicated program for multiple variables displays a three dimensional solid comprehensible to the less technical person. Statistical qualities

of collected data can be extracted and displayed visually in a penetrating manner.

Visual arts. Computer animation is a part of our lives. Yet we hardly recognize it as such. Many television programs use computer animation for logos and advertisements. Most news broadcasts begin with a computer animated display. Computer animation is also the principal medium for cinema science fiction *(Tron, 2001, Star Wars).*

Serious artists use graphics as a medium for pictures and three dimensional sculpture models.

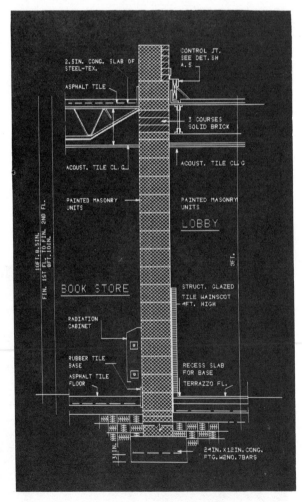

Figure 41.8. Architectural drawing. (Courtesy Lexidata Corporation)

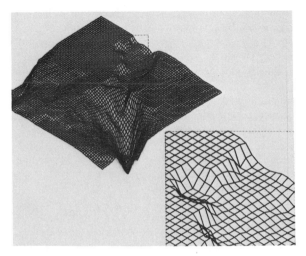

Figure 41.9. Cartography: mapped area with detail. (Courtesy Calma)

CAD/CAM. Computer aided design (CAD) and computer aided manufacture (CAM) have come a long way due to computer graphics. The entire design process can be performed on the terminal. Programs take designs and convert them to other programs to run milling machines, boring machines, multiple hole drillers and the like—a portion of an assembly line.

41.2 THE GRAPHIC SYSTEM

A graphic system enables the user to perform these functions:

- Enter graphics data;
- Create graphic images;
- View the images;
- Manipulate images in complex ways to augment them;
- Produce graphic output, for example, a record on paper or film;
- Record images on some machine-readable medium to recreate them later.

Not all graphic systems provide all these facilities.

The Overall System

Figure 42.11 is a block diagram of a graphic system. It always includes a digital computer. The equipment at the left of the dashed line is part of the basic computer; additional devices on the right make this a graphic system.

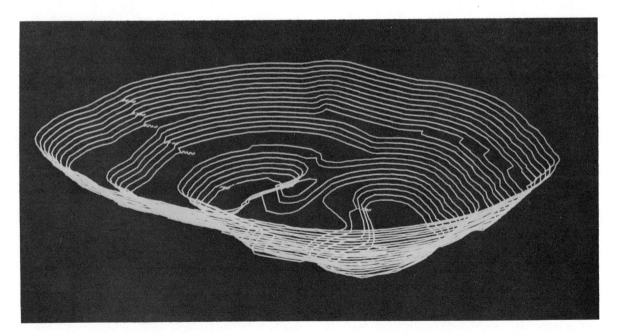

Figure 41.10. Cartography: an open-pit mine. (Courtesy Evans & Sutherland)

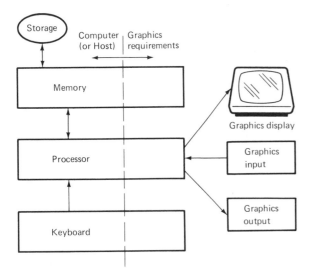

Figure 41.11. The graphics system.

The dividing line between the computer and the graphic system is rarely clear. We discuss alternative system configurations later.

Additions for graphics.   Additional hardware is necessary for graphics. The most important is the visual display which shows the image via technology which emits light. The display usually consists of a screen comparable to a television set in technology and size. Note that the terminals associated with many micros, personal computers and main frames are *not* satisfactory for graphic display because they can show only text.

Next we require an image memory made from the same RAM components as the main memory of the computer. However, the format of graphic information stored there is different. The image memory and the display must coordinate so that the pictorial information appears as planned.

Next there is an optional graphic input device to convey pictorial information to the system. Although a terminal keyboard suffices, it is designed for textual entry and is less than ideal for pictorial input.

The terminal displays the picture being created, which disappears when the equipment is turned off. The picture itself is rarely the end result. Most of us are not satisfied unless the picture is captured on paper or some intransigent medium. Most computer output devices do not handle graphics. The exception is certain dot matrix printers.

Equipment to produce an image as a drawing or a set of dots (hard output) may be expensive; the price of such equipment varies with the amount of detail to be produced and whether color is included.

Finally, as suggested at the upper left of Figure 42.11, storage, usually a floppy disk, may be provided to hold programs and data. Graphic images or command sequences or data stored there can reproduce images dot for dot or line for line.

Levels of systems.   Systems are marked by capability and price as described shortly in more detail. They can be categorized something like this:

- The **home** or **hobby system** is available for a few hundred dollars and requires a television set for display;
- The **semiprofessional** or **managerial system** costs a few thousand to an upper limit of $10,000 and includes a monitor;
- The **professional terminal** consists of a keyboard monitor and a computer for image generation in a single terminal. Although capable of creating some images on its own, it usually depends upon a host computer.

The Hobby System

Figure 41.12 is a block diagram of a typical hobby system. The whole computer is housed in a small box a couple of inches high and about 9 by 12 inches in its other dimensions. Half of the box's surface is a keyboard to enter data and commands. Within is a processing chip on a printed circuit board and RAM (random access memory) ranging from 16K to 64K. A read-only memory (ROM) may also be present.

Part of the RAM is devoted to storing the image. Since the graphics are low resolution, only a small amount of memory is required. The television screen shows either a black and white or a three or four color image (but sometimes 16 or more). The colors displayed are fixed, usually red, blue and green.

The computer contains a convertor which receives digital signals, and puts them in analog form, which is often nothing more than the turning on or off of analog voltages. This **modulates** a radio frequency carrier to produce a complete television signal.

Although conversion from digital input to a complete television signal is a complex activity, a large investment has been made by semiconductor manufacturers to put all the circuitry on a single chip. This technology has

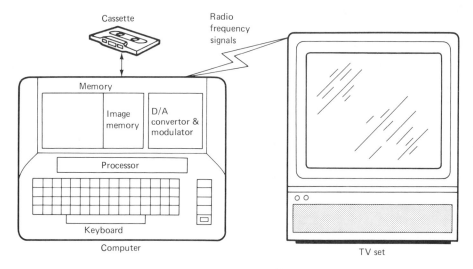

Figure 41.12. Low cost graphics system.

made possible today's inexpensive and highly popular video games.

The output television signal feeds directly to the antenna input of a television set, usually through a switch which chooses among the roof antenna, cable television and a game or computer. For some, an optional cassette input brings in different games or programs.

No other output device is shown in Figure 41.12, a reason being that a dot matrix printer costs more than the entire computer. For most, the system is a source of entertainment; what appears on the screen is sufficient.

The Management Work Station

This system is intended for the serious but occasional computer user. The services received from the computer in other areas are supplemented by graphics features available (and sometimes not even used).

The configuration shown in Figure 41.13 might be found in a typical micro or personal computer. Two floppy disks provide program and data. The printer *should* have graphics capability. A monitor in the terminal shows either black and white or color images. A conventional keyboard with additional function keys helps produce graphic images.

Image display.   Part of RAM holds the image created by the user. There are two ways that this image may dis-

play. The older system keeps the image in digital form in main memory. Each refresh cycle of the monitor examines RAM and recreates the image many times a second on the screen as described in Section 41.4. This type of cycle is used for Apple graphics and also text.

For the second method, the monitor with its own memory can be put in *graphics mode* or *character mode*. In graphics mode, data sent to the monitor is interpreted by the monitor as an image; in character mode, the same data is interpreted as text.

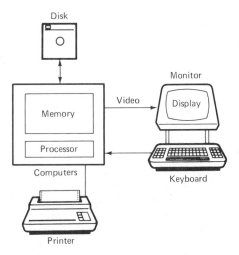

Figure 41.13. Manager's PC graphics.

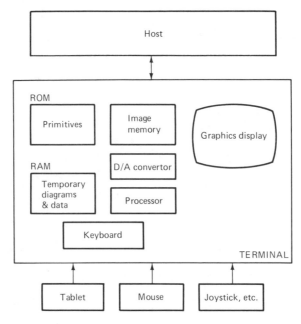

Figure 41.14. Graphics work station.

Professional Graphics Work Terminal

The professional terminal is illustrated in block form in Figure 41.14; it is almost self-sufficient. One can sit and create images at the keyboard or through special input devices. They are immediately displayed on the monitor. Usually, though, the images have some purpose outside of enjoyment or creativity and are related to problems in the real world. Therefore hard copy output and a medium for storage during the creation cycle, which may cover several sessions, are needed. The work station is connected to a host—a mini, supermini or mainframe—for additional processing. The large host may support several work terminals.

The terminal contains its own large image memory (100K bytes or more) and its own processor; programs to run the processor are contained in terminal ROM, RAM or both. A monitor may be included in the keyboard cabinet or if may be separate. Circuitry in the terminal converts the memory image to display on the monitor.

The graphics work station is designed to create complex images with speed and efficiency. Its keyboard can be used to enter data and commands into most conventional computers or micros when not used for graphics.

Applications

The hobby system is intended for entertainment regardless of the advertisements. However, many educators are working on programs to help youngsters to think, learn and develop visual concepts. Programs such as LOGO are expanding students' horizons.

The personal computer can provide useful graphic output depending on the amount of graphic facility incorporated in the overall system. Tables, figures, bar and pie charts and even a certain amount of drawing can be done with some equipment. The Lisa computer introduced by Apple Computer in the beginning of 1983 is meant to help the manager in most kinds of office planning as displayed on a black and white screen of medium resolution. LisaDraw, implemented on the Lisa computer, enables the manager to draw simple objects and move them around as described later in this chapter. This $8,000 computer is intended specifically as a management work station. There are a few others, at the same or a lower price, that perform this kind of function.

The professional graphics work station is required for most applications described in this chapter and may cost $20,000 to $40,000. However, the price for some had dropped to $10,000 by mid-1983. Makers of this type of terminal have combined them into a complete computer run by a Motorola 68000 microprocessor with extensive capabilities in the $15,000 to $20,000 range. The Apollo computer, for example, contains a complete high resolution graphics facility of the type discussed; the low end of the line sells for $10,000.

New and more powerful processor chips are constantly emerging. Memory prices are plummeting. In no time, high quality graphics will be available to all who want it. It is important to be aware of this formcoming power.

41.3 THE IMAGE AND ITS DISPLAY

Graphics equipment produces pictorial images rather than text. To be useful, the equipment must help the operator to create and manipulate images. Regardless of the final form of the representation, creation almost always involves an image on a CRT which may be edited many times over. This section is devoted to how the image is created, stored and displayed. Later sections describe how to enter, modify and put the image onto external media and to produce hard copy.

Hardware Image Generation: Strokes

There are two ways to create the picture on the screen. The first is called the **vector** or **stroke** method. It works as does the artist who makes strokes with pen or brush to paint a picture as black (or colored) lines on white paper.

This method is illustrated in Figure 41.15. To display the church, a figure of five lines with a cross on the top, the beam traces out the lines which compose the **closed figure;** here the end of one stroke is the beginning of the next. To display the closed figure, the equipment does the following:

1. While the beam is off, changes the potential on the deflection plates (moves the beam as shown by the dashed arrow) to the beginning of the first line;
2. Turns on the beam and displays the first line;
3–6. Creates the other lines similarly.

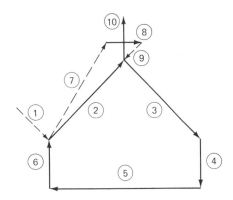

Figure 41.15. Image of church created by strokes.

To create the "cross" at the top of the church, after tracing out the building, it moves the beam to the beginning of one edge of the cross with the beam turned off (7), draws the line (8), moves to the end of the other line with the beam off (9) and draws it (10).

Many applications for which computer generated images replace mechanical drawings occur throughout industry. The stroke method of image generation is especially applicable here. It mates well with the plotting board (Section 41.8).

The stroke method has been very effective in the past. Many systems based on this concept are in use and more are being sold. Still, its share of the market is decreasing steadily. The newest technology seems to be entirely based on the *raster scan,* probably because color is difficult and expensive to achieve with the stroke method. Since the preponderance of new systems uses raster scan, the rest of this chapter is based on that technology. Table 41.1 contrasts the characteristics of the two methods.

Table 41.1. Contrast of CRT Display Characteristics

Characteristic	Stroke	Raster
Resolution	Very high	Low to high
Drawing Speed	Slow	Fast
Brightness	Low	High
Ease of correction	Poor	Great
Color	Monochrome	Full
Flicker	Low	Moderate

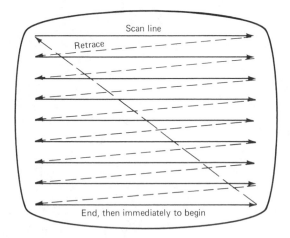

Figure 41.16. Raster scan.

Raster Scan

The raster scan display method is by far the most popular for several reasons. Most importantly, television sets and monitors used for text, programming and word processing use this technology.

The **raster scan** is so-called because the CRT beam sweeps out the entire screen in a rectangular pattern or raster, writing the image as it goes along. This is shown in Figure 41.16.

The beam sweeps across one horizontal line of the picture at a time, a **scan line.** Each pass of the beam traces out a line at a successively lower level. The beam writes in only one direction—from left to right. The beam is turned on wherever there is a white area in the picture; it is kept off otherwise. (It is *always off* on the downward trip from right to left, dashed in the figure.) Figure 41.17 shows how the church with the cross is produced by a raster scan.

When the beam has traced out one line, it moves over to the left side again and down by a small amount so that it is ready to trace out the next lower line. As the beam passes along each scan line, it is turned on to produce a **dot** or kept off to produce an **undot.** The beam is kept off on the way back from the right side to the left and moves much faster. This is called the **retrace.**

As the beam sweeps along the line, at places called **resolution elements,** or **rels,** the beam is either turned on or off to make a dot or undot (no spot). The number of such rels along the scan line is predetermined. Thus we consider the screen as a **grid,** or **raster,** a number of horizon-

tal and vertical lines; at each line intersection there is a *rel* for either a *dot* or an *undot*.

Resolution. Resolution is the amount of detail, the **definition** which the screen displays in this graphics system. The raster defines the screen as a number of lines, or rows, and a number of columns. The home television set provides 512 lines with somewhat fewer rels on the line (about 300). This is the maximum resolution that can be achieved using a television set or a conventional monitor. Anything with greater definition is said to be **high resolution graphics.**

Image. The image is composed of dots and undots, perhaps one for each rel on the screen. The ideal situation provides memory for one or more bits for each rel. For high resolution, this amounts to millions of bits. A separate memory may be provided for the image only or part of main memory may be used; in either case, this is called **image memory.**

The pixel. Pixel, contraction of *picture element*. The use of this term varies from one author or discussion to another and can mean two things:

- A single rel on the screen;
- A single element in the image memory.

A **rel** is an element of resolution on the screen, a *place* a dot or undot *may* appear. Hence **pixel** is reserved here for an element in image memory. The distinction makes it clear that a pixel *may* represent a number of rels. This is the case for low resolution graphics, as illustrated in Figure 41.18.

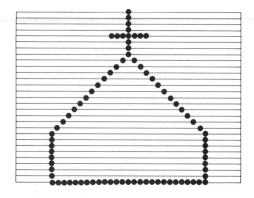

Figure 41.17. Raster scan of church.

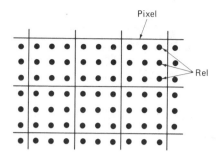

Figure 41.18. A pixel can represent several sites.

The pixel represents an image area which does not overlap with other pixels where the pixels cover all the screen. For instance, a pixel can represent a 3 × 3 square of rels on the screen as shown in Figure 41.17. An image is composed of a number of such squares. For **monochrome** (black and white), one bit per pixel suffices. This means that fewer bits are required to store the screen image at low resolution.

The size and shape of a pixel may be under the control of the host computer. The Atari 400 and 800 have several different graphic modes which define differently shaped pixels.

Creating the Image: the CRT

There are several alternate methods of producing a light image, including those that use planes of light emitting diodes and storage tubes. The most important method for image display uses the **cathode ray tube (CRT)**. Millions of such tubes are produced each year for television sets, game arcades and now personal computers. This keeps the cost of CRTs at a minimum. Because of their overwhelming dominance in computer and terminal technology, the following discussion is restricted to CRTs.

The CRT consists essentially of two parts: a gun and a screen, The user faces the screen, which is configured as a rectangle. The inside tube face is coated with a material which **fluoresces,** or emits light when hit by a stream of electrons. The **gun** creates an extremely narrow beam of electrons, focused to bombard the screen at a precisely defined point: the rel. This beam of electrons is moved about the screen and turned on and off to create an image.

The gun.   The gun creates a narrow beam of electrons and directs it at a particular spot. It is shown in Figure 41.19. At the left (the bottom of the gun) is the **filament,**

an electrical coil which heats the cathode to a high temperature. The cathode emits large quantities of electrons when heated. (Since the cathode takes time to reach this temperature, we have to wait for an image to appear on the CRT).

Vacuum. The CRT is evacuated to make it ideal for electrons to transverse. There is nothing for them to hit as they travel. Electrons emitted from the cathode are guided by an accelerator and focusing plates to the screen at the other end of the tube. They are "bundled" into a fine beam by a magnetic focusing system shown as the cylinder in Figure 41.19. Electrons leave the focusing system as a thin beam aimed dead center at the screen.

Positioning. It is possible to make a spot of light appear anywhere on the face of the screen by **deflecting** the beam either magnetically or electrostatically. The *electrostatic* method was developed first and is easiest to understand. For *magnetic* deflection, a magnetic yoke surrounds the neck of the tube; this method has replaced the electrical method almost completely. The explanation below describes electrostatic deflection, but the signals are actually converted electronically to drive the yoke magnetically to achieve the same effect.

For electrostatic deflection, two pairs of electrically charged plates perform this function:

- A potential on the **vertical deflection plates** moves the beam up or down;
- The potential on two **horizontal deflection plates** moves the beam left or right.

The effect of applying vertical and horizontal potentials is additive in a vector sense. The spot can be positioned

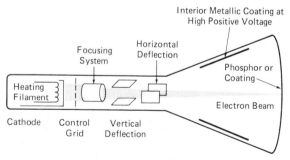

Figure 41.19. Gun for cathode ray tube. (Adapted from J. D. Foley and A. Van Dam, *Fundamentals of Interactive Computer Graphics.* Copyright © 1982 by Addison-Wesley Publishing Company, Reading, Massachusetts. Fig. 3.14. Reprinted by permission of the publisher.)

anywhere on the screen by varying these voltages. The deflection plates set up an X and Y coordinate system.

So far we have seen how to position the intense narrow beam of electrons to create a spot of light on the screen at the other end of the tube. A picture consists of a combination of light and dark areas. How do we get the dark areas? By turning off the beam of electrons so that none hit the screen and no light is produced; that is the purpose of the **control grid.** In fact, a gradation between black and white light may be produced by changing the grid potential continuously. In this section we are only concerned with producing dots or undots. Later, with respect to color we examine producing light of varying intensity.

Linearity. To reproduce a picture accurately on the screen, even if just a line drawing, it is important to control the beam *accurately.* Nonlinear relationships in the tube geometry cause image distortion. All the causes of distortion are well known to CRT design engineers. Many forms of compensation are provided in the CRT electronics so that the picture is accurately reproduced. Realism in the home television set attests to this.

41.4 THE SCREEN

This section discusses properties of the screen, its phosphor and methods for color formation. **Persistence** is the length of time that a spot continues to emit visible light after the electron beam is turned off. CRT screens for raster scan have a persistence of only a fraction of a second and therefore they must be **refreshed**—the image must be recreated many times per second or it disappears. Hence **refresh memory** is another name for the image memory, the aggregation of bits which store the image in pixel form.

To create the image, a **refresh register** is filled with a number of bits from image memory, each conveying one pixel, as shown in Figure 41.20. The scan line is synchronized with access to this register. As a line is swept out, the bits in the register activate the grid in the gun to turn the beam on and off and thus to create the image on the screen. For low resolution graphics, the refresh register may be used for several scan lines where a pixel spans several lines. Figure 41.20 shows refresh memory, the screen, the refresh register and the scan beam and suggests how they are all synchronized. Here the pixel represents a 3×3 square of rels; the small triangle shows the current scan position with reference to the screen, refresh register and image memory.

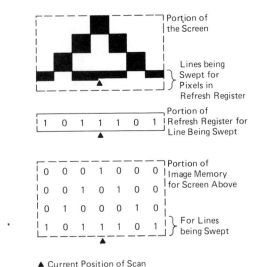

▲ Current Position of Scan

Figure 41.20. Display synchronization.

Phosphors

A **phosphor** coats the inside of the screen. When hit by the beam of electrons, it flouresces to produce light. A single chemical compound when bombarded by an electron stream produces **monochromatic light,** or light of a single wave length—a spectral color. It is pure light, not a mixture. Only a few of the colors that we encounter in our daily existence are spectral colors, such as pure blue, green, red, violet, and so forth. Most colors are mixtures, such as aquamarine, coral, or fuschia.

Persistence. A pure phosphor produces monochromatic spectral light which has persistence associated with it. A **low persistence phosphor** stops emitting light a few microseconds after the electron beam stimulating it is shut off. **High persistence phosphors** can continue to emit light for minutes, even hours. Neither of these is optimal for presenting a changing image on the screen.

With the low persistence phosphor, the image disappears as soon as it is created. Thus the time the image is visible is short compared to the time it is invisible. This unfavorable relationship results in **flicker,** often disturbing to the observer.

With a high persistence phosphor, it is impossible to change images quickly because the old image persists after the screen is refreshed with a new version.

A **medium persistence** phosphor is ideal; the image lasts a fraction of a second, leaving a residual image when the next refresh image appears on the screen. This slight overlap provides continuity from one image to the next and reduces flicker, yet the image does not last too long for changes to be made.

Mixed phosphors. A **monochrome screen** provides a single color light, usually white, green, or amber. It should be a color pleasing to the operator over long periods of continuous use. White is a mixture of spectral phosphors. Most monochromatic phosphors are also mixtures to get pleasing colors and ideal persistence to make a flickerless changeable image on the screen.

Intensity

The grid turns the beam on and off, creating dots and undots, black and white in the screen image. A photograph or pictorial image contains **gradations,** greys. A picture is reproduced on the black and white television screen by varying the control grid voltage continuously from one extreme to another to produce black, greys and white.

To present a pictorial image with gradations of black and white and to store that image in the computer, either in memory or externally, the image is first **digitized.** Now, instead of representing only black or white, each pixel records a level between 0 (black) and a maximum (white); greys are converted to intermediate levels. The accuracy of the image depends upon the number of levels employed.

For example, a photo is digitized and each pixel is represented with one of four levels of intensity (two bits): black, white and two shades of grey. More levels can be provided; the number of levels is a power of two to be efficiently stored by an integral number of bits.

A digitized image is stored as pixels in image memory. Usually a pixel represents a square area. For black and white, a pixel is a single bit. For multilevel pictorial reproduction, a pixel is a set of bits depending on the number on levels. The pixel determines the voltage applied to the grid when scanning the rel it represents. Sixteen levels (four bits) will hold enough photographic detail for most purposes.

Color

Visible colors are made of spectral colors. That is, a single nonspectral color such as aquamarine is a combination of light of several wave lengths. An important question is, "Can we find a *set* of spectral color components, which when added in the proper proportion, can make any conceivable color?" If this is answered positively, the next question is, "Can we find phosphors to produce them?"

To answer both questions, phosphors are now available which, in combination produce *almost* all conceivable colors. The minimum number of components required is three. Several different sets of three components have been found and used in the color CRT. The most popular set is red, green and blue, sometimes simply abbreviated RGB. Before we examine the technology, we look into the qualities of color.

Color Qualities

Chromatologists, people who deal with color, call the three qualities of color perception hue, saturation and brightness.

Hue is the combination of spectral colors which produces a particular color. **Brightness** is the intensity of the color. Thus a spot of color with a given hue emits an amount of light proportional to its intensity.

When a color is pure, no white light is included and it is said to be **saturated.** When white light is mixed with the color, it reduces the amount of color relative to the overall light produced and so that the color is less saturated.

The Color CRT

The tube itself. The color CRT is several times more expensive than the CRT for black and white because of its extra technology. A front view of the screen appears in Figure 41.21. Each rel consists of a **color triad:** three

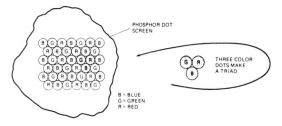

Figure 41.21. Color screen with triads. (From M. Kiver and M. Kaufman, *Television Electronics: Theory and Service,* 8th Ed., Van Nostrand Reinhold, 1983. Copyright © 1983 by Delmar Publishers Inc.)

tiny light emitting spots are arranged in a triangle, one for each primary color—red, green and blue. The screen is laid out extremely accurately so that the center of each triad is at the center of the rel.

Just behind the screen is a **color mask** which is also precisely laid out, a plate of material opaque to the electron beam with holes centered above each rel. Thus a beam of electrons sent through the hole should hit the center of the triad. But this is *not* done.

At the base of the tube, instead of the single gun as explained in Section 41.3, there are three guns, one gun for each color. A gun is aligned so that when its beam passes through a hole in the mask, it hits the color dot in the triad for which it is intended, the beam from the "red" gun hits the red dot, and so forth.

Producing color.

Each gun has a grid to control the intensity of the electron beam it projects. If the guns were aimed separately, this would defeat the purpose. Deflection aims all three guns at the same hole: if one gun points at a particular mask hole so do the other two. This should be clear from Figure 41.22. During raster scan, the guns are aimed at successive holes on a line. Then each gun's grid is activated separately to provide a different intensity electron beam for each spot of the triad at that rel. Each spot of the triad contributes a different quantity of its color and the mixture produces the desired color.

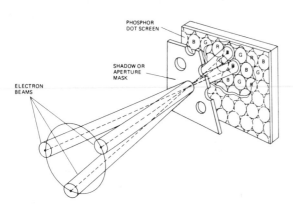

Figure 41.22. Each beam hits the right triad. (From M. Kiver and M. Kaufman, *Television Electronics: Theory and Service*, 8th Ed., Van Nostrand Reinhold, 1983. Copyright © 1983 by Delmar Publishers Inc.)

Controlling the color.

What determines the three qualities of a color at a rel—hue, saturation and brightness? How can they be controlled simultaneously by the voltages on the grids of the three guns?

View this as three actions, the production of hue, saturation and brightness one after the other. (In actuality the three are controlled simultaneously.) To construct a hue, provide the right combination of red, green and blue. For instance, for pure spectral red, only the grid on the red gun is on and the other two off. To get a fully saturated nonspectral hue, activate the grids proportionally for the three primary colors.

To reduce saturation, add white light, an exact combination of the three primaries. The more white is added, the less saturated the color becomes. To **tint** the color, increase the voltage on the grids proportionally, so that the ratio is that for white. Thus saturation is the ratio of the desired pure color intensity to the total intensity.

Consider a color, A, a pure hue consisting of three components, A_R, A_G and A_B in a fixed ratio.

$$A_R : A_G : A_B = a_R : a_G : a_B \qquad (41.1)$$

or put another way,

$$A_R = ka_R; \quad A_G = ka_G; \quad A_B = ka_B \qquad (41.2)$$

The color is seen brightest on the screen when at its highest intensity. At full brightness, k is such that one of A_R, A_G or A_B is 1 and k is some multiplier.

White is produced by a combination of red, green and blue as. It is a ratio of these components given as

$$W_R : W_G : W_B = kw_R : kw_G : kw_B \qquad (41.3)$$

A tint is a combination of the color and white. A tint of A, call it AT, is a combination like

$$AT_R = ka_R + tw_R; \quad AT_G = ka_G + tw_G; \qquad (41.4)$$

$$AT_B = ka_B + tw_G$$

Thus the ratio k to t is the ratio of the color to white and indicates how "pale" the color is, its saturation.

We have produced the required tint of the desired color. To increase the brightness of the color, increase the amplitude of each beam keeping the proportion constant. The more intense the beams, the brighter the color spot.

To summarize:

1. Hue is determined by the intensities of the R, G and B beam *relative to each other* with no white light present.

2. Saturation is determined by the ratio of the color with no white light added to total light present.

3. Brightness is the overall light intensity.

Storing the Image

Pixels again. The colored image is stored by recording a code for a color for each pixel. The number of pixels provided depends on the memory available. Low resolution displays such as the Apple II or Atari may use a few thousand pixels of two bits each. High resolution graphics can use a screen of 1024×1280 pixels, well over a million pixels!

For each pixel a **color packet (CP)** is stored. (This is not a standard term, but it is convenient.) Its size determines how many colors can be displayed simultaneously, the palette size. A byte size CP provides a palette of 256 colors. A high resolution display with this palette size requires 1M byte of image memory, an impressive figure.

Ways to set up the CP for each pixel in image memory differ. We examine one particular method called *multiple bit planes.*

The bit plane. Consider a **bit plane** with one bit for each pixel: put together several to form a **bit plane array.** Then add a technique which addresses all bit planes simultaneously for the CP for that pixel.

The palette size depends on the CP size. Two bits provide combinations of four colors, sufficient for making three-color graphs, bar charts and pie displays. Three bits provide eight colors. Eight bits provide 256 colors, sufficient for most applications except textile design, animation and art, where subtle changes in shading demand an even greater palette.

Color tables. The CP alone is not enough to specify hue, saturation and brightness. How is the meaning of each CP fixed? A convenient method is a **color table** such as shown in Table 41.2. It contains one entry for each CP combination. The entry consists of four parts a CP and a color intensity value for each of the three guns. The **granularity,** the number of levels of control for each gun, varies with the design. A typical figure is 256 levels, controlled by one byte.

Thus a high resolution display color is determined by 256 settings for *each* of the three guns: the number of colors from which you may make your palette is 256^3, or 16 million colors. Image memory for the high resolution

Table 41.2. A Color Table

Entry Number	Red	Blue	Green
0	0A	00	00
1	0A	04	04
2	0A	08	08
⋮	⋮	⋮	⋮
253	CA	D0	D0
254	D0	D0	D0
255	D8	D8	D8

terminal requires one byte per pixel. As the scan proceeds along a scan line

1. Image memory is accessed for the applicable CP;
2. It designates an entry in the color table;
3. Those three bytes are applied to digital to analog converters;
4. The D/A converter produces three voltages;
5. They are sent to the RBG guns;
6. They generate the color spot for this pixel.

Moving images. To set up a palate, one color is assigned to each CP combination. This creates one entry in the color table.

An image created with one palette (one particular color table) can be "recolored" by resetting the color table. One way to produce animation or the illusion of motion is to set up a design and then to change the color table so that the colors move or change in each area. Section 42.7 describes a way to do this from a menu.

41.5 MAKING THE PICTURE

Graphics equipment presents a screen image or sequence of images to meet specifications. There are several ways to enter the image:

1. Point by point (not very efficient);
2. By primitive commands using software;
3. By more complicated software programs which manipulate existing images;
4. By high level programs which give level choices for specification of the image;
5. With facilitating hardware (Section 41.6).

These topics are now discussed.

The Software

To create an image, directions are given either at the terminal keyboard or with input devices (Section 41.6). Commands are interpreted by the terminal software and hardware to place bits into the image memory, the basis for the image generated. This software or firmware is included in the high priced terminal; otherwise a graphics software package is brought from auxiliary storage to the host memory to set the image into the image memory section to drive the display. Wherever the software resides, only the principles of *image generation* are important.

Pixel-by-Pixel Image Generation

To write a point on the screen you need the following kinds of commands:

1. *Move* the **cursor,** a visible screen marker, to a particular position.
2. *Set* where applicable, color or intensity.
3. *Enter* the point here.

Action takes place at a point designated hereafter as the **current access position (CAP)** and conveyed by the **cursor.** For textual display, a cursor ideally occupies and highlights a character position. Spotlighting a pixel or rel with a **cross-hair,** a pair of lines intersecting at a right angle, each line perhaps a quarter- or half-inch in length, is more appropriate for graphics. This is the CAP.

Motion.   To change the CAP, the cursor is moved. A direct command with reference to an imaginary superimposed grid moves the cursor quickly and precisely. The coordinates of a pixel, its row and column number, is determined by the **pixel resolution. Absolute positioning** identifies each pixel by an X and Y coorindate, its row and column number.

A **normalized scale** makes references independent of terminal resolution and X and Y coordinates are specified on a scale of 0 to 1. If H is the number of pixels in the horizontal direction (number of columns) and V in the vertical (rows), then the absolute position (X,Y) is divided by the pixel resolution (H,V) to get the normalized coordinates (x,y). For $V = 512$ and $H = 400$, we have

$$X = 375, Y = 217; x = 0.938, y = 0.424   (41.5)$$

It is sometimes easier to use **relative positioning.** Motion is requested in terms of an increase (or decrease) in the number of pixels in each direction. **Normalized relative positioning** expresses increments in a normalized scale.

Setting color and position.   Color can be requested by reference to the palette by number: for 16 entries, a color with a number from 0 to 15 is specified. A point is set into the display with a simple mnemonic like **SET-POINT.** This marks the current color at the CAP into the image memory, which displays at once.

Primitives

With 10,000 or more pixels, it could be very tedious to enter each point of a complete image as described above. An alternative implements primitive functions in software (firmware). The number and type of these **primitives** varies with the terminal. There are several "standard" primitive sets, but none are universally accepted. A few primitives are now examined.

Draw a line.   A simple request is to connect two points by a line of a designated color or **texture** (dotted, dashed, solid, etc.). With the cursor at a starting position, a command is issued to specify the terminal point. The software sets to 1 all the intervening points which make up the line.

A second means names the X and Y *displacement* relatively—how many pixels to move in each direction, rather than in terms of an absolute terminal point. In a third method, one marks the initial point, moves the cursor to the terminal point and makes a request; *arrow* keys move the cursor.

The **line drawing routine** does geometry and smoothing to connect an imaginary line between the points. An exact line might actually intersect few, if any, pixels. One type of routine chooses points closest to the line in the hope that this displays convincingly. This unsophisticated routine results in an illness sometimes called the **jaggies,** because it produces a jagged line like the blade of a saw.

The cure of the jaggies is **antialiasing.** High priced displays include this feature, which picks points or pixels so that the line does not have rough edges. An example of the disease and its cure appears as Figure 41.23. A common approach uses grey level averaging (for monochrome) for points close to the line. Points with lower intensity do this for colored lines. Of course, higher resolution also helps.

Circles.   A routine draws a circle with a specified radius in the current color or line pattern at the CAP. Some routines use an angular starting and stopping radius to

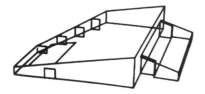

Figure 41.23. Jaggies and antialiasing. With antialiasing, left; without, right. From Henry Fuchs and Jose Barros, "Efficient Generation of Smooth Line Drawings on Video Displays," SIGGRAPH '79 Proceedings, published as *Computer Graphics*, 13 (2), Aug. 1979, pp. 260-69.

draw an arc for a rounded corner at intersecting lines. If there is no terminal primitive, to simulate it draw a complete circle tangent to the lines; connect the ends of the desired arc by a chord; paint the unwanted sector black; only the tangent arc remains visible.

Polygonal fill.   The **polygonal fill** establishes colored or shaded areas but only for *closed* polygons or *closed* irregular figures. The routine refers to the boundary at each side of the figure to terminate line segments it generates. To color a closed figure, the cursor is positioned within it and the request made. The current color fills this area as shown in Figure 41.24. Monochrome displays provide fill with a designated line pattern, such as diagonals, cross hatching, and so forth.

The fill routine searches for the topmost (or bottommost) point in the closed area, finds the left boundary and draws a colored horizontal line segment to the right boundary. It steps down a line and continues the process until it finds the bottonmost (topmost) point of the closed area.

Partial Displays and Windows

An important set of primitive routines is **zoom, pan** and **scroll.**

These functions allow an area described visually to be magnified and a window to this area viewed and moved about within the "field of vision." To achieve this objective, the terminal must do either or both of these:

1. Provide a memory plane with overall dimensions in pixels considerably larger than the raster size for the display;
2. Provide less definition in the magnification mode so that a portion of the screen becomes enlarged. Since the same definition need not be maintained for this portion of the object, pixels get larger.

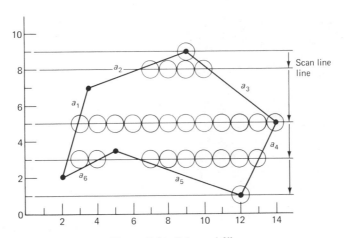

Figure 41.24. Polygonal fill.

Using the memory plane. The number of pixels is usually fewer than the number of rels for low resolution graphics. Now let us reverse the situation and provide more pixels than rels. The memory plane(s) describes an object or scene with greater detail than can be displayed on the screen. There are several pixels per rel. To **zoom in** and look at the detail available in a particular area of memory for the scene reduce the number of pixels per rel, perhaps even reversing the ratio. This appears as a magnification of a particular area of the scene. Figure 41.25 shows examples before and after zoom.

To **zoom out** is to view a *larger* portion of the image plane by increasing the number of pixels per rel. The dis-

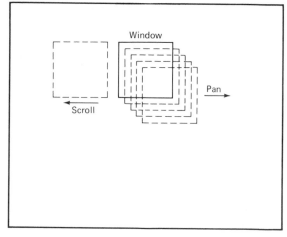

Figure 41.26. Scroll and pan.

play routine has rules for choosing pixels to display for an unmagnified or intermediate image (several pixels per rel).

To **zoom in,** the routine is told the magnification factor to use and the origin of the (magnified) **window.** An integer multiple (1 to 16) is specified to give greater detail and the magnified view jumps to the screen. However, the difference between $\times 1$ and $\times 2$ is considerable while that between $\times 15$ and $\times 16$ is hardly noticeable. A more sophisticated scaling is logarithmic, where each change is about $\times 1.1$, for instance, of the previous one.

Once zoomed, it may be desirable to move the window to a different area keeping the same magnification: to **scroll** is to change the origin of the window, to move in a jump to a new position within the scene. **Pan,** continuous scroll, moves the window at a constant rate in a designated direction as shown in Figure 41.26, until stopped.

Host Based Routines

Routines which require elaborate manipulations are based in the host. A sampler of these follows.

Object defintion. We have described how to draw a set of lines, create a polygon and fill a closed figure with color. One may **define absolutely** (at a particular spot on the screen), or **relatively** (starting anywhere by giving drawing commands relatively [see below]). Commands (or actions with input devices, Section 41.6) **define an object.** This is comparable to defining a processing *proce-*

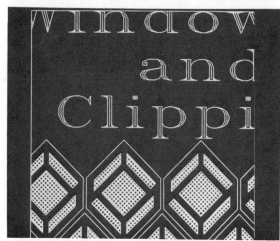

Figure 41.25. Zoom. Before (top) and after.

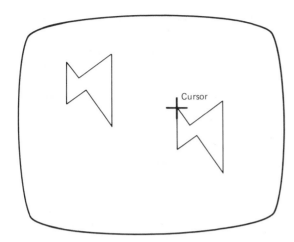

Figure 41.27. Copy an object.

dure in a higher level language or a *macro* in assembly language.

An object is defined relatively by the set of operations to produce the object beginning at any CAP (current cursor position); such sets of operations may be stored in memory, and also incorporated into a graphics library from which they may be recalled.

Now, in a high level graphics program, one can move the cursor anywhere and request a copy. The procedure is performed relative to the CAP to produce an image of the object as shown in Figure 41.27. To *destroy* an object, one starts at its origin and requests that the object be drawn again in black.

Rotation. With a defined object and a center of rotation, a routine can rotate the object through a designated angle. Alternatively, the object may rotate slowly but continuously until the routine is directed to stop. The routine

1. Calculates the starting and ending position of *each* line segment after rotation;
2. Creates a new object by drawing lines between the vertices it has just calculated;
3. Erases the old object by writing over it in black;
4. Stores the directions relatively, to translate the rotated object later if desired.

Figure 41.28 shows a scene (top), an object copied there (middle) and then rotated (bottom).

For continuous rotation the object is erased and rede-

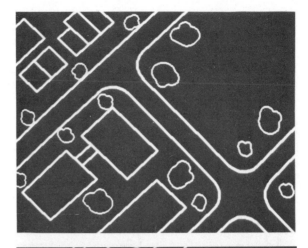
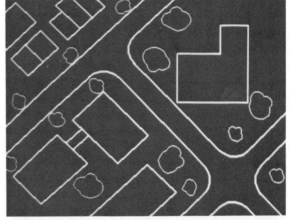
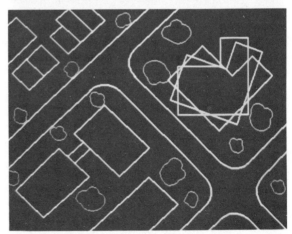

Figure 41.28. Copy and rotate an object. (Courtesy Carl Machover Associates)

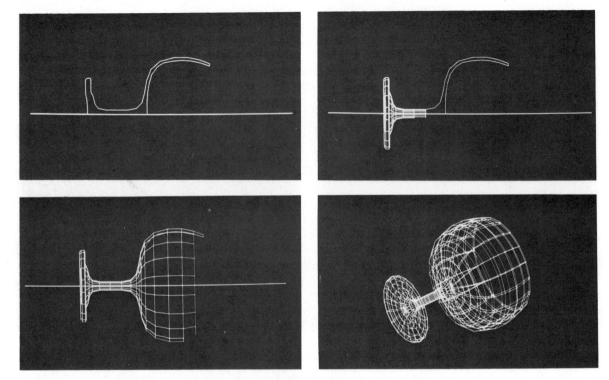

Figure 41.29. A mesh figure development. (Courtesy Megatek)

fined at incremental angular rotations until directed to stop.

Three dimensional objects.

Programs to handle three dimensional objects are complex and consume considerable computer time. Many such applications use the assistance of a mainframe or minicomputer but powerful micros are coming into their own. Steps to deal with three dimensional objects are the following:

1. Specify the object completely in three dimensions;
2. Show the object viewed from a particular direction;
3. Rotate the object about some axis and show its appearance after rotation;
4. Keep track of all the hidden lines;
5. Hide lines which should not display and show only those visible from this aspect.

Entering the detailed dimensions of the object is formidible. A wire mesh figure as shown in Figure 41.29 is described by giving its cross-section (for a figure of rev-

olution), then software aids in further describing and drawing the object. Figure 41.30 shows a more complicated mesh figure "eye".

A mesh figure is easy to rotate because no line is ever hidden; surfaces do not display. A familiar display on television is wire mesh automobiles rotated and frequently zoomed rapidly, sometimes in a time lapse sequence to produce multiple images.

Calculations of a view of the figure after rotation may take seconds on a high speed computer. Once made, a new image is formed by a sequence of commands to generate each line for the new position. This command sequence can be stored and the image regenerated at will in a fraction of a second. It is one "photo" of the rotating object. "Photos" can be calculated and stored separately, each as a command sequence. Then the sequence, the rotating figure, can be presented much more rapidly since the time for calculations is eliminated. What you see on television may have been speeded up hundreds of times.

To show a *solid* three dimensional car, visible surfaces are colored in and hidden surfaces eliminated. This takes

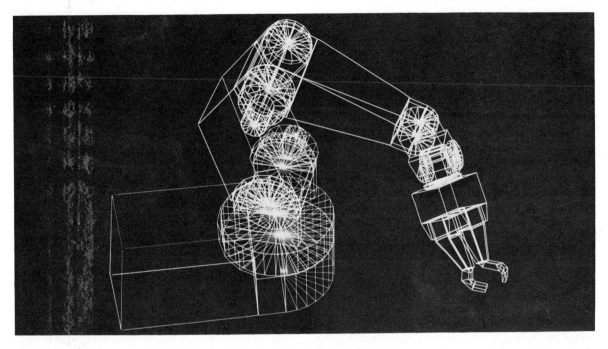

Figure 41.30. A more complicated mesh figure. (Courtesy Evans & Sutherland)

additional time for polygonal fill. To make an object appear more realistic, each surface can be colored differently.

Shading. Yet additional complexity is required to shade and light each surface. A sophisticated program calculates shading for curved surfaces and complicated objects. The object is tinted as though light from a point source were hitting it. In this way realistic interpretations of *imaginary* objects are produced.

41.6 INPUT DEVICES

We have noted how to control the display from the keyboard: *arrow* keys move the cursor; other keys in command mode initiate activity.

The system described works to create a complex image from the keyboard. However there is a discrepancy between how the image is entered and how it is presented. While the display is visual and two dimensional, entry is verbally or conceptually oriented (MOVE thus, MAKE a line). Why not make the construction technique more similar to the presentation which it affects?

Input devices help provide a simple and natural way to control the display without knowing command mnemonics or what is going on behind the scenes. Drawing or moving one's hand on a tablet, smooth surface or the screen itself is the method. It gives tactile/visual feedback in a realistic way.

To exploit the technology at hand, only a slight additional cost buys an entry method more compatible to the screen and coordinated with the display. This facilitates the operation, expedites decisions and speeds up image creation.

Classification

Input methods in order of the operator's facility to interact with the screen (in the reverse order of presentation) are the following:

1. **Direct**—the operator interacts with the screen.
2. **Indirect**—the operator interacts with a model of the screen.
3. **Conceptual**—the operator performs actions at the terminal which obviously affect the screen, but the ac-

tions themselves are tactilely and kinesthetically different.

Input is discussed without regard to whether signals go to the terminal or the host computer. Where the terminal is elaborate and provides firmware for implementing primitives, the action is taken there and a "note" sent to the host computer. A subsection below is devoted to that topic.

Direct and indirect input techniques lend themselves to menu selection, which is indeed powerful. The operator selects from a myriad of alternatives on the screen.

This section examines conceptual, indirect and direct input devices in that order. Within each category, devices are discussed in approximate order of complexity.

Conceptual Input

For **conceptual input,** actions needed to create a set of lines are in the operator's mind as an idea or concept. But instead of drawing, the operator hits a key sequence, turns knobs, and so on, alternatives which are now described.

Commands.   We have seen how to command the cursor to move to an absolute position. The operator uses a

set of letters, a **mnemonic.** For instance, MOV 35,45 moves the cursor to column 35, row 45. Relative commands in the form MOVR 3,−8 move the cursor 3 pixels right and 8 pixels up from there.

Cursor key.   Four *arrow* keys request horizontal and vertical cursor movement. The cursor responds by moving a fixed increment in the indicated direction. This increment is often under operator control (1 rel, 5 rels, etc.). Four more keys with arrows pointing in diagonal directions are sometimes combined with another command code key, such as HOME, to position quickly to the screen's limits.

Positioning with an arrow key alone is slow, even with **repeat action:** hold it down a second and it begins to emit character codes at the rate of 10 per second. The cursor responds accordingly.

Knobs.   Turning a **knob,** as shown at the left of the keyboard of Figure 41.31, varies the voltage output of a potentiometer. A **digitizer** converts this into digital form picked up in turn by the software. It finds the desired pixel and moves the cursor to the corresponding position. The angular rotation of *two* knobs determine the horizontal vertical position of the cursor. A **vernier** knob is sometimes provided.

Figure 41.31. Keyboard with knobs and joystick. (Courtesy Megatek)

Figure 41.32. Roller ball. (Courtesy Measurement Systems, Inc.)

Joy stick. The **joy stick**, a lever, is a popular device in television and arcade games to find a pixel. The joy stick has two degrees of freedom, left or right and up or down. The stick is attached to two potentiometers which produce voltages digitized for angle of tilt in two planes. A joy stick is at the right of the keyboard in Figure 41.31.

For the **positional joy stick,** one combination of rotation and tilt corresponds to one position on the screen. The cursor moves quickly but *positioning accurately* is difficult. Only a slight stick motion causes the cursor to jump about considerably.

The **incremental joy stick** is an improvement: its direction of motion determines the *direction of cursor motion;* deviation from the vertical determines the *rate of motion.* We have

1. A vertical dead spot (with the joy stick upright) where the cursor is not moving;
2. Tilting the joy stick, which makes the cursor move in that direction;
3. The rate of cursor motion determined by the amount of tilt.

Thus tilting the joy stick steeply to the right moves the cross hair quickly rightward. As it approaches the destination, easing up on the joy stick slows the cursor down. At the objective, returning the joy stick to dead center stops the motion.

Roller ball. A roller ball, about the size of a golf ball, is seated in a square container, as shown in Figure 41.32. Slapping it with the hand rotates it rapidly in any direction. Rotation is digitized for direction and speed to move the cursor. When the cursor arrives, the operator simply stops the ball.

The mouse. The mouse, shown in Figure 41.33, is a small, handheld device with a roller ball underneath. Placing the mouse on the table and moving it in any direction causes the cursor to move accordingly. This is an inexpensive yet effective device that provides feedback of the order found with the tablet, discussed below. The mouse is becoming very popular.

Entry. Once the cursor is at the site of a new activity, there should be some way to report this as the new CAP: an additional key—a button on the joy stick or on the top of the mouse—usually serves for this purpose.

The Tablet

The **tablet,** an indirect input device, is a square or rectangle, generally the shape and size of the screen. It may be used with a mouse as seen in Figure 41.33 or with a stylus as seen in Figure 41.34. In the latter case, the **stylus** matches the tablet design. Built into the tablet is a **coordinate grid** to sense stylus position and convert it into digital X and Y coordinates. The resultant digital signal is returned to the terminal to position the cursor.

Methods for detecting stylus position on tablets include

- An electrical grid;
- A capacitive effect;
- A sound source and several microphone pickups.

Positioning. The stylus position on the tablet is reflected immediately by the cursor on the screen. As the stylus moves, so does the cursor. Tactile/visual feedback quickly and clearly establishes the direction to move the stylus to reach a destination: keeping an eye on the screen and adjusting the direction of stylus motion make the cursor go where it is supposed to. Pressing the stylus button gives the desired position to the software, which displays a confirming marker on the screen.

Continuous mode. This mode is particularly effective for entering sketches, maps and line drawings affixed to the tablet. Rear illumination through translucent glass helps one trace a sketch with the stylus.

Figure 41.33. Mouse and tablet. (Courtesy Summagraphics)

Figure 41.34. Stylus and tablet. (Courtesy Summagraphics)

Continuous mode reports a sequence of short line segments to the program which then displays them on the screen as an apparently continuous curve. The rate of line segment generation is adjustable by the user. The continuous mode turns on or off with the button on the stylus, from the menu (Section 41.7) or with a function key.

To terminate a curve in the drawing, the operator presses the stylus button. Now further stylus movement does not produce lines. The operator moves on to the next line position, presses the button and begins a new line. Erasing mistakes and reentering corrected lines is easy. (Note that the mouse works in about the same way, but on a neutral surface.)

Light Pen

The light pen is true **direct entry.** The operator puts the stylus directly on the CRT screen; the stylus's position is reported to software in either the terminal or the host gives the operator both visual and tactile feedback. The stylus CAP is reported anywhere on the screen that is lit.

Stylus.   The stylus is often called a light pen, but this is a misnomer. The stylus does not *emit* light; it *detects* light. At its base is a photosensitive detector; on top is one or more buttons. A light pen is shown in Figure 41.35; here it can be used to select displayed objects or menu items, or to place objects and indicate dimensions.

The light pen must be coupled to software synchronized with raster generation. The pen position emits light only during a fraction of each raster scan. The photocell detects the light and emits a signal to the terminal software. The software notes the time the signal arrives relative to the raster scan and this determines the X and Y coordinates of the stylus. If the stylus is in motion, its position on each raster scan is reported as fast as rasters are produced. Raster scan rates, either 30 or 60 times a second, are fast enough for most purposes.

Note that this method fails if the screen is not lit where the stylus is put. Light cannot be picked up from a black screen.

Positioning with a grid.   A superimposed grid overcomes this last difficulty. An additional (ninth) memory image plane produces a faint light grid of horizontal and vertical lines on the screen. Any point on the grid can be reported.

Cursor feedback loop.   A cursor stylus feedback makes it possible to move the cursor through a dark area on the screen. This works because the stylus picks up light in an area rather than from a point. The photocell covers a number of rels on the screen.

It appears as though the stylus drags the cursor across the screen. Actually, the software picks up a new position as long as the stylus overlaps *part* of the cursor. The next raster scan presents the cursor at the last previous detected position of the stylus. An adjustment is made on each scan as the stylus moves.

Figure 41.36 makes this clear. At the left is the crosshair produced on the screen by a set of dots, a vertical and horizontal line segment each about a half-inch long. The stylus's circular area is centered and intersects most of the cross-hair. When the stylus is in motion, its last previous position displays. Its pickup area, the circle, is not concentric with the intersection of the cross-hair but it still picks up some light, enough for an accurate fix. Such positioning is seen in the right portion of the figure.

The software receives signals from the photosensitive stylus during several different parts of the raster scan.

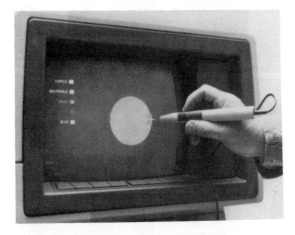

Figure 41.35. Light pen. (Courtesy Hewlett-Packard)

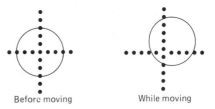

Before moving   While moving

Figure 41.36. Cursor feedback.

The feedback module averages out signals received and calculates the new position of the stylus for *this* scan. The position calculated displays as a cross-hair projected on the *next* screen. As the stylus moves further, a new calculation is made to present the next position of the cursor on the subsequent raster scan.

This system works well as long as the stylus does not move too fast. If the stylus is out of range of the cursor, the latter detects *no* light and there is no way to figure out the stylus's position. A solution to this is to **flood the screen.** When the cursor is lost, ask for FLOOD and *all* the screen is lit for an instant; the software finds the photo-cell and the cursor appears.

Text

Some visual images communicate without including text. Others require labels, names and directions, especially true for business applications; bar charts and pie charts make no sense unless each bar of each sector of the circle is labeled. Most mechanical and architectural drawings need text, also.

Creating text.   A character generator is included in the terminal with one or more ROMs, one per character set. These character sets could also be acquired by the host and downloaded.

A simple command to the terminal software resets the keyboard. Instead of functioning as graphic generation commands, keystrokes are now recognized as character codes. Control sequences still convey certain requests such as changing the character set, or size, or to switch to menu control. One command sequence is reserved to return to graphics mode.

Commands in the text mode enable one to select

- The typeface used for text;
- The size of the characters;
- The characteristic of the characters used—italic, bold, underline, etc.;
- The orientation—horizontal or rotated;
- The color of the presentation.

An extra plane.   Sometimes an *extra* image plane holds text. Characters keyed at the cursor are placed in this plane, to appear as an overlay, generally in white.

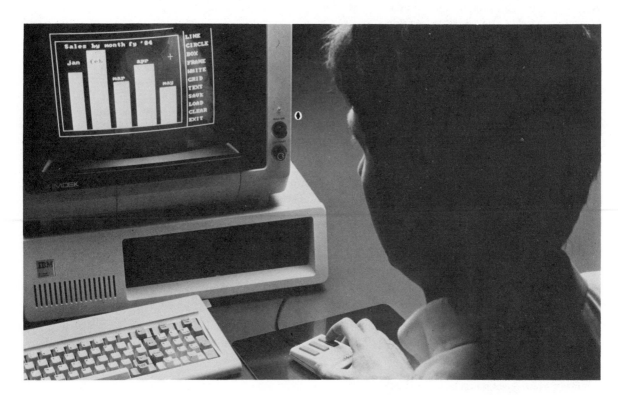

Figure 41.37. Menu and image (at the menu's left). (Courtesy Summargraphics)

The beauty of an additional plane is that its color can be set to black and the text disappears so that one can alter an image without distraction. It also allows alternation between this text and other text for menus, a much easier way to give commands which we now examine.

41.7 MENU DRIVEN GRAPHICS

A **menu** is a set of text alternatives presented on the screen. It expedites response for one simple reason: the operator need not remember a command mnemonic nor a command key sequence. Each alternative includes a letter or number. The operator conveys a choice by hitting that key.

When considerable graphics work is done at the terminal, an interactive entry device such as that described in Section 41.6 is usually available. Program activation is indeed facilitated with a **graphics menu;** the operator chooses action by "pointing" at a labeled square, putting the cursor there. But only *some* graphic systems work this way.

General Description

Let us see how menu driven graphics work in the middle of a session, creating a complicated color image which is now on the screen.

The menu is an overlay. For high resolution graphics, it is easy to make the menu an inch or two wide along one margin of the screen. Figure 41.37 shows how the menu and picture share the screen. A white menu overlay does not detract much from the image.

A menu may also be an overlay applied to a tablet and activated by a mouse or, as in Figure 41.38, by a stylus. There are many things that one might do in the graphics environment; it is impossible to put all of them on a single menu. Instead, a number of **submenus** are often available. A submenu lists actions for a particular type of function and may name other submenus.

Here is a small sample of actions which a submenu might offer:

- Construction by line segments and circles;
- Sketching with continuous lines;
- Color table definition and fill;
- Object naming, definition and manipulation;
- Zoom, pan and scroll.

These are *simple* activities. Even so, they may not be available in all systems. Constructing three dimensional objects, moving them and rotating them are complex actions which require multiple submenus.

Action.   The operator "points" at an action choice on a submenu to set it in motion. **Pointing** consists of moving the cursor to the associated box and pressing the stylus button. A tablet, light pen, joy stick or mouse does the trick.

Figure 41.38. Menu activated from tablet overlay. (Courtesy Hewlett-Packard)

Scenarios

A few scenarios for different submenus shows how simple this method is to use.

Straight line figures. We might call this **formal sketching,** with straight line segments and arcs of circles.

One mode for creation is **polygon** generation. A phrase in the menu displays this alternative; move the cursor there and press the button. Move the cursor to the first point of the figure and press the button. A dot or symbol called an **icon** appears at the initial point. Move the cursor to the next point and press the button. A line segment now appears between the initial point and this terminal point.

To create the next line segment, move the cursor, press the button and a line appears between the previous position and the new one. Continue thus until finished. To exit this mode, move the cursor to a box in the menu for a new mode or submenu, and press the button.

Color fill. The color terminal provides a palette of 4 to 256 colors. The palette itself is chosen from a much larger range of colors, sometimes as many as one million. (For some small color micros and PCs, the palette is fixed.) Such a large range tends to confuse. To help, the system provides a **default palette,** a preselected set of colors.

Try to describe a color; nothing is as effective as seeing it. To make color choice simple, the palette is reproduced within the submenu. Let us see how to fill a closed area with a chosen color:

1. Select the *color fill* option from the color submenu;
2. Put the stylus someplace in a closed figure and press the button;
3. A cross-hair appears within the figures;
4. Put the stylus on one of the variegated color bars of the palette to select a color;
5. Press the button;
6. The area is filled with the chosen color;
7. Turn off the fill feature to do something else.

Changing the palette. To add new colors to the palette, select an empty place there. (An existing color can be altered by the same method.) Setting up a larger square may help to see the color better. Three squares containing the primary colors, red, blue and green, are also on the menu to mix into the square.

Select one primary color, choose to *add* color to the square and indicate an increment rate using the menu. Now touch the square and press the button. Color fills the

square at a low intensity. The color becomes more intense changing at the rate called for earlier. Hit the stylus button to stop. Mix in a second and third spectral color, watching the result. If too much of one color is present, then *subtract* that color.

The menu lets you increase or decrease the *brightness* of the color when it is the right hue by *proportionately* increasing the amount of each primary color.

This is probably a *saturated* color. To get a tint, add white. Simply place the stylus on the white square and press the button to add increments of white. Should the color become too pale, reduce the tint by *decrementing* white. Thus by touching boxes on the menu, a box on the palette shows the hue, intensity and saturation you desire.

A palette change can alter an existing image. Any color in the image is on the palette. An *existing* palette can be changed: alter intensity or tint by touching one of a pair of squares ($+$ or $-$) for each; alter hue by adding or subtracting a primary.

Creating a new color or resetting an existing color resets an entry in the color table. Each bar on the menu palette represents an entry in the table. One can choose the entry affected by pointing at a palette box in the menu. We have the following

- Adding (subtracting) a primary color increments (decrements) the byte for that primary in the entry and changes hue;
- Increasing (decreasing) the intensity of the color increases (decreases) each primary byte proportionately;
- Changing tints adds (subtracts) *white*.

If areas in the image are colored by this CP, the color changes simultaneously as the palette is altered. A change takes effect on the very next scan.

Menu Requirements

Requirements for a graphics menu system may not be obvious; the facility is *not* built into the terminal. It is run by a specialized program in the host.

Communication. When in menu mode, the operator talks *to the program* via the screen and stylus and so the keyboard is inoperable except for some control sequences.

Suppose that input is a tablet stylus with one entry button. Both a scene and a menu display. Move the stylus on the tablet to move the cursor. Talk to the terminal only via the tablet. The terminal picks up the stylus coordinates and immediately activates image memory to display the cursor in a corresponding position. The host is not involved yet.

When the cursor is in a position relevant to the image, press the button. The cursor might be in a square of the menu or at some point of interest on the image. Pressing the button causes the terminal to return the present stylus (and cursor) position to the program which is thereby activated. The program interprets the stylus position and directs the terminal what to do next by issuing one or more graphic primitives.

The program then resets the terminal to

- Respond to tablet input internally via the moving cursor;
- Transmit the next position *only* when the operator hits the entry button.

Implementation Program for a Submenu

To elucidate further, examine a typical submenu program invoked from the main menu or an initial submenu. A block diagram appears as Figure 41.39. If it is not in memory, the submenu program is brought from the system disk.

Submenu image. The first submenu program action is to find the submenu image, a data file on the system disk, and to project it on the screen. The file is a set of commands; the program gives the commands to the ter-

minal to create the menu image in the ninth image plane (to superimpose it on the margin or near the current graphic image). The commands clear the previous submenu and *create* the new submenu: they make boxes, write text on the screen and enter colors in boxes where appropriate.

Executive routine. An executive routine is the part of the submenu program which accepts and interprets a choice. It activates the stylus and awaits input from the operator. When no operation is in progress, the operator *must* make a choice to get something going. The operator finds a choice box, puts the stylus there and presses the button. This transmits an *X, Y* coordinate pair through the terminal to the executive routine.

An **analysis routine** examines the coordinate pair. Each choice corresponds to a range of both *X* and *Y* coordinates. Each range pair has a meaning. The executive routine notes the choice and passes to the analysis routine. It responds by

- Calling in another appropriate routine to take over the computer and terminal to fulfill the chosen function;
- Displaying an error message if the stylus is not in a choice box and returning to the executive routine.

Line segment routine. To draw line segments, the LS routine gets control from the executive. The stylus and tablet are used as described to position the cursor and transmit point coordinates to the routine.

When the user *marks* a coordinate in the image area, the LS routine takes over. It sends a command to the terminal to mark the first point with an icon (a special symbol). Then it reactivates the tablet for cursor display. For the second (or other successive) button press, after the terminal sends the coordinate pair to the host, the LS routine sends a *line draw* command to the terminal and enables cursor display again.

Any screen pixel is a legal terminal point for a *line draw* command. However, pixels on the menu may be out of bounds because, at any time, the operator may stop drawing lines and do something else; simply activate a square on the submenu for that purpose. The active routine screens out messages for a function change from directions to the routine itself. If it detects a function request, it gives control to the executive routine to fulfill.

Sketching Aids

Just as the word processor provides help constructing text, the "graphics processor" helps sketch figures on the

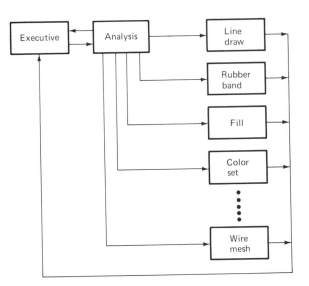

Figure 41.39. Interrelation of menu routines.

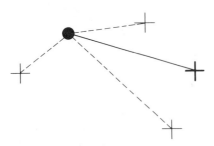

Figure 41.40. Rubber band effect.

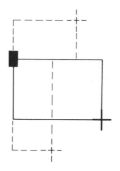

Figure 41.42. Rubber rectangle.

screen. A few instances below show it is possible to *construct* your own aid to help you in almost any way.

Rubber band.   Figure 41.40 illustrates **rubber band** aid for creating a line segment. A diagram hardly does justice to how simple it is to position a straight line anyplace on the screen—one has to experience it.

In rubber band mode, place the cursor at the initial point and press the stylus button; an icon appears. Now move the cursor. This seems to pull a line away from the point, like pulling out taffy. The line follows the cursor like a rubber band but remains straight; stretch it way out or bring it back, and it follows. To *set* the line on the screen, press the button.

The rubber band routine uses the line segment primitive to create and erase lines. It *continuously* monitors the signals from the stylus sent via the terminal once per raster scan and indicating the CAP. The routine compares each coordinate pair with the last received CAP. If the two are the same, nothing happens; the line remains displaying. Should the two differ, the routine issues a *black* line command to erase the current line; then another line

command in the current color writes a *new* line from the icon to the latest CAP. When the line is in place, pressing the button causes the visible line to remain there. The routine turns off rubber band mode and the executive awaits the next menu choice.

Rubber circle.   A "rubber circle" is one which permits a continuous change of the radius. Enter this mode through the menu; establish the center of the circle by pointing. Move the cursor outward from the center and an ever enlarging concentric circle appears with its circumference passing through the cursor as shown in Figure 41.41. Moving the cursor towards or away from the center changes the circle's radius accordingly.

The rubber circle routine uses the circle primitive. For each new CAP, the routine calculates the distance between the cursor and the center and compares it to the previous radius. If the radius changes, a black circle erases the current one and a new circle is created to pass through the cursor.

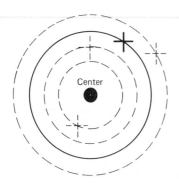

Figure 41.41. Rubber circle.

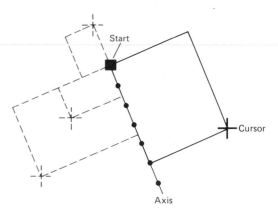

Figure 41.43. Rotated rubber rectangle.

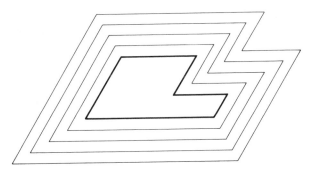

Figure 41.44. Making an object grow.

Rubber rectangle. Enter this mode and establish an origin. Now move the cursor. The *diagonal* is a line from the origin to the CAP. The routine draws a rectangle based on this diagonal, with sides parallel to the *X* and *Y* axes as shown in Figure 41.42. Moving the cursor establishes a new terminal point for the diagonal; the rubber rectangle is erased and another constructed in the new position.

Rotated rubber rectangle. This is a simple extension of the rubber rectangle. The user establishes an origin *and* an axis as shown in Figure 41.43. Moving the cursor defines a diagonal between the origin and the CAP. The rectangle is constructed with two sides parallel to the axis and two perpendicular to it.

Grow. The "grow" (or scaling) routine changes the size of an object defined relatively. Choose a grow factor, greater than 1 to enlarge the object, less than 1 to reduce it. Make the object grow continuously by the factor or in single steps of the factor as the button is pressed. Figure 41.44 illustrates this effect.

The routine reworks all lines by progressively determining the vertices of the enlarged object. To find the

Figure 41.46. Multiple image draw action.

next vertex, find the angle and length of this line segment; increase the length of the segment by the growth factor.

Drag. We have seen how to create, name and duplicate an object. Another alternative is called "drag." Start with the cursor on the origin of a copy of the object as shown in Figure 41.45. Move the stylus and the object is *dragged* across the screen.

The routine for drag is like that for the rubber band. If the CAP changes, the routine erases the current copy (by writing it in black) and replaces it with a new copy beginning at the CAP. To *fix* the object, press the button; the routine exits to the executive.

Multiple images. Alter the *drag* procedure above: instead of erasing each image, let it stay on the screen. Now, as the object is dragged across the screen, multiple images are produced as shown in Figure 41.46. Set an image production rate into the routine; at known intervals copies appear. Move the stylus faster and fewer copies of the object appear.

Brush stroke. Instead of using a thin line to sketch with, one can define a **brush** as a short line segment. As the user *drags* the line across the screen (at continuous repetition rate), this action produces a brush stroke of the predefined color and width. Irregularities in the brush can be created by making it a dashed, dotted or irregular line as shown in Figure 41.47. The brush can even work as an object as in the multiple image presentation above.

Once how these routines work is reasonably apparent, it is a straightforward matter to construct one's own. Use the high level language in which the routines are written.

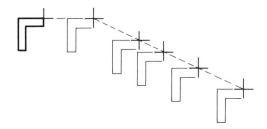

Figure 41.45. Dragging an object.

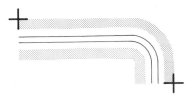

Figure 41.47. Brush stroke.

Then describe the logic of generation and finally put it into language form.

41.8 OUTPUT

General Considerations

We have discussed the production of a visual image on the CRT screen. Actually the screen is itself a form of output immediately consumed by the observer. However, it is transient; when the computer is turned off, the image disappears. Memory planes used in the computer and the terminal have volatile storage. On powering up, nothing is left of the image one has worked so hard to develop.

The image can be preserved in two forms:

- Digitally recorded on a storage medium such as a disk, for reproduction when needed on the CRT screen;
- As hard copy generated now and examined later without need for the computer.

These two kinds of output are defined first and then examined in detail.

Digital storage.   An image in progress is held in image planes. It can be dumped onto a magnetic storage medium and later returned to these planes for recreation. A whole floppy disk may be needed to store a single high resolution color image. This process **backs up** the image. If done bit by bit, storage may take considerable time—several minutes. *Compression* reduces the space required.

An alternative keeps track of the commands required to produce the image. If these commands are issued again they provide a new image produced in exactly the same sequence before your eyes.

Hard copy   for graphics includes photographs, plots and printouts on vellum, mylar or paper.

Digital Storage

Bit by bit.   After a session of creating and revising, a pictorial image is in two forms:

- Presented visually on the screen;
- Stored in the image plane in the terminal or in computer memory.

When the computer is turned off, both forms of image disappear. It is impossible to recreate the image for viewing or for further editing without storing it.

The picture in image memory is a pattern of 0s and 1s. If stored in this form on a floppy disk or a similar medium, it can be recovered and reentered later.

For the monochrome image, a single plane stores the pattern. The terminal on request transmits a byte at a time from the plane to the host, which puts the pattern in a named serial file. The time to store or retrieve the pattern depends upon the number of pixels involved. For monochrome, backup can take a few seconds to a minute.

For high resolution color graphics, an image may consist of as many as a million bits. Additional information is necessary, such as the color table, to preserve the color values. It may take several minutes to store this on a floppy (a fraction of a minute for a hard disk).

Data compression.   A monochrome line drawing shows as a black screen with just a few white areas. Image memory contains mostly 0s and very few 1s. Instead of recording all the bits, why not compress the data? One method, **run length encoding,** writes the current bit value (1 or 0), followed by a *number* indicating the successive bits that have this value. An area which contains a thousand 0s can be encoded in a few bytes. For line drawings, the data reduction factor may be of an order of magnitude or more. Compression is equally applicable for recording color.

Recalling.   To reproduce the image, one reads it into memory from disk and concurrently transmits it to the terminal to fill the bits of the memory planes. For compressed data, the host notes string lengths and creates corresponding strings to pass to the terminal (at a transmission rate of 19 kilobaud or more). The terminal puts the bits into image memory and the picture is painted on the screen from the top to the bottom (or vice versa).

Storing commands.   An image is created by issuing commands at the terminal. Or a menu invokes routines to issue commands to the terminal. A graphics package can record all commands it (or the user) sends to the terminal. If these are reissued later, starting with a clear screen, the drawing sequence produces the same result, only speeded up many times.

Why not record these commands onto an external medium? Then read back the commands from the medium, send them to the terminal and the image is generated as created.

As a graphics package sends commands to the terminal, a routine can also assemble an edited command list. When finished, the main menu may have a choice to write this command list to disk. Usually the space required to store primitives is much smaller than that for the image bits, even in compressed form.

An intelligent recording routine can cull out unnecessary commands, of which there are several classes ranging from obvious to subtle:

1. Communication commands that turn on and off stylus control and accept information passed back and forth.
2. Intermediate commands, as produced for rubber banding. These routines send commands to display and then to erase lines or forms until *set* into the picture.
3. Decisions made along the way to move or remove an object, i.e. destroy an old image segment and create a new one.

The executive makes a command file omitting directives about both transmission (1) and intermediate commands, as for the rubber band features (2).

A set of commands to destroy or move an existing object (3) corresponds to a previous set of commands which created the object and appears earlier in the command file. The executive routine searches the command file to see if an *erase* command set has an equivalent *create* command set. These erase commands are forwarded to the terminal to effect the display. But instead of being entered into the command file, comparable creation commands are removed.

Compressing the command file thus has two effects: the command file uses less storage, and the time to create the drawing is shorter.

An image created from a command file looks like a drawing produced by an invisible hand on the screen. This process is especially dramatic if the action is slowed down with a programmed time delay. Otherwise, for a small drawing, the entire command file is read back and all commands are issued to the terminal in a fraction of a second; the image jumps onto the screen without showing a production sequence.

Sometimes a host has a command file collection program built into the graphics package. It provides automatic backup; at frequent intervals the memory copy of the command history file is rewritten to disk, an impor-

tant safeguard. Otherwise, a power failure could wipe out as much as a full day's work on an important drawing. Automatic backup allows one to go back to the last backup image.

Photographic Images

This subsection discusses not only photographic images of the screen but alternatives which work with television signals.

Photography. The CRT showing an image is a source of light which can be captured by a camera. The problem is to get a high quality photographic image. The CRT has a glass face which reflects visible light. The camera captures the reflections. Hence the CRT and camera combination must be shielded from light, or the lights in the room must be turned off or made very dim.

Other factors to consider include exposure, focusing and focal length of lenses. It is difficult for an amateur to get a good photograph of a CRT image. An attractive but somewhat costly alternative is the selfcontained photographic unit. It attaches to the terminal like an external supplementary monitor. It consists of a miniature high intensity color CRT built around a camera holder and a light excluding hood. When the screen image is satisfactory, this unit is activated and the picture snapped.

The photographic medium can be Polaroid, color negative, monochrome or slide film. Slides are by far the most popular. Slides of bar charts, pie charts, and so forth, with captions formatted attractively, are the handiest for executive briefings.

VCR. **Video cassette recorders** are popular and inexpensive. They can record a single image, a set of images or an entire production session from a source which produces a television signal. Some terminals feed a monitor directly without having to create the complex signal required to drive a television set. Others, such as low cost micros, provide (only) a television output signal. A VCR records whatever is on the screen, whether it changes or moves or not. This is a good medium for computer controlled animation.

Hard Copy

Graphics hard copy is produced by printing or drawing with ink on paper or vellum. In attempting to produce a faithful image, three difficulties arise:

1. Pigment and light mixing do not obey the same rules.
2. Raster presentation, scanning from the top of the page to the bottom in a sequence of lines, may need to be adapted to stroke drawing or vice versa.
3. Large areas of intense color are not easily produced on the output medium.

Hence hard copy is never quite as good as photography for full color fidelity.

Mixing colors.   The CRT, by activating differentially the three spots which comprise the triad, can produce almost all conceivable colors. This action is **additive;** light produced by the three spots is spectrally pure and combines to produce the desired color.

With pigments the action is **subtractive.** A pigment absorbs all light except those frequencies which produce the characteristic color perception. Thus pure red pigment absorbs all light except red. For example, a red dress appears almost black in blue light; the red pigment in the dress absorbs the blue light so there is little light left to reflect to the viewer.

Almost everyone has experimented with pigments in the form of paint, watercolor, crayon or coloring pencils. Mixing rules for pigments are not the same as for light. For example, when painting a picture in oil or watercolor and a violet hue is desired but that pigment is lacking, one mixes red and blue. However, when red and blue *light* are mixed in equal proportions magenta is produced, which contrasts considerably with violet.

Metering pigments.   Assume that there are rules to generate pigment mixtures for each color on the palette. How do we actually mix the pigments in the proper proportions as printing takes place? None of the printing methods described shortly allows effective **metering,** which controls the relative quantities of pigment accurately enough to produce the desired color. Keep this in mind as you read these subsections.

Image generation technique.   The methods to be examined create an image as

• A sequence of dots; or
• A line drawn by a pen.

These correspond respectively to raster scan and vector stroke image production. A raster scan image is easy to convert into a sequence of dots, but not into strokes to control a pen-type output. Similarly, a vector stroke method easily produces pen-type output, but it requires programming to convert to a dot sequence.

Solid colors.   When a broad expanse of color appears on the screen, it is impressive. An expanse of color produced on paper as a sequence of dots or horizontal and vertical lines is often dull and insipid. Viewing by reflected light makes the apparent intensity even duller.

Dot matrix printer.   The dot matrix printer produces a line of text by scanning the paper from left to right or on faster machines, in both directions. The print head consists of a number of print needles; each needle is activated individually to print a dot which is part of a vertical line segment. As the head passes through a character position, the print needles lay down a pattern of dots for the character. The needles hit a black ribbon and leave an impression on the paper. (See Chapter 6)

This printer is readily adapted to print graphics; *each* needle is responsible for printing successive dots of *one* line of the raster. For a print head of ten needles, the top 10 lines of the display print in one pass of the print head. The paper is advanced (by 10 scan lines) and the next pass prints the next 10 lines.

It would waste time to require that the printhead always start at the left. It is simple for the program to send dots for the reverse path in the reverse order. Dot matrix printers have reached a high stage of development and are inexpensive; they are ideal for business graphics in monochrome. Although the output does not show solid black areas well, their output is acceptable in other respects.

Color dot matrix printers use ribbon which has several color components. These printers work on different principles. Some use a separate pass for each color; others activate the ribbon separately at different vertical positions. In any case, the printer lays down a matrix of dots of up to three colors.

Color matrix printout cannot produce an accurate rendition of screen colors. If hue, saturation and tint are important, this method is useless. If color only distinguishes one kind of box from another, as with bar and pie charts, then color rendition is not important and the matrix printer serves well.

Ink jet printer.   The ink jet printer is essentially similar to the dot matrix printer, with jets of ink substituting for

Figure 41.48. Pen plotter for business applications. (Courtesy Hewlett-Packard)

print needles. Drawing on multiple color reservoirs, jets of two or three colors provide color output. Quality tends to be better as contrasted with dot matrix output because the ink is fluid and distributes itself evenly to produce well formed lines. Metering colors is still a problem, however; expect only a few colors to display on the copy.

Plotter.   These important devices come in a wide range of sizes from that of a pad of paper to 12 feet long. Figure 41.48 shows a small-format plotter, and Figure 41.49 shows example typical for a drafting facility capable of producing large engineering drawings.

A flat bed or a cylinder holds the sheet of paper firmly as the drawing is made. A pen is held in an arm which moves in two directions. Commands from the computer lower or raise the pen from the paper; other commands cause the pen to move as directed by the computer program. Straight and curved lines of all sorts are sketched by the pen. The pen is raised, repositioned and lowered to start a new line; lines need not be continuous.

To change colors, the device returns the pen to its holder and chooses another. A variety of colors, perhaps a dozen or more, may be available according to plotter design. A long straight or curved line of any pen color is drawn in a fraction of a second.

It is easy to see the distinction between this method of producing the image and the others. It is not comparable to raster methods. A program to produce a drawing from a raster image memory must be connected to line drawing primitives. Any irregular line segment can be produced by a number of short straight line segments. There is little problem in convering terminal primitives to plotter primitives. Similar methods produce text characters on the drawing.

Although a range of colors is provided by multiple pens, it is impossible to meter color to produce hues accurately. An area of solid color is produced by a series of straight lines with wide pens that make overlapping strokes. This proves satisfactory in many cases, but does not produce the dramatic image found on the CRT.

Figure 41.49. Drafting plotter. (Courtesy Calcomp)

REFERENCES

Foley, J. D., and A. Van Dam, *Fundamentals of Interactive Computer Graphics.* Reading, MA: Addison-Wesley, 1982.

Machover, C., and R. E. Baluth, Eds., *The CAD/CAM Handbook.* Bedford, MA: Computervision Corp., 1980.

Newman, W. M., and R. F. Sproull, *Principles of Interactive Computer Graphics,* 2nd Ed. New York: McGraw-Hill Book Co., 1979.

Scott, J. E., *Introduction to Interactive Computer Graphics.* New York: John Wiley & Sons, 1982.

42
CICS-VS: An On-Line Software Monitor

Paul Gubitosa

National Council on Compensation Insurance

42.1 INTRODUCTION

This chapter is written with the assumption that the reader has some understanding of IBM data processing terminology and procedures. The purpose of the chapter is to familiarize the reader with the **CICS-VS** environment and provide an understanding of related components and facilities. The chapter represents a small subset of many manuals written on CICS-VS. More specific and technical details can be found by checking references at the end of the chapter.

Traditionally, data processing may occur in batch or on-line mode. In the batch environment, transactions are grouped and processed by a single stream of program steps that perform the common functions of data editing, data manipulation, file updating, summarization and output reporting. The batch job stream is usually scheduled to run routinely as required. Output is available at a later time, after processing, printing and distribution.

The on-line environment provides immediate access for data inquiry and updating interactively. If need be, an on-line application can approach the maximum availability of 24 hours, if the business needs this and if the facility can support backup functions.

An on-line facility is similar to an operating system: it manages tasks through multitasking and multithreading. Furthermore, the on-line system is usually accessed through a network of locally or remotely connected terminals by which the user expects a fast response to an inquiry. Thus the user's request is handled when it is made rather than later as with the batch processing system. Let us look at a scenario to further illustrate the on-line environment.

This scenario illustrates the on-line environment. Suppose a manager wants to check the status of the accounts for the firm's biggest customers. In the batch mode, a job stream is configured, scheduled, processed, printed and distributed for the results to be obtained. This may take hours. In the on-line environment, the manager logs on to the system, keys a transaction number and receives an initial menu of functions to be performed. By means of selecting a function and entering the account codes, the information is made available in seconds. The advantages of on-line processing over batch processing are significant, but the complications and costs involved in the design and implementation of the on-line environment are equally significant.

On-line software is a group of complex interacting programs capable of

- Serving a myriad of terminals and terminal types;
- Handling all file I/O for application programs;
- Providing rapid response to inquiries;
- Handling and managing multiple tasks and requests according to predefined rules;
- Coordinating the sharing and distribution of resources.

In addition, on-line software must provide efficient and easy-to-use data recovery and security features. If each application programmer had to include these functions in every online application program, an on-line system would be impossible to implement.

In the late 1960s and early 1970s, IBM's laboratories developed an on-line data communications facility which IBM called the **Customer Information Control System,** or **CICS** (often pronounced "kicks"). The latest version, called **CICS-VS** *(VS = Virtual Storage),* is a program product available via a licensing agreement. This chapter gives an overview and examines the modular components and related functions of CICS-VS. The various optional features are considered. A discussion provides a typical transaction flow, defines the steps for configuring and tailoring and examines the programming languages available. An example follows with an interface call, diagnostic tools and special features, such as intersystem communication and multiregion facilities.

42.2 USING CICS-VS

Using an on-line system is a matter of business objectives and service requirements set by the organization. Many organizations use CICS-VS (or simply CICS hereafter) to handle the functions of data manipulation and information processing. The *CICS/VS General Information Manual* [4] mentions the use of CICS for inventory control, manufacturing control, credit card services, banking and finance, insurance, hospital administration, educational services, retail, and so on. CICS aids the organization in controlling information, maintaining current and accurate information and disseminating information responsively.

CICS provides management modules to pass terminal requests to user applications, which in turn effect file access and transfer of data back to the terminal. Further, as a record is being updated, its access is denied to others to ensure data integrity and accuracy. Thus, a reservations control clerk may receive a phone call for an airline seat, a rental car or hotel room, and needs to supply an immediate response to the customer. A fast inquiry service using CICS returns a screen detailing the openings and choices for the customer. Once the customer chooses the date, time, and so on, the clerk enters the reservation. CICS locks out the record while making the update, and when done, returns a visual confirmation to the clerk who informs the customer. All these actions can happen in less than a minute.

An international organization communicates information globally in seconds, using CICS message switching capabilities. Messages can be stored and viewed later at sign-on or received at once on an active terminal.

Finally, a CICS data entry application prompts the operator to enter data, which is then batched into a file and processed later. Thus, CICS supports many typical business applications, using interactive data entry and inquiry terminals.

42.3 A SYSTEM OVERVIEW

CICS is a general data communications monitor that services a network of mixed terminals providing on-line access to a group of files or a collection of related files called a **data base.** The CICS monitor performs functions similar to an operating system. For example, CICS dynamically allocates storage to tasks and dispatches tasks according to preassigned priorities. A user signs on to the system by entering a user identification (user id) and password. Since CICS can service many different applications, the user identifies the one desired by typing a preassigned 4 character code, called a **transaction code.** All transactions can be protected with a security key so that each user must be authorized for a particular application or else the request is rejected.

Once CICS has validated the code, control is passed to the **task manager,** which schedules the transaction request as a unit of work known as a **task.** If additional operators enter the same transaction code, one task per terminal is created. The task manager creates a control block that contains information about the task, including the task's **dispatching priority,** its priority among competing CICS tasks. A task's priority is determined by combining assigned priority values for the operator, the terminal and the transaction code. The task eventually gets control and, as with the majority of on-line applications, a series of file accesses commences. Then through the basic mapping support (BMS) facility, a formatted screen is sent to the user.

Modes

Usually the first screen is a menu of functions from which the operator chooses. Now the task can

1. Remain in execution, exchanging information (messages) back and forth with the operator in a dialogue;
2. Terminate and be automatically reinvoked with each choice by the operator.

The first case, the **conversational mode,** ties up many resources for the duration of the dialogue. An operator command (**transaction**) followed by a series of single message prompts for response is an example of conversational processing. Since many other functions can be performed by the computer while the operator is reacting, the second case, **pseudoconversational,** is more efficient and preferred in most environments. Here, control passes back and forth between the application program, and CICS management modules and other users. Once the application outputs a formatted screen, the program exits setting a transaction code to be automatically initiated at the terminal when the operator hits <u>enter</u>.

Control

The task control program, called KCP, passes control among the different modules or tasks. This is **multitasking,** managing a number of tasks concurrently. Multitasking is how an operating system manages partitions or regions. CICS handles its subtasks similarly. Along with multitasking, CICS uses **multithreading,** in which sections of a single program are executed concurrently [2].

In COBOL terms, several transactions are allocated discrete areas in dynamic storage (the CICS pool of working storage) for their own working storage sections, but the tasks share the same copy of procedure division code. Multithreading contributes to the efficiency of CICS because more tasks can reside in memory. When a transaction is initiated, if the program exists already in

dynamic storage, there is no need for an I/O to load it again. Furthermore, a frequently used application program can be made resident.

CICS services are classified in distinct categories of functionality by IBM [4]. These are depicted in Figure 42.1:

- *Data communication functions* include those functions that handle terminal control and interface: BMS for easier screen manipulation, intersystem communication (ISC), and multiregion operation (MRO).
- *Data handling functions* include the interfaces to data sets, data bases, and CICS control areas. Aside from file access methods, CICS uses facilities to insure data integrity like transaction backout and recovery via journaling and logging.
- *Application programming services* provide the interface to CICS facilities in assembler, COBOL, RPG-II, and PL/I through the command translator and execution interface program. In addition, there are programmer aids like the execution diagnostic facility (EDF), and trace and dump facilities.
- *System services* include task control functions, program control functions (associating a transaction with a specific application program), storage management, and interval control, i.e., time dependent function initiation.

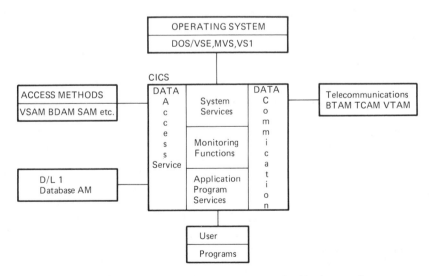

Figure 42.1. An overview of the CICS services and interrelationships to operating components (adapted from IBM GC33-0155).

- *Monitoring functions* collect data for performance and accounting purposes. Included are transaction oriented data, such as frequency of use and CPU time, terminal oriented data, application program data and file access data.

It is beyond the scope of this chapter to detail all of these facilities, but emphasis is placed on some of the more important facilities as well as the modular structure of CICS.

42.4 MODULARIZED MANAGEMENT FACILITIES

CICS is modular and is tailored to the user's needs. CICS executes in a single operating system (OS) region/partition. It functions through a collection of software modules, programs and tables. These components manage access to terminals, data and program resources through a preset standardized system level and through application specifications. The management modules are named by three characters ending with a P (e.g. FCP for file control program). The CICS systems programmer selects the various file access methods for the on-line files with FCP. The CICS tables are named by three characters ending with a T, (e.g. FCT for file control table which lists the resources used in this environment by the on-line programs). All files for the on-line system are included in one control table, the FCT, shared by all the different applications. Thus the FCP uses the information in the FCT to handle file access requests from an active task.

File Control Program/Table (FCP/FCT)

The **FCP** handles files, whether organized for VSAM, ISAM, BDAM/DAM or DL/1. Sequentially organized files are handled by another program. In the on-line environment, several operators may key a transaction code to access a single file. So tasks can share a file. FCP provides exclusive control when more than one operator tries to update the same record. **Exclusive control** permits only the first arriving request to access with update, locking out others until the update is done.

FCP services read, write, add, update and delete records for the application. FCP can deblock, retrieve sequential records starting from a designated point, interface to DL/1 (data base), and handle segmented records (consisting of several sets of adjacent fields) [2]. FCP finds the file characteristics in the FCT. The **FCT** contains definitions of all files opened upon CICS initializa-

tion. Definitions are reviewed and updated at task termination. The FCT contains the name of the file, the access method to use, how the file is used for processing (read-only, write, rewrite, browse, and so forth) and how many concurrent requests can be outstanding against the file.

Terminal Control Program/Table (TCP/TCT)

The **TCP** removes the burden of terminal communication from the application programmer, who merely codes *send* and *receive* calls in the program which enables data transfer to and from the terminal under TCP control. The TCP searches the **TCT** for an entry for the terminal with which it is communicating. When an operator enters a transaction, TCP validates the terminal through the TCT. Then it accepts submitted data and stores them in the terminal input/output area (TIOA). Control then passes to the task control manager. In the event of a terminal malfunction, the TCP can pass control to the terminal error program, which attempts recovery without causing the whole network to be affected. The TCP interfaces with the communications access methods in the operating system (VTAM, TCAM or BTAM), which handle functions such as polling.

For all lines and terminals, the TCT lists attributes such as line protocol (SDLC, bisynchronous), keyboard types, screen sizes. The TCT is configured using selection macros and can be large, taking some time to assemble for a large network.

Basic Mapping Support (BMS)

BMS removes the tedious work of programming the terminal device to display preformatted screens. BMS helps the programmer to develop maps with macros to form a two dimensional screen layout. The map can include the format of input and output data, fixed data such as page and screen headings, variable data fields and the device type to which the map relates [4]. The map (or screen format) uses attribute bytes whereby the programmer controls the way a field is displayed. For example, a password entry can be *nondisplay* as keyed and *must enter* fields can be highlighted.

BMS is available for most terminals supported by CICS. BMS provides **device independence;** a terminal may send or receive data without regard to physical terminal type [4]. BMS checks the device types with which it communicates and converts the data streams to device dependent requirements. BMS also provides **format independence;** on the screen, references to data are symbolic names, which allow maps to be changed dynamically [2].

All maps are defined, then assembled and stored in a load module library in the **processing program table (PPT)** prior to use. Here is a sample extract of map source code for line 1 of a 24 line screen:

```
FMS020T DFHMSD TYPE = DSECT,
                CTRL = (FREEKB),
                LANG = COBOL,
                MODE = INOUT,
                TIOAPFX = YES
FMS0205 DFHMDI COLUMN = 1,
                LINE = 1,
                SIZE = (24,80)
        DFHMDF POS = (1,3),
                INITIAL = 'DATE:',
                LENGTH = 5
DATE    DFHMDF POS = (1,10),
                LENGTH = 8,
                ATTRB = (ASKIP,BRT)
        DFHMDF POS = (1,26),
                INITIAL = 'REINSURANCE POOLS
                -P/L DATA'
                LENGTH = 30
        DFHMDF POS = (1,60),
                INITIAL = 'FUNCTION',
                LENGTH = 8
FUNCTN  DFHMDF POS = (1,71),
                LENGTH = 8,
                ATTRB = (ASKIP,BRT)
```

the macros define the map to be assembled and stored in the load library.

BMS provides terminal **paging** or **scrolling** so that the operator can move back and forth through the multiple presentation screens for the duration of the task. The application programmer can send a group of maps, called a **map set,** to the terminal. CICS handles this by storing the overflow (to the terminal) maps in temporary storage. Message routing sends maps to other terminals and/or printers (if hardcopy is required).

Task Control Program/Program Control Table (KCP/PCT)

The traffic cop of the CICS system is the **task control manager; KCP** supervises multitasking by controlling task dispatching. KCP validates a transaction initiated by the operator against the **program control table (PCT).** If

it is not a valid transaction, a message is returned with a prompt to resubmit a valid transaction. To be valid, the transaction code must be coded in PCT.

If the request *is* valid, KCP obtains the name of the associated application program and asks the **storage control program (SCP)** for memory to build the task control area. KCP also handles task termination, at which time all resources used by the task are freed. For a pseudoconversational task, KCP tries to initiate the next transaction automatically.

While tasks are processing, KCP maintains task synchronization, offers stall recovery, synchronizes resources, adjusts task priorities and prevents runaway tasks. Task synchronization places tasks in a *wait* or *suspend* state when they are waiting for an event (I/O) to complete; it resumes such tasks when the event(s) has completed. Resource synchronization is handled through enqueuing and dequeuing resources. KCP tracks all the enqueues against a single server (serial) resource, thus ensuring proper servicing. A system stall occurs when an overload of requests is made against a resource such as main storage, so that no task can process and no new task can be initiated [2]. KCP searches the PCT for purgeable tasks (noted by SPURGE = YES) and flushes them from the region in lowest priority order until the system can satisfy the pending request. Notification is made to the master terminal operator and the system designer might take note to increase the size of the parti tions to prevent a future stall.

The PCT contains the 4 character transaction codes used by operators. The characteristics for a particular code or group of codes are specified with parameters in the DFHPCT macro. A few of the attributes specified in the PCT follow:

- Association of task to an application program.
- Task security code.
- Task priority.
- Purgeability.
- Transaction work area.

Program Control Program/Processing Program Table (PCP/PPT)

Program management facilities control and coordinate the activities of each application program. The **PCP** saves and restores registers when control passes from one module to another. It checks each request to see if the applicable program is in the CICS dynamic storage area; otherwise, the program is loaded from the CICS load module library or a separate user library. Applications link to PCP through the command level handler called the execute interface program (EIP), described in the Section 42.7, on programming facilities. PCP gives control to requested services through standard system macros LINK, ATTACH, LOAD, DETACH, DELETE and XCTL.

The **PPT** contain definitions of all modules available under CICS. It provides the program name, the source language, program status (reusable or not reusable, resident or not resident), the security level and whether the module is a map or a program.

Storage Control Program (SCP)

The SCP handles all of the storage related requests (GETMAIN/FREEMAIN): I/O areas, buffers, or work areas for control blocks and intermediate storage for user application programs. Other functions include storage initialization storage accounting (reporting on all chain storage areas for a user application), conditional storage requests and system overload detection [5]. When an overload occurs, the SCP uses a storage cushion or reserve. A control block, common system area (CSA), records how often this cushion is used. If it is used often, then more storage should be allocated.

Interval Control Program (ICP)

Interval or time management functions include exit time, system stall detection, runaway task protection, time of day, time dependent task synchronization and time ordered transaction initiation. These intervals are set at initialization. CICS releases control to the operating system when no tasks are ready to resume processing after the **exit time interval.** When the system storage resource becomes overloaded, ICP detects this and directs KCP to start purging low priority tasks. ICP provides the time of day to the application program via the execute interface block (EIB), a control block available to an application program which contains accounting and time of day data in read-only mode.

ICP permits a task to

- *wait*—temporarily suspend itself for a given period of time;
- *post*—when a specified interval has elapsed the task is notified;

- *cancel*—allow a task to terminate its own or another task request for a post or wait.

Finally, automatic time ordered initiation will start a transaction at a specific time of day.

Transient Data Program/Destination Control Table (TDP/DCT)

Transient data are created or collected by one or more tasks and passed on to another task for processing. These data are stored by the transient data program (**TDP**) in sequential data sets called **transient data queues.** Since the data are processed sequentially at a later time, the queues are also called **destinations.**

Queues are classified by the TDP as intrapartition or extrapartition destinations. **Intrapartition destinations** are direct data sets accessible only by tasks executing within the CICS region/partition. Several tasks may write to the same destination but only one task can process it. An **extrapartition destination** is a sequential data set on tape or disk to be processed by a batch program after the CICS system has terminated.

Another function of the TDP is automatic transaction initiation on a predefined trigger level. When data in an intrapartition queue reaches a specified level, a task is initiated by the TDP to process the queue.

The **DCT** provides information to the TDP about the data transient to CICS. Automatic statistics, terminal I/O error messages, abend messages and sign on/off data are written to transient queues. The DCT describes data set control information, such as record format, record length, buffers, and so forth.

Temporary Storage Program/Temporary Storage Table (TSP/TST)

The **TSP** provides a facility for the application program to store data temporarily in dynamic storage or on a direct access storage device. The data set is a disk VSAM file. A temporary storage area buffers multiple screens of data received by an application. Each record written is labeled with a name and task association identification, available through the execute interface block (EIB), which contains accounting data. The program issues a READQ, WRITEQ, or DELETEQ to access the data [12]. Basic mapping support (BMS) and execution diagnostic facility (EDF) use temporary storage.

The **TST** is an optional table used for recovery at an abnormal termination of CICS.

Journal Control Program/Journal Control Table (JCP/JCT)

JCP is an optional feature which tracks all activity against a file. If files are not updated on-line but updated later in a batch mode, then journaling can be omitted. When files are updated on-line, then special purpose data sets called journals are recommended to act as audit trails, to record data base updates, additions and deletions for backup or to track transaction activity in the system [5]. Journaling is an involved management function performed for recovery purposes with some overhead to the environment.

JCP performs the following functions:

- Creating and managing journal files;
- Handling application service requests for journaling;
- Making records changes to the data base;
- Keeping an activity log;
- Facilitating reconstruction of the original files.

The logging function records information to back out the effects of a record add, update and delete.

JCP records a **before** image of the record (prior to change), an **after** image, and a synchronization point written to the output volume every time a logical unit of work (KCP detaches task) is completed. Synchronization points permit CICS recovery to find the last complete unit of work to ensure file integrity. During recovery from a CICS abnormal termination, the recovery program reads to **end of file** and proceeds backwards to the last sync point. From that point forward, all transaction updates are backed out and all before images are restored. JCP also adds the following to the output journal record:

1. A journal record identification prefix to identify the source and time of the update;
2. Output scheduling the collection of several journal records, while the journal is processing another output operation;
3. Volume identification for operational control [5].

The JCT desribes two types of journals and their characteristics. The *system log file* is used for the emergency restart facility, user logging, or automatic journaling. Emergency restart is needed when it is to recover infor-

mation in temporary storage, transient data queues, and terminal messages [5]. Otherwise the system designer may only choose to log updates from application programs. Thus *specific journal files* (up to 98) can be chosen to record file update data. JCT provides the following journal file attributes for **JCP**:

1. Disk or tape file;
2. Device type;
3. Buffer space allocation prior to the write;
4. Options such as retry I/O errors, input operations against the file, open status at initialization time, and the nature of the file (crucial or noncrucial) [11].

System Initialization Table (SIT)

The SIT is a list of all the management modules used in this CICS environment. The SIT enables system designers to call up new versions of modules, such as FCP or FCT, and quickly back out the changes by pointing the SIT list to the old versions. Each module is stored in the CICS with a suffix appended to the module name. Thus different SIT versions can be stored in the program library at the same time. The SIT may also have a user suffix so that the user can call a different SIT by simply changing a JCL parameter. The SIT is also used to initialize control block areas and temporary storage areas.

42.5 TRANSACTIONAL FLOW

Figures 42.2–42.9 illustrate and explain how the CICS management modules handle a typical transaction. They were adapted and modified from [12]. The events represent an overview of the transactional flow rather than the detailed steps. More detailed information can be found in [7].

42.6 INSTALLATION AND TAILORING

A well planned CICS project is constructed prior to configuration required for any program product. One should investigate fully the scope of its use, by whom, for what business purposes and how to convert the existing applications. Assuming that planning, design, implementation, testing and training have been completed, the installation process commences.

The CICS system is shipped on a multifile tape, accompanied by a maintenance tape to bring the system up to the most current release level. A cover letter and several manuals are provided. Prior to installation, the cover letter and manuals [10, 11], should be thoroughly reviewed. After the allocation of files, downloading the modules and application of the fixes, the tailoring or generating process begins. The result of generation is an executable load module library of user and vendor configured CICS management modules.

Macrocoding

The CICS systems programmer codes stage 1 macros to select options, if any, to be included for all management modules such as the FCP, the terminal control program (TCP), basic mapping support (BMS), and so on. To save time in generation, IBM supplies preassembled modules with default options included. Only modules with different option choices are assembled during stage 2 processing. Coding consists of writing CICS system generation macros with parameters which specify the

management modules and the desired options. Here are two examples:

DEFAULT DFHSG PROGRAM = KCP,   (42.1)
    STAGE2 = SELECTIVE

CONFIG DFHSG PROGRAM = FCP,
    FILSERV = (INDA,DAUPD,VSADD,VSUPD),
    AUTOJRN = YES,
    SUFFIX = 01

(42.2)

In the first case, the system programmer selects a preassembled module for the KCP, that is, the task control manager; no options are required. The CONFIG example selects specific file access techniques which are to be available to the online applications programmer; BDAM and VSAM are selected with update and add capabilities.

Automatic journaling of all file changes is provided. The suffix parameter enhances the modularity of the sys-

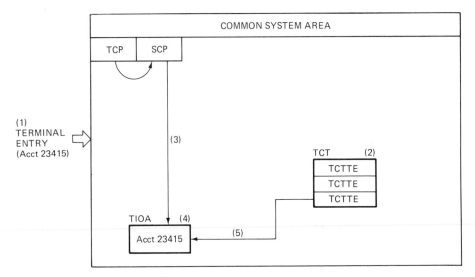

Figure 42.2. In the first illustration of a typical transaction flow through the CICS environment, the operator enters a transaction code and search key (1). The (2) terminal address is validated through the TCT terminal entry (TCTTE). TCP invokes the storage control program (3) to acquire an area for the terminal input output area (TIOA). SCP acquires memory for the TIOA, the TCP is informed and the entry is then stored in the TIOA (4). A pointer from the TCTTE to the TIOA is set in the TCT (5).

The common system area (CSA) is a CICS major control block area allocated at system initialization time and remains available until CICS termination. The CSA contains system constants, register save areas, statistical work areas pointers to CICS management modules, and tables.

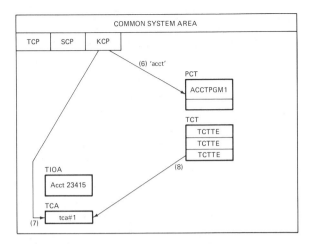

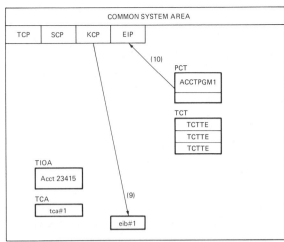

Figure 42.3. Next, control passes to KCP to validate the entered transaction code. The task control manager checks the PCT (6). If the transaction code 'acct' is valid, KCP acquires the name of the associated program to process the transaction. Once acquired, KCP creates a task and sets up a task control area (TCA). The TCA (7) contains information that assists all modules during the processing cycle of the task. The TCA contains storage addresses and facilitates communication between the application and CICS modules. KCP associates the terminal with its TCA by setting up a pointer in the TCTTE (8).

Figure 42.4. KCP creates the execute interface block (EIB), a read-only control block to which the application would not normally have access (9). Information such as task number, terminal identification, transaction identification, and date are found here. The application program uses the execute interface program (EIP) to translate its CICS function calls, such as terminal send and receive, read, write, and so on (10).

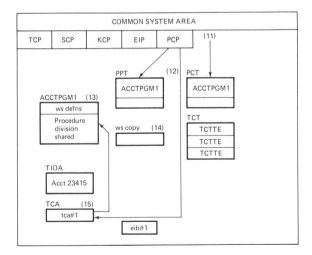

Figure 42.5. After validation (11), and setting up of the various control blocks and linkages, control is passed from KCP to PCP to select and initiate the program. PCP uses the information in the PPT (12). The PPT informs the PCP as to the application programs status (Does it need to be loaded from the program library on disk or is a copy of the code already resident in the CICS region?). If not resident, **ACCTPGM1** is loaded (13 into the region and a copy of the working storage for that specific task is created (14). Linkage to the TCA (15) is established by PCP and control is passed to **ACCTPGM1**. If **ACCTPGM1** is needed to service a transaction from another terminal, the code resides in memory and all that would be needed is a setup of another working storage area and the necessary linkages for task 2.

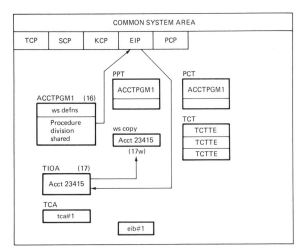

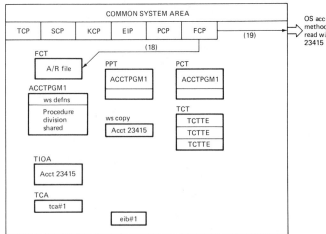

Figure 42.6. Upon entry into the application program (16), the CICS call to EIP, usually requests a terminal receive to get the data from TIOA into the program's working storage area. EIP moves the data from the TIOA (17) into the working storage area (17w).

Figure 42.7. The program, **ACCTPGM1**, has the data, and typically issues another call specifying the file and providing the key (23415). EIP passes the request to file control. FCP checks the FCT (18) to validate the request and obtain the file characteristics to give control to the proper access method. If the request is validated, FCP transfers the request to the OS access method to do a read (19) of the file. FCP also asks KCP to put the task in a wait until the I/O is complete, so that other ready tasks can gain control.

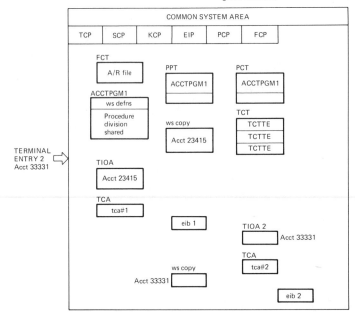

Figure 42.8. Since CICS is a multitasking system, another request can be received from a second terminal (acct 33331). CICS performs steps 1–17 again for this specific terminal transaction. As FCP transfers control to the OS access method for this task, assuming the first task's I/O is complete, the original task regains control. Note that there is only one copy of **ACCTPGM1**'s procedure code, and each task has its own copy of working storage.

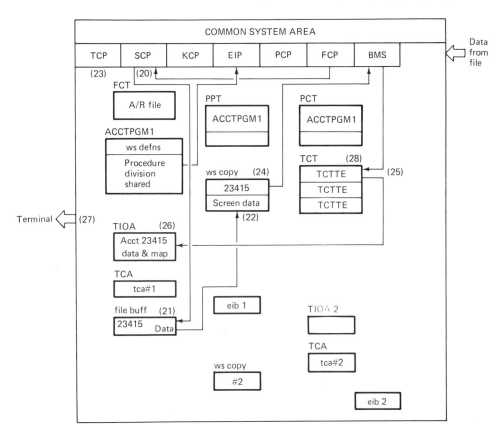

Figure 42.9. The access method returns the record for the first task. FCP requests a file buffer from SCP (20), and places the record there (21). The completion of the request results in data moved to the task's working-storage area (22). The application program formats a screen with the record information and informs TCP via an EIP call for a terminal send (23). The program issues an output mapping command which causes BMS to retrieve the physical map and merge it with the program data (24). The appropriate TCTTE entry is scanned to find the terminal type information so that the map can be converted (25) to the proper data stream, which is placed in the TIOA (26) to be sent by TCP to the terminal (27). TCP gets the address of the TIOA and marks the TCTTE the terminal has output pending (28).

For efficiency, programs are kept small, and after the terminal map and send, a return is issued to release control and free storage areas for new tasks. When TCP has sent the message stream to the terminal, the SCP is informed and the related I/O areas are released. The application program code remains in the region until its PPT entry is marked "not in use" and CICS needs the memory for other tasks.

tem since several versions of FCP can be stored in the load module library. (This one is FCP01.) A specific version is selected at CICS initialization time. The suffix technique facilitates testing different options and environmental configurations (e.g., new terminals) with a simple job control language (JCL) change.

Two assembly jobs are run to create the management programs and service modules and to put them in the CICS program library.

Table Selection

Next, the systems programmer selects the tables by coding more macros with parameters. The following control tables are mandatory:

1. The system initialization table (SIT);
2. The terminal control table (TCT);
3. The program control table (PCT);
4. The processing program table (PPT).

These are not mandatory but are coded in most installations:

5. The file control table (FCT);
6. Destination control table (DCT);
7. Sign-on table (SNT) of authorized users and security levels;
8. Temporary storage table (TST);
9. Journal control table (JCT).

There are several other tables that should be considered:

10. The system recovery table (SRT), which contains a list of abnormal conditions from which CICS can recover and may be tailored to include exits for specific user abends.
11. The nucleus load table (NLT), a rarely used table that controls the ordering, alignment and loading of modules forming the CICS nucleus.
12. The application load table (ALT), similar to the NLT but serving for loading of application modules and maps, helping to reduce virtual storage fragmentation and paging.
13. The terminal list table (TLT) which logically relates and controls a group of terminals and operators.
14. The transaction list table (XLT), listing transactions to be executable during the first stage of a system quiesce.
15. The program list table (PLT), listing programs to be executed at initialization time.
16. The terminal error program/table (TEP/T) providing a list of actions in the event of terminal errors—retrying the terminal command, placing the terminal out of service rather than the the whole line, branching to a user exit to handle the error condition, and so on.

The system programmer selects tables to satisfy the CICS environment, codes the macros and associated parameters, then assembles and links the tables into the program libraries.

Libraries and Files

The next step is to construct a list of required libraries and files. This facilitates constructing the JCL stream for initialization. The JCL stream consists of many data def-

inition (DD) cards that specify the libraries and files. Terminal, dump, statistical, trace, temporary storage, log, journal, transient and user file DD cards are found in a typical JCL stream; following is an extract of JCL from a typical installation.

```
//JS10       EXEC PGM = DFHSIP,PARM = ('SIT = 53,TCT = 51')
//*       ****** CICS SEARCH LIBRARIES********
//STEPCAT    DD DSN = VSAMUCAT.VSAM01,DISP = SHR
//          DD DSN = VSAMUCAT.VSAM02,DISP = SHR
//          DD DSN = VSAMUCAT.VSAM03,DISP = SHR
//STEPLIB    DD DSN = CICS.LOADLIB2,DISP = SHR
           DD DSN = CICS.LOADLIB1,DISP = SHR
//SYSUDUMP   DD SYSOUT = D
//*       ****** CICS LOAD MODULE LIBRARIES********
//DFHRPL     DD DSN = IDMS.R570.LOADLIB,DISP = SHR
//          DD DSN = CICS.LOADLIB2,DISP = SHR
//          DD DSN = CICS.LOADLIB,DISP = SHR
//*       ******   TERMINAL DATASETS      ********
//L3270      DD UNIT = 080
//          DD UNIT = 082
//R3270T1    DD UNIT = 035
//R3270T2    DD UNIT = 034
//*       ******   DUMP DATASETS    ********
//DFHDMPA    DD DSN = CICS.DUMPA,DISP = SHR
//DFHDMPB    DD DSN = CICS.DUMPB,DISP = SHR
//*       ******   LOG   DATASETS JSI ********
//JSILOGX    DD DSN = JSI.LOGX,DISP = MOD
//JSILOGY    DD DSN = JSI.LOGY,DISP = MOD
//DFHSNAP    DD SYSOUT = D,OUTLIM = 0
//*       ****** AUTOMATIC STATISTICS DATASET ******
//DFHSTM     DD DSN = CICS.STATSM,DISP = SHR
//DFHSTN     DD DSN = CICS.STATSN,DISP = SHR
//*       ******  AUXILIARY TRACE DATA SET      *******
//DFHAUXTR   DD DSN = CICS.TRACE1.DATA,DISP = (OLD,KEEP)
//DFHBUXTR   DD DSN = CICS.TRACE2.DATA,DISP = (OLD,KEEP)
//*       ******  INTRAPARTITION DATA SET      *******
//DFHNTRA    DD DSN = DFHNTRA,DISP = OLD
//*       ******   TEMPORARY STORAGE DATA SETS     *******
//DFHTEMP    DD DSN = DFHTSDS,DISP = OLD
//*       *EXPRT* USER DATA SETS (SEE FCT)      *******
//EERNMDIR   DD DSN = P35330.EXPNMDIR,DISP = SHR
//EERALDIR   DD DSN = P35330.EXPALDIR,DISP = SHR
//*       *ACCT*  USER DATA SETS (SEE FCT)      *******
//PLMASTR    DD  DSN = P35730.PLDATA.MASTER,DISP = SHR
//POOLST     DD  DSN = POOL.DIRECTORY,DISP = SHR
//PLMTKSDS   DD  DSN = P35730.PLMTKSDS,DISP = OLD
//*       ******   EXTRAPARTITION DATA SET     *******
//PRINTER    DD SYSOUT = &SYSOUT
//PRINT01    DD DSN = PRINT01.CICS,DISP = (OLD,KEEP)
```

All the DD cards in this figure refer to existing data sets and are part of the JCL for initialization of CICS. The step card (EXEC) points to DFHSIP, the system initialization program (SIP). SIP uses the SIT (system initialization table) with suffix 53 to select modules to be loaded. The TCT parameter has SIP override the SIT entry for TCT (terminal control table). With these parameters, different modules can be selected at initialization time, providing considerable flexibility. Initialization produces many messages during the initialization phase to let the user know what is happening. At the bottom of the page are messages from a typical console log.

Now users can sign onto their terminals and enter transaction codes.

42.7 PROGRAMMING FACILITIES

The application programmer and/or analyst, using CICS, designs and codes on-line programs. There are several facilities and languages available to help.

CICS on-line program logic is not significantly different from that of a batch program. However, unlike batch programs, on-line programs need to pass control to management modules for file access, terminal management, storage allocation, and so forth. There are two ways an on-line program can invoke these services: the **command level interface (CLI)** and the **macro level interface (MLI).**

Command Level Interface (CLI)

CLI is available to COBOL, PL/I, BAL, and RPG-II. It isolates the programmer from the internal structure of CICS and removes the burden of knowing the control blocks and their fields. It works like this:

1. The programmer puts CICS commands with parameters in the program where needed;

2. At precompile time, the CLI preprocessor replaces them with a series of moves and calls and a parameter listing;
3. The result of step 2 is compiled into machine language;
4. At execution time, the **executive interface program (EIP)** is called when this translated command stream is reached.

Now EIP receives the parameter listing with pointers to the actual parameters that represent the original command. EIP then passes control to the appropriate management module which returns control to the application program after its original request is satisfied.

EIP does allow the program to have access to some control block fields by setting up a read-only control block called the **execute interface block (EIB).** From the EIB, the programmer can acquire the time the task was started, the task number, the transaction identification, the terminal identification, the last CICS function executed, the return code and several other fields.

Three examples of COBOL command level coding are taken from [12]. A receive command for acquiring terminal input is:

EXEC CICS RECEIVE INTO (DATA-AREA)
LENGTH (DATA-SIZE) END-EXEC

(42.3)

```
LOG DFH1500 - CICS START-UP IS IN PROGRESS; VERSION 1.5, PTF LEVEL 0150
LOG DFH1501 - DFHSIT53 IS BEING LOADED
LOG DFH1500 - LOADING CICS NUCLEUS
LOG DFH1542 - CICS SVCS ARE INOPERATIVE
LOG DFH1500 - RELOCATABLE PROGRAM LIBRARY IS BEING OPENED
LOG DFH1500 - TRANSIENT DATA SETS ARE BEING OPENED
LOG DFH1500 - DATA BASE DATASETS ARE BEING OPENED
LOG DFH1500 - TERMINAL DATA SETS ARE BEING OPENED
LOG DFH1500 - DUMP DATA SET IS BEING OPENED
LOG DFH1500 - INITIALIZING TEMPORARY STORAGE
LOG IEC070I 104-203,CICSYS02,PS010,DFHTEMP,436,VSAMT1,DFHTSDS.TEST,
LOG IEC070I TB21A890.VSAMDSET.DFD82257.T945A9E0.TB21A890,VSAMUCAT.TEST
LOG DFH1500 - LOADING RESIDENT APPLICATION MODULES
LOG DFH1500 - SUBPOOL SIZE FOR THIS START-UP IS 164K
LOG DFH1500 - SPIE AND (E)STAE MACROS ARE BEING ISSUED
LOG JSICXP10 JSI CICS/VS INTERFACE NOW LOGGING ON JSILOGX.
LOG JSICXP60 JSI CICS/VS INTERFACE LOG 000% FULL.
LOG JSICXP70 JSI CICS/VS INTERFACE WARM START RECOVERY COMPLETE.
LOG DFH1500 - CONTROL IS BEING GIVEN TO CICS
```

The length of **DATA-AREA** is initialized to the maximum length expected, **DATA-SIZE**, and CICS places the data in the field, **DATA-AREA**.

A link to another program is handled thus:

EXEC CICS LINK PROGRAM (PROGRAM2) END-EXEC

(42.4)

PCP searches for the **PROGRAM2** entry in the PPT, and if this entry is found, the program gets control after several setup functions.

A file read command obtains data from a disk file:

EXEC CICS READ INTO (DATA-AREA)
    LENGTH (DATA-SIZE) DATASET (FILE-NAME)
        RIDFLD (KEY-NO) END-EXEC

(42.5)

FCP gains control and passes parameters **KEY-NO** and **FILE-NAME** to the access method to obtain the data placed into **DATA-AREA**.

The CLI enjoys wide use in many CICS environments due to its simplicity. IBM supplies an interactive CLI for the programmer to check individual **EXEC CICS** commands for syntax prior to use in a program. This is helpful especially for introducing application programmers to command level coding. Thus, in this environment, the beginning programmer can execute commands, check fields, check the EIB, and modify variables without having to code a full program.

Macro Level Facility

The macro level facility invokes CICS through a series of CICS macros, of the form **DFHXXX** and obtains information from the control blocks. The MLI is difficult to use because the user must understand the content and format of the CICS control blocks, maintain addressability to the blocks, and manage storage. MLI is available directly to the BAL programmer, and indirectly, via a preprocessing program to COBOL and PL/I users.

An example of a terminal control macro is

DFHTC TYPE = (ERASE,WRITE,READ,WAIT)   (42.6)

Unlike command level, the programmer must establish addressability to the TIOA, TCTTE, CSA, and TCA prior to issuing the terminal control macro. Without addressability, the data entered is impossible to retrieve. The macro (Eq. 42.6) causes an erase, then a write of

data to the terminal, an implied wait (for the enter key), a read, and a requested wait so that the program does not get control until the read is completed [2].

One of the advantages of macro level programming is the use of built-in functions through the **DFHBIF** macro. The programmer uses **DFHBIF** to perform table search, field verification (i.e., alphabetic, numeric, and so on), various field edits, bit manipulation, input formatting, and weighted retrieval (selects a group of records in a VSAM data set according to prescribed selection criteria). However, because of its complexity and lack of use, IBM plans to discontinue enhanced support of MLI in future releases of CICS.

Programs

Since the on-line environment typically uses many shared resources such as code, files and storage, many tasks can be active concurrently. Thus, there are several points the CICS programmer must consider. First, the programs should be **serially reusable.** In COBOL terms, this is the ability of several tasks to execute the same procedure division code concurrently. Hence, variables within the COBOL module should not be altered. Second, all I/O is handled by CICS modules so that no file definitions are coded in the Data Division. The FCT (File Control Table) is used for this function. Third, since the program executes in a paging environment, the main line execution code should have related functions close to each other. Finally, COBOL verbs that expand into subroutines and require additional memory should be avoided. Programs should be modular, quick and efficient.

42.8 DIAGNOSTIC TOOLS

To be useful, a package should include tools to support problem determination so that quick, effective solutions can be obtained. CICS contains components to help both the applications programmer and the systems programmer.

Manuals

The CICS Messages and Codes [6] provides system messages grouped according to specific CICS modules. Messages go to the console operator at initialization time, during execution, and in response to operator requests. Messages can appear on the console log as well as in extrapartition transient data queues which are usually printed at job end. The message code is formatted with the following: DFH prefix which identifies it as a CICS module; a component number (for example, 15 refers to SIP); a number, 00-99, that conveys the particular message within the cluster. Initialization messages (such as displayed in Section 42.6) are an example of this. These messages are informational, requiring no operator action.

Some messages reflect error situations which require operator action. The *CICS/VS Messages and Codes* manual [6] also show abend codes that identify the transaction, the program and the nature of the error. If an error explanation and action requested are not sufficient to resolve the problem, then further information can be obtained from the snap dump and formatted trace table.

IBM provides a *CICS/VS Problem Determination Guide* [8] to assist in trace and dump reading. It provides problem analysis with respect to performance, wait states, terminal errors, and, in addition, discusses the interfaces with BTAM, VTAM, and DL/1. Finally, Online Software International supplies a very good CICS handbook of data areas and control blocks [15].

Trace Facility

The trace facility consists of two components. The **internal trace table** is kept in main storage. At system initialization, CICS determines the size of the table according to a SIT parameter called TRT=XXXXX, where XXXXX equals the number of trace table entries. This number should be kept to a reasonable length (200–300 entries) so that storage is not constrained. Each fixed length trace table entry supplies useful debugging information about a transaction prior to system or task abend. The table is wraparound, so that when it is full, the top entry is overlaid with the current entry. The trace table is found through a pointer in the CSA when the dump is unformatted.

The second component is the auxiliary trace feature, **Auxtrace.** As the name implies, the information produced by Auxtrace is stored on secondary storage in two datasets; when one fills, the other is automatically activated. To check the task flow over a longer time interval, Auxtrace is invoked through an operator command. The Auxtrace data sets accommodate many trace entries and should be used sparingly; otherwise performance degrades due to additional I/Os. Another advantage of Auxtrace, aside from volume tracing, is the ability to print only selected entries based on terminals, transactions or time periods.

With either component, the entries point to the executing module, show the type of request it is servicing, provide task identification so that like entries can be grouped, and supplies data fields to assist in the diagnosis. The *CICS/VS Problem Determination Guide* details all the table entries and assists in interpretation. Trace tables often preclude dump reading to solve problems.

Dumps

To look at internal storage and control block details (to get to the root of some complex problem situations), one can take a snap dump dynamically through an operator command or request a full formatted dump at abend time via the SIT parameter. Transaction abends (abnormal termination) which do not take the system down usually produce a snap dump. Dump data is written to a dump data set on disk. The DFHDUP program prints a formatted dump giving a brief reason for the dump, segregates the major control blocks, like CSA and TCA, and formats the internal trace table, PSW/registers, and storage areas. The *CICS/VS Problem Determination Guide* shows how to read the dump.

Statistics

Statistics allow environmental service levels or patterns of performance to be established. Statistics help prevent problems because they alert the analyst when acceptable limits have been exceeded. Then action can be taken (for example, increase storage capacity or reduce disk contention).

The program DFHSTUP gathers statistics about system activity, stores them on disk data sets (two are available in the event of an overflow) and prints them after termination. The print program can produce interval or summary data. A listing may show the following:

- Task statistics, such as peak number of tasks, number of times at maximum task, total tasks and maximum number of active tasks;
- Storage acquisiton and release counts;
- Transaction statistics, such as count of individual use, program calls, and times stalled;
- Program statistics, such as times used and times fetched;
- Terminal statistics, such as message counts, transmission and transaction errors;
- File requests, number of adds browses, deletes, contention, overflows.

Execution Diagnostic Facility (EDF)

Problems arise during command level program development. A tool to aid in testing and debugging of program problems without making modifications to the source code, EDF runs as a transaction under CICS. EDF can be used in **single** or **dual terminal mode;** in the latter, one terminal serves for EDF informational displays and the other terminal for transaction entry and screens. EDF functions as an interactive tool that intercepts execution of the program at various points and displays a screen of program information.

The *CICS/VS Systems Design Guide* (9) names those times when EDF intercept may take place:

1. During transaction initiation, after the EIB is set up, but before the program is given control;
2. After the trace entry for the **EXEC** command but before the action is performed;
3. After the requested action is performed;
4. At program termination;
5. At normal task end;
6. At abend.

The following information is then displayed on the terminal screen:

- The **EXEC** command with all keywords and parameter values;
- The EIB fields;
- The program's working storage in hex or character format;
- The contents of any address within CICS;
- Up to five previous **EXEC** commands.

With EDF one can interact with the application to examine values after specific commands are executed. Thus, by rerunning the task you can modify values at the intercept point to effect a different course of events. You effect branches to different sections of the program by changing branch points of CICS exception commands. In addition, working storage can be viewed and modified prior to command execution.

Figures 42.10 and 42.11 [12] illustrate EDF displays before and after a command is executed. The displays show the task transaction name, program name, task identification, display status, the **EXEC** command and parameters, and program functions (PF) available to the programmer.

Online Software International (OSI) markets a competitive product, called Intertest, which is more flexible and powerful for testing and debugging. It permits setting symbolic breakpoints, instruction stepping, breakpoints, instruction stepping, checking program reentrancy and providing more detailed displays [1]. In addition, Intertest supports MLI and CLI (the macro and command level interface), and breakpointing is to the instruction level rather than to CICS commands. But Intertest incurs an extra cost, whereas EDF is included in the price of CICS.

42.9 PERFORMANCE TOOLS

A key element of CICS is the responsiveness of the online monitor in servicing user requests. Aside from the system response perceived by the terminal operator, there are measures in the form of system statistics that reflect system resource usage. These include transaction load, I/

```
TRANSACTION: NCCI    PROGRAM: EERO905P    TASK NUMBER: 0000026    DISPLAY:
STATUS:   ABOUT TO EXECUTE COMMAND
EXEC CICS READ
   DATASET('PLMKSDS')
   INTO('. . . . . . . . . . . . . . . . . . . . . . . . . . . . . . . . . .)
   LENGTH(+00090)
   RIDFLD(ACCTNUM)
   EQUAL


OFFSET:   X'000736'    LINE:   00043    EIBFN = X'0602'
ENTER:  CONTINUE

PF1:    END EDF SESSION     PF2:    RE-DISPLAY          PF3:    SWITCH HEX/CHAR
PF4:    EIB DISPLAY         PF5:    WORKING STORAGE     PF6:    USER DISPLAY
PF7:    SUPPRESS DISPLAYS   PF8:    ABEND USER TASK     PF9:    STOP CONDITIONS
PF10:   OLDEST DISPLAY      PF11:   PREVIOUS DISPLAY    PF12:   UNDEFINED
```

Figure 42.10. EDF display before execution of command.

```
TRANSACTION:  FC01     PROGRAM: FCEXCOB1     TASK NUMBER:  0001592     DISPLAY:
STATUS:    COMMAND EXECUTION COMPLETE
EXEC CICS READ
   DATASET('CLASSDS')
   INTO('LS012GR54 5BAND SHORTW RECEIV CHI177 78 0130LAX 78177 0295NYC10' . . .)
   LENGTH(+00075)
   RIDFLD('LS012')
   EQUAL


OFFSET:   X'000736'     LINE:    00043       EIBFN = X'0602'
RESPONSE: NORMAL                              EIBRCODE = X'000000000000'
ENTER: CONTINUE

PF1:     END EDF SESSION      PF2:    RE-DISPLAY           PF3:    SWITCH HEX/CHAR
PF4:     EIB DISPLAY          PF5:    WORKING STORAGE      PF6:    USER DISPLAY
PF7:     SUPPRESS DISPLAYS    PF8:    ABEND USER TASK      PF9:    STOP CONDITIONS
PF10:    OLDEST DISPLAY       PF11:   PREVIOUS DISPLAY     PF12:   UNDEFINED
```

Figure 42.11. EDF display after execution of command.

O utilization, processor utilization, storage demands, network utilization and task response time. The *CICS/VS Systems Programmer's Guide* [10] identifies potential bottlenecks that can affect perceived response rate and recommends solutions to these and other problems. For example, if the response is bad at all transaction loads, then check the paging rates, CPU utilization, line utilization, and so on.

In addition to the statistical data recorded and written to the statistics datasets by DFHSTUP, CICS can record performance data in greater detail at specified collection intervals. The monitoring programs DFHCMP, DFHCMON, and DFHCCMF can record accounting, performance, and detailed exception data by scanning control blocks, and tracking information through counters and calculations. They use the monitor control table (MCT) to decide how often to sample, what classes of data to record, and to what journal files to log the data. The *CICS/VS Systems Programmer's Reference Manual* [11] details the three performance oriented classes and what data is included in each class.

Briefly, the accounting class includes transaction identification, terminal identification, operator identification, transaction type and count, transaction abend count, and number of input messages. The performance class includes some accounting data as well as user transaction elapsed time, dispatched time, real CPU time, and I/O wait times. In addition, system tasks, such as KCP, JCP and TCP, are tracked for dispatched time and CPU time. Storage usage and paging statistics are also available.

The exceptional class highlights potential problem areas such as waits for VSAM files (wait for strings),

waits for shared buffers, waits for main storage and temporary storage, and ISAM overflow conditions.

Note that monitoring facilities entail system overhead through periodic reading and writing of control block information. They should be used sparingly to establish trends, then dynamically deactivated through an operator command and reactivated only during slow response or problem situations.

Monitor data is recorded in a journal file but no analysis program is provided to list them. The user can write an analysis program or license IBM's **CICS Performance Analysis Reporting System (PARS)**. PARS provides performance analysis and monitor reports, as well as on-line displays of dynamic storage, OS storage requirements, and virtual storage maps. In addition, graphs of CPU utilization, file requests, terminal control requests, transaction rates, and transient data requests are available.

Johnson Systems International (JSI) markets an alternative approach. The JSI facility is called the **CICS Utilization Monitor and Chargeback System (UMAX)** and replaces MCT and PARS. UMAX is an interface program, configured and generated according to selected user options. It includes an accounting table with the capability of merging organizational cost centers in the data used for reporting to facilitate charging CICS users for service.

The interface program collects data in basic mode (after every transaction) or in interval mode. It records accounting data, system and CPU data, program and file I/O data. It can be activated or deactivated through a transaction request. In addition, current record accumulations and use statistics can be examined dynamically, through **graphic on-line display (GOLD)** at different

Table 42.1. Output: Segregation of User Area by Usage and Charges Over a Three-Day Span

USER CHARGEBACK SUMMARY

BEGIN DATE: - 11/21/82   RUN DATE: - 11/26/82
END DATE: - 11/24/82   PAGE   1

........USER........	USE COUNT	FILE+DL/1 I/O COUNT	FILE I/O CHARGE	PROCESS TIME	PROCESS CHARGE	TOTAL CHARGE?
SIGN-ON USAGE	344	5,449	$49.46	1.03894	$103.97	$354.77
ACCOUNTING	132	108	$.63	.10920	$10.95	$132.00
APPL. PROGRAMMING	581	1,986	$9.94	.63485	$63.58	$581.00
PLANNING & CONTROL	107	0	$.06	.01339	$1.33	$107.00
OPERATIONS	58	0	$.03	.01898	$1.93	do58.00
EXTERNAL OPERATIONS	10,654	64,662	$342.38	16.08192	$1,608.81	$10,654.00
MAILING	10,495	43,012	$263.70	15.43858	$1,543.98	$10,495.00
INDEX GROUP	42,389	461,295	$2,317.76	64.33782	$6,435.39	$42,389.00
RISK ANALYSIS	7,322	46,162	$307.18	15.23596	$1,523.90	$7,348.97
RISK CONTROL	894	9,994	$50.06	2.56922	$256.92	$894.00
RATING ADMINS	896	3,757	$19.78	.90685	$90.79	$896.00
FIELD SERVICES	1,002	5,526	$28.00	1.15668	$115.71	$1,002.00
	74,874	641,951	$3,388.98	117.54239	$11,757.26	$74,911.74

points during the on-line session. GOLD displays statistics that reflect system task CPU usage, paging, number of records collected, the active log file, current number of active tasks, and resource utilization graphs.

The interface records data to a VSAM or SMF log file. The data is dumped daily to an intermediate log file which is used as input to the **resource utilization graph (RUG)** reporting facility. RUG produces graphs of line, CPU, terminal and file usage, and storage demands. In addition, user accounting cost centers are integrated into the data and the output serves as input to the reporting program which can produce user configured detail or summary reports, two samples of which appear as Tables 42.1 and 42.2.

42.10 ADDITIONAL FEATURES

Security

Unauthorized access to company information is a major organizational concern in an on-line environment. CICS restricts access by requiring users to sign on. The SNT contains a list of operator identifications, associated passwords and a security key parameter that restricts the type of transactions. Several key values from 1 to 24 appear in each operator's entry in the SNT. Each transaction has a security value between 1 and 24 in the PCT. When an operator enters a transaction, its security key is found in the PCT; if this key is not listed in the SNT entry for the operator, the transaction is refused. Every time an operator logs on and off or causes a security violation, the event is logged via a message sent to an extrapartition transient data queue.

A second level of security extends to specific resources through the use of **resource security level codes (RSLC)**. RSLC is used by the Command Level Interpreter, EIP, and EDF to validate access to files and queues for each operator and transaction. The PCT contains a parameter to turn on RSLC for that particular transaction. Resources, such as files defined in the FCT which are used by the secured transaction, are assigned a security code that is validated against the operator's security code.

Table 42.2. A Graph of CPU Utilization by Time of Day

NOVEMBER PRODUCTION DATA

TIME OF MEASUREMENT IS FROM 82/11/24 AT 07.30.58
TO   82/11/24 AT 16.06.47

CPU UTILIZATION

TIME HHMM	TRANSACT COUNT	CPU SECONDS	PCT	0	342.84	685.66	1028.48	1371.30
				+ --------- + --------- + --------- + --------- +				
0730	434	66.12	4.8	**				
0800	577	86.17	6.2	***				
0830	350	46.89	3.4	**				
0900	488	68.30	4.9	**				
0930	421	63.75	4.6	**				
1000	464	89.87	6.5	***				
1030	688	105.10	7.6	****				
1100	845	154.17	11.2	*****				
1130	523	102.87	7.5	****				
1200	2	0.78	0.0	*				
1230	0	0.00	0.0	*				
1300	507	67.60	4.9	**				
1330	706	92.42	6.7	***				
1400	999	141.51	10.3	*****				
1430	488	63.85	4.6	**				
1500	699	99.40	7.2	***				
1530	813	122.39	8.9	****				
1600	1	0.11	0.0	*				
1630–0730	• • • • • NO DATA • • • • •							
SUMMARY								
MAX OBSERVED		154.17	11.2	*****				
AVG	529	80.66	5.8	***				
TOTAL	9005	1371.30		+ --------- + --------- + --------- + --------- +				
				0	342.84	685.66	1028.48	1371.30

One final level of security is an external security interface (user written or vendor supplied, like IBM's RACF for OS/MVS). In the SNT, if the entry contains an **EXTSEC = YES** parameter, the sign-on validation request is passed to the external security program. In addition, transactions via a PCT entry can be subjected to external security checking.

Multiregion Operation (MRO)

Most CICS installations segregate production, testing and development functions. This is possible within a single system CICS through security levels. But the draw-

back to this approach is the overhead. Furthermore, much planning and thought must be given to design so that test functions (file access, for example) do not impact production functions.

A programmer may decide that file redefinintion source code changes and recompilation are necessary as a result of interactive testing such as the execution diagnostic facility. But then the next testing session can not commence until CICS is terminated and reinitialized, particularly if the program is resident. There is always the possibility that a new transaction test may abend CICS. This will delay restarting CICS due to verification and recovery of files. Thus many organizations have a test

CICS region and a production CICS region running on the same system. Typically, an organization might look toward VM/370 which supports multiple virtual machines to run multiple CICS systems. But VM/370 does not support CICS directly; CICS is only supported by DOS and OS systems.

The primary function of MRO is to share resources, such as transient data queues, temporary storage, DL/1 data bases, files, transactions and terminals among *multiple* CICS regions within a *single* processor. Without MRO, there would be duplication of resource management within each region and the processor, if underutilized, could be overtaxed. Multiple regions assist in load balancing by sharing task loads, and provide operational flexibility, since applications can be segregated according to time constraints.

MRO is facilitated through three functions:

- Transaction routing;
- Function shipping;
- Module sharing.

Transaction routing. Terminals used in CICS regions are defined in the TCT. However, with the transaction routing facility, a terminal defined for region A can run a transaction in region B. A user can segregate applications by CICS regions, with one more region used as a front end to handle all terminal requests and route them to the proper region.

Transaction routing is accomplished through a **relay program.** The region's PCT contains an entry that determines whether the transaction is serviced by the local or remote region. If remote, the relay program passes the request to the TCP in that region, which sets up a TCTTE defined as remote and initiates the transaction. The remote TCP and the relay program continue to pass information from region to region until task termination or abend.

Function shipping. Function shipping enables file sharing, transient data queues, temporary storage and DL/1 data bases among multiple regions. As the name implies, a command level function (for example, a read file) is passed to EIP, which uses the MRO program and FCT to determine the locality of the referenced resource. A file request to another region is shipped there; a *mirror* transaction executes it and sends the reply back.

Shared management modules. One problem with running multiple regions is the duplication of management module code in both virtual and real memory, which may well result in more paging. A pageable area called the *linkpack area* holds code shared by all regions. Management modules kept in pageable linkpack result in less virtual storage and smaller working sets and reduces paging.

To summarize, MRO presents the user with a single CICS system image and handles cross-region CICS communication.

Intersystem Communication (ISC)

The ISC facility provides communication among CICS regions in different local and/or remote CPUs. ISC requires VTAM (virtual storage telecommunication access method) with the multisystem network facility and uses function shipping. Thus for every file request, temporary storage access, and so on, MRO's function shipping finds where the resources are, effects an access and returns. ISC provides the **distributed transaction processing (DTP)** facility, an enhancement to MRO's function shipping.

DTP can split the transaction logic, with part of it executing in one CPU (front end) and the rest executing in a remote CPU (back end). Thus, rather than incurring the overhead of MRO function shipping while the application is performing a browse (multiple reads), the back end logic handles the file accesses and only communicates with the front end logic when the record is found (or not found). Function shipping facilities are used with ISC, but with DTP only one request is sent and one reply returned.

More complex designs are possible with ISC's alternate facility and parallel sessions capabilities. The alternate facility allows the back end transaction, once initiated, to function independently and start another remote transaction. Thus a file search can be routed through multiple CPUs. A front end transaction can also initiate multiple back end transactions (sessions), which exist in parallel. Through ISC, transactions can acquire and free sessions according to their needs. Information, such as a search argument, is passed to the sessions, and the front end transaction waits for the reply.

If the user considers an increase in CICS capabilities, the increase in resource requirements and costs should be carefully reviewed. MRO and ISC are two powerful and complex facilities, but the demands placed on resources reflected by higher CPU utilization, increased virtual and real memory, enhanced OS and communications software, and employee education may not warrant its use in every organization.

42.11 SUMMARY

CICS provides the vehicle for an organization to process data on-line and retrieve information to assist in management decisions. CICS supports local and remote terminals, and manages their task (transaction) access to the CPU, memory, and auxiliary storage. It accomplishes task management through its component modules and related tables. An applications program interfaces to CICS management modules through command level calls from COBOL, PL/I, BAL and RPG-II, or invokes CICS macros from BAL, COBOL and PL/I.

A systems programmer discusses the user applications, selects the required components and generates the facilities (journaling, access method support, and so forth) to satisfy objectives. Diagnostic tools are available to aid problem resolution and monitoring facilities which supply data for off-line tuning analysis. As the DP environment becomes more complex (multiple CPUs and a requirement for multiple CICS regions), CICS provides features like multiregion operation and intersystem communication to accommodate these requirements.

IBM continues to provide enhanced support for CICS/VS as evidenced by their recent announcement of the new release (CICS/VS Release 1.6). The enhancements include the capability of running CICS transactions beyond the 16 megabyte boundary (the latest IBM architecture allows 31 bit addressing instead of 24 bit addressing), improved and simplified installation procedures, more security features including additional keys, user exits and transaction restriction by operator and terminal, journal control through operator commands, improved publications and manuals, and much more.

REFERENCES

[1] Datapro Research Corp. (ed.), "Intertest," *Datapro,* July 1981, 70E-672-01a/01b.
[2] *IBM CICS/VS Application Programmer's Reference Manual.* SH20-9003, 1975.
[3] *IBM CICS/VS Concepts and Facilities Version 1 Release 5.* SR20-4673, 1980.
[4] *IBM CICS/VS General Information Manual.* GC33-0155, 1982.
[5] *IBM CICS/VS Introduction to Program Logic.* SC33-0067, 1978.
[6] *IBM CICS/VS Messages and Codes.* SC33-0081, 1982.
[7] *IBM CICS/VS Program Logic.* SY28-0685, 1982.
[8] *IBM CICS/VS Problem Determination Guide.* SC33-0089, 1982.
[9] *IBM CICS/VS Systems Application and Design Guide.* SC33-0068, 1982.
[10] *IBM CICS/VS Systems Programmer's Guide.* SC33-0070, 1982.
[11] *IBM CICS/VS Systems Programmer's Reference Manual.* SC33-0069, 1982.
[12] *IBM Command Level Coding for CICS/VS.* SR20-7341, 1982.
[13] *JSI CICS/VS Utilization Monitor and Chargeback System: Data Collection,* Vol. I. JS003-002, 1982.
[14] *JSI CICS/VS Utilization Monitor and Chargeback System: Report Program,* Vol. II. JS003-002, 1982.
[15] *The CICS/VS Reference Handbook.* Online Software International, 1982.

43
Simulation

Julian Reitman

United Technologies

43.1 INTRODUCTION

Simulation is difficult to define. A few examples show the range of items which might be construed under this heading. At one extreme are **simulators**—hardware/software systems that permit, for example, airplane pilots to be trained in a "cockpit" firmly planted on the ground. The cockpit instruments and controls are coupled to a computer that produces responses as though the pilot were flying an aircraft instead of being firmly fixed on the ground. At the other extreme, models designed to predict the economic performance of the entire world for the next 20 years use software languages and data bases.

Limited Subsystems

Rather than to attempt to cover such a broad range of simulation activity, this chapter is limited to an intermediate topic, the simulation of **limited subsystems.** This is the class of application that a system analyst is most likely to be called on to solve. The focus is on the tools of the simulation practitioner, the higher order simulation languages.

Simulation techniques are commonly required where there are limited facilities to handle traffic, material, communication, or banking transactions. For example, how many bank tellers are needed to serve customers so that the average (or median) wait is less than x minutes? Alternatively stated, how do you provide services to keep the maximum waiting time for 90 percent of the customers to less than y minutes? Note some of the variables:

- Is there a common line waiting for service, or are there individual lines for each teller?
- If there are individual lines, what conditions cause an individual to switch lines?
- And of course, how often does one transaction require ten times the average time to be completed?

Analysis. As the customer/bank teller situation is investigated, several characteristics emerge. Customers do not arrive at the bank at regular intervals, nor do they arrive as described by a mathematically convenient relationship. Instead, their demand is keyed to transportation schedules, lunch hours, holidays, and the response to their previous transactions. Under such circumstances, the usually bell shaped curve based on an average time between customers may not be bell shaped at all; then simulation is a convenient way to represent the problem more accurately by utilizing as input actual historical data. Of course, there are many situations for which data are not available. In those cases, **pseudodata,** made up data, may be used; the sensitivity of the system performance to various sets of input data provides insight to critical values. After all, nowhere is it stated that analyzing complex systems was an easy task.

Difficulty. Another reason analysis may be difficult is that systems often have several transactions going on simultaneously. That is, there are many items being processed simultaneously to the point it is implausible to separate out one item from another; and what happens to one may influence another or all others. For example, customers are certainly free to change from one queue to another.

Several additional examples provide an estimate of the scope and variety of problem areas suitable for analysis and simulation.

Suppose one were asked to evaluate the cost of maintenance for a large number of items. If there were only the usual questions of how often there are failures and how long it takes to repair them, then a simple analysis would suffice. However, consider this frequent occurrence. A repair action is made which causes yet another repair action. Consequently, interrelationships get quite complex. Simulation offers an alternative approach to predicting the system uptime, number of maintenance actions and the advantage of alternative repair, initial quality, and location of resource strategies.

In cases where neither production nor consumption follows well defined rules, the question of what size reservoir is needed to ensure an adequate supply is understood through sensitivity analysis. Different strategies for varying intervals are compared. Again, an increased insight is all that is expected.

Suitable Problems

What are the characteristics of problems suitable to simulation? First, there is usually no other convenient approach. If a mathematical solution is obvious, it takes less effort and provides greater accuracy. Simulation is undertaken because analytic alternatives are *not* available.

Second, the system may be composed of numerous poorly understood interactions. Decompose the system into partitions and the solution for each partition is different from that obtained for the system as a whole. Simulation provides an opportunity to analyze the system and preserve its interactions.

Third, if a system is poorly understood, it is difficult to conduct *any* analysis. One possibility is to develop a simplified simulation that is known to be less than correct. Various classes of data are used to test the system hypothesis. The sensitivity analysis of results directs the acquisition of additional data to modify the system hypothesis; iteration of this procedure often results in a system definition quite different from that initially stated.

There are a variety of reasons to use simulation. After these reasons are evaluated, one conclusion, again, emerges: simulation is used when there is no convenient alternative. It should be the last method chosen to produce the desired results.

43.2 SIMULATION APPROACH

Simulation has a number of distinct functions in the design of complex systems. Among the advantages gained in using simulation are:

1. The problem definition becomes clearer;
2. Design uncertainties are reduced;
3. Problem definition is more complete, and the influences of data uncertainties are lessened;
4. A dynamic representation of the system is produced.

An initial benefit from simulation accrues even before the simulation is actually run. There may be a number of people working on the design at one time and it is important for the group to have a problem definition. Even when the definition is only an agreement to disagree, the boundaries of the disputed area are identified, focused upon and quantified—not a trivial achievement.

Language structure has an important role in determining the clarity of problem definition. If each language expression is readily understood by the design team, the statement of the problem is clarified. Thus, the simulation language may be put to its most important use before the computer is even used.

The major expectations from simulation are viewed as an aid in system synthesis and analysis. The choice of simulation over conventional methods goes back to the inability to make the real world conform to classical mathematical techniques. Simulation provides a convenient means for the analyst to participate in the design process by using the computer **iteratively:** the design process converges through a series of steps toward an adequate system representation.

Simulation requires input data. Where there is an abundance of data, statistical analysis may extract the trends. However, historical data may also be used. In fact, a simulation can accept statistical distributions for some data and historical records for other data.

Analytical and mathematical disciplines provide specific answers to appropriate questions or set of questions. Ambiguity in the problem relationships leads to using statistical techniques in the expectation that a mathematical relationship may be found when enough individual events are examined. The system analyst operates in yet a different environment. As contrasted with seeking a single optimum solution, alternative solutions are investigated in the search for an adequate system.

An answer does not require that all possible situations

be explored thoroughly. Many possible solutions can be ruled out on the basis of simple analysis. Meaningful comparisons among the remaining alternatives can be evaluated against sets of requirements and boundary conditions, such as traffic density, average waiting time, mission profiles, or a combination of factors. When results are quantitative, consistent with established criteria, and indicative of possible system behavior, they can be compared to an ideal case or to each other on a relative basis. Care must be exercised before extrapolating.

Simulation proceeds through well defined steps. First, the overall possibilities are investigated with a coarse overview model. Then comes the evolutionary process of system design.

Somehow the validity of the initial or derivative model becomes established or altered accordingly. The simulation model becomes more and more detailed in areas determined by the sensitivity analysis. Eventually, the model is composed of both detailed and coarse parts. The coarse parts remain coarse when the range of possible data indicates that they have little effect on system outcome.

The statistical significance of the results also depends on many factors. Often it is preferable to compare alternative systems directly and determine what causes them to diverge. Statistical significance sometimes becomes itself a factor in simulation. For example, radio communication can become unsatisfactory due to sun spot activity; how often this occurs can be important, for instance, in a communication simulation. When the behavior of a specific system is being analyzed, comparative results of alternative assumptions are preferred to complete statistical tests of significance because of the large amount of computer time required for adequate test results. Where necessary, the system configuration can be examined comparatively, using, for example, a worse case contrast. As the level of confidence changes, the model is exercised with different inputs for evolving uses.

43.3 WHO CREATES THE MODEL?

Two skills are required to develop a simulation. First and foremost, some individual should know the problem situation thoroughly. Or if knowledge of the problem is limited, someone should be prepared to set down an initial system hypothesis. Second, analytical skills are required to convert the system definition into a working, computer based simulation model that hopefully will provide results.

There is a contrast between these skills: system definition calls for a broad overview; computer models are based on attention to minute detail. If two separate groups handle these tasks, then effective communication between them is of primary concern. Historically, this has not happened. The common flaw occurs when programmers misinterpret a system definition established by system analysts. To compound the problem, the system analysts may not be aware of the programmers' misreading of their intent. They may not have provided the level of detail needed to make the discrepancy obvious. Far fetched? Not when one considers that candidate systems for simulation are extremely complex.

The Importance of Language

One way to reduce communication failure is to reduce the quantity of effort required to program the model. Then, if the system analyst also programs the simulation, communication is preserved. How can this come about? The key is to use an efficient and terse high level simulation language instead of a common procedure oriented language such as FORTRAN. If one line of code in a high level simulator language replaces twenty lines of FORTRAN code, then the total effort is proportionately reduced. Evidence accumulated over the last two decades supports this conclusion.

The unfortunate fact remains that most simulations are still being programmed in FORTRAN. People know FORTRAN because it is an established computer language, a familiar way to program. That it consumes critical resources and skilled system analyst time is overlooked in the normal reluctance to enter into the unknown, using a "new" language. Another way to express the same view is that one cannot be criticized for selecting FORTRAN for simulation, but one is extremely vulnerable to criticism if any other language is used.

As a consequence, we see the successful development of simulation models of complex systems by a few groups using simulation languages and a large body of negative experience by those who did not use simulation languages.

Simulations should be flexible, quick and efficient. When these criteria are met, the simulation becomes modified as the understanding of the problem grows. The alternative, to attempt to understand the problem fully before the simulation begins, is doomed to fail. Also to the point, the amount of up-front funding necessary to acquire complete mastery of the problem is never available.

In the ideal situation, the system analyst also develops the simulation. The problem of communication is minimized. Timeliness is inherent. Equally important is the insight gained from the construction of the simulation, which serves to review the system definition. To achieve this, the system analyst *must* learn a simulation language and gain confidence in its use.

43.4 HOW A MODEL IS PRODUCED

The first rule is clear—use a simulation language. Discrete event simulation is effective and economical when GPSS, SIMSCRIPT or SLAM is used. Continuous simulation is best done in CSSL, CSMP or MIDAS. These languages provide flexibility to build a model which reflects the problem and they are **portable** in the sense that many different computers will compile the simulation. While cited for its portability, the effort to model a complex system in FORTRAN requires considerable "reinventing of the wheel." Today there are books (see References) which clearly explain how to build a model with most simulation languages.

Simulation languages help the user to develop a model because of their internal structure which is designed to define, interpret and implement general simulation models. In addition, they provide facilities which reduce the need for the user to be familiar with list processing, logic, data retrieval and statistical testing. Experience has shown that these languages do allow the modeller to represent a complex system accurately, quickly, conveniently, economically and without having to adopt simplifying assumptions.

The speed of building the model is heavily influenced by the debugging aids which the language provides. Interactive systems, efficient housekeeping and clear presentation of results are vitally needed to limit the efforts required. With large systems, one should start with a small coarse overall model and let it grow or add to it subsystem by subsystem until the entire problem is modelled. Since the simulation language can act as the problem definition language, either choice of methodology should succeed. Much experience has demonstrated though, that when funding is limited, only the coarse model approach can be implemented.

The best approach to the coarse overview model defines the entire system, noting the boundaries and constraints. The functional aspects of the problem should be examined and the level of detail kept intentionally coarse. With a full definition of the problem in place, the next step is to implement the limited model. Implementation uses sample input data and tests the results obtained for accuracy and sensitivity.

How well these results compare to the historical data dictates the next step. The place to put the most effort is where there are factors that are not well understood. Increased detail in these limited areas should provide the greatest payback. Eventually, all areas will require a full level of detail, but it is better to concentrate on the uncertain aspects rather than those that contribute less to understanding the system.

43.5 EXAMPLE

The foregoing approach of constructing a model of a complex system, a lengthy and detailed process, can be appreciated through a limited example: a plant or facility performing a number of tasks to produce a product or service, namely a job shop. The simulation language used is GPSSV. The functions to be performed in a generic sense are as follows:

1. Define each new job as it enters the facility (the job shop). How many such jobs will there be during the period being modeled? What is the interval between jobs? Are there priorities of one job over another?
2. Establish the characteristics of the tasks to be performed at each process step. What facilities are required? What labor is involved? How long does each task take? In the coarse view, each task is performed according to a specific capability. In the real world, one capability can substitute for another for reasons of economics or convenience. This additional complexity should be included in the model.

The generic model in GPSSV is shown in the flow diagram, Figure 43.1. The implementation is listed in Figure 43.2. A matrix shown in Table 43.1 provides specific data inputs for the generic model. The flow chart illustrates the generic nature of the model. There are a number of sources for the tasks to be performed, each of which may be treated as independent. The frequency of task generation and average intervals between tasks are described individually for each source.

Questions

When a source generates a task, input data describe what is required for that task: the processes to be performed, the particular skills needed.

Each task with its associated parameters then enters

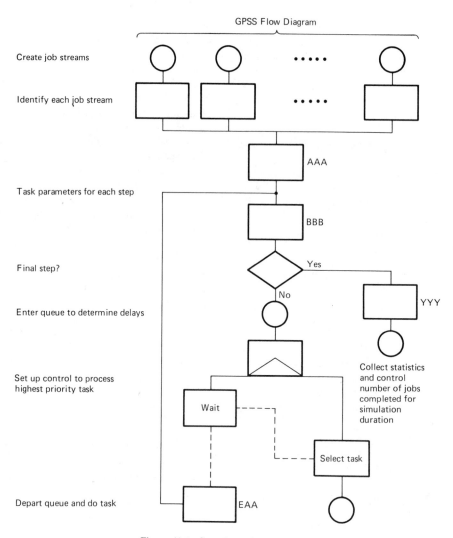

GPSS Flow Diagram

Create job streams

Identify each job stream

AAA

Task parameters for each step

BBB

Final step?   Yes

No

Enter queue to determine delays   YYY

Collect statistics and control number of jobs completed for simulation duration

Set up control to process highest priority task

Wait

Select task

Depart queue and do task   EAA

Figure 43.1. Genetic model of GPSS.

the process competition for resources. At completion, the task statistics are collected:

- How long the process took;
- The extent of delay due to conflict for resources;
- The degree of utilization of the various resources.

These are the basic parameters. In addition, it is possible to acquire **stratified data,** a comparison of the elapsed time for all tasks and the mean and median values. **Historical data,** such as the sequences of tasks per-

formed by specific resources, can also be maintained for later retrieval. While the basic structure of the model may be generic, the actual parameters and job shop needs can produce enhancements in the model to focus on a particular requirement of the simulation study.

Data for a Task

The easiest way to associate the input data with a particular task and the sequence of task requirements is via **input data matrices** such as those shown in Table 43.2.

```
GPSS/H VM/370 RELEASE 1.0 (AY142)        29 JUN 82   6:22:54     FILE: SHOP
LINE# STMT#  IF DO  BLOCK# *LJC  OPERATION  A,B,C,D,E,F,G     COMMENTS
         1                          SIMULATE    2
         2              1           MATRIX      X,100,4
         3              2           MATRIX      X,100,4
         4              3           MATRIX      X,100,4
         5                          INITIAL     MX1(1,1),1
         6                          INITIAL     MX1(1,5),6
         7                          INITIAL     MX1(1,3),300
         8                          INITIAL     MX1(1,4),1
         9                          INITIAL     MX1(2,1),2/MX1(2,2),1/MX1(2,3),20/MX1(2,4),2
        10                          INITIAL     MX1(3,1),3/MX1(3,2),2/MX1(3,3),200/MX1(3,4),3
        11                          INITIAL     MX1(4,1),1/MX1(4,2),1/MX1(4,3),30/MX1(4,4),2
        12                          INITIAL     MX1(5,1),999
        13                          INITIAL     MX2(1,1),2/MX2(1,2),1/MX2(1,3),10/MX2(1,4),2
        14                          INITIAL     MX2(2,1),2/MX2(2,2),1/MX2(2,3),20/MX2(2,4),2
        15                          INITIAL     MX2(3,1),3/MX2(3,2),3/MX2(3,3),35/MX2(3,4),3
        16                          INITIAL     MX2(4,1),999
        17                          INITIAL     MX3(1,1),2/MX3(1,2),1/MX3(1,3),440/MX3(1,4),2
        18                          INITIAL     MX3(2,1),999
        19              1           FUNCTION    RN1,C2
        20     0,200/1,800
        21              2           FUNCTION    RN1,C2
        22     0,100/1,900
        23              3           FUNCTION    RN1,C2
        24     0,400/1,600
        25                          STORAGE     S1,5/S2,2/S3,1
        26           *
        27              1           GENERATE    800,,,1,10PH
        28              2           ASSIGN      1,1,PH
        29              3           TRANSFER    ,AAA
        30              4           GENERATE    800,800,400,,1,10PH
        31              5           ASSIGN      1,2,PH
        32              6           TRANSFER    ,AAA
        33              7           GENERATE    2000,,,1,10PH
        34              8           ASSIGN      1,3,PH
        35              9           SPLIT       3,AAA
        36             10           TRANSFER    ,AAA
        37           *
        38             11  AAA      ASSIGN      7,20,PH
        39             12  BAA      ASSIGN      2+,1,PH
        40             13           ASSIGN      3,MX*PH1(PH2,1),PH
        41             14           TEST NE     PH3,999,YYY
        42             15           ASSIGN      4,MX*PH1(PH2,2),PH
        43             16           ASSIGN      5,MX*PH1(PH2,4),PH
        44                 MOD      VARIABLE    MX*PH1(PH2,3)*FN*PH5/1000
        45             17           ASSIGN      6,V$MOD,PH
        46             18           ASSIGN      7-,1,PH
        47             19           ASSIGN      8,0,PH
        48             20           QUEUE       PH3
        49             21           GATE LR     1
        50             22           LOGIC S     1
        51             23           SPLIT       1,DAA
        52             24           LINK        PH7,FIFO
        53           *
        54             25  DAA      ASSIGN      8+,1,PH
        55             26           SELECT G    8PH,PH6,21,0,CH,LAX
        56                 RES      BVARIABLE   (FN0*PH3)*(SNF*PH4)
        57             27  DAB      UNLINK      PH6,EAA,1,BV$RES,,DAA
        58             28           PRIORITY    0,BUFFER
        59             29           TRANSFER    ,DAB
        60             30  DAX      LOGIC R     1
        61             31           TERMINATE
        62           *
        63             32  EAA      DEPART      PH3
        64             33           SEIZE       PH3
        65             34           ENTER       PH4
        66             35           ADVANCE     PH6
        67             36           RELEASE     PH3
        68             37           LEAVE       PH4
        69             38           TRANSFER    ,DAA
        70           *
        71             39  YYY      TABULATE    PH1
        72             40           TABULATE    10
        73             41           TERMINATE   1
        74              1           TABLE       M1,100,100,50
        75              2           TABLE       M1,100,100,50
        76              3           TABLE       M1,100,100,50
        77             10           TABLE       M1,100,100,50
        78                          START       40
        79                          START       40
        80                          END
```

RELATIVE CLOCK: 18792   ABSOLUTE CLOCK: 18792

BLOCK	CURRENT	TOTAL	BLOCK	CURRENT	TOTAL	BLOCK	CURRENT	TOTAL	BLOCK	CURRENT	TOTAL	BLOCK	CURRENT	TOTAL
1		23	AAA		84	21		200	31		200	41		80
2		23	BAA		280	22		200	EAA		197			
3		23	13		280	23		400	33		197			
4		25	14		280	24		200	34		197			
5		25	15		200	DAA		566	35		197			
6		25	16		200	26		566	36		196			
7		9	17		200	DAB		563	37		196			
8		9	18		200	28		197	38		196			
9		36	19		200	29		197	YYY		80			
10		9	20		200	DAX		200	40		80			

FACILITY	--AVG-UTIL-DURING-- TOTAL TIME	AVAIL TIME	UNAVL TIME	ENTRIES	AVERAGE TIME/XACT	CURRENT STATUS	PERCENT AVAIL	SEIZING XACT	PREEMPTING XACT
1	.205			45	85.844	AVAIL	100.0		
2	.490			106	87.018	AVAIL	100.0	270	
3	.333			46	136.326	AVAIL	100.0		

Figure 43.2. Model simulation based on Figure 43.1.

STORAGE	--AVG-UTIL-DURING--			ENTRIES	AVERAGE	CURRENT	PERCENT	CAPACITY	AVERAGE	CURRENT	MAXIMUM
	TOTAL TIME	AVAIL TIME	UNAVL TIME		TIME/UNIT	STATUS	AVAIL		CONTENTS	CONTENTS	CONTENTS
1	.169			128	74.554	AVAIL	100.0	3	0.507	1	2
2	.158			45	125.311	AVAIL	100.0	2	0.300	0	2
3	.222			24	174.000	AVAIL	100.0	1	0.222	0	1

QUEUE	MAXIMUM CONTENTS	AVERAGE CONTENTS	TOTAL ENTRIES	ZERO ENTRIES	PERCENT ZEROS	AVERAGE TIME/UNIT	$AVERAGE TIME/UNIT	QTABLE NUMBER	CURRENT CONTENTS
1	1	0.028	45	39	86.6	12.066	90.500		
2	9	2.823	108	39	36.1	491.240	768.898		2
3	3	0.533	47	22	46.8	213.468	401.320		1

USER CHAIN	ENTRIES	AVERAGE TIME/XACT	AVERAGE CONTENTS	CURRENT CONTENTS	MAXIMUM CONTENTS
16	22	24.681	0.028	0	1
17	47	213.468	0.533	1	3
18	47	126.957	0.317	0	1
19	84	560.559	2.505	2	6

FULLWORD MATRIX SAVEVALUE 1

ROW/COL	1	2	3	4
1	1	2	300	1
2	3	1	20	2
3	3	1	200	3
4	1	1	30	
5	999	0	0	6

FULLWORD MATRIX SAVEVALUE 2

ROW/COL	1	2	3	4
1	2	1	100	2
2	2	3	20	2
3	3		350	3
4	999	0	0	0

FULLWORD MATRIX SAVEVALUE 3

ROW/COL	1	2	3	4
1	2	1	440	2
2	999	0	0	0

STATUS OF COMMON STORAGE

2992 BYTES AVAILABLE
7008 BYTES IN USE
7488 BYTES USED (MAX)

START   40

RELATIVE CLOCK: 10471   ABSOLUTE CLOCK: 10471

BLOCK	CURRENT	TOTAL	BLOCK	CURRENT	TOTAL	BLOCK	CURRENT	TOTAL	BLOCK	CURRENT	TOTAL	BLOCK	CURRENT	TOTAL
1		13	AAA		143	21		103	31		103	41		40
2		13	6AA		143	22		103	LAA		103				
3		13	13		143	23		208	33		130				
4		13	14		143	24		103	34		130				
5		15	15		103	DAA		280	35		130				
6		15	16		103	26		260	36		98				
7		5	17		103	DAL		277	37		98				
8		25	18		103	28		100	38		98				
9		5	19		103	29		130	YYY		40				
10		5	20		103	DAX		103	40		40				

FACILITY	--AVG-UTIL-DURING--			ENTRIES	AVERAGE	CURRENT	PERCENT	SEIZING	PREEMPTING
	TOTAL TIME	AVAIL TIME	UNAVL TIME		TIME/XACT	STATUS	AVAIL	XACT	XACT
1	.192			25	80.520	AVAIL	100.0	127	
2	.453			52	91.346	AVAIL	100.0	135	
3	.288			23	131.008	AVAIL	100.0		

STORAGE	--AVG-UTIL-DURING--			ENTRIES	AVERAGE	CURRENT	PERCENT	CAPACITY	AVERAGE	CURRENT	MAXIMUM
	TOTAL TIME	AVAIL TIME	UNAVL TIME		TIME/UNIT	STATUS	AVAIL		CONTENTS	CONTENTS	CONTENTS
1	.156			64	76.625	AVAIL	100.0	3	0.468	1	2
2	.142			25	116.960	AVAIL	100.0	2	0.284	1	2
3	.180			11	171.727	AVAIL	100.0	1	0.180	0	1

QUEUE	MAXIMUM CONTENTS	AVERAGE CONTENTS	TOTAL ENTRIES	ZERO ENTRIES	PERCENT ZEROS	AVERAGE TIME/UNIT	$AVERAGE TIME/UNIT	QTABLE NUMBER	CURRENT CONTENTS
1	1	0.035	25	21	84.0	15.040	94.000		0
2	7	2.321	55	19	34.5	442.000	675.277		3
3	3	0.424	23	12	52.1	193.391	404.363		0

USER CHAIN	ENTRIES	AVERAGE TIME/XACT	AVERAGE CONTENTS	CURRENT CONTENTS	MAXIMUM CONTENTS
16	12	31.333	0.035	1	1
17	23	193.391	0.424	0	3
18	23	145.130	0.316	1	1
19	45	466.044	2.002	3	6

Figure 43.2. Model simulation based on Figure 43.1. (*continues*)

```
FULLWORD MATRIX SAVEVALUE 1
   ROW/COL          1              2             3             4
                    1             2           300            1
   1                2             1            20            2
   2                3             2           200            3
   3                1             1            30            2
   4              999             0             0            0
   5
```

```
FULLWORD MATRIX SAVEVALUE 2
   ROW/COL          1              2             3             4
                    2             1           100            2
   1                2             1            20            2
   2                3             3           350            3
   3              999             0             0            0
   4
```

```
FULLWORD MATRIX SAVEVALUE 3
   ROW/COL          1              2             3             4
                    2             1           440            2
   1              999             0             0            0
   2
```

```
STATUS OF COMMON STORAGE

    3060 BYTES AVAILABLE
    6920 BYTES IN USE
    7240 BYTES USED (MAX)

       END

TOTAL BLOCK EXECUTIONS:        7436
```

GPSS/H IS A PROPRIETARY PRODUCT OF, AND IS USED UNDER A LICENSE
GRANTED BY, WOLVERINE SOFTWARE AND JAMES O. HENRIKSEN.

Figure 43.2. Model simulation based on Figure 43.1. (*continued*)

For each different product there is a unique matrix. Each step in the process has input data which indicate the equipment, labor skill and time involved. The extent of use of each resource may not be the same for a particular task; it may vary over a small or large range that depends on the modifier selected. The crucial point of this model is that it reflects the assumptions of how the system works

Table 43.1. Input Data Matrix

Step Number	Facility Number	Labor Code	Nominal Task Duration	Function Used to Modify Task Duration
1	1	2	300	1
2	2	1	20	2
3	3	2	200	3
4	1	1	30	2
.				
.				
.				
N	999			

Table 43.2. Input Matrices for Three Different Products

FULLWORD MATRIX SAVEVALUE 1

ROW / COL	1	2	3	4
1	1	2	300	1
2	2	1	20	2
3	3	2	200	3
4	1	1	30	2
5	999	0	0	0

FULLWORD MATRIX SAVEVALUE 2

ROW / COL	1	2	3	4
1	2	1	100	2
2	2	1	20	2
3	3	3	350	3
4	999	0	0	0

FULLWORD MATRIX SAVEVALUE 3

ROW / COL	1	2	3	4
1	2	1	440	2
2	999	0	0	0

and produces a reasonable approximation with little additional effort.

Expansion

If the model is expanded so that a product fabrication could use one of several facility types to perform each task, then for each step number the data is added for the second and third equipment choices. During the model execution, supposing the initial equipment or labor category to be unavailable, the acquisition of the second and third choices is attempted before the process task becomes delayed.

One other embellishment, interrupting the task in progress and substituting another, as shown in the implementation, can also be accomplished within the model structure. Additional logic accomplishes this function. The duration of each task is expressed in integral time units. One convenient unit is hundredths of an hour.

The Code

At this point, it is appropriate to examine the model in its actual GPSSV format as shown in Figure 43.2, which extends from page 741 through page 743. To aid in understanding, each important line of GPSSV code is presented below, preceded by its statement and block number. The explanation of the statement follows.

The transactions.   The initial section of the model introduces the task in the form of transactions which the logic of the model processes to simulate the job shop.

| 27 | 1 | | GENERATE | 800,,,,10PH | (43.1) |

A task stream is created at the start of the simulation and thereafter every eight hours. Since time is described in hundredths of hours, 800 specifies 8 hours. It has 10 half-word parameters.

| 28 | 2 | | ASSIGN | 1,1,PH | (43.2) |

Parameter 1 is defined to indicate the product identification. This is product type 1.

| 29 | 3 | | TRANSFER | ,AAA | (43.3) |

There are several task streams. The **TRANSFER** block sends each tributary to location AAA, where the main stream of the model logic begins.

| 30 | 4 | | GENERATE | 800,800,400,,,10PH | |
| | | | | | (43.4) |

More streams.   A second task stream is created. In this case the first entry is 4 hours after the start, and there are 0 to 16 hours between successive entries.

| 31 | 5 | | ASSIGN | 1,2,PH | (43.5) |

Now parameter 1 is defined as product type 2.

| 32 | 6 | | TRANSFER | ,AAA | (43.6) |

Again the job is sent to the dispatching area.

| 33 | 7 | | GENERATE | 2000,,,,1,10PH | |
| | | | | | (43.7) |

This task stream represents a weekly input.

| 34 | 8 | | ASSIGN | 1,3,PH | (43.8) |

Product 3 is identified.

| 35 | 9 | | SPLIT | 3,AAA | (43.9) |

Three additional transactions are created by the original one (Eq. 43.6).

| 36 | 10 | | TRANSFER | ,AAA | (43.10) |

These are sent for dispatching to AAA in the mainstream.

The above commands comprise a reasonable representation of possible ways to generate competing traffic. In practice, any deterministic or probabilistic method or a combination can be used.

Mainstream.   The mainstream of the model starts at location AAA where all the transactions are joined into one logic path.

| 38 | 11 | AAA | ASSIGN | 7,20,PH | (43.11) |

Any of the 10 available parameters may be used as desired. Here parameter 7 sets an incoming job to the lowest priority in the model, 20. Later, each transaction will accomplish its task and the parameter used to set priority will be decremented until it reaches the highest (1) priority. This completes the transaction initialization. After this point, transactions representing all stages of completion are being processed by the same set of statements.

| 39 | 12 | BAA | ASSIGN | 2+,1,PH | (43.12) |

Starting with 0, parameter 2 is increased by 1 every time a transaction passes by. This parameter identifies the step to be processed in the logic which follows and locates the appropriate datum in the matrix. For each step, a number of task descriptors are needed.

| 40 | 13 | | ASSIGN | 3,MX•PH1(PH2,1),PH | |
| | | | | | (43.13) |

Parameter 3 contains the facility code for the equipment to be used to process the task in this step. Parameter 1 (PH1) selects the matrix (MX); parameter 2 (PH2) is the row number and column 1 (the 1 in (PH2,1)) is always used.

| 41 | 14 | TEST NE PH3,999,YYY | (43.14) |

To identify the last step, the value of 999 is placed in parameter 3. The TEST block passes any value other than 999. For value of 999, the transaction goes to address YYY, where statistics are gathered.

| 42 | 15 | ASSIGN 4,MX*PH1(PH2,2),PH | (43.15) |

Parameter 4 is assigned the labor code required for this step. This is obtained from column 2 of the proper row (PH2) of the matrix (MX*PH1).

| 43 | 16 | ASSIGN 5,MX*PH1(PH2,4),PH | (43.16) |

The modifier code for the task duration deviation obtained from the matrix is placed into parameter 5. These task duration modifiers are a series of cumulative probability distributions representing the choice for modifying the average task duration.

| 44 | MOD | VARIABLE MX*PH1(PH2,3)*FN*PH5/1000 | (43.17) |

A **variable statement** performs the evaluation of the expression: the nominal duration is multiplied by the value of the modifier (PH5) and is divided by 1000.

| 45 | 17 | ASSIGN 6,V$MOD,PH | (43.18) |

The duration for the task on this particular occasion is put into parameter 6.

| 46 | 18 | ASSIGN 7-,1,PH | (43.19) |

Since there is competition for resources, some form of separation of tasks according to priority is a useful strategy. Each task starts with a priority of 20 (Eq. 43.11). Now as each step is processed, that priority number is decremented to increase the job's priority.

At this point, the input data describing each step have been transferred to the transaction that represents the task.

| 47 | 19 | ASSIGN 8,0,PH | (43.20) |

Parameter 8 is used as a temporary address register. Since there may be entries left over from old transactions in this parameter, it is necesary to reset parameter 8 to 0.

Since the object of this model is to analyze competition for resources, a statement is introduced to collect statistics on the delay experienced by each transaction. There are several ways these data may be of interest. An example of this is the delay required before each step's resources become available. A QUEUE statement is used thus:

| 48 | 20 | QUEUE PH3 | (43.21) |

This gather statistics for each equipment facility required.

| 49 | 21 | GATE LR 1 | (43.22) |

This allows a single transaction to go through this point and continues on.

| 50 | 22 | LOGIC S 1 | (43.23) |

We shut the gate behind us. The purpose is to allow only one transaction to move through the system at this instant. The case in which two transactions arrive at the same instant is resolved by letting one through (arbitrarily) and detaining the other until the first had gone far as possible. At that point LOGIC R 1 (statement 60) resets the GATE and allows the second transaction through.

Access to resources. The strategy employed to select which transaction has access to resources is controlled to prevent a transaction just entering from automatically getting first crack at the available resources. Instead, the entering transaction acts as a trigger to review all waiting transactions with a greater priority. If none are found, then it is able to compete for the resources.

If the required resource is not available, then lower priority transactions are allowed to compete for the remaining resources. The GPSS statements to accomplish this set of functions take advantage of the transaction flow from statement to statement. The guiding rules are that a transaction will flow until

1. It has to wait for a future time.
2. It is blocked because of a restriction.
3. It is placed on a user chain.
4. The model logic allows other transactions to precede it at the same clock time.

The logic of one possible implementation is:

1. Create a temporary control transaction;
2. Have it manipulate the transactions representing tasks;

3. When its function has been accomplished, destroy the control transaction.

This logic is now examined.

51   23   SPLIT 1,DAA   (43.24)

This statement creates the control transaction.

52   24   LINK   PH7,F1F0   (43.25)

The original task transaction is placed on a user chain according to its priority. Once it is on the user chain, the control transaction becomes active and leaves SPLIT to appear at DAA. Other transactions active at the same clock time also get their turn to be processed.

54   25 DAA ASSIGN 8+,1,PH   (43.26)

Parameter 8 is used to start the selection of transactions at the chain with the highest priority. At first the value is 1, but since there are no transactions on chain 1, the parameter is updated to provide the number of the chain with transactions.

55   26   SELECTG 8PH,PH8,21,0,CH,DAX

(43.27)

The SELECTG statement locates the user chain with a transaction and places the number of that chain in parameter eight. The first time through, the chain number of the task transaction is selected. In a congested system, however, a higher priority chain is selected first to give that transaction the opportunity to acquire the available resources.

The availability of the required resource is assessed by evaluating a Boolean expression. The required resources are either available or they are not. The facility is or is not used and the storage is or is not full.

56   RES BVARIABLE (FNU∗PH3)∗(SNF∗PH4)

(43.28)

If both equipment and labor are available, the expression evaluates to 1; otherwise, it becomes 0.

57   27 DAB UNLINK PH8,EAA,1,BV\$RES,,DAA

(43.29)

The UNLINK statement is activated by the control transaction to look at the selected user chain of task transactions and determine the first transaction which is able to use the available resources. Therefore the Boolean variable will be evaluated to 1. That task transaction is sent to EAA, where the status of those resources is changed from available to unavailable. If none of the

transactions on the chain can use the available resources, the control transaction goes back to the SELECT statement and updates parameter 8 with the number of the next user chain with transactions.

58   28   PRIORITY 0,BUFFER (43.30)

To cover the situation where more than one task could be removed from the task user chain, the control transaction relinquishes its activity until one task transaction has completely secured the resources. Then the control transaction repeats the attempt to UNLINK another task transaction from the same chain.

59   29   TRANSFER,DAB
60   30 DAX LOGIC R 1   (43.31)

When the control transaction can no longer locate a user chain with task transactions, its function is finished. The next transaction is allowed through.

61   31   TERMINATE   (43.32)

This statement is the means of removing the control transaction from the model.

63   32 EAA DEPART   PH2
64   33   SEIZE   PH3 (43.33)

The task transaction goes to EAA, where the queues are flushed (DEPART) and the resources allocated.

The facility for the task identified in parameter 3 is used by the transaction.

65   34   ENTER   PH4 (43.34)

This takes care of labor.

66   35   ADVANCE PH6 (43.35)

This keeps the transaction in control of both the equipment and labor for the time specified in parameter 6.

67   36   RELEASE   PH3
68   37   LEAVE   PH4
69   38   TRANSFER ,BAA (43.36)

This returns the equipment and labor to be available for the next user. The task transaction goes back to location BAA, where its priority is increased and the process repeated until all the steps required are finished. Before the transaction leaves the model, some statistics are collected.

71   39 YYY TABULATE PH1
72   40   TABULATE 10 (43.37)

Data is collected for the task transactions, namely the elapsed time from start to finish for each product and for all products.

| 73 | 41 | TERMINATE 1 | (43.38) |

This ends the completed task but enables the model to run until the required number of tasks have completed.

74	1	TABLE	M1,100,100,50	
75	2	TABLE	M1,100,100,50	
76	3	TABLE	M1,100,100,50	
77	10	TABLE	M1,100,100,50	(43.39)

These statements provide the definitions for the tables used to collect the elapsed time statistics. The GPSS system also collects statistics for how long each queue was occupied and the utilization of the equipment and labor categories.

| 78 | START 40 | (43.40) |

The model is run until the first 40 tasks have been finished.

| 79 | START 40 | (43.41) |

This continues the simulation until another 40 transactions have been finished. In addition, there is an optional printout of all the transactions in the model at the count of transaction 40.

Data Entry

Data entry for the model is performed by a number of statements located at the beginning of the listing.

| 1 | SIMULATE 2 | (43.42) |

This is needed to request the simulation and limit the amount of computer time on a not-to-exceed basis.

| 2 | 1 | MATRIX | X,100,4 | (43.43) |

There are up to 100 rows and 4 columns in MATRIX 1.

There are three MATRIX statements starting with (Eq. 43.43) which define the maximum size of each MATRIX and allow full-word data to be stored.

| 5 | INITIAL | MX1(1,1),1 | (43.44) |

The initial item to be stored in each MATRIX cell is introduced through a series of INITIAL statements, starting with this one.

The three FUNCTION statements which follow allow random numbers selected from a starting seed to vary the duration of the tasks. Each FUNCTION has a different shape.

Output statistics are gathered by the GPSS system and produced after each START statement. A comparison between the two sets of output data shows that the utilization of labor and equipment does not vary significantly from one period to the next. However, the QUEUE statistics show a significant increase in the delay until the lowest priority transaction is processed. Further running of the model would determine whether the value stabilizes or continues to increase. Obviously, if it continues to increase, either more resources should be made available or the number of tasks needed to be performed should be reduced.

The execution of this simple model enables the analyst to visualize the constraints in the system, sense the bottlenecks and then determine the most satisfactory way to overcome them. This is accomplished in a GPSS model of 80 statements. The model is general in nature and is controlled by the entry of data into its matrices; conflict between tasks is resolved by priority. The entire run consumes minor computer time.

43.6 CONCLUSIONS

Simulation is a tool for the analysis of complex systems. It is the tool to be used when other tools cannot provide the insight required required to predict system performance. However, like most tools it has advantages and disadvantages. Each potential use has to be evaluated independently. Simulation may in the long run be the quickest and cheapest way to obtain the required estimate of system performance. Still, there is considerable effort required to obtain results. The following factors help to reduce the effort a useful simulation demands.

1. Use a simulation language. It will help in problem definition. The total cost for the simulation will be significantly less. The results will be available sooner, and there will be considerably less effort required to change the simulation to reflect the progress in system synthesis.
2. Limit your objectives. To model the *complete* system accurately will require more time and money than is available. Use both coarse and fine levels of detail. In so far as practicable, limit the use of detailed subsystem models.
3. Select those areas of greatest sensitivity for investigation. The results from early versions of the model

point out the areas that require concentration and greater detail.

4. Anticipate the methods of model validation. Select what is considered appropriate for the system. Be aware of the limitations inherent problem definition, input data, and representational faithfulness.

REFERENCES

The literature for simulation does not appear in a single field. Instead, most papers involving simulation appear in the field that pertains to the application. The result is that a considerable amount of effort is involved to become familiar with what has been previously done in a particular application area. There are three publications which are helpful as a starting point.

Simulation—Journal of the Society for Computer Simulation, P.O. Box 2228, La Jolla, CA 92038.
Summer Computer Simulation Proceedings, AFIPS Press, 1815 North Lynn Street, Arlington, VA 22209.
Winter Simulation Conference Proceedings, IEEE, 445 Hoes Lane, Piscataway, NJ 08854.

The next item to be resolved is which simulation language to use. Since most people prefer to use the language they are familiar with, it is difficult to find an unbiased comparison of simulation languages. The practical approach is to use the language someone is willing to teach. Then ask for a recommended reading list. Since GPSS was used in this chapter, there is a responsibility to mention some of the books that focus on GPSS:

Gordon, G., *The Application of GPSS V to Discrete System Simulation.* Englewood Cliffs, NJ: Prentice-Hall, 1975.
Henriksen, J. O., and R. Crain, *GPSS/H User's Manual,* 2nd Ed. Annandale, VA: Wolverine Software.
General Purpose Simulation System V User's Manual, IBM Form SH20-0851-1, 2nd Ed. (Aug. 1971).
Reitman, J., *Computer Simulation Applications.* Malabar, FL: Krieger, 1981 (reprint).
Schriber, T. J., *Simulation Using GPSS.* New York: John Wiley & Sons, 1974.

For a sampling of other approaches to simulation, the following is a small fraction of the available literature:

Dahl, O.-J., B. Myhrhaug and K. Nygaard, *Simula 67 Common Base Language.* Oslo: Norwegian Computing Center, 1970.
Fishman, G. S., *Principles of Discrete Event Simulation.* New York: Wiley-Interscience, 1978.
Franta, W., *A Process View of Simulation.* Amsterdam: Elsevier North Holland, 1977.
Kiviat, P., R. Villaneuva and H. Markowitz, *The SIMSCRIPT II Programming Language.* Englewood Cliffs, NJ: Prentice-Hall, 1969.
Pritsker, A. A. B., *The GASP IV Simulation Language.* New York: John Wiley & Sons, N.Y., 1974.
Pritsker, A. A. B., and C. D. Pegden, *Introduction to Simulation and SLAM.* New York: Halsted Press, 1979.
Pugh, A. L., III, *Dynamo User's Manual,* 5th ed, Cambridge, MA: The MIT Press, 1976.
Russell, E., *Simulation with Processes and Resources in SIMSCRIPT II.5.* Arlington, VA: CACI Inc., 1974.

VI
PROCEDURES

44
Numerical Methods

Martin Weinless

Baruch College
City University of New York

44.1 INTRODUCTION

In this chapter, a brief survey of numerical methods is presented that are of importance in the solution of engineering problems. Numerical methods are concerned with the use of algorithms for problem solving. Numerical analysis is concerned not only with the development and implementation of these algorithms but, in addition, with an analysis of errors that are intrinsic in the use of a particular algorithm. In this chapter, only numerical methods are considered.

Numerical methods are important to an engineer for a very specific reason. The problems that he or she have to solve are often nonlinear. Consequently, an exact solution is generally impossible. The use of algorithms to generate approximate solutions is necessary. It is not surprising that rapid advances in numerical methods have coincided with the increased availability of digital computers since the early 1960s.

44.2 TAYLOR SERIES

Many of the techniques of numerical analysis have their foundations in the Taylor series expansion of a function. The Taylor series of a function is an infinite power series that converges within its radius of convergence to the function it represents. For practical (i.e., numerical) purposes, however, we must truncate the series after a finite number of terms. Taylor's theorem gives us an estimate of the error made in approximating the function by a finite sum (in fact, a polynomial), rather than its infinite series representation. The statement of Taylor's theorem is

If the function f is continuous on the closed interval determined by the points a and x, and has derivatives up to order $(n + 1)$ on this interval, then

$$f(x) = f(a) + f'(a)(x - a) + \frac{f''(a)}{2!}(x - a)^2$$
$$+ \frac{f'''(a)}{3!}(x - a)^3 \qquad (44.1)$$
$$+ \cdots + \frac{f^{(n)}(a)}{n!}(x - a)^n + R_n(x)$$

where $R_n(x)$ is the remainder term, and in Lagrange's form, is given by

$$R_n(x) = \frac{f^{(n+1)}(t)}{(n + 1)!}(x - a)^{n+1} \qquad (44.2)$$

for some t where $a \le t \le x$.

For example, if $a = 0$,

$$e^x = \sum_{n=0}^{\infty} \frac{x^n}{n!}$$
$$= 1 + x + \frac{x^2}{2!} + \frac{x^3}{3!} + \cdots + \frac{x^n}{n!} \qquad (44.3)$$

$$\sin x = \sum_{n=0}^{\infty} (-1)^n \frac{x^{2n+1}}{(2n+1)!}$$
$$= x - \frac{x^3}{3!} + \frac{x^5}{5!} - \frac{x^7}{7!} + \cdots + (-1)^n \frac{x^{2n+1}}{(2n+1)!} \qquad (44.4)$$

751

$$\cos x = \sum_{n=0}^{\infty} (-1)^n \frac{x^{2n}}{(2n)!}$$

$$= 1 - \frac{x^2}{2!} + \frac{x^4}{4!} - \frac{x^6}{6!} + \cdots + (-1)^n \frac{x^{2n}}{(2n)!} \quad (44.5)$$

In each instance, the remainder that results from truncating the series after the nth term can be estimated by

$$R_n(x) \le \frac{3^x}{(n+1)!} \cdot x^{n+1} \quad (44.3a)$$

$$R_n(x) \le \frac{|x|^{2n+2}}{(2n+2)!} \quad (44.4a)$$

$$R_n(x) \le \frac{|x|^{2n+1}}{(2n+1)!} \quad (44.5a)$$

EXAMPLE 44.1. Compute sin 3 with an error less than 10^{-5}.

SOLUTION:

$$\sin 3 = 3 - \frac{3^3}{3!} + \frac{3^5}{5!} - \cdots + (-1)^n \frac{3^{2n+1}}{(2n+1)!} + R_n$$

where we require $|R_n| < 10^{-5}$. We must therefore determine n so that $(3^{2n+2})/(2n+2)! < 10^{-5}$. Using a table of factorials or a calculator, we find that $n = 6$ suffices. We can write therefore

$$\sin 3 = 3 - \frac{3^3}{3!} + \frac{3^5}{5!} - \frac{3^7}{7!} + \frac{3^9}{9!} - \frac{3^{11}}{11!} + \frac{3^{13}}{13!} + R$$

with $|R| < 10^{-5}$.

EXAMPLE 44.2. Calculate $e^{0.1}$ using the first 5 terms of the Taylor expansion of e^x, and find an upper bound for the error.

SOLUTION:

$$e^x = 1 + x + \frac{x^2}{2!} + \frac{x^3}{3!} + \frac{x^4}{4!} + R_n$$

with $R < \dfrac{3^x x^{n+1}}{(n+1)!} = \dfrac{3^x x^5}{5!}$.

At $x = 0.1$, $R_n < 9.3 \times 10^{-8}$, so that

$$e^{0.1} = 1 + (0.1) + \frac{(0.1)^2}{2!} + \frac{(0.1)^3}{3!}$$
$$+ \frac{(0.1)^4}{4!} = 1.10517083$$

to 8 decimal places. The actual error in our estimate of $e^{0.1}$ is 8.4×10^{-8}.

At this point, it is useful to introduce terminology that will be used throughout the rest of the chapter. If we terminate the Taylor series for a function after the nth term, we say that our approximation of f is accurate to order $(x - a)^{n+1}$, which we will write as $\mathcal{O}(x - a)^{n+1}$. Equivalently, we say the **truncation error** is of order $(n + 1)$; i.e., $|R_n| < $ constant $|x - a|^{n+1}$. The more terms of the series we retain, the smaller the truncation error. Furthermore, the closer that a is to x, R converges to zero quite rapidly for large n. A useful alternative form of Taylor's theorem can be obtained by setting $h = x - a$, so that

$$f(a + h) = f(a) + hf'(a) + \frac{h^2}{2!} f''(a)$$
$$+ \cdots \frac{h^n}{n!} f^{(n)}(a) + R_n \quad (44.6)$$

44.3 ITERATION AND THE SOLUTION OF EQUATIONS

Another idea that recurs in numerical analysis is **iteration**, or **successive approximation.** This consists in the repeated application of a numerical scheme to successively improve an approximation to the solution of a problem. We must choose a starting value, and then the scheme generates a sequence of numbers, each of which (under suitable circumstances) is a better approximation to the solution than its predecessor.

The question that immediately comes to mind is how do we know how accurate each approximation is, since in fact, we do not even know the actual solution to the problem? What we must do is devise a criterion that allows us to decide when to stop the iteration process. For example, we might decide that the difference between two successive iterates be less than some given number. If we let x_n and x_{n+1} be the nth and $(n + 1)^{st}$ approximations to the solution, we require $|x_{n+1} - x_n| < \epsilon$. We would then say that to the desired degree of accuracy, x_n is the solution of the problem.

For an example of the technique of iteration, let us solve the equation $x^2 = c$, i.e., find the square root of the positive number c. The algorithm that generates the sequence of approximations to $\sqrt{c}$ is

$$x_{n+1} = \frac{1}{2} \left(x_n + \frac{c}{x_n} \right) \quad n = 0, 1, 2, \ldots \quad (44.7)$$

To use the algorithm, we choose a starting value x_0, and repeatedly apply the algorithm to generate the sequence of iterates $x_0, x_1, x_2 \ldots$, which converges to $\sqrt{c}$.

It is a simple exercise to show that if we set $\lim\limits_{n\to\infty} x_n = \alpha$, then $\alpha = \sqrt{c}$.

EXAMPLE 44.3. Compute $\sqrt{7}$ using different starting values.

SOLUTION:

First Choice	Second Choice	Third Choice
$x_0 = 2.5$	$x_0 = 1.0$	$x_0 = 11.0$
$x_1 = 2.65$	$x_1 = 4.0$	$x_1 = 5.818181820$
$x_2 = 2.645754717$	$x_2 = 2.875$	$x_2 = 3.510653410$
$x_3 = 2.645751311$	$x_3 = 2.654891305$	$x_3 = 2.752292111$
$x_4 = 2.645751311$	$x_4 = 2.645767045$	$x_4 = 2.647813400$
	$x_5 = 2.645751311$	$x_5 = 2.645752114$
		$x_6 = 2.645751311$

It is worth noting that this algorithm is insensitive to a wide range of positive starting values, converging to the root in a few steps. In the first and third cases, the convergence is monotonic, while in the second case, the convergence is oscillatory.

The most frequently used method for finding the roots of an equation $F(x) = 0$ is **Newton's method.** This method is based on truncating the Taylor series expansion of $F(x)$ after the second term. If x_0 is sufficiently close to a root x of $F(x) = 0$, then, we have

$$F(x) = F(x_0) + (x - x_0)F'(x_0)$$
$$+ (x - x_0)^2 \frac{F''(x_0)}{2!} + \cdots$$

Truncating the series after the first derivative term, and setting $F(x) = 0$, we can write

$$x = x_0 - \frac{F(x_0)}{F'(x_0)}$$

which we take as a first approximation to the root of F. Using this first approximation, we repeat the process, and obtain a sequence of points:

$$x_2 = x_1 - \frac{F(x_1)}{F'(x_1)}$$

$$x_3 = x_2 - \frac{F(x_2)}{F'(x_2)}$$

In general,

$$x_{n+1} = x_n - \frac{F(x_n)}{F'(x_n)} \qquad n = 0, 1, 2, \ldots \quad (44.8)$$

Using our previous convergence criterion, we terminate the iterations when $|x_{n+1} - x_n|$ is less than some preassigned value. The convergence of the iterates generated by Newton's method is guaranteed by the following theorem:

If α is a root of $F(x) = 0$, and if $F'(\alpha)$ and $F''(\alpha)$ exist with $F'(\alpha) \neq 0$ in some neighborhood of α, then there exists an interval I containing α such that for any initial approximation x_0 in I, the sequence of iterates will converge to α.

For example, if we apply Newton's method to $F(x) = x^2 - c = 0$, we obtain

$$x_{n+1} = x_n - \frac{(x_n^2 - c)}{2x_n} = \tfrac{1}{2}\left(x_n + \frac{c}{x_n}\right)$$

which is our original square root algorithm. The theorem asserts that for any x_0 in the neighborhood of $\sqrt{c}$, the sequence of iterates will converge. In fact, any positive x_0 will generate a convergent sequence of Newton iterates.

A geometric analysis of Newton's method illustrates an important technique in the solution of nonlinear problems. As a first approximation to its solution, the problem is linearized. Graphically, for an initial approximation x_0 (Figure 44.1), we construct the tangent line to the graph of $F(x)$ at the point $(x_0, F(x_0))$. The equation of this line is

$$y = F'(x_0)(x - x_0) + F(x_0) \qquad (44.9)$$

This line intersects the x-axis in the point x_1, given by

$$x_1 = x_0 - \frac{F(x_0)}{F'(x_0)} \qquad (44.10)$$

Continuing this process generates the sequence of points $x_1, x_2, \ldots, x_n$, which converges to the root α of $F(x) = 0$.

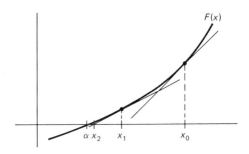

Figure 44.1. Geometric illustration of Newton's method.

EXAMPLE 44.4. Find the roots of

$$F(x) = x^3 - 1.473x^2 - 5.738x + 6.763 = 0.$$

SOLUTION:

Because $F(x)$ changes sign in the intervals $(-3,-2)$, $(1,2)$, and $(2,3)$, a judicious choice of starting values for Newton's method would be a value for x_0 which is in each of these intervals. The algorithm becomes

$$x_{n+1} = \frac{2x_n^3 - 1.473x_n^2 - 6.763}{3x_n^2 - 2.946x_n - 5.738}$$

With initial approximations for $x_0 = 1.5$, 2.5 and -2.5, we find:

$x_0 = 1.5$	$x_0 = 2.5$	$x_0 = -2.5$
$x_1 = 0.9765923$	$x_1 = 2.7059943$	$x_1 = -2.3172817$
$x_2 = 1.0957949$	$x_2 = 2.6739636$	$x_2 = -2.3002175$
$x_3 = 1.0999698$	$x_3 = 2.6730977$	$x_3 = -2.3000728$
$x_4 = 1.0999757$	$x_4 = 2.6730971$	$x_4 = -2.3000727$
$x_5 = 1.0999757$	$x_5 = 2.6730970$	$x_5 = -2.3000727$

EXAMPLE 44.5. Find the root of $\sin x - x/2 = 0$ on the interval $(\pi/2, \pi)$.

SOLUTION:

With $x_{n+1} = \dfrac{x_n \cos x_n - \sin x_n}{\cos x_n - \tfrac{1}{2}}$

and a starting value of $x_0 = \pi$, we have

$x_0 = \pi$	$x_3 = 1.895672$
$x_1 = 2.094395$	$x_4 = 1.895494$
$x_2 = 1.913223$	$x_5 = 1.895494$

The advantage of Newton's method is the rapidity of convergence of the iterates to a root of $F(x)$. If we set $\epsilon_n = x_n - \alpha$ (where α is a root of $F(x) = 0$) then, we can show that ϵ_{n+1} is proportional to ϵ_n^2, i.e., the convergence is said to be quadratic. There are instances, however, in which Newton's method fails to converge quadratically, or fails to converge at all. If, for example, a root of $F(x)$ occurs at an inflection point of F, the sequence of iterates will fail to converge. Suppose $F(x) = (x - 1)^{1/3}$. For no choice of x_0 will the sequence of iterates converge to the root at $x = 1$ (Figure 44.2). If we choose our starting value near a local extremum of F, the sequence of iterates will not converge to the root (Figure 44.3).

Finally, if $F(x)$ is a polynomial, then at a multiple root of F, the convergence of Newton's method becomes linear as x_n approaches α because $F'(x)$ is approaching zero. In the event that F does have a multiple zero, we can modify Newton's method in order to restore the quadratic convergence property. We replace $F(x)$ in the algorithm by $u(x) = F(x)/F'(x)$, so that the algorithm becomes

$$x_{n+1} = x_n - \frac{u(x_n)}{u'(x_n)} \qquad n = 0, 1, 2, \ldots \quad (44.11)$$

$$u(x) = \frac{F(x)}{F'(x)} \qquad (44.12)$$

EXAMPLE 44.6. Find the roots of

$$F(x) = x^3 + x^2 - x - 1.$$

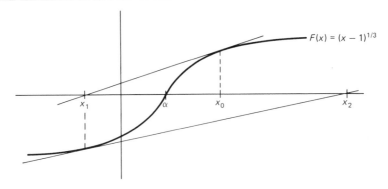

Figure 44.2. Convergence of $F(x) = (x - 1)^{1/3}$.

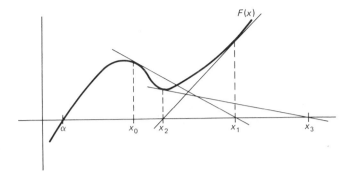

Figure 44.3. An example of nonconvergence to a root.

SOLUTION:

$F(x)$ has a double root at $x = -1$. The ordinary Newton's method requires 19 iterations to converge to this root. If we use the modified algorithm,

$$x_{n+1} = \frac{-x_n^4 + 4x_n^3 + 10x_n^2 + 4x_n - 1}{3x_n^4 + 4x_n^3 + 2x_n^2 + 4x_n + 3}$$

Choosing $x_0 = -0.5$, the sequence of iterates is

n	x_n	$|x_{n+1} - x_n|$
0	-0.5	
1	-0.894736842	0.394736842
2	-0.996918343	0.102181501
3	-1.000000000	0.003081657

For the same starting value, a representative portion of the iterates of the unmodified Newton's method, together with $|x_{n+1} - x_n|$, are

n	x_n	$|x_{n+1} - x_n|$
5	-0.988734618	0.011396005
6	-0.994383301	0.005648683
7	-0.997195616	0.002812315
8	-0.998598742	0.001403126
9	-0.999299625	0.000700883

Observe that each value $|x_{n+1} - x_n|$ is approximately one-half of the preceding value.

The quadratic convergence of Newton's method is obtained at the expense of more computations per iteration, but this is balanced by the rapidity of convergence compared to methods which converge linearly. One lesson which ought to be stressed is that before attempting to solve an equation, it is important to obtain some knowledge of the behavior of the function near its zeros.

44.4 NUMERICAL INTEGRATION

In this section, our concern is developing techniques to approximate the value of

$$\int_a^b f(x)\, dx$$

for finite values of a and b. We shall consider two basic methods for approximating a definite integral: the trapezoidal rule, and Simpson's ⅓ rule.

Trapezoidal Rule

The trapezoidal rule results from approximating the area under the graph of f by the sum of areas of trapezoids. More precisely, if the interval $[a,b]$ is partitioned into subintervals of uniform width, say $h = (b - a)/n$, with

$$a = x_0 < x_1 < x_2 \cdots < x_{n-1} < x_n = b$$

(Figure 44.4), the area of two adjacent trapezoids is

$$(h/2)[f(x_{i-1}) + 2f(x_i) + f(x_{i+1})]$$

Thus,

$$\int_{x_{i-1}}^{x_{i+1}} f(x)\, dx \approx (h/2)[f(x_{i-1}) + 2f(x_i) + f(x_{i+1})]$$

If we extend this analysis to the whole of $[a,b]$, we find

$$\int_a^b f(x)\, dx \approx (h/2)\left[f(a) + f(b) + 2\sum_{i=1}^{n-i} f(x_i) \right]$$

$$(44.13)$$

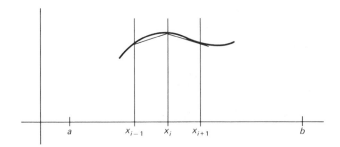

Figure 44.4. Illustrating trapezoidal rule.

Owing to the approximate nature of this result, we need a quantitative estimate of the error involved by approximating the integral by this sum. By use of Taylor's series, we can show that the local error, i.e., the error resulting from approximating the integral in each subinterval, is $\mathcal{O}(h^3)$, while the global error is $\mathcal{O}(h^2)$:

$$\int_a^b f(x)\, dx = T_n(f)$$
$$- \frac{h^2}{12}(b-a)f''(t) \qquad a \le t \le b$$

where $T_n(f)$ is given by the approximation (44.13).

EXAMPLE 44.7. Using the trapezoidal rule, evaluate $\int_2^4 (x^3 - x^2 - x + 1)\, dx$ (exact value = 37⅓).

SOLUTION:

n	h	T_n	**Global Error Estimate**		$|I - T_n|$
2	1	40	$E_{max} = 3.\overline{6},$	$E_{min} = 1.\overline{6}$	$2.$
4	½	38	$E_{max} = 0.91\overline{6},$	$E_{min} = 0.41\overline{6}$	$0.\overline{6}$
8	¼	37.5	$E_{max} = 0.229,$	$E_{min} = 0.104$	$0.1\overline{6}$
16	⅛	37.375	$E_{max} = 0.0573,$	$E_{min} = 0.0260$	0.0417

The global error estimates were computed by noting that in the interval [2,4], the integrand is increasing. Point t was chosen in each case, therefore, as the initial and terminal point of the interval.

Simpson's Rule

Simpson's rule attempts to improve the accuracy of the trapezoidal rule by using a second degree curve to approximate f, rather than the secant line. As before, the interval [a,b] is partitioned into subintervals. This time, however, we require an even number of subdivisions. A parabolic arc is passed through the points $[x_{2i}, f(x)_{2i}]$, $[x_{2i+1}, f(x_{2i+1})]$ and $[x_{2i+2}, f(x_{2i+2})]$. For each pair of subintervals, we have

$$\int_{2i}^{x_{2i+2}} f(x)\, dx \approx (h/3)[f(x_{2i})$$
$$+ 4f(x_{2i+1}) + f(x_{2i+2})].$$

Extending this result to [a,b], we obtain

$$\int_a^b f(x)\, dx \approx (h/3)[f(a) + 4f(x_1) + 2f(x_2)$$
$$+ 4f(x_3) + \cdots + 4f(x_{2i-1}) + f(b)] \qquad (44.14)$$

with global error estimate

$$I - S_{1/3}(f)$$
$$= -\frac{h^4(b-a)}{180} f^{(4)}(t) \qquad \alpha \le t \le b \quad (44.15)$$

where $S_{1/3}$ is the approximation (44.14).

Simpson's rule and the trapezoidal rule can be applied not only to approximating the integral of a given function, but also to the situation in which data is presented in tabular form at equally spaced intervals of the independent variable.

EXAMPLE 44.8. Approximate

$$\int_{0.301}^{0.311} f(x)\, dx$$

by the trapezoidal rule and by Simpson's rule.

SOLUTION:

x	f(x)
0.301	0.351209
0.302	0.352561
0.303	0.353914
0.304	0.355269
0.305	0.356625
0.306	0.357982
0.307	0.359341
0.308	0.360701
0.309	0.362062
0.310	0.363425
0.311	0.364789

With $h = 0.001$, using the trapezoidal rule,

$$I \approx (0.001/2)[0.351209 + 2(0.352561) + \cdots + 2(0.363425) + 0.364789] = 3.579879 \times 10^{-3}.$$

Using Simpson's rule,

$$I \approx (0.001/3)[0.351209 + 4(0.352561) + 2(0.353914) + \cdots + 4(0.363425) + 0.364789]$$
$$= 3.579978 \times 10^{-3}$$

In neither case can we estimate the global error because we have no explicit representation for $f(x)$.

44.5 SYSTEMS OF LINEAR EQUATIONS

The solution of linear systems falls into two categories: direct methods and iterative methods. **Direct methods** are extensions of the technique of successive elimination of variables from a system of equations, as taught in high school. The version that we will consider is **Gauss-Jordan elimination** with partial pivoting. **Iterative methods** involve choosing a starting value that is inserted in an iterative scheme (in our case the Gauss-Seidel algorithm) and then generating a sequence of approximations which, under suitable conditions, converges to the solution of our system of equations.

For the purpose of simplicity, we will resort to matrix notation in this section. A matrix is a rectangular array of numbers, with each entry indexed by a row and column subscript. We denote the element in the ith row and jth column by a_{ij}, where i denotes the row and j the column of this entry. We will write a matrix A as (a_{ij}), $i = 1, \ldots, m$; $j = 1, \ldots, n$. If $m = n$, the matrix is called *square*. Hence, matrix A appears as

$$A = \begin{pmatrix} a_{11} & a_{12} & a_{13} \cdots a_{1n} \\ a_{21} & a_{22} & a_{23} \cdots a_{2n} \\ \cdots\cdots\cdots\cdots\cdots \\ a_{m1} & a_{m2} & a_{m3} \cdots a_{mn} \end{pmatrix}$$

Two matrices of the same size can be added or subtracted, the operation defined by

$$(a_{ij}) \pm (b_{ij}) = (a_{ij} \pm b_{ij})$$

A $(1 \times n)$ matrix is called a **row vector,** and an $(n \times 1)$ matrix is called a **column vector.** If we set

$$\mathbf{a}_i = (a_{i1} \quad a_{i2} \quad a_{i3} \cdots a_{in})$$

and

$$\mathbf{b} = \begin{pmatrix} b_{1j} \\ b_{2j} \\ b_{3j} \\ \vdots \\ b_{nj} \end{pmatrix}$$

we can define the product of $\mathbf{a}$ and $\mathbf{b}$ as

$$\mathbf{a}_i \cdot \mathbf{b}_j = a_{11}b_{11} + a_{12}b_{21} + \cdots + a_{1n}b_{n1} = \sum_{k=1}^{n} a_{ik}b_{kj} \tag{44.16}$$

Using this notation for the product of a row vector and a column vector, we can define the product of two matrices. Let $A = (a_{ij})$ be an $m \times n$ matrix, $B = (b_{ij})$ be an $n \times r$ matrix. Note that the number of columns in A is equal to the number of rows in B (in this case we say that the matrices A and B are *conformable* for multiplication). We define the product of A and B as

$$AB = \begin{pmatrix} \mathbf{a}_1 \cdot \mathbf{b}_1 & \mathbf{a}_1 \cdot \mathbf{b}_2 & \mathbf{a}_1 \cdot \mathbf{b}_3 \cdots \mathbf{a}_1 \cdot \mathbf{b}_r \\ \mathbf{a}_2 \cdot \mathbf{b}_1 & \mathbf{a}_2 \cdot \mathbf{b}_2 & \cdots\cdots \mathbf{a}_2 \cdot \mathbf{b}_r \\ \vdots & \vdots & \vdots \quad \vdots \\ \mathbf{a}_m \cdot \mathbf{b}_1 & \mathbf{a}_m \cdot \mathbf{b}_2 & \cdots\cdots \mathbf{a}_m \cdot \mathbf{b}_r \end{pmatrix}$$

where $\mathbf{a}_l \cdot \mathbf{b}_k$ is the product of row l of A with column k of B; $l = 1, \ldots, m$ and $k = 1, \ldots, r$.

EXAMPLE 44.9. Multiply matrices A and B where

$$A = \begin{pmatrix} 2 & 4 \\ -1 & 3 \\ 5 & 7 \end{pmatrix} \quad B = \begin{pmatrix} 1 & -1 & 3 & 4 \\ 6 & 2 & 7 & -8 \end{pmatrix}$$

SOLUTION:

AB =

$$\begin{pmatrix} 2(1) + 4(6) & 2(-1) + 4(2) & 2(3) + 4(7) & 2(4) + 4(-8) \\ -1(1) + 3(6) & (-1)(-1) + 3(2) & -1(3) + 3(7) & -1(4) + 3(-8) \\ 5(1) + 7(6) & 5(-1) + 7(2) & 5(3) + 7(7) & 5(4) + 7(-8) \end{pmatrix}$$

$$= \begin{pmatrix} 26 & 6 & 34 & -24 \\ 17 & 7 & 18 & -28 \\ 47 & 9 & 64 & -36 \end{pmatrix}$$

In this example, the product **BA** is not defined.

If **A** and **B** are square matrices, it is important to note that, in general, matrix multiplication is not commutative. Considering a square matrix **A**, we call the elements $a_{11}, a_{22}, \ldots a_{nn}$ the *main diagonal* of **A**. A matrix with all elements zero except those on the main diagonal is called a *diagonal matrix*. If $a_{11} = a_{12} \ldots = a_{nn} = 1$, the matrix is called the $n \times n$ *identity matrix*, denoted by I_n. In the case that **A** is an $n \times n$ matrix, and **B** is an $n \times n$ matrix,

$$\mathbf{AB} = I_n = \mathbf{BA}$$

then matrix **B** is called the *inverse* of **A**, and is denoted by $\mathbf{A}^{-1}$. For example, if

$$\mathbf{A} = \begin{pmatrix} 0 & 2 \\ 2 & -1 \end{pmatrix}, \text{ then } \mathbf{A}^{-1} = \begin{pmatrix} \frac{1}{4} & \frac{1}{2} \\ \frac{1}{2} & 0 \end{pmatrix}$$

In the event that the inverse of a matrix exists, the matrix is called *nonsingular;* otherwise, *singular*.

Returning to systems of equations, let us write n equations in n unknowns in the following form:

$$a_{11}x_1 + a_{12}x_2 + a_{13}x_3 + \cdots + a_{1n}x_n = b_1$$
$$a_{21}x_1 + a_{22}x_2 + a_{23}x_3 + \cdots + a_{2n}x_n = b_2$$
$$\vdots \qquad \vdots \qquad \vdots \qquad \vdots \qquad \vdots$$
$$a_{n1}x_1 + a_{n2}x_2 + a_{n3}x_3 + \cdots + a_{nn}x_n = b_n$$

If we define a matrix **A** (the *coefficient matrix*) by

$$\mathbf{A} = \begin{pmatrix} a_{11} & a_{12} & \cdots & a_{1n} \\ a_{21} & a_{22} & \cdots & a_{2n} \\ \vdots & \vdots & & \vdots \\ a_{n1} & a_{n2} & \cdots & a_{nn} \end{pmatrix},$$

a column vector **b** (the *right hand side vector*) by

$$\mathbf{b} = \begin{pmatrix} b_1 \\ b_2 \\ \vdots \\ b_n \end{pmatrix}$$

and the solution vector **x** by

$$\mathbf{x} = \begin{pmatrix} x_1 \\ x_2 \\ \vdots \\ x_n \end{pmatrix},$$

we can write our system in matrix form as $\mathbf{Ax} = \mathbf{b}$. By adjoining vector **b** to matrix **A** as the $(n + 1)$'st column, we form the *augmented matrix* $(\mathbf{A}|\mathbf{b})$ of the systems of equations.

Gaussian elimination is a procedure by means of which we reduce the system of equations (equivalently the augmented matrix) to the form

$$a_{11}x_1 + a_{12}x_2 + \cdots + a_{1n}x_n = b_1$$
$$a'_{22}x_2 + \cdots a'_{2n}x_n = b'_2$$
$$a''_{33}x_3 + \cdots a''_{3n}x_n = b''_3$$
$$\vdots$$
$$\hat{a}_{nn}x_n = \hat{b}_n$$

$$\begin{pmatrix} a_{11} & a_{12} & a_{13} \cdots & a_{1n} & b_1 \\ 0 & a'_{22} & a'_{23} \cdots & a'_{2n} & b'_2 \\ 0 & 0 & a''_{33} \cdots & a''_{3n} & b''_3 \\ \vdots & \vdots & & \cdots a_{nn} & \vdots \\ 0 & \cdots & & & b_n \end{pmatrix}$$

by a sequence of elementary row operations. The fact that the coefficients in the modified system are labelled with primes and double primes, etc., stems from the fact that they are altered from the original coefficients during the elimination procedure. An elementary row operation is one of the following:

1. Interchanging two equations.
2. Multiplying one equation by a nonzero constant.
3. Adding a nonzero multiple of one equation to another equation.

The resulting system of equations can be solved by back substitution, i.e., $x_n = \hat{b}_n / \hat{a}_{nn}$ from the last equation is to obtain x_{n-1} from the next to last equation, and finally arrive at x_1.

EXAMPLE 44.10. Solve:

$$2x_1 - 5x_2 + 4x_3 = -3$$
$$x_1 - 2x_2 + x_3 = 5$$
$$x_1 - 4x_2 + 6x_3 = 10$$

SOLUTION:

The sequence of steps that leads to the back substitution phase starts with forming the augmented matrix and then by a sequence of elementary row operations converting it to "triangular" form:

$$\begin{pmatrix} 2 & -5 & 4 & -3 \\ 1 & -2 & 1 & 5 \\ 1 & -4 & 6 & 10 \end{pmatrix} \rightarrow \begin{pmatrix} 2 & -5 & 4 & -3 \\ 1 & -2 & 1 & 5 \\ 0 & -\frac{3}{2} & 4 & \frac{23}{2} \end{pmatrix}$$

$$\rightarrow \begin{pmatrix} 2 & -5 & 4 & -3 \\ 0 & \frac{1}{2} & -1 & \frac{13}{2} \\ 0 & -\frac{3}{2} & 4 & \frac{23}{2} \end{pmatrix} \rightarrow \begin{pmatrix} 2 & -5 & 4 & -3 \\ 0 & \frac{1}{2} & -1 & \frac{13}{2} \\ 0 & 0 & 1 & 31 \end{pmatrix}$$

At this point, the matrix corresponds to the system

$$2x_1 - 5x_2 + 4x_3 = -3$$
$$\tfrac{1}{2}x_2 - x_3 = \tfrac{13}{2}$$
$$x_3 = 31$$

which can be solved (back substitution) to yield

$$x_3 = 31, \quad x_2 = 75, \quad x_1 = 124$$

There are numerous examples to demonstrate that this procedure can lead to untenable results. For example, if we attempt to solve the system

$$2x_2 + 4x_3 = 0$$
$$x_1 + 4x_2 + 2x_3 = 0$$
$$2x_1 + x_2 = 2$$

by Gaussian elimination, our first step would be to subtract some multiple of the first equation from the second, in order to produce a zero coefficient of x_1 in the second equation. However, this is impossible. Gaussian elimination fails if $a_{11} = 0$.

Gauss-Jordan elimination with partial pivoting is one method to alleviate this shortcoming of ordinary Gaus-

sian elimination. The method incorporates the back substitution in the elimination procedure by normalizing the diagonal elements of the coefficient matrix to unity. At the same time, the super and subdiagonal elements in each column are reduced to zero. The partial pivoting aspect of the method consists in interchanging equations so that the element of largest magnitude in each column becomes the diagonal element in each step of the reduction procedure.

EXAMPLE 44.11. The system whose augmented matrix is

$$\begin{pmatrix} -0.0038 & 6.000 & 6.000 & 11.997 \\ -3.000 & 4.305 & -2.937 & -1.632 \\ 5.000 & -6.027 & -2.393 & -3.420 \end{pmatrix}$$

has exact the solutions $x_1 = 1.000$, $x_2 = 1.000$, and $x_3 = 1.000$. Solve for x_1, x_2 and x_3 using Gauss-Jordan elimination without partial pivoting and then resolve with Gauss-Jordan elimination with partial pivoting.

SOLUTION:

If we work to 3 decimal place accuracy and use the diagonal elements as pivots (normalizing elements), we obtain the following sequence of transformed matrices:

$$\begin{pmatrix} -0.003 & 6.000 & 6.000 & 11.997 \\ -3.000 & 4.305 & -2.937 & -1.632 \\ 5.000 & -6.027 & -2.393 & -3.420 \end{pmatrix}$$

$$\rightarrow \begin{pmatrix} 1.000 & -2000.000 & -2000.000 & -3999.000 \\ 0.000 & -5995.695 & -6002.937 & -11,995.308 \\ 0.000 & 9993.973 & 9997.607 & 19,998.420 \end{pmatrix}$$

$$\rightarrow \begin{pmatrix} 1.000 & 0.000 & 2.000 & 3.000 \\ 0.000 & 1.000 & 1.001 & 2.001 \\ 0.000 & 0.000 & -6.360 & 0.480 \end{pmatrix}$$

$$\rightarrow \begin{pmatrix} 1.000 & 0.000 & 0.000 & 3.150 \\ 0.000 & 1.000 & 0.000 & 2.076 \\ 0.000 & 0.000 & 1.000 & -0.075 \end{pmatrix}$$

Values of $x_1 = 3.150$, $x_2 = 2.076$, and $x_3 = -0.075$ differ greatly from the exact solution.

If we solve the system using partial pivoting, we would first rewrite the augmented matrix (the maximum element in the first column is the pivot) as

$$\begin{pmatrix} 5.000 & -6.027 & -2.393 & -3420 \\ -3.000 & 4.305 & -2.937 & -1.632 \\ -0.003 & 6.000 & 6.000 & 11.997 \end{pmatrix}$$

The sequence of transformed matrices is

$$\begin{pmatrix} 1.000 & -1.205 & -0.479 & -0.684 \\ 0.000 & 0.690 & -4.374 & -3.684 \\ 0.000 & 5.996 & 5.999 & 11.995 \end{pmatrix}$$

At this point, we interchange row 2 and 3 to put 5.996 in the pivot position (it is the element of largest magnitude in the second column).

$$\begin{pmatrix} 1.000 & -1.205 & 0.727 & 1.727 \\ 0.000 & 1.000 & 1.001 & 2.001 \\ 0.000 & 0.000 & -5.065 & -5.065 \end{pmatrix}$$

$$\begin{pmatrix} 1.000 & 0.000 & 0.000 & 1.000 \\ 0.000 & 1.000 & 0.000 & 1.001 \\ 0.000 & 0.000 & 1.000 & 1.000 \end{pmatrix}$$

In this case, $x_1 = 1.000$, $x_2 = 1.001$, and $x_3 = 1.000$, which is a remarkable improvement over our previous solution. The partial pivoting technique helps to minimize the inherent roundoff error that occurs, because we are not working in the rational number system.

An interesting byproduct of G-J elimination is that we can compute the inverse of a matrix and, by keeping track of the pivot elements, the determinant of a matrix at the same time we are computing the solution to a system of equations.

EXAMPLE 44.12. Solve the following system of equations:

$$2x_2 + 4x_3 = 0$$
$$x_1 + 4x_2 + 2x_3 = 0$$
$$2x_1 + x_2 = 2$$

Compute the inverse of the coefficient matrix and its determinant.

SOLUTION:

Write the augmented matrix in the form

$$\begin{pmatrix} 2 & 1 & 0 & 2 & 1 & 0 & 0 \\ 1 & 4 & 2 & 0 & 0 & 1 & 0 \\ 0 & 2 & 4 & 0 & 0 & 0 & 1 \end{pmatrix}$$

Note: we have adjoined the 3×3 identity matrix to the augmented matrix $(\mathbf{A}|\mathbf{b})$ to form the augmented matrix $(\mathbf{A}|\mathbf{b}|\mathbf{I}_3)$. This matrix will be converted by the elimination procedure to $(\mathbf{I}_3|\mathbf{x}|\mathbf{A}^{-1})$.

The sequence of transformed matrices is

$$\begin{pmatrix} 1 & \frac{1}{2} & 0 & 1 & \frac{1}{2} & 0 & 0 \\ 0 & \frac{7}{2} & 2 & -1 & -\frac{1}{2} & 1 & 0 \\ 0 & 2 & 4 & 0 & 0 & 0 & 1 \end{pmatrix}$$

$$\begin{pmatrix} 1 & 0 & -\frac{2}{7} & \frac{8}{7} & \frac{4}{7} & -\frac{1}{7} & 0 \\ 0 & 1 & \frac{4}{7} & -\frac{2}{7} & -\frac{1}{7} & \frac{2}{7} & 0 \\ 0 & 0 & \frac{20}{7} & \frac{4}{7} & \frac{2}{7} & -\frac{4}{7} & 1 \end{pmatrix}$$

$$\begin{pmatrix} 1 & 0 & 0 & \frac{42}{35} & \frac{3}{5} & -\frac{1}{5} & \frac{1}{10} \\ 0 & 1 & 0 & -\frac{2}{5} & -\frac{1}{5} & \frac{2}{5} & -\frac{1}{5} \\ 0 & 0 & 1 & \frac{1}{5} & \frac{1}{10} & -\frac{1}{5} & \frac{7}{20} \end{pmatrix}$$

The solution of the system is $x_1 = 1.2$, $x_2 = -0.4$, and $x_3 = 0.2$. The inverse of the coefficient matrix is:

$$\begin{pmatrix} \frac{3}{5} & -\frac{1}{5} & \frac{1}{10} \\ -\frac{1}{5} & \frac{2}{5} & -\frac{1}{5} \\ \frac{1}{10} & -\frac{1}{5} & \frac{7}{20} \end{pmatrix}$$

The sequence of pivot elements is 2, $\frac{11}{2}$, $\frac{20}{7}$, and if we multiply, we find the determinant of $\mathbf{A}$ is 20, which in fact is the case.

Gauss-Seidel Method

The most important iterative method for solving linear systems is the Gauss-Seidel method. If our system is

$$a_{11}x_1 + a_{12}x_2 + a_{13}x_3 = b_1$$
$$a_{21}x_1 + a_{22}x_2 + a_{23}x_3 = b_2$$
$$a_{31}x_1 + a_{32}x_2 + a_{33}x_3 = b_3$$

the first step in the Gauss-Seidel method is to rewrite the system as

$$x_1 = (b_1 - a_{12}x_2 - a_{13}x_3)/a_{11}$$

$$x_2 = (b_2 - a_{21}x_1 - a_{23}x_3)/a_{22}$$

$$x_3 = (b_3 - a_{31}x_1 - a_{32}x_2)/a_{33}$$

As in any iterative method, we choose an initial approximation to the solution $\mathbf{x}_0 = (x_{1,0}\ x_{2,0}\ x_{3,0})$ and compute successive iterates until some predetermined convergence criterion is satisfied. The distinguishing feature of the Gauss-Seidel method is that the most recent approximation to $\mathbf{x}_i$ is used at each step of the iteration. Thus, with $(x_{1,0}\ x_{2,0}\ x_{3,0})$ as our initial approximation vector, the first step in the solution of the above system is:

$$x_{1,1} = (b_1 - a_{12}x_{2,0} - a_{13}x_{3,0})/a_{11}$$

$$x_{2,1} = (b_2 - a_{21}x_{1,1} - a_{23}x_{3,0})/a_{22}$$

$$x_{3,1} = (b_3 - a_{31}x_{1,1} - a_{23}x_{2,1})/a_{33}$$

Note that in the second and third equations the most recent value of $\mathbf{x}_i$ is used.

A sufficient criterion for the Gauss-Seidel iterates to converge to a solution of the system is that the coefficient matrix $\mathbf{A}$ be diagonally dominant:

$$|a_{ii}| > \sum_{j=1}^{n} |a_{ij}|\ i \neq j, i = 1, 2, \ldots, n \quad (44.17)$$

If the system is not diagonally dominant, then rearrangement of the equations is called for. We can write the Gauss-Seidel algorithm in the form:

$$x_{i,n+1} = \frac{b_i}{a_{ii}} - \sum_{j=1}^{i-1} \frac{a_{ij}}{a_{ii}} x_{j,n+1} - \sum_{j=i+1}^{N} \frac{a_{ij}}{a_{ii}} x_{j,n} \quad (44.18)$$

where $n = 0, 1, 2, \ldots$ and N is the number of equations.

EXAMPLE 44.13. Using the Gauss-Seidel method, solve the system:

$$\begin{pmatrix} 4 & -1 & -1 & 0 \\ -1 & 4 & 0 & -1 \\ -1 & 0 & 4 & -1 \\ 0 & -1 & -1 & 4 \end{pmatrix} \begin{pmatrix} x_1 \\ x_2 \\ x_3 \\ x_4 \end{pmatrix} = \begin{pmatrix} 1 \\ 2 \\ 0 \\ 1 \end{pmatrix}$$

SOLUTION:

The system is diagonally dominant, so no rearrangement is necessary. We thus rewrite our system in the form

$$x_1 = \tfrac{1}{4}(1 + x_2 + x_3)$$

$$x_2 = \tfrac{1}{4}(2 + x_1 x_4)$$

$$x_3 = \tfrac{1}{4}(x_1 + x_4)$$

$$x_4 = \tfrac{1}{4}(1 + x_2 + x_3)$$

If we choose $x_0 = (0,0,0,0)$ as our initial approximation, we generate the following sequence of iterates:

$$x_1 = (\tfrac{1}{4}, \tfrac{9}{16}, \tfrac{1}{16}, \tfrac{13}{32})$$

$$x_2 = (\tfrac{13}{32}, \tfrac{45}{64}, \tfrac{13}{64}, \tfrac{61}{128})$$

$$x_3 = (\tfrac{61}{128}, \tfrac{189}{256}, \tfrac{61}{256}, \tfrac{253}{512})$$

If we tabulate these results, we obtain,

n	$x_{1,n}$	$x_{2,n}$	$x_{3,n}$	$x_{4,n}$
0	0.0	0.0	0.0	0.0
1	0.25	0.5625	0.0625	0.40625
2	0.40625	0.703125	0.203125	0.4765625
3	0.4765625	0.7382813	0.2382813	0.4941406
4	0.4941406	0.7470703	0.2470703	0.4985352

The iterates are converging to $x_1 = 0.5$, $x_2 = 0.75$, $x_3 = 0.25$, and $x_4 = 0.5$, which is the exact solution.

A useful convergence criterion for the Gauss-Seidel method is given by

$$|x_{i,n+1} - x_{i,n}| < \epsilon$$

This is the allowable change in the value of an element of the solution vector from one iteration to the next and is at most ϵ. Two other points worth remembering are the following:

1. Diagonal dominance is only a sufficient criterion for convergence. Systems that are not diagonally dominant may have iterates that converge to the solution.
2. A diagonally dominant system will converge to the solution vector no matter the choice of the initial vector.

44.6 DIFFERENTIAL EQUATIONS

In this last section, we shall briefly look at the numerical solution of ordinary differential equations. In particular, we will be interested in the approximate solution to the initial value problem which consists of an ordinary differential equation and a condition which must hold at one point of the domain of the independent variable. The typical initial value problem takes the form: Solve

$$dy/dx = f(x,y) \text{ subject to } y(a) = y_0 \text{ for } a \leq x \leq b$$

We will approximate the solution at discrete points in the interval $[a,b]$. Each computed approximation will serve as a new initial value to be used at the next step of the approximation. This implies that the only exact value we have of the solution is $y(a)$—the initial value of y.

If we introduce a partition $a = x_0 < x_1 < x_2 < \cdots < x_n = b$ of $[a,b]$ of uniform step size $h = (b - a)/n$ at each point x_i, we can introduce the concept of local truncation error. Let $y(x_i)$ be the exact solution of the differential equation at x_i, and let y_i be the approximate solution at the same point. The quantity $y_i - y(x_i)$ measures the error in approximating the exact solution by the approximation. The global truncation error is $y_n - y(x_n)$ —the accumulated error at the last step of the approximation procedure.

The two techniques we will discuss are single step methods. We advance the solution one step at a time, from x_i to x_{i+1}, by using the approximation to the solution at x_i as a new starting value to compute the approximation at x_{i+1}. **Euler's method** is the simplest of the single step methods and can be derived by use of Taylor series methods.

If we expand the solution function $y(x)$ in a Taylor series about the point x_i and truncate the series after two terms, we obtain

$$y(x_i + h) = y(x_i) + hy'(x_i) + \mathcal{O}(h^2)$$

Because $x_{i+1} = x_i + h$, we have

$$y_{i+1} = y_i + hf(x_i,y_i) \qquad i = 0, 1, 2, \ldots, n \quad (44.19)$$

which is the algorithm for Euler's method. The local truncation error is $\theta(h^2)$ while the global truncation error at the nth step is $\theta(h)$. This decrease in accuracy stems from the fact that the algorithm uses the value of y at x_i as the initial value for the next step in the solution. Thus, an error at an early step will propagate through the iterations in such a manner as to decrease global accuracy.

The geometry underlying Euler's method has an intrinsic error built into it right at the beginning. The solution across the first step $[x_0,x_1]$ follows the tangent line to the solution curve at the point (x_0,y_0) as shown in Figure 44.5. The starting value for the next step is y_1, *not* $y(x_1)$.

EXAMPLE 44.14. The differential equation $dy/dx = y \cos(x)$, $y(0) = 1$, has the exact solution $y = e^{\sin(x)}$. Determine the solution to this equation by Euler's method with step size $h = 0.1$ and compare at each step with the exact solution.

SOLUTION:

i	x_i	y_i calculated	$y(x_i)$ exact
1	0.1	1.1	1.104986830
2	0.2	1.209450458	1.219778556
3	0.3	1.327984655	1.343825244
4	0.4	1.454851875	1.476121946
5	0.5	1.588852606	1.615146296
6	0.6	1.728287540	1.758818846
7	0.7	1.870929266	1.904496534
8	0.8	2.014025829	2.049008650
9	0.9	2.154344360	2.188741913
10	1.0	2.288260553	2.319776825

Note that the agreement between the computed and the exact solution is not very good because of the propagation of error from step to step. One way to improve the accuracy of our approximate solution is to decrease the step size, i.e., try $h = 0.01$, $h = 0.001$.

A better way to improve the accuracy of our approximate solution is to keep more terms of the Taylor expansion of the solution function. This is the rationale behind the higher order **Runge-Kutta methods.** The most widely used single step method for the solution of ordinary differential equations is the fourth order Runge-Kutta method given by

$$y_{n+1} = y_n + (h/6)(k_1 + 2k_2 + 2k_3 + k_4)$$

$$k_1 = f(x_n, y_n)$$

$$k_2 = f(x_n + h/2, y_n + hk_1/2)$$

$$k_3 = f(x_n + h/2, y_n + hk_2/2)$$

$$k_4 = f(x_n + h, y_n + hk_3)$$

Locally, this method has accuracy of $\mathcal{O}(h^5)$, while globally, its accuracy is $\mathcal{O}(h^4)$.

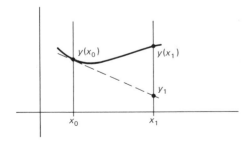

Figure 44.5. Application of Euler's method.

$h = 0.1$

x_i	$y_{1,i}$	$y_1(x_i)$	$y_{2,i}$	$y_2(x_i)$
0.0000	0.00000000	0.00000000	1.00000000	1.00000000
0.1000	0.11033333	0.11033299	1.09965000	1.09964967
0.2000	0.24265610	0.24265527	1.19705668	1.19705602
0.3000	0.39891203	0.39891055	1.28957032	1.28956937
0.4000	0.58094621	0.58094390	1.37406271	1.37406154
0.5000	0.79044242	0.79043908	1.44689032	1.44688904
0.6000	1.02885024	1.02884567	1.50386080	1.50385954
0.7000	1.29730114	1.29729511	1.54020405	1.54020303
0.8000	1.59651304	1.59650534	1.55054983	1.55054930
0.9000	1.92668290	1.92667330	1.52891351	1.52891381

$h = 0.01$

x_i	$y_{1,i}$	$y_1(x_i)$	$y_{2,i}$	$y_2(x_i)$
0.0000	0.00000000	0.00000000	1.00000000	1.00000000
0.0500	0.05254166	0.05254166	1.04995728	1.04995728
0.1000	0.11033299	0.11033299	1.09964967	1.09964967
0.1500	0.17362234	0.17362234	1.14878810	1.14878810
0.2000	0.24265527	0.24265527	1.19705602	1.19705602
0.2500	0.31767297	0.31767297	1.24410818	1.24410818
0.3000	0.39891055	0.39891055	1.28956937	1.28956937
0.3500	0.48659515	0.48659515	1.33303333	1.33303333
0.4000	0.58094390	0.58094390	1.37406154	1.37406154
0.4500	0.68216175	0.68216175	1.41218216	1.41218216
0.5000	0.79043908	0.79043908	1.44688904	1.44688904
0.5500	0.90594922	0.90594922	1.47764070	1.47764070
0.6000	1.02884567	1.02884567	1.50385954	1.50385954
0.6500	1.15925927	1.15925927	1.52493102	1.52493102
0.7000	1.29729511	1.29729511	1.54020303	1.54020303
0.7500	1.44302927	1.44302927	1.54898535	1.54898535
0.8000	1.59650534	1.59650534	1.55054930	1.55054930
0.8500	1.75773084	1.75773083	1.54412749	1.54412749
0.9000	1.92667331	1.92667330	1.52891381	1.52891381
0.9500	2.10325633	2.10325633	1.50406358	1.50406358

$h = 0.001$

x_i	$x_{1,i}$	$y_1(x_i)$	$y_{2,i}$	$y_2(x_i)$
0.0000	0.00000000	0.00000000	1.00000000	1.00000000
0.0250	0.02563021	0.02563021	1.02499473	1.02499473
0.0500	0.05254166	0.05254166	1.04995728	1.04995728
0.0750	0.08076554	0.08076554	1.07485402	1.07485402
0.1000	0.11033299	0.11033299	1.09964967	1.09964967
0.1250	0.14127498	0.14127498	1.12430725	1.12430725
0.1500	0.17362234	0.17362234	1.14878810	1.14878810
0.1750	0.20740566	0.20740566	1.17305176	1.17305176
0.2000	0.24265527	0.24265527	1.19705602	1.19705602
0.2250	0.27940117	0.27940117	1.22075680	1.22075680
0.2500	0.31767297	0.31767297	1.24410818	1.24410818
0.2750	0.35749987	0.35749987	1.26706229	1.26706229
0.3000	0.39891055	0.39891055	1.28956937	1.28956937
0.3250	0.44193315	0.44193315	1.31157765	1.31157765
0.3500	0.48659515	0.48659515	1.33303333	1.33303333
0.3750	0.53292339	0.53292339	1.35388060	1.35388060
0.4000	0.58094390	0.58094390	1.37406154	1.37406154
0.4250	0.63068192	0.63068192	1.39351612	1.39351612
0.4500	0.68216175	0.68216175	1.41218216	1.41218216
0.4750	0.73540672	0.73540672	1.42999532	1.42999532
0.5000	0.79043908	0.79043908	1.44688904	1.44688904
0.5250	0.84727996	0.84727996	1.46279451	1.46279451
0.5500	0.90594922	0.90594922	1.47764070	1.47764070
0.5750	0.96646541	0.96646541	1.49135426	1.49135426
0.6000	1.02884567	1.02884567	1.50385954	1.50385954
0.6250	1.09310561	1.09310561	1.51507857	1.51507857
0.6500	1.15925927	1.15925927	1.52493102	1.52493102
0.6750	1.22731894	1.22731894	1.53333420	1.53333420
0.7000	1.29729511	1.29729511	1.54020303	1.54020303
0.7250	1.36919637	1.36919637	1.54545003	1.54545003
0.7500	1.44302927	1.44302927	1.54898535	1.54898535
0.7750	1.51879820	1.51879820	1.55071667	1.55071667
0.8000	1.59650534	1.59650534	1.55054930	1.55054930
0.8250	1.67615046	1.67615046	1.54838609	1.54838609
0.8500	1.75773083	1.75773083	1.54412749	1.54412749
0.8750	1.84124114	1.84124114	1.53767153	1.53767153
0.9000	1.92667330	1.92667330	1.52891381	1.52891381
0.9250	2.01401635	2.01401635	1.51774756	1.51774756
0.9500	2.10325633	2.10325633	1.50406358	1.50406358
0.9750	2.19437611	2.19437611	1.48775034	1.48775034
1.0000	2.28735529	2.28735529	1.46869394	1.46869394

Figure 44.6. Calculated solutions using Runge-Kutta algorithm for $h = 0.1$, $h = 0.001$, and $h = 0.001$.

EXAMPLE 44.15. Using the Runge-Kutta method, repeat Example 44.14 and compare the approximate solution with the exact solution.

SOLUTION:

i	x_i	y_i calculated	$y(x_i)$ exact
1	0.1	1.104986746	1.104986830
2	0.2	1.219778374	1.219778556
3	0.3	1.343824954	1.343825244
4	0.4	1.476121544	1.476121946
5	0.5	1.615145781	1.615146296
6	0.6	1.758818221	1.758818188
7	0.7	1.904495808	1.904496534
8	0.8	2.049007833	2.049008650
9	0.9	2.188741016	2.188741913
10	1.0	2.319775860	2.319776825

Single step methods can also be used to solve systems of ordinary differential equations. This is of particular importance because second order differential equations can be reduced to a system of first order equations and the Runge-Kutta algorithm then applied.

For example, the second order differential equation $y'' - (1 - y^2)y' + y = 0$ can be converted into a system of first order equations by setting $y = y_1$ and $y_1' = y_2$. We have

$$y_1' = y_2$$
$$y_2' = (1 - y_1^2)y_2 - y_1$$

The general initial value problem for systems of first order differential equations is

$$y_1' = f_1(x, y_1, \ldots, y_n) \quad y_{1,0} = y_1(x_0)$$
$$y_2' = f_2(x, y_1, \ldots, y_n) \quad y_{2,0} = y_2(x_0)$$
$$\vdots$$
$$y_n' = f_n(x, y_1, \ldots, y_n) \quad y_{n,0} = y_n(x_0)$$

The Runge-Kutta algorithm for systems is

$$y_{j,i+1} = y_{j,i} + \frac{h}{6}(k_{j1} + 2k_{j2} + 2k_{j3} + k_{j4})$$

$$k_{j1} = f_j(x_i, y_{1,i}, y_{2,i}, \ldots, y_{n,i})$$

$$k_{j2} = f_j\left(x_i + \frac{h}{2}, y_{1,i} + \frac{1}{2}hk_{j1}, \ldots, j_{n,i} + \frac{1}{2}hk_{j1}\right)$$

$$k_{j3} = f_j\left(x_i + \frac{h}{2}, y_{1,i} + \frac{1}{2}hk_{j2}, \ldots, y_{n,i} + \frac{1}{2}hk_{j2}\right)$$

$$k_{j4} = f_j(x_i + n, y_{1,i} + hk_{j3}, \ldots, y_{n,i} + hk_{j3})$$

EXAMPLE 44.16. Using the Runge-Kutta algorithm, solve the following system of first order differential equations:

$$y_1' = y_1 + y_2 \quad y_1(0) = 0$$
$$y_2' = -y_1 + y_2 \quad y_2(0) = 1$$

The exact solution is $y_1 = e^x \sin(x)$ and $y_2 = e^x \cos(x)$.

SOLUTION:

Figure 44.6 (p. 763) shows the calculated solutions together with the exact solutions for 3 different values of h. Observe the improvement in the calculated solution at corresponding points as the step size is decreased.

REFERENCES

Carnahan, B., H. A. Luther and J. Wilkes, *Applied Numerical Methods.* New York: John Wiley & Sons, 1979.

Cheney, W., and D. Kincaid, *Numerical Mathematics and Computing.* Monterey, CA: Brooks/Cole, 1980.

Conte, S. D., and C. de Boor, *Elementary Numerical Analysis—An Algorithmic Approach.* New York: McGraw-Hill Book Co., 1972.

Dahlquist, G., and A. Björk, *Numerical Methods.* Englewood Cliffs, NJ: Prentice-Hall, 1974.

Gerald, C. F., *Applied Numerical Analysis,* 2nd Ed. Reading, MA: Addison-Wesley, 1980.

Ralston, A., and P. Rabinowitz, *A First Course in Numerical Analysis,* 2nd Ed. New York: McGraw-Hill Book Co., 1978.

45
Documentation

Edward L. Averill
Honeywell Aerospace Defense Group

45.1 INTRODUCTION

We consider documentation to be a relatively new phenomenon, but it has roots which are older than literature, indeed, which probably reach back to the beginning of writing and pictorial art. Today, documentation appears to be restricted to library science courses and is a word as yet without much significance in the academic world. In this chapter, we establish what documentation is, and show its place in the world of technology.

We therefore explore the human causes which produced documentation in the first place. Then from a review of the relationship between documentation and science and engineering (with particular emphasis on system products and software) we project how documentation may be developed in the future. As a result, we hope documentation will be viewed as a vital discipline that enables technological progress as a whole.

Documentation, which has been with us since we first notched a twig to keep a tally, is a technology in its own right. Scientific enquiry and engineering activity into documentation, still in the preliminary stages, are being spurred on by the recent resources and insights provided by computer technology.

Current Attitudes

Let us start by noting what **documentation** means to us now. The chances are most people will define it in terms of their working experience. Engineers involved with product development or manufacture, or both, may imagine all the documents with which they are required to be knowledgeable, or alternatively all the documents they have to produce, alone or jointly with technical writers. To the scientist, documentation might be all the papers and texts that define the particulars of his or her special field. A lawyer or insurance agent may imagine the file or papers that have to do with one client. Whatever the working experience, the word "documentation" in normal use refers to the "paper" of that environment.

Engineers have gained a reputation of being producers or poor documentation, even to the point of having their literacy level questioned. In fact, doing any form of writing has not been part of the engineer's job image. There are technical writers and editors to fulfill this need. However, engineering is changing because engineers suffer from having to read other engineers' poor documentation. Collectively, they now recognize that documentation is both valuable and necessary.

However, imagine being a computer programmer 25 to 30 years ago, having to perform a task for which there was no precedent. Having spent inordinate hours getting a program to work, you the programmer are then asked to document it. At that time you barely understand how you have done it. To be asked to document the program appears to be both unkind and unnecessary. You have, from your point of view, earned a respite. Where, you might ask, are the nouns and verbs and the sentence constructs to be found for this documentation? Where are the concepts and whole infrastructure of ideas that are available for other descriptive writing? This kind of experience may be why the word "documentation" has such a negative association for some people.

This handbook covers an area of engineering in which

we can hope to be masters of only a small fraction. Even if we are software engineers, can we personally code in all programming languages? Can we master the art of designing operating systems, compilers and also microcode instruction operation? No matter what our field is, we cannot be instant masters in all parts of it. We may feel we are prepared and sufficiently experienced to become masters of any part of it. But how do we go about extending our mastery?

When we move from what we know to what we do not know, we can experiment and follow a path of trial and error. However, if others have already done this work, they can give us a conducted tour. If we have the necessary prerequisites, we can cover the same path in a fraction of the time. *Documents* can become the conducted tour.

Today, no technology is isolated; every field of endeavor is an interacting set of technologies. In no field does the state of the technological art progress faster than in computer science. This field, like many others, is too big for a person to learn through hands-on experience or word of mouth. Hence we find we do not have a real choice—we have to get information from documents. We have to be readers, and many also have to be authors to record their progressive discoveries. In spite of the common experience summed up by the saying, "When all else fails, read the instructions" (which testifies both how poorly they are often written and how reluctant we are to read if we do not have to), it turns out that we depend on documentation to be effective as professional people.

The Term "Documentation"

Th. P. Loosjes [1] speaks for people whose special concern is documents. In the first chapter of his book on documentation, he records the many different definitions found in the literature. Basically he finds two views. Some limit the term to librarianship and others recognize no such limit, which is, in fact, the normal colloquial usage. Librarianship refers to such things as literature service, library service, literature reviews, abstract service, and the dissemination of information.

We are going to use the term documentation to refer to all that is recorded (written) about a particular subject area. This includes the traditional books, journals and periodicals. There are also technical reports from institutions of learning and research centers of all types. Our need for documentation and our need to produce it depend on what we are doing (the role we are playing).

Hence our special focus for documentation is to refer to all available written material which could make what we are doing more productive.

In time, computer systems will change our ideas and concepts of how we go about doing our daily work. But documents in some form will continue to be increasingly important in every work activity. Current experience shows that today's ideas and standards of documentation cannot stay where they are for a number of reasons related to work inefficiency and volume explosion. Documentation must become a technology in which we all participate, because it plays an important role making the application of the state of the technological art cost-effective.

The next two sections examine the relationships between documentation and the human being, and then between documentation and science and engineering. A third section looks ahead to possible future changes.

45.2 A HUMAN SETTING FOR DOCUMENTATION

Documentation began when humankind first found that the collective memory was inadequate. It became necessary to make a record at once to preserve and also to depersonalize memory. This necessity presented two problems. How should the record be formulated in the mind? And what means could be used to represent the internal mind's formulation?

Since this beginning, there has been a constant human struggle to develop *mental constructs* (concepts, and the means of holding inner mental knowledge), as well as to develop more effective ways of *representation,* i.e. make records (see Figure 45.1). These two problems continue to present themselves anew with every step we take into new experience. Software is a new experience, and we show, in a later section, the significance of addressing these broad issues in terms of our ability to make progress in software technology.

Figure 45.1 presents an outline of how to relate documentation to how people think and the support they need for their job. On the left are human documentation skills; in the middle is the record of some sort; and on the right are the technologies that influence the form, style and content of the record. Before documentation, there was the tribal storyteller, the source of historical information. Documentation is now the principal means of conveying information between people.

A record must communicate. In communication there

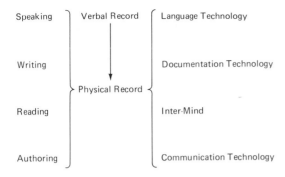

Speaking — Verbal Record — Language Technology

Writing — Documentation Technology

Physical Record

Reading — Inter-Mind

Authoring — Communication Technology

Figure 45.1. Relationship between the need for a record and technology.

are always three things: "the communication" itself, a meaning and a protocol. The communication, for documentation, has most often been inscriptions on paper. James L. Kinneavy [2] calls "the communication" the **signal.** The meaning is what the record is intended to convey to the reader (to Kinneavy, this "meaning" is reality). The **protocol** is what the creator uses to encapsulate the meaning into the inscriptions. This protocol has to be fully known to the reader if the encapsulated meaning is to be the meaning extracted. Protocol as used here is what Kinneavy calls *encoding* and *decoding,* via syntactics, morphology, graphology and semantics.

Communication has the structure shown in Figure 45.2. The author of documentation intends the reader to extract the meaning from word and picture inscriptions.

Figure 45.2 represents the situation in which the meaning being conveyed does not involve mentally digested understanding derived from direct experience. As people started to think about their environment, they began to develop ideas, concepts and knowledge structures (collectively, mind structures). When they possessed such structures within their minds, they started to use them as part of "the communication" within their records. When mind structures are referred to within the record inscriptions (i.e. the document), it is necessary for the reader not only

to use the same protocol, but also the same mind structures if the *intended* meaning is to be the *extracted* meaning when comprehension occurs.

Word Invention and Meaning

In Figure 45.2, meaning is conveyed by words. The set of possible meanings associated with a word is directly related to our environment; that is each meaning in the set relates to an experience that we encounter as part of our environment. The words we use in our language reflect the scope of things commonly encountered. For example, Arabic has more than 30 words for *camel,* and Eskimos have a similar number for *ice.* Intelligence, however, involves mental things based not just upon some encountered thing but upon a constructed understanding of what an encountered thing *is.* For instance, "mammal" pulls together things into a set in accordance with, in turn, a common set of attributes and properties by which any member of the group can be recognized. This makes "mammal" a mental idea that has been derived from encountered things. By this means, we are able to build a structure of meaning (knowledge) which we can draw upon in our writing and speaking.

New technological territory requires new words, new ideas and new concepts. The engineer/scientist explorer attempts to explain the new territory with existing words, existing ideas and concepts; the object is to make the new understood by means of the old. Known words and ideas are extended to carry new connotations. For instance, "protocol" until recently referred almost exclusively to the formal procedures of statesmanship. However, in the development of communication systems, "protocol" has also come to represent the forms and courtesies to be observed while communicating via a communication channel. To make such a transfer, the ideas associated with a word have to be abstracted to a more general level so they can apply to the extended environment.

Sometimes no words or concepts are readily available. Then there is need to invent jargon and acronyms, some

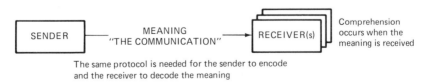

SENDER — MEANING "THE COMMUNICATION" → RECEIVER(s) — Comprehension occurs when the meaning is received

The same protocol is needed for the sender to encode and the receiver to decode the meaning

Figure 45.2. The communication within all documentation.

of which—like radar, which first appeared as *radio detecting and ranging*—slip quietly into dictionaries as a new word acceptable in formal discourses.

Mind Structures as Conveyors of Technical Meaning

Figure 45.3 illustrates how the reader interprets what he or she reads by knowledge, concepts and information data bases already possessed.

In fact, every reader has a different base set. An author has to be aware that readers interpret all references according to their own mind structures, not according to the author's.

Persuasion into new or different thinking is the principal objective of **rhetoric,** which has been part of the motivational use of language from the earliest civilization. When writing technical documentation, we have to recognize that the reader's mind structures may prohibit extraction of the meaning intended. Such readers will therefore have to make some mind structure changes to comprehend what we are communicating; rhetoric is the agent enabling such changes. Because people are the way they are, and because engineers and scientists are people first, we cannot omit rhetoric from technical documentation.

Figure 45.3 does not complete the whole human scenario that applies to the reader. It leaves out the reader's skill, intelligence and motivation. These factors, of course, have been working throughout the reader's life and therefore are well entrenched in his or her mind structures; these factors are the only resources we have to effect mind structure change. This potential exists in the reading process. When mind restructuring occurs through reading, we may experience an uplift and a satisfying burst of energy.

Figure 45.3 does introduce mind structures into the picture of documentation technology, while Figure 45.1 addresses mind structures via "inter-mind communication technology." As of now there is no recognized technology with that name. Even so, psychologists, linguists and others [3,4,5] interested in education are in effect establishing a basis for a technology that could bear that name. This chapter goes into inter-mind communication only far enough to examine the relationship between science as a whole and mind structures in general.

Carl G. Hempel, in an excellent monograph [6], talks about mind structures in the form of definitions, concepts, hypotheses, theories, systems and classifications; he examines the logical relationship between these and observables (which we have referred to as "things encountered"). Following this line of understanding, one could say, ideally, that the ultimate technical document would represent an explicit and objective mind structure such as

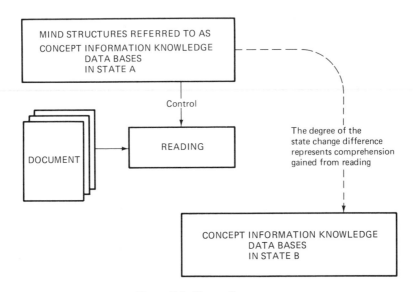

Figure 45.3. The reading process.

we might like to possess. It would have the property of enabling us actually to perform and do just what science indicates we can potentially perform and do; it would represent our ultimate understanding of reality.

In this regard, we should note that a person can possess complex mind structures which may or may not relate to reality in any way. Mind structures do not have to be real. What is true is that meaning is extractable only in terms of the structures that we possess. We find that our mind structures may facilitate communication between two or more minds, or may prevent it.

However, we who are concerned with science and engineering strive to tie technical ideas and structures to a reality that is available for all to demonstrate. Having looked at the relationship between documentation and how people think, we now focus on the people who need effective documentation the most.

Problems for the Professional in a Technological or Scientific Field

No one is more dependent upon documentation than the professional, and no one has such motivation to find and use an effective documentation technology. We use the word **professional** in its large sense: it refers to someone having significant experience and effective skill in a specific role, ideally, someone to whom we could go for advice or a service.

The professional in this setting needs to be informed about what other workers in the same field are doing; conversely, the professional has the responsibility to make known the results of work he or she may have accomplished, and from which other professionals could benefit.

The only means for the collective communication of such information is documentation. However, with the increase in the number of people in the world doing significant things in science and technology, there is an equivalent increase in the volume of documentation. Bourne [7] as long ago as 1962 reported for natural sciences and technology the production of some 41,000 periodicals with over 1,000,000 articles a year. Abstract services for a particular field will produce more than 200,000 abstracts a year. Estimates are that more than 10 million different books were produced in the 100 years before 1950, and that the increase is exponential, with a doubling time of 15 years (Price [8]).

Analysis of documentation reveals that the real knowledge increase is by no means comparable in rate with the documentation explosion. The useful life of a document

can, in fact, be very short. There are, however, no measures or standards available by which, for example, a librarian can judge who needs a given document and for how long it would be pertinent.

The problem is summed up by Kent [9] as having three dimensions of frustration: (1) it is impossible to read and remember all the literature one could use; (2) the cost of an extensive service to make available a given section of the literature is beyond the financial capability of even large organizations; and (3) library methods cannot provide efficient services by which a person can make contact with all the information that is available and pertinent to his or her need.

However, in spite of the problems, on-line retrieval services, through communication networks and time sharing computer systems, have emerged from the experimental stage and become commercially available to all. Networks such as Telenet and Tymnet connect the user's office terminal to the time-share system. Companies such as Lockheed Information Systems (with DIALOG) and System Development Corporation (with ORBIT) based in California, and Brodart Inc. (with OLAS) based in Pennsylvania, provide time share services to connect the user to data bases searches. Library services create data bases containing indexes and abstracts. Time share software provides the user with search commands to connect to data base files. Document delivery can be ordered. Hawkins and Caruso [10] report on on-line information retrieval systems and on computer aids for helping the user learn how to search and obtain information required.

Personal responsibility. If a professional's work extends mastery of an existing technology, or breaks new technological ground through basic research, chances are that he or she will be called upon to document progress within the supporting organization via internal reports. No worker contributing to the technological age can escape being an author of some sort.

W. A. Mambert [11], in addressing the problem of presenting technical ideas which are foundational to one's work, identifies thirteen ways by which ideas can be supported: testimony, reasoning via premises and conclusions, explanation, description, emotion, sensory reinforcement, analogy, example, statistics, demonstration, action, restatement and definition of the units of expression (glossary of terms). These become a checklist which can stimulate our thinking about our own work.

Authors should be as controlled by the needs of their readers as it is possible for them to be. As we have noted, learning takes place when a person, by reading, is able to add to or reform one or more of his or her current knowledge, information and concept bases. In a technological society, there is a wide variety of job activities for which the prerequisite skills are the same, but also for which the prerequisite knowledge/information/concept sets are very different. This means that today the demand for documentation is ever increasing—a situation markedly different from the days when all job learning was via apprenticeship in which documentation was unnecessary.

Activities Influencing Documentation Technology

Part of the basis upon which the technology of documentation is being founded is current investigations into learning, linguistics, and English composition. This work is still recent and is in the process of being assimilated by those not directly working in these areas. Here we will not attempt to summarize or abstract, but will make a few references in passing to original works themselves. This work is significant because it awakens people who want to communicate effectively, to thinking that will develop their written and spoken communication capabilities.

The time spent by readers is by far the greatest time element in the communication between author and reader. Because of the overwhelming amount of documentation on most desks, it is likely that a reader cannot afford to devote much time to any one document. The author's meaning has to be immediately available.

Cognitive psychology and learning. This work focusses upon what the reader does. The view of the learning process in Figure 45.3 is supported by F. J. Taylor [12], who describes the activity of a learner who busily works upon incoming material, scans it, searches for clues and meaning, draws heavily upon past knowledge, forms mental pictures to aid recall, uses the total context to get understanding, and finally organizes the new material to fit in with his or her own way of structuring knowledge. Taylor identifies three components which determine the learning outcome of reading.

1. Initial knowledge level and cognitive structure.
2. Existing special aptitude in the particular field.
3. The method of communication—the organization, the extent of internal and external connectedness; the strategy of presentation, which provides or fails to provide advance organizers for subsequent details of information (advance organizers being the intellectual

scaffolding to both support and organize coming detail)

Taylor notes that the best organizers are concepts and principles. J. G. Greeno [13] identifies internal connectedness as a function dependent on word order, grammar, semantic prerequisites, the number of major clustering foci and the degree of discrimination between them, and finally, the complexity of the sentence structures. He identifies external connectedness as the degree of correspondence between the internal organization of the material and the cognitive structure of the reader.

English composition. Good writing is the product of well digested subject matter and unremitting review and effort. No one who has to become the author of a document should feel that the skills needed to communicate effectively cannot be learned. Linda Flower [14] addresses the needs of any student who would take a noncredit course in writing because of a felt need to develop this ability in the furtherance of a career. Her book looks at the process of writing and presents a problem-solving approach. She focusses on composing, adapting to the needs of the reader, and evaluating and editing one's own writing. Flower shows us through plentiful examples (and references) that writing is a thinking process.

Style and revision. In technical documents, there is a tendency to present information in a flat uninteresting style. It may be we feel that style implies art and therefore cannot be scientific or technical. Joseph Williams [15] presents an analysis of style that shows it should be a developed aspect of technical writing.

Another approach to style, by R. A. Lanham [16], comes in a very readable text with meaningful examples for business, but equally applicable to technical documentation. Lanham proposes eight rules to use when revising prose so as to improve its readability. These rules apply to the writer's expression rather than to organization and subject matter preparation, and hence are for refining and polishing. J. C. Lane [17] and D. S. Davis [18] give examples of things authors should avoid. A few hours spent reading such works will improve and cultivate one's own style.

Programmed learning. Those who have developed tutorial texts, or programmed learning exercises that can be "read" via a device of some sort, have had to work much harder preparing their material as compared with authors of standard texts. Learning here implies building an effective mind structure. The reader is guided through the prepared material according to his or her comprehension, which is measured by the reader's selection of an answer from a set of possible answers to a question.

J. Hartley [19] reviews the programmed instruction techniques in use between 1954 and 1974. A significant thrust throughout programmed learning techniques is reader participation. The material is structured from the reader's point of view, and the author has to estimate with a high degree of precision the reader's grasp of the subject matter at every step taken through the prepared material.

Readability. Some have tried to measure the reading skill level needed for various types of document. Readability is approached quite mechanically in this context, as opposed to the readability criteria of Joseph Williams [15], in which a long sentence can still be very readable. Another influence of readability, to be discussed below, is document style and format.

G. R. Klare, in his article on assessing readability [20], reviews the published formulas to calculate the grade level the reader needs to comprehend meaning as a function of such things as the following:

1. Average sentence length in words.
2. Number of prepositional phrases per 100 words.

3. Number of "hard" words that do not occur within a specific limited vocabulary.
4. Number of words per punctuated pause.
5. Number of words per paragraph.
6. Number of syllables per 100 words.

Computer programs have been written for most of these formulas to aid in the evaluation of individual texts.

The USAF, for example, assesses its instructional documents by calculating the Reading Grade Level (RGL) to be one tenth of twenty minus the average number of one syllable words found within each consecutive 150 words. This is compared against the target audience's assigned RGL, which is based upon the audience's occupational code.

45.3 DOCUMENTATION AND THE TECHNOLOGICAL AGE

No one doubts that we are in a technological age, but what does that involve? Figure 45.4 shows the basic technological cycle to be the cause of change in the human environment. Amidst change, the human need for record and communication is itself changing. Documentation is still our principal means of record. But the need for communication in the technological process is as significant as the need for records, and inseparably wedded to it. In

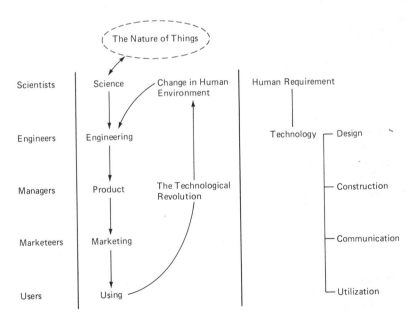

Figure 45.4. The technological cycle.

this section, we are going to explore this double record/communication need by turning our attention to system products and software.

The technological age is characterized by an ongoing spiral of change driven by science and engineering. As scientists acquire new knowledge and understanding about the nature of things, engineers exploit the discoveries by making new products under the control of human need as perceived by financiers and marketeers. The use of the new products changes the human environment and the resulting experience stimulates the perception of new human need. It is argued here that this process, this human and technological revolution, is enabled by documentation. For documents to play their enabling role, we first have to determine how the human mind holds the new "technical" knowledge, and second, how to represent it effectively to other people. So the creation of an effective documentation technology becomes the means for collective assimilation for human experience.

Documentation for System Products

Computer technology has turned most engineered products into system products—that is, products containing software. Effectively a mental engine dimension has been added to the physical engines which produced the industrial era some 100 years ago. In this section, we explore the relationship between documentation and system product cost. And we examine the special documentation needs for current software. In the final section, we will project this base into a future for documentation.

A considerable volume of documentation is needed to contain all the information associated with an engineered system product. Currently a massive volume of documentation is required for system products procured by the Department of Defense. The total documentation for one product may be tens of feet high.

When designing and developing products, we have to consider the requirements of the user, and the potential resources we have to satisfy these requirements. Manuals guide use and define maintenance, and for software, enable the extension or adjustment of the product's functional capability. Documents are required to record the current status for every avenue of investigation, planning, analysis and work task definition. The documentation required to keep the status record current and to communicate the status to workers and managers according to the role they play is obviously formidable.

New product of a new type.   Part of the reason new products of a new type (such as tactical equipment) are

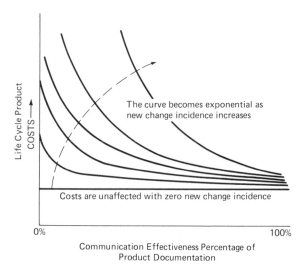

Figure 45.5. Relationship between communication effectiveness costs, and incidence of new change.

so costly is that internal documentation does not communicate sufficiently to ensure a minimum of wasted engineering effort. And once a product is produced, comprehensive documentation must be available if users and maintenance engineers are to realize the design goals and mission of the product.

In this scenario, a small adjustment in the stated requirement for the product can cause a considerable ripple of change throughout the entire documentation set. Inability to keep documentation up to date so as to maximize utility and minimize time delays also boosts costs. Engineering, maintenance and operational effectiveness is too often reduced to an unacceptably low level for complex modern system products because of our inability to solve the communication problem with the documentation techniques we employ. The direct relationship between the need for documentation and the incidence of new change is shown in Figure 45.5.

DOD Standards for Embedded Computer Systems

The acquisition of products has to be managed. Where the product is specially made under contract, there is the great need to specify exactly what it is and to control every step of its development. Nowhere is the challenge to describe greater than in government acquisition of real time systems. It is not surprising therefore that technical systems, and the software they require, are subject to many standards.

The Department of Defense (DOD) recognizes that documentation forms the foundation for controllable, usable and supportable software for embedded computer system products. In the last several years, there has been an effort by the Army, Air Force and Navy to standardize their documentation standards. This effort has been carried out by a triservice initiative under the direction of the Joint Logistic Commanders. A. J. Fletcher [21] in a report on recommendations presented to the Joint Logistic Commanders identifies 23 different documents that are needed for software documentation and which are required for an orderly and practical acquisition of software for "embedded computer system" products.

Of the 23,

  2 are government/contractor baseline documents;
  4 describe the management of the development process;
 11 describe the requirements and the design;
  6 describe the test and support activities.

In the bibliography of this report are 23 triservice standards and directive documents which are directly concerned with embedded computer system software.

Documentation standards—a protocol for communication.
The need for documentation standards arises primarily from the need to manage transactions between people who are engaged in the process of acquiring and of supplying system products. At one time, few formalized records were used to communicate business transaction information. When it was necessary to send some written description of a transaction, a letter was the means. It took time for letters to be replaced by forms. Forms on which business transactions are described are, in fact, a kind of documentation.

Clearly, volumes of documentation are meant to communicate something to someone. If several feet of documents have to be read to find the few pages one must access, then the logical organization in the documentation record is inappropriate. For documentation, the word "protocol" is extended to include the logic by which the reader knows how to extract needed information. Documentation is analogous to a map which allows the reader to find out what he or she wants to know. Other writing can be more like a description of a specific journey the writer wants the reader to take. Standards in documentation define what record is required to declare the current status of an ongoing process at each progress point (eg. milestone) in the process. The acquisition, development and supply of system products is a process with a network of communication which documentation serves.

One should not think of documentation standards as something imposed after work has been done. That is the old engineering attitude. The pragmatic reality is that real engineering progress is made only when there is a record of that engineering task in the hands of the next person who needs to know, so that person can now carry out further tasks on the same project. The documentation serves as a vital synergistic control for all the people in the process. This is analogous to a set of connected relay races which relate to each other in a tree structure.

DOD documentation standards measure and make visible real progress in the acquisition of new engineered products from the acquirer's viewpoint. However, outside these standards, considerable documentation is also required by the supplier to coordinate managers and engineers in the design and development stages. Industry is only just beginning to recognize the cost implications of effective internal communication through documentation. Currently there are no products which enable internal documentation to be the source of external deliverables. Many managers in industry feel they have to support the cost of two separate documentation flows: one for internal communication and operational control, and the other for deliverables. Until internal documentation drives the production of document deliverables, we will be blocked from gaining the synergistic control which would improve overall operational efficiency and productivity in the development of system products.

Life cycle documentation associated with a new product.
Let us look at how we become aware of the need for a new product. First come reports within an organization that it is experiencing some difficulty. Then these are formulated into specifications of things needed to help the organization fulfill its mission within its cash flow constraints. The user defines what is wanted from an operational viewpoint. To begin with, these are *internal* documents, reports of some sort. At this point a systems engineer (one who can look at operations via structural analysis along lines described by Yourdon [22], DeMarco [23], and so on) should review the mission in terms of the whole operation.

To give an example, the Air Force currently produces technical orders as its method for defining the work of a maintenance engineer. Automatic trainer products are designed to teach the technical orders. A systems engineer first examines the data flow of the technical order and finds out its exact role and origin. The first task before designing the automatic trainer is to decide whether the technical order itself is the proper vehicle for keeping equipment maintained in the field. It is very unusual if an investigation of this type does not considerably modify the user's thinking about operational needs. In this example, one modification could be to use design to simplify the maintenance of new equipment.

In the development of a new product, once the **foundational operational analysis** is properly done, a **system specification document** can be written. This document should talk only in terms of the operational needs, and not in terms of how those needs should be met. Usually (and unfortunately) the system specification liberally mixes up the need itself and preconceived ideas of how the need should be satisfied.

The system specification document then becomes the basis for a **Request For Quote (RFQ)** or a **Request For Proposal (RFP) document.** Potential suppliers reply with **proposal** and **quotation documents.** The supplier who wins the contract negotiates the **Contract document,** which often is accompanied by a **rewritten system specification.** It is then that the supplier's internal communication defines what is required by whom. In a company with ongoing contract activity, many groups of people play a role in a new contract. The role they actually play can be in fact no better than the *documented* internal communication. Internal *verbal* communication cannot be effective in this environment because the volume of detail is too great and changes too frequent to be remembered without written memoranda. Digestion of documented information takes time, but leads to a better and greater understanding which introduces a ripple of adjustment through the documentation.

Unless the internal documentation record is kept up to date, work may continue on the incorrect information; when this is discovered there will be another ripple of change. The number of people and the total incidence of change from all sources are such that automated on-line documentation support is required with real time terminal access for connection to the engineers and managers. Such a system needs to handle diagrams, tables and text with equal facility. As yet no complete system is available, but some suppliers are extending their offerings and in time a comprehensive documentation package will become standard, one that integrates documentation into the minute by minute workings of engineers.

From the system specification, a **document of software requirements** is produced. Associated are the **communication interface specifications** and the **data base documents.** The software requirements at this stage should not contain application detail (defining how the product is to meet the user's needs). However, this level of software requirement probably defines the language and the operating system.

The software is partitioned into major units called **configuration items.** For each item, detailed requirements are formalized into a **specification document.** This in turn leads into **detailed requirement specifications** for each software component (which is usually made up of discrete software modules). The degree and formalism with which this flow of documented communication and record is carried out depend upon the company, who the customer is, and the size of the undertaking. But for each *requirement* document there must be a *design* document. This design document controls the implementation of the software.

Documentation for Software

Software is created as a list of declarative, imperative and conditional statements that are addressed not to a person but to a compiler (or equivalent) which itself is a software program. The statements are turned into more primitive statements which are addressed to the computer (called the **hardware**). When the software is "run by the hardware," the hardware executes each primitive statement that is pertinent (as determined by the conditional statements) for that execution. Because of the contained conditional statements in any software, any one execution run of the software will not follow all the statement pathways that exist in the program. In fact there are so many such pathways in software that, for a large software program, it can take years of regular use before a particular pathway is followed in the execution; and if that pathway has an error, or "bug," in it, then the program can fail. For some software, the number of potential pathways is so large that one can confidently state that some will never be followed during the life cycle of the product software.

Writing software. The original software document written by the software engineer is called the **source.** The **compiler** is the generic name for the software which turns the source into the **object** document. Before the software can be executed the object document has to be "loaded" into the hardware. Today it is possible for hardware to be constructed to execute directly from the source document. It is also possible that the source document can be written in the most primitive machine language (30 or more years ago, this was the only way).

Declarative statements define the **environment** and **data objects** that the imperative statements work within and upon respectively. Imperative statements define operations performed by the hardware upon the data objects or their primitive derivatives. **Conditional state-**

ments act as guards to sequences of imperative statements; those sequences are executed if and only if the guarding conditions are found to be true. **Identification points** throughout the software document (address points) mark nodal points in the network of pathways that is the structure for all software at its execution level. Upon this base a module structure can be superimposed. A network structure with a superimposed module structure will have address nodal points which are the only way into a modular unit of software.

The network structure can be modified in another way. Some groups of statements can be brought together and replaced by one call statement. The **call statement** causes the execution to leave the network, and to execute a **subroutine** of selfcontained software that returns to the network at the place it left it. Imagine the network to exist in a plane; then subroutines are like bunches of grapes hanging down from the plane. However, there is no constraint to attach the subroutine to one part of the network; each subroutine can be entered from any point in the network. In general, there is one "main" module which contains and connects a whole set of modules. This modular and subroutine structure should be explicitly defined in the source document.

Writing comments within software. The software writer has to "look up" to see what needs to be accomplished by the software, and then "look down" at the software language being employed to decide how these needs may be defined using the language. If the writer finds that the software contains no record of what is needed to be accomplished (when looking up), or of why a particular statement set was selected (when looking down), then the source document becomes progressively more unintelligible even to the original writer, as his or her memory fades (a matter of weeks). When software is unintelligible, it is quicker to rewrite than to work out all the missing comment information. So we learn two lessons about software documents from bitter experience:

1. Software that is used will always need to be modified to meet new needs *even* if errors (bugs) do not occur (but they always have).
2. Without comments even the original author can get sadly lost, and another software engineer can only cope by extensively rewriting.

This experience led to a tremendous plea to software engineers that they must **document** their software source (meaning they must include proper *comments*). The **comment statements** introduced into their source statements

(code) are for other software engineers and must be ignored by the compiler or program that turns the source document into an object document. It was further found that by "raising the level" of the language resource, the volume of comment statements could be reduced. Comment statements should explain what each language statement (or statement set) is achieving and, equally important, it should explain structure. At one time, program structures were unintelligible; Dijkstra [24] and others are responsible for introducing **structured programming** techniques into source documents, which, among other advantages, reduces the volume of structure comments needed.

Software design document. As the scope of the problem addressed by the software increased, it became necessary to break up the software into component pieces. The description of the software is the **software design document** (or **document set**), which identifies the various software components and defines how they interface with each other and the outside world. This world includes such elements as the user, the data base structures (which house the data objects), and communication between software in one hardware resource and software in another hardware resource. Data flow between the software components, and how the users relate to the changing functional state of the system, also have to be explicitly and rigorously defined in this design document (set).

For each software module (and subroutine) there is a section called a "preamble" which describes the module and its connection to the outside. The software structure within the module is defined overall by a more or less formal set of program design language (PDL) statements which grew out of structured programming techniques.

To make a computer system work, one has to communicate comprehensive instructions in the form of documents that the system can read. Software engineering is a specialized form of document writing.

Effect of change. We have indicated (Figure 45.5) the relationship between documentation and product cost. There is also a relationship between documentation and product life cycle; this resembles an analogous relationship between the language we use and the way we think. We encapsulate what we mean to say within our language; looking from the other side, we can observe that our language constrains how and what we can think. Similarly, the documentation associated with a system product reflects how we think about that product. The effect of the changes described below either causes the whole document to be rewritten, or causes only pertinent parts of the document to be modified. Documentation technology should be organized so that it not only facilitates change but also minimizes it.

Two basic factors are a source of continual change. First, the required need for an engineered product is in process of change within the user's operation. Indications are that the incidence of this change is increasing and will continue to do so. Second, new technology enables new or improved resources to be utilized in engineered products. It appears that the incidence of significant technology improvement and change is also increasing.

When these two rates of change reach a critical level for a particular product, design and development costs have to be amortized over such a short period that production costs will rise significantly. Because everything does not change, but only a small—though significant— percentage, engineers will be forced to maximize the reuse of the engineering that does not have to change. New internal design and development documentation standards are needed to keep effective records by which the cost of changes can be minimized.

The lessons being learned by developing new systems for DOD apply to a wider and wider range of engineered products as the incidence of requirement and technology change increases. This makes documentation, and the communication for which it is the protocol, a very significant factor (perhaps *the* significant factor) in economically successful engineering operations.

Analysis of the Components within a Document

Documentation for an engineer/scientist is a complete set of documents required for a particular use and user. The subject matter in the documents depends upon what the user needs to know, which in turn depends upon his or her background knowledge and the particulars of the use. Structure and organization vary depending on subject matter, but there are four basic structures for a document.

1. **Reference** or **catalog.** The user is assumed to know the subject matter well enough to find the information required by looking up some name or code in the document.
   Examples are reference manuals, journals, directories, etc.
   Generic structure: Look-up table.
2. **Guidelines** (for some activity or procedure). The user needs to know how to use something, or how to carry out a process. The guidelines may review the reason the document exists, but the reader is expected to know the environment of the activity.
   Examples are instructions, users' guides, rules of play etc.
   Generic structure: Sequence.
3. **Tutorial** (a document highly structured for self instruction). Usually it contains the same information as a reference manual, but is organized to enable readers to proceed step by step at their own pace, providing questions and answers which enable the reader to verify that the subject matter has been correctly interpreted and assimilated.
   Examples are tutorial text, programmed text.
   Generic structure: special sequence, organized for self teaching. It may contain extra structure that leads the reader to the sections matching his or her level of comprehension.
4. **Text** a general form in which to present information about a particular subject.
   Examples are textbooks, reports, specifications.
   Generic structure: hierarchical sequence.

B. H. Weil [25] notes two types of *science report*. One type, designated S1, represents science in the making, with its own vocabulary and modes of progress. The second type, S2, is more institutionalized, being based upon an inherited world of accepted concepts.

Internal engineering reports have a similar profile. Some reports deal with new technical concepts and are informal. These are of text type (above). The others are written to a defined format within a standard structure.

In all documents, there are three major *modes* of communication:

- Text—normal language sentence structures within paragraphs, which are formatted with headings and indentation.
- Table—a formal presentation of partitioned space. The partitions are marked off with lines and hold elements belonging to a list or matrix.
- Figure—diagrams and pictures.

The logical document.   Whereas the subject matter for a document usually employs all three modes of communication (text, table, and figure), there is always a *hierarchical pattern* for the document (portrayed in the table of contents), no matter what generic structure is used for the subject matter. The levels in the hierarchy may be named in descending order as follows:

Document;
Part;
Subpart;
Block;
Subblock;
Sub-subblock;
Line.

Figure 45.6 shows the three top levels in the document hierarchy. In specifications, the sections and appendices are *parts* of the document; typically these are organized into *text blocks, table blocks* and *figure blocks*. Each block has a reference number and title which, together with the number of the page on which the block is to be found, are entered into the table of contents, or list of tables, or list of illustrations.

In text blocks, the subject matter often consists of lists of paragraphs which are highlighted by indenting the paragraphs from the lefthand margin. The use of white space and typography gives specific subblocks and sub-subblocks a distinctive appearance, called **format.** Format plays a role in written communication analogous to that of body language in spoken communication. The collective formats associated with different types of subblocks and sub-subblocks are called the **style** of the document. Format and style are essential aspects of reading, whether the document is presented on a screen or on paper. Format and style can greatly affect document readability and they can convey relationships which are independent of the organization of the written subject matter.

Factors that cause the form and medium of documentation to change include the costs of producing, distributing and storage. The information in many documents is volatile and regularly changing. The time readers spend on documents is collectively much greater than that spent by authors; awareness of user costs attributable to poor documentation is becoming recognized.

The physical document.   A document is a string of symbols presented within a sequence of lines which themselves fall within a sequence of pages. The magnetic form of a document is typically represented by a string of ASCII (American Standard Code for Information Interchange) characters, each character being an 8 bit byte, with a byte representing up to 256 symbols. The ASCII standard associates particular symbols, for example, the lower case letter 'a' with the eight bit binary value 97 (decimal), which in octal representation is 141. The ASCII values associated with all the normal alphabetic, numeric, and punctuation symbols are fixed by the standard. There is, however, some variability in the values associated with the rarer symbols, as there is variability in placing these symbols on a typewriter keyboard. There is also variability in the selection of symbols that are available on a typewriter or printer.

For a document in magnetic form to be printed, there is need to embed into the string of symbols special ASCII characters (control characters) to represent such things as the end of a line and the end of a page.

Physical layout and special symbols.   Language in words alone lacks enough communication power to satisfy the needs of technical literature. To communicate meaning efficiently, it is necessary to introduce the following:

1. Typographical skills, which include layout structure and the use of white space.
2. "Shorthand" symbols such as $>$ $=$ $<$ %, etc.
3. Special relationships such as superscripts and subscripts.

Hartley [26] reports upon current research by typographic designers and psychologists. Communication of the message within the "written word" can be greatly facilitated by typographical design and the structural use of white space.

Automated support for documentation.   Software can supply considerable assistance to engineering and science by providing systems (over and above word processing) to assist in

• The capture of subject matter to go into a document;
• Formatting of the captured matter;

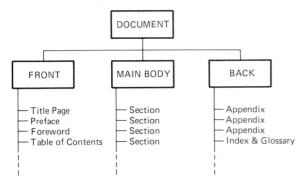

Figure 45.6. The top levels of the document heirarchy.

- Storage and retrieval of documents;
- Presentation and examination of stored documents.

How can a document be defined so that it can be represented in a computer system? One way is to use a syntactic definition language to describe the constituent parts of the document. The following illustrates the technique by partially defining a document using N. Wirth's [27] notation:

$$document = \langle part \rangle$$

A document is made up of one or more parts.

$$part = \langle subpart \rangle$$

A part is made up of one or more subparts.

$$subpart = \langle block \rangle$$

A subpart is made of one or more blocks.

$$block = [coded\text{-}identifier]\ title\ \langle subblock \rangle$$

A block may be labeled with a coded-identifier, has a title and is made up of one or more subblocks.

$$subblock = text \mid table \mid figure$$

A subblock may be a text subblock, a table subblock or a figure subblock.

A full specification of document would include all the possible things a document could be. In the above notation, the { } (curly braces) indicate that the contained object can be repeated; the [ ] (square brackets) indicate that the contained object is optional; and the ¦ -interrupted vertical line is a Boolean **or.**

Computer systems that deal with technical documentation do not currently address the whole problem. The magnetic media do not easily capture the physical typographical features or the special symbols. Further, few display screens are document paper size. Only very recently have computer driven printers put most of the technical document printing needs together. Considerable software and hardware capability as well as system flexibility are required to print diagrams and ruled tables with lettering running both vertically and horizontally. The package needs routines by which to paginate files and to show the style and format of the subject matter on

the selected pages. Further, this software should automate the production of the table of contents and the index.

Typically, computer driven printers are not of sufficient quality for original document production. However, a mixture of xerography and laser techniques has achieved both the needed speed and quality. The requisite flexibility is attained with dot matrices, but full quality graphics require hundreds of dots per inch. Such printers need detailed instructions to be embedded within the subject material; thus the necessary software is so large. However, the demand for sophisticated engineering documentation support systems on a par with CAD/CAM systems is definitely there. Its realization awaits only recognition by engineering management and an affordable price.

45.4 DOCUMENTATION TECHNOLOGY— FUTURE TRENDS

The discovery of the nature of things is enabled by the way we think about what we observe. For instance, the system of Roman numerals shows how the Romans thought about numbers, and quantities. Had such thinking continued, it would have severely restricted if not prevented outright the growth of mathematics. Similarly, the act of documentation forces us to make explicit and objective our inner mental knowledge, which in turn influences how we think and how we represent our concepts.

The science which probes how humankind thinks and holds knowledge leads to documentation engineering that is concerned not only with on-line availability and documentation services but also with how the human mind assimilates new knowledge in relation to the knowledge already held. We can expect to see significant changes which will make it easier for us to acquire knowledge and understanding, and give us more effective ways to represent those gains. Finally, computers will provide services to make it easier to access, store, retrieve, read and comprehend records, as well as to communicate and thus enable us to know about and make contact with technological advances in a form more suited to our needs.

Changes in Documentation Issues

We have examined a number of fundamental issues which underlie documentation. They start with the need to establish a record and continue with a person's need to know. Next comes the means of communication by which the need to know is satisfied by access to the record. Then there is the issue of the infrastructure of concepts and knowledge so as to facilitate the effective flow of meaning via communication. The more clearly understood and widely accepted is meaning, the greater is the use of formalism in terms of structure at all levels. Structure itself includes, for instance, the formulation of new words such as "radar." Formulation of documentation standards is also structure, and this becomes the essential protocol for clear and efficient communication. These standards are issues.

We can see that all these issues are in the process of change; the effects of different changes interact and affect the resolution of the other issues.

As we have shown, software engineering is a form of documentation. Software involves specialized use of language. As we come to grips with a software system, we have to tell it what we want to do. The usual approach is reading a user's guide. Alternatively, the user's guide can be placed on-line (incorporated within the system) and we can make requests until we find out what we need to know.

The latter approach is an example of a document changing from a conventional paper volume to a computer document. What actually changes is how we use the document. We turn pages of the paper volume; we enter commands to extract information from the computer document. Such commands are in a special language, and the form of that language is a structure. Gradually, standards for such structures emerge and often become part of some curriculum.

Each year many of these issues are addressed within the volume published by the American Society for Information Science [28]. This volume reviews information science and technology and deals with what is being done to provide accessibility of pertinent information from available literature.

Documentation Technology—Our Work Interface

The development of computer systems and software provides new means by which every person on the work force will be enabled to perform. Eventually a "paperless society" will emerge in which most recording and communicating will be done by machine media. It is doubtful that paper will disappear all together, but it will not be nearly as necessary as it is today. Lancaster [29] discusses this trend in regard to the intelligence community. Computer systems will change all our methods of storing, manipulating and transferring data.

Computer systems on their own, however, will not address the real problem, which is the exponential growth of documents. Everyone has had the experience of feeling that, within a given area, the knowledge inside the human mind is at least two orders of magnitude more compact than it appears possible to achieve within any document.

Some interesting research has been carried out at the Jet Propulsion Laboratory [30] which showed the possibility of creating a formal data base and then from it deriving a document with a selected set of information such as a specific person may require. It would be possible therefore to hold the information in a very structured form and then use routines to extract particular views of this base for specific readers. The computer processing involved in JPL's experiment was considerable, but then their experimental demonstration of the method was the very first attempt.

We have indicated how computer systems will have to address the user's need to know how to use the systems themselves, and we have indicated that the documentation to satisfy this need will be part of the magnetic storage, in which case a system will then have to provide the user with a standard way to "leaf" through the document's contents. JPL's research suggests an extension of this technique. They have demonstrated there could be an organization with which it is possible to hold all the data about an object such as a computer system. And they have gone on to show how a person who has a particular need for information about that object could call upon software by means of a command language to obtain the information in the format desired.

Even if the practical realization of such a facility should be many years away, we have a clear indication that methods will be found to shrink the documentation volume as we now know it.

45.5 SUMMARY

Documentation preserves knowledge and information to serve as our collective civilized memory. The record is dynamically updated, extended and revised. Without effective contact with this collective record, as many feel is today's case, we find technological society in danger of killing itself with its own toxins. Yesterday's technology has ushered in today's problems, which in turn will be resolved by tomorrow's technology (inherent in the technological revolution, Figure 45.4). The underlying stability of this revolution is based upon our collective ability to learn and respond. It is not that today's problems are caused by yesterday's technology. The problems are a result of what we are as human beings, which causes us to develop and use the technology in the way we do. The technology progression therefore becomes a catalyst for revealing the deeper levels of what we are.

Our ability to learn and respond (to deal with today's problems) depends almost entirely upon how connected we are to each other and on how our collective knowledge base is connected to reality. It is the thesis of this chapter that documentation technology is a key to technological stability, and therefore to our own stability, as a society, as individuals.

The human being is very much at the center of the scientific enquiry into documentation, because documentation is not only responding directly to human need, but in this technological age is becoming part of the human process itself.

Basic to human endeavor is current experience and knowhow. Documentation addresses the knowledge and concept bases that are prerequisite for assimilation of the information to enable the learning of the pertinent knowhow. The objective of documentation is equally the recording and the communication of knowledge and concepts. In the communication process, from a document record to a human being, the knowledge and concepts already held within the human mind play a primary role in what meaning the reader extracts.

The author(s) of documentation must deal with the necessity that the knowledge and concept base of individual readers be up to a given state before they can successfully extract the intended information. Perhaps the most promising avenue of research is study of how the human mind learns and holds assimilated information.

As engineers and scientists, we must realize we are intimately involved with documentation and deeply concerned with its progress as a technology.

REFERENCES

[1] Loosjes, Th. P., *On Documentation of Scientific Literature*. London: Butterworth, 1973.

[2] Kinneavy, James L., *A Theory of Discourse* (Figs. 1.1–1.4 in Ch. 1). Englewood Cliffs, NJ: Prentice-Hall, 1971.

[3] Hartley, James, *The Psychology of Written Communication* (Sec. 3, 4: "Information by Design and Technology," "Beyond Print"). New York: Nichols, 1980.

[4] Moffett, James, *Coming on Center* (Ch. 12: "Inner Speech Writing, and Meditation"). Upper Montclair, NJ: Boynton/Cook, 1981.

[5] Olson, David R., "Writing: Divorce of the Author from the Text," in Barry Kroll and Roberta J. Vann, *Exploring*

[6] Hempel, Carl G., "The Fundamentals of Concept Formation in Empirical Science," in *International Encyclopedia of Unified Science*. Chicago: University of Chicago Press, 1952.

[7] Bourne, C. P., "The World Technical Journal Literature: An Estimate of Volume Origin, Language, Field, Indexing and Abstracting," *American Documents* 13,2,159 (1962).

[8] Price, D. J. de Solla, *Little Science, Big Science*. New York: Columbia University Press, 1965.

[9] Kent, A., *Information Analysis and Retrieval* New York: Becker and Hayes, 1971.

[10] Hawkins, D. T., and E. Caruso, Ch. 6, 11, respectively, in *Annual Review of Information Science and Technology,* Vol. 16 (1981). American Society for Information Science:

[11] Mambert, W. A., *Presenting Technical Ideas*. New York: John Wiley & Sons, 1968.

[12] Taylor, F. J., "Acquiring Knowledge from Prose and Continuous Discourse," in Michael. J. A. Howe, *Adult Learning: Psychological Research and Applications*. New York: John Wiley & Sons, 1977.

[13] Greeno, J. G., "On the Acquisition of a Simple Cognitive Structure," in Endel Tulning and Wayne Donaldson, *Organization of Memory*. New York: Academic Press, 1972.

[14] Flower, Linda, *Problem Solving Strategies For Writing*. New York: Harcourt Brace Jovanovich, 1981.

[15] Williams, Joseph, and Timothy Shopen, *Style and Variable in English*. Cambridge, MA: Winthrop, 1981.

[16] Lanham, R. A., *Revising Business Prose* (Scribner English Series). New York: Charles Scribner's Sons, 1981.

[17] Lane, J. C., "Writing the Technical Progress Report," in Benjamin Henry Weil, *The Technical Report*. New York: Van Nostrand Reinhold, 1958.

[18] Davis, D. S., "Common Faults and Recommended Practice in Writing Technical Reports," in Benjamin Henry Weil, *The Technical Report*. New York: Reinhold, 1954.

[19] Hartley, J., and I. Davies, "Programmed Learning and Educational Technology," in Michael. J. A. Howe, *Adult Learning: Psychological Research and Applications*. New York: John Wiley & Sons, 1977.

[20] Klare, G. R., "Assessing Readability, *Reading Research Quarterly* X,1,62 (1974–75).

[21] Fletcher, A. J., *Embedded Computer System Software Documentation Standardization:* A Tri-service Initiative. NSIA Software Conference Proceedings, Washington, D.C., Oct. 1981.

[22] Yourdon, E., and L. L. Constantine, *Structyred Design*. New York: Yourdon Press, 1978.

[23] DeMarco, T., *Structured Analysis and System Specification*. New York: Yourdon Press, 1978.

[24] Dahl, O. J., E. W. Dijkstra, and C. A. R. Hoare, *Structured Programming*. New York: Academic Press, 1972.

[25] Weil, B. H., *The Technical Report*. NY: Reinhold, 1954.

Speaking–Writing Relationships. Urbana, IL: National Council of Teachers of English (NCTE), 1981.

[26] Hartley, J., and P. Burnhill, "Understanding Instructional Text Typography, Layout and Design," in Michael Howe, *Adult Learning: Psychological Research and Applications.* New York: John Wiley & Sons, 1977.

[27] Wirth, N., "What Can We Do About the Unnecessary Diversity of Notation Syntactic Definitions." *Communications of the ACM,* Vol. 20, No. 11 (Nov. 1977).

[28] American Society For Information Science. (1981) *Annual Review of Information Science and Technology,* Vol. 16 (1981). Knowledge Industry Publications Inc.

[29] Lancaster, E. W., *Toward Paperless Informations Systems.* New York: Academic Press, 1978.

[30] Hartsough, C., Y. Yamamoto, and E. D. Callender, "Documentation Production from a Formal Data Base Jet Propulsion Laboratory," *ACM Sigdoc SIGOA,* International Conference on Systems Documentation, Jan. 1982.

46
Ergonomics

Roy L. Chafin

Human Factors Specialist

46.1 INTRODUCTION

The purpose of this chapter is to assist the computer system designer in creating a system which is "user friendly." This is accomplished by matching the system characteristics to the user characteristics. Both user cognitive and user physiological characteristics should be matched. User cognitive skills and limitations are addressed in the user-computer dialogue design. User physiological characteristics are addressed in the workstation design and are principally issues of physical comfort and glare reduction.

Ergonomics, or human factors, are system characteristics which influence the user's interaction with the system. They may be designed into the system using good human factors practices, or they may be the inadvertent result of neglect. However they are obtained, they determine whether the system is easy or hard to use, and, ultimately, how well the system is accepted. Which human factors are most appropriate depends upon the characteristics of the user and the characteristics of the tasks that are being performed.

This chapter discusses user analysis and task analysis to identify user and task characteristics. A set of human factors principles is presented for the designer to use in human factors design. The complex interaction between user and task characteristics and human factors issues precludes specific guidelines for system design except for very narrow applications. The intent of this chapter is to provide the designer with a basic understanding of human factors which will bring good judgment to the development of specific system requirements.

46.2 USER ANALYSIS

The object of user analysis is to identify the user characteristics which affect system design decisions. Although there are several dimensions on which users can be analyzed, the most useful is skill. We expect a user-computer dialogue designed for an expert user to be different from one designed for a novice user. This section presents a user skill level model along with several models of users interacting with system.

User Skill Level Model

The knowledge required to operate a system can be equated to user skill level. Shneiderman [1] suggests that two kinds of knowledge are required to operate a system. The first is **semantic knowledge,** the general knowledge of how a system works. It is the understanding of the system which allows the user to apply the system to the solution of a problem; it is the knowledge of the relationships between a system and the tasks being attempted.

The second kind of knowledge is **syntactic.** This is the specific and detailed knowledge of the actions and activities which allow the user to control and operate the system. A user who lacks both semantic and syntactic knowledge is defined as a **naive user** [2]. A user who has extensive semantic and syntactic knowledge is defined as an **expert user.** These are the two extremes of the user skill dimension. In between are **novice users** and **competent users.** More specific definitions for user skill levels follow.

Naive. The naive user lacks both semantic and syntactic knowledge. This user must determine both what the system can do in accomplishing a task and the specific commands to use. A system designed for a naive user should be easy to understand. It should provide semantic aids to the user by explaining each function, and syntactic aids by providing the alternatives available for system control. A menu command system is appropriate for the naive user.

Novice. The novice user generally understands the system (his semantic knowledge is adequate), but he doesn't know how to control the system effectively (his syntactic knowledge is weak). Again, the system should be easy to understand. A system designed for a novice user would not need the system explanations, in fact they would tend to become tedious. But he does need syntactic aids, such as menus, to guide him through its operation.

Competent. The competent user has good semantic and syntactic knowledge. The system designed should be easy to use; that is, it should require minimum effort. This user does not need either the semantic or the syntactic aids. A direct command system is appropriate at this level.

Expert. The expert user knows the system so well that he operates it automatically. At this level, the user does not have to think about how the system works or what to do to make it work. A system designed for an expert operator must be easy to use. Menus or prompts disturb automatic operations and are therefore disliked. It follows that a direct command system is essential for an expert user.

User Oriented Models

Other user dimensions relate to how the user interacts with the system.

Casual/dedicated. A **casual** user uses the system only once in awhile. The **dedicated** user needs the system to perform the duties of an occupation. The casual user tends, of course, to be less skilled than the dedicated user. Often the casual user is novice or competent where the dedicated user is competent or expert.

Committed/discretionary. A **committed** user *must* use the system; this user has no option for another way of accomplishing the task. A **discretionary** user may elect not to use the system if it is too difficult at his or her level. The effect of poor human factors is different for these two kinds of users. A committed user cannot avoid using the system, so any dissonance developed by a poor human factors design will emerge as lowered morale, higher absenteeism, higher labor turnover rates, or increased supervisory problems. A discretionary user will react to a poor human factors design by electing not to use the system, and find another way to accomplish a task.

Continuous/interrupted. Some users are on a system **continuously** (data entry, for example) and can apply all their attention to operating that system. Other users are **interrupted** by other activities (secretaries on word processors, for example). When the user is likely to have frequent interruptions, the system must be easy to put on hold and resume later.

46.3 TASK ANALYSIS

Task analysis describes in detail the sequence of the operation of the system. Its objective is to expose specific human factors issues. Task analysis is typically much more detailed than system functional requirements. **Functional requirements** relate to overall system objectives, whereas **task analysis** relates to the specific actions required of the user to accomplish the system objectives. Task analysis is best illustrated with an example.

A limited partnership in real estate is setting up an investment support program. The functional requirements of the program are

- Record individual transactions.
- Maintain a subscriber file.
- Maintain a selling agent file.
- Output reports on request.

Only one of the many possible operator sequences is presented in the following breakdown.

Data Input Task Analysis

Each case is entered as a complete transaction.

1. A new case is established when the operator enters a new subscriber's name.
2. Data from the subscription form is keyed in. At the same time, errors detected in previous entries in the

same case can be rectified by backing up to that prior entry and reentering the data.

3. At the conclusion of the case forms entry, the operator approves the writing of the data record on the case file.
4. After a case has been entered, the operator may suspect data problems. The case record is called up and displayed for review.
5. When errors are detected in the recorded data, the operator corrects them by using the program change mode.

Three important human factors issues are embodied in the preceding task analysis example.

1. The input data sequence in step 2 should follow the data sequence on the subscription form. (see Section 46.7)
2. Errors detected in step 2 require the capability of immediate recovery. (see Section 46.4)
3. In steps 4 and 5, the operator needs the capability of reviewing the data records and changing them as required. (see Section 46.4)

46.4 SYSTEM CAPABILITY

Human Factors Principle 1

Provide the user with the system capabilities needed to do the job.

Besides the clear functional capabilities required to accomplish the basic task, a set of background capabilities is required to support the user's specific needs. A user will find it very frustrating, for example, if a mistake cannot be rectified without starting over from the beginning of the system operation.

Display System States

One of the first things that a user needs is to know the present location of the command in the program which is now executing. Often this is inherent in the flow of dialogue, particularly for simple systems. For large systems, highly structured systems, or systems with similar operating modes, a specific display is necessary to identify the present state of the system. This display should be in some consistent location on the display screen, at the top for instance; it should relate to how the user understands the system structure (see Section 46.6). A printing terminal should identify a new state when it is entered. The state display does not have to be repeated because the user can look back through the printout for further reference.

Display Data

On a video display unit (VDU), the user often will lose track of previously entered data because it has rolled off the screen. The user should have the option of recalling previously entered data for verification. Again, this is typically not an issue with printing terminals because the input can be verified from the printout.

Data Editing

It is inevitable that mistakes will be made in entering data or command arguments. The user must have a convenient method for rectifying these mistakes.

Input Data Precision

Most input data is accurate and complete because it stands by itself. Some inputs, however, have special precision requirements. For example, keywords used for file access have to match the file keyword exactly. Or input data may have to match some internal data word, such as a count for a data categorizing accumulation. When the input data has accuracy requirements, the systems designer has several options in implementing the user-computer dialogue.

The simplest option to implement is to require that the input be exact. If the input data doesn't match the required accuracy, the user is informed and required to correct it or to input the data again. This mechanization tends to be very frustrating for a user, and unless the input data is quite simple, another method should be used.

Another mechanization is for the program to check the input data, then, if the data does not meet the precision requirements, make a best guess as to what the input should be. This approach is good if the consequence of the program making the wrong guess is not severe.

For example, in calling up display formats, if the wrong display is chosen, the consequence is a delay while the operator calls up the correct display. But if the consequence is that a file is inadvertently erased, then this technique should be avoided. If this system correction method is chosen, the system could tell the operator the choice that it has selected and ask the operator to confirm. But this procedure can become tedious to the operator and should be used only when the consequence of the action warrants it.

For extreme accuracy requirements, the most appropriate technique is first to check the input for the necessary match, then if the match is not obtained, present the operator with a list of choices. Let the operator pick one from that list, to retain a feeling of control.

Error Recovery

Errors are inevitable, so an error recovery capability is essential. In addition to user frustration, the lack of a convenient error recovery will significantly slow the operation of the system, since the user tends to become very cautious.

Control errors are commands which take the system into an undesired state. Special care is needed in the menu and prompt systems to allow the user to navigate out of an erroneous system state. Typically, one menu selection should be provided to take the system back to the previous state for control error recovery.

Data errors are the result of either keying errors or selection of the wrong data. Data error recovery entails going back to the entry point for that specific datum and reentering it. With a direct command system, corrections typically are easy because the correct data (or datum) can be entered reusing the command. Prompt systems require a way of going back to the previous prompt. A back-up key or back-up command can be included in the command repertoire to accomplish data error recovery.

HELP Function

HELP functions are on-line documentation that aids the user in operating the system. The appropriate level of on-line HELP depends on the user's skill level. Naive users need both semantic and syntactic aids. The on-line HELP function should explain the basic nature of the system (semantic knowledge) as well as the specific commands needed to control the system (syntactic knowledge).

Novice users may find an operating memory jogger helpful (semantic knowledge). This would be a short display of the basic functional elements of the system. The novice user also needs syntactic aids. These aids take the form of a command list with arguments. Competent users do not have a use for system aids but find a quick reference to the command list helpful as a memory jogger. An expert user will not need a HELP function, either semantic or syntactic.

The HELP function design should also reflect the anticipated frequency of use. Lesser used functions should have greater HELP availability. When there is a diversity of user skills, the HELP function should reflect the lowest skill level expected. It should also be unobtrusive, to avoid disturbing more skilled users.

An effective way of implementing HELP functions is to tailor the HELP display to the system state. Only that information which applies to the system function being performed should be displayed. After HELP has been called, the program should return to the same place in the operation that it left.

Variable depth HELP functions are also very effective for diversified user populations. The first HELP call displays an abbreviated command memory jogger (syntactic aid). The second HELP call displays a more detailed command list with argument definitions organized to provide some system understanding (extensive syntactic aid with small semantic aid). The third HELP call displays a description of the system functions (extreme semantic aid).

The user continues to request HELP functions until reaching the level that will provide the aid needed.

46.5 SYSTEM CHARACTERISTICS

Human Factors Principle 2

Match the system's characteristics to the user's characteristics.

The principal system characteristic which system designers need to consider is whether the system should be "easy to understand" or "easy to use".

An "easy to understand" system is designed so that the user can perceive what the system does and what has to be done to make it work. It has aids to understanding such as a HELP function, which is presented with sufficient text so that the user can easily understand what the system can do and what to do to make it work.

An "easy to use" system requires the least activity from the user, either cognitive or physical. Typically, an "easy to use" system translates to *minimum key strokes*. Whether the system is "easy to understand" or "easy to use" is essentially determined by the command format. Menu and prompt command formats should be "easy to understand" and direct command formats "easy to use". The primary concern of the system designer is to match the command format to the needs of the user as determined by user analysis.

The recommended command formats for users follow:

Naive user. The menu format is most appropriate for the naive user; it provides the semantic aids in the menu selection items. For naive users, each menu selection item should explain in some detail the functional aspects of that choice. The menu also allows the naive user to avoid command syntax. The user evaluates the function of each item in the menu and selects the appropriate one.

The menu format handles program control functions and a limited number of discrete data values very well, but it does not handle continuous variables well at all; a prompt format should be used for that kind of data. Again, for a naive user, the prompt should be very explanatory.

Novice user.   The menu format is also appropriate for the novice user. However, the novice user does not need extensive semantic aids, so the menu select items can be abbreviated. The prompt format is also appropriate, particularly for data entry oriented programs or serial control sequences. The prompts can be abbreviated because the novice user understands the function being performed and needs only a hint as a memory refresher to establish the program's current location. A direct command format can also serve the novice, provided the system is relatively simple.

Competent user.   The direct command format is most appropriate for the competent user, who can immediately key in the specific command. This user does not have to evaluate each item in a menu format, for example. The important issue in designing a direct command repertoire for a competent user is to make the commands mnemonic, since the selection of a command is a cognitive process. Each command should relate well to its function to aid as a memory recall. The prompt format should be used when a strict sequence of commands is required, so that the competent user needs not remember the actual sequence.

Expert user.   Direct command format is essential for the expert user. It fits the automatic mode of operating. The expert user is in complete control of the dialogue, both in sequence and in pacing. A mnemonic command is not as important because the expert user does not have to think about the command; it is accomplished as an automatic response. Menu and prompt formats are inappropriate because they tend to disrupt the expert user's automatic actions.

Combination.   A wide range in the user population calls for mixed command formats. Typically, menus are provided for the lower skill levels with menu bypass to direct commands for the higher skill level users. This arrangement is appropriate for users on a large system where the users' skill levels will vary over the range of functions (due to different frequencies of use). A mixed format is also appropriate for users who start at the naive or novice level and progress to the competent or expert level.

System Messages

The messages from the system to the operator should also match the users' characteristics. Messages for naive or novice users should be long enough to be self-explanatory. Messages for competent or expert users should be short for rapid display; they do not need to be self-explanatory because the user already understands them, needing only an identifier and a memory jogger. Messages for competent users should be mnemonic to aid in memory recall. *Coded* messages, however, should be avoided on all levels because they place a heavy burden on the user's memory.

Decision Span

Decision span is the number of items in the selection process. In a menu format, it is the number of items in the menu. In a direct command format, it is the number of separate commands in the command repertoire. A good rule of thumb is to limit the decision span to 10; command formats with decision spans greater than 10 should have built-in aids. For menu formats, a large decision span means that, most likely, the menu will extend to more than one display page. So some mechanism is needed to go back and forth between pages, since the user cannot be expected to remember matter from a page other than the one being displayed. For a direct command format, the user should be provided with a memory aid such as an abbreviated command list (HELP function).

Short Term Memory

Short term memory can be described as the cognitive process of reading or hearing an item and holding it in memory just long enough to transfer it to a keyboard entry. Human beings are information channels limited in this kind of cognitive processing, and for short term memory are limited as a rule to 5 to 7 items. For example, a 12 digit number (12 items) typically exceeds an individual's short term memory capacity.

An operation which exceeds a user's short term memory is error prone. That is, we can expect that the user will make errors in handling the data. A way of accommodating lengthy character strings is to "chunk" them into groups of more manageable size. For example, a long

distance telephone number (10 digits) is too large by itself, but chunked into area code (3 digits), exchange (3
digits), and line number (4 digits), it becomes manageable. Character strings greater than 5 to be processed by
a user's short term memory should be avoided. If they
cannot be avoided, then they should be chunked.

Consistency and Standardization

Whatever command format and message structure are
chosen, the individual commands and messages should
follow a consistent syntax philosophy. Commands which
do the same thing in different parts of the system should
be the same. For example, HALT, TERM, END and
STOP typically mean the same thing, but only one should
be used throughout the system. Also, functions which are
different should not have the same or even similar commands for different parts of the system.

46.6 USER MODELS

Human Factors Principle 3

The system should be compatible with the user's internal model.

Each individual approaching a system develops a mental model for that system. This internal model helps the
user to decide which commands to issue to cause the system to take a desired action. The user's success in effectively operating the system depends on how realistically
the model matches the system.

The user's internal model is developed from previous
experience with the system or other similar systems, abet-
ted by training and documentation. Often the user's internal model is a result of an understanding of a natural
process. For example, turning a car steering wheel clockwise causes the car to turn right—a natural motion. The
model can also have cultural origins. Moving a light
switch up to turn the light on is a cultural pattern in the
United States.

The system designer's task, then, is to determine the
user's likely internal model and design the system to
match that model as closely as possible. This is usually
done in the user-computer dialogue design.

The nature of the user's model is not always obvious to
the designer. The system designer can estimate the most
likely models for the population of users by examining
their previous experiences with similar systems, and by
looking at the "natural" attributes of the system and any
cultural patterns that might apply.

For inexperienced users (typically, naive and novice),

the system designer can expect that the user's internal
model will not be well developed. Therefore, the system
should be designed so that it can be presented to the user
in small, easy to understand increments. At first, the user
should be able to employ just a small part of the system
to accomplish a useful task, then as his or her internal
model expands through exposure to the system, expand
use of the system. The designer's task is to design the system in a segmented manner to emphasize such incremental operation and to provide understandable ways for the
user to accommodate new functions.

For experienced users (typically, competent and expert), the system designer can expect a well developed internal model. Again, aids to understanding are not as important as they are to naive/novice users. The system
should be presented to the competent/expert user as an
integrated package, so that the user can effectively employ the system over its entire range of functions. The
system should be designed for ease of navigation through
the range of functions rather than for ease of understanding the functions.

Documentation. Documentation aids in developing
the user's model (semantic knowledge) as well as providing the details for commanding the system (syntactic
knowledge). Documentation for naive/novice users
should contain significant semantic content. Documentation for competent/expert users should have much less
semantic content, emphasizing reference material as
memory refreshment.

Training. Training for the naive/novice user should
concentrate on internal model development (semantic
knowledge). Such training is most effective when it is incremental. That is, the user gains the semantic and syntactic knowledge and practice needed to accomplish a
small task first, then goes on to attempt additional tasks.
Training for the competent/expert should establish the
semantic knowledge needed to differentiate the new system from prior systems, that is, to adjust the user's internal model. It should then concentrate on the syntactic
knowledge needed to operate the system.

46.7 SYSTEM OPERATIONAL FLOW

Human Factors Principle 4

System operational flow should match the user's thought
processes.

A user will develop a line of thought which is related
to the problem at hand. It corresponds to the *model* of

the problem solving process that he or she has in mind. When system operation does not correspond to that line of thought, the user's thinking is interrupted; the user has to stop thinking about the problem being solved and start thinking about the system itself. This disturbs the user and tends to be frustrating. It requires extra mental effort and should be avoided.

For example, the system control sequence should correspond to the user's natural problem solving sequence. This would require minimum user attention to the operation of the system.

For data entry tasks, the data sequence requested by the system should follow the same sequence as the raw data. For example, when the data comes from a form, the system should sequence data requests to match the sequence of the form so the operator can go directly down the form from line to line and not have to jump around the form. Deviation from the natural data flow requires the operator to exert extra effort to locate data items, which generally violates the user's sense of what is right and how the system should work. The user tends to become dissatisfied with the system and the probability of error increases.

System response should match the user's mental pacing. The user prefers to apply continuous attention to the problem at hand until a closure point is reached; **closure** is the sense that a task has been accomplished, the objective has been reached, and the user can disconnect attention. Data entry typically requires an unbroken attention span until the data record is complete and recorded.

Within this restriction, short lapses by the system due to system response can be tolerated by the user, who can readily accommodate response times up to 1 second without losing attention. Further, although 5 second delays will register as a definite interruption, the user can normally bridge these without a break in attention span. But it is very difficult for a user to bridge a system response delay of greater than 10 seconds without disconnecting attention. Here, extra mental effort is required to reconnect after an excessive system response delay before a natural closure point is reached. Systems which thus break the user's natural attention span are looked upon as unfriendly.

The designer's responsibility is to determine user attention spans from detailed task analyses, identify closure points, and design systems to avoid interrupting attention spans.

A system should inform its user when a response is going to require more than 10 seconds, and give an estimate of the delay length. This allows the user to legiti-

mately disconnect his attention and apply it to something else without the stress of constantly monitoring the system for its return. It is also very helpful for the system to inform the user when it has returned; a soft bell signal is appropriate.

At times anomalous conditions, data input errors for example, force the system to interrupt the user. When the data is outside its expected range, the data entry sequence should be stopped immediately so that the user can rectify the mistake. The user must also be interrupted for system faults and errors which require a user reaction.

Several attention getting devices are available; the one chosen is determined by how closely the user is interacting with the display. For instance, if the user is paying close attention to the display, then an error message is appropriate because it will likely be seen. If the user looks at the display occasionally, then some form of blinking, bold patch, or color is appropriate to call the user's attention to the error message. If applying attention primarily to the task and operating in an automatic mode (expert user), the user may miss the error message on the display screen, even when it is emphasized. In this case, an audio alarm should be activated to break the user's concentration.

46.8 USER DISCOMFORT

Human Factors Principle 5

The system should avoid making the user physically uncomfortable.

User comfort at a terminal workstation is determined by two primary factors: unnatural body positions and eye strain. Awkward body positions typically have to be maintained by tensed muscles, which, over time, produces fatigue and discomfort. Restricted blood flow caused by poorly fitting furniture also results in fatigue and discomfort.

Physical comfort for a variety of users is obtained by adjustable furniture and equipment. The workstation chair should be adjustable in seat height, back height, and back inclination. A critical issue is that the individual's feet should be on the floor. If the chair adjustment is not sufficient, a short box for a foot rest can be provided. Also, the individual's seat and thighs should be roughly equally supported by the chair seat, a problem primarily for tall people. The seat height adjustment should accommodate user variability; chair back height

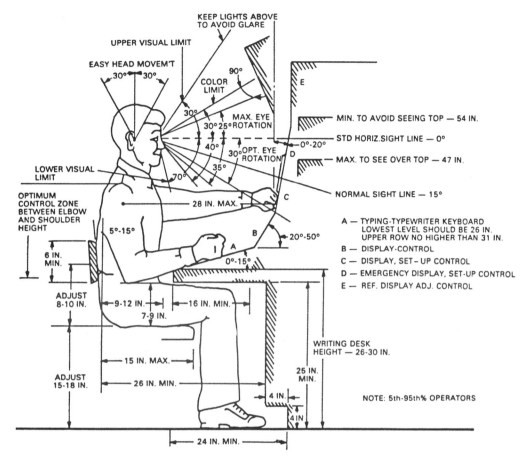

KEEP LIGHTS ABOVE
TO AVOID GLARE

UPPER VISUAL LIMIT

EASY HEAD MOVEM'T
30° 30°

90°

COLOR
LIMIT

30°

MAX. EYE
30° 25° ROTATION

40°

OPT. EYE
30° ROTATION

35°

70°

LOWER VISUAL
LIMIT

OPTIMUM
CONTROL ZONE
BETWEEN ELBOW
AND SHOULDER
HEIGHT

5°-15°

6 IN.
MIN.

ADJUST
8-10 IN.

9-12 IN.

7-9 IN.

16 IN. MIN.

B

A

0°-15°

28 IN. MAX.

C

20°-50°

15 IN. MAX.

ADJUST
15-18 IN.

26 IN. MIN.

24 IN. MIN.

E

MIN. TO AVOID SEEING TOP — 54 IN.

STD HORIZ.SIGHT LINE — 0°

0°-20°

D

MAX. TO SEE OVER TOP — 47 IN.

NORMAL SIGHT LINE — 15°

A — TYPING-TYPEWRITER KEYBOARD
LOWEST LEVEL SHOULD BE 26 IN.
UPPER ROW NO HIGHER THAN 31 IN.

B — DISPLAY-CONTROL

C — DISPLAY, SET-UP CONTROL

D — EMERGENCY DISPLAY, SET-UP CONTROL

E — REF. DISPLAY ADJ. CONTROL

WRITING DESK
HEIGHT — 26-30 IN.

25 IN.
MIN.

4 IN.

4 IN.

NOTE: 5th-95th% OPERATORS

Figure 46.1. The ideal ergonomic work station allows adjustment for maximum efficiency and comfort. (Courtesy Design West, Irvine, CA)

and inclination adjustability provides back support for people of different sizes (Figure 46.1).

The table height should place the keyboard in a natural position for the user's hands. An important terminal feature, a detachable keyboard, allows the user to sit at a convenient distance from the screen and position the keyboard for comfort. This flexibility is particularly important for users wearing bifocal glasses, which can be extremely uncomfortable if screen distance and keyboard positioning cannot be adjusted separately.

The other major factor is eye strain due to glare from incident light sources. There are three basic methods of reducing glare:

1. A tiltable screen allows adjustment for minimum reflection from incident light.

2. An antireflective coating or screen fitted onto the CRT can effectively reduce glare (but care must be taken in maintaining the proper contrast between the screen characters and the CRT background).

3. Lights can be placed relative to the CRT screen so that reflections are avoided.

The normal eye line of sight for a user looking at a VDU is approximately 15–20 degrees below the horizontal (see figure). The screen should be placed normal to the line of sight, between 16 and 24 inches from the eye. Any incident light from light fixtures or windows should be beyond a 20 degree angle from the normal line of sight.

The comfort issue is important for all users. It is particularly critical for dedicated users who spend full working days at a terminal workstation. Sitting at a terminal for an extended time is usually fatiguing, even in a well designed and well adjusted workstation. The operator's work schedule should provide adequate rest periods for moving around to counteract body stiffness from relatively fixed operational positions. Five minutes' rest every hour is recommended for extended work schedules.

46.9 SUMMARY

Ergonomics in computer systems is the application of human factors principles and practices to the design of the systems. The objective is to match computer systems to user populations to create "user friendly" systems. The first step in applying human factors practice is to perform a user analysis which will characterize a user population. The next step is to perform a task analysis to identify the human factors issues involved with the system of interest. Human factors principles 1 through 5 are applied to the user characteristics and the system human factors issues to determine the specific human factors characteristics which are most appropriate.

REFERENCES

[1] Shneiderman, B., *Software Psychology Human Factors in Computer and Information Systems.* Cambridge, MA: Winthrop, 1980.

[2] Chafin, R. L., "A Model for the Control Mode Man-Computer Interface Dialogue," 17th Annual Conference on Manual Control, UCLA, Los Angeles, June 16–18, 1981.

[3] Loftus, G. R., and E. F. Loftus, *Human Memory: The Processing of Information.* Hillsdale, NJ: Lawrence Erlbaum Associates, 1976.

[4] Miller, G. A., "The Magic Number Seven, Plus or Minus Two: Some Limits on Our Capacity for Processing Information", *Psychological Review,* 63 (1956), pp. 81–97.

[5] Cheriton, D. R., "Man-Machine Interface Design for Time-Sharing Systems," *Proceedings of the ACM Annual Conference,* October 20–22, 1976, Houston, Texas.

[6] McCormick, E. J., and M. S. Sanders, *Human Factors in Engineering and Design,* 5th Ed. New York: McGraw-Hill Book Company, 1982.

[7] Rohlfs, R., "User Interface Requirements," in *Infotech State of the Art Report: Convergence: Computers, Communications and Office Automation,* Vol. 2, Invited Papers. Infotech International Limited, Maidenhead, Berkshire, England, 1979.

47
Computer Security

Rita C. Summers

IBM Los Angeles Scientific Center

47.1 INTRODUCTION

As organizations automate their record keeping and their operations, computer security becomes vital to their functioning.

The computer has become the main repository for all kinds of records. Some of the records represent or control resources, such as money and inventory—resources that can be stolen through manipulation of the records. Some of the records are essential to the operation of an organization, some contain trade secrets and some describe persons whose privacy must be protected. Thus one aspect of computer security is the protection of information against inappropriate manipulation, destruction or disclosure.

Equally critical is the role of the computer in processes and on-line applications: process control at a chemical plant, for example, or airline reservations. These processes must be carried out correctly; the data they need must be protected; and the computing system must be available to carry them out in a timely way. So another aspect of computer security is maintenance of the integrity and availability of the computing system and of the applications.

An additional impetus for security comes from legal requirements. Laws in a number of countries and states prescribe how personal records are to be handled and other laws and regulations require organizations to control their assets properly—including assets maintained or controlled by a computing system.

In this chapter, we define **computer security** broadly to include all concepts, techniques, and measures relating to the protection of the computing system and the information that it maintains against either deliberate or accidental threats. We first consider in more detail the motivations for security measures, then list different possible strategies for computer security, such as controlling access to information. Next we consider actions and events that threaten security, and we describe technical problems that can prevent the computer from adequately dealing with the threats.

Since a conceptual framework is essential for research in security as well as for intelligent application of security techniques, formal models of security have been developed. We survey some important ones, and also consider informal models that are implicit in many software systems and application environments.

Having developed the necessary framework, we then consider specific measures for promoting security. These can be divided into two classes: technical measures implemented within the computing system, and nontechnical (usually administrative) measures implemented outside the computing system. We deal first with the measures taken within the system, summarizing general principles that have proved useful in designing systems to be secure. We describe techniques used in hardware and in operating systems to protect programs and data. We survey ways of identifying users who attempt access to a computing system. We describe encryption, a technique that can be used to guard against a wide variety of security threats. We discuss software packages that can control access to data and other resources.

Turning to the outside measures, we consider personnel, the physical security of the computing system and

791

auditing and controls as they relate to computerized systems. We then describe how an organization can establish a security program using the measures discussed.

Computing systems are accessed over communication lines and are connected into networks. We review the special security problems introduced by communications and networks and discuss the use of encryption as a security measure. Security aspects of local networks are also discussed.

Data base systems have their own special requirements; these are discussed. Security features of data base management systems are introduced, and research on the security of statistical data bases is summarized.

47.2 MOTIVATIONS AND STRATEGIES FOR COMPUTER SECURITY

A primary reason for security measures is to protect the *privacy* of individuals; that is, to give individuals some control over information about themselves that is maintained in computerized systems. Personal information appears in banking, credit, medical, and tax records and in many other kinds of records. More and more such information is being collected and kept, and there have been abuses, such as crucial decisions based on inaccurate information, or the revelation of sensitive personal data. A number of countries now have privacy legislation. In the U.S., the Privacy Act of 1974 applies to all federal record systems and other laws apply to specific areas of the private sector, such as credit and banking. Many states also have privacy laws. (More information about privacy can be found in References [13], [31], and [47].)

Although privacy laws differ considerably from country to country, they are underlain by some common principles. We describe here the principles adopted by the Organization for Economic Cooperation and Development (OECD), which has 24 member nations [29]:

- There should be limits on the collection of personal data, and the data that is collected should be obtained lawfully and fairly, with the knowledge or consent of the subject where appropriate. (In this context the **subject** is the person the data is about.)
- Data should be relevant to the purposes for which it is collected and accurate, complete and up to date.
- The purposes for collecting the data should be specified when the data is collected and again whenever the purposes change (and the new purposes must be compatible with the old ones).
- The data must not, in general, be used for other purposes.

- Data should be protected by reasonable safeguard against "loss or unauthorized access, destruction, use, modification, or disclosure . . ." (In other words, data security should be provided.)
- It should be possible to find out what personal record systems exist, their main purposes, and the persons responsible for them (the controllers).
- Individuals should be able to find out whether a data bank has information about them and, if so, gain access to the information. A subject should also be able to challenge the data and, if successful, have it erased or corrected.
- A data controller should be accountable for complying with measures that implement these principles.

As another motivation for security related controls, U.S. legislation (the Foreign Corrupt Practices Act of 1977 [1]) requires all publicly held corporations to maintain internal accounting controls to ensure that transactions are executed in accordance with management's authorization, transactions are properly recorded, and access to assets is permitted only in accordance with management's authorization.

Computer related crime as a motivation for computer security is perhaps better publicized than documented [44], but there is reason to believe that it causes substantial losses [30].

There is no single strategy for achieving security. One approach is **access control,** ensuring that data is accessed only by authorized persons, in authorized ways. Access control is not concerned with how the authorized person uses information legitimately obtained. With a general strategy of access control, there is still a choice as to whether to try to *prevent* all unauthorized access, or to allow it to occur, but to *detect* it and take action against the violator.

Information flow control goes further: it attempts to control the flow of information within the computing system and as it leaves the computing system. A longer range goal, rarely aimed at in current systems, is **inference control** [9]. **Data integrity** means ensuring that data is not destroyed or improperly modified and that it is correct or reasonable, accurately reflecting the real objects that it describes. **Application integrity** means ensuring that an application (typically viewed as a system) continues to operate according to its specifications and to be available, and **system integrity** aims at the availability and correct operation of the entire computing system.

Clearly, these different strategies require different kinds of security techniques. Information flow control, for example, is much more demanding of an operating system than is access control and may also involve special programming languages. It is also true, however, that one security measure can contribute to more than one strategy. For example, preventing access by an unauthorized user also helps to protect the integrity of data, since such a user is more likely to change the data improperly.

A section of this chapter discusses models of access control and information flow control. Inference control is discussed as applied to statistical data bases. Measures to protect application and system integrity are discussed in various sections. This chapter does not deal specifically with data integrity, but Reference [13] can introduce the reader to this very important topic.

47.3 SECURITY THREATS AND PROBLEMS

Threats to the security of a computing system come from many sources; the following examples show how varied the sources are.

First, there are threats from *outside* the computing system. Computing system hardware (including data storage devices) can be physically damaged by flood, fire, earthquake, sabotage, traffic accident, or other disaster. The same events can also damage data stored away from the system on tapes, disks, or diskettes. If the wrong volume is used on the system, information may be accidentally destroyed. Off-line storage can be stolen or copied, as can printed output. Communication lines are vulnerable to eavesdropping or to insertion of unauthorized messages.

A person can get unauthorized access to data by masquerading as someone else. An application program can be improperly modified (using the normal procedures for changing programs). If an application lacks adequate safeguards, even its authorized users can perform improper actions, either deliberately or by accident. An authorized user may act as a spy, passing restricted information outside the system.

Thus people who are sources of threats may have legitimate access to the system—as application user, application programmer, system programmer, operator, system administrator—or may be outsiders who succeed in penetrating the system.

Within the computing system, we can have errors in application programs or operating systems, inadequate protection mechanisms in the hardware and operating system (resulting in failure to isolate user programs properly), or hardware failures. The immediate result is usually unauthorized reading or writing of data in memory or on disk. That in turn may lead to a system crash (with consequent **denial of service**), theft or improper modification of data, theft of proprietary software, or many other possible results.

Generic problems in system software may cause it to fail in its protection against threats. One of these is known as the TOCTTOU problem—time of check to time of use [24]. Some information (for example a parameter of a request to the operating system) is checked and found valid, but the information is *changed* by the user before the system actually carries out the request. Another class of problem is **residues.** When an area of memory is released by a user, or a file is deleted, the information stored in memory or on the disk may remain there, although it is inaccessible in the normal way. The information can then be read by the *next* user to whom the space is allocated.

Another problem, not guarded against by current systems, is the passing of information by **covert channels**— that is, by some means other than the normal channels provided by the computing system. For example, a program could convey information to the operator by varying its speed of reading a tape; or a program could convey information to another program by varying its amount of computation and use of memory, thus changing the rate of progress of the other program.

Before discussing security measures that can be taken to counter the various threats, we introduce models of security which are useful in describing the measures.

47.4 SECURITY MODELS

The Access Matrix Model

The best known security model is the access matrix model described by Lampson [19]. The basic elements of the model are **subjects, objects,** and **access types.** The model grew out of work on operating systems and each element can be interpreted in terms of operating system concepts. A subject is an active entity capable of accessing objects; in the operating system context, the subject is a **process** (sometimes defined as a program in execution). In a time sharing system, for example, a number of processes run concurrently on the same computer, sharing the memory and processor; each process represents a different user. An object is anything to which access is controlled; examples of objects known to an operating system are files, programs, and segments of memory. An access type is simply a kind of access to an object; for each type of object there is a set of possible access types. Files, for example, have access types such as READ, WRITE, or ERASE.

The access matrix $\mathcal{M}$ relates the three types of ele-

Table 47.1. Access Matrix

	Program 1	Segment A	Segment B
Process 1	READ EXECUTE	READ WRITE	
Process 2			READ

ments of the model. In this matrix the rows represent subjects and the columns represent objects. The cell $\mathcal{M}_{ij}$ contains the list of access types permitted to subject i for object j. (These are sometimes called *access rights, privileges,* or *permissions.*) Table 47.1 shows an access matrix, where Process 1 can read and execute Program 1, and can read and write Segment A, but has no access at all to Segment B; Process 2 can read Segment B, but has no access to Program 1 or Segment A. Since operating system subjects and objects can be created and destroyed dynamically, and access rights change continually, the dimensions and contents of the access matrix also change.

The elements of the access matrix model can also be given interpretations at a different level. The subjects then become the users of a computing system and they have rights to persistent resources such as application programs or data base objects.

For *implementing* access control (as opposed to using a model), it is generally inefficient to represent access control information with a matrix, since the matrix is typically sparse (there are many objects and subjects and relatively few rights). Two ways are commonly used to store access control information. An **access control list,** associated with an object, lists all the subjects who can access the object, along with their rights. The information of Table 47.1 is shown in access list form:

Access Control List for Program 1:
    Process 1 (READ, EXECUTE)
Access Control List for Segment A:
    Process 1 (READ, WRITE)
Access Control List for Segment B:
    Process 2 (READ)

A **capability list,** associated with a subject, lists all that subject's rights to all objects. Two capability lists based on Table 47.1 follow:

Capability List for Process 1:
    Program 1 (READ, EXECUTE)
    Segment A (READ, WRITE)

Capability List for Process 2:
    Segment B (READ)

Models Using Levels and Compartments

A different model was developed because the U.S. military wanted systems that would enforce military security policy. According to that policy, as described by Landwehr [20], information is either unclassified, or classified into **sensitivity** levels (confidential, secret, and top secret). People are given **clearance** to access information up to a certain sensitivity level. Thus a person cleared for secret information could also access confidential and unclassified information, but not top secret. The person must also have a **need to know** for the specific information. In addition, some information also has one or more **compartment** designations, such as NUCLEAR, and access to such information requires clearance for all of its compartments. A **security level** consists of both a sensitivity or clearance level and a set of compartments.

This policy has been formally specified as a first step toward the goal of demonstrating convincingly that computing systems correctly enforce the security policy, whatever the actions of programs and users. The best known model was developed by Bell and LaPadula [2, 26]. The subjects in this model again usually represent processes and the objects represent files or other containers of information. One security level (call it A) **dominates** another level B when (1) A's classification or clearance level is greater than or equal to B's, and (2) A's set of compartments contains B's.

The access types are the following: READ (observe only), APPEND (alter only), and WRITE (observe and alter). The state of the system is described by (1) the **current access set,** where each access is (subject, object, access type); (2) an access matrix (representing need to know); and (3) the security levels of all subjects and objects. The system state is changed by a **request.** The system's response to the request, and the new state, are determined by a **rule.** If it can be proved that each rule preserves security, so that any request results in a new secure state, then the system is secure.

A secure state is defined by the **simple security property,** and the **∗-property.** The simple security property is the following: for an "observe" access type, the level of the subject dominates the level of the object; in other words, "no reading upward in level".

The simple security condition would not prevent a spy with secret clearance from reading information from a secret object and writing it into a confidential object. The

*-property, which prevents such "writing downward," is defined as follows:

For READ the subject's level dominates the object's;
For APPEND the object's level dominates;
For WRITE the levels are equal.

A third property, **discretionary security,** requires every access to be authorized by the access matrix.

Information Flow Models

As Landwehr points out, the Bell and LaPadula model is still formulated in terms of access to objects, rather than in terms of information flow. The **lattice model,** described by Denning [7], treats information flow more directly and also generalizes levels and categories and their relationships. This model provides a basis for eventually analyzing source programs to determine whether they violate the information flow properties of a specific security structure.

Models Implied by Commercial Systems

Many operating systems, data base management systems and application systems provide access control facilities, and these usually imply an access matrix model. Some user or group of users has the authority to specify the contents of the access matrix. Since the number of objects may be very great, this authorization function is usually distributed among different people. That is, for any object, some user has the right to specify the column in the access matrix (or equivalently, the object's access control list).

A more detailed survey of security models can be found in Reference [20].

47.5 SECURITY MEASURES: WITHIN THE COMPUTING SYSTEM

This section describes technical measures that can be taken within the computing system to promote security. Some measures have to do with the structure and design of the system; they can be called **passive** measures. Other measures are **actively** taken specifically for security reasons.

Principles of Secure Systems

Some quite general principles can be stated about how to design security measures in hardware, in various levels of software, and also in system administration. The discus-

sion here is based on an influential 1975 article by Saltzer and Schroeder [36].

The design should be simple and small, to allow careful checking of its accuracy.

The default situation should be *no access,* with access requiring explicit permission. This principle is known as **fail-safe defaults;** it describes a *closed* system as opposed to an *open* one.

Every access must be checked against the access control information, including those occurring outside normal operation (as in recovery or maintenance). This is the principle of **complete mediation.**

A mechanism (a "lock") that demands two "keys" for access is safer than one requiring only a single key. (Saltzer and Schroeder use the analogy of the two keys required to open a bank safe deposit box.) Each key can be in the custody of a different component of the system. Then a single failure does not result in a security breach. This principle is known as **separation of privilege.**

The principle of **least privilege** states that "Every program and every user of the system should operate using the least set of privileges necessary to complete the job" [36, p. 1282].

According to the principle of **least common mechanism** (first stated by Popek [32]), the design should minimize the amount of mechanism that is shared by different users and which all users depend on for security. Such shared mechanism is crucial; keeping it small and isolated helps to keep it correct.

Security mechanisms must be psychologically acceptable. They should not interfere unduly with the work of users, and they should meet the needs of those who authorize access.

A final principle differs from the others in addressing not the design but its dissemination. It is generally believed that the design of a system should be *open* rather than secret. Although encryption keys, for example, must be secret, the encryption *mechanisms* that use them should be open to public scrutiny. They can then be reviewed by many experts, and users can therefore have more confidence in them. (In practice, encryption mechanisms are not completely public, and attempts are being made to control the dissemination of encryption research [10].)

Protection Techniques in Hardware and Operating Systems

Computing systems are typically shared by many users and many applications. The needs and privileges of these users and applications vary, and they differ as a whole from the needs and privileges of system components, such as the operating system. The hardware provides **protection features** that isolate executing programs from one another, protect the operating system from user programs, and allow only the operating system to perform sensitive operations such as physical I/O.

We begin our discussion with two of the most important and most universal of such features: **states of privilege** and **virtual memory.** The discussion makes use of the *process* concept that was introduced earlier.

States of privilege.   Certain machine instructions are intended for use only by the operating system. These include, for example, I/O instructions and the instructions that control the protection features themselves. In most computers, these instructions are valid only when the processor is executing in a **privileged state.** On System/370 [16] for example, supervisor state contrasts with problem state, which is used for application programs. A machine can have a number of privileged states, and these can be used for different operating system functions that themselves vary in privilege. The VAX-11/780 [42] has four states (called **access modes**): KERNEL, the most privileged, which is used for interrupt handling and physical I/O; EXECUTIVE, for higher-level I/O functions; SUPERVISOR, for command interpretation; and USER. Multics [35] generalizes the state concept, providing a number of **rings** of privilege.

Virtual memory.   Virtual memory, although having as its primary function the expansion of memory available to programs, is a valuable protection feature. The (real) memory of a computer provides a numbered sequence of cells that must be shared by all processes and all operating system components. A virtual memory is a corresponding sequence that can be used by a program as if it were real. The virtual memory seen by one process is not the same as that seen by another process. For example, real memory might provide 1 million bytes, while *each process* sees a virtual memory of 16 million bytes. The virtual memories of the different processes either do not overlap at all, or overlap at one end to allow the processes to share system code that resides there. Thus one process has absolutely no access to the private data and code of another process.

Virtual memory is considered as divided into **pages;** the page size is 2,048 or 4,096 bytes on the System/370 and 512 bytes on the VAX-11/780. Real memory is divided into **frames** of the same size. Page tables keep track of where each page is—either in a frame of real memory or on a storage device. On each memory reference, either the virtual address is translated by hardware into the corresponding real address, or (if the page is not in real memory) an interrupt occurs, so that the needed page can be brought in. Many systems (S/370, for example) also use a larger unit than the page, the **segment.** With a segmentation scheme, the page tables do not have to be in real memory at all times.

States of privilege and virtual memory can be used together to enforce appropriate access rights for processes. In the VAX-11, the page-table entry for each page specifies what kind of access (WRITE, READ, or none) is allowed from each access mode. As the mode of a process changes during execution (because it calls or returns from system procedures), different pages become accessible.

Virtual machine systems.   A still more powerful concept is the **virtual machine.** With a virtual machine system, such as VM/370 [39], each user has the illusion of commanding an entire computer, including a processor, memory, and I/O devices, but all of these virtual machines are implemented by a single real computing system. This structure provides an even higher degree of isolation among users.

Capability systems.   A different approach to protection uses capabilities. A **capability** can be described as a *ticket* that allows its holder to gain access to some object. The ticket specifies the object and the type of access. Capability protection is usually implemented by special hardware or microcode that interprets capabilities when they are used and prevents them from being wrongly copied or manufactured. Since capabilities can be passed around and even stored, they make it possible to implement quite flexible protection schemes. This very flexibility also leads to difficulty in controlling and auditing what capabilities have been given out, and in selectively revoking capabilities. An example of a capability machine is the Cambridge CAP system [48].

The Kernel Approach

A line of research that has resulted in several experimental operating systems is based on the concept of a **security kernel**—a relatively small portion of the operating system that is responsible for enforcing security policy. Flaws in other portions of the operating system can never threaten security because the kernel mediates *all* accesses. The kernel itself must be tamper proof; that is, there must be no way to modify it or interfere with its behavior. The kernel must be *verifiable;* it should be possible to demonstrate convincingly that the design implements the system's security policy correctly and that the programs of the kernel implement the design correctly. It is of course essential to the kernel approach that the security policy be concretely, even formally, stated. Nearly all of the kernel based systems use the Bell and LaPadula model.

One way of verifying a kernel is to *prove* that it is correct; special languages and verification programs have been developed for this purpose [4]. Other ways involve careful scrutiny of the code by experts, or penetration attempts by "tiger teams." (It is not necessary to demonstrate that the kernel is correct in all respects, but only that it correctly implements security policy.)

Hardware support for the kernel approach includes

- Checking each memory access, with independent control for different types of access;
- Ways to isolate the kernel (such as a kernel mode, or implementation of the kernel in read only memory);
- Support for the process concept;
- Efficient switching between modes and between processes.

One of the kernelized operating systems is KVM/370 [15], which is based on the VM/370 virtual machine system. The functions of the VM/370 monitor (the component that implements virtual machines) are split between a security kernel and a set of nonkernel monitors, one per security level. Each nonkernel monitor supports all the virtual machines at its level, and the kernel enforces the military security policy.

User Authentication Techniques

A prerequisite for almost any kind of security is accurate identification of users. By **authentication** the system verifies the user's claim of identity.

The most widely used technique is the **password,** a string of characters that the user must provide to gain access to a system. The system stores each password for comparison with the string presented by the user. (Often a one way transformation is used for the stored passwords, so that they are not intelligible if accidentally printed. The same transformation is applied to the password supplied by the user before it is compared with the stored password.)

A password scheme is economical, acceptable to most users and easy to implement. It has a number of problems, however. Although the method depends on the secrecy of the password, it is common for users to write down passwords in exposed places or divulge them to others. Other persons can observe the keying in of a password. If the terminal is itself a computer, it can try many passwords in a relatively short time (although a system can guard against this by allowing only a few erroneous attempts).

Another method that has been used to learn a password is **spoofing.** A user of a time sharing system writes a program that generates a display exactly like the system's sign-on display. The program is started and the terminal is then left to be used by a victim, who unknowingly communicates his or her password to the first user's program.

Other authentication techniques involve some machine readable object possessed by the user, such as a card or badge. But here, there is the danger of loss, theft or forgery of the object.

Promising techniques that are still primarily in the research stage involve recognizing some characteristic of the user, such as the voice, hand, fingerprint or signature. The technology to do this must be both accurate and cheap if it is to be widely used.

Logging

Logging consists of recording events so that they can be monitored at a later time. Logging is a valuable technique for both deterring and detecting unauthorized actions; it does not *prevent* such actions. Logging can be performed by applications, by data base management systems, or by special access control software. Operating systems sometimes provide basic logging facilities that can be used by these other components.

A typical entry in a log (sometimes also called an **audit trail**) might include the following

- User's identity;
- Transaction or job identifier;
- Name of the object being accessed (a file, for example);
- Type of access;
- Data values actually read or written;
- Date and time.

Useful features in a logging facility include

- Ways to specify the events to be logged without actually programming the logging;

- Ways to dynamically start and stop logging of selected events;
- Programs to generate reports from the log.

Encryption

The technique of encryption predates computers by many centuries. **Encryption** consists of transforming (encrypting or enciphering) data into a form that cannot be understood. The data are useful only to someone who possesses the special knowledge needed to restore them to their original form. Encryption can be used for data stored on external media (such as tapes or removable disk volumes), for data transmitted over communication lines, and also for data stored in the computing system.

The process of encryption takes a sequence of **plaintext,** P, applies to it an encryption procedure, $\mathscr{E}$, controlled by a **key,** K, to produce a **ciphertext** C. To recover the original plaintext, we apply a **decryption** procedure $\mathscr{D}$, controlled by the same key K. This may be written as follows:

$$\text{Encryption: } C = \mathscr{E}_K(P) \qquad (47.1)$$

$$\text{Decryption: } P = \mathscr{D}_K(C) \qquad (47.2)$$

In conventional encryption systems, the key K must be kept secret; the procedures $\mathscr{E}$ and $\mathscr{D}$ are normally public.

The strength of an encryption system (its resistance to being broken) can be described in terms of the kinds of attacks that it can survive. The strongest type of attack is the **chosen plaintext attack,** in which the attacker can submit any amount of any plaintext and determine the corresponding ciphertext. Current encryption systems are designed to withstand chosen plaintext attacks.

In 1977, the U.S. National Bureau of Standards adopted a standard encryption algorithm known as the **DES** [5]. The DES uses the same algorithm for both encryption and decryption. It uses a 64 bit key (of which 8 bits are for parity checking) to encrypt 64 bit blocks of plaintext. One reason for adopting a standard was to encourage inexpensive implementations of the algorithm, and a number of hardware DES devices are now marketed.

The DES is a **private key system;** that is, the keys must be kept secret. One of the problems in such systems is finding a way to securely distribute and maintain the keys. There have been proposed **public key systems** which make use of *two* keys (or procedures), a public one, $\mathscr{E}$, for encryption and a private one, $\mathscr{D}$, for decryption. A public procedure $\mathscr{E}$ is associated with each subscriber to the system. The two procedures must have the property that for any plaintext P, $\mathscr{D}(\mathscr{E}(P)) = P$, and it must not be feasible to derive $\mathscr{D}$ from $\mathscr{E}$. To send a message to subscriber A, we encrypt with $\mathscr{E}_A$. This encrypted message can be decrypted only by the possessor of $\mathscr{D}_A$, namely A. Public key systems are quite promising and have important applications (such as digital signatures), but research is still needed to develop practical algorithms that meet the requirements of the method.

Encryption, although an extremely valuable technique, does not solve all security problems. It cannot prevent destruction of data and it is difficult to apply to data as used within the computing system. Its application in network security is described in a later section. Surveys of cryptography can be found in References [11] and [21].

Software Packages for Access Control

A number of software packages provide access control and related functions. The market for these programs appears to be growing as users become more concerned about security. Three important ones are ACF2, RACF and SECURE [17], all intended for use with IBM operating systems. The functions provided by such packages typically include authentication of users, maintenance of access control information, checking of authorization to use files or other objects, logging, and production of reports. RACF, for example, allows files, storage volumes, applications, data base transactions, or user defined resources to be specified as protected objects. RACF maintains the access control list for each object. Users may belong to groups and receive all the privileges of their groups. RACF is basically an open system, in that resources not defined to RACF are not protected, whereas ACF2 is a closed system. RACF can however provide closed system protection for any specified set of resources.

47.6 SECURITY MEASURES: OUTSIDE THE COMPUTING SYSTEM

This section surveys some practices, primarily nontechnical and administrative, that are considered useful for security. Such practices are covered in some detail in Reference [18].

Physical Security

Physical security practices include controlling access to sensitive areas, such as the computing facility and even the data processing department as a whole. Many organizations have a policy of not allowing programmers, or anyone but operators, in the computer room. Access to terminals, especially those used for sensitive applications, may also be controlled. Employee cooperation in enforcing the access restrictions is often preferable to elaborate locks and fences. Libraries for storage of tapes and disks need their own area, and their own authorized personnel.

Classification of Data

An organization needs an explicit policy about confidentiality of data. Some companies define three or four levels of sensitivity and prescribe handling and disclosure procedures for data in each level. The policy should be made known in writing to each employee at hiring and periodically.

Personnel Considerations

Appropriate care in hiring and dealing with employees is of course important for security. Practices discussed in Reference [18] include:

- Ensuring vacations are taken;
- Rotating assignments periodically with an unpredictable schedule;
- Providing grievance channels that allow employees to discuss sources of dissatisfaction without jeopardizing their positions;
- Periodic performance evaluations, with supervisors trained to recognize danger signals (such as refusal of vacations or promotions, alcohol, or gambling);
- Employment termination procedures (avoiding layoffs if possible and carrying them out fairly, exit interviews, changing of passwords, notification of other employees).

In general, these practices are directed at avoiding situations where employees are motivated to misuse computers or where they have continuous access. Security advisors usually advocate prosecution of employees who have embezzled and dismissal of those who have violated security policy, but many employers hesitate to take such action, usually for fear of exposing the vulnerability of their systems or to avoid looking foolish.

Since security is not an organization's only objective, it may be a valid choice to sacrifice some security for other goals, such as better employee relations.

Auditing and Controls

The auditing profession is deeply involved with security, and there is a specialty within auditing (called EDP audit) which deals with computerized aspects of systems. Internal auditors, employed by an organization, maintain the organization's system of internal controls, and external auditors conduct periodic audits of those controls. Controls include a wide variety of measures, many of which can be viewed as security measures. More information about audit and control in computer environments can be found in References [13] and [43].

Computer security auditing aims at identifying and evaluating the security measures for a specific installation. Rahden [34] lists five types of computer security auditing:

1. **System development audit** of the procedures intended to ensure that only secure systems are developed;
2. **Application review** of the security controls in the design of a specific application;
3. **Installation security review** of all controls of the installation (administrative, technical, or physical);
4. **Security function review** of all generalized security functions that apply to multiple departments or applications (such as those of a data base management system);
5. **Controlled test** or **penetration study** to demonstrate security weaknesses.

Implementing a Security Program

Given some understanding of security threats and problems, and also of the measures available to counter them, how does an organization set up a realistic security program?

One important step is to classify data according to its sensitivity, and to establish a written policy about how data of each type is to be handled. As another step, data should have an *owner* who is responsible for managing its protection. Many organizations tend to leave the responsibility for security with the data processing organization. This is inappropriate, since it is the owners and users of the data who suffer the losses if something happens to their data. A security program works best if higher level management is involved.

Once management support has been obtained, the first step is usually a **risk analysis** [14, 34]. Risk analysis, as described in Reference [3], has two main aspects: (1) analyzing threats, and (2) identifying the undesirable events that can result. The threat analysis also identifies the security weaknesses that can permit each threat. Consider, for example, the threat of an unauthorized user accessing the system from a remote terminal using a password found on a printout in the trash. The corresponding security weaknesses would be the following: inadequate physical security of the terminal, failure to suppress printing of passwords, and inadequate physical security of sensitive trash. The undesirable events are usually categorized as follows: unauthorized disclosure, manipulation and use of data, and denial of service.

Once the risks have been analyzed, a **risk assessment** is carried out. The undesirable events are rated and ranked according to severity. (These ratings cannot, of course, be precise.) The *likelihood* of each event is then estimated, as is its acceptability. A program of security measures is then developed, with the cost of each measure being considered in relation to the losses it is intended to prevent. All of this information can then be used as the basis for management decisions about the security program. After the program is implemented, it needs to be monitored continuously for effectiveness and periodically evaluated.

47.7 COMMUNICATION AND NETWORK SECURITY

Security Problems

Since users increasingly access computing systems from remote locations, careful attention must be given to problems of **communication security.** Also increasingly important are security problems deriving from the connection of computers into **networks.** We consider communication and network security together.

The transmission mechanisms used for data communication are vulnerable to two types of intrusion. A **passive** intruder "listens" to the communications; an **active** intruder can alter or insert messages, or retransmit valid messages. Both types of intrusion can be accomplished through wiretapping; passive intrusion can be done by picking up microwave or satellite transmissions. Vulnerabilities also exist at switching centers (themselves computing systems) and in the interfaces of computing systems (**nodes**) to the network. These vulnerabilities are of great practical importance in applications such as electronic funds transfer (EFT), in which billions of dollars are transferred daily, and a single message can involve millions.

Some of the objectives of network security measures are the following:

• To protect privacy by preventing unauthorized listening to messages;

• To authenticate users and messages;
• To prevent disruption of network operation (which can occur through blocking of message delivery, alteration of messages, or overloading of the network);
• To assist in access control.

Physical security measures can help (buried cables, for example), but the most important measure is encryption.

Use of Encryption

One issue in encryption of messages is the level of the computing system at which encryption is done. Encryption is the most efficiently done just before the message goes out on the communication line; here, encryption can be done in conjunction with other manipulations, such as compression, packet formation, or checksum calculation. Encryption at this level is **data link encryption** [45]. A problem with this method is that either a single key must be used for all communications of a pair of nodes, or some central authority must be entrusted with all the users' keys. Also, the security of a message depends on the correct functioning of all levels of system software that intervene between the user and the communication line. In **end to end encryption,** the key is chosen by the user or application and not divulged to other system components (except the encryption mechanism itself); the key can be changed whenever there is a possibility of compromise.

One of the most difficult problems in managing network security is **key distribution.** With conventional (secret key) systems, a key is typically needed for each potential pair of communicators, so that the number of keys is large. The keys must be distributed in some secure way. One approach is a central **key distribution center (KDC),** which maintains all the keys and has (by prearrangement) a special key for communicating with each node on the network. When one node wants to communicate with another, it asks the KDC to send both participants the appropriate keys. Such an approach is vulnerable to failure of the KDC, and the KDC itself may become a bottleneck. Refinements are possible, such as keeping frequently used keys at each node, or distributing the key distribution function among all the nodes.

Public key systems have similar problems. Here there is no need to distribute secret keys, but there is a need to keep the public listing of keys correct and up to date. The keeper of this listing must authenticate all changes. A sender who has been given the public key of a potential receiver needs assurance that it is correct. Key distribution is discussed in References [23, 27, and 33].

Authentication

An extremely important communication security problem is authentication of users. We have noted some drawbacks of password techniques; in addition, passwords can be compromised by passive intrusion if they are communicated in plaintext. One technique to prevent such compromise is for the system to call back the user, using a list of telephone numbers that it keeps. This at least restricts access to authorized locations.

Messages must also be authenticated. How does a receiver of a message validate it, in the face of possible message alteration or insertion? Digital signatures offers a means to authenticate both users and messages.

Digital Signatures

A paper transaction (such as a check or order) is typically authenticated by a handwritten signature. Electronic transactions need *digital* signatures. Various schemes have been developed to use encryption for this purpose. A digital signature scheme has these minimum requirements:

- It should not be possible to forge a signature.
- The receiver must be able to validate the signature at the time the message is received and also to demonstrate at a later time that a valid message was received.
- The sender should not be able to repudiate the message later.

Both public key and conventional encryption have been proposed as the bases for signature schemes, which are summarized in References [22] and [33]. In the public key proposal, the sender encrypts the message with his or her own private key, and the receiver decrypts it with the sender's public key. If the message is then intelligible, it is valid. Without additional refinements, however, this scheme does not prevent repudiation of messages (by a claim that a key was compromised and someone forged the message in question) and it does not allow validation at a later time. The conventional scheme requires that a central authority encrypt and later authenticate signatures. Development of digital signature schemes is continuing (see, for example, Reference [25]). Their practical success will depend not only on the technology but on the entire environment (legal and procedural) in which they are used.

Security of Local Networks

A local network consists of computers and other devices that are connected within a limited geographical area (such as one building or a few buildings). Typically the network is privately owned. Although not as vulnerable as long haul networks, local networks cannot be regarded as secure. The cable or other transmission medium is spread throughout the local area and thus should be treated as subject to intrusion. Each node in the network needs some way to authenticate the messages arriving from other nodes, especially if these messages are requests for the recipient node's data and services.

Proposed solutions to this problem use encryption to provide for authentication and access control. Encryption creates **protected identifiers** that behave something like capabilities and which cannot be forged, or used if stolen. One proposal [12] uses public key encryption and another [28] uses conventional encryption.

47.8 DATA BASE SECURITY

Special Requirements

Data bases contain structured data that is maintained by a **data base management system (DBMS)**. The DBMS is usually a separate software component that runs on top of the operating system and provides the additional functions needed to enable use of the data base. A DBMS may also include functions to manage transactions. A DBMS assumes one or more **data models** according to which the data is structured. For example, the data may be structured as relations (tables), as hierarchies, or as networks. For briefness we consider here only tables; an example is Table 47.2.

Data base applications typically require a fine **granularity** of access control. That is, access is controlled not to tables as a whole but to certain columns and rows of tables. This is sometimes called **field level access control.** The DBMS (which understands the data model) usually provides its own access control, using the operating sys-

Table 47.2. Employee Table

Name	Dept.	Salary	Manager
Ball	Computer	35000	Chan
Chow	Shipping	18000	Diaz
Fox	Computer	39000	Chan
Katz	Mail	19000	Roth
Wood	Building	27000	Lee

Table 47.3. Employee Table (Restricted View)

Name	Dept.	Manager
Ball	Computer	Chan
Fox	Computer	Chan

tem only to protect the large containers (segments or files) in which the data is stored.

A way to provide field level control is through **views.** A view of the data base can be constructed from one or more of the basic data base tables. A view can eliminate columns or rows. The view in Table 47.3, for example, eliminates the salary column and all rows except those for employees in the computer department from the employee table, Table 47.2. Each user is given access only to those views that are needed in his or her job assignment. Views that eliminate *rows* provide **data dependent** access control (so-called because the user's access to a specific row depends on the data values in that row).

Another way to provide fine granularity of access control is to encapsulate sets of allowed accesses in precompiled transactions, and to grant users access to only certain transactions.

DBMS Authorization Facilities

A DBMS provides facilities that allow some users to specify access control information. The **authorizer** may be a central person or group, or authorization may be decentralized, with each group or individual owning or controlling a portion of the total data base. For example, in SQL/DS [41] the user who creates a new table can perform any operation on that table, can grant another user any of these privileges, and can revoke the grant. The grant can also allow the recipient to grant the privileges to still another user.

Since the complex validations required in data base systems could degrade performance if not carefully implemented, designers of these systems have given considerable attention to reducing overhead by having some of this work done prior to execution time (at compile time, for example). More information about authorization and enforcement of data base security can be found in Reference [13].

Security of Statistical Data Bases

This section summarizes research on the security of statistical data bases. What characterizes a statistical data base? It contains information about individual people; statistical summaries (such as counts or sums) are freely available, but data about individuals is confidential. Examples of statistical data bases are census data and medical research data.

A threat to confidentiality comes from the **inference problem.** That is, the user may be able to correlate the statistical summaries with some prior knowledge. The result may be **compromise** or **disclosure.**

The data model assumed in research on statistical data bases is of a set of **records** for n individuals. Fields contain values of **attributes** (such as sex or age or salary). Users can query the data base, and there is assumed to be no change to the data base between the related queries of a potential intruder.

Some terminology:

n: the number of records in the data base;
C: a "characteristic formula"—such as

$$\text{SEX} = \text{'MALE' and AGE} < 30$$

Query: for example, "What is the average age of all males in the data base?"
Query set: the set of records satisfying C.

It is obviously very easy to compromise a data base when the query set size is small. For example, we can ask for the *average age* where (NAME = 'JOE') and learn Joe's age; user Dave can ask for the average age of Joe and Dave. It might seem reasonable to control this problem by requiring the query set size to be greater than some minimum. Any queries having appropriate query set sizes are *answerable.*

It turns out that this is not enough, however; an intruder can develop a formula called the **tracker** that allows compromise in spite of limits for answerable queries. A tracker for a specific individual can be developed quite easily if the intruder has prior knowledge of an answerable query that uniquely characterizes the individual. And even a *general* tracker, which works for anyone in the data base, can be guessed in a reasonable number of tries.

Certain defenses can be used against compromise. One is to **perturb** the data, by adding to it (either before or after computing the statistic) a pseudorandom value that depends on the data. Another defense is to release only a random sample of the original data base. This technique is used successfully for census data, but is not practical for a rapidly changing data base. Audit trails can detect (but not prevent) sequences of queries that attempt compromise. Data swapping, a technique under research, attempts to build a new data base that produces the same statistics as the original data base, but that contains different records. Another technique, random sample queries, randomly determines which records are in a *sampled* query set and computes the statistic from this sampled set. More information about these techniques can be found in References [8, 37, and 38].

In summary, most statistical data bases are easy to compromise. A growing body of research has been revealing the bad news; useful defenses are now beginning to emerge.

47.9 CONCLUSION

This chapter has summarized the main threats to computer security, introduced models that provide a conceptual framework, and surveyed the technology that is developing to counter the threats. It has also outlined practical steps that organizations can take to protect their data and systems.

There is increased awareness of the necessity for security, and there has been considerable success in developing solutions for security problems. However, security rarely receives the priority that it warrants. Computers have become central in our social and economic lives, and rapidly changing technology is introducing new vulnerabilities with new uses. The sponsors and designers of the new uses need to foresee and avoid these vulnerabilities. Computer security has taken on new importance.

REFERENCES

[1] Baruch, H., "The Foreign Corrupt Practices Act," *Harvard Business Review,* Vol.**57**, No. 1 (Jan.–Feb. 1979), pp. 32–50.

[2] Bell, D. E., and L. J. LaPadula, "Secure Computer System: Unified Exposition and Multics Interpretation," Report ESD-TR-75-306. Bedford, MA: MITRE Corp., March 1976.

[3] Campbell, R. P., and G. A. Sands, "A Modular Approach to Computer Security Risk Management," *AFIPS Conference Proceedings 48,* 1979 NCC, AFIPS Press, 293–303.

[4] Cheheyl, M. H., M. Gasser, G. A. Huff, and J. K. Millen, "Verifying Security," *Computing Surveys,* Vol. 13, No. 3 (Sept. 1981), pp. 279–339.

[5] Data Encryption Standard, National Bureau of Standards, FIPS Pub. 46, January 1977.

[6] Davies, D. W. (ed.), *Tutorial: The Security of Data in Networks.* Los Angeles: IEEE Computer Society, 1981.

[7] Denning, D. E., "A Lattice Model of Secure Information Flow," *Communications of the ACM,* Vol. 19, No. 5 (May 1976), pp. 236–43.

[8] Denning, D. E., "Secure Statistical Databases with Random Sample Queries," *ACM TODS,* Vol. 5, No. 3 (Sept. 1980), pp. 291–315.

[9] Denning, D. E., and P. J. Denning, "Data Security," *Computing Surveys,* Vol. 11, No. 3 (Sept. 1979), pp. 227–49.

[10] Denning, P. J., "A Scientist's View of Government Control over Scientific Publication," *Communications of the ACM,* Vol. 25, No. 2 (Feb. 1982), pp. 95–97.

[11] Diffie, W., and M. E. Hellman, "Privacy and Authentication: An Introduction to Cryptography," *Proceedings of the IEEE,* Vol. 67, No. 3 (Mar. 1979), pp. 397–427. Reprinted in [6], pp. 18–48.

[12] Donnelly, J. E., and J. G. Fletcher, "Resource Access Control in a Network Operating System," *ACM Pacific Regional Conference, 1980,* pp. 115–26.

[13] Fernandez, E. B., R. C. Summers and C. Wood, *Database Security and Integrity.* Reading, MA: Addison-Wesley, 1981.

[14] Fordyce, S., "Computer Security: A Current Assessment," *Computers and Security* Vol. 1, No. 1 (Jan. 1982), pp. 9–16.

[15] Gold, B. D., et al., "A Security Retrofit of VM/370," *AFIPS Conference Proceedings,* Vol. 48, 1979 NCC, pp. 335–44.

[16] IBM System/370 Principles of Operation. IBM Corporation Form No. GA22-7000.

[17] Johnston, R. E., "Security Software Packages—A Question and Answer Comparison of the 'Big 3,'" *Computer Security Journal,* Vol. 1, No. 1 (Spring 1981), pp. 15–38.

[18] Krauss, L. I., and A. MacGahan, *Computer Fraud and Countermeasures.* Englewood Cliffs, NJ: Prentice-Hall, 1979.

[19] Lampson, B. W., "Protection," Proceedings 5th Annual Princeton Conference on Information Sciences and Systems, 1971, pp. 437–43. Reprinted in *ACM Operating Systems Review,* Vol. 8, No. 1 (January 1974), pp. 18–24.

[20] Landwehr, C. E., "Formal Models for Computer Security," *Computing Surveys,* Vol. 13, No. 3 (Sept. 1981), pp. 247–78.

[21] Lempel, A., "Cryptology in Transition," *Computing Surveys,* Vol. 11, No. 4 (Dec. 1979), pp. 285–303.

[22] Matyas, S. M., "Digital Signatures—An Overview," *Computer Networks,* Vol. 3, No. 2 (April 1979), 87–94.

[23] Matyas, S. M., and C. H. Meyer, "Generation, Distribution and Installation of Cryptographic Keys," *IBM Systems Journal, Vol.* **17**, No. 2 (1978), pp. 126–37.

[24] McPhee, W. S., "Operating-System Integrity in OS/VS2," *IBM Systems Journal,* Vol. 13, No. 3 (1974), pp. 230–52.

[25] Meijer, H., and S. Akl, "Digital Signature Schemes for

Computer Communication Networks," in *Proceedings 7th Data Communications Symposium,* 1981, pp. 37–41. Available from ACM.

[26] Millen, J. K., "Security Kernel Validation in Practice," *Communications of the ACM,* Vol. 19, No. 5 (May 1976), pp. 243–50.

[27] Needham, R. M., and M. D. Schroeder, "Using Encryption for Authentication in Large Networks of Computers," *Communications of the ACM,* Vol. 21, No. 12 (Dec. 1978), pp. 993–99.

[28] Nessett, D. M., "Identifier Protection in a Distributed Operating System," *Operating Systems Review,* Vol. 16, No. 1 (Jan. 1982), pp. 26–31.

[29] "OECD Guidelines Governing the Protection of Privacy and Transborder Flows of Personal Data," *Computer Networks,* Vol. 5, No. 2 (Apr. 1981), pp. 127–41.

[30] Parker, D. B., "Vulnerabilities of EFTs to Intentionally Caused Losses," *Communications of the ACM,* Vol. 22, No. 12 (Dec. 1979), pp. 654–60.

[31] *Personal Privacy in an Information Society.* Report of the Privacy Protection Study Commission. U.S. Govt. Printing Office, Stock No. 052-003-00395-3, July 1977.

[32] Popek, G. J., "A Principle of Kernel Design," *AFIPS Conference Proceedings 43,* 1974 National Computer Conference, pp. 977–978.

[33] Popek, G. J., and C. S. Kline, "Encryption and Secure Computer Networks." *Computing Surveys,* Vol. 11, No. 4 (Dec. 1979), pp. 331–56.

[34] Rahden, H. R., "Computer Security Auditing," *WESCON 1979 Conference Record,* Vol. 14, No. 3. Reprinted in [46], pp. 345–51.

[35] Saltzer, J. H., "Protection and the Control of Information Sharing in Multics," *Communications of the ACM,* Vol. 17, No. 7 (July 1974), pp. 388–402.

[36] Saltzer, J. H., and M. D. Schroeder, "The Protection of Information in Computer Systems," *Proceedings of the IEEE,* Vol. 63, No. 9 (Sept. 1975), pp. 1278–1308.

[37] Schlörer, J., "Disclosure from Statistical Databases: Quantitative Aspects of Trackers," *ACM TODS,* Vol. 5, No. 4 (Dec. 1980), pp. 467–92.

[38] Schlörer, J., "Security of Statistical Databases: Multidimensional Transformation," *ACM TODS,* Vol. 6, No. 1 (Mar. 1981), 95–112.

[39] Seawright, L. H., and R. A. MacKinnon, "VM/370—A Study of Multiplicity and Usefulness," *IBM Systems Journal,* Vol. 18, No. 1 (1979), pp. 4–17.

[40] Shankar, K. S., "The Total Computer Security Problem: An Overview." *Computer,* Vol. 10, No. 6 (June 1977), pp. 50–73.

[41] SQL/Data System: Planning and Administration. IBM Corporation Form SH24-5014, Feb. 1982.

[42] Strecker, W. D., "VAX-11/780—A Virtual Address Extension to the DEC PDP-11 Family," in D. P. Siewiorek, C. G. Bell and A. Newell (eds.), *Computer Structures: Principles and Examples.* New York: McGraw-Hill, 1982.

[43] "Systems Auditability and Control Study." Altamonte Springs, FL.: Institute of Internal Auditors, 1977.

[44] Taber, J. K., "A Survey of Computer Crime Studies," *Computer/Law Journal,* Vol. 2, No. 2 (Spring 1980), pp. 275–327.

[45] Tanenbaum, A. S., *Computer Networks.* Englewood Cliffs, NJ: Prentice-Hall, 1981.

[46] Turn, R., (ed.), *Advances in Computer System Security.* Dedham, MA: Artech House, 1981.

[47] Turn, R., *Trusted Computer Systems: Needs and Incentives for Use in Government and the Private Sector.* Santa Monica, CA: The Rand Corporation, June 1981.

[48] Wilkes, M. V., and R. M. Needham, *The Cambridge CAP Computer and Its Operating System.* New York: Elsevier North Holland, 1979.

48
Algorithms

Kurt Maly

University of Minnesota

48.1 INTRODUCTION

According to the dictionary, an **algorithm** is a "rule of procedure for solving a mathematical problem that frequently involves repetition of an operation." The word is derived from the name of the Arab mathematician al-Khuwarizmi. In computer science, the term algorithm is somewhat more encompassing and refers to a broader concept. For instance, one possible definition is as follows:

An algorithm is a finite sequence of well defined instructions, each of which can be carried out mechanically within a finite amount of time; furthermore, an algorithm always halts.

An algorithm is the means to specify the solution of a problem. The important aspects of the above definition are:

1. The solution has to be obtained in finite time;
2. The instructions are unambiguous.

To avoid ambiguity, we insist in the definition that instructions can, at least in principle, be carried out mechanically. For example, the instruction

Tell me the result of dividing 7 by 2   (48.1)

given to two humans might produce either 3 or 3.5 as answers. In practice, then, we have to define a language such that sentences in the language—instructions—are completely unambiguous. For informal purposes (for instance, a general outline of the solution), it is quite acceptable to use a natural language such as English; but English is definitely not appropriate as the main language to state algorithms within computer science. In brief, the development of an algorithm is one of the major first steps in designing a computer program which, when executed, provides the solution to a given problem.

To obtain a proper perspective of the relevance of algorithms to computer science, study Figure 48.1 which shows some of the steps involved in the construction of a program and the application of various areas of computer science in this process. From this diagram, we can infer that the concept of an algorithm permeates the whole process, and that understanding algorithms and related issues forms an integral part of computer science.

In the following sections, we shall strive to provide a thorough explanation of algorithms and directly related concepts. We do assume that the reader has had a minimal exposure to computer science such as might be given in an introductory class. More precisely, in Section 48.2 we define an algorithmic language to be used in subsequent discussions. Following that, in Section 48.3, we address the issue of optimality, how to find "best" algorithm among those which solve the given problem. And finally, in Section 48.4 we present several techniques—ranging from simple to sophisticated—which lead to a good algorithm when applied to a well specified problem statement. However it should be clear that these techniques are only aids in the design and cannot replace the "spark of creation" in finding the solution to a problem.

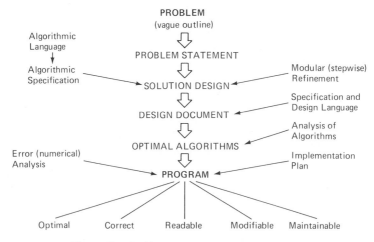

Figure 48.1. Problem-to-program development process.

48.2 AN ALGORITHMIC LANGUAGE

A language may be defined in several ways. In one approach we describe the language more or less informally using English which is the path we shall pursue in this paper; another, more formal approach defines the syntax of the language with a grammar and the semantics of the language with an interpreter, which defines the changes in the state of a hypothetical machine caused by executing a statement in the language. Before we describe the actual algorithmic language to be used, we shall discuss some of the design principles for, and goals of, an algorithmic language to make it a practical tool.

One of the main characteristics of an algorithmic language is that it should provide for a higher level of abstraction than a regular programming language. One should not have to worry about such implementation issues as whether an object is implemented as a packed array of characters or as an integer representing a character string. As a rule, algorithms should be general enough to be implemented in a variety of programming languages on a variety of computers. Hence most algorithmic languages do not have declarative statements; they use context and, if necessary, comments to describe data types.

However, an algorithmic language has to have a formal syntax which rejects ambiguous statements. Thus, an algorithm has to satisfy three criteria:

- It should be formal and specific enough to enable the implementer to develop a program;

- It should also be of a level high enough to let the implementer fully utilize all the features of the programming language selected as the implementation vehicle;
- It should be simple and openly supportive of modern problem-solving methodologies.

Simplicity means that one should be able to learn and use the language by reading a one or two page summary. As it is, the majority of algorithms published today in journals and books can be read by anybody familiar with PASCAL (indeed, most modern algorithmic languages can be traced back to a subset of ALGOL, from which PASCAL itself derives). Supportiveness rests on the observation that languages influence the thought process. For instance, if a language does not allow the expression of certain solutions, the language's user will not even think of these solutions. Since modern problem solving methodologies all involve structured processes (i.e. modular refinement, structured programming, stepwise refinement) a language to describe these and only these solutions should have judiciously selected control structures to support such ideas.

Before an example of an algorithm written in AL is given, a few comments on the above definition are appropriate. The assignment statement is actually more powerful than the definition might lead one to believe. Mainly this is because in this context a variable may represent any addressable entity which can be implemented on a computer. In the broadest sense, this includes functions over arbitrary domains. In most programming languages, functions (which can be used on both the lefthand and

Table 48.1. Summary of an Algorithmic Language*

1. DECLARATION
   Comments   /*this is an AL comment*/
   Assignment   **variable ← expression**

   Variable names
   Any string of alphabetic or numeric characters (including-,_), the first character of which must be alphabetic.

   Expression
   Any legal combination of constants, variables, operators, etc.

   Operators
   Include addition ($+$), multiplication($*$), subtraction($-$), division($/$), etc. The *logical operators* (which return a truth value) include equal ($=$), not equal ($\neq$), less than ($<$), less than or equal to ($\leq$), greater than ($>$), greater than or equal to ($\geq$), etc. Logical connectives include *and* ($\wedge$), *or* ($\vee$), etc. Either the symbolic form or the written expression of the operator is allowed.

   Input/Output   **input** variable list
        output variable list
   Where the variable list is a list of the variables whose values are to be printed or read. Items in the list are separated by commas.

   Compound statement   **begin**/*comment*/
        S_1;
        .
        .
        .
        S_n
        end/*comment*/
        or[S_1; S_2]
   Where the S_i are AL statements, either simple or compound.

   Halt statement   **halt**

2. CONTROL STRUCTURES
   If-then-else   **if** P **then** S_1
        if P **then** S_1 **else** S_2
   Where P is a predicate which evaluates to true or false.

   Case statement   **case** E **of**
        α_1 :S_1 ;
        .
        .
        .
        α_n :S_n ;
        error: S_{n+1}
        end/*case name*/
   Where E is an AL expression which evaluates to one of the α_i. Each α_i is any legitimate value of the expression E. S_i is an AL statement, either simple or compound.

   While statement   **while**(P) S
   Where P is a predicate and S a statement.

   Procedure definition   **procedure** name($f_{i1}, \ldots , f_{in}; f_{o1}, \ldots , f_{om}$)S
   Where the f_i's and f_o's represent formal input and output parameters.

   Procedure call   **name**($a_{i1}, \ldots , a_{in}; a_{o1}, \ldots , a_{om}$)
   Where the a_i's and a_o's represent actual input and output parameters.

3. CONVENIENCE FEATURES
   Terminate statement   **terminate**
   Error branch in case statement   See case statement above.

*See Maly and Hanson (listed in the references).

righthand sides of an assignment operator) are restricted to domains of consecutive integers—vectors or arrays—and the values of the functions have to be the same type. In AL we allow arbitrary domains and ranges and justify the use by giving an implementation scheme. Any function, for instance the one defined by:

$$\text{telephone\_number('joe')} \leftarrow 1234567;$$
$$\text{telephone\_number('ann')} \leftarrow 2345678$$
(48.2)

can be represented by two corresponding tuples, for instance:

$$\text{t\_n\_domain} := (\text{'joe', 'ann'})$$
$$\text{t\_n\_range} := (1234567, 2345678).$$
(48.3)

The correspondence between domain and range value is ordinal by position in the respective tuples. To set a function value, the domain tuple is searched for the matching domain value and, if found, the corresponding range value is entered. If no matching domain value is found, a new entry is added at the end. Thus we have defined, at least informally, the concept of a function (as opposed to a simple variable) in AL.

The next concept in AL in need of elaboration is the label in a case statement. The label may be any constant of a data type defined and used in the algorithm. To emphasize the importance of well specified input/output communications for a module, we separate the input and output parameters in the header of a procedure definition. The meaning of a name occurring in both lists (input, output) is that the corresponding entity in the calling procedure is actually modified (i.e. call by reference). If a name occurs only in the input list, only the value is transmitted and no change occurs in the corresponding entity in the calling procedure (i.e., call by value).

Finally, we have two convenience features. One, the terminate statement, is a bit dangerous in the sense that it can somewhat obfuscate clear flow of control. When a terminate statement is encountered while the body of a procedure or while statement is executing, control is transferred out of the body to the following statement. This requires a test, after the compound statement has executed, to decide which form of exit has occurred. The **error** label in the case statement allows us to specify corrective actions when an out-of-range condition occurs in evaluating the expression.

EXAMPLE Consider the following simple problem: given a text and a set of legal characters, determine the

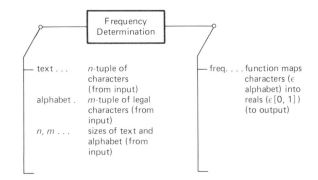

Figure 48.2. Problem statement for "frequency" problem.

frequency of these characters in the text. According to this informal specification, the problem statement in Figure 48.2 may be the one we think the user wants.

In the input/output specification of Figure 48.2 we give names to the major data structures, but at this point we are not committed to any particular implementation of them. The following simple algorithm solves this particular problem:

```
begin /*determine frequency of characters in given text*/
    input n, m, text, alphabet;
    i ← 1; /*initialize freq*/
    while (i ≤ m) [freq(alphabet(i)) ← 0; i ← i+1];
    det_freq(text, n, freq, alphabet, m; freq);
    output freq;
    procedure det_freq(text, n, freq, alpha, m; freq)
    begin
        i ← 1; count ← 0;
        while (i ≤ n) /*keep count of number of occurrences*/
        begin
            char ← text(i);
            if char ϵ alpha then [freq(char) ←freq(char)+1;
                                        count ← count + 1];
            i ← i + 1
        end;
        i ← 1; /*normalize*/
        while(i ≤ m) [freq(alpha(i)) ← freq(alpha(i))/count;
        i ← i + 1]
    end
end
```
(48.4)

This algorithm is not completely self-evident and cannot stand alone. It has to be considered in conjunction with the problem statement (Figure 48.2), and normally additional design specifications such as communication and solution structure have to be provided.

To elaborate some of the constructs used in the algorithm, we look first at the procedure heading for "det freq." Note that in the parameter list only the structure called "freq" can cause any change in the calling block. The actual parameters corresponding to text, alpha, n, and m cannot be modified from this procedure. Next, an unfamiliar sight might be the high-level operator ϵ, which appears in the test "char ϵ alpha." The value of this expression is true if the value of char is a member of the tuple alpha.

This operator (ϵ) illustrates one of the differences between algorithms and programs. In the algorithm, we only wish to specify concisely that we have to test whether or not a character is legal. At this point we are not concerned with whether or not the programming language used in the implementation features such an operator. For PASCAL we have the operator in when alpha is a set. The only other operation on alpha in the algorithm is an iteration over its elements, which PASCAL provides with the successor function. However, for FORTRAN, no ϵ operator exists and we have to write a small in-line function.

Analysis of Algorithm

To discuss the subject of algorithm analysis, we have to understand that in general a problem has many solutions and corresponding algorithms and that it is our decision which algorithm to implement. To see this, consider the problem described above. Another solution is described by the following algorithm segment:

```
begin
    .
    .  } initializations
    .
    i ← 1; count ← 0;
    while (i ≤ m)
    begin
        j ← 1; charcount ← 0; char ← alphabet(i);
        while (j ≤ n)
            [if char = text(j) then charcount ← charcount + 1;
            j ← j + 1];
        freq(char) ← charcount;
        i ← i + 1; count ← count + charcount
    end
    .
    .  } normalization
    .
end                                                    (48.5)
```

Analysis of the two algorithms will show that the first solution is far superior. The question we are faced with is essentially: how do we measure the "goodness" of an algorithm? Unfortunately, goodness is such a vague term

and open to different interpretations in different circumstances. For example, an algorithm which finds the necessary rocket adjustments for a vehicle landing on the moon takes a definition of "goodness" different from that assumed by an algorithm which computes the taxes for a single person to be run once a year on a microcomputer. In the first example, fast execution time is all important whereas in the second the major criteria will probably be the limited amount of space available in a microcomputer. Since these two objectives frequently are in an inverse relationship, one measures the time and space complexities of an algorithm separately and makes the selection dependent on the environment in which an algorithm is to be implemented.

Both complexities, time and space, require that we define a unit of measure. The analysis we describe in this section, *order analysis*, does not concern itself with actual running times of programs but with overall performance of algorithms. As such, we wish the analysis to be as independent as possible of the machine, the language and the compiler. Accordingly, we define as the unit of time complexity one execution of the "dominant" instruction. We cannot give a universal definition of *dominant*, since this depends very much on the type of problem to be solved. In general, the dominant instruction is an intrinsic part of the solution and not one which occurs because of the language or computer used. For instance, if the problem is sorting a list of keys, an appropriate dominant instruction is that which compares two keys. Instructions such as those for incrementing an index are only incidental and normally are provided in conjunction with the dominant instruction.

In the frequency problem discussed earlier, we may select the character test as the dominant instruction. In terms of space complexity, matters are much simpler. As the unit of space complexity we select the basic addressable entity of the data area of the algorithm. For example, if we select as a unit the amount of bits needed to store an integer, a 10-tuple of integers then consumes 10 units, and a complex number consumes 2 units.

One main ingredient for a practical analysis is still missing. When programs are executed with different inputs, they have different running times and different memory requirements. Some changes in input values will not greatly affect performance; for instance, the performances of the same sorting program executed with two different lists of 100 integers will be comparable; but execute first with a list of 100 integers and then with a list of 10,000 integers and the difference is immediately apparent.

To capture this behavior, we define a measure(s) of the

input called the *size* of the input and express the complexity of the algorithm as a function of this measure(s).

The performance of the algorithm changes as the other values of the input change and one defines the complexity of an algorithm as the **average performance** or the **worst performance** over all possible values and calls them *expected case complexity* or *worst case complexity* respectively. Sometimes the two are equal.

Let us now summarize the process of analyzing an algorithm to obtain its complexity.

Worst (average) case time complexity:

1. Determine "dominant" instruction (depends on problem).
2. Define input size parameter(s), call it(them) n(m, . . .).
3. Determine the number of times the dominant instruction(s) is to be executed in the worst (average) case as a function of n(m, . . .).

Worst (average) case space complexity:

1. Determine storage unit.
2. Define input size parameter(s).
3. Determine the number of times the dominant instruction(s) is to be executed in the worst (average) case as a function of n(m, . . .).

As an example, we analyze the two algorithms to solve the frequency problem. It turns out there is no difference in worst and average case complexities and we refer only to the complexity C. First, we select the character test instructions, char ϵ alphabet and char = text(j) respectively as the dominant instruction. Second, the parameters which influence program performance are obviously the lengths of the text and the alphabet, namely n and m. In the first algorithm, the character test operation is executed exactly n times, hence, we have

$$C(n,m) = n; \qquad (48.6)$$

whereas in the second algorithm this operation occurs in a doubly nested **while** iteration and we therefore have for the second algorithm

$$C(n,m) = n*m; \qquad (48.7)$$

From which analysis we conclude that for any $m > 1$, the second algorithm is inferior.

In the field of algorithm analysis, a sequence of standard measuring functions has been established and the complexities of algorithms are classified according to as to which of these functions has the same order.* The most important functions are: log n, n^α, α^n, α^{n^n} for $\alpha > 0$ and any combinations of these basic functions. Algorithms whose complexity functions are of the same order as these functions are said to have logarithmic, polynomial, exponential and hyperexponential complexity respectively. The special polynomial case with $\alpha = 1$ is referred to as *linear*. Thus, the first solution to the frequency problem is of linear order with respect to the length of the text.

48.3 ALGORITHM DEVELOPMENT TECHNIQUES

At this point, we are able to describe solutions algorithmically for problems amenable to execution on a computer. Further, we are able to analyze algorithms and, depending on the results, select that algorithm which works best in a given set of circumstances. What is missing is an aid (tools) to develop these solutions. Over the years, techniques have been developed which are applicable in certain well defined circumstances and which frequently lead directly to good algorithms. The list of techniques presented below is by no means inclusive but serves as an introduction.

Induction

The induction technique is based on the well known method in mathematics to prove theorems for integers called *induction proof*. In brief, to prove a theorem $T(n)$ for integers, show first that it holds for $n = 1$; that is, show that $T(1)$ is true. Next, assume (the induction hypothesis) that $T(1), \ldots, T(k - 1)$ are all true and show that it follows that $T(k)$ must also be true. Proving only those two statements, one can then conclude that T is true for all integers. The translation into terminology for algorithms is as follows:

Assuming the input x (of size n) to a problem T can be represented as n individual components, $x = (x_1, \ldots, x_n)$, and the output of T on an input of size k is denoted as $\bar{x}_k$, then

1. Write an algorithm, A, to obtain $\bar{x}_1$, i.e., solve the problem for inputs of size 1;
2. Write an algorithm, B, to obtain $\bar{x}_k$, given as input

---

*A function $f(n)$ is said to be of the same order as another function $g(n)$, $f(n) = 0(g(n))$, if there exist constants c_1, c_2, n_0 such that $c_1|g(n)| \leq |f(n)| \leq c_1|g(n)|$ for all $n > n_0$.

$\overline{x}_{k-1}$ and x_k, i.e., the induction hypothesis states that the problem of size $k - 1$ is already solved;

3. Place the algorithm A and B in the following framework algorithm to obtain the solution to T:

```
begin
    input n,x;
    x(1) ← A(x(1)); k←2;
    while(k≤n)[x̄(k)←B(x̄(k−1),x(k)); k←k+1];
    output x̄
end                                              (48.8)
```

As an example, we take T to be the problem of sorting an n-tuple of keys, of positive integers into ascending order. That is, n in the algorithm is the input size parameter, x is the tuple of keys and to represent $\overline{x}_k$ we use the k elements of keys rearranged in a tuple to have the property that any two consecutive elements x_i, x_{i+1} have the proper ordering relationship, that $x_i < x_{i+1}$ for all i from 1 to $k - 1$.

The algorithm in the first step is empty since any 1-tuple is sorted by default. The algorithm in the second step gets as input a sorted $(k - 1)$-tuple and a positive integer and has to produce as output a sorted k-tuple containing all the input elements. One informal solution to this problem compares the input integer successively to the sorted tuple until the proper insertion point is found and adjusts the position of the remaining elements accordingly. Formalizing this outline and placing it in the framework algorithm result in the following solution:

```
begin /*sort the n-tuple keys of positive integers*/
    input n,keys; keys(0) ← 0;
    k ← 2;
    while(k≤n)
    begin /*induction step-algorithm B*/
        safe ← keys(k); i←k − 1;
        while(safe < keys(i)) [keys(i+1)←keys(i);
                                        i←i−1];
        keys (i+1) ← safe;
        /*end of algorithm B*/
        k←k+1
    end
end                                              (48.9)
```

In the above algorithm we incorporated the concept of a 'fence' which is useful whenever we have to search a list of items for the occurrence of a given value. We can save the index test for the end of the list by adding such an element to the end of the list that the regular comparison of items will terminate the search. In the above example all the values are positive integers, hence we can guarantee that the test in the innermost iteration causes termination when we reach keys(0) which equals 0.

If we take the key comparison as our dominant instruction and let n be the input size parameter than the worst case complexity for this algorithm (called the insertion sort) is:

$$C(n) = \sum_{k=2}^{n} k$$

$$= n(n + 1)/2 - 1$$

$$= n^2/2 + 0(n). \qquad (48.10)$$

To understand this formulation, observe that, for a fixed k in the algorithm, the innermost iteration might have to compare safe against keys($k - 1$), key($k - 2$), ... , keys(1), keys(0); that is in the worst case, k comparisons will be performed. Since we add the complexities of each iteration through the outer while loop to arrive at the above formulation.

Divide-and-Conquer

This technique has arisen from the observation that twice the half is sometimes less than the total. In particular, this holds for functions of an order greater than linear. For example, let $f(n) = n^2$ then

$$f(n) > 2f(n/2) \qquad (48.11)$$

since

$$n^2 > 2n^2/4 = n^2/2. \qquad (48.12)$$

In terms of algorithm development, the applicability of this observation is obvious if we let $f(n)$ be the complexity of an algorithm. The proper interpretation of this observation leads us to the following statement. Assume, we have already an algorithm, A, for the problem T and further assume we can partition the input $x = (x_1, \ldots, x_n)$ into the two halves $y = (x_1, \ldots, x_{n/2})$ and $z = (x_{(n/2)+1}, \ldots, x_n)$, apply A to y to obtain $\overline{y}$, and apply A to z to obtain $\overline{z}$. Unfortunately, in most cases having $\overline{y}$ and $\overline{z}$ does not necessarily imply that we have $\overline{x}$ the output of A, and an additional merging process is required to produce the output of the original problem. Formally stated, we obtain algorithm B from applying divide-and-conquer to algorithm A as follows:

```
begin /*input x to problem can be represented as x =
            (y,z)*/
    ȳ ← A(y);
    z̄ ← A(z);
    x̄ ← M(ȳ,z̄)
end                                              (48.13)
```

The complexity of the new solution, $C_B(n)$, is then given by:

$$C_B(n) = 2C_A(n/2) + C_M(n) \qquad (48.14)$$

and the following two necessary conditions for making B the better algorithm can be derived:

1. $C(n) \geq 0(n)$,   That is, the complexity of algorithm A should at least be linear.
2. $C_M(n) < C_A(n)$,   That is, it should not cost more to merge the two partial solutions than to solve the original problem with A.

As an example, let us apply this technique to the sorting problem solved in the previous section. We select for algorithm A the insertion sort described in that section. We have to modify the algorithm slightly to enable it to work on parts of an input tuple as implied by the following procedure heading:

procedure insort(x, left, right; x)
    /∗sort x(left), x(left + 1), . . . , x(right)∗/   (48.15)

(*Caveat* - the concept of a fence is not applicable.)

Following the above framework algorithm, the new algorithm is given by:

       begin
          input n, keys;
          insort (keys, 1, n/2; keys);
          insort (keys, n/2+1, n; keys);
          merge (keys, 1, n/2+1, n; keys);
          output keys
       end   (48.16)

It is left as an exercise to write the procedure "merge," which merges the first $n/2$ elements of keys (which are sorted) with the second $n/2$ elements of keys (also sorted), and to show that the worst case complexity of this procedure is of $0(n)$. Given this fact we can determine the complexity of the new algorithm as:

$$
\begin{aligned}
C(n) &= C_A(n/2) + C_A(n/2) + C_M(n) \\
     &= n^2/8 + n^2/8 + 0(n) \\
     &= n^2/4 + 0(n).
\end{aligned}
$$

Thus the new algorithm (48.16) is about twice as fast as the original algorithm (48.9). In the next section, we shall see how this technique can be built into one which does not rely on an already existing algorithm A.

Recursion

One point of view regards recursion as an extension of divide-and-conquer. More specifically, recursion is one way of representing repeated application of divide-and-conquer. Since commonly problems of size 1 can be solved trivially, after we have divided the input often enough we are left only with repeated application of the merging process to increasingly larger partial solutions. Recursion as an algorithm specification technique allows us to describe the rather intricate process of dividing input and then recombining the partial solutions quite concisely. However, the underlying set of conventions has to be made explicit to define the execution of a recursive algorithm.

Actually, recursion as a general technique does not insist on a balanced division; frequently the division is made with parts of size $n - 1$ and 1 respectively. The technique itself can be described quite easily as follows (however, the novice should be warned that many find it difficult to apply it to a given problem):

1. Specify the problem and give a name to the procedure which solves it;
2. Identify the parameter of the input to be divided;
3. Provide a solution to the problem with input of size 1 and a test for detecting that such a situation has occurred.
4. Find a relation between solutions to the problem of smaller sizes and the original problem, and express this relation algorithmically.

Before we go into a further discussion, let us immediately illustrate the formulation used in the above steps on the sorting problem. The first two steps are satisfied by defining the following procedure heading:

     procedure recursive_sort (x,left,right;x).   (48.17)

The third step is satisfied by

       if right $\leq$ left **then terminate**.   (48.18)

Lastly, if we decide to partition keys into halves then the relation between the solution to sorting the first $n/2$ keys, recursive sort (keys,1,n/2;keys), the solution to sorting the second $n/2$ keys, recursive_sort (keys,n/2 + 1,n; keys) and the solution to the original problem is given by

      mid ← (right−left+1)/2;
      recursive_sort(x,left,mid; x);
      recursive_sort(x,mid+1,right; x);
      merge(x,left,mid+1,right; x)   (48.19)

where we have expressed the actual arguments in terms of the formal arguments of the procedure heading. The procedure "merge" is the same as the one in (48.16). Combining the various steps, we obtain the following recursive formulation of a sorting algorithm:

procedure recursive_sort(x,left,right; x)

begin

    if right $\leq$ left **then** terminate;

    mid $\leftarrow$ (right-left+1)/2;

    recursive_sort(x,left,mid; x);

    recursive_sort(x,mid+1,right; x);

    merge(x,left,mid+1,right; x)

end   (48.20)

To make this recursive formulation a valid feature of AL, we define the semantics of a recursive call as follows. A **recursive call** is a call, directly or indirectly, to the procedure of the same name as the procedure from which the call originates and has the same effect as a call to a copy of the recursive procedure. We do not examine how this effect can be implemented effectively. To illustrate this definition, we trace the sorting algorithm with the call

    keys $\leftarrow$ (4,3,2,1);

    recursive_sort(keys, 1, 4; keys).

- In copy 1, we calculate mid as 2 and call copy 2 with (4,3,2,1), 1, 2;
- In copy 2 we calculate mid as 1 and call copy 3 with (4,3,2,1), 1, 1, which returns to copy 2 after executing the termination test;
- Back in copy 2, we call copy 4 with (4,3,2,1), 2, 2 which returns after testing;
- Back in copy 2 we call merge (nonrecursively) with (4,3,2,1), 1, 2, and merge modifies keys to (3,4,2,1);
- Copy 2 then returns to copy 1 which calls copy 5 with (3,4,2,1), 3, 4 which after several recursive calls (exercise) returns to copy 1 having modified keys to (3,4,1,2).
- The final call to merge produces the proper answer, (1,2,3,4).

Backtracking, Preprocessing and Dynamic Programming

With the exception of backtracking, these techniques, rather sophisticated, warrant only a brief outline.

Backtracking. In contrast with the previous techniques, backtracking is only applicable if we can partition the output $\bar{x}$ into n individual components, $\bar{x} = (\bar{x}_1, \ldots, \bar{x}_n)$. Specifically, we have to be able to transform the problem statement such that it can be viewed as a search in an n-dimensional solution space for those points which satisfy a certain predicate, $C(\bar{x}_1, \ldots, \bar{x}_n)$. We have to specify the solution space for each component $\bar{x}_i$ either by enumeration or provide a function which computes the possible values for $\bar{x}_i$ in an ordered sequence. In addition, we have to be able to specify a partial predicate $C_i(\bar{x}_1, \ldots, \bar{x}_i)$ which, if false, implies that $C(\bar{x}_1, \ldots, \bar{x}_n)$ is false.

For example, a famous problem is to place eight queens on a chessboard such that no queen attacks any other queen. We can view this problem as amenable to backtracking if we select $\bar{x}$ to be an 8-tuple, each element of which records the position (rows 1 through 8) of a queen in one of the columns on the chessboard. The final predicate, C, is true if any row or diagonal contains no more than one queen and C_i is the same predicate involving the i queens placed in the first i columns. It should be clear that the falseness of the partial predicate implies the falseness of the final predicate.

The ad hoc method of solving problems of this nature is simply to check all points of the solution space against the final predicate. Backtracking uses the partial predicates to eliminate whole subspaces from this search. For example, assume we have the partial solution $(\bar{x}_1, \ldots, \bar{x}_i)$ and select the value z for $\bar{x}_{i+1}$. Testing $(\bar{x}_1, \ldots, \bar{x}_i, z)$ against C_{i+1}, we find it violates the partial predicate and we can eliminate all elements of the solution space which have $(\bar{x}_1, \ldots, \bar{x}_i, z)$ as their first $i + 1$ coordinates. The name *backtracking* comes from the fact that the algorithm—after it has not found any value for the $i + 1$st component which satisfies C_{i+1}—backtracks to the ith component and selects another value. Applying this technique to the eight queens problem results in an algorithm which investigates a few thousand possibilities as opposed to the ad hoc method which investigates a few million possibilities.

Preprocessing. The technique of preprocessing applies to problems which have to be solved repeatedly for various inputs. In particular, if one part of the input values remains the same over a number of runs, we may be able to preprocess this constant part and obtain an algorithm of lower complexity. For example, it is known that the best algorithm for evaluating a polynomial of degree

$n, p(x) = \sum_{i=0}^{n} a_i x^i$ takes n multiplications. The input to this problem are the coefficients $a_0, \ldots, a_n$ and x_0 the point of evaluation. If we want to evaluate the same polynomial repeatedly at various points, then one part of the input $a_0, \ldots, a_n$ is constant and preprocessing them leads to an algorithm which takes only about $n/2$ multiplications.

Dynamic Programming. Dynamic programming originated in the area of decision problems. These are problems in which many feasible solutions, depending on the state of decision variables, exist and we wish to find a solution which is optimal according to some specified cost criteria. The central idea in dynamic programming is to view the problem such that it can be represented as a linear sequence of independent subproblems, each of which contains only one decision. A problem, frequently used to illustrate the applicability of this technique, is that of finding the cheapest route from A to B with several stopovers selected from various sets of cities.

48.4 SUMMARY

This purpose of this brief introduction to the world of algorithms has been to establish the framework of computer science in which algorithms play such a central role. The most important concept addressed in this chapter is not that of an algorithm per se, but the part an algorithm plays in problem solving and, more specifically, in finding the "best" solution. One needs a great amount of experience with the various algorithm development techniques we have discussed to become an expert problem solver in computer science. Probably the *art* in being a computer scientist involves the ability to see underlying patterns in problems, to recognize the applicability of a certain technique, and to transform the problem into one one has already handled.

REFERENCES

Aho A., J. E. Hopcroft and J. D. Ullman, *Theory of Algorithms*. Reading MA: Addison-Wesley, 1974.

Knuth, D. E., *The Art of Computer Programming*, Vol I. Reading MA: Addison-Wesley, 1974.

Maly, K. and A. Hanson, *Fundamentals of the Computing Sciences*. Englewood Cliffs, NJ: Prentice-Hall, 1978.

Horowitz, E., and S. Sahni, *Fundamentals of Computer Algorithms*. Rockville, MD: Computer Science Press, 1978.

49
Software Performance

Boris Beizer

Data Systems Analysts, Inc.

49.1 GENERAL

System performance can be *predicted* by analytical models or by simulation, but measurement can provide an accurate *assessment* of performance. **Instrumentation** here denotes hardware or software or a combination used to gather performance related data. Performance measurements can be undertaken to determine a system's performance, to tune the system or to determine the hardware and/or software elements that limit the system's performance.

Determining the factors that affect program execution time is of primary importance in batch processing systems. Load handling capacity is a more significant performance measure for on-line systems. In either type of system, measurements are often undertaken in support of **tuning**, the optimal balance of system resources. Because the application, the software, the load and, to a lesser extent, the hardware, undergo continual change over a system's life, tuning and associated measurement are a continual, ongoing process rather than a singular event. Consequently, while considerable effort may be expended the first time measurements are attempted, there is a payoff throughout the system's (or the application's) life.

Effective measurement presupposes a working, debugged, stable system. Bugs induce uncertainties in measurement that can invalidate analysis based on them. Furthermore, bugs can induce symptoms that mask the true cause of poor performance. Finally, there are bugs which do not affect the functions of a system but which can impact its performance. Given a smoothly running, reliable and stable system of hardware and software, performance measurement has the following aspects:

1. A clear statement of performance objectives.
2. A source of transactions to drive the experiment.
3. A controlled experimental process.
4. A method for gathering data.
5. Analytical tools to process and interpret the data.

Each of these subjects is now discussed further.

49.2 PERFORMANCE OBJECTIVES

General

Time is an implicit part of every notion of system performance. Other than memory size, the only fundamental difference between small and large computers is processing time. In principle, given sufficient memory, the smallest microcomputer can be programmed to do the work done by a supercomputer. What makes one system adequate and another inadequate is the time elapsed between the submission of a task and its completion. That elapsed time is called the **processing delay,** or **delay** alone when the context is clear. In primitive **batch processing,** when systems work on one task at a time, processing delay is equal to the sum of the CPU execution time for the task, overhead processing and waiting time for completion of input or output operations. In a multiprogramming, multitask, on-line system, the processing delay is longer than the CPU execution time because sharing system resources among many tasks induces queueing delays. The delay, then, is the sum of all actual execution time for the task and the time spent on all queues.

Processing delay depends on the total number of active tasks, which in turn depends on the rate at which those tasks are submitted to the system. In most multiprocessing systems, **load** is the simultaneous number of active tasks. Each active task is a source of internally generated transactions that occur at a statistically specifiable rate. The number of active users can therefore be translated into an equivalent job submission/job completion rate. The rate at which jobs are submitted and completed (they must, on the average, be the same) is called the **throughput** and is measured in transactions per second.

Evaluating system performance can be reduced to establishing a relationship between throughput and delay for all systems. System performance is adequate if it does not reject or lose transactions when they are submitted at a rate lower than or equal to the design rate and when the delay at the rated throughput is within the margin deemed acceptable for a given application. An "acceptable" delay is application dependent: a few milliseconds is likely to be intolerable in an aircraft autopilot, whereas several hours would be acceptable for a monthly payroll; weeks may be reasonable for an annual inventory run.

Resources

A system consists of **hardware resources,** fixed characteristics of the system. Examples of resources are computer instruction execution rates, memory access rates, bus and channel transfer rates and processing rates for devices such as tapes, printers, card readers, communication channels, terminals and discs. Each transaction makes a statistically determinable demand on these rate resources. If a resource is available at, say, 100,000 units per second, and each task requires an average of 10,000 units of processing per second, the system cannot handle a throughput rate of more than 10 tasks per second.

Memory is a second kind of resource. In principle, all memory must be included—that is, main memory, registers, cache memory, disks, tapes and so forth. In practice, only main memory and mass memory such as disk need be considered in the majority of cases. Memory assignment is called *static* and *dynamic*.

Static memory includes most operating system overhead and program space, fixed tables, fixed portions of a data base, and application program space. Its use does not depend on throughput.

Dynamic memory supports processing tasks. It is configured in pools of fixed or variable length blocks; it is allocated to a task as it enters the system and is returned to the pool when the task has been processed.

What constitute static and dynamic memory can be subjective and is application dependent. For example, if the performance of a time shared operating system is considered, user program space and tables constitute "dynamic memory": it is continually being allocated and deallocated to support several users. From the user's point of view, all space used may be static. Given a fixed context for dynamic and static, performance measurements are also concerned with determining the amount of dynamic memory allocation; tuning involves trades between dynamic and static memory.

Utilization of Resources

At any instant, a resource may be gainfully employed or unused. Dynamic memory in a pool, but not allocated to a task, is not in use. If time passes without a disk transfer, then during that period the disk is not in use. If a CPU is in an exerciser mode or in a supervisory wait state because there are no other tasks to process, it is not in use. Resource *utilization* varies with throughput between no use and fully occupied.

A fully occupied resource is **saturated**. This is a statistical concept which implies a sample period. For example, a bus transfers data. During the actual data transfer, the bus is saturated because it transfers data at the maximum rate possible. However, this is followed by a hiatus when no transfers occur. If the transfer takes an average of 10 milliseconds, one would not draw conclusions on resource saturation based on a few milliseconds during which the bus is in use.

Resource utilization should be averaged over a period of time which is long compared with the typical duration of a task in the system. If the typical task enters and leaves the system in a few seconds, then the sample period should be in the order of a minute. Similarly, in a batch processing system with sojourn times measured in hours, the sample should be taken over a period of days.

Resource utilization p is a function denoted by p_n for the resource n. When $p_n = 1$, the resource is saturated.

Binding Resources

One can perform a simple but revealing conceptual experiment on which all measurement and tuning is based. Suppose a program uses the CPU, a printer and a moving head disk to achieve a processing objective. One should analyze the system three different ways, once for each separate resource (or n ways for n resources) under the assumption that all other resources are infinite. Each analysis yields a different execution time and the system as a whole exhibits a different processing delay at different throughputs. In this example, the conceptual analysis yields three distinct processing times; for the CPU alone, the printer alone and the disk alone. The resource for which the system has the longest execution time is called the **binding resource.**

In a hypothetically perfect system, all nonbinding resources are fully overlapped with the binding resource and therefore *only* the binding resource determines the delay. The binding resource, however, is not fixed and depends on throughput. Thus, at low throughput, disk transfer time may bind the system, while at high throughputs, it is CPU execution that binds. As a first approximation, most systems behave at a given throughput as if the delay is determined by the resource which binds at that throughput.

Full overlap of the nonbinding resources with the binding resource is generally not achievable. Consequently, there must be periods during which a given resource is not gainfully employed, even though for the most part *it* is the binding resource. Whenever the execution time for a single task exceeds the execution time for the binding resource alone, full overlap has not been achieved and the binding resource is, to some extent, wasted. The binding resource is said to have a **gap**.

A major objective of performance measurement and tuning is the identification and elimination of gaps. Achievement is complicated because the identity of the binding resource is dynamic and can vary from task to task, in addition to varying with throughput. At best, one can only identify which resource is most often bound and which resources are most often gapped. The entire approach must be statistical.

The Objectives of Tuning

Tuning is the identification of binding resources and the elimination of gaps. Gaps can be eliminated by several means:

1. Rearranging the order of processing.
2. Rearranging the priority of processing and/or resource allocation.
3. Making the binding resource faster, i.e. less binding through more efficient code.
4. Trade between equivalent resources (main memory for disk, buffered channel for unbuffered channel, and so forth).
5. Trade between unequivalent resources (increase program space to achieve faster code, tighten code to save space at the cost of time, and so forth).

6. Use of more or faster hardware (a faster CPU, more channels, a disk with a shorter seek time, more memory).

Corrective action without knowledge of what the binding factor is and the extent to which it is gapped may yield little or no improvement. Suppose that a system is disk bound and that it is well tuned. It is so well balanced in fact, that memory utilization is almost always at maximum. Furthermore, the CPU is gainfully employed 90 percent of the time. A new disk twice as fast as the old one offers no noticeable improvement because memory has become the binding factor. Now add to the memory, but the system's load handling capacity is not improved because CPU binding asserts itself.

Improvements in gapped binding resources shift the binding resource to the cause of the gap, again with little improvement. Only careful measurements properly interpreted identify the binding resource, the gaps, if any, the relation to other resources, and the extent to which alleviation of the binding resource or reduction of the gaps might improve system performance.

System Behavior

Measurement of resource utilization for a single program in a uniprogramming environment is simple compared to a multiprogramming on-line system simultaneously handling transactions from many different sources. Therefore most models of system behavior deal with more complex, general cases.

Figure 49.1 shows typical behavior when the system is

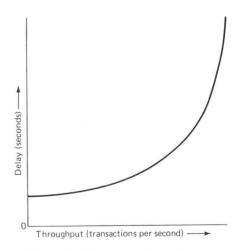

Figure 49.1. Typical throughput delay curve.

subjected to different steady state transaction arrival rates. Only steady state conditions are considered. With few exceptions, analysis of dynamic systems subjected to time varying loads is beyond the practical state of the art and experimentally difficult. The processing delay depicted in Figure 49.1 is small at low loads but increases nonlinearly with increasing loads—typically as $1/(1-p)$. At some loads, at least one resource becomes saturated and the delay becomes infinite. In practice, this does not happen because properly designed systems automatically take preventive measures such as limiting the input rate to forestall true saturation.

The same principle can be used for batch processing although the concept might not seem to apply at first. Jobs are submitted to the computer, a single server queueing system. A queue builds up for the computing facility as a whole, even though not within the computer itself. The facility as a whole experiences a behavior like that shown in Figure 49.1.

Memory as a Resource

Memory is a tricky resource to analyze and interpret. The amount of dynamically allocated memory required to support a given transaction mix and arrival rate is affected by

1. Memory required to process the transaction.
2. Time during which blocks are held for processing the transaction, the **holding time**.

The number of memory blocks required to process a transaction is typically independent of the load. If a transaction requires an average of 10 buffer blocks, it requires them whether transactions arrive at 1, 10 or 100 per second. Holding time, however, is proportional to the processing delay rather than to the execution time for a single transaction. It is the sum of execution times and time spent on queue. Therefore, the amount of memory required to handle a steady state load is approximately proportional to the product of the transaction arrival rate and the delay. But the processing delay is proportional to $1/(1-p_n)$, where n is the binding resource. Consequently, buffer utilization experiences faster increase with load than does processing delay.

It is not unusual for buffer demand to follow linearly with increased load, and then to appear to zoom upwards discontinuously with an insignificant further increase in load. This phenomenon makes memory depletion a sensitive indicator of binding in other resources. Unfortunately, although symptomatic of binding in other re-

sources, memory is often erroneously seen as the cause rather than the symptom. Additional memory (main, disk, and so forth) is purchased, but because it is not the *true binding factor*, the result is an insignificant improvement in system performance.

Memory is correctly identified as the binding factor only after other factors are ruled out. For example, the system is channel bound because it is used to swap between main memory and disk to compensate for inadequate memory. The key to memory binding is to separate its components—the amount of memory required (number of blocks) to process a transaction and the holding time for these blocks. The number of blocks per transaction should be constant and the holding time should be proportional to processing delay. If a significant component of the delay is attributable to the alleviation of memory scarcity, then memory *is* probably the binding factor. Otherwise some other factor binds the system and memory binding is only a symptom.

49.3 SIMPLE MODELS OF SYSTEM BEHAVIOR

General

Which are the true binding resources; how do they affect one another; how to experimentally determine those effects; how does one interpret the results of measurements; how does one adjust the system to alleviate a binding resource? Answering these questions requires some notion of how the system behaves. Detailed analytical or simulation models can be constructed, but such models are rarely needed in support of an experimental determination of performance. Experimental performance models are simple and should be based on a black box approach, independent of the implementation details of the operating system or the application programs.

A Simple Model

Most practical models of system behavior can be reduced to the form,

$$D \sim 1/(1 - f(p)) \qquad (49.1)$$

where D is the expected processing delay;
p is the utilization of the binding resource;
f is a positive, nondecreasing function of the utilization.

The function is dominated by a linear term proportional to the transaction arrival rate, R. Therefore (49.1) can be restated as

$$D = k_1/(1 - k_2R + \epsilon) \qquad (49.2)$$

where k_1 and k_2 are constants (or nearly so) and ϵ represents the contribution of nonlinear higher order terms in the resource utilization. Note that if we invert this expression and consider the reciprocal of the delay (call it S), the resulting expression becomes linear:

$$S = 1/D = (1 - k_2R + \epsilon)/k_1 = S_0 - k_3R \quad (49.3)$$

The right side is obtained by renaming the constants and dropping negligible terms. Redefining the constants once again, we obtain

$$S/S_0 + R/P = 1 \qquad (49.4)$$

where S is the reciprocal of the delay;

S_0 is the delay at zero load experienced by a single transaction in an otherwise empty system;

R is the transaction arrival rate in transactions per unit time;

P is the rate at which the system is capable of processing transactions.

Generally, P is a function of load and varies with the binding factor shifts. Note that R/P is the utilization (p). S is called the **subjective arrival rate** (in distinction to R, the **objective arrival rate**) because it is the rate at which the system *appears* to be capable of processing transactions when viewed by a single user.

For example, if the system has a 10 second delay, it appears to be able to process transactions every 10 seconds. A plot of S/S_0 versus R/P for an ideal system is a straight line sloping downward at a 45° angle. Comparisons of systems can be made by normalizing the delay to

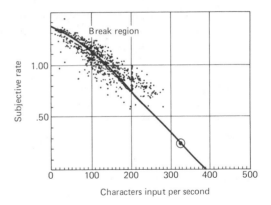

Figure 49.3. Subjective rate curve of actual system.

the zero load delay and the transaction arrival rate to the maximum arrival rate. Figure 49.2 plots an ideal system's (dotted line) and a real system's throughput against a subjective rate. Figure 49.3 shows the same functions plotted from data taken from a real system.

Interpretation of the Model

Consider a well tuned system, without resource gaps but with several different binding resources. Under these assumptions, the processing delay is dominated by the most binding resource at any given throughput. We could plot a function like (49.4) for each resource separately with a result like that in Figure 49.4. Delay is determined by resource 1 in the low load region. As throughput increases, resource 2 becomes the binding factor. The system's ultimate load handling capacity, however, is determined by resource 3.

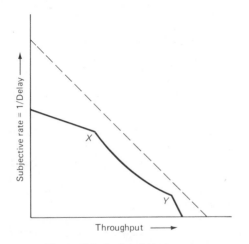

Figure 49.2. Real and ideal systems.

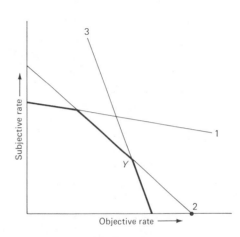

Figure 49.4. Several resources.

In each region, the system's behavior is linear (or almost so) and can be modeled by (49.4). Note the break in the points in the experimental data of Figure 49.3, which shows the shift in binding resources. Note also that, because the binding factor shifts with load, experimental data taken at low load (resource 1 in Figure 49.4) may have no bearing on the system's capacity, because it is resource 3 that limits the system. Therefore, determination of the system's handling capacity should only be based on measurements taken over the entire range of loads from minimum to maximum to determine the true binding factor rather than low load binding factors.

Figure 49.2 can now be interpreted. It consists of three different behavior regions. The first region, with the gentle slope, is disk latency binding. A transition occurs to a second region at point X. The curvature in this second region is typical of a resource that has a high initial overhead which is amortized over many more transactions as load increases (program initialization, overlay overheads, and so on). A positive curvature indicates that processing time per unit transaction $(1/p)$ increases with increasing load. This might occur with a queue scanning process, a sort, or similar processes with nonlinear increases in unit transaction processing time. The break at Y is indicative of the ultimate binding factor asserting itself.

Danger Points

Performance analysis based on experimental data consists of gathering data, plotting values, fitting a curve and extrapolating system behavior. Ideally, all experimentation should be based on a fixed testbed in which all loads, from minimum to maximum, are measured so that no extrapolation is necessary.

Unfortunately, a controlled testbed for a system is often a luxury. Most often, measurements must be taken on a live system where it is impossible to explore extremes of range. A prediction of load handling capacity for Figure 49.4 based on extrapolating from data taken in the resource 1 region would be optimistic, as would be prediction based on resource 2. The solution to this dilemma, when a controlled experiment is not possible, is to take data over a long period (days and weeks if necessary) in the hope that the system will hit its peak, a near saturating load, for a few minutes.

Bugs and Tuning

With careful measurement of throughput and delays, we can occasionally see curves such as that of Figure 49.5.

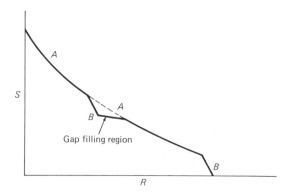

Figure 49.5. A notch.

The notch is typical of bugs or ill tuning. The slope of the subjective rate curve is a good indicator of the binding factor. Over a small range, the slope tends to be constant for any given factor. Therefore, regions with comparable slopes probably represent the same binding factor. The initial binding resource is A. The curve then shifts discontinuously to a new binding resource, B. The A slope subsequently reasserts itself, indicating that the binding resource is once again A. Finally, the B slope dominates.

This kind of notch is indicative of a bug in the processes that dominate the A binding factor. Typically, such occurs when there is a discontinuous increase in overhead that forces the entire curve down to a lower region. The overhead is consumed (the gaps are filled in) until the true binding factor is again asserted. Some examples are instructive:

1. A system has a hardware bug in its fixed head disk. The disk should be capable of processing up to 64 read/write operations per revolution, but at approximately 50 transactions per revolution, transfers are missed, forcing an additional revolution. The increase of processing delay by one revolution at about 50 transactions per second shows up as a notch. Beyond that point, because more revolutions are committed to handling fewer transactions, the delay remains constant, until either the true binding factor dominates or yet another superfluous spin is forced.
2. A system has many task queues. When the load is low, the queues are examined by a sequential scan. At higher loads, in the interest of efficiency, the queues are sorted prior to examination. But the sorting process itself is time consuming. The shift to the sort routine is apparent as a notch. It should be noted that if

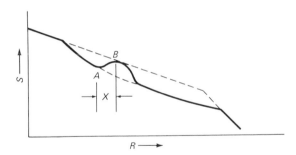

Figure 49.6. A bump.

sort or scan time is not the binding factor, it is better to stick to the simpler nonsorting approach. In either case, invoking the sort should be delayed to a higher load region to provide a continual and gradual change in system performance, because a discontinuous change in the system behavior is always disturbing.

A definite indicator of bugs is a subjective rate curve that increases at any point, shown in Figure 49.6. The delay at B is less than the delay at A, despite the fact that at B the system has to handle X more transactions per second. This is contrary to common sense because it tells us that in order to improve the system's performance we should pump in X extra, useless transactions per second. At worst, it should be possible to improve the system by invoking earlier whatever is happening so that the system will follow the dotted curve in Figure 49.6.

Usually the discovery and identification of the source of the anomalous behavior allow a redesign which extends the system's performance throughout the range and increases the ultimate throughput as well.

Typical systems have simple subjective rate curves that consist of one, two or three regions. Most systems have two regions. The first region is flat and corresponds to disk or I/O binding. A sharp drop follows when processing binding takes over. Either the first region or the central region has a slight negative curvature caused by improved efficiency and increased amortization of overhead functions with increasing load.

Summary

System behavior is characterized by a simple subjective rate function. The objective of any experiment is to gather enough data for an accurate representation of the entire curve, not just a segment. Given the curve we should

1. Identify the dominant factor in each segment;
2. See every break as a transition from one binding resource to another;
3. Identify negative curvature with a factor whose efficiency improves with increasing load due to amortization of overhead functions;
4. Identify a positive curvature with a factor that increases with increasing load, such as queue scanning operations, sorting or interprocess interference;
5. Investigate notches as targets for improvements and indicators of potential bugs and/or poor tuning;
6. Investigate lumps in detail because they must be caused by bugs or ineffectual load management strategies.

49.4 TRANSACTION SOURCES

General

Performance measurement is an experimental process in which as many variables as possible are under the experimenter's control. The primary control over the loads is obtained by several means:

1. Load generators and simulators.
2. Cogeneration.
3. Self-generation.
4. Real loads.

These are listed in order of increasing experimental complexity and instrumentation requirement.

Load Generators and Simulators

These range from a simple predetermined set of transactions presented to the system under a job control language to the entire, real time simulation of a complex environment. One of the most elaborate load generators is the FAA test facility at Pomona, New Jersey. This facility can provide realistic loads for an entire air traffic control system, including the simulation of pilots and air traffic controllers. An air traffic control program can be tested in this environment under a wide variety of situations. Different elements may be provided by other programs or by people who act as pilots or controllers. Elaborate test facilities and load generators are used in the space program and with military applications.

A load generator is a source of statistically specified transactions which may be generated on-line. Or various components may be produced off-line and run on-line.

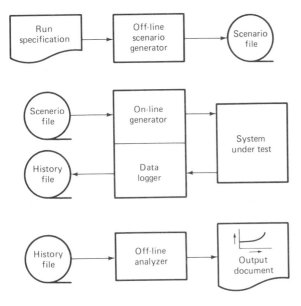

Figure 49.7. Load generator block diagram.

Because a load generator often incorporates hardware to measure a system's behavior under load, it can be as complex as the system for which it is generating a load. Furthermore, the resources required to support a load generator (the computer in which it is run) can be massive. How do we distinguish load generator saturation, should it arise, from system saturation?

Elaborate load generators can test many different systems or simulate many environments when no other approach is safe. For example, a process control system might use a load generator to simulate processes to which it might be applied. A telecommunications system might be tested with a load generator to simulate the different communications environments.

Figure 49.7 is a block diagram of a typical load generator with three components: an off-line scenario generator, an on-line system and an off-line analyzer. The scenario generator accepts a statistical specification of the transactions to be generated. It constructs a file which contains the transactions, the time each is to be submitted (if possible) and its channel or communications line. The generator is application specific. For example, a generator for telephone systems specifies numbers to be called, misdial percentages, waiting time between digits, wrong numbers, incomplete calls, and so on.

The on-line portion of the system is designed under the assumption that there is a response to every stimulus. For example, every inquiry has a response. If no response oc-

curs, then additional software may be needed in the system under test to create one artificially. The on-line generator portion issues the transactions in accordance to the times scheduled. If the system under test does not accept a transaction because it is backlogged, then the on-line generator should react realistically: try again; or try n times and then quit.

The reaction may itself be part of the scenario. Whenever the generator issues or attempts to issue a transaction, it logs that fact for subsequent analysis. Similarly, it measures system reaction (time stamp) and provides sufficient information to match the stimulus to the response and to record delays in a history file.

Matching stimulus to response is done off-line. The time stamp determines the transaction arrival rate and the processing delay, resulting in the system throughput delay function.

Cogeneration

Cogeneration uses a system to provide load for another copy of the system. Here the requirements of the load simulator and the system tested are almost identical, as in communications systems. For process control, the act of execution control and the software required to create control responses can be modified to provide the responses that the process itself would provide. Cogeneration is useful when it requires only small modifications of the system under test.

An inherent difficulty in cogeneration is disentangling cause and effect—distinguishing between delays produced by the system tested and those internal to the generator (resulting in time stamp errors). One solution bypasses all processing in the generator not required for load generation or data logging.

Self-Generation

Self-generation is applicable when input and output transactions are indistinguishable (in communications systems). Because an output message from one system could be an input message to some other communications line, a combination of routing information in the data base and physical patches of lines in a loop forces messages to circulate in the system. Stable, controlled loads can be generated in this way. Communications systems do extensive data logging as a byproduct of normal message processing. In process control, stability problems at nearly saturated loads can invalidate the results of self-generation.

Real Loads

For a real load, there is no compromise with reality. It provides a proper measure of error conditions, anomalous cases, bursts, and so forth. But monitoring requires far more data logging and instrumentation. Further, it is hard to obtain reliable data over the entire load range. However, because most systems, once put into operation, are not likely to be released for experimentation, the analysis of real loads becomes a part of most experimental programs and tuning efforts at some point in system life. To obtain data over the entire load range, it may be necessary to monitor a system around the clock for a week so that flows like Friday afternoon rushes can be measured.

With real loads, forcing systems into saturation is often impossible. The operators of a system used for checking credit cards, say, would not tolerate artificially induced overloads in the interest of experimentation. Furthermore, because of the typical break at high loads, where the ultimate binding resource takes over, proper extrapolation of the system's capability may not be possible. Thus it is dangerous to extrapolate linearly from the highest measured load if the binding resource has not been identified. One way out of this dilemma briefly injects an artificial load over the real load so that the system is momentarily driven close to the limit.

With real loads the data are scattered, while data taken on a test bed tend to follow subjective rate curves to within a fraction of a percent. The realism of the load provides considerable variation in the statistical characteristics of the system's behavior and only techniques like regression analysis (see Section 49.7) can determine what has actually occurred. Breaks and gaps show as changes in regression coefficients and the overall scatter in the data may make this hard to see.

The ideal situation is to have the ability to run real loads, gather statistics on them, obtain crude indications of system behavior and then to set up a controlled test bed to simulate the loads.

49.5 INSTRUMENTATION

General

Instrumentation takes two principal forms: hardware and software. Hardware instrumentation is almost always augmented by software. The combination is more effective than either alone. There are four functions:

1. Event logging.
2. Counts of events.
3. Duration of events and processes.
4. Sampling of events and states.

Event Logging

Events of interest in the context of system performance include interrupts, I/O operations, execution of specific programs or their parts and calls to subroutines. An event occurrence can be detected and recorded by imbedded software. **Logging** records all data pertinent to the event, including the time it occurred, register contents, system state, and the contents of memory.

If software is used to log the event, then the processing time and resources are required. These resources distort the measurement. Such a distortion is called an **artifact**; it is most noticeable in event logging because it consumes more resources than most other forms of instrumentation.

Event Counting

If an event can be identified easily, then instead of logging, one may count the number of events in a time period. For example, a log might contain the time at which each disk access occurs, whether it is a read or a write, the size of the transfer, and number of cylinders traversed. Alternatively, one could count the accesses to given cylinders or ranges of cylinders in a given time period. Information is lost but artifacts are reduced. Typically, event counts are accumulated either until counters fill up or until a specified time.

Duration of Events or Processes

Duration can be measured when the system has a hardware timer, software access to an external real-time clock, or a periodic clock interrupt. The start and end of the event must be recognizable.

Sampling Events

Periodically (at a high priority level triggered by a clock interrupt) hardware states or software states can be examined to see if an event is in progress. Artifacts can be controlled by reducing the sample rate. For example, to determine the elapsed time for the execution of a routine, one can sample the program counter every 100 milliseconds and count the number of samples during which the program counter is within the range of the routine. The sample rate and the percentage of hits determine the percentage of time in that routine. Examining the execution time for the entire program enables one to determine the execution time for the sampled program. Sampling methods presume a predictable program which statistically repeats itself.

49.6 SOFTWARE INSTRUMENTATION

General

Logging, counting, timing and sampling can be accomplished by software by inserting code. Logging is most artifact prone because many instructions are needed to move data to an output buffer for transfer to another medium.

Controls

Software instrumentation is artifact inducing and cannot be inserted wholesale into a program. As a result, it is necessary to turn the software instrumentation probe on and off. Examples follow.

Conditional logic. Instrumentation code is fitted with bypass control logic (flags) and control software to turn the flags on or off. To obtain the measurements with minimum artifact, all but one probe is turned off. The run is repeated for each probe. This method is relatively artifact free, but caution must be used in systems with cache memories and instruction look ahead. Such systems may have different execution times with the probe active versus inactive. Paged systems may also provide distorted measurements because the activation or deactivation of the probe may increase or decrease page boundary crossings or working set statistics.

Conditional assembly or compilation. Some compilers permit tagging statements for conditional assembly or compilation. The source code contains the software instrumentation, but only a specified part is assembled or compiled. The user prepares as many object versions of the program or system as there are cases to measure and repeats the runs. An optimizing compiler may take a different strategy with the conditionally compiled probe, active or inactive; cache memory operations may change; page boundaries may change, as may the working set, and therefore induce measurement uncertainty.

Patching. Object code patching provides the greatest control but with considerable effort. An unconditional branch is replaced by a branch to a patch area where instrumentation software is implemented. Because patching is done at the object level, page boundary changes, register usage changes, working set changes, and so on can be avoided (although cache memory artifact might not be avoided) and the additional processing time and resources consumed by the instrumentation software identified and analyzed.

Event Logging

Events are logged by inserting code at points in the program where events are recognized. Logged information can be anything from a simple event count to an entire memory dump (as an extreme). A time tag may identify single events or an entire buffer filled with event logs. A buffer minimizes artifact by taking advantage of the efficiency of large block transfers to disk.

Elaborate logging is to be avoided in software instrumentation because it distorts the system's behavior. In many systems, accounting information (as in a time shared system) can provide much of the data that would be obtained by elaborate special logs. Often, logging is available as a byproduct of the operating system's normal functions. When logging is not inherent in the system's operation, it is best kept simple even if this means extensive off-line processing.

Event Counting

Event counting is a simple form of a log. Each time the event of interest occurs, a counter is incremented. For a single program, counter sizes can be set for the worst case expected. A simple routine or declarations in the source code initializes the counter values prior to the run, and the incremented values are recorded at the end of the run.

In on-line programs, counters are either periodically reset and recorded or the time at which a counter overflows is recorded and logged as an event. In periodic resetting, all counter values are recorded in a buffer for logging and then reset to the initial value after recording, under control of a real-time clock. More elaborate systems classify counters for different sample or reset rates. The overflow method logs the time of overflow and consequently consumes more time, and off-line analysis is more complicated. If counters are maintained in a single block or array, then a single block transfer records all counters.

Event Duration Measurements

Here the beginning and the end of the event are detected. Event duration can be measured by modifying the clock interrupt handler. Suppose the program operates at a low priority level, while a clock interrupt routine operates at a high priority level. When the event is initiated at the low priority level, a flag is set in a control array. When the event is concluded, the flag is reset. The clock interrupt routine now increments a corresponding counter for every active flag. The counters are then treated as event counters. When the event is concluded, the counter value is logged and the counter reset to await the next event. The more accurately one times the event, the more frequent is the clock interrupt and therefore the more artifact it induces.

One inherent weakness of software event duration measurements is uncertainty. Most events occur at low priority levels. There is no assurance (unless measures have been taken in the operating system or supervisory program) that the time recorded is the time at which the event took place. In event logging, this is not important; but when a pair of event logs are used to measure the elapsed time of an event, the unknown time spent in higher priority processing may induce additional uncertainties between recorded time and actual time. A method based on counting clock interrupts does not have an uncertainty greater than the interclock pulse duration.

Sampling Methods

Sampling methods for counting, logging and timing can be accurate and minimize artifact. Software samples events, counters, and so forth, although not at all at the same rate. The software instrumentation codes and resets event flags, and increments and resets event counters. A sample is triggered by a clock interrupt whereupon memory locations of interest are recorded.

Computers and operating systems with subroutines and/or priority stacks are particularly amenable to sampling methods. A clock at a high priority level samples the stack top and identifies the active routine. Typically, this is a program counter value. Subsequent off-line analysis determines the executing subroutine. Sufficient samples determine elapsed time for all routines in the system.

One can focus on individual routines, segments of programs, etc. For example, consider three routines in locations 1776–2004, 2005–2151, and 2152–2200. Over a specified period of time, 23 percent of stack samples are in the first range, 54 percent in the second, and the rest in the third.

Accuracy can be increased by increasing the number of accumulated counts. From the execution time of the program, the elapsed time for three routines is accurately determined. Artifact level is constant and depends only on the processing at the clock interrupt level. However, considerable off-line software time may be needed to map the recorded program counter ranges onto the routines. When software is relocatable, load information converts absolute stack values into program identities. Similarly, virtual memory systems complicate the issue if the stack contains physical rather than virtual addresses.

Sampling provides accurate information and minimizes artifact, but it requires cooperation with utility software, operating systems, compilers, loaders, linkage editors and complex off-line analytical packages to convert the sampled information into a useful form.

Hardware Instrumentation

Hardware monitors.   A hardware monitor is typically a mini or a micro with high impedance connectors to sample hardware elements within the computer. A probe connector on the system bus monitors all bus events. Connectors or probes may be attached to the bus, I/O channels, data and address ports, interrupt lines, and so forth. A high impedance device does not affect system operation. A hardware monitor operates like software instrumentation but without artifact.

Event detection.   Hardware monitors detect events by wired (plugboard) or programmed logic. A programmed logic device or microcode evaluates truth functions of a bit pattern. A hardware monitor recognizes events that occur at system bus speed or memory speed. It monitors bit patterns on probe lines for a hit. The logic can be simple masking, ranges of values, combinations or sequences of values, such as:

1. Any memory address above 17777777.
2. A data line value between 234 and 236.
3. A memory data value of 12345671.
4. A bus sequence of Z C Z C.
5. A Boolean expression of line values.

The detected event is logged and recorded. What happens subsequently depends on how the monitor has been programmed.

Hardware implemented logic is limited. Consequently, events with elaborate criteria are recognized partially by the hardware and partially by software within the monitor. Product line monitors are provided with extensive "front end" software to detect events. While the execution of programs within the hardware monitor to extend the limited hardware logic is possible, such programs consume monitor resources. And even though the hardware monitor's operation does not create artifact in the program being measured, the hardware monitor is susceptible to saturation. For example, if it takes 20 microseconds of monitor CPU time to record an event, the monitor cannot record more than 50,000 events per second. If the hardware monitor is operated close to saturation, it runs out of buffers, falls behind in time tagging events, or otherwise fails to keep up. This is an indirect form of artifact. The answer may lie in splitting the measurements over several runs with different probes activated in each run.

Event logging. Event logging consists of detecting an event, time tagging and recording it. In the first two parts of this operation, the hardware monitor is superior. No artifact is associated with time tagging. Typically, a memory address is modified or accessed as a byproduct of the measured system's processing; the event causes a jump to a specified location. The monitor detects the jump on the memory address lines. At worst, one inserts a single instruction to write data to a memory location reserved for the purpose.

If the data to be logged with the event are contiguous and appear on a channel, say, or are transferred to contiguous memory locations, then recording has little artifact. If it is necessary to move the data, then the overhead remains. Hardware monitors are best suited to the detection and capture of data for simple events. Complex events are better handled with software.

Event counting. Here the hardware monitor is superior. The monitor increments (or decrements) specified counter(s) in its memory when an event is detected. Monitor software resets the counters in accordance with programmed schedules and criteria.

Event duration measurement. The event initiates a timer; its completion stops the timer. The timer is updated at specified rates by the monitor software. For ex-

ample, the first action is the detection of the I/O instruction that initiates the disk seek operation on the disk channel. The second action is the detection of the seek-complete interrupt associated with the same channel. While most counters are programmed and implemented in monitor memory, some monitors use hardware counters and are consequently fast but limited.

Internal events. The typical monitor is a minicomputer. It can therefore detect and record its own actions. For example, one can receive event duration measurements on a set of counters. On-line monitor software checks the range of each time interval and increments associated counters. As with software monitors, there is no limit to sophistication other than monitor resources and its saturation.

Sampling methods. Sophisticated monitors turn probes on and off and sample events, thereby reducing the probability of saturation. Sampling depends on monitor logic and the monitored system's architecture. Microcomputers offer few opportunities to insert probes. Mainframes may be fitted with probes on ALUs, cache memory, and so on, including hardware elements not monitorable by software.

Monitor data processing. On-line processing and reduction of data gathered by a hardware monitor are minimized to prevent monitor saturation. A typical approach records data on industry compatible media and then runs analytical software off-line.

49.7 THE EXPERIMENTAL PROCESS

Software performance measurement is experimental and success depends on the extent to which it is controlled.

Preparation

Measurement should be scheduled in advance. Most systems require several thousand data points sampled over a typical operational cycle. Most systems operate on a weekly cycle with low activity at night and peak towards the end of the week. Hence only a full week's data assures meaningful results. Unusual activities such as special runs, operating system changes and major data base changes should be avoided.

All hardware and software instrumentation should be debugged in advance. Short test runs of instrumentation and data logging should be carried through to final data reduction prior to actual measurements. Before measurements are undertaken, the system patch log should confirm that no changes have been made that could affect the data validity.

Conduct of Tests

The extent to which a test observer is required depends on the quality of the operation logs. If logs are detailed and explicit and include operator actions, then it is not necessary to have an observer. There may be some data points that must be discarded because of unusual circumstances which do not reflect a typical load.

A backup copy should be made of the source data even though considerable processing may follow. Errors may creep into the analysis and it may be necessary to go back to the raw data to validate it. Data gathered for the first time should be examined daily for reasonableness. Part of the analysis should be carried out to assure that what is gathered is what is wanted. A preliminary analysis of this kind may reveal gross problems that obviate the need for further data gathering because conclusions regarding the system's performance or tuning may be obvious. Similarly, erratic behavior may indicate hardware or software problems that must first be rectified.

How Much Data and How Often

Some measurements should be accumulated and averaged (on-line) to yield a data point. Data points should be recorded at long intervals compared with the typical transaction time. A recording interval of 10 to 20 times the length of a transaction's sojourn is a useful rule of thumb. For example, a data base inquiry system clears a typical transaction in 10 seconds—accumulate the data over a 2 minute interval and store the summary every 2 minutes. The sojourn must be measured from the initiation of the transaction to its conclusion. If, for example, a terminal operates at 10 characters per second, and the typical input consists of 1000 characters, then the sojourn time should include the 100 seconds it takes to get the transaction in and the 100 seconds to get it out.

Long sample periods smooth the data and make it easier to interpret. Short periods of peak activity are smeared over and valuable peak data are lost. The long period also reduces the number of data points gathered and this can affect the conclusions. Very short sample periods capture crucial peaks, with a lot of noise. Furthermore, the resulting data is so scattered that it is difficult to draw "eyeball" conclusions.

Enough data points (i.e. one minute samples, for example) should be gathered to allow a statistically valid analysis whose results vary by less than 10 percent at 90 percent confidence—typically, from 500 to 1,000 points. For reasons discussed below, more than half of the raw data points are discarded. Consequently, 2,000 data points are needed at the beginning. In a controlled test bed, valid results can be achieved with a few hundred points. Some systems have such regular behavior on the test bed that it is possible to evaluate performance on the basis of a few dozen points.

Data Format and Transformation

Almost all analyses are based on regression and curve fitting. When the analysis computer is not the one being measured, the data may need to be formatted or converted. When a hardware monitor is used, the data gathered by it is invariably incompatible in format with the computer being measured and the computer being used for analysis.

49.8 DATA REDUCTION AND ANALYSIS

Tools

A small computer is indispensable. The computer should have the following capabilities:

1. Memory of at least 100K characters;
2. A scientific language and associated processors such as extended BASIC, FORTRAN or PASCAL;
3. High quality graphics with hard copy printing;
4. The ability to store and invert at least two or more 10 $\times$ 10 matrices;
5. Ten digit floating point arithmetic;
6. A library of statistical and graphic packages;
7. Means for inputting or translating the source data.

The importance of good software cannot be overstated. Otherwise, the results of analysis may be meaningless.

Preliminary Analysis

General. A typical set of data consists of several hundred to a few thousand points. Each data point consists of a dependent variable, such as the transaction delay or its reciprocal, and several independent variables, such as arrival rates for transactions and resource utilization counts. The analysis establishes a relation between throughput and delay. But throughput is usually the sum of several different transaction types, each of which makes different demands on a system's resources.

Is the data sensible? Add throughput transaction rates to get overall throughput. Plot the reciprocal of the delay (subjective rate) and resource utilization versus throughput.

This preliminary examination assures that the data make sense. Gross computational errors are caught at this stage. If the data exhibit several different isolated populations, there may be data problems or the system may be ill-tuned. Any systematic grouping of points, such as repeating gaps in either the dependent or independent variable or sawtooth data, should be investigated for potential problems.

Does the data make sense and represent physicaly realizable behavior? Look for outlying data that appear to stand out from the crowd to check against the operations log for something unusual. Groupings of data that correspond to different operational modes make it necessary to split the analysis and evaluate system performance separately in each mode.

When data are scattered, more than one factor influences system response. Scatter appears because a function of two or more variables is forced onto a two dimensional plane.

Eyeballing. The throughput delay curve can be extrapolated by drawing an "eyeball" regression line as in Figure 49.3. Unfortunately, this is often the point where some analyses stop. Such "eyeball" curves are unreliable. If there is a lot of scatter to the points, "eyeball" regression lines can lead to an extrapolation which is valid only over a 4-to-1 range. If the object of analysis is to show the limiting throughput or that minimal performance can be met, then "eyeballing," while dangerous, may be adequate.

Eyeballing achieves a qualitative understanding of system behavior. It establishes upper and lower bounds on performance and the importance of various parameters. It may show that additional data must be gathered or that previously unsuspected behavioral anomalies or system bugs must be investigated and corrected before further analysis is possible.

Data Transformation and Scaling

Initial processing scales or transforms the data or both. The hardware and software monitors do not measure

data in the same way. The two sets of data are merged and made compatible. Outlying points caused by abnormal system operation verified by the logs are removed. For data input manually, keypunch errors are corrected; further transformation may format them for regression analysis. A transformation and extraction package should have capabilities to

1. Examine any source point by number;
2. List data associated with a point or with a specified range of points;
3. Edit any point;
4. Do simple linear transformations to scale;
5. Extract data based on the values of any variable from the source file;
6. Plot the results of extraction.

If a typical analysis requires 1,000 points, each of 10 numbers using 8 characters of storage, one such data set uses 80,000 characters of storage. An analysis may require 10 such files.

First Cut Regression

Regression analysis. Linear regression analysis fits a straight line through a set of data points. If the dependent variable is a function of two independent variables, then linear regression analysis fits a plane through the set of points. Almost all regressions are based on **least squares:** the line (plane, hyperplane), the sum of the squares of the differences between the line and point values, is minimized. A linear regression analysis, therefore, expresses the value of the independent variable (say, subjective rate) as a function of the various independent variables.

$$Y = a_0 + a_1X_1 + a_2X_2 + a_3X_3 \cdots \quad (49.5)$$

where a_1 are the regression coefficients. Regression analysis measures how well the regression surface fits the data.

First cut analysis. First cut analysis does a linear fit to establish which coefficients are important. The coefficients, when scaled, define the mean processing time for each transaction type. The constant term a_0 is a measure of overhead. The coefficients of the first cut analysis should be reconciled with system behavior. These coefficients are an agglomeration of CPU time, wait time, I/O time, and so forth.

This initial analysis is qualitative. Does it make sense

that transaction type 2 takes five times longer to process than transaction type 5? Often, such a situation identifies binding factors.

In addition to the major regression, subjective rate versus throughput, the following regression analyses should be done:

1. I/O time divided by throughput versus throughput;
2. Disk activity time versus throughput;
3. Resource utilizations versus throughput.

These additional analyses measure unit transaction utilization of all factors and variation with increasing throughput. Unit transaction resource utilization should remain constant over a wide throughput range. There is a slight tendency for it to decrease with increasing throughput as the system gains efficiency by amortizing overhead over more transactions.

Data Culling

Ideal data consist of points uniformly distributed over the throughput range. But most systems exhibit large diurnal load variations. Consequently, the data tend to be biased toward low throughput regions, leading, because of the typical system behavior, to an optimistic extrapolation of the system capacity. The data should be culled to remove the surplus of low throughput points, but not manually lest inadvertant bias creep in.

A data extraction program selects points at random based on the distribution of values for the variable used as a selection key. Suppose that throughput is the selection criterion. Plot the probability frequency function for throughput, typically an exponential distribution. Establish a cutoff probability and extract points using a random number generator. Points for which distribution probability is less than cutoff probability are retained. Throughput values that have an excess of points are reduced in proportion to make the values tend to a uniform distribution. A typical file of 2,000 points can be culled to 750. Very low and high throughput values are not lost.

Piece Wise and Polynomial Fits

Piece wise fits. Systems tend to exhibit breaks as different binding resources assert themselves. Hence a single linear fit is rarely adequate. The typical system may be fit with two or three segments thus:

1. The break is evident in the plotted area. When breaks are evident, subdivide the data file into regions and analyze each separately.
2. Search for a break. A break may not be obvious because of excessive scatter. Split the file in half and analyze each separately. Note significant differences in the coefficients, particularly the constant term (a_0) because it is the most sensitive indicator. If a difference is found, split one side and try again. Continuing this way, one will find the break by successive halving. Packages work here.
3. Use polynomial regression to determine the point of maximum curvature to detect the presence of a break.

Polynomial regression. Some regression analysis packages do nonlinear curve fit of a restricted kind. New, created variables are a function of the original variables; the resulting analysis is linear in the new variables. For example, to fit a polynomial of the form

$$Y = a_0 + a_1X + a_2X^2 + a_3X^3 \cdots \quad (49.6)$$

transform the problem to a new set of variables,

$$Y = a_0 + a_1Z_1 + a_2Z_2 + a_3Z_3 \cdots \quad (49.7)$$

where

$$Z_1 = X, Z_2 = X^2, Z_3 = X^3 \cdots \quad (49.8)$$

While Y is not a linear function of X, it is a linear function of the transformed variables Z_1, Z_2, Z_3. Similar transformations such as $Z = \ln(X)$, e^X, and so on, can linearize many functions. Regression packages contain facilities for making the common transformations. Polynomial regression programs contain additional capabilities that select a polynomial of best fit. Polynomial regressions find breaks which are not obvious. They can also track nonlinear increases in resource utilizations or in processing that may result from bugs.

If analysis is based on throughput versus delay, which is nonlinear, one will be forced to use polynomial regressions. The subjective rate function (reciprocal of delay), a linearizing transformation, is preferable to a polynomial fit because the former eliminates unnecessary variables, leaving room in the analysis for additional variables.

It is important to plot the entire polynomial over the range of throughput. Polynomials are amoral and produce phyically meaningless coefficients that fit the data well. This danger increases with the number of terms. Inherent nonlinearities in computer systems take the form of a square law (as in an inefficient sort or search routine), $N \ln (N)$, or $1/(1 - p)$. Cubic behavior of transaction processing time with increasing throughput is rare. Generally, even-numbered exponents are better than odd, except for the linear term. A good polynomial regression package indicates which terms dominate and how the fit is improved through the incorporation of higher terms.

Nonlinear fits.   Nonlinear fits, such as $N \ln (N)$, $1/(1 - p)$, or e^x, should be based on a preliminary analysis of the system. Exponentials, while a favorite of the novice, rarely have a real basis. A regression package based on linearized variables can select the linearization function that yields the best fit. A combination of direct linear, polynomial and nonlinear transformations may establish a better model of system behavior. Nonlinear regression should be used sparingly because

1. Each transformation adds variables in the regression equations. Processing increases by the second or third power of the number of variables. A simple analysis based on a half-dozen variables which takes a few seconds of processing time could take days using a fourth order polynomial for each variable.
2. More variables increase the danger of roundoff errors and meaningless results. The typical regression analysis package, even with double precision arithmetic, is marginally accurate for more than 20 variables.
3. A sensible analysis is more useful than a good fit. N data points can always be fit perfectly by an $N - 1$ order polynomial.

Fine Grained Analysis and Tuning

A good model which fits the known data within 15 percent at 50 percent confidence is a prerequisite to tuning. The initial analysis obtains the relation between delay and resource utilization as a function of throughput. Tuning is based on resource utilization per unit transaction for each throughput rate. Tuning problems exhibit an erratic behavior in unit resource utilization, for instance, increasing and then decreasing processing time per transaction, discontinuous changes in resource utilization per transaction, and so forth.

Once overall behavior is established, consider more detailed data. For example, having measured overall processing time for several of the more important processing jobs, remove it from the analysis to be replaced by several subsidiary processing components. Separate regressions can determine how each fares with increasing load. The same can be done for I/O time and memory utilization.

The possibilities are unlimited; however, most tuning problems can be spotted without resort to complicated analysis.

Dangers of Extrapolation

Extrapolation is required when there is insufficient high load data. Extrapolation is an act of faith that the system's behavior continues linearly. Because low throughput may mask the real binding factor, we have no real assurance that there is no sharp break in a region lacking data. Statistical methods establish a degree of confidence in extrapolations on the assumption of no sharp behavioral break, contrary to the observed behavior of many systems.

Suggestions.   If extrapolation is the objective, the following suggestions can be helpful:

1. Be aware of the direct and consequential damages associated with extrapolation.
2. Be careful regarding conclusions drawn from an extrapolation. Statistical meticulousness is not enough.
3. Take additional data during peak periods, if necessary.
4. Do additional runs with a shorter sample time, using the previous analysis to see through the noise induced by the shorter sample.
5. Inject artificial loads during peak periods to force saturation and eliminate extrapolation altogether. But it is difficult to get users to agree to that kind of experiment.

REFERENCES

Organizations and Periodicals

Computer Measurement Group, Bethesda, MD. Professional society that sponsors annual conventions and symposia, local chapter meetings, and so forth. Journal devoted to performance analysis and measurement.

Computer Performance, IPC Science and Technology Press, Haywood Heath, Sussex, UK. Journal devoted to performance analysis, measurement and modeling.

EPD Performance Review, Applied Computer Research, Phoenix, AZ. Monthly journal that publishes abstracts, reviews and short articles devoted to computer performance. Valuable annual survey of performance related hardware and software products lists several hundred products from 100 vendors. Accessible and complete guide to available products.

IEEE (Institute for Electrical and Electronic Engineers). Performance related articles published by IEEE Computer Society in *IEEE Transactions on Computers* and in *IEEE Transactions on Software Engineering*. See also the *IEEE Transactions on Communications* and *IEEE Transactions on Reliability*.

Performance Evaluation, North Holland, Amsterdam. Quarterly journal devoted to system and network performance.

Performance Evaluation Review, ACM Special Interest Group on Measurement and Evaluation (SIGMETRICS). Quarterly newsletter covering performance analysis, simulation, and modeling. Announcement of pertinent conferences. Case studies.

Books

Beilner, H., and Gelenbe, E. (Eds.), *Modeling and Performance Evaluation of Computer Systems*. Amsterdam: North Holland, 1977. Conference proceedings of an international workshop on performance evaluation, 1976. Statistical methods and many case studies.

Beizer, Boris, *Micro Analysis of Computer System Performance*. New York: Van Nostrand Reinhold, 1978. General text on analytical modeling of systems with emphasis on models derived from program code. Treatment of cyclic systems, queueing network models, latency models, tuning, and measurement.

Benwell, Nicholas, *Benchmarking: Computer Evaluation and Measurement*. New York: John Wiley & Sons, 1975. A conference proceedings.

Borovits, Israel, and Seev Neumann, *Computer System Performance Evaluation*. Lexington, MA: Lexington Books, 1979. Readable introduction to performance measurement, analysis, organization of studies and cost-benefit analyses.

Bunyan, C. J. (Ed.), *Computer Systems Measurement: Infotech State of the Art Report No. 18*. Infotech Internation LTD., Maidenhead, Berks., UK., 1974. A panel of experts discussing system performance, analysis, simulation and tuning. An excellent overview.

Carnahan, B., H. A. Luther and J. O. Wilkes, *Applied Numerical Methods*. New York: John Wiley & Sons, 1969. A big book with lots of information on regression analysis methods. Programs, flowcharts, listings. A good source book.

Daniel, C., F. S. Wood and J. W. Gorman, *Fitting Equations to Data*. New York: Wiley Interscience, 1971. An excellent introduction to regression analysis with many examples. This book goes beyond the likely needs of most performance studies.

Draper, N., and H. Smith, *Applied Regression Analysis*, 2nd Ed. New York: John Wiley & Sons, 1981. A big book (more than 700 pages) and a primary reference.

Drummand, M. E., Jr., *Evaluation and Measurement Techniques for Digital Computer Systems*. Englewood Cliffs, NJ: Prentice-Hall, 1973. Introduction to performance analysis and measurement. Use of benchmarks, simulation, and hardware and software instrumentation is discussed in detail.

Ferrari, D., *Computer System Performance Evaluation*. Englewood Cliffs, NJ: Prentice-Hall, 1978. Overview of the field including measurement, simulation, analytical models, computer selection, tuning and design.

Freiberger, W. (Ed.), *Statistical Computer Performance Evaluation*. New York: Academic Press, 1972. Collection of articles from 1971 conference proceedings on statistical computer performance evaluation.

Gilb, T., *Software Metrics*. Cambridge, MA: Winthrop, 1977. Measurement of software performance in the broad sense including reliability, and maintainability in addition to throughput delay. Much philosophy and guidance related to the value of additional performance vis-à-vis its actual or potential cost.

Helleran, H., and T. F. Conroy, *Computer System Performance*. New York: McGraw-Hill Book Co., 1975. Survey of the field, strong statistical introduction, queueing theory, modeling, application to OS-360, time sharing, and virtual memory systems.

Kuo, S. S., *Numerical Methods and Computers*. Reading, MA: Addison-Wesley, 1965. Source book on numerical analysis aimed at computer solutions; flowcharts and listings.

Morris, M., and P. F. Roth, *Computer Performance Evaluation*. New York: Van Nostrand Reinhold, 1982. Management of performance evaluation activity, monitors, benchmarking, with a commercial data processing orientation.

Spirn, J. R., *Program Behavior: Models and Measurement*. New York: Elsevier North-Holland, 1977. Emphasis on analysis, measurement, and modeling of page fault problems, thrashing and other virtual memory system performance problems.

Svobodova, L., *Computer Performance Measurement and Evaluation Methods: Analysis and Application*. New York: American Elsevier, 1976.

50
Installation Management

Ben Klein

City University of New York

50.1 INTRODUCTION

This chapter covers a wide range of topics relating to computer installation management:

- The function and composition of the center;
- The concerns of the computer installation regarding the service it provides;
- The relationship of the center to the parent company.

We first review the function of a computing facility, called a **computer center, data center, data processing center, information services unit,** or simply the **center**. The center should be recognized as an indispensable part of the modern corporation. It provides services to virtually all units of the corporation. For example, the center may

- Keep the accounting records for the accounting department;
- Keep inventory records for the production department;
- Provide records on sales for the sales department;
- Combine all this information to assist corporate management with planning.

The computer center management is responsible for serving all corporate departments and thus assists them in performing their own functions. So that it may serve the needs of the corporation now and in the future, the center should plan for its own staffing, the career development of its employees and its physical requirements.

50.2 MANAGEMENT

Good planning requires knowledgeable management. The center has its own organizational structure. Most data processing (**DP**) facilities (another of the many names by which a center may go) are headed by a **director of data processing.** He should be knowledgeable in all aspects of computing, including hardware, software, capacity planning and personnel requirements. No one is an expert in all these areas; therefore the director is assisted by a staff, the next level of management, with titles of associate or assistant director or manager of units of the center, typically systems, operations and applications.

Director

The center director's responsibilities include

- Being responsive to corporate management in serving their needs;
- Directing the center's staff by setting their goals to mesh with those of the corporation;
- Directing the center so that it retains its identity within the corporate structure and is not under the thumb of other units.

While these goals may seem at odds, the director balances them to satisfy both the corporate organization and the data center. If either is dissatisfied, the result is an inefficient department; everyone suffers. Here are two examples:

A DP center that does not respond adequately to the requests of user departments (corporate departments that make requests for DP work) finds itself constantly fighting for survival within the corporation. User departments complain to corporate management and claim that the DP center is not serving their needs and therefore is a waste of money. They may request that the DP center budget be reallocated to the user departments to assist them in performing their tasks.

A DP center that deals ineffectively with its own staff experiences many problems. DP people are usually sensitive to poor management direction. They have marketable skills; if they are discontent, they resign and go elsewhere. While some leave for monetary rewards, others do because there is a problem with DP management. A DP director faced with a dwindling staff finds it difficult to run the "shop." More staff can be hired, but they require a relatively long training period before they become productive. There are companies that rate DP management based upon staff turnover.

Second Echelon

The next level of management includes the associate and assistant directors. They:

- Supervise day to day operations at the center;
- Implement center policies;
- Manage the staff;
- Advise the director.

They assemble proposals from the input of their staffs and present the proposals to the director. Sometimes the director himself proposes a new idea to be evaluated by them. It may even be vetoed by them. The more this happens, though, the less respect the staff has for the director.

50.3 PLANNING

Proposals from second level managers include requests for more hardware or specialized software and implementations of policy issues such as the order in which user department requests should be accepted when there is a lack of resources. Each department manager makes requests to allow his or her own group to do its job better or easier, sometimes at the expense of the other groups. It is the director's responsibility to balance requests so that the company may profit, not an individual group.

Planning is an important director function; here the director is assisted by the staff. Planning includes plotting the center's growth and anticipating new projects that benefit the company as a whole. New applications that run on the computer are sometimes suggested by users who benefit directly from them; but a well run computer center will also suggest new applications to departments that do not realize how the computer could assist them.

There are a number of questions to be considered within this planning function:

1. Can the center support new applications with the current resources—software and hardware?
2. Does the manager want to start a new project if it endangers the progress of current projects?
3. Should new software be written or purchased for a new application?
4. Is existing hardware support sufficient?
5. Will the newly developed system be worth the new resources required?
6. Will the computer center expenditures be justified?

Once a new project is accepted for implementation, the computer staff determines what new software and hardware are required to support it and specifies its nature. One way is to write a **request for proposal (RFP)** to submit to the computer hardware and software vendors. They respond with a proposal that should include a detailed report on what is to be acquired, how much it will cost, how long will it take, and so forth.

Another method of selecting resources is to research the published literature, which includes

- *EDP Solutions*, published by the Datapro Research Corporations.
- *The Auerbach Information Management Series,* and
- The *Auerbach Data Processing Manual,* both from Auerbach Publishers.

These manuals contain case histories, sample scenarios and user evaluations of software and hardware products, along with general methods of project design.

Once the selection is made, the computer installation manager should project the useful life of these products. Newly introduced computer software may perform the function needed for this project more efficiently or economically. The price of computer hardware is dropping, so what will hardware acquired today be worth next year? Experience at large installations indicates that computer hardware retained for more than five years drops in value so quickly that it cannot be given away!

Other project decisions follow the initial one to acquire a new system, or parts to upgrade a current system:

- Should the new system be run on the current computer or should new hardware be acquired specifically for it?
- Should it be compatible with existing hardware and software or could this new system be developed using a different manufacturer's hardware?
- If hardware compatibility *is* required, should the center stay with the same hardware manufacturer or go to a competitor who manfactures **plug compatible** equipment (hardware that performs identically with that of the present installations vendor).

When the DP director makes these decisions, they are usually repackaged as a proposal to upper corporate management. The director convinces them that this decision is best with respective corporate goals. It is cost effective, easy and fast to implement.

After management approval, hardware and software are scheduled to be acquired. The purchasing department provides administrative help for the purchases. Contracts are drawn up by the legal department; they should be reviewed thoroughly by both DP management and the corporate legal staff. Until all angles are covered to everyone's satisfaction, no contract should be signed. There are many books on computer contracts that will show all involved parties how to retain their rights and what their obligations are (two are listed in this chapter's References).

Once acquired, the new system is

1. Installed, either by inhouse staff or by vendor's representatives;
2. Tested by the DP staff;
3. Accepted by a written statement that the system performs as requested; and
4. Finally put into production status.

The director is ultimately responsible for the smooth running of the center during the transition, with the assistance of general management, and the purchasing and legal departments.

50.4 OPERATIONS

The associate director for operations has a number of groups that report to him, including operations, teleprocessing and production control. The manager of operations, assisted by shift supervisors, is responsible for the day to day running of the computer center. They are on the front line: if the computer system **goes down** (becomes unavailable), at once they get phone calls from concerned and, usually, irritated users. Malfunctions in the system are usually blamed on operations. Indeed, users generally view the operations group as responsible for all problems, even hardware faults.

If the system does **crash** (fail), the operators must restart it. Since computing time is expensive, it is imperative that it is restarted quickly.

The operators are responsible for dealing with the **customer engineers** (CEs, or repair people) whenever the hardware goes down. CEs do **preventive maintenance** on the hardware to avoid potential problems. Scheduling repair periods (when the computer is unavailable for production work) and the installation of new or updated equipment are also handled by the operations staff.

Operators mount tapes and disks as requested by the operating system and make sure that paper and ribbon is installed on the printing equipment. These are not trivial tasks! They are indispensable to the continued operation of the system. If tape or disk mount requests are ignored, the computer eventually goes into a wait state because it lacks data to work on; so do all the users who expect output from their runs. If printers are not monitored closely, the paper may tear or the ribbon wear out, with unusable computer generated reports the result.

The media librarian keeps computer tape and disk catalogs up to date and provides maintenance, cleaning, repair and replacement of media and devices—again, routine but vital tasks. Damage to disks or tapes means the loss of data vital to the operation of the company. Ordering and maintaining stocks of paper and other special printer forms (such as checks, invoice blanks) are also the responsibility of operations.

50.5 TELEPROCESSING

More corporations are going on-line, using interactive terminals to communicate with the computer. Terminals require cable connections to the computer. The **teleprocessing group** is responsible for acquiring terminals, ensuring that they are compatible with the computing system and establishing connections to the computing system. Planning and contracting for cables to be run through the building is a considerable project.

A nationwide teleprocessing network is of an order of magnitude more complicated than a local network. It is not uncommon for a corporation to have terminals throughout the country (or world) linked by telephone or satellite communications. With distributed computing, small local computers do specific types of processing and are connected to other computers and the central computer. Proper communications facility availability is the concern of the teleprocessing group. The group may be distributed, with personnel located in distant cities to deal with that portion of the network.

The teleprocessing group, in conjunction with other installation groups, selects the **teleprocessing systems (TP)**. An evaluation determines which operations are needed on-line. The cost associated with an on-line system is higher than for a batch system; they consume resources faster than batch systems. There are two basic types of TP systems:

- **Remote batch** with one or more data entry and printing workstation at a remote part of the company.
- **Interactive,** with terminals placed in offices and areas of plants where workers interact in real time with the computer.

An example of remote batch is **remote job entry,** the small dedicated computer that allows users to submit computer jobs from a remote location and receive results back at a printer installed there.

The **interactive terminal** is more common. The user, a clerk or manager in a nonDP department, makes queries to the computer to retrieve data from the data base system and receives the responses at that terminal.

The communications system uses communications lines, rented or leased from a common carrier, such as the Bell System. For **dedicated lines,** the connection is permanently made and never broken, ensuring that data can be transmitted at any time without dialing. They may use access to a **switched network,** which is dialed up and connected when needed and the connection broken when not in use.

The satellite is a relatively new communication medium exclusively for communications.

The criteria for determining which mode of communication to use depend upon many factors:

- Amount of traffic;
- Hours when lines are needed (night vs. prime time);
- Transmission speed (the switched network is not suitable for high speed).

There is another question about these lines: Should these be public communications lines, subject to intercep-

tion and possible data modification, or should they be private leased lines at greater cost? There are a number of scrambler products currently on the market that provide encryption of data signals transmitted on public lines.

50.6 PRODUCTION

Production describes functions done repetitively. Examples are billing, accounts payable, general ledger and payroll. Production programs and large complex systems are written, debugged and tested by the applications programming group. When functioning properly, they are turned over to the production group, which is then responsible for running them against data periodically. The production group, too, is important to the corporation; without accounts receivable or payable systems running in a timely fashion, the company would suffer. Production control is looked down upon by programming professionals because it involves repetitive work and requires little of the creativity that DP people seem to value.

Production runs are frequently done at night, even after midnight. The programming staff uses the computer during the day to develop new programs and systems and test them. Large amounts of production work may keep the computing system busy both day and night; two complete computers, one exclusively for production, the other for test and development systems, alleviate this condition.

Production runs done at night (third shift, 12:00PM to 8:00AM) are usually completed by morning; reports and output are ready at 9:00AM. If a run does not complete, a procedure manual tells the production group how to recover and repair the programming system to continue the run. Unfortunately, not all cases are covered in the manual. It is common for programmers to be "on call" like doctors. A phone call at 3:00AM may get a programmer out of bed to sign on to a computer terminal in the home to repair the system. If the home effort fails (or if there is no terminal at home), a ride to work is necessary.

Being on call is the task that programmers hate most. In some companies, this duty is delegated to a junior programmer; in others, it rotates among the staff. It is a frequent reason for resignations of top notch programmers who feel it is beneath their dignity. The beeper you may hear in a theatre may not be a doctor as one would suppose, but a computer programmer on call!

50.7 SYSTEMS

The systems group, the elite of the programming professions, is composed of the programmers responsible for managing the operating system (see Chapter 30, on operating systems). **Systems programmers** make alterations in the operating system in assembler language to suit specific needs of the installation. They are the most highly trained and expensive personnel on the DP staff. There is a dearth of such experienced professionals; consequently there are numbers of applications programmers who are more than willing to make the transition to systems programmer.

An operating system (OS) is a complex program prone to bugs, which may prevent the computer from functioning properly. The operations staff is responsible for restarting the machine if the system crashes due to operating system failure, as contrasted with a malfunction of the computing hardware handled by the CEs. But the system staff fixes the operating system itself whenever possible.

Sometimes putting in a **fix,** an alteration to correct a difficulty encountered by the installation of the OS, actually causes the system to crash. There must be a good working relationship between operations and systems since they function together so often.

As an example, the computer crashes and the operations group cannot restart it using normal recovery procedures in their procedures manual. The faulty component may be identified by error messages that appear on the system console. A call is made to the systems programmer responsible for the failing component. Sometimes operations cannot diagnose the failing component and seeks assistance from *any* systems programmer to get the system operational again.

Though management usually decides which operating system runs the computer, systems has a voice in that decision. Factors such as the job mix influence the decision, for instance, few long running jobs as opposed to many short jobs or jobs that spend most of their time I/O bound or compute bound. On-line requirements are a consideration. IBM's Time Sharing Option (TSO), one on-line system, is available only under the Multiple Virtual Storage (MVS) operating system. MVS is primarily a production and development tool. The Virtual Machine (VM) operating system uses the Conversational Monitor System (CMS), another on-line system preferable for nonprogrammers also. The systems group chooses between the two, TSO and CMS.

The procedures manual, usually a joint effort between operations and systems, contains information to restart the computer system in the event of a crash. It also contains backup information: how to restart when various units of the computer are inoperative. Alternate hardware units are defined so that in the event of a failure of the primary unit, the staff can bring the system up in the alternative mode.

Another system function is to install **program temporary fixes,** called **PTFs,** to the operating system. PTFs are sent to the installation by the operating system supplier, usually the computer vendor. The systems staff, along with management, decides if and when to apply these fixes. PTFs are maintenance patches to remedy known or potential problems; they are not applied to a running system since this may cause other problems. They are applied to a test version of the operating system.

A number of programs facilitate the application of fixes. SMP (System Maintenance Program) for System/370 running MVS is a simple but powerful program that allows fixes to be applied, tested, backed out if necessary and then permanently installed. Another fix program called VMSERV (for VM Service) performs the same function as SMP for VM.

Testing requires a **dedicated computer.** The computer system is used only for the test; any other user might be adversely affected. Testing cannot be done during the day, when the applications staff are running development programs. It cannot be done at night, when production systems are running. System tests are usually scheduled for early morning hours (4:00AM to 8:00AM), early evening hours (6:00PM to 11:00PM), or for weekends, depending on when the computer is used for regular processing.

VM can run several operating systems concurrently under its direction. One of these can be the system under test. Thus operating systems test and production runs can proceed at the same time.

Computer Performance Evaluation

A shared responsibility of systems and operations is **computer performance evaluation (CPE).** A computer is expensive; its work should be maximized. An installation calculates the work performed in order to bill user departments proportionately. They want to receive the most for their money, the "biggest bang for the buck." The CPE staff may include members from operations, and/or systems, or it may be an independent group. They evaluate hardware and its performance. Both hardware and software monitor the CPU, its peripheral devices and attachments to observe and report to management the CPU's work rate. Bottlenecks may indicate too few disk storage devices, for example. There may not be enough paths to one set of disks. The monitors may observe a failing component within the computer that the machine has detected and has automatically put out of service but which is still causing degraded performance.

Software monitors track running programs and display those in wait states at a given moment. They keep track of I/O activity and time spent in supervisor routines. This information may indicate why production runs are taking excessive time, even though the computer seems fast enough to handle them. The information reported by the CPE group may be used by management as a justification for more hardware based on the facts of system utilization.

Software and Security

The systems staff installs general purpose software and language compilers for the applications staff. General purpose software are program products not written by the computer center staff. They perform general tasks such as security checking, accounting of computer utilization, disk and tape management, sorts, dumps and program verification.

Security is a concern for two reasons. First, the computer system contains sensitive data about the corporation which could be used by competitors to sabotage the company. For example, a customer list including orders and payments could be used by a competitor to undercut sales the company makes, or personnel data could be used to hire away talent.

Security programs marketed by reputable companies help the installation restrict access to the computer to authorized users. They further restrict user access to specified files and data; employees with read access only view data but cannot manipulate or change them.

Security programs are selected by the systems group in conjunction with the computer auditing group, part of the company's accounting function. In large organizations, a separate group, **quality assurance,** may select security software and also be responsible for the CPE function and thus monitor the computing installation's efficiency and procedures.

The second concern is for the physical security of the center. Computing hardware, if damaged, could cripple company operations. Management would not have access to data on customers, accounts receivable and payable, inventory, and so forth. Besides the replacement cost of a large computing center, lost time is also costly. Insurance is obviously a necessity.

Management addresses these concerns through disaster recovery plans and backup for natural disaster, mali-

cious fire and bombing. Disaster recovery plans include creating backup copies of vital data at regular intervals. Off-site storage facilities are rented from a company specializing in this service. Their vaults store copies of disks and tape at a distance from the computer center. In case of wide spread disaster, both the data and its backup should not be lost. Another service alternative is complete computing facilities backup. Even if the entire computer center is destroyed, personnel can move backup copies to another computing facility and continue processing.

Proper disk and tape management enables the systems staff to monitor the use of these media. The staff removes old, obsolete disk files by copying them to tape for long term storage. The staff should know how much disk space is in use and for what. Tape management systems keep track of what data are on tape and to which programmer and user department the tape belongs. Some media management systems also interface with the security system to control access to tapes.

Chargeback

A joint concern of the operations and systems groups is computer chargeback systems. Although the computing facility is owned and operated by the parent company, a charging (or billing) system for service departments internal to the company is common practice. This is necessary to

- Ascertain who is using the computing resource and to what degree;
- Help the computing center justify its budget.

The computer chargeback or accounting system accounts to the center for all resources:

- Central processing unit time;
- Number of input/output operations (I/O);
- Number of lines printed on a high speed printer.

Personnel time—programmers, operators, and so on—can be included in this cost or broken out.

Some information on CPU time and I/O operations is collected through the operating system of most large scale computing systems. The IBM System/370 provides the System Management Facility (SMF), which writes records periodically to a designated device to give the assignment and use of each computing resource. These records can be the input to a statistics gathering and accounting system.

These data may then be related to each user and department according to job card account number (furnished in the JCL). At the end of an accounting period (usually one month), detailed and summary reports are prepared for each user department manager describing computing resources used. The computer center management reviews the reports and the general summary to determine trends and spot excessive facility use by an individual or group. Computer chargeback identifies all users, including suspicious ones. Unauthorized use of the computer can sometimes be spotted—either an attempt to use the computer without a valid charge code or illegal use of a charge code.

Processing raw SMF data can be cumbersome and time consuming. A chargeback package can be installed in a few hours. It collects data from a running system and produces reports tailored to the installation. Collection parameters may be set differently for each. For example, CPU time is not meaningful when applied to different machine types (faster or slower CPUs). An installation sets different accounting (or dollar) units for each CPU model. In multiple CPU shops (with CPUs of different speeds), the center equates the cost of doing the same work on each. For example, a job that takes 1 CPU second on one machine may take 10 CPU seconds on a slower machine. Therefore, the accounting unit charge for the slower machine should be about 1/10 the unit charge for the faster machine.

Staff time to maintain the system environment and also operating costs, including air conditioning, electricity, security and rent, are sometimes included in chargeback.

Priority for computer runs influences charging. Normal jobs are executed in first-in, first-out sequence. There are occasions when certain runs must go to the head of the queue. For example, a payroll run which aborts for some reason gets rerun after the problem is diagnosed and fixed. But paychecks must be produced immediately to be signed and distributed to the employees. The computer has other jobs queued up, so the payroll job would normally wait to run later. Increasing the scheduling priority of the payroll job sends it to the top of the queue so that it starts next. When used correctly, a flexible scheduling priority scheme is very useful.

When everyone submits work at top priority, all the work falls back to a first-in, first-out scheme. **Priority charging** may control this: high priority work is charged at a higher rate. Since management reviews billing reports, anyone misusing priority is identified.

Some systems also allow low priority, low cost jobs that go to the bottom of the queue. Work not needed immediately is run when the computer is underutilized. Priority cost schemes are widely used in computer service bureau environments where priority also helps load balancing. There should be a lock in the accounting system so that work cannot be submitted at high priority and charged at a lesser rate because the user or operator later lowers its priority for that very purpose. Once the job is already executing, the OS is no longer concerned about its scheduling priority.

Systems accounting is usually done nightly. SMF records created for work done that day are placed into the accounting data base. In service bureau organizations, which sell services to other companies, the scheme is usually more complex. Two types of accounting are used: debit or additive. In **debit accounting**, a budget is allocated to a charge code and the accounting system debits the account for the cost of each job upon completion. There are **hooks** in the operating system, accounting exits, that allow the OS job manager to determine if there still is a positive balance in the job's account. As with a checking account, if the balance is insufficient, the job is rejected. Upon completion, another hook has the job manager debit the account with the charges for the run.

With **additive accounting**, the OS job manager puts the charges for each job to the account's bill. A total is posted at the end of each billing period and the account is zeroed out.

Accounting software is installed by the systems group, who attach their routines to the operating system hooks. Reporting and maintenance are done by application programmers. In organizations in which the accounting function is essential to computer center operation (a computer service bureau, for example), a separate accounting group has this responsibility.

50.8 APPLICATIONS

An applications group is sometimes part of the computing staff. It may be one (or more) complete department under a management separate from that for the computer center. When the applications group reports to the installation manager, they work with user departments, analyze needs and develop computer programs to fulfill them. This task looms large when there are many user departments, each with unique needs. The group is composed of junior and senior programmers, data base programmers and systems analysts. It can also contain specialists in a new area called the Information Center.

Also, maintenance programmers modify existing programs to satisfy changing needs. They learn about the programs and systems of the company from the inside. Once they have learned a system, they may be moved into a development group writing code for new applications supervised by a project leader. Each team member is responsible for a part of the system under development.

A system is conceptualized by a systems analyst, who meets with the user department in response to a specific problem. The implementation of the solution is done by the programming team (see Chapters 33–35).

With the advent of large data base systems, programmers now write programs to retrieve or manipulate data stored in the data base. The data base administrator (DBA) and his or her group administer the data base. They load the data, define it and make it available to the programming staff.

The supply of computer professionals is substantially less than the demand and the prospect of this changing in the near future is very slim. Hence a new concept called the **information center** is here. Its personnel help the nonDP user to access data and to produce reports without the intervention of a DP staff member. A high level, English-like computer language can request these services through a terminal situated in the manager's office.

Such a center reduces the demand for professional programmers, but certainly not entirely. The DP staff sets up the data base system. They instruct the user on accessing data and using the query and report language. DP staff is also available for later assistance, should users encounter a problem or need a new function not previously encountered. These DP staff members are called **information specialists** or **internal consultants.**

50.9 PERSONNEL

Staffing the computing facility is a responsibility of the installation management. Candidates are interviewed by the group manager. As noted, finding qualified staff is difficult. There is a demand for trained computer professionals which schools and colleges are trying to fulfill. The number of college computer majors has increased considerably. Adult education classes, extension courses and private schools are also producing graduates in droves. But they have no work experience. When a company hires them, it must give them further training in both computing and the installation procedures. Therefore they are not fully productive for a long time.

Requirements for new employees vary. Operations staff must have either a two year college degree (Associate in Applied Science), or be graduates of a private school course in computer operations. Companies seek people with experience with their particular hardware and software systems. Colleges offer internship programs in which students spend a term or two working for a company for course credit. A good student serving as intern in a company is often offered a position in that company upon graduation.

Application programmers with a B.S. in computer science or data processing are hired as programmer trainees. They advance to programmer or programmer/analyst. Computer programming aptitude is also required. Exams, such as the Wold Computer Programmer Aptitude Test, are given by the Institute for Certification of Computer Professionals, which also bestows the Certificate in Data Processing.

Systems programmers are required to have four-year college degrees. After a number of years as applications programmers or computer operators, they are eligible for promotion to systems programming. They code in assembly language and take training courses offered by the hardware manufacturers and on the job.

Personnel agencies locate prospective staff, or a firm seeking computer staff may advertise directly for applicants. Advertising may seem less expensive, but to evaluate relatively unscreened applicants is time consuming. Many applicants have an impressive resume and a vocabulary of "buzz" words but lack real knowledge or experience. Weeding out such applicants may cost more than an agency fee for persons actually employed.

Many agencies specialize in locating and qualifying data processing professionals. Fees can range up to 20 percent of each hired prospect's yearly salary. These "head hunters" assist in staffing, but they also contribute to loss of staff. They check with an employee after he or she has been with the company for a year to fill other vacancies (and thus get another fee). Many companies now require the employee to remain some time (sometimes up to a year) before the agency gets its fee. Before "hiring" an agency to fill a vacancy, the prospective employer should check how good their record is and how well they weed out the true professionals from "buzz word" applicants.

How does one evaluate a computer programmer, analyst or operator? Their work cannot be quantified by productivity like that of an assembly line worker. Rating programmers by number of lines of code written and tested per unit time does not take into account the complexity of the assignment. The best way to rate a professional is close observation by a supervisor.

Operations staff can be observed and rated how smoothly their area runs and how accurately and quickly they respond to emergencies. The computer usually runs itself. But a job may hang or a group of TP lines drop; users are affected but operators may not notice. They should monitor the system consoles watching for an abnormality: no new jobs starting; no terminal users. Thus they can remedy any problem as soon as possible. Operator rating is based upon *the amount of time lost by users*. Operator intervention is required on modern computers only to change disk packs and tape reels, fill card hoppers and install paper.

Advancement

For all employees the inevitable question arises: "Where do I go from here?" Professionals look for advancement in the form of money, greater responsibility and freedom to do what they feel needs doing.

A career path plan with salary reviews at known intervals and based upon performance is important. It should be established in conjunction with corporate personnel. A programmer trainee advances to full programmer after a year or two of satisfactory performance. Requirements for higher titles may include academic achievement, demonstration of competence in other areas and a given number of years of experience in the current title. To balance the number of employees in certain titles, some companies may fix the number of positions available and thus advancement from a lower title may be possible only upon the availability of an open position. This holds down costs and provides a more rigid organizational structure for the company, but may also cause the resignation of bright people in a hurry to advance.

50.10 SUMMARY

The computer installation is a service department. It is composed of

1. An operations group, responsible for operating the computer hardware;
2. A systems group, which maintains the computer operating system;
3. An applications group, which does programming for the rest of the corporation.

It is administered by a hierarchy of managers.

The installation has the problems of a service department along with those of running and maintaining a computer system, a complex collection of machines.

The center staff is hired and evaluated on the basis of technical knowledge and ability to solve problems, both in computing and for user departments.

Software is acquired by the center staff to provide security, backup, performance evaluation and accounting. These are unique to the center and no other department is involved in their acquisition or implementation.

The center management balances corporate goals against its own needs. As technology changes, the center remains current while attempting to squeeze the most utility from its current equipment. It is responsive to the user community while also providing new challenges to its staff.

Installation management performs these functions while providing mandated service to the company and so contributes to the company's growth and expansion.

REFERENCES

Auer, J., and C. Harris, *Computer Contract Negotiations.* New York: Van Nostrand Reinhold, 1981.

Auerbach Information Management Series. Pennsauken, NJ: Auerbach, 1977.

Brandon, Dick H., *Data Processing Contracts: Structure, Content, and Negotiations.* New York: Van Nostrand Reinhold, 1976.

EDP Solutions. Delran, NJ: Datapro Research Corp., 1979.

Rubin, M., *Handbook of Data Processing Management.* Pennsauken, NJ: Auerbach, 1971.

Schaeffer, H., *Data Center Operations.* Englewood Cliffs, NJ: Prentice-Hall, 1981.

Index